International Conflict and Security Law

Sergey Sayapin · Rustam Atadjanov ·
Umesh Kadam · Gerhard Kemp ·
Nicolás Zambrana-Tévar · Noëlle Quénivet
Editors

International Conflict and Security Law

A Research Handbook

Volume 1

Editors
Sergey Sayapin
School of Law
KIMEP University
Almaty, Kazakhstan

Umesh Kadam
National Law School of India
Pune, India

Nicolás Zambrana-Tévar
School of Law
KIMEP University
Almaty, Kazakhstan

Rustam Atadjanov
School of Law
KIMEP University
Almaty, Kazakhstan

Gerhard Kemp
Law and Social Sciences
University of Derby
Derby, UK

Noëlle Quénivet
Bristol Law School
University of the West of England
Bristol, UK

ISBN 978-94-6265-517-1 ISBN 978-94-6265-515-7 (eBook)
https://doi.org/10.1007/978-94-6265-515-7

Published by T.M.C. ASSER PRESS, The Hague, The Netherlands www.asserpress.nl
Produced and distributed for T.M.C. ASSER PRESS by Springer-Verlag Berlin Heidelberg

© T.M.C. ASSER PRESS and the authors 2022
No part of this work may be reproduced, stored in a retrieval system, or transmitted in any form or by
any means, electronic, mechanical, photocopying, microfilming, recording or otherwise, without written
permission from the Publisher, with the exception of any material supplied specifically for the purpose of
being entered and executed on a computer system, for exclusive use by the purchaser of the work.
The use of general descriptive names, registered names, trademarks, service marks, etc. in this publication
does not imply, even in the absence of a specific statement, that such names are exempt from the relevant
protective laws and regulations and therefore free for general use.

This T.M.C. ASSER PRESS imprint is published by the registered company Springer-Verlag GmbH, DE,
part of Springer Nature.
The registered company address is: Heidelberger Platz 3, 14197 Berlin, Germany

Foreword

For much of the history of international law, the distinction between war and peace affected the laws that applied to a given situation, but was not a legal question itself. Oppenheim's magnum opus, for many editions, came in two volumes: the first on 'peace' and the second on 'war and neutrality'. Of the various transformations in the course of the twentieth century—including the end of colonialism, the rise of human rights, the shift to multilateralism—the prohibition on the use of force arguably affected the structure of international law in the most fundamental way.

As this important new work demonstrates, international conflict and security law today has gone far beyond the jus ad bellum and the jus in bello. Much as the United Nations Security Council's brief to address 'threats to international peace and security' expanded considerably in the euphoric 'new interventionism' of the early 1990s, the contributors interpret threats to human well-being broadly. It is now two decades since the September 11, 2001 attacks led the USA to conclude that it had more to fear from failing states than from conquering ones. Our own insight at this moment of pandemic is that shared biology renders us all vulnerable to diseases that pay no heed to borders. And, at least in the back of our minds, we know that the greatest threat our children will face is the sickening of the Earth itself.

Solving or resolving these and other problems demands cooperation, and the editors are to be congratulated for bringing together authors that span literal and metaphorical boundaries of geography and discipline. The resultant work—coincidentally, also published in two volumes—will be of interest to lawyers and diplomats, but also activists and officials, as well as anyone seeking to understand the evolving dangers confronting our shared world, and the tools and institutions needed to avert, mitigate, or survive them.

Singapore   Simon Chesterman
October 2021

Preface

As this two-volume book was being conceptualized in late 2017, it was the co-editors' starting point that threats to international peace and security were numerous and not necessarily military, and therefore, our exposition of international conflict and security law should go beyond the narrowly defined classical areas such as the use of force, the law of armed conflict, peacekeeping, refugee law, and international criminal law. Surprisingly enough, few book-length works have been written on the subject. One, edited by Burchill et al., is a collection of essays on selected topics of the conflict and security law.[1] Another one is a research handbook edited by White and Henderson focusing mostly on conflict prevention and the legality of resorting to the use of force.[2] The third book, written by White, constitutes an introduction to international conflict and security law dealing with the use of force, conflict situations, and peacetime security.[3] We departed from earlier approaches by highlighting a few key values protected by international law and then proceeding to discuss some of the most relevant aspects of international conflict and security law in an interdisciplinary manner. In the first volume, we examine values protected by relevant legal rules, as well as some key international institutions enforcing those rules, whereas the second volume deals with a few challenges to established rules, crimes under international law, and a handful of illustrative case studies. We believe that the ensuing developments, including the COVID-19 pandemic, confirmed the relevance of our basic perception and editorial approach.

We were lucky to assemble a team of contributors from literally all continents and all major legal systems of the world, in order to make the project truly international. In order for international law to be deserving of its name, it must be reflective of a

---

[1] Burchill R et al. (2005) International conflict and security law. Essays in memory of Hilaire McCoubrey. Cambridge University Press, Cambridge.

[2] White N, Henderson C (2015) Research handbook on international conflict and security law: Jus ad bellum, jus in bello and jus post bellum. Edward Elgar Publishing, Cheltenham, Northampton.

[3] White N (2014) Advanced introduction to international conflict and security law. Edward Elgar Publishing, Cheltenham, Northampton. Most recently, Geiß R, Melzer N (2021) The Oxford Handbook of the International Law of Global Security (Oxford University Press, Oxford) covered a broader range of topics.

variety of legal traditions and perspectives. Also, in order for international law to be effective, especially in such a sensitive area, as international security, it should take account of lawful interests of as many actors concerned as possible, including states, international institutions, and non-state actors. On account of the contemporary world realities, increasing attention is being paid to issues concerning international conflict and security from a variety of perspectives, such as political, legal, sociological, philosophical, economic, and cultural. One aspect of such renewed attention is that a sizable number of academic institutions have introduced either stand-alone courses that revolve around the general theme of international conflict and security, or integrated elements of these studies in general courses on public international law, international relations, political science, journalism, etc. Undergraduate and postgraduate students pursuing such studies will benefit from these volumes. Undoubtedly, even non-lawyers are often required to delve into legal dimensions of these issues. Apart from students, the present work will also profit those who work for think tanks, intergovernmental and non-governmental organizations dealing with peace, conflict and security related issues as well as armed forces, military academies, governments, and media houses.

The first volume is organized into three parts. Part I ("Protected Values") makes the point that mankind's security and welfare are based upon fundamental values both of a natural and positive character. The three inaugural chapters deal with the philosophy and sociology of international law: Rustam Atadjanov (Chap. 1) reflects on the idea of humanity, which transcends all international law, followed by Boris Kashnikov (Chap. 2) who dwells on the concept of self-determination, and Anthony Cullen with Kostiantyn Gorobets (Chap. 3) who introduce the rule of law theory. The next chapter (Chap. 4) written by Victor Ventura and Eduardo Filho, discusses the common heritage of mankind. Part I concludes with Anicée Van Engeland's chapter (Chap. 5) on the concept of cultural relativism in international human rights law.

Part II ("Law") explores the main areas of international conflict and security law. In Chap. 6, Onder Bakircioglu offers a useful overview of the legal regulation of the use of force. In the three following chapters, the UN Security Council is discussed: Rossana Deplano in Chap. 7 explores the Security Council's evolving role in the maintenance of international peace and security, Ben Murphy in Chap. 8 analyses the modalities of the Security Council sanctions, and Sabine Hassler in Chap. 9 explains the formalities of peace operations mandated by the Security Council. Joop Voetelink's following chapter (Chap. 10) on the Status of Forces Agreements explains the regime of extraterritorial deployment of state armed forces. Next, Melanie O'Brien (Chap. 11) introduces readers to international human rights law (IHRL), before international humanitarian law (IHL) is expounded on in a few chapters. In Chap. 12, Christine Byron explains the key concept of direct participation in hostilities (DPH). Jeroen van den Boogaard highlights the operational perspectives of the conduct of hostilities (Chap. 13) and explains the legal regime of the prohibition of chemical and biological weapons (Chap. 14). Next, Rustam Atadjanov (Chap. 15) turns to the status of nuclear weapons under international law, and Evhen Tsybulenko analyses the regulation of blinding laser weapons (Chap. 16) and vacuum weapons (Chap. 17). In Chap. 18, Evhen Tsybulenko and Anastassiya Platonova

Preface ix

dwell on the legal regulation of new types of weapons, and Kubo Mačák in Chap. 19 completes the overview of Hague Law in his chapter on military space operations. In the next two chapters, Tara Smith (Chap. 20) analyses the effects of armed conflicts on the environment and natural resources, and Marina Lostal (Chap. 21) focuses on the protection of cultural property in armed conflicts. Next, after Sergey Sayapin's general introduction to international criminal law (ICL) (Chap. 22), Thomas Kruessmann (Chap. 23) goes into the particulars of anti-corruption law and action. Katja Samuel and Silvia Venier (Chap. 24) complete Part II with their chapter on the due diligence obligations of international organizations engaged in disaster management.

Part III ("Institutions") is devoted to universal and regional institutions, both intergovernmental and non-governmental, which are instrumental in enforcing international conflict and security law, and maintaining international and regional peace and security. Since such institutions are numerous, we had to be selective, and our approach to peace and security was broad and comprehensive enough to include institutions dealing with economic cooperation, education and culture, health care, and development. The first three chapters in this part relate to representative regional organizations with broad competences, including security issues: Ioannis Tzivaras' chapter (Chap. 25) on the Organization for Security and Cooperation in Europe (OSCE) is followed by Lehte Roots' chapter on the European Union (EU) (Chap. 26), and then by Ondrej Hamulak and Josef Valuch's overview (Chap. 27) of the Association of East Asian Nations (ASEAN). In the next chapter, Sultan Sakhariyev (Chap. 28) explains the mandate of the Collective Security Treaty Organization (CSTO). Whereas an overview of the International Criminal Court (ICC) is offered in the chapter on international criminal law, two chapters exemplify the action of "hybrid" tribunals: Olivier Beauvallet and Jeanne-Thérèse Schmit (Chap. 29) explain the operation of the Extraordinary Chambers in the Courts of Cambodia (ECCC), and Michail Vagias (Chap. 30) analyses other "hybrid" tribunals. Alison Bisset (Chap. 31) adds to the discussion an overview of post-conflict justice mechanisms. The next few chapters are devoted to universal institutions such as INTERPOL (Chap. 32 by Evhen Tsybulenko and Sebastian Suarez), UNESCO (Chap. 33 by Umesh Kadam), UNICEF and the WHO (Chaps. 34 and 35 by Nataliia Hendel), and the UNDP (Chap. 36 by Julio P. F. H. de Siqueira, Andrew Mtewa, and Daury César Fabriz). The part concludes with Heike Spieker's chapter (Chap. 37) on the International Red Cross and Red Crescent Movement, and a chapter on human rights NGOs and humanitarian NGOs (Chap. 38) written by Nataliia Hendel, Tymur Korotkyi and Roman Yedeliev.

The purpose of the second volume consists in placing the first volume's theory in practical contexts. Part IV ("Challenges") exemplifies a few threats calling for a creative and innovative application of existing rules. Tara Smith's inaugural chapter (Chap. 39) discusses the problem of climate change and is followed by a chapter on wildlife poaching as a threat to international peace and security by Federico Dalpane and Maria Baideldinova (Chap. 40). The next two chapters discuss the use of force in specific contexts: Elizabeth Chadwick in Chap. 41 discusses the use of force in pursuance of the right to self-determination, and Eki Omorogbe in Chap. 42 explores the African Union's action against mercenaries. Each of the final three chapters in

Part IV addresses an individual issue: Julio P. F. H. de Siqueira, Daury César Fabriz and Junio G. Homem de Siqueira in Chap. 43 discuss the rights of elderly and disabled persons in the context of security challenges, Stefanie Bock and Nicolai Bülte in Chap. 44 explore the politics of international justice, and Evelyne Schmid in Chap. 45 addresses the problem of poverty.

Part V ("Crimes") is devoted to crimes under international law and some transnational crimes. The "core" crimes under international law are addressed in accordance with Article 5 of the ICC Statute: in Chap. 46 Olivier Beauvallet with Hyuree Kim and Léo Jolivet discuss genocide, followed by Rustam Atadjanov (Chap. 47, on crimes against humanity), Gerhard Kemp (Chap. 48, on apartheid), Ewa Sałkiewicz Munnerlyn and Sergey Sayapin (Chap. 49, on war crimes), and Annegret Lucia Hartig (Chap. 50, on aggression). The subsequent chapters address military ecocide (Chap. 51 by Peter Hough), religious extremism (Chap. 52 by Sherzod Eraliev), human smuggling and human trafficking (Chap. 53 by Natalia Szablewska), and organized crime (Chap. 54 by Thomas Kruessmann).

Finally, Part VI ("Case Studies") discusses a few conflicts from geographic and thematic perspectives. The country case studies discussed are Cambodia (Chap. 55 by Natalia Szablewska), Myanmar (Chap. 56 by Melanie O'Brien), Northern Cyprus and the former Yugoslavia (Chaps. 57 and 58 by Ioannis Tzivaras), and Northern Ireland (Chap. 59 by Lauren Dempster). The thematic case studies include the "war on terror" (Chap. 60 by Rumyana Van Ark (nee Grozdanova)), an assessment of the Boko Haram crisis from Islamic and international humanitarian law perspectives (Chap. 61 by Muhammad-Basheer A. Ismail), reflections on the accountability of religious actors for religiously motivated conflicts, and on the accountability of the Catholic Church for clergy sex abuse (Chaps. 62 and 63 by Nicolás Zambrana-Tévar), and the role of international law in the prevention and resolution of possible conflicts over water in Central Asia (Chap. 64 by Hafeni Nashoonga).

As mentioned above, in international law the concepts of conflict and security are often understood narrowly. Such an approach fails to take into consideration a wider spectrum of situations and factors that create or mitigate conflicts or change their nature. Espousing this narrow stance often leads commentators to failing to grasp some of the intricacies of a specific conflictual situation and, consequently, to offer concrete, valuable legal solutions. Whilst in international affairs scholars have long accepted the multifaceted aspects of conflicts, legal pundits, constrained by the straightjacket of a rigid, often doctrinal interpretation of international law and a conservative United Nations Security Council, have been unable to move beyond the military/human/environmental security discursive framework. A broader view, as adopted by this book, is thus warranted. This endeavour is further met by bringing together scholars who are not only specialists in their field but also whose views reflect a worldwide variety of approaches towards the subject-matter.

Liberation from the conventional notions of "human security" and "conflict", as well as the legal, political, and social paradigms that inform them, requires humility and a sense of history. It also demands serious work on, and recognition of, the roles that the marginalized, the oppressed, and the colonized have played in the formation of an essentially hegemonic and triumphalist international system. For

Preface xi

instance, not recognizing the crime of apartheid as a settler-colonialist continuity that fundamentally destroyed any sense of security and humanity of entire populations (and the dignity and self-respect of an entire continent), and by analysing *that* crime through a narrower (Western!) lens of twentieth century, post-Second World War human rights sensibilities, exposes the flaw at the heart of international (criminal) law. Our approach (as evidenced throughout the book, including the chapter on the crime of apartheid) is thus informed by perspectives from the marginalized (for instance, the disabled and the elderly in the context of IHL), gender perspectives, and a sense that we must with this book, in all humility and with critical awareness of its own limitations, create avenues that will lead to further debate, discussion, and serious intellectual work on the construction and deconstruction of notions of law, security, and human interests in the twenty-first century.

Social stability and the protection of individual rights, especially the right to life and property are considered common, probable, and desirable goals of any moral and legal system. The very existence of moral and legal norms presupposes and leads to the absence of arbitrariness, which is often present in any community where laws are replaced by the will and self-interests of those who have power and can impose it on those who have not. Law, therefore, leads in itself to security and to the absence of conflict. However, the more we learn about the causes of conflict and violence, the more we can tailor our legal system to ensure that conflicts are appropriately tackled, eliminating their exact causes, sensibly approaching those opposing interests in the community which are often behind outbursts of violence or present in any sustained situation of injustice and deprivation of individual and collective rights. Books on conflict and security law—such as this one—contribute to this study of how to remedy violence and attacks on human rights by examining specific types of conflicts and how the law can contribute to long-standing solutions.

We take this occasion to thank all contributors for their reflection and hard work. They made this book possible. Very special thanks are due to Prof. Simon Chesterman, Dean and Professor at the National University of Singapore, for his endorsing Foreword. English language editors at Scribendi (www.scribendi.com) were very helpful in proofreading selected chapters. KIMEP University (Almaty, Kazakhstan) should be credited for taking over the English language editing costs. We thank Dr. Chan Young Bang, President of KIMEP University, Dr. Joseph Luke, Acting Vice President for Academic Affairs, Mr. Yuri Fidirko, Vice President for Finance, Dr. Fred M. Isaacs, Associate Professor and Dean of KIMEP University's School of Law, and Dr. Claudio Lombardi, Assistant Professor and Research Director at the School of Law, for their continued support. We also thank Mr. Frank Bakker, Ms. Kiki van Gurp, and other colleagues at T.M.C. ASSER PRESS and the law team at Springer for their support for this project since its inception. Ms. Anna Margatova was helpful in formatting the manuscript and putting together the List of Abbreviations, and Ms. Dilnaz Israilova provided administrative assistance. We dedicate this book to our students and all friends of international law, in the hope that they will contribute to building a better and safer world.

Almaty, Kazakhstan	Sergey Sayapin
Almaty, Kazakhstan	Rustam Atadjanov
Pune, India	Umesh Kadam
Derby, UK	Gerhard Kemp
Almaty, Kazakhstan	Nicolás Zambrana-Tévar
Bristol, UK	Noëlle Quénivet
August 2021	

Contents

Part I Protected Values

1 **Humanity** 3
Rustam Atadjanov

2 **Self-determination of Peoples** 27
Boris Kashnikov

3 **The International Rule of Law** 47
Anthony Cullen and Kostiantyn Gorobets

4 **The Common Heritage of Mankind** 67
Victor Alencar Mayer Feitosa Ventura
and Eduardo Cavalcanti de Mello Filho

5 **Human Rights: Between Universalism and Relativism** 93
Anicée Van Engeland

Part II Law

6 **The Use of Force in International Law** 117
Onder Bakircioglu

7 **The UN Security Council: From Preserving State
Sovereignty to Protecting Humanity** 149
Rossana Deplano

8 **UN Security Council Sanctions and International
Peace and Security: Context, Controversies and (Legal)
Challenges** 171
Ben L. Murphy

9 **Peace(keeping) Operations: Soldiers Without Enemies?** 201
Sabine Hassler

xiii

xiv | Contents

10 **The Status of Forces Agreements** 229
Joop Voetelink

11 **International Human Rights Law** 255
Melanie O'Brien

12 **Direct Participation in Hostilities** 277
Christine Byron

13 **The Conduct of Hostilities** 301
Jeroen C. van den Boogaard

14 **Chemical Weapons** 317
Jeroen C. van den Boogaard

15 **Nuclear Weapons** 337
Rustam Atadjanov

16 **Blinding Laser Weapons** 367
Evhen Tsybulenko

17 **Fuel Air Explosive Weapons** 379
Evhen Tsybulenko

18 **Current Issues of Hague Law** 389
Evhen Tsybulenko and Anastassiya Platonova

19 **Military Space Operations** 399
Kubo Mačák

20 **The Protection of the Environment and Natural Resources
in Armed Conflict** 421
Tara Smith

21 **The Protection of Cultural Property in Armed Conflict
and Occupation** 443
Marina Lostal

22 **Transnational and International Criminal Law** 469
Sergey Sayapin

23 **International Anti-corruption Law** 503
Thomas Kruessmann

24 **The Due Diligence Obligations of International
Organisations Engaged in Disaster Management** 527
Katja L. H. Samuel and Silvia Venier

Contents

Part III   Institutions

25   Organization for Security and Co-operation in Europe (OSCE) 555
Ioannis P. Tzivaras

26   European Union (EU): Security, Conflict and Migration 575
Lehte Roots

27   Association of Southeast Asian Nations (ASEAN) 595
Jozef Valuch and Ondrej Hamuľák

28   Collective Security Treaty Organization (CSTO) 609
Sultan Sakhariyev

29   The Extraordinary Chambers in the Courts of Cambodia 619
Olivier Beauvallet and Jeanne-Thérèse Schmit

30   Other "Hybrid" Tribunals 633
Michail Vagias

31   Post-conflict Justice Mechanisms 651
Alison Bisset

32   INTERPOL 673
Evhen Tsybulenko and Sebastian Suarez

33   United Nations Educational, Scientific and Cultural Organization (UNESCO) 693
Umesh Kadam

34   United Nations International Children's Emergency Fund (UNICEF) 719
Nataliia Hendel

35   World Health Organization (WHO) 733
Nataliia Hendel

36   United Nations Development Programme (UNDP) 761
Julio Homem de Siqueira, Andrew G. Mtewa
and Daury César Fabriz

37   The International Red Cross and Red Crescent Movement 779
Heike Spieker

38   Human Rights NGOs and Humanitarian NGOs 813
Nataliia Hendel, Tymur Korotkyi and Roman Yedeliev

Part IV   Challenges

39   Climate Change and Armed Conflict 841
Tara Smith

Contents

40 Poaching and Wildlife Trafficking as Threats to International Peace and Security 861
Federico Dalpane and Maria Baideldinova

41 The Use of Force in Pursuance of the Right to Self-determination 885
Elizabeth Chadwick

42 The African Region's Pushback Against Mercenaries 917
Eki Yemisi Omorogbe

43 International Humanitarian Protection to Disabled and Elderly People in Armed Conflict Zones 941
Julio Homem de Siqueira, Daury César Fabriz
and Junio G. Homem de Siqueira

44 The Politics of International Justice 957
Stefanie Bock and Nicolai Bülte

45 Poverty 981
Evelyne Schmid

Part V   Crimes

46 Genocide 1005
Olivier Beauvallet, Hyuree Kim and Léo Jolivet

47 Crimes Against Humanity 1031
Rustam Atadjanov

48 The Crime of Apartheid 1073
Gerhard Kemp

49 War Crimes 1093
Ewa Sałkiewicz-Munnerlyn and Sergey Sayapin

50 The Crime of Aggression: The Fall of the Supreme International Crime? 1111
Annegret Lucia Hartig

51 Military Ecocide 1139
Peter Hough

52 Religious Extremism 1161
Sherzod Eraliev

53 Human Smuggling and Human Trafficking 1181
Natalia Szablewska

54 Organized Crime 1207
Thomas Kruessmann

Contents   xvii

Part VI Case Studies

55 Cambodia 1229
Natalia Szablewska

56 Myanmar 1257
Melanie O'Brien

57 Northern Cyprus 1285
Ioannis P. Tzivaras

58 Former Yugoslavia 1309
Ioannis P. Tzivaras

**59 Northern Ireland: The Right to Life, Victim Mobilisation,
and the Legacy of Conflict** 1333
Lauren Dempster

60 The "War on Terror" 1359
Rumyana van Ark

**61 Jihad Misplaced for Terrorism: An Overview of the Boko
Haram Crisis from Islamic and International Humanitarian
Law Perspectives** 1389
Muhammad-Basheer A. Ismail

**62 Accountability of Religious Actors for Conflicts Motivated
by Religion** 1421
Nicolás Zambrana-Tévar

**63 The Children vs the Church: Human Rights and the Holy
See in the Sex Abuse Crisis** 1443
Nicolás Zambrana-Tévar

**64 The Role of International Law in the Prevention
and Resolution of Possible Conflicts over Water in Central
Asia: A Comparative Study with Special Reference
to the European Union (EU)** 1473
Hafeni Nashoonga

Editors and Contributors

About the Editors

Sergey Sayapin LLB, LLM, Dr. iur., Ph.D., is Associate Professor and Associate Dean at the School of Law, KIMEP University (Almaty, Kazakhstan). In 2000–2014, he held various posts at the Communication Department of the Regional Delegation of the International Committee of the Red Cross (ICRC) in Central Asia. His current research focuses on Central Asian and post-Soviet approaches to international law, international and comparative criminal law, human rights, and sociology of law. He regularly advises the Central Asian Governments as well as UNODC and the ICRC on international and criminal law and has recently joined Chatham House's expert pool. He is Sub-Editor for Central Asia of the *Encyclopedia of Public International Law in Asia* (Brill, 2021).

Rustam Atadjanov LLB, LLM, Dr. iur., Ph.D., is Assistant Professor of Public and International Law at KIMEP University School of Law (Almaty, Kazakhstan) since 2019 and Director of the Bachelor in International Law Programme. He is Graduate of the Karakalpak State University, Uzbekistan (2003), University of Connecticut School of Law, USA (2006), and University of Hamburg, Faculty of Law, Germany (2018). He formerly worked as Programme Responsible and Legal Adviser at the Regional Delegation of the International Committee of the Red Cross (ICRC) in Central Asia (2007–2014), dealing with international humanitarian law, public international law, and criminal law issues. His areas of expertise and research include public international law, international human rights law, international criminal law, international humanitarian law, theory of law and state, and constitutional law. He authored a monograph entitled *Humanness as a Protected Legal Interest of Crimes against Humanity: Conceptual and Normative Aspects* (T.M.C. ASSER PRESS/Springer, 2019) and published 20 academic and publicist articles, encyclopedic entries, and book reviews in a number of European and Asian academic journals. At KIMEP University's School of Law, he teaches public law and international law-related courses.

Umesh Kadam holds a LLM, M.Phil. (Education) and Ph.D. in International Law from Shivali University, Kolhapur, India, and LLM in International Law from University of London. From 1980 to 1998, he taught international law in various Indian law schools. From 1998 until 2008, he worked for the International Committee of the Red Cross (ICRC) as Regional Legal Adviser for the promotion and implementation of International Humanitarian Law in South Asia, Southeast and East Asia, and East Africa. Currently, he works as Visiting Professor in some Indian law schools. His areas of interest include international humanitarian law, international criminal law, and international migration law.

Gerhard Kemp obtained the BA, LLB, LLM, LLD degrees (Stellenbosch) and the International Legal Studies Certificate (Antwerp). He is Professor of international and transnational criminal justice at the University of Derby in the UK and serves on the executive committee of the Institute for Justice and Reconciliation in Cape Town, South Africa. He has published widely in the fields of international and transnational criminal justice, transitional justice, international humanitarian law, and comparative criminal law. He is Recipient of the Alexander von Humboldt research fellowship.

Nicolás Zambrana-Tévar studied law at the Complutense University in Madrid. He received an LLM degree from the London School of Economics and a Ph.D. from the University of Navarra. He worked as Lawyer for Freshfields Bruckhaus Deringer and Garrigues Abogados. He has been Member of several research groups on Business and Human Rights. He has also published in the field of law and religion in the *Journal of Church and State*, the *Oxford Journal of Law and Religion*, and *Ius Canonicum*.

Dr. Noëlle Quénivet (LLM Nottingham; Ph.D. Essex) is Associate Professor in International Law at the Bristol Law School of UWE (UK) where she has been working since 2006. Prior to that, she was Researcher at the Institute for International Law of Peace and Armed Conflict (Germany). She has extensively published in the field of International Humanitarian Law, International Criminal Law, and more specifically Gender and Children in Armed Conflict.

Contributors

Rustam Atadjanov School of Law, KIMEP University, Almaty, Kazakhstan

Maria Baideldinova School of Law, KIMEP University, Almaty, Kazakhstan

Onder Bakircioglu Leicester Law School, University of Leicester, Leicester, UK

Olivier Beauvallet Supreme Court Chamber, Pre-Trial Chambe, Extraordinary Chambers in the Courts of Cambodia, Phnom Penh, Cambodia

Alison Bisset Faculty of Law, University of Reading, Reading, UK

Editors and Contributors

Stefanie Bock Department of Law, Philipps University Marburg, Marburg, Germany

Christine Byron Cardiff University, Cardiff, Wales, UK

Nicolai Bülte Department of Law, Philipps University Marburg, Marburg, Germany

Eduardo Cavalcanti de Mello Filho Graduate Institute of International and Development Studies, Geneva, Switzerland;
University of Geneva, Geneva, Switzerland

Elizabeth Chadwick (Retired) Nottingham Trent University, Nottingham, UK

Anthony Cullen Middlesex University, London, UK

Federico Dalpane School of Law, KIMEP University, Almaty, Kazakhstan

Julio Homem de Siqueira Institute of Criminal Law Studies Alimena, University of Calabria, Rende, Italy

Junio G. Homem de Siqueira Rio Grande do Norte Federal Justice, Rio Grande do Norte, Brazil

Lauren Dempster School of Law, Queen's University Belfast, Belfast, Northern Ireland, UK

Rossana Deplano University of Leicester, Leicester, UK

Sherzod Eraliev Aleksanteri Institute, University of Helsinki, Helsinki, Finland

Daury César Fabriz Vitoria Law School, Vitoria, Brazil;
Brazilian Academy of Human Rights, Vitoria, Brazil

Kostiantyn Gorobets University of Groningen, Groningen, The Netherlands

Ondrej Hamuľák Faculty of Law, Palacký University Olomouc, Olomouc, Czech Republic;
TalTech Law School, Tallinn, Estonia

Annegret Lucia Hartig University of Hamburg, Hamburg, Germany

Sabine Hassler Bristol Law School, University of the West of England, Bristol, UK

Nataliia Hendel International Law and Comparative Law Department, International Humanitarian University, Odessa, Ukraine

Peter Hough Department of Politics, Middlesex University, London, UK

Muhammad-Basheer A. Ismail School of Law, University of Hull, Hull, England, UK

Léo Jolivet Organised crime, white collar crime and international cooperation division, Office of the Prosecutor, Orléans, France

Umesh Kadam Independent Consultant, Pune, India

Boris Kashnikov National Research University Higher School of Economics, HSE University, Moscow, Russian Federation

Gerhard Kemp Faculty of Law, University of Derby, Derby, United Kingdom; Humboldt Universität zu Berlin, Berlin, Germany

Hyuree Kim Supreme Court Chamber, Pre-Trial Chamber, Phnom Penh, Cambodia

Tymur Korotkyi Department of International Law and Comparative Law, National Aviation University, Kyiv, Ukraine

Thomas Kruessmann King's College London, London, UK; Global Europe Centre, University of Kent, Canterbury, UK

Marina Lostal School of Law, University of Essex, Colchester, UK

Kubo Mačák Law School, University of Exeter, Exeter, UK

Andrew G. Mtewa Malawi University of Science and Technology, Thyolo, Malawi

Ben L. Murphy School of Law and Social Justice, University of Liverpool, Liverpool, UK

Hafeni Nashoonga Independent Legal Consultant, Windhoek, Namibia

Eki Yemisi Omorogbe Law School, University of Leicester, Leicester, UK

Melanie O'Brien University of Western Australia, Perth, Australia

Anastassiya Platonova Tallinn University of Technology, Tallinn, Estonia

Lehte Roots School of Law, Governance and Society, Tallinn University, Tallinn, Estonia

Sultan Sakhariyev KIMEP University School of Law, Almaty, Kazakhstan

Katja L. H. Samuel GSDM, Southampton, UK

Sergey Sayapin School of Law, KIMEP University, Almaty, Kazakhstan

Ewa Sałkiewicz-Munnerlyn Akademia Krakowska AFM, Krakow, Poland

Evelyne Schmid Faculty of Law, Criminal Justice and Public Administration, University of Lausanne, Lausanne, Switzerland

Jeanne-Thérèse Schmit Paris Bar, France

Tara Smith School of Law, Bangor University, Wales, UK

Heike Spieker German Red Cross, Berlin, Germany

Sebastian Suarez Equinord—International Law Counsellors, Tallinn, Estonia

Natalia Szablewska The Open University Law School, Milton Keynes, United Kingdom;
Royal University of Law and Economics, Phnom Penh, Cambodia;
Humanitarian and Development Research Initiative, Western Sydney University, Sydney, Australia

Evhen Tsybulenko Faculty of Law, Tallinn University of Technology, Tallinn, Estonia;
Kyiv International University, Kyiv, Ukraine

Ioannis P. Tzivaras Department of Economics and Management, Open University of Cyprus (OUC), Nicosia, Cyprus

Michail Vagias The Hague University of Applied Sciences, The Hague, The Netherlands

Jozef Valuch Faculty of Law, Comenius University, Bratislava, Slovakia

Rumyana van Ark T.M.C. Asser Instituut, The Hague, The Netherlands;
University of Amsterdam, Amsterdam, The Netherlands

Jeroen C. van den Boogaard Ministry of Foreign Affairs, The Hague, The Netherlands;
University of Amsterdam, Amsterdam, The Netherlands

Anicée Van Engeland Defence Academy of the UK, Shrivenham, Swindon, UK

Silvia Venier GSDM, Southampton, UK;
Scuola Superiore Sant'Anna, Pisa, Italy

Victor Alencar Mayer Feitosa Ventura Brazilian National Agency for Agriculture, João Pessoa, Paraíba, Brazil;
Humberto Bezerra Law Firm LLP, João Pessoa, Brazil;
Center for Political-Strategic Studies of the Brazilian Navy, Rio de Janeiro, Brazil;
Brazilian Institute for the Law of the Sea (BILOS), Belo Horizonte, Brazil

Joop Voetelink Netherlands Defence Academy (NLDA), Breda, The Netherlands

Roman Yedeliev International Law Department, Taras Shevchenko National University of Kyiv, Kyiv, Ukraine

Nicolás Zambrana-Tévar School of Law, KIMEP University, Almaty, Kazakhstan

Abbreviations

AAA	American Anthropological Association
ACHPR	African (Banjul) Charter of Human and Peoples' Rights
ACWG	Working Group on Anti-Corruption
ANC	African National Congress
AP	Additional Protocol
APIM	Association Professionnelle Internationale des Médecins
ARSIWA	Articles on Responsibility of States for Internationally Wrongful Acts
ASA	Association of South East Asia
ASEAN	Association of Southeast Asian Nations
ASP	Assembly of States Parties
AU	African Union
AUC	African Union Commission
BWC	Biological Weapons Convention
CAH	Crime(s) against Humanity
CAJ	Committee on the Administration of Justice
CAR	Central African Republic
CAT	Convention against Torture
CBM	Confidence-building Measures
CCE Statute	Continuing Criminal Enterprise Statute
CCF	Commission for the Control of INTERPOL's Files
CEDAW	Convention on the Elimination of All Forms of Discrimination against Women
CEPPs	Childhood and Early Parenting Principles
CERD	Convention on the Elimination of Racial Discrimination
CERN	European Organization for Nuclear Research
CESCR	Committee on Economic, Social, and Cultural Rights
CFSP	Common Foreign and Security Policy
CHM	Common Heritage of Mankind
CIS	Commonwealth of Independent States

CITES	Convention on International Trade in Endangered Species of Wild Fauna and Flora
CIVCOM	Committee for Civilian Aspects of Crisis Management
CJEU	European Court of Justice
CNR	Council of National Nursing Association Representatives
COPs	Conferences of the Parties
COPUOS	Committee on the Peaceful Uses of Outer Space
CPP	Cambodian People's Party
CR(O)C	Convention on the Rights of the Child
CRPD	Convention on the Rights of Persons with Disabilities
CSCE	Conference on Security and Cooperation in Europe
CSDP	Common Security and Defence Policy
CSTO	Collective Security Treaty Organization
CTA	Central Tracing Agency
CTBT	Comprehensive Nuclear Test Ban Treaty
CTC	Counter Terrorism Committee
CWC	Chemical Weapons Convention
DARIO	Draft Articles on the Responsibility of International Organizations
DCCIT	Draft Comprehensive Convention on International Terrorism
DK	Democratic Kampuchea
DPH	Direct Participation in Hostilities
DRC	Democratic Republic of the Congo
EAC	Extraordinary African Chambers
EC	European Commission
ECCC	Extraordinary Chambers in the Courts of Cambodia
ECHR	European Convention on Human Rights
ECOSOC	United Nations Economic and Social Council
ECtHR	European Court of Human Rights
EDC	European Defence Community
EEAS	European External Action Service
EFA programme	'Education for All' programme
EIAP	Ebola Interim Assessment Panel
EITI	Extractive Industries Transparency Initiative
ENMOD	Convention on the Prohibition of Military or Any Other Hostile Use of Environmental Modification Techniques
ENVSEC	Environment and Security Initiative
EOKA	National Organization of Cypriot Fighters
EPHA	European Public Health Alliance
ESDP	European Security and Defence Policy
ESS	European Security Strategy
EU	European Union
EUMC	Military Committee of the European Union
FAE weapons	Fuel Air Explosive Weapons
FBI	Federal Bureau of Investigation

FCPA	Foreign Corrupt Practices Act
FPA(s)	Framework Partnership Agreement(s)
GA	General Assembly
GAERC	General Affairs and External Relations Council
GC(s)	Geneva Convention(s)
GCPCA	Global Coalition to Protect Education from Attack
GDP	Gross Domestic Product
GNA	Government of National Accord
HCNM	High Commissioner on National Minorities
HDR	Human Development Report
HLRM	High-Level Reporting Mechanism
HRC	Human Rights Council/Human Rights Committee
HRCe	Human Rights Committee
HRW	Human Rights Watch
HVDP	High-Value Detainee programme
HVO	Croatian Defence Council
IAC(s)	International armed conflict(s)
IACHR	Inter-American Convention on Human Rights
IAComHR	Inter-American Commission on Human Rights
IAEA	International Atomic Energy Agency
IARC	International Agency for Research on Cancer
ICC	International Criminal Court
ICCPR	International Covenant on Civil and Political Rights
ICCWC	International Consortium on Combating Wildlife Crime
ICESCR	International Covenant on Economic, Social, and Cultural Rights
ICI	Imperial Chemical Industries
ICIDH	International Classification of Impairments, Disabilities, and Handicaps
ICJ	International Court of Justice
ICL	International Criminal Law
ICN	International Council of Nurses
ICPC	International Criminal Police Commission
ICPR	International Commission for the Protection of the Rhine
ICRC	International Committee of the Red Cross
ICSL	International Conflict and Security Law
ICTR	International Criminal Tribunal for Rwanda
ICTY	International Criminal Tribunal for the Former Yugoslavia
IDP(s)	Internally Displaced Person(s)
IED	Improvised Explosive Device
IFOR	NATO's Implementation Force
IFRC	International Federation of the Red Cross and Red Crescent Societies
IHL	International Humanitarian Law
IHR	International Health Regulations

IHRL	International Human Rights Law
ILA	International Law Association
ILC	International Law Commission
ILO	International Labour Organization
IMT	International Military Tribunal
IMTFE	International Military Tribunal for the Far East
INTERPOL	International Criminal Police Organization
IO(s)	International Organization(s)
IOCTA	Internet Organized Crime Threat Assessment
IOM	International Organization for Migration
IRM	Implementation Review Mechanism
ISA	International Seabed Authority
ISIL	Islamic State of Iraq and the Levant
ISIS	Islamic State of Iraq and Syria
ISU	Implementation Support Unit
JNA	Yugoslav People's Army
JTJ	Jama'at al-Tawhid wal-Jihad
KIA	Kachin Independence Army
KIO	Kachin Independence Organization
KKK	Ku Klux Klan
KNLA	Karen National Liberation Army
KNU	Karen National Union
KR	Khmer Rouge
LNA	Libyan National Army
LoAC	Law of Armed Conflict
LRA	Lord's Resistance Army
MDBs	Multilateral Development Banks
MDGs	Millennium Development Goals
MILAMOS	Manual on the International Law of Military Space Operations
MSF	Médicins Sans Frontières
NAPs	National Adaptation Plans
NATO	North Atlantic Treaty Organization
NCA	Nationwide Ceasefire Agreement
NCB(s)	National Central Bureau(s)
NESG	Nigerian Economic Summit Group
NGO(s)	Non-governmental organization(s)
NHRIs	National Human Rights Institutions
NIAC(s)	Non-international Armed Conflict(s)
NIEO	New International Economic Order
NIO	Northern Ireland Office
NLD	National League for Democracy
NNAs	National Nursing Associations
NP/APN Network	Nurse Practitioner/Advanced Practice Network
NSAG	Non-State Armed Group
NSs	National Red Cross or Red Crescent Societies

NSW	New South Wales
NTC	Nuclear Terrorism Convention, International Convention for the Suppression of Acts of Nuclear Terrorism
OAU	Organization of African Unity
OCCRP	Organized Crime and Corruption Reporting Project
OCG(s)	Organized Criminal Group(s)
ODIHR	Office for Democratic Institutions and Human Rights
OECD	Organization for Economic Cooperation and Development
OHCHR	Office of the High Commissioner for Human Rights
OLAF	European Anti-Fraud Office
OP	Optional Protocol
OPCW	Organization for the Prohibition of Chemical Weapons
OPG	Open Government Partnership
OPONI	Office of the Police Ombudsman for Northern Ireland
OSB	Operation Sovereign Borders
OSCE	Organization for Security and Cooperation in Europe
OTP	Office of the Prosecutor
PAC	Pan Africanist Congress
PCIJ	Permanent Court of International Justice
PESCO	Permanent Structured Cooperation
PMCs	Private Military Companies
POW(s)	Prisoner(s) of War
PRK	People's Republic of Kampuchea
PSC	Political and Security Committee/Private security company
PTBT	Partial Nuclear Test Ban Treaty, Treaty Banning Nuclear Weapon Tests in the Atmosphere, in Outer Space and Under Water
PTC	Pre-Trial Chamber
R2P	Responsibility to Protect
RAF	Royal Air Force
RICO	Racketeer Influenced and Corrupt Organizations Act
RSS	Rashtriya Swayamsevak Sangh
RUSI	Royal United Services Institute for Defence and Security Studies
SAARC	South Asian Association for Regional Cooperation
SADF	South African Defence Force
SAR	International Convention on Maritime Search and Rescue
SAS	Special Air Service
SC	Security Council
SCO	Shanghai Cooperation Organization
SCSL	Special Court for Sierra Leone
SDGs	Sustainable Development Goal(s)
SGBV	Sexual and Gender-based Violence
SIS	Schengen Information System
SMCC	Strengthening Movement Coordination and Cooperation

SMM	Special Monitoring Mission
SOCTA	Serious and Organized Crime Threat Assessment
SOFA	Status of Forces Agreement
SPSC	Special Panels for Serious Crimes
STL	Special Tribunal for Lebanon
TEIA	Transboundary Environmental Impact Assessment
TEU	Treaty on the European Union
TFEU	Treaty on the Functioning of the European Union
TFSC	Turkish Federated State of Northern Cyprus
TMT	Turkish Resistance Organization
TOCTA	Transnational Organized Crime Threat Assessment
TPNW	Treaty on the Prohibition of Nuclear Weapons
TRC	Truth and Reconciliation Commission
TRNC	Turkish Republic of Northern Cyprus
TSK	Turkish Armed Forces
UDHR	Universal Declaration of Human Rights
UK	United Kingdom
UN	United Nations
UN.GIFT	United Nations Global Initiative to Fight Human Trafficking
UNAKRT	United Nations Assistance to Khmer Rouge Trials
UNBRO	United Nations Border Relief Operation
UNCAC	United Nations Convention against Corruption
UNCAT	United Nations Convention against Torture
UNCC	United Nations Compensation Commission
UNCDF	United Nations Capital Development Fund
UNCED	United Nations Conference on the Environment and Development
UNCHE	United Nations Conference on the Human Environment
UNCLOS	United Nations Convention on the Law of the Sea
UNCOPUOS	United Nations Committee on the Peaceful Uses of the Outer Space
UNCRC	United Nations Convention on the Rights of the Child
UNCTED	United Nations Counterterrorism Executive Directorate
UNDAF	United Nations Development Assistance Framework
UNDP	United Nations Development Programme
UNDRD	United Nations Declaration on the Right to Development
UNDS	United Nations Development System
UNEF	United Nations Emergency Force
UNEP	United Nations Environment Programme
UNESCO	United Nations Educational, Scientific and Cultural Organization
UNFCCC	United Nations Framework Convention on Climate Change
UNFICYP	United Nations Peacekeeping Force in Cyprus
UNFPA	United Nations Population Fund
UNGA	United Nations General Assembly

UNGPs	United Nations Guiding Principles on Business and Human Rights
UNHCR	United Nations High Commissioner for Refugees
UNICEF	United Nations International Children's Emergency Fund
UNMIK	United Nations Mission in Kosovo
UNODC	United Nations Office on Drugs and Crime
UNPOs	United Nations Peace Operations
UNPROFOR	United Nations Protection Force
UNSC	United Nations Security Council
UNSDG	United Nations Sustainable Development Group
UNTAC	United Nations Transitional Authority in Cambodia
UNTAET	United Nations Transitional Authority for East Timor
UNTOC	United Nations Convention against Transnational Organized Crime
UNV	United Nations Volunteers
UPR	Universal Periodic Review
US	United States
VCS	Vatican City State
VHP	Vishnu Hindu Parishad
VSS	Victims Support Section
WCESKT	World Commission on the Ethics of Scientific Knowledge and Technology
WCO	World Customs Organization
WHO FCTC	World Health Organization Framework Convention on Tobacco Control
WHO	World Health Organization
WMA	World Medical Association
WMD	Weapons of Mass Destruction
WTO	World Trade Organization
WWI	First World War
WWII	Second World War

Part I
Protected Values

Part I
Protected Values

Chapter 1
Humanity

Rustam Atadjanov

Contents

1.1 Introduction 4
1.2 Brief Observations on the Role of the Concept of Humanity in International Law 6
1.3 Humanity as 'Humanness' and International Criminal Law 8
    1.3.1 Conceptual Aspects: Content and Constituent Elements 9
    1.3.2 Normative Aspects: Protected Legal Interest 10
1.4 Humanness and the Principle of Humanity in International Humanitarian Law 17
1.5 Humanity in International Human Rights Law: Human Dignity as Its Manifestation 20
1.6 Conclusion 22
References 25

Abstract The discussion of values protected by international law will not diminish in significance. Those are quite diverse and heterogeneous as is the extent to which they have been established or clarified in law. If some of them have already been legally well defined, this is not so for others. The concept of humanity belongs to such yet undefined concepts. While it is hard to imagine a more compelling and global idea for appeal in the modern public discourse worldwide than the idea of humanity it is also difficult to find a more ambiguous category. No explicit definition of 'humanity' currently exists in international legal documents or in relevant case-law. The chapter argues that without understanding this basic underlying value many important questions will continue arising on the precise nature of key relevant legal categories in different branches of international law. It then offers several observations on the role of humanity in international law: first, there has been no comprehensive formulation for the concept of humanity, in international law or beyond; second, the notion of humanity found itself constantly reinstated in different civilizations and societies, always carrying with it the same fundamental and basic values, or humanitarian sentiments; third, the concept of humanity does not represent an autonomous source of international law. Subsequently, the chapter discusses the concept (value) of humanity in light of several legal branches constituting an integral part of ICSL: international criminal law, international humanitarian law and international human rights law, with a view to demonstrating the role of humanity for the pertaining legal categories and its relationship with those (e.g., humanity as a central protected

---

R. Atadjanov (✉)
KIMEP University, Almaty, Kazakhstan

© T.M.C. ASSER PRESS and the authors 2022
S. Sayapin et al. (eds.), *International Conflict and Security Law*,
https://doi.org/10.1007/978-94-6265-515-7_1

interest of crimes against humanity at both domestic and universal levels). A comprehensive view of humanity as 'humanness', or status of being human, is offered as instrumental in the understanding of the protective scope of the examined branches of law. In conclusion, a recommendation is made to secure a holistic definition of humanity at the international treaty level.

Keywords Humanity · Humanness · Principle of humanity · Human dignity · Crimes against humanity · International law · International criminal law

1.1 Introduction

The discussion of values and principles protected by law, in particular, international law, will never lose its significance. This is rightly so and needs no specific explanation as legal norms function on behalf of and for the sake of protection of those very values and principles. They are quite diverse and heterogeneous as is the extent to which they have been established or clarified in law: while the concepts of, for example, self-determination, territorial integrity or common heritage of mankind[1] have been recognised as principles of international law under customary law (even if their imperative character is sometimes contested) the case is not so clear for other concepts considered within present textbook's first Part such as the one discussed here. However, the difficulty of properly defining the content of those concepts need not necessarily stop the effort since the law requires as clear and non-ambiguous conceptual formulations as possible.

Moreover, this effort even becomes a critical task if one takes into account the influences of rising populist ideas in the modern world which often (mis-)use or pretend to act on behalf of many of the values introduced in this part of the textbook. In fact, the so-called value-based scrutiny is being now definitely observed including in the judicial practice, for example, in the sphere of international criminal law (ICL).[2] Furthermore, denying the recognition and subsequent protection of global values (or legal goods) loses its meaning and becomes dangerous in the ever-more globalised world.[3]

One of such undefined values is humanity. It is hard to imagine a more compelling and global idea for appeal in the modern public discourse worldwide than the idea of humanity. A broad range of circumstances and situations where humanity may be invoked demonstrates the category's universal and fundamental nature. It permeates each and every societal culture. Thinkings and discussions involving some sort of implied notion of humanity can be traced back to ancient times. And yet, it is also difficult to find a more ambiguous or multifaceted category than the concept of

---

[1] See the subsequent chapters for the discussion of those values in international conflict and security law (ICSL).

[2] Laverty 2018.

[3] For a deserving analysis of how the global legal values are protected in different legal systems see generally Santarelli 2013.

1 Humanity

humanity. This is all the more so striking considering its widespread appearance in legal, political, ethical, social and cultural spheres, expressly or otherwise. A study throughout history shows that there has not been a systematic analysis of the concept applied universally, with a view to suggesting an integral comprehensive interpretation. There are simply too many diverse understandings of humanity.[4]

There are several contemporary definitions of the word in common knowledge. The first, and apparently the most widespread understanding of it is humanity as 'humankind' or 'mankind', i.e., the aggregation of all human beings, as a collectivity. The second definition encompasses the quality of being human, or humanness, or the very human condition itself. These first two figure prominently in various legal scholarly works dealing with international criminal law.[5] The third definition foresees the set of strengths focused on tending others, or humanity as a virtue (benevolence). Yet another meaning represents a combination of natural human characteristics (such as ways of thinking, feeling and acting), or humanity as 'human nature'; this one may serve as a distinguishing characteristic of human beings as opposed to animals.[6]

While this was not the case with the generally used common term of 'humanity' which has several notions embedded under the one umbrella term, no explicit and accepted definition of 'humanity' currently exists in international legal documents or in international or domestic case-law. It appears that since the beginning of the formation of international law, the precise intrinsic meaning of humanity has been left to an intuitive understanding in a big measure conditioned by political, social, cultural, or possibly some other important factors.

Logically, it is not entirely satisfying to accept the idea that 'humanity' cannot be defined using, first of all, legal analytical approaches. To study a concept in a detailed manner does not mean to reject the legal constructions of which the concept forms a part. The question of clear conceptual definitions becomes critical when one tries to analyse what exact role those concepts played in the formation of legal categories including in international law. Without understanding this basic underlying concept many important questions will continue arising on the precise nature of the key relevant legal categories. Correspondingly, several observations as to the role played by idea of humanity in the evolution of international law[7] are first offered in this chapter, before proceeding to the intra-disciplinary analysis of humanity as a protected value of international conflict and security law (ICSL).

For the purposes of such an inclusive legal discipline as ICSL, it would be useful to discuss the concept (value) of humanity in light of several legal branches directly pertinent to ICSL and constituting its integral part. Those would be ICL,[8] international humanitarian law (IHL) and international human rights law (IHRL). In

---

[4] Feldman and Ticktin 2010, at 1–2.

[5] See, e.g., Luban 2004; Bassiouni 2011; May 2005; Werle and Jessberger 2014.

[6] As explained in Beauvallet 2017, at 524–527.

[7] Manske 2003, at 220–221.

[8] While international peace and security undoubtedly constitute a central protected value of ICL (see also Chap. 6 by Onder Bakircioglu), humanity belongs to the list of legal interests to be ensured by ICL, too.

case of the first, the relevant category of law where a properly explained notion of humanity could contribute with a useful conceptual clarification would be crimes against humanity.[9] In the same section an inclusive definition of humanity as 'humanness' will be offered which will also be used for the subsequent analysis. In case of the second discipline, such a category would be the principle of humanity, one of the cornerstone principles upon which IHL is based. And in the third case, the notion of human dignity, the central concept of IHRL could well be served by a comprehensive understanding of humanity as shown in the following sections.

1.2 Brief Observations on the Role of the Concept of Humanity in International Law

It was once suggested that the concepts of humanity and international law "go hand in hand as universal necessities for human existence".[10] A corresponding historical look reveals that this process of mutual 'walk' underwent sometimes very significant ups and downs. It also makes clear that many unresolved questions remain concerning the exact (legal) nature of 'humanity', its content as well as related *legal developments* in different human societies onto which this comprehensive concept have exerted at times a considerable influence. For example, if some recognize 'humanity' expressed through the famous resonating "laws of humanity" as a source of international law,[11] others deny it the important role it plays in international law, for example, in IHL via its principle of humanity.[12] Equally, even if one assumes that the concept of humanity has acquired an increasingly significant meaning and has eventually become a recognized legal concept, in particular through the international prosecutions of war crimes after World War II, the substantive elements of the concept still remain largely unexplained or divergent at best.

The following short observations may be made. First, there has been no comprehensive formulation for the concept of humanity, in international law or beyond. It appears sometimes so multi-faceted that the task of setting a satisfactory definition for the purposes of international law or the law of crimes against humanity in particular becomes very difficult. That is so especially given the subjective nature of the concept. Martens' "laws of humanity" have never been defined in any declarative or binding instrument;[13] instead, it appears that the exercise of their clarification was purposefully avoided, as the history of drafting the Nuremberg Charter reveals.

---

[9] For the discussion of crimes against humanity, see Chap. 47 by Rustam Atadjanov.

[10] Coupland 2001, at 989.

[11] Coupland 2001, at 969–970.

[12] Cooper et al. 2013, at 73.

[13] The Martens Clause reads as follows: "Until a more complete code of the laws of war is issued, the High Contracting Parties think it right to declare that in cases not included in the Regulations adopted by them, populations and belligerents remain under the protection and empire of the principles of international law, as they result from the usages established between civilized nations, from the *laws of humanity*, and the requirements of the public conscience" [emphasis added]. Convention

1 Humanity

Second, the notion of humanity found itself constantly reinstated in different civilizations and societies, under various formulations and containing sometimes starkly differing elements but always carrying with it the same fundamental and basic values, or humanitarian sentiments. Thus viewed, it includes within its purview all the relevant phenomena, i.e., the ancient ideas of *Humanitas* (Ancient Rome) and *Ren* (Ancient China), 'moral' elements of the natural law doctrine, Kantian philosophy, the humanism of the Renaissance intellectuals, and humanitarian considerations pertinent to the law of armed conflict (LoAC).[14] All these principles, doctrines and considerations have developed over several millennia, spanning across continents, covering human conduct both during peace and wartime; they evolved in one same direction.

Third, with respect to the legal nature of the idea of humanity, it turns out that the concept of humanity did not and does not represent the appearance of an autonomous source of international law, distinct from the customary process. The "laws of humanity" have not been recognized as a new and independent legal rule. It would be difficult to refer to 'humanity' either as a general principle of law or as a general principle of international law. Instead, "elementary considerations of humanity" have been carefully viewed as belonging to certain *general and well-recognized principles*, which are even more exacting in peace than in war, and on which state obligations are to be based upon.[15]

In any case, one should not underestimate the significance of 'humanity' for the development of international law. It served (and continues to serve, as is demonstrated by the inclusion of a modified version of the Martens' Clause in the draft Convention on crimes against humanity[16]) as a strong rhetorical code language which, by and in itself, have clearly exerted a strong pull toward normativity. And importantly, the concept of the "laws of humanity" provided a convenient starting point for the thinking behind crimes against humanity and corresponding initiatives during the twentieth century thus positively influencing the dynamic evolution of ICL.

Moreover, the combined progress and increasing interaction of ICL, IHL, IHRL and the law of State responsibility provides evidence of the increasing importance of the concept, or value of humanity partly informed in its content by the so-called "humanitarian considerations". To discard them or to downgrade to mere 'background thinkings' would undermine the significance of protecting the civilian population, be it in peace or war.

(II) with Respect to the Laws and Customs of War on Land (Hague II), 29 July 1899; Convention (IV) Respecting the Laws and Customs of War on Land (Hague IV), 18 October 1907 as reprinted in Schindler and Toman 1996.

[14] The pertaining legal concepts which were affected by or themselves affected the idea of humanity include Roman Law, *ius gentium*, natural law, criminal law and others.

[15] *Corfu Channel Case* (UK vs. Albania), Merits, ICJ Reports 4 (1949), para 22; see also Brownlie 2008, at 27.

[16] Proposed International Convention on the Prevention and Punishment of Crimes Against Humanity, August 2010, Preamble, published in Sadat 2011, at 360.

1.3 Humanity as 'Humanness' and International Criminal Law

The concept of humanity plays a critical role in the substantive ICL,[17] even if it has not been yet positively defined. The category of crimes against humanity forms an integral important part of material ICL where 'humanity' represents the category's central object, in the sense that it constitutes the main protected interest (value) of these crimes. However, the doctrinal treatment of this central element is very uneven, with humanity being interpreted in many different ways in various legal or even interdisciplinary theories purporting to explain crimes against humanity. As for the judicial review, the existing relevant case-law is very scarce; the pertaining cases mostly avoid systematic discussion of humanity as a concept or a value— within or out of the context of crimes against humanity, and include *Einsatzgruppen Case* (Subsequent Proceedings under the Allied Control Council Law № 10)[18] and *Erdemović Case* (The International Criminal Tribunal for the Former Yugoslavia).[19]

According to Renzo,[20] any account of crimes against humanity has to provide an answer to the two main questions: (1) a *conceptual question* of how one should understand the notion of crimes against humanity, and (2) a *normative question* of what exactly justifies the international prosecution of those who commit the crimes.[21] In other words, the first question deals with the nature of crimes against humanity and its attacked object (i.e., "what do we mean when we label certain crimes as 'against humanity'?"). And the second tries to explain on what basis the international community has the right to prosecute and punish crimes against humanity.[22]

Indeed, any comprehensive explanation of crimes against humanity must be able to provide an adequate answer to both of these fundamental questions. These crimes are harmful to human beings' most fundamental interests. Moreover, humanity as a value itself is a fundamental concept. Therefore, to properly describe crimes against humanity the umbrella concept encompassing all their protected interests has to be fundamental and comprehensive, too. A theory based on such holistic conceptual reading can better provide satisfactory answers to the question of how exactly we should understand the notion of crimes against humanity as well as to the question of what justifies the domestic AND international criminalization, prosecution and punishment of these crimes (in turn dividing the answer to the second question into two important parts).

---

[17] For a description of ICL, see Chap. 22 by Sergey Sayapin.

[18] *United States v. Otto Ohlendrof*, reprinted in VI Trials of War Criminals Before the Nuremberg Military Tribunals Under Control Council Law No. 10 (IV) 411 (1950).

[19] *Prosecutor v. Dražen Erdemović* (IT-96-22-T), Sentencing Judgement, 29 November 1996, paras 27–28.

[20] Renzo 2012, at 448.

[21] Ibid.

[22] Ibid.

1.3.1 Conceptual Aspects: Content and Constituent Elements

This theory builds upon the reach and strong content of 'humanity' seen as '*humanness*'. That content consists of several important elements some of which represent already well-known ideas in ICSL while others are considered as belonging to the fields outside of legal discipline. Without taking into account all of them it is difficult to perceive humanness in its entirety, to see it as a whole. This 'whole' comes up as a comprehensive multi-elemented concept which can best describe what comes under threat by the commission of crimes against humanity. To explain how, all the elements need to be systematically considered, and then be taken as one coherent notion.

A logical deconstruction allows us to see that there are main five elements, with each incorporating in itself a sister sub-concept, or sub-concepts. I am in no way offering new or alternative definitions for the elements. Each one of them has been countlessly discussed elsewhere. What follows is a brief description of each constituent elements of humanity (humanness), highlighting the main points which made them relevant for the discussion of the protected interest of crimes against humanity.

1. *Freedom.* Freedom is indispensable for the (inherent) notion of humanity as understood by Kant and defined as follows: "*Freedom is the only one and original right of every man inherent in him by virtue of his humanity, provided it can coexist with the freedom of others, in accordance with one universal law.*"[23]

2. *Human dignity.* The notion of human dignity is fundamental for the whole classical understanding of human rights: "*Firstly, human dignity is the value that explains why all human beings can be said to have human rights: it is in virtue of their intrinsic dignity, however we understand the notion, that human beings are in possession of these rights. Secondly, human dignity constitutes the ultimate value that human rights are supposed to protect. These rights protect human dignity by placing limits on how human beings can be treated.*"[24]

3. *Civilized attitude.* This element can be defined as "*the quality of civilized and cultural behaviour that is inculcated in people by education and training*".[25] it incorporates in itself the following notions: culture, civilization, and education. It can also be said that through this civilized and universally uniting element a connection to common mankind is present.

4. *Humaneness.* Humaneness is best understood as a sentiment of active good will towards mankind.[26] The concept of humaneness lies at the core of so-called "humanitarian considerations" which influenced greatly the development of IHL and its main principles, first of all, its principle of humanity. It includes

---

[23] Translated from German by the author and taken from Gierhake 2005, at 273.

[24] Renzo 2012, at 450.

[25] Bauman 2003, at 2.

[26] Pictet 1979, at 143.

within its purview the following synonymous notions: compassion, empathy, mercy, benevolence, philanthropia and chivalry.

5. *Reason*. Out of all the elements, reason is perhaps most closely connected to human nature—as the fundamental feature which distinguishes us from other, non-human beings. Unlike emotions or feelings, this particular characteristic is the one which allows human beings to live by and employ their comprehensive humanity which is void without reason. All the constituent elements of humanity—even humaneness that is often associated with benevolent feelings rather than mind, are based on reason.

Now, the answer to the conceptual question, i.e., what do we mean when we label certain crimes as 'against humanity', thus would be the following.

The protected interest (value) of crimes against humanity is humanity as humanness. Humanness is a human status, or condition, or quality of being human. It is what makes us human. Crimes against humanity are inhuman acts which attack each and every element of humanity. The inhuman acts include inhumane acts as the former are more serious in their degree of gravity than the latter. The commission of these acts eventually aims at rendering their victims 'inhuman', in the sense of depriving them of that very status. All parts of this status come under attack:

1. the victims' individual freedom is denied;
2. they are deprived of their human dignity;
3. the civilized attitude is negated removing the link between the victims and mankind;
4. the sentiment of active good will, or humaneness, ceases to exist by the commission of inhumane acts, and
5. the victims' human nature in the form of reason is denied as well since those acts do not allow them the status of reasonable creatures anymore.

From this conceptual definition it becomes clear what exact objects are under threat when these international crimes are committed. Some elements represent the values that are fundamental for human beings as such (freedom, human dignity). Others represent the basic foundations for these or other values (humaneness, civilized attitude, reason). While some crimes—either international or domestic, may be said to be encroaching upon one or more of these elements, I maintain that crimes against humanity breach all of them. This breach is inflicted upon the whole humanity—as humanness, or human condition. That is why they are crimes against, precisely, humanity as such.

1.3.2 Normative Aspects: Protected Legal Interest

1.3.2.1 Domestic Level

When it comes to the analysis of concepts relevant to a particular branch of law it is important that such analysis remains consistent with the relevant principles of

1 Humanity

that branch. The concept of crimes against humanity is, first of all, a criminal legal concept. It belongs to the category of crimes against international law and forms a significant part of the material content of ICL. Therefore, it is only logical to apply in the research of this category the fundamental principles of criminal law dealing with justification for crime and punishment.

Now, in order to deal with the normative aspects of humanness in ICL, an important criminal law theory is instrumental. Why use a criminal law doctrine? The answer appears to be quite obvious: the category of crimes against humanity lies as much in the sphere of criminal law as it does in the area of international law.

The theory under the question represents a fundamental principle of criminal law in the continental legal system which has not been yet much invoked in order to try to justify the penalization of international crimes. It is called the *Rechtsgutstheorie*, or the theory of protected legal interest (otherwise known as protected legal good). One of the foundational concepts underpinning the German criminal law system, the *Rechtsgutstheorie* lies at the core of German theory of crime.[27] But for the purposes of present discussion, what is truly important is not the question of which exact domestic legal system is represented by the doctrine but rather *which philosophical construct it employs in order to reach its goals*. The doctrine of protected legal interest uses the social contract theory which is critical for both domestic and international levels of criminalization of crimes against humanity.

According to the classical description of *Rechtsgutstheorie*, the sole function of criminal law is the protection of legal goods and nothing else; thus, anything that does not qualify as a legal good falls outside of the scope of criminal law and cannot be criminalized. In other words, a criminal statute which does not seek to protect a legal good (i.e., interest) is *prima facie* illegitimate.[28]

To be able to apply the doctrine to crimes against humanity's protected interest, one needs to determine whether or not humanity a.k.a. humanness represents a fully valid legal interest, i.e., *Rechtsgut* as such. For that, we have to first define *Rechtsgut*. The classical progressive description of legal good is proposed by Claus Roxin. The reasons for choosing this particular view over the others are, very shortly: its comprehensiveness, normative and progressive nature, value-based foundation, preciseness and clarity. According to Roxin,

> the legal goods are to be understood as all the conditions or purposes necessary for the free development of the individual, the realization of his/her fundamental rights and the functioning of a state system based on these objectives.[29]

The following several constituent elements are discerned from this definition: the legal goods are (1) conditions or (2) purposes (3) that are necessary for (4) the free development of the individual(-s), (5) the realization of his/her fundamental rights, as well as (6) the functioning of a state system based on these objectives. Following the logic of legal analytical argumentation, we now have to establish if

---

[27] Dubber 2005, at 683.

[28] Ibid., at 684.

[29] Roxin 2006, at 16.

and how 'humanity', in its conceptual understanding of *'humanness'*, satisfies these elements.

Humanity as a Condition (element 1). Can we claim that humanity as humanness serves as a condition which must ensure (and so is necessary) that either the individuals freely develop, or that the individuals' basic rights are realized, and/or that the state system, which aims at such development and realization, properly functions? To answer this, we need to look at the specific aims separately.

Free development of the individual (element 4). The answer to the question of how humanity (humanness) is a condition necessary for the free development of individuals can be deduced from two central notions: the free (and full) development of individuals may not be possible without the component of freedom—the fundamental and original albeit not an absolute component. But the freedom itself is inherently present in people because of the element of humanness ("by virtue of his/her humanity"). Freedom represents an indispensable (sub-)element of humanity while without the inherent notion of humanity there can be no truly ensured freedom. Thus, if freedom is necessary for the actual development of one's personality, so is— in a more global sense—humanness. And if the latter is necessary for each individual members of the society in order to develop freely, then it does constitute a condition.

Humanity as a Purpose (element 2). In order to prove that humanness is a necessary legal interest, needed to ensure one of these particular aims, we will now have to look at this element from another perspective, i.e., not from the condition-based point of view but from the purpose-based, or teleological, perspective.

The realization of the individual's fundamental rights (element 5). The second element is another objective for the achievement of which the legal interest is necessary in *Rechtsstaat* (or 'state of law'). To prove the reverse relationship as well, namely, that to realize basic rights would mean to ensure humanness, we need to consider another sub-component of the latter: human dignity. This is because to analyse issues such as the objectives developed by Roxin, one has to apply the human rights law rationale: the realization of fundamental rights is based on and aimed at ensuring dignity.[30]

A useful description of human dignity (also already quoted above) has been offered by a legal philosopher who used it as part of his own explanation of crimes against humanity:

> Firstly, human dignity is the value that explains why all human beings can be said to have human rights: it is in virtue of their intrinsic dignity, however we understand the notion, that human beings are in possession of these rights. Secondly, human dignity constitutes the ultimate value that human rights are supposed to protect. These rights protect human dignity by placing limits on how human beings can be treated.[31]

---

[30] See in general Braarvig et al. 2014. For a discussion of human rights as a protected value under ICSL, see Chap. 5 by Anicée Van Engeland.

[31] Renzo 2012, at 450.

1 Humanity

If human rights aim at protecting dignity as a value (and in fact are based on the need to ensure human dignity), then, by extension, their proper observation, implementation and realization do, too. What is the point of discussing the foundations of human rights if no corresponding realization of those rights is implied?

Now, the concept of dignity is closely connected to the more general notion of humanness. It would be wrong to separate these two, as it would be wrong to separate humanness from its other elements such as freedom or civilized attitude. The conceptual part of the theory of humanness holds that humanity must be viewed as one comprehensive 'umbrella' concept since crimes against humanity attack each and every element of humanity. If so, human dignity is an inseparable component of humanness. It is as fundamental for humanity and human beings as is freedom.

Then, if we agree that the realization of human rights has as its eventual purpose the upholding of human dignity indispensable for those rights (and this is what the leading human rights law instruments say), it does the same with respect to humanity as humanness which incorporates the daughter concept of human dignity. Therefore, humanity represents a 'purpose' as a particular *Rechtsgut*, providing justification for the second objective of Roxin's definition.

Humanity as Both a Condition and a Purpose (elements 1 and 2). While the first two objectives for the achievement of which a legal good is considered necessary in Roxin's description represent the individual dimension of the theory, the last one, i.e. the functioning of a state system based on these objectives, adds a collective dimension to the *Rechtsgut*'s definition. It is essential and it is based on Roxin's liberal understanding of the social contract theory.

The functioning of a state system based on the individuals' free development and realization of their rights (element 6). According to Roxin, the main object of criminal law is to enable individual (citizens) to live together, or co-habit in peace and freedom whilst all constitutionally guaranteed rights are assured.[32] With its role thus understood, the criminal law fits well within Roxin's overall view of the social contract model which he describes in the following way:

> One therefore acts on the hypothetical assumption that all the inhabitants of a certain territory enter into an agreement in which they consign to certain institutions the role of safeguarding their cohabitation. They create an organization – the State – and assign the right to safeguard the citizens by enacting criminal laws and other regulations to it. But since a criminal law restricts the individual in his or her liberty of action, nothing that is not necessary to achieve a peaceful and liberal co-existence may be prohibited.[33]

In order to safeguard the peaceful and liberal cohabitation of its individual subjects, via its available means and system resources (including criminal law), the sovereign, i.e., the State, must clearly realize the purposes, or objectives, which are needed for such cohabitation. Roxin identifies those objectives in line with the logic of the social contract theory (at least the liberal contractual reading of it) as well as the concept of *Rechtsstaat* where the citizens share legally based civil liberties: those

---

[32] Roxin 2006, at 16; Lauterwein 2010, at 9.

[33] Lauterwein 2010, at 9.

objectives include the free development of the individuals of that State and the full realization of their fundamental rights.

What remains is the application of pure logical reasoning. If we accept the first two premises, then for the last element of the definition—which is necessarily based on the first two—both rationales hold no less true. Humanity (humanness) is necessary as a condition and it is necessary as a valid purpose for the State in its pursuit of the two main objectives. Those are in turn needed to fulfil its main task assigned to it by the individuals who entered into a social agreement with that State: to safeguard their peaceful and liberal cohabitation and provide for their essential human rights.

Furthermore, the concept of humanity as a valid *Rechtsgut* satisfies both the critical (limiting) function as well as the methodological function of the doctrine. It does so because, first, it represents a legitimate legal interest which needs to be protected by criminal law whose main task is to ensure a peaceful co-existence of members of the society. Without the humanity such co-existence does not seem plausible. Second, it may not be considered as a simply abstract object of protection but rather as a more global value (similar to international peace and security, or human rights, or the common heritage of mankind) of ICL and law of crimes against humanity; thinking otherwise would put the whole value-based foundation of ICL under a question mark.

Hence, humanity (humanness) does constitute a fully valid and legitimate *Rechtsgut* in its own right and it must be included under the protection of criminal law. But if it is so, then such protection will be foreseen to ensure that the grave transgressions upon humanity such as crimes against humanity are criminalized, prohibited, and if need be—prosecuted and correspondingly punished.

1.3.2.2 International Level

The next imperative issue to be addressed at this stage is to look at the extent to which the social contract theory and the *Rechtsgut* doctrine borrowed from Roxin's liberal view may be exploited with a view to justifying the penalization of crimes against humanity. While the argumentation laid out in Sect. 1.3.2.1 aims at providing such a justification with respect to domestic criminalization, it must also be demonstrated whether it holds true for *international criminalization*. That requires further serious clarification and substantiation in its own right. The main question here would be: whereas the legal interest doctrine based on the social contract theory is related to the State-centred system, how exactly the doctrine can justify the *international repression* of crimes against humanity? Correspondingly, it is important to make clear to whom precisely the *Rechtsgut* of 'humanness' should be attributed. The response will also necessitate the clarification of the meaning of the concept of 'international community' as well as its relation to the notion of 'mankind'.

The following argumentation tries to respond to these critical questions. First of all, one has to keep in mind that the discussion needs to stay on the normative plane, instead of using an empirical, moral, formal, descriptive or other approaches. This is because the social-contract theory—in its contractualist interpretation—can best work in a *normative* international order as the former itself builds upon a system

1 Humanity 15

established on a normative basis. This is not to say that the national community is equal to international; there are certainly important differences. Now, in order to employ the logic of Roxin's *Rechtsgut* doctrine, we need to first envisage whether the contractual basis may be transferred onto the international arena.

In fact, such efforts have been undertaken; they are cumulatively known as "global social contract". Proposed by Rousseau,[34] Kant[35] and Rawls,[36] and based on Grotius's outline of international justice,[37] it describes a system where States replace citizens as the parties to the social contract.[38] The justice component (principles that bind the States) in this system may be seen in terms of international treaties. The legitimacy component (or the legitimate power of the sovereign) can be used to justify the alienation of power to the International Criminal Court or the United Nations.

However, here the differences between national and international come into play. Absence of a sovereign, the governmental system and political features typical to national communities, enforcement mechanisms—these are all the elements not found at the international level. The criminal law of an international order, or ICL, lacks a consolidated punitive power and it has been called "a penal system without a State and a sovereign".[39] But this, in my view, need not be discouraging. Here, the so-called value-based explanation of the world order noted in the chapter can be of help. In order to apply it, the concept of international community has first to be determined.

Accordingly, the following definition of 'international community' could be useful: "*a major group of States bound together by common values*". There are certainly risks inherent in describing this phenomenon since it has often been criticized as mainly a West-oriented body promoting primarily the national interests of politically powerful States. Hence the attempt of a universalist description. International community is NOT to be equated with 'mankind': while the latter represents a collective aggregate of all human beings, the former is the aggregate of States. It strives, or must strive, to represent the whole mankind to which it is connected by the common values.

Now, using this definition, we may deploy it onto the global social contract view of the international order. By entering into agreements (i.e., treaties), the individual members of the international community (i.e., States) create a general collective will in pursuit of common interests and values. Those represent the values protected under international law and include international peace and security, fundamental human rights and many others discussed in the present textbook as well. These values are worthy of being defended by a universal and inter-culturally recognized criminal law. But how? That is where Roxin's theory of *Rechtsgut* may be helpful. The State, in his doctrine, would be replaced by the value-bound 'international community'. This

---

[34] Masters and Kelly 2005, at 48–49.

[35] Kant 1999, at 151.

[36] Rawls 1999, at 4.

[37] In general, Grotius 2005.

[38] For a useful explanation of the theory of global social contract see Neidleman 2012.

[39] Ambos 2013, at 298.

community, just like the State, is based on similar (not all!) imperative objectives, and the legal interests to be protected by the supra-national criminal law are the similar conditions and purposes without which the international realization of the rights' protection is not possible.

The difference between this view and that of some other scholars (such as Ambos[40]) lies in the nature of those values. If they put forward the realization and protection of human rights and human dignity as the central value to be ensured by ICL, the theory of humanness would propose humanity as the basic intrinsic concept denoting the very human status of individuals. In that connotation, it serves as a foundational concept for all the human rights since it incorporates in itself the crucial elements needed for the protection and realization of the rights: freedom, dignity and reason. Because of that intrinsic or inherent nature of humanity, the universal or international normative order based on common values is possible without all those features named above: sovereign, government, legislator, etc. Such a value-based approach links humanity with the idea of a normative international order. It constitutes a value judgement that expresses the legal necessity to punish criminal conduct at the macro level, in order to protect the fundamental legal interest, the *Rechtsgut*. At the same time, it avoids the possible accusations in being too idealistic or utopian: it does not call into picture the radical cosmopolitanism, trying to avoid, instead, the loud rhetoric of world citizenship and *Weltbürgerrecht*; thus the existing system of the Nation-states still holds.

Lastly, the individual should not be lost in the collective: the rights are carried by the individuals, and the peaceful coexistence is to be ensured for natural persons. And it is this individualistic dimension that allows us to trace the attribution of the *Rechtsgut* 'humanness': using its (supra-)national criminal law, the international community has to protect the humanity (as humanness) by way of criminalizing the most serious attacks against it, and it does so for the members of mankind whom it strives to represent. Thus, humanness is not something possessed by the entities like international community or collectivities such as mankind but it is something that inherently belongs in the individual members of the latter.

Based on the foregoing analysis it may be concluded that the concept of humanity as a protected value under ICL can be well clarified if viewed as a comprehensive 'humanness', namely the status or quality of being human. It constitutes a central element of an important material part of ICL, i.e., crimes against humanity, the prohibition of which is aimed at ensuring and restoring this element. The proposed conceptual and normative explanation of humanity (humanness) allows one to understand how one of the significant components of ICSL protects this value and the role it plays even if the concept has yet to be positively defined in law.

---

[40] See Ambos 2013.

1.4 Humanness and the Principle of Humanity in International Humanitarian Law

The principle of humanity has hugely influenced IHL—a set of rules which seek for humanitarian reasons to limit the effects of armed conflict also known as the law of war or the law of armed conflict (LoAC),[41] which itself serves as the basis for the law of war crimes.[42] The concept of humaneness lies at the core of the so-called "humanitarian considerations"[43] informing the key principles of humanitarian law, first of all, its principle of humanity which in turn provides the balancing basis for the other key principles of the law of armed conflict: principles of distinction, military necessity, proportionality and prohibition of unnecessary suffering. The concept of humaneness is properly understood as a sentiment, or attitude, of active good will towards mankind, as offered by Jean Pictet.[44]

The phenomenon of war has accompanied human societies since prehistoric times[45] and is as old as mankind itself—as are rules on how to behave in war. For reasons of space and purpose, the chapter does not dwell on how exactly considerations of humaneness, mercy, etc., shaped out the long evolution of LoAC. It suffices to say that humanitarian considerations have influenced those rules since ancient history, with the result that some significant restraints must be observed even under the extreme conditions of armed conflicts.[46] Thus, the very occurrences of inhumanity and brutality in war have prompted the basic humanistic values to rise and impose limitations on the use of force and violence against civilians.

Similar to the cases of humanity and the "laws of humanity", the principle of humanity has not been explicitly defined in law. So, how best to formulate it for the purposes of the present discussion?

The following working definition could be useful: *"The requirement that each and every individual must be treated humanely and with respect under all circumstances, out of humanitarian considerations and fundamental standards of humanity"*.[47] This definition relies on the concept of humaneness seen in accordance with Pictet's proposal, via the inclusion of "humanitarian considerations". As for "fundamental standards of humanity", an irreducible core of non-derogable humanitarian norms

---

[41] For a useful working definition of IHL, see ICRC Manual 2013, at 13.

[42] See Chap. 49 by Ewa Sałkiewicz Munnerlyn and Sergey Sayapin for an overview of war crimes.

[43] According to Pictet, the term 'humanitarian' characterizes any action beneficent to man. Pictet 1979, at 143. The word denotes 'concerned with or seeking to promote human welfare', see the contemporary English definition in the 'Oxford Dictionaries Online' (UK English), at http://www. oxforddictionaries.com/definition/english/humanitarian (accessed 17 August 2018). Both are in full accord with Pictet's earlier definition of humanity as a sentiment of active goodwill towards mankind. For both terms the ultimate object is the human being.

[44] Pictet 1979, at 143; also Condé 2004, at 110–111.

[45] Sayapin 2014, at 4.

[46] Cooper et al. 2013, at 3.

[47] The project of "fundamental standards of humanity" is well described in Oberleitner 2015, at 64–68.

and human rights to be respected at all times and in all situations,[48] it provides a resonating and underlying value basis to the requirement of humane treatment.[49]

Although the project of "fundamental standards of humanity" (or FSH) understood as core protective rules (both humanitarian and fundamental) for all conflict scenarios and representing a bridge between humanitarian law and human rights law[50] did not eventually succeed the integration of "fundamental standards of humanity" in the definition above makes sense. It serves as a reminder that the main rules and principles which protect individuals during conflict situations and situations of violence stem not only from one particular set of norms but derive from a more inclusive range of minimum standards. Moreover, judging by the listing of those standards in the Turku Declaration itself,[51] it becomes clear that they represent an interplay between various corpora of law including IHL, ICL, IHRL, international refugee law and other relevant branches—which constitute ICSL proper, thus highlighting their comprehensive and inter-disciplinary nature.

As with the case of other positively undefined notions mentioned before, the term 'humanity' within the "fundamental standards of humanity" is nowhere explained in the draft Turku Declaration or any other document relevant to FSH project for that matter.[52] However, it is clear that the principle(-s) of humanity referred to in the Declaration and borrowed from Martens Clause implies in particular humanitarian considerations (or alternatively, considerations of humaneness) if one looks at the text of the Declaration. In turn, the proposed formulation of the principle of humanity relies heavily on one constituent element of the theory of humanness described in the preceding section: the concept of humaneness ('... must be treated humanely...', '...out of humanitarian considerations...'). The question is: how the value of humanity (humanness) is protected under IHL if the principle of humanity enshrines the protection of humaneness? Another way of asking it could be in a negative form: how is 'humanity' injured by the commission of violations of IHL?

Humanitarian considerations have had a tremendous impact on the development of IHL which in turn formed the basis for the law of war crimes (serious violations of IHL which entail direct individual criminal responsibility under international law). The desire to reduce the negative humanitarian consequences of armed conflict, among others, by way of criminally prohibiting their most serious transgressions of the law regulating the conflict flows out from those considerations.[53] A more or less simple answer to the question(-s) posed above can be extrapolated using the example of war crimes.

---

[48] Id., at 66.

[49] This is so even if the eventual adoption of a respective declaration by the UN General Assembly has come to a halt in the mid-1990s. Id., at 66–68.

[50] Id., at 64–66.

[51] United Nations 1991.

[52] Ibid.

[53] The *ad hoc* International Criminal Tribunals have put an emphasis on humanitarian considerations. Boot 2002, at 537.

War crimes represent serious violations of not only the norms of IHL but necessarily and by extension the very principles of humanitarian law contained and enshrined in those norms. Each war crime violates the whole "principle + norm/rule" structure of the treaty and customary provisions of law applicable during the time of armed conflict. Every time a serious violation of LoAC occurs the principle of humanity as informed by the ideas of humaneness and mercy is breached. A criminal violation of any of the above key principles (distinction, military necessity, proportionality and prohibition of unnecessary suffering) results in the cessation of Pictet's sentiment of active good will towards other human beings.

If by violating the norms and rules of IHL crimes committed in the context of armed conflict also breach the key principles ensured by those norms, then values endorsed by those principles are injured, too. As argued above, the principle of humanity is based on the concept of humaneness. Therefore, it is safe to state that one of the values attacked by war crimes is the value of humaneness.[54] But humaneness constitutes an integral element of humanity as 'humanness' as demonstrated in Sect. 1.3.1 (humanness must be seen in its entirety). If so, then it can logically be concluded that the perpetrators of war crimes attack humanity understood as humanness.

Using the reverse logic: by criminalising the serious violations of IHL and reinforcing its principle of humanity and other key principles, the applicable international law ensures the protection of the value of humanity.[55] Here, one can notice a combined protection of law since the category of war crimes based on IHL belongs in the material part of ICL.

Compared to later crystallization of other principles of LoAC, the principle of humanity carries a rather vague nature. Furthermore, it is difficult to disagree with the statement that unlike the other principles, the principle of humanity does not constitute a set of obligations *per se* in written humanitarian law; there is no explicitly overarching and binding norm of humanity telling what one ought to do or not to do during war. It can be said that at the current stage of the development of humanitarian law the principle of humanity has not yet acquired a fully independent and autonomous status as such. It has not been recognized as a full-fledged legal principle of international law, nor does it set up any list of positive obligations written black and white in a binding legal instrument.

However, its role and validity continue to remain crucially important—as a guiding interpretative tool, via Martens Clause's provisional construction, ensuring a proper interpretation of legal rules in otherwise unclear cases in accordance with the principle of humanity, for example, in 'grey' non-regulated areas of law (e.g., in non-international armed conflicts). Moreover, despite the stall of some important humanitarian projects such as FSH, the combined progress and increasing interaction of IHL,

---

[54] For the discussion of other values protected by criminalisation of war crimes, see Werle and Jessberger 2014, at 409, paras 1073–1074.

[55] A keen observation in this regard has been made by one of the human rights researchers: 'Notwithstanding the intricacies of the interplay of human rights and humanitarian law, humanity is always the '*telos*' of all regulatory activities in armed conflict.' Oberleitner 2015, at 233.

ICL, IHRL and the law of State responsibility provides evidence of the increasing importance of the principle of humanity[56] informed by humaneness and humanitarian considerations. It is through these elements that the existing corpus of IHL may be said to be safeguarding and ensuring the protection of humanity.

1.5 Humanity in International Human Rights Law: Human Dignity as Its Manifestation

As with the case of the concept of humanity in international law in general, it has never been defined within the instruments of IHRL.[57] While in other branches of law the concept has direct links with important legal categories, either in material part (crimes against humanity in ICL, negative protection) or in terms of underlying principles (principle of humanity in IHL, positive protection), this is not so for the international law of human rights. There exists no 'right to humanity' or 'right of humanity' or, for example, 'humanity as a fundamental right, or interest, or freedom'. Likewise, 'humanity' is not known to be a 'formally' protected value of IHRL, the branch of public international law which sets forth the international legal norms, rules and principles for the protection of human rights and fundamental freedoms of every individual human being.[58]

Certainly this fact should not be surprising as the whole philosophical idea of human rights is based on another, related concept: the concept of human dignity. It is fundamental first of all for the global idea of human rights and human rights law, and it has been acknowledged at both international treaty level and in many domestic legal systems.[59] Despite its central role as a fundamental protected value of IHRL, human dignity continues to remain a source of much debate and disagreement, not in the least because of the lack of precise universal definition of dignity. As a result, there exists a number of different understandings of the notion.

"A Handbook of International Human Rights Terminology" provides the following authoritative description of human dignity:

> The innate value or worthiness of a human being, existing by the very nature of humanity and recognised as the juridical philosophical basis of all human rights. This human dignity

---

[56] As noted in Brus et al. 2013, at 90.

[57] For a detailed description of IHRL, see Chap. 11 by Melanie O'Brien.

[58] Condé 2004, at 109. These rules and principles establish the legally acceptable and (at least in theory) enforceable minimum standards of conduct for governments to protect the inherent human dignity of individuals. Ibid.

[59] The notion of human dignity is mentioned in numerous domestic constitutions, has been included into major international human rights instruments such as the Universal Declaration of Human Rights, the International Covenant on Civil and Political Rights and many others, and it is often used in relation to the oppressed or vulnerable persons and groups. Fomerand 2014, at 210. For a useful analysis (and listing) of different legal instruments adopted at various levels (international, domestic, regional) incorporating or mentioning in that or another manner the notion of human dignity, see McCrudden 2008.

1 Humanity

is preserved and enhanced by the setting of international human rights standards that limit the state from committing acts or failing to act in such a way as to violate human dignity. Human rights protect human dignity. Every human being possesses human dignity, which is inherent and inalienable. The basis of human rights is often referred to as "inherent human dignity".[60]

This exact but also comprehensive definition represents a viable view on human dignity since it looks at it as *a value*. Indeed, any human being is worthy as such because of human dignity he or she inherently carries, and human rights protect, preserve and enhance this dignity. But formulation above is useful for this chapter, too, as it helps to see the connection between human dignity and 'humanity'. The logical reading allows one to see that what is meant by humanity here appears to be the *status of being human (humanness)* and not *mankind* or *humaneness*. That in turns helps us to recognize the dependence between the two discussed concepts: human dignity is contingent upon the very nature of humanity suggesting that without this intrinsic humanity there would be no human dignity.[61]

All the definitional and doctrinal problems notwithstanding, one aspect of human dignity does not seem to cause much disagreement: dignity as being something inherent or intrinsic to human beings.[62] That all human beings are equal in their inherent dignity does not appear disputed either. The inherent and inalienable nature of dignity is upheld in the above definition, too. The use of the value-based understanding of human dignity is justified. Respect for the inherent worth of every human being means that individuals are not to be treated, or even perceived, as some instruments that serve the will of others.[63] Such a position fully corresponds to the Kantian value-based ethical philosophy starting with the rules of the categorical imperative.

The concept of dignity is closely connected to the more general notion of humanness as discussed in Sect. 1.3.2.1 above. Moreover, that these two ideas are strongly linked is not a new observation. The proponents of influential philosophical schools such as the Kantian ethical philosophy as well as the legal scholars who based their conceptual theories of the most serious violations of human rights law and gravest criminal transgressions on value-based grounds all seem to agree on, or at least silently acknowledge, the said connection.[64] The underlying notion of inherent humanity is as critical for human dignity as it is for the former's other elements, e.g., human freedom. If the most serious human rights breaches deprive their victims of their intrinsic dignity, they equally strip them of their inherent humanness.

---

[60] Condé 2004, at 109. Another explanation of human dignity (by Renzo) is used in Sect. 1.3.1 above as well. The Handbook's definition has been employed in this section thanks to its more comprehensive coverage and at the same time a more detailed approach.

[61] This understanding of the connection between human dignity and humanity is confirmed by other scholars, too. See, for example, Oberleitner who states the following: "The ultimate benchmark for all law is human dignity as expressed in international human rights law and no other possible manifestation of humanity." Oberleitner 2015, at 233.

[62] Also Schachter 1983, at 848–852.

[63] Ibid., p. 849.

[64] See generally Radbruch 1947; Manske 2003; Gierhake 2005; Geras 2011; Renzo 2012.

Then, if we agree that the respect for and realization of human rights has as its eventual purpose the upholding of human dignity indispensable for those rights (and this is what the leading human rights law instruments say), it does the same—albeit more generally, with respect to humanity as humanness which incorporates the daughter concept of human dignity. Therefore, one may safely say that humanity represents an indirectly protected value of IHRL.

1.6 Conclusion

One thing must be remembered when dealing with conceptual issues similar to the present one: a history of the idea is not a history of the word. Many significant factors have contributed to the development of the considerations of humanity pertinent to the evolution of legal theories. Those factors go beyond purely conceptual definitions and include: realities of life and politics in any given society, in addition to legal developments; individual influences including philosophical contributions; social factors; globalization, and international developments. This contextual aspect must always be realised when trying to understand the nature of the concept of humanity.

It needs also to be kept in mind that trying to tackle all problematic aspects of such fundamental and complicated concept as humanity in one small chapter is all but impossible and also not requisite for the purposes of the textbook. Hence the chapter's effort to delineate the most topical issues pertaining to the value of 'humanity' and its role in international law in general and in ICSL in particular.

The foregoing overview and analysis suggested several important conclusions.

First, there has been no comprehensive formulation for the concept of humanity, in international law or beyond. Second, the notion of humanity found itself constantly reinstated in different civilizations and societies, under various formulations and containing sometimes starkly differing elements but always carrying with it the same fundamental values, or humanitarian sentiments. Third, with respect to the legal nature of humanity, it has not been recognized as an independent legal rule, principle of law or as a general principle of international law.

Yet it continues to serve as a strong ethical code language which have exerted a strong pull toward normativity. The concept of the "laws of humanity" provided a convenient starting point for the thinking behind crimes against humanity and corresponding initiatives during the twentieth century hence positively affecting the dynamic evolution of ICL, thus, by extension, international law. The role and influence of the 'humanity', all its ambiguity and subjectivity notwithstanding, may not be exaggerated.

The three legal branches in whose contexts humanity is considered in the chapter have been chosen because different manifestations of humanity and humanitarian considerations have obviously played the most obvious or direct part in the formation of those branches. Be it in peacetime or during armed conflict 'humanity' with its daughter concepts such as humaneness, human dignity, or freedom, constantly figures in the various instruments as well as their scholarly interpretations even if often in different wording and even if not yet positively defined.[65]

As shown in Sect. 1.3, a comprehensive view of 'humanity' is key when one tries to better understand the critical but still unclarified categories in law, such as crimes against humanity. The latter are harmful to human beings' most fundamental interests. Therefore, to describe them the umbrella concept encompassing all those interests has to be fundamental and comprehensive, too. Such a concept avails itself in the form of 'humanity' understood as 'humanness'. It allows to reflect and explain all the elements characteristic for these crimes' protective scope.

The first purpose of the theory of humanness consists in describing and clarifying the protective scope of crimes against humanity and thus contributing to a proper understanding of this category of core crimes. It does so by answering the question "What is humanity?", with the answer being 'humanness'.

In responding to the second—normative—question, i.e., "Why should crimes against humanity be criminalized and prosecuted?", the theory of social contract and German criminal law doctrine of the protected legal interest are instrumental. For the domestic level, the definition of *Rechtsgut* and the ensuing analysis concluded that humanity as humanness represents a fully valid *Rechtsgut* because it is necessary for all the specific objectives on which the social contract-based system is dependent. This legal interest must be protected by criminal law.

With respect to the criminalisation at the universal level, the so-called "global social contract" view of the international order is key. By entering into agreements (treaties), the individual members of the international community (States) create a general collective will in pursuit of common interests and values. These are worthy of being defended by a universally recognized criminal law. The State (as viewed in *Rechtsgutstheorie*) would be replaced by the value-bound 'international community'. This community, just like the State, is based on similar imperative objectives, and the legal interests to be protected by the supra-national criminal law are the similar conditions and purposes without which the international realization of the rights and their protection is not possible. The theory of humanness proposes 'humanity' as a central value to be ensured by ICL. This value-based approach constitutes a value judgement that expresses the legal necessity to punish criminal conduct at the macro level, in order to protect the fundamental legal interest.

This criminalisation should be present in the relevant legal instruments. This is already the case with respect to the Rome Statute; but no legal instrument of the International Criminal Court contains any definition clarifying the concept of humanity. Furthermore, no particular separate treaty specifically on crimes against humanity has so far been adopted. The international efforts led by the UN International Law Commission are underway but not yet concluded.[66] Equally, no comprehensive legal

---

[65] But this is not to say that they have not exerted their influence on other constituent parts of ICSL.

[66] Update information on the work of the International Law Commission on crimes against humanity and the draft Convention may be found at http://legal.un.org/ilc/summaries/7_7.shtml (accessed 17 August 2018).

definition of humanity, either as a protected interest in terms of criminal law, or as a legal principle for the purposes of international law currently exists.

Securing the definition of humanity—as humanness—at international treaty level would turn out instrumental for much-needed criminalizations at the domestic level as well. States and governments would be able to refer to such provisions in the process of implementation of the Rome Statute's substantive part, specifically as concerns crimes against humanity, and become positively affected in favour of opting for their national criminalization and prohibition. Moreover, using the rationale of humanness as a valid legal interest under the liberal view of social contract would contribute to the justification of the laws and codes which implement the dispositions of crimes against humanity.

In IHL, the principle of humanity is based on the concept of humaneness. Therefore, we would not err in maintaining that one of the values attacked by war crimes is the value of humaneness. But humaneness constitutes an integral element of humanity as 'humanness' as demonstrated in Sect. 1.3.1 (humanness must be seen in its entirety). If so, then it can logically be concluded that the perpetrators of war crimes attack humanity understood as humanness. Furthermore, it appears logical to sustain that by criminalizing the serious violations of IHL and reinforcing its principle of humanity and other key principles, the applicable international law ensures the protection of the value of humanity.

As concerns IHRL, 'humanity' is not known to be a 'formally' protected value of the law. However, here, too, a comprehensive understanding of humanity could well serve in the explanation of the notion of human dignity, a central concept and a protected value of IHRL. That is so because of the strong connection between human dignity and 'humanity' and the dependence of the former upon the latter. If the eventual purpose for the realization of human rights is the upholding of human dignity indispensable for those rights, it does the same with respect to humanity as humanness which incorporates the daughter concept of human dignity. Therefore, we may conclude that humanity represents an indirectly protected value of IHRL, too.

It has been stated back in 1995 that it is "the spirit of humanity that gives international law its philosophical foundation".[67] No matter how broadly this spirit may be understood it fully conforms to the undeniable processes which have characterized the evolution of international law during the last several decades in the history of mankind: the so aptly called process of humanization.[68] This is despite the fact that the positive influence of this phenomenon might seem somewhat diminished of late, due to the global negative processes ongoing in the world and affecting, among others, the legal developments: the rise of nationalistic thinking and populist ideas, religious extremism and increasing number of human rights violations.

The overarching concept of humanity is what has been driving the humanization processes. It has informed the development of ICL, and it remains of no lesser significance for other branches of international law such as IHL, IHRL and others.

---

[67] Cited in Brus et al. 2013, at 70.

[68] See Meron 2006.

1 Humanity

The value-based approaches in developing the doctrinal part of the law are justified since they take into account the role of the concepts like humanity and humanitarian considerations in shaping it out.

References

Ambos K (2013) Punishment without a sovereign? The ius puniendi issue of international criminal law: A first contribution towards a consistent theory of international criminal law. 33 Oxford J. Legal Studies 293

Bassiouni M (2011) Crimes against humanity: Historical evolution and contemporary application. Cambridge University Press, Cambridge

Bauman R (2000) Human rights in ancient Rome. Routledge, London/New York

Beauvallet O (2017) Dictionnaire encyclopédique de la justice pénale internationale. Berger-Levrault, Boulogne-Billancourt

Boot M (2002) Genocide, crimes against humanity, war crimes: Nullum crimen sine lege and the subject matter jurisdiction of the International Criminal Court. Intersentia, Antwerp/Oxford/New York

Braarvig J, Brownsword R, Düwell M, Mieth D (2014) The Cambridge handbook of human dignity: Interdisciplinary perspectives. Cambridge University Press, Cambridge

Brownlie I (2008) Principles of public international law, 7th edn. Oxford University Press, Oxford

Brus M, Matthee M, Toebes B (2013) Armed conflict and international law: In search of the human face. T.M.C. Asser Press, The Hague

Condé V (2004) A handbook of international human rights terminology, 2nd edn. University of Nebraska Press, Lincoln

Cooper C, Larsen K, Nystuen G (2013) Searching for a 'principle of humanity' in international humanitarian law. Cambridge University Press, Cambridge

Coupland R (2001) Humanity: What is it and how does it influence international law? Int'l Rev. Red Cross 844:969–989

Dubber M (2005) Theories of crime and punishment in German criminal law. Am. J. Comp. Law LIII(3):679

Feldman I, Ticktin M (2010) In the name of humanity: The government of threat and care. Duke University Press, Durham, London

Fomerand J (2014) Historical dictionary of human rights. Rowman and Littlefield, Lanham

Geras N (2011) Crimes against humanity: Birth of a concept. Manchester University Press, Manchester

Gierhake K (2005) Begründung des Völkerstrafrechts auf der Grundlage der Kantischen Rechtslehre. Duncker and Humblot, Berlin

Grotius H (2005) The rights of war and peace. Liberty Fund, Indianapolis

International Committee of the Red Cross (ICRC) (2013) The domestic implementation of international humanitarian law: A manual. International Committee of the Red Cross https://www.icrc.org/eng/assets/files/publications/icrc-002-4028.pdf Accessed 17 August 2018

Kant I (1999) The metaphysics of morals. Hackett, Indianapolis

Lauterwein C (2010) The limits of criminal law: A comparative analysis of approaches to legal theorizing. Routledge, London/New York

Laverty C (2018) What lies beneath? The turn to values in international criminal legal discourse. https://www.ejiltalk.org/what-lies-beneath-the-turn-to-values-in-international-criminal-legal-discourse/comment-page-1/#comment-257442 Accessed 17 August 2018

Luban D (2004) A theory of crimes against humanity. Yale J. Int'l L. 29:85–167

Manske G (2003) Verbrechen gegen die Menschlichkeit als Verbrechen an der Menschheit: Zu einem zentralen Begriff der Internationalen Strafgerichtsbarkeit. Dunker & Humblot, Berlin

Masters R, Kelly C (2005) The collected writings of Jean-Jacques Rousseau. Vol. 11. Dartmouth College Press, Lebanon, New Hampshire

May L (2005) Crimes against humanity: A normative account. Cambridge University Press, Cambridge

McCrudden C (2008) Human dignity and judicial interpretation of human rights. 19 EJIL 655–724

Meron T (2006) The humanization of international law. Martinus Nijhoff Publishers, Leiden/Boston

Neidleman J (2012) The social contract theory in a global context. E-International Relations (E-IR) http://www.e-ir.info/2012/10/09/the-social-contract-theory-in-a-global-context/ Accessed 17 August 2018

Oberleitner G (2015) Human rights in armed conflict: Law, practice, policy. Cambridge University Press, Cambridge

Pictet J (1979) The fundamental principles of the Red Cross: Commentary. Int'l Rev. Red Cross 19:130–149

Radbruch G (1947) Zur Diskussion über die Verbrechen gegen die Menschlichkeit, in Humanitätsverbrechen und ihre Bestrafung. Sondernummer, Süddeutsche Juristenzeitung-2

Rawls J (1999) The law of peoples. Harvard University Press, Cambridge

Renzo M (2012) Crimes against humanity and the limits of international criminal law. 31(4) Law & Phil. 31(4):443–448

Roxin C (2006) Strafrecht: Allgemeiner Teil. Grundlagen: der Aufbau der Verbrechenslehre, Band 1, 4th edn. C.H. Beck, Munich

Sadat L (2011) Forging a convention for crimes against humanity. Cambridge University Press, Cambridge

Santarelli N (2013) The protection of global legal goods. 13 Anuario Mexicano de Derecho Internacional 405, 405–450

Sayapin S (2014) The crime of aggression in international criminal law: Historical development, comparative analysis and present state. T.M.C. Asser Press, The Hague

Schachter O (1983) Human dignity as a normative concept, 77 Am. J. Int'l L. 4, 848–854

Schindler D, Toman J (1996) Des conflits armés: Recueil des conventions, résolutions et autre documents. Comité international de la Croix-Rouge, Geneva

United Nations (1991) Declaration of Minimum Humanitarian Standards, UN. Doc. E/CN.4/Sub.2/1991/55, reprinted in 31(282) Int'l Rev. Red Cross 330

Werle G, Jessberger F (2014) Principles of international criminal law, 3rd edn. Oxford University Press, Oxford

Rustam Atadjanov LLB, LLM, Dr. iur., Ph.D. is an Assistant Professor of Public and International Law at KIMEP University School of Law (Almaty, Kazakhstan) since 2019, and Director of the Bachelor in International Law Programme. He is a Graduate of the Karakalpak State University, Uzbekistan (2003), University of Connecticut School of Law, USA (2006), and University of Hamburg, Faculty of Law, Germany (2018). Rustam formerly worked as a Programme Responsible and Legal Adviser at the Regional Delegation of the International Committee of the Red Cross (ICRC) in Central Asia (2007–2014), dealing with international humanitarian law, public international law and criminal law issues. His areas of expertise and research include public international law, international human rights law, international criminal law, international humanitarian law, theory of law and state, and constitutional law. Rustam authored a monograph entitled *Humanness as a Protected Legal Interest of Crimes against Humanity: Conceptual and Normative Aspects* (T.M.C. Asser Press/Springer, 2019), and published 20 academic and publicist articles, encyclopedic entries and book reviews in a number of European and Asian academic journals. At KIMEP University's School of Law, Rustam teaches Public Law and International Law-related courses.

Chapter 2
Self-determination of Peoples

Boris Kashnikov

Contents

2.1 Introduction 28
2.2 Self-determination as a Value 29
2.3 Historical Transformations of the Principle and the Mythology
    of Self-determination 32
2.4 Self-determination in Two Post-War Movements 34
2.5 The Third Movement: Self-determination as a Universal Moral Value and the Theories
    of Secession 37
    2.5.1 Choice Theory 37
    2.5.2 The Nationalist Theories 38
    2.5.3 Just Cause Theories 39
2.6 The Critique of the Right to Self-determination and the Possibility of Further
    Developments 40
    2.6.1 What Comprises a People? 41
    2.6.2 The Critique of the Language of Rights 42
    2.6.3 The Return of the Great Powers Rule 43
2.7 Conclusion 43
References 44

Abstract Self-determination of peoples is one of the fundamental principles of contemporary international law and a human right. Nevertheless, it is full of gaps and inconsistencies. In what follows, I give an account of the historical origin of the principle, its normative logic, its development and the problems of practical implementation. The principle simultaneously belongs to three overlapping realms: politics, law and ethics. As a political principle, it serves the interests of the groups seeking security and power. As a legal norm, it guarantees the collective right to determine political status and pursue social and cultural development. As a moral principle, it is supposed to be universal, coherent and promote the common good. Human rights norms can only be valid if they are firmly embedded in corresponding valid moral

---

The research that led to this chapter was carried out within the framework of a research project called "Applied Ethics" and funded by the National Research University Higher School of Economics.

B. Kashnikov (✉)
National Research University Higher School of Economics, HSE University, Moscow, Russian Federation
e-mail: bkashnikov@hse.ru

© T.M.C. ASSER PRESS and the authors 2022
S. Sayapin et al. (eds.), *International Conflict and Security Law*,
https://doi.org/10.1007/978-94-6265-515-7_2

principles or stem from the general and unambiguous moral consensus of international agents. This is not the case with self-determination. It fails dramatically as a moral principle of international relations. This principle invariably succumbs to political whirlwinds, and its moral standing is doubtful. In each of the three movements related to the principle, it progressively revealed itself as unethical and predominantly political. The principle, which was forged in the 20th century to serve the political purposes of either political settlement of post-World War I Europe or dismantling the colonial system after World War II, has outlived its moral validity and should be regarded as a harmless anachronism at best, a harmful atavism at worst.

Keywords self-determination · war · nationalism · ethnic groups · sovereignty · democracy · colonialism

2.1 Introduction

Self-determination is one of the fundamental principles of contemporary international law and one of the collective rights of people aspiring to self-rule. The principle of self-determination is enshrined in the UN Charter and is legalized though the United Nations' Declaration on the Granting of Independence to Colonial Countries and Peoples in 1960: "All peoples have the right to self-determination; by virtue of that right, they freely determine their political status and freely pursue their economic, social and cultural development."[1] The International Covenant on Civil and Political Rights (Article 1) and the International Covenant on Economic, Social, and Cultural Rights (Article 1) adopted by the General Assembly resolution of 1966 promulgate the right of self-determination in identical terms.[2] Many official international documents, including UN resolutions and the decisions of the International Court of Justice, refer either to the principle or to the right of self-determination. Nevertheless, the principle is full of gaps, inconsistencies and ambiguities:

> Under the present legal order, there is no clear basis in law for criticizing an intervener's subjective decision regarding the legitimacy of a group's claim to self-determination or for criticizing its judgment in giving priority in its normative hierarchy to the principle of self-determination over non-intervention and the prohibition of force.[3]

---

[1] General Assembly Resolution 1514 (XV), 14 December 1960.

[2] 1. All peoples have the right of self-determination. By virtue of that right they freely determine their political status and freely pursue their economic, social and cultural development.

2. All peoples may, for their own ends, freely dispose of their natural wealth and resources without prejudice to any obligations arising out of international economic co-operation, based upon the principle of mutual benefit, and international law. In no case may a people be deprived of its own means of subsistence.

3. The States Parties to the present Covenant, including those having responsibility for the administration of Non-Self-Governing and Trust Territories, shall promote the realization of the right of self-determination, and shall respect that right, in conformity with the provisions of the Charter of the United Nations.

[3] Buchheit 1978, p. 37.

2 Self-determination of Peoples

The principle is evidently at loggerheads with another cardinal principle—the principle of the inviolability of the borders of sovereign states. The principle triggers an array of political issues, one of which is the problem of unilateral secession. The Westphalian doctrine, to which we still belong, is founded on sovereign states and may allow self-determination only as a corrective principle, if at all. The self-determination of one people residing on a territory competes with the corresponding self-determination of other people claiming the same territory. It invokes a desire to assert one's identity by means of excluding others. Even if self-determination is short of secession, it may work as a stepping-stone for future outright secession. It is true that self-determination may often prove necessary, and an emerging political state may become a new subject of international law in good standing. If self-determination is a value, it is an ambiguous, unpredictable, jealous and envious value—but one that is often necessary. In what follows, I give a critical analysis of the principle of self-determination. My conclusion is that for many reasons, the principle in its totality has outlived its usefulness. It was forged for the definite political purpose of dismantling the colonial system and, when this purpose was accomplished, it became an anachronism if not an atavism in contemporary international law.

2.2 Self-determination as a Value

Let us compare self-determination with its conceptual siblings. Self-determination of a collective people has an intuitive appeal similar to that of individual self-determination. A mature and reasonable individual is typically a self-determining one, deemed capable of moral freedom. The dominant ideology of liberalism promulgates self-determination as a norm. Liberal man is a Kantian moral individual endowed with autonomous will. At first glance, the principle of self-determination of a people is simply a carbon copy of the same principle writ large. The problem is that the moral status of the collective agent is not similar to the status of the individual agent, and collective decision-making is not similar to individual decision making.[4] The rational moral agency rests in an individual and not in a congregate, even if it is a congregate of saints. The collective moral choice can only perfectly correspond to the choices of individuals of the collective when all the members unanimously agree to the choices of the group, which rarely happens. In social practice, we facilitate collective decision-making by applying some clumsy mutually agreed upon device; usually it is a majority rule. In the majority of cases, social decision-making is accomplished by dire coercion, propaganda and manipulation. This means that there is no strict analogy between individual self-determination and self-determination of the group.

It is evident that the principle of self-determination is at best a hybrid principle, a combustible mix of two diametrically opposite systems of values—liberalism and collectivism. The values of liberalism—individual autonomy, freedom and

---

[4] See Gaertner 2010.

equality—are individualistic to the very core. There is no direct analogy between individual determination and collective determination. If collective self-determination is regarded as a vehicle to promote the core values of liberalism, it cannot be done in any straightforward way. It can only be accomplished in a roundabout fashion that would require a great deal of moral indoctrination, if not outright coercion. Nationalistic collectivism is a completely different set of values that does not necessarily merge with liberalism. The core values of nationalism tend to suppress individual autonomy and freedom. The true value of nationalism is the community with its specific culture, language, and institutions, including a political state itself, which can only flourish as a collective venture. The two systems of values often conflict. Both may come to extremes. Nationalism gives rise to fascism and totalitarianism; liberalism to colourless individualism. As an individualistic principle, self-determination clings to individual autonomy; as a nationalist principle, it is more at home in the principle of collectively stemming from the mysterious "Volksgeist" of Hegelian philosophy and 19th century romanticism.

Self-determination also draws from democracy. It is evident that the surge of democratic state-making in the late 1980s was accompanied by a surge in self-determination. The fact that the two political processes have occurred at the same time raises the question whether the spread of democracy and secessionism are related. Democracy is more or less the right of a people to political freedoms. In Philpott's view, democracy and the rights to self-determination are the same: both derive from internal autonomy:

> The democratic intuition in international relations is that just as self-governing people ought to be unchained from kings, nobles, churches, and ancient customs, self-determining people should be emancipated from outside control—imperial power, colonial authority, Communist domination, self-determination is inextricable from democracy; our ideas commit us to it.[5]

In this conception, democracy itself gives rise to self-determination. David Copp, in a similar vein, assumes that the commitment to democracy is founded on equal respect for persons.[6] At the same time, it is hard to deny that commitment to democracy is consistent with a constraint on self-determination and secession. This is why an open season to secession can hardly strengthen democracy if democracy is not only the majority rule but also reconciliation, dialogue and compromise.

Another concept that has much to do with self-determination is popular sovereignty, often termed "internal self-determination". In fact, self-determination is simply an aspect—perhaps the most significant aspect—of popular sovereignty, which may be called collective freedom, self-rule, general will, etc. Self-determination is about self-rule while collectively sharing similar values. Self-determination as popular sovereignty has a militant nature and often provides just cause for wars and conquests, not to mention terrorism, genocide and displacement. Still, self-determination is of little value if instead of foreign rule, we are getting homemade, domestic, national dictatorship, which is no less grasping and even more

---

[5] Philpott 1995, p. 353.

[6] Copp 1997.

2 Self-determination of Peoples

corrupt. There is every reason to believe that self-determination is only valuable when it promotes people's will to freedom, compatible with popular sovereignty and with freedom of other peoples. This is not a self-evident truth, and it is often claimed that a benevolent national dictator, charismatic leader, or traditional authority provide sufficient legitimation for supreme power, endowed with the power to "force individuals to be free".

Self-determination is enshrined in international law as a human right. In this capacity, it exists alongside other collective rights. These are the collective rights to cultural development, as well as social, political and civil rights of the groups, all of which stem from the inalienable right of a group to exist and a right to resist. These twin rights are not the same and cannot be reduced to individual rights. The group right to exist may be violated without murdering a single individual belonging to the group. As soon as the group is deprived of its culture and modes of expression, of its unique cultural codes as well as the ways of transmission of these codes, the existence of people as collective entities is threatened. At the same time, the emergence of almost all nations was only possible through the subjugation of many local cultural communities, which constituted both actual and potential people. This process usually went hand in hand with the establishment and crystallization of national language and political institutions. Nobody knows what makes one people submissive and another resistant. At the same time, nobody knows exactly what truly makes self-determination. Is it the expansion of national cultures at the expense of local ones, or the resistance of local cultures and the defeat of cultural imperialism? This contradictory right to exist transmits its contradictory nature to the right of self-determination. The right of a group to exist as well as the right for self-determination is the right to exist at the expense of some other group. The principle of self-determination inherits these contradictions of more basic rights and does not resolve its core problems. On the contrary, the right of self-determination prompts the right to resist, even when there is no threat to the right to exist. It triggers suspicion when there is no threat to the right of a group to exist, even when there is in fact no group. Self-determination creates a paranoia, an atmosphere of constant and persistent alert. The right of a group to exist does not need any special pronouncement, if it is truly a group. If the right is violated, it triggers the right to resist violence if necessary.

Another basic conceptual value, which provides a context for a possible understanding of self-determination, is the value of global distributive justice. This is a relatively new approach, stemming from globalism.[7] It is possible to regard sovereignty, emerging from self-determination, as one of the basic goods under global distribution. Some people have it, others do not. Those who do not cast an envious glance on those who do. Even if one does not need it, it is still rational to claim it, for the only purpose of bargaining and trading it for some other basic good. Some are rather indifferent to the goal of obtaining the good that is sovereignty; some are keen on getting it. Who exactly gets this good and who is deprived of it is a matter of both historical chance and decision making by global players. This aspect of self-determination has perhaps

---

[7] Young 2007.

always been present, but it is only now that it is progressively taken into account. If we approach the problem of self-determination in the light of global justice, we adopt a very specific understanding of the value. If it is a good under distribution, it is distributed according to the proper principle of justice, establishing a link between the principle of distribution and the special character traits of the subjects, who may or may not be provided with self-rule. If we regard sovereignty as a basic global good under global distribution, we will have to establish some principles of distribution based on merit, need or equality, and we will have to find an agent responsible for this distribution, which could only be some other sovereign power or international body. We can only hope that the prize of self-determination is distributed only to those who truly deserve it and who may become members of the Westphalian system in good standing. By proclaiming the right of self-determination, we prompt the multiplication of grasping groups, competing for the resources of the planet.

Self-determination is a many-faceted principle, belonging simultaneously to three overlapping realms: the realm of politics, of international law and of morals. These are completely different realms. As a political principle, self-determination serves the purpose of domination and empowerment. It is the product of fear and desire of gaining power over this or that group. As a legal principle, it stems from the consent of states that make international law. Many states emerged due to succession, which they claim to be morally valid for this particular case, but often deny for other cases. Therefore, the final authority on the validity of self-determination could only be universal and unambiguous moral reason. However, self-determination fails as a universal moral principle. It cannot be conceptualized as such without fallacy, and the consequences it triggers are ruinous for international morality. The legal norm of self-determination thus remains predominantly and disproportionally a political principle even if proclaimed as a legal right.

2.3 Historical Transformations of the Principle and the Mythology of Self-determination

The principle of self-determination emerged at the beginning of the 20th century. It was brought to the table by Woodrow Wilson in his 14-point address to the American Congress on the eve of World War I.[8] The principle was not a complete novelty. The seemingly new principle of self-determination had evolved out of an array of existent political ideas. Aristotle deemed collectivity the most important propensity of human nature. "Gregarious animals" as they are, humans flock into political states and form groups.[9] If individuals have value, so must groups have value and be endowed with inalienable rights of primary importance, such as the right to exist and the right to resist. Aquinas came to this conclusion in the 13th century. In the 15th century, the idea that peoples, even if they are not Christians, not only have the right to exist, but

---

[8] Heater 1994, p. 1.

[9] Aristotle 1999.

also to organize themselves into political states that could not be easily dismissed, was promulgated in the writings of Francisco de Vitoria and the Salamanca school of law. The idea that sovereign states are the products of the self-organization and self-protection of peoples was promoted in the writings of Hobbes and Grotius in the early 17th century. According to the Peace of Westphalia (1648), political states were not supposed to interfere in each other's agendas, and international law itself was founded on the will of states that represented different peoples. In the 18th century, the dominant political theory, developed in the writings of Burke and Rousseau, was that the idea that the general will of peoples should be expressed. It was Kant who coined the idea of individual self-determination, and the analogy could be drawn to collective self-determination, although Kant only took into consideration the self-determination of states. The notion of a nation as a collective individual and the actuality of the ethical idea were introduced by Herder and Hegel. So, we can see that the pieces of the mosaic from which self-determination is constructed existed long before the term itself was coined. At a certain moment, a special political project plucked the notion of self-determination from the boiling cauldron of concepts and threw it on the table of political negotiations, where it still lives on; but there is no guarantee that a different political wind will not blow it back to where it came from in the course of time.

The first paradigmatic case of obtaining self-rule for people, which provided the point of departure for what was later called self-determination, was the case of America breaking away from the British Empire in the 18th century, although the American Revolution was never called self-determination. It was rather an exercise of a much more fundamental right to exist. This included the moral right to exist as a free nation and to resist unjust tyranny (real or imagined) by the English crown. It was a case of unilateral secession, triggered by the growing economic burden imposed by the British Empire and little political self-rule ("taxation without representation"). It was a bloody and violent act, not only because of the subsequent war with the British, but also because of the harassment, expulsion and displacement of the so-called "legalists" (the people who wanted to remain loyal to the British). At the same time, the subjective and frivolous nature of self-determination was soon revealed. When the Confederate States of America decided to secede on the same terms from the United States of America, they were prevented by the sword.[10] Another foundation for future self-determination was laid down by the French revolution, which not only claimed to be based on the idea of general will, but which engaged in referenda that were used as a yard stick to measure the people's will to join revolutionary France.[11] The referenda, of course, were ill arranged and to a great extent manipulated, because the revolutionaries knew perfectly well what the people's will was even without holding a referendum, and of course those provinces and peoples who did not demonstrate the desire for self-determination in the right direction, were swiftly "forced to be free". This kind of violence is still demonstrated whenever it comes to the practical application of self-determination.

---

[10] Buchanan 1991.

[11] Heater 1994, pp. 4–10.

2.4 Self-determination in Two Post-War Movements

As mentioned above, the principle of national self-determination surfaced within international legal discourse only in the 20th century. Before that, international law simply equated self-determination with sovereignty or secession. All in all, there are two stages in the implementation of the principle of self-determination in international relations, which are in fact worlds apart. At each of the stages, the principle adopted a completely different meaning, and the common name is deceptive. Self-determination never performed the role of a universal moral principle, although it might be causing such an illusion.[12] It was originally forged as a political and even pragmatic principle to meet the political problem of dealing with the empires defeated in World War I. In what follows, I will give an account of the two acts of the drama that was self-determination in the 20th century. Self-determination was proclaimed as the working principle of the new world order, which Woodrow Wilson suggested for the Paris Peace Accord of 1919. There is no doubt that the principle itself stemmed from the bringing together of the mythology of the American Revolution and American philosophical pragmatism. All peoples were supposed to choose the sovereignty under which they should live, and the world itself should be made safe for every peace-loving nation. These nations would create their own autonomous states on the ruins of former empires. The principle implemented the idea that state boundaries should respect the self-determining identities of nations.

Not all nations, only "great nations", were taken into account, which is, of course, a shaky criterion, and the peace accord had winners and losers. The Poles were formally the winners; they managed to build up their own state at the expense of other nations. There is every indication that this favour was promulgated by the strong Polish lobby in the US. In turn, Silesia was partitioned in a similar manner as Poland itself had been in the 18th century. The Paris Peace Conference and its aftermath gave birth to new states. New state boundaries emerged, and the political entities, old and new, were now supposed to respect the self-determining identities of liberated nations. In reality, it was little more than a radical political redistribution of sovereign power wrapped up in political demagogy, carried out by the winners of World War I and on their behalf. It is necessary to admit that even though a limited amount of political self-determination was generally regarded as excessive and the principle was defeated by other delegates to the Paris Peace Conference as a legal principle of international law, it sounded too dangerous for the sovereign states. As for the principle of self-determination, it was restricted to Europe and to peoples deemed to be sufficiently developed to merit recognition. The system, validating the colonization of "peuple sauvage," remained untouched until the end of the next World War. Even those closest to Wilson regarded the principle as "loaded with dynamite".

Another possible formulation of the principle of self-determination was proclaimed simultaneously by Vladimir Lenin in his famous article, "On the Right

---

[12] The major feature of the moral principle is universalizability, which is consistency in terms of subject, application and agent of the principle. The principle cannot be regarded as ethical if it is inconsistent by its very nature. See Fotion 2014, p. 276.

of Peoples to Self-Determination". This version was much more radical and presupposed total and complete free self-determination of political and social status for all peoples irrespective of their geographical location or current political status. Of course, this proclamation can only be regarded as part of the Bolshevik agenda of the "World Revolution". It equalled the total annihilation of the current world order and the destruction of the bourgeois political states. Lenin's project was consistent, perfectly logical, and at the same time totally destructive. Lenin and the Bolsheviks did not care about the existence of political states. On the contrary, the complete devastation of the bourgeois states was on the agenda, because communism does not need political states and is above politics:

> The result may also be anarchy, but a kind of capitalist, not socialist, anarchy in the global setting. The proletariat is opposed to such practicality. While recognizing equality and equal rights to a national state, it values above all and places foremost the alliance of the proletarians of all nations, and assesses any national demand, any national separation, from the viewpoint of the working-class struggle.[13]

The second coming of the principle in the new attire took place after World War II. This time it was much more radical and was stemming directly from the Leninist version of self-determination. The principle emerged as an attempt to decolonize, which was triggered by massive national-liberation movements and enjoyed support from the Soviet Union. Soon after the war and the UN Charter's enactment, international law performed a reversal on the legal status of colonialism. What happened was a transition from a political principle of self-determination into a legal right of self-determination that coincided with international law's decolonization project. Self-determination now meant something different. The colonized peoples acquired the right to determine their political fate—at the expense of the former colony. In this capacity, the principle of self-determination was enshrined in the United Nations Charter and subsequent documents. One of the proclaimed purposes of the UN was "to develop friendly relations among nations based on respect for the principle of equal rights and self-determination of peoples". The 1960 Declaration on the Granting of Independence to Colonial Countries and Peoples stated that all peoples possess the right of self-determination and declares that alien subjugation, domination and exploitation constitute violations of fundamental human rights. The declaration was, of course, inconsistent. It stated at the same time that "any attempt aimed at the partial or total disruption of the national unities and the territorial integrity of a country is incompatible with the Purposes and Principles of the Charter of the United Nations." The principle of self-determination was espoused further in the Covenant on Economic, Social, and Cultural Rights and the Covenant on Civil and Political Rights of 1966. Article 1 of both Covenants provided that all peoples have the right to self-determination. This time, the principle adopted evident decolonization overtones and had some bite.

Outside the decolonization paradigm, the existence of any general self-determination rights, not to mention the right to secession, was not considered. Only colonized peoples acquired the right to form an independent state or to remain a part

---

[13] Lenin 1951.

of their existing colonizer or to associate with another state. The so-called "salt water test" was introduced, according to which the territory endowed with the right of self-determination was supposed to be separated from the host country by an ocean and be linguistically and culturally different from the metropolis. The second movement of self-determination had little relevance to the first movement. This time, it was not about political rearrangement of sovereignty on winner's terms. Self-determination was imposed exclusively on the former colonies by the mighty national liberation movements. Still, the scope and meaning of self-determination remained as narrow and as egotistical as it was before. Self-determination was supposed to take place within the administrative borders of the former colonies, which had little to do with ethnic divisions.[14] The new states stubbornly clung to their artificial borders and were ready to subdue national liberation movements within it. The right to self-determination could only be exercised within the boundaries established by the colonial power, and thus in a way of paradox, the self-determination entity was defined by colonialism itself. The principle could be used to both promote the emancipation of some and confirm the subjugation of others.

The colonial liberation was more or less complete by the 1970s. Few formal colonies remain in the world. The salt-water colonialism and closely analogous cases of conquest no longer exist. Does that mean that the right of self-determination should be dismissed? Can we still apply the principle to settle some other problems? Some scholars are confident:

> There is still every reason to believe that classical self-determination, narrowly conceived in the colonial context, cannot contribute to the resolution of the presently ongoing self-determination conflicts around the word.[15]

Still, the genie of self-determination has already left the bottle. As Antonio Cassese holds, "[t]o explore self-determination… is also a way of opening a veritable Pandora's Box" because "[i]n every corner of the globe peoples are claiming the right to self-determination."[16] The problem of self-determination became acute by the end of 1980s due to the demise of the Soviet Union and the surge of democratic state-makings, accompanied by a wave of state-breakings. As could be expected, the rush for self-determination was accompanied by a war of self-determination. In the words of Moore:

> Between 1947 and 1991, only one instance of secession occurred (Bangladesh). In that period, the superpowers were committed to upholding existing state boundaries, and they encouraged the development of international law and practice in which borders were viewed as permanent—non-negotiable—features of the international state system. Since 1989, there have been at least a dozen secessionist attempts, and more than twenty-five new states have been formed out of fragments of old ones. Since 1991, however, numerous multinational states have disintegrated along national lines—the Soviet Union, Yugoslavia, Czechoslovakia, Ethiopia and the process may not have exhausted itself yet, as many of the successor states are as multinational as the states they left behind.[17]

---

[14] The principle is known as *uti possidetis juris*.

[15] Weller 2008, p. 9.

[16] Cassese 1995, p. 1.

[17] Moore 1998, p. 1.

2 Self-determination of Peoples

The question of to what extent, if at all, the principle of self-determination is applicable to non-colonial settings and unilateral secessions remains actual and needs practical solutions.

2.5 The Third Movement: Self-determination as a Universal Moral Value and the Theories of Secession

The third movement of self-determination was started in earnest in the 1990s, and it was worlds apart from the first two movements. This time, self-determination came into play as a presumably moral principle, regulating the right of secession. The death knell to the decolonization illusions of the right to self-determination sounded with the Yugoslavian debacle of the 1990s and the secessionist wars that followed. Self-determination must be forged anew as a moral principle outside of the scope of 'salt-water colonialism'. Only in this case may self-determination have any chance to remain as a legal right beyond the decolonization paradigm. It is no wonder that, since the 1990s, there has been a resurgence of ethical theories for justified secession. Broad rubrics of the types of ethical theories of secession that have been crystallized to date are *choice theories, national self-determination theories,* and *just-cause theories.* Most disagreements between the theories are about which groups possess the right to secede, under what circumstances, and who is to decide. The theories are raising important strategic, sociological and legal issues, as well as ethical questions, and paving the way for political and legal rearrangements globally.

2.5.1 Choice Theory

Choice theories typically require that territorially concentrated groups may secede from the political state, if they so desire.[18] The majority vote is sufficient for the secession, and there is no requirement that the group have a historical right to the territory or be a nation. Different choice theorists may develop different prerequisites for secessions. By and large, choice theory is an extension of the democratic theory, and democracy is closely related to the right to secession. They are both founded on the idea of individual decision making about the institutional structure of society. In the words of Kei Nielsen:

> The right of secession should be treated like the right to a no-fault divorce […] No prior or imminent injustice need be shown in either case. If the parties want to split in either case, they have the right to split provided certain harms (not all harms) do not accrue to the other party. If Mary wishes to split with Michael she should have the right to do so provided there is a fair settlement of their mutual properties, adequate provision and care of any children

---

[18] See Philpott 1995; Wellman 2005; Gauthier 1994.

they may have is ensured, and the like. Similarly, if Quebec wishes to split with Canada it should have the right to do so provided a fair settlement of mutual assets and debts is made and the like.[19]

This theory makes an easy target for criticism. It ignores the fact that most secessionist movements do not arise out of the blue but are propelled by nationally mobilized groups and stem from a long history of ethnic grievances. In addition, this theory fails to explain and justify the territorial claim that these groups make. Land is not simply a territory but the location of sacred places, tombs of ancestors, and glorious battle sites. Besides, the practical consequences of the implementation of these theories are indeed ruinous to both democracy and self-determination. This theory is the most Leninist of all. Buchanan holds:

> If a plebiscitary right to secede were recognized (either as a matter of constitutional or international law or by a widespread moral consensus), a territorially concentrated minority could use the threat of secession as a strategic bargaining tool.[20]

One more consequence to consider is the potential for blackmail. Norman holds:

> The most serious and commonly recurring objections include doubts about the usefulness of consent to justify the legitimacy or illegitimacy of states; doubts that the value of individual autonomy is necessarily enhanced by having sweeping powers to decide collectively with others the frontiers of one's state; concerns about the undemocratic and unjust consequences of secession (i.e. that the right to secede would corrupt democratic politics by allowing pseudo-secessionists to make threats in order to receive preferential treatment); concerns about the fate of minorities within the seceding regions; and perhaps most importantly, concerns about secessionist anarchy in a world of legalized no-fault secession, which would be to the detriment of liberal-democratic values.[21]

2.5.2 The Nationalist Theories

The nationalist theories hold that any territorially concentrated group may secede by virtue of being a national community.[22] David Miller is perhaps the most eloquent contemporary promoter of this theory.

> Let me say, very briefly, what I take a nation to be: a group of people who recognize one another as belonging to the same community, who acknowledge special obligations to one another, and who aspire to political autonomy—this by virtue of characteristics that they believe they share, typically a common history, attachment to a geographical place, and a public culture that differentiates them from their neighbours.[23]

According to this theory, the right to self-determination does not belong to individuals even if they organize themselves into a group, but is held collectively by

---

[19] Nielsen 1993, p. 365.

[20] Buchanan 1998, p. 21.

[21] Norman 1998, p. 38.

[22] Margalit and Raz 1990; Miller 1995; Nielsen 1998; Tamir 1993.

[23] Miller 1998, p. 65.

2 Self-determination of Peoples

nations. In this regard, the theory is communitarian, rather than individualistic. At the same time, a nation must be politically autonomous to be able to implement justice and protect culture. Nielsen toes the line claiming that nationality is instrumentally important to individual self-identity and human flourishing.[24] According to Tamir, the principle of nationality protects us from excessive globalization. This conception has the merit of acknowledging that nationalism underlies most secessionist movements and attempts to give ethical significance to this fact, but it does not escape thorough criticism.

Gelner provides a pragmatic criticism of this theory, positing that since there are at least 5000 ethnic groups across the globe that may have a right to secede according to nationalist theory, if they all decide to claim a political state it would result in calamity.[25] There may also be endless secessions within secessions. Besides, it is not only the nation state with matters. Kedourie, in his indictment of nationalism, holds:

> The only criterion capable of public defence is whether the new rulers are less corrupt and grasping, or more just and merciful, or whether there is no change at all, but the corruption, the greed, and the tyranny merely find victims other than those of the departed rulers.[26]

Further, nationally mobilized groups may be eager to apply violence, and the nationalistic conception does not take seriously the possibility of national conflict. The principle of national self-determination is unproblematic only in ideal cases. In addition, these theories are rather anachronistic; they are moored to romantic notions of popular sovereignty and the desire to shake off foreign domination—real or imaginary.[27]

2.5.3 Just Cause Theories

The just cause (or remedial) theory holds that the right to secede arises only in response to serious and persisting grievances.[28] Just-cause theorists argue that the right to secession is analogous to a just cause principle of just war theory. Different just-cause theorists focus on different kinds of injustices. One advantage of this theory is that it suggests a strong connection between injustice and the right to self-determination.

> In my version of the remedial right only position, injustices capable of generating a right to secede consist of persistent violations of human rights, including the right to participate in democratic governance, and the unjust taking of the territory in question, if that territory previously was a legitimate state or a portion of one (in which case secession is simply the taking back of what was unjustly taken).[29]

---

[24] Nielsen 1998.

[25] Gellner 1983.

[26] Kedourie 1960, p. 140.

[27] Teson 2016.

[28] Buchanan 1998, p. 25.

[29] Ibid.

The list of flaws in this theory is no less long. One evident fault is the subjectivity of the claims to justice. In practice, it depends on the group's choices of what to consider injustice and technically may resemble choice theories. Besides, the claims of justice may be blown out of proportion. More often than not, people exaggerate their grievances and even provoke governmental repressions for the only reason of calling in international armed assistance, like it happened in Kosovo in 1999. Another problem with this theory is that many secessionist movements are not primarily about justice or injustice and are not seeking remedy. People want to be free and often claim sovereignty for no other reason. The very dynamic of the nationalist movement, which is usually behind secessionist claims, is normally above any claims of justice. What is at stake is cultural and especially national identity. Justice is not the primary factor in understanding the quest to secede nor is an understanding of the massive movement to decolonize in the 1960s. In any case, the just cause theory tends to deal with the right to exist rather than with the right to self-determination. The international community may protect the group from genocide by endowing it with sovereignty, even if it has no desire for self-determination. This mode of reasoning puts the cart of self-determination before the horse of people, who are usually supposed to move it, not the other way around.

All three of these theories deserve more detailed consideration than can be provided here. The criticism they pose on each other is convincing. It is very easy to merge these three theories into one metatheory. If there is a group of people dwelling on a certain territory, they may share a sense of justice stemming from some grievances. As soon as they forge a common conception of justice, they may be regarded as a nation, since a nation is a subjective construction based on a sense of community. Being a nation, they will be even more susceptible to a feeling of humiliation and thus will easily submit to the propaganda of their elite that they are being mistreated and deprived of their rights. It is true that some of the newest theories of succession are extremely sophisticated.[30] Nevertheless, it does not make them less naïve. They all share one grand illusion, very typical of the 1990s—the illusion of a benevolent sole superpower who will apply one of the three theories in moral rearrangement of the world order, very similar to what Wilson once did. All these theories are forged to facilitate the rearrangement of the international order on the terms of victors in the Cold War.

2.6 The Critique of the Right to Self-determination and the Possibility of Further Developments

What is really an issue is to find a moral principle that could govern unilateral secession. The principle of self-determination as we know it is a child of the early 20th century at best, with its romanticism and the myth of popular sovereignty. The principle and a corresponding right can provide little support in guiding the justified

---

[30] See Wellman 2005.

succession. Desperate results of self-determination struggle to have demonstrated the tremendous difficulty of applying this theory to real-life situations. The problem of finding a firm ethical background to both political principles and the legal right to self-determination has so far failed dramatically. In what follows, I will try to find the key reasons for that. I also want to shatter some common illusions, firmly embedded in the current theories of just secession. I will refer to these illusions as the illusion of the subject, the illusion of rights, and the illusion of the agent. I do not see a way to overcome these predicaments in the near future, and these predicaments make the principle of self-determination in its present formulation redundant at best and harmful at worst.

2.6.1 What Comprises a People?

The first illusion, which besets the theories of justified secession and the conceptions of self-determination in more general terms, is the indeterminacy of the concept of *a people*. There is no answer to the question of what really makes a people. To establish secession as an effective right, it is necessary to reach a scientific and objective definition of its bearers, the people, since there is no clear definition of people in international law. Jennings holds:

> On the surface, it seemed reasonable: let the people decide. It was in fact ridiculous because the people cannot decide until somebody decides who is a people.[31]

One can find at least three versions of what may be referred to as a people. These three versions bluntly correspond to the three major movements related to the principle of self-determination mentioned above. First, by people we may understand politically mobilized ethnic groups residing in historic or ancestral territory. As the second option, we may understand people as the citizens of political units, including those who happen to live within the boundaries drawn by the colonial power. In this case, we may be less interested in ethnicity and more interested in administrative borders. This understanding of peoples was common to the second movement. Third, we may put a stress on territorial belonging of the group sharing a conception of justice. The conception that people are in fact any collection of individuals residing in a certain territory and enjoying the feeling of mutual recognition is promulgated by choice theory of secession. Almost all these theories in one way or another share the major premises developed in the influential article by Margalit and Raz. They provide a list of six points as a set of character traits of the people, entitled as 'encompassing community'.[32] I do not consider this finding invigorating, since the core of these traits is still a subjective sense of belonging or mutual recognition. Even with this thorough explication, the net is cast too wide. The encompassing group is again an attempt to run before one can walk. One possible way to deal

---

[31] Jennings 1956, p. 56.
[32] Margalit and Raz 1990, p. 87.

with the problem of people is to deny the necessity of the existence of people as the founding act of self-determination. It is possible to claim that it is not people who seek self-determination, but it is through self-determination that a group can emerge as people. Frederic Megret rightfully claims: "Self-determination, therefore, does not as much flow from the existence of a people as it is its founding act."[33] The people become people through the sequence of acts of self-determination and not the other way around. As a result, sovereignty must be deserved and self-determination is not an inalienable right, which one possesses simply in light of being a people. The way to deserve is by treating others morally, recognizing individual rights, and proving that the group may create a political state in good standing in a community of respectful states.

2.6.2 The Critique of the Language of Rights

The second common illusion of self-determination is related to the means-end dialectic of self-determination. What are the means available for the overarching cause of self-determination? Is it terrorism, war or negotiations? The problem remains unresolved. The core of this problem is the problem of the very language of rights. The language of rights itself is a wrong language to proceed with when discussing secession. Whenever one approaches someone with a claim of rights, it is usually a language of unilateral demand and not of compromise of mutual recognition, including the construction of identity. The people searching for their identity may find it by way of constructive dialogue, during which they can prove and assure the international community that they are not only willing but also deserving of self-determination. They deserve it because they are capable of honouring the needs and legitimate demands of other people as well. Strictly speaking, the language of rights, which suited the era of colonial domination, does not really correspond to the current situation, not only because there are no more colonies and very few conquered or oppressed people, but because the other people may have similar rights and a similar claim to the same territory.[34] It may be much more productive simply to drop the language of rights and adopt the language of duty or responsibility. Self-determination in the current situation is more related to the obligation of a group to take additional moral responsibility to uphold the global order. In this respect, self-determination should not be regarded as the desire of the elite to grab the territory and resources, but as a collective obligation to ameliorate the world. Probably, if self-determination adopts this meaning, there will be very few volunteers to proceed with it, and the term 'self-determination' will lose its contemporary attractiveness.

---

[33] Megret 2016.
[34] Beiner 1998, pp. 158–181.

2.6.3 The Return of the Great Powers Rule

The third illusion is the illusion of agency. The theories of secession remain by and large ideal moral theories and, to a very small extent, institutional moral theories. They tend to ignore the agent providing self-determination or making it possible. At the same time, there is always some specific agent of self-determination at each of the three movements. The first movement was propelled by the political states—the winners of World War I. The second movement was promoted by the Soviet Union and national-liberation movements worldwide. What may be regarded as the third movement, secessionism, which started in earnest in the 1990s, coincided with the initial illusion of universal international morality, promoted by a benevolent sole superpower—the United States of America—and it was the major agent of both self-determination and secession in the 1990s. However, the illusions are shattered. The sobering reality, which progressively crystallizes, is the reality of a multipolar world of diverse great powers rule. The obliteration of legal international norms by the great powers is a reality. It happened in Kosovo, it happened in Crimea, and it is happening everywhere. Any people seeking self-determination will have to obtain the great powers mandate for their cause. Milena Steiro refers to this process as the return of the great powers rule:

> The great powers' rule has replaced normative international law in the field of self-determination; politics have effaced law. What may remain of the theory of self-determination in the future is uncertain (unless the International Court of Justice was to choose to address self-determination issues within the context of a future case). At the start of the new millennium, the great powers' rule dictates the results of self-determination quests. External self-determination rights exist if they fit within the parameters of the great powers' rule. An entity will become an independent state through the exercise of external self-determination if the great powers approve of such a result.[35]

I do not think that it is a cynical conclusion, and the great powers may be moved by moral considerations. Nevertheless, these are very diverse and incompatible moral considerations. This means that the processes of self-determination will now be taking place in completely different settings, which is not yet taken into account by the major theories of self-determination or secession, and the agreement of the great powers on the application of the principle of self-determination as the common right is hardly possible in the near future.

2.7 Conclusion

Self-determination of peoples is one of the most important political principles of the early 20th century and one of the basic legal collective rights of the middle of the 20th century. Nevertheless, at closer inspection, both the principle and the right are full of gaps, uncertainties and contradictions, which makes the principle impotent as

---

[35] Steiro 2013, p. 22.

a moral principle in the contemporary setting. These gaps and contradictions stem from both the legacy of the normative foundation of the idea of self-determination as a compromise of liberalism and nationalism and its nature as a pragmatic instrument of political rearrangements. When the principle obtained the status of an inalienable political right, the inherent inconsistencies of the principle were not in fact resolved. It was only in the early 1990s that attempts to develop the principle of self-determination as a universal moral principle through the theories of justified secession took place. These attempts coincided with the massive secessionist movements and the processes of democratization. Nevertheless, the attempts did not gain much success. The principle of self-determination can hardly be translated into a universal moral principle. As a result, the right of self-determination can have only limited applicability and little moral value. Three misconceptions prevent self-determination from obtaining the status of universal moral principle. I refer to these misconceptions as the illusion of people, illusion of rights, and illusion of agent. Since there is still no theoretical or practical solution to the three problems besetting justified secession, the principle of self-determination is more reminiscent of anachronism of decolonization epoch or an atavism of the post-World War political arrangements. It can hardly provide a morally instructed legal compass. It is at the disposal of any unprincipled political undertaking.

References

Aristotle (1999) (transl. Ross WD) Nicomachean ethics. Batoche Books, Kitchener

Beiner RS (1998) Democracy and Secession. In: Moor M (ed) National Self-Determination and Secession. Oxford University Press, Oxford, pp 158–181

Buchanan A (1991) Secession: the morality of political divorce from Fort Sumter to Lithuania and Quebec. Westview Press, Boulder, San Francisco/Oxford

Buchanan A (1998) Democracy and Secession. In: Moor M (ed) National Self-Determination and Secession. Oxford University Press, Oxford, pp 14–34

Buchheit L (1978) Secession: The Legitimacy of Self-Determination. Yale University Press, New Haven, CN

Cassese A (1995) Self-determination of peoples: A legal reappraisal. Cambridge University Press, Cambridge, NY

Copp D (1997) Democracy and Communal Self-Determination. In: McMahan J, McKim R (eds) The Morality of Nationalism. Oxford University Press, New York/Oxford, pp 277–300

Fotion N (2014) Theory VS Anti-Theory in Ethics. A Misconceived Conflict. Oxford University Press, Oxford

Gaertner W (2010) A primer in social choice theory. Oxford University Press, Oxford

Gauthier D (1994) Breaking Up: An Essay on Secession. Canadian Journal of Philosophy, 24:357–72

Gellner E (1983) Nations and Nationalism. Cornell University, Ithaca, NY

Heater D (1994) National Self-Determination. Woodrow Wilson and his Legacy. The Macmillan Press, Houndmills/London

Jennings I (1956) The Approach to Self-Government. Cambridge University Press, Cambridge

Kedourie E (1960) Nationalism. Hutchinson, London

Lenin V (1951) The Right of Nations to Self-Determination https://www.marxists.org/archive/lenin/works/1914/self-det/ Accessed 12 August 2020

Margalit A, Raz J (1990) National Self-Determination. The Journal of Philosophy, 87 (9): 439–461

2 Self-determination of Peoples

Megret F (2016) The Right to Self-Determination. Earned, not Inherent. In: Teson FR (ed) A Theory of Self-Determination (ASIL Studies in International Legal Theory). Cambridge University Press, Cambridge, pp 44–69

Miller D (1995) On Nationality. Oxford University Press, Oxford

Miller D (1998) Secession and the Principle of Nationality. In: Moor M (ed) National Self-Determination and Secession. Oxford University Press, Oxford, pp 62–79

Moore M (1998) Introduction. In: Moor M (ed) National Self-Determination and Secession. Oxford University Press, Oxford, pp 1–14

Nielsen K (1993) Secession: The Case of Quebec. Journal of Applied Philosophy. 10:365

Nielsen K (1998) Liberal Nationalism and Secession. In: Moor M (ed) National Self-Determination and Secession. Oxford University Press, Oxford, pp 103–134

Norman W (1998) The Ethics of Secession as the Regulation of Secessionist Politics. In: Moor M (ed) National Self-Determination and Secession. Oxford University Press, Oxford, pp 34–62

Philpott D (1995) A Defense of Self-Determination. Ethics, 105(2): 352–385

Steiro M (2013) The Right to Self-Determination under International Law. "Selfistans", secession, and the rule of the great powers. Routledge, London/New York

Tamir Y (1993) Liberal Nationalism. Princeton University Press, Princeton, NJ

Teson FR (2016) Introduction. In: Teson FR (ed) A Theory of Self-Determination (ASIL Studies in International Legal Theory). Cambridge University Press, Cambridge, pp X11–12

Weller M (2008) Escaping the Self-Determination Trap. Martinus Nijhoff Publishers, Leiden/Boston

Wellman C (2005) A Theory of Secession. Cambridge University Press, Cambridge

Young IM (2007) Global Challenges. War, Self-Determination and Responsibility for Justice. Polity Press, Cambridge

Boris Kashnikov is a professor at the National Research University "Higher School of Economics" (Moscow, Russian Federation). Retired colonel. In 1989, he served in Soviet peacekeeping forces during the Nagorno-Karabakh separatist crisis, and in 1993–1994, he took part in peacekeeping operations in the Former Yugoslavia as a United Nations civilian police station commander. His research interest is in moral and political philosophy, especially in the problematic of war and peace. He published widely in both Russian and English. With Nick Fotion and Joanne Lekea, Dr. Kashnikov coauthored *Terrorism: The New World Disorder* (London, Continuum, 2007).

Chapter 3
The International Rule of Law

Anthony Cullen and Kostiantyn Gorobets

Contents

3.1 Introduction 48
3.2 Delineating the International Rule of Law 48
3.3 The International Rule of Law, International Legality, and Values of Humanity 50
    3.3.1 Formal Side of the International Rule of Law 51
    3.3.2 The International Rule of Law and Global Values 54
3.4 The International Rule of Law in Practice: Conflict and Security Context 56
    3.4.1 The Use of Force and the Conduct of Hostilities 57
    3.4.2 Issues of Transparency and Accountability 57
    3.4.3 Issues of Compliance with Substantive Values Shared by the International
        Community 60
3.5 Conclusion 63
References 64

Abstract The chapter explores the significance of the international rule of law for international conflict and security law. The first section of the chapter investigates how the international rule of law is conceptualised, unpacking its formal and substantive requirements. The second section applies the concept in the context of international conflict and security law, focusing in particular on the implications for the use of lethal force. In doing so, an argument is advanced for the prioritisation of compliance with both formal and substantive requirements of the international rule of law. Necessary for the maintenance of international peace and security, and for the prevention and punishment of international crimes, emphasis is placed on the importance of the international rule of law for the integrity of the international legal order and for the future development of international conflict and security law.

Keywords international rule of law · international human rights law · international humanitarian law · use of force · international legality · substantive values ·

A. Cullen
Middlesex University, London, UK
e-mail: a.t.cullen@mdx.ac.uk

K. Gorobets (✉)
University of Groningen, Groningen, The Netherlands
e-mail: k.v.gorobets@rug.nl

© T.M.C. ASSER PRESS and the authors 2022
S. Sayapin et al. (eds.), *International Conflict and Security Law*,
https://doi.org/10.1007/978-94-6265-515-7_3

extraterritoriality · *jus ad bellum* · *jus in bello* · armed conflict · drones · UN Charter · *jus cogens* · customary international law

3.1 Introduction

A foundational principle of the international legal order, the international rule of law is a requisite for the maintenance of international peace and security and for the prevention and punishment of international crimes. This chapter will explore the relevance of the international rule of law to international conflict and security law by first describing how the rule of law is conceptualised. It will then examine the formal requirements of the principle and consider some of the substantive values protected by the international rule of law. In doing so, the significance of the principle will be unpacked, focusing in particular on the challenges presented by the use of lethal force. In this way, the chapter will seek to demonstrate the applicability of the international rule of law as a pre-condition of international conflict and security law.

3.2 Delineating the International Rule of Law

The concept of the international rule of law belongs to the most complicated and debatable topics in international legal scholarship.[1] One of the central issues regarding the nature and importance of the international rule of law is the question of the sense in which it is 'international' and whether the rule of law is ever possible in international law as such. For domestic jurisprudence, the idea of the rule of law is connected with what B. Tamanaha calls 'the three main themes':[2] government limited by law, formal legality, and the rule of law, not man. Even though a specific meaning of these three themes depends on a context, they determine the general frames for the rule of law discourse. However, things are less apparent in international law. First, there is no centralised government to be limited by law; second, the threshold of formal legality in international law is less clear than in national law; third, states are officials in themselves, which makes it challenging to pursue the superiority of rules over the particular interests of powerful states and alliances. As a result, it is widely accepted that a direct analogy between the domestic and the international rule of law is counterproductive.[3]

There are several approaches to understanding the essence of the rule of law as 'international.' First, the international rule of law can be seen as a result of the 'internationalisation' of the rule of law as known in domestic legal systems.

---

[1] During recent decades, the international rule of law has become a widely-discussed topic. We base our analysis on works by Beaulac 2009, Chesterman 2008, Hurd 2014, 2015a, 2015b, Nardin 2008, Nollkaemper 2009 and others.

[2] Tamanaha 2004, pp. 114–126.

[3] See Hurd 2015b; Nardin 2008.

3 The International Rule of Law

Thus, the international rule of law is supplementary to the domestic rule of law in the sense that international institutions become actively involved in promoting and strengthening the rule of law within states. This understanding of the rule of law is commonly (although not exclusively) used by the United Nations, the Council of Europe, and other international organisations. The influential definition of the rule of law suggested by the UN Secretary-General in 2004,[4] 'is a statement about how the rule of law should operate in *national* systems and it is *not* a definition of the rule of law at the global level.'[5] Such a vision of the international rule of law implies a focus on states as the primary addressees of rule of law requirements which must be implemented within their legal systems. It is worth noting that this approach to the international rule of law does not imply its perception as a genuine phenomenon of the international legal system, or as a legal ideology applicable to international law as such. The international rule of law here is merely an additional layer of promoting and strengthening the rule of law within states.

Second, the international rule of law may be treated as an independent set of principles relevant to the international legal system. Thus, the international rule of law is not merely a result of international cooperation on promoting the rule of law amongst states, but a specific version or a branch of the rule of law as a universal legal ideal. It implies that a concept of the international rule of law should not be a deduction (or reduction) of the rule of law known domestically; both versions of the rule of law (domestic and international) are conceptually self-reliant. The international rule of law constitutes a set of principles which ensure compliance with and accountability under international law of all relevant actors, as well as a transparent and procedurally appropriate way of the creation and application of the rules of international law.[6] Such an understanding of the international rule of law traces back to the Grotian tradition of international law and implies that the international rule of law is not a weaker or defective version of the rule of law but its independent manifestation.[7]

Third, there are attempts to provide an integral vision of the international rule of law which would combine its 'internationalised' and 'genuinely international' sides. Thus, M. Kanetake argues that the international rule of law concerns three levels of relations: horizontal state-to-state relations; relations in respect of the execution of governmental authority in regard to individuals and non-state actors; and relations

---

[4] 'A principle of governance in which all persons, institutions and entities, public and private, including the State itself, are accountable to laws that are publicly promulgated, equally enforced and independently adjudicated, and which are consistent with international human rights norms and standards. It requires, as well, measures to ensure adherence to the principles of supremacy of law, equality before the law, accountability to the law, fairness in the application of the law, separation of powers, participation in decision-making, legal certainty, avoidance of arbitrariness and procedural and legal transparency.'

The rule of law and transitional justice in conflict and post-conflict societies: Report of the Secretary-General (S/2004/616), para 6.

[5] McCorquodale 2016, p. 286.

[6] See Beaulac 2007.

[7] Nijman 2015, p. 135.

in respect of the execution of authority by international institutions.[8] According to this approach, the international rule of law gains its integrity as a legal ideology that highlights both formal and substantive aspects of how international law should operate and how states should apply it both within their domestic legal systems and in relations with each other. The international rule of law is, therefore, the ideological core of the international legal system and also a key principle of international law's interplay with domestic law in securing and guaranteeing the values of humankind.

In the context of international conflict and security law, the international rule of law has a twofold nature: first, it advocates compliance, transparency, and accountability of international decision-making regarding the maintenance of international peace and security; second, it serves a guide to the substantive values shared by the international community.

3.3 The International Rule of Law, International Legality, and Values of Humanity

The rule of law is commonly discussed through the opposition and complementarity of its 'thin' and 'thick' versions.[9] The 'thin' version of the rule of law is concerned with the principles of formal legality requiring laws to be made, applied, adjudicated, and enforced equally, consistently, and within a due and transparent procedure. This version of the rule of law also contains such requirements as 'no-one can be a judge in his own cause', 'laws should not prescribe the impossible', etc.[10] The 'thick' version of the rule of law goes beyond these formal requirements and also includes substantive values and goals which should be furthered; mere legality is not enough to speak of the rule of law. Commonly, in the context of international law, these are human dignity, peace and security, social progress and development, self-determination of peoples, and the like.[11]

The metaphor of 'thin' and 'thick' rule of law implies that in order to get thicker, one must first be thin, that is, the 'thin', formal rule of law is a necessary precondition for going further in pursuing substantive goals. The 'thin' rule of law is therefore about 'doing things right', whereas the 'thick' rule of law is about 'doing the right thing'.[12] Even though these two aspects of the rule of law go hand-in-hand, its formal side is a common starting point for analysis, and the international rule of law is no exception.[13] At the same time, the formal version of the (international) rule of law does not exist separately or independently from its substantive version; they often

---

[8] Kanetake 2016, p. 16.

[9] Bingham 2010; Gowder 2016; Tamanaha 2004.

[10] The idea behind the 'thin' version of the rule of law is that law is considered to be morally indifferent. See Raz 1979, pp. 212–218.

[11] See, for example, Spijkers 2011.

[12] Westerman 2018, pp. 141–167.

[13] See Beaulac 2009; Hurd 2015b.

3 The International Rule of Law

presuppose each other in rule of law discourses.[14] They always intertwine, and in the case of the international rule of law, it is not always feasible to perceive one in detachment from the other.

3.3.1 Formal Side of the International Rule of Law

The formal, or 'thin' version, of the international rule of law is linked to the principles of international legality. It primarily requires a basic level of legal ordering of international affairs, meaning not only the existence of international law but also compliance with it, that is, its minimal effectiveness. The international rule of law is hence based on international actors' treatment of international law as authoritative, that is, as a normative order capable of guiding and constraining their actions.[15] For such a normative order to become authoritative, there exist several sets of requirements for its elements and structure.[16] The first set of requirements relates to the qualities of the rules that constitute such a normative order; they should be stable, predictable, certain, etc. The second set, to the scope and conditions of their application: the rules of international law are to be applied equally and consistently. The third set, to the status and limits of discretion of the agencies authorised to enforce these rules.

3.3.1.1 Stable, Predictable, and Certain Rules

A basic legal ordering of international affairs requires the rules of international law to be stable, predictable, and certain,[17] otherwise they cannot effectively guide actors' behaviour. This primarily implies that the international rule of law is rooted in the idea that maintaining global peace and security, as well as the resolution of conflicts, should be based on rules, not on the particular actors' motives and wishes. The international rule of law therefore becomes undermined by uncertainty, indeterminateness, or change in the normative and institutional structure of the international legal order. Such uncertainty and indeterminateness is directly linked to the (il)legality of

---

[14] Gowder insists that the 'thin' and 'thick' rule of law are better called the 'weak' and the 'strong' versions of the rule of law. Formal legality is 'weak' exactly because it does not encompass substantive values represented by the rules of law. For instance, the requirement of equality can be treated formally through the formula 'treat like cases alike', yet to determine which cases are indeed 'like' and which are not, one must always consider the substance of the rules. Gowder 2016, Chapters 2–3.

[15] Kumm 2003–2004, p. 19.

[16] As noted by Raz, these requirements do not exist for their own sake. They simply determine some minimal qualities any law must possess so that its addressees can be guided by it, see Raz 1979.

[17] This list of formal qualities of legal rules is not exhaustive. One of the most widely recognised lists of such formal qualities of law is offered by Fuller (see Fuller 1964; for the application to international law, see also Kumm 2004; Brunnée and Toope 2010). It is beyond the scope of this chapter to discuss all the intricacies of formal legality in international law.

the most dangerous threats to the international order, such as war. This is exactly why today's concept of the international rule of law is based on the general prohibition of the threat or use of force established by Artticle 2(4) of the United Nations Charter.[18] Such a general prohibition, which only provides for an exception in cases of self-defence and actions with respect to threats to the peace, breaches of the peace, and acts of aggression,[19] serves the purpose of establishing a stable and predictable world order.

As with most of the formal requirements of the rule of law, the stability, predictability, and certainty of rules are merely the means employed to enable conditions for the peaceful coexistence of states and peoples. Yet the fundamental status of these requirements shapes their greater importance which reaches beyond a pure instrumentalist vision of the international rule of law. It is especially visible against the background of the debates around humanitarian intervention.[20] From the perspective of the international rule of law, even a legitimate aim cannot be furthered by the illegal use of available means; hence for humanitarian interventions to avoid undermining the international rule of law, they must be conducted within a set of existing rules. The maintenance of international peace and security, as well as the resolution of conflict, are to be constructed and governed by legal rules; otherwise the international rule of law is undermined.

The formal qualities of the rules of international law certainly go beyond the issues of international peace, security, and conflict resolution. The international legal order, in general, should consist of rules that provide for clear and reliable guidance for the subjects of international law, and in this regard, international legality as such is of instrumental *and* substantive value.

3.3.1.2 Equally Applicable and Justiciable Rules

For the rules of international law to fulfil the requirements of the rule of law, mere stability, predictability, and certainty are not enough as they mean little if these rules are not equally applicable and justiciable. Moreover, it is rare that a rule is clear and unequivocal to the extent that all affected subjects interpret it uniformly.

Equal application of international law has several dimensions. *Ratione loci*, it implies the universality and generality of the international legal order, that is, its validity for all states regardless of their political, cultural, religious or other identities. *Ratione personae*, the equal applicability of international law requires the fulfilment of the principle of the sovereign equality of states in their international relations. Finally, *ratione materiae*, this requirement is widely known as the principle 'treat like

---

[18] Randelzhofer and Dörr 2012. See also Hathaway and Shapiro 2017 for a discussion of the interplay between rule of law rhetoric and outlawing war.

[19] It is beyond the scope of this contribution to discuss whether Article 51 and Ch. VII of the UN Charter constitute exceptions from the general prohibition of the use of force. For discussion, see de Hoogh 2015.

[20] See for discussion Chesterman 2001; Hurd 2011; Rodley 2015; Simma 1999; Tesón 2005; Koh 2016.

3 The International Rule of Law 53

cases alike' and implies consistency and uniformity in the application of international law.

The requirement of equal application raises the most significant concerns regarding the basic ability of international law to conform to the rule of law. However, the mere difficulties in reaching equal applicability of international law should not be treated as a sign of the irrelevance or unattainability of the international rule of law. The international rule of law is a legal ideal, and, as in the case of any other ideal, its value must not be measured against practical obstacles to its achievement.

The justiciability of rules, also, constitutes an integral part of the (international) rule of law, and it has been referred to as such throughout the whole history of this doctrine.[21] In the case of international law, however, this crucial requirement of the rule of law is amongst the most challenging in the present structure of the international legal order. Even though the creation of the International Court of Justice is often seen as a significant achievement of the international rule of law,[22] its jurisdiction is far from what might be considered as satisfactory in the light of the rule of law's requirements. The proliferation of international courts and tribunals in recent decades has provided for a more comprehensive justiciability of rules, since different fields of international relations are increasingly covered by the jurisdiction of one or another judicial authority.[23] Yet the existing limitations upon the international judiciary are still of concern, insofar as courts remain the crucial institutional guards for the rule of law.

3.3.1.3 Governance Limited by Law

No formal concept of the international rule of law can be complete without the idea of procedural limitations on the powers of authorities. Such a limitation strongly relates to the idea that discretionary powers must be subjected to the requirements of due procedure, a fair trial, the right to be heard, inclusion, etc. Taken broadly, the international rule of law can only be a meaningful concept if it applies to institutions set up to shape and maintain the international legal order, that is, to international organisations, and primarily to the United Nations given its exceptional mission and functions. It is at the core of the meaning of the rule of law that power should not be exercised arbitrarily, and that authorities, especially those enforcing law, must be bound by procedural rules guaranteeing transparency and accountability. To ensure accountability, there must be legal mechanisms for holding the law-applying and law-enforcing agencies accountable.[24]

---

[21] See Bingham 2010; Dicey 1897; Hayek 2012.

[22] Jessup 1945; Lauterpacht 2011; for a recent inquiry, see Feinäugle 2016a.

[23] See Simma 2004, 2009.

[24] This ratio stands behind the Draft Articles on the Responsibility of International Organizations. ILC, 'Report of the International Law Commission on the Work of its 43rd Session' (26 April–3 June and 4 July–12 August 2011) UN Doc A/66/10.

The United Nations, as the most representative international organization, set up to maintain international peace and security, has declared that, 'the rule of law applies to [...] the United Nations and [...] should guide all of [its] activities.'[25] In the light of the international rule of law, the UN and its bodies can indeed be considered as exercising public authority regarding its member-states,[26] and, as became apparent after *Kadi*, even over particular individuals,[27] which is of extreme importance in relation to Security Council powers under Chapter VII of the UN Charter. Thus, the intricacies of Security Council procedure also play a significant role in determining its conformity with the principles of the international rule of law. In this light, the right of the five permanent members to veto raises many concerns regarding the Security Council's practical commitment to the formal legality which gives rise to criticism of the Council in general.[28] Remarkably, some of the members of the Security Council do not regard the right to veto as one of the Council's working methods thus taking it out of the context of the procedural requirements of the rule of law.[29] The practice of the UN Security Council is also quite illustrative of the value of procedural limitations as an element of the international rule of law: these limitations should not exist for the sake of procedure, they should exist to make the practice of the authorities more predictable. The right to veto—taken as a procedural working method or not—undermines this principle, and in most cases in relation to the authorization of the use of force the practice of the Council is not consistent. In this way, the Security Council, while being designed as the principled organ for maintaining and restoring the international rule of law, can also be a threat to it.

Overall, the formal side of the international rule of law as encompassing the principles relating to the qualities of rules, mode of their application and enforcement, as well as to the procedural limitations of the authorities, unlike in domestic law, is a value in itself. The international rule of law cannot be seen as formal legality alone, as it is not enough for maintaining the authority of international law. This is why the substantive side of the international rule of law is not something additional or supplementary in respect to formal legality, but rather a necessary counterpart which enables the international rule of law as such.

3.3.2 The International Rule of Law and Global Values

Even a brief analysis of the international rule of law cannot be complete without some consideration of the substantive side of this concept and doctrine. One of the critical

---

[25] General Assembly (GA) Res 67/1 UN Doc A/RES/67/1, 30 November 2012, para 2.

[26] Feinäugle 2016b, p. 161.

[27] Joined Cases C-402/05 P and C-415/05 P *Yassin Abdullah Kadi and Al Barakaat International Foundation v Council of the European Union and Commission of the European Communities* [2008] ECR 461, paras 323–325.

[28] See Bailey and Daws 2003, pp. 379–412.

[29] See Harrington 2017, p. 42 ff.

3 The International Rule of Law

breaking points in the theory of the rule of law has always been the issue of whether the rule of law includes requirements as to the *content* of law, and not only its formal features. This, to a significant degree, relates to a teleological understanding of the rule of law, that is, that the rule of law is by definition incompatible with tyranny, oppression and violations of human rights, and should thus indicate a path to a better and more just law, not only to a formally proper law. Therefore, substantively, the rule of law is not always distinguishable from the other merits a legal order may have, and the rule of law often, though not always, includes and assumes an idea of the rule of *good* law. Such a view links to the idea that, at least to some extent, the doctrine of the international rule of law must be aligned to the substantive values underlying contemporary international legal order.

One of the problems with broadening the idea of the (international) rule of law, though, is that it is not always clear what kind of values must be taken into account as relevant for the rule of law. Moreover, in case of international law, it is even more complicated since consensus on universal values cannot be assumed. Yet as highlighted by Spijkers, 'the identification of global values is motivated by an urgent sense of what is lacking, a sense that the state of the world could—and should be—better than it is now.'[30]

Traditionally, the mere idea of the international rule of law has always been tightly related to the value of maintaining peace, which in the modern era has been transformed into the main purpose of the United Nations.[31] This, to a significant degree, has its roots in the idea that international law as a normative system is chiefly legitimised by its ability to prevent wars, or at least to mitigate their consequences. Hence, the international rule of law is often associated with an image of international law as the only normative framework available as an alternative to the chaos of war.[32] Such connotations are also evident in the preamble to the UN Charter, where adherence to international law is linked to the necessity of saving future generations from the sorrow of war.

Apart from being substantively connected to the fundamental value of international peace and security, the international rule of law can also be conceptualised through the prism of human rights and dignity. From this perspective, the formal requirements of the international rule of law 'have to be constrained by, and balanced against the more fundamental goal of an international rule of law, the protection of the autonomy of individual persons, best realized through the entrenchment of basic human rights.'[33] Such an approach links to the idea that at its core, the international rule of law is needed as a safeguard for the autonomy of the subject of law. And if international peace and security are the values reflecting the autonomy of the primary subjects of international law, namely states, then human dignity and

---

[30] Spijkers 2012, p. 365.

[31] See Wolfrum 2012, pp. 109–115.

[32] This goes back to Hobbesian conceptions of law- or rule-based order as opposed to the natural condition states would inevitably fall into if there were no international law. See Dyzenhaus 2014.

[33] Pavel 2019, p. 3.

human rights reflect the autonomy of individuals who are directly affected by international law more and more often. From this perspective, the discourse relating to the international rule of law is indistinguishable from the discourse of human dignity and autonomy; hence international law may only comply with the rule of law if it respects and promotes them.[34]

In recent decades, the idea of development has also turned into one of the values determining the content of the international rule of law. The paradigm of sustainable development that is designed to comprehensively cover all critical spheres of the world community and integrate them into one overarching policy, though not always translated into legal language, has had a major impact on the international rule of law. Promotion of the rule of law at national and international levels is one of the SDGs' targets,[35] but the relations between the SDGs and the international rule of law are much deeper than this. The SDGs' policies tend to 'leak' into the legal field by impacting the ways international law is perceived and interpreted. Because of the SDGs, more and more domains covered by, or incorporated into, Agenda-2030 get directly or indirectly subjected to the authority of international law. As a consequence, the interrelation between the global policy of the SDGs and the international rule of law is twofold. First, the mere existence and implementation of this policy increases the importance of international law and its 'coverage'; second, the strengthening of the international rule of law is itself an element of this global policy.

Inclusion of global values into the structure of the international rule of law provides a more comprehensive picture of this normative ideal and shows its relevance for the international legal order not only from the side of its formal features, but also from the side of its development towards a better and more just future. From these two perspectives, the nature of the international rule of law appears as a merit of the international legal order that grounds its authority and legitimacy.

3.4 The International Rule of Law in Practice: Conflict and Security Context

As mentioned above, in the context of international conflict and security law, the international rule of law has a twofold nature: first, it advocates compliance, transparency, and accountability of international decision-making regarding the maintenance of international peace and security. Second, it serves as a guide to the substantive values shared by the international community, including in relation to the means and methods of warfare. The sections that follow explore the significance of each aspect, focusing on the use of lethal force.

---

[34] Also see Fasbender 2018, pp. 771–72. McCorquodale emphasises the importance of human rights for the definition of the international rule of law through the arguments of legal pluralism, McCorquodale 2016, pp. 292–94.

[35] Transforming our world: the 2030 Agenda for Sustainable Development: UN General Assembly Resolution (A/RES/70/1), para 59, target 16.3.

3.4.1 The Use of Force and the Conduct of Hostilities

The use of lethal force is regulated at an international level by international humanitarian law, international human rights law, and rules governing the resort to the use of armed force. As a principle of the international legal order, the international rule of law provides a framework that supports each of these different bodies of law in their distinctive functions. While the use of lethal force is often undertaken covertly, the international rule of law requires transparency and accountability with regard to its legal basis. It also requires—reflecting the substantive values shared by the international community—compliance with fundamental guarantees that protect the inherent dignity of an individual. When either requirement is not fulfilled, the efficacy of the regulation provided for by the different bodies under international law is undermined. To illustrate this, it is instructive to consider the debate generated by the use of lethal force in extraterritorial counter-terrorism operations.

3.4.2 Issues of Transparency and Accountability

In a report issued on use of lethal force through armed drones, the UN Special Rapporteur on extrajudicial, summary or arbitrary executions, Christof Heyns, highlighted the implications of the practice for the rule of law: 'A lack of appropriate transparency and accountability concerning the deployment of drones undermines the rule of law and may threaten international security.'[36] Emphasising the importance of compliance with international standards, Heyns stated that 'Accountability for violations of international human rights law (or international humanitarian law) is not a matter of choice or policy; it is a duty under domestic and international law.'[37]

Issues of transparency and accountability—fundamental requirements of the international rule of law—have been recurring themes in the debate concerning the use of armed drones. A concern that has been frequently raised is the lack of clarity on the legal basis for the extraterritorial use of armed force. Amnesty International have emphasized:

> States must ensure transparency in the use of armed drones, publicly disclose the legal criteria governing their lethal targeting operations, specify the safeguards in place to ensure compliance with international law, and conduct prompt, independent and impartial investigations whenever there is credible information about a possible violation of international law caused by their use of armed drones.[38]

---

[36] Report of the Special Rapporteur on extrajudicial, summary or arbitrary executions, Christof Heyns, UN Doc A/68/382, 13 September 2013, para 97.

[37] Report of the Special Rapporteur on extrajudicial, summary or arbitrary executions, Christof Heyns, UN Doc A/68/382, 13 September 2013, para 97.

[38] 'Oral Intervention by Amnesty International in the UN Human Rights Council's panel discussion on "Ensuring use of remotely piloted aircraft or armed drones in counterterrorism and military operations in accordance with international law, including international human rights and humanitarian

The conduct of prompt, independent and impartial investigations requires clarity concerning the legal framework for the extraterritorial use of force. In the absence of such clarity, the non-disclosure by State authorities of the basis for the use of lethal force raises significant issues for the rule of law at both national and international levels. To comply with this principle as a matter of national law, the laws enabling such operations must be accessible. As noted by Lord Bingham, the rule of law requires that 'the law must be accessible and so far as possible intelligible, clear and predictable. This seems obvious: if everyone is bound by the law they must be able without undue difficulty to find out what it is.'[39] The lack of transparency on the part of states such as the United States and the United Kingdom also has significant implications for accountability and compliance with applicable rules of international law. In 2014, the UN Human Rights Council convened an interactive panel discussion of experts on the use of armed drones and issues of compliance with international law. The report that summarises the discussion of the panel highlights the importance of transparency for the rule of law:

> Many delegations emphasized that lack of transparency created an accountability vacuum and prevented access to an effective remedy for victims. Transparency played an important role in assessing and enhancing respect for the rule of law. It was required for an evaluation of the consequences of the use of armed drones, a determination of the applicable legal framework and, consequently, a determination of the lawfulness of each strike. States that were using drones were urged to be as transparent as possible concerning the use of armed drones, as a significant step towards ensuring accountability.[40]

As a requirement of the rule of law at national and international levels, accountability presupposes access to an effective remedy. For example, the decision-making process at some level should be amenable to judicial review. The lack of clarity concerning the applicable law undercuts the legal basis for judicial review in the event of violations. In a resolution adopted at its 55th meeting, the UN Human Rights Council called upon 'States to ensure transparency in their records on the use of remotely piloted aircraft or armed drones and to conduct prompt, independent and impartial investigations whenever there are indications of a violation to international law caused by their use.'[41] The European Parliament made a similar call in a resolution adopted on the use of armed drones, calling on the European Union 'to promote greater transparency and accountability on the part of third countries in the use of armed drones with regard to the legal basis for their use and

---

law",' statement by Amnesty International, UN Human Rights Council, Geneva, 22 September 2014.

[39] Bingham 2007, p. 69–70.

[40] Summary of the Human Rights Council interactive panel discussion of experts on the use of remotely piloted aircraft or armed drones in compliance with international law: Report of the Office of the United Nations High Commissioner for Human Rights, UN Doc. A/HRC/28/38, 15 December 2014, para 46.

[41] UN Human Rights Council, Resolution 25/22, Ensuring use of remotely piloted aircraft or armed drones in counterterrorism and military operations in accordance with international law, including international human rights and humanitarian law, adopted on 28 March 2014, UN Doc. A/HRC/RES/25/22, 15 April 2014.

3 The International Rule of Law

to operational responsibility, to allow for judicial review of drone strikes and to ensure that victims of unlawful drone strikes have effective access to remedies.'[42] The lack of access to an effective remedy undermines guarantees provided for under national and international law and weakens the rule of law at national and international levels. Both international human rights law and international humanitarian law obligate State authorities to investigate possible violations. The importance of such investigations has been emphasised by a number of UN Special Rapporteurs, including Ben Emmerson, a UN Special Rapporteur on the promotion and protection of human rights and fundamental freedoms while countering terrorism; he urged states to ensure that 'in any case in which there is a plausible indication from any apparently reliable source that civilians have been killed or injured in a counter-terrorism operation, including through the use of remotely piloted aircraft, the relevant authorities conduct a prompt, independent and impartial fact-finding inquiry, and provide a detailed public explanation.'[43]

As requirements of rule of law at national and international levels, transparency and accountability protect the integrity of national and international legal orders. In doing so, they support the rights of victims as subjects of national and international law. The lack of transparency and accountability in the use of lethal force has implications not only for victims, but also for those involved in facilitating the execution of such operations. This was highlighted in a report issued in 2016 by the UK Parliament Joint Committee on Human Rights. Following the killing of Reyaad Khan by an RAF drone strike in Syria in 2015, concerns regarding the lack of clarity in the UK government's legal position were raised before the Committee. The Committee's report on its enquiry into the use of drones for targeted killing states that the 'ongoing uncertainty about the Government's policy might leave front-line intelligence and service personnel in considerable doubt about whether what they are being asked to do is lawful, and may therefore expose them, and Ministers, to the risk of criminal prosecution for murder or complicity in murder.'[44] Under such conditions, it is clear that the efficacy of rules and regulations that exist to support compliance with the law are weakened in the absence of transparency on the part of State authorities. The section that follows considers the significance of compliance for the international rule of law and for the substantive values shared by the international community in the field of conflict and security law.

---

[42] European Parliament resolution on the use of armed drones, 2014/2567(RSP), 25 February 2014, para 4. It is instructive to recall the rule of law as one of the fundamental values upon which the European Union is based. See: Treaty on European Union, 31 I.L.M. 253 (1992), Article 6(1): 'The Union is founded on the principles of liberty, democracy, respect for human rights and fundamental freedoms, and the rule of law, principles which are common to the Member States.' See Pech 2009, 2010.

[43] Report of the Special Rapporteur on the promotion and protection of human rights and fundamental freedoms while countering terrorism, Ben Emmerson, UN Doc A/HRC/25/59, 11 March 2014, para 73.

[44] UK Parliament Joint Committee on Human Rights, The Government's policy on the use of drones for targeted killing: Second Report of Session 2015–16, HC 574, HL Paper 141, 10 May 2016, p. 6.

3.4.3 Issues of Compliance with Substantive Values Shared by the International Community

In addition to the formal requirements of transparency and accountability, the international rule of law presupposes adherence to the substantive values shared by the international community. These are reflected in customary international law, in particular the rules of *jus cogens*. This section will focus on the significance of the international rule of law for compliance with such rules in relation to the use of lethal force. It will consider how the formal and substantive aspects of the international rule of law are inter-related and how the principle imposes positive and negative obligations on States and international organisations.

3.4.3.1 International Human Rights Law

The preamble of the Universal Declaration on Human Rights states: 'it is essential, if man is not to be compelled to have recourse, as a last resort, to rebellion against tyranny and oppression, that human rights should be protected by the rule of law.'[45] In as much as human rights are to be protected by the rule of law, it is clear that the rule of law at the national and international levels cannot be sustained without the protection of fundamental human rights. A right of particular significance to international conflict and security law is the right to life. As noted by Christof Heyns and Thomas Probert, 'The right to life has been described as the "supreme" or "foundational" right. Efforts to ensure other rights can be of little consequence if the right to life is not protected.'[46] The customary status of the right is beyond debate:

> The right to life is a well-established and developed part of international law, in treaties, custom, and general principles, and, in its core elements, in the rules of *jus cogens*. Its primacy and the central features of the prohibition on arbitrary deprivations of life are not contested. Nonetheless, in practice, life remains cheap in many parts of the world. This is true in the many armed conflicts that are raging, but also outside such conflicts, where police and others authorised or tolerated by states often use excessive force, or there is a failure to investigate homicides.[47]

When the prohibition on the arbitrary deprivation of life is not enforced, the rule of law is undermined. As a substantive value shared by the international community, respect for the right to life is a fundamental prerequisite of the international rule of law. As a norm of international human rights law, the right to life implies not only a prohibition on the arbitrary deprivation of life but also a duty to investigate violations. Here the substantive and formal aspects of the rule of law dovetail into accountability, highlighting the fundamental importance of prompt, independent and impartial investigations. Although the protection provided by international

---

[45] Universal Declaration of Human Rights, G.A. res. 217A (III), U.N. Doc A/810 at 71 (1948), preamble.

[46] Heyns and Probert 2016.

[47] Heyns and Probert 2016.

3 The International Rule of Law

human rights law is clear, the continued use of lethal force in extraterritorial counter-terrorism operations presents significant challenges to compliance with the right to life. As noted by a panel of experts convened by the UN Human Rights Council on the use of armed drones:

> The lack of accountability for violations of international human rights law, in particular the right to life, must be addressed. Where there were credible allegations of violations of international law, States were under an obligation to carry out prompt, independent and impartial investigations, and to make the results publicly available. States had a duty of public explanation to victims and to the international community. States should permit judicial review of the claims alleging grave violations of domestic and international law, and should be more transparent in their use of drones as a precondition to any meaningful accountability, including by providing information about the legal basis for the use of drones and facts about specific strikes.[48]

3.4.3.2 International Humanitarian Law

The duty to investigate violations is also provided for under international humanitarian law. The ICRC Study on Customary International Humanitarian Law states that: 'States must investigate war crimes allegedly committed by their nationals or armed forces, or on their territory, and, if appropriate, prosecute the suspects. They must also investigate other war crimes over which they have jurisdiction and, if appropriate, prosecute the suspects.'[49] Another rule of customary international law which is significant for the international rule of law is that which pertains to ensuring respect for international humanitarian law *erga omnes*: 'States may not encourage violations of international humanitarian law by parties to an armed conflict. They must exert their influence, to the degree possible, to stop violations of international humanitarian law.'[50] Compliance with the substantive values enshrined in international humanitarian law also entails an obligation to prevent violations, to 'ensure respect' for the law. For instance, the UN General Assembly has urged states to 'ensure that any measures taken or means employed to counter terrorism, including the use of remotely piloted aircraft, comply with their obligations under international law, including the Charter of the United Nations, human rights law and international humanitarian law, in particular the principles of distinction and proportionality.'[51] The issue here for the rule of law at national and international level is one of compliance. Speaking on the 70th anniversary of the Diplomatic Conference which drafted the Geneva Conventions of 1949, the President of the International Committee of

---

[48] Summary of the Human Rights Council interactive panel discussion of experts on the use of remotely piloted aircraft or armed drones in compliance with international law: Report of the Office of the United Nations High Commissioner for Human Rights, UN Doc. A/HRC/28/38, 15 December 2014, para 54.

[49] Henckaert and Doswald-Beck 2005, p. 607.

[50] Henckaert and Doswald-Beck 2005, p. 509.

[51] UN General Assembly Resolution 68/178, Protection of human rights and fundamental freedoms while countering terrorism, adopted on 18 December 2013, UN Doc A/RES/68/178, 28 January 2014, para 6(s).

the Red Cross stated that 'in conflicts across the world we see enormous violations of IHL... Our collective challenge today is to find ways to ensure greater respect within the changing dynamics of conflict.'[52]

The challenge of ensuring greater respect for international humanitarian law cannot be realized without strengthening the international rule of law. While institutions of international criminal justice have a role to play, 'international criminal law as a whole can only provide a remedy for crimes that shock the conscience of mankind after the fact—it cannot operate so as to prevent such injustice from occurring in the first place.'[53] Prevention supposes frameworks of rules, procedures and processes reinforcing the rule of law at national and international levels. While international humanitarian law regulates the use of force in the context of armed conflict, the law prohibiting resort to the use of force has been described as the cornerstone of the UN Charter system.[54] The section that follows considers the significance of this area of international law for the international rule of law.

3.4.3.3 Legal Regulation of Resort to the Use of Force

The international rule of law is substantively connected to the fundamental value of international peace and security. Although the term is not used in the Charter of the United Nations, the rule of law is implicit in the framework of the rule-based international legal order established by the Charter. As with international human rights law and international humanitarian law, the most significant concern with rules governing resort to the use of force is one of compliance. However, the fact that violations exist does not render the law obsolete. The international rule of law is a legal ideal the value of which is not to be measured against impediments to its realisation. It can only be understood in terms of the formal and substantive requirements of the international legal order.

One of the most widely debated issues in regard to the international rule of law and the use of force is humanitarian intervention and related doctrines (such as the responsibility to protect). The question of whether or not a state or a group of states may resort to armed force using the humanitarian justification reveals an important inner tension in the concept of the international rule of law. On the one hand, the requirements of legality as one of the core elements of the international rule of law imply that rules of positive international law must be obeyed. Positive international law is clear on the matter: use of force is prohibited under the UN Charter; it can only be legitimate when authorised by the Security Council or in situations of self-defence. Humanitarian intervention, therefore, cannot be a legitimate ground for the use of force, and many attempts to argue otherwise suffer from a lack of justification as a matter of *lex lata*. On the other hand, the substantive side of the international

---

[52] Maurer 2019.

[53] Crawford 2014, p. 492.

[54] Armed Activities on the Territory of Congo, ICJ Reports (2005) 168 at para 148, 45 ILM (2006) 271.

rule of law, which links it to the fundamental values of the international community, including human dignity, peace, and self-determination, makes it possible to argue in favour of humanitarian intervention in the context of *lex ferenda.*

This ambivalence of the international rule of law in regard to humanitarian intervention, however, only reinforces the point made earlier, namely that the logic of the (international) rule of law has entailed a movement from 'thin' to 'thick', that is, from formal requirements to substantive values, not the other way around. This logic prioritises the importance of substantive values such as peace or human dignity—typical justificatory devices for humanitarian intervention—over the formal requirements of legality. The logic of the thickening of the rule of law to further morally justifiable goals depends on the *modus operandi* of institutional arrangements supporting such ends. If the institutional arrangements do not comply with the formal requirements of the rule of law, the sustainability of such an approach is questionable. At the same time, not furthering such goals and values does not mean non-conformity with the rule of law. This is precisely why reversing the idea of the international rule of law in justifying the doctrine of humanitarian intervention substantially risks weakening rather than strengthening the current legal regime prohibiting the use of force. The strengthening of this legal regime would require institutions of global governance to be reformed to effectively secure the primacy of the international rule of law. Until this is realised, compliance with the prohibition on the threat or use of force will continue to be an issue.

3.5 Conclusion

There is no concept more fundamental to the integrity of the international legal order than the international rule of law. It is the foundation upon which international conflict and security law is based. As a value protected by the international community, the international rule of law requires transparency, accountability and compliance with the various rules of international law applicable to the use of lethal force. It serves not only as a measure of progress but also as an indicator of threats and challenges to international peace and security, which are often reflected in the level of protection accorded to the right to life.

The substantive values embodied in the international rule of law are intertwined with the formal requirements of the principle. For example, laws protecting human rights cannot be enforced without the provision of access to an effective remedy. Access to an effective remedy presupposes the existence of transparency and accountability. These are prerequisites for judicial review and the conduct of prompt, independent and impartial investigations. Here the formal and substantive requirements of the international rule of law provide a framework of rules that are fundamental not only to the current efficacy of international conflict and security law, but also its future development.

The formal and substantive aspects of the international rule of law provide important indicators illuminating the state of health of the international legal order. International conflict and security law is dependent upon the integrity of this legal order in fulfilling its functions. In this context, the challenge that currently faces the international community is one of prioritising compliance, in particular with regard to the rules of international law governing the use of lethal force. In the absence of such compliance, the future development of international conflict and security law will rest on weak foundations.

References

Bailey D, Daws S (2003) The Procedure of the UN Security Council. Oxford University Press, New York

Beaulac S (2007) An inquiry into the international rule of law. EUI Working Paper MWP 1–35. http://hdl.handle.net/1814/6957

Beaulac S (2009) The Rule of Law in International Law Today. In: Palombella G, Walker N (eds) Relocating the Rule of Law. Hart Publishing, Oxford, pp 197–223

Bingham T (2007) The Rule of Law. Camb. Law J.66:67–85

Bingham T (2010) The Rule of Law. Allen Lane, London

Brunnée J, Toope S (2010) Legitimacy and Legality in International Law. Cambridge University Press, New York

Chesterman S (2001) Just War or Just Peace: Humanitarian Intervention and International Law. Oxford University Press, Oxford

Chesterman S (2008) An International Rule of Law? Am. J. Com. Law 56:331–62

Crawford J (2014) Chance, Order, Change: The Course of International Law. Brill, The Hague

Dicey A (1897) Introduction to the Study of the Law of the Constitution, 5th edn. Macmillan, London

de Hoogh A (2015) *Jus Cogens* and the Use of Armed Force. In: Weller M (ed) The Oxford Handbook of the Use of Force in International Law. Oxford University Press, Oxford, pp 1161–86

Dyzenhaus D (2014) Hobbes on the International Rule of Law. Ethics Int. Aff. 28:53–64

Fasbender B (2018) What's in a Name? The International Rule of Law and the United Nations Charter. Chinese Journal of International Law 17:761–97

Feinäugle C (2016a) The International Court of Justice and the Rule of Law. In: Feinäugle C (ed) The Rule of Law and Its Application to the United Nations. Hart Publishing, Oxford

Feinläuge C (2016b) The UN Declaration on the Rule of Law and the Application of the Rule of Law to the UN: A Reconstruction from an International Public Authority Perspective. Goet. J. Int. Law 7:157–85

Fuller L (1964) The Morality of Law. Yale University Press, New Haven

Gowder P (2016) The Rule of Law in the Real World. Cambridge University Press, New York

Harrington J (2017) The Working Methods of the United Nations Security Council: Maintaining the Implementation of Change. ICLQ 66:39–70

Hathaway O, Shapiro S (2017) The Internationalists: How a Radical Plan to Outlaw War Remade the World. Simon & Schuster, New York

Hayek F (2012) Law, Legislation and Liberty: a New Statement of the Liberal Principles of Justice and Political Economy. Taylor and Francis, Hoboken

Henckaerts J-M, Doswald-Beck L (eds) (2005) Customary International Humanitarian Law, Volume I: Rules. Cambridge University Press, New York

Heyns C, Probert T (2016) Securing the Right to Life: A Cornerstone of the Human Rights System. EJIL:*Talk!* https://www.ejiltalk.org/securing-the-right-to-life-a-cornerstone-of-the-human-rights-system/

Hurd I (2011) Is Humanitarian Intervention Legal? The Rule of Law in an Incoherent World. Ethics & Intern. Aff. 25:293–313

Hurd I (2014) The International Rule of Law: Law and the Limit of Politics. Ethics and International Affairs 28:39–51

Hurd I (2015a) Three Models of the International Rule of Law. Eidos 23:37–48

Hurd I (2015b) The International Rule of Law and the Domestic Analogy. Global Constitutionalism 4:365–95

Jessup P (1945) The International Court of Justice and the Rule of Law. World Aff. 108:234–38

Kanetake M (2016) The Interfaces Between the National and International Rule of Law: A Framework Paper. In: Nollkaemper A, Kanetake M (eds) The Rule of Law at the National and International Levels: Contestations and Deference. Hart Publishing, Oxford/Portland, OR, pp 11–41

Koh H (2016) The War Powers and Humanitarian Intervention. Houst. L. Rev. 53:971–1033

Kumm M (2003-2004) International Law in National Courts: The International Rule of Law and the Limits of the Internationalist Model. Va. J. Int. Law 44:19–32

Kumm M (2004) The Legitimacy of International Law: A Constitutionalist Framework of Analysis. EJIL 15:907–31

Lauterpacht H (2011) The Function of Law in the International Community. Oxford University Press, Oxford

Maurer P (2019) Changing world, unchanged protection? 70 Years of the Geneva Conventions. https://www.icrc.org/en/document/changing-world-unchanged-protection-70-years-geneva-conventions

McCorquodale R (2016) Defining the International Rule of Law: Defying Gravity? ICLQ 65:277–304

Nardin T (2008) Theorising the International Rule of Law. Rev. Int'l Stud. 34:385–401

Nijman J (2015) Images of Grotius, *or* the International Rule of Law beyond Historiographical Oscillation. Journal of the History of International Law 17: 83–137

Nollkaemper A (2009) The Internationalized Rule of Law. HJRL 1: 74–78

Pavel C E (2019) The International Rule of Law. CRISPP 22:1–20

Pech L (2009) The rule of law as a constitutional principle of the European Union. Jean Monnet working paper series 4: 1–79

Pech L (2010) 'A Union Founded on the Rule of Law': Meaning and Reality of the Rule of Law as a Constitutional Principle of EU Law. European Constitutional Law Review 6: 359–396

Randelzhofer A, Dörr O (2012) 'Article 2(4).' In: Simma B et al (eds) The Charter of the United Nations. A Commentary, 3rd edn. Oxford University Press, Oxford, pp 201–34

Raz J (1979) Authority of Law. Essays on Law and Morality. Oxford University Press, New York

Rodley N (2015) Humanitarian Intervention. In: Weller M (ed) The Oxford Handbook of the Use of Force in International Law. Oxford University Press, Oxford, pp 775–96

Simma B (1999) NATO, the UN and the Use of Force: Legal Aspects. EJIL 10:1–22

Simma B (2004) Fragmentation in a Positive Light. Mich. J. Int. L. 25:845–48

Simma B (2009) Fragmentation of International Law From the Perspective of a Practitioner. EJIL 20:265–97

Spijkers O (2011) The United Nations, the Evolution of Global Values and International Law. Intersentia, Cambridge

Spijkers O (2012) Global Values In the United Nations Charter. Neth. Int'l L. Rev. 59:361–397

Tamanaha B (2004) On the Rule of Law: History, Politics, Theory. Cambridge University Press, Cambridge

Tesón F (2005) Humanitarian Intervention: An Inquiry into Law and Morality, 3rd edn. Transnational, Ardsley

Westerman P (2018) Outsourcing the Law: A Philosophical Perspective on Regulation. Edward Elgar Publishing, Cheltenham

Wolfrum R (2012) Article 1. In: Simma B et al (eds) The Charter of the United Nations. A Commentary, 3rd edn. Oxford University Press, Oxford, pp 107–20

Anthony Cullen BA, MA, LLM, Ph.D., SFHEA is a Senior Lecturer in Law at Middlesex University, London. Prior to taking up this position, he was a Research Fellow at the School of Law, University of Leeds (2011–2013) and a Research Fellow at the Lauterpacht Centre for International Law, University of Cambridge (2007–2011). His research focuses on the areas of international humanitarian law, international human rights law, the use of contemplative methods in higher education, and student wellbeing. In addition to his position at Middlesex University, Dr Cullen is also a Visiting Professor at the University of Bordeaux.

Kostiantyn Gorobets is a Ph.D. student at the University of Groningen, the Netherlands. His research interests lie at the overlap of analytical jurisprudence and theory and philosophy of international law. He is interested in particular in the international rule of law, authority of international law, and theory of customary international law.

Chapter 4
The Common Heritage of Mankind

Victor Alencar Mayer Feitosa Ventura ⓘ
and Eduardo Cavalcanti de Mello Filho

Contents

4.1 Introduction 68
4.2 The Genesis of the Common Heritage of Mankind Principle in International Law 70
4.3 The Normative Nature of the Common Heritage of Mankind Principle 75
4.4 The Elements of the Common Heritage of Mankind Principle 82
    4.4.1 Prohibition of Private and Public Appropriation or Sovereignty 82
    4.4.2 Designation for Peaceful Uses 84
    4.4.3 Equitable Distribution of Benefits 86
    4.4.4 Concerted Management and Exploitation by All Nations 87
4.5 Recent Developments and the Future of the Common Heritage of Mankind
    Principle 88
4.6 Conclusion 90
References 91

Abstract This chapter analyses the Common Heritage of Mankind (CHM) principle as applied to areas beyond national jurisdiction in international law. By examining its genesis, normative nature, elements, recent developments and challenges, this work presents a comprehensive study on this complex and often misunderstood topic. The first section highlights the CHM principle's aptitude for (i) preventing conflicts, (ii) promoting a common interest of mankind as international law moves its focus from bilateral interests to community interests, and (iii) offering a solution to the wider North-South divide in terms of material inequality. The second section examines the normative nature of the CHM principle and its sub-norms—both in general international law and in special regimes—approaching the interplay of sources of international law regarding the subject and special normative statuses (e.g., norms

---

V. A. M. F. Ventura (✉)
Brazilian National Agency for Agriculture, João Pessoa, Paraíba, Brazil

Humberto Bezerra Law Firm LLP, João Pessoa, Brazil

Center for Political-Strategic Studies of the Brazilian Navy, Rio de Janeiro, Brazil

Brazilian Institute for the Law of the Sea (BILOS), Belo Horizonte, Brazil

E. Cavalcanti de Mello Filho
Graduate Institute of International and Development Studies, Geneva, Switzerland

University of Geneva, Geneva, Switzerland

© T.M.C. ASSER PRESS and the authors 2022
S. Sayapin et al. (eds.), *International Conflict and Security Law*,
https://doi.org/10.1007/978-94-6265-515-7_4

erga omnes and *jus cogens*). The third section focuses on the elements and sub-norms of the CHM principle, which encompass the prohibition of appropriation, the reservation for peaceful purposes, equitable benefit sharing, and the concerted management of the area and its resources. The fourth section delves into recent developments of the CHM principle and what is reasonable to expect for it in the future, especially concerning the seabed, biodiversity beyond national jurisdiction, and outer space. Finally, concluding remarks sum up the previous sections in an intertwined and holistic fashion, highlighting the fundamentals of the Common Heritage of Mankind principle.

Keywords Common Heritage of Mankind · outer space · seabed · areas beyond national jurisdiction · public commons

4.1 Introduction

The Common Heritage of Mankind (CHM) principle has been used in respect to areas beyond national jurisdiction in which the international community has a special interest, such as the international seabed area, the moon and other celestial bodies and, to a lesser extent, Antarctica.[1] Notable commentators have linked the concept to the Spanish school of international law, especially to the work of Francisco de Vitoria.[2] Some even suggest that its embryonic manifestations may have been found in the 1912 Draft Convention on the Svalbard Archipelago.[3]

This chapter, however, is not concerned with its exact historical and distant origins. Instead, it focuses on the elements and the normativity of the Common Heritage of Mankind principle as it stands in the 21st century. In order to address these issues, one must go back to 1967. In this key year, not only did Maltese Diplomat Arvid Pardo make a historic speech at the United Nations General Assembly (UNGA) demonstrating the ocean space to be the Common Heritage of Mankind, but earlier that year Argentine Ambassador Aldo Cocca also introduced the same concept for outer space in the United Nations Committee on the Peaceful Uses of the Outer Space (UNCOPUOS).

The context in which the CHM principle emerged in the 1960s and 1970s was marked by three main historical processes: (i) the post-World War II shift from a state-centred international law based mainly on the realistic advancement of national interests, to a community interests/justice/humanity-focused regime grounded in rules to promote human rights and the environment via institutional cooperation; (ii) the Cold War, which augmented the potential for conflicts involving areas beyond national jurisdiction (ABNJ); and (iii) the decolonisation process, putting the spotlight on developing countries not satisfied with their reigning regimes, undisputedly

---

[1] Although some reports prefer the gender-neutral equivalent "common heritage of humankind", the expression is widely quoted as "of mankind", and so it will be used in this chapter.

[2] Isa 1993, p. 4.

[3] Isa 1993, p. 10.

4 The Common Heritage of Mankind

favourable to developed states' interests, alongside the "New International Economic World Order".[4]

It is generally agreed that the idea of a CHM emerged from an ideologically and politically conditioned background, one which cast shadows on the concept's normativity. On the one hand, for that reason, the constitutive elements and normative status of the CHM principle were not exactly clear for a while. For instance, is the peaceful uses requirement a necessary and exclusive characteristic of the CHM regime? Does this requirement stipulate complete demilitarisation or only the prohibition of aggression? Are benefit-sharing provisions compensatory or based on preferential status (toward developing states, for instance)? How should the rational management of areas beyond national jurisdiction and its resources be achieved? Is such achievement more likely to occur through an international organization, such as the International Seabed Authority (ISA)? These and other questions will be addressed in the present assessment of the CHM principle.

On the other hand, the principle's normativity has been a question mark since the beginning, as the adhesion to international legal instruments was timid, the provisions were vague, and state practice and *opinio juris* did not seem to favour the idea of a particular set of resources lying beyond sovereign reach and exclusive exploitation. Nonetheless, it is now indisputable that the CHM, in the realm of the law of the sea, for instance, possesses strong normativity. In fact, the principle has clearly defined elements; both the United Nations Convention on the Law of the Sea (UNCLOS) and the 1994 Implementing Agreement have been adhered to and constantly developed by the International Seabed Authority (ISA) and other relevant stakeholders.

Therefore, this chapter will initially revive the rather recent genesis of the norm, delimiting the principle's scope according to different international legal regimes, such as the law of the sea and outer space law. The principle's normativity will also be investigated, i.e., whether it is a philosophical idea, soft law, binding rule, customary international law, *erga omnes* obligation or *jus cogens*. Then, the elements—basic rules and constitutive parts—of the CHM will be explained and assessed. Finally, the chapter will both analyse recent normative developments concerning the principle and speculate on the principle's future, particularly in light of its challenge in preventing conflicts on the international stage.

Regarding the material extent of the CHM principle, this chapter will examine the principle in the specific context of resources and areas beyond national jurisdiction. Although it has been associated with UNESCO's 1972 Convention on Cultural

---

[4] For further details on the "New International World Economic Order", *see* generally Makarczyk 1988. In the wake of the decolonization process, the Group of 77 advocated a more radical form of the "common heritage of mankind" principle, based on the ideology underpinning the so-called New International Economic Order (NIEO), designed to rebalance economic relations between industrialized countries of the North and poorly developed States of the global South.

and Natural Heritage,[5] human rights, the environment,[6] and even the internet,[7] and while these may be common concerns of humanity, they are not subject to the rules pertaining to the CHM legal concept. Hence, applying the concept indistinctly would risk jeopardizing the analysis of its elements and its already controversial normative status.

4.2 The Genesis of the Common Heritage of Mankind Principle in International Law

To understand the idea of a common heritage of mankind in international law, one must explain the concept of areas beyond national jurisdiction, the most notable of which happen to be the ocean and the outer space.[8] Since medieval times, conflicting views regarding the seas have shaped the laws applicable to those spaces: on the one hand, the freedom of the seas, as defended by Grotius; on the other, territorial sovereignty over the waters, as posited by Welwood. Since Grotius' *The Free Seas*, the high seas have shifted from *res nullius*, owned by no one and subject to appropriation, towards *res communis omnium*, a common good that shall not be enclosed by a single nation.[9] To a large extent that remains valid: community interests concerning the oceans prevail over particular aspirations by coastal states.[10]

---

[5] The notion of Common Heritage of Humanity is to be found in the Preamble of the 2005 UNESCO Convention on the Protection and Promotion of the Diversity of Cultural Expressions: "Conscious that cultural diversity forms a *common heritage of humanity* and should be cherished and preserved for the benefit of all." Paris, 20 October 2005.

[6] Concerning the environment, ICJ Judge Cançado Trindade considers in an avant-gardiste fashion: "That international law is no longer exclusively State-oriented can be seen from reiterated references to humankind, not only in extensive doctrinal writings in our days, but also and significantly in various international instruments, possibly pointing towards an international law for mankind, pursuing preservation of the environment and sustainable development to the benefit of present and future generations." ICJ, *Pulp Mills* case (Argentina v. Uruguay), Cançado Trindade, Separate Opinion, 2006, p. 195.

[7] Applying the concept of common heritage of mankind to the internet is a proposal put forward by Malta's Special Envoy to the United Nations, Dr. Alex Trigona, according to whom the concept should apply to the internet's critical infrastructure, so as to, among others, narrow the "digital divide" between developing and developed countries. World Summit on Information Society Review Process, New York, 15 December 2015.

[8] Edith Brown made the famous analogy between hydrospace and outer space, both of which shared a vastness, inaccessibility and a challenge for space-age technology; economic potential and strategic importance; and difficult boundary problems. In her words, humankind ought to invest more in deep-sea research than in outer space projects. For further details, *see* Brown 1973, p. 7.

[9] *See* Casella 2014, p. 534. Also, Vicente Marotta Rangel, former Judge at the International Tribunal for the Law of the Sea, emphasizes Grotius' position that "it would threaten the interests of the international community to subject the ocean to the sovereignty of a certain state". Rangel 1979, p. 104.

[10] The concept of "community interests" can be found in Bruno Simma, in a clear link to the Common Heritage of Mankind concept. Simma 1998, p. 266.

4 The Common Heritage of Mankind

Still, on the high seas, Grotius famously stated that the ocean and its resources are so vast that they suffice for all uses that every people may want or need. A century later, Wolff and Vattel proposed similarly that *mare vastum res usus inexhausti est.*[11] The validity of this premise is fundamental to the doctrine of freedoms of the seas since these freedoms had long been considered non-excludable and non-rivalrous. Very soon, however, it became clear that the ocean resources were not infinite, which rendered a purely freedom-based *res communi omnium usus* regime unsustainable.[12]

As early as 1960, Latin American states spread the conception that unlimited access to marine living and non-living resources beyond the territorial sea would perpetuate an unequal international economic order and feed the so-called "tragedy of the commons".[13] Combined with maritime powers' great influence on the seas and technological advancements, this led to a territorialist haste by Latin-American and African States in the decades preceding the Third Conference on the Law of the Sea. Such movement confirms that areas beyond national jurisdiction are not a novel concept and neither is the interest of the international community in them. Furthermore, states' *creeping jurisdiction*[14] is not a mere manifestation of national interest, as it dismisses the unlimited freedoms of the seas' regime—based on the high seas as *res communi omnium usus*—as inadequate.

A regime grounded in complete freedom (or "open access") allowed for overexploitation and degradation, to the point that what began as a doctrine suited to the needs of traditional maritime empires had become a right to overfish and a license to pollute.[15] As a consequence, international quarrels and conflicts regarding marine resources emerged, such as the 1951 Fisheries Case between the United Kingdom and Norway,[16] and the 1963 Lobster War between Brazil and France.[17] In sum, action was needed to prevent the emergence of further conflicts.

In 1967, Arvid Pardo made a historic speech at the United Nations, criticizing the liberalism of the *res communi*, in order to focus on communitarian perspectives that consider the interests of present and future generations, as well as the equal sharing

---

[11] Rangel 1979, p. 105.

[12] Venezuelan international lawyer Andrés Bello, considering the exhaustibility of the resources of the sea, affirmed in 1832 that it would be legitimate for a nation to appropriate parts of the sea where it is located, which are not already owned by another nation. Dupuy and Vignes 1991, p. 48.

[13] See generally Hardin 1968.

[14] For a critique on the misleading use of the phrase "creeping jurisdiction", see generally Ventura 2020.

[15] Taylor 2019, p. 143.

[16] International Court of Justice, Fisheries Case (UK v. Norway), Order of 18 December 1951.

[17] The economic potential and relevance of marine resources for Brazil was at the core of the so-called "Lobster War" against France in 1963, due to French vessels capturing lobsters and other crustaceans of the Brazilian continental shelf.

In addition to traditional sedentary fisheries, one ought also to bear in mind the still unknown potential of the genetic resources of some of the species inhabiting the depths of the continental margin.

of benefits among rich and poor nations.[18] Moreover, Pardo also drew attention to the fact that the race for the seabed had already started:

> Surpassing in magnitude and in its implications last century's colonial scramble for territory in Asia and Africa. Between the very few dominant powers, suspicions and tensions would reach unprecedented levels.[19]

It is worth noting that in the 1960s there was no clearly established limit for national claims over the sea and, specifically, the 1958 Convention on the Continental Shelf provided that the continental shelf would extend up to the point where it reached a 200-m depth or wherever the coastal state proved capable of exploiting. So, there was no real limit to state territorialism at the time, meaning that in the future there could be no international seabed area. It was a true state of disorder.

The Maltese alert came when the existing legal order of the seas had already begun to collapse.[20] Considering the ecological unity of ocean space, the protection of the marine environment, the fair sharing of the riches of the sea, and the need to avoid conflicts, the Common Heritage of Mankind was introduced. The principle came to be applied to the Area, but philosophically it was proposed that the whole ocean space is a common heritage of mankind—this is actually the content of Malta's 1971 Draft Ocean Space Treaty—and it does not mean a derogation of the sovereignties and rights over the sea, but it does mean that the governance of the sea, made by the competent authorities, should take into consideration the interest of mankind.[21]

Even though the final formulation of the CHM principle in the UN Convention on the Law of the Sea did not apply to the "ocean environment as a complex and interconnected whole", thus leaving the ocean vulnerable to traditional notions of state sovereignty,[22] the application of the CHM principle to the Area greatly inhibited the extension of continental shelves to commons involving the interests of mankind. Moreover, the peaceful uses element was ruled as essential, given that the seabed had a great potential for military purposes and tests.[23] Also, the then imminent potential for exploration and exploitation of the international seabed, especially by developed states, became a symbol of the unequal benefits of marine wealth to different nations.

---

[18] Kiss 1982, p. 123.

[19] *Note verbale* of the Permanent Mission of Malta to the United Nations addressed to the Secretary-General to the United Nations, A/6695, 18 August 1967.

[20] Tuerk 2017, p. 260.

[21] Taylor 2019, p. 146.

[22] According to Taylor, "Elisabeth and Arvid worked tirelessly to champion CHM and its legal implementation in the law of the sea and, ultimately, UNCLOS. Where they perhaps differed was in their response to the outcome of the negotiations. A combination of political and economic factors greatly restricted the scope of CHM to mineral resources on the deep seabed and ocean floor in areas outside of national jurisdiction. UNCLOS did not apply CHM to the entire ocean environment as a complex and interconnected ecological whole. This created an 'ecological nonsense' that left much of the oceans vulnerable to traditional notions of state sovereignty (including creeping claims of sovereign jurisdiction), common property, and freedom of the high seas. Arvid expressed grave disappointment with this outcome". Taylor 2019, p. 143.

[23] In 1971, the Seabed Arms Control Treaty was signed, banning the emplacement of weapons of mass destruction beyond the 12 nautical miles measured from the baselines.

4 The Common Heritage of Mankind

Therefore, a compensatory regime (or one that attributed a preferential status towards developing states) was sought by these countries.

The application of the CHM principle to the whole ocean space made and still makes sense from a philosophical and scientific perspective. The political setting considering developing states, maritime powers, landlocked and geographically disadvantaged countries, amongst others, welcomed the CHM regime applicable to the Area. Despite the regime's reform in 1994, the general aspects of the CHM principle had already crystalized as customary international law.[24]

When the CHM idea made it into international law, the following instruments were adopted: (i) the 1968 UNGA Resolution 2467A, which created the Committee on the Peaceful Uses of Seabed; (ii) the 1971 Declaration of Principles Governing the Seabed and the Ocean Floor, and the Subsoil Thereof, beyond the Limits of National Jurisdiction adopted by the UNGA Resolution 2749; (iii) the 1982 UNCLOS, which provided that the Area and its resources are the Common Heritage of Mankind (Article 136); and (iv) the 1994 Implementation Agreement. Apart from those, recent norms enacted by the International Seabed Authority (ISA), as mandated by the UNCLOS, help complete the circle of international rules that shape and define the normative silhouette of the CHM principle regarding the law of the sea.

In the meantime, the Soviet Union's Sputnik was set into orbit, inaugurating the space race. The Cold War context demanded new laws, especially in order to avoid the risk of militarization of outer space. Already in 1958, an *ad-hoc* committee on the peaceful uses of outer space was established by the UNGA, and, in 1959, it became the permanent Committee on the Peaceful Uses of Outer Space (COPUOS). Then, in 1962, the Declaration of Legal Principles Governing the Activities of States in the Exploration and Use of Outer Space was adopted.[25] For almost five years, this had been the main reference of outer space law, and in 1966, American president Lyndon Johnson suggested a treaty to the Soviet Union based on the freedom of exploration and use of outer space, on the principle of non-appropriation, freedom of scientific research, peaceful uses and protection of the space environment.[26]

In January 1967, the Treaty on Principles Governing the Activities of States in the Exploration and Use of Outer Space, including the Moon and Other Celestial Bodies (OST), was opened for signatures. This instrument stated that "the exploration and use of outer space, including the moon and other celestial bodies, shall be carried out for the benefit and in the interests of all countries, irrespective of their degree of economic or scientific development, and shall be the province of all mankind".[27]

The CHM principle is not mentioned in the OST. Instead, the term used in Article 1 is "province," which carries no specific legal content.[28] In the preamble, the expression *common interest of all mankind* appears, just like in international instruments

---

[24] Wolfrum 1983, p. 335.

[25] UNGA Resolution 1472 (XIV), 1962.

[26] Isa 1993, p. 151–4.

[27] Preamble and Article 1.

[28] Smouts 2005, p. 56.

concerning human rights and the environment, which refer abstractly to this expression, with no binding legal implications. In fact, whereas an interest is no more than an aspiration or concern, the "common heritage" reaches a step beyond in legal terms, amounting to a subjective right.

Alexander Kiss suggests that the Common Heritage of Mankind be the materialization of the common interest of mankind in a situation of dual need: to maintain peace in certain areas, considering the interests of mankind, and to in concert manage the resources of such areas in order to conserve them. The CHM principle—as the materialization of the CIM—would presuppose a specific legal structure. According to Kiss:

> In fact, the common heritage is the complete territorial expression, the materialization of the common interest of mankind. This means that the states suspend or do not assert rights or claims to territorial jurisdiction, or in some cases exercise such jurisdiction only within set limits, for the benefit of the whole human community, without any immediate return, and conserve and if necessary manage areas in conformity with the common interest for the benefit of all mankind.[29]

Ergo, such perception considers the CHM equally applicable to areas within national jurisdiction, in conformity with Borgese and Pardo's aspirations. Nonetheless, this conceptualization does not properly consider the *lege lata*—the law as it is. Therefore, the authors of this chapter understand that it is more appropriate to delimit the CHM principle's scope solely to areas beyond national jurisdiction.[30]

Still, in 1967, Argentinian Ambassador Aldo Cocca claimed that the international community had recognized *humanity* as a subject of international law, to which *res communi humanitatis* would be endowed. Among these *common things of humanity*, Cocca highlighted outer space, including the moon and other celestial bodies.[31] Only in 1979, the Agreement Governing the Activities of States on the Moon and Other Celestial Bodies (Moon Agreement, or MA), in Article 11(1), provided that "the Moon and its natural resources are the common heritage of mankind, which finds expression in the provisions of this agreement, in particular paragraph 5 of this article".

Two observations are needed regarding the phrase "which finds expression in the provisions of this agreement". First, it seems appropriate to say that, given the lack of normativity of the CHM principle *per se*, its specific regime should be further defined through treaty provisions.

In 1983, Wolfrum argued that the CHM regime, as delimited in UNCLOS, was not part of customary international law, except for its most general terms, such as non-appropriation and peaceful uses.[32] Yet, today the CHM principle (as applied to the seabed) seems undisputed, respected even by non-state parties, including the United States; today some may argue more reasonably that it is Customary International

---

[29] Kiss 1985, p. 428.

[30] This is the most adopted position by commentators and States. Noyes 2012, p. 449.

[31] Cocca 1981, p. 13.

[32] Wolfrum 1983, p. 335.

4 The Common Heritage of Mankind

Law.[33] Without specific and concrete treaty provisions, this would probably not be the case. The second observation, based on the first one, is that, because Article 11(1) MA creates an abstract principle and an obligation to establish an undefined international regime—almost an open clause—the number of ratifications is lower than expected (less than 20), none of them being a great space power.

Prior to all these legal and political developments regarding the idea of a common heritage of mankind, the international community had already discussed it in relation to the sixth continent: Antarctica. Some commentators assessed the Antarctic Treaty (1959) System as non-explicitly applying the CHM principle—although not perfectly. After all, the continent's landmass lies beyond national jurisdiction (where sovereignty claims are suspended), is reserved for peaceful uses, and counts on extensive environmental protection, among other proofs of a true "common heritage".[34]

In light of the above, one realizes that the genesis of the CHM in the initial decades of the second half of the 20th Century was due to a number of reasons. First, there was a pressing need to avoid conflicts. The preamble of the Antarctic Treaty declared that "it is in the interest of all mankind that Antarctica shall continue forever to be used exclusively for peaceful purposes and shall not become the scene or object of discord". Similarly, avoiding conflict was also at the epicentre of the law of the sea—as applicable to the international seabed—and outer space law, given that the OST clearly forbade the employment of weapons of mass destruction in outer space. Second, the CHM principle aimed at fulfilling the interests of mankind in exploring and better understanding these largely uncharted places. Third, there was a need to rethink the terms of a reasonable and equitable management of the resources found in areas beyond national jurisdiction. This factor manifested differently depending on the specific area, as will be seen in the next topic.

4.3 The Normative Nature of the Common Heritage of Mankind Principle

To discuss the normative nature of the CHM principle is to dwell on the sources of international law. Any assessment of the principle's normativity must take into account that the CHM is a broad and comprehensive concept, comprised of a number of elements, norms and sub-norms. Furthermore, according to Baslar,

---

[33] Noyes 2012, p. 456.

[34] Kiss 1982, p. 144. Such a view is not prevalent though, as other commentators have contended that the CHM principle is hardly compatible with the Antarctic Treaty System (ATS) considered as a whole. This position, with which the authors of this chapter agree, seems more reasonable, as there is a profound political interest by 12 States, which render the ATS more an oligarchy than a democratic organization representing the humankind. They do that in pursuing mainly their national interests. There are indeed some similarities with the CHM concept, but the very foundation leads to this inevitable conclusion: the Antarctic Treaty System is not subject to the CHM principle. *See* Altemir 1992, p. 197.

Care is needed as to whether one is discussing its nature and meaning under a particular discipline of international law, or whether one is referring to the concept in the context of public international law as a whole. Care is also needed as to by whom (i.e., politician or international lawyer), when (i.e., pre or post-Cold War periods), in which context (i.e., international spaces or the global environment), according to which description (i.e., *res communis omnium* or public trust), according to which school of thought (i.e., positivism or naturalism), the common heritage of mankind is being judged in order to come to a conclusion whether it is a principle of international law or merely transcendental nonsense.[35]

In light of Baslar's considerations, this chapter adopts the following key premises. As seen in the previous topic, the discussion on the CHM nature and meaning is held under particular disciplines of International Law, as it is not *ipso facto* applicable to every area beyond national jurisdiction or common concern of humankind, but to treaty-based areas. In addition, this chapter contains a legal analysis, so the political aspect of the term and its philosophical content, albeit relevant, are not central. Third, this chapter takes into account the international juncture of the early 2020s, before the last session of the Intergovernmental Conference on an international legally binding instrument under UNCLOS on the conservation and sustainable use of marine biological diversity of areas beyond national jurisdiction (BBNJ).[36] Fourth, this chapter deals specifically with areas beyond national jurisdiction, given that in applying to some of them the CHM principle carries a manifest minimum normativity.[37] Fifth, the *res communi* paradigm is certainly not the most appropriate one for the CHM concept, and some may argue that it is a public trust, but its structure and on whose behalf it is established remain to be examined in this work. Sixth, and finally, almost every analysis of the normative nature of the CHM takes into consideration a positivist perspective, and even if a naturalist one is considered, its application is usually limited to *general principles of law* and *jus cogens* norms. Either way, as will be seen, the CHM is not susceptible to a discussion on whether it is a general principle of law and/or a *jus cogens* norm.

Regarding the wide-ranging nature of the CHM principle, it should be noted that broad concepts are neither good nor bad, but difficult to handle and impossible to control. John Noyes has analysed this matter with exceptional clarity when he suggested that

---

[35] Baslar 1997, p. 342.

[36] In its resolution 72/249 of 24 December 2017, the General Assembly decided to convene an Intergovernmental Conference to elaborate the text of an international legally binding instrument under the United Nations Convention on the Law of Sea on the conservation and sustainable use of marine biological diversity of areas beyond national jurisdiction.

[37] Smouts is categorical thereon, considering that it applies only to the moon and other celestial bodies, the orbit of geostationary satellites, the spectre of radioelectric frequencies, and the international seabed. In his words, "Le patrimoine commun de l'humanité est pauvre. Juridiquement, ni l'espace extra-atmosphérique, ni les eaux de haute mer, ni l'Antarctique n'en font partie, encore moins la foret Amazonie. Les seuls espaces relevant de cette catégorie sont la lune et les corps célestes, l'orbite des satellites géostationnaires et le spectre des frequences radioelectriques, les grand fonds marins. Le reste est de l'ordre de l'incantation et n'engage pas les Etats, ou bien fait l'objet de déclarations peu contraignantes, telle la liste des biens inscrits au patrimoine culturel et naturel de l'Unesco, et, plus récemment, le génome humain". Smouts 2005, p. 54.

4 The Common Heritage of Mankind

Legal principles have value even if left in general terms. Indeed, it is not always desirable to convert broad principles into more concrete or determinate rules. Principles of international law may fill gaps in rules and provide decision makers with a guiding mindset—a reminder of basic objectives of the law—when they interpret or apply rules. […] That is, they may accord different States discretion to pursue a common objective in different ways, in line with particular domestic political and legal arrangements. A legal principle need not be incorporated into treaty law in order to have significance. Indeed, even as soft law, political concept, or "emerging customary international law," a principle may be used to influence debates and shape legal developments.[38]

Nonetheless, treaty rules seem to be the best instrument for accommodating the CHM principle in international law. The adoption of the CHM regime implies a number of sub-norms that could not be minimally specific and operational if the principle were provided for only in customary international law. Concerted management and benefit sharing provisions, for instance, may establish determined rules on decision-making, on what resources should be shared, and on how they should be shared.[39] As Noyes would put it, this "may suggest the desirability of more determinate language to guide States and other actors operating under the principle."[40]

Indeed, the International Law Association's 1986 Seoul Declaration stated that the CHM principle was to be specified by internationally agreed-upon regimes.[41] Take, for instance, the relevant provisions of the Declaration of Principles Governing the Seabed and the Ocean Floor, and the Subsoil Thereof, beyond the Limits of National Jurisdiction (1970)[42] and of the Moon Agreement (1979),[43] it seems undeniable that the CHM principle may only attain a "strong normativity"[44] once internationally agreed upon. General and vague expressions without specific developments, such as common concern of humankind, common interest of humankind or even Common

---

[38] Noyes 2012, p. 460–1.

[39] In this sense, UNCLOS Part XI, on the Area, contains specific provisions on competence and procedures. The latter are further elaborated within the work of the International Seabed Authority, which counts on rules of procedure for its main organs (Assembly, Council, Legal and Technical Committee, and Financial Committee) and detailed regulations on the exploration of determined types of mineral—all developed with the participation of member States and relevant stakeholders. This is evidence of the level of consolidation the CHM principle, as applied to the Area, has reached.

[40] Noyes 2012, p. 461.

[41] *See* Declaration on the Progressive Development of Principles of Public International Law Relating to a New International Economic Order, 1986, para 7.1.

[42] The 9th paragraph of the 1970 Declaration of Principles: "On the basis of the principles of this Declaration, an international régime applying to the area and its resources and including appropriate international machinery to give effect to its provisions shall be established by an international treaty of a universal character, generally agreed upon".

[43] Article 11(5) MT: "States parties hereby undertake to establish an international regime, including appropriate procedures, to govern the exploitation of natural resources of the moon as soon as such exploitation becomes feasible".

[44] A norm with strong normativity is a minimally specific and concrete legal command that allows subjects to request and demand compliance with it—to whoever is bound by this norm. If there is only a norm stating that a certain area beyond national jurisdiction is CHM, what specific conduct may one demand from States? See note below.

Heritage of Mankind—when used without a legal support—would have no or low normativity, limiting its effects in the political arena.[45]

Furthermore, beyond Article 26 of the Vienna Convention on the Law of Treaties—*pacta sunt servanda*—, another crucial question is whether the CHM principle is a norm of Customary International Law or not. Preliminarily, one should note the distinction between the CHM principle, generally speaking, and its sub-norms/elements, e.g., prohibition of appropriation, reservation for peaceful uses, concerted management, and equitable benefit-sharing.

To answer that question, one must fulfil three qualifying preconditions, as described by Joyner:

> First, the legal content of the CHM must be so distinct and well-defined that the concept can be fully integrated into the corpus of international law. Second, resultant State practice must comply with the development of the CHM notion and, additionally, evidence of *opinio juris* (i.e., consensus) must be demonstrated and evident. Third, the customary acceptance of the CHM as determined by State conduct and behaviour must be manifest, or at least sufficiently broad-based to attest to the CHM's widespread acceptance. State practice carries within it certain norm-creating effects that may give rise to the evolution and crystallisation of a new principle of law.[46]

In the 1980s, Joyner was adamant that the CHM doctrine had not been transformed into a legal principle and, as such, did not amount to international custom. With respect to the first precondition, the vagueness of the principle might have rendered it not so well defined. This precondition is still valid. But, especially in respect to the development of the Seabed Regime, one can say that the principle became well-defined, counting on clear elements. Regarding the Moon and other celestial bodies, as exploitation is not feasible yet, its CHM regime is not well defined. Under this perspective, only the very general terms of the CHM principle, collected using a holistic approach, could be considered CIL—these general terms will be revisited in the next topic about the elements of the CHM principle.

The second precondition is a traditional definition of a CIL norm, perhaps too traditional and too simplistically put. Already in the 1960s, influential scholars[47] suggested that the *opinio juris* requirement is the crucial one, as state practice should be understood as a manifestation of that *opinio juris*.

It has been emphasized in scholarly literature on CHM that "the process has been reversed in such a way that *opinio juris* takes precedence over the material element of State practice."[48] And this should be the case for regimes where effective practice is still limited, but by no means negligible. In recent years, scholars and practitioners have had great advances in the understanding of the elements of CIL, but deepening

---

[45] Here, it is useful to understand soft law's two traditional meanings. (i) A hard law provision with low normativity (i.e., an undeveloped CHM treaty regime or a vague norm of CIL stating that a determined area is CHM) and (ii) a non-hard law provision to which one may attribute a certain degree of normative strength. Weil 1983, p. 414.

[46] Joyner 1986, p. 198.

[47] Cheng 1965, p. 23.

[48] Baslar 1997, p. 351.

4 The Common Heritage of Mankind

on this subject would be inappropriate in this chapter.[49] Made these considerations, it should be highlighted that:

> Widespread acceptance of a treaty may also bolster support for the CH principle as a norm of customary international law. [...] the LOS Convention/Implementation Agreement regime — our only example of a widely accepted treaty regime specifically incorporating the CH principle —appears stable, despite the United States not being a party. Indeed, the practice of states and international institutions operating under this regime reinforces the CH principle as applied to deep seabed mining.[50]

In addition, as of July 2020, the ISA has entered into 15-year exploration contracts with 21 contractors, state and state-sponsored private entities. Among these are Germany, Japan, the United Kingdom, France, Russia,[51] which were, alongside the United States and the Soviet Union, the ones who unilaterally adopted national legislation on the concession of exploration and exploitation licenses in the Area. Moreover, the UK and Germany had chosen to abstain from signing the UNCLOS in 1982.[52]

In light of the above, the entire seabed regime may be taken as Customary International Law, the United States being the only state entitled to raise the *persistent objector* exception. As mentioned earlier, in these cases the *opinio juris* element plays a more important role—and the American objection to the Part XI regime is historic, persistent and notorious. Furthermore, it is relatively clear that the CHM principle is not a *jus cogens* norm, so the American objection is valid. Notice, nevertheless, that the United States is not a persistent objector to the CHM as a whole, but to the CHM rules present in the UNCLOS' normative edifice. This means that it is bound to essential elements of the CHM principle, such as the non-appropriation rule, as applicable to the oceans and to celestial bodies.

In order to depict the whole international seabed regime as CIL, it should be taken into consideration that state practice must be consistent (uniform), widespread (extensive) and representative.[53] First, state practice is consistent. Except the United States, those who had differing national legislation all contracted with the ISA and no records exist of blatant violations of UNCLOS' seabed regime. Second, state practice is also extensive. The very number of parties to UNCLOS and the absence of blatant disregard in general prove this point. Third, and most important, it is representative, since there is virtually no state (except for the United States) interested in and powerful enough to explore and exploit the international seabed against the current regime, through conducts or declarations—those states who lack the power tend to agree with the regime, especially due to the benefit-sharing provisions.

---

[49] Focus should be given to the 2000 ILA Report on Formation of Customary International Law and to the 2018 ILC Draft Conclusions on Identification of Customary International Law.

[50] Noyes 2012, p. 468.

[51] See ISA Contracts, https://www.isa.org.jm/deep-seabed-minerals-contractors. Accessed 29 July 2020.

[52] Isa 1993, p. 172.

[53] These are the three criteria used to assess State practice, according to the 2000 ILA Report (Article 12) and the 2018 ILC Draft Conclusions (Conclusion 8), largely influenced by the 1969 North Sea Continental Shelf Cases, before the International Court of Justice.

On the other hand, the Moon Agreement, which states that the Moon and other celestial bodies are CHM, lacks recognition. Actually, the range of its states parties is neither extensive nor representative, as no great space explorer state is a party to it. Because we consider that the CHM should have its specific terms internationally agreed upon, this would render the CHM in outer space law and in the Antarctic System a mere political or philosophical concept—except for the parties to the Moon Agreement. Nevertheless, some provisions in the OST (and the correspondent norms of CIL) are compatible with the CHM as a philosophical concept applied to the Moon and other celestial bodies, such as the prohibition of appropriation.

Finally, this topic will approach *erga omnes* and *jus cogens* norms—these are characteristics of international law norms, not a source—leaving aside discussions of the so-called and controversial *objective regimes*. Because of its own nature, the CHM principle ought to be regarded as an *erga omnes* norm as it reflects a collective interest, meaning that its observance is owed to the international community as a whole.[54] Following this rationale, the International Law Commission has already affirmed that the common heritage of mankind as applied to the deep seabed expresses a collective interest that may be brought before international courts and tribunals by any party to the UNCLOS.[55] The same conclusion could be valid for the Moon and other celestial bodies. However, one must bear in mind that the norms of the Moon Treaty bind few states, and very few norms of outer space law are CIL.

While it is true that the CHM principle may be opposable *erga omnes*, one must determine in whose favour it is opposable. In other words, what does *mankind* mean?[56] It is debatable whether *mankind* is a subject of international law. The reference made by Cocca in 1967 to the CHM explicitly considered it so, but the internationally agreed upon terms of the Principle are not explicit in this sense. Regarding the CHM principle as applicable to the Seabed Regime, in answering the question raised above, one may bring Article 140 UNCLOS onto the spotlight, because, in determining that activities in the Area shall be carried for the benefit of mankind as a whole, it states that the interests of "peoples who have not attained full independence or other self-governing status recognized by the United Nations in accordance with General Assembly Resolution 1515 (XV) and other relevant GA Resolution" should be given particular consideration.

Hence, the interests of mankind may be similar, but not identical to all states' interests. Even though this provision recognizes no active subjectivity, mankind does play a certain role on the passive side as beneficiaries of the deep seabed regime, and its interests should be considered. On the active side, one might refer to Article 137(2) UNCLOS, according to which "all rights in the resources of the Area are vested in mankind as a whole on whose behalf the Authority shall act", and Article

---

[54] Barcelona Traction Case (Belgium v. Spain), International Court of Justice, Judgement of 5 February 1970, p. 32.

[55] Report of the International Law Commission of the Work of its 37th session (1985). Yearbook of the International Law Commission, part 2, 1M 27, UN Doc. A/CN.4/SER/A/1985/Add.1. Today, an *actio popularis* in international law is enshrined in Article 48 of the 2001 ILC Draft Articles on the Responsibility of States for Internationally Wrongful Acts.

[56] For more on the related concept of humanity, see Chap. 1.

4 The Common Heritage of Mankind

157(1), which states that "the Authority is the organization through which States Parties shall organize and control activities in the Area". This said, the subjectivity in the international law of mankind is to be considered too limited or inexistent. Nevertheless, the Authority—and states parties through the Authority—should act on its behalf.[57] It should be highlighted that although considering it a subject seems a legally reckless position, the tendency towards its strengthening is so powerful that it cannot be preliminarily rejected.[58]

As to a potential peremptory character, special attention must be devoted to the distinction between the CHM principle and its sub-norms. It seems undisputed that certain sub-norms, such as the prohibition of appropriation and of non-peaceful uses, have reached the status of *jus cogens* norms.[59] However, in the Third Conference, attempts to declare the principle a *jus cogens* norm failed.[60] Therefore, Article 311(6) UNCLOS emerges as a compromise resulting from these attempts and their objectors, limiting the amendment to the Common Heritage of Mankind, specially not to undermine it—and States Parties should not be a party to any agreement in derogation thereof. This compromise reflects the importance of the principle and leaves it clear that the CHM principle is not to be considered a part of *jus cogens* in its entirety. According to Baslar, the peaceful uses and the non-appropriation principles are peremptory norms.[61] Considering the CHM principle, a peremptory norm in outer space law seems acceptable only to the extent it encompasses the prohibition of appropriation. As will be seen in the next topic, it is also controversial to determine whether non-appropriation is a part of the CHM regime in outer space law or not.

To sum up, the preliminary conclusions on the normative nature of the CHM principle in international law are the following: (*i*) the CHM regime governing the seabed is CIL; (*ii*) concrete provisions in treaty norms (on the seabed) brought stronger normativity to their correspondent customary norms; (*iii*) only general aspects of the CHM principle as applied to the seabed may be considered peremptory norms, not the whole regime; (*iv*) the outer space is not considered CHM under any source of international law, although the regime governing it may present some similarities with the CHM principle; (*v*) the moon and other celestial bodies may be CHM only to parties to the MT [non CIL]; and (*vi*) the norms contained in the CHM regime are opposable *erga omnes*—only insofar as the subjects concerned are bound by it.

---

[57] Wolfrum 1983, p. 319.

[58] Rodriguez Carrión 1987, p. 369 (*apud* Isa 1993, p. 187).

[59] Tuerk 2017, p. 264.

[60] Chilean proposal, UN DOC.A/Conf. 62/122. For more, *see* Baslar 1997, p. 364. *See* also Wolfrum 1983, p. 314.

[61] Baslar 1997, p 365.

4.4 The Elements of the Common Heritage of Mankind Principle

A broad legal principle such the common heritage of mankind is composed of elements, or sub-norms, which collectively constitute what became known as the CHM principle. The normative nature of these elements varies; not all of them oblige every state in the same manner. The following four elements are found in the UN Law of the Sea Convention: (i) prohibition of private and public appropriation or sovereignty; (ii) designation for peaceful uses; (iii) equitable distribution of benefits; and (iv) concerted management and exploitation by all nations.[62] Despite the relevance of other important "elements" to the CHM principle, such as environmental protection and scientific research, this chapter is limited to the analysis of those elements which are essential to the characterization of the principle as applicable to areas beyond national jurisdiction. In addition, because the principle in outer space law is not as developed as in the law of the sea, the examination concerning the Moon and other celestial bodies follows a holistic approach, not attached to a particular instrument. This justifies the adoption of UNCLOS as the basis for the elements analysed below.

4.4.1 Prohibition of Private and Public Appropriation or Sovereignty

As explained above, the application of the CHM principle is limited to areas beyond national jurisdiction, and customary international law has established that these areas

---

[62] Pardo added to the above mentioned four elements just the freedom of scientific research with regard to the deep seas and ocean floor, not directly connected with defence, and the availability to all of the results of such research. In his words, "we are strongly of the opinion that the following, among other principles, should be incorporated in the proposed treaty: (a) The Seabed and the ocean floor, underlying the seas beyond the limits of national jurisdiction as defined in the treaty, are not subject to national appropriation in any manner whatsoever; (b) The sea-bed and the ocean floor beyond the limits of national jurisdiction shall be reserved exclusively for peaceful purposes; (c) Scientific research with regard to the deep seas and ocean floor, not directly connected with defence, shall be freely permissible and its results available to all; (d) The resources of the sea-bed and ocean floor, beyond the limits of national jurisdiction, shall be exploited primarily in the interests of mankind, with particular regard to the needs of poor countries; (e) The exploration and exploitation of the sea-bed and ocean floor beyond the limits of national jurisdiction shall be conducted in a manner consistent with the principles and purposes of the United Nations Charter and in a manner not causing unnecessary obstruction of the high seas or serious impairment of the marine environment [...] a widely representative but not too numerous body should be established in the first place to consider the security, economic and other implications of the establishment of an international regime over the deep seas and ocean floor beyond the limits of present national jurisdiction". Pardo. United Nations General Assembly First Committee, 1967, Official Records, Twenty-Second Session, Doc. A/C.1/PV.1516, para 10 and 15.

4 The Common Heritage of Mankind

shall not be subject to private or public appropriation.[63] This rule is explicitly found in Article 137(1) UNCLOS, which determines that states cannot claim sovereignty or sovereign rights over any part of the Area (international seabed), nor its resources. This provision marks a difference between the regime of the high seas and that of the CHM principle as applied to the Area, namely because while there can be no claim over any part of the high seas (Article 89, UNCLOS), its resources may be freely appropriated.

Regarding outer space law, it is undisputed that the prohibition of private and public appropriation of outer space, the Moon and other celestial bodies is a norm of CIL,[64] some commentators having pushed it to the status of *jus cogens*.[65] What about the natural resources of the moon and other celestial bodies—are they subject to this norm?

Article 11(1), MA, states that the Moon and its resources are the CHM. These resources, under the CHM legal framework, would lie beyond appropriation, just like the Area's, which requires abiding by a specific regime to effectively explore and exploit them.[66] Yet, such legal treatment cannot be considered customary, and the terms of Article 1 of the OST prevail, in that it provides that "the outer space shall be free for exploration and use for all States without discrimination".

Still, on outer space law, three points deserve to be mentioned. First, there was some controversy as to the prohibition of private appropriation regarding the OST, because Article 2 prohibits solely "national appropriation by claim of sovereignty, by means of use or occupation or by any other means". While Article 11(2) MA adopted a similar wording, paragraph 3 of that provision did set a comprehensive prohibition, including to natural and legal persons, to the point that the most common interpretation of Article 2 OST is the expansive one, which extends the prohibition to private appropriation.

Second, the geostationary orbit is not subject to appropriation either. The geostationary orbit is an orbit above the Equator line, about 36,000 km from Earth, where artificial satellites are placed that rotate around the planet in such a way that they would appear stationary to an observer from the earth. It is limited, given that there can be no more than approximately 180 satellites. In 1973, the Telecommunications Convention underlined the necessity of allowing equitable access to different countries, based on necessity and technological means. At the time, this norm clearly benefitted the most developed ones. As a consequence, in 1976, eight Equatorial States (Colombia, Brazil, Indonesia, Ecuador, Kenya, Uganda and Zaire) claimed sovereignty over the geostationary orbit corresponding to their geoposition,[67] so as to oppose the *first come, first served* approach that benefited developed states. The

---

[63] Some scholars suggest it is a peremptory norm. *See* Baslar 1997, p. 365; Hoof 1986, p. 64.

[64] Lyall and Larsen 2009, p. 71; Vereschetin and Danilenko 1985, p. 22.

[65] Christol 1994, p. 33.

[66] For part of the literature, lunar and other celestial bodies' resources are subject to appropriation if the regime provided for Article 11(5) MT is abided by. Isa 1993, p. 158.

[67] 1976 Declaration of Bogota.

move, however, went against Article 2 OST, on non-appropriation of outer space, and ended up not prospering.[68]

Third, it remains to be seen how the non-appropriation rule would be compatible with human settlements on the Moon.

4.4.2 Designation for Peaceful Uses

Both the seabed and outer space were pivotal points of potential conflicts in the 1960s amidst the Cold War. The designation of these areas for peaceful purposes would probably happen even without the CHM Concept. In 1958, the UNGA created an *ad hoc* committee to deal with the peaceful uses of outer space, which later became the Committee on the Peaceful Uses of the Outer Space. After many UNGA Resolutions in the same fashion, in 1963, the United States, Great Britain, and the Soviet Union signed the Moscow Treaty, prohibiting thermonuclear experiments in outer space—currently with more than 100 signatory parties.

Then, in 1967, the OST was opened to signature, and it contained specific clauses on the prohibition of non-peaceful uses. The Preamble's second paragraph considered it to be in the interest of mankind that the progress of exploration and use of outer space be carried out for peaceful purposes. Article 3 provides that activities in outer space shall be carried out in the interest of maintaining international peace and security. The most important provision on this subject, Article 4, determines that: (i) States undertake not to put nuclear weapons or weapons of mass destruction (WMD) into space, whether in orbit or otherwise stationed in space, or on the Moon or other celestial bodies; (ii) the Moon and other celestial bodies shall be used by all States exclusively for peaceful purposes; (iii) the establishment of military bases, installations and fortifications, the testing of any type of weapons and the conduct of military manoeuvres on celestial bodies shall be forbidden; (iv) the use of any military equipment or facility necessary shall not be prohibited. On the basis of these provisions, some observations can be made. The first one is that it prohibits aggressive uses of outer space—given the wording of Article 3 OST and Article 3(2) MT. Second, states cannot station WMD anywhere in outer space.

Article 4 OST and Article 3(1) MT mention that the Moon and other celestial bodies shall be used exclusively for peaceful purposes. The peaceful uses clause concerning the Moon and other celestial bodies seems clear, as it emphasizes the prohibition of establishing military bases, installations and fortifications, the testing of any type of weapons and the conduct of military manoeuvres. It makes an exception to the general rule determining clear limits to militarization: the use of military personnel for scientific research or for any other peaceful purposes. Nevertheless, conventional weaponry (non WMD) is permissible in outer space, apart from the Moon and other celestial bodies, and so are military satellites and weapon testing.[69]

---

[68] Isa 1993, p. 158–9.

[69] Bourbonniete and Lee 2007, p. 901.

4 The Common Heritage of Mankind

As recollected above, the genesis of the contemporary seabed regime is also intimately intertwined with potential conflicts during the Cold War. Moreover, there were two basic assumptions: non-peaceful uses usually take into account national interests, not envisaged by a regime aiming at the interests of mankind, and they can actually hinder the exploration and the exploitation of the deep sea.[70] Pardo's historic speech was at the UNGA's first committee on disarmament and security to examine the question of the reservation exclusively for peaceful purposes of the seabed and the use of its resources in the interests of mankind. In 1970, the Declaration of Principles was adopted already containing provisions on the peaceful uses principle.[71] The 1971 Treaty on the Prohibition of the Emplacement of Nuclear Weapons and Other Weapons of Mass Destruction on the Sea-Bed and the Ocean Floor and in the Subsoil thereof represented another development in the peaceful uses principle.

Concerning the seabed, UNCLOS contains three relevant provisions: Articles 138, 141, and 301. Articles 138 and 301 share a similar language, the difference being that the latter is applicable to the entire ocean space while the former exclusively applies to the area. Article 301 determines that states, in exercising rights and performing duties, shall refrain from any threat or use of force against the territorial integrity or political independence of any State, or in any other manner inconsistent with the principles of international law in the UN Charter. Article 138 does not mention the use of force, as it is very similar to the sixth paragraph of the 1970 Declaration, described above.

Article 141, on the other hand, provides that the Area shall be open to use exclusively for peaceful purposes. There is again some controversy as to the exact meaning of peaceful purposes: non-aggressive or non-military uses? Some commentators suggested that Article 301 on the "peaceful uses of the seas" served as an interpretation of the phrase "peaceful uses/purposes" throughout the Convention, prohibiting the illegal threat or use of force, as it is in Article 2(4) of the UN Charter.[72] Others consider that the peaceful purposes clause concerning the Area means the prohibition of aggression, and not complete demilitarization, particularly in light of UNCLOS' final wording: "The Area shall be open to use exclusively for peaceful purposes by all States Parties, whether coastal or land-locked, without discrimination, in accordance with the provisions of this Convention, and regulations made thereunder".[73] Thus, had the negotiating States agreed to specify the peaceful purposes clause as to encompass the complete demilitarisation, they would probably have done so.

---

[70] Wolfrum 1983, p. 319.

[71] Paragraphs 4, 5, and 8, Preamble.

[72] Wolfrum 1983, p. 320.

[73] Vöneky and Höfelmeier 2017a, b, p. 984.

4.4.3 Equitable Distribution of Benefits

Here, great differences emerge between the regimes of outer space and the seabed. Regarding the Moon Agreement, Article 11(5) calls upon states parties to establish an international regime as soon as exploitation becomes feasible. This regime, among others, shall include the equitable sharing of the benefits derived from exploitation, taking into account the interests and needs of developing states and efforts of the ones involved in the exploration—Article 11(7) (d). One might say that the Moon Agreement framework provides for an effort-based—and not needs-based—distribution.[74] However, there is no such regime yet, and because of the low adhesion to the MT, Article 1 OST prevails in every circumstance, according to which the outer space, including the Moon and other celestial bodies, shall be free for exploration and use by all states without discrimination, *for the benefit and in the interests of all states.* Given the absence of a space international organization, such as the ISA for the seabed, each state may, alone or in cooperation with others, explore and use the outer space, bearing in mind that this should be for the benefit and in the interests of all States. The question remains, however, how to effect this benefit. The 1976 Declaration of Bogota expressed dissatisfaction with the unjust state of space affairs. Later, in 1996, the UNGA passed the "Declaration on International Cooperation in the Exploration in Use of Outer Space for the Benefit and in the Interests of all States Taking into Particular Account the Needs of Developing Countries".[75]

The benefit-sharing structure in the seabed regime has witnessed important changes through the 1994 Implementation Agreement to UNCLOS Part XI, concerning the Area.[76] The key UNCLOS provision is Article 140, as it determines that activities in the Area be regulated by the ISA and carried out for the benefit of mankind as a whole. In practical terms, the Authority is given the power to provide for the equitable sharing of financial and other economic benefits derived from activities in the Area through any appropriate mechanism, on a non-discriminatory basis.

Other Articles of UNCLOS Part XI regulate benefit sharing. It is the case of Article 160(2) (f) (i), according to which the Assembly—the most important and democratic body within the ISA—will assess and approve the rules and procedures for the equitable sharing of benefits after recommendation by the Council—the executive body. Moreover, Article 160(2) (g) entrusts the Assembly with the decision on the actual distribution.

During the Third Law of the Sea Conference (1973–1982), there was stark opposition between developed and developing states regarding the methods to achieve

---

[74] Khatwani 2019.

[75] UNGA Res. 51/122, 1996. Notwithstanding the apparently weak normativity of Article 1 OST—with respect to the benefit sharing part, it has been claimed that developing countries have indeed benefited from the use of space by the space-competent, especially regarding direct broadcasting, satellite telecommunications, global positioning, and remote sensing, while it is true that commercial considerations have entered in.

[76] *Agreement Relating to the Implementation of Part XI of the UNCLOS*, UNGA, A/RES/48/263, 17 August 1994.

4 The Common Heritage of Mankind

such distribution and equitable sharing of benefits. The former favoured a licensing regime for exploration and exploitation of the Area, whereas the latter fought for the creation of an internationally managed enterprise, the profit of which would be distributed equitably. However, the 1994 Implementation Agreement postponed the creation of the Enterprise, in a certain way killing it before birth. Section 2 (3) of the Agreement provides that States Parties do not have the obligation to fund the Enterprise for the operation in one mine site specifically provided for it, thus revoking Article 11(3), Annex IV UNCLOS. Section 2 (3) also cancels any other form of financing of operations of the Enterprise in a mining site. Presently, the perspectives for benefit sharing rely on the royalties on the revenue of exploitation contracts with the Authority[77] and royalties on the revenue of activities on extended continental shelves worldwide (Article 82 UNCLOS),[78] none of which are yet in place.

4.4.4 Concerted Management and Exploitation by All Nations

Whoever ends up entitled to manage the common heritage and regulate activities concerning it will not act solely in its own interest, but in the interest of mankind, as a sort of international trustee. Because all nations presumably have an interest in that common heritage, *concerted management* seems unavoidable.

Regarding the seabed, the ISA shall act on behalf of mankind, in which all rights in the resources of the Area are vested.[79] Moreover, under Article 157(1), "the Authority is the organization through which States Parties shall, in accordance with this Part, organize and control activities in the Area, particularly with a view to administering the resources of the Area".

However, when it comes to outer space law, the *concerted management* concept is rather weak as of 2020. As examined above, Article 11(5) MT provides that when the exploitation of natural resources of the Moon becomes feasible, states parties shall establish an international regime. This far and unlikely contingency—for reasons already mentioned—does not obfuscate some kind of concerted management without a central authority. There are important fora and organizations dealing with the issue, the UN Committee on the Peaceful Uses of the Outer Space being the most important one thus far.

---

[77] As of July 2020, there are no regulations on any kind of deep-sea mineral exploitation.

[78] Tuerk 2017, p. 267.

[79] According to UNCLOS Article 137(2).

4.5 Recent Developments and the Future of the Common Heritage of Mankind Principle

In the last three decades, the international community has witnessed a mature International Seabed Authority performing its duty not only to effectively regulate activities in the Area, but also to foster permanent dialogue between stakeholders (states, companies, and civil society). To date, the ISA has signed 30 contracts of exploration with multiple states or state-sponsored companies. Thus far, there has been no account of direct violations to the UNCLOS' seabed regime, namely concerning peaceful uses, access and benefit sharing, and environmental protection of the deep-sea habitats. Indirectly, some may raise cases of allegedly undue extension of continental shelves worldwide to the detriment of the common heritage of mankind. The ISA "Mining Code," which comprises regulations and procedures with respect to the scientific exploration of each class of deep-sea minerals, is constantly updated.

As for the legal framework for the actual commercial exploitation of the deep seabed, the ISA has been consulting with interested parties in experts' workshops, and prepared studies and discussion papers, a process which culminated in the so-called draft regulations, currently under scrutiny by the Authority's Legal and Technical Commission.[80] Efforts are currently directed at minimizing ecological degradation, as well as on implementing UNCLOS Article 82 (revenue-sharing mechanism).[81] Such is an illustration of how a collectively managed area/resources offers the international community a chance to comprehend and regulate potentially damaging activities before they occur.

Nevertheless, the development of the seabed regime is not due exclusively to the work of the Authority. In 2011, the International Tribunal for the Law of the Sea, through its Seabed Disputes Chamber, issued a landmark advisory opinion on the responsibility and obligations of states sponsoring persons and entities with respect to activities in the Area. After inviting several states, including Russia, China, Germany and the United Kingdom, to formally manifest on the issue at stake, the Tribunal stated that:

> The role of the sponsoring state, as set out in the Convention, contributes to the realization of the common interest of all states in the proper application of the principle of the common heritage of mankind, which requires faithful compliance with the obligations set out in Part XI.[82]

That is further evidence of the consolidation of the CHM principle as applied to the international seabed area, recognizing States' obligations and responsibilities

---

[80] For more on ISA's latest regulations on polymetallic nodules, sulphides and cobalt-rich ferromanganese crusts, visit: https://www.isa.org.jm/mining-code/regulations. Accessed 1 August 2020.

[81] To that end, there have also been official proposals for a joint venture with the still non-existent Enterprise, Article 170 UNCLOS. It was the case of the Canadian company, Nautilus Minerals Inc.

[82] Responsibilities and obligations of States sponsoring persons and entities with respect to activities in the Area (request for Advisory Opinion submitted to the Seabed Disputes Chamber), International Tribunal for the Law of the Sea, Advisory Opinion of 1 February 2011, para 76.

4 The Common Heritage of Mankind

under Part XI of UNCLOS as instruments of an international community-centred approach.

Regarding outer space law, in the wake of major developments concerning outer space anthropogenic activities, such as the Chinese achievements in successfully launching rovers to Mars, or the United States' plans to man the moon until 2030, mankind is soon to witness a run to Earth's natural satellite. Reasonably, questions emerge as to the adequacy of the current legal regime applicable to the Moon in preventing international conflicts. Although some elements of the wider CHM principle are present in outer space law, it remains to be seen how states will apply them, considering that the OST privileges a rather liberal regime. Spacefaring and moon exploration, as in the seabed, are economic activities backed by interests that favour precisely a more liberal approach to access and exploitation, thus benefiting the most technologically advanced states. In light of recent news, one ought to exercise a certain degree of scepticism concerning the ideal that the morality-driven notions of the CHM will be preserved, i.e., that the world will jointly explore space as egalitarian nations.

The CHM principle, as it stands, may be perceived as too restrictive of states' actions in outer space, particularly with regard to the access and benefit-sharing feature. Such a feature is not expected to prevail in international norms concerning the moon, as the current political momentum does not seem to favour states' voluntary giveaway of technological and military edge in the name of community interests. The principle, as applied to the moon, other celestial bodies or the outer space, assumes the shape of a philosophical or political tool. The Moon Agreement binds no more than 11 states and it does so with quite low normativity levels (i.e., based on norms that can hardly be invoked before courts); the main players in space exploration—the United States, China and Russia—are not among those it binds. Effective implementation of the Treaty's provisions remains another major challenge since it depends on the incorporation of international documents into the domestic legal order of signatory countries.

Interestingly, the CHM concept has also been in the spotlight of the Intergovernmental Conference on the Conservation and Sustainable Use of Biodiversity in Areas Beyond National Jurisdiction (BBNJ). For more than a decade, states have debated on the adequacy of the regime governing marine genetic resources in waters beyond national jurisdiction, especially those of the deep seas, to protect ecosystems such as hydrothermal vents. The fact that the CHM principle applies only to the Area and its mineral resources led to the dissatisfaction of several countries, which oppose the application of the freedoms of the high seas to access and exploit genetic resources in those regions. After vivid debates on whether a legally binding treaty on BBNJ would be due, a Preparatory Committee to the Conference was established,[83] a solution to the tradition polarization between the freedom of the seas *versus* the CHM principle has been a so-called "pragmatic approach," which handpicks the element of equitable access and benefit-sharing of the CHM and applies it to the waters beyond

---

[83] UNGA Resolution 69/292, 19 June 2015.

national jurisdiction. There is some risk to that approach, though, including that of focusing solely on the intragenerational facet of the CHM principle.[84]

To apply the CHM principle to the waters beyond national jurisdiction is to foster both the intragenerational and intergenerational aspects of the principle. Intra, due to the benefit sharing mechanisms, which would offer immediate relief to developing states not actively exploiting the resources of those regions. Inter, due to the limitations aimed at achieving sustainability, environmental protection and the peaceful purposes of activities. The central idea is the conservation and sustainable use of marine biodiversity beyond national jurisdiction, a remarkable common concern of mankind. Yet, the probability that the CHM be prioritized in a possible legally binding treaty is rather low. In fact, the PrepCom has been pushed forward with loads of scepticism and reluctance from different countries belonging to different informal groups, such as large-coast countries, those with powerful fishing fleets, and those with extensive marine scientific technology, among others.

4.6 Conclusion

The common heritage of mankind is a popular concept, but it should not be adopted recklessly. Expressions such as the common concern of humankind and international community interests are familiar with the CHM Principle because of their focus on the interest of mankind, but they clearly do not share the same normative status. In fact, the legal construct of the common heritage of mankind differs substantially from correlated notions, such as "common interest", "common concern of mankind", or "cultural heritage of humanity". Occasionally, the careless and alternated use of those phrases in relation to different subject-matters may produce more confusion than clarity and may prove to be a potent rhetorical tool—in the worst possible meaning of "rhetorical". Also, references to the environment (as a whole), as well as to cultural heritage, or the internet, as common heritage of mankind often aim at borrowing some of the CHM principle's normativity, in order to strengthen a particular argument or to make a specific point.

The normative nature of the CHM principle and its elements should not be hastily assessed. Considering that it may attain stronger normativity if it is present in treaty provisions, UNCLOS and the Moon Treaty play a paramount role in making the CHM principle effective. The latter is because outer space, the Moon and other celestial bodies are not CHM under international customary law. The former, because it counts on great adhesion and a high level of detailing, and, upon influence of the previous ones, inspires CIL. The regime of the CHM principle as applied to the Area is wholly customary international law. However, since only general aspects of it are peremptory norms, persistent objections to the remaining elements, notably by the US, cannot simply be dismissed.

---

[84] Tladi 2017, p. 109.

4 The Common Heritage of Mankind 91

Regarding the sub-norms of the CHM principle, this chapter has adopted a treaty-based approach: the main provisions on the principle as applied to the Area, according to UNCLOS. The most fundamental ones are the following: prohibition of appropriation, reservation for peaceful purposes, equitable benefit-sharing, and concerted management. Essentially, all of them are only present in the international seabed regime. The parties to the Moon Treaty are to develop its CHM regime once exploitation becomes feasible. Some norms similar to CHM elements, however, are applicable not only to the Moon and other celestial bodies, but to all of outer space.

From the above examination, one may notice that international law is shifting from a state-oriented paradigm towards a community-oriented one, in the sense that current principles and rules already acknowledge (or tend to do so) values relevant for humanity as a whole, and not just to traditional elements of statehood. These are values such as peaceful uses of areas and resources beyond national jurisdiction, equitable benefit-sharing of those resources, sustainable productivity and intergenerational equity, among others. The Common Heritage of Mankind regime (and its multiple sub-norms) represents an important tool for materializing such a shift. Should international lawyers turn a blind eye to the imperatives of human health and the well-being of peoples while managing areas beyond national jurisdiction, odds are that it may fail to achieve its ultimate *raison d'être*: the prevention of conflicts.

References

Altemir A (1992) El Patrimonio Común de la Humanidad: Hacia un régimen jurídico para su gestión. Bosch, Barcelona

Baslar K (1997) The Concept of the Common Heritage of Mankind in International Law. Martinus Nijhoff Publishers, Leiden

Bourbonniete M, Lee R (2007) Legality of the Deployment of Conventional Weapons in Earth Orbit: Balancing Space Law and the Law of Armed Conflict. European Journal of International Law, 18:873–901

Brown ED (1973) Maritime Zones: A Survey of Claims. In: Lay SH, Churchill RR, Nordquist MH (eds) New Directions in the Law of the Sea. Oceana, New York, 157–192

Casella P (2014) Direito Internacional no Tempo Moderno de Suárez a Grócio. Atlas, São Paulo

Cheng B (1965) United Nations Resolutions on Outer Space: 'Instant' International Customary Law? Indian Journal of International Law, 5: 23–112

Christol C (1994) Judge Manfred Lachs and the Principle of Jus Cogens. Journal of Space Law, 22: 33–45

Cocca A (1981) The Advances in International Law through the Law of Outer Space. Journal of Space Law, 9:13 et seq

Dupuy R J, Vignes D (1991) A handbook of the new Law of the Sea. Volume 1, Brill Nijhoff, Dordrecht

Hardin G (1968) Tragedy of the commons. Science 162 (3859): 1243–1248

Hoof G (1986) Legal Status of the Concept of the Common Heritage of Mankind. Grotiana New Series, 7: 49

Isa F (1993) Patrimonio Común de la Humanidad. Estudios de Deusto, 41:119–192

Joyner C (1986). Legal Implications of the Concept of the Common Heritage of Mankind. The International and Comparative Quarterly 35: 190–199

Khatwani N (2019) Common Heritage of Mankind for Outer Space. The International Journal for Space Politics and Policy, 17:1–15

Kiss A (1982) La notion de patrimoine commun de l'humanité. R.C.A.D.I, The Hague

Kiss A (1985) The Common Heritage of Mankind: Utopia or Reality. International Journal, 40:423–441

Lyall F, Larsen B (2009) Space Law.; LARSEN, P. B. Space Law. Routledge, Abingdon

Makarczyk J (1988) Principles of a New International Economic Order: a study in international law-making. Nijhoff, Boston

Noyes J (2012) The Common Heritage of Mankind: Past, Present, and Future. Denver Journal of International Law and Policy, 40: 447–471

Rangel V (1979) O Novo Direito do Mar e a America Latina. Revista da Faculdade de Direito de Sao Paulo, 75:97–108

Rodriguez Carrión AJ (1987) Lecciones de Derecho Internacional Publico. Tecnos, Madrid

Simma B (1998) The 'International Community': Facing the Challenge of Globalization. European Journal of International Law, 9:266–277

Smouts MC (2005) Du Patrimoine Commun de l'Humanité aux Bien Publics Globaux. In: Cormier-Salem MC et al (eds) Patrimoines naturels au Sud : territoires, identités et stratégies locales. IRD Éditions, Paris, pp. 53–70

Taylor P (2019) The Common Heritage of Mankind: Expanding the Oceanic Circle. In: Boudreau PR et al (eds) The Future of Ocean Governance and Capacity Development: Essays in Honor of Elisabeth Mann Borgese (1918-2002). Brill Nijhoff, Leiden, pp. 142–150

Tladi D (2017) The Pursuit of a Brave New World for the Oceans: The place of Common Heritage in a proposed Law of the Sea Treaty. In: Maluwa T et al (eds) The Pursuit of a Brave New World in International Law: An Essay in Honor of John Dugard. Brill Nijhoff, Leiden, pp. 87–113

Tuerk H (2017) The Common Heritage of Mankind after 50 Years. Indian Journal of International Law, 57:259–283

Ventura V A M F (2020) Environmental Jurisdiction in the Law of the Sea: The Brazilian Blue Amazon. Heidelberg, Springer

Vereshcetin V, Danilenko G (1985) Custom as a Source of International Law of Outer Space. Journal of Space Law, 13:22–35

Vöneky S, Höfelmeier A (2017a) Article 136. In: Proelss A et al (eds) United Nations Convention on the Law of the Sea: A Commentary. C.H. Beck/Nomos/Hart, Munich, pp. 949–957

Vöneky S, Höfelmeier A (2017b) Article 141. In: Proelss A et al (eds) United Nations Convention on the Law of the Sea: A Commentary. C.H. Beck/Nomos/Hart, Munich, pp. 982–986

Weil P (1983) Towards Relative Normativity in International Law. American Journal of International Law 77:413–442

Wolfrum R (1983) The Principle of the Common Heritage of Mankind. Zeitschrift fur Auslandisches Offentliches Recht und Volkerrecht, 43:312–337

Victor Alencar Mayer Feitosa Ventura Ph.D. is a licensed lawyer before the Brazilian Bar Association, in the practices of Environmental and Maritime Law. He is Legal Advisor to the Brazilian National Agency for Agriculture of Paraíba, Brazil; Partner at Humberto Bezerra LLP for Environmental and Maritime Law; founding member of the Brazilian Institute for the Law of the Sea (BILOS); and Consultant to the Center for Political-Strategic Studies of the Brazilian Navy. Dr. Ventura deals with environmental law, maritime and port law, marine governance and renewable resources.

Eduardo Cavalcanti de Mello Filho is a student of the Master in International Law at the Graduate Institute of International and Development Studies, Geneva, and a Research Auxiliary at the University of Geneva.

Chapter 5
Human Rights: Between Universalism and Relativism

Anicée Van Engeland

Contents

5.1	Introduction	94
5.2	Universality and Cultural Relativism: Human Rights Law as a Battleground	95
	5.2.1 The Principle of Universality of Human Rights	95
	5.2.2 Questioning Universality	97
5.3	Contesting the Liberal Model	100
	5.3.1 Shades of Disagreement Within the International Community	101
	5.3.2 The Issue with the Liberal World Order	104
5.4	Transcending the Tensions: New Developments Resulting from Current Challenges and Possible Ways Forward	105
	5.4.1 Accommodating Universalism	105
	5.4.2 Accepting Cultural Relativism Within Universalism	108
5.5	Conclusion	110
References		111

Abstract The connection between human rights, peace and security highlights the stakes attached to the respect and enforcement of the principle of universality. Yet the 1948 Universal Declaration of Human Rights and all subsequent international conventions have been questioned by States and communities: they are believed to be reflective of euro-centric values. This is why cultural relativism has emerged as an alternative to the principle of universality of human rights. This raises security questions: if a state questions universality of human rights, does it undermine the whole UN peace and security system? Is cultural relativism a threat to universality, leading to fragmentation and insecurity? The book chapter seeks to address such issues while looking at transcending the dichotomy between universalism and relativism. Scholars' views and strategies to overcome the tensions and ensure the respect of human rights while promoting peace and security are consequently examined.

Keywords Universality · Human Rights · Security · Relativism

A. Van Engeland (✉)
Defence Academy of the UK, Shrivenham, Swindon SN6 8LA, UK
e-mail: a.van-engeland@cranfield.ac.uk

© T.M.C. ASSER PRESS and the authors 2022
S. Sayapin et al. (eds.), *International Conflict and Security Law*,
https://doi.org/10.1007/978-94-6265-515-7_5

5.1 Introduction

The linkage between human rights, peace and security is established in the United Nations (UN) Charter. The 1948 Universal Declaration of Human Rights (UDHR) and all subsequent international conventions were drafted with the aim of maintaining peace and security in the post-World War II (WWII) world. Consequently, in the liberal peace and security matrix, human rights are approached as an inhibitor of conflict.[1] This raises questions with regards to States and communities following other standards than universal norms: for example, Asian countries have their human rights particularism, with a focus on the community, an emphasis on the family and the priority given to economic, social and cultural rights.[2] Other examples are to be found in regions of the world such as Africa where individualism, that is inherent to the Enlightenment period and to universal human rights law, is superseded by the dichotomy between rights and duties of the individual vis-à-vis the community.[3]

Human rights charters existed well before the 1948 UDHR, as illustrated by the Cyrus Cylinder. The reference to the past but also to different beliefs, values and practices with regard to, for example, equality between men and women, has constituted grounds for challenging the principle of universality of human rights as encompassed in UDHR. Some States and communities consider that universal human rights law is a neo-colonial enterprise[4] and that the UDHR reflects Judeo-Christian values.[5] It has also been said that the UDHR is euro-centric in its drafting since most of the world states were still under colonial rule after World War II and could not effectively contribute to the drafting of the Declaration. Now that these countries have become States in their own right, they challenge the universality of the UDHR. The UDHR is also defied in the interpretation and its implementation and is denounced as impacting civilisations negatively.

These different approaches to human rights are often regrouped under the cultural relativism umbrella. Yet, it is to avoid the fragmentation of a universal vision of human rights that the UN Charter links human rights, peace and security and that the UDHR was drafted. This idealistic endeavour has not prevented many States and communities to adopt a relativist stance on the topic of human rights. As the universality of human rights is embedded in the security discourse, it is legitimate to question whether such stance on relativism leads to insecurity.

The discussion about the universality of human rights in relation to security is extremely relevant in a post-colonial context: most States and communities seek to position themselves with regard to their identity while seeking to abide by the UDHR, to be in line with the UN Charter. This is a balancing act that does not always bear fruits; the discrepancies between the UDHR and local, state or regional interpretations and practices of human rights are sometimes too big. This is why it is

---

[1] Lekha Sriram et al. 2017, p. 589.

[2] Huong et al. 2018, p. 302.

[3] Cobbah 1987, p. 309; Mutua 2011, p. 84.

[4] Alzubairi 2019; Hilsdon et al. 2000; Ibhawoh 2017; Ingiyimbere 2017.

[5] Féron 2014, p. 190.

necessary to include a chapter on the debate on universality, examining relativists' claims as the whole UN system is now built on the premise that the respect and implementation of human rights is a condition for security, at least in the universal liberal model of governance.[6] The question to be asked, and that this chapter will seek to address, is to know whether rights can truly be universal, and, if one adopts cultural relativism, will this alignment lead to insecurity and conflict. The first part of the paper will examine universality and cultural relativism looking at the main sources of law applicable. The second part will seek to illustrate the tensions so that the stakes are well understood. The last part will engage with ways forward, including transcending the opposition between universalists and relativists. Each section looks at security issues.

5.2 Universality and Cultural Relativism: Human Rights Law as a Battleground

It is, firstly, necessary to understand the principle of universality of human rights, and how the protection and the implementation of universal human rights is key to maintaining peace and security. This section goes further by engaging with the discontent surrounding the principle of universality.

5.2.1 The Principle of Universality of Human Rights

The principle of universality is found in Article 2 of the UDHR but also the Preamble of the International Covenant on Civil and Political Rights (ICCPR) and of the International Covenant on Economic, Social and Cultural Rights (IECSR). Affirming the principle of universality of human rights means that those rights apply to everyone, everywhere. Human rights are therefore values that transcend borders and cultures. The 1993 Vienna Declaration states that the universality of human rights is "beyond question".[7] The principle is therefore essentially entrenched into human rights law. The respect and implementation of universal human rights law ensures in turn peace and security. From its inception post WWII, it was clear that the very purpose of the UDHR would be to transcend all differences, including cultural and religious,[8] without denying their existence. As a result, Henkin speaks of the UDHR as an "authoritative catalog of rights".[9]

---

[6] Buchan 2013, p. 81.

[7] Vienna Declaration and Programme of Action 1993, para 1.

[8] Glendon 2001, p. 301.

[9] Henkin 1989, p. 11.

To be as universal as possible, independent experts from China and Lebanon participated to the drafting of the UDHR;[10] the drafting committee was varied, representing different cultures. The American Law Institute issued the Statement of Essential Human Rights to present the Latin American perspective. Cuba, Panama, Lebanon and Egypt proposed amendments to the Draft Declaration. As summed up by Norchi, the UDHR then emerged as a consensus.[11] It is believed that this consensus among nations has become, with time, "binding as part of customary international law, legal principles of the so-called civilized nations".[12] Consequently, universal human rights as encompassed in the UDHR and other conventions is believed to reflect the diversity of the world. In that regard, human rights have become a yardstick by which all abide, overriding other benchmarks that might be ethical, cultural, religious, traditional or customary. The norm to measure compliance with universal human rights law is the very object that seeks to be measured: human rights. The best example of that endeavour is the Rainbow Constitution of South Africa where customary or religious matters are assessed to ensure compliance with the Constitution's human rights declaration.[13] Concretely, the respect and the implementation of human rights are measured by looking at the respect and the implementation of human rights. This belief that human rights are de facto and de lege normal is in itself a weakness in the universal human rights system. It ignores that, for other civilisations, human rights might be anchored in a different realm of legitimacy, such as the divine or traditional leading authorities enforcing customary law.

This premise that human rights are universal then links in with peace and security: the respect for universal human rights helps to prevent conflicts, to mitigate the impact of conflicts and to negotiate the end of conflicts. As stated by Hathaway, "promoting human rights promotes security and promoting security promotes human rights."[14] The question of the universality of human rights is pertinent here, as the compliance with human rights to maintain peace and security is understood as referring to the UDHR and other conventions. If a State abides by another set of human rights, for example the Asian set of values, the idea that security equals human rights and vice-versa could be nullified in the eyes of the proponents of universality. Supporters of the principle of universality believe that attempts at fragmenting human rights undermine security and demonstrate the need for common human rights values: how could parties to a conflict agree on mitigating the impact of war if they both follow different sets of human rights law, one secular—that is the UDHR—and the other religious—that is the Quran—and find common grounds? Yet, as demonstrated by the legal narrative during the 1980–88 conflict with Iraq, Iran relied on both universal human rights law and Islamic law.[15] As a result, universalists and relativists have been working together to improve international, regional and domestic respect and

---

[10] Dundes Renteln 1990, p. 28.

[11] Ayton-Shenker 1995, p. 2.

[12] Dundes Renteln 1990, p. 32.

[13] Sachs 1990, p. 10.

[14] Hathaway n.d.

[15] Van Engeland 2017, p. 61.

enforcement of universal human rights, seeking to maintain peace and security; even the most convinced universalists acknowledge either the challenges inherent to universality in a world of pluralism, or the rejection of universality.[16] Yet, these human rights scholars and practitioners believe that the principle of universality constitute the very soul of human rights and that we should prevent cultures from interfering at the risk of having relative human rights.[17]

Indeed, after anchoring this principle of universality of human rights in the Enlightenment period, Henkin proceeded, well before Fukuyama claimed to end of history for democracy, to state the end of history for universality: he considered that universality of human rights was a fact and was achieved in the twentieth century.[18] Thirty years after this statement was made, the principle of universality is still being challenged. The engagement with the debate on "universality vs relativity" of human rights is often framed in political terms: it is understood that States or communities challenging the principle of universality do it in quest of political gains.[19] The challenge to the principle of universality cannot and should not be reduced to a political game: States or communities that engaged with relativism have produced elaborated legal narratives. While most of these narratives do not challenge the internationality of human rights, they challenge their universality, as internationality does not guarantee universality. Internationality is a characteristic of human rights that some advocates have been trying to put forward so that the international community would make human rights applicable everywhere to everyone. Internationality is illustrated by the existence of international courts. However, the existence of Asian, African or Muslim human rights values demonstrates that there are regional or national specificities putting forward an alternative discourse. It is therefore safe to claim that while human rights are international, they are not universal, and will never be. This helps re-framing the debate as to how different visions of human rights could function together to ensure the respect of the UDHR. Yet, before engaging with how to transcend the universality-relativism debate, the first step is to understand how and why the principle of universality is being questioned.

5.2.2 Questioning Universality

Questioning the universality of human rights and the values of the UDHR is not new: in 1947, the American Anthropological Association (AAA) issued a statement cautioning the panel working on the UDHR, stating that "values and standards are relative to the culture from which they derive."[20] Herskovitz, one of the authors of the AAA statement, believed that the UN Charter and the 1948 UDHR to be too

---

[16] Henkin 1989, p. 10.

[17] Freeman 2010, pp. 125–126; Howard 1995, p. 2.

[18] Henkin 1989, p. 10.

[19] Mayer 1999, p. 3.

[20] American Anthropological Association 1947.

western-oriented.[21] The AAA predicted the struggle to come between those advocating for universal human rights and the proponents of cultural relativism. Indeed, many believe that universal human rights values are not universal and that the human rights regime is generalised at the expenses of alternative understandings, may they be cultural or religious, of the concept. For example, Dr. Hossein Mehrpoor, former representative of Iran to the UN, addressed the lack of consideration of religious values by the international organisation:

> The Human Rights Commission and other UN institutions have no consideration for religious values; we can even say it is the forum where, under a variety of pretexts, there is some sort of struggle against some beliefs and religious values.[22]

Proponents of relativism believe that cultural, religious, traditional and customary values, beliefs and norms dictate the approach and content to human rights.[23] A community, a society or a State select what human rights are from a chosen perspective that is anchored in religious, cultural or social beliefs, values and practices. There is then a bottom-up or top-bottom selection of human rights principles that can be based on ethics, customs, religion or culture and that take precedence over universal human rights law. An example of this is the argument in support of the practice of female circumcision: it is argued by some that the women who do not undergo the procedure will not be able to marry and as a result will be side-lined from the community; they could, at worse, be exiled.[24] In such tight-knit communities, the advocacy for women's rights is inefficient as the stakes are high for those who challenge customs. There are new voices challenging the universal human rights' approaches to female circumcision in a post-colonial fashion: it is believed that universal human rights activists have under-estimated the stakes and have essentialised women bodies in their quest to have universality respected. Ahmadu expressed her

> concern about the negative psychosexual ramifications of anti-female genital mutilation (FGM) campaigns and stereotypes for circumcised African women, particularly vulnerable teenagers and young adults, many of whom are struggling with all sorts of conflicting messages regarding their bodies and sexuality.[25]

Ahmadu builds on Shweder's questioning of the anti-female genital mutilations campaigns that has endorsed universality of human rights and body integrity as their core argument.[26] She engages with the human rights' narrative of the liberal world order, side-lining the issue of assessing circumcision with regard to human rights law. Instead, she confronts the outcomes of such bias that are based on a universal perception of human rights law; she reflects on how expectations of respect of universal norms turn universalists into zealots who are prejudiced. Ahmadu and Shweder's work demonstrates that there is more to relativism than the mere anchoring

---

[21] American Anthropological Association 1947.

[22] Mehrpoor 1995, pp. 37–38.

[23] Musalo 2015.

[24] Berg and Denison 2013, p. 837.

[25] Ahmadu 2007, pp. 278–79.

[26] Schweder 2009, p. 14.

5 Human Rights: Between Universalism and Relativism

of rights into an alternative: relativism is also about post-colonialism and the respect of the Other's voice.

The tensions between universalists and relativists reached a peak, such that in 1993, an international conference was organised in Vienna. There were concerns that the principle of universality was eroded. The representatives of 171 States present adopted by consensus the Vienna Declaration and Programme of Action to strengthen human rights around the world. The aim of the conference was to innovate in terms of promotion and protection of human rights, addressing underlying issues such as the fragmentation principle of universality. While the outcome of this conference is often praised, the fact that such an event was needed to re-affirm the principle of universality while considering "national and regional particularities and various historical, cultural and religious backgrounds"[27] is telling of the tensions that exist between universalism and cultural relativism. Besides, the 1993 Conference gave the opportunity to States to formalise their disagreements with regard to the principle of universality: the 1993 Asian Regional Meetings in Bangkok for the World Conference on Human Rights produced a document stating "while human rights are universal in nature, they must be considered in the context of a dynamic and evolving process of international norm-setting, bearing in mind the significance of national and regional particularities and various historical, cultural and religious backgrounds."[28] Therefore, far from constituting a new base to implement universal norms, the conference shed light on divisions. One can find more recent examples of relativism looking at the Universal Periodic Review process: China has used it to declare that the authorities will "respect the principle of the universality of human rights" but

> given differences in political systems, levels of development and historical and cultural backgrounds, it is natural for countries to have different views on the question of human rights. It is therefore important that countries engage in dialogue and cooperation based on equality and mutual respect in their common endeavour to promote and protect human rights.[29]

The debate is, consequently, still ongoing.

The challenges to the principle of universality are varied. Some challenge the very idea of universality while others believe that the principle of universality needs to be mitigated. Some cultural relativists denounced the UDHR as a neo-imperialist endeavour.[30] Others believe that the UDHR is not reflective of all approaches to human rights and the cultural specificities should supersede the Declaration.[31] Cultural relativists but also advocates of alternative readings believe the UN human rights documents to reflect Western values, with an emphasis on the Enlightenment's

---

[27] Vienna Declaration and Programme of Action 1993, para 5.

[28] Declaration Regional Meetings for the Asia of the World Conference on Human Rights 1993, para 8.

[29] A/HRC/WG.6/4/CHN/1 of 10 November 2008, para 6.

[30] Ibhawoh 2017; Shaheed and Richter 2018.

[31] Packer 2002, p. 90; Shah 2006, p. 209.

understanding of human rights. This means, for example, that the focus is on indi-vidualism when the Banjul Charter insist on community rights take precedence over individual rights. Cultural relativists take issue with the lack of consideration of beliefs, values and practices others than those set in the UDHR: "[T]he universalist position completely denies that the existing universal standards may be themselves culturally specific and allied to dominant regimes of power."[32] The double standard practiced by States that "predict that even the slightest 'dilution' of universalism will give the green light to tyrannical governments, torturers, and mutilators of women"[33] while using human rights to interfere or invade other countries. Security makes an apparition in the debate on universality when States like the United States and its allies justified the intervention in Afghanistan to protect women's rights: interna-tional security then partly depends on the respect of their rights, bringing in the liberal security narrative.[34] Another illustration is to be found in the design and implementation of the principle of responsibility to protect: while some believed that this principle would enhance the promotion and protection of human rights around the world,[35] cultural relativists see it as a powerful tool to impose a liberal and western understanding of human rights as a ground to go to war.[36]

The principle of universality of human rights has been contested since its incep-tion. The debate now gives the impression that there is, on the one hand, a liberal democratic world where human rights are universal and security is maintained opposed to other governance models or transitioning democracy that seek to maintain their beliefs, values and practices, including their own perspective on human rights. The debate is however more complex than this opposition, as demonstrated in the next part of this chapter.

5.3 Contesting the Liberal Model

In the realm of cultural relativism, there are different trends, ranging from those who advocate for cultural relativism to those supporting particularism, including cross-relativists. There are therefore shades of disagreement, with different outcomes for security. The heart of the issue remains the contestation of the current human rights system that is perceived as being western-oriented due to the its roots or its tendency to link human rights with democracy, liberalism and capitalism.

---

[32] Otto 1998, p. 8.

[33] Otto 1998, p. 8.

[34] Gassama 2012, p. 408.

[35] Donnelly 1984, pp. 414–15.

[36] Barša 2005, p. 5.

5.3.1 Shades of Disagreement Within the International Community

As a result of the tensions, the UHDR is sometimes accommodated while, in other settings, it is rejected as constituting a threat to local values, beliefs and practices. For example, in 1977, the Saudi delegate to the UN Jamil Murad Baroody denounced the UDHR as an "exclusively Western approach to the human rights questions."[37] In 1997, Mahathir bin Mohamad, the Prime Minister of Malaysia urged for the reform of the UDHR.[38] Universality of human rights is also challenged by some regional declarations such as the 1990 Cairo Declaration on Human Rights in Islam. Then, the challenges to the principle of universality are not uniform. There are obviously shades of universality as some scholars and practitioners argue for a complete takeover of local values to supplant them with the UDHR;[39] there are also shades of cultural relativism with some states or communities sometimes rejecting universal values altogether, and other times also proceed to a choice *à la carte* of the human right they feel are relevant, rather than proceeding *au menu*.

One of the best examples of the tensions between universality and cultural relativism is the Convention of the Elimination of All Forms of Discrimination against Women (CEDAW). While it has been well ratified, the implementation of this Convention has faced a number of challenges and obstacles due to reservations. Some articles of the Convention are perceived to reflect Western cultural imperialism or attempts by the West to demean and alter traditional, religiously-based practices.[40] Consequently, some States have ratified the Convention with reservations that protect their religiously or culturally-sanctioned customs. Egypt stated the following:

> The Arab Republic of Egypt is willing to comply with the content of [Article 2], provided that such compliance does not run counter to the Islamic Sharia....This is out of respect for the sacrosanct nature of the firm religious beliefs which govern marital relations in Egypt and which may not be called in question and in view of the fact that one of the most important bases of these relations is an equivalency of rights and duties so as to ensure complementarity which guarantees true equality between the spouses...

Iraq's reservation stated: "Approval of and accession to this Convention shall not mean that the Republic of Iraq is bound by [certain of its] provisions... [Iraq's accession] shall be without prejudice to the provisions of the Islamic Shariah according women rights equivalent to the rights of their spouses so as to ensure a just balance between them...." These reservations demonstrate how religious values take precedence over universal norms. The case of women's rights in Islam is of particular interest to the debate on universality. Muslim women are, like all believers, expected to fulfil duties before benefiting from rights.[41] Yet, the rights they benefit from are

---

[37] Burke 2011, p. 138.

[38] Churchill 2016, p. 44.

[39] Caney 2005, p. 93; Nussbaum 2006, p. 78.

[40] Brems 1997, p. 160.

[41] Kar 2001.

mostly construed through their family status as a married woman, a daughter or a mother. For example, a woman should benefit from good spousal treatment if she is obedient. From the onset, women are then limited to the performance of duties, which in turns, reduces their access to rights if the duties are not performed properly. As stressed by Smail Salhi, women find themselves subjected to patriarchal culture and misinterpretations of religion.[42] The other issue with Islamic human rights law, and that is to be found in the general reservation made by Saudi Arabia to CEDAW. It stated:

> in case of contradiction between any term of the Convention and the norms of Islamic Law, the Kingdom [of Saudi Arabia] is not under the obligation to observe the contradictory terms of the Convention.[43]

The justification is that Shari'a is fluid and depends on interpretations made of the holy scriptures. Several countries, including the United Kingdom criticised this reservation precisely because of the fluidity of the content of Shari'a. There is no clear prescribed content of the Islamic values and Islamic law, as norms are left to human beings to interpret the scriptures. This flexibility leads again to a selection of which rights would be applied, raising the issue of arbitrariness and political whims. In terms of human security, it leaves Muslim women at the mercy of a patriarchal political establishment and a patriarchal society that leaves no doubt to the desire to control them, from their bodies to their thoughts. Yet, would universality of human rights be the answer to those old and deeply anchored beliefs, values and practices?

When examining cultural relativism, Donnelly divides the trend into strong or weak.[44] He assesses a case of strong cultural relativism when culture becomes the primary referent for human rights, thereby effectively rejecting the UDHR or selecting the right that matches the culture, and filling them with the relevant localised content. Weak cultural relativism considers culture as an important normative source, and is to be understood as creating exceptions within universality. In the case of a Muslim woman living in a country where the authorities and society seek to control her, there would be a strong cultural relativism. The issue with such argument is that it denies the disagreements over the principle of universality that are specific to each culture. As an illustration the Islamic republic of Iran's approach to universality is not divided into strong and weak and is not solely based on culture. Instead, there are a multiple of approaches to human rights, ranging from hardliners who reject the idea that human rights are universal and who embrace an Islamic Iranian vision of human rights, to those who advocate for liberal approaches to human rights; the shades of perspectives in between transcend the strong or weak measure of assessment.[45] It makes the challenge of universality of the world even more complex.

This complexity is further illustrated with the engagement with the UDHR, ranging from full rejection to accommodation. Particularists believe that universal

---

[42] Smail Salhi 2008, p. 304.

[43] See specific reservations by country: https://www.unwomen.org/en.

[44] Donnelly 1984, p. 401.

[45] Van Engeland 2011.

5 Human Rights: Between Universalism and Relativism

human rights should be riddled with exceptions. The explanation of this argument is that universality is an impossible utopia because all norms are relative.[46] This is exemplified by the above Shari'a debate. There is no uniformity in the way human rights are approached. In Europe and North America, it is acceptable to have human assemblies decide of the content and meaning of human rights. In Islam, trusting human beings with human rights is to err as humans are fallible; only Allah can decide what human rights are, how they apply and to whom they apply.[47] Muslim scholars have approached the human rights paradigm through a conditional stance: one has human rights granted by God once they have fulfilled their religious obligations. A believer's responsibility towards Shari'a and Shari'a law therefore supersedes commitment to international human rights. This approach is partly at the root of the disengagement of some Muslims from universal human rights.[48] This duties/rights pattern is problematic for all citizens when seeking to reconcile Muslimness and universal human rights law, and goes well beyond of a categorisation between strong and weak particularism. The issue is one of legitimacy, where universal human rights are man-made while Islamic human rights are divinely ordered.

The impact on security as approached in the UN Charter and by the international community is the following: it is understood that having multiple states and communities advocating for different readings of human rights undermines the world order.[49] The Rahman case is a good illustration of the linkage between universal human rights law and security: Abdul Rahman, an Afghan citizen, was condemned to death for apostasy.[50] Hanafi law as interpreted by Afghan authorities stated that a Muslim who rejects Islam shall be sentenced to death. This decision of the courts to rely on Hanafi jurisprudence was grounded in Article 130.2 of the new Constitution. Yet, Article 7 of the same Constitution affirms the obligation for the country to abide by international law and the UDHR. Afghanistan is also a party to the ICCPR which in its Article 18.2 states that obligation to respect freedom of religion and belief. Article 6 of the Constitution which states that "the state is obliged to create a prosperous and progressive society based on social justice, protection of human dignity, protection of human rights, realization of democracy, and to ensure national unity and equality among all ethnic groups and tribes and to provide for balanced development in all areas of the country." This case demonstrates the complexity of including a religious perspective on human rights alongside universal human rights law: the judges working on the case had different constitutional directives to work with, some stating that Hanafi law is the base law while others claim universal human rights need to be implemented. This case study also shows that the liberal model that marries human rights with democracy and liberalism is difficult to export and the Afghan constitution could not provide a solution to the tension between Islamic law and universal

---

[46] Churchill 2016, p. 44.

[47] Qurbani 1996, 10.

[48] Al Mawudi 1978, p. 5; Amuli 1998, p. 89; Merad 1984, p. 127.

[49] Van Engeland 2014, p. 1337.

[50] Afshar 2006, p. 591.

human rights.[51] The Afghan constitutional experiment failed to encompass the challenges and difficulties of reconciling a religious system of law with a secular one. In security terms, this means that the protection of minorities in Afghanistan is undermined by another reading of human rights law that gives the priority to the majority community's religious values. This creates grounds for greed and grievances that are known for being causes of conflict.[52] The Afghan Hanafi perspective on human rights is consequently problematic from a security perspective.

It could also be argued that the problem is not with local specifities when it comes to human rights, but rather with the way the principle of universality is advocated and has become anchored to liberalism.

5.3.2 The Issue with the Liberal World Order

One of the premises of this book chapter is that universal human rights law is linked to liberal peace. The outcome is that the respect of universal human rights becomes a primary referent to be considered as peaceful or threatening: the Islamic Republic of Iran, under these terms, become a threat to peace and security as it advocates for another reading of human rights. The argument could and should be turned on its head to question whether insecurity is not caused by the refusal to accommodate or even include alternative human rights voices. The principle of universality that claims to merge all human rights' culture into one is, in that regard, an ideal but also an encouragement to the international community to assess the world security through a biased lens. This has led to justifying interventions and invasions in countries and within communities on the ground of universal human rights, without addressing human rights violations "at home" such as the existence of Guantanamo Bay camp. The stakes attached to the double standard approach to human rights had been understood early on by the AAA when it "cautioned the U.N. Commission on Human Rights about this danger [of erasing cultural diversity] during the drafting of the UDHR. The Society pointed to the West's history of 'ascribing cultural inferiority' to non-European peoples."[53] Yet, the UN approach to peace and security that, in its philosophy but also in its practice, liberal often appears to side-line cultural values, beliefs and practices. Universality of human rights then risk being seen as a crusade against other values.

The association between liberal peace, democracy and human rights has strengthened the position of cultural relativists. This combination has slowly crept onto universal human rights law, and some have now claimed the end of history when it comes to human rights, using responsibility to protect as a paradigm to do so. This is how and why Zeid Ra'ad Al Hussein, then UN High Commissioner for Human Rights, declared:

---

[51] Van Engeland 2014, p. 1337.

[52] Collier and Hoeffler 2004; Fearon and Laitin 2003.

[53] Otto 1998, p. 8.

5 Human Rights: Between Universalism and Relativism

The universality of rights is being contested across much of the world. It is under broad assault from terrorists, authoritarian leaders and populists who seem only too willing to sacrifice, in varying degrees, the rights of others, for the sake of power. Their combined influence has grown at the expense of liberal democratic order, peace and justice.[54]

He then endorsed the narrative that liberalism produces human rights and that the sole governance model to sustain universal human rights is that of the liberal democracy.

Yet, in a post-colonial world, it is key to listen to alternative human rights' voices. This is why there are now calls to reclaim human rights. In that regard, human rights constitute a field for de-colonisation but also for contestation where it can be advocated that a bottom-up approach is to put forward when it comes to the principle of universality: it could either be a societal bottom-up approach,[55] a community bottom-up approach or a States to international community approach. In that regard, envisioning universality as a concept being built and "not yet" completed as suggested by McNeilly, gives room to challenge the mainstream dominant discourse.[56] The question then becomes to know how flexible the international community can be when it comes to including other perspectives without negating the very soul of universal human rights and ensuring liberal peace and security?

5.4 Transcending the Tensions: New Developments Resulting from Current Challenges and Possible Ways Forward

Scholars have worked on a third approach to human rights, one that would go beyond the *face-à-face* between universality and relativism. Different strategies are proposed and some of them are discussed in this book chapter.

5.4.1 Accommodating Universalism

Not all communities, countries and regions that voice an alternative approach to human rights struggle with the principle of universality. Some accommodate human rights quite well while others have become drivers in seeking ways of working on commonalities between universality and specificity. The African Commission on Human and Peoples' Rights has produced ground-breaking case law in the domain of social and economic rights. Its judges have sought to make the best use of universal human rights to encourage a liberal development agenda. For example, the Commission observed in *Purohit and Moore v. The Gambia* that it was:

---

[54] Al Hussein 2017.

[55] Van Engeland 2011, p. 74.

[56] McNeilly 2015, p. 256.

aware that millions of people in Africa are not enjoying the right to health maximally because African countries are generally faced with the problem of poverty which renders them incapable to provide the necessary amenities, infrastructure and resources that facilitate the full enjoyment of this right. Therefore, having due regard to this depressing but real state of affairs, the African Commission would like to read into Article 16 the obligation on part of States party to the African Charter to take concrete and targeted steps, while taking full advantage of its available resources, to ensure that the right to health is fully realised in all its aspects without discrimination of any kind.[57]

The Court thereby sought to implement the universal right to health. The judges' methodology has been to focus on less controversial rights as they address the need of the community rather than those of individuals. This contribution to the second generation of human rights is therefore rather logical: judges have found a field where they can reconcile African values and universal values. Another example is to be found in Latin America where courts have used the same strategy: in the case *Asociación Civil por la Igualdad y la Justicia c/GCBA* in Argentina, the judges conducted a budget analysis to show that the State did not use its resources efficiently in order to implement the right to education.[58] Yet, this methodology seems to fail when addressing individual rights, considered to reflect western-centric concerns. Regional courts have consequently not been able to address the issue of the differences between local human rights' readings and universal human rights law.

Muslim scholars have largely contributed to another methodology, as demonstrated by Iranian scholars. The contribution to the debate on human rights in Iran relates primarily to the principle of universality but also to establishing strategies to enforce religion and the universality of human rights together. As an illustration, scholars have worked toward the enforcement of universal human rights by reaching a balance between interpretation of the scriptures and the universality of human rights.[59] Ayatollah Javadi Amuli discusses the distribution of rights and duties, seeking to reach a balance between divine law and natural law: he defines both divine law and natural law as a source of human rights. He tries to give an Islamic consistency to the theory of natural rights by explaining that divine law came first and God set natural law on earth. He concludes that human beings deserve claiming rights in respect to man's nature and status and it is only religion that can ensure human rights.[60] Another example is Hojjat-ol eslam Mohsen Saidzadeh who believes that human rights are superior to religion and to the Islamic system:

> Fundamental rights do not fall within the realm of *fiqh* (Islamic jurisprudence) [...] because they are essential and are not subject to debate or explanations. It does not matter if a jurist declares a fatwa, that he agrees or not, humanity has a right to life. Human beings have an essential dignity.[61]

---

[57] Purohit and Moore v. The Gambia, para 84.

[58] Sigal and Antúnez 2010, p. 317.

[59] Mir Hosseini 1999, p. 202.

[60] Amuli 1998.

[61] Saidzadeh 2002, pp. 239–240.

5 Human Rights: Between Universalism and Relativism

According to Saidzadeh, Islamic sources recognise universal rights and it is consequently necessary to enforce them.[62] The issue is rather with how scripture is being interpreted to socially construct roles. He speaks, in particular, of women's rights and explains why conservative interpretations of the scriptures limit women to a traditional role, limiting their access to human rights. He goes further than Amuli, stating that natural law supersedes divine law, which does not mean the end of the influence of Islamic law. This shows how scholars have tried to embrace universality without betraying their roots.

On their end, universalists have sought to consider, accommodate or embrace cultural relativism as a contribution rather than a threat. A seminar organised in Geneva in 2001, entitled "Enriching universality of human rights: Islamic perspectives on the UDHR" is an example as to how relativism has been considered: the purpose of the meeting was to ensure a better understanding of the Muslim reading of human rights and apprehend issues with universal norms. In the closing speech, Mary Robinson insisted on the creative power of diversity, thereby reminding that, while no concession is possible when it comes to the principle of universality in itself, there is a desire to accommodate other values, beliefs and practices. However, Robinson also raised key questions when she questioned whether universality was not only accessible to a group of privileged individuals.[63] By raising the issue of ownership, she then challenged the international community to question how the principle of universality is being approached.

Such questions have resonated within the international community as shown by the United Nations' commitment to respect cultural diversity. Cultural diversity has been embraced as an inclusive instrument to ensure representations of others' beliefs, values and practices. The 2001 Universal Declaration on Cultural Diversity links cultural diversity and human rights, as "the defence of cultural diversity implies a commitment to human rights and fundamental freedoms." The relationship between cultural diversity and universal human rights has not been clarified; Pollis and Schwab have still concluded to the existence of a new universalism.[64] While there is a new universalism, the recognition that a diversity of beliefs, values and practices exists does not provide an in-depth answer to cultural relativists' claims: cultural diversity solely acknowledges other culture, customs or religions but does not include or embrace them, let alone accommodate them. This raises the issues of similarities and differences: similarities between the UDHR and a specific culture will be celebrated as falling under cultural diversity. Differences are left to States and communities to navigate through a margin of appreciation, creating the same issues observed above with the regional courts' approaches.

This recognition of cultural differences remains a major step forward, and it has led to a reflection on multiculturalism. As a result of the emphasis on cultural rights, Lenzerini speaks of the culturalization of human rights: he suggests that

---

[62] Saidzadeh 1998.

[63] U.N.Doc.HR/98/85 (9 November, 1998).

[64] Pollis and Schwab 2000, pp. 1–2.

the rise of collective rights and cultural rights is a major change in the universality narrative, embracing the idea of the margin of appreciation. This argument supports the European Court of Human Rights or the African Court on Human and Peoples' Rights methodology. He then argues that principle of universality could be re-engineered through a culturally-based approach, embracing multi-culturalism.[65] Lenzerini thereby argues that a multi-cultural relativism maximises the effectiveness of human rights while respecting a certain universalism.

The tension is therefore dynamic and productive, but finding compromises is a difficult task, in theory and in practice. Shall we compromise in practices that lead to lowering the threshold of protection granted to the most vulnerable ones? For advocates of universal human rights, the issue is clearly the reference to religion or culture in any human rights documents: those conventions, declarations and texts are meant to be religiously and culturally neutral so that all can identify with universal norms and benefit from them. This is an issue in Muslim countries abiding by the principle of dhimmis, according to which non-Muslims have less rights than Muslims. The fact that Islam provides for non-Muslims via the law of dhimmitude has led to a special law for religious minorities which is seen as discrimination in the eyes of the international community. There is therefore a fundamental tension that is inherent to the nature of religion and culture: Islam and Muslim culture is applicable to those who believe in it and those who chose to be part of that community. All other segments of a society will not benefit from Islamic human rights because of their choice to opt-out because they believe in other religions or because they are non-believers. It is consequently clear that human rights are conditioned to religion. Among those who denounce this situation is Huntington who believes Islam by nature lacks the capacity to integrate universal human rights. In his all-too famous book, he devotes a chapter to Islam in which he explains that Islam is anti-democratic by nature and cannot adopt human right, liberalism and secularism.

This perhaps demonstrates that accommodating other beliefs, values and practices could endanger the principle of universality. The question is then raised as to the methodologies used to consider culture, religion, customs or traditions in the international arena.

5.4.2 Accepting Cultural Relativism Within Universalism

Human rights operate at the local, regional and international levels: it constitutes a "paradoxical intersection between the universal and the specific".[66] This is a result of globalisation as noted by Pollis and Schwab.[67] Most authors agree that some consideration of values and beliefs are therefore necessary to maintain peace and security. Yet, working on similarities and leaving differences to the margin of appreciation is

---

[65] Lenzerini 2014.

[66] Stern and Straus 2014, p. 4.

[67] Pollis and Schwab 2000, pp. 1–2.

5 Human Rights: Between Universalism and Relativism

problematic from a universality perspective, and consequently for peace and security: would it mean that the international community should approach female circumcision as part of a culture? Should we accept child labour as part of a liberal reality? Should we compromise on the prohibition to torture in case of terrorism? To what extent is the international community ready to accept different beliefs, values and practices that not only undermine the principle of universality by promoting fragmentation but also endorse violations of those very same universal human rights? And how would we measure what is acceptable due to a high level of similarity while leave the "rest" to the margin of appreciation? Would accepting specifities endanger liberal peace?

Those questions and the divide between universality and cultural relativism seem almost overridden by another issue: it is key to discuss the principle of universality in relation to liberalism. To fully apprehend human rights in the twenty-first century, it is necessary to re-imagine the principle of universality of human rights and this goes through a discussion on the linkage with liberal peace. Scholars using different methods have engaged with the issues. One of the strategies has been to acknowledge the need to re-define universality in a post-colonial world: in his controversial book, Kennedy states

> I worry, moreover, that human rights, given its origins, its spokesmen, its preoccupations, has often been a vocabulary of the centre against the periphery. A vehicle for empire rather than an antidote to empire.[68]

He outlines clearly his concern that human rights are a vehicle for imperialism. It is indeed to be noted that in the UN perception of peace and security, human rights are at the heart of the global governance project. Interventions and invasions conducted in the name of human rights carry a neo liberal agenda. In that regard, ensuring that human rights are universal would then internationalise the Fukuyama's agenda of liberalism. Orford alerts us to the same issue when she says:

> I want to suggest that human rights discourse offers resources for attempting to create a universalist ethic that is not premised upon a denial of difference or a nostalgia for a lost, imagined wholeness. Human rights has the potential to found an international law that is not limited to supporting the fantasy life of nations and the international community through recreating the violent exclusion of the alien or the foreign.[69]

She then seeks solutions to re-imagine human rights differently. In that regard, Mutua, who criticises human rights as a neo colonialist enterprise,[70] proposes an alternative. He not only transcends the universalist-cultural relativist debate; he also finds a solution to the use and ownership of universal human rights law: he proposes to re-build universality from the bottom-up, based on cross-culturalism. For his project, he builds on the work of An Na'im who supports cross cultural approaches to human rights law.[71]

---

[68] Kennedy 2006, p. 133.

[69] Orford 2003, p. 214.

[70] Mutua 2001, p. 201.

[71] An-Na'im 1995, p. 20.

I believe that the current human rights corpus has no answers to these questions. It does not have the tools to deal with these deeply embedded questions. That will only be possible, I believe, if we re-open debate on the entire normative scheme of the human rights corpus and reconstruct it from the ground up. The participation of all societies and cultural milieus must be required if the corpus is to claim genuine universality.[72]

Mutua criticises the approach of the principle of universality that seeks to be inclusive of others and wishes instead to promote a new universalism. This method transcends the debate of inclusion and benchmarking as universality would be built brand new, from the bottom-up by those who live human rights. This new universalism would reject Western hegemony, thereby questioning the liberal peace and security agenda.[73] In that regard, McNeilly's approach, building on Butler, is to constantly re-imagine the principle of universality of human rights, making it a "not yet" domain. Universality becomes a space for contest, adapting to the political reality of the moment:

I seek to think through the possibility of exploring the universality of human rights as a process of ongoing universalisation. This approach considers universality not as a static attribute or characteristic of human rights to be either endorsed or rejected, but as a process, an action, a doing which takes place through politico-legal engagements with rights and is the very lifeblood of human rights.[74]

The question as to how link between universal human rights and security can be broken is therefore addressed, indirectly: a new principle of universality will lead to a re-definition of international priorities in the domain of peace and security.

5.5 Conclusion

The search for a new universalism builds on the work done by post-colonial scholars seeking to transcend the tensions between universalism and cultural relativism. While new ideas and approaches are emerging, the strategy to ensure a co-existence of different cultures, religions, traditions and customs remain a challenge. The re-framing of the debate on the principle of universality is key: it has enabled a post-colonial critique of the principle of universality and a questioning of the liberal aim of universal human rights when it comes to peace and security. Such work is now powering the emergence of a new universalism.

The association between universal human rights on the one hand and peace and security on the other hand also need to be questioned in other terms: post-colonialism alone will not help sort out this matrix on which the post-World War II world is built. Liberal peace should either be dismantled at the risk of creating more conflicts or peace and security need to re-frame and re-imagined as well to accommodate the new universality paradigm.

---

[72] Mutua 2008, xi.

[73] Mutua 2008, p. 156.

[74] McNeilly 2015, p. 265.

References

Afshar MKR (2006) The Case of an Afghan Apostate: The Right to a Fair Trial Between Islamic Law and Human Rights in the Afghan Constitution. Max Planck UNYB 10:591–605

Ahmadu F (2007) Ain't I a woman too? Challenging myths of sexual dysfunction in circumcised women. In: Hernlund Y, Shell-Duncan B (eds) Transcultural Bodies: female genital cutting in global contexts. Rutgers University Press, New Brunswick, pp 278–310

Al Hussein Z (2017) Values enshrined in Universal Declaration of Human Rights under assault, must be defended. https://www.ohchr.org/FR/NewsEvents/Pages/DisplayNews.aspx?NewsID= 22507&Lan. Accessed 27 October 2020

Al Mawudi M (1978) Human rights in Islam. Islamic Foundation, Leicester

Alzubairi F (2019) Colonialism, Neo-Colonialism, and Anti-Terrorism Law in the Arab World. Cambridge University Press, Cambridge

American Anthropological Association (1947) Statement on human rights. Am Antropol 49(4): 539–543

Amuli J Ayatollah (1998) Falsafe-ye Hoquq-e Bashar. Markaz-e Nashr-e Isra, Qom

An Na'im A (1995) Toward a Cross-Cultural Approach to Defining International Standards of Human Rights: The Meaning of Cruel, Inhuman, or Degrading Punishment. In: An Na'im A (ed) Human Rights in Cross-Cultural Perspectives: A Quest for Consensus. University of Pennsylvania Press, Philadelphia, pp 19–43

Ayton-Shenker D (1995) The challenge of human rights and cultural diversity. United Nations Department of Public Information, New York

Barša P (2005) Waging War in the Name of Human Rights? Fourteen Theses about Humanitarian Intervention. Perspectives 24:5–20

Berg RC, Denison E (2013) A tradition in transition: factors perpetuating and hindering the continuance of female genital mutilation/cutting (FGM/C) summarized in a systematic review. Health Care Women Int doi: https://doi.org/10.1080/07399332.2012.721417

Brems E (1997) Enemies or Allies? Feminism and Cultural Relativism as Dissident Voices in Human Rights Discourse. HRQ 19-1:136–164

Buchan R (2013) International law and the construction of the liberal peace. Hart Publishing, London

Burke R (2011) Decolonization and the Evolution of International Human Rights. University of Pennsylvania Press, Philadelphia

Caney S (2005) Justice beyond borders: a global political theory. Oxford University Press, Oxford

Churchill RP (2016) Human Rights and Global Diversity, Routledge, London

Cobbah E (1987) African Values and the Human Rights Debate: An African Perspective. HRQ doi: https://doi.org/10.2307/761878

Collier P, Hoeffler A (2004) Greed and Grievances in Civil War. Oxf Econ Pap doi:https://doi.org/ 10.1093/oep/gpf064

Donnelly J (1984) Cultural Relativism and Universal Human Rights. HRQ 6:4: 400–419

Dundes Renteln A (1990) International human rights: universalism versus relativism. Sage Publications, New York

Fearon JD, Laitin D (2003) Ethnicity, Insurgency, and Civil War. Am. Political Sci. Rev doi https:// doi.org/10.1017/S0003055403000534

Féron H (2014) Human rights and faith: a 'world-wide secular religion'? Ethics Glob. Politics doi: https://doi.org/10.3402/egp.v7.26262

Freeman M (2010) Human Rights. Polity Press, Oxford

Gassama I (2012) A World Made of Violence and Misery: Human Rights as a Failed Project of Liberal Internationalism. BJIL 37(2):408–458

Glendon MA (2001) A world made new: Eleanor Roosevelt and the Universal Declaration of Human Rights. Random House, New York

Hathaway OA (n.d) Security and Human Rights, https://law.yale.edu/sites/default/files/documents/ pdf/Faculty/SecurityandHumanRights.pdf. Accessed 27 October 2020

Hathaway OA (2007) Why do countries commit to human rights treaties? J Conflict Resolut. doi: https://doi.org/10.1177/0022002707303046

Henkin L (1989) The Universality of the Concept of Human Rights. Annals Am. Acad. Pol. & Soc. Sci. Doi: https://doi.org/10.1177/0002716289506001002

Hilsdon AM, Mackie V, Stivens M, Macintyre M (2000) Human Rights and Gender Politics: Asia-Pacific perspectives. Routledge, London/New York

Howard RE (1995) Human Rights and the Search for Community. J Peace Res. doi: https://doi.org/10.1177/0022343395032001001

Huong NTM, Vu GC, Nguyen TM (2018) Asian Values and Human Rights: A Vietnamese Perspective. JSEAHR. doi: https://doi.org/10.19184/jseahr.v2i1.7541

Ibhawoh B (2017) Imperialism and Human Rights: Colonial Discourses of Rights and Liberties in African History. SUNY Press, Albany

Ingiyimbere F (2017) Domesticating Human Rights: A Reappraisal of their Cultural-Political Critiques and their Imperialistic Use. Springer, Cham

Kar M (2001) Kudum Huqquq? Kuddum Taqlif? Darhbarah-ye vahziat-ye huqquq-e zan dar Khanevadeh Jamiyah-ye Iraniyan. Zanan, Tehran

Kennedy D (2006) Reassessing International Humanitarianism: The Dark Sides. In: Orford A (ed) International Law and its Others. Cambridge University Press, Cambridge, pp 131–155

Lekha Sriram C, Martin-Ortega O, Herman J (2017) War, Conflict and Human Rights. Routledge, Abingdon/New York

Lenzerini F (2014) The culturalization of human rights law. Oxford University Press, Oxford

Mayer AE (1999) Islam and Human Rights: Tradition and Politics. Westview Press, Boulder

McNeilly K (2015) Reclaiming the Radical in Universal Human Rights: Universality as Universalisation. INT'l HUM. Rts. L. REV doi https://doi.org/10.1163/22131035-00402007

Mehrpoor H (1995) Hoquq-e Bashar dar Asnad-e Binalmellali and Muzeh-e Jomhurri-ye Islami-ye Iran. Ihilahat, Tehran

Merad A (1984) Droits de Dieu, Droits de l'Homme en Islam. In: Meyer Birsch P (ed) Universalité des Droits de l'Homme et Diversité des Cultures. Editions Universitaires Fribourg, Fribourg, pp 127–139

Mir Hosseini Z (1999) Islam and Gender: The Religious Debate in Contemporary Iran. Princeton University Press, Princeton

Musalo K (2015) When Rights and Cultures Collide. https://www.scu.edu/ethics/ethics-resources/ethical-decision-making/when-rights-and-cultures-collide/. Accessed 27 October 2020

Mutua M (2001) Savages, Victims, and Saviors: The Metaphor of Human Rights. Harv. Int. Law J 42(1): 201–245

Mutua M (2008) Human Rights: A Political and Cultural Critique. University of Pennsylvania Press, Philadelphia

Mutua M (2011) Human rights: a political and cultural critique. University of Pennsylvania Press, Philadelphia

Nussbaum MC (2006) Frontiers of justice. Belknap Press of Harvard University Press, Cambridge

Orford A (2003) Reading Humanitarian Intervention: Human Rights and the Use of Force in International Law. Cambridge University Press, Cambridge

Otto C (1998) Rethinking the 'Universality' of Human Rights Law. HRQ 29-1:49–60

Packer C (2002) Using Human Rights to Change Tradition: Traditional Practices Harmful to Women's Reproductive Health in sub-Saharan Africa. Intersentia, Oxford

Pollis A, Schwab P (2000) Human Rights: New Perspectives, New Realities. Lynne Rienner, Boulder

Qurbani ZA (1996) Islam va Hoqquq-e Bashar. Office for Islamic Culture, Tehran

Sachs A (1990) Protecting human rights in a new South Africa. Oxford University Press, New York

Saidzadeh H (1998) Zanan dar Jamiyat-e Madani: Chi Andazeah Sahm Darand? Barras-e fiqh-e va Kalami Nasr-e Qahrah. Tehran

Saidzadeh M (2002) Fiqh et Fiqaha. JINEL 1(2):239–258

Shah NA (2006) Women, the Koran and International Human Rights Law: The Experience of Pakistan. Martinus Nijhoff Publishers, Leiden/Boston

5 Human Rights: Between Universalism and Relativism

Shaheed A, Richter RP (2018) Is human rights a western concept https://theglobalobservatory.org/2018/10/are-human-rights-a-western-concept/. Accessed 27 October 2020

Shweder RA (2009) Disputing the Myth of the Sexual Dysfunction of Circumcised Women: An Interview with Fuambai S. Ahmadu. Anthropo Today 25(6):14–17

Sigal M, Antúnez D (2010) Budget Analysis and the Right to Education in the City of Buenos Aires. EHRLE 3:317–319

Smail Salhi Z (2008) Gender and Diversity in the Middle East and North Africa. Br. J. Middle East. Stud 35(3):295–304

Stern S, Straus S (2014) The human rights paradox: universality and its discontents. University of Wisconsin Press, Madison

Van Engeland A (2011) Human Rights and Strategies to avoid Fragmentation as a Threat to Peace: Iran as a case-study. IJHR 5(1):25–47

Van Engeland A (2014) The balance between Islamic Law, Customary Law and Human Rights in Islamic constitutionalism through the prism of legal pluralism. CILJ 3(4): 1321–1348

Van Engeland A (2017) Be Karbala Miravim!: Iran and the Challenges of Internalizing International Humanitarian Law in a Muslim Country. In: Evangelista M, Tannenwald N (eds) Do the Geneva Conventions Matter? Oxford University Press, Oxford, pp. 250–280

Dr. Anicée Van Engeland is an Associate Professor of International Security & Law, Cranfield University. She holds a Ph.D. in Politics & Law (Muslim World) (Institut d'Etudes Politiques, Paris, 2006), LLM (Harvard Law School, 2004), an MA in International relations (Université Paris II Assas, 2002), and an MA in Iranian Studies (Université Paris III Sorbonne, 2002). Prior to becoming an academic, Anicée was a human rights worker and an aid worker. She acts as a consultant for several international organisations and NGOs such as UNDP, ICRC, UNHCR, ILO and IOM. She also serves as an expert witness to courts in the UK and the USA. Anicée's main areas of research and practice are in the fields of security, governance, rule of law and human rights law in relation to Islam.

Part II
Law

Chapter 6
The Use of Force in International Law

Onder Bakircioglu

Contents

6.1 Introduction 118
6.2 The Use of Force Regime Under the League of Nations 119
6.3 The Use of Force Regime Under the United Nations 123
6.4 Exceptions to the Prohibition on the Use of Force 129
    6.4.1 General Observations 129
    6.4.2 Collective Security Measures 132
    6.4.3 The Right to Self-defence 134
6.5 Conclusion 144
References 144

Abstract War and other forms of collective violence have been omnipresent in human history. While the idea of perpetual peace has always been an aspiration since time immemorial, the rejection of aggression to resolve international disputes is peculiar only to modern times. Indeed, only after World War II had the international community prohibited unilateral aggression. While the rules regulating the use of force are of critical importance in international law, the political dynamics of international relations often engender self-interested conduct apropos security-related matters. Thus, the maintenance of international peace and security is in large measure hinged on the control and restriction of military force. After examining the evolution of the laws governing use of force under the League and United Nations systems, this chapter will argue that despite the emergence of new threats to international security, stemming from new actors and modern military technologies, the international community must remain attentive to unjustified attempts to downplay the principles of *jus ad bellum*.

Keywords war · use of force · self-defence · League of Nations · United Nations · Security Council · unwilling and unable doctrine · anticipatory self-defence

---

O. Bakircioglu (✉)
Leicester Law School, University of Leicester, Leicester LE1 7RH, UK
e-mail: onder.bakircioglu@le.ac.uk

© T.M.C. ASSER PRESS and the authors 2022
S. Sayapin et al. (eds.), *International Conflict and Security Law*,
https://doi.org/10.1007/978-94-6265-515-7_6

6.1 Introduction

Humankind has fought wars for myriad reasons since time immemorial. But evidence suggests that various moral and religious considerations had often been invoked to limit the outbreak or devastation of collective fighting.[1] Restrictions on warlike conduct involved such humanitarian considerations as the protection of non-combatants, the inviolability of places deemed sacred (e.g. wells, graves, oases, and places of worship), exchange or good treatment of prisoners and envoys, proper burial of the dead, as well as the conclusion of truces or peace treaties.[2] Such restrictions were generally in tune with what was considered as 'honourable' bellicose conduct. Evidently, however, since what constitutes 'honourable' has usually been culturally specific and temporally contingent, warfare and its limits had been contextually, historically and relationally structured, along changing axes of ethical principles and military interests. Hence, as the Prussian general and military theorist Von Clausewitz famously put it, 'every age had its own kind of war, its own limiting conditions, and its own peculiar preconceptions'.[3]

The rules regulating the use of force are of critical significance in international law. These rules are related with other crucial principles including territorial sovereignty, political independence and equality of States. Although the maintenance of international peace and security is in large measure hinged upon the control and restriction of military force, there exists no international government capable of exerting monopoly on aggression. At its inception, the Security Council was meant to exercise such a monopolistic function; but its divided political structure made this largely impracticable. Hence, as Shaw points out, in international law controlling military force is not only dependent on legal factors, but also on political factors, which means that 'reliance has to be placed on consent, consensus, reciprocity and good faith' of States.[4]

Legal norms governing the use of force have undergone dramatic changes particularly over the past century. Indeed, as this chapter will show, the international community has attempted, first with the League of Nations (the League) and later with the United Nations (UN), to curb State aggression. Before the League system, created after the First World War (WWI), international relations operated in a decentralised system, where each State could claim the right to judge the merits of its own case. In situations of war, this phenomenon blurred any clear demarcation line between *bellum justum* and *bellum injustum*. Hence, Hall, observing in 1890, stressed that 'as international law is destitute of any judicial or administrative machinery, it leaves States, which think themselves aggrieved, and which have exhausted all peaceable methods of obtaining satisfaction, to exact redress for themselves by force'.[5] States, in other words, had the power to invoke forceful measures of self-help when their

---

[1] See Brownlie 1963, p. 3; Best 1997, p. 14; Blank and Noone 2019, p. 63ff.

[2] Phillipson 1911, p. 64ff.

[3] Von Clausewitz 1976, p. 593.

[4] Shaw 2017, p. 851.

[5] Hall 1890, p. 65.

6 The Use of Force in International Law

demands were not met to their satisfaction. The first legal breakthrough on limiting aggression came with the establishment of the League, followed by the more sophisticated UN system. This chapter will trace the evolution of the laws governing the use of force under the League and UN regimes. It will in particular discuss some of the major recent politico-legal challenges surrounding the use of force discourse under the UN system, with specific attention devoted to suggested changes to the law of self-defence in relation to non-State actors. The chapter in a nutshell will argue that despite the emergence of new threats to international peace and security, it is imperative that the international community remain vigilant against unjustified attempts to downplay laws governing *jus ad bellum* embodied in customary international law and the United Nations Charter.

6.2 The Use of Force Regime Under the League of Nations

In the practice of States until the end of the nineteenth century, wars had been fought as a valid form of dispute settlement. The acceptance of aggression as a tool of statecraft meant that there existed a 'right of conquest' under international law.[6] Such thinking partly survived within the League system that was created in the wake of WWI. The hitherto unparalleled atrocities of WWI surely compelled the drafters of the League Covenant to introduce certain innovations; but these in the main constituted procedural constraints on the manner in which hostilities could be initiated.[7]

The League essentially aimed at facilitating amicable settlement of international disputes. To this end, it envisaged some basic provisions to limit the 'right' of States to wage wars. The members of the League, in this context, undertook 'to respect and preserve as against external aggression the territorial integrity and existing political independence of all Members'.[8] The Covenant also set forth a mandatory three-month 'cooling off period' for disputants before they could go to war to settle their differences. Hence, whilst the Covenant did not outlaw offensive wars, it did oblige Member States to avoid military confrontations as long as the dispute was under consideration by the Council of the League.[9] The Covenant further empowered the Council to impose a variety of collective sanctions on States that resorted to war in disregard of their Covenant obligations. In such cases, Members of the League pledged to consider an attack on a fellow Member an act of aggression against all, in

---

[6] Korman 1996, p. 7ff.

[7] Crawford 2012, p. 744.

[8] The Covenant of the League of Nations, Article 10.

[9] Article 12 of the Covenant reads thus: 'The Members of the League agree that, if there should arise between them any dispute likely to lead to a rupture they will submit the matter either to arbitration or judicial settlement or to enquiry by the Council, and they agree in no case to resort to war until three months after the award by the arbitrators or the judicial decision, or the report by the Council. In any case under this Article the award of the arbitrators or the judicial decision shall be made within a reasonable time, and the report of the Council shall be made within six months after the submission of the dispute'.

which case they were to subject the aggressor to various economic, diplomatic, or, where necessary, military sanctions.[10]

Clearly, therefore, while the Covenant put in place a number of instruments to restrict warfare, it ultimately did not prohibit warfare as a means of national policy. Instead, Member States were encouraged to invoke certain dispute settlement mechanisms; and where these processes failed, disputants could 'take action as they ... [considered] necessary for the maintenance of right and justice'.[11] In other words, the chief objective of the League was to restrict, and not to outlaw, recourse to warfare.

As regards whether the right of self-defence existed under the League system, while the Charter did not contain any specific provision in this respect, it was generally recognised that self-defence was an 'inherent' right of States that was not curtailed in any manner whatsoever,[12] provided that the customary rules of 'necessity' and 'proportionality' of force had been satisfied. In fact, such customary status and qualifying rules of self-defence had been confirmed by the *Caroline* affair of 1837,[13] where it was affirmed that a State could resort to defensive military measures when there was 'a necessity of self-defence, [which was] instant, overwhelming, leaving no choice of means and no moment for deliberation'.[14] Under the *Caroline* criteria, therefore, a State invoking anticipatory self-defence would need to show that defensive force against a putative aggressor was absolutely necessary to forestall an imminent threat of harm. While the *Caroline* criteria were later employed by the International Military Tribunal (IMT) at Nuremberg,[15] its place in contemporary international law has remained controversial.[16] The International Court of Justice (ICJ) has hitherto refrained from referring to *Caroline* in its rulings on self-defence, arguably because such concepts as 'instant,' 'overwhelming,' 'leaving no choice of means,' and 'no moment for deliberation' are so ambiguous as to invite potential abuse. As shown in the following pages, today it is often the advocates of the anticipatory war strategy that make frequent reference to *Caroline* in their attempts to relax the traditional rules governing the use of force discourse.

Relegating the question of self-defence to customary law, rather than to legal norms, was in tune with the overall ethos of the League, which essentially sought to serve as a political institution to facilitate a peaceful reorganisation of the international order which was seriously unsettled after WWI. Considering the asymmetrical power structure and colonial legacy of the post-war order,[17] what the League

---

[10] The Covenant of the League of Nations, Article 16.

[11] The Covenant of the League of Nations, Article 15(7); also see Kennedy 2006, p. 75ff.

[12] See Weightman 1951, p. 1102.

[13] See D. Webster, 'Letter from US Secretary of State Daniel Webster to British Minister Henry Fox (24 April 1841)' 29 *British and Foreign State Papers* 1841.

[14] Ibid.

[15] The IMT at Nuremberg held that Germany's attack against Norway on grounds of forestalling an allied invasion was illegal. IMT (Nuremberg), *The Trial of German Major War Criminals*, Proceedings of the International Military Tribunal sitting at Nuremberg, Germany, Part 22, Judgment of 1 October 1946, p. 435.

[16] See Green 2009, pp. 75–80.

[17] For an analysis, see Anghie 2006, p. 739ff; Koskenniemi 2001, p. 98ff.

6 The Use of Force in International Law

Covenant sought to achieve was not to outlaw the war altogether, but rather to restrict permissible grounds on which legitimate wars could be fought.[18] Despite such limitations, war remained an acceptable instrument of national policy. True, the Covenant obliged Member States 'to respect and preserve as against external aggression the territorial integrity and existing political independence of all members of the League'.[19] However, when read in conjunction with subsequent provisions (particularly Articles 12, 13, and 15), this obligation did not amount to an unqualified prohibition of interstate aggression. Instead, the founders of the League articulated their preference for amicable resolution of international disputes before States could make war. The chief achievement of the League system, therefore, lay in the fact that wars became a matter for international concern, in that 'illegitimate' wars were sought to be deterred through collective measures. Lawrence Lowell, a leader of the League to Enforce Peace, spelled out the rationale for such collective measures:

> We feel that the only thing that will prevent war is the certainty that the country going to war will have to meet the world in arms, and we believe that any country which is fully convinced that if it commits acts of hostility towards another before submitting the question in dispute to arbitration it will have to fight all the world, will never commit such acts of hostility, and hence that such a universal war will never be needed.[20]

But such optimism was to be short-lived, as in the series of crises that led up to World War II (WWII) the League could not exercise its peacekeeping functions effectively, which eroded its credibility. Indeed, even before Hitler's aggressive policies on the European status quo, the failure of the League to curb the expansionist policies of Japan and Italy disheartened its supporters, who had once looked upon the League as a workable mechanism for protecting international peace and security.

Despite the failure of the League, during the interwar period a radical legal idea was conceived—namely, the renouncement of warfare as an instrument of national policy. This once-unthinkable notion came with the Kellogg-Briand Pact of 1928.[21] Initially signed by the United States (US), France, the British Empire, Germany, Belgium, Ireland, Italy, Japan, Poland and Czechoslovakia, the Pact was acceded to by 63 States by 1938, thus attaining a near universal support. This mere three-articled treaty condemned 'recourse to war for the solution of international controversies' and renounced 'warfare as an instrument of national policy'.[22] The signatories further agreed that 'the settlement or solution of all disputes or conflicts of whatever nature or of whatever origin they may be ... shall never be sought except by pacific means'.[23] Again, the Pact did not address the question of self-defence, although the parties, prior to the conclusion of the Pact, agreed that the 'inherent' right of self-defence

---

[18] See, for instance, Articles 12, 13 and 15 of the Covenant.

[19] Article 10 of the Covenant.

[20] Quoted in Egerton 1983, p. 98.

[21] General Treaty for Renunciation of War as an Instrument of National Policy (Kellogg-Briand Pact or Pact of Paris), 27 August 1928, 46 Stat. 2343; Treaty Series 796.

[22] Ibid., Article 1.

[23] Ibid., Article 2.

had remained unimpaired.[24] What is meant by 'inherent' was not defined; yet the reference suggested that self-defence was a natural right, which was thus beyond the domain of positive law.

Likewise, because the concept of 'war' was not clarified by the Pact, it was not clear whether forcible measures 'short of war' were permissible. It was evident that warfare as an instrument of 'national policy' was prohibited, but the question of whether States could wage international wars of, for instance, political, ideological or religious character also remained open.[25] Relatedly, it was obscure whether States could engage in armed hostilities in pursuit of executing an arbitral award or a judicial decision—given that such rationale did not strictly qualify as wars of 'national policy'.[26]

Leaving aside such imprecision concerning legal contours of wars untaken in pursuit of national interest, the Pact's renunciation of war was to live short anyhow, not least due to the rise of fascist dictatorships in Germany, Italy and Spain, and of authoritarian regimes in new States of Central and Eastern Europe, such as Poland, Hungary, Romania and Yugoslavia. The collective security system of the interwar period further lost strength when Germany and Japan left the League in the early 1930s, and as Russia was expelled from the League on account of its aggression against Finland in 1940. Nonetheless, by that time the Covenant was practically a dead letter, in large measure because neither Britain nor France pursued their foreign policies in accordance with the liberal principles of the League. And, ironically, the US Senate, adopting a policy of isolationism, had never ratified the Covenant. The League system proved particularly impotent concerning the Japanese invasion of Manchuria in 1931, the Italian conquest of Ethiopia in 1936, the German reoccupation of the Rhineland in 1936 and its annexation of Austria in 1938, Czechoslovakia and Poland in 1939, as well as the Russian attack on Finland in 1939.[27] In short, the ruthless pursuit of national interest had overborne Woodrow Wilson's idealistic vision of peace through global institutions, democratic mechanisms and international cooperation.

Notwithstanding the failure of the League to forestall the outbreak of hostilities culminating in the outbreak of WWII, principles set by the Covenant and the Pact had nonetheless sowed the seeds for a more sophisticated collective security system under the UN framework. The League was indeed the precursor of the legal regulation of the use of force under the UN Charter, in that it required, albeit with little success, international actors to resolve their differences by peaceful means, to present peace-threatening matters to the League Council (the forerunner of the Security Council), and to undertake collective measures against those States which made recourse to war outside the parameters of the League system.

---

[24] Weightman 1951, p. 1108.

[25] See Wehberg 1931, p. 99.

[26] For a discussion, see Dinstein 2017, p. 88.

[27] See Harley 1943, p. 9ff.

6.3 The Use of Force Regime Under the United Nations

The unprecedented atrocities of WWII altered the basic configuration of international relations, in that the legal regulation of force for maintaining peace and security became the top priority of the international community. Indeed, following the untold devastation of WWII, victorious States pledged to maintain international order by creating a scheme that restricted the ability of States to wage aggressive wars. The drafters of the UN Charter, in this context, placed explicit emphasis on peace as their key priority, expressing a determination 'to save succeeding generations from the scourge of war' by creating 'conditions under which justice and respect for the obligations arising from treaties and other sources of international law ... [could] be maintained'.[28]

The preamble of the UN Charter is accordingly categorical in its tone that 'armed force shall not be used, save in the common interest'.[29] The Charter with its unequivocal prohibition on the use of force is thus unmistakably distinguished from the League Covenant, because for the first time in history Member States had agreed to put in place far-reaching legal limitations on their once sovereign prerogative to use, or threaten to use, force. The wording of Article 2(4) of the Charter confirms this: 'All members shall refrain in their international relations from the threat or use of force against the territorial integrity or political independence of any state, or in any other manner inconsistent with the purpose of the United Nations'. As the ICJ recognised in its *Nicaragua* judgement, which was confirmed in its *Armed Activities* ruling, the prohibition against unilateral use force (or its threat) to resolve disagreements constitutes a peremptory norm of contemporary international law from which States cannot derogate.[30]

Having thus acquired a peremptory norm status, the prohibition on aggression is no longer a mere treaty obligation. Again, whilst the UN Charter started its life as a treaty, it is now considered to be a universally subscribed constitutional instrument of the international community; and as such its norms are of a higher legal order.[31] The prohibition of unilateral force hence forms the highest level of State obligation toward the international community—a rule of *jus cogens*[32] which rests on the rationale that State aggression must be avoided at all costs to prevent mass destruction of life and property. Indeed, perhaps the most prominent goal of the UN Charter, whose drafters had experienced the unprecedented devastation of World Wars, is to promote peaceful settlement of disputes among States as reflected in Article 1(1) of the UN Charter.

---

[28] Charter of the United Nations (24 October 1945), Preamble.

[29] Ibid.

[30] *Case Concerning the Military and Paramilitary Activities in and against Nicaragua* (*Nicaragua v United States of America*) (Judgement of 27 June 1986) ICJ Rep 14, para 190; *Case Concerning Armed Activities on the Territory of the Congo* (*Democratic Republic of the Congo* v. *Uganda*) [Judgement of 19 December 2005], ICJ Reports 116, paras 148–65.

[31] For an analysis, see Fassbender 2009, p. 34ff.

[32] The concept of *jus cogens* places a categorical limitation on States to contract out of, or derogate from, peremptory norms. For a discussion, see Hoogh 2015, p. 1170ff.

124   O. Bakircioglu

Notably, therefore, unlike the League Covenant and the Kellogg-Briand Pact, the UN Charter's prohibition of aggression applies universally, which means that all States, irrespective of their membership to the UN, are bound by it.

Such a dramatic attempt to remould the entire edifice of international relations is unsurprisingly related with the unspeakable horrors of WWII that jeopardised the very existence of humankind. The apprehension about global annihilation, in other words, spurred States to bring their political tensions within the realm of law and renounce their prerogatives to wage aggressive wars. Yet it is worth noting that the only reference to war in the Charter is found in its preamble, where the drafters denounced the 'scourge of war'. Since there has been no agreed definition of 'war,' the Charter appears to have deliberatively avoided the term, preferring instead the concept of 'use of force'.[33] Elsewhere in the Charter such concepts as 'threat or use of force,' 'armed attack,' 'threat to the peace,' 'breach of the peace,' and 'act of aggression' are also used in reference to situations where self-defensive or collective security measures might be undertaken. It is generally accepted that war denotes military action taken by States for reasons of national interest, which is distinct from other forms of force undertaken for 'altruistic' motives, such as international peace-keeping missions or humanitarian interventions.[34]

The controversial and restricted meaning of war hence appears to have led the drafters to prefer the concept 'use of force' to cover all conflicts and forcible measures short of war. In this sense, conflicts in which one of the parties is a non-State actor (e.g. an armed conflict between a State and a terrorist organisation), or conflicts that are wars in essence, but not formally declared or so recognised fall under this category. However, some scholars argue that there is a certain 'gravity threshold' which must be reached for the general prohibition on the use of force to apply.[35] The argument that Article 2(4) is subject to such a gravity threshold has gained further traction when the Independent International Fact-Finding Mission on the Conflict in Georgia stated in its 2009 report that the 'prohibition of the use of force covers all physical force which surpasses a minimum threshold of intensity;' and that '[o]nly very small incidents lie below this threshold, for instance the targeted killing of single individuals, forcible abductions of individual persons, or the interception of a single aircraft'.[36] While the ICJ has already distinguished the concepts of 'use of force' and 'armed attack' for the purposes of self-defence under Article 51 of the Charter,[37] the idea of 'minimum gravity' may render the prohibition under Article 2(4) susceptible to abuse. Indeed, as Ruys stresses, the possible acceptance of such minimal threshold of gravity 'may well open Pandora's box by making it far easier for states to justify

---

[33] See Henkin 1995, p. 114.

[34] Johnson 2003, pp. 3–4.

[35] See Corten 2010, p. 403.

[36] Report of the Independent International Fact-Finding Mission on the Conflict in Georgia, September 2009, Vol. II, 242. Available at: http://www.mpil.de/files/pdf4/IIFFMCG_Volume_II1.pdf.

[37] See *Military and Paramilitary Activities in and against Nicaragua* (*Nicaragua vs US*), Merits, Judgement of 27 June 1986, ICJ Rep. 14, para 195; *Iran vs US*, para 51.

6 The Use of Force in International Law

targeted killings, counterterrorist operations, and the like by reference, for example, to necessity, countermeasures, or distress'.[38] To avoid such problems, it appears preferable to proceed on the premise that Article 2(4) covers all intentional lethal attacks targeting other States.

There has, however, been further controversy concerning the scope of 'use of force'.[39] The word 'force' conventionally denotes military force; yet the reach of Article 2(4) goes beyond actual recourse to force by covering 'threats' of force, too. But how are we to measure whether a threat would fall under the general prohibition of force? This question was answered pithily by the ICJ in its Advisory Opinion on the *Legality of the Threat or Use of Nuclear Weapons*:

> The notions of 'threat' and 'use' of force under Article 2, para 4, of the Charter stand together in the sense that if the use of force itself in a given case is illegal—for whatever reason—the threat to use such force will likewise be illegal.[40]

Hence, in order for a threat of force to be unlawful, the threatened force itself must be illegal to begin with. In the final analysis, though, the Advisory Opinion does no more than reaffirming the Charter law, in that the use or threat of force is prohibited unless it qualifies as self-defence under Article 51, or falls within the collective security paradigm under Chapter VII of the Charter.[41]

In 1970, a UN Declaration on Friendly Relations sought to further delimit the bounds of legitimate force by throwing some light on the scope of the prohibition. Accordingly, (1) a war of aggression is deemed a crime against peace; (2) States are to refrain from the threat or use of force to violate international borders; (3) they are to refrain from acts of reprisals involving armed measures; (4) they are to avoid forcible acts to deprive peoples of their right of self-determination; (5) they are to refrain from supporting irregular armed groups seeking to breach sovereign rights of other States; (6) they are neither to get involved in organising, instigating, supporting or participating in civil wars or acts of terrorism in other States, nor are they to allow their territories to be used in such a manner as to endanger other States; and (7) they must not occupy the sovereign territory of other States by either using or threatening to use armed force.[42]

Significantly, the Declaration made it clear that the prohibition on the use of force applies to both military and paramilitary force, whether through direct or indirect military involvements. There remains an unanswered question, however: What forms or levels of overt or covert military acts may amount to a violation of Article 2(4) that may justify the right to self-defence under Article 51 of the Charter? The ICJ made several pronouncements regarding this point. In its *Nicaragua* judgement, it held that

---

[38] Ruys 2014, p. 210.

[39] See Bokor-Szego 1986, p. 461ff.

[40] Advisory Opinion of 8 July 1996, ICJ Rep. 226, para 246.

[41] For a discussion whether possession of nuclear weapons itself is an unlawful threat of force, see Grimal 2013, p. 61ff.

[42] Declaration on Principles of International Law Concerning Friendly Relations and Cooperation Among States in Accordance with the Charter of the United Nations, UNGA, Resolution 2625 (XXXV), 24 October 1970.

military operations amounting to use of force may not qualify as an 'armed attack,' against which self-defensive measures may be undertaken. In order to qualify as an armed attack for the purposes of Article 51, the Court reasoned, an operation must satisfy a minimum scale of gravity.[43] The ICJ in *Oil Platforms* confirmed this stance, concluding that for a bellicose act to amount to an 'armed attack,' it was 'necessary to distinguish "the most grave forms of the use of force (those constituting an armed attack) from other less grave forms'.[44] In other words, the existence of an armed attack (which needs to be attributed to a State)[45] is deemed an absolute requisite for the legitimate exercise of self-defence.[46]

The ICJ in its *Nicaragua* decision distinguished between an 'armed attack on a significant scale' and 'assistance to rebels in the form of the provision of weapons or logistical or other support'.[47] By drawing a line between 'unlawful use of force' and 'armed attack,' the Court held that while providing armed bands with weapons or other forms of logistical support could amount to use of force or intervention in domestic affairs, such assistance was insufficient to constitute an 'armed attack'.[48] However, given that States, while ostensibly denouncing aggression, often engage in covert forms of lethal force, it is doubtful whether it is prudent to take such an unqualified stance. In recognising that a direct or organised military offensive may not be the only form of an armed attack, Judges Schwebel and Jennings hence dissented from the majority view. Depending on the gravity of such logistical or other forms of support, they reasoned, a military campaign conducted through armed bands or irregulars might amount to an armed attack for the purposes of the right to self-defence.[49] Jennings noted that for the ICJ 'to say that the provision of arms, coupled with "logistical or other support" is not armed attack is going much too far, [as] logistical support may itself be crucial'.[50] It indeed appears plausible to adopt a case-by-case approach to assess whether indirect forms of military support in a given scenario is of such gravity as to constitute an armed attack. To tie the right to self-defence only to gravest forms of military attacks might in practice render the right devoid of true content, in particular absent timely Security Council interventions.

Viewed in this light, the architects of the Charter arguably acted wisely in not defining the precise contours of the concepts of aggression, use of force and armed attack, lest such definitions would fall short of covering various cases of military force in distinct settings, and lest all-encompassing definitions be turned into an

---

[43] See *Nicaragua vs US*, para 195.

[44] *Oil Platforms (Iran vs US)*, Merits, Judgement of 6 November 2003, ICJ Rep. 161, para 51.

[45] Ibid., para 161.

[46] The Court clearly stressed that 'the United States has to show that attacks had been made upon it for which Iran was responsible; and that those attacks were of such nature as to be qualified as "armed attacks" within the meaning of that expression in Article 51 UN Charter, and as understood in customary law on the use of force'. Ibid., para 51.

[47] *Nicaragua vs US*, para 195.

[48] Ibid.

[49] 'Dissenting Opinion of Judge Schwebel' and 'Dissenting Opinion of Judge Jennings,' *Nicaragua vs US*, 321–331.

[50] Ibid., 543.

avenue of manipulation for would-be aggressors. Flexibility might prove advantageous considering the rich variety and ever-changing techniques of warfare. It thus appears prudent to leave it to the Security Council to determine, under Article 39 of the Charter, in each case which forms of military, economic or other forms of coercive measures constitute a threat to the peace or violation of the peace.[51] Evidently, the Council might not act objectively in cases where its permanent members express disagreement on the characterisation of the matter.

Relatedly, the prohibition of aggressive force principally applies to interstate conflicts as opposed to intrastate clashes.[52] States must accordingly avoid employing force against each other and at the same time refrain from intervening in domestic politics of other States.[53] Intrastate conflicts, in this sense, are generally deemed to fall within the jurisdiction of a State wherein conflict takes place. It follows that States are allowed to resort to legitimate measures against insurgent groups or liberation movements claiming to fight against various forms of oppression or colonialism. During the decolonisation period, this narrow reading of the Charter paved the way for colonial powers to quell national liberation movements without technically violating Article 2(4). Such injustice eventually prompted the so-called 'Third World' to seek the support of the then Socialist Block to challenge the prevailing framework of international law. The ensuing clash between the demands of the western and those of socialist as well as developing bloc resulted in a compromise that was crystallised in the Declaration on Friendly Relations.[54] The Declaration envisaged that the prohibition of force applied not merely to States, but also to *peoples* that had a representative body (i.e. a national liberation movement), and to those who were thought to possess the right of self-determination. In other words, since *peoples* could 'determine their political status and freely pursue their economic, social and cultural development'[55] like other sovereign entities, any lethal effort to subdue force against them is held to violate Article 2(4).[56]

While the Declaration specified that *peoples*' subjection to alien subjugation constitutes a denial of human rights, and that *peoples* were entitled to resist any forcible action that deprives them of their right to liberty, the questions of who such *peoples* are and whether they could resort to self-defensive armed resistance

---

[51] For the drafting history of Article 39 of the Charter, see Goodrich and Hambro 1946, p. 155ff.

[52] Dinstein 2017, p. 89ff.

[53] Article 2(7) of the UN Charter.

[54] Declaration on Principles of International Law Concerning Friendly Relations and Cooperation Among States in Accordance with the Charter of the United Nations, UNGA Resolution 2625 (XXV) 24 October 1970.

[55] The right to self-determination has found expression in identical terms in common Article 1 of the International Covenant on Civil and Political Rights (ICCPR) and International Covenant on Economic, Social and Cultural Rights (ICESCR).

[56] The Declaration read: 'Every State has the duty to refrain from any forcible action which deprives peoples referred to in the elaboration of the principle of equal rights and self-determination of their right to self-determination and freedom and independence'. Declaration on Principles of International Law Concerning Friendly Relations and Cooperation Among States in Accordance with the Charter of the United Nations, UNGA Resolution 2625 (XXV) 24 October 1970.

to end foreign domination or internal oppression (in cases of minority groups) have remained controversial ever since.[57] That said, the least contentious formulation of self-determination portrays the right as a collective aspiration of the colonised peoples to achieve independence with a view to pursuing their full political, economic and cultural potential.[58]

Again, while intrastate conflicts are said to fall within States' domestic jurisdiction, Article 2(7) of the UN Charter does not preclude the implementation of collective security measures in such conflicts that have the potential of disrupting international peace and security.[59] But, as Wittke notes, 'the concrete conditions under which the [Council] may use these particular powers under Chapter VII remain vague, mainly because of the open-endedness of the terms and formulas used in the UN Charter as well as throughout subsequent practices'.[60] Be that as it may, it is worth recalling that as early as 1961 the Council determined a threat to international peace concerning the conflict in the Congo, which was predominantly intrastate in character.[61] In the wake of the Cold War, the Council's inertia was somewhat overcome by the recognition that an internal strife could amount to a threat to international peace and security for the purposes of Article 39 of the Charter. The increased preparedness of the Council to interfere with intrastate conflicts became more visible in peace-keeping missions undertaken under Chapter VII.[62] In the case of *Tadic*, the Appeals Chamber of the International Criminal Tribunal for the Former Yugoslavia (ICTY) confirmed such expanding preparedness of the Council to consider internal armed conflicts as potential threats to international security thus:

---

[57] Indeed, international law is not explicit on whether any group may claim to be a 'people' on grounds of common language, culture, common heritage, shared beliefs and values; or whether, if it satisfies some of such criteria, it can claim the right to secede from colonial rule or from the dominant political community (in cases of minority groups). The controversy gets more complicated by dint of often vague and contradictory references to self-determination in international law, whether concerning colonial people, minority groups or indigenous peoples. See further Cassese 2008; Crawford 1988; Jones 2018.

[58] Not surprisingly, during the era of decolonisation this view was not shared by some powerful States that opposed to extending the authority to use force beyond the traditional exceptions set out in the UN Charter. For a discussion, see Wilson 1988, pp. 91–137.

[59] Article 2(7) clearly states that the principle of non-intervention 'shall not prejudice the application of enforcement measures under Chapter VII'.

[60] Wittke 2018, p. 169.

[61] See S/RES/161, 21 February 1961, where the Security Council urged that 'the United Nations take immediately all appropriate measures to prevent the occurrence of civil war in the Congo, including arrangements for cease-fires, the halting of all military operations, the prevention of clashes, and the use of force'.

[62] As underlined by the report of the then UN Secretary-General 'of the five peace-keeping operations that existed in early 1988, four related to inter-state wars and only one (20 per cent of the total) to an intra-state conflict. Of the 21 operations established since then, only 8 have related to inter-state wars, whereas 13 (62 per cent) have related to intra-state conflicts, though some of them, especially those in the former Yugoslavia, have some inter-state dimensions also. Of the 11 operations established since January 1992 all but 2 (82 per cent) relate to intra-state conflicts'. See Supplement to an Agenda for Peace: Position Paper of the Secretary-General on the Occasion of the Fiftieth Anniversary of the United Nations, A/50/60-S/1995/1 (03/01/1995).

6 The Use of Force in International Law

Indeed, the practice of the Security Council is rich with cases of civil war or internal strife which it classified as a 'threat to the peace' and dealt with under Chapter VII, with the encouragement or even at the behest of the General Assembly, such as the Congo crisis at the beginning of the 1960s and, more recently, Liberia and Somalia. It can thus be said that there is a common understanding, manifested by the 'subsequent practice' of the membership of the UN at large, that the 'threat to the peace' of Article 39 may include, as one of its species, internal armed conflicts.[63]

What this means in practice is that States are bound to avoid using aggressive force in a variety of international and domestic settings, for the prohibition of force, while originally envisaged in response to international conflicts, must encompass serious intra-state conflicts, which in recent decades have outnumbered inter-state hostilities. The increasing number of cross-border terrorist attacks or civil wars with spill-over effect to neighbouring countries also prompts new thinking on the use of force discourse and its exceptions.

6.4 Exceptions to the Prohibition on the Use of Force

6.4.1 General Observations

While the preamble to the Charter expresses an aspiration 'to save succeeding generations from the scourge of war,' the Charter does not rule out legitimate forms of war. Such exceptions to the prohibition of force are stipulated against unlawful uses of force that are grave enough to threaten international peace and security. Any legitimate resort to force, however, is meant to be a tool of final resort; for Article 2(3) of the Charter obliges States to 'settle their international disputes by peaceful means'. As detailed below, the prohibition of force is subject to two exceptions: (a) the Council may authorise collective enforcement measures under Chapter VII; and (b) a State may invoke its right to self-defence as per Article 51.

Although the overall framework of the Charter encourages a narrow reading of the exceptions,[64] some States seek to broaden the scope of self-defence and other forms of self-help including the right to protect nationals abroad, humanitarian intervention, and the 'responsibility to protect' (R2P). As self-defence has elicited a great deal of controversy, particularly since the atrocities of 11 September 2011 (9/11), this chapter will pay closer attention thereto in the following pages. Among other attempts to relax the contours of the use of force discourse, this chapter, owing to space constraints, will briefly examine the doctrines of humanitarian intervention and the R2P.

The advocates of humanitarian intervention largely maintain that international community should not stand idly by while mass atrocities, such as the ethnic cleansing in the Balkans and Rwanda, occur absent Security Council action. Apart from the

---

[63] ICTY, *The Prosecutor v. Dusko Tadić*, IT-94-1-AR72, Appeals Chamber, Decision of 2 October 1995, para 30.

[64] Williamson 2018, p. 280ff; Krisch 2003, 150ff.

absence of Security Council authorisation, a key obstacle to humanitarian invention in conflicts taking place within the boundaries of a State is the principle of non-interference as envisaged in Article 2(7) of the Charter. There are certainly compelling moral reasons to undertake humanitarian action to protect populations from egregious human rights violations committed by governments hiding behind State sovereignty.[65] However, such expansive reading of the Charter has not elicited strong support largely for fear of abuse.[66] Rodley, in this context, stresses the *jus cogens* character of the prohibition of unilateral force and rhetorically asks thus:

> [W]e might ... ask ourselves how, if regional enforcement action can only be lawful when authorised by the Security Council, unilateral intervention can be lawful absent the same authorisation. Surely, a fortiori the latter, not contemplated by the Charter, needs at least the same authority as the former?[67]

While the principle of sovereignty no longer affords protection to governments that violate the human rights of their citizens, no State is permitted to take unilateral action to stop such abuses. Absent an independent and impartial international body to decide whether such 'humanitarian' intervention has indeed been imperative, States might well hide behind humanitarian motives to disguise their pursuit of self-interested goals.[68] Another serious concern is that mostly powerful States would be able act upon such humanitarian crises.

The Security Council, as discussed below, is technically the sole authority to authorise the use of force and other coercive measures in such humanitarian catastrophes. The Council in such cases might also act within the context of the R2P. In fact, the discourse of humanitarian intervention has in recent years been largely replaced by the so-called R2P. A major step in this direction was taken with the International Commission on Intervention and State Sovereignty's 2001 report, *The Responsibility to Protect*.[69] This report stressed that should a State commit egregious human rights violations, its sovereignty cannot provide a legal shield against an international response.[70] It further stated that due to its extraordinary character,

---

[65] See, generally, Moore 1998; Holzgrefe and Keohane 2003; Luban 1980.

[66] It is beyond dispute that military force under 'humanitarian intervention' does not empower a State to forcefully intervene in a State to depose its government and occupy its territory. See Henkin 1989, pp. 41–42.

[67] Rodley 2015, p. 794.

[68] As argued by Franck and Rodley as early as 1973, 'the general rule [on the prohibition of aggression] is already so shaky that it needs reinforcement, not further caveats;' and 'the facts do not indicate the existence of conditions warranting the incorporation of exceptions to a general prohibition'. Franck and Rodley 1973, p. 305.

[69] Report of the International Commission on Intervention and State Sovereignty, 'The Responsibility To Protect,' December 2001. Available at: http://responsibilitytoprotect.org/ICISS%20Report.pdf.

[70] The language of the report was clear: 'where a population is suffering serious harm, as a result of internal war, insurgency, repression or state failure, and the state in question is unwilling or unable to halt or avert it, the principle of non-intervention yields to the international responsibility to protect'. Ibid., XI.

6 The Use of Force in International Law

'there is no better ... body than the UN Security Council to authorize military intervention for human protection purposes'.[71] The report hence reaffirmed the principle prohibiting unilateral resort to force by noting that 'the task is not to find alternatives to the Security Council as a source of authority, but to make the Security Council work better than it has'.[72]

The theme of protecting populations from such grave atrocities as genocide, war crimes, ethnic cleansing and crimes against humanity was revisited by a UN Panel on Threats, Challenges and Change,[73] which in its ensuing report, published in 2004, endorsed the emerging norm that there is an international responsibility to protect a population from grave violations of human rights, a task that is solely 'exercisable by the Security Council authorising military intervention as last resort'.[74] Likewise, at the 2005 World Summit of Heads of States and Governments it was once again reiterated that the international community would take all necessary measures to protect populations from grave violations of human rights. It was further observed that:

> [The international community was] prepared to take collective action, in a timely and decisive manner, *through the Security Council* [alone],[75] in accordance with the Charter, including Chapter VII, on a case-by-case basis and in cooperation with relevant regional organizations as appropriate, should peaceful means be inadequate and national authorities are manifestly failing to protect their populations from genocide, war crimes, ethnic cleansing and crimes against humanity.[76]

The World Summit therefore unambiguously confirmed that enforcement action under Chapter VII to protect populations from international crimes remains within the remit of the Council, and hence the doctrine of R2P does not introduce any modifications to the UN Charter. The Summit Outcome does not, however, consider circumstances where the Council might fail to react to such grave international crimes due to potential political stalemate between the veto-wielding powers. Instead, it only suggested that States were prepared to take action through the Security Council, without clarification as to how this would transpire. In practice, the doctrine of R2P has largely failed to translate into decisive action, as the Council in most cases remains politically paralyzed, and thus unable to do much about humanitarian crises.[77]

---

[71] Ibid., XII.

[72] Ibid.

[73] UN Doc, A/59/565, 2 December 2004.

[74] Ibid., para 203.

[75] Emphasis added.

[76] 2005 World Summit Outcome, General Assembly Resolution A/RES/60/1, 24 October 2005, para 139.

[77] See Burke-White 2012, p. 17ff; Bellamy and Luck 2018.

6.4.2 Collective Security Measures

The founders of the UN sought a decisive departure from the League legacy by trying to inject a working system of collective security into international relations. The idea of collective security envisages a variety of forcible and non-forcible measures in response to violations of law in order to maintain or restore international peace and security. More specifically, the collective security system is designed to counter unlawful attempts to alter the political status quo through coercive means.[78] In this context, if a State resorts to forcible forms of self-help to resolve a dispute, the Charter pledges that collective measures may be taken 'for the prevention and removal of threats to the peace, and for the suppression of acts of aggression or other breaches of the peace'.[79]

At the helm of the collective security machinery stands the Security Council, which, under Article 24 of the Charter, is responsible for ensuring international peace and order. Chapter VII provides the Council with specific powers to achieve this objective. The Council, pursuant to Article 39, is the only authority to determine whether any threat to the peace, breach of the peace, or act of aggression has taken place. Since the Charter does not clarify what precisely constitutes a threat to the peace or act of aggression, the Council has a broad measure of discretion to decide whether a situation under its consideration is serious enough to qualify as such a threat or aggression.[80]

When the Council determines that a given situation constitutes a threat to the international peace, it is authorised to order either provisional measures to prevent the aggravation of the crisis,[81] or enforcement measures, including economic, diplomatic and/or military sanctions, to resolve the matter.[82] Evidently, forceful measures must be invoked as a last resort. Article 42, in this respect, stipulates that if peaceful means have not been effective, the Council 'may take such [military] action by air, sea or land forces as may be necessary to maintain or restore international peace and security'. The Council may therefore authorise coercive measures against an offending State without prejudice to the principle of non-interference in domestic affairs envisaged under Article 2(7).

The Council should in principle make every effort to resolve a dispute by peaceful means before it could authorise forceful measures. Nonetheless, since the Council is mandated to deal with any 'threat to the peace,' it does not need to await until

---

[78] For a discussion, see Hsiung 1997, p. 53ff.

[79] Article 1 of the UN Charter.

[80] At the San Francisco Conference on International Organisations, the Committee observed that it would be wiser 'to leave the evaluation of the situation to the Council'. See The Documents of UN Conference on International Organisation, Vol. XII, Committee 3 Enforcement Arrangements, 1945, 380. Also see Kapungu 1974, p. 104ff.

[81] Such measures, under Article 40, might include a call for dialogue, negotiation, cease-fire, withdrawal of regular troops or mercenaries, release of hostages, and other convenient measures to prevent the deterioration of the matter. See Kooijmans 1998, p. 296ff.

[82] See Articles 41 and 42 of the UN Charter.

6 The Use of Force in International Law

an 'actual breach of the peace' has taken place to invoke coercive measures—albeit it generally steps in after the hostilities actually break out.[83] Putting otherwise, the Council has the prerogative to turn to military sanctions without resorting to non-military means first. Its discretion in choosing the type of measures is hence absolute.

The exercise of such discretion has no doubt a political character. The fact that the maintenance of international order is left to such a Council, which is dominated by five veto-wielding powers, reflects the relevance of power politics within the configuration of international relations. The composition of the permanent, veto-wielding members is indeed reflective of the power balance, which emerged in the wake of WWII. Today, the Council remains under the indisputable sway of these powers. According to Article 27(3) of the Charter, decisions on all but procedural matters 'shall be made by ... the concurring votes of the permanent members'. This means that a group of powerful States is granted a privilege to veto any decision about matters of high international significance.

In as early as 1945, at the San Francisco Conference, some States in fact expressed concerns that veto power infringed the idea of sovereign equality, and that a rigid designation of permanent members in the Council would eventually render the UN system unresponsive to ever-changing political realities.[84] In response, the major powers gave reassurance that their voting privileges would not be used 'to wilfully obstruct the operation of the Council'.[85] But the apprehension about the potential abuse of veto power to the detriment of international peace was not baseless. During the Cold War, the Council's exclusive authority to intervene in serious international crises was practically unusable owing to political differences between the permanent members. The permanent powers generally cast veto to defend or further their national interests, or to uphold a tenet of their foreign policies. Prior to the fall of the so-called iron curtain, therefore, the Council had made very little resort to collective enforcement measures. Mandatory sanctions were imposed on only two occasions: Southern Rhodesia in 1966,[86] and South Africa in 1977.[87] The use of force was explicitly authorised only against North Korea in 1950,[88] where the Council 'recommended' that Member States should defend South Korea against the invasion of the North. Interestingly, such authorisation became possible due to the fortuitous USSR's

---

[83] For a discussion, Dinstein 2017, p. 59ff.

[84] Sievers and Daws 2014, p. 279.

[85] Statement by the Delegations of the Four Sponsoring Governments on Voting Procedure in the Security Council, S/Procedure/79 (04 May 1946).

[86] In Rhodesia, where a racist white minority group unilaterally declared independence in contradiction to the will of the majority population, the Security Council, acting under Chapter VII, called upon the international community not to recognise the regime, imposing oil and arms embargoes on Rhodesia. S/Res/216, 12 November 1965; S/Res/217, 20 November 1965; S/Res/221, 9 April 1966; S/Res/232, 16 December 1966.

[87] Acting under Chapter VII, the Security Council condemned the apartheid regime in South Africa and established a mandatory arms embargo against the same. S/Res/418, 4 November 1977; S/C/Res 421, 9 December 1977.

[88] S/Res/83, 27 June 1950.

134   O. Bakircioglu

boycotting of the Council meetings in reaction to the representation of nationalist China over Mao's communist regime.[89]

The fall of the Berlin Wall in 1989, in this context, marked the termination of sharp ideological confrontations, generating high expectations for global cooperation. Indeed, in the course of the 1990s, big-power cooperation grew, and the Council began to exercise its Charter functions in a more satisfactory manner. Apart from peacekeeping missions, there was more frequent resort to collective security measures to compel compliance with the UN sanctions and resolutions. The Council, for instance, authorised member States to use 'all necessary means' (a euphemism for the use of force) for Kuwait (1990), Bosnia and Herzegovina (1992), Somalia (1992), Rwanda (1994), Haiti (1994), East Timor (1999), Afghanistan (2001), Congo (2003), the Ivory Coast (2003), Darfur (2004), Libya (2011), Iraq and Syria (here identifying a non-State actor—ISIS—as a serious global threat in 2015) and Yemen (2018).[90]

The post-Cold War period, in other words, signified a sea change in international law and relations. But this was not to last for long. Ever since the atrocities of 9/11, and ensuing controversial US military operations, followed by such cases as the Russian intervention in South Ossetia (2008), the seizure of Crimea by pro-Russian separatists with the support of Russian forces (2014), and many ongoing civil wars in various parts of the world, international community appears to have politically split. Once again, the Council is unable to carry out its primary functions, because any permanent member can block any course of action on collective security, particularly when such a State is directly or indirectly involved, whether politically, militarily or otherwise, in a situation constituting a threat to international peace and security. Perhaps it is a cliché, but a true one, to state that international law has hitherto been enforced in a rather selective manner which is contingent on power politics, where hegemonic powers generally eschew international sanctions.[91]

6.4.3 The Right to Self-defence

Self-defence is morally and legally hinged on the idea that aggression is impermissible. However, not until the general prohibition of war, which gained tangible traction with the Charter, had the concept of self-defence become more than a political excuse to engage in hostilities. The right of self-defence, as laid down in Article

---

[89] See Forsythe and Weiss 2014, p. 49ff.

[90] See S/Res/678, 29 November 1990; S/Res/770, 13 August 1992; S/Res/794, 3 December 1992; S/Res/929, 22 June 1994; S/Res/940, 31 July 1994; S/Res/1272, 25 October 1999; S/Res/1386, 20 December 2001; S/Res/1413, 23 May 2002; S/Res/1493, 28 July 2003; S/Res/1807, 31 March 2008; UNSC Res. 1464 (4 February 2003); S/RES/1556 (30 July 2004); S/RES/1973 (17 March 2011); S/RES/2249 (20 November 2015); S/RES/2402 (26 February 2018).

[91] For an analysis of how power relations are in one form or another inscribed into international law, see Krisch 2005, p. 369ff.

6 The Use of Force in International Law

51 of the Charter, permits States to launch defensive military operations against aggressor States:

> Nothing in the present Charter shall impair the inherent right of individual or collective self-defence if an armed attack occurs against a Member of the United Nations, until the Security Council has taken measures necessary to maintain international peace and security. Measures taken by Members in the exercise of this right of self-defence shall be immediately reported to the Security Council and shall not in any way affect the authority and responsibility of the Security Council under the present Charter to take at any time such action as it deems necessary in order to maintain or restore international peace and security.

Article 51, in this context, contains a notable exception to the general obligation of States not to use armed force under Article 2(4) of the Charter. While the Charter refers to the inherent quality of the right, it does not elaborate on what 'inherent' actually means. Although it is controversial among scholars, reference to the inherent character of self-defence is generally said to highlight the customary roots of the right.[92] Thus, where Article 51 lacks specificity, a clarification of its content may be obtained from customary international law. In its Nicaragua judgement, the ICJ hence stresses the indispensability of customary law for elucidating the scope and content of self-defence:

> Article 51 ... is only meaningful on the basis that there is a 'natural' or 'inherent' right of self-defence, and it is hard to see how this can be other than of a customary nature, even if its present content has been confirmed and influenced by the Charter. Moreover, the Charter, having itself recognized the existence of this right, does not go on to regulate directly all aspects of its content. ... [Hence] customary international law continues to exist alongside treaty law.[93]

On this account, since the elements of imminence, necessity and proportionality are not regulated by the UN Charter, but are relevant to the correct interpretation of the right to self-defence, resort to customary international law might prove indispensable.[94] Likewise, although Article 51 does not expressly require an armed attack to be *unlawful* in order to trigger a legitimate exercise of self-defence, one may plausibly deduce this from customary law. Customary norms may further be invoked to deduce the principle that States may only employ defensive force as a measure of last resort when all peaceful alternatives have been exhausted. Read in line with Article 51, one may additionally infer that self-defensive measures are of temporary

---

[92] See Goodrich and Hambro 1946, pp. 177–178; Duffy 2005, p. 155ff. The natural law connection of the right to self-defence goes back to ancient times. There is a well-known passage by Cicero wherein he bears witness to nature to prove the inalienable quality of self-defence: 'Who has given us this law, which is not written, but innate, which we have not received by instruction, hearing or reading, but the elements of it have been engraven in our hearts and minds with her own hand: a law which is not the effect of habit and acquirement, but forms a part in the original complexion of our frame: so that if our lives are threatened with assassination or open violence from the hands of robbers or enemies, any means of defence would be allowed and laudable'. Quoted in Grotius 1901, Bk. I/II/III.

[93] *Nicaragua v US*, para 176.

[94] Ibid.

character aimed at thwarting a material or immediate attack until the Council has taken measures to contain the situation.

Having clarified that self-defence is not created out of vacuum, but merely recognised by Article 51, it should further be observed that the exercise of the right does not require prior authorisation from the Council, which might, however, endorse acts of self-defence. Notably, States should act in self-defence as a necessary and proportionate reaction to an 'armed attack'. It will be recalled that under ICJ jurisprudence an attack warranting self-defensive reaction must satisfy a minimum level of gravity.[95] Accordingly, self-defence is only allowed in response to an actual or imminent armed attack, and not to ordinary uses of force. Relatedly, because the right to self-defence is an exceptional tool, its objective must be narrowly construed. To illustrate, in cases of self-defence against material attacks, defensive measures should be geared toward repelling the attack as well as the invading forces (if any) with a view to restoring the status quo ante.

The main role of self-defence, then, is to thwart an unlawful aggression and its authors. But what about the legitimacy and scope of self-defence against an anticipated attack? Are putative victims entitled to use anticipatory force against impending dangers, particularly when the threat of harm, as stressed in *Caroline*, is such that is 'instant, overwhelming, leaving no choice of means, and no moment for deliberation?'[96] In such cases, imminence of the anticipated attack should arguably be subjected to rigorous scrutiny by having regard, among others, to the nature of the threat faced, the capabilities of the putative aggressor and the victim, the type of military technology involved, the feasibility of amicable dispute resolution mechanisms, and the potential speed with which the Council could take charge prior to, or during, the hostilities.[97] Plausibly, the State purporting to be acting in anticipatory defence is required to prove beyond reasonable doubt that there has been an imminent threat of an armed attack.[98] This burden of providing credible evidence to showcase the necessity of defensive measures is critical, for otherwise States might well exploit the doctrine of anticipatory self-defence to mask their aggression.

It has been stressed above that any self-defensive force must remain within the limits of necessity and proportionality. This means, more specifically, that the defending State must bear the burden of proof that lethal force has been absolutely necessary and proportionate to ward off a material or imminent danger of aggression. It follows that if military force is deemed the sole alternative to fend off an armed attack, the defender must show that its deployed force was necessary, absent less drastic means, and proportionate relative to the harm threatened.[99] Necessity, then, not only demands that the putative victim had no less harmful alternative to prevent or

---

[95] Ibid., para 195.

[96] Supra note 12.

[97] For a discussion, see Sofaer 2003, p. 220ff.

[98] See Falk 2003, p. 592ff.

[99] Thus, as Cassese argues, 'the victim of aggression must use an amount of force strictly necessary to repel the attack and proportional to the force used by the aggressor'. Cassese 2005, p. 355.

6 The Use of Force in International Law

thwart the attack, but also had no chance to make effective recourse to the Council.[100] Self-defence, in this sense, constitutes the only justified unilateral aggression to be invoked as a measure of last resort absent Council action against an unlawful armed attack.[101] The element of proportionality, on the other side, requires a balancing exercise between the interests of the aggressor and the defender. This suggests that defensive force must neither be disproportionate to the expected harm,[102] nor should any incidental injury or collateral damage be excessive in comparison with the military advantage expected from the defensive attack.[103]

Evidently, the customary elements of necessity and proportionality are inextricably connected to the objective of ensuring that defensive lethal force is not abused. Accordingly, defensive force should be used responsibly to bring about the desired goal, which is simply to thwart aggression until the Council has stepped in to contain the situation. This distinguishes the modern conception of self-defence from the traditional just war theory, under which wars may be launched to inflict punishment and vindicate justice. Indeed, the essence of self-defence, as Grotius observed, is that it is a right of self-preservation against a direct threat in the absence of alternative solutions, and thus not of punishment of the perceived wrongdoer.[104] That said, there are very few wars of self-defence which entirely exclude punitive elements. The punishment of the enemy generally occurs with intent to deter potential future aggression.[105]

Likewise, in the fog of war principles of necessity and proportionality may be totally or partially suspended. While the right of self-defence normatively permits the defending State to secure the 'submission of the enemy with the least possible expenditure of time, life and money,'[106] mitigating the brutality of hostilities is hardly possible in reality. Simply put, self-defensive wars, for a variety of complex psychological, religious, political, economic and cultural reasons, are rarely limited to fending off unjustified aggression. Rather, as Dinstein points out, 'force is often used tenaciously with a view to bringing about the ... collapse of the aggressor's armed forces'.[107] It, therefore, behoves the international community, in particular the Council, to assure that States do not resort to self-defence as a means of inflicting punishment or retribution; for this would go against the grain of self-defence—a type of restricted warfare where not all is fair.

---

[100] The UN Charter reserves to the Council the full authority to use military force. The Council is conferred with the primary responsibility for the maintenance of international security and monopoly on force to this end. Furthermore, Article 2(5) expressly provides that '[a]ll Members shall give the United Nations every assistance in any action it takes in accordance with the present Charter, and shall refrain from giving assistance to any state against which the United Nations is taking preventive or enforcement action'.

[101] For an analysis, see Rodin 2002, p. 107ff.

[102] See Bakircioglu 2009a, p. 9.

[103] See Brownlie 1963, 261; Moir 2010, pp. 68–70.

[104] Grotius 2012, 82ff.

[105] For an analysis, see Brown 2014, p. 29ff; Wagner and Werner 2018, p. 313ff.

[106] *US v List* (American Military Tribunal, Nuremberg, 1948) 11 NMT 1230, 1253.

[107] Dinstein 2017, p. 285.

6.4.3.1 The Challenges of 9/11 on Self-defence

The 'Unable or Unwilling' Doctrine

After the 9/11 attacks, the purported need to undertake anticipatory force against putative attacks has become subject of heated controversy. The 9/11 atrocities have further fuelled such debates as whether an attack of the scale of 9/11 may qualify as an armed attack proper against a State, and whether the imminence rule may be relaxed to allow self-defence against modern threats posed by terrorist groups[108] and 'rogue States,' armed with weapons of mass destruction.[109] While self-defence is traditionally considered a responsive measure against an armed attack emanating from a State, the Council in its resolutions 1368 and 1373 suggested the possibility of individual or collective self-defence against acts of international terrorism.[110] This was the first time where the Council had insinuated that self-defensive acts could be exercised against a non-state actor.

The Council, however, did not categorically state that a victim State could always treat a grave terrorist act as an 'armed attack' against which defensive military measures may be invoked. Nor did the Council deal with the question whether the nexus between the Taliban and al-Qaeda was of such a nature as to trigger State responsibility for the armed attack. The Council, put another way, did not resolve the moot questions concerning the requisite scale of non-State actor attacks as well as the degree to which State control needs to be exercised over a non-State group.[111] For the purposes of self-defence, it was traditionally reasoned that the link between a State and non-State actor had to be direct and manifest. Thus, the ICJ in *Nicaragua* adopted a narrow approach, confirming that armed attacks by a State could legitimate self-defensive force.[112] In cases of non-State aggression, however, the Court—having relied on the UN General Assembly's Definition of Aggression[113]—ruled that this might constitute an armed attack if it can be attributed to a State 'by clear evidence'.[114] The Court further reasoned that for such a proxy attack to give rise to State responsibility, 'it would in principle have to be proved that [the State in question] had effective control [over] the military or paramilitary operations in the course

---

[108] Before 9/11, the legitimacy of defensive force against terrorism had been highly contested, in that only very few states, such as the US, Israel and Turkey, had expressly claimed to exercise self-defence against acts of terrorism. See Franck 2002, pp. 56–68; Gray 2018a, pp. 614–619.

[109] See Brown 2003, p. 29ff.

[110] S/RES/1368 (12 September 2001); S/RES/1373 (28 September 2001).

[111] See Moir 2010, p. 59ff; Murphy 2002, p. 41; Watkin 2004, p. 1.

[112] *Nicaragua vs US*, para 195.

[113] UNGA Res. 3314 (XXIX) (14 December 1974).

[114] *Nicaragua vs US*, paras 109 and 195.

6 The Use of Force in International Law

of which the alleged violations were committed'.[115] In its later judgments, the Court has maintained its restricted reading of self-defence against non-State actors.[116]

It thus appears that both States and non-State actors (sent by or acting on behalf of a State) can commit armed attacks against which the right to self-defence may be resorted to.[117] Nonetheless, since the 9/11 attacks, the USA has sought to develop a broad doctrine of self-defence that allows States to launch attacks against other States' sovereign territory on grounds that the targeted State has been *unwilling* or *unable* to prevent the exploitation of its territory by a belligerent non-State actor. The drone warfare initiated by the Bush Administration, which was later expanded by the Obama Administration, was based on such a reading of self-defence. In fact, the targeted killings of many al-Qaeda members (including its leader Osama bin Laden) and affiliated groups in such States as Pakistan, Somalia and Yemen have thus far transpired under the 'unwilling and unable' doctrine.[118] It is worth adding that the 2006 Israeli military action against the Hezbollah was also based on the same ground, where Israel asserted that the 'responsibility for [Hezbollah's bellicose acts lay with] ... Lebanon, from whose territory these acts have been launched into Israel'.[119] The Turkish attacks on PKK targets in Northern Iraq was similarly grounded on the premise that Iraq was either unwilling or unable to prevent the attacks of PKK against Turkey launched from Iraqi soil.[120]

Notably, the unable and unwilling doctrine has been invoked by the US to legitimate its bombings of ISIS targets in Syria. In 2014, the US Permanent Representative to the UN sought to justify the US and its allies' use of force in Syria thus:

> ISIL and other terrorist groups in Syria are a threat not only to Iraq, but also to many other countries ... States must be able to defend themselves, in accordance with the inherent right of individual and collective self-defence ... when ... the government of the State where the threat is located is unwilling or unable to prevent the use of its territory for such attacks. The Syrian regime has shown that it cannot and will not confront these safe havens effectively itself. Accordingly, the United States has initiated necessary and proportionate military actions in Syria in order to eliminate the ongoing ISIL threat ...[121]

Taken together, the rationale of this doctrine rests on the assumption that if a State does nothing, whether intentionally or not, to neutralise a threat posed by a non-State actor operating from its own territories, it cannot hide behind the legal shield

---

[115] Ibid., 115.

[116] See *Legal Consequences of the Construction of a Wall in the Occupied Palestinian Territory (Advisory Opinion)* [9 July 2004] ICJ Rep. 136; *Congo v. Uganda; Case Concerning Application of the Convention on the Prevention and Punishment of the Crime of Genocide (Bosnia and Herzegovina v Serbia and Montenegro)* [Judgement of 16 February 2007], ICJ Rep. 43.

[117] For an analysis of attribution, see Tsagourias 2016, p. 813ff.

[118] See Gray 2018a, p. 616.

[119] Letter from the Permanent Representative of Israel to the Security Council, A/60/937-S/2006/515, 12 July 2006.

[120] However, Turkey did not provide an elaborate legal justification for its action. See further Steenberghe 2010, pp. 187–194.

[121] Samantha J. Power, The Permanent Representative of the US to the UN addressed to the Secretary-General to the UN, U.N. Doc. S/2014/695, 23 September 2016.

of territorial sovereignty. It is consequently argued that in a world where non-State actors have access to potent weapons, capable of posing grave threat to the lives of innocent people, it would be unrealistic to espouse a threshold of direct attribution for armed attacks, as envisaged in *Nicaragua v US*.[122] The proponents of the unwilling and unable doctrine, in other words, reject the attribution rule on the ground that this would limit the ability of States to use self-defensive force in such cases where it would be fatal to wait until the question of State responsibility could satisfactorily be addressed.[123] Where a host State, so the argument runs, proves unable or unwilling to prevent its territory from being exploited as a launch pad for terrorist operations, the victim State is left with a limited array of alternatives: (a) to respect the territorial integrity of the host State at its own peril; and (b) to violate the territorial integrity of the host State in a 'limited and targeted fashion, using force against ... the very source of the terrorist attack'.[124] Advocates of this thinking often analyse the threat or use of force within the narrow matrix of necessity, arguing that the doctrine does not replace the law on self-defence. Rather, the unwilling and unable test is argued to be a component of the necessity rule.[125] Moir, in this context, notes that 'armed action against armed groups where the host State cannot take preventive action certainly appears to meet the "necessity" criteria for lawful self-defence in that, given the host State's failure to control its own territory, there is no reasonable and/or effective alternative to the use of force'.[126]

Plausible though these arguments are, the unwilling and unable doctrine ultimately introduces a new paradigm to the traditional understanding of self-defence, in that it severs the attribution link between the non-State conduct and the host State. Thus, where the failure of States to prevent the use of their territories as a base for non-State armed activities could potentially give rise to State responsibility,[127] it is now asserted that this could further legitimate self-defensive wars.[128] This is because the doctrine does not distinguish between whether the host State has been deliberately unwilling or simply unable to contain the armed group. It is likewise not clear from State practice whether the alleged defending State should now legitimize its lethal measures by reference to the 'harbouring the terrorists' argument, or the 'unable and unwilling' doctrine.[129] Apparently, the defending State, under this doctrine, may in both settings claim the right to self-defence against the host State, whose consent for intrusive defensive acts is not required.

Worse still, the unwilling and unable test subjectivises the doctrine of self-defence by removing independent and objective judgement from the normative framework

---

[122] For a discussion, see Michael 2009, p. 133ff; Steenberghe 2010, p. 194ff.

[123] See, generally, Weller 2015, p. 109ff.

[124] See Trapp 2007, p. 147.

[125] See Lubell 2017, pp. 219–220.

[126] Moir 2015, p. 735.

[127] *Corfu Channel Case (United Kingdom of Great Britain and Northern Ireland v Albania)* [1949] ICJ Rep. 22.

[128] See Brunnée and Toope 2018, p. 264.

[129] Paulussen et al. 2016, 87ff.

6 The Use of Force in International Law

of self-defensive force. In this respect, Brunnée and Toope correctly stress that the notion of 'inability' is more complicated than meets the eye: 'In the case of Syria itself,' they rhetorically ask, 'how can it be said that the Syrian government is unable to act when it is itself engaged with its ally, Russia, in attacks on IS-controlled areas?'[130] Gray voices similar scepticism by arguing that the unwilling and unable doctrine 'does not impose effective constrains on a State's use of force, and one that is difficult to reconcile with the prohibition on the use of force in Article 2(4) and with the Charter principle of the equality of States'.[131] Gray's stress on nominal State equality is especially noteworthy, for the unwilling and unable doctrine is realistically applicable only against militarily weak States that are unable to react to what is claimed to be self-defensive measures. The imbalance of power between conflicting States would prove particularly critical in cases where there exists no clear nexus between the host State and activities of the non-State actor. In such scenarios, the putative victim must ideally not employ force against any target other than those belonging to the bellicose non-State actor. Yet, in the absence Security Council intervention (an organ which is dominated by powerful States), the host State would clearly be at the mercy and good faith of the (powerful) State using defensive force.

Anticipatory Self-defence

The atrocities of 9/11 also opened the floodgates for anticipatory self-defence claims. In the wake of the attacks, the then US President, George W. Bush, declared that these 'were more than acts of terror; they were acts of war;'[132] and that the military response, styled as 'war on terror', was to involve 'far more than instant retaliation and isolated strikes'.[133] 'Americans should not expect one battle,' Bush further stressed, 'but a lengthy campaign, unlike any other we have ever seen. It may include dramatic strikes … and covert operations, secret even in success. We will starve terrorists of funding, turn them one against another, drive them from place to place, until there is no refuge or no rest'.[134]

This approach unmistakably stretched the traditional contours of self-defence by envisioning an unlimited time frame for any defensive military action, and holding governments responsible for lethal operations emanating from their territories irrespective of whether they actually supported terrorist groups, or had the capability to prevent them from operating within their borders. This approach somewhat correlates with the unwilling and unable doctrine, as it too permits defensive force without

---

[130] Brunnée and Toope 2018, p. 285.

[131] Gray 2018a, p. 616.

[132] See Seelye and Bumiller 2001.

[133] G. W. Bush, "Address to a Joint Session of Congress and the American People" (20 September 2001). Available at: https://georgewbush-whitehouse.archives.gov/news/releases/2001/09/20010920-8.html.

[134] Ibid.

attributional link between a state and non-state actor. But anticipatory self-defence claims goes further in its subjectivity, and its temporal and spatial implications. Significantly, the 'war on terror' discourse favours anticipatory use of force to arrest *incipient* threats posed by the so-called 'rogue States,' or 'terrorists' that operate globally.[135] According to this preventive war strategy, therefore, unilateral force may be employed to arrest nascent threats (that potentially target US interests, allies and friends) before they have fully matured. President Bush in his 2002 speech to the US Military Academy summarised this doctrine by noting that the US 'must take the battle to the enemy, disrupt his plans, and confront the worst threats before they emerge'.[136] This sweeping interpretation of self-defence has, in other words, sought to reduce the imminence rule to merely establishing necessity. Accordingly, if war seems necessary to prevent the enemy from striking first, it is considered absurd to require the defending State to absorb the fatal blow before acting in self-defence. It has also been argued that the traditional law of self-defence does not match the realities of modern military technology readily available to terrorists, who should not be allowed to have the military upper hand by attacking first.[137]

As stressed above, the downplaying of imminence has so far served to legitimate targeted killings and drone attacks within the context of war on terrorism, whereby it is possible to strike suspected terrorists anytime and anywhere on grounds that they continuously pose military threats.[138] Since this policy no longer places sufficient emphasis on the imminence requirement, such other factors as the likelihood of a would-be attack or the scale of estimated injury are given more weight.[139] However, such conjectural thinking about the probability and nature of an anticipated aggression undercuts the central importance of the notion of 'armed attack' for the purposes of self-defence. Such a reinterpretation of the imminence rule, as Gray stresses, 'clearly offers an extremely wide discretion to the State claiming the right to use force in self-defence'.[140]

Worse still, jettisoning the requirement of imminence would eventually weaken the UN system, whereby each (potentially powerful) State could claim entitlement to act in self-defence with the alleged intention of warding off putative threats of aggression.[141] In fact, the danger of according exclusive, unilateral competence to States in ascertaining what is necessary for their own security was noticed soon after the conclusion of the Kellogg-Briand Pact. Lauterpacht argued as early as 1933 that a claim that the right to self-defence could not be subject to objective assessment would

---

[135] See Acharya 2004, pp. 203–205; Cohen 2005, pp. 37–47; Snauwaert 2004, p. 121.

[136] G. W. Bush "Graduation Speech at West Point" West Point, New York (1 June 2002). Available at: https://georgewbush-whitehouse.archives.gov/news/releases/2002/06/20020601-3.html.

[137] *The National Security Strategy of the United States of America*, September 2002. Available at: http://georgewbush-whitehouse.archives.gov/nsc/nss/2002/. See, generally, Rockefeller 2005; Nagan and Hammer 2004.

[138] This corresponds with the increased attribution of armed attacks to non-State actors in areas where territorial States have lost effective control. See De Wet 2019, p. 1ff.

[139] See Yoo 2003, p. 563; Wedgwood 2003, p. 576.

[140] Gray 2018a, pp. 616–617.

[141] For a detailed critique of the attempt to discard imminence, see Bakircioglu 2011, pp. 134–188.

run counter to the very idea of law. For 'such a claim is self-contradictory inasmuch as it purports to be based on legal right and at the same time, it dissociates itself from regulation and evaluation of the law'.[142] Also, in response to Germany's claim of self-defence in the events leading up to WWII, the Nuremberg Tribunal made a similar point: 'whether action taken under the claim of self-defence was in fact aggressive or defensive must ultimately be subject to investigation or adjudication if international law is ever to be enforced'.[143] It is hence plausible to argue that if a State is intent on invoking anticipatory self-defence, it should bear the burden of proof as to the necessity of such an action, so that the international community could scrutinize the justifiability of its claim. This State should further show that there had been no peaceful alternative to military action. Above all, the existence of an unavoidable and palpable, or imminent threat of an armed attack must be supported by evidence based on facts and solid intelligence. Such evidence should not only demonstrate the destructive capacity, but the hostile intention of the putative aggressor. In the case of Iraq War, where the purported need to discard imminence was ardently advocated by the US, such evidentiary requirements were not met. Instead, hearsay evidence was presented as credible to muster domestic and international support for the war.[144]

Another pitfall of discarding imminence is the near impossibility of duly measuring the elements of proportionality and necessity in defensive force. In non-confrontational settings, necessity and proportionality cannot serve as reliable yardsticks to assess the justifiability and aptness of lethal measures, for the anticipated harm might never materialize, or be serious enough to legitimate force in self-defence. Again, the US war in Iraq is a case in point, where neither the necessity of the US anticipatory attack, nor the potential scale of the alleged Iraqi threat could realistically be measured, nor the proportionality between the interests preserved (in the US) and harm inflicted (on Iraq) could be assessed.

Undoubtedly, as with the unwilling and unable doctrine, a broad construction of anticipatory self-defence is tantamount to a dramatic reinterpretation of Article 51; which is why it has not elicited sufficient backing from the general international community. State practice suggests that except in pressing circumstances the international community in the main expresses disagreement with uses of lethal force in anticipation of a material armed attack.[145] More significantly, anticipatory self-defence claims are predominantly made in the absence of stronger arguments to justify force. Even then, such claims are principally made by powerful States against militarily weaker States.

---

[142] Schachter 1989, p. 261.

[143] *International Military Tribunal* (Nuremberg), Judgment of 1 October 1946, p. 436; also see Waldock 1963, pp. 407–408.

[144] See Bakircioglu 2009b, p. 1297ff.

[145] For an analysis, see Bakircioglu 2011, 164ff; Gray 2018b, pp. 170–175.

6.5 Conclusion

War and other forms of collective violence have been omnipresent in human history. The idea of rejecting military force as a means of resolving disputes is peculiar only to modern times, though. As Maine remarks, 'war appears to be as old as mankind, but peace is a modern invention'.[146] Indeed, whilst the ideal of peace among nations has been an aspiration since time immemorial, only during the past century has it been deemed a politically and legally desirable objective.[147] It is thus telling that it took the unprecedented devastation of WWII to finally make the prohibition of unilateral aggression a reality. Today, the prohibition of the use of force is the cornerstone of modern international law. But the political dynamics of international relations, mainly dominated by superpowers, often engender self-interested State conduct about security-related matters. This chapter has shown that despite the emergence of new threats to international peace and security, the international community must be vigilant against attempts to unduly relax the rules governing the use of force, lest subjectivist, self-serving and biased approaches render unilateral aggression once again a valid instrument of resolving international disputes.

References

Acharya A (2004) The Bush Doctrine and Asian Regional Order: The Perils and Pitfalls of Preemption. In: Gurtov M, Ness PV (eds) Confronting the Bush Doctrine: Critical Views from the Asia-Pacific. Routledge-Curzon, New York

Anghie A (2006) The Evolution of International Law: Colonial and Postcolonial Realities. Third World Quarterly 26:739–753

Bakircioglu O (2009a) The Right to Self-Defence in National and International Law: The Role of the Imminence Requirement. Indiana International & Comparative Law Review 19:1–48

Bakircioglu O (2009b) The Future of Preventive Wars: The Case of Iraq. Third World Quarterly 30:1297–1316

Bakircioglu O (2011) Self-Defence in International and Criminal Law: The Doctrine of Imminence. Routledge, London

Bellamy AJ, Luck EJ (2018) The Responsibility to Protect: From Promise to Practice. Polity Press, Cambridge

Best G (1997) War and Law since 1945. Clarendon Press, Oxford

Blank L, Noone G (2019) International Law and Armed Conflict. Wolters Kluwer, New York

Bokor-Szego H (1986) The Attitude of Socialist States towards the International Regulation of the Use of Force. In: Cassese A (ed) The Current Legal Regulation of the Use of Force. Martinus Nijhoff Publishers, Dordrecht, 455–470

Brown D (2003) Use of Force against Terrorism after September 11th: State Responsibility, Self-Defence and Other Responses. Cardozo Journal of International and Comparative Law 11:1–29

Brown D (2014) Judging the Judges: Evaluating Challenges to Proper Authority in Just War Theory. In: Brown D (ed) The Just War Tradition: Applying Old Ethics to New Problems. Routledge, London

---

[146] Quoted in: Howard 2000, p. 1.

[147] Ibid., 2; also see Howard 1997, p. 31ff.

6 The Use of Force in International Law

Brownlie I (1963) International Law and the Use of Force by States. Oxford University Press, Oxford

Brunnée J, Toope SJ (2018) Self-Defence against Non-State Actors: Are Powerful States Willing but Unable to Change International Law? International and Comparative Law Quarterly 67:263–286

Burke-White WW (2012) Adoption of the Responsibility to Protect. In: Genser J, Cotler I (eds) The Responsibility to Protect. Oxford University Press, Oxford

Cassese A (2005) International Law, 2nd edn. Oxford University Press, Oxford

Cassese A (2008) Self-Determination of Peoples: A Legal Reappraisal, 2nd edn. Cambridge University Press, Cambridge

Cohen EL (2005) National Security Strategy and the Ideology of Preventive War. In: Artz L, Kamalipour YR (eds) Bring'em on: Media and Politics in the Iraq War. Rowman & Littlefield Publishers, Maryland

Corten O (2010) The Law against War: The Prohibition on the Use of Force in Contemporary International Law. Hart Publishing, Oxford

Crawford J (ed) (1988) The Rights of Peoples, Clarendon Press, Oxford

Crawford J (2012) Brownlie's Principles of Public International Law, 8th edn. Oxford University Press, Oxford

De Wet E (2019) The Invocation of the Right to Self-Defence in Response to Armed Attacks Conducted by Armed Groups: Implications for Attribution. Leiden Journal of International Law 32:91–110

Dinstein Y (2017) War, Aggression and Self-Defence, 6th edn. Cambridge University Press, Cambridge

Duffy H (2005) The War on Terror and the Framework of International Law. Cambridge University Press, Cambridge

Egerton GW (1983) Great Britain and the League of Nations: Collective Security as Myth and History. in: The League of Nations in Retrospect. Proceedings of a Symposium organized by the United Nations Library, New York, 98–110

Falk RA (2003) What Future for the UN Charter System of War Prevention? American Journal of International Law 97:590–598

Fassbender B (2009) The United Nations Charter as the Constitution of the International Community. Martinus Nijhoff Publishers, Leiden

Forsythe DP, Weiss TG (2014) The United Nations and Changing World Politics, 7th edn. Westview Press, Oxford

Franck TM (2002) Recourse to Force: State Action against Threats and Armed Attacks. Cambridge University Press, Cambridge

Franck TM, Rodley NS (1973) After Bangladesh: The Law of Humanitarian Intervention by Military Force. The American Journal of International Law 67:275–305

Goodrich LM, Hambro E (1946) Charter of the United Nations: Commentary and Documents. World Peace Foundation, Boston

Gray C (2018a) The Use of Force and the International Legal Order. In: Evans MD (ed) International Law, 5th edn. Oxford University Press, Oxford

Gray C (2018b) International Law and the Use of Force. Oxford University Press, Oxford

Green JA (2009) The International Court of Justice and Self-Defence in International Law. Hart Publishing, Oxford

Grimal F (2013) Threats of Force: International Law and Strategy. Routledge, London

Grotius H (1901) The Rights of War and Peace (Campbell AC (translator)). M. Walter Dunne Publisher, London

Grotius H (2012) On the Law of War and Peace (Neff S (ed)). Cambridge University Press, Cambridge

Hall WE (1890) Treatise on International Law, 3rd edn. Clarendon Press, Oxford

Harley JE (1943) The Coming Revival of the League of Nations. In: Johnsen JE (ed) Reconstituting the League of Nations. The H. W. Wilson Company, New York, 7–14

Henkin L (1989) Use of Force: Law and U.S. Policy. In: Henkin L et al (eds) Right v. Might. Council on Foreign Relations Press, New York, 61–70

Henkin LV (1995) International Law: Politics and Values. Martinus Nijhoff Publishers, Dordrecht

Holzgrefe JL, Keohane RO (eds) (2003) Humanitarian Intervention: Ethical, Legal and Political Dilemmas. Oxford University Press, Oxford

Hoogh A (2015) Jus Cogens and the Use of Armed Force. In: Weller M (ed) The Oxford Handbook of the Use of Force in International Law. Oxford University Press, Oxford, 1161–1186

Howard M (1997) Land of War, Land of Peace. Wilson Quarterly 21:30–36

Howard M (2000) The Invention of Peace: Reflections on War and International Order. Profile Books, London

Hsiung JC (1997) Anarchy & Order: The Interplay of Politics and Law in International Relations. Lynne Rienner Publishers, London

Johnson JT (2003) Aquinas and Luther on War and Peace: Sovereign Authority and the Use of Armed Force. Journal of Religious Ethics 27:3–20

Jones P (2018) Human Rights and Collective Self-Determination. In: Etinson A (ed) Human Rights: Moral or Political. Oxford University Press, Oxford, 441–460

Kapungu LT (1974) Economic Sanctions in the Rhodesian Context. In: Ayouty Y, Brooks HC (eds) Africa and International Organisation. Martinus Nijhoff Publishers, The Hague

Kennedy D (2006) Of War and Law. Princeton University Press, Oxford

Kooijmans P (1998) Provisional Measures of the UN Security Council. In: Denters E, Schrijver N (eds) Reflections on International Law from the Low Countries: In Honour of Paul de Waart. Martinus Nijhoff Publishers, The Hague

Korman S (1996) The Right of Conquest: The Acquisition of Territory by Force in International Law and Practice. Clarendon Press, Oxford

Koskenniemi M (2001) The Gentle Civilizer of Nations: The Rise and Fall of International Law: 1870-1960. Cambridge University Press, Cambridge

Krisch N (2003) More Equal than the Rest? Hierarchy, Equality and US Predominance in International Law. In: Byers M, Nolte G (eds) United States Hegemony and the Foundations of International Law. Cambridge University Press, Cambridge, 135–175

Krisch N (2005) International Law in Times of Hegemony: Unequal Power and the Shaping of the International Legal Order. The European Journal of International Law 16:369–408

Lauterpacht (1933) The Function of Law in the International Community. Cited in: Schachter O (1989) Self-Defence and the Rule of Law. American Journal of International Law 83:259–277

Luban D (1980) Just War and Human Rights. Philosophy and Public Affairs 9:160–181

Lubell N (2017) Fragmented Wars: Multi-Territorial Military Operations against Armed Groups. International Law Studies 93:215–249

Michael B (2009) Responding to Attacks by Non-State Actors: The Attribution Requirement of Self-Defence. Australian International Law Journal 16:133–159

Moir L (2010) Reappraising the Resort to Force: International Law, jus ad bellum and the War on Terror. Hart Publishing, Oxford

Moir L (2015) Action against Host States of Terrorist Groups. In: Weller M (ed) The Oxford Handbook of the Use of Force in International Law. Oxford University Press, Oxford, 720–736

Moore J (ed) (1998) Hard Choices: Moral Dilemmas in Humanitarian Intervention. Rowman & Littlefield Publishers, New York

Murphy S (2002) Terrorism and the Concept of Armed Attack in Article 51 of the UN Charter. Harvard International Law Journal 43:41–51

Nagan WP, Hammer C (2004) The New Bush National Security Doctrine and the Rule of Law. Berkeley Journal of International Law 22:375–438

Paulussen C et al (eds) (2016) Fundamental Rights in International and European Law: Public and Private Law. T.M.C. Asser Press, The Hague

Phillipson C (1911) The International Law of Ancient Greece and Rome, Vol I. MacMillan & Co., London

Rockefeller ML (2005) The 'Imminent Threat Requirement for the Use of Pre-emptive Military Force: Is it Time for a Non-Temporal Standard. Denver Journal of International Law and Policy 33:131–160

Rodin D (2002) War and Self-Defence. Oxford University Press, Oxford

Rodley N (2015) Humanitarian Intervention. In: Weller M (ed) The Oxford Handbook of the Use of Force in International Law. Oxford University Press, Oxford

Ruys T (2014) The Meaning of Force and the Boundaries of the Jus Ad Bellum: Are Minimal Uses of Force Excluded from UN Charter Article 2(4)? American Journal of International Law 108:159–210

Seelye KQ, Bumiller E (2001) After the Attacks: The President Bush Labels Aerial Terrorist Attacks Acts of War. The New York Times, September 11, A16

Shaw M (2017) International Law, 8th edn. Cambridge University Press, Cambridge

Sievers L, Daws S (2014) The Procedure of the UN Security Council, 4th edn. Oxford University Press, Oxford

Snauwaert DT (2004) The Bush Doctrine and Just War Theory. The Online Journal of Peace and Conflict Resolution 6:121–135

Sofaer AD (2003) On the Necessity of Pre-emption. European Journal of International Law 14:209–226

Steenberghe R (2010) Self-Defence in Response to Attacks by Non-State Actors in the Light of Recent State Practice. Leiden Journal of International Law 23:183–208

Trapp KN (2007) Back to Basics: Necessity, Proportionality, and the Right of Self-Defence against Non-State Terrorist Actors. International and Comparative Law Quarterly 56:141–156

Tsagourias N (2016) Self-Defence against Non-State Actors: The Interaction between Self-Defence as a Primary Rule and Self-Defence as a Secondary Rule. Leiden Journal of International Law 29:801–825

Von Clausewitz C (1976) On War (Howard M, Paret P (translators)). Princeton University Press, Princeton

Wagner W, Werner W (2018) War and Punitivity under Anarchy. European Journal of International Security 3:310–325

Waldock H (1963) The Law of Nations: An Introduction to the International Law of Peace. Oxford University Press, New York

Watkin K (2004) Controlling the Use of Force: A Role for Human Rights Norms in Contemporary Armed Conflict. American Journal of International Law 98:1–34

Webster D (1841) Letter from US Secretary of State Daniel Webster to British Minister Henry Fox. British and Foreign State Papers 29:1841

Wedgwood R (2003) The Fall of Saddam Hussein: Security Council Mandates and Preemptive Self-Defense. American Journal of International Law 97:576–585

Wehberg HW (1931) The Outlawry of War: A Series of Lectures Delivered before the Academy of International Law at the Hague and in the Institut Universitaire De Hautes Études Internationales at Geneva (Zeydel EH (translator)). Carnegie Endowment for International Peace, Washington

Weightman MA (1951) Self-Defence in International Law. Virginia Law Review 37:1095–1115

Weller M (2015) Striking ISIL: Aspects of the law on the use of force. American Society of International Law 19, available at: https://www.asil.org/insights/volume/19/issue/5/striking-isil-aspects-law-use-force

Williamson M (2018) Operation Litani-1978. In: Ruys T, Corten O, Hofer A (eds) The Use of Force in International Law: A Case-Based Approach. Oxford University Press, Oxford

Wilson HA (1988) International Law and the Use of Force by National Liberation Movements. Clarendon Press, Oxford

Wittke C (2018) Law in the Twilight: International Courts and Tribunals, the Security Council and the Internationalisation of Peace Agreements. Cambridge University Press, Cambridge

Yoo J (2003) International Law and the War in Iraq. American Journal of International Law 97:563–576

Onder Bakircioglu LLB, MA, LLM, Ph.D. is an Associate Professor of Law at the University of Leicester. Dr. Bakircioglu's research interests are in the fields of public international law and human rights law. He is particularly interested in the use of force discourse in international and national settings. In 2011, he published his first monograph entitled *Self-Defence in International and Criminal Law: The doctrine of Imminence* (Routledge, 2011). In 2014, he completed his second monograph entitled *Islam and Warfare: Context and Compatibility with International Law* (Routledge, 2014).

Chapter 7
The UN Security Council: From Preserving State Sovereignty to Protecting Humanity

Rossana Deplano

Contents

7.1   Introduction 150
7.2   The Security Council's Practice Unpacked (1946–2017) 152
      7.2.1   Tracing International Law in the Text of Resolutions 155
      7.2.2   Significance and Limits of the Thematic Resolutions 158
7.3   The Security Council and the International Rule of Law 162
7.4   Conclusion 168
References 169

Abstract This chapter examines the extent to which international law shapes the politics of the Security Council and vice versa. By providing an empirically-grounded analysis of the quantity and quality of international legal instruments referred to in the text of resolutions, the chapter reconstructs patterns of the Security Council's behavioural regularities and assesses them against the scope of its mandate. An argument is made that while international law plays an important role in shaping the politics of the Security Council, its resolutions do not contribute significantly to the development of international law. However, a closer look at the role the thematic resolutions are increasingly playing in the practice of the Security Council reveals that there is "another", more democratic, Security Council which runs in parallel with the Leviathan. The empirical findings suggest that the Security Council's action has progressively moved from preserving state sovereignty to only protecting humanity as a whole, albeit with certain limitations.

Keywords Security Council · resolutions · customary international law · human rights · civilians

---

The findings of the original database of the Security Council's practice are adapted from an article that appeared in vol. 60 of the German Yearbook of International Law.

R. Deplano (✉)
University of Leicester, Leicester, UK
e-mail: rossana.deplano@leicester.ac.uk

© T.M.C. ASSER PRESS and the authors 2022
S. Sayapin et al. (eds.), *International Conflict and Security Law*,
https://doi.org/10.1007/978-94-6265-515-7_7

7.1 Introduction

Achieving perpetual peace is the biggest utopia ever conceived by mankind. The United Nations (UN) is the modern institution charged with the task of realising such utopia: essentially, a world without war. Accordingly, Article 24 of the Charter of the United Nations (UN Charter)[1] establishes the Security Council as the institution in charge of maintaining international peace and security. However, the Security Council is often portrayed as a Leviathan: an institution above the law, unwieldy, biased and tremendously powerful.[2] Yet 70 years after the creation of the United Nations, it is still up and running, and largely supported by Member States.

The discourse about international peace has an inherent utopian flavour, since it ultimately concerns human social co-existence at the international level.[3] In the League of Nations, the Council was conceived as the guardian of world order.[4] As it is well known, it failed because of the combination of the rule of unanimity and the lack of enforcement power.[5] The shortcomings of the League's Council prompted the creation of an institution revolutionary both in composition and functions: the United Nations Security Council. Thus, in the United Nations the guardian of international peace is a creation of the victorious powers of World War II, its composition comprising five of the major powers of the time and its action being endowed with largely discretionary powers bestowed on it by the UN Charter itself.[6]

Some scholars argue that the Security Council's decision-making process is not subject to the rule of law, in terms of transparency, equitable participation and predictability of its actions.[7] Likewise, other scholars maintain that its enforcement powers are unfettered by international law. Conversely, many scholars recognise that the powers of the Security Council, albeit largely discretional, are limited by customary international law norms,[8] and especially *jus cogens*.[9] The latter position seems more convincing. Much less discussed is the issue of whether certain violations of international law—first and foremost, customary international law and *jus cogens*—as such amount to a threat to the peace and, under certain circumstances, provide sufficient ground to demand Security Council's intervention. The wording

---

[1] Charter of the United Nations, 26 June 1945, UNCIO 15, 335 (UN Charter).

[2] See, for instance, Oosthuizen 1999, p. 549.

[3] Allott 2017, p. viii.

[4] Pedersen 2015; Conwell-Evans 1929.

[5] Riches 1933.

[6] Article 39, UN Charter.

[7] Elgebeily 2017, pp. 9–15.

[8] Tsagourias and White 2013, pp. 281–317. See also De Wet 2003, p. 19 (focusing on the right to a fair hearing).

[9] Orakhelashvili 2005, p. 59. For a contrary position, see Oosthuizen 1999, pp. 558–563; Schwaigman 2001, pp. 195–202.

of Article 39 of the UN Charter does not provide any guidance in this respect, effectively leaving the decision in the hands of the five permanent members.[10] A possible answer may nonetheless come from a different approach to the study of collective security: namely, one that is not grounded on strict positivism.

Building on the considerations above, this chapter aims at clarifying the extent to which recourse to the language of international law in the text of resolutions has become part of the politics of the Security Council and influences its behaviour. The underlying assumption is that, although the resolutions are addressed to States and increasingly non-State actors, it is expected that the Security Council will not violate the principles and rules it itself establishes or recognises in its own resolutions. If the premise is correct, it should be possible to observe that international law contributes to effectively shaping Security Council's practice to the extent that the Security Council resorts to it. The most direct way of ascertaining whether this is the case is to analyse the text of the resolutions adopted.

For the purposes of this chapter, the focus of the inquiry remains on the Security Council's decision making, rather than enforcement, powers. Specifically, the analysis aims at shedding light on the factors that may contribute to the identification of a given situation as a potential threat to international peace and security, as such able to prompt Security Council's action. In the absence of both a definition of international peace and security in the UN Charter and a duty of the Security Council to give reasons for its actions,[11] Article 39 of the UN Charter leaves the task of determining the specific content of actual or potential breaches of international peace and security to the Security Council itself. This justifies the focus on resolutions—that is to say, the decisions taken. Moreover, in the text of several resolutions the Security Council has denounced violations of international law by both States and non-State actors, thus presenting it as one of the reasons justifying intervention. Whether this stance is developing into a more concrete attitude remains to be established. If so, the immediate implication would be that resort to international law could be used to hold the Security Council politically accountable for inaction.

The systematic analysis of the use of international law in the text of the resolutions adopted over seven decades provides the first step to understand the breadth, scope, limits and implications of an often-overlooked benchmark of legitimacy of Security Council action. However, providing an empirically-grounded type of analysis does not mean proceeding to an unmethodical examination of the Security Council's practice. Quite the contrary, the strategy adopted calls for a specific method of investigation of social phenomena: one that arrives at the production of knowledge, and therefore theory, through the pragmatic, inductive and systematic observation of how the practice of the Security Council has unfolded over time. If we can only criticize,

---

[10] Article 39, UN Charter reads: "The Security Council shall determine the existence of any threat to the peace, breach of the peace, or act of aggression and shall make recommendations, or decide what measures shall be taken in accordance with Articles 41 and 42, to maintain or restore international peace and security".

[11] Moeckli and Fazel 2017, p. 13.

and therefore reimagine, what we know,[12] then the starting point of the investigation must be the empirical observation of the practice of the Security Council in action, chiefly in the form of resolutions, as opposed to the practice of the Security Council in books.[13]

Section 7.2 provides an overview of the composition by subject area of the resolutions adopted between 1946 and 2017. While demonstrating the presence of selection bias, it points out the significance of the thematic, as opposed to country-specific, resolutions in the practice of the Security Council. Section 7.2.1 reconstructs discernible patterns of reliance on international legal instruments in the text of resolutions and places the thematic resolutions in context of such shifting paradigm. Using the group of resolutions on the protection of civilians in armed conflict as a case study, Sect. 7.2.2 then illustrates the main features of the thematic resolutions with a view to reconsidering the accuracy of the assumption that the Security Council is unbound by law. Section 7.3 gathers up the threads of the empirical analysis and speculates about a possible Security Council conception of the international rule of law. Section 7.4 concludes.

7.2 The Security Council's Practice Unpacked (1946–2017)

The ensuing analysis of the seven decades of Security Council's practice is informed by an original database. Political scientists have performed quantitative analysis of resolutions. *Schlesiger's* study, for instance, provides evidence that the Security Council is concerned about collective security and, to a lesser extent, human security. However, the database is limited to showing the frequency with which certain elements of the UN Development Programme's human security index appear, directly or indirectly, in the text of a limited number of randomly selected resolutions.[14] As far as legal scholars are concerned, studies about the practice of the Security Council abound.[15] None of them, however, has been designed to specifically, and systematically, trace the evolution over time of patterns of reliance on international legal instruments by the Security Council. The customised database created for the present study fills the gap in the academic literature.

At first sight, the practice of the Security Council appears like an uncategorised batch of documents. The official website of the United Nations contains a chronological list of the Security Council's working documents, of which resolutions are only one category.[16] It is also widely accepted that the latter are the category of

---

[12] Allott 1990, p. xxvii.

[13] The distinction is taken from Pound 1910, p. 12.

[14] Schlesiger 2008.

[15] See, among many, Sievers and Daws 2014.

[16] Security Council decisions comprise resolutions, press statements as well as statements, letters, and notes by the Council's President. The full list is available at: www.un.org/en/sc/documents/ (accessed on 1 October 2018).

7 The UN Security Council: From Preserving State Sovereignty to …

decisions endowed with the greatest political importance.[17] More generally, it has become commonplace to argue that the decision-making at the Security Council is ultimately governed by reasons of political convenience.[18] The main argument to support this view is that the presence of five permanent members endowed with veto power entails that situations representing actual or potential breaches of international peace and security are likely to be overlooked whenever they involve a direct interest of any of them.[19]

Piecing together the information available from the UN website,[20] it emerges that in the period between 1946 and July 2017, the Security Council has adopted 2369 resolutions. The figure in itself is not that relevant, but the distribution over time of resolutions warns against generalisations in the assessment of Security Council's practice. One point, however, must be made: By admission of the Security Council itself,[21] the relationship among the permanent members greatly affects its functioning. It is indeed striking that during the Cold War period (1948–1991) the Security Council has adopted 688 resolutions while in the post-Cold War period (1991–2017) their number amounts to 1644. Equally striking is the fact that statements stressing the role of the five permanent members as the sole judges of disputes concerning threats to international peace and security are not infrequent. A passage from Resolution 668 (1990), for example, reads:

> [The Security Council] Endorses the framework for a comprehensive political settlement of the Cambodia conflict and encourages *the continuing efforts of China, France, the Union of Soviet Socialist Republics, the United Kingdom of Great Britain and Northern Ireland and the United States of America in this regard.*[22]

The United Nations website does not elaborate on the composition of the body of resolutions, in terms of quantifying how many resolutions have been adopted within a certain subject area. I have therefore created a code book comprising three categories of resolutions using the descriptive formulation provided for each resolution in the UN digital archive.[23] They include: country-specific resolutions, thematic resolutions and a residual category of resolutions regulating aspects of both the internal functioning of the United Nations, including the Security Council, and country-specific operations conducted by the United Nations and seconded by the Security Council. The category of country-specific resolutions has been further divided into four sub-categories in order to reconstruct clusters of resolutions on the same subject-matter, some of which span across decades and seem to be ongoing issues on the

---

[17] Zimmermann 2012, p. 1820. On the interpretation of Security Council resolutions, see Wood 1998, p. 73; Orakhelashvili 2007, p. 143; Yee 2012, p. 613.

[18] Barnett and Finnemore 2008, p. 41.

[19] Ibid.

[20] On the UN website, the resolutions, which are freely available, are listed only chronologically by year of adoption.

[21] Security Council (SC) Res. 135 of 27 May 1960.

[22] SC Res. 668 of 28 September 1990, para 1 (emphasis added).

[23] UN SC, Security Council Resolutions, available at: www.un.org/en/sc/documents/resolutions/ (accessed on 1 October 2018).

Security Council's agenda. They are: resolutions on Africa, amounting to 45% of all the country-specific resolutions adopted between 1946 and 2017; the Middle East, amounting to 27%; Europe, amounting to 18%; and other regions of the world, amounting to 10%.

The empirical reconstruction confirms that the relationships between the five permanent members condition the area of activity of the Security Council. Tellingly, the resolutions adopted during the Cold War period, especially during the 1980s, are almost entirely dedicated to addressing the situation in the territories occupied by Israel. It is also noticeable that after the end of the Cold War the attention radically shifts to the humanitarian situation in Africa and the conflict in Europe following the dismemberment of the former Yugoslavia while the rest of the world virtually disappears from the geographical map of the Security Council. Equally striking is the fact that situations representing potential or actual breaches of international peace and security are not dealt with whenever they involve a direct interest of a permanent member. For instance, up to date not a single resolution has been adopted on the situation in Tibet or Chechnya while only one resolution has been adopted on Cuba.[24] The ongoing civil conflict in Syria and the annexation of Crimea by Russia in 2014 also add up to the list of politically charged conflicts that have paralysed Security Council's action, at least partially.

The considerations above suggest a marked presence of bias in the practice of the Security Council, thus supporting the general perception that the Security Council is an institution unbound by law.[25] In this respect, the language of numbers turns out to be particularly hard to deny or contradict. However, an argument is made that this is not the only possible way of reading the numbers of the practice of the Security Council. The gradual appearance of the thematic resolutions as an established feature of Security Council's practice reveals another, and relatively overlooked, face of the Security Council as a standard setting institution.

The thematic resolutions have two distinctive characteristics: Firstly, they are largely framed in the language of international law. Secondly, they attribute a number of rights to groups of individuals which are usually caught up in situations of armed conflict, whether internal or international, thus providing a principled approach to collective security without addressing any conflict in particular.

Taken at face value, the presence of the thematic resolutions in the practice of the Security Council suggests that the Security Council is the opposite of an institution unbound by law. Unless the meaning attached to the use of international law in the text of resolutions is only symbolic, it appears that the Security Council has progressively become bound by international law at its own initiative, culminating in the adoption of thematic, as opposed to country-specific, resolutions. The following sub-sections will test this assumption by assessing the significance, as well as the limits, of the role of the thematic resolutions in the practice of the Security Council. Specifically, they will further elaborate on the two characteristics of the thematic

---

[24] SC Res. 144 of 19 July 1960 (complaint by Cuba).

[25] See, for instance, Oosthuizen 1999, p. 549; Joyner 2012, pp. 225 and 251. See also note 7 above.

7 The UN Security Council: From Preserving State Sovereignty to …

resolutions abovementioned with a view to assessing the extent to which they are able to contain the discretionary powers of the Security Council.

7.2.1 Tracing International Law in the Text of Resolutions

This sub-section provides a systematic assessment of Security Council's practice. Such method presents one main advantage compared to the traditional case study approach: It adds a temporal dimension that allows the international law scholar to appreciate different dynamics related to the politics of the Security Council and, on the basis of that, formulate a theory. At the same time, it has a disadvantage: By focusing on broad thematic areas, it lacks the depth of analysis of a case study. Recourse to empiricism should therefore be seen as supplementing, rather than replacing, the traditional normative and doctrinal analysis typical of the case study approach. Bearing this caveat in mind, the following analysis aims at providing an account of the interplay between law and politics in Security Council's practice as it transpires from the text of the resolutions adopted.

To that end, the specific research method adopted consists of the content analysis of the text of the 2369 resolutions adopted between 1946 and 2017.

During the Cold War period, much importance was attached to the purposes and principles of the UN Charter in assessing the actual or potential breach of the peace posed by a given conflict. The cluster of resolutions on the situation between Angola and South Africa, for example, continuously refers to the purposes and principles of the UN Charter.[26] Although not so prominent, referral to the formal sources of international law was not infrequent either. On the one hand, groups of resolutions such as those on Angola and the situation between Afghanistan and Pakistan cite international treaties,[27] with the resolutions on hostage-taking containing the highest number of citations.[28] On the other hand, rules of customary international law are referred to only in Resolution 620 (1988) on the situation between Iraq and Iran.[29]

Sporadically, the resolutions of the Cold War period also contain a generic reference to international law, sometimes establishing that certain situations violating international law or international legal standards constitute a breach of international peace and security, while at other times requiring the parties involved in a dispute to take action according to international law.[30] Among such groups of resolutions, those on the situation between Iraq and Iran contain the highest number of references

---

[26] See, for instance, SC Res. 545 of 20 December 1983, Preamble, para 2 ("in flagrant violation of the principles and objectives of the Charter of the United Nations and of international law").

[27] SC Res. 696 of 30 May 1991; SC Res. 647 of 11 January 1990.

[28] SC Res. 638 of 31 July 1989.

[29] SC Res. 620 of 26 August 1988, para 2.

[30] See, for instance, SC Res. 395 of 25 August 1976, Preamble, para 6 (referring to "the need of the parties […] to respect each other's international rights and obligations").

to international law.[31] Other resolutions, like those on the situation between Iraq and Israel and those on Israel and Tunisia, contain expressions such as "norms of [international] conduct" and "internationally accepted objectives" whose interpretation is ambivalent, thus denoting that recourse to international law in the text of resolutions during the Cold War was neither systemic nor systematic.[32]

The selective use of international law by the Security Council is also evidenced by the generic reference to international humanitarian law in the resolutions on hostage-taking, the situation between Iraq and Iran, and especially those on Iraq and Kuwait.[33] International human rights law is never mentioned, although a restricted group of resolutions contains multiple references to the Universal Declaration of Human Rights, which, in this specific period of time, was taken as the reference document in the field of human rights.[34] Noteworthy is also Resolution 497 (1981), which refers to the UN Charter provisions, principles of international law, and Security Council resolutions as if they were on an equal footing,[35] thus *de facto* conferring the status of formal sources of international law on the Council's resolutions.

During the post-Cold War period, the attention previously given to the purposes and principles of the UN Charter progressively fades away and is replaced by a consistent reference to international legal instruments. For instance, certain treaties are recognised as the standards of international legality in certain fields. Prominent examples are the Treaty on the Non-Proliferation of Nuclear Weapons,[36] the UN Convention on the Law of the Sea,[37] and the 1949 Geneva Conventions (see).[38] Other resolutions have a more local focus and address situations classified as breaches of international peace and security. The resolutions on Somalia and Sudan/South Sudan,[38] in particular, represent the cusp of a trend in which resolutions addressing situations taking place in Africa rely heavily upon international legal instruments as the preferred means for eliciting compliance of their addressees.[39] The text of such

---

[31] SC Res. 685 of 31 January 1991 and previous ones.

[32] See, for instance, SC Res. 487 of 19 June 1981, para 1 ("norms of international conduct") and 4 ("the internationally accepted objective of preventing nuclear weapons proliferation"); and SC Res. 611 of 25 April 1988, para 1 ("international law and norms of conduct").

[33] SC Res. 660 of 2 August 1990.

[34] See, for example, the group of resolutions on Namibia, South Africa, the territories occupied by Israel, and West Africa.

[35] SC Res. 497 of 17 December 1981, Preamble, para 2.

[36] SC Res. 1887 of 24 September 2009, Preamble, para 6 ("Underlining that the NPT remains the cornerstone of the nuclear non-proliferation regime and the essential foundation for the pursuit of nuclear disarmament and for the peaceful uses of nuclear energy").

[37] SC Res. 2018 of 31 October 2011, Preamble, para 6 ("Affirming that international law, as reflected in the United Nations Convention on the Law of the Sea of 10 December 1982, in particular its Articles 100, 101 and 105, sets out the legal framework applicable to countering piracy and armed robbery at sea, as well as other ocean activities"). [38] SC Res. 1894 of 11 November 2009, Preamble, para 4 ("the Geneva Conventions of 1949, which together with their Additional Protocols constitute the basis for the legal framework for the protection of civilians in armed conflict").

[38] SC Res. 2184 of 12 November 2014; SC Res. 2075 of 16 November 2012.

[39] See the group of resolutions on the Democratic Republic of the Congo, Ivory Coast, Mali, peace and security in Africa, and Sudan/South Sudan. *Contra* see those on Liberia and Sierra Leone.

7 The UN Security Council: From Preserving State Sovereignty to …

resolutions contains a generally well-proportioned amount of references to various sources of international law, both in the preamble and the operative part of resolutions. Sources referred to include specific treaties and United Nations documents as well as international law, international humanitarian law, and human rights law in general.

In contrast with the resolutions adopted during the Cold War period, customary international law is explicitly recognised as a source of international obligation. A passage from Resolution 1067 (1996), for example, reads:

> [The Security Council] Condemns the use of weapons against civil aircraft in flight as being incompatible with elementary considerations of humanity, *the rules of customary international law as codified in article 3*bis *of the Chicago Convention*, and the standards and recommended practices set out in the annexes of the Convention.[40]

The same resolution also refers to "the principle, *recognized under customary international law*, concerning the non-use of weapons against [civil] aircraft in flight"[41] while Resolution 937 (1994) on the UN Observation mission in Georgia refers to "established principles and practices of the United Nations," which may be regarded as evocative of *usus* and *opinio juris*.[42] In addition, Resolution 2292 (2016) goes as far as to recognise that Security Council resolutions may themselves constitute custom. The relevant passage reads:

> [T]he authorization provided by paragraph 5 of this resolution applies only with respect to vessels that are the subject of a designation made by the Committee pursuant to paragraph 11 and shall not affect the rights or obligations or responsibilities of Member States under international law, including rights or obligations under the United Nations Convention on the Law of the Sea, including the general principle of exclusive jurisdiction of a flag state over its vessels on the high seas, with respect to other vessels and in any other situation, and underscores in particular that *this resolution shall not be considered as establishing customary international law*.[43]

However, not all resolutions rely on international law as a parameter of legitimacy adopted by the Security Council to justify its action. For example, in the groups of resolutions on the Central African Republic,[44] the Democratic Republic of the Congo,[45] and Haiti[46] reference to international treaties is virtually absent, with scattered reference to UN documents only in both the preamble and the operative part. Instead, such groups of resolutions tend to supply the paucity of reference to international treaties and customs with constant reference to the Security Council's thematic resolutions on women, children, and civilians as well as those on threats to international peace and security caused by terrorist acts. The thematic resolutions contain abundant references to international law in general and international

---

[40] SC Res. 1067 of 26 July 1996, para 6 (emphasis added).

[41] Ibid., Preamble, para 5 (emphasis added).

[42] SC Res. 937 of 21 July 1994, para 4.

[43] SC Res. 2292 of 14 June 2016, para 9 (emphasis added).

[44] SC Res. 2239 of 27 January 2017 and previous ones.

[45] SC Res. 2360 of 21 June 2017 and previous ones.

[46] SC Res. 2350 of 13 April 2017 and previous ones.

humanitarian and human rights law in particular. They are the object of the following sub-section.

Finally, other resolutions, such as those establishing a date of election to fill a vacancy in the International Court of Justice do not contain any reference to international legal materials at all.[47]

The considerations above suggest that although the powers of the Security Council to intervene are entirely discretionary, once the Security Council decides to act it does so by taking the provisions of international law seriously. There is abundant evidence of an increasing reliance by the Security Council on the primary sources of international law, moving from a sporadic use of them during the Cold War period to a consistent, almost systematic, presence of citations in the text of the post-Cold War period resolutions. Such a trend has culminated in the adoption of thematic resolutions, which are largely formulated in the language of international law. In this sense, the increasing reliance on international law in the practice of the Security Council appears to provide a degree of legitimacy to its actions in terms of elaborating on certain aspects of the scope of its mandate, as established in Articles 24 and 39 of the UN Charter.

7.2.2 Significance and Limits of the Thematic Resolutions

The thematic resolutions amount to only 6% of the Security Council's practice, consisting of 145 resolutions out of 2369. However, the numbers as such are not particularly relevant and, to a certain extent, can be deceptive. From a legal perspective, what is interesting about the empirical reconstruction is the distribution over time of the thematic resolutions.

Three main patterns of Security Council's behaviour are clearly discernible. Firstly, from 1946 to the end of the 1970s, the Security Council has adopted a limited number of thematic resolutions mainly addressing the two related issues of regulation of armaments and the use of atomic energy for peaceful uses.[48] This is hardly surprising since those issues represent the two main concerns of the international community in the post-World War II period, along with the economic reconstruction of post-war Europe. Secondly, throughout the 1980s until the end of the 1990s, the Security Council has passed a handful of resolutions addressing issues variously related to the idea of international peace and security,[49] international terrorism,[50] and the issue of hostage-taking.[51] Thirdly, in 1999 the Security Council adopted resolutions 1261 on children in armed conflict and 1265 on the protection of civilians in

---

[47] SC Res. 2034 of 19 January 2012.

[48] See SC Res. 97 of 30 January 1952 and previous ones (armaments); SC Res. 255 of 19 June 1968 and previous ones (nuclear-weapon and non-nuclear-weapon States).

[49] SC Res. 1172 of 6 June 1998.

[50] SC Res. 1189 of 13 August 1998.

[51] SC Res. 638 of 31 July 1989.

armed conflict.[52] From that moment onwards, the thematic resolutions have become the hallmark of the twenty-first century practice of the Security Council.

The thematic resolutions have become an established pattern in the practice of the Security Council not only for the consistency with which they are now adopted year after year, but also because groups of thematic resolutions have developed a systemic character, building progressively on the previous ones and cross-referencing each other, thus forming wider thematic areas. As of today, patterns of thematic resolutions providing a principled approach to issues related to international peace and security clearly exist. The main ones are: the resolutions protecting specific categories of civilians in armed conflict, which include the clusters of resolutions on civilians as well as those on women and children; the resolutions on international peace and security, which include the resolutions on international terrorism, non-proliferation of weapons of mass destruction, and the role of the Security Council in maintaining international peace and security. Other groups of less developed thematic resolutions regulate issues of cooperation between the United Nations and regional and sub-regional organisations, post-conflict peace-building, general issues relating to sanctions, small arms and light weapons, and UN peacekeeping operations.

A shared characteristic of all the thematic resolutions is that, compared to the country-specific ones, they are more democratic and representative of the international community, since non-members of the Security Council as well as representatives of relevant UN institutions, governmental and non-governmental organisations (NGOs) are customarily invited to contribute to the debate of draft resolutions. The group of resolutions on the protection of civilians in armed conflict, for example, have been introduced and supported by the Secretary-General,[53] the UN High Commissioner for Human Rights,[54] the UN Under-Secretary-General for Humanitarian Affairs and Emergency Relief Coordinator,[55] the President of the International Committee of the Red Cross,[56] NGO representatives,[57] and the near totality of the UN Member States. Moreover, as a consequence of the more participatory nature of the process of adoption, the thematic resolutions have all been adopted unanimously. Taken together, these observations portray the Security Council as an idealised, and largely utopian, institution.

However, a closer look at the text of the resolutions on civilians, for example, reveals that a significant part of the normative propositions referred to therein has been introduced into the debate through Statements of the President of the Security Council, which are another type of working document of the Security Council

---

[52] SC Res. 1261 of 30 August 1999; SC Res. 1265 of 17 September 1999.

[53] UN SC, Report of the 4046th Meeting, UN Doc. S/PV.4046 (1999), 3–4; *id.*, Report of the 6216th Meeting, UN Doc. S/PV.6216 (2009), 4–5; *id.*, Report of the 7685th Meeting, UN Doc. S/PV.7685 (2016), 2–4.

[54] Id., Report of the 4046th Meeting (note 63), 4-6; *id.*, Report of the 6216th Meeting (note 63), 7–9 (Deputy High Commissioner).

[55] Id., Report of the 6216th Meeting (note 63), 5–7.

[56] Id., Report of the 4130th Meeting, UN Doc. S/PV.4130 (2000), 4–7.

[57] Id., Report of the 7374th Meeting, UN Doc. S/PV.7374 (2015), 6–7; *id.*, Report of the 7450th Meeting, UN Doc. S/PV.7450 (2015), 3–6; *id.*, Report of the 7685th Meeting (2016), 7–8.

endowed with a lesser degree of political importance than resolutions.[58] This move may signify that the resolutions on civilians, and the thematic resolutions in general, are intended to be ancillary to the country-specific resolutions. An alternative interpretation is that, as long as Presidential Statements are statements by the President on behalf of the Security Council which are previously discussed with the Security Council's members and subsequently adopted at a formal meeting,[59] they are intended to be technical, rather than political, documents. The latter consideration seems more plausible since all the Presidential Statements on the protection of civilians in armed conflicts, to stay within the example, have been discussed by the same actors who have partaken in the resolutions' debates. Taken together, the considerations above on the resolutions on civilians can reasonably be extended to the thematic resolutions in general and suggest that the adoption of thematic resolutions follows a rather transparent voting procedure.

Another shared characteristic of the thematic resolutions is that they clearly spell out legal rights and duties of State and non-State actors alike. In order to perform this function, they rely heavily on the language of international law. The group of resolutions on the protection of civilians in armed conflict, for instance, aims at facilitating the effective implementation of existing humanitarian law.[60] A passage from Resolution 1894 (2009) states: "[T]he Geneva Conventions of 1949 [...] together with their Additional Protocols constitute the basis for the legal framework for the protection of civilians in armed conflict."[61]

The legal basis of the commitment of the Security Council to the protection of civilians in armed conflict also includes other relevant international instruments such as the Hague Conventions (1899 and 1907),[62] the UN Convention on the Rights of the Child (1989),[63] and the Convention on the Safety of United Nations and Associated Personnel (1994).[64] Violations of relevant rules of applicable international humanitarian and human rights law are therefore regarded as a condition sufficient to justify Security Council actions.[65] Equally, other factors such as the proliferation of arms, in particular small arms and light weapons,[66] and disarmament are

---

[58] United Nations, The Security Council: Working Methods Handbook (2012), 90.

[59] UN SC, Note by the President of the Security Council, UN Doc. S/2010/507 (2010) Annex, Section VII, para 42.

[60] Id., Presidential Statement, UN Doc. S/PRST/2015/23 (2015), para 3; SC Res. 2286 of 3 May 2016, Preamble, para 2.

[61] SC Res. 1894 of 11 November 2009, Preamble, para 4.

[62] Hague Convention (II) with Respect to the Laws and Customs of War on Land and Its Annex: Regulations concerning the Laws and Customs of War on Land, 29 July 1899; Hague Convention (IV) Respecting the Laws and Customs of War on Land and Its Annex: Regulations Concerning the Laws and Customs of War on Land, 18 October 1907.

[63] SC Res. 1738 of 23 December 2006, Preamble, para 5.

[64] SC Res. 1265 of 17 September 1999, para 9.

[65] UN SC, Presidential Statement, UN Doc. S/PRST/2013/2 (2013), para 9 ("The Council reaffirms its readiness to adopt appropriate measures aimed at those who violate international humanitarian and human rights law").

[66] See, for instance, SC Res. 1894 (note 47), 29.

7 The UN Security Council: From Preserving State Sovereignty to …

flagged as contributing to exacerbate the negative impact of conflicts on civilians.[67] Consequently the thematic resolutions establish that the implementation of relevant international instruments, such as the Convention on the Use, Stockpiling, Production and Transfer of Anti-Personnel Mines and Their Destruction (1997), may have beneficial effects on the safety of civilians.[68]

At the same time, none of the thematic resolutions create new legal obligations. They only recognise the Security Council's commitment to the protection of civilians in armed conflict. They nonetheless suggest that international law represents the benchmark of legitimacy of Security Council actions.[69] For example, a passage from resolution 1296 (2000) reads:

> [The Security Council] Notes that the deliberate targeting of civilian populations or other protected persons and *the committing of systematic, flagrant and widespread violations of international humanitarian and human rights law in situations of armed conflict may constitute a threat to international peace and security.*[70]

In light of the preceding, the issue of the effectiveness of this set of resolutions turns out to be of paramount importance in determining whether international law is able to contain, wholly or partially, the discretionary power of the Security Council to take action. Considering that the rationale behind Security Council intervention is represented exclusively by violations of rules and principles of international law,[71] two issues emerge.

Firstly, as part of its consideration of the protection of civilians, the Security Council has adopted an Aide Memoire. Primarily aimed at facilitating Security Council deliberations on the establishment, change, or close of peacekeeping operations,[72] the Aide Memoire may also provide guidance in circumstances outside the scope of peacekeeping operations which may require the urgent attention by the Security Council.[73] However, the Preamble to the Aide Memoire provides that its adoption is without prejudice to the provisions of Security Council resolutions and other decisions.[74]

Secondly, the Aide Memoire states that the consideration of issues pertaining to the protection of civilians in armed conflict must be decided where appropriate and on a case-by-case basis,[75] taking into consideration the particular circumstances.[76] This,

---

[67] UN SC, Presidential Statement, UN Doc. S/PRST/2004/46 (2004), paras 6 and 10.

[68] SC Res. 1296 of 19 April 2000, paras 20–21.

[69] SC Res. 1894 (note 47), 8.

[70] SC Res. 1296 (note 79), 5 (emphasis added).

[71] UN SC, Presidential Statement, UN Doc. S/PRST/2008/18 (2008), para 2 ("The Security Council condemns all violations of international law, including international humanitarian law, human rights law and refugee law committed against civilians in situations of armed conflict").

[72] SC Res. 1894 (note 47), para 30.

[73] UN SC, Presidential Statement, UN Doc. S/PRST/2014/3 (2014), Annex, para 5.

[74] *Id.*, Presidential Statement, UN Doc. S/PRST/2010/25 (2010), Annex, para 4.

[75] SC Res. 1674 of 28 April 2006, 16; UN SC, Presidential Statement, UN Doc. S/PRST/2014/3 (2014), Annex, para.

[76] UN SC, Presidential Statement, UN Doc. S/PRST/2014/3 (2014), Annex, para 5.

however, leads to the awkward conclusion that while all actors involved in armed conflict are strictly bound by the obligations applicable to them under international law, the Security Council is allowed to choose which situations address, and redress, for violations of international law.

The way the group of thematic resolutions on civilians has been used in practice confirms the appearance of selection bias in the practice of the Security Council. For instance, the overwhelming majority of cross-references to the thematic resolutions (and accompanying Presidential Statements) on the protection of civilians in armed conflict contained in country-specific resolutions can be located in the preamble of resolutions, suggesting that reference to binding international law instruments has a largely symbolic value in the practice of the Security Council. Moreover, as Table 7.1 shows, the existent citations of thematic resolutions on civilians in armed conflict are modest and mostly confined to a handful of conflicts taking place in Africa.

The numerical evidence yielded by the empirical reconstruction suggests that the resolutions on civilians in particular, and the thematic resolutions in general, are not able to qualify the discretionary powers of the Security Council. Moreover, the fact that the thematic resolutions are entirely framed in the language of international law but applied in a selective, and arguably biased, way eventually disempowers the Security Council as the twenty-first century guardian of international peace and security. A plausible consequence is that States may be more and more tempted to take unilateral or regional action to address humanitarian situations whenever the Security Council is deadlocked and political convenience so suggests, on the basis that the Council has failed to implement the international obligations stated in its own resolutions.

7.3 The Security Council and the International Rule of Law

The empirical reconstruction of the practice of the Security Council brings to the fore three main themes. The first one is that there is strong evidence of bias in the practice of the Security Council: The fact that 72% of all the country-specific resolutions adopted so far address conflicts in Africa and the Middle East alone leaves no doubt about that. The findings are aligned with scholarly positions arguing that the Security Council's discretionary powers cannot be constrained[77] and that the Security Council has gradually developed its powers beyond the text of the UN Charter and probably in violation of international law.[78] However, the distribution over time of the thematic resolutions suggests that we are witnessing the beginning of what appears to be a new wave in Security Council practice. Nobody in 1945 would

---

[77] See Oosthuizen 1999.

[78] For a recent account, see Powell 2007, p. 157. *Contra* see Tsagourias and White 2013, pp. 297–318 (arguing that the discretionary powers of the Security Council have been created by the UN Charter and, as such, are both legal and indispensable for the Security Council to dispense its mandate effectively).

7 The UN Security Council: From Preserving State Sovereignty to ...

Table 7.1 Number of citation of thematic resolutions on civilians (1999–2014)

Non-thematic resolutions	Women		Children		Civilians	
	Pream.	Op. part	Pream.	Op. part	Pream.	Op. part
Afghanistan	18	11	15	7	22	0
Burundi	8	2	7	1	7	1
Chad, Central African Republic and the sub-region	4	0	3	0	4	0
Children in armed conflict	3	0	–	–	3	0
Cooperation between the UN and regional and sub-regional organizations	1	0	1	0	0	0
Democratic Republic of the Congo	17	7	18	4	17	0
General issues relating to sanctions	0	0	0	0	0	0
Great Lakes region	1	0	1	0	0	0
Guinea-Bissau	3	5	0	0	0	0
Haiti	3	13	1	10	1	4
High-level meeting of the SC: combating international terrorism	0	0	0	0	0	0
Implementation of the report of the Panel on UN Peace Operations (S/2000/809)	1	0	0	0	1	0
Iraq	3	0	2	0	0	0
Ivory Coast	23	11	21	6	19	0
Letters from the Secretary-General	7	0	6	0	0	0
Liberia	6	1	1	1	0	0
Libya	5	0	5	0	5	0
Maintenance of international peace and security	1	0	1	0	0	0
Maintenance of international peace and security: conflict prevention	1	0	0	0	0	0
Maintenance of international peace and security: security sector reform	1	0	1	0	1	0
Mali	0	4	0	4	0	4
Middle East	9	0	1	1	2	0
Non-proliferation of weapons of mass destruction	0	0	0	0	0	0
Peace and security in Africa	1	1	2	1	0	1
Protection of civilians in armed conflict	3	0	2	1	–	–
Protection of UN and associated personnel	0	0	1	0	1	0

(continued)

Table 7.1 (continued)

Non-thematic resolutions	Women		Children		Civilians	
	Pream.	Op. part	Pream.	Op. part	Pream.	Op. part
Reports of the Secretary-General on Sudan and South Sudan	23	13	19	1	20	1
Sierra Leone	0	6	0	0	1	0
Situation between Iraq and Kuwait	1	0	0	0	0	0
Small arms and light weapons	1	0	0	0	1	0
Somalia	8	7	8	5	8	7
Sudan	12	2	12	0	12	0
Sudan sanctions	1	0	1	0	0	0
Sudan and South Sudan	2	2	3	0	2	0
Threats to international peace and security caused by terrorist acts	1	0	1	0	0	0
Timor-Leste	2	0	0	0	1	2
UN Peacekeeping operations	2	0	2	0	1	1
Women and peace and security	–	–	5	2	5	1

Source Deplano 2015, pp. 36–37

have possibly predicted an evolution of the Security Council's sphere of competence of this kind: from a country-specific to a thematic focus, accompanied by a more democratic type of decision-making process open to actors other than the members of the Security Council.

This reading of the empirical findings appears to contradict certain established scholarly positions. One of the finest scholars in the field of collective security, for example, argues that "it is difficult to envisage developments of the Security Council in the direction of an institution effectively promoting and sustaining a global community *based on the values proclaimed by the UN Charter*".[79] The statement accurately captures the unwieldy use the Security Council has made of its discretionary powers. Yet the text itself of the thematic resolutions delineates a different aspirational trajectory to maintain international peace and security and ultimately achieve the goals of the UN Charter. An argument is therefore made that it is both realistic and normatively desirable to create, and consolidate, theoretical frames providing a principled approach to collective security in the text of resolutions with a view to invoking them as the threshold of legitimacy of State and non-State actors' actions.

Equally, such normative frames could be utilised as the benchmark of legitimacy of Security Council action (or inaction). Doing so would create forms of political accountability of the Security Council before the international community for failure to implement the principles of international peace and security it itself has elaborated in the resolutions, thus circumventing potential deadlocks caused by the power to veto resolutions. In other words, putting the Security Council under constant pressure

---

[79] Fassbender 2012, p. 52 (emphasis added).

would force it to be more proactive, and less speculative, in reaffirming *de facto*, and not only *de jure*, its status of guardian of international legality on a daily basis.

The second theme is that the thematic resolutions represent the cusp of a decades-long process of progressive reliance on international law as an objective language of communication. However, the majority of scholars argue that the Security Council has adopted resolutions embracing the language of human rights as a reaction to outside pressure coming mainly from NGOs and the media, especially in the aftermath of humanitarian disasters that could have been stopped or prevented from happening.[80] As a result, the engagement of the Security Council with human rights has been mostly perceived in the negative as insufficient and inefficient.[81] For example, in relation to the resolutions on civilians, *Brooks* acknowledges that to a certain extent the Security Council has always concerned itself with the protection of civilians. She nonetheless concludes that: "Ultimately, improving Security Council civilian-protection efforts will depend more on the evolution of norms and practices external to the Council [...] *than on anything internal to the Council.*"[82]

The statement above criticises the inconsistent patterns of behaviour of the Security Council in the field of human rights protection. This view finds confirmation in the number of resolutions adopted to address selected conflicts only taking place on the African continent, and after much outside pressure. However, by focusing on the emerging role of the thematic resolutions, the findings of the empirical study appear to point to the opposite direction: namely, that the Security Council has progressively committed itself to protect human beings, in addition to preserving State sovereignty, as a matter of principle rather than convenience.

The third theme is that the presence of the thematic resolutions as an established feature of the twenty-first century practice of the Security Council reveals an inherent tension between the formal commitment of the Security Council to uphold international law, as recognised in the text of resolutions, and the concrete steps taken to actualise it. On the one hand, the fact that the thematic resolutions mostly appear in the text of a handful of country-specific resolutions suggests that the reliance on international law by the Security Council is largely based on convenience. Specifically, it seems that the references to international legal instruments contained in the text of resolutions serve the purpose of justifying Security Council intervention in relation to selected conflicts rather than activating it as a matter of law. In this sense, international law turns out to be a form of apology.[83] On the other hand, the fact that the thematic resolutions do not address any conflict in particular means that they lack concreteness, and thus resemble a form of utopia.[84]

The two conceptual oppositions, however, are not irreconcilable. Between "the infinite flexibility of international law (apologism)" and "the 'moralistic' nature of

---

[80] Genser and Stagno Ugarte 2014, p. 29.

[81] Fassbender 2012, p. 7; Bailey 1994.

[82] Brooks 2014, p. 67 (emphasis added).

[83] Koskenniemi 2005a, pp. 17 and 21.

[84] Ibid.

the law (utopianism)"[85] it is possible to assess the new roles the Security Council is carving out for itself to cope with the twenty-first century threats to international peace and security against a different background: one that reimagines the relationship between facts and norms in international law as a means to rethink the idea of an international rule of law. Accordingly, understanding the prospects offered by the innocent use of international law by the Security Council requires appreciating the Security Council's conception of the rule of law, which in turn informs its conception of collective security.

Looking at its seven decades of practice, it appears that the Security Council neither recognizes nor adheres to the idea of an international rule of law. Indeed, no resolution deals explicitly with this issue. However, three Presidential Statements on the item entitled: "The promotion and strengthening of the rule of law in the maintenance of international peace and security" acknowledge that, on the one hand, the idea of rule of law has, in itself, a national dimension only.[86] On the other hand, they establish that certain violations of international law committed by the parties to an armed conflict directly affect the (domestic) rule of law and, as a result, international peace and security.[87] Taken together, such considerations justify the Security Council's commitment to "an international order based on the rule of law and international law".[88]

Practical steps taken by the Security Council to translate its commitment to preserving the rule of law into reality include a series of activities, such as providing operational support to national police enforcement agencies and supporting the security sector reform, as part of the mandates of peacekeeping operations.[91] On top of that, gross violations of the rights of civilians caught in armed conflict—especially women and children—are qualified as unacceptable violations of international law, since they bear direct consequences for the establishment and preservation of an international order based on the rule of law.[89] From this perspective, serious violations of international humanitarian and human rights law, including refugee law, amount to violations of the rule of law. For this reason, the Security Council applies to itself, in the form of peacekeeping and missions, certain restraints in the conduct admissible by peacekeepers on the ground. For instance, following widespread condemnation, a zero-tolerance policy towards sexual exploitation of women and vulnerable people by peacekeepers is now rigorously enforced.[90]

Taken together, the considerations above suggest that the commitment of the Security Council to preserve the rule of law turns out to have a particular narrow

---

[85] Ibid., 24.

[86] They are: UN SC, Presidential Statement, UN Doc. S/PRST/2006/28 (2006); UN SC, Presidential Statement, UN Doc. S/PRST/2012/1 (2012); and UN SC, Presidential Statement, UN Doc. S/PRST/2014/5 (2014).

[87] UN SC, Presidential Statement, UN Doc. S/PRST/2014/5 (2014), paras 11–12; UN SC, Presidential Statement, UN Doc. S/PRST/2012/1 (2012), paras 11–12; and UN SC, Presidential Statement, UN Doc. S/PRST/2006/28 (2006), para 4.

[88] UN SC, Presidential Statement, UN Doc. S/PRST/2014/5 (2014), para 2.

[89] UN SC, Presidential Statement, UN Doc. S/PRST/2012/1 (2012), para 5.

[90] See, for instance UN SC Res. 2275 of 11 March 2016.

scope: namely, the one of promoting the rule of law in those conflict and post-conflicts situations under its consideration rather than as a matter of principle.[91] It thus appears to be a discretionary, discriminatory and in part contradictory conception of what constitutes a threat to international peace and security rather than a firm commitment to take action whenever gross violations of human rights or serious violations of international humanitarian law occur, irrespective of whether or not an instance of armed conflict is inscribed on the Security Council agenda. However, such a superficial assessment of the consideration of humanitarian issues by the Security Council does not account for the political element of Security Council's action.

Specifically, the idea of humanitarian assistance to vulnerable populations in conflict or post-conflict situations attaches to the discretionary powers of the Security Council in the same way recourse to international law as a means for delineating what is (un-)acceptable state behaviour attaches to the idea of universality of law as a source of justification and compliance.[92] The use of international law in the Presidential Statements on the rule of law and in the thematic resolutions performs an explanatory function allowing the Security Council to justify the legitimacy of its choices on a case-by-case basis through the language of legalism. It does not, however, create international obligations on the Security Council. Quite the opposite, it creates a flexible platform of principles open to interpretation by the five permanent members: by virtue of their *de facto* powers coupled with those bestowed on them by the UN Charter, they shape the meaning of international rules and obligations through practice, interpretation and compromise.

Viewed from this angle, the content of the Presidential Statements on the rule of law and the thematic resolutions on civilians, women and children present a striking resemblance in terms of normative content. This in turn suggests that the Security Council's conception of the rule of law has an enabling and constraining function: it allows the Security Council to justify its actions and at the same time constrains the spectrum of available choices on the ground, since they are all aimed at achieving the same goal of creating the right conditions for the maintenance of a peaceful world order. In this sense, although the practice of the Security Council is selective, recourse to the language of international law in the text of the resolutions confers legitimacy to Security Council's action while at the same time imposing certain limits to otherwise unlimited discretionary powers. This leads to the further conclusion that the emergence of the thematic resolutions in the practice of the Security Council represents a new shade of meaning of the idea of international peace and security.

---

[91] UN SC, Presidential Statement, UN Doc. S/PRST/2014/5 (2014), para 15 and UN SC, Presidential Statement, UN Doc. S/PRST/2012/1 (2012), para 17.

[92] Hurd 2017, p. 133.

7.4 Conclusion

It is widely accepted that the Security Council is, at least to a certain extent, an institution above the law by virtue of the discretionary powers bestowed on it by the UN Charter. However, this Chapter has demonstrated that while there is consonance between the doctrinal assumption about the breadth and scope of the Security Council's powers and their unwieldy use in practice, they do not always sing at unison. The inductive inquiry into the behavioural patterns of the Security Council shows that there is another, more democratic Security Council, which functions in parallel with the Leviathan. The increasing reliance on international legal instruments over time culminating in the adoption of thematic, as opposed to country-specific, resolutions is strong evidence of the emerging humanitarian soul of the Security Council.

The longitudinal observation of the practice of the Security Council suggests that the Security Council is re-creating itself through the language of international law. The fact that the Security Council has started to recognise the protection of individuals as the ultimate end of the UN system of collective security and, albeit inconsistently, has acted upon it, confirms that ideas are a form of power inasmuch as power is ideas translated into reality. As *Koskenniemi* points out:

> *Ideas and institutional power cannot be detached from each other* [...] Revolution in the mind calls for a revolution in the streets just as the latter can only take place if the former is already under way. The battle is not between power and ideas but between *ideas and ideas, between power and power.*[93]

Looking systematically into the practice of the Security Council invites the researcher to transcend the boundaries of the legal discipline and look at extralegal factors that may affect the behaviour of both the Security Council and other international actors concerned.[94] There is always an underlying relationship between power and ideas, and it is constantly changing.

The thematic resolutions provide solid evidence that the Security Council has become an important standard setting institution.[98] They also reveal that a proper revolution in the mind of the Security Council is under way. The thematic resolutions of the Security Council embody community values such as the principle of humanity and human rights and, in this limited sense, embody utopian values. An argument is therefore made that the increasing reliance on the language of international law is the pragmatic means through which such utopian values becomes tangible and concretises in practice, thus contributing to elucidate the content and scope of the Security Council's peculiar conception of the international rule of law.[95]

The original, bespoke database of seven decades of practice I have created clearly shows that the legal mind of the Security Council is slowly but relentlessly moving from protecting State sovereignty only to protecting humanity as an end in itself.

---

[93] Koskenniemi 2005b, p. 329 (emphasis in the original).

[94] Feichtner 2012, p. 1156; Bhuta 2012, pp. 66–75.

[95] See also Feichtner 2012, pp. 1155–1156.

The balance of action between the two ends of the spectrum is still inconsistent and in the process of gaining a distinctive identity, which is an issue scholars could, and should, contribute to clarifying. This, however, requires a methodological shift in the traditional way the practice of the Security Council, and that of international organisations in general, has been examined and interpreted by international legal scholars.

By moving beyond the realm of doctrinal analysis of legal phenomena, this article has provided a first step toward a much-needed methodological change in international legal scholarship. It has uncovered certain aspects of the untold story behind the numbers of Security Council practice, showing how the use of international law in the text of resolutions at the same time empowers and disempowers the legitimacy of its action. In doing so, it has created a new pathway for "thinking the unthought"[96] about the evolving idea of collective security.

References

Allott P (1990) Eunomia: New Order for a New World, 2001 paperback edn. Oxford Scholarship Online

Allott P (2017) Eutopia: New Philosophy and New Law for a Troubled World. Cambridge University Press

Bailey SD (1994) The UN Security Council and Human Rights. Palgrave Macmillan

Barnett M, Finnemore M (2008) Political Approaches. In: Daws S, Weiss TG (eds) The Oxford Handbook on the United Nations. Oxford University Press

Bhuta N (2012) The Role International Actors Other than States Can Play in the New World Order. In: Cassese A (ed) Realizing Utopia: The Future of International Law. Oxford University Press

Brooks R (2014) Civilians and Armed Conflict. In: Genser J, Stagno Ugarte B (eds) The United Nations Security Council in the Age of Human Rights. Cambridge University Press, New York

Conwell-Evans TP (1929) The League Council in Action. Oxford University Press

De Wet E (2003) The Role of Human Rights in Limiting the Enforcement Power of the Security Council: A Principled View. In: De Wet E, Nollkaemper A (eds) Review of the Security Council by Member States. Springer

Deplano R (2015) The Strategic Use of International Law by the United Nations Security Council: An Empirical Study. Routledge

Elgebeily S (2017) The Rule of Law in the United Nations Security Council Decision-Making Process: Turning the Focus Inwards. Oxford University Press

Fassbender B (2012) The Security Council, Progress Is Possible but Unlikely. In: Cassese A (ed) Realizing Utopia: The Future of International Law. EJIL 23:4, pp 1143–1157

Feichtner I (2012) Realizing Utopia through the Practice of International Law. EJIL 23

Genser J, Stagno Ugarte B (2014) The United Nations Security Council in the Age of Human Rights. Cambridge University Press

Gowlland-Debbas V (2017) The Security Council as Enforcer of Human Rights. In: Fassbender B (ed) Securing Human Rights?: Achievements and Challenges of the UN Security Council. Oxford University Press

Hurd I (2017) How To Do Things with International Law. Princeton University Press

Joyner DH (2012) The Security Council as Legal Hegemon. Georgetown Journal of International Law 43

---

[96] Scobbie 2005, p. 313.

Koskenniemi M (2005a) From Apology to Utopia: The Structure of International Legal Argument. Cambridge University Press

Koskenniemi M (2005b) International Law as Therapy: Reading the Health of Nations. EJIL 16

Moeckli D, Fazel R (2017) A Duty to Give Reasons in the Security Council: Making Voting Transparent. International Organizations Law Review 14

Oosthuizen G (1999) Playing the Devil's Advocate: The United Nations Security Council is Unbound by Law. Leiden Journal of International Law 12 (1999) 549

Orakhelashvili A (2005) The Impact of Peremptory Norms on the Interpretation and Application of United Nations Security Council Resolutions. European Journal of International Law (EJIL) 16

Orakhelashvili A (2007) The Acts of the Security Council: Meaning and Standards of Review. UNYB 11

Pedersen S (2015) The Guardians: The League of Nations and the Crisis of Empire. Oxford University Press

Pound R (1910) Law in Books and Law in Action. American Law Review 44

Powell C (2007) The Legal Authority of the United Nations Security Council. In: Goold BJ, Lazarus L (eds) Security and Human Rights. Hart Publishing

Ramcharan BG (2012) The Security Council and the Protection of Human Rights. Martinus Nijhoff Publishers

Riches CA (1933) The Unanimity Rule and the League of Nations. Johns Hopkins Press

Schlesiger M (2008) Human Security vs. Collective Security: An Empirical Study of Security Council Resolutions. Verlag

Schwaigman D (2001) The Authority of the Security Council under Chapter VII of the UN Charter: Legal Limits and the Role of the International Court of Justice. Martinus Nijhoff Publishers

Scobbie I (2005) Slouching the Holy City: Some Weeds for Philip Allott. EJIL 16

Sievers L, Daws S (2014) The Procedure of the UN Security Council. Oxford University Press

Shraga D (2011) The Security Council and Human Rights – From Discretion to Promote to Obligation to Protect. In: Fassbender B (ed) Securing Human Rights?: Achievements and Challenges of the UN Security Council. Oxford University Press

Tsagourias N, White N (2013) Collective Security. Cambridge University Press

Wood M (1998) The Interpretation of Security Council Resolutions. Max Planck Yearbook of United Nations Law (UNYB) 2

Yee S (2012) The Dynamic Interplay between the Interpreters of Security Council Resolutions. Chinese Journal of International Law 11

Zimmermann A (2012) Voting: Article 27. In: Simma B et al (eds) The Charter of the United Nations: A Commentary, 3rd edn. Oxford University Press

Dr. Rossana Deplano is Lecturer in Law at the University of Leicester (UK). She holds an LLB and LLM from the University of Cagliari (Italy) and a Ph.D. from Brunel University London (UK). Her main research interests lie in the field of public international law. She has been Scholar-in-Residence at the Library of Congress, Washington DC (2018, 2019) as well as Visiting Researcher at the University of Cambridge (2017) and Georgetown University, Washington DC (2016). Rossana presented at the 12th Stanford International Junior Faculty Forum (2019) and is currently writing a monograph for Cambridge University Press entitled *Empirical and Theoretical Perspectives on International Law: How States Use the UN General Assembly To Create International Obligations.*

Chapter 8
UN Security Council Sanctions and International Peace and Security: Context, Controversies and (Legal) Challenges

Ben L. Murphy

Contents

8.1 Introduction 172
8.2 The Nature of Security Council Sanctions 174
    8.2.1 Terminological Considerations 174
    8.2.2 Article 41 in Context 177
8.3 From Blanket to (Not So) Smart Sanctions 179
8.4 (Individual) Rights and (UN) Responsibilities 183
    8.4.1 Specific Rights Engaged 183
    8.4.2 Legal Limitations on Security Council Sanctions 185
8.5 Challenging Sanctions Inside and Outside the Courtroom 192
    8.5.1 The ICJ 192
    8.5.2 Regional and Domestic Courts 193
    8.5.3 The Ombudsperson Procedure 196
8.6 Conclusion 198
References 199

Abstract The focus of this chapter is UN Security Council sanctions; that is, coercive measures short of the use of military force taken under Article 41 of the UN Charter. Since the late 1990s, the Council has undergone a seismic shift in its sanctioning practice, from imposing blanket sanctions against states towards targeting individuals apparently implicated in global terrorism. As a result of this shift, this area of the Security Council's practice has, in recent times, courted a high degree of controversy. Criticisms centre on the lack of due process guarantees provided to those targeted, which culminated in the now notorious *Kadi* litigation before the courts of the European Union, and other high-profile decisions of regional and domestic courts. This chapter situates these developments, first in light of the Council's 'primary responsibility for the maintenance of international peace and security' and, secondly, in the context of a broader conversation on the legality and legitimacy of Security Council decision-making under Chapter VII.

B. L. Murphy (✉)
School of Law and Social Justice, University of Liverpool, Liverpool, UK
e-mail: B.L.Murphy@liverpool.ac.uk

© T.M.C. ASSER PRESS and the authors 2022
S. Sayapin et al. (eds.), *International Conflict and Security Law*,
https://doi.org/10.1007/978-94-6265-515-7_8

Keywords Security Council · Article 41 · Sanctions · Legal limits · Legitimisation · *Kadi*

8.1 Introduction

As the primary political organ of the organisation, the Security Council sits at the apex of the UN collective security regime. Its power stems from Article 24(1) of the UN Charter, through which member states have conferred to the Council 'primary responsibility for the maintenance of international peace and security'. In order to fulfil this responsibility, the Charter provides two main mechanisms: the pacific dispute resolution and socio-economic cooperation contained in Chapters VI and X, and the coercive powers of the Security Council acting under Chapter VII. Under Chapter VII, upon a determination that a situation constitutes a 'threat to the peace, breach of the peace, or act of aggression'[1] (and the Council enjoys a wide degree of discretion in this regard) the door is opened for the Council to invoke a wide range of forcible or non-forcible measures. In relation to the former, in light of the general prohibition of the use of force in international law, unless a state has a claim to be acting in self-defence the Security Council essentially holds a monopoly on the authorisation of military force.[2] In relation to the latter, Article 41 captures the range of enforcement measures which fall short of the use of force. Often referred to as 'sanctions', these measures are the subject of the present chapter.

It is interesting to note that if this publication was compiled thirty years ago it would almost certainly be the case that there would be no space for a chapter on this topic. For the majority of the Cold War era, the Security Council was stuck in almost perpetual political paralysis, its sanctioning power rarely invoked. However, since the Council was rejuvenated during the mid-1990s its sanctioning practice has undergone a number of seismic shifts. The contemporary importance of this practice is demonstrated by the fact that, to the present author, 'sanctions' sit at the top of two important lists: by some distance, they simultaneously constitute *the most commonly invoked and the most controversial aspect* of the Council's recent practice.

The rationale underpinning the increased use of sanctions is clear. The power to sanction a recalcitrant state (or, increasingly, non-state groups or even individuals) is a key tool at the Council's disposal in fulfilling its peace and security mandate. When employed effectively, sanctions can exert significant pressure on those targeted. When designed and applied astutely, they can serve as the basis for a bargaining dynamic in which the promise of lifting sanctions becomes an incentive to encourage political concessions and cooperation.[3] There is also a strong argument to suggest that non-forcible measures are more likely to receive the support and required unanimity of

---

[1] UN Charter (1945), Article 39.

[2] UN Charter (1945), Article 42.

[3] Cortright et al. 2008, p. 206.

the Council's permanent, veto-wielding members than resolutions which authorise the use of force, thus enhancing the Council's overall effectiveness.[4]

There is a stark difference, however, between the laudable goals of Security Council sanctions, in theory, and the way that they are implemented in practice. It is impossible to understate the controversy attached to these regimes, especially the 1267 sanctions regime, established in response to the threat posed by Al-Qaida and associated groups and recently extended to include ISIL (Da'esh).[5] Consider the following (not so hypothetical) situation: you wake up, walk downstairs and make your morning coffee. In collecting your mail, buried within the usual collection of pizza menus and bills there is a letter with a government postmark. You open the letter with heightened expectation. As you read the letter, you learn that you have been designated a terrorist suspect by the 1267 Sanctions Committee (you were most probably previously unaware that the entity even existed). You learn that all of your assets have been frozen and that you are not permitted to leave the country during the investigation. No further explanation is offered. Whether or not the Sanctions Committee has evidence of your links to terrorist organisations, it will likely be years until you are delisted (if you are at all).[6] The situation of an individual listed under the 1267 regime has been compared to that of Josef K. in Kafka's *The Trial*, 'who awakens one morning and for reasons never revealed to him or the reader is arrested and prosecuted for an unspecified crime'.[7]

Considering the contentious nature of targeted sanctions, it is important, as a standalone consideration, to appreciate their position in the UN collective security regime. More broadly, Security Council sanctions offer a particularly fruitful lens through which to consider wider issues relating to the legal and political framework governing Security Council decision-making under Chapter VII of the UN Charter. The present chapter proceeds with these dual objectives in mind. After a few preliminary remarks about the terminological misnomer of 'sanctions' in order to locate its meaning and its relationship with Article 41 of the Charter (Sect. 8.2), I will provide a more detailed account of the Council's historic and contemporary sanctioning practice briefly touched upon above (Sect. 8.3). I will then situate this practice within a broader conversation about the potential legal constraints imposed on the Security Council by the UN Charter (the *lex specialis*) and general international law (the *lex generalis*) (Sect. 8.4), with specific reference to the role played by regional and domestic courts in protecting the individual rights of those targeted (Sect. 8.5).

By way of conclusion, I will offer some thoughts on what is, to my mind, an underconsidered distinction between recent attempts to legalise (or formalise) Security Council sanctions and accounts that are more concerned with the broader question of the legitimisation of Security Council decision-making (Sect. 8.6). It is not that questions of legitimacy have not been discussed.[8] The real issue is that, too often, the

---

[4] On the Security Council's voting procedures, see UN Charter (1945), Article 27(3).

[5] UNSC Res 1267 (1999); UNSC Res 1989 (2011); UNSC Res 2253 (2015).

[6] See similarly Hooper 2018, p. 613.

[7] Hovell 2016a, p. 114.

[8] See e.g., ibid.; Hurd 2007; Bianchi 2006.

174 B. L. Murphy

question of the legitimacy of sanctions decisions is folded into a narrower enquiry of its legality. I argue that the effectiveness of the contemporary sanctions regime is predicated on the broadest possible conception of legitimacy, one which transcends a purely positivist legal analysis.

As a final introductory remark, it is important to clarify the scope of the chapter. In a general sense, all measures designed to enforce the law can be categorised as sanctions. This is especially true in the context of the decentralised international legal system, where international law is effectuated in a plurality of different ways. For example, the question of whether states are permitted to 'auto-enforce' the rules of international law in the form of countermeasures, reprisals or acts of retorsion (in other words, 'sanctions') is an important one. However, the focus of this chapter is limited to Security Council imposed economic sanctions. Unilateral sanctions in this sense will not be considered.[9] For the same reason, neither will economic sanctions imposed by regional organisations under Article 53 of the Charter. White captures the distinction well. He suggests that unilateral sanctions relate to the 'private enforcement of bilateral norms', whereas collective sanctions are deployed for the 'public enforcement of community-based norms'.[10]

It should also be noted that the term 'collective sanctions' covers a range of other measures which fall under the general rubric of Article 41. The Security Council has used its Article 41 powers in the field of criminal justice, to establish the International Criminal Tribunals for the Former Yugoslavia (ICTY) and Rwanda (ICTR) and the Special Tribunal for Lebanon. The Council has also ventured into dispute settlement, for example when mandating the settlement of compensation claims after the Iraqi invasion of Kuwait and the determination of the territorial boundary between the same.[11] Finally, although the Council's purported dalliances into global 'legislating' clearly overlap with its sanctioning practice, linked as this phenomenon is with the theme of counter-terrorism, so too the Council's sweeping resolutions on terrorist financing and the proliferation of weapons of mass destruction are deemed outside the scope of this chapter.[12]

8.2 The Nature of Security Council Sanctions

8.2.1 Terminological Considerations

The term 'sanction' is among the most 'polarising' and 'antagonising' of all concepts in international law,[13] not least because it is associated with some of the discipline's

---

[9] See instead van Aaken et al. 2019.

[10] White 2018, p. 7.

[11] UNSC Res 687 (1991) and UNSC Res 773 (1992).

[12] UNSC Res 1373 (2001) and UNSC Res 1540 (28 April 2004).

[13] Pellet and Miron 2013, para 1.

most fundamental questions. In the Kelsenian tradition, the ability to sanction an actor for violating a legal obligation is deemed to be the very essence of what gives a legal order its 'legal' status.[14] For this reason, the lack of compulsory sanctions in international law hung, for a long time, as a dark cloud over the discipline; it threatened its very existence.

Of course, as international law has 'matured', its status as legal order is no longer seriously questioned. Nevertheless, the Kelsenian orthodoxy lingers in another way: whereas the status of a legal order is no longer predicated on the existence of sanctions in the sense of compulsory enforcement of its rules, the meaning of the term 'sanctions' still seems to carry this conceptual baggage, in the sense that it is still rooted in the idea of law enforcement. Thus, according to Pellet and Miron, the broadest acceptance 'of the word 'sanctions' designates all types of consequences triggered by the violation of an international legal rule'.[15] The implication is that if we were to suggest that 'sanctions' can be triggered by something other than a violation of international law this would stretch the meaning of the term too far.

While non-forcible measures imposed under Article 41 have long been referred to as 'sanctions', the term itself is mentioned nowhere in the Charter. In an attempt to ascertain whether the expression is suitable in this context, guidance can be sought in the precursor to Article 41, Article 16(1) of the League of Nations Covenant. The economic measures to be imposed against states under this provision were triggered in the event that a member of the League should 'resort to war in disregard of its covenants'. That is, explicitly as a response to a breach of an international obligation. Enforcement measures under Article 41, conversely, are triggered by the Security Council's designation of a situation as a 'threat to the peace' under Article 39 of the Charter. It is true that in most cases a determination of a 'threat to the peace' is prompted by a prior violation of international law.[16] This has led some scholars to suggest that Article 41 measures 'thus become, beyond any doubt, a form of law enforcement'.[17] Schachter perhaps puts this in the strongest terms, describing collective sanctions as 'the quintessential type of international enforcement'.[18] He continues that the 'language of Article 41 is broad enough to cover any type of punitive action not involving the use of armed force'.[19]

However, the categorisation of Article 41 measures as sanctions *par excellence* should give us reason to pause. The reference to punitive action is particularly telling. The Security Council's relationship with international law is much more complex and contested than this implies. The Council takes on different faces—from law-maker,

---

[14] Kelsen 1950, p. 706. 'Law is, by its very nature, a coercive order. A coercive order is a system of rules prescribing certain patterns of behaviour by providing coercive measures, as sanctions, to be taken in case of a contrary behaviour…'.

[15] Pellet and Miron 2013, para 4.

[16] Ibid., para 16.

[17] ibid., para 23.

[18] Schachter 1994, p. 12 (emphasis added). See further Cassese 2005, p. 339. Cassese follows a similar line of reasoning as Schachter in categorising Article 41 measures as sanctions 'properly so-called' or sanctions 'stricto sensu'.

[19] Schachter, Ibid.

law-clarifier, law-applier, law-enforcer—in different contexts. One thing is clear though: the rationale underpinning Security Council imposed enforcement measures is not, first and foremost, punitive. The primary purpose of the UN is not to enforce compliance with international law, *per se*, but 'to maintain international peace and security, and to that end: to take effective collective measures for the prevention and removal of threats to the peace',[20] which is not the same thing. Likewise, the purpose of Security Council enforcement 'is not: to maintain or restore the law, but to maintain, or restore peace, which is not necessarily identical with the law.'[21] From this, it follows that:

> The Security Council has the power to take enforcement actions even in case no obligation expressly imposed on the members has been violated, provided that the Security Council considers such action necessary for the maintenance of international peace and security.[22]

While usually stating a breach of an international obligation when resorting to sanctions, the Council is under no obligation to and sometimes does not offer any precise determination of the existence of an internationally wrongful act. Furthermore, the Council may act pre-emptively to prevent a threat to the peace, without the need to identify that a certain international obligation incumbent upon a state has been breached.[23] It is not clear, therefore, that Article 41 measures constitute 'sanctions' according to the classical Kelsenian definition.

Perhaps in an attempt to square this circle, some scholars have argued that the wording of Article 39 and the Security Council's subsequent practice together point to a general obligation incumbent upon member states not to conduct themselves in a way which constitutes a threat to the peace.[24] If this was the case, the imposition of sanctions would always be a response to illegality. It would address the non-compliance of a state with this derivative obligation, enforced by the Council through a binding decision.[25] However, this is not altogether persuasive. Correlation does not imply causation. The fact that conduct which amounts to a 'threat to the peace' often coincides with the breach of an international obligation does not warrant the conclusion that Article 39 itself amounts to a binding norm in positive international law. The claim that states should be under a general obligation not to act in a way that threatens international peace and security has some merit *de lege*

---

[20] UN Charter (1945), Article 1(1).

[21] Kelsen 1950, p. 294. For an alternative view, see Gowlland-Debbas 1994. Gowlland-Debbas examines the Security Council's role in the enforcement of international obligations from the framework of analysis provided by the doctrine of state responsibility. Her central point is that the Security Council has become increasingly involved in the enforcement of international law (e.g. the establishment under Chapter VII of Tribunals for the Enforcement of Humanitarian Law in the former Yugoslavia and Rwanda). However, it is not clear that this signifies that the Council's primary function has become that of an international law enforcement agency. On this point, see Gill 1995, p. 33. 'The enforcement activities of the Council are adjective to its primary function as a collective security organ'.

[22] Kelsen 1948, p. 788.

[23] Tzanakopoulos 2011, p. 77; Krisch 2012, p. 1310.

[24] E.g. Tzanakopoulos 2011, p. 78.

[25] Ibid.

ferenda. Nevertheless, it does not follow, in the absence of a clear violation of some other obligation, that Article 39 provides a catch-all obligation not to threaten the peace. The question of whether a 'threat to the peace' has occurred is a judgement that appears to be based primarily on a factual (subjective) finding and the weighing of political considerations. It would be very difficult to measure these considerations against legal criteria.[26]

Other commentators have attempted to conceptualise 'sanctions' in a more nuanced way. Abi-Saab refers to 'coercive measures taken in execution of a decision of a competent social organ, i.e. an organ legally empowered to act in the name of the society or community that is governed by the legal system'.[27] Note here that compliance with international law is important in the sense that the Security Council must maintain the legal competence to enact collective sanctions, but it does not mean that sanctions can only be imposed in the name of the enforcement of international law *per se*. The commentary to the Articles on the Responsibility of International Organizations uses the term sanctions in a similar way, referring to measures 'which an organization may be entitled to adopt against its members according to its rules'.[28] On the one hand, this dispels the restrictive definition of sanctions as only relating to law enforcement. However, on the other hand, the recent practice of targeting individuals would not fit this definition. The decision to ignore the significance of contemporary sanctions practice is perhaps surprising considering the amount of publicity targeted sanctions receive and were already receiving at the time of the drafting of the Articles. The definition is nevertheless helpful as it moves away from the classical connection between sanctions and law enforcement.

In sum, there is no harm in utilising the term 'sanctions' in the context of Article 41 measures; in fact, it is at this stage necessary considering that it has clearly been adopted as the term of art. It is imperative though that caution is taken not to use an overly restrictive construction of the term.

8.2.2 Article 41 in Context

As noted, the antecedent to Article 41 was Article 16(1) of the League of Nations Covenant. According to this provision, member states who acted in breach of the Covenant would be subject 'to the severance of all trade or financial relations'. When, in October 1935, the Italian government invaded Ethiopia in violation of its obligations under Article 12[29] the Assembly of the League of Nations established a coordinating committee, which recommended a prohibition on the supply of weapons

---

[26] See, e.g., *Lockerbie (Libya V US)* (Provisional Measures) [1992] ICJ Rep 114 (separate opinion of Judge Weeramantry), para 176.

[27] Abi-Saab 2001, p. 32.

[28] ILC, 'Draft Articles on the Responsibility of International Organizations, with Commentaries' (2011) UN Doc A/66/10, p. 47.

[29] 'The Members of the League agree that, if there should arise between them any dispute likely to lead to a rupture they will submit the matter either to arbitration or judicial settlement or to enquiry

to Italy, an abstention from financial dealings and later a ban on the import of Italian commodities and an embargo on certain products. Although Article 16(1) was not invoked again, it serves as an important precedent, as measures taken under Article 41 typically take a remarkably similar form to those imposed against Italy. Most notably, Article 16(1) mandated for the 'prevention of all financial, commercial, or personal intercourse between the nationals of the covenant-breaking State and the national of any other State'. As such, the Covenant foresaw the fact that the impact of collective sanctions will inherently be felt by the citizens of a state, and not only the government thereof. The difference was that Article 16 was explicit on this point, and the impact was direct. In the Charter era, the impact on individuals has been more implicit and indirect, but no less apparent.

There are other differences in the use of economic sanctions in the pre- and post-Charter eras. For example, the sanctions listed in Article 16(1) represented measures to be taken by states unilaterally, not by the League of Nations collectively. The League's Council, in fact, was not expected to play any role at all.[30] The key sea change, then, is that sanctions have been centralised and collectivised under the auspices of the UN Security Council. Also, we have already noted the fact that the Security Council's competence is engaged by a determination of a 'threat to the peace' and not a violation of international law as such. Finally, the range of measures available to the Security Council under Article 41 would appear broader than those anticipated under the League's Covenant. In this light, it is telling that the Soviet Union's proposal during the Dumbarton Oaks negotiations to include a conclusive catalogue of economic enforcement measures was rejected. The USA and the UK, in particular, regarded this as an unnecessary and inappropriate imposition on the authority of the Security Council.

The final formula of Article 41 should be read, therefore, as something of a compromise:

> The Security Council may decide what measures not involving the use of armed force are to be employed to give effect to its decisions, and it may call upon the Members of the United Nations to apply such measures. These may include complete or partial interruption of economic relations and of rail, sea, air, postal, telegraphic, radio, and other means of communication, and the severance of diplomatic relations.

The wording of Article 41 calls for four observations. First, the term 'may' is doing quite a lot of work in the construction of Article 41. On the one hand, it speaks to the scope of the Security Council's discretion under Chapter VII. Upon a determination of a 'threat to the peace', the Council *may decide* to take enforcement measures, but it is under no legal obligation to do so. On the other hand, it speaks to the fact that the potential sanctioning measures listed therein are illustrative, but not

---

by the Council, and they agree in no case to resort to war until three months after the award by the arbitrators or the judicial decision, or the report by the Council.'

[30] Even when, in 1921, the Assembly of the League adopted guidelines stipulating that the Council could recommend to States that economic enforcement measure would be appropriate, this did not change the essentially hortatory nature of the Council's role, and unilateral nature of the implementation of sanctions.

comprehensive.[31] It follows that the Council may take measures that are not included in the wording of Article 41. To evidence this, we need to look no further than the contemporary practice of targeting individuals as opposed to member states, a practice that is not explicitly covered by Article 41.

Secondly, while the breadth of measures available under Article 41 is seemingly infinite, there should be no doubt as to the upper limits of the provision. The measures available under Article 41 explicitly exclude the use of force, which should be construed in the broadest sense.[32] At the San Francisco conference, the US delegation described the Security Council's involvement with crises as a process of graduated stages justifying the Council's intervention to the extent necessary.[33] On a gradient scale, therefore, sanctions may be said to be less severe than measures taken under Article 42. That said, the third observation is that reference to the 'scale' or 'ladder' of measures under Chapter VII should not be misconstrued. There is no obligation for the Council to formally progress through the stages, this is a matter of discretion. Non-forcible measures are not a prerequisite before the Council authorises the use of force under Article 42. In the same way, there is no need to exhaust provisional measures under Article 40 before non-forcible measures are imposed under Article 41.

The final point relates to the wording of 'calls upon' ('*inviter*' in the French version), which might appear relatively informal and hortatory, but this is misleading.[34] On the contrary, the mandatory force of Security Council sanctions has been widely recognised.[35] After all, these measures are contrasted with mere recommendations in the text of the provision itself. They are 'decisions' for the purposes of Article 25 of the Charter, thus states have no room for deliberation in terms of implementing sanctions. The International Court of Justice (ICJ) has also declared that such decisions of the Security Council fall within the scope of obligations under the Charter, and thus prevail over other obligations in international law by virtue of Article 103.[36]

8.3 From Blanket to (Not So) Smart Sanctions

The Council invoked Article 41 for the first time in 1966, in imposing an embargo against Southern Rhodesia after the Smith regime declared independence of the UK

---

[31] *Prosecutor v Tadic* (Jurisdiction) [1995] IT-94-AR72, para 35.

[32] Ibid.

[33] Orakhelashvili 2011, p. 26.

[34] Krisch 2012, p. 1310.

[35] *Prosecutor v Tadic* (Jurisdiction) [1995] IT-94-AR72, para 31; *Lockerbie (Libya v UK)* (Provisional Measures) [1992] ICJ Rep 3, paras 35–40.

[36] *Case Concerning Paramilitary Activities in and against Nicaragua (Nicaragua v USA)* [1984] (Jurisdiction and Admissibility) ICJ Rep 132, para 107.

in order to establish white majority rule.[37] Later, in 1977, having regard to the acts of the apartheid government, the Council imposed an arms embargo on South Africa.[38] These two instances were exceptions rather than the rule of the time, as during the Cold War the Security Council found itself strangled in political deadlock, with the permanent members unable to reach the unanimity required to take enforcement action with any regularity.

Since the fall of the Berlin Wall, an invigorated Security Council has demonstrated a seismic quantitative and qualitative expansion of its sanctions practice. Quantitatively, economic sanctions have now been used in more than thirty cases. There are currently fourteen ongoing sanctions regimes. The Council's response to the Iraqi invasion of Kuwait in 1990, in particular, brought forth a 'sanctions decade',[39] during which time mandatory sanctions were also imposed against the former Yugoslavia,[40] Somalia,[41] Libya,[42] Liberia,[43] Haiti,[44] Rwanda,[45] Sudan,[46] Sierra Leone,[47] and Afghanistan.[48]

A defining aspect of these initial sanctions regimes is that they were addressed to states. This is logical; after all, the UN has no formal authority over any entity other than its members. However, the practice of comprehensive, blanket sanctions against the state as a whole came to be increasingly criticised on the basis of humanitarian considerations.[49] Specifically, blanket sanctions tend to disproportionately impact the civilian population of targeted states. As former Secretary-General Boutros Boutros-Ghali observed:

> Sanctions, as is generally recognized, are a blunt instrument. They raise the ethical question of whether suffering inflicted on vulnerable groups in the target country is a legitimate means

---

[37] UNSC Res 232 (1966). See further, UNSC Res 253 (1968); UNSC Res 277 (1970).

[38] UNSC Res 418 (1977).

[39] Van den Herik 2014, p. 431.

[40] UNSC Res 713 (1991) and UNSC Res 757 (1992) (arms embargo and economic sanctions following military involvement in Bosnia and Herzegovina); UNSC Res 1160 (1998) (arms embargo concerning activities in Kosovo).

[41] UNSC Res 733 (1992) (arms embargo following outbreak of civil conflict).

[42] UNSC Res 748 (1992); UNSC Res 883 (1993) (arms and air traffic embargo in context of refusal to extradite perpetrators of the Lockerbie bombing).

[43] UNSC Res 788 (1992) (arms embargo following ceasefire violations).

[44] UNSC Res 841 (1993) (arms embargo and petroleum sanctions in response to the failure of the military regime to restore the legitimate government).

[45] UNSC Res 918 (1994) (arms embargo in context of systemic internal violence).

[46] UNSC Res 1054 (1996); UNSC Res 1070 (1996) (restrictions on Sudanese officials abroad following an assassination attempt against the Egyptian President).

[47] UNSC Res 1132 (1997) (arms embargo and petroleum sanctions following military coup).

[48] UNSC Res 1267 (15 October 1999) (travel restrictions and asset freeze against Taliban regime, following failure to extradite Usama bin Laden).

[49] E.g. O'Connell 2002; Craven 2002.

8 UN Security Council Sanctions and International Peace and ... 181

of exerting pressure on political leaders whose behaviour is unlikely to be affected by the plight of their subjects. Sanctions also always have unintended or unwanted effects.[50]

Initially, the permanent members of the Security Council seemed to be attuned to this dilemma. In 1995, their ambassadors wrote collectively to the President of the Council, agreeing that 'future sanctions regimes should be directed to minimize unintended adverse side-effects of sanctions on the most vulnerable segments of targeted countries'.[51] However, reform was slow to come. After nearly a decade of sanctions against Iraq, which one commentator provocatively described as 'sanctions of mass destruction',[52] in 2000, the UN Human Rights Commission's Sub-Commission on the Promotion and Protection of Human Rights suggested that the sanctions against Iraq were 'unequivocally illegal' under existing international human rights law and humanitarian law.[53] The monitoring body for the International Covenant on Economic, Social and Cultural Rights also repeatedly expressed concern in its general comments about the impact of economic sanctions on the enjoyment of human rights.[54]

In an important move, this pressure led directly to a more qualitative shift in Security Council policy. Today, it is more common for the Council to target sanctions measures against specific individuals or entities within states, as opposed to states as a whole. Sanctions had already been imposed against a non-state entity in the form of UNITA forces in Angola.[55] However, the 1267 and 1333 counter-terrorism sanctions regimes, adopted in light of the suspected involvement of Osama Bin Laden in attacks on US embassies in Kenya and Tanzania, which saw a surge after the events of 9/11, are most symptomatic of this shift.[56]

Contemporary sanctions are often described as 'smart sanctions', in the sense that they are more targeted and circumscribed. To some, they are evidence of a 'sea change that significantly advanced the sophistication of the sanctions instrument'.[57] However, it is not clear that this description is justified. Somewhat paradoxically, considering they were established against a backdrop of human rights concerns relating to blanket sanctions, so too targeted sanctions have been criticised for their

---

[50] 'Report of the Secretary-General on the Work of the Organization: Supplement to an Agenda for Peace' (1995) UN Doc A/50/60-S/1995/1, para 70.

[51] UN Doc S/1995/300 (1995).

[52] O'Connell 2002, p. 63; Mueller and Mueller 1999, p. 49. 'No one knows with any precision how many Iraqi civilians have died as a result [of the sanctions], but various agencies of the United Nations ... have estimated that they have contributed to hundreds of thousands of deaths.'

[53] UN Commission on Human Rights, Sub-Commission on the Promotion and Protection of Human Rights, 'The Adverse Consequences of Economic Sanctions on the Enjoyment of Human Rights' (2000) UN Doc ECN.4/Sub.2/2000/33, at para 6.

[54] E.g. UN Committee on Economic, Social and Economic Rights General Comment 8, 'The Relationship between Economic Sanctions and Respect for Economic, Social and Cultural Rights' (1997) UN Doc E/C.12-1997/8.

[55] UNSC Res 864 (1993) (arms embargo and petroleum sanctions, following UNITA's failure to observe a ceasefire agreement).

[56] See UNSC Res 1267 (1999); UNSC Res 1333 (2000).

[57] Cortight et al. 2008, p. 207.

potentially far-reaching encroachments on the rights and freedoms of those targeted. It quickly became clear that the 'state-orientated institutional framework was architecturally unprepared to accommodate the individual as a new target of sanctions'.[58] Those caught in the Council sanctions net have only very limited possibilities to seek reasons and redress.

Accountability questions arise specifically concerning the procedures for listing and delisting individuals. With regards to listing, although the formal responsibility for the creation of sanctions lists lies with the 1267 Sanctions Committee, which comprises all fifteen members of the Council, names are submitted by individual member states. Decisions are generally made on a 'no-objection procedure'; that is, a proposed name will be added to the list if no committee member objects to the listing within ten working days.[59] In practice, 'there is little or no independent evaluation of the evidence',[60] which gives 'an almost unlimited latitude of discretionary powers to member states'.[61]

This practice benefits permanent members of the Council disproportionately, who are normally the states that submit the name to the Committee. Permanent members have always been 'careful to maintain the ad hoc nature' of the listing process, 'so as to keep maximum control'.[62] The same degree of discretion is not afforded to the targeted individual's state of residence or their state of nationality, or the states of incorporation or location for entities. This is problematic, for it is precisely these states who are tasked with the implementation of sanctions decisions. These same states frequently complain that the Committee has added or removed a name without consulting them. This has led to accusations of double standards and elitism within the Council. There is a 'sense that the sanctions regime reflects the concerns of Committee members more than those of other Member States, including those that face the greatest threat' from terrorist groups.[63]

The lack of transparency relating to listing procedures is exasperated by the difficulty that individuals and entities face in challenging a decision. Initially, there was no obligation for the Committee or member states to even notify those affected. Although mandatory notification was introduced in 2008,[64] this did little to quell criticisms, for it was not coupled with an obligation to give reasons. To seek a justification to explain their listing, or ultimately to seek delisting, those targeted have no direct access to the Sanctions Committee. Until 2009, they were dependent on the agreement of their state of nationality or residence taking up their case on their behalf. If the relevant state was either unable or unwilling to take up the case or if

---

[58] Van den Herik 2014, p. 431.

[59] The ISIL (Da'esh) and Al-Qaida Sanctions Committee, 'Guidelines of the Committee for the Conduct of its Work' (2018), para 6(n).

[60] Hovell 2016a, p. 14.

[61] Ibid., p. 16.

[62] Van den Herik 2014, p. 4.

[63] 'Report of the Analytical Support and Sanctions Monitoring Team' (2010) UN Doc S/2010/497, para 24.

[64] See UNSC Res 1822 (2008), para 19.

Council members were unwilling to negotiate, this was the end of the road.[65] The Council has since established an Ombudsperson procedure, which is discussed in more detail below, but the fact remains that individuals cannot access the Sanctions Committee directly.

If evidence was to be sought that international law has been slow to respond to the controversies of Security Council sanctions, initially the only restrictions on the Security Council were self-imposed, there were no external constraints. With blanket sanctions, self-imposed restrictions took the form of exempting certain goods from its measures, such as those intended for medical purposes.[66] As the policy shifted towards targeted measures, decisions typically make an exception from asset freezes for certain 'basic expenses', or allow for travel out of 'humanitarian need'.[67] Article 50 of the Charter does grant third states that are confronted with economic problems arising from economic sanctions a right to consult with the Council.[68] However, exceptions based on such consultation remain voluntary and the Council maintains the discretion to disregard them on a case by case basis. The question lingered (and to some extent still lingers) as to whether, beyond political and diplomatic accountability mechanisms, the Council itself is subject to any legal limitation in its sanctioning practice.

8.4 (Individual) Rights and (UN) Responsibilities

8.4.1 Specific Rights Engaged

Security Council sanctions raise several questions concerning their compatibility with international human rights law. They may give rise to rights claims for individuals caught up in the Council's sanctions net. It is also worth pointing out that Security Council sanctions also potentially engage the rights of persons or entities who are not directly targeted by sanctions, but who may be affected consequentially, for example, if their business interests are affected by financial restrictions or trade embargoes, or who may have a claim to property that has been seized.[69] If the individuals directly affected had no access to redress, however, traditionally these third parties had no leg to stand on.

The first category of rights engaged relates to the principle of 'due process'. The gulf between Security Council decision-making and the individuals affected, in terms of access to information, participation and redress, raises a significant red flag. The internationally recognised right to due process refers to the general 'right of a person

---

[65] Hovell 2016a, p. 20.

[66] See Krisch 2012, p. 1315.

[67] See, e.g., UNSC Res 1988 (2011).

[68] See further Security Council Provisional Rules of Procedure, rule 37.

[69] Krisch 2012, p. 1318.

or entity to an effective remedy against an individual measure before an impartial institution or body'.[70] At the most abstract level, the principle *audi alteram partem* (hear the other side) is generally accepted as a principle of procedural justice.[71] This principle, in its more substantive form, is generally taken to encompass two elements. The first is the 'right to be heard', or the right to challenge any measure which might adversely affect an individual. If the challenge is successful, the second element is the 'right to redress', or the right to an effective remedy before an impartial tribunal or other body. A majority of judicial and scholarly authority contends that together these rights constitute customary international law. In light of constitutional recognition in the great majority of domestic and regional jurisdictions, there is also a strong argument that the 'right to a fair trial' is protected as a general principle of international law.[72]

We can also trace the importance of due process rights in specific human rights instruments. Article 10 of the Universal Declaration of Human Rights, for example, provides for the 'right to be heard'. It states that '[e]veryone is entitled in full equality to a fair and public hearing by an independent and impartial tribunal, in the determination of his rights and obligations and of any criminal charge against him'. Article 8 provides for 'the right to an effective remedy by the competent national tribunals for acts violating the fundamental rights granted him by the constitution or by law'. Articles 10 and 8 can be read together as crystallising the two constitutive elements of due process. In turn, Article 14(1) of the International Covenant on Civil and Politics Rights similarly pronounces that '[i]n the determination of ... his rights and obligations in a suit at law, everyone shall be entitled to a fair and public hearing by a competent, independent and impartial tribunal established by law'.

In turn, these international human rights instruments have clearly influenced their regional counterparts. Article 6(1) of the European Convention on Human Rights provides that '[i]n the determination of his civil rights and obligations or of any criminal charge against him, everyone is entitled to a fair and public hearing within a reasonable time by an independent and impartial tribunal established by law'. This provision served as a protocol for similar provisions in other regional human rights instruments, in the Americas and Africa in particular.

More specific rights may be engaged in certain, but not all, instances. *Inter alia*, the freezing of an individual's assets may touch upon the presumption of innocence.[73] Travel bans may impinge an individual's freedom of movement,[74] or rights and freedoms such as the freedom of religion if the particular religion requires pilgrimages, for example.[75] It has also been suggested that, in the extreme, sanctions could conceivably violate the right to life,[76] for instance, if a travel ban prevents a targeted

---

[70] Fassbender 2006, p. 28.

[71] Ibid., p. 11.

[72] In accordance with the Statute of the ICJ (1945), Article 38(1).

[73] ECHR (1950), Article 6(2).

[74] ICCPR (1966), Article 12; ECHR (Protocol 4) (1963), Article 2.

[75] ICCPR (1966), Article 18; ECHR, Article 9.

[76] ICCPR (1966), Article 6; ECHR, Article 2.

person from leaving the country to seek medical treatment, or when financial sanctions are so stringent that a targeted person does not have the resources to buy basic goods such as food.[77]

Finally, the seizure of property could engage a range of privacy, reputation and family rights,[78] or the right to property more generally. Article 1 of the First Additional Protocol to the European Convention enshrines the right accordingly: 'Every natural or legal person is entitled to the peaceful enjoyment of his possessions. No one shall be deprived of his possessions except in the public interest and subject to the conditions provided for by law and by the general principles of international law'. It is notable, however, that the relevant case law offers a significant margin of appreciation to states regarding freezing orders regarding property rights, especially as compared to due process rights. That said, the two considerations are far from mutually exclusive. For example, the question of whether the restriction of the right to property is justified should be read in light of the individual's right to be heard.[79]

8.4.2 Legal Limitations on Security Council Sanctions

While it is relatively straightforward to identify the individual rights that are potentially in play in the context of Security Council sanctions, whether these rights can be directly enforced against the Council is more questionable. To challenge a sanctions resolution, it would have to be shown that the resolution engages the international legal responsibility of the UN. There are three main points to consider: whether the UN Charter itself provides legal constraints upon the Council, whether the Council is obliged to comply with general international law, most notably customary human rights law and, in any event, whether international courts and tribunals may judicially review Council decision-making. The first two will be addressed in this section, the final section will discuss challenging the legality of sanctions decisions.

8.4.2.1 The *Lex Specialis*

The UN Charter, as the organisation's *lex specialis*, is the logical place to begin when considering the Council's legal obligations. In a general sense, the Security Council should respect the text and spirit of the UN Charter, the 'constitutional' treaty from which it derives its power. This follows from the proposition that the Council's power is not inherent but is in the nature of delegated power. Thus, any specific competence must be either explicitly or implicitly conferred via the Charter. The ICJ has made clear that the Council must respect the 'treaty provisions established by the Charter when they constitute limitations on its powers or criteria for its judgment.

---

[77] For this argument, see De Wet 2004, pp. 219–220.

[78] ICCPR (1966), Article 17; ECHR, Article 8.

[79] *AGOSI v UK* [1987] (ECrtHR, Chamber) App no 9118/90.

To ascertain whether an organ has freedom of choice for its decision, reference must be made to the terms of its constitution'.[80] Although the specific source of these limitations can, at times, be difficult to pinpoint, the International Criminal Tribunal for the Former Yugoslavia found, surely correctly, that 'neither the text nor the spirit of the Charter conceives the Security Council as *legibus solutus* (unbound by law)'.[81] In identifying the relevant rules, the Council is under an obligation to comply with a number of procedural rules under the Charter, particularly those referring to the right of the veto. Beyond that, three provisions of the Charter might plausibly (but not altogether persuasively) be interpreted to impose more substantive constraints on sanctions decision-making.

Article 39 serves, at the very least, as a necessary precondition before the Council may impose Chapter VII measures.[82] Considering the functional connection between Articles 39 and 41, we might ask whether the obligation to first make a determination that a situation constitutes a 'threat to the peace', 'a breach of the peace' or an 'act of aggression' before imposing sanctions coincides with an obligation to ensure that such a determination is objectively and legally verifiable. In other words, whether an arbitrary determination of the same would render a resolution *ultra vires*.

To answer this question, we have to ask whether the terms themselves carry any juridical meaning. To a certain extent, the notion of a 'breach of the peace' is straightforward, for it implies that a state is responsible for breaching the peace, read as 'the serious outbreak of armed hostilities'.[83] Likewise, although the nature of an act of aggression is slightly more contested, guidance can be sought from the Definition of Aggression adopted by the General Assembly in 1974.[84] The 1974 definition was largely followed at Kampala in a meeting of the state parties of the ICC. While the ICC, by definition, focusses on individual liability, it views aggression through the prism of the Charter, with its definition echoing Article 2(4) almost verbatim.[85] There is a strong argument to suggest, therefore, that a determination of either a 'breach of the peace' or an 'act of aggression' that does not involve armed hostilities would be to stretch the ordinary meaning of these terms too far.

In keeping with the links to Article 2(4), we might be tempted to suggest that a 'threat to the peace' constitutes a threat of the use of force. However, this doctrinal link should not be assumed. On numerous occasions, the Council has determined a situation as a 'threat to the peace' which does not involve the use of force at all. Article 2(4) therefore provides no guidance when ascertaining the legality of a finding of a 'threat to the peace', in the way that it could be said for the other terms within

---

[80] *Conditions of Admission* (Advisory Opinion) [1948] ICJ Rep 57, para 64.

[81] *Prosecutor v Tadic* (Jurisdiction) [1995] IT-94-AR72, para 28.

[82] See *Behrami* (General Court) (ECrtHR) [2007] App Nos 7142/01 and 78166/01, para 128.

[83] De Wet 2004, p. 144.

[84] UNGA Res 3314 (XXIX) (1974).

[85] After decades of negotiations, the Court now has jurisdiction over the crime of aggression. See ICC Assembly of States Parties, 'Draft resolution proposed by the Vice-Presidents of the Assembly Activation of the jurisdiction of the Court over the crime of aggression' (2017) UN Doc ICC-ASP/16/L.10.

8 UN Security Council Sanctions and International Peace and …

Article 39. In comparison, the concept of a 'threat to the peace' appears somehow less tangible, more open to interpretation.

The elastic nature of the term 'threat to the peace' is potentially problematic, for it is this notion that the Council invariably refers to in the course of imposing sanctions.[86] From one perspective, while the Council's discretion in deciding what situations constitute a 'threat to the peace' is considerably wide, it is not unfettered, as a 'discretion can only exist within the law'.[87] Tzanakopoulos argues that the Council has discretionary power to select any of a range of possible alternative meanings to the term 'threat to the peace' as long as the meaning remains, but does not exceed, the 'interpretative radius of the provision'.[88] The argument is based on the presumption that the term 'threat to the peace' has to mean something, that it cannot be interpreted *contra legem*. Such an interpretation would be contrary to the well-established principle that if two interpretations of a provision are possible, but one of them would render the provision redundant, the other interpretation is to be preferred.[89] Taken to its logical conclusion, Tzanakopoulos contends that this 'moulds a procedural obligation into a substantial one'.[90]

This would seem to be an overly formalistic argument. While one could disagree on the facts with the Council's determination of a threat to the peace, it is practically very difficult to conceive a situation in which a determination of the Council explicitly contravenes the Charter and is thus invalid on the grounds that the Council is acting *ultra vires*.[91] In the *Kanyabashi* case, the International Criminal Tribunal for Rwanda concluded (I submit authoritatively), that the Council 'has a wide margin of discretion in deciding when and where there exists a threat to international peace and security. By their very nature, however, such discretionary assessments are not justiciable since they involve the consideration of social, political and circumstantial factors which cannot be weighed and balanced objectively'.[92]

The second provision of relevance to our enquiry is Article 25, pursuant to which member states 'agree to accept and carry out the decisions of the Security Council in accordance with the present Charter'. From one standpoint, Article 25 might be read as qualifying the mandatory nature of Council decisions, in the sense that member states are not obliged to carry out decisions that are outside the scope of the Charter.[93] Support for this view might be found in Article 2(5), which obliges states to respect Chapter VII resolutions that are adopted in accordance with the Charter. If it is the case that states are not bound to do so where a resolution contravenes the Charter,

---

[86] The Council has never made a determination of an 'act of aggression' and has only made a determination of a 'breach of the peace' on four occasions.

[87] Tzanakopoulos 2011, p. 61.

[88] Ibid., p. 62.

[89] Ibid., p. 63.

[90] Ibid., p. 62.

[91] Kelsen 1950, p. 727.

[92] *Prosecutor* v *Joseph Kanyabashi* (Decision on the Defence Motion for Interlocutory Appeal on Jurisdiction) [1997] ICTR-96-15-T, para 20.

[93] Tzanakopoulos 2011, p. 58 (emphasis in original).

it would be strange to suggest that states are bound under Article 25 to follow *ultra vires* decisions.[94]

However, we should treat this assumption with caution. The alternative view that Article 25 is merely a cross-reference to the fact that member states accept Chapter VII decisions as binding and not merely recommendatory remains compelling. From this perspective, the final stanza of Article 25 is descriptive as opposed to qualitative: it merely explains that the obligation to comply with all decisions derives from the Charter. If the wording of Article 25 must be taken to imply some constraint on the Council's decision-making, it might be read as confirming that decisions must comply with the formal voting procedures; that is, be supported by nine member states including the affirmative vote or abstention of all permanent members. There is less evidence, in practice, that Article 25 implies a substantive constraint further to this procedural requirement.

The most explicit constraint on Security Council conduct is found in Article 24(2), which mandates that in discharging its duties the Security Council must respect the purposes and principles of the UN contained in Articles 1 and 2.[95] However, these purposes are notoriously broad and vague, to the point that their utility in serving as a constraint on the Council is doubtful. The first purpose of the UN is the most important:

> ... to take effective collective measures for the prevention and removal of threats to the peace, and for the suppression of acts of aggression or other breaches of the peace, and to bring about by peaceful means, and in conformity with the principles of justice and international law, adjustment or settlement of international disputes or situations which might lead to a breach of the peace.[96]

Two points can be elucidated from the wording of Article 1(1). First, it is important to note that reference to 'the principles of justice and international law' is limited to where the Security Council is acting to settle disputes 'by peaceful means', in other words under Chapter VI. The first part of Article 1, the taking of 'effective collective measures' relates to Chapter VII decisions, and it is not similarly qualified. The implication is that it would appear that, when acting under Chapter VII, the Council is permitted to derogate from the existing rules of international law. Indeed, this omission is no coincidence, but instead represents a conscious decision on the part of the drafters. In San Francisco, several attempts were made to explicitly require Chapter VII measures to respect general international law, but these were rejected.

Secondly, the argument that the purposes of the UN constrain the Council in substantive terms is further undermined by the position of the purposes relative to one another. It might be argued that enforcement measures should not undermine the essence of self-determination,[97] or international human rights or humanitarian

---

[94] See, e.g., De Wet 2004, p. 377.

[95] 'The duty is imperative and the limits are categorically stated'. *Lockerbie (Libya v USA)* (Provisional Measures) [1992] ICJ Rep 114 (Dissenting Opinion of Judge Weeramantry), p. 171.

[96] UN Charter (1945), Article 1(1).

[97] UN Charter (1945), Article 1(2).

law, as these are also listed among the purposes of the UN.[98] However, Article 24(2) refers to the purposes and principles collectively, which implies that Security Council conduct would only violate them if it failed to correspond with all of them. It is very difficult, is not impossible, to argue that enforcement action can simultaneously violate all of the purposes of the UN, considering that Article 1(1) of the Charter lists the maintenance of international peace and security as its first purpose. As the ICJ confirmed in the *Certain Expenses* case:

> The primary place ascribed to international peace and security is natural, since the fulfilment of the other purposes will be dependent upon the attainment of that basic condition. These purposes are broad indeed, but neither they nor the powers conferred to effectuate them are unlimited.[99]

Of course, it does not follow that in the realisation of this goal the Council can disregard the other purposes of the Charter altogether. The structure of the purposes and principles is, therefore, in the nature of a hierarchy as opposed to supremacy. The Security Council must balance the maintenance of international peace and security with the realisation of the secondary goals of the Charter.[100] However, it is submitted that, by virtue of its position at the head of the purposes of the UN, the maintenance of international peace and security is the most important and, as a result, 'all other objectives can be related to this purpose'.[101] The Council will, in practice, always frame its decisions to be in line with Article 1(1). Since the specific formula of invoking Chapter VII requires a determination that a situation constitutes a threat to the peace, all Chapter VII decisions will *de facto* be said to be furthering the purposes, as opposed to conflicting with the same. The purposes are, therefore, so broad that almost any decision could be said to further them.[102]

The influence of the principles, under Article 2, is even more circumscribed. The main reason for this is that respect for state sovereignty, reiterated in various ways by Articles 2(1), 2(4) and 2(7), cannot apply to Security Council enforcement action under Chapter VII The very nature of enforcement action implies that it is not predicated on a state's consent, which is a core element of state sovereignty. Enforcement measures are thus explicitly listed as an exception in the principle of domestic jurisdiction in the final part of Article 2(7).

All in all, there can be little doubt that the Charter does provide some limitations on Council decision-making, but these limitations are notoriously ambiguous, making it very difficult to use the Charter to construct a meaningful regime to constrain the Council.

---

[98] UN Charter (1945), Article 1(3).

[99] *Certain Expenses of the United Nations* (Advisory Opinion) [1962] ICJ 151, p. 168.

[100] De Wet 2004, p. 193. See further Peters 2012, p. 812. 'The 'purposes' as enumerated in Article 1 are so sweeping and abstract that [it] is hardly conceivable that the Council take any decision which cannot be said to further them'.

[101] Peters 2012, p. 812.

[102] Ibid.

8.4.2.2 The *Lex Generalis*

The question as to whether the Council is bound by sources external to the Charter is even more contested. As Daugirdas contends, 'the answers that scholars have given to the question of whether general international law binds [international organisations] include: maybe, sometimes, and always'.[103] That said, the answer is rarely 'never', which necessitates an analysis of the arguments traditionally put forward to test their persuasiveness. As the Council is not directly party to any international human rights instruments, the consensus view is that it cannot be directly bound by them. Instead, it has been suggested that the Council is bound indirectly. There are four potential lines of argument. We will consider each in turn.[104]

The first suggests that it is implausible that member states forego their own human rights obligations when transferring competences to international organisations, so the member's responsibility continues even after the transfer. This reasoning resonates with Reinisch's proposal of a 'functional treaty succession' by international organisations to the position of their member states. That is, it suggests that the Council is bound 'transitively' by international human rights standards as a result and to the extent that its members are bound.[105] However, there is nothing in this argument to suggest that the organisation itself is responsible. The proposition that the Council is bound simply because most of its members are bound is only plausible upon a conception of the Council as a mere vehicle for its member states, and it would make a mockery of the separate legal personality of the UN.

Alternatively, it might be argued that the Council has bound itself to respect human rights in its own declarations and practice.[106] This might be taken to demonstrate that the Council does not intend to violate human rights in its resolutions. That said, it is one thing for the Council to acknowledge, rhetorically, the importance of human rights compliance in its decision-making.[107] It is quite another thing to suggest that this manifests in a conclusive undertaking to do so in all instances. It is another thing altogether to read in an acceptance that when the Council departs from human rights compliance its international legal responsibilities are engaged. In any event, the Council is under no legal obligation to follow its own previous decisions and statements.

Thirdly, some scholars have argued that the UN is under a particular obligation with respect to treaties concluded under its auspices. However, the operationalisation

---

[103] Daugirdas 2016, p. 335.

[104] These arguments draw heavily on Peters 2012, pp. 822–825.

[105] Reinisch 2001, p. 143.

[106] See, e.g., UNSC Res 1456 (2003), para 6. 'States must ensure that any measure taken to combat terrorism comply with all their obligations under international law, and should adopt such measures in accordance with international law, in particular, international human rights, refugee, and humanitarian law.'

[107] See, e.g., 'Statement by the President of the Security Council' (29 June 2010) UN Doc S/PRST/2010/11, at 2: 'The Council reiterates the need to ensure that sanctions are carefully targeted in support of clear objectives and designed carefully so as to minimize possible adverse consequences'.

of this rule would be extremely problematic; there is no general rule in international law that specifies that facilitating the conclusion of a treaty, or being a beneficiary of a treaty, helps to create duties. Therefore, finally, the only possible argument is that the Council might be said to be bound by those human rights norms that have passed over into general international law (customary international law and general principles of law). Indeed, the ICJ has long maintained that 'international organizations are subjects of international law, and, as such, are bound by any obligations incumbent upon them under general rules of international law'.[108]

However, while many human rights norms have surely crossed over into customary international law, it does not automatically follow that there has been a shift in the primary addressees of these rules from states to international organisations.[109] Thus, for the Council to be bound by customary international human rights, this would require a structural change: the relevant obligations to respect, protect and fulfil would need to be extended to the UN, and such a 'normative evolution would have to be based on [state] practice and *opinio juris*'.[110] So far it is difficult to identify such an evolution.

While the argument that all human rights law binds the Security Council is ultimately unpersuasive, the lowest common denominator is that, at the very least, those customary human rights norms that constitute peremptory norms of international law do conclusively bind the Council in its sanctions decision-making.[111] The peremptory norms of international law represent those norms that have been 'accepted and recognized by the international community of States as a whole as a norm from which no derogation is permitted'.[112] While it may be possible to argue that certain other rules of general international law are incumbent upon the Council in certain circumstances, it will always be open to members of the Security Council to launch some other argument to show that the breach is covered by an exception to that rule. The illegality emanating from the breach of *jus cogens* is, conversely, immediate and objective. As such, the basis of the illegality is the breach of the rule as such, regardless of the attitude of specific actors. The result is that the applicability of peremptory norms to a given situation—or the legality of a given fact, or action—would not be prejudiced by how the Council treats that act or situation.[113]

To be sure, the application of *jus cogens* to Security Council decisions technically removes the concept from its natural heritage. Article 53 of the Vienna Convention on the Law of Treaties, after all, reads: 'a *treaty* is void if, at the time of its conclusion, it conflicts with a peremptory norm of general international law'. Responsibility indeed falls, first and foremost, on states to bring their mutual relations in conformity with *jus cogens* norms. However, the state-centric heritage of *jus cogens* norms is not

---

[108] *Interpretation of the Agreement between the WHO and Egypt* (Advisory Opinion) [1980] ICJ Rep 73, pp. 89–90.

[109] Peters 2012, p. 824.

[110] Ibid.

[111] De Wet 2004, pp. 187–191; Orakhelashvili 2005, p. 59; Tzanakopoulos 2011, pp. 70–72.

[112] Vienna Convention on the Law of Treaties (1969), Article 53.

[113] Orakhelashvili 2005, pp. 77–78.

necessarily an insurmountable hurdle. If peremptory norms permit no derogation, it follows that states should not be permitted to delegate out of their own peremptory obligations.[114]

The Charter is itself a treaty, so where the implementation of a binding Council decision would result in a violation of a *jus cogens* norm, 'member states would be relieved from giving effect to the obligation in question'.[115] The relief that Article 103 of the Charter may offer the Security Council in the case of a conflict between one of its decisions and an operative treaty obligation cannot—as a matter of simple hierarchy of norms—extend to a conflict between a Security Council resolution and *jus cogens*.[116] As de Wet notes, the stakes are extremely high: if the Charter can override the peremptory norms of *jus cogens*, then 'states could instrumentalise the collective security system in order to engage in slavery, apartheid or even genocide, provided that the requisite majority in the Security Council can be secured'.[117] Such a position cannot be supported.

In short, whether the Charter itself constrains the Security Council's ability to impose sanctions and, if so, to what extent, is extremely contested. I have suggested that doctrinal attempts to identify such constraints in the Charter often overplay the role that Articles 1 and 2 can play in this regard. There is some consensus that the Council is obliged to comply with customary international law, especially customary human rights law, but it is less clear *why* and *how* this is the case as a matter of legal doctrine. There is almost unanimous agreement, however, that the Security Council must at the very least respect the peremptory norms of international law in its sanctioning practice.

8.5 Challenging Sanctions Inside and Outside the Courtroom

8.5.1 The ICJ

The ICJ is 'the principal judicial organ' of the UN.[118] The question arises, based on the discussion of the legal limitations on the Security Council's sanctioning practice above, as to whether the ICJ has the power to 'judicially review' sanctions resolutions and to declare decisions null and void if they are deemed incompatible with the Council's legal obligations. However, the ICJ is not formally conferred this role. In

---

[114] Orakhelashvili 2005, p. 68.

[115] De Wet 2004, p. 188.

[116] *Application of the Convention on the Prevention and Punishment of the Crime of Genocide (Bosnia & Herzegovina v Serbia & Montenegro)* (Provisional Measures) (Separate Opinion of Judge Lauterpacht) [1993] ICJ Rep 407, para 440.

[117] De Wet 2004, pp. 189–190; Tzanakopoulos 2011, p. 71. '…if States cannot escape the operation of *jus cogens*, they certainly cannot create an [international organisation] which is unbound by it'.

[118] Statute of the ICJ (1945), Article 1.

fact, the court tends to operate on the general presumption of the legality of actions of the Security Council,[119] and traditionally extends a good deal of discretion to the Council to determine the extent and breadth of its own powers. In any event, judgments and advisory opinions of the Court do not enjoy general binding force 'except between the parties and in respect of that particular case'.[120] The Security Council cannot be a party to a case before the court,[121] and although its sanctioning practice could be relevant to a case involving a state that is mandated to implement its resolutions, or could arise in the course of ICJ advisory proceedings, such review of the Council's practice would be incidental to the case at hand. Any accountability function that the court might exercise would, by definition, be indirect.

8.5.2 *Regional and Domestic Courts*

The ambiguity surrounding limits to Security Council sanctions in international law, coupled with the lack of direct judicial review at the ICJ, opens up something of a lacuna in terms of the judicial protection (or lack thereof) afforded to those implicated in the Council's sanctions net. Interestingly, this void has been filled primarily by regional and domestic courts. In recent times, we have witnessed an increasing use of extremely strong language to communicate judicial disapproval of the sanctions regime. The UK Supreme Court has used the powerful term 'prisoners of the state' to characterise the plight of those targeted, concluding that the 'draconian nature of the [sanctions] regime ... can hardly be over-stated'.[122] The Canadian Federal Court criticised the 'denial of basic legal remedies' for targeted individuals as 'untenable under the principles of international law'.[123]

Crucially, the formal source for rights claims before regional and domestic courts lies not in international law but constitutional law, as constitutional courts may block the implementation of sanctions resolutions in their local jurisdictional sphere.[124] The European Court of Human Rights and the Court of Justice of the European Union, in particular, have developed judicial strategies in an attempt to minimise (or avoid altogether) conflicts between international law and the regional legal order. One technique favoured by the Strasbourg court in *Nada*, contrary to the conventional wisdom that member states enjoy almost no discretion in implementing sanctions,[125]

---

[119] *Certain Expenses* (Advisory Opinion) [1962] ICJ Rep 151, p. 168.

[120] UN Charter (1945), Article 59.

[121] Statute of the ICJ (1945), Article 34(1).

[122] *HM Treasury v Ahmed and others* [2010] UKSC 2, para 4.

[123] *Abelrazik v Canada* [2009] FC 580, para 51.

[124] Krisch 2012, p. 1318.

[125] UN Charter (1945), Articles 25 and 103.

is to suggest that states do have some latitude to harmonise, where possible, obligations under Security Council resolutions with their human rights obligations under the Convention.[126]

A similar avoidance strategy was utilised by the same court in the *Al-Dulimi* and *Al-Jedda* cases. The court suggested that legal analysis should start from 'a presumption that the Security Council does not intend to impose an obligation on member states to breach fundamental rights'.[127] From this point of departure, the court surmised that 'it is to be expected that clear and explicit language would be used were the Security Council to intend States to take particular measures which would conflict with their obligations'.[128] In the absence of such explicit language, the court held that it must choose the interpretation most in line with the requirements of the Convention. The method of harmonising member state's conflicting obligations is normatively appealing, it offers relief to the appellant in the instant case but does not rule specifically on the question of the supremacy of obligations that derive from Security Council resolutions. This is only possible, however, when such harmonisation is conceivable.

An alternative approach was evidenced in the now infamous *Kadi* case before the courts of the European Union. In the first iteration of the case, the Court of First Instance followed a conventional deferential approach to the Security Council. It held that, under Article 103 of the Charter, the obligation to implement Security Council sanctions prevails over every other obligation, even those provided under the European Union treaties.[129] From this, it followed according to the court that EU institutions had no 'autonomous discretion' to alter the content of the resolutions at issue to ensure that the individual's rights were protected.[130] The court concluded that it had no jurisdiction to review the lawfulness of Security Council decisions 'according to the standard of protection of fundamental rights as recognised by the [European] Community legal order ... such jurisdiction would be incompatible with the undertakings of member states under the Charter'.[131]

However, on appeal, the European Court of Justice took an altogether different, remarkably interventionist approach. It invalidated the regulation giving effect to the relevant Security Council sanctions resolutions, specifically on the basis that the regulation violated fundamental rights protected by the European legal order.[132] In something of a judicial sleight of hand, the court went to great lengths to emphasise that it was not engaging in a review of the lawfulness of the resolution, but rather 'the Community act intended to give effect to that resolution'.[133] It suggested that

---

[126] *Nada v Switzerland* (Grand Chamber) [2012] App no 10593/08, paras 175–180.

[127] *Al-Dulimi & Montana Management v Switzerland* (Grand Chamber) [2016] App no 5809/08, para 140; *Al-Jedda v UK* (Grand Chamber) [2011] App no 27021/08, para 102.

[128] Ibid.

[129] *Kadi v Council and Commission* [2005] ECR II-0000, para 181.

[130] Ibid., paras 213–214.

[131] Ibid., paras 221–222.

[132] *Kadi v Council of the European Union* [2008] ECR I-0000.

[133] Ibid., para 278.

the relevant assessment was the compatibility of the implementing EU regulation with 'principles of liberty, democracy and respect for human rights and fundamental freedoms enshrined in Article 6(1) [of the Treaty on European Union] as a foundation of the union'.[134] The decision to annul the implementing regulation on this basis was subsequently upheld in 2010 by the then renamed General Court and in 2013 by the Court of Justice of the European Union.

On the whole, the activism demonstrated by regional and domestic courts has to be welcomed, after decades of unwillingness on the part of the Security Council to engage thoroughly with the accountability critique by reforming its own decision-making procedures. It serves as a useful counteractive to the inability of the international legal framework to hold the Security Council to account. Where international legal rules to constrain the Security Council seem somehow too nebulous, and where the principal judicial organ of the UN lacks jurisdiction to directly review Council decisions, the *Kadi* approach at least offers genuine judicial protection of due process rights.

That said, it is important to take a step back and reflect critically upon the true impact of this judicial trend, both from the perspective of fairness for targeted individuals but also from the Security Council's own perspective. If it continues, this trend has potentially dramatic implications for how we should understand the Council's authority vis-à-vis member states and, considering its 'primary responsibility for the maintenance of international peace and security', in relation to the overall effectiveness of the sanctions regime. It must first be acknowledged that from the standpoint of the individual, notwithstanding its normative appeal, review by domestic and regional courts does not offer a panacea for the range of controversies and other (non-legal) challenges to sanctions decisions. It is important to maintain caution when we consider the fragmented nature of such oversight, and the fragmented nature of the rules being applied, making it difficult to envisage a more unified and systematic approach. As Hovell notes, if we were to attempt to universalise this model of protection it might risk further contributing to the 'distorted conception of procedural fairness already present in the international sphere'.[135] It is surely no coincidence, for example, that Mr. Kadi, a Saudi-Arabian businessman born in Egypt, challenged his listing before European courts. In other jurisdictions, the regime of human rights protection may not be as robust, and judicial institutions may not feel as empowered to conduct this type of review.

In terms of the Security Council's authority, it is important to note that the *Kadi* approach represents a very particular view of the relationship between the European legal order and the international order. The court essentially determined this relationship in accordance with its own internal values and priorities rather than in light of any common principles or norms of international law. To some commentators, conceptualising the relationship in this way is highly reminiscent of a traditional dualist position.[136] However, in almost completely ignoring the international legal

---

[134] Ibid., para 303.

[135] Hovell 2016a, pp. 31–32.

[136] E.g. Isiksel 2010, p. 559.

framework that it is operating within, it may be more appropriate to talk of monism in reverse. While monism in this context traditionally relates to the privileging of international law at the expense of domestic or regional legal orders, under the *Kadi* approach the latter is privileged at the expense of—almost in ignorance of—international legal commitments. From the perspective of international law, the decision to disapply regulations implementing binding sanctions resolutions is technically unlawful. The orthodox position adopted by the Court of First Instance, which the apex court overturned, was surely correct: the mandatory nature of Security Council decisions technically prevails 'over every other obligation under the ECHR and ... under the EC Treaty'.[137] Again, this conclusion is not to deny the positive implications of this approach in the specific cases for the protection of individual rights. Instead, it is simply to draw attention to quite how bold this judicial intervention actually was.

In disregarding the supremacy of international law, therefore, the court's decision constitutes no less than 'an act of open judicial revolt against years of fruitless political dialogue'.[138] The decisions are thus best conceptualised as civil disobedience, defined as 'a conscientious yet political act contrary to law usually done with the aim of bringing about a change in the law or policies'.[139] From the perspective of civil disobedience, the series of cases have had a dramatic impact. We need only recall that the decision obliged some twenty-seven states to (indirectly) refuse compliance with Council sanctions. This is a not inconsiderable portion of the UN's membership. It is also important as the Council relies disproportionately on European states for the implementation of its decisions. The Council is not likely to risk a subsequent resolution again being ruled incompatible with fundamental rights protected by the EU treaties.

8.5.3 The Ombudsperson Procedure

Ultimately, the most significant consequence of the *Kadi* litigation is not so much the enhanced judicial protection of due process rights, but the response that it triggered in the Security Council itself. The Council had already established a 'focal point' initiative, a non-state-based forum to which designated individuals and entities could submit a request for delisting, in 2006. If anything, however, the focal point merely added an additional bureaucratic layer. Upon receiving a request for delisting, the focal point sent it to the designating state, the state of residence and the state of nationality. It was only if one of those states supported the request that the delisting

---

[137] *Kadi v Council & Commission* [2005] ECR II-0000, para 181.

[138] Hovell 2016b, pp. 157–158.

[139] Rawls 1971, p. 364.

request was placed on the Committee's agenda.[140] The impact of the focal point on the due process rights of individuals was extremely marginal.[141]

The inadequacy of the focal point as a procedural safeguard for individuals, coupled with the felt need to respond directly to the European judicature, led to the establishment of the Office of the UN Ombudsperson in 2009. The Ombudsperson reviews the claims of those who were listed under the 1267 regime. Although the Council has not yet established a similar procedure for other regimes that impose similar measures, it has had a significant impact.[142] Mirroring the institutional role of the Ombudsperson in other contexts, the role is not adjudicatory as much as it is inquisitorial. The Ombudsperson receives de-listing requests and engages in a process of information gathering which culminates in the production of a comprehensive report which lays out the principal arguments concerning the de-listing request. In a fundamental change, if the Ombudsperson recommends de-listing, the individual or entity is removed unless, within sixty days, the Sanctions Committee decides by consensus to maintain the listing. In practical terms, the process is cheaper for applicants, is relatively quick, and does not require legal representation.

To be sure, the Ombudsperson's decisions are non-binding and require voluntary compliance from the Security Council. But the Council normally does comply with the recommendations. The success is seen in its own nascent record: unlike a court-based process, the Ombudsperson can definitively secure the delisting of suspects. Of the 79 cases which have concluded through the Ombudsperson process, 54 individuals and 28 entities have been delisted and one entity has been removed as an alias of a listed entity. In addition, four individuals were delisted by the Committee before the Ombudsperson process was completed. The figures themselves illustrate the positive impact of the Ombudsperson procedure, but perhaps the best illustration is found in the most high-profile of all delisting requests, that of Mr. Kadi himself. Despite securing the judgment in his favour, this did not directly secure his delisting. Courts have no more of a direct influence on the Sanctions Committee than the states that they represent. It was the Office of the Ombudsperson that ultimately secured his delisting.

All this considered, in light of the Council's rather unique position in international society, which straddles international law and politics, the Ombudsperson framework appears a more appropriate locus for procedural protection than a court-based process.[143]

---

[140] UNGA Res 60/1 (2005), paras 106–109.

[141] Hovell 2016a, p. 21.

[142] UNSC Res 1904 (2009). The Resolution acknowledged in its preamble that the Office had been established as a direct result of the 'challenges, both legal and otherwise, to the measures implemented by member states'.

[143] For a compelling defence of the Ombudsperson procedure, see, generally, Hovell 2016a.

8.6 Conclusion

In the first part of this contribution, I attempted to place UN Security Council sanctions in their conceptual, institutional and historical context. The post-Cold War era can justifiably be labelled the 'sanctions era'. During the 1990s, the Council courted controversy after controversy, principally due to the disproportionate impact that blanket sanctions wielded on the civilian populations in targeted states. The Council responded, towards the end of that decade, by pivoting to more targeted sanctions against specific individuals and entities deemed to be responsible for 'threats to international peace and security', with a particular focus on those believed to be implicated in global terrorism. However, the defining feature of this shift has been not less but more controversy. Targeted individuals initially found themselves in something of a black hole: their assets frozen, a ban on travel, and yet they were provided with no or very little information as to why this was the case, and how to challenge their listing.

This situation clearly engaged certain well-established rights in international human rights law, not least those rights relating to procedural guarantees of a fair process. However, in fulfilling its 'primary responsibility for international peace and security', the Security Council has traditionally weighed effectiveness over other considerations (for example human rights compliance). Secure in the comfort blanket provided by Articles 25 and 103 of the Charter, which ensures that member states have very little wriggle-room in their obligation to implement sanctions, and safe in the knowledge that their own legal obligations under the *lex specialis* of the Charter and in general international law are nebulous at best, the Council was extremely slow to reform its practices. The final complicating factor is that the principal judicial organ of the UN, the ICJ, does not explicitly have the competence to review Security Council decisions, and this is not a role that it has shown any eagerness to take on for itself.

It is no surprise, based on the above, that subsequent debates have centred on how best to ensure fairness for targeted individuals by allowing them to challenge sanctions decisions, without compromising the Security Council's ability to effectively fulfil its peace and security mandate. What is perhaps more surprising, however, is how forcefully (and successfully) domestic and regional courts have stepped into the void left by the ICJ, most notably in the *Kadi* litigation before the courts of the European Union. In annulling regulations implementing Security Council sanctions, the Court of Justice of the European Union directly ensured that fundamental rights would be upheld for individuals targeted, and indirectly prompted the Council to reform its procedures by establishing the Office of the Ombudsperson to hear challenges to sanctions decisions. The Ombudsperson is a much more robust mechanism than the previous iteration, the 'focal point' framework.

As a final word, it is illustrative to take a step back from these developments and appreciate them in context, particularly in light of the principles of legality and legitimacy. The preceding analysis has shown that recent developments in Security Council sanctioning practice actually say very little about the Council's relationship with the former, the principle of legality. While it was a court of law that ultimately prompted the Council to reform its decision-making procedures, and even as the protection for individuals caught up in the Council sanctions net has improved, it does not appear that the Council is any more concerned with ensuring that its decisions comply with international (or, for that matter, regional and domestic constitutional) law, than it has been in the past.

Instead, the Council's primary focus remains to ensure that member states comply with sanctions decisions, which is pivotal to the effective fulfilment of its 'primary responsibility for the maintenance of international peace and security'. Everything else is tangential to this goal. To this end, what does emerge is a picture of a Security Council that is increasingly concerned with the *legitimisation* of its procedures, as opposed to the *legalisation* of the same. Legitimate decisions, in the words of Franck, exert a 'compliance pull' towards their addressees.[144] It appears that the Council's rationale to reform its procedures was no more and no less than to ensure the perception of fairness (legitimacy) in the eyes of the international community, in order to ensure the continued effective implementation of its sanctions decisions. Thus, it follows that a holistic understanding of the contemporary sanctions regime and, for that matter, the effective realisation of the Council's peace and security mandate more broadly, is predicated on a broader conception of legitimacy, one which transcends a purely positivist legal analysis.

References

Abi-Saab G (2001) The Concept of Sanction in International Law. In: Gowlland-Debbas V (ed) United Nations Sanctions and International Law. Brill: 29–41

Bianchi A (2006) Assessing the Effectiveness of the UN Security Council's Anti-Terrorism Measures: The Quest for Legitimacy and Cohesion. European Journal of International Law 17(5): 881–919

Cassese A (2005) International Law, 2nd edn. Oxford University Press

Cortright D et al (2008). In: Lowe et al (eds) The United Nations Security Council and War. Oxford University Press, pp 205–225

Craven M (2002) Humanitarianism and the Quest for Smarter Sanctions. European Journal of International Law 31(1): 43–61

Daugirdas K (2016) How and Why International Law Binds International Organizations. Harvard International Law Journal 325–381

De Wet E (2004) The Chapter VII Powers of the United Nations Security Council. Hart

Fassbender B (2006) Targeted Sanctions and Due Process. Study Commissioned by the UN Office of Legal Affairs

Franck TM (1990) The Power of Legitimacy Among Nations. Oxford University Press

Gill TD (1995) Legal and Some Political Limitations on the Power of the UN Security Council to Exercise its Enforcement Powers under Chapter VII of the Charter. Netherlands Yearbook of International Law 26: 33–138

Gowlland-Debbas V (1994) Security Council Enforcement Action and Issues of State Responsibility. International and Comparative Law Quarterly 43(1): 55–98

Hooper H (2018) Between Power and Process: Legal and Political Control over (Inter)national Security. Oxford Journal of Legal Studies 38(3): 613–634

---

[144] Franck 1990, p. 24.

Hovell D (2016a) The Power of Process: The Value of Due Process in Security Council Sanctions Decision-Making. Oxford University Press

Hovell D (2016b) Kadi: King-Slayer or King-Maker? The Shifting Allocation of Decision-Making Power between the UN Security Council and Court. Modern Law Review 79(1): 147–166

Hurd I (2007) After Anarchy: Legitimacy and Power in the United Nations Security Council. Princeton University Press

Isiksel NT (2010) Fundamental Rights in the EU after *Kadi* and *Al Barakaat*. European Law Journal 16(5): 551–577

Kelsen H (1948) Collective Security and Collective Self-Defense under the Charter of the United Nations. American Journal of International Law 42: 783–796

Kelsen H (1950) The Law of the United Nations: A Critical Analysis of its Fundamental Problems. Praeger

Krisch N (2012) Article 41. In: Simma B et al (eds) The Charter of the United Nations: A Commentary, Volume II, 3rd edn. Oxford University Press

Mueller J, Mueller L (1999) Sanctions of Mass Destruction. Foreign Affairs 78(3): 43–53

O'Connell ME (2002) Debating the Law of Sanctions. 13(1) European Journal of International Law 13(1): 63–79

Orakhelashvili A (2005) The Impact of Peremptory Norms on the Interpretation and Application of United Nations Security Council Resolutions. European Journal of International Law 16(1): 59–88

Orakhelashvili A (2011) Collective Security. Oxford University Press

Orakhelashvili A (2015) The Impact of Unilateral EU Economic Sanctions on the UN Collective Security Framework: The Cases of Iran and Syria. In: Marossi A et al (eds) Economic Sanctions under International Law. Springer

Pellet A, Miron A (2013) Sanctions. Max Planck Encyclopaedia of International Law

Peters A (2012) Article 25. In: Simma B et al (eds) The Charter of the United Nations: A Commentary, Volume II, 3rd edn. Oxford University Press

Rawls J (1971) A Theory of Justice. Oxford University Press

Reinisch A (2001) Securing the Accountability of International Organizations' Global Governance 7(2): 131–149

Schachter O (1994) United Nations Law. American Journal of International Law 88: 1–23

Tzanakopoulos A (2011) Disobeying the Security Council: Countermeasures against Wrongful Sanctions. Oxford University Press

Van Aaken A et al (2019) Symposium on Unilateral Sanctions. American Journal of International Law Unbound 113: 130–168

Van den Herik LJ (2014) Peripheral Hegemony in the Quest to Ensure Security Council Accountability for Its Individualized UN Sanctions Regimes. Journal of Conflict and Security Law 19(3): 427–450

White ND (2018) Autonomous and Collective Sanctions in the International Legal Order. Italian Yearbook of International Law 27(1): 1–32

Dr. Ben L. Murphy is a Lecturer in Law and Deputy Director of the International Law and Human Rights Research Unit at the School of Law and Social Justice, University of Liverpool. His research interests lie in the fields of collective security law, international institutional law and international legal and political theory. Ben holds Ph.D. and LLM degrees in international law from the University of Liverpool. Prior to this, he received his undergraduate degree in Politics with French from Loughborough University.

Chapter 9
Peace(keeping) Operations: Soldiers Without Enemies?

Sabine Hassler

> Peacekeeping is a risky activity (dos Santos Cruz 2017, Executive Summary).

Contents

9.1 Introduction 202
9.2 The UN Charter Framework and the Necessity of Security Council Authorisation 204
    9.2.1 The Pacific Settlement of Disputes|Chapter VI 206
    9.2.2 Authorising Enforcement Action|Chapter VII 207
    9.2.3 Innovation Through Straddling the Divide|Chapter VI½ 209
9.3 Peacekeeping Operations—An Overview 211
    9.3.1 Terminology 212
    9.3.2 Underlying Principles 212
    9.3.3 Legal Basis 213
    9.3.4 How is a Peacekeeping Operation Created? 214
    9.3.5 The Evolution Post-Cold War 215
9.4 What are the Next Challenges? 217
    9.4.1 Proposals for Change 218
    9.4.2 What is the Future of Peace Operations? 219
9.5 Conclusion 221
References 223

Abstract Peacekeeping as an operative tool has existed almost for as long as the United Nations (UN) and while its value is recognised, indeed it has become an all-encompassing means to building, securing and maintaining peace, it was never meant to exist. The drafters of the UN Charter and its framework had envisaged a system of collective security that was very much built on the experiences of the past. Yet, events immediately evidenced that the new world order was not going to be easily managed by the rules and regulations that proved already out of step with the

---

This is with reference to Fabian's work of 1971.

S. Hassler (✉)
Bristol Law School, University of the West of England, Bristol, UK
e-mail: Sabine2.Hassler@uwe.ac.uk

© T.M.C. ASSER PRESS and the authors 2022
S. Sayapin et al. (eds.), *International Conflict and Security Law*,
https://doi.org/10.1007/978-94-6265-515-7_9

times. The UN, however, proved that there is room for innovation and interpretation within its system; so much so that a tool could be created that had been neither envisaged nor does it have, to this day, a legal foundation in the UN Charter. Rather, peacekeeping was put under the auspices and authority of the UN Security Council which administers missions with reference to UN Charter terminology but without generally anchoring them to any particular Chapter or Article. Despite their flexible and versatile nature, peacekeeping has over the years faced a variety of challenges and suffered from a range of drawbacks that might under different circumstances have caused calls for abolition of the whole initiative. Peacekeeping, however, has endured and is undergoing a renewed transformation to make the future of peace operations part of the continued UN narrative.

Keywords Peacekeeping · peacekeeping operations · source of authority · legitimacy · Security Council · mandate · contemporary challenges · future of peace operations

9.1 Introduction

Peace is at the heart of the United Nations (UN)[1] whose genesis as an international organisation traces the horrors of early 20th century conflicts that not only bore evidence of technological advancements[2] but also of the increasingly global nature of conflict. Its predecessor, the League of Nations which itself was born of the Great War and so the first conflict of truly international character, laid the foundations for the UN in a vow 'not to resort to war' and 'to achieve international peace and security'.[3]

The pursuit of peace is the UN's mandate and it is doubtlessly the most successful international organisation to date with (at the time of writing in 2019) 193 member-states.[4] Nonetheless, 'peace' on a global scale remains an ideal and yet elusive. Indeed, it must be acknowledged that 'peace' as an objective is aspirational[5] and the UN as an organisation can only work towards creating the conditions, in cooperation with and support of the international community, in which the use of force as part of conflict must become the choice of last resort.

In an effort to focus UN member states on this aspiration, the obligation to settle disputes of an international nature peacefully is a fundamental commitment.[6] To

---

[1] Preamble, Charter of the United Nations 1945 (henceforth UN Charter).

[2] The Hague Conferences of 1899 and 1907 recognised the increasing threat posed by new, more sophisticated weaponry. See UNIDIR Resources 2017.

[3] See Preamble, The Covenant of the League of Nations 1919.

[4] United Nations undated.

[5] 'Peace' is a term subject to differentiation as it can at best connote the absence of strife or armed conflict. See UN News 9 September 2014.

[6] Article 2(3), UN Charter. For more discussion on the scope of settling international disputes, see Mani and Ponzio 2018.

create the supporting conditions to 'maintain international peace and security',[7] the founders of the UN and authors of the UN Charter allocated to the organisation's principal organs[8] a variety of tasks and equipped them with tools in an effort to collectively pursue, if not attain, its primary purpose. Today, the UN is much more than about the maintenance of peace but, for the purposes of this chapter, we shall concentrate on 'peace', its nature in the context of the achievable, its attainment and its maintenance through so-called peace operations under the aegis of the Security Council.

With six principal organs set to work towards peace, each organ with its own purpose, remit and tools at its disposal, the Security Council is the organ tasked with the 'primary responsibility for the maintenance of international peace and security'.[9] To that end and to be able to discharge this duty, the Security Council was granted specific powers as elaborated in Chapters VI, VII, VIII and XII of the UN Charter,[10] subject to overview by the General Assembly.[11] As such, the Security Council should have, and in theory does have, at its disposal a number of avenues and measures ranging from the 'Pacific Settlement of Disputes' under Chapter VI, 'Action with Respect to Threats to the Peace, Breaches of the Peace, and Acts of Aggression' under Chapter VII, to the use of 'Regional Arrangements' under Chapter VIII. Yet, as the first part of this chapter will show, the original aspirations could not be realised with the tools provided, leading to compromises on the one hand and the creation of measures not envisaged by the UN Charter on the other. Combined, these now fall within the definition of 'peace operations'. Peace operations are about 'working towards peace' and a look at United Nations Peace Operations (UNPOs) reveals that the term combines both 'peacekeeping operations' and 'political missions and good offices engagements',[12] with the former led by the United Nations Department of Peacekeeping Operations,[13] and the latter led by the United Nations Department of Political Affairs.[14]

The terminology elicits reactions ranging from hopeful to despondent to unequivocally critical and even dismissive. Hopeful because peace is the aspirational ideal but also despondent because attaining and maintaining peace is elusive and fraught with difficulties. Critical voices have long accused peacekeeping of severe failings[15] and thereby, directly and indirectly, cast doubt on peacekeeping operations' rationale, purpose and, ultimately, their usefulness. With peace as elusive as ever, 'peace operations' that are subject to a Security Council mandate have faced an uphill

---

[7] Preamble, UN Charter.

[8] Article 7, UN Charter.

[9] Article 24(1), UN Charter.

[10] Article 24(2), UN Charter.

[11] Article 24(3), UN Charter.

[12] United Nations Peace Operations undated.

[13] United Nations Department of Peacekeeping Operations undated.

[14] United Nations Department of Political Affairs undated. Note that while the text identifies 'peace operations', the focus of this chapter will be on peacekeeping operations.

[15] Notably Boot 2000.

struggle, not least plagued by the organ's contentious composition and ongoing reform discussions.[16]

In order to understand the nature of such operations under the auspices of the Security Council, this chapter will briefly introduce the Security Council as the pertinent UN organ in charge of administering peace and relevant processes, and the tools at its disposal in that regard (Sect. 9.2). We will examine how peacekeeping came to be within the purview of the Security Council and where, if at all, peacekeeping operations fit within the UN Charter framework. Further, in Sect. 9.3, we will take a more detailed look at peacekeeping operations, their purpose and objectives, the basis for such operations and how they have evolved. Finally, in Sect. 9.4, the chapter will identify current challenges and proposals for change and then provide an outlook on the future of peacekeeping operations.

9.2 The UN Charter Framework and the Necessity of Security Council Authorisation

The Security Council is one of the six principal UN organs.[17] With each organ tasked with a specific objective and remit, the Security Council's functions and powers are outlined in Article 24. Accordingly, the Security Council is tasked by the UN member states with the 'primary responsibility for the maintenance of international peace and security' on their behalf,[18] and, in discharging its duties, it is subject to the 'Purposes and Principles of the United Nations' as outlined in Chapter I.[19] Crucially, to provide the Security Council's primary responsibility with the necessary weight, its decisions are binding on the UN member states, underlining and ensuring their commitment to the purposes and principles.[20] This central position in the UN framework coupled with the fact that its membership is limited to a total of 15, with 5 positions already, and seemingly irreversibly, occupied[21] makes the Security Council, for better or worse, 'first among equals' and consequently the centre of much attention.

The Security Council was created as a 'powerful executive committee'[22] that, it was expected, had the military backbone to deliver a realistic response to a potential

---

[16] Reform discussions are beyond the remit of this chapter. For discussions, see e.g. Fassbender 1998; Hurd 2002; and Hassler 2013.

[17] The other organs are the General Assembly, the Economic and Social Council, the (defunct) Trusteeship Council, the International Court of Justice, and the Secretariat (notably represented by the UN Secretary-General). See Article 7, UN Charter.

[18] Article 24(1), UN Charter. Arguably, primary does not mean exclusive responsibility as the General Assembly's 'secondary' role was highlighted in the case of the 'Uniting for Peace' resolution, see n. 56 below.

[19] Article 24(2), UN Charter.

[20] See Article 25, UN Charter.

[21] Article 23(1), UN Charter. The remaining 10 members are non-permanent, Article 23(2), and are elected for two-year terms.

[22] Finkelstein and Finkelstein 1966.

9 Peace(keeping) Operations: Soldiers Without Enemies?

threat to the UN's peace and security framework.[23] This security framework is built on two Chapters both of which are under Security Council remit and offer incremental alternatives to action. First, Chapter VI which offers means and measures for the peaceful settlement of disputes or situations whose continuance is 'likely to endanger the maintenance of international peace and security' and should, by all accounts, be the first port of call in any dispute or situation.[24] Secondly, Chapter VII, which acknowledges that a dispute or situation has become a threat to the peace, breach of the peace or an outright act of aggression and therefore requires more forceful, active intervention.

The UN Charter's in-built protection mechanism to prevent arbitrary external intervention in a State is provided in Article 2(7): anything 'essentially within the domestic jurisdiction of any State' remains off-limits. This is an acknowledgement to the fact that while the member states submit to the UN as an international organisation they do remain sovereign States. Thus, means and measures under Chapter VI are part of voluntary dispute resolution and the Security Council is, at most, in a position to offer non-binding recommendations only.[25] Crucially, however, this does not apply to 'enforcement measures under Chapter VII', specifically decisions under Articles 41 and 42, which are taken by binding Security Council decisions.[26]

Another in-built protection mechanism to prevent arbitrary external intervention through the use of force is the ban on the same by virtue of Article 2(4). This ban on the use of force by a State[27] has, under the UN Charter framework, been limited to two exceptions: self-defence within the meaning of Article 51 and action mandated under Chapter VII, notably with reference to Article 39 as the 'trigger' provision and Article 42 as the enforcement provision. Accordingly, force can only be used either by a State (or States, in a collective response) in response to an 'armed attack'[28] against a member state and only until the Security Council has taken relevant measures to maintain peace and security, or by member states acting on the authorisation of the Security Council, following a determination under Article 39 and taking (or authorising the taking) of relevant action under Article 42.

---

[23] The permanent members' continued tenure at the centre is subject to much debate. It is not within the scope of this chapter to discuss this, however.

[24] Article 33, UN Charter.

[25] Article 38, UN Charter.

[26] Article 25, UN Charter. On the force of binding Security Council resolutions, see Delbrück 2002, p. 457, para 11.

[27] This has been confirmed as being of ius cogens status and therefore not simply only applicable to UN member states: see Case Concerning Military and Paramilitary Activities in and against Nicaragua (Nicaragua v United States of America), Merits, Judgment of 27 June 1986, ICJ Reports (1986) 99.

[28] The debate on whether an armed attack is a necessary prerequisite or whether a pre-emptive or even preventive use of force in self-defence is permissible with reference to customary international law is not within the scope of this chapter.

9.2.1 The Pacific Settlement of Disputes\Chapter VI

Turning to the pacific settlement of disputes under Chapter VI first, the focus is on any disputes that are likely to endanger *international* peace and security.[29] The Security Council's role is one of providing support and acting as independent facilitator.[30] While it does have the power to investigate under Article 34, at no point in Chapter VI does the Charter confer on the Security Council greater powers other than referral, e.g. to the ICJ,[31] or the making of non-binding recommendations.

Referrals to the Security Council can come from other UN organs such as the General Assembly under Articles 11 and 12, the Secretary-General under Article 99, and both member-states and non-member-states.[32] Nonetheless, the expectation is primarily upon the parties to the dispute to find a pacific solution. They are called upon to choose from a range of measures from the dispute resolution toolkit in Article 33(1), including 'means of their own choice'.[33] If they are unable to settle by the means listed in Article 33, the parties do have a duty as per Article 37 to submit their dispute to the Security Council. Submission of the dispute to the Council, however, does not add it automatically to its perennially crowded agenda but is rather subject to a procedural decision requiring a majority of nine votes whether to place it on the agenda *in the first place*.[34] If adopted onto the agenda, Article 32 requires that the parties to the dispute are invited to participate in, but not vote on, discussions.

While the parties are called upon to resolve their disputes without recourse to the use of force, even have a duty to refer their dispute to the Security Council, any of its recommendations in the pursuit of pacific settlement entail no legal obligation to comply on part of the parties.[35] Therefore, action under Chapter VI very much leaves the parties to the dispute in charge as to their preferred course of action in resolving their dispute making use of the resources available but with the Security Council taking a supporting rather than leading role. Crucially, at this point, their dispute is not deemed to be of a nature to make it subject to mandatory external intervention. This approach supports not only the notion of States as sovereign entities that act as equals on the international stage,[36] it also underlines the fundamental ideal that

---

[29] Emphasis added. The point at which the relevant threshold has been reached when disputes are or should be referred has been the subject of debate from the start. See Eagleton 1946.

[30] For an overview of the Security Council's practice in the pacific settlement of disputes see Repertoire of the Practice of the Security Council, Pacific Settlements of Disputes (Chapter VI).

[31] Article 36(3), UN Charter. See e.g. Corfu Channel Case (United Kingdom v Albania) Judgment of 9 April 1949 ICJ Rep. (1949) 4.

[32] Article 35, UN Charter.

[33] These methods are 'supplementary to those methods traditionally established in international law'. Sands and Klein 2001, p. 43.

[34] Article 27(2), UN Charter. For information on the Security Council's procedures, see Repertoire of the Practice of the Security Council, Provisional Rules of Procedure, Rules 6–12.

[35] The binding nature of Article 25 does not apply to recommendations under Chapter VI. See above n. 22 and 28.

[36] See Article 2(1), UN Charter.

peace can only be achieved and maintained through peaceful means.[37] Disputes and situations are resolved regularly without much publicity.[38] Once peacefully resolved they rarely, if ever, make it into the public's conscience. After all, if something works well, little notice is taken of its successes.

9.2.2 Authorising Enforcement Action\Chapter VII

With the pacific settlement of disputes to be pursued in preference, enforcement action under Chapter VII was meant to constitute the exception rather than the rule. Despite this aspiration, it rarely takes long before (public) attention shifts to Chapter VII and intervention is either being deliberated or actively taken.[39]

Under this Chapter, the focus shifts either directly onto a brewing conflict or away from any, failed, attempts at dispute resolution, with the Security Council as the central organ with the power to make a determination under Article 39 as to the 'existence of any threat to the peace, breach of the peace or act of aggression'. Hence, at this point a conflict or a dispute between parties is deemed to have, or has in fact, become a matter of international concern, and any attempts, if any, at resolving the conflict or dispute have failed (or are seen to have failed). States' right to have their sovereignty respected in terms of external non-intervention, while explicitly recognised in Article 2(7), is no longer effective. The matter has now moved within Chapter VII remit; accordingly, member states accept derogations to their sovereignty in an effort to subscribe to international conflict management.

For a matter to come within the remit of Chapter VII, it has to satisfy the "trigger criteria" as per Article 39 mentioned above. With this, the Security Council effectively 'provides an authoritative statement regarding the seriousness of an event'[40] although it should also be noted that 'not every violation of the peace produces an automatic response from the Council'.[41] Once a situation has satisfied the Article 39

---

[37] This endeavour is reflected in a multitude of instruments such as the 'Friendly Relations Declaration' (A/RES/2625 (XXV), October 1970); the Manila Declaration on the Peaceful Settlement of International Disputes (A/RES/37/10, November 1982); the 'Declaration on the Prevention and Removal of Disputes and Situations Which May Threaten International Peace and Security and on the Role of the United Nations in this Field, A/RES/43/51 (December 1988); or the 2005 World Summit Outcome document, A/RES/60/1 (24 October 2005).

[38] For a record of Chapter VI dispute resolution, see Repertoire of the Practice of the Security Council, Pacific Settlements of Disputes (Chapter VI).

[39] For an overview of the Security Council's practice under Chapter VII, see Repertoire of the Practice of the Security Council, Actions with Respect to Threats to the Peace, Breaches of the Peace, and Acts of Aggression (Chapter VII).

[40] Hassler 2013, p. 14.

[41] Hassler 2013, p. 14.

criteria, having caught the Security Council's attention and having been included in its agenda,[42] there is a range of tools available within Chapter VII.

The Chapter is said to depict a non-sequential 'sanctions ladder',[43] from resorting to measures not involving the use of force in an effort 'to prevent an aggravation of the situation',[44] to economic and other non-forcible measures,[45] to finally the authorisation of enforcement action.[46] It is, of course, the latter that attracts most attention as it may involve, and has become synonymous with, the use of armed force.[47] It is this 'use of armed force', however, that caused some consternation early on.

In order to provide the UN collective security system with the necessary teeth to repel potential aggressors and prevent potential conflicts from escalating, the Security Council was to be supported by all UN members in its efforts by 'armed forces, assistance, and facilities' to be made available to it 'on its call'.[48] The application of such armed force was to be made 'with the assistance of the Military Staff Committee'[49] which was to consist of the Chiefs of Staff of the five permanent members 'to advise and assist the Security Council on all questions relating to the Security Council's military requirements [...]' and 'the employment and command of forces placed at its disposal'.[50] Agreements subject to Article 43 have never been signed[51] and the Military Staff Committee in Article 47 remained ineffectual owing to disputes among the permanent members. This rendered this potentially most potent tool in the Security Council's armour a paper tiger.

As the Security Council was not provided with standing forces at its disposal within the meaning of the UN Charter, alternative arrangements had to be agreed on. How pressing this need for improvisation and flexibility was is well illustrated by the action in Korea in 1950 when the Security Council, in order to have its decisions enforced, approved military action under US command.[52] While to some extent reactionary in that the Security Council merely approved and legitimised the action the US would have taken in any case, it provided the footing to allow for the Security Council to function in accordance with its primary responsibility; command may no longer be in the Security Council's hands as originally envisaged, but as member

---

[42] For a record of Chapter VII actions, see Repertoire of the Practice of the Security Council Actions with Respect to Threats to the Peace, Breaches of the Peace, and Acts of Aggression (Chapter VII).

[43] Miller 1999.

[44] Article 40, UN Charter.

[45] Article 41, UN Charter.

[46] Article 42, UN Charter.

[47] For an analysis of the use of Article 42 as a means of ensuring the collective security framework, see e.g. Rumage 1993, also Vidmar 2017.

[48] See Article 42, UN Charter.

[49] Article 46, UN Charter.

[50] Article 47, UN Charter.

[51] Relevant arrangements as per Article 43, UN Charter, have never been implemented and the article remains, to all intents and purposes, ineffective. See Rossman 1994.

[52] S/RES/83 (27 June 1950) and S/RES/84 (7 July 1950).

states are provided with authorisation by the Security Council to enforce its decisions, the requisite legitimacy is conferred on the action nonetheless.[53]

Arguably, Security Council authorisation for enforcement action not under its command but with its blessing is a "success story" as without this cloak of legitimacy a multitude of enforcement actions would simply have fallen outside the UN's collective security framework and thus undermined its founding purposes and principles. As would become evident, early instances of adaptive flexibility and interpretive ingenuity were only the beginning.

9.2.3   Innovation Through Straddling the Divide\Chapter VI½

The UN may have been conceived in the spirit of war time efforts to assure future generations that recourse to armed conflict would become a thing of the past through the use of a sophisticated reciprocal security system. Yet, the conciliatory tone and cooperative atmosphere, especially among the permanent five members, soon evaporated. With the Cold War came power struggles that more often than not thwarted effective Security Council action. No other event evidenced this ultimate deadlock and thus failure on part of the Security Council in its primary responsibility to take effective action than the events that led to the adoption of the Uniting for Peace resolution.[54]

While initially an instance of illustrating the flexibility within the framework, the Korean experience (above) also brought into sharp relief the disabling disagreements between the permanent five that would affect the Security Council's functioning for decades to come. One of the most disabling illustrations of such disagreements, without any doubt, is the use, or threat, of the permanent member "veto".[55] While the word "veto" does not appear in the text of the UN Charter, the permanent members are effectively afforded one.[56]

With the Security Council deadlocked, the passing of the Uniting for Peace resolution evidenced that the international community was not prepared to let the UN as an organisation fail in its objectives because they had conceded the most central position of power to five member states. Flexibility and improvisation consequently proved an essential feature of the UN system. As would become clear: the UN was nothing if not adaptable. Its Charter, while framed in the language and experience of World War II, proved to be amenable to interpretation to the point of implying terms

---

[53] The extent to which this has now been developed, especially the controversies surrounding the authorisation practice, is beyond the scope of this chapter.

[54] A/RES/377 (V), 3 November 1950. This is the one, and only, instance in which the General Assembly stepped up to taking the place as the alternative organ.

[55] To ensure the backing of the permanent members a non-procedural vote is required. This requires a majority of nine, including the concurring votes of the permanent members as per Article 27(3), UN Charter.

[56] For a discussion on the veto and its place within Security Council decision-making, see e.g. Fassbender 1998.

arguably neither intended nor foreseen by its drafters. This is further evidenced by the fact that even interpretive lines between clearly separate Chapters would have to be blurred in order to achieve the UN's objectives.

While priority was to be given to solving disputes through Chapter VI, the focus started to shift to Chapter VII. However, as seen above, while the focus did shift, it also became clear that the Security Council would not be able to function as envisaged if the Charter and its language were to be read in their literal sense only. Measures were developed and devised to deal with situations that had not been contemplated, and thus did (and do) not neatly fit within either Chapter. Prime examples of such measures are peacekeeping operations.

As will be elaborated in more detail in the next section below, peacekeeping as we now know it was not originally contemplated. While the terminology appears intuitive in light of the primary objective to maintain and keep the peace, it is not found in the UN Charter and had to be developed in response to the needs at the time. An early example in 1947,[57] while now listed as a peacekeeping operation,[58] did not even come within the terminology, which was yet to be coined.It was Dag Hammarskjöld, the second UN Secretary-General and a firm believer in the power of diplomacy,[59] who defined it within the framework of the UN Charter as a response to the Suez crisis in 1956.[60] The United Nations Emergency Force (UNEF) was the first of its kind and was conceived as an impartial and armed UN force to stabilise fragile situations.[61] Because of its nature and the fact that peacekeeping operations consist of a combination of elements, Hammarskjöld described them as falling under "Chapter VI and a half" of the Charter, that is 'somewhere between traditional methods of resolving disputes peacefully (outlined in Chapter VI), on the one hand, and more forceful, less "consent-based" action (Chapter VII), on the other.'[62]

Peacekeeping operations are no doubt a prime example of the desire to see the UN and its objectives succeed against permanent member divisions and in light of constraints, both internal and external.[63] As a tool, peacekeeping has evolved, and keeps evolving, to keep meeting the demands of a changing landscape.[64] While originally limited to maintaining ceasefires and acting as a stabilising force, more complex tasks have been added since UNEF. UN peacekeeping operations have become the only globally-recognised means to credibly and impartially keep and build the peace.

---

[57] Following the endorsement by the General Assembly in November 1947 of a plan for the partition of Palestine, providing for the creation of an Arab State and a Jewish State, in 1948, unarmed UN military observers were deployed to the Middle East to monitor the Armistice Agreement. UNTSO (UN Truce Supervision Organisation) was established by S/RES/50 (1948).

[58] See, e.g. United Nations undated-a.

[59] Bildt 2011.

[60] See Hammarskjöld 1958.

[61] Bildt 2011.

[62] United Nations undated-a, Background.

[63] There is a range of constraints, including lacking financial and logistical support. See e.g. Press Release 2000; NYU Center on International Cooperation undated; and Langholtz 2010.

[64] For an overview of the developments, see Fetherstone 1994.

9 Peace(keeping) Operations: Soldiers Without Enemies?

9.3 Peacekeeping Operations—An Overview

There is no easy 'one size fits all' definition.[65] Even attempts at doing so are contentious, as Kofi Annan admitted:

> [P]eacekeeping appears as "the use of multinational military personnel, armed or unarmed, under international command and with the consent of the parties, to help control and resolve conflict between hostile states and between hostile communities within a state." Clear as that definition seems, events are now rendering parts of it contentious.[66]

Owing to its very nature, peacekeeping must be flexible and adaptable. Operations have consequently been deployed in a variety of combinations and configurations. They are increasingly multi-dimensional and are called upon 'not only to maintain peace and security, but also to facilitate the political process, protect civilians,[67] assist in the disarmament, demobilization and reintegration of former combatants; support the organization of elections, protect and promote human rights and assist in restoring the rule of law.'[68] In order to achieve lasting peace, therefore, peace operations encompass a range of multi-dimensional, multi-functional and complex operations.[69] Notably, they involve 'not only military but also various civilian and police components'.[70] The underlying mandate is situation-specific, depending on the nature of the conflict and the specific challenges it presents.[71]

While certainly flawed, as discussed below, peacekeeping operations have proven to be one of the most effective and enduring tools available in assisting in the difficult path from conflict to peace. Its various means of engagement are undoubtedly a strong point and represent much of UN practice.[72] In the following, this section will address the difficulties surrounding the use of terminology, outline the underlying principles and legal basis of operations, describe the steps to the creation of an operation and cover the evolution of operations post-Cold War.

---

[65] Indeed, peacekeeping operations are but one means in the wider spectrum of the UN's peace and security activities. See United Nations Department of Peacekeeping Operations 2008, Chapter 2.

[66] Annan 2017.

[67] For an assessment of the uncertainty with respect to the use of force to protect civilians with a particular view of missions' rules of engagement, see Blocq 2006.

[68] United Nations Peacekeeping undated-f. See also United Nations Department of Peacekeeping Operations 2003.

[69] Hatto 2013 charts the developments and considers the challenges.

[70] Aoi et al. 2007, p. 4.

[71] United Nations Department of Peacekeeping Operations 2008, p. 16.

[72] Useful and instructive guidance is provided in the United Nations Department of Peacekeeping Operations 2008.

9.3.1 Terminology

Peacekeeping as a term includes under its heading a variety of operations. It is commonly used for reasons of simplicity and convenience, yet this belies the complexity of operations subsumed under the umbrella term. While peacekeeping operations traditionally were to monitor ceasefire agreements and to provide a secure environment for the delivery of humanitarian action as an immediate response, as they developed, they also were to address the root causes of conflicts[73] to eventually 'lay the foundations for social justice and sustainable peace'.[74] Clearly, a tall order for any operation. Additionally, peacekeeping operations, irrespective of size, mandate and objectives, are to conform to and apply underlying principles that were designed to ensure their acceptability.

9.3.2 Underlying Principles

To achieve each operation's purpose and objectives, three 'inter-related and mutually reinforcing'[75] principles underlie UN peacekeeping:

1. Consent of the parties
2. Impartiality
3. Non-use of force except in self-defence and defence of the mandate.[76]

Consent of the parties: Ideally, consent is gained from the main parties to the conflict, necessitating commitment to the wider political process and 'acceptance of a peacekeeping operation mandated to support that process'.[77] While this is a reasonable expectation, it is also riddled with controversies and contradictions, not least in situations where the 'main parties to the conflict' consist of a multitude of factions.[78]

Impartiality: Mandates are to be implemented 'without favour or prejudice to any party'.[79] This is both crucial and complementary to obtaining both consent

---

[73] Although, arguably, many if not all peace operations mandates have failed in effectively tackling, managing and eradicating the root causes owing to complex scenarios on the ground. For more detailed analyses see e.g. Woodward 2007, Annan 2014, and United Nations Meetings Coverage 2017.

[74] Aoi et al. 2007, p. 5.

[75] United Nations Department of Peacekeeping Operations 2008, p. 31.

[76] United Nations Peacekeeping undated-c. For a more detailed outline of each principle, see United Nations Department of Peacekeeping Operations 2008, Chapter 3. See also Clemons 1993–1994. Clemons charts the historical developments of peacekeeping principles.

[77] United Nations Department of Peacekeeping Operations 2008, Chapter 3, p. 31.

[78] For further details, see United Nations Department of Peacekeeping Operations 2008, Chapter 3, pp. 31–33. For a more detailed consideration and discussion of the issues surrounding host-State consent see Sebastián and Gorur 2018.

[79] United Nations Department of Peacekeeping Operations 2008, Chapter 3, p. 33.

and cooperation from the main parties yet is 'not be confused with neutrality or inactivity'.[80] However, this principle is equally subject to controversy as it has, on occasion, become 'an excuse for inaction'.[81]

Non-use of force: This principle dates back to UNEF.[82] While principally 'not an enforcement tool', it is acknowledged that owing to the circumstances into which operations are deployed, force may have to be used at 'the tactical level', including 'resistance to attempts by forceful means to prevent the peacekeeping operation from discharging its duties'.[83]

Needless to say, the three underlying principles appear somewhat simplistic out of context and have, each in their own way but also when looked at holistically, drawn widespread criticism which led to calls for clarification and adaptation in light of the changing nature of conflicts. Not only that, it is also accepted that, by themselves, they are not enough to contribute to operation success.[84] In fact, peacekeeping needs to be embedded in a much more detailed and integrated peacebuilding system.[85]

9.3.3 Legal Basis

Strictly speaking, there is no legal basis for peace operations in the UN Charter as they were not provided for in the language of the Charter. Rather, they are the result of ongoing improvisation and interpretation. Traditionally, peacekeeping operations have been rooted in Chapter VI, yet practice has shown that the Security Council does not need to refer to a specific Chapter or indeed Article when passing a resolution that authorises a peacekeeping mission. As a tool, peacekeeping 'has largely been used in situations where application of Chapter VI of the Charter was not adequate and utilization of Chapter VII was not possible.'[86] It is only more recently that the Security Council has started invoking Chapter VII when authorising a mission into settings where the State has shown itself to be unable to maintain security and public order.[87]

---

[80] United Nations Department of Peacekeeping Operations 2008, Chapter 3, p. 33.

[81] United Nations Department of Peacekeeping Operations 2008, Chapter 3, p. 33. For further details, see United Nations Department of Peacekeeping Operations 2008, Chapter 3, pp. 33–34. For a more detailed consideration and discussion of the issues surrounding impartiality, see Rhoads 2016.

[82] See text to n. 63 above.

[83] United Nations Department of Peacekeeping Operations 2008, Chapter 3, p. 34. For further details, see United Nations Department of Peacekeeping Operations 2008, Chapter 3, pp. 34–35. For a more detailed consideration and discussion of the issues surrounding the non-use of force, see Berdal 2019.

[84] For further details, see United Nations Department of Peacekeeping Operations 2008, Chapter 3, pp. 36–40. See de Coning and Peter 2019.

[85] For extensive analyses of the underlying principles and theories, see Ryan 2000; Sitkowksi 2001.

[86] Annan 2017.

[87] United Nations Department of Peacekeeping Operations 2008, p. 14.

9.3.4 How is a Peacekeeping Operation Created?

Peacekeeping is resource-intensive. The path to creating, setting up, financing and maintaining such an operation is longwinded and depends on a variety of UN actors (such as the General Assembly and the Secretary-General). During initial consultations on a situation that is either developing or has worsened, a variety of actors, including relevant UN actors, the potential host government and the parties on the ground, member states that are likely to contribute troops and other logistical support, regional and other intergovernmental organisations as well as other relevant key external partners, is called upon to determine the most appropriate response.[88] Following a technical field assessment that analyses 'the overall security, political, military, humanitarian and human rights situation on the ground, and its implications for a possible operation', a report is sent to the Security Council outlining 'options for the establishment of a peacekeeping operation as appropriate including its size and resources'.[89] This report will also outline financial implications and a statement of preliminary estimated costs.[90]

However, it is only if and when the Security Council determines that deploying an operation is appropriate that it will formally pass a resolution authorising the mission.[91] While not embedded in the UN Charter, peacekeeping operations do depend on a Security Council resolution which will not only authorise the mission, but will also provide its mandate, its size and its scope.[92] Crucially, as the UN has no standing army,[93] and so the Security Council has no recourse to a deployable force, member states are called upon to contribute troops.[94]

While the mandates themselves are influenced by the nature and content of the agreement reached by the parties to the conflict,[95] regular reports to the Security Council will update it on the implementation of the mission and, based on these reports, the future of the mission is decided. Ultimately, it is Security Council

---

[88] United Nations Peacekeeping undated-b.

[89] United Nations Peacekeeping undated-b.

[90] It is here that the General Assembly plays a key role in assessing the feasibility of a peacekeeping operation. See United Nations Peacekeeping undated-e.

[91] Notably, in 'its first 40 years, the Security Council authorized only 13 peacekeeping operations'. For an overview of how this tool became revitalised and acquired a new drive under then Secretary-General Boutros Boutros-Ghali, see Meisler 1995, p. 187.

[92] Staffing, especially with regard to senior officials, is within the remit of the Secretary-General's office. This is alongside the Department of Peacekeeping Operations and the Department of Field Support.

[93] Peacekeepers are only identifiable as such owing to the UN blue helmet or beret and a badge; as military personnel, they continue wearing their own countries' uniform. See United Nations Peacekeeping undated-b.

[94] This in itself has proven a major barrier to operations in the past owing to dwindling support and a failure to provide troops when needed. See Meisler 1995, p. 193. Also, as Hurd pointed out, the Security Council has 'enormous formal powers' yet has no direct control with which to enact them. Hurd 2002, p. 35.

[95] United Nations Department of Peacekeeping Operations 2008, p. 14.

9 Peace(keeping) Operations: Soldiers Without Enemies?

authority that not only provides the mandate but also imbues the operation with legitimacy. As the UN's bearer of primary responsibility to maintain peace and security, its support is essential.[96]

9.3.5 The Evolution Post-Cold War

The end of the Cold War substantially affected both practice and scale of peacekeeping operations and brought about nothing less than conceptual change.[97] While peacekeeping operations had proven to be a workable solution in inter-State conflicts, with the advent of intra-State conflicts where 'the lines of hostility are not so neatly drawn', vulnerabilities of the set-up were drawn sharply into focus.[98] Operations had evolved from the original military model of observing ceasefires and separating forces after inter-state wars to incorporating a complex mix of military, police and civilian elements working together to help lay the foundations for sustainable peace.[99] As part of the UN's 'peacebuilding architecture',[100] peacekeeping missions increasingly have a role to play in conflict prevention, peace-making, peace enforcement[101] and, ultimately, peacebuilding.[102] In fact, the language of conflict prevention[103] only entered practice with the end of the Cold War.[104] Consequently, in an *Agenda for Peace*, the central importance of "preventive diplomacy", including confidence-building measures, fact-finding, early warning, preventive deployment, and demilitarized zones was underlined.[105] This was defined as 'action to prevent disputes from arising between parties, to prevent existing disputes from escalating

---

[96] Increasingly, Security Council mandates also reflect the broader normative debates shaping the international environment and there are a number of landmark Security Council resolutions. See S/RES/1325 (2000) on women, peace and security; S/RES/1612 (2005) on children and armed conflict; or S/RES/1674 (2006) on the protection of civilians in armed conflict. United Nations Department of Peacekeeping Operations 2008, p. 14.

[97] Annan 2017.

[98] Clemons 1993–1994, p. 120.

[99] United Nations Department of Peacekeeping Operations 2008, p. 18.

[100] United Nations Department of Peacekeeping Operations 2008, p. 20.

[101] Although peace enforcement 'may involve the use of force at the strategic or international level, which is normally prohibited for Member States under Article 2(4) of the Charter unless authorized by the Security Council.' See United Nations Department of Peacekeeping Operations 2008, p. 19.

[102] For a brief and useful overview of how peacekeeping developed and which phases can be discerned, see Goulding 1993.

[103] Successive Secretaries-General advocated a more activist approach to conflict prevention, notable among these were *An Agenda for Peace* and *In Larger Freedom*. Kofi Annan, e.g., called for a 'culture of prevention' within the UN. Press Release 1999.

[104] The peaceful settlement of disputes and conflict prevention are closely related concepts. However, while the former concentrates on "damage limitation", the latter seeks to go deeper by addressing both more immediate and the root causes of conflict. For an excellent overview, see Mani and Ponzio 2018.

[105] Report of the Secretary-General 1992.

into conflicts and to limit the spread of the latter when they occur.'[106] This presented opportunities but also challenges as while the 'world has united behind peacekeeping in principle, it has failed in many respects to take commensurate steps in practice.'[107]

Increasingly, mandates included the authority to use force (with the consent of the host authorities) to both defend themselves and their mandate.[108] True, originally peacekeepers were deployed to keep peace, not to make war; their major weapon was moral authority, not military strength.[109] However, the change in mandate to include a more robust use of force stems from hard-learned lessons in Somalia, Rwanda and the former Yugoslavia to name but a few.[110] These operations 'were deemed to have been flawed in their adherence to outdated neutrality and their lack of correct operational design and competence for dealing with identifiable "enemies"'[111] while at the same time highlighting that warring factions increasingly perceived peacekeepers as "intrusive meddlers" and can both, in their own right, be seen as gamechangers.[112]

Somalia was the first instance in which 'both greater involvement in conflicts occurring within borders, as well as a wider use of force was required'.[113] Consequently, the Security Council, for the first lime, found that a humanitarian disaster constituted a threat to peace and security.[114] Action was initiated by a traditional peacekeeping force, the United Nations Operation in Somalia (UNOSOM I), which was subsequently replaced by UNISOM II and backed up with a more substantial military operation, the Unified Task Force (UNITAF) which had been comprised of contributions from many member states. The violence persisted despite UNITAF's mandated effort to create a secure environment and limited the success of efforts to deliver humanitarian aid and alleviate suffering in the region.[115] The Protection Force (UNPROFOR) that was sent to the former Yugoslavia was also largely unsuccessful in its efforts to bring about an end to the conflict.[116] As an immediate reaction, the UN 'decided to remain distant from dangerous regions and narrow down the objectives for peacekeeping in general'[117] while seemingly re-evaluating its position.

The problems faced by UN peacekeepers highlighted that such missions cannot be tasked in isolation.[118] It became clear that peacekeeping operations are unlikely

---

[106] Report of the Secretary-Genera 1992, para 20.

[107] Annan 2017.

[108] Blocq 2006 further picks up the issue that there is ambiguity in the law guiding peacekeepers in their missions.

[109] Annan 2017.

[110] For a useful overview of the development of peacekeeping with regard to the use of force, see Sloan 2014

[111] Pugh 2004, p. 39.

[112] Clemons 1993–1994.

[113] Annan 2017.

[114] See S/RES/733 (23 January 1992).

[115] Annan 2017.

[116] For an overview that outlines the issues at the time, see Clemons 1993–1994, pp. 123–135.

[117] Blocq 2006, p. 202.

[118] Note from the Editor to Annan 2017.

9 Peace(keeping) Operations: Soldiers Without Enemies?

to succeed in multi-party intra-State conflicts when the parties on the ground are not genuinely committed to resolving the conflict through a political process; a lack of supportive attitude of neighbouring states; a divided Security Council as disagreements within are likely to send mixed messages to the parties; and a mandate that is both unclear and unrealistic.[119] Moreover, the changing landscape and conditions brought to the fore that the practice developed during the Cold War 'suddenly seemed needlessly self-limiting' and that there was 'increasing support for "peacekeeping with teeth".'[120]

Official recognition of the need for change came with the *Brahimi Report.*[121] The report found that 'peacekeeping operations were increasingly deployed not in post-conflict situations, but in stalemate situations where at least one of the parties was not seriously committed to ending the confrontation.'[122] Consequently, peacekeeping operations, while remaining impartial and adhering to the principles of the UN Charter, would need to be prepared to 'confront the lingering forces of war and violence' and have 'the ability and determination to defeat them'[123] lest they become 'complicit with evil'.[124] Consequently, a UN peacekeeping operation's authority to use force should be 'specified and its rules of engagement should be sufficiently robust to prevent UN contingents from ceding the initiative to peace spoilers.'[125]

This point was also picked up by the *New Horizon* initiative.[126] This UN Secretariat 'non-paper' took stock of the increasing scale and complexity of UN peacekeeping operations and emphasised the need for a stronger political consensus, shifting the focus from quantity to quality and capabilities of troops, enhancing the accountability among the stakeholders of UN peacekeeping, and developing a coherent strategy for the United Nations field support system.[127] Undoubtedly, owing to the range of and changes in expectations and demands, the evolutionary changes brought forth a variety of different types of peace operations. While responsive to immediate needs, it created new challenges.

9.4 What are the Next Challenges?

The range of tasks assigned to peacekeeping operations has expanded significantly in response to shifting patterns of conflict. Although each operation is different,

---

[119] United Nations Department of Peacekeeping Operations 2008, pp. 49–51.

[120] Annan 2017.

[121] Report of the Panel on United Nations Peace Operations 2000.

[122] Bildt 2011.

[123] Report of the Panel on United Nations Peace Operations 2000, p 1.

[124] Bildt 2011.

[125] Bildt 2011.

[126] Department of Peacekeeping Operations and Department of Field Support, A New Partnership Agenda 2009.

[127] Bildt 2011.

there is a considerable degree of consistency in the types of mandated tasks assigned by the Security Council. At the same time, success is never guaranteed, because each mission is unique and goes into the most physically and politically difficult environments.[128] This final section will outline the initial proposals for change to then consider the future of peace operations by delving deeper into the steps identified as necessary to ensure demands are met.

9.4.1 Proposals for Change

Proposals for change and improvement initially focused on three main areas. First, to address issues of feasibility and viability of operations, the carrying out of independent and ongoing reviews of peacekeeping missions was proposed, aimed at refining priorities and configuration, while assessing the viability of mandates and political processes.[129] This included appeals to more effective political engagement and enhanced accountability and transparency.[130]

Secondly, proposals identified peacekeepers' safety and security through measures that improve the preparedness and response of missions by strengthening training, reviewing medical support, and addressing performance issues.[131] Indeed, while peacekeeping operations have improved the lives of millions of people in 'countries that have found stability and durable peace through the support of multidimensional peacekeeping',[132] since 2013 casualties among peacekeepers have spiked,[133] making the practice of peacekeeping increasingly dangerous with peacekeepers being 'targeted more and more frequently'.[134] This has led to calls for change in practice and expectations or risk 'damaging the instrument of peacekeeping'.[135] While efforts have been made to strengthen peacekeeping operations by acknowledging the challenges faced and offering solutions,[136] they equally have shone a harsh light on peacekeepers being 'under-equipped, under-prepared and unready for the dangerous environments in which they now operate'.[137] This may be because of troops being

---

[128] United Nations Peacekeeping undated-f.

[129] Review teams, which are being led by independent experts, have been charged with questioning fundamental assumptions. Where required, they will aim for a "strategic reset" of operations in need of new direction. Haeri 2018.

[130] UN Secretary-General 2018.

[131] In terms of training needs, it is worthwhile looking at Blocq 2006.

[132] Haeri 2018.

[133] dos Santos Cruz 2017, Executive Summary.

[134] Press Release 2018.

[135] UN Secretary-General 2018. For a discussion on whether the High-Level Panel can deliver reform, see Whalan 2016.

[136] See Report of the High-Level Independent Panel on United Nations Peacekeeping Operations 2015.

[137] UN Secretary-General 2018.

9 Peace(keeping) Operations: Soldiers Without Enemies?

poorly equipped,[138] because of 'poor troop quality',[139] or because of both. This, linked with 'gaps in command and control, in culture, in equipment and in training', renders peacekeepers vulnerable and targets for attacks[140] while also potentially acting as aggressors and exploiters as well.[141] In reaction, a new approach to sexual exploitation and abuse was launched[142] to ensure that allegations can be followed up and victims have a clear way to report them.[143]

As has become obvious, the UN flag 'no longer offers natural protection' to either side.[144]

9.4.2 What is the Future of Peace Operations?

It is the prerogative of the Security Council, acting in its capacity as the organ with primary responsibility for the maintenance of international peace and security, to determine when and where a peacekeeping operation should be deployed.[145] The Security Council responds to crises on a case-by-case basis and it has a wide range of options at its disposal. Nevertheless, without prejudice to its ability to do so and to respond flexibly as circumstances require, the Security Council has indicated that it may take a number of factors into account when the establishment of a new peace-keeping operation is under consideration.[146] This has taken on a new meaning as peacekeeping operations are more frequently deployed in volatile, highly stressed environments that are characterised by the collapse or degradation of State structures with lawlessness and insecurity prevalent and opportunists present who are willing to exploit any political and security vacuum.[147] It is here that peacekeeping oper-ations are 'operating at the outer limits of peacekeeping. They are deployed in the face of weak or stalled political processes, diminished consent, and direct attacks on personnel, sometimes by transnational actors'[148] where they are tested for 'weakness and division by those whose interests are threatened by its presence, particularly in

---

[138] See Autesserre 2019.

[139] See Haass and Ansorg 2018.

[140] UN Secretary-General 2018.

[141] See, e.g. Oswald 2016; Kihara-Hunt 2017.

[142] United Nations undated-b.

[143] UN Secretary-General 2018.

[144] Williams 2018.

[145] This also highlights a fundamental issue at the heart of such operations: they depend on the Security Council with that organ itself being dominated by five permanent members and attendant power struggles at a political level. For a fundamental assessment and critique of peace operations as part of a 'global governance' that 'is not neutral but serves the purpose of an existing order' and therefore can be seen as a form of 'riot control directed against the unruly parts of the world to uphold the liberal peace', see Pugh 2004, p. 41.

[146] United Nations Department of Peacekeeping Operations 2008, p. 47.

[147] United Nations Department of Peacekeeping Operations 2008, p. 37.

[148] Haeri 2018.

the early stages of deployment'.[149] In the light of high-risk environments, casualties and the costs of failed and failing missions, questions arose as to whether the UN can continue to afford being caught in a 'trilemma',[150] pursuing 'three principal goals': the maximisation of success, the minimisation of risk, and the maximisation of efficiency. However, 'for logical and practical reasons only two of them can be achieved simultaneously'.[151] Inevitably, this has revived discussions about the viability of mandates in contemporary settings.[152]

However, as conflicts change in nature, scope and reach, the future will demand an even greater involvement in conflicts occurring within borders, as well as a wider use of force.[153] This necessitates questioning traditional approaches such as obtaining the consent of the parties involved.[154] Moreover, 'how should we define a party?'[155] While Article 2(7) UN Charter warns against infringing upon sovereignty, it becomes 'difficult to apply in situations where there is no recognized or recognizable sovereign.'[156]

Further action is needed to future-proof peacekeeping operations and the UN is keenly aware that reform is required as part of an ongoing, evolutionary approach.[157] Steps to making peacekeeping 'stronger, safer and more effective' came with the *Santos Cruz Report*[158] and the *Action for Peacekeeping* (A4P) initiative[159] which was launched in 2018.[160] The *Cruz Report* put it quite starkly: unless mindsets are changed troops will be consciously sent into harm's way.[161] Above all, the report is quite clear that a real and a realistic commitment is required to adapt to the changed, and continuously changing, requirements of modern peacekeeping and calls for more proactive, even pre-emptive, action and the preparedness to use force when necessary. While the report picks up some uncomfortable truths, there have been criticisms of its militaristic approach and goals in focussing too narrowly on security responses to the threats that kill peacekeepers instead of concentrating on the political processes that should be at the heart of UN peacekeeping.[162] The fundamental question of whether peacekeeping should deploy to such dangerous and problematic environments in the first place is being sidestepped.[163] This remains a fundamental question and a first and

---

[149] United Nations Department of Peacekeeping Operations 2008, p. 37.

[150] Williams 2018.

[151] Williams 2018.

[152] Haeri 2018.

[153] Annan 2017.

[154] See above Sect. 9.3.2.

[155] Annan 2017.

[156] Annan 2017.

[157] United Nations Peacekeeping undated-d.

[158] UN Secretary-General 2018, and dos Santos Cruz 2017

[159] United Nations Peacekeeping undated-a.

[160] Press Release 2018. For the launching speech, see UN Secretary-General 2018.

[161] dos Santos Cruz 2017, p. 10.

[162] Williams 2018.

[163] Haeri 2018.

9 Peace(keeping) Operations: Soldiers Without Enemies?

most formidable obstacle facing peacekeeping generally: translating commitment into action.[164] This is true all the more so if such actions are to have the necessary 'teeth' in terms of mandate and means,[165] not only to deal with contemporary threats but also to react flexibly to future challenges with factors, factions, and characteristics as yet unclear or not envisaged.

Additionally, many peacekeeping operations face crises that are political at their core. Even perfect performance by UN military and police would leave many missions reckoning with a fundamental obstacle: the lack of durable political solutions.[166] 'Peace operations cannot succeed if they are deployed instead of a political solution, rather than in support of one.'[167] Politics and security are mutually reinforcing, creating the very comparative advantage that is the hallmark of multidimensional UN peacekeeping.[168]

A4P[169] attempts to make strides in that direction by outlining six main requirements on the future of peacekeeping operations: (i) for the Security Council to sharpen and streamline mandates,[170] (ii) for Member States to sustain their political engagement and push for political solutions and inclusive peace processes, including through bilateral diplomacy and sanctions if necessary, (iii) to foster and reinforce the relationships with regional organisations; (iv) for those responsible to maintain the peace for their personnel (civil, military and police) to keep themselves at the ready to deliver their mission,[171] (v) for those responsible to assume their responsibility and to allocate the missions the necessary human and financial resources to attain the mandates,[172] and (vi) for the host countries to provide their consent to the operations to maintain peace and to cooperate actively in their attainment.[173]

9.5 Conclusion

The drafters of the UN Charter's collective security framework had divided it into two Chapters to deal with disputes, situations or conflicts that either are likely to impact or have already negatively impacted on international peace and security. This

---

[164] Annan 2017.

[165] Annan 2017.

[166] Haeri 2018.

[167] UN Secretary-General 2018.

[168] Haeri 2018.

[169] United Nations Peacekeeping undated-a.

[170] The Secretary-General called for an end to 'mandates that look like Christmas trees' in UN Secretary-General 2018.

[171] Particularly pertinent as peacekeeping as we know it has no capital fund, no reserve of equipment, and no reserve force. Annan 2017.

[172] Member states call for lower budgets while the world expects greater results to prevent violence and atrocities. See Haeri 2018.

[173] UN Secretary-General 2018.

was conceived at a time when conflicts were rather more neatly categorised and by powers whose reach was still able to manage, even suppress, conflicts within their 'sphere of influence'. However, as had become rather quickly clear in the immediate aftermath of the UN's creation, implementation of its goals was inevitably hampered by great power politics. What had not been envisaged was the decolonisation process and the civil strife that came with it. With the pursuit for independence, including from each other as well as from their colonial powers, came armed conflicts of a nature not previously experienced or, indeed, envisaged. The classic assumption of State versus State dispute that could escalate into an inter-State conflict, while still valid, has increasingly been supplanted by intra-State disputes and conflicts that involve so-called non-State actors,[174] alongside the State, that have traditionally not been part of the dispute resolution discourse. Therefore, in addition to the traditional definition of international (armed) conflicts,[175] we have to acknowledge conflicts that fall outside the inter-State conflict paradigm as intra-State, non-international armed conflicts,[176] with potentially a variety of non-State actors whose aims and objectives are not necessarily aligned with those classically pursued by the State and its representatives.

'Classic' or 'traditional' means of conflict resolution as inscribed in the UN Charter proved increasingly 'unfit for purpose' or simply not appropriate necessitating flexible and innovative thinking and approaches. Consequently, the lines between Chapters VI and VII became increasingly blurred with measures being developed out of a need to respond to situations on the ground in a credible, effective and efficient manner. To some extent, the UN system and its constitutive document, the UN Charter, have been able to adapt and respond. While the UN Charter as originally designed did not cater for such developments,[177] there is, arguably, a fair amount of flexibility within the UN as an organisation and the Charter's language to allow for interpretation, growth and adaptation.[178] No other practice bears witness to this better than peacekeeping operations, which, without being mentioned or provided for in the UN Charter, filled a void. From inception onwards, they have remained a 'remarkable and constantly evolving tool for international cooperation, burden sharing and the promotion of global security.'[179] That is not to say that the UN has not struggled in its efforts to neutralise 'vengeance wherever and whenever it could.'[180] But the UN's

---

[174] For a detailed analysis of the issue non-State actors represent in classic international law, see Noortmann et al. 2015.

[175] See, e.g., Protocol Additional to the Geneva Conventions of 12 August 1949, and relating to the Protection of Victims of International Armed Conflicts (Protocol I), 8 June 1977.

[176] See, e.g., Protocol Additional to the Geneva Conventions of 12 August 1949, and relating to the Protection of Victims of Non-International Armed Conflicts (Protocol II), 8 June 1977.

[177] But then, neither had it catered for the process of decolonisation that started only a few years after the organisation's creation. Originally, most members of today fell within the remit of the Trusteeship Council.

[178] As was acknowledged in Certain Expenses of the United Nations (Article 17, para 2, of the Charter), Advisory Opinion, 20 July 1962, I.C.J. Reports (1962) 151.

[179] Haeri 2018.

[180] Annan 2017.

9 Peace(keeping) Operations: Soldiers Without Enemies?

strength lies in its flexibility and adaptability. It is a key actor in the development of the international legal framework for codes of conduct and rules of engagement, and in dealing with the consequences of armed conflicts.[181]

For peacekeeping operations to effectively promote peace and security, all those who have a stake in them—the UN Secretariat, Security Council, General Assembly, troop and police contributors, host-states, financial contributors, and regional organizations—need to fulfil their roles respectively, take a hard look collectively at peacekeeping and ask whether it has the mandate, resources, political support, mindset, and human capital needed to meet the very high expectations.[182] Above all, and to paraphrase former Secretary-General Kofi Annan, '[T]he will to attain peace can be neither compelled nor coerced; it must be expressed by the [affected parties] themselves.'[183] Ultimately, parties to the conflict must want peace.[184]

References

Annan K (2017) The Path of Peace-Keeping. Harvard International Review (online edition), http://hir.harvard.edu/article/?a=14530. Accessed 24 June 2019.

Annan N (2014) Violent Conflicts and Civil Strife in West Africa: Causes, Challenges and Prospects. Stability: International Journal of Security and Development 3:1, https://doi.org/10.5334/sta.da. Accessed 24 June 2019.

Aoi C, de Coning D, Thakur R (2007) Unintended Consequences of Peacekeeping Operations. United Nations University Press, New York

Autesserre S (2019) The Crisis of Peacekeeping: Why the UN Can't End Wars. Foreign Affairs 98:1:101–116

Berdal M (2019) What Are the Limits to the Use of Force in UN Peacekeeping? In: de Coning C, Peter M (eds) United Nations Peace Operations in a Changing Global Order. Palgrave Macmillan, Cham

Bildt C (2011) Dag Hammarskjöld and United Nations Peacekeeping UN Chronicle XLVIII: 2 (online edition). https://unchronicle.un.org/article/dag-hammarskj-ld-and-united-nations-peacekeeping. Accessed 24 June 2019.

Blocq DS (2006) The Fog of UN Peacekeeping: Ethical Issues regarding the Use of Force to Protect Civilians in UN Operations. Journal of Military Ethics 5:3:201–213

Boot M (2000) Paving the Road to Hell: The Failure of U.N. Peacekeeping, Foreign Affairs (online edition) (March/April 2000). https://www.foreignaffairs.com/reviews/review-essay/2000-03-01/paving-road-hell-failure-un-peacekeeping. Accessed 24 June 2019.

Clemons E (1993–1994) No Peace to Keep: Six and Three-Quarters Peacekeepers. N.Y.U. J. Int'l L. & Pol. 26:107–141

de Coning C, Peter M (eds) (2019) United Nations Peace Operations in a Changing Global Order. Palgrave Macmillan, Cham

Delbrück J (2002) Article 25. In: Simma B (ed) The Charter of the United Nations – A Commentary. Oxford University Press, Oxford

Department of Field Support (undated) https://peacekeeping.un.org/en/department-of-field-support. Accessed 24 June 2019.

---

[181] Bildt 2011.

[182] Haeri 2018.

[183] Annan 2017.

[184] Haeri 2018.

Department of Peacekeeping Operations (undated) https://peacekeeping.un.org/en/department-of-peacekeeping-operations. Accessed 24 June 2019.

Department of Peacekeeping Operations and Department of Field Support (2009) A New Partnership Agenda: Charting a New Horizon for UN Peacekeeping. https://peacekeeping.un.org/sites/def ault/files/newhorizon_0.pdf. Accessed 24 June 2019.

dos Santos Cruz CA Lt Gen (ret.) (2017) Improving Security of United Nations Peacekeepers: We Need to Change the Way we Are Doing Business. https://peacekeeping.un.org/sites/default/files/ improving_security_of_united_nations_peacekeepers_report.pdf. Accessed 24 June 2019.

Eagleton C (1946) The Jurisdiction of the Security Council over Disputes. A.J.I.L. 40:3:513–533

Fabian LL (1971) Soldiers without Enemies: Preparing the United Nations for Peacekeeping. The Brookings Institution, Washington, DC

Fassbender B (1998) UN Security Council Reform and the Right of Veto: A Constitutional Perspective. Kluwer Law International, The Hague

Fetherstone AB (1994) Towards a Theory of United Nations Peacekeeping. Macmillan, London

Finkelstein MS, Finkelstein LS (eds) (1966) Collective Security. Chandler Publishing, San Francisco

Goulding M (1993) The Evolution of United Nations Peacekeeping. International Affairs 69:3:451–464

Haas F, Ansorg N (2018) Better Peacekeepers, Better Protection? Troop Quality of United Nations Peace Operations and Violence against Civilians. Journal of Peace Research 55:6:742–758

Haeri, D (2018) Strengthening UN Peacekeeping: Placing the Santos Cruz Report in Context, IPI Global Observatory. https://theglobalobservatory.org/2018/02/strengthening-peacekeeping-cruz-report-context/. Accessed 24 June 2019.

Hammarskjöld D (1958) United Nations Emergency Force, Summary Study of the Experience Derived from the Establishment and Operation of the Force. United Nations General Assembly, New York

Hassler S (2013) Reforming the UN Security Council Membership: The Illusion of Representative-ness. Routledge, Oxon

Hatto R (2013) From Peacekeeping to Peacebuilding: The Evolution of the Role of the United Nations in Peace Operations. I.R.R.C. 95:495–515

Hurd I (2002) Legitimacy, Power, and the Symbolic Life of the UN Security Council. Global Governance 8:35–51

Kihara-Hunt A (2017) Addressing Sexual Exploitation and Abuse: The Case of UN Police – Recom-mendations. Journal of International Peacekeeping 21:62–82

Langholtz HJ (2010) Logistical Support to United Nations Peacekeeping Operations: An Introduc-tion. Peace Operations Training Institute. http://www.ccopab.eb.mil.br/images/stories/cursos_est agios/logistica/1.%20LOG1_EN.100524.pdf. Accessed 24 June 2019.

Mani R, Ponzio R (2018) Chapter 18: Peaceful Settlement of Disputes and Conflict Prevention. In: Weiss TG, Daws S (eds) The Oxford Handbook on the United Nations. Oxford University Press, Oxford

Meisler S (1995) Dateline U.N.: A New Hammarskjöld? Foreign Policy 98:180–197

Miller LH (1999) The Idea and the Reality of Collective Security. Global Governance 5:303–332

Noortmann M, Reinisch A, Ryngaert C (eds) (2015) Non-State Actors in International Law. Hart Publishing, Oxford

NYU Center on International Cooperation (undated) Peacekeeping Overstretch: Symptoms, Causes, and Consequences - Background Paper for the Thematic Series "Building More Effective UN Peace Operations". https://cic.es.its.nyu.edu/sites/default/files/overstretchen.pdf. Accessed 24 June 2019.

Oswald BO (2016) Sexual Exploitation and Abuse in UN Peace Operations: Challenges and Developments. Journal of International Peacekeeping 20:143–170

Press Release (1999) Secretary-General Stresses Shift from Culture of Reaction to One of Prevention in 1999 Report on Work of Organization, SG/2059 – GA/9587. https://www.un.org/press/en/1999/ 19990909.sg2059.doc.html. Accessed 24 June 2019.

Press Release (2000) Challenges of United Nations Peacekeeping Operations Reviewed By Countries with First-Hand Experience, GA/SPD/201. https://www.un.org/press/en/2000/20001109.gaspd201.doc.html. Accessed 24 June 2019.

Press Release (2018) Peacekeeping Remains Defining Activity of United Nations, Secretary-General Says during Dag Hammarskjöld Medal Ceremony, SG/SM/19062-HQ/723-PKO/735. https://www.un.org/press/en/2018/sgsm19062.doc.htm

Provisional Rules of Procedure, Repertoire of the Practice of the Security Council. http://www.un.org/en/sc/repertoire/rules/overview.shtml. Accessed 24 June 2019.

Pugh M (2004) Peacekeeping and Critical Theory. International Peacekeeping 11:1:39–58

Report of the High-Level Independent Panel on United Nations Peacekeeping Operations (2015) Uniting Our Strengths For Peace – Politics, Partnership and People. https://peaceoperationsreview.org/wp-content/uploads/2015/08/HIPPO_Report_1_June_2015.pdf. Accessed 24 June 2019.

Report of the Panel on United Nations Peace Operations (2000) A/55/305 – S/2000/809

Report of the Secretary-General (1992) pursuant to the statement adopted by the Summit Meeting of the Security Council on 31 January 1992, An Agenda for Peace, A/47/277

Repertoire of the Practice of the Security Council, Actions with Respect to Threats to the Peace, Breaches of the Peace, and Acts of Aggression (Chapter VII). http://www.un.org/en/sc/repertoire/actions.shtml. Accessed 24 June 2019.

Repertoire of the Practice of the Security Council, Pacific Settlements of Disputes (Chapter VI). http://www.un.org/en/sc/repertoire/settlements.shtml. Accessed 24 June 2019.

Repertoire of the Practice of the Security Council, Provisional Rules of Procedure. http://www.un.org/en/sc/repertoire/rules/overview.shtml. Accessed 24 June 2019.

Rhoads EP (2016) Taking Sides in Peacekeeping: Impartiality and the Future of the United Nations. Oxford University Press, Oxford

Rossman JE (1994) Article 43: Arming the United Nations Security Council. NYU J. Int'l L. & Pol. 27:227–263

Rumage S (1993) The Return of Article 42: Enemy of the Good for Collective Security. Pace Int'l L. Rev. 5:1:211–286

Ryan S (2000) United Nations peacekeeping: A Matter of Principles? International Peacekeeping 7:1:27–47

Sands Ph, Klein P (2001) Bowett's Law of International Institutions, Thomson, Sweet & Maxwell: London

Sebastián S, Gorur A (2018) UN Peacekeeping and Host-State Consent: How Missions Navigate Relationships with Governments. Stimson Center. https://www.stimson.org/sites/default/files/file-attachments/UN-PeacekeepingAndHostStateConsent.pdf. Accessed 24 June 2019.

Sitkowksi A (2001) Reflections on The Peacekeeping Doctrine. Journal of International Peacekeeping 7:181–196

Sloan J (2014) The Evolution of the Use of Force in UN Peacekeeping. The Journal of Strategic Studies 37:5:674–702

United Nations (undated) About the UN http://www.un.org/en/sections/about-un/overview/index.html. Accessed 24 June 2019.

UN News (2014) Peace Means Dignity, Well-being for All, not Just Absence of War – UN officials. https://news.un.org/en/story/2014/09/476992-peace-means-dignity-well-being-all-not-just-absence-war-un-officials. Accessed 24 June 2019.

UN Secretary-General (2018) Secretary-General's Remarks to Security Council High-Level Debate on Collective Action to Improve UN Peacekeeping Operations. https://www.un.org/sg/en/content/sg/statement/2018-03-28/secretary-generals-remarks-security-council-high-level-debate. Accessed 24 June 2019.

UNIDIR Resources (2017) The Role and Importance of the Hague Conferences: A Historical Perspective. http://www.unidir.org/files/publications/pdfs/the-role-and-importance-of-the-hague-conferences-a-historical-perspective-en-672.pdf. Accessed 24 June 2019.

United Nations (undated-a) Honouring 60 Years of United Nations Peacekeeping. http://www.un.org/en/events/peacekeepersday/2008/1948.shtml. Accessed 24 June 2019.

United Nations (undated-b) The Compact on Preventing Sexual Exploitation and Abuse. https://www.un.org/preventing-sexual-exploitation-and-abuse/content/voluntary-compact. Accessed 24 June 2019.

United Nations Department of Peacekeeping Operations (undated) https://peacekeeping.un.org/en. Accessed 24 June 2019.

United Nations Department of Peacekeeping Operations (2003) Handbook on United Nations Multidimensional Peacekeeping Operations. https://peacekeeping.un.org/sites/default/files/peacekeeping-handbook_un_dec2003_0.pdf. Accessed 24 June 2019.

United Nations Department of Peacekeeping Operations (2008) Department of Field Support, United Nations Peacekeeping Operations (Capstone Doctrine): Principles and Guidelines. https://peacekeeping.un.org/sites/default/files/capstone_eng_0.pdf. Accessed 24 June 2019.

United Nations Department of Political Affairs (undated) https://www.un.org/undpa/en/overview. Accessed 24 June 2019.

United Nations Meetings Coverage (2017) General Assembly, Plenary, GA/11884 Speakers Urge Focus on Root Causes of Conflict as General Assembly Debates Strategies for Linking Sustainable Development, Lasting Peace (24 January 2017) https://www.un.org/press/en/2017/ga11884.doc.htm. Accessed 24 June 2019.

United Nations Peacekeeping (undated-a) Action for Peacekeeping (A4P). https://peacekeeping.un.org/en/action-for-peacekeeping-a4p. Accessed 24 June 2019.

United Nations Peacekeeping (undated-b) Forming a New Operation. https://peacekeeping.un.org/en/forming-new-operation. Accessed 24 June 2019.

United Nations Peacekeeping (undated-c) Principles of Peacekeeping. https://peacekeeping.un.org/en/principles-of-peacekeeping. Accessed 24 June 2019.

United Nations Peacekeeping (undated-d) Reforming Peacekeeping. https://peacekeeping.un.org/en/reforming-peacekeeping. Accessed 24 June 2019.

United Nations Peacekeeping (undated-e) Role of the General Assembly. https://peacekeeping.un.org/en/role-of-general-assembly. Accessed 24 June 2019.

United Nations Peacekeeping (undated-f) What is Peacekeeping? https://peacekeeping.un.org/en/what-is-peacekeeping. Accessed 24 June 2019.

United Nations Peace Operations (undated) https://www.unmissions.org/. Accessed 24 June 2019.

United Nations Truce Supervision Organisation (undated) https://untso.unmissions.org/backgr ound. Accessed 24 June 2019.

Vidmar J (2017) The Use of Force as a Plea of Necessity. A.J.I.L. 111:302–306

Whalan J (2016) Reforming UN Peace Operations: Will the High-Level Panel's Report Make a Difference for Human Rights? Journal of International Peacekeeping 20:5–20

Williams PD (2018) Cruz Report: The Politics of Force and the United Nations' Peacekeeping Trilemma. https://theglobalobservatory.org/2018/02/cruz-report-peacekeeping-tri lemma/. Accessed 24 June 2019.

Woodward SL (2007) Do the Root Causes of Civil War Matter? On Using Knowledge to Improve Peacebuilding Interventions. Journal of Intervention and Statebuilding 1:2, 143–170

Cases, Advisory Opinions and Other Documents

Case Concerning Military and Paramilitary Activities in and against Nicaragua (Nicaragua v United States of America), Merits, Judgment of 27 June 1986, ICJ Reports (1986) 99

Certain Expenses of the United Nations (Article 17, paragraph 2, of the Charter), Advisory Opinion, 20 July 1962, ICJ Reports (1962) 151

Charter of the United Nations 1945

Corfu Channel Case (United Kingdom v Albania), Judgment of 9 April 1949, ICJ Reports (1949) 4

Covenant of the League of Nations 1919

9 Peace(keeping) Operations: Soldiers Without Enemies?

Sabine Hassler LLB (Hons), LLM, Ph.D. is a Senior Lecturer in Law at the Bristol Law School, University of the West of England, Bristol. Her PhD was published as a monograph with Routledge, *Reforming the UN Security Council Membership: The Illusion of Representativeness* (2012). She has published on and researches into aspects of the UN Security Council's future, the responsibility to protect and peacekeeping, hybrid threats and asymmetric warfare, and aspects of nationality, in particular the means by which nationality is conferred.

Chapter 10
The Status of Forces Agreements

Joop Voetelink

Contents

10.1 Introduction 230
10.2 Historical Overview 232
    10.2.1 Introduction 232
    10.2.2 19th and 20th Century General Practice 232
    10.2.3 NATO Status of Forces Agreement 234
    10.2.4 Status of Forces and Crisis Management Operations 235
10.3 International Law Perspective 237
    10.3.1 Introduction 237
    10.3.2 Jurisdiction of States over Armed Forces Personnel Stationed Abroad ... 238
    10.3.3 Immunity of State Officials 240
10.4 Operational Law Perspective 242
    10.4.1 Introduction 242
    10.4.2 Military Operational Law 242
    10.4.3 Operational Law Perspective on SOFAs 244
10.5 Synthesis and Conclusion 249
References 251

Abstract A key element of the framework as regards the extraterritorial deployment of State armed forces is the legal status of its service personnel present on the territory of another State. Today, this matter is mostly dealt with in international agreements, generally referred to as Status of Forces Agreements (SOFAs). International law, including customary law, is at the heart of this practice and continues to affect the scope and further development of these agreements. SOFAs cannot be fully appreciated without acknowledging the operational context in which armed forces are deployed abroad. A legal analysis of SOFAs, therefore, includes an assessment of the operational requirements that define the extraterritorial deployment of forces, making SOFAs a unique instrument defining the legal position of a particular group of State officials abroad.

J. Voetelink (✉)
Netherlands Defence Academy (NLDA), Breda, The Netherlands
e-mail: jed.voetelink@mindef.nl

© T.M.C. ASSER PRESS and the authors 2022
S. Sayapin et al. (eds.), *International Conflict and Security Law*,
https://doi.org/10.1007/978-94-6265-515-7_10

Keywords Sovereignty · Jurisdiction · Immunity · Privileges · State official · Armed forces · Extraterritorial operations · Military operational law · Visiting forces · Status of Forces Agreement · Claims

10.1 Introduction

Armed forces are key State organs tasked with upholding the external security of the State.[1] When a government has deployed elements of its armed forces abroad this unique position will remain unchanged. The military units and service members continue to be part and parcel of the State, carrying out their tasks under the ultimate command and control (in military terms: Full Command[2]) of the State that sends them abroad (the Sending State), even, for example, when deployed as part of an international force in a crisis management operation. Consequently, the Sending State can order the deployed forces to return to their home bases at all times, whenever the government decides national interests so demand.

Being a key organ of the Sending State, the deployed forces' legal position and that of its service members when present abroad is an issue of utmost concern for the Sending State. Also, as the presence of foreign forces on the territory of the State receiving the forces (the Host State) impacts its sovereignty,[3] the legal status of the visiting forces will be equally of interest to that State. Today's practice shows that the mutual concerns with respect to visiting forces are typically covered in some sort of international arrangement, often an international agreement or treaty,[4] generally referred to as a Status of Forces Agreement (SOFA).[5] Failure to come to an agreement on the terms of a SOFA may prevent the deployment of forces abroad or hinder[6] or even terminate ongoing military cooperation or operations.[7] The latter happened in

---

[1] Voetelink 2015, p. 151.

[2] "The military authority and responsibility of a commander to issue orders to subordinates. It covers every aspect of military operations and administration and exists only within national services"; AAP-6 2017, p. 51.

[3] Cf. Heefner 2017, 51–52, referring to US efforts to reactivate an airbase in Libya in 1948.

[4] Occasionally SOFAs are laid down in a non-legally binding Memorandum of Understanding (MOU, e.g., MOU between the North Atlantic Treaty Organization and the Government of the Hashemite Kingdom of Jordan on the Status of NATO Personnel Present on the Territory of the Hashemite Kingdom of Jordan (11 April 2016), on file with author); a Security Council Resolution (e.g., UN Doc S/RES/2100, 25 April 2013 with respect to the UN Multidimensional Integrated Stabilization Mission in Mali, or a unilateral document (e.g., Coalition Provisional Authority Order Number 17 (revised): Status of the Coalition Provisional Authority, MNF-Iraq, Certain missions and Personnel in Iraq; 27 June 2004. Available at: www.iilj.org/wp-content/uploads/2016/08/Order-17-Section-4.pdf.

[5] At times, the term Status of Mission Agreement (SOMA) is used.

[6] E.g., the delayed conclusion of a SOFA for the Kosovo Force, KFOR (1999) seriously hampered the initial phase of the mission; Fleck 2018b, p. 40.

[7] Cf. Rule 8.1 of the List of Rules in the Leuven Manual, p. 335: "Rights and obligations of an organisation deploying military and civilian personnel in a Peace Operation, and those of such personnel, should be specified in Status of Forces or Status of Mission Agreements".

December 2011 when the SOFA between Iraq and the US[8] could not be renewed as Iraq was not prepared to meet US demands for full immunity for US troops from prosecution in Iraqi courts. Consequently, the US forces withdrew its armed forces before expiration of the SOFA on 31 December 2011.[9]

Clearly, in situations where armed forces find themselves in another State without that State's consent, no SOFA will apply and the status of the troops will then be part of another legal framework. For example, a unit accidentally crossing a neighboring State's borders because of a map reading error during a military exercise, may invoke the rules on international responsibility. In an international armed conflict, in which State armed forces intentionally breach another State's territorial integrity, the laws of war, including the law on belligerent occupation, will be applicable. These types of actions are outside the scope of the present chapter, which will only address situations where armed forces operate extraterritorially with Host State consent.

Although contemporary SOFAs are comprehensive documents covering a broad set of subjects,[10] the core notion of status of forces centers around jurisdictional issues and is deeply rooted in public international law, including international customary law. Although international law thus gives SOFAs a common basis, so far no universal regime has emerged, covering the status of visiting forces worldwide. Consequently, deployment of forces invariably leads to the conclusion of new SOFAs between, on the one hand, Sending States or international organizations acting on behalf of Sending States and, on the other hand, Host States. Still, this wide array of SOFAs share some common characteristics, making the agreements a unique and effective instrument to set out the legal position of this particular group of State agents.

The present chapter will provide an insight in contemporary SOFA practice by exploring criminal jurisdiction over visiting forces and other the key provisions of these agreements taking into account the military operational context in which SOFAs apply. By way of an introduction, the chapter starts with a historical overview of SOFAs focusing on the exercise of criminal jurisdiction over visiting forces (Sect. 10.2). As the latter aspect has its roots in public international law, Sect. 10.3 examines the position of sovereign States under international law and the jurisdictional powers reflecting that position in relation to visiting forces. Section 10.4. introduces military operational law to take a closer look at the operational side of SOFAs and their provisions; in particular the jurisdictional provisions. Finally, this chapter offers a brief synthesis and conclusion.

---

[8] Agreement between the United States of America and the Republic of Iraq on the withdrawal of US forces from Iraq and the organisation of their activities during their temporary presence in Iraq (17 November 2008), KAV 8551, www.state.gov/documents/organization/122074.pdf.

[9] The new US-Iraq SOFA should have served as a template for a new SOFA between Iraq and NATO regarding the NATO Training Mission in Iraq. As no SOFA was signed, NATO had to discontinue the mission.

[10] Modern SOFAs may also address the status of other groups, such as civilians associated with the armed forces, family members, and contractors (See Fleck 2018a, Chs. 9–11). The present chapter will deal with military personnel only.

10.2 Historical Overview

10.2.1 Introduction

The term 'Status of Forces Agreement' was not in use until the start of the Cold War. Well before that period, however, a number of agreements were concluded that today would qualify as SOFAs. The first series of SOFAs were the agreements concluded by Allied States fighting the Central Powers in World War I. Within weeks of the outbreak of the conflict Belgium and France reached an agreement on jurisdiction over their armed forces present on the other State's territory.[11] The agreement the UK and France concluded the next year included a provision that would serve as a sort of template for most of the subsequent agreements,[12] recognizing the exclusive jurisdiction of Sending States over their service members operating on the territory of the other State.[13] Although the World War I SOFAs were the first of their kind, the jurisdiction arrangements built on long-standing practices and experiences were developed further in and after World War II leading to, *inter alia*, the NATO-SOFA and crisis management SOFAs.

10.2.2 19th and 20th Century General Practice

In the 19th century the consensual presence of armed forces on the territory of other States was not as wide-spread as it is today, yet it was not uncommon either. Individual service members or small groups would visit other States for various reasons, e.g. observing exercises in befriended States or participation in international events.[14] Also, naval vessels frequently called at foreign ports for resupplying or repair. As a rule, these visits were brief and as they hardly affected the Host State, no formal agreements were needed. On land regiments passed through the territory of foreign States quite regularly, at times based on bilateral agreements. Most of the agreements dealt with the practical and operational aspects of the transit of the regiments, such as the number of troops and supplies, frequency of transit, routes etc. Only occasionally, the status of the troops in transit was touched upon. An example is an agreement between Austria and Saxony of 1813 in which it was stipulated that the commanders of the troops were to maintain strict discipline and order over their troops, implying that the Host State would not exercise jurisdiction over the foreign forces.[15]

---

[11] Agreement between Belgium and France relative for the better prosecution of acts prejudicial to the armed forces; Brussels, 14 August 1914 (Parry 1969b, p. 274).

[12] Declaration between France and Great Britain respecting military penal jurisdiction; London, 15 December 1915 (Parry 1969c, p. 227)

[13] For an overview of these agreements, see Voetelink 2015, p. 37.

[14] E.g., Moore 1906, Sect. 213.

[15] Article VI, Convention between Austria and Saxony respecting the passage of troops; Vienna, 8 April 1813 (Parry 1969a, p. 213 ff).

10 The Status of Forces Agreements

Absent formal agreements, ideas on status of forces issues, in particular on criminal jurisdiction over service personnel abroad, developed in case law and literature. In 1812 the topic was for the first time addressed by a court in The Schooner Exchange v. McFaddon case in the US.[16] In this particular case dealing with the question whether a citizen of a State could claim ownership over another State's warship, Chief Justice Marshall, interpreting the facts in accordance with general legal principles, came to the conclusion that in general jurisdiction of a State is exclusive and absolute and that exceptions thereon must be traced to that State's consent. One of these exceptions, he argued, is the transit of armed forces. Where the State allowing foreign armed forces to pass through its territory, the transit State "… waives his jurisdiction over the army to which the right of passage has been granted without any express declaration to that effect".

Although this line of reasoning had been relied on in a number of US court cases dealing with the presence of members of the armed forces on the territory of another State,[17] its exact scope remained somewhat unclear. Most 19th century authors did not consider the Host State's waiver to be absolute and felt that visiting forces were "in a greater or less degree" exempted from the jurisdiction of the Host State courts.[18] An example of these ideas can be found in de 1868 Affaire Der-case. When a sailor, embarked on a British warship, committed a crime in Saigon, the French *Cour de Cassation* decided that the sailor was not exempted from local jurisdiction. As the crime had not taken place on board the ship, the Host State authorities could exercise their jurisdiction. Later, this view was included in a regulation of the 'Institut de Droit International'.[19]

In the literature, the focus was on the exercise of jurisdiction by Sending State authorities over their deployed forces, rather than the precise extent of the Host State's waiver. In general, authors seemed to take as a starting point the command relationship between a military commander and the armed forces deployed abroad. That commander, acting as the Sending State authority, could exercise jurisdiction *vis-à-vis* service members who were part of a military unit under his command and control. That would include situations where a crime had been committed by a member of the armed forces inside a military camp under control of the visiting forces, or outside the camp when the service member was on duty.[20]

Elements of these ideas can be found in a number of 20th century SOFAs. Still, at the start of that century international practice showed that Sending States would often be granted the right to exercise full and exclusive jurisdiction over their deployed

---

[16] U.S. Supreme Court 24 February 1812, The Schooner Exchange v. McFaddon 11 U.S. 116 (1812). supreme.justia.com/us/11/116/case.html.

[17] E.g., U.S. Supreme Court, Coleman v. Tennessee, 97 U.S. 509 (1878), supreme.justia.com/us/97/509/case.html>; U.S. Supreme Court, Dow v. Johnson, 100 U.S. 158 (1879), supreme.justia.com/us/100/158/case.html and U.S. Supreme Court, Tucker v. Alexandroff, 183 U.S. 424 (1902).

[18] E.g., Lawrence 1885, p. 47

[19] Article 18, Règlement sur le régime légal des navires et de leurs équipages dans les ports étrangers of 1898; Institut de Droit International; The Hague, 23 August 1898.

[20] Cf. Moore 1906, p. 560, Hall 1895, p. 206 and Oppenheim 1905, p. 483.

armed forces. In other words, the Host States had waived their jurisdiction over the visiting forces altogether, as was the case in the World War I SOFAs mentioned above. In the interwar period only a limited number of arrangements on the status of forces were negotiated. Two of the arrangements are SOFA-type agreements concluded by the United Kingdom with Iraq (1924)[21] and Egypt (1936).[22] The agreements granted British authorities the exclusive right to exercise criminal jurisdiction over all members of the British armed forces stationed in Iraq and Egypt. The status of international forces established by the League of Nations was not set out in international agreements but was part of the resolution establishing the mission, exempting the participating forces from the jurisdiction of the local courts.[23] Other examples are agreements as regards US military advisory missions in South and Central America. Members of these missions were granted equivalent rights as diplomatic personnel enjoyed and were, therefore, exempted from local jurisdiction.[24]

In World War II Allied States deployed an unprecedented number of troops throughout the world for an extended period of time. As deployments became more complex, a growing number of SOFAs were concluded covering a wide array of subjects. The principal issue of these often comprehensive documents still was criminal jurisdiction over the visiting forces. Also, the majority of the agreements continued the World War I and the interwar period practice with respect to criminal jurisdiction, granting Sending States exclusive rights over their forces. Yet, not all Allied States that received foreign forces on their soil were prepared to fully waive their rights. The Soviet Union, France, and the United Kingdom, for instance, stipulated in a number of SOFAs that their domestic courts would exercise jurisdiction over certain type of crimes committed by visiting forces, limiting the scope of the Sending States' jurisdiction over their deployed troops.

10.2.3 NATO Status of Forces Agreement

After World War II international tensions led to the start of the Cold War, resulting in the semi-permanent extraterritorial stationing of massive amounts of troops both

---

[21] Military Agreement made under Article VII of the Anglo-Iraq Treaty Baghdad, 25 March 1924 (Vol. 35 LNTS 1925, No. 892).

[22] Convention between his Majesty's government in the United Kingdom and the Egyptian government concerning the immunities and privileges to be enjoyed by the British forces in Egypt; London, 26 August 1936 (Vol. 173 LNTS 1936-1937, No. 4032).

[23] E.g., Resolution of the Council of 11 December 1934, League of Nations Official Journal, December 1934, p. 1762–1763.

[24] E.g., Article 21, Agreement between the United States of America and the United States of Brazil, concerning a military mission of the United States of America to Brazil; Washington, 10 May 1934 (Vol. 150 LNTS 1934, No. 445).

10   The Status of Forces Agreements

in the East and the West. In Western Europe, building on the efforts of five European States to create a common defence (the Brussels Treaty Powers),[25] the North Atlantic Treaty Organisation (NATO) was established in 1949. In order to regulate the presence of armed forces of the member States on one another's territory within the framework of this alliance, a new agreement was negotiated, drawing on, *inter alia*, a US text that was based on the draft SOFA intended for the armed forces of the Brussels Treaty Powers.[26]

The talks resulted in the NATO-SOFA,[27] which stood apart from earlier status agreements. Not only was it the first multilateral and reciprocal SOFA but, more important, it also adopted an innovative and balanced approach to the issue of criminal jurisdiction by respecting the rights and interests of Sending States as well as Host States. Acknowledging the territorial rights of the Host State and the rights of the Sending State to be in control of its national armed forces abroad, Article VII of the NATO-SOFA provides for shared (or concurrent) jurisdiction over the members of these forces. Within this system of shared jurisdiction, either the Sending State or the Host State has primary jurisdiction over a specific offence, depending on the nature of the offence and the circumstances of the case, while the State not having primary jurisdiction can request the State having primary jurisdiction to waive this right.[28] If an offence is only punishable under the laws of one of the States, obviously, this State retains exclusive jurisdiction.[29]

10.2.4   *Status of Forces and Crisis Management Operations*

Because of its balanced approach to the issue of criminal jurisdiction this particular SOFA-provision still serves as an example for quite a few contemporary SOFAs world-wide.[30] Nevertheless, article VII of the NATO-SOFA has not become a

---

[25] To that end, Belgium, France, Luxembourg, the Netherlands and the UK had adopted the Treaty for collaboration in economic, social and cultural matters and for collective self-defence; Brussels, 17 March 1948 (Vol. 19 UNTS 1948, No. 304).

[26] Status of members of the armed forces of the Brussels Treaty Powers; Brussels, 21 December 1949 (Department of State Bulletin, 20 March 1950). This treaty did not enter into force.

[27] Agreement between the parties to the North Atlantic Treaty regarding the status of their forces; London, 19 June 1951 (Vol. 199 UNTS 1954, No. 2678).

[28] The US has negotiated with a number of States supplementary agreements whereby the Host State agrees to waive its primary right to exercise jurisdiction; International Security Advisory Board 2015, p. 18.

[29] Article VII (2)(a)-(c) NATO-SOFA.

[30] E.g., the SOFA between EU member States (Agreement between the Member States of the European Union concerning the status of military and civilian staff seconded to the institutions of the European Union, of the headquarters and forces which may be made available to the European Union in the context of the preparation and execution of the tasks referred to in Article 17(2) of the Treaty to the European Union, including exercises, and of the military and civilian staff of the Member States put at the disposal of the European Union to act in this context (EU SOFA); Brussels, 17 November 2003 (OJ 2004, C 321); not in force yet) and over half of the SOFAs the US

universal standard and in many SOFAs States adopted a different position. A case in point are SOFAs concluded with regard to today's crisis management operations.[31] When the United Nations (UN) continued the practice started by the League of Nations of establishing international forces, it was not clear whether the UN Privileges and Immunities Convention[32] would cover the legal status of the members of the military contingents that UN-member States contributed to these UN-missions. So when in 1956 the UN established its first so called peacekeeping operation in response to the Suez crisis, the UN Emergency Force (UNEF), it also concluded a SOFA with Egypt, Host State of the mission, in order to avoid any uncertainty about the status of the troops.[33]

Because of the exclusive international nature of the mission requiring it to operate independently of its Host, immunity of the forces was felt to be essential.[34] Consequently, Para 11 of the UNEF-SOFA read: "Members of the Force shall be subject to the exclusive jurisdiction of their respective national States in respect of any criminal offences which may be committed by them in Egypt". This particular provision has been included in other mission specific UN-SOFAs and is now part of the Model UN-SOFA that forms the template for negotiations between UN and Host States with respect to new UN-missions.[35] As a result, in all UN missions Sending States have exclusive criminal jurisdiction over their forces.[36] Moreover, other international organisations involved in crisis management operations, such as the African Union (AU), the European Union (EU),[37] and NATO, are now taking a similar approach

---

has concluded (International Security Advisory Board 2015, p. 18), such as the SOFA with Japan (Agreement under article VI of the Treaty of Mutual Co-operation and Security between Japan and the United States of America, regarding facilities and areas and the status of United States armed forces in Japan; Washington, 19 January 1960 (TIAS 4510) and South Korea (Agreement under Article IV of the Mutual Defense Treaty between the United States of America and the Republic of Korea, regarding facilities and areas and the status of United States Armed Forces in the Republic of Korea (with agreed minutes, agreed understandings and exchange of letters); Seoul, 9 July 1966 (Vol. 674 UNTS 1971, No. 9605), and

[31] The term crisis management operation is used in this chapter as a generic term for any multilateral military operation taking place with Host State consent and includes notions, such as peacebuilding, peace support, peace operations, peace-keeping operation and peace-enforcement operations.

[32] Convention on the Privileges and Immunities of the United Nations; 13 February 1946 (UNTS 1946-1947, No. 4).

[33] Exchange of letters constituting an agreement between the United Nations and the Government of Egypt concerning the status of the United Nations Emergency Force in Egypt; New-York, 8 February 1957 (Vol. 260 UNTS 1957, No. 3704).

[34] UN Secretary-General 1958, para 14.

[35] Model Status of Forces Agreement for Peace-Keeping Operations, Report of the Secretary-General, UN Doc A/45/594, 9 October 1990. Based on this model mission specific SOFAs are adopted.

[36] Today, the UN Security Council includes in its Resolutions establishing a new mission a provision to the effect that pending the conclusion of the SOFA the Model UN-SOFA will apply provisionally.

[37] The EU is the only other organization that has a Model SOFA like the UN has: Revised Draft Model Agreement on the Status of the European Union Led Forces between the European Union and a Host State, EU Doc. 12616/07, 6 September 2007 in conjunction with EU Doc. 11894/07, 20 July 2007 and EU Doc. 11894/07 COR1, 5 September 2007.

10 The Status of Forces Agreements

and secure in their SOFAs that States contributing armed forces to missions led by them will have exclusive jurisdiction over their forces.[38] The same applies to crisis management operations set up by a coalition of States, such as the Resolute Support Mission in Afghanistan.[39]

Today, with only very few exceptions, States participating in crisis management operations are granted the right to exercise exclusive jurisdiction over their forces deployed in the States where a particular operation is taking place.[40] Whether this practice amounts to a customary rule under international law is still a subject of debate. While some authors have made a positive statement to that effect,[41] others are more reluctant to make that step yet[42] or are clearly not convinced that such a rule has emerged.[43]

The right of Sending States to exercise full criminal jurisdiction over their forces abroad is sometimes criticized. When a service member of the visiting forces commits a crime that affects the local population and the Sending State authorities put him on trial after return to his home State, it may not be clear for the local community that justice has been done. Therefore, and to facilitate access to local witnesses, it has been suggested that Sending States conduct on-site courts martial in the Host State. One of the few SOFAs that have incorporated this idea is the agreement reached between South Sudan and Uganda on deployment of Ugandan troops to South Sudan. Article 4.2 states that "A member of a visiting Force alleged to have committed the offence of murder, manslaughter or rape, shall be tried at the scene of the alleged crime".

10.3 International Law Perspective

10.3.1 Introduction

The previous section's emphasis on the fact that today the status of armed forces present abroad is generally set out in specific international agreements, may give

---

[38] For an overview see Voetelink 2015, Chapter 4.

[39] Agreement between the North Atlantic Treaty Organization and the Islamic Republic of Afghanistan on the Status of NATO Forces and NATO Personnel Conducting Mutually Agreed NATO-Led Activities in Afghanistan; Kabul (30 September 2014), NATO Doc PO(2014)0652 (1 October 2014), mfa.gov.af/Content/files/SOFA%20ENGLISH.pdf.

[40] One of the exceptions concerned the SOFA for the Regional Assistance Mission to Solomon Islands (RAMSI) that accorded the participating forces functional immunity: Article 10(2), Agreement between Solomon Islands, Australia, New Zealand, Fiji, Papua New Guinea, Samoa and Tonga concerning the operations and status of the police and armed forces and other personnel deployed to Solomon Islands to assist in the restoration of law and order and security; Townsville, 24 July 2003 (2003 ATS 17; 2003 PITSE 12).

[41] Voetelink 2015, p. 186.

[42] Leuven Manual 2017, pp. 120–121 and Fleck 2018a, p. 11.

[43] Liivoja 2017, p. 152.

the impression that the law of visiting forces is fully based on conventional international law, separated from international law in general. The subject is, however, deeply rooted in international law and closely related to some of its fundamental principles, e.g. sovereignty and immunity, which are fundamental to understand the principles underlying SOFAs, in particular the provisions on criminal jurisdiction. This section examines the position of sovereign States under international law and the jurisdictional powers reflecting that position in relation to visiting forces.

10.3.2 Jurisdiction of States over Armed Forces Personnel Stationed Abroad

From the 16th century onwards, the concept that States were subordinate to a higher worldly and ecclesiastic authority, gradually gave way to the idea that States constitute the highest sovereign authority, administering their respective territories independently and as equals.[44] These ideas reside in the *Westphalia Peace Treaties* of 1648,[45] which are considered the inception of the modern State system.[46] The Permanent Court of Arbitration described the sovereign position of States in the *Island of Palmas* case: "Sovereignty in the relations between States signifies independence. Independence in regard to a portion of the globe is the right to exercise therein, to the exclusion of any other State, the functions of a State".[47]

Thus sovereignty is reflected in the notion of jurisdiction,[48] referring to a State's legislative, enforcement and adjudicative powers.[49] Legislative, or prescriptive, jurisdiction is the power of a State to apply its laws to "the activities, relations or status of persons, or interests of persons in things, whether by legislation, by executive act, or by determination of a court",[50] while adjudicative jurisdiction refers to the authority to: "subject persons or things to the process of its courts or administrative tribunal, whether in civil or criminal proceedings, whether or not the State is a

---

[44] The equality of States is laid down in the maxim '*par in parem non habet imperium*' (an equal has no power over his equal), which originates from Canon law and was later applied to feudal emperors, who were considered to be each other's equals; Schneider 1964, p. 15.

[45] Instrumentum Pacis Osnabrugensis; Osnabrück, 14/24 October 1648. Available at www.lwl.org/westfaelischegeschichte/portal/Internet/finde/langDatensatz.php?urlID=740&url_tabelle=tab_quelle and Instrumentum Pacis Monasteriensis; Münster, 24 October 1648. Available at avalon.law.yale.edu/17th_century/westphal.asp.

[46] Wessel 2007, p. 3.

[47] PCA 4 April 1928, The Island of Palmas case (or Miangas), United States v. The Netherlands, Award of the tribunal, p. 8. Available at www.pca-cpa.org (accessed November 2014).

[48] Mann 1964, p. 30: "Jurisdiction is an aspect of sovereignty, it is coextensive with and, indeed, incidental to, but also limited by, the State's sovereignty". Bowett 1982 regards jurisdiction as a "manifestation of state sovereignty".

[49] Restatement of the Law, Third, Foreign Relations Law of the United States 1986, p. 230 ff.

[50] Ibid., p. 232.

10 The Status of Forces Agreements

party to the proceedings".[51] Enforcement jurisdiction allows a State "to induce or compel compliance or to punish noncompliance with its laws or regulations, whether through the courts or by use of executive, administrative, police, or other non-judicial action".[52]

Extraterritorial exercise of a State's jurisdiction finds its limits in "the sovereign territorial rights of other States"[53] as, in principle, jurisdiction and the exercise thereof is territorial in nature.[54] Hence, States can only exercise their jurisdiction extraterritorially insofar as international law permits.[55] Consequently, a State can apply its laws extraterritorially, extending its prescriptive jurisdiction, provided that a genuine and significant link or interest exists between the regulating State and a specific act or person abroad or in international space, e.g., the high seas. As a rule this nexus is reflected in provisions in national laws, which are based on established principles of jurisdiction under international law.[56]

Based on the principles of active nationality and passive nationality a State may extend the reach of its laws to nationals abroad and, in limited cases, to foreign citizens who breach their nationals' interest. Based on the protective principle a State can also establish legislative jurisdiction when its interests are at stake. In addition, a State can assert extraterritorial legislative jurisdiction based on the universality principle that flows from the idea that specific criminal offences, or the circumstances under which they may take place, justify the exercise of jurisdiction by any State, as they impact the international community as a whole.[57]

A number of States also make their laws applicable to military personnel serving abroad,[58] making them, figuratively speaking, carry national criminal law in their backpacks abroad.[59] This principle is often referred to as the "law of the flag"[60] (*la loi suit le drapeau*).[61] This type of jurisdiction has a unique character and cannot

---

[51] Idem.

[52] Idem.

[53] ECHR, 12 December 2001, Banković and others v. Belgium and 16 others, App no 52207/99, §59.

[54] PCIJ 7 September 1927, The case of the S.S. Lotus, Series A. No. 10, p. 19.

[55] Ryngaert 2008, p. 21 ff. I.e., a permissive rule of international law or the other State's 'consent, invitation or acquiescence'; Banković and others v. Belgium and 16 others, App no 52207/99, §60.

[56] I.e., next to the nationality principle: the protective principle, the universality principle, and the passive personality principle, Introductory comment on the 1935 Harvard Draft Convention, Harvard Draft Convention on Jurisdiction with Respect to Crime, Vol. 29 *A.J.I.L.* Supplement: Research in International Law (1935), p. 445. Today, commentators often refer to effects principle as well, e.g., Ireland-Piper 2017, p. 34.

[57] The classical example, of course, is piracy. Because of the threat of pirates to all seafaring nations and international trade, all States can exercise jurisdiction

[58] Liivoja 2010, p. 310, mentions, *inter alia,* Australia, Denmark, Germany, the United Kingdom and the United States. Other States, like Canada and Ireland, are more reticent: Odello 2010, p. 377.

[59] Liivoja 2017, p. 1, paraphrasing an Israeli judge.

[60] Lazareff 1971, p. 11.

[61] According to Napoleon Bonaparte, the French army was never actually abroad as on foreign territory it continued to operate under its national flag: "Il faut regarder le drapeau comme le domicile. Partout où est le drapeau, là est la France"; Fenet 1827, pp. 427–428.

be exclusively based on principles mentioned above. Liivoja refers to it as 'service jurisdiction' and, after analysing the traditional principles of jurisdiction, comes to the conclusion it "... should be recognized as jurisdictional principle in its own right, based on membership in or substantive connection with the armed forces of a State".[62] Sari, drawing on the ideas of Seyersted,[63] focuses on a State's competence to regulate and control its organs and officials, using the term 'organic jurisdiction'.[64]

Extraterritorial application of national laws does not necessarily impact the legal order of other States, which explains why international law allows for this exemption from the territorial jurisdiction of a State. Extraterritorial enforcement and adjudication of a State's laws are more intrusive and in general will affect another State's sovereign rights.[65] Consequently, a State cannot subject other sovereign States to its adjudicative and enforcement jurisdiction (*par in parem non habet judicium*)[66] without the other's consent[67] or a permissive rule under international law,[68] making State borders the geographical boundaries of enforcement and adjudicative jurisdiction.[69]

As a result, a State's national abroad is subject to the legislative jurisdiction of the State where he is present, as well as to his home State's legislative jurisdiction to the extent it has extended its jurisdiction beyond its borders. Furthermore, that person is subject to the exclusive adjudicative and enforcement jurisdiction of the foreign State. In other words: his home State cannot exercise its adjudicative and enforcement jurisdiction in a foreign sovereign State *vis-à-vis* its national while abroad.

10.3.3 Immunity of State Officials

This jurisdictional regime would seriously hamper international relations when rigorously applied to State officials abroad. If fully subjected to foreign jurisdiction these officials could become liable to politically motivated legal procedures threatening the effective performance of their official functions. In order to facilitate international relations international law accords State officials privileges and immunities, based on and inspired by international customary rules on state immunity and diplomatic

---

[62] Liivoja 2017, p. 263.

[63] Seyersted 2008, pp. 81–105.

[64] Sari 2015, p. 19.

[65] Ryngaert 2008, p. 144.

[66] Kokott 2007, p. 6, para 35.

[67] E.g., a Host State can give its consent in a SOFA, allowing the Sending State to exert enforcement powers over its service personnel abroad.

[68] Mann 1964, pp. 129–131 and 138 on enforcement jurisdiction.

[69] Boister 2018, p. 3.

immunity.[70] Privileges exempt persons from application of specific foreign State legislation, by and large in the field of customs, fiscal law, and social security law. Privileges are substantive in nature contrary to immunities, which are exceptions to the enforcement and adjudicative jurisdiction of the Host State and as such are procedural rules.

The scope of immunities generally depends on the position and function of State officials and the nature of their acts. High-ranking officials, such as Heads of State and Government, and Ministers for Foreign Affairs, and diplomatic agents have to discharge their functions without any interference of the Host State. Hence, they enjoy immunity *ratione personae* exempting them from the enforcement and adjudicative jurisdiction of the host State with respect to official acts as well as private act, thus effectively shielding them from exercise of jurisdiction of a foreign State during their tenure.

All State officials can be considered instruments of their States, as a State itself is a legal abstraction.[71] Therefore, their official acts are to be attributed to the State[72] and as the State enjoys immunity, State officials cannot be held accountable before a foreign court. In other words, they enjoy immunity for acts carried out during the course of official duties: immunity *ratione materiae* or functional immunity.[73] Armed forces are key State organs and consequently, members of the armed forces qualify as State officials. When they are deployed abroad with the consent of the Host State and are on duty, in accordance with general international law they enjoy immunity *ratione materiae*, just like any other State official.[74] Thus, even without a SOFA members of the armed forces are entitled to functional immunity under customary international law. The notion that without a SOFA military personnel has the same legal status as tourist, which until recently could be found in the literature, is, therefore, misleading.[75] Functional immunity is the minimal legal requirement

---

[70] Diplomatic law has been codified in the Vienna Conventions on Diplomatic Relations; Vienna, 18 April 1961 (Vol. 500 UNTS 1964, No. 7310) and on Consular Relations; Vienna, 24 April 1963 (Vol. 596 UNTS 196, No. 8638).

[71] Voetelink 2015, p. 131 and Liivoja 2017, p. 87.

[72] See UN Doc A/CN.4/631 (2010), ILC Second report on immunity of State officials from foreign criminal jurisdiction, 10 June 2010, para 26 and ICTY Appeals Chamber 29 October 1997, Prosecutor v. Blaskić, IT-95-14-AR108bis, Judgement on the request of the Republic of Croatia for review of the decision of the trial chamber II of 18 July 1997, paras 38 and 41. Available at: <www.icty.org/x/cases/blaskic/acdec/en/71029JT3.html>.

[73] E.g., Ronzitti 2015, p. 60–62; Liivoja 2017, p. 89. Further, see the work of UN International Law Commission on 'Immunity of State officials from foreign criminal jurisdiction'; <legal.un.org/ilc/guide/4_2.shtml>, in particular draft articles 5 ("State officials acting as such enjoy immunity ratione materiae from the exercise of foreign criminal jurisdiction" and 6(1) ("State officials enjoy immunity ratione materiae only with respect to acts performed in an official capacity").

[74] Ronzitti 2012, p. 21, Voetelink 2015, p. 158–162; Liivoja 2017, p. 163, Fleck 2015, p. 111–112, and Fleck 2018a, p. 881 ff. and Conderman and Sari 2018, p. 217.

[75] E.g., the remark "In the absence of a status of forces agreement which has to be transformed by law, the status of foreign military personnel travelling to a host country is essentially that of foreign tourists" made in the 1st edition of the Handbook of Visiting Forces did not return in the 2018, 2nd edition, Fleck 2018b, p. 86.

for forces to operate abroad as it "...ensures an unimpeded cooperation between sovereign States in protecting the official functions of the personnel involved."[76]

So indeed, as Chief Justice Marshall concluded in The Schooner Exchange v. McFaddon-case, the jurisdiction of a Host State is not unrestricted, *inter alia*, because under general international law visiting armed forces are exempt from the enforcement and adjudicative jurisdiction of the Host State. This exemption is, however not complete, and only applies as regards to offences committed while on duty.

10.4 Operational Law Perspective

10.4.1 Introduction

Well over a century after conclusion of the first set of SOFAs in World War I, States and international organisations continue to conclude SOFAs in order to balance the interest of Sending States and Host States with respect to the criminal jurisdiction over visiting forces. Model-SOFAs and SOFAs such as the NATO-SOFA notwithstanding, no universal regime covering the consensual extraterritorial presence of armed forces has emerged yet. Moreover, even though jurisdiction provisions form the core of all SOFAs, a host of other issues can be part of the agreements as well; the exact nature and scope thereof depending on the situation at hand.

Another interesting feature of SOFAs is that while the legal status of State officials is in general expressed in terms of immunity, SOFAs often focus on the exercise of jurisdiction, granting Sending States more legal authority over their deployed forces than could be expected based on the functional immunity rule discussed in the previous section. In order to examine these issues in more depth it is useful to also take the operational perspective into account. Hence, this section introduces military operational law, a specialized field of law that focuses on legal aspects of military action, to take a closer look at the operational side of SOFAs and their provisions; in particular the jurisdictional provisions.

10.4.2 Military Operational Law

As principal State organs armed forces are subjected to the international rule of law. Applied in a military context rule of law implies that military activities have to have a clear legal basis under international law and have to be executed in accordance with the law, taking into account the pertinent legal basis. Legal basis and applicable rules together cover all legal aspects pertaining to the preparation and execution

---

[76] Fleck 2015, p. 111.

10 The Status of Forces Agreements 243

of operations and today is often referred to as military operational law.[77] It is a relatively young and still-developing sub-discipline of law that, depending on the situation at hand, can include international law, as well as domestic and foreign law. As these interacting areas of law regulate and impact all phases of an operation[78] they constitute its legal framework.

Still, military operational law is not a rigid construct forcing the military in a legal straitjacket when conducting an operation. It has a certain degree of flexibility and can make law a non-physical capability enabling a commander to achieve his operational objectives.[79] This instrumental character of military operational law in its most far-reaching form is reflected in the notion of lawfare, (re)defined as: "The concept of using or misusing law by a participant in a military operation, or an entity acting under its control, with its consent or in coordination with it, as a substitute for traditional military means deliberately designed to achieve an operational military goal in an ongoing military operation".[80] Although, obviously, not all aspects of military operational law amount to lawfare, many can be constructive to mission accomplishment.[81]

SOFAs are a case in point. As any extraterritorial operation entails questions regarding the status of the visiting forces, SOFAs are an integral part of the military operational law. These agreements covering the rights and obligations of foreign forces when present within another State's territory are part of the *jus in praesentia*.[82] As such, they do not necessarily address the right of the forces to be present on the territory of another State. That right is part of a closely connected field of law: the *jus ad praesentiam*[83] that covers the legal basis for the extraterritorial presence of armed forces. Moreover, it not only justifies that presence, but defines the functions the forces are allowed to perform during their stay on Host State territory as well.

It is important to note that by granting armed forces of another sovereign State access to its territory, a Host State in fact accepts a breach of its territorial integrity. It will only do so for a very good reason while at the same time limiting the impact of the visiting forces' presence. Hence, a Host State will, in principle, not give those forces blanket permission to exercise all their military functions within its territory. Access will be granted for a specific purpose, such as transit of forces or equipment, conduct of training or exercises, or participation in a crisis management operation. In addition, further conditions can be set out in a formal arrangement, for instance as regards the size of the force and duration of their presence. These arrangements may come under various names often referring to the visiting forces' principal activity in the Host State, such as basing or stationing agreement, training agreement or exercise agreement. These agreements formalize the Host State's consent with the presence

---

[77] Voetelink 2017, p. 240.

[78] Gill and Fleck 2015, p. 3.

[79] Voetelink 2017, p. 239.

[80] Voetelink 2017, p. 252; building on Dunlap original definition in Dunlap 2008, p. 146.

[81] Dunlap 2010, p. 128.

[82] E.g. Spies 2008.

[83] Together both fields of law comprise the law of visiting forces.

of the visiting forces and establish the legal basis for their entry in and presence on Host State territory.

The *jus in praesentiam* then takes over and delineates the legal position of the visiting forces while present on the territory of the Host State by setting out its rights and obligations in SOFAs.[84] These agreements build, therefore, on the *jus ad praesentiam* and consequently, a SOFA is impacted by the nature and scope of the pertinent legal basis.[85] Viewed from a Sending State's perspective, the legal basis for the extraterritorial presence is reflected in the operational objective of the visiting forces. The mission specific SOFA must be geared towards that objective enabling the military commander of the visiting forces to accomplish the Sending States mission abroad. SOFA-provisions, or the lack thereof, limiting the visiting forces to reach their operational objective, would defy the very purpose of the forces' presence the Host State has agreed to. A SOFA can support the visiting forces by expediting their entry into Host State territory and facilitating daily operations of the units during their foreign presence.[86] As operations benefit from a balanced relationship with Host State authorities and acceptance by the local population, conclusion of a SOFA should not only be led by the Sending States' requirements, but take Host States' interests into account as well.

10.4.3 *Operational Law Perspective on SOFAs*

10.4.3.1 General

A SOFA dealing with criminal jurisdictional matters only does not fit the needs of modern armed forces. Hence, SOFAs often have become comprehensive documents dealing with a host of issues depending on the nature of the foreign forces' presence in the Host State. That helps explain why no universal SOFA has been developed yet. Other State officials, like diplomats, for instance, carry out their functions world-wide in a uniform way. The nature of the official duties of the staff of a diplomatic mission in the Netherlands is not fundamentally different from the tasks performed by their colleagues in, say, Kazakhstan, although the issues they have to attend to may differ, of course. Their status is the same around the world based on customary international law and international agreements, such as the Vienna Convention on Diplomatic Relations.[87] Such a convention could be helpful to set out some issues regarding visiting forces in general, but would lack details of the jobs the visiting

---

[84] Sometimes agreements as stationing agreements are combined with SOFAs into one overarching document.

[85] Cf. Spies 2008, p. 240.

[86] Voetelink 2015, Chapter 10.

[87] Vienna Convention on Diplomatic Relations; Vienna, 18 April 1961 (Vol. 500 UNTS 1964, Nr. 7310).

10 The Status of Forces Agreements   245

forces need to perform efficiently. So, notwithstanding some Model-SOFAs and an agreement such as the NATO-SOFA, a wide variety of SOFAs is in force today.

Nevertheless, many SOFAs have a number of subjects in common, although the details may be worked out in different ways depending on the visiting forces' duties in the Host State. Apart from criminal jurisdiction, these subjects include, but are certainly not limited to: personnel covered by the SOFA,[88] respect for Host State law, claims, entry and exit, right to operate equipment, exemptions from Host State duties, fees, tariffs and taxes,[89] acceptance of permits and licenses, use of infrastructure, carrying of arms, and wearing of national uniforms. The next paragraphs will address some of the subjects that are also of interest from an international law perspective. The final part of this section will again look at criminal jurisdiction now taking military operational law as starting point.

10.4.3.2 Claims

Whenever armed forces are deployed abroad injury to local persons and damage to their property is inevitable.[90] However, State immunity prevents an injured local citizen to bring his case to a local court as exceptions under international law to State immunity in case of wrongful acts,[91] do normally not apply to acts of the armed forces.[92] If an injured person would end up bearing the loss himself it would not only be unfair,[93] but, from an operational point of view, undesirable as well, as it could jeopardize the good rapport the visiting forces have established with local authorities and population. Therefore, from World War I on visiting forces have established formal procedures to settle claims, often in accordance with local regulations.[94] Based on these practices claims provisions are now part and parcel of modern SOFAs. An example is Article VIII of the NATO-SOFA that provides that intergovernmental claims are waived, third-party claims related to official duty are settled by the Host State and partly reimbursed by the Sending State and third-party claims related to non-official activities are reviewed by the Host State and may be

---

[88] E.g. civilian component of the armed forces, family members, and civilian contractors.

[89] These should be distinguished from charges for services rendered, which will in general be paid.

[90] Prescott 2018, p. 278.

[91] See Article 11, European Convention on State Immunity; Basel, 16 May 1972 (Vol. 1495 UNTS 1988, No. 25699) and Ar. 12, United Nations Convention on jurisdictional immunities of states and their property; New-York, 17 January 2005 (UN Doc A/RES/59/38 (2004) van 16 December 2004).

[92] Voetelink 2015, p. 241.

[93] A general principle of law "requires that those who cause an injury to others compensate them"; Reisman and Sloane 2000, p. 514; also see Leuven Manual 2017, p. 288.

[94] E.g., In World War I Claims Commissions of the British forces in France settled claims in accordance with French rules; Morris 1916, p. 320 and in World War II the UK settled claims against US forces based in the UK using local laws; Exchange of notes constituting an agreement between the United States of America and the United Kingdom relating to claims for damages resulting from acts of armed forces personnel; London 29 February and 28 March 1944 (Vol. 15 UNTS 1948, No. 104).

settled by an *ex gratia* payment[95] by the Sending State. As this type of provision meets the interests of the injured party while respecting the Sending State's immunity, many SOFAs follow a similar approach.[96]

There is one major exception to this practice, which is closely related to the operational environment in which the visiting force may have to operate. As in armed conflict, visiting armed force may have to resort to armed force when participating in a crisis management operation. Whenever they act out of operational necessity and in accordance with the applicable rules, in particular the right to self-defence, the mission's mandate, and the Rules of Engagement, their conduct is lawful. As a consequence, they cannot be held liable for any damage resulting from these forceful, yet legitimate acts.[97] This notion builds on international humanitarian law conventions that stipulate that parties to a conflict are liable to pay compensation when they have violated the laws of armed conflict.[98] The UN even regards operational necessity[99] as a legal principle[100] and, consequently, does not include in UN SOFAs provision exempting operational damage from liability. In many other SOFAs, however, provisions to that effect are included.[101] It must be noted, however, that often injured persons nevertheless do receive an *ex gratia* payment,[102] because of operational considerations, such as force protection and confidence building.

10.4.3.3 Respect for Host State Law

Another recurring topic is respect for local law. Many SOFAs state the duty to respect Host States' laws and regulations.[103] Respect does not merely imply the commitment to pay due regard to Host State law, rather it reflects the duty to obey these laws[104] based on the principle of territorial sovereignty. As mentioned above, while jurisdiction of a State is in principle territorial, a State may extend application of its laws beyond its borders in accordance with general accepted principles of jurisdiction.

---

[95] Voluntary payment without accepting any liability or other legal obligation.

[96] Voetelink 2015, p. 242.

[97] Cf. Leuven Manual 2017, p. 304 ff.

[98] E.g. Article 3, Convention (IV) respecting the Laws and Customs of War on Land and its annex: Regulations concerning the Laws and Customs of War on Land. The Hague, 18 October 1907; The Hague, 18 October 1907 and Article 91, Protocol Additional to the Geneva Conventions of 12 August 1949, and relating to the Protection of Victims of International Armed Conflicts (Protocol I); Bern, 12 December 1977 (Vol. 1125 UNTS 1979, No. 17512).

[99] Leuven Manual 2017, p. 304.

[100] Schmalenbach 2004, p. 277 and 392.

[101] E.g. Article 15, Model Agreement on the status of the European Union-led forces (Revised Model EU-SOFA EU Doc (11894/07), corrigendum of 5 September 2007, EU Doc 11894/07 COR 1).

[102] Sometimes referred to as 'goodwill', 'solatia', 'condolence' or 'battle damage' payments.

[103] E.g. Para 7, Model UN-SOFA, Article 2, EU-SOFA, and Article II, NATO SOFA. A similar provision can also be found in the Vienna Convention on Diplomatic Relations (Article 41(1)).

[104] Denza 2016, p. 374.

10 The Status of Forces Agreements

Extraterritorial application of these laws does not affect, however, operation of the other States' laws. So when a Sending State deploys its armed forces abroad, its service members become subjected to Host State law the moment they enter its territory, even if the laws of the Sending State continue to apply *vis-à-vis* its soldiers abroad.

10.4.3.4 Privileges

Full application of Host State law could, however, be detrimental to mission accomplishment. Therefore, States will agree on certain privileges and immunities facilitating the visiting forces operations. As discussed above, by granting immunities the Host State accepts to refrain from exercising its enforcement and adjudicative jurisdiction with respect to the privileged persons, while its laws continue to apply. By providing visiting forces privileges, the Host State exempts them from the application of certain rules, often in the field of taxes and customs.[105] Hence, most SOFAs include provisions exempting visiting forces from paying local taxes and customs duties. The notion underlying these privileges is the idea that a State should not profit from governmental activities of another State on its territory. Respect for local law means, therefore, that the visiting forces are subjected to Host State law, as discussed above, except insofar privileges and immunities apply.

10.4.3.5 Jurisdiction versus Immunity

As noted above, SOFAs often deal with status of armed forces personnel stationed abroad in terms of exercise of jurisdiction, while under general international law it is common practice to refer to immunities when addressing the legal position of State officials. Indeed, there are very few SOFAs that explicitly grant visiting forces immunity,[106] while in some jurisdiction and immunity are combined in one provision.[107] A number of SOFAs build on existing agreements that address immunities of State officials abroad, such as the Vienna Convention on Diplomatic Relations. The jurisdiction provisions of these SOFAs offer visiting forces immunities equivalent to

---

[105] Voetelink 2015, p.

[106] E.g., Exchange of letters between the government of New Zealand and the government of the Solomon Islands constituting an agreement on the deployment of New Zealand personnel to the Solomon Islands as members of the International Peace Monitoring Team; Honiara, 9–10 November 2000 (2000 Pacific Islands Treaty Series 7).

[107] The SOFA between the Netherlands and Burkina Faso grants visiting forces immunity, adding that the Sending State has exclusive jurisdiction over the forces; Accord entre le Gouvernement du Royaume des Pays-Bas et le Gouvernement du Burkina Faso sur le statut des personnels civils et militaires du Ministère de la Défense du Royaume des Pays-Bas sur le territoire du Burkina Faso; Ouagadougou, 9 June 2015 (Dutch Treaty Series 2015, No. 96 ; UNTS No. 53067).

those received by the administrative and technical staff of a diplomatic mission,[108] without having diplomatic status though.[109]

The reason for emphasizing jurisdiction in the military context is the somewhat 'passive' nature of the system of immunities. Immunity rules only exempt a privileged person from the exercise of the Host State's enforcement and adjudicative jurisdiction.[110] Immunity does not grant the privileged person's home State the right to use its enforcement and adjudicative jurisdiction *vis-à-vis* a privileged national abroad. As a result, only on the official's return home States can act and exercise its sovereign rights over him.

Such an approach does not always meet the Sending States' need to continue to exercise control over its forces abroad. One of the basic military principles is unity of command implying that a commander must lead his personnel without interference from outside the military chain of command and independent from the Host State authorities. Especially during operations in a (potentially) non-benign environment, like in a crisis management operation, a commander must have direct control over its personnel without undue outside interference. To some extent such interference can be avoided by claiming immunity for the visiting forces. Functional immunity, as recognized under international law, is indeed a *sine qua non* for deployed forces. It does not, however, grant Sending States authorities full legal control over their forces. Of course, they can exercise administrative and disciplinary powers *vis-à-vis* their service members with respect to internal matters that do not affect the legal order of the Host State, but they cannot exercise enforcement powers over their troops without Host State consent.

Therefore, SOFAs grant Sending States the right to exercise jurisdiction *vis-à-vis* their service members, which includes enforcement jurisdiction.[111] Consequently, Sending State authorities can, for instance, investigate a crime committed by one of its service members, using coercive powers with respect to the suspect on Host State territory.[112] For mission accomplishment it is essential that any form of misconduct by the armed forces is promptly acted upon by the Sending States' authorities demonstrating resolve to deal with any breach of rules. Also, if an offence is committed breaching a person's right to life the Sending State may have an obligation under human rights law to conduct an effective investigation.[113] From an operational perspective prompt action is essential to maintain order and discipline within the

---

[108] Brakel 2016, p. 230.

[109] E.g., Article 6(1), Agreement between the Kingdom of the Netherlands and Ukraine on the International Mission for Protection of Investigation, Kiev, 28 July 2014 (Dutch Treaty Series 2014, No. 135) and Agreement between the Russian Federation and the Syrian Arab Republic on the Stationing of an Air Force Unit of the Armed Forces of the Russian Federation on the Territory of the Syrian Arab Republic; Damascus, 26 August 2015 (on file with author).

[110] van Hoek et al. 2012, p. 242.

[111] In general, SOFAs address jurisdiction in a generic way without distinguishing between the different forms of jurisdiction (legislative, adjudicative, and enforcement); Voetelink 2018, p. 266.

[112] A Host State will not allow a Sending State to independently exercise enforcement powers with respect to Host State citizens.

[113] E.g., ECHR 20 November 2014, Case of Jaloud v. The Netherlands, Appl. No. 477/08.

10 The Status of Forces Agreements

deployed unit and, in particular when Host State interests are involved, to show that a SOFA granting the visiting forces extensive rights, will not lead to impunity of its service members.

However, not under all circumstances do Sending States need to have exclusive jurisdiction over their forces. In peacetime situations where there is not much chance of the visiting forces having to resort to armed force to execute their tasks, less strict control may be sufficient. A case in point is the elaborate NATO-SOFA provision on criminal jurisdiction, that, basically, grants visiting forces jurisdiction over their forces while on duty and with respect to *inter se* offences. In the event of hostilities, however, parties to the NATO-SOFA will immediately review Article VII on criminal jurisdiction,[114] as during the negotiations the US expressed the opinion that under those conditions Sending States had to have exclusive criminal jurisdiction over its forces.[115]

10.5 Synthesis and Conclusion

Today, SOFAs are part and parcel of foreign military activities affecting visiting forces as well as the local community. Nevertheless, in general international law this particular type of international agreement does not receive wide attention, even though its core provisions on criminal jurisdiction are firmly rooted in that field of law. Within the sub-discipline of military operational law, on the other hand, SOFAs are one of the main themes as they are regarded as a cornerstone of the legal framework applicable to armed forces stationed abroad. This chapter has provided an insight in contemporary SOFA practice by exploring criminal jurisdiction over visiting forces as key feature of the agreements, bringing together the international law and military operational law perspective.

Over a period of more than 200 years, SOFAs have evolved around the key issue of criminal jurisdiction over visiting forces, into the comprehensive documents concluded today, addressing a wide variety of subjects. Which issues each SOFA covers largely depends on the purpose of the visiting forces' presence on Host State territory. A short training period abroad of a limited number of troops in a befriended State will not need too much detail, whereas a UN crisis management operation, for instance, requires a comprehensive arrangement on the rights and obligations of the visiting forces. It may even be necessary to reach additional agreements with a Host State regarding certain aspects of complex and protracted operations. The Model UN-SOFA includes a provision facilitating the conclusion of supplemental arrangements between UN-mission and Host State government (para 55).[116]

---

[114] Article XV(2), NATO SOFA.

[115] Voetelink 2015, p. 109.

[116] Recently, the provision has been used to secure the fair and humane treatment by Host State of persons detained by a UN mission and transferred to the Host State authorities; e.g., Arrangement to the Agreement between the United Nations and the Government of the Republic of Mali regarding

In international law the status of State officials abroad is referred to in terms of immunity. SOFAs, however, in general use jurisdiction to define the status of armed forces. This practice can be explained by taking the military operational law perspective into account as well. From an operational point of view it is mandatory that visiting forces remain under the command and control of their commanders. Immunity merely prevents Host State authorities from taking legal action against members of the visiting forces, but does not, on the other hand, allow the Sending States' authorities to enforce national rules in the Host State. Granting visiting forces the right to exercise jurisdiction includes the right to use enforcement powers *vis-à-vis* their personnel, allowing the commanders to exercise control over their troops.

To what extent Sending States can exercise jurisdiction over their armed forces abroad will depend on the visiting force's purpose and task. In general, modern SOFAs respect the rule that all State officials enjoy immunity for official acts (immunity *ratione materiae*). SOFAs do not, however, explicitly grant military personnel functional immunity, rather they authorize Sending States to exercise jurisdiction *vis-à-vis* their personnel while on duty. Often Sending States are allowed to exercise even broader authority over their forces. The most far-reaching scheme is the right of Sending States to exercise exclusive jurisdiction over their forces. It is common practice now that States contributing forces to a crisis management operation have that level of jurisdiction over their forces, which, in terms of immunity, amounts to full immunity.

Only on rare occasions do States agree to deviate from the functional immunity rule, denying the visiting forces even functional immunity. An example is Article 12(2) of the 2014 Netherlands-Qatar SOFA.[117] Under this provision, Courts of Qatar have jurisdiction over offences committed by Dutch personnel, whereas the "…the Netherlands authorities are entitled to exercise their jurisdiction over their personnel in cases of offences (crimes, felonies, and misdemeanors), as well as civil cases committed by its own personnel against their property, safety, fellow personnel or equipment".[118]

Status of armed force serving abroad with the consent of the States receiving the troops on their territory will continue to be of interest in the future as international military cooperation is critical in times of conflict or crisis as well as peace-time. Although a universal SOFA could benefit the expedient deployment of the forces, at the end of the day, operational requirements of these forces in relation to the particular tasks at hand will determine the contents of the SOFA. Criminal jurisdiction over the service members involved is a key issue for Sending States as well as Host States and will remain the central issue of these agreements.

---

the treatment of persons arrested by personnel of the Multidimensional Integrated Stabilization Mission in Mali (MINUSMA) and handed over to the Government of the Republic of Mali; Bamako, 1 July 2013 (on file with author).

[117] Status of forces agreement for military personnel and equipment for the forces between the State of Qatar and the Kingdom of the Netherlands; Doha, 16 December 2014 (Dutch Treaty Series 2015, No. 12).

[118] However, the Netherlands can request Qatar to waive its criminal jurisdiction (Article 12(4)).

References

AAP-6 (2017) NATO Glossary of terms and definitions.

Boister N (2018) An introduction to transnational criminal law. Oxford University Press, Oxford

Bowett DW (1982) Jurisdiction: Changing patterns of authority over activities and resources. 53.1 British Yearbook of International Law

Brakel YS (2016) Developing better U.S. status of forces protections in Africa. The AF L Rev 76:207–266

Conderman PJ, Sari A (2018) Chapter 20. Jurisdiction. In: Fleck D (ed) The Handbook of the Law of Visiting Forces, 2nd edn. Oxford University Press, Oxford

Denza E (2016) Diplomatic Law: Commentary on the Vienna Convention on Diplomatic Relations. Oxford University Press, Oxford

Dunlap CJ (2008) Lawfare today. Yale Journal of International Affairs 3(1):146–154

Dunlap CJ (2010) Does lawfare need an apologia? Case Western Reserve Journal of International Law 43(1):121–143

Fenet PA (1827) Recueil complet des travaux préparatoires du Code Civil Vol. 8. Impr. de Ducessois, Paris 46–48

Fleck D (2015) Status of forces in enforcement and Peace enforcement operations. In: Gill TD, Fleck D (eds) The Handbook of the International Law of Military Operations, 2nd edn. Oxford University Press, Oxford, 110–127

Fleck D (2018a) The Handbook of the Law of Visiting Forces, 2nd edn. Oxford University Press, Oxford

Fleck D (2018b) The Immunity of Visiting Forces and Their Headquarters (Chapter 5). In: Fleck D (ed) The Handbook of the Law of Visiting Forces, 2nd edn. Oxford University Press, Oxford

Fleck D, Grenfell K, Newton MA (2018) Multinational Military Operations (Chapter 3). In: Fleck D (ed) The Handbook of the Law of Visiting Forces, 2nd edn. Oxford University Press, Oxford

Gill TD, Fleck D (2015) Concept and sources of the international law of military operation. In: Gill TD, Fleck D (eds) The Handbook of the International Law of Military Operations, 2nd edn. Oxford University Press, Oxford, 3–13

Hall WE (1895) A Treatise on international law. Stevens & Sons, Oxford

Heefner G (2017) "A slice of their sovereignty": Negotiating the U.S. empire of bases, Wheelus Field, Libya, 1950–1954. 41 Diplomatic History, 1:50–77

International Security Advisory Board (2015) Report on Status of Forces Agreements. Washington. www.state.gov/t/avc/isab/236234.htm

Ireland-Piper D (2017) Accountability in extraterritoriality: A comparative and international law perspective. Edward Elgar, Northampton

Kokott J (2007) States, sovereign equality, In: Max Planck Encyclopedia of Public International Law

Lawrence TJ (1885) A handbook of public international law. Deighton, Bell and Co., Cambridge

Lazareff S (1971) Status of Military Forces under Current International Law. Sijthoff, Leiden

Leuven Manual on the International Law Applicable to Peace Operations (2017) Cambridge University Press, Cambridge

Liivoja R (2017) Criminal Jurisdiction over Armed Forces Abroad. Cambridge University Press, Cambridge

Liivoja R (2010) Service jurisdiction under international law. 11 Melbourne Journal of International Law

Mann FA (1964) The doctrine of jurisdiction in international law. Vol. 111 Hague Academy Collected Courses

Moore JB (1906) A digest of international law as embodied in diplomatic discussions, treaties and other international agreements, international awards, the decision of municipal courts, and the writings of jurists, Vol II. Washington

Morris WF (1916) Claims against the British Army in France. How dealt with. International Law Notes May 1916, p. 74

Odello M (2010) Tackling criminal acts in peacekeeping operations: The accountability of peacekeepers. Vol. 15 J.C.S.L.

Oppenheim L (1905) International law, a treatise, Vol I, peace. Longmans, Green and Co, London

Parry C (ed) (1969a) The Consolidated Treaty Series (with annotations), Vol. 62, 1812–1818. Oceana Publications

Parry C (ed) (1969b) The Consolidated Treaty Series (with annotations), Vol. 220, 1914–1915. Oceana Publications

Parry C (ed) (1969c) The Consolidated Treaty Series (with annotations), Vol. 221, 1915-1916. Oceana Publications

Prescott JM (2018) Claims. In: Fleck D (ed) The Handbook of the Law of Visiting Forces, 2nd edn. Oxford University Press, Oxford

Reisman WM, Sloane RD (2000) The Incident at Cavalese and strategic compensation. 94 AJIL 505–515

Restatement of the Law, Third, Foreign Relations Law of the United States (1986) American Law Institute Publishers, Washington

Ronzitti N (2012) The Enrica Lexie incident: Law of the sea and immunity of State officials issues. Italian Yearbook of International Law, Vol. XXII

Ronzitti N (2015) The immunity of State organs – A reply to Pisillo Mazzeschi. Questions of International Law, Zoom out

Ryngaert C (2008) Jurisdiction in International Law. Oxford University Press, Oxford

Sari A (2015) The Status of armed forces in public international law: Jurisdiction and immunity. In: Orakhelashvili A (ed) Research handbook on jurisdiction and immunities in international law. Edward Elgar, Cheltenham/Northampton

Schmalenbach K (2004) Die Haftung Internationaler Organisationen im Rahmen von Militäreinsätzen und Territorialverwaltungens. Peter Lang, Frankfurt am Main

Schneider G (1964) Die Exterritorialität der Truppen in strafrechtlicher Hinsicht, unter besonderer Berücksichtigung der das deutsche Territorium betreffenden Truppenverträge. Albert-Ludwig Universität, Saarbrücken

UN Secretary-General (1958) UN Doc A/3943, Summary study of the experiences derived from the establishment and operation of the Force, report of the Secretary-General, 9 October 1958.

Seyersted F (2008) Jurisdiction over organs and officials. In: Seyersted F (ed) Common Law of International Organizations. Brill, Leiden

Spies SC (2008) On the legal status of foreign armed forces, with a focus on the interrelation of ius ad praesentiam and ius in praesentia. Military Law and the Law of War Review 47/1–2, 235–251

van Hoek B, Nijhof J, Voetelink J (2012) The scope of jurisdiction provisions in status of forces agreements related to crisis management operations. Military Law and the Law of War Review 51/2:335–359

Voetelink JED (2015) Status of forces: criminal jurisdiction over military personnel abroad. T.M.C. Asser Press, The Hague

Voetelink JED (2017) Chapter 13, Reframing lawfare. In: Ducheine PAL, Osinga FPB (eds) Netherlands Annual Review of Military Studies 2017 - Winning Without Killing: The Strategic and Operational Utility of Non-Kinetic Capabilities in Crises. T.M.C. Asser Press, The Hague, pp 237–254

Voetelink JED (2018) Chapter 21, Enforcement Jurisdiction, In: Fleck D (ed) The Handbook of the Law of Visiting Forces, 2nd edn. Oxford University Press, Oxford

Wessel R (2007) Internationaal recht in ontwikkeling. In: Horbach N, Lefeber R, Ribbelink O (eds) Handboek internationaal recht. T.M.C. Asser Press, The Hague

Joop Voetelink a former Air Force Lawyer, is Associate Professor of Law at the Faculty of Military Sciences of the Netherlands Defence Academy (NLDA). His primary scholarly interest centres around export control law and military law in general, with a particular focus on the law of military operations. In 2012 Col Voetelink defended his PhD thesis on the legal status of military forces stationed abroad at Amsterdam University. He is the author of *Status of Forces: Criminal Jurisdiction over Military Personnel Abroad*.

The present chapter is part of the author's research under the auspices of the Amsterdam Center for International Law and the NLDA as part of the research program The Role of Law in Armed Conflict and Peace Operations. The author has written it in a personal capacity and it does not necessarily reflect the views of the Dutch Ministry of Defence.

Chapter 11
International Human Rights Law

Melanie O'Brien

Contents

11.1 Introduction 256
11.2 Civil and Political Rights 258
11.3 Economic, Social and Cultural Rights 258
11.4 Limitations and Derogations 259
11.5 The UN Human Rights System 262
    11.5.1 Treaty Bodies 262
    11.5.2 Human Rights Council 263
    11.5.3 Office of the High Commissioner for Human Rights 265
11.6 Extraterritorial Application of Human Rights 265
11.7 Conflict- and Security-Related Human Rights Case Studies 266
    11.7.1 Right to Life 266
    11.7.2 Cultural Rights 270
11.8 Conclusion 274
References 274

Abstract This chapter provides an introduction to international human rights law. After introducing human rights generally, the chapter goes on to provide an overview of civil and political rights and of economic, social and cultural rights. A subsequent outline of the limitations and derogations that can be put on human rights provides understanding of the limits of human rights law. Following this, an overview of the United Nations human rights system is given, examining the three main agents of human rights within the United Nations: the treaty bodies (who oversee the implementation of the human rights treaties); the Human Rights Council (which undertakes the Universal Periodic Review); and the Office of the High Commissioner for Human Rights (which oversees incorporating human rights into all United Nations entities and actions). The chapter looks at the extraterritorial application of human rights, before concluding with two conflict- and security-related human rights case studies.

Keywords Human rights law · United Nations · Right to life · Cultural rights · Human Rights Council · Derogations

---

M. O'Brien (✉)
University of Western Australia, Perth, Australia
e-mail: melanie.obrien@uwa.edu.au

© T.M.C. ASSER PRESS and the authors 2022
S. Sayapin et al. (eds.), *International Conflict and Security Law*,
https://doi.org/10.1007/978-94-6265-515-7_11

11.1 Introduction

Human rights are freedoms that are inherent to all persons, which trigger obligations on states to protect those rights. Human rights are traditionally thought of as beginning with the Magna Carta in 1215. A document issued by King John of England, the Magna Carta was the first text to establish the principle that nobody, including the king, was above the law. Within the document were included rights such as the right of free men to justice and fair trial.

Modern day human rights began at the conclusion of World War II. The atrocities of that war, in particular the persecution and annihilation of six million Jews in The Holocaust,[1] shocked the global community into the creation of today's human rights legal system. Traditionally, international law was concerned with the rights and regulations of states. After The Holocaust, the push for including other actors in international law began, motivated by the perspective that states should not be free to treat persons within their territory as they wish, and in particular, should not be free to persecute and kill. Rather, people should be respected and accorded rights, to be able to live life with dignity and liberty, within a broader desire for democratic rule of law.[2] 'Human security… is a concern with human life and dignity.'[3] Dignity and freedom are the essence of human rights, and are to be enjoyed by all without discrimination as to race, gender, religion, ethnicity, sexuality, nationality, language, political or other opinion, disability, or any other reason. This is the universality and inalienability of human rights, in that everyone, everywhere is entitled to them.

Human rights were categorised into 'civil and political rights' and 'economic, social and cultural rights' ('ecosoc' rights). These categories were initially termed first and second generation rights (with group right the third generation rights), with priority given to first generation civil and political rights. This distinction was based on the idea that civil and political rights required little work for implementation and therefore could be implemented immediately, while ecosoc rights would take greater time and were dependent on state resources.[4] The difference was also based on civil and political rights being concerned with 'freedom from State interference while economic, social and cultural rights represent objectives or aspirations for a State to pursue in promoting the well-being of its people'.[5] However, while the categorisation still exists, the hierarchy of rights has been eliminated, as all rights are indivisible, inter-dependent and interrelated.[6] All rights contribute to dignity and freedom; denial of one right usually impedes enjoyment of other rights, while fulfilment of one right

---

[1] See e.g. Friedländer 2007.

[2] Mill 1991.

[3] UNDP, *Human Development Report 1994: New Dimensions of Human Security* (1994), http://www.hdr.undp.org/en/content/human-development-report-1994, p. 22. Accessed 13 August 2020.

[4] Conte and Burchill 2016, pp. 2–3.

[5] Ibid., p. 2.

[6] UN GA Res 32/120 (1977), paras 1(a)–(c). '[H]uman rights in international law share a common purpose: to mitigate injustices produced by the ways in which international law brings legal order to global politics'; Macklem 2015, p. 62.

11 International Human Rights Law

is generally dependent on the attainment of other rights. Rule of law plays a role in human rights through the obligation of duty-bearers such as states to respect, observe, guarantee and implement human rights; and the subsequent accountability for breaches of that obligation.

Under the United Nations (UN) Charter, all member states pledge to cooperate with the UN for the purposes of promoting 'universal respect for, and observance of, human rights and fundamental freedoms for all without distinction as to race, sex, language, or religion'.[7] The UN was established in 1945, and by 1948 the Universal Declaration of Human Rights (UDHR) was drafted and adopted. The UDHR is the founding document of the modern human rights system. Despite its status as a declaration and not a convention, initially intended not to be binding,[8] at least many of the rights enshrined in the UDHR are generally perceived to have attained customary law status, thus rendering those rights binding on all states.[9] At a minimum, the UDHR is deemed to enshrine fundamental principles of human rights.[10]

The international human rights law regime is principally governed by the hard law of treaties, with soft law including UN resolutions and treaty body findings and comments. This chapter will discuss some examples of substantive rights, as well as the relevant treaty law and the UN human rights system as it functions to ensure implementation of human rights worldwide. The main treaties discussed in this chapter are:

- International Covenant on Civil and Political Rights (ICCPR)
- International Covenant on Economic, Social and Cultural Rights (ICESCR)
- Convention on the Elimination of All Forms of Discrimination Against Women (CEDAW)
- Convention on the Rights of the Child (CROC)
- Convention on the Rights of Persons with Disabilities (CRPD)
- Convention on the Elimination of Racial Discrimination (CERD)
- Convention Against Torture (CAT)[11]

---

[7] 1945 Charter of the United Nations 1 UNTS XVI, articles 55–56; *Legal Consequences for States of the Continued Presence of South Africa in Namibia (South West Africa) notwithstanding Security Council Resolution 276 (1970)*, ICJ, Advisory Opinion of 21 June 1971, p. 45 para 131; see also Schwelb 1972.

[8] Samnøy 1999, p. 10.

[9] Or 'as an authoritative interpretation of the Charter's human rights provisions'. Alston and Goodman 2013, p. 82.

[10] *Case concerning United States diplomatic and consular staff in Tehran (United States v. Iran)*, ICJ, Judgment of 24 May 1980, p. 42.

[11] The 1976 International Covenant on Civil and Political Rights 999 UNTS 171; the 1976 Covenant on Economic, Social and Cultural Rights 993 UNTS 3; the 1981 Convention on the Elimination of All Forms of Discrimination against Women 2131 UNTS 83; the 1990 Convention on the Rights of the Child 1577 UNTS 3; the 2008 Convention on the Rights of Persons with Disabilities 2515 UNTS 3; the 1966 International Convention on the Elimination of All Forms of Racial Discrimination 660 UNTS 195; the 1987 Convention against Torture and Other Cruel, Inhuman or Degrading Treatment

258　　　　　　　　　　　　　　　　　　　　　　　　　　　　　　　　　M. O'Brien

The human rights system was a catalyst for the inclusion of other agents within the international law system.[12] Within the human rights system, we see individuals and civil society organisations play a direct role in international law, which is a striking change from the traditional perspective of international law as regulating states only. That said, the human rights system still imposes obligations on states. Human rights are owed to individuals by states; states must ensure these rights are guaranteed and respected, and that any violations are ceased, rectified or repaired. Through the human rights treaty system, states' obligations are clarified, implemented and monitored.

11.2　Civil and Political Rights

Civil rights are about the protection of an individual's physical and mental integrity, while political rights ensure full participation in civil society. Civil rights include freedom from torture and fair trial rights; political rights include the right to vote; freedom of religion; and freedom of thought.

Civil and political rights are found in the UHDR, the ICCPR, and a range of other human rights treaties. As is clear from its treaty name, the ICCPR is the key treaty dealing with civil and political rights. However, there are many civil and political rights not found in the ICCPR, resulting in the need for other treaties to provide for rights such as racial discrimination, child rights or refugee rights.

11.3　Economic, Social and Cultural Rights

Economic, social and cultural ('ecosoc') rights were initially deemed 'second generation' rights, with civil and political rights give 'priority' for fulfilment over ecosoc rights. Political and economic factors drove this differentiation and prioritisation, with states unwilling to commit to upholding rights that were more costly to implement (e.g. providing social security vs freedom from torture) and persecuted peoples prioritising rights such as freedom from slavery and torture over rights perceived as less important such as the right to form and join trade unions. Another perception was that civil and political rights were 'negative' rights, and ecosoc rights 'positive rights'- meaning that the former only required a government to avoid certain behaviour (e.g. not torture, not have slavery) and the latter required specific action to ensure their fulfilment (thereby requiring resources).[13] This is an inaccurate depiction, as many civil and political rights require action (e.g. fair trial rights require significant law enforcement and judicial institution education and structure), and not

---

or Punishment 1465 UNTS 85. For a summary discussion of a number of human rights treaties, see Egan 2011, Chapter 3.

[12] Moyn 2010, p. 176.

[13] Haas 2008, p. 113.

11 International Human Rights Law 259

all ecosoc rights require positive action (e.g. not prohibiting people from participating in cultural life or in trade unions). Further, civil and political rights 'were largely seen as immediately applicable and largely justiciable, whereas [ecosoc] rights were viewed as subject only to progressive realization through measures of state policy'.[14] Certainly, time and action has demonstrated that ecosoc rights are certainly justiciable.[15] Despite these differentiations, over time, the interdependency and inter-relatedness of rights has been recognised, and it has been acknowledged that economic, social and cultural rights are vital and equal to civil and political rights (e.g. right to adequate standard of living, right to education). In addition, the focus on development in recent decades, such as through the Millennium and Sustainable Development Goals, has demonstrated that ecosoc rights are central to international politics and law, particularly finance and economics.[16]

Ecosoc rights are found in the majority of human rights conventions. While the principle treaty is the International Covenant on Economic, Social and Cultural Rights (ICESCR), ecosoc rights emerge in many other instruments such as the UDHR, the ICCPR, CEDAW, CROC, and many International Labor Organization (ILO) treaties.[17] The UDHR grants the rights to social security; work (including just and favourable conditions of work) and equal pay; form and join a trade union; rest and leisure; adequate standard of living; education; participate in cultural life; protection of intellectual property; and social and international order.[18]

Most of these rights also appear in the ICESCR, in addition to which is included the rights to protection and assistance to the family, and maternity leave; and physical and mental health.[19] The ILO has adopted many treaties on employment issues, such as forced labour, child labour, collective bargaining, discrimination, equal pay, minimum employment age, and trade unions.[20]

11.4 Limitations and Derogations

In a 'time of public emergency which threatens the life of the nation and the existence of which is officially proclaimed', states are permitted to derogate from most rights.[21]

---

[14] Saul et al. 2014, p. 1.

[15] King 2012; Lazarus 2014.

[16] United Nations, News on Millennium Development Goals, http://www.un.org/millenniumgoals/. Accessed 5 March 2020. United Nations, Sustainable Development Goals, https://www.un.org/sustainabledevelopment/. Accessed 5 March 2020.

[17] For a list of international and regional instruments dealing with ecosoc rights, see King 2012, p. 326; for a comprehensive collection of resources, see Leckie and Gallagher 2006.

[18] Articles 22–28.

[19] Articles 10 and 12.

[20] See e.g. 1999 Convention concerning the Prohibition and Immediate Action for the Elimination of the Worst Forms of Child Labour (ILO No. 182) 2133 UNTS 161; 1957 Convention Concerning the Abolition of Forced Labor (ILO No. 105) 320 UNTS 291.

[21] ICCPR, article 4(1); ICESCR article 4.

Given that derogations are only allowed in a state of emergency, such interference with rights must be 'of an exceptional and temporary nature'.[22] A public emergency is 'an exceptional situation of crisis or emergency which afflicts the whole population and constitutes a threat to the organised life of the community of which the community is composed',[23] and thus must go beyond 'low-level civil disturbance'.[24] The Siracusa Principles on derogations refer to a 'threat to the organized life of the community' and a danger which 'concerns the whole population', and that 'internal conflict and unrest that do not constitute a grave and imminent threat to the life of the nation cannot justify derogations'.[25] Danger must be 'actual or imminent, not merely potential, latent, or speculative'.[26]

A public emergency includes armed conflict, genocide, riots, insurrections and public health emergencies, during which time states are also required to comply with other international law obligations.[27] These obligations include adherence with international humanitarian law (IHL), the law regulating the means and methods of warfare during armed conflict. Under customary law, IHL must be applied without "adverse distinction… based on race, colour, sex, language, religion or belief, political or other opinion, national or social origin, wealth, birth or other status, or on any other similar criteria".[28] Therefore, both human rights law and IHL underscore the essential, fundamental nature of non-discrimination, regardless of whether in peacetime or emergency. Other situations in which derogations have been enacted in recent years include terrorist attacks and coups, although the legality of these derogations have been questioned by scholars and considered by human rights courts.[29]

---

[22] Human Rights Committee, CCPR General Comment 29: States of Emergency, Seventy-second Session, 31 August 2001, UN Doc. CCPR/C/21/Rev.1/Add.11, para 2 (hereinafter HRC General Comment No. 29). See generally, United Nations Sub-Commission on Prevention of Discrimination and Protection of Minorities, Siracusa Principles on the Limitation and Derogation of Provisions in the International Covenant on Civil and Political Rights, Annex, E/CN.4/1984/4 (1984) (hereinafter Siracusa Principles). For a discussion of derogations specifically in the context of the ICCPR, see Conte and Burchill 2016, Chapter 3.

[23] *Lawless v. Ireland (No 3)* (1961) 1 EHRR 15, p. 31.

[24] Hartman 1981, p. 16.

[25] Siracusa Principles, Principles 39 and 40.

[26] Hartman 1981.

[27] Force majeure may also be an applicable justification for derogation from human rights treaty obligations, as under treaty law. See Alston and Goodman 2013, p. 402.

[28] International Committee of the Red Cross, Customary IHL Database, Rule 88, https://ihl-databa ses.icrc.org/customary-ihl/eng/docs/v1_rul_rule88. Accessed 5 March 2020. See also Pejic 2001.

[29] Note the European Court of Human Rights cases *Ireland v. the United Kingdom* (5310/71) [1978] ECHR 1; *Aksoy v. Turkey* (21987/93) [1996] ECHR 68; and *A. and Others v. the United Kingdom* (3455/05) [2009] ECHR, in which the Court observed that a state of emergency did exist due to terrorist attacks. See also *Şahin Alpay v. Turkey* (16538/17) [2018] ECHR and *Mehmet Hasan Altan v. Turkey* (13237/17) [2018] ECHR, in which the Court concluded that a military coup amounted to a public emergency constituting a threat to the life of the nation. For discussion, see Nugraha 2018; Müller 2018.

Derogations, however, are only permitted within specific limitations.[30] The first is that derogations should satisfy the condition of legality and be consistent with obligations under international law. That is, while derogations are permitted, they must not breach the state's other international obligations under treaty or customary law. The second limitation on derogations is the condition of legitimacy, where any derogation from rights must by justified by a legitimate aim, responding to a pressing social or public need. Thirdly, any interference with a human right must be only what is necessary to accomplish the legitimate aim. This is the principle of proportionality: a state applies only 'such measures [as] are limited to the extent strictly required by the exigencies of the situation', and a state must be able to justify that such measures were necessary.[31] Finally, reinforcing the important of the right to freedom from discrimination, derogations are prohibited if they discriminate on the basis of race, colour, sex, language, religion or social origin.[32]

States are obligated to notify persons within their territory of derogations (through proclamation) and to inform other state parties to the ICCPR and the UN Secretary-General of any limitations imposed on human rights, any extension of these derogations, and the termination of derogation.[33] This ensures oversight and, if necessary, accountability, for state derogations from rights, which should only occur during public emergencies that threaten 'the life of the nation'. This conforms to the principles balancing derogations: ensuring that fundamental rights are not abused during times of social or political upheaval or tension, but acknowledging that enjoyment of individual rights cannot be unlimited.[34]

There are some human rights from which no derogation is permitted. These are expressly listed in Article 4(2) of the ICCPR: right to life; prohibition of torture or cruel, inhuman or degrading punishment, or of medical or scientific experimentation without consent; prohibition of slavery, slave-trade and servitude; prohibition of imprisonment because of inability to fulfil a contractual obligation; the principle of legality in the field of criminal law; the recognition of everyone as a person before the law; and freedom of thought, conscience and religion. These absolute rights are guaranteed because it is considered that derogating from these particular rights will never be required to protect 'the life of the nation', rather than being a confirmation of the peremptory nature of these particular rights.[35]

---

[30] ICCPR, article 4(1). Similar provisions are found in other human rights treaties. For more detail on the limitations placed on derogations, see de Schutter 2014, pp. 339–426.

[31] HRC General Comment No. 29, paras 4–5.

[32] ICCPR, article 4(1); HRC General Comment No. 29, para 8.

[33] ICCPR, article 4(3); HRC General Comment No. 29, para 17.

[34] Hartman 1981, p. 11; Hafner-Burton et al. 2011.

[35] HRC General Comment No. 29, para 11.

11.5 The UN Human Rights System

There are several components to the UN human rights system: the treaty bodies, the Human Rights Council, and the Office of the High Commissioner for Human Rights.

11.5.1 Treaty Bodies

Human rights treaties have affiliated treaty bodies within the UN. These bodies are commissions or committees tasked with monitoring implementation of their particular treaty.[36] The main task of these bodies is to receive periodic reporting, which is the only mandatory supervision of treaty parties. Period reporting requires a state party to report to the treaty body on the measures the state has taken to implement its treaty obligations, such as, for example, amending laws to remove discriminatory provisions. Non-governmental organisations are also permitted to make submissions to the treaty body for these reports. The treaty body assesses the state and NGO reports, making non-binding suggestions and recommendations to assist the state meet its treaty obligations.

Other responsibilities of the treaty bodies are optional inquiry and inter-State or individual complaint mechanisms. The inquiry system allows a treaty body to initiate an investigation into particular human rights issues on the ground in a state. An 'inquiry procedure' provides for the body to respond to 'reliable information on systematic abuses in a particularly country by conducting a dedicated inquiry into such allegations'.[37] The inquiry may include field visits to the state, if possible, and will result in the treaty body issuing conclusions and recommendations. Treaty bodies may also investigate implementation of treaty obligations on the ground, which is a form of preventive inquiry separate from the periodic reporting, and does not require the existence of systematic abuses.

Individual complaint mechanisms are commonly used, and enable an individual (or an organisation on their behalf) to bring a complaint or petition before a treaty body alleging breaches of their rights under the relevant treaty. This process can result in a remedy for the victim of rights violations, may bring about changes in law and practice (which will not only benefit the victim but also others), and provide a form of jurisprudence on the interpretation of the rights under the relevant treaty.[38] In comparison to the individual complaint system, the inter-State complaint system has been unsuccessful and unused.[39]

The treaty bodies also issue 'general comments', which are interpretations of individual provisions of the relevant treaty. These are seen as authoritative guidance on

---

[36] For detailed discussion of the different treaty bodies and their procedures, see e.g. Egan 2011; Alston and Crawford 2000.

[37] Egan 2011, p. 179.

[38] Ibid., p. 253.

[39] Bayefsky 2001, p. 71.

11 International Human Rights Law

the definitions of specific rights, and may be updated as definitions and societal structures (for example, technology) evolve. Combined with the findings for individual complaints, the general comments add to the jurisprudence of human rights law.

These functions of the treaty bodies have been seen to have successes and limitations. For example, the individual complaints allow human rights issues to come to light that may not otherwise be heard, and can lead to state action to undo or provide restitution for violations.[40] On the other hand, accessing the UN system can be highly challenging, particularly given the requirement to exhaust domestic remedies first, especially for those who are most vulnerable and therefore most need the system; and individual complaint mechanisms are optional, resulting in many states who do not allow individual complaints against them.[41] Thus, there is room for some reform in the system, although this is unlikely to occur in the near future.[42]

11.5.2 Human Rights Council

Established in 2006 as a 'cooperative mechanism',[43] the Human Rights Council rose from the ashes of the Commission on Human Rights, which was established in 1946 but was ultimately dismantled due to criticisms that its integrity had been compromised to political considerations.[44] Yet the Human Rights Council is a state-driven process, and thus, also 'inevitably politicised'.[45] It is a subsidiary body of the General Assembly (GA), which elects the Council's 47 Member States. Members are elected for staggered three-year terms on a regional basis.

Within the Human Rights Council, an Advisory Committee provides expertise and advice on thematic human rights issues. Eighteen Committee members are experts nominated by government and elected by the Council, with regional distribution. Each member serves for three years and may be re-elected once. Advice stems from studies and research-based evidence, and may consult with NGOs and civil society.

A Complaint Procedure is also open to individuals, groups and organisations to raise issues of violations of human rights. Through the Complaint Procedure, the Human Rights Council has reviewed human rights situations in many states, including the Maldives, Iraq and the Democratic Republic of Congo.[46] Special Procedures also

---

[40] Egan 2011, p. 253.

[41] O'Flaherty 2010.

[42] There is much debate around the successes and limitations of human rights treaties. See e.g. Kanter 2019; Simmons 2012; Goodman and Jinks 2003; Hathaway 2002.

[43] Human Rights Council, Institution-building of the United Nations Human Rights Council, HRC Res. 5/1, Fifth Session, 18 June 2007, Annex, UN Doc. A/HRC/RES/5/1, para 3(b). Establishment document, Human Rights Council, 15 March 2006, GA Res 60/251.

[44] Egan 2011, pp. 27–35.

[45] Collister 2015, p. 111.

[46] See Human Rights Council, List of Situations Referred to the Human Rights Council under the Complaint Procedure since 2006 (October 2014), https://www.ohchr.org/Documents/HRBodies/ComplaintProcedure/SituationsConsideredUnderComplaintProcedures.pdf. Accessed 5 March 2020.

form part of the Council's mandate, where special rapporteurs, special representatives, independent experts and working groups are created and allocated to examine, advise and report on human rights thematic issues or situations in specific states.[47] Issues under the Special Procedure mandate include arbitrary detention, the right to food, human rights defenders, Indigenous peoples, rights of migrants, privacy, and violence against women. Countries include Cambodia, Eritrea, Myanmar, Somalia, Sudan and Syria.

The main process of the Human Rights Council is the Universal Periodic Review (UPR), which reviews the human rights record of all UN Member States. Each year 42 States are reviewed, with every State reviewed in each 4.5-year cycle (the third cycle is 2017–2022). While the UPR is conducted by the UPR Working Group (the 47 Council members), any UN Member State can participated in the UPR dialogue. For the review, the Working Group will take into account a national report from the state, reports of human rights treaty bodies and other UN entities, and submissions from other bodies such as NGOs and national human rights institutions (NHRIs). A 3.5-hour discussion takes place for the review, including questions from states for the state under review. The review assesses compliance with human rights under the UN Charter, the UDHR, any human rights treaties to which the state is a party, voluntary pledge and commitments made by the state, and applicable international humanitarian law. After the review, an 'outcome report' is issued, summarising questions, comments and recommendations from states, and the responses of the reviewed state. Before the report is adopted, the reviewed state may make comments and choose to either accept or note recommendations. At a plenary Council session, the state may address any issues not covered during the UPR time, and the report is adopted. At this time, NGOs, NHRIs and others may make comments. Subsequent UPRs follow up on issues from previous reviews, where states have been expected to take action to develop human rights in between review periods. In the case of persistent non-cooperation with the Human Rights Council, the President of the Council takes up the issue.[48]

The UPR is not without criticism, particularly due to the state-centric nature of the process, which results in states playing a role in the negotiation and rejection of the recommendations included in their own final UPR report.[49] In addition, the UPR process is extremely limited in time, resulting in little to no real discussion with states about human rights issues, and recommendations that are not adopted by consensus but rather 'remain the recommendations of individual states to their peers'.[50]

---

[47] See OHCHR, Special Procedures of the Human Rights Council, https://www.ohchr.org/EN/HRB odies/SP/Pages/Welcomepage.aspx. Accessed 5 March 2020.

[48] Human Rights Council, Report of the Human Rights Council on its Seventh Organizational Meeting, 4 April 2013, Seventh Organizational Meeting, 14 and 29 January 2013, A/HRC/OM/7/1; Human Rights Council, Decision adopted by the Human Rights Council at its seventh organizational meeting, 4 April 2013, Seventh Organizational Meeting, 29 January 2013, OM/7/101.

[49] Collister 2015, p. 77.

[50] Ibid., p. 115.

11 International Human Rights Law

11.5.3 Office of the High Commissioner for Human Rights

The Office of the High Commissioner for Human Rights (OHCHR) is mandated with the promotion and protection of all human rights around the globe, which also includes safeguarding peace and security, and development. The OHCHR focuses on the practical side of human rights standard-setting, monitoring and implementation. OHCHR assists governments implement their human rights obligations and supports individuals with any claims for rights. The Office also speaks out publicly on human rights violations, and provides support to the Human Rights Council and the treaty bodies. The OHCHR particularly supports the Special Procedures of the Human Rights Council, such as through assisting Special Rapporteurs to carry out investigations in the field; and provides legal research and secretariat support to the treaty bodies.

While the OHCHR is based in Geneva, the Office also has field offices around the world, to enable the OHCHR to conduct on the ground monitoring and implementation of human rights. These may be stand-alone offices, offices within a peace operation, regional offices or human rights advisers in UN Country Teams.[51] These field office activities may include working with governments to provide technical training and support 'in the areas of administration of justice, legislative reform, human rights treaty ratification, and human rights education'.[52] Through this work, the OHCHR seeks to mainstream human rights, coordinating UN human rights activities and 'lead[ing] efforts to integrate a human rights approach within all work carried out by United Nations agencies'.[53] Due to its broad mandate, the OHCHR works with UN entities, governments, NGOs, national human rights institutions, individuals, and other international organisations.

11.6 Extraterritorial Application of Human Rights

It is traditional that jurisdiction only applies within the territory of a state, as jurisdiction is linked to state sovereignty.[54] This would result in human rights obligations of a state only being applicable to individuals within that state's territory. However, an exception exists to this rule, for human rights law, and it is an exception that is highly relevant in armed conflict situations. In fact, much case law around the

---

[51] Field offices are listed at OHCHR, OHCHR in the World: making human rights a reality on the ground, https://www.ohchr.org/EN/Countries/Pages/WorkInField.aspx. Accessed 5 March 2020.

[52] OHCHR, What we do, https://www.ohchr.org/EN/AboutUs/Pages/WhatWeDo.aspx. Accessed 5 March 2020.

[53] OHCHR, Mandate, https://www.ohchr.org/EN/AboutUs/Pages/Mandate.aspx. Accessed 5 March 2020.

[54] *Lotus Case*, Permanent Court of International Justice, Judgment of 7 September 1927, PCIJ ser. A no. 10 (1927), p. 20.

extraterritoriality of human rights stems from situations of armed conflict, where a state is engaged in conflict outside its territory.

In 2004 the International Court of Justice (ICJ) held that the ICCPR 'is applicable in respect of acts done by a State in the exercise of its jurisdiction outside its own territory', and that 'the drafter of the Covenant did not intend to allow States to escape from their obligations when they exercise jurisdiction outside their national territory'.[55] The ICJ followed this reasoning in 2005, declaring that the 'conduct of individual soldiers and officers... is to be considered as the conduct of a State organ... a party to an armed conflict shall be responsible for all acts by persons forming part of its armed forces'.[56] The Human Rights Committee, the treaty body for the ICCPR, in its General Comment 31, noted that 'a State party must respect and ensure the rights laid down in the Covenant to anyone within the power or effective control of that State Party, even if not situated within the territory of the State Party...'.[57] These findings are also echoed by regional human rights bodies and by domestic courts.[58] Human rights are considered so fundamental that a state cannot escape its obligations, even when violations occur outside of its territory. It would defeat the purpose of human rights law if a state could violate human rights simply because its agents were acting outside of the territory of that state. Agents of a state party are considered to be acting on the part of the state and thus have an obligation to respect human rights of all individuals, anywhere.

11.7 Conflict- and Security-Related Human Rights Case Studies

11.7.1 Right to Life

The right to life is an interesting right, in that it is a fundamental right: after all, no other right can be enjoyed without the right to life.[59] The right to life is enshrined in many human rights instruments, including the UDHR, which affords everyone 'the right to life, liberty and security of person' (Article 3). This is expanded in

---

[55] *Legal Consequences of the Construction of a Wall in the Occupied Palestinian Territory*, ICJ, Advisory Opinion of 9 July 2004, p. 178 para 106, p. 179 para 109.

[56] *Armed activities on the territory of the Congo (Democratic Republic of the Congo v. Uganda)*, ICJ, Judgment of 19 December 2005, paras 213–214.

[57] Human Rights Committee, CCPR General Comment No. 31 [80] The Nature of the General Legal Obligation Imposed on State Parties to the Covenant, Eightieth Session, 26 May 2004, UN Doc CCPR/C/21/Rev.1/Add.13. The Human Rights Committee also made this conclusion in individual complaints cases: Human Rights Committee, *Delia Saldias de Lopez v. Uruguay*, Views: Communication No. 52/1979, UN Doc. CCPR/C/OP/1 at 88 (1984), para 12.

[58] For more details on extraterritorial application of human rights, see, e.g, Milanović 2011; O'Brien 2010–2011; Miller 2010; Coomans and Kamminga 2004.

[59] Human Rights Committee, 'General comment No. 36, Article 6: right to life', CCPR/C/GC/36, 3 September 2019, para 2.

Article 6 of the ICCPR, which guarantees every human being 'the inherent right to life', while also imposing the obligation to enshrine this right in law and noting that no person 'shall be arbitrarily deprived of his [sic] life'. This protection of life appears in other conventions, such as the Convention on the Rights of the Child, the Genocide Convention and the International Convention for the Protection of All Persons from Enforced Disappearance, and is intertwined with other conventions such as the Convention Against Torture (where torture or ill treatment creates risk of deprivation of life).

It is a right that must be interpreted broadly, as it 'concerns the entitlement of individuals to be free from acts and omissions that are intended or may be expected to cause their unnatural or premature death, as well as to enjoy a life with dignity'.[60] States are obligated to respect and ensure the right to life, including protecting the right by law and refraining from 'engaging in conduct resulting in arbitrary deprivation of life'.[61] The Human Rights Committee defines deprivation of life as 'intentional or otherwise foreseeable and preventable life-terminating harm or injury, caused by an act or omission. It goes beyond injury to bodily or mental integrity or a threat thereto'.[62]

Thus, one would assume that no derogation from this crucial right is permissible. However, while generally one can say that no official derogation from this right is allowed, there are exceptions to the right in particular circumstances- and these circumstances relate directly to conflict and security. The key indicator of this is the phrasing of the right to life: that it is the prohibition on *arbitrary* deprivation of life. Thus, the right permits killing under specific circumstances, namely, armed conflict and law enforcement actions.[63] The European Convention on Human Rights goes some way to clarifying the parameters of permissible deprivation of life, allowing deprivation of life if 'in defence of any person from unlawful violence'; 'in order to effect a lawful arrest or to prevent the escape of a person lawfully detained'; or 'in action lawfully taken for the purpose of quelling a riot or insurrection'.[64] Other UN documents also regulate the framework of the right to life, dealing with use of force and firearms by law enforcement officials and extra-judicial executions, including

---

[60] General Comment No. 36, para 3.

[61] Ibid., paras 7, 18–31.

[62] Ibid., para 6.

[63] The right also allows for the death penalty, although protocols to human rights treaties take an abolitionist stance in a slow progression to the rejection of the death penalty. See, e.g., 1989 Second Optional Protocol to the International Covenant on Civil and Political Rights, Aiming at the Abolition of the Death Penalty, GA Res. 44/128, annex, 44 UN GAOR Supp. (No. 49) at 207, UN Doc. A/44/49 (1989).

[64] 1950 European Convention for the Protection of Human Rights and Fundamental Freedoms, ETS 5, 213 UNTS 222, Article 2(2).

'preventing the perpetration of a particularly serious crime involving grave threat to life' as a permissible use of potentially lethal force.[65]

Prominently, while human rights law and IHL both apply during armed conflict, IHL is regarded as *lex specialis*, meaning that it applies over and above human rights law, because IHL is specifically designed to apply only during armed conflict.[66] One way in which IHL overrides human rights law is that IHL permits violations of the right to life. That is, it is permissible to kill people in armed conflict. The ICJ has held that:

> The Court observes that the protection of the International Covenant of Civil and Political Rights does not cease in times of war, except by operation of Article 4 of the Covenant whereby certain provisions may be derogated from in a time of national emergency. Respect for the right to life is not, however, such a provision. In principle, the right not arbitrarily to be deprived of one's life applies also in hostilities. The test of what is an arbitrary deprivation of life, however, then falls to be determined by the applicable *lex specialis*, namely, the law applicable in armed conflict which is designed to regulate the conduct of hostilities. Thus whether a particular loss of life, through the use of a certain weapon in warfare, is to be considered an arbitrary deprivation of life contrary to Article 6 of the Covenant, can only be decided by reference to the law applicable in armed conflict and not deduced from the terms of the Covenant itself.[67]

Thus, killing people is a legitimate activity within armed conflict, insofar as that killing is a military objective or it is carried out in self-defence, as regulated under IHL.[68]

The right to life has also been at issue in context of targeted killings, which may or may not be related to armed conflict, but are most controversial in human rights when carried out outside the context of armed conflict. Targeted killings are those carried out against an individual who poses a threat to security, even if that individual is not engaging in hostile activities at the time. They are usually enacted against terrorist targets, particularly by the United States and Israel.[69] Targeted killings have become more common due to the development of drones, which serve as a weapons-delivery system that do not require risking a human life in the delivery of the weapon. Criticism of US targeted killings (particularly in Yemen and Somalia) is focused on the lack of transparency in the program, under which statistics on the true number of people

---

[65] Principle 9 of the 1990 Basic Principles on the Use of Force and Firearms by Law Enforcement Officials, UN Doc. A/CONF.144/28/Rev.1 at 112. See also 1989 Principles on the Effective Prevention and Investigation of Extra-Legal, Arbitrary and Summary Executions, UN Doc. E/1989/89.

[66] For discussion on the relationship between IHL and human rights law, see e.g. Gill 2013; Heintze 2013; Milanović 2010; Doswald-Beck 2006.

[67] *Legality of the Threat or Use of Nuclear Weapons*, Advisory Opinion of 8 July 1996, para 25.

[68] Killings must also comply with general IHL principles, such as the principles of distinction and military necessity; see ICRC Casebook, Principle of Distinction, https://casebook.icrc.org/law/principle-distinction, and Military necessity, https://casebook.icrc.org/glossary/military-necessity. Accessed 13 August 2020.

[69] The Israeli Targeted Killings case is a prominent case on the issue: *The Public Committee against Torture in Israel and Palestinian Society for the Protection of Human Rights and the Environment v. The Government of Israel [et al.]*, HCJ 769/02, 13 December 2006.

11 International Human Rights Law

killed in drone strikes is unknown, particularly due to the use of civilian agencies such as the Central Intelligence Agency (CIA).[70] The number of civilian casualties from the strikes is also a concern. Human rights groups have concluded that some components of US targeted killing practices and policies amount to a violation of the right to life, being intentional use of lethal force in non-conflict zones outside of the limitations permitted in international law.[71] An example is the killing of Iranian General Soleimani in Iraq by the USA on 3 January 2020, carried out through a targeted drone attack.[72] This was an act that the Special Rapporteur on extrajudicial, summary or arbitrary executions has deemed an arbitrary killing in violation of human rights law.[73]

The Human Rights Committee has stated that targeted killings should not be used as a deterrent or punishment, and that a state should 'ensure that the utmost consideration is given to the principle of proportionality in all its responses to terrorist threats and activities... Before resorting to the use of deadly force, all measures to arrest a person suspected of being in the process of committing acts of terror must be exhausted'.[74] The UN Special Rapporteur on extrajudicial, summary or arbitrary executions has noted: 'For a particular drone strike to be lawful under international law it must satisfy the legal requirements under all applicable international legal regimes... The right to life can be adequately secured only if all the distinct requirements posed by the various constitutive parts of international law are met.'[75] Thus, it is clear that targeted killings are not unlawful per se, provided they comply with international law. However, their increased use due to drone technology developments has resulted in the perpetration of a significant amount of targeted killings that do not comply with international law, whether that be human rights law or international humanitarian law.[76]

---

[70] See e.g. NGO Statement on Reported Changes to US Policy on Use of Armed Drones and Other Lethal Force, 7 March 2018, https://www.hrw.org/news/2018/03/07/ngo-statement-reported-changes-us-policy-use-armed-drones-and-other-lethal-force. Accessed 13 August 2020.

[71] Amnesty International 2012.

[72] For comprehensive reporting of the killing, see Al Jazeera's Soleimani Assassination News page, https://www.aljazeera.com/topics/events/200103131449509.html. Accessed 13 August 2020.

[73] 'Extrajudicial, summary or arbitrary executions', Report of the Special Rapporteur on extrajudicial, summary or arbitrary executions, 29 June 2020, UN Doc A/HRC/44/38, Advanced Unedited Version.

[74] Concluding Observations of the Human Rights Committee: Israel, 21 August 2003, UN Doc. CCPR/CO/78/ISR, para 15. The requirement to take measures to arrest before more serious action does not apply in armed conflict.

[75] Report of the Special Rapporteur on extrajudicial, summary or arbitrary executions, 13 September 2013, UN Doc. A/68/382, para 24.

[76] Ibid., discussing the relevant rules of both fields of international law as applicable to targeted killings.

11.7.2 Cultural Rights

Cultural rights are protected in the UDHR, the ICCPR, the ICESCR, as well as instruments such as the 1960 Convention Against Discrimination in Education and the 1972 Convention Concerning the Protection of the World Cultural and Natural Heritage (both sponsored by UNESCO), and the 1954 Convention for the Protection of Cultural Property in the Event of Armed Conflict (Cultural Property Convention).[77] "The full promotion of and respect for cultural rights is essential for the maintenance of human dignity and positive social interaction between individuals and communities in a diverse and multicultural world."[78] Article 15 of the ICESCR provides for the right to participate in cultural life, to obtain benefits from authored works, and freedom of scientific research and creativity activity. This right is closely related to the right to education, where values, religion, customs, language, and other cultural references are transmitted through generations.[79]

Cultural life "is an explicit reference to culture as a living process, historical, dynamic and evolving, with a past, a present and a future".[80] Culture is interpreted broadly, encompassing,

> inter alia, ways of life, language, oral and written literature, music and song, non-verbal communication, religion or belief systems, rites and ceremonies, sport and games, methods of production or technology, natural and man-made environments, food, clothing and shelter and the arts, customs and traditions through which individuals, groups of individuals and communities express their humanity and the meaning they give to their existence, and build their world view representing their encounter with the external forces affecting their lives.[81]

Participating or taking part in cultural life includes the freedom of every person to choose their identity (including identifying with a particular community); being part of political life; engaging in cultural practices; exercising expression in a chosen language; seeking, developing and sharing cultural knowledge and expressions; and acting creatively. Contributing to cultural life means being "involved in creating the

---

[77] 1960 Convention Against Discrimination in Education and the 1972 Convention Concerning the Protection of the World Cultural and Natural Heritage 429 UNTS 93; 1972 Convention Concerning the Protection of the World Cultural and Natural Heritage 1037 UNTS 151; 1954 Convention for the Protection of Cultural Property in the Event of Armed Conflict 249 UNTS 215.

[78] CESCR, General Comment No. 21: Right of everyone to take part in cultural life (article 15, para 1(a), of the International Covenant on Economic, Social and Cultural Rights), 21 December 2009, Forty-third Session, 2-20 November 2009, UN Doc. E/C.12/GC/21, para 1 (hereinafter General Comment No. 21).

[79] A part of the protection of cultural rights is the right of everyone to enjoy the benefits of scientific progress and its applications. This is obviously deeply connected to the right to education, and includes freedom of scientific research and communication, enjoyment of the benefits of scientific progress, and protection from adverse effects of science. For more, see Saul et al. 2014, pp. 1212–1224.

[80] General Comment No. 21, para 11.

[81] Ibid., para 13.

11 International Human Rights Law

spiritual, material, intellectual and emotional expressions of the community", an inherent aspect of community development.[82]

The CESCR has specifically interpreted the right to include the right of minorities to conserve, promote and develop their own culture. This expressly includes "cultural diversity, traditions, customs, religion, forms of education, languages, communication media (press, radio, television, Internet) and other manifestations of their cultural identity and membership".[83] Access to culture must be provided without discrimination. States must respect, recognise and protect minority cultures, and are prohibited from enacting forced assimilation.

There are positive obligations for states with regards to cultural rights, including ensuring access to all persons to cultural institutions such as libraries, museums, cinemas, theatres, sport venues, parks, streets, and natural sites; and to intangible culture such as traditions, beliefs, knowledge and history. The "obligations to respect and to protect freedoms, cultural heritage and diversity are interconnected".[84] Cultural heritage is to be understood as the resources enabling the cultural identification and development processes of individuals and groups, which they, implicitly or explicitly, transmit to future generations.[85] Cultural heritage is tangible, such as sites, structures and remains of archaeological, historical, religious, cultural or aesthetic value. It is also intangible, as evidenced through traditions, customs and practices, aesthetic and spiritual beliefs, vernacular or other languages, artistic expressions and folklore. Cultural rights are inter-related to rights such as freedom of expression; freedom of thought, conscience and religion; the right to education and the right to development.

The protection of cultural rights is particularly relevant in armed conflict, during which there can be a significant theft and destruction of cultural property.[86] Prominent examples of theft or destruction of cultural property include the wide-scale looting of European cultural artefacts by the Nazis, the desecration of Buddhist temples and artefacts in Cambodia by the Khmer Rouge, the shelling of the Old Town of Dubrovnik in 1991 by JNA forces, the destruction of Timbuktu mausoleums and shrines by Ansar Dine, and the destruction of Palmyra in Syria by Daesh.[87] The connection between this protection of cultural property in conflict and the right

---

[82] Ibid., para 15.

[83] Ibid., para 32.

[84] Ibid., para 50.

[85] Report of the Special Rapporteur in the field of cultural rights on the intentional destruction of cultural heritage as a violation of human rights, Human Rights Council, Thirty-first Session, 3 February 2016, UN Doc. A/HRC/31/59, para 47.

[86] Cultural property 'refers to buildings and other monuments of historic, artistic or architectural significance, to archaeological sites, to artworks, antiquities, manuscripts, books, and collections of the same, to archives, and the like'; O'Keefe 2014, p. 492. Cultural destruction is a significant element of genocide, although a discussion of this is outside the scope of this chapter; see e.g. O'Brien 2022, Chapter 3 Education and Culture Rights.

[87] Destruction of cultural heritage can occur outside of the parameters of conflict, as evidenced by the destruction of the Bamiyan Buddhas in Afghanistan, by the Taliban, the connection of which to armed conflict is debated. See e.g. Francioni and Lenzerini 2003, whose analysis appears to assume war crimes were committed; compared with O'Keefe 2010, p 4, who expressly states that

to culture is demonstrated through the importance of sites of cultural significance, which are attacked 'as part of attacks against civilian populations based on religion, nationality, ethnicity and/or race',[88] and can play a positive role in post-conflict reconstruction.[89]

The intersection between protection of cultural rights and conflict is demonstrated through the existence of cultural protections in other areas of international law, particularly including international humanitarian law. The Cultural Property Convention was specifically drafted to protect cultural property during armed conflict, and it is supplemented by Regulations and two Protocols.[90] This regime draws on human rights language in its presentation of cultural property, perceiving damage to cultural property as 'damage to the cultural heritage of all mankind [sic], since each people makes its contribution to the culture of the world'.[91] The Cultural Property Convention was drafted because the Geneva Conventions of 1949 did not contain any specific provisions protecting cultural property (only civilian property generally). However, in 1977, the two Additional Protocols to the Geneva Conventions included provisions relating to the protection of cultural property in armed conflict.[92] Article 53 of Additional Protocol I and Article 16 of Additional Protocol II prohibit, without prejudice to the Cultural Property Convention, 'acts of hostility directed against the historic monuments, works of art or places of worship which constitute the cultural or spiritual heritage of peoples', the use of 'such objects in support of the military effort', and making 'such objects the object of reprisals.' The protection of cultural property is also considered to be customary international law, under which attacks on cultural property are prohibited unless 'imperatively required by military necessity' and parties to a conflict are required to protect cultural property.[93] Under the latter requirement, seizure or destruction or wilful damage to 'institutions dedicated to religion, charity, education, the arts and sciences, historic monuments and works of art and science is prohibited', as is '[a]ny form of theft, pillage or misappropriation of, and any acts of vandalism directed against, property of great importance to the cultural heritage of every people'. In accordance with these rules, the Rome Statute of

---

the destruction 'did not constitute a war crime' because 'the Buddhas were not destroyed in the course of fighting' because there were no hostilities in the Bamiyan Valley.

[88] Brammertz et al. 2016, p. 1145.

[89] Pratt 2018, p. 1050.

[90] Regulations, 14 May 1954; 1954 Protocol to the Hague Convention for the Protection of Cultural Property in the Event of Armed Conflict 249 UNTS 215; 1999 Second Protocol to the Hague Convention for the Protection of Cultural Property in the Event of Armed Conflict 2253 UNTS 172.

[91] Cultural Property Convention, Preamble.

[92] 1977 Protocol Additional to the Geneva Conventions of 12 August 1949, and Relating to the Protection of Victims of International Armed Conflicts 1125 UNTS 3; and 1977 Protocol Additional to the Geneva Conventions of 12 August 1949, and Relating to the Protection of Victims of Non-International Armed Conflicts 1125 UNTS 609.

[93] Customary International Humanitarian Law Rule 38 (Attacks Against Cultural Property) https://ihl-databases.icrc.org/customary-ihl/eng/docs/v1_rul_rule38 and Rule 40 (Respect for Cultural Property) https://ihl-databases.icrc.org/customary-ihl/eng/docs/v1_rul_rule40. Accessed 13 August 2020.

11 International Human Rights Law

the International Criminal Court criminalises 'intentionally directing attacks against buildings dedicated to religion, education, art, science or charitable purposes, [and] historical monuments', unless they are military objectives, rendering such actions war crimes.[94] The inclusion in these laws of references to religious institutions, and buildings dedicated to education and the arts and sciences links these protection with other human rights, namely the right to education and freedom of religion. It also connects the tangible nature of culture (property) with intangible cultural concepts such as art and science.[95]

There has been a number of cases in which persons have been prosecuted for the war crime of attacks against cultural property, at the International Criminal Tribunal for Yugoslavia (ICTY), the International Criminal Court (ICC). Before the ICTY, the significant destruction of the Old Town of Dubrovnik was prosecuted in several cases, including *Strugar* and *Jokić*.[96] The ICTY also charged attacks on cultural property as crimes against humanity, under which it was held that such attacks 'when perpetrated with the requisite discriminatory intent, amounts to an attack on the very... identity of a people. As such, it manifests a nearly pure expression of the notion of "crimes against humanity", for all of humanity is indeed injured by the destruction of a unique... culture and its concomitant cultural objects'.[97] The ICC saw its first guilty plea in the case of *Al Mahdi*, in which the charges related to the destruction of cultural property in Timbuktu.[98] Al Madhi pled guilty under overwhelming evidence (including video evidence of his personal involvement in the destruction of the mausoleums and shrines) to the war crime of intentionally directing attacks against religious and historical buildings.[99] He received a sentence of nine years' imprisonment, which is comparative to ICTY sentences of seven or eight years' imprisonment. The ICC found that Al Madhi's crimes were committed for discriminatory religious motives, and that the sites were of 'symbolic and emotional value' to the local population, 'at the heart of Mali's cultural heritage', 'among the most cherished buildings of the city'.[100] The Trial Chamber also ordered reparations, the first ordered by an international criminal court.[101] Reparations focused on the significance of access to cultural heritage for the effective enjoyment of human rights, through the contribution to the reconstruction of the cultural property. Inhabitants of Timbuktu were the priority, with an order of collective reparations for the protection and maintenance of the UNESCO protected sites, and payments to individuals whose

---

[94] 1998 Rome Statute of the International Criminal Court 2187 UNTS 90, Article 8(2)(b)(ix) and (e)(iv).

[95] See above n 62.

[96] *Prosecutor v Strugar*, IT-01-42; *Prosecutor v Jokić*, IT-01-42/1. See Brammertz et al. 2016 for an overview of the ICTY cultural heritage cases.

[97] *Prosecutor v Kordić and Čerkez*, Trial Judgement, 26 February 2001, IT-95-14/2, para 207.

[98] *Prosecutor v Ahmad Al Faqi Al Madi*, ICC-01/12/01/15.

[99] For further detail on the sentencing and judgment, see Pratt 2018 and Vrdoljak 2018.

[100] *Prosecutor v Ahmad Al Faqi Al Madi*, Judgment and Sentence, 27 September 2016, ICC-01/12/01/15-171, paras 78–79.

[101] *Al Madhi*, Reparations Order, 17 August 2017, ICC-01/12-01/15-236.

274   M. O'Brien

livelihoods depended on the protected sites. Al Madhi also made an apology, which
was translated into local languages.

Given the extensive protection of culture and cultural heritage under human rights
law, international humanitarian law and international criminal law, it is evident that
this is one of the most important components of humanity. There is a harmony
in the language used and the specific protection obligations in all three fields of
international law with regards to the importance of culture to the global community
and to human identity. The relationship between culture and identity is fundamental,
and international law seeks to safeguard the many unique identities of different
peoples around the globe.

11.8 Conclusion

The current international human rights law system may have begun in 1948 with a
declaration adopted through a non-binding resolution, but today human rights are an
inherent part of international law, with the majority of rights contained in the UDHR
deemed customary international law, and thus binding on all states.[102] Human rights
are seen as part of the general principles of international law, and superior to other
treaty obligations (where treaty obligations would be contrary to human rights). Some
rights have attained *jus cogens* status, giving them priority in the international hierarchy of norms: the prohibitions on slavery, genocide, torture, racial discrimination
and apartheid, and the right to self-determination.[103] The human rights law system
has fundamentally changed the structure and functions of international law, incorporating individuals, international organisations and civil society organisations into
this previously state-centric field of practice. The creation of the United Nations led
to the establishment of a relatively comprehensive legal system to ensure the promotion, protection, respect and monitoring of human rights throughout the globe. The
extraterritorial nature of human rights obligations emphasises the crucial nature of
rights, as they overcome traditional notions of sovereignty. International law's structural evolution in the 20th century was because of human rights, flowing from a
desire to ensure that a state's power is not unlimited, and that individuals deserve
liberty, dignity and respect.

References

Alston P, Crawford J (eds) (2000) The Future of UN Human Rights Treaty Monitoring. Cambridge
    University Press, Cambridge

---

[102] de Schutter 2014, pp. 63–66.

[103] At least these rights, and possibly all human rights, are obligations *erga omnes*. See e.g.
Barcelona Traction, Light and Power Company Ltd (Belgium v. Spain), ICJ, Judgment of 5 February
1970, p. 32 paras 33–34; de Schutter 2014, pp. 113–118.

Alston P, Goodman R (2013) International Human Rights. Oxford University Press, Oxford

Amnesty International (2012) United States of America: 'Targeted Killing' Policies Violate Right to Life, AMR 51/047/2012. https://www.amnesty.org/en/documents/AMR51/047/201 2/en/. Accessed 13 August 2020

Bayefsky A F (2001) Direct Petition in the UN Human Rights Treaty System. Proceedings of the Annual Meeting (American Society of International Law) 95:71-75

Brammertz S, Hughes K, Kipp A, Tomljanovich W (2016) Attacks against Cultural Heritage as a Weapon of War. Journal of International Criminal Justice 14: 1143–1174.

Collister H (2015) Rituals and Implementation in the Universal Periodic Review and the Human Rights Treaty Bodies. In: Charlesworth H, Larking E (eds) Human Rights and the Universal Periodic Review: Rituals and Ritualism. Cambridge University Press, Cambridge, pp 109–125

Conte A, Burchill R (2016) Defining Civil and Political Rights : The Jurisprudence of the United Nations Human Rights Committee. Routledge, Farnham

Coomans F, Kamminga M T (eds) (2004) Extraterritorial Application of Human Rights Treaties. Intersentia, Antwerp/Oxford

de Schutter O (2014) International Human Rights Law: Cases, Materials, Commentary, 2nd edn. Cambridge University Press, Cambridge

Doswald-Beck L (2006) The right to life in armed conflict: does international humanitarian law provide all the answers? International Review of the Red Cross 88:881–904

Egan S (2011) The United Nations Human Rights Treaty System: Law and Procedure. Bloomsbury Professional, Haywards Heath

Francioni F, Lenzerini F (2003) The Destruction of the Buddhas of Bamiyan and International Law. European Journal of International Law 14: 619–651

Friedländer S (2007) The Years of Extermination: Nazi Germany and the Jews, 1939–1945. Harper Perennial, New York

Gill T D (2013) Some Thoughts on the Relationship Between International Humanitarian Law and International Human Rights Law: A Plea for Mutual Respect and a Common-Sense Approach. Yearbook of International Humanitarian Law 251

Goodman R, Jinks D (2003) Measuring the Effects of Human Rights Treaties. European Journal of International Law 14:171–83

Haas M (2008) International Human Rights: A Comprehensive Introduction. Routledge, Abingdon

Hafner-Burton E M, Helfer L R, Fariss C J (2011) Emergency and Escape: Explaining Derogations from Human Rights Treaties. International Organization 65:673–707

Hartman J F (1981) Derogation from Human Rights Treaties in Public Emergencies: A Critique of Implementation by the European Commission and Court of Human Rights and the Human Rights Committee of the United Nations. Harvard International Law Journal 22:1–52

Hathaway O (2002) Do Human Rights Treaties Make a Difference? Yale Law Journal 111:1935–2042

Heintze H-J (2013) Theories on the relationship between international humanitarian law and human rights law. In: Kolb R, Gaggioli G (eds) Research Handbook on Human Rights and Humanitarian Law. Edward Elgar Publishing Limited, Cheltenham, pp 53–64

Kanter A (2019) Do Human Rights Treaties Matter: The Case for the United Nations Convention on the Rights of People with Disabilities. Vanderbilt Journal of Transnational Law 52:577–609

King J (2012) Judging Social Rights. Cambridge University Press, Cambridge

Lazarus L (2014) Reasoning Rights: Comparative Judicial Engagement. Hart Publishing, Oxford

Leckie S, Gallagher A (2006) Economic, Social, and Cultural Rights: A Legal Resource Guide. University of Pennsylvania Press, Philadelphia

Macklem P (2015) Human Rights in International Law: Three Generations or One? London Review of International Law 3:61–92

Milanović M (2010) A Norm Conflict Perspective on the Relationship between International Humanitarian Law and Human Rights Law. J Conflict Secur Law 14:459-483

Milanović M (2011) Extraterritorial Application of Human Rights Treaties. Oxford University Press, Oxford

Mill J S (1991) On Liberty and Other Essays. Oxford University Press, Oxford (orig. 1806–1873)

Miller S (2010) Revisiting Extraterritorial Jurisdiction: A Territorial Justification for Extraterritorial Jurisdiction under the European Convention. European Journal of International Law 20:1223–1246

Moyn S (2010) The Last Utopia: Human Rights in History. Harvard University Press, London

Müller J (2018) European Human Rights Protection in Times of Terrorism – the State of Emergency and the Emergency Clause of the European Convention on Human Rights (ECHR). Zeitschrift für Politikwissenschaft 28:581–91

Nugraha I Y (2018) Human Rights Derogation During Coup Situations. The International Journal of Human Rights 22:194–206

O'Brien M (2010-2011) From Sexual Exploitation to Srebrenica: State Responsibility for Criminal Misconduct by Peacekeepers. New Zealand & Australian Armed Forces Law Review 10 & 11:125–47

O'Brien M (2022) From Discrimination to Death: Genocide Process through a Human Rights Lens. Routledge, London (forthcoming)

O'Flaherty M (2010) Reform of the UN Human Rights Treaty Body System: Locating the Dublin Statement. Human Rights Law Review 10:319–35

O'Keefe R (2010) Protection of Cultural Property under International Criminal Law. Melbourne Journal of International Law 11: 339

O'Keefe R (2014) Protection of Cultural Property. In: Clapham A, Gaeta P (eds) The Oxford Handbook of International Law in Armed Conflict. Oxford University Press, Oxford, pp 492–520

Pejic J (2001) Non-Discrimination and Armed Conflict. International Review of the Red Cross, No. 841. https://www.icrc.org/eng/resources/documents/article/other/57jqzq.htm. Accessed 5 March 2020

Pratt L (2018) Prosecution for the Destruction of Cultural Property - Significance of the al Madhi Trial. International Criminal Law Review 18: 1048–1079

Samnøy Å (1999) The Origins of the Universal Declaration of Human Rights. In: Alfredsson G, Eide (eds) The Universal Declaration of Human Rights. Martinus Nijhoff Publishers, The Hague, pp 3–22

Saul B, Kinley D, Mowbray J (2014) The International Covenant on Economic, Social and Cultural Rights: Commentary, Cases, and Materials. Oxford University Press, Oxford

Schwelb E (1972) The International Court of Justice and the Human Rights Clauses of the Charter. American Journal of International Law 66:337–351

Simmons B (2012) Mobilizing for Human Rights: International Law in Domestic Politics. Cambridge University Press, Cambridge

Vrdoljak A F (2018) Introductory Note to Prosecutor v Ahmad Al Faqi Al Madhi: Judgment and Sentence & Reparations Order (Int'l Crim. Ct.). International Legal Materials 57: 17–20

Melanie O'Brien (BA/LLB, GDLP, LLM, Ph.D., GCTT) is Associate Professor of International Law at the University of Western Australia, an award-winning teacher of International Humanitarian Law, Public International Law, and Legal Research. Her research examines the connection between human rights and the genocide process; and sexual exploitation by peacekeepers. She is President of the International Association of Genocide Scholars (IAGS) and co-convened the 2017 IAGS conference at University of Queensland. Melanie has conducted fieldwork and research across six continents. She is an admitted legal practitioner, and a long-term member of the International Humanitarian Law Committee of the Australian Red Cross. Melanie has previously worked at several Australian universities; the National Human Rights Institution of Samoa; and the Legal Advisory Section of the Office of the Prosecutor at the International Criminal Court. She is the author of *Criminalising Peacekeepers: Modernising National Approaches to Sexual Exploitation and Abuse* (2017, Palgrave) and tweets @DrMelOB.

Chapter 12
Direct Participation in Hostilities

Christine Byron

Contents

12.1 Introduction 278
12.2 The Emergence of DPH in Treaty Law 278
12.3 Treaties, Commentaries, Reports and Cases 279
    12.3.1 The ICRC Customary Study on IHL and DPH 282
12.4 The Interpretive Guidance on the Notion of DPH—Introductory Comments 283
    12.4.1 Temporal Scope of the Loss of Protection 286
    12.4.2 The Interpretive Guidance on the Notion of DPH—Elements of DPH 287
    12.4.3 Threshold of Harm 287
    12.4.4 Direct Causation 288
    12.4.5 Belligerent Nexus 290
    12.4.6 Beginning and End of DPH 290
    12.4.7 Precautions and Presumptions in Situations of Doubt 291
    12.4.8 Restraints on the Use of Force in Direct Attack 291
    12.4.9 Consequences of Regaining Civilian Protection 293
    12.4.10 Conclusion to the Interpretive Guidance 293
12.5 The Application of DPH by the ICC in *Ntaganda* in 2019 294
12.6 Conclusion 296
References 298

Abstract Direct participation in hostilities (DPH) was created as a concept in Additional Protocol I, developed in human rights and national case law and discussed briefly by the International Committee of the Red Cross (ICRC) Customary Law Study. However, it was not clearly defined at the time. The Interpretive Guidance on the Notion of Direct Participation under International Humanitarian Law (Interpretive Guidance) developed by the ICRC requires a threshold of harm, direct causation and a belligerent nexus as well as suggesting that civilians should be captured rather than killed if possible. However, there have been many controversies about the precise modalities of DPH. This chapter, which offers a rare practical-facing analysis of the Interpretive Guidance and contestation surrounding it, argues that the Guidance is inadequate for the realities of warfare, and that a human rights-based approach offers better, more meaningful protection to civilians taking a DPH.

C. Byron (✉)
Cardiff University, Cardiff, Wales, UK
e-mail: byronc@cardiff.ac.uk

© T.M.C. ASSER PRESS and the authors 2022
S. Sayapin et al. (eds.), *International Conflict and Security Law*,
https://doi.org/10.1007/978-94-6265-515-7_12

Keywords belligerent · civilian · direct participation in hostilities (DPH) · International Committee of the Red Cross (ICRC) · international humanitarian law (IHL) · Interpretive Guidance

12.1 Introduction

This chapter initially analyses the emergence of the notion of civilians taking a DPH. The concept of an individual taking a direct part in hostilities is a detailed aspect of International Humanitarian Law (IHL), whereby civilians can lose their normal protection and be targeted. In addition to analysing the development of DPH before the Interpretive Guidance and international and national cases on the subject, substantial attention will be paid to the Interpretive Guidance itself, which has proven controversial in parts. In addition to analysing the controversy, improvements will be proposed.[1] Finally, the effect of the concept of DPH in *Ntaganda* before the International Criminal Court (ICC), and worrying developments in that case, which took place after the Interpretive Guidance's launch in 2009 are analysed. It must be remembered that the concept of DPH has to be applied by soldiers in combat and so should be as practical as possible. Since the ICRC suggests that civilians taking a DPH should be captured rather than killed if possible, but as it does not consider how such civilians should be treated, the chapter concludes with an alternative suggestion for the protection of civilians taking a DPH.

12.2 The Emergence of DPH in Treaty Law

The first mention of a similar phrase to 'direct part in hostilities' was in Common Article 3 to the four Geneva Conventions of 1949,[2] in the context of addressing when the protections of Common Article 3 would apply in a non-international armed conflict (NIAC): among those protected were "[p]ersons taking no active part in the hostilities". The Commentary to the Geneva Conventions did not discuss this phrase at all.[3] Nevertheless, the equally authentic French text to Common Article 3 renders it as "*directement aux hostilités*", so 'active part in hostilities' is synonymous with 'direct part in hostilities'.[4] With respect to Article 15 of Geneva Convention IV which mentioned 'taking part in hostilities', the International Criminal Tribunal for the former Yugoslavia (ICTY) in the *Strugar* Appeal commented that holding

---

[1] See the ICRC Reports and Documents 2008, (henceforth Interpretive Guidance), pp. 1013–1014.

[2] Common Article 3 to all four Geneva Conventions, 75 UNTS (1950) 31, 85, 135 and 287.

[3] See Pictet ed. 1952 Geneva Convention I, pp. 38–61; 1960 Geneva Convention II, pp. 32–39; 1960 Geneva Convention III, pp. 28–44 and 1958 Geneva Convention IV, pp. 26–44.

[4] See Commentary on Geneva Convention I 2016, para 525 and *Prosecutor v Strugar*, Appeal Chamber Judgment, 17 July 2008, IT-01-42-A, para 173. See also, HPCR Manual 2013, p. 132 and the International Institute of Humanitarian Law 2006, p. 4, para 2.

12 Direct Participation in Hostilities

everything in support of military operations as amounting to DPH "would in practice render the principle of distinction meaningless".[5] Clearly the paucity of treaty law and the mere caution in *Strugar* not to consider every support for military operations to amount to DPH provides scant guidance from a professional military point of view. It is important, therefore, to further analyse the evolution of the expression 'direct part in hostilities' for the purposes of the present chapter. This analysis starts by addressing the evolution of the terminology prior to the Interpretive Guidance being issued.

12.3 Treaties, Commentaries, Reports and Cases

The actual expression 'direct part in hostilities' was first used in the 1977 Additional Protocols to the 1949 Geneva Conventions,[6] and the ICRC Commentaries took the approach that hostile acts forming part of DPH should be understood to be acts intended to cause "actual harm to the personnel and equipment of the armed forces",[7] which requires a nexus or sufficient causal relationship between participation and its immediate consequences.[8] The Commentaries also stated that several delegations were of the opinion that DPH "included preparations for combat and the return from combat" and required a clear distinction between DPH and participating in the war effort more generally, in order to protect civilians not taking a DPH.[9] The Commentaries emphasised that once a civilian ceased to take a DPH they no longer represented a danger and could not, therefore, be attacked.[10] Provided that the person has returned to civilian life, this seems to be a reasonable point, but until that point the guidance offered is too brief to be practical for soldiers on the ground to apply.[11]

The Inter-American Commission on Human Rights (IAComHR) considered DPH in *Abella v Argentina*, in which it likened civilians who attacked the Tablada base to

---

[5] *Prosecutor v Strugar*, Appeal Chamber Judgment, 17 July 2008, IT-01-42-A, para 176. Note that the Commentary to Article 15 assumed that civilians taking a DPH would either be part of a *levée en masse* or part of an organized resistance movement within Article 4(2)–(6) of Geneva Convention III and so would have Prisoner of War status if captured, Pictet ed. 1958 Commentary Geneva Convention IV, pp. 131–132.

[6] Additional Protocol I, Article 51(3), UNTS 1125 (1979) 3 and in a NIAC Additional Protocol II, Article 13(3), UNTS 1125 (1979) p. 609.

[7] Sandoz et al eds. 1987, p. 618.

[8] Ibid., p. 1451. See Henckaerts and Doswald-Beck 2005, in their Rule 6, p. 20 in respect of the UK view of Article 53(1).

[9] Sandoz et al. 1987, pp. 618–619. This issue will be returned to later in the context of the ICRC Interpretive Guidance.

[10] Ibid., p. 619 and Commentary to Protocol II, p. 1451, but see Schmitt 2010a, p. 711.

[11] Controversies on this will be discussed in the Interpretive Guidance at Sect. 12.4 below.

combatants,[12] although it held that they were only legitimate targets whilst actually fighting and so did not go so far as to suggest that the attacking civilians would have had prisoner of war (POW) status if captured.[13] Indeed, the Commission only dealt with the question of whether the civilians could be legitimately attacked, not their status or protection once captured.

It is clear that civilians taking a DPH do not actually become combatants and that their only similarity to combatants is that they can be targeted.[14] Nevertheless, it is certainly arguable that on a practical basis, to a soldier, there is no real difference between attacking combatants or civilians taking a DPH. Indeed in the report on Columbia the view was expressed that when taking a DPH becomes the "principal daily activity" of an individual", they could be attacked to the same extent as members of regular armed forces.[15] This was a similar approach to the Israeli *Targeted Killings Case*,[16] which considered that a civilian who makes a terrorist organisation his "home" and as part of that organization commits a "chain of hostilities", with only short periods of rest between them, loses his immunity from attack "for such time" as he is committing the "chain of acts".[17] Indeed both the IAComHR and the *Targeted Killing Case* agreed that if civilians are captured they can be tried and punished.[18] However, the only reference to the *treatment* of captured civilians who have taken a DPH is given in a few lines in the *Targeted Killings Case*. Such a brief comment is wholly inadequate to protect such civilians.[19]

The *Targeted Killings Case* was unusual in that the Supreme Court of Israel considered that the law that applied to the armed conflict between Israel and the terrorist organisations in the area was the IHL applicable in an international armed conflict (IAC), on the basis that "[a]t times… [terrorist organisations] have military capabilities that exceed those of States".[20] It is submitted that the military capacity of terrorist or other non-State actors is not relevant to the determination of whether a conflict is international or non-international and is, in fact, only relevant to intensity of the fighting if no other State party is involved.[21] Furthermore, despite the fact that

---

[12] *Abella v Argentina*, Case 11.137, 18 November 1997, OEA/Ser.L/V/II.98, para 178. The Inter-American Commission on Human Rights took the same approach in the third report on the human rights situation in Colombia, 26 February 1999, OAE/Ser.L/VII.102, para 61.

[13] *Abella v Argentina*, ibid., para 189.

[14] Crawford 2015, p. 81.

[15] Third report on the human rights situation in Colombia, n.13 *supra*, para 61.

[16] *The Public Committee against Torture in Israel et al v The Government of Israel et al*, The Supreme Court sitting as the High Court of Justice, HCJ 769/02, 11 December 2006 (hereafter *Targeted Killings Case*). Note, although this case was decided before the publication of the Interpretive Guidance; it was decided after the expert meetings on DPH, so it may have been influenced by them.

[17] *Targeted Killings Case*, para 39, making reference to Statman 2004, p. 195.

[18] The third report on the human rights situation in Colombia, n.13 *supra*, para 55 and the *Targeted Killings Case*, para 25.

[19] See *Targeted Killings Case*, para 25, this will be returned to in the conclusion at Sect. 12.6 below.

[20] *Targeted Killings Case*, para 21, referring to Judea, Samaria and the Gaza Strip.

[21] ICRC 2016 and its Commentary to Article 3, especially paras 431–432 and 420–430.

12 Direct Participation in Hostilities

Israel is not a party to API, the Court stated that it saw Article 53(1) as representing customary international law and that it was therefore part of the law of Israel.[22] Its definition of DPH included, apart from those acts intended to cause damage to the army, acts intended to cause damage to civilians.[23] The Court gave examples of civilians taking a DPH (including using weapons, gathering intelligence or preparing for hostilities) and emphasised that "[i]t is possible to take part in hostilities without using weapons at all".[24] It also considered that DPH should not be read too narrowly and includes, in addition to the person committing the physical act, those who sent them as well as the person deciding on the act, and the person who planned the act.[25] This latter point explains the Court's concept of DPH as including those without weapons as they read DPH widely and this interpretive ambit would necessarily include those without weapons if the definition were to include all those in the planning stage. It is highly unfortunate that the Court did not even consider DPH in a NIAC, especially as no other State was involved at that stage.[26]

When reading the *Targeted Killings Case*, it is important to remember the context. The Court was dealing with terrorism and, therefore, explained DPH in the context of terrorism. The aim was not to offer more general comments about DPH. This explains why, unlike the Interpretive Guidance, the Court considered civilians serving as voluntary human shields for terrorists to be taking a DPH,[27] whereas civilians forced to do so were victims of terrorism and not taking a DPH.[28] However, it must be said that when suspected terrorists are targeted by drones or other aerial bombardment it is hard to see how, short of excellent intelligence, it would be possible to tell the difference between voluntary and involuntary human shields for the purposes of applying the principle of proportionality or indeed, whether, as a political issue, targeting civilians in these circumstances would be helpful in defeating terrorists.[29] It is also interesting that the Court expressly went so far as to include those who, in non-terrorist cases, would be called 'commanders',[30] although this was part of the Court's broad interpretation of DPH. The Court also expressly stated that terrorists taking a DPH are not combatants and are not, therefore, entitled to POW status.[31]

---

[22] *Targeted Killings Case*, para 30 and see para 19 for an explanation as to why customary international law is part of the law of Israel.

[23] *Targeted Killings Case*, para 33.

[24] Ibid., paras 33 and 35 and see para 12 on sending out a person to commit a terrorist attack.

[25] Ibid., para 37.

[26] Note that the Palestinian representation at the UN was not upgraded to UN 'non-Member Observer State' status until 29 November 2012 in General Assembly Resolution A/RES/67/19.

[27] Note that this is a different view than that taken by the ICRC Interpretive Guidance, see Sect. 12.4.5 below.

[28] *Targeted Killings Case*, para 36.

[29] See generally Dixon 2009.

[30] Targeted Killings Case, para 37.

[31] Ibid., para 25.

The issue of DPH also arose in a US terrorism case, on a reconsideration to dismiss for lack of jurisdiction.[32] In this case the Military Commission found that that the accused took a DPH as he drove a vehicle containing two surface-to-air missiles in what they termed "temporal and spatial proximity" to ongoing combat; it emphasised Hamdan's past history of delivering munitions to the Taliban and al-Qaeda fighters.[33] It is significant that they took the past history of the individual into account when deciding whether he was taking a DPH as well as the fact that he was heading towards "a battle already underway" with his missiles.[34] Although the ICRC Customary Study did not make reference to past behaviour as such, and the Interpretive Guidance expressly denied that this could be taken into account,[35] the US case took into account past history when deciding if an individual had taken a DPH.

The analysis thus far amply illustrates the complexities involved in deciding whether or not a civilian is taking DPH. The guidance offered by the various treaty commentaries and case reports discussed above is woefully inadequate to guide the difficult, high-pressured and practical decision-making demanded of soldiers in combat. What then, of the ICRC Customary Study on IHL and DPH?

12.3.1 The ICRC Customary Study on IHL and DPH

The ICRC Customary Study on IHL was written before the Interpretive Guidance on DPH, but contemporaneously with the expert meetings that resulted in the Customary Study.[36] Therefore, the Study did not go into any great detail about DPH, presumably because it did not want to risk contradicting the forthcoming Interpretive Guidance; it only commented that a precise definition of the term DPH did not exist.[37] The Study used the IACHR view in *Abella*, other reports by the IACHR, and military manuals to cover this issue. In particular, it made some reference to the US view expressed, in the *Commander's Handbook on the Law of Naval Operations*, that civilians serving as lookouts, guards or intelligence agents for military forces might

---

[32] *United States of America v Salim Ahmed Hamdan*, On Reconsideration Ruling on Motion to Dismiss for Lack of Jurisdiction, 19 December 2007, AE 084, at www.mc.mil/Portals/0/pdfs/Hamdan/Hamdan%20(AE084).pdf accessed at 3 March 2019. The reversal of this case was on a different basis by the Supreme Court, see *Hamdan v Rumsfeld*, 548 U.S. 557 (2006) at https://casebook.icrc.org/case-study/united-states-hamdan-v-rumsfeld accessed at 28 August 2019.

[33] See *United States of America v Salim Ahmed Hamdan*, ibid., page 6.

[34] Ibid.

[35] Interpretive Guidance, p. 1035.

[36] The ICRC Customary IHL Study was published in 2005, whilst the Interpretive Guidance was published in 2009. As some experts disagreed with the final advice and would not sign it, the Interpretive Guidance was published purely under the name of the ICRC.

[37] Henckaerts and Doswald-Beck 2005, Rule 6, p. 22.

12 Direct Participation in Hostilities

be taking a DPH.[38] The *Handbook* has some similarities to the approach that the Israeli court took in the *Targeted Killings Case* with respect to the argument that it is possible to take a DPH without using weapons at all.[39] It should be noted, however, that the *Handbook* continued that combatants must "make an honest determination as to whether a particular person is or is not taking a direct part in hostilities based on the person's behavior, location and attire, and other information available at the time".[40] This was also the approach taken by the Commission in *Hamdan* above, where the accused's behaviour (driving surface-to-air missiles), location (heading towards an ongoing battle) and the other information available (the Americans had intelligence that he had previously delivered munitions to Taliban and Al Qaeda fighters), were seen as sufficient for him to have taken a DPH.[41] This similarity indeed suggests that the Commission could have been influenced by this *Handbook* (or possibly its 1995 predecessor), although the book's guidance was not directly applicable to a conflict not involving the US Navy.

Therefore, the Study adds little to the interim conclusion drawn by the analysis: the guidance offered by the sources considered so far remains inadequate for effective practical deployment by soldiers in combat.

The analysis now turns to the Interpretive Guidance in order to assess its adequacy as a practical guide.

12.4 The Interpretive Guidance on the Notion of DPH—Introductory Comments

The ICRC published its 'Interpretive Guidance on the Notion of Direct Participation in Hostilities Under International Humanitarian Law' in the International Review of the Red Cross in December 2008.[42] Although the Interpretive Guidance was 'informed' by the expert discussions at the five meetings held from 2003 to 2008, the final document reflects, not the experts' views, but the ICRC's own preferred position.[43] Indeed, Nils Melzer, a legal adviser for the ICRC, who guided the Expert Meetings from 2004 and authored the Interpretive Guidance, accepted that the final position did not reflect a unanimous view or even a majority position of the participating experts but rather the ICRC's own view.[44] He claimed that "the Guidance

---

[38] The Commander's Handbook 2007, para 8.2.2. Note that the earlier edition was from 1995 and it must have been this that Henckaerts and Doswald-Beck 2005 were citing.

[39] See *Targeted Killings Case*, para 37.

[40] Commander's Handbook 2007, n.40, *supra*.

[41] See Sect. 12.3.1 above.

[42] See Interpretive Guidance, pp. 991–1047.

[43] See the expert discussions at https://www.icrc.org/en/doc/resources/documents/article/other/dir ect-participation-article-020709.htm accessed on 6 September 2019, Interpretive Guidance, p. 992.

[44] Melzer 2010, pp. 853–856. Note that it is not possible to tell if the ICRC selected the military participants or their countries nominated them.

constitutes a holistic and carefully balanced 'package deal'".[45] Whilst in conferences 'a package deal' might indeed be used to gain consensus agreement, it is a rather odd turn of phrase for something that should have practical application for soldiers involved in armed conflict and in respect of which the ICRC, in places, ignored the majority of experts, including those with military experience.[46]

As far IACs are concerned, the Interpretive Guidance accepted as a basic position the definition of Article 43 of API, accepting that this was a "broad and functional concept of armed forces".[47] The ICRC view was that whilst membership of regular State armed forces is regulated by national law, membership of irregular armed forces, such as militia, volunteer corps and resistance movements 'belonging to a party to the conflict', can only be dependably determined on the basis of "functional criteria".[48] The ambit of 'functional criteria' is contentious, and for example seems to allow the targeting of military lawyers in the State forces, but not civilian lawyers who support irregular armed forces without reference to a specific attack, as they would then qualify as civilians not taking a DPH. It was also clear that the Interpretive Guidance reference to membership in irregular armed forces was only in order to see if a person was targetable and not in order to see if such a person would gain POW status if caught taking a DPH. In fact, the Interpretive Guidance explicitly only deals with targeting issues,[49] leaving the question of how to classify civilians who are caught when they are taking a DPH a matter of conjecture. Importantly the Interpretive Guidance does not mention how civilians caught taking a DPH should be treated if captured.[50]

One of the initial contentious comments in the Interpretive Guidance relates to members of organised armed groups. This is understood to refer mainly to NIACs where the ICRC contrasted civilians directly participating in hostilities on a merely unplanned, infrequent or unorganised basis, with those having a "continuous combat function", who have a more permanent integration into an organised armed group and effectively serve as the armed forces of a non-State party to an armed conflict.[51] The Interpretive Guidance emphasised that "individuals whose continuous function involves the preparation, execution, or command of acts or operations amounting to direct participation in hostilities are assuming a continuous combat function".[52]

The purpose of this new concept was clearly practical. It was intended to allow some civilians to be targeted at all times, rather than in a purely reactive way only

---

[45] Ibid.

[46] Note that the former military members of the expert group, Boothby, Schmitt, Watkin and Hays Parks have all made comments very critical of the ICRC Interpretive Guidance. It is not possible to tell if the ICRC selected the military participants or their countries nominated them.

[47] Interpretive Guidance, pp. 998–999. See also Schmitt 2010b, p. 15.

[48] Interpretive Guidance, p. 1001, but see Watkin 2010, pp. 671–672.

[49] Interpretive Guidance, p. 993.

[50] This issue will be returned to in the conclusion at Sect. 12.6 below.

[51] Interpretive Guidance, p. 1007. The expression of making the group their 'home' potentially has the same effect in the *Targeted Killings Case*, para 35.

[52] Interpretive Guidance, p. 1007.

12 Direct Participation in Hostilities 285

when they are actually taking a DPH.[53] Nevertheless, Philip Alston, the Special Rapporteur to the Human Rights Council, has described the concept of continuous combat function as "questionable" and argued that the specific treaty language limits DPH to "for such time" that civilians take a DPH as opposed to "all the time".[54] It is certainly the case that the continuous combat function has been criticised by academics for a variety of reasons.[55] Hampson, for example considers that DPH could only be established by a behaviour test, pointing out that such people "lose civilian immunity from attack but do not gain the privileges of a combatant", although the Interpretive Guidance fails to comment on this issue.[56] It is submitted, moreover, that those who, according to the ICRC, can always be targeted because of their continuous combat function, are unlikely to apply IHL enthusiastically if they would be vulnerable to prosecution simply for taking part in the conflict.

There is a difference between most military publications, the ICRC and most human rights-influenced publications. The ICRC considers that the best way to protect non-State actors in a NIAC is to apply as much of the law of IAC as possible.[57] The military and retired military commentators mainly consider that it is efficient and necessary for the security of a State to be able to target non-State actors, even if the latter are not attacking at the time.[58] However, many human rights actors and courts as well as some academics take the approach that the victims of NIACs can best be protected by applying human rights law as much as is possible in a NIAC.[59] The concept of 'continuous combat function' in a NIAC thus represents a stark fault line between the three types of commentator in this area.

The fact that the Interpretive Guidance excludes from continuous combat function those who recruit, train and carry out propaganda or purchase, smuggle or maintain

---

[53] See Sassòli 2019, p. 359 at 8.317.

[54] Alston P., 'Report of the Special Rapporteur on extrajudicial, summary or arbitrary executions: Addendum: Study on targeted killings', A/HRC/14/24/Add.6, 28 May 2010, para 65, and see Crawford 2018, p. 24.

[55] For example, see Solis 2016, p. 585 and Sassòli 2019, p. 360 at 8.318.

[56] Hampson 2011, pp. 200–201, although Tsagourias and Morrison 2018, p. 287, disagree.

[57] This is demonstrated by the fact that the ICRC Customary IHL Study has 136 of 161 rules based on API that they argue are a norm of customary international law applicable in both IACs and NIACs. The online edition of Sassòli et al undated, see the development of the law of NIAC closer to the law of IAC as a "good thing for the victims of such conflicts".

[58] For example, Watkin 2010, p. 656; Corn and Jenks 2011, p. 338 and McBride 2012, p. 50.

[59] Most have the opinion that it applies at the same time as humanitarian law, for example the International Court of Justice Advisory Opinion on the *Legality of the Threat or Use of Nuclear Weapons*, (1996), para 25 and in its Advisory Opinion on *Legal Consequences of the Construction of a Wall in the Occupied Palestinian Territory*, (2004), para 106. Compare the law of IAC in *Hassan v UK*, Application no. 29750/09, Grand Chamber Judgment in 2014, para 104 with the law of NIAC in a British Court of Appeal case in *Serdar Mohammed* [2015] EWCA Civ 843, para 246 (note that the Supreme Court did not deal with IHL). See comments of Kretzmer 2009, particularly p. 39 in which he argues that the development of human rights law means that it is unnecessary to resort to IHL in a non-international armed conflict and see Martin 2001, where he argues that human rights law and IHL should be merged.

weapons, along with the fact that it, even, comments that such persons are civilians and therefore "benefit from protection against direct attack",[60] means that the continuous combat function or even DPH would not necessarily cover the actions of part-time planners or individuals involved at the tactical or operational levels of war carrying out "campaign functions".[61] The ICRC's interpretation of DPH, therefore, is unquestionably narrower than that of the Supreme Court of Israel on this issue.[62]

12.4.1 Temporal Scope of the Loss of Protection

To some extent it looks uncontroversial to say that civilians lose their protection against attack when they deploy to take a DPH, before returning, and then regain protection when they withdraw sufficiently and take up their normal civilian lives.[63] Nevertheless, the Interpretive Guidance caused controversy by stating that civilians who regularly carry out attacks regain protection in each pause between them, stating that the effect of Article 51(3) necessarily includes the so-called "revolving door" of civilian protection.[64] Their argument, that a civilian repeatedly having taken a DPH previously does not necessarily mean that they will do so again, contradicts *US v Hamdan*.[65] It is submitted that short of excellent intelligence, in a NIAC it would be very difficult for a State to tell the difference between civilians taking a continuous combat function (who could be attacked at all times, including in their beds) and those who frequently took a DPH and then disengaged in a 'revolving door' situation, and thus had regained civilian protection.[66] Such high quality intelligence is unlikely to be available. In Afghanistan, for example, intelligence from three sources was still insufficient to prevent innocent civilians from being mistaken for taking a DPH.[67] Excellent intelligence may be the exception rather than the rule, a probability leaving civilians insufficiently protected by the 'revolving door' concept's lack of practical clarity.

---

[60] Interpretive Guidance, p. 1008.

[61] See Watkin 2010, p. 661 and *Targeted Killings Case*, para 21, which makes the same point.

[62] See discussion of the *Targeted Killings Case* in Sect. 12.3.1.

[63] The issue of deploying and returning from attacks is discussed in Sect. 12.4.7 below.

[64] Interpretive Guidance, p. 1035.

[65] Ibid., and see the *US v Hamdan* On Reconsideration Ruling on Motion to Dismiss for Lack of Jurisdiction, discussed in Sect. 12.3.1 above.

[66] See Melzer 2010, pp. 899–890; Watkin 2010, p. 688 and Crawford 2018, p. 39.

[67] See Marchant 2020, especially pp. 60–61 and Chandrasekaran 2009.

12 Direct Participation in Hostilities

12.4.2 The Interpretive Guidance on the Notion of DPH—Elements of DPH

The Interpretive Guidance, over 15 pages, considers what constitutes DPH.[68] The definition applies irrespective of the nature of the conflict and requires three elements to qualify as DPH, namely: a threshold of harm, direct causation and a belligerent nexus.[69] Each of these elements shall be analysed in turn. Again, it is doubtful that the elements and the definition overall are practical enough to be applied by a soldier on the battlefield.

12.4.3 Threshold of Harm

To reach this threshold the Interpretive Guidance states that "a specific act must be likely to adversely affect the military operations or military capacity of a party to an armed conflict" or, alternatively, "to inflict death, injury or destruction on persons or objects protected against direct attack".[70] It is clear that the former does not require a specific outcome and would not necessarily constitute a violation of IHL, whereas the latter requires an outcome that would amount to a war crime if the consequences resulted from the act in the circumstances.[71] Nevertheless, *Strugar* at the ICTY only referred to the former as a requirement for taking a DPH—and not the latter.[72] Since the concept of DPH is only relevant to whether a civilian can be targeted or not, civilians do not have to commit a war crime in order to be legally targetable.

Examples of actions that would or would not meet the threshold of harm are given by the Interpretive Guidance,[73] although it was admitted that some of the latter would still breach IHL, such as "the interruption of electricity, water or food supplies".[74] It is submitted that such actions could potentially kill any vulnerable civilians, but the ICRC stated that in the absence of adverse military affects these actions would not suffice to reach the threshold of harm required for DPH.[75] Needless to say, it is unclear why the Interpretive Guidance concludes that attacking civilians in one, direct, way would meet the threshold of harm, whereas attacking them in an indirect way would not.

---

[68] Interpretive Guidance, pp. 1016–1031.

[69] Ibid., p. 1016.

[70] Ibid.

[71] Ibid., p. 1017.

[72] *Prosecutor v Strugar,* Appeal Chamber Judgment, 17 July 2008, IT-01-42-A, para 68.

[73] Interpretive Guidance, pp. 1017–1019 and also see the examples of DPH in HPCR 2013, Rule 29, pp. 135–140.

[74] Interpretive Guidance, p. 1019.

[75] Ibid.

12.4.4 Direct Causation

The Interpretive Guidance discusses direct as opposed to indirect participation in hostilities and requires causation "in one causal step".[76] This strict concept fails to fully protect civilians as has been shown above,[77] and shows "insensitivity to the nature of modern combat operations".[78] The Interpretive Guidance gives the example of assembly and storage of an improvised explosive device (IED) and agrees that they may have a connection with the resulting harm, "but unlike the planting and detonation of that device, do not cause that harm directly".[79] By discussing IEDs the ICRC demonstrates some understanding of the devastation in terms of life and life changing injuries caused by these devices in Afghanistan, although their requirement of direct harm is clearly an unfortunate limitation.

In fact, there are examples that suggest that the ICRC view on the significance of indirect harm is indeed insufficient. If there were good intelligence that a house contained IEDs, obviously the IEDs would be a target and, depending upon the quality and content of the intelligence available, the proportionality equation might allow an attack.[80] Even if the builder or the person who stores IEDs amounted to taking a DPH, their families, which could include young children, must in any case, be factored in as part of the proportionality equation.[81] However, the Interpretive Guidance does differentiate between the tactical elements of a group who carry out specific attacks and the strategic elements of a large group who are unlikely to be engaged in carrying out a specific attack.[82] This need for involvement in a specific attack is problematic: the recruiter of suicide bombers, for example, would be seen as having a civilian status unless the suicide bombers were recruited for a specific attack.[83] It is submitted that to assign civilian status to persons heavily involved in a group's activities targeting the military of a State, unless they are involved in an individual attack, is indeed "counter intuitive".[84]

Even the discussion of direct causation in what the Interpretive Guidance terms "collective operations", (those carried out by a group of civilians taking a DPH) does not silence its critics.[85] The Interpretive Guidance allows for direct causation

---

[76] Ibid., 1021.

[77] See Schmitt's argument.

[78] See argument of Schmitt 2010b, p. 29 and Melzer's reply, Melzer 2010, p. 867. See also Schmitt 2010a, p. 725.

[79] ICRC Interpretive Guidance, p. 1022 and see McBride 2012, p. 56.

[80] See Additional Protocol I, Article 51(5)(b) and in Article 57(2)(b), accepted by the ICRC Customary IHL Study in their Rule 14 as customary international law in both international and non-international armed conflicts.

[81] Ibid., See also Schmitt 2010b, p. 38.

[82] See McBride 2012, p. 56.

[83] See McBride 2012, p. 50.

[84] Ibid., and was not the approach of the Supreme Court in the Targeted Killing Case, see the discussion in Sect. 12.3.1 above.

[85] Interpretive Guidance, p. 1022 and Schmitt 2010a, p. 731.

12 Direct Participation in Hostilities

to be "interpreted to include conduct that causes harm only in conjunction with other acts" but still requires the act of each person to be an "integral" part of a particular coordinated tactical operation which directly causes the required harm, such as the delayed harm caused by computer network attacks.[86] However, it seems likely that it would be difficult for cyber weapons to satisfy the required direct causation since the number of steps in the classic chain of causation as well as the high probability of unintended consequences makes it unlikely that such causal elements will satisfy the required 'one causal step' to count as DPH.[87]

The Interpretive Guidance demonstrates the ICRC's view on what amounts to direct participation and indirect participation, by giving further examples. A contrast is set up between physical and legal obstacles; first, civilians who voluntarily obstruct land forces physically, which amounts to DPH and secondly, civilians who act as voluntary human shields, who are only a legal obstacle to aerial bombardment. Surprisingly the Interpretive Guidance views the latter as not taking a DPH.[88] This position has caused confusion and concern.[89] Schmitt comments that from the position of the attacker it makes no difference whether the civilian action is considered to be physical or legal and adds that whilst a physical obstacle can often be removed or countered, "a legal prohibition is absolute".[90] He argues that voluntary human shields should be treated as taking a DPH, thus precluding their inclusion in the proportionality equation.[91] However, Melzer responds to such criticisms on this by questioning how much 'free will' is expressed by 'voluntary human shields' and challenges the extent to which coercion or social pressure would make such shields 'involuntary'.[92] Melzer's argument, however, shifts the issue from whether voluntary human shields are to be treated as civilians at all times and deals with a different issue; namely, how 'voluntary' such human shields are. The same question could be posed over civilians physically obstructing soldiers, yet he does not question their voluntariness. It is possible that Melzer is merely emphasising the problem of sufficiency of intelligence to know whether human shields are indeed involuntary, as was submitted earlier;[93] nevertheless, he does not deal with the substance of Schmitt's criticisms.

---

[86] Interpretive Guidance, pp. 1022–1023.

[87] See Turns 2012, p. 296 and Boothby 2010, p. 752.

[88] Interpretive Guidance, p. 1024.

[89] This is a different interpretation from that taken in the *Targeted Killings Case* discussed in Sect. 12.3.1 above.

[90] Schmitt 2010b, p. 32.

[91] Schmitt 2010b, p. 33.

[92] Melzer 2010, p. 871.

[93] See comments on the problem of telling whether human shields were voluntary or involuntary in Sect. 12.3.1 above and see also comments of Fenrick 2009, p. 294.

12.4.5 Belligerent Nexus

The Interpretive Guidance states that the third element of DPH, belligerent nexus, means that the acts must be so closely related to one of the parties to a conflict that they are an integral part of them: the required harm must be *"in support of a party to an armed conflict and to the detriment of another".*[94] It is clear that who the parties are fighting for or against should not be relevant to determination of civilian status.[95] The Interpretive Guidance does state that organised armed groups operating within the broader concept of an IAC but not 'belonging' to a party to the conflict could still be regarded as parties to a separate NIAC if they meet the conditions relating to that.[96] However, "[t]his difference is one certain to be lost on both those being attacked and those mounting attacks".[97] This lack of clarity would certainly cause confusion from the practical point of view of soldiers carrying out the attacks—not least because there is less law applicable in a NIAC than in an IAC.

The Interpretive Guidance, having dealt with their essential elements of civilians taking a DPH, turned to other aspects of this issue.

12.4.6 Beginning and End of DPH

The ICRC Commentary to Article 51(3) API stated that many delegations agreed that the expression "hostilities" used in this article included preparations for combat and the return from combat.[98] This definition was reflected in the Interpretive Guidance which limited the concept of preparation to a specific attack.[99] It could be argued in relation to this that the text of Article 51(3) does not mention preparations for combat and return and only mentions their losing protection "for such time" as civilians take a DPH. The *Harvard Manual on International Law Applicable to Air and Missile Warfare* acknowledges that there is a division between those experts who believe that only concrete preparations for a specific attack and immediate withdrawal amount to DPH and those who believe that it is much broader, going as far as the causal connection would stretch.[100] It is submitted, however, that as preparations and return from combat never made it into API, this part of the Interpretive Guidance should not be criticised for not going further than it does.

---

[94] Interpretive Guidance, p.1026, original emphasis. See Schmitt 2010a, p. 736.

[95] See also Schmitt 2010b, p. 17.

[96] Interpretative Guidance, p. 1000.

[97] Schmitt 2010b, p. 18.

[98] Sandoz et al eds. 1987, p. 618. Note that modern states have not made a declaration about this according to the ICRC state party database.

[99] Interpretive Guidance, pp. 1031–1033.

[100] HPCR 2013 p. 133, commentary to Rule 28 and see Boothby 2010, p. 750.

12.4.7 Precautions and Presumptions in Situations of Doubt

The part of the Interpretive Guidance that deals with feasible precautions and the presumption of civilian status in cases of doubt is uncontentious.[101] It does not expect the 'standard of doubt' applicable to targeting decisions to be as precise as that for criminal prosecutions, and simply expects "the level of certainty that can reasonably be achieved in the circumstances".[102] The presumption of civilian status where there is doubt and only expecting 'reasonable' intelligence could form the basis of a practical standard for military officers on the ground. However, the concept of extra restraints when dealing with civilians taking a DPH is contentious and less practical for professional military soldiers.

12.4.8 Restraints on the Use of Force in Direct Attack

Without doubt Part IX of the Interpretive Guidance is the most contentious part of the whole document.[103] There are whole academic articles addressing just this one issue.[104] This level of controversy has caused consternation among retired military and civilian academics alike.[105] Part IX states that the loss of protection for civilians who take a continuous combat function or DPH does not mean that they fall outside the law.[106] Part IX acts without 'prejudice' to international law relating to other branches of law, such as human rights law,[107] and states that the type of force used against those taking a DPH "must not exceed what is actually necessary to accomplish a legitimate purpose in the prevailing circumstances".[108] Even Melzer has admitted that this position was "highly controversial" and did not express the "majority opinion" of the experts in the ICRC process, but nevertheless argued that Part IX "ensures a clear and coherent interpretation of the law consistent with the purposes and principles of IHL".[109]

---

[101] Interpretive Guidance, pp. 1037–1040.

[102] Ibid., p. 1039.

[103] Although it has support in the *Targeted Killings* Case, para 40.

[104] See Hays Parks 2010, 35–52 and Kleffner 2012, 35–52.

[105] See for example Akande 2010, p. 192 and Fenrick 2009, p. 299.

[106] Interpretive Guidance, p. 1040.

[107] Ibid., p. 1044 states that "international human rights law or the law governing the use of international State force (*jus ad bellum*)" may apply, though the latter only seems relevant to the type of the armed conflict.

[108] Interpretive Guidance, p. 1040 and see pp. 1043–1044.

[109] Melzer 2010, p. 896. From the ICRC expert meeting notes, after Part IX was introduced, it is impossible to tell if the minority of experts who supported this. were those who worked for the ICRC currently or formerly, or if they included any independent academics. It is only possible to know which experts opposed Part IX if they criticised this part of the ICRC Interpretive Guidance in book chapters or articles. It is impossible to know what the majority of experts who remained silent on this issue actually thought.

The initial criticism of Part IX comes from Hays Parks who complains that it was introduced without warning in the 2007 expert meeting and that neither the participating experts nor the co-sponsor, the TMC Asser Institute, were consulted.[110] This is a criticism of form, rather than content. A criticism of the content is presented by the argument that, notwithstanding the famous Pictet comment on the gradation of the use of force,[111] State practice has not revealed any "use of force continuum" when engaging enemy combatants or civilians taking a DPH.[112] Meron makes the point that the Martens Clause allows the principles of humanity to help interpret IHL in cases where there is doubt, but even he affirms that the Martens Clause does not allow building "castles of sand".[113] It is arguable that this part of the Guidance creates a castle built of sand, and so cannot be supported, especially in the light of the practical problems it creates for soldiers on the ground. Goodman's support for this part of the Interpretive Guidance which he describes as a "moderate or compromise position",[114] notwithstanding the other analysis in his article, still falls short of making a convincing case that Part IX represents current (as opposed to emerging) IHL and simply does not deal with the practical problems for the military generated by this part of the Interpretive Guidance.

Practical problems include the fact that "military personnel do not have an unlimited choice of weapons",[115] most being intended to kill or disable the enemy and the fact that those involved in a conflict may not be aware that it is possible to disable a threat by capturing rather than by killing.[116] These problems are accentuated by the fact that the Interpretive Guidance states that civilians taking a DPH should be given an opportunity to surrender and potentially to be detained even if they refuse to surrender.[117] Hays Parks accepts the concession to practicality inherent in the fact that the principles of military necessity and humanity are unlikely to restrict the use of force in large-scale confrontations against normally legitimate military targets beyond "what is already required by the specific provisions of IHL",[118] but Part IX suggests that the normally applicable provisions of IHL do not apply in other situations, which is a curious position for the ICRC to take.

Kleffner considers that human rights law may be the reason for the concepts arising in this part of the Guidance, and is willing to consider that human rights law

---

[110] Hays Parks 2010, p. 783.

[111] Pictet 1985, p. 75, stating that the minimum use of force to put soldiers out of action must be used, capturing, wounding and only then killing if necessary.

[112] Hays Parks 2010, p. 799, Schmitt 2010b, p. 41 and see Fenrick 2009, p. 299. Note that Schmitt does not footnote this claim about State practice and Fenrick, in a footnote, admits that he has not done any empirical work on State practice, but argues that his claim is "substantiated to a degree by wide and relevant reading over the years". See also Kleffner 2012, p. 39 and the opposing view of Goodman 2013, p. 836, referring to the 1868 St Petersburg Declaration.

[113] Meron 2000, pp. 87–88 and Kleffner 2012, pp. 40 and 45.

[114] Goodman 2013, pp. 829–830.

[115] Fenrick 2009, p. 299.

[116] See Akande 2010, p. 192.

[117] Interpretive Guidance, pp. 1043–1044 and see Schmitt 2010b, p. 42.

[118] Ibid., p. 1043.

12 Direct Participation in Hostilities 293

"clearly establishes a least harmful means requirement" similar to that discussed in the Interpretive Guidance, although he is concerned that non-State actors would not be "subject to the same restraints" as States.[119] It is submitted that this is a valid concern, but that an additional problem is that States are a party to different human rights laws and whilst the same is the case for IHL, the latter body of law is open to all, whereas some of the instruments in the former are regional treaties. Nevertheless, it seems that the application of current human rights law was not the basis of Part IX the Interpretive Guidance,[120] which makes this part of the Guidance most perplexing.

12.4.9 Consequences of Regaining Civilian Protection

This part of the Interpretive Guidance is not controversial, although it confirms that the DPH of civilians is not prohibited by IHL or by international criminal law and confirms that civilians taking a DPH must comply with IHL or risk being held responsible for war crimes.[121] The Interpretive Guidance ends by asserting that as civilians taking a DPH do not have a combatant's privilege to engage in conflict, "they are not exempted from prosecution under national criminal law for acts committed during their direct participation or membership".[122] This position does makes one wonder why such people would comply with the law of armed conflict, which this part of the Interpretive Guidance affirms that they must do, if they have nothing to gain from so doing in terms of their status.

12.4.10 Conclusion to the Interpretive Guidance

The Interpretive Guidance has created the concept of 'continuous combat function' and discussed the 'revolving door of civilian protection'. These concepts are contentious, ambiguous in application to practical complexities and have been described as "difficult to justify" conceptually.[123] Another problem is that when the Interpretive Guidance discusses NIACs they do not define what level of NIAC they mean and their concept of continuous combat function could operate at a low level of conflict of a Common Article 3 nature.[124] In short, the Interpretive Guidance solves few, if any, of the problems afflicting the concept of civilians taking DPH as guidance for soldiers on the ground, while generating further complexities of its own.

---

[119] Kleffner 2012, pp. 47 and 50.

[120] Interpretive Guidance, p. 1044, footnote 222.

[121] Ibid., pp. 1045–1046.

[122] Ibid., p. 1047.

[123] Watkin 2010, p. 693.

[124] See Hampson 2011, pp. 201 and 205, who is concerned that Human Rights bodies would not accept "the application of a status test in low-intensity conflicts".

A practical example of the problems in applying DPH in a conflict is illustrated by the case of *Ntaganda*, heard before the ICC *after* the Interpretive Guidance was issued.[125]

12.5 The Application of DPH by the ICC in *Ntaganda* in 2019

This case arose from the conduct of Bosco Ntaganda in Ituri in the Democratic Republic of the Congo. He was in charge of some Hema ethnic fighters and they were attacking, in particular, the Lendu ethnic group in a NIAC.[126] When considering this case, it must be remembered that Article 66 of the Rome Statute of the ICC requires that the accused be presumed innocent and that the onus is on the prosecution to demonstrate the guilt of the accused beyond reasonable doubt.[127] This room for reasonable doubt explains—why—despite being in control of men who committed serious sexual atrocities,[128] Ntaganda was able to use the excuse that some individuals targeted could have been taking an active part in hostilities to avoid those parts of the charges. The Trial Chamber reinforced the reasonable doubt by holding that fighting members of the Lendu ethnic group were not uniformly dressed and included some women and children.[129] In the case of one attack on civilians in Sayo village, the fact that no weapons were found on the bodies after the attack was still not taken to mean that the Trial Chamber had any evidence as to "whether these persons may have been armed *at the time* when they were killed" and so it could not exclude the reasonable possibility that the dead civilians may have been taking a DPH when killed.[130] As a result Ntaganda was found not guilty on that part of the charge.[131]

In some cases, alleged Lendu fighters were captured before being killed and the Trial Chamber rightly held that, whether or not they had been fighters, they were *hors de combat* at the time at which they were killed.[132] It is clearly a war crime to kill combatants or civilians taking a DPH after capture.[133] In another instance, a civilian man not believed to be taking a DPH was nevertheless killed, simply because, he was singing an anti-Hema song as he fetched water.[134] Neither the *Targeted Killings*

---

[125] *Prosecutor v Ntaganda*, ICC Trial Chamber Judgment, 8 July 2019, No.ICC-0104-02/05.

[126] Ibid., paras 701 and 730.

[127] This was held to apply to every element charged, ibid., para 44.

[128] *Prosecutor v Ntaganda*, n.125 *supra*, paras 805–808.

[129] Ibid., para 885.

[130] Ibid., para 886, original italics.

[131] Ibid., para 886.

[132] Ibid., paras 890–892.

[133] See Common Article 3(1) and (1)(a) in addition to *Prosecutor v Tadić*, Decision on the Defence Motion for Interlocutory Appeal on Jurisdiction, 2 October 1995, No.IT-94-1, paras 119 and 126.

[134] *Prosecutor v Ntaganda*, n. 125 *supra*, para 895.

12 Direct Participation in Hostilities

case, nor the Interpretive Guidance consider that support for a party to the conflict alone, amounts to the DPH of a civilian.[135]

It is most concerning that the Trial Judgment held that women who were singing, shouting and hitting pots and pans, before being fired upon by Ntaganda's men in order to make them disperse, might have been taking a DPH.[136] This was in the context of an attack on Kobu, where Lendu fighters, armed with rifles, attacked the camp of Ntaganda's men, whilst the women, who were further away, carried out their demonstration.[137] The Interpretive Guidance considers that civilians who are protesting and, merely expressing dissatisfaction with one party, are not taking a DPH.[138] Nevertheless, the Trial Chamber stated that the Prosecution had not proven that the civilians were not taking a DPH,[139] giving credence to the argument that they were trying to distract the soldiers from an attack by the Lendu fighters, which was taking place at the same time as the women were making a loud noise.[140] However, the only exception given by the Interpretive Guidance for civilians taking a DPH, in the context of an attack, is when they "voluntarily and deliberately position themselves to create a physical obstacle to fighting personnel".[141] The women were not accused of doing this.[142] It is submitted—in response to this—that it is a serious concern when women who are only making a noise are considered to be taking a DPH. Whether under the expanded version of DPH in the *Targeted Killings Case* or the more restrictive Interpretive Guidance, it is hard to imagine that either the Court or the ICRC would have found that these women took a DPH.[143] Therefore, it is very disappointing that the Appeal Brief of the Officer of the Prosecutor in the case of *Ntaganda* did not challenge this interpretation of DPH.[144] Although it is for the Prosecutor to prove each point of each crime beyond reasonable doubt, it is surprising that the Trial Chamber was of the opinion that a reasonable doubt had been raised in this situation by the women.

The central problem demonstrated by this case is that DPH, due to its interpretive ambiguity and lack of clear guidance, is sometimes used as an *ex post facto* excuse, rather than as a guide to future behaviour. This underlines the lack of a clear, practical version of DPH to guide professional soldiers on the ground in an armed conflict.

---

[135] *Targeted Killings* Case, para 35 and the Interpretive Guidance, p. 1006.

[136] *Prosecutor v Ntaganda*, n. 125 *supra*, para 910.

[137] Ibid., para 925.

[138] Interpretive Guidance, p. 129.

[139] *Prosecutor v Ntaganda*, n. 125 *supra*, para 925.

[140] Ibid., para 925.

[141] Interpretive Guidance, p. 1024.

[142] *Prosecutor v Ntaganda*, n. 125 *supra*, para 925.

[143] See Sect. 12.3.1 and Sects. 12.4.2, 12.4.3, 12.4.4, 12.4.5, 12.4.6, 12.4.7 and 12.4.8 above.

[144] Prosecution Appeal Brief, in the case of *Prosecutor v Ntaganda*, 7 October 2019, No.ICC-01/04-02/06.

12.6 Conclusion

This analysis of DPH demonstrates just how important the concept is.[145] From early human rights and national cases to a 56-page document created by the ICRC as its Interpretive Guidance and then to a more recent case before the ICC, it has never been more important for professional military soldiers to understand the concept.

This importance is why it is so problematic that the guidance in treaty law is insufficient to guide soldiers on how they should behave in any armed conflict and why it is so worrying that the ICRC Interpretive Guidance is not practical enough for soldiers to apply on the battlefield. In situations where soldiers can be advised, it will be in the interests of States to pressurise any military lawyers guiding their military in a NIAC to say that civilians are taking a continuous combat role (invented by ICRC Interpretive Guidance[146]) so that soldiers can target such civilians at all times, even when asleep in their village, rather than only reactively to their taking a DPH. This is a deeply unsatisfactory situation. It will also be in States' interests to find that civilians repeatedly taking a DPH, in what has been called the 'revolving door' of civilian protection,[147] are actually taking a continuous combat role, whether they are or not; and it will be in States' interests to maintain that they do not accept this concept,[148] so such civilians can also be targeted at all times, instead of recovering civilian immunity between each time they take a DPH.

Many States use military lawyers to advise on targeting,[149] and this advice should include the proper consideration of targeting those civilians taking a DPH However, the first question is whether such lawyers could confidently and accurately interpret the scant treaty law on DPH and secondly, whether they would consider non-binding ICRC commentaries or Interpretative Guidance as representing customary international law.[150] Thirdly, there is the question of whether or not such advisors would have the necessary quality of military or other intelligence to confirm that a civilian was in fact taking a DPH. These problems should be mitigated for soldiers on the ground by the construction of ambiguous or vague laws into specific and practically applicable rules of engagement.[151] Nevertheless, the military lawyers would not be able to give sufficiently fast guidance to soldiers on the ground, who are suddenly confronted with an unclear situation as to DPH such as that of civilians blocking their way as they attack enemy fighters.[152] Soldiers in the field need a default rule so

---

[145] Schmitt 2010a, p. 700.

[146] See Interpretive Guidance, p. 1007.

[147] See Ibid., pp. 1035–1036.

[148] Department of Defense Law of War Manual 2015, 5.8.4.2, pp. 235–236.

[149] See Henckaerts and Doswald-Beck 2005, Rule 141.

[150] UK Ministry of Defence 2004, 5.33 at p. 54 deals with DPH in one short paragraph. The US Department of Defense Law of War Manual 2015 covers DPH in over 10 pages, 226–236 with dense footnotes, and is too detailed to be practical. Both are authoritative guidance for all services.

[151] Haque 2019, p. 127. Note that rules of engagement are always classified so it is not possible to compare between them here.

[152] See Haque 2019, pp. 127–128.

12 Direct Participation in Hostilities

that they do not end up in court accused of attacking civilians who were not taking a DPH,[153] but in reality, this does not currently work well as the Kunduz case shows.[154]

For the future, there is clearly an important need to deal with the issue of the status and treatment of civilians if they are caught when taking a DPH. Indeed, as has been noted, a controversial part of the ICRC guidance, states that civilians taking a DPH should be captured rather than killed, if possible.[155] The inclusion of this section makes it all the more incomprehensible that the Interpretive Guidance does not deal with the treatment of detained civilians taking a DPH at all. It seems accepted that such individuals are most likely to be prosecuted domestically,[156] but a few scant lines from the *Targeted Killings Case*, suggest that Article 75 of API would be relevant to civilians taking a DPH.[157]

The fundamental principles of humane treatment and fair trials for civilians taking a DPH are merely skeletal in IHL. Therefore, it is necessary that civilians who are captured following taking a DPH are protected as much as possible by human rights law in addition to IHL.[158] Human rights bodies can only deal with States and so, despite the argument that human rights standards are applicable to non-State actors,[159] only States could be addressed by human rights bodies.[160] If two non-State actors are fighting in a NIAC, human rights law is not useful; so human rights law has limitations in protecting civilians taking a DPH which IHL does not have.[161]

An important question is whether the various human rights law treaties will apply in both IACs and NIACs.[162] It is uncontentious that human rights treaties will apply to military prisons in their own jurisdiction,[163] but the question is whether such treaties will apply to civilians who are held in a State's military prisons in another jurisdiction.[164] Caselaw and decisions suggests that the International Covenant for Civil and Political Rights (ICCPR), the Inter-American Convention on Human Rights (IACHR) and the European Convention on Human Rights (ECHR) will apply, *inter*

---

[153] See Sect. 12.5 above.

[154] See Haque 2019, p. 128 on erring on the legally safe side and Sect. 12.4.2 above.

[155] Interpretive Guidance, pp. 1040–1044.

[156] See, for example, the *Targeted Killings Case*, para 40 and Department of Defense Law of War Manual 2015 5.8.5, p. 236.

[157] *Targeted Killings Case*, para 25; generally considered customary international law in this case and by the US, see Milanovic 2011. On the equivalent in a NIAC, Articles 4 and 6 as customary international law, see Henckaerts and Doswald-Beck 2005, rule 87and rule 100.

[158] See Sassòli 2019, 10.14.41-10.305, pp. 617–623, mainly considering detention under human rights law.

[159] See generally Clapham 2006.

[160] See Kleffner 2012, pp. 47 and 50 and Sect. 12.4.9 above.

[161] See Byron 2007, pp. 883–884.

[162] See Byron 2007, p. 848.

[163] See Article 2, ICPPR, 999 UNTS 171; Article 1 ECHR, 213 UNTS 221, Article 1 ACHR, 144 UNTS 123 and note that the African Charter on Human and People's Rights (ACHPR) 1520 UNTS 217, assumes in Article 1 that each state will take legislative measures to give effect to the rights and duties.

[164] Either as an 'exported' NIAC or in an IAC.

alia, to civilians who have taken a DPH held in military prisons in countries other than their own.[165] Whilst some of the fair trial rights may be derogated from in an emergency, the prohibitions against ill treatment cannot be derogated from.[166] Further research on the protection under human rights law of civilians taking a DPH is needed.

Further research is also needed for civilians taking a DPH in the future of warfare. More complex tasks, including controlling drones and carrying out cyber warfare are increasingly carried out by civilians. The issue of autonomous weapons complicates matters. If autonomous weapons fire upon innocent civilians, are the designers of those weapons systems, if civilian, taking a DPH? Presumably, according to the Interpretive Guidance they would not be so doing if the weapons were designed with no specific conflict in mind.[167] Article 36 API reviews of new weapons is nowhere near a complete answer to this problem. It is in the future of warfare that the concept of civilians taking a DPH will need to be made relevant.

Finally, Crawford and Pert claim that *Prosecutor v Strugar* takes the most measured approach in requiring "acts of war which by their nature or purpose are intended to cause actual harm to the personnel or equipment of the enemy's armed forces".[168] It is submitted, however, that despite their argument that this reflects current state practice, this is too brief to guide soldiers on the ground.

References

Akande D (2010) Clearing the Fog of War? The ICRC's Interpretive Guidance on Direct Participation in Hostilities. International and Comparative Law Quarterly 59:180–192

Boothby B (2010) "And for Such Time as": The Time Dimension to Direct Part in Hostilities. NYU Journal of International Law and Policy 42:741–768

Byron (2007) A Blurring of the Boundaries: The Application of International Humanitarian Law by Human Rights Bodies. Virginia Journal of International Law 47:839–896

Chandrasekaran R (2009) Washington Post Foreign Service, NATO Orders Probe of Afghan Airstrike Alleged to Have Killed Many Civilians at https://www.washingtonpost.com/wp-dyn/content/article/2009/09/04/AR2009090400543.html?sid=ST2009090400002. Accessed 1 July 2020

Clapham A (2006) Human Rights Obligations of Non-State Actors. Oxford University Press, Oxford

Commentary on the First Geneva Convention (2016) Convention (I) for the Amelioration of the Condition of the Wounded and Sick in Armed Forces in the Field, ICRC and Cambridge University Press, Cambridge

Corn J, Jenks C (2011) Two Sides of the Combatant Coin: Untangling Direct Participation in Hostilities from Belligerent Status in Non-International Armed Conflicts. University of Pennsylvania Journal of International Law 33:313–362

---

[165] See Byron 2007, pp. 848–864 and the more recent cases before the European Court of Human Rights in respect of Iraq, for example, *Al-Jedda v UK*, Application No.27021/08, 7 July 2011, para 85.

[166] See Articles 4, 6, 7, 10 and 14 ICCPR; Articles 2, 3, 5, 6, 7 and 15 ECHR; Articles 4, 5, 7, 8, 9 and 27 ACHR and Articles 3, 4, 5, 6 and 7 ACHPR.

[167] See Interpretive Guidance, pp. 1021–1022 on direct and indirect causation.

[168] *Prosecutor v Strugar*, n. 5 *supra*, para 178 and see Crawford and Pert 2020, p. 123.

12 Direct Participation in Hostilities

Crawford E (2015) Identifying the Enemy: Civilian Participation in Armed Conflict. Oxford University Press, Oxford

Crawford E (2018) Who is a Civilian? Membership of Opposition Groups and Direct Participation in Hostilities. In: Lattimer M, Sands Ph (eds) The Grey Zone: Civilian Protection between Human Rights and the Laws of War. Hart Publishing, Oxford, 19–40

Crawford E, Pert A (2020) International Humanitarian Law, 2nd edn. Cambridge University Press, Cambridge

Department of Defense Law of War Manual (2015) (updated 2016) Office of General Council Department of Defense, Pentagon, Washington at https://dod.defense.gov/Portals/1/Documents/pubs/DoD%20Law%20of%20War%20Manual%20-%20June%202015%20Updated%20Dec%202016.pdf?ver=2016-12-13-172036-190. Accessed 6 July 2020

Dixon P (2009) 'Hearts and Minds'? British Counter-Insurgency from Malaya to Iraq. The Journal of Strategic Studies 32:353–381

Fenrick W (2009) ICRC Guidance on Direct Participation in Hostilities. Yearbook of International Humanitarian Law 12:287–300

Goodman R (2013) The Power to Kill or Capture Enemy Combatants. European Journal of International Law 24:819–853

Hampson F (2011) Direct Participation in Hostilities and the Interoperability of the Law of Armed Conflict and Human Rights Law. International Law Studies 87:187–213

Haque A (2019) Indeterminacy in the Law of Armed Conflict. International Law Studies 95:118–160

Hays Parks W (2010) Part IX of the ICRC "Direct Participation in Hostilities" Study: No Mandate, No Expertise, and Legally Incorrect. NYU Journal of International Law and Politics 42:769–830

Henckaerts J-M, Doswald-Beck L (2005) Customary International Humanitarian Law, Volume I: Rules. ICRC and Cambridge University Press, Cambridge

HPCR (Humanitarian Policy and Conflict Research) (2013) Manual on International Law Applicable to Air and Missile Warfare. Cambridge University Press, Cambridge

International Institute of Humanitarian Law (2006) The Manual on the Law of Non-International Armed Conflict with Commentaries at https://www.fd.unl.pt/docentes_docs/ma/jc_MA_26125.pdf. Accessed 29 June 2020

ICRC (2016) Commentary on the First Geneva Convention (2016) Convention (I) for the Amelioration of the Condition of the Wounded and Sick in Armed Forces in the Field, 2nd edn. Available at https://ihl-databases.icrc.org/ihl/full/GCI-commentary. Accessed 7 July 2020

ICRC Reports and Documents (2008) Interpretive Guidance on the Notion of Direct Participation under International Humanitarian Law. International Review of the Red Cross 90 (872): 991–1047

Kleffner J (2012) Section IX of the ICRC Interpretive Guidance on Direct Participation in Hostilities: The End of *Jus in Bello* Proportionality as we Know it? Israel Law Review 45:35–52

Kretzmer D (2009) Rethinking the Application of IHL in Non-International Armed Conflicts. Israel Law Review 42:8–45

Marchant E (2020) Insufficient Knowledge in Kunduz: The Precautionary Principle and International Humanitarian Law. Journal of Conflict and Security Law 25:53-79

Martin F (2001) Using International Human Rights Law for Establishing a Unified Use of Force Rule in the Law of Armed Conflict. Saskatchewan Law Review 64:347–396

McBride D (2012) Who is a Member? Targeted Killings against Organised Armed Groups. Australian Yearbook of International Law 30:47–91.

Melzer N (2010) Keeping the Balance Between Military Necessity and Humanity: A Response to Four Critiques of the ICRC's Interpretive Guidance on the Notion of Direct Participation in Hostilities. NYU Journal of International Law and Politics 42:831–916

Meron T (2000) The Martens Clause, Principles of Humanity, and Dictates of Public Conscience. American Journal of International Law 78:78–89

Milanovic M (2011) Article 75 and US Opinio Juris, EJIL:Talk! blog of the European Journal of International Law at https://www.ejiltalk.org/article-75-ap-i-and-us-opinio-juris/. Accessed 8 July 2020

Pictet J (ed) (1952) Commentary Geneva Convention I for the Amelioration of the Condition of the Wounded and Sick in Armed Forces in the Field. ICRC, Geneva

Pictet J (ed) (1960) Commentary Geneva Convention II for the Amelioration of the Condition of Wounded, Sick and Shipwrecked Members of Armed Forces at Sea. ICRC, Geneva

Pictet J (ed) (1960) Commentary Geneva Convention III Relative to the Treatment of Prisoners of War. ICRC, Geneva

Pictet J (ed) (1958) Commentary Geneva Convention IV Relative to the Protection of Civilian Persons in Time of War. ICRC, Geneva

Pictet J (1985) Development and Principles of International Law. Nijhoff, The Hague

Sandoz V, Swinarski C, Zimmerman B (eds) (1987) Commentary on the Additional Protocols of 8 June 1977 to the Geneva Conventions of 12 August 1949. Martinus Nijhoff Publishers, Geneva

Sassòli M (2019) International Humanitarian Law: Rules, Controversies and Solutions to Problems Arising in Warfare. Edward Elgar, Cheltenham

Sassòli M, Bouvier A, Quintin A, Grignon J (eds) (undated) How Does Law Protect in War? Cases, Documents and Teaching Materials on Contemporary Practice in International Humanitarian Law. ICRC, Geneva, available at https://casebook.icrc.org/law/non-international-armed-conflict. Accessed 8 January 2020

Schmitt M (2010a) Deconstructing the Direct Participation in Hostilities: The Constitutive Elements. NYU Journal of International Law and Policy 42:697–739

Schmitt M (2010b) The Interpretive Guidance on the Notion of Direct Participation in Hostilities: A Critical Analysis. Harvard National Security Journal 1:5–44

Solis G (2016) The Law of Armed Conflict: International Humanitarian Law in War, 2nd edn. Cambridge University Press, Cambridge

Statman D (2004) Targeted Killing. Theoretical Inquiries in Law 5:179–198

Tsagourias N, Morrison A (2018) International Humanitarian Law: Cases, Materials and Commentary. Cambridge University Press, Cambridge

The Commander's Handbook (2007) on the Law of Naval Operations. NWP 1-14M at https://www.jag.navy.mil/documents/NWP_1-14M_Commanders_Handbook.pdf. Accessed 30 August 2019

Turns D (2012) Cyber Warfare and the Notion of Direct Participation in Hostilities. Journal of Conflict & Security Law 17:279–297

UK Ministry of Defence (2004) The Manual of the Law of Armed Conflict. Oxford University Press, Oxford

Watkin K (2010) Opportunity Lost: Organized Armed Groups and the ICRC "Direct Participation in Hostilities" Interpretive Guidance. New York University Journal of International Law and Politics 42:641–695

Christine Byron received her Bachelor of Law (LLB) from Newcastle University in 1993, she then received her Master in Law (LLM) from the University of Liverpool in 1998 and her PhD on the International Criminal Court from the University of Liverpool in 2003. She currently works at Cardiff University. Her research interests are mainly in International Humanitarian Law, Genocide, War Crimes and the Extraterritorial Application of the ECHR. Between her Masters and PhD Christine completed a six-month internship with the ICTY and has also taught Military Lawyers on an International Course in Vienna for ten years.

Chapter 13
The Conduct of Hostilities

Jeroen C. van den Boogaard

Contents

13.1 Introduction 301
13.2 Targeting 302
13.3 Fundamental Rules of the Conduct of Hostilities 306
    13.3.1 Distinction 306
    13.3.2 Precautions 308
    13.3.3 Proportionality 310
13.4 Specific Prohibitions and Restrictions 312
13.5 Conclusion 313
References 314

Abstract This chapter assesses the rules of international humanitarian law (IHL) regulating the conduct of hostilities. To that end, a short description of the notion of targeting is provided, as well as an analysis of the interrelated IHL rules and principles of distinction, precautions in attack and proportionality.

Keywords Conduct of hostilities · targeting · distinction · precautions in attack · proportionality

13.1 Introduction

War is a messy affair. At its core lies the armed confrontation between human beings, killing and wounding each other on purpose. This is "the unique and defining characteristic of war that makes it different from any other human activity."[1] To regulate this activity is nothing new. The reason for adopting rules during the conduct of hostilities is captured in the text of the preamble to the 1868 St. Petersburg Declaration, which states that "the only legitimate object which States should endeavour to accomplish

---

[1] Smith 2005, p. 73.

J. C. van den Boogaard (✉)
Ministry of Foreign Affairs, The Hague, The Netherlands
e-mail: j.c.vandenboogaard@uva.nl

University of Amsterdam, Amsterdam, The Netherlands

© T.M.C. ASSER PRESS and the authors 2022
S. Sayapin et al. (eds.), *International Conflict and Security Law*,
https://doi.org/10.1007/978-94-6265-515-7_13

during war is to weaken the military forces of the enemy [and that] for that purpose it is sufficient to disable the greatest possible number of men"[2] This statement shows the inherent balance required between military necessity and humanitarian considerations embodied in the rules regulating the conduct of hostilities.[3] The rules of international humanitarian law (IHL) dealing with the treatment of those not, or no longer, participating in the hostilities were codified in regularly updated detailed rules. From the adoption of the first Geneva Convention of 1864 until Additional Protocol III in 2005, 'Geneva Law' regulates the protection of persons *hors de combat* in great detail during armed conflict, but mostly outside actual combat. Most current rules for the conduct of hostilities followed a different path. 'Hague law' consists of the rules with regard to the methods of warfare, or *how* the armed force may be used against the opponent, as well as the rules with regard to the means of warfare. These rules were codified in the 1899 and 1907 Hague Conventions, numerous weapons conventions, such as the Certain Conventional Weapons Convention of 1980 and its Protocols as well as the 1977 Additional Protocols to the Geneva Conventions. Particularly the 1977 Additional Protocol I (API) contains the most complete codification of the rules regulating the conduct of hostilities, including its core concepts such as the definition of military objectives, precautions in attack and the IHL rule on proportionality. API may be seen as a merge of the strands of Geneva Law and Hague law, containing rules that may be placed in both categories. The distinction between Hague law and Geneva law is not of particular practical importance, although in the interpretation of IHL rules it may be useful to be mindful of its origin.

This chapter first discusses the nature of targeting, followed by a short discussion of the fundamental principles and rules of the conduct of hostilities: the principles of distinction and precautions and the IHL proportionality rule. Next, some of the specific prohibitions relevant to the conduct of hostilities are discussed. The concluding remarks briefly comment on the adequacy of the IHL rules on the conduct of hostilities.

13.2 Targeting

The conduct of hostilities is a broader notion than only the launch of attacks towards the enemy. First, this is because also defensive operations are part of the definition of an attack under IHL.[4] Second, the term 'targeting' may be viewed as broader than only the use of kinetic armed force.[5] Nonetheless, this chapter views the conduct of

---

[2] St. Petersburg Declaration Renouncing the Use, in Time of War, of Explosive Projectiles Under 400 Grammes Weight, opened for signature 11 December 1968, 138 CTS 297 (entered into force 11 December 1868), para 3.

[3] Kalshoven 1984, p. 370.

[4] The term "attack" is defined in Article 49 (1) API as "violence against the adversary, whether in offence or in defence".

[5] For non-kinetic targeting, see Ducheine 2016, pp. 201–230.

13 The Conduct of Hostilities

hostilities as the activities of armed forces involving kinetic targeting. In that context, targeting may be defined as:

a broad process encompassing planning and execution, including the consideration of prospective targets of attack, the accumulation of information to determine whether the attack of a particular object, person, or group of persons will meet military, legal and other requirements, the determination of which weapon and method should be used to prosecute the target, the carrying out of attacks, including those decided upon at short notice and with minimal opportunity for planning, and other associated activities.[6]

The conduct of hostilities cannot be done without other types of military operations. Particularly, advancing troops attacking the enemy will at one point or another be stopped if their supply lines become too long, or when there is no possibility to bring new supplies such as food, munition and other necessities to the troops involved in the actual combat. Logistical military operations are thus required. Information is also crucial to any military operation, thus intelligence operations must be integrated in operations on different levels of command. Accordingly, effective communication to distribute and acquire information between units and their headquarters, as well as units from other services enables the effective coordinated execution of an operation. Military forces especially assigned to maintaining contact between different components are thus also required. If in the course of an offensive operation casualties occur on either side of the conflict, (military) medical personnel and equipment is required to take care of wounded, sick or shipwrecked persons. Furthermore, opposing military fighters as well as civilians who pose a threat to the advancing forces may be detained and must consequently be guarded, registered, transported to and held in appropriate locations, where they must receive medical aid and be fed, etcetera. Thus, detention operations are also part of any military operation that may be branded as conducting hostilities. Furthermore, kinetic attacks executed by ground operations may be supported not only by these land-based supporting operations, but also by operations from other dimensions. This includes air assets such as attack helicopters providing close air support; assets placed in outer space, such as communication satellites providing datalinks between units and their headquarters; cyber operations affecting or damaging the functionalities of the enemy's computer systems and operations at or from the sea, blocking the access into enemy ports and launching missiles towards targets on land.

The core concept of targeting is nonetheless launching attacks. Attacks may have different objectives. It may consist of advancing ground forces, aiming to gain control over (parts of) territory, or military action in defence against these advancing troops. It may also consist of the release of projectiles (bullets, bombs, missiles, grenades) aiming to destroy military objectives or put the opponent *hors de combat*, often, but not always, through the use of kinetic force. In short, the term 'attack' equals 'combat action': "[t]his should be taken into account in the instruction of armed forces who should clearly understand that the restrictions imposed by humanitarian law on the use of force should be observed both by troops defending themselves and by those

---

[6] Boothby 2012, p. 4.

who are engaged in an assault or taking the offensive."[7] Some controversy emerged during the drafting of the definition of attacks concerning the phrase 'against the adversary'.[8] The reason for this is that a literal interpretation of the definition of an attack would infer that it excludes using force against the civilian population, whereas that is manifestly prohibited. It must be understood that using armed force against civilians or civilian objects is nonetheless included in the definition of attacks for the purpose of the applicability of the principles and rules of IHL.[9]

Attacks may originate from land forces, air assets, warships on or under water, but may also be conducted through cyber means[10] or, at least theoretically, from space. As soon as targeting affects any objects or persons on land, the law is indifferent as to whether the origin of the attack was from land, air, sea, space or cyberspace.[11]

The law is identical for combat operations subjected to pre-planned procedures involving well-staffed military headquarters on different operational levels, and for attacks by a single soldier in the midst of a chaotic fire-fight. IHL rules on the conduct of hostilities are generally addressed to the 'military commander'. This military commander may be the on-scene commander of a small unit, or a high-ranking military commander at a headquarters far away from the location where the targeting is intended to generate effect.[12] Obviously, the responsibility to acquire and develop new means of warfare is usually not placed with lower level military commanders, because these decisions are usually reserved for strategic and political levels of armed forces. Nonetheless, when it comes to developing innovative methods of warfare, it may be that commanders on the ground develop these in the course of their mission to attain the objectives they were ordered to accomplish. In those circumstances, they need to take into account that certain use of means of warfare may be subject to specific prohibitions or restrictions. An example could be the prohibition to use of incendiary projectiles to attack a military objective within a concentration of civilians, even though these projectiles were designed to conceal troop movements from enemy observers by creating smoke-screens.[13]

The conduct of hostilities in the different domains obviously results in practical differences of how the operations are conducted and which rules are of particular importance. For example, the application of the IHL proportionality rule is less relevant in an autonomous weapons systems loitering in the deep seas, searching for enemy submarines, because there is simply no civilian presence in the deep sea.

---

[7] ICRC Commentary on API, see Sandoz et al. 1987, p. 603.

[8] ICRC Commentary on API, see Sandoz et al. 1987, pp. 602–603.

[9] See for example the discussion in Van Den Boogaard 2018, pp. 198–199.

[10] Rule 92 of the Tallinn Manual 2.0 defines a cyberattack as "a cyber operation, whether offensive or defensive, that is reasonably expected to cause injury or death to persons or damage or destruction to objects." Schmitt et al. 2017, p. 415.

[11] Article 49 (3) API: "The provisions of this Section apply to any land, air or sea warfare which may affect the civilian population, individual civilians or civilian objects on land. They further apply to all attacks from the sea or from the air against objectives on land but do not otherwise affect the rules of international law applicable in armed conflict at sea or in the air."

[12] Corn and Corn 2012, p. 344.

[13] Article 2 (2) Protocol III CCW.

13 The Conduct of Hostilities

Kinetic attacks in the domain of outer space on the other hand, even though the presence of civilians is virtually non-existent in outer space, may still raise fundamental issues of proportionality and precautions in attack. Indeed, the destruction of an enemy's military satellites may not cause direct collateral damage, but the resulting space debris may potentially cause long-lasting secondary effects as the debris would affect satellites used exclusively for civilian purposes, potentially crippling vital civilian uses such as GPS and communications.[14]

The way targeting is conducted as such does generally not differ during international armed conflicts or non-international armed conflicts. The common goal is to defeat the military capability of the enemy, usually through attacks involving kinetic means. The IHL rules on the conduct of hostilities applicable to these two types of armed conflict are mostly identical.[15] However, the type of actors involved does differ, because the IHL rules for international armed conflicts apply to armed conflicts between States or during the situation of occupation. By its nature, at least one of the parties to a non-international armed conflict is a non-state armed group (NSAG), which often possess a lower level of sophistication in terms of the available weapon systems and other military capabilities. Special IHL targeting rules for less sophisticated armed forces do however not exist.

The targeting process is well-defined by certain States.[16] For sophisticated armed forces, there are different types of targeting processes, namely deliberate and dynamic targeting.[17] The difference between these processes is the fact that in the case of deliberate targeting, the military objective was known in advance, leaving usually ample time to assess whether the target may be struck in accordance with IHL rules. The process for dynamic targeting is shorter and is used for targets popping up. This means that the dynamic targeting process is used where time simply does not permit using the more elaborate and thorough deliberate targeting process. Within the deliberate targeting process, sophisticated forces use varying assets and sensors to analyse the situation surrounding a possible target.[18] Headquarters may be able to co-ordinate land operations with air strikes and use standardized procedures to assist in maximizing the effect of the operation and in determining its possible impact on the civilian population.[19] NSAGs however need to rely on different and often more rudimentary sources of information in the planning of their attacks.

The targeting process thus involves a thinking exercise in which military commanders are dependent on many different factors and circumstances. These circumstances include for example weather conditions; the weapons systems available; ongoing

---

[14] For further details concerning the military use of outer space, see Chap. 19 by Kubo Mačák.

[15] See the customary rules with regard to targeting as identified in the ICRC Customary Law Study, rules 5-22. Henckaerts and Doswald-Beck 2005, pp. 17–71.

[16] See for example the US Joint Chiefs of Staff, Joint Publication 1-02 2010, which is available online: www.dtic.mil/doctrine/new_pubs/jp1_02.pdf.

[17] Pratzner 2016, p. 81. See also Jachec-Neale 2015, pp. 200–204.

[18] Pratzner 2016, p. 82.

[19] For a description of the specifics for targeting in the context of joint operations, see generally De Cock 2016, pp. 231–259.

operations of the adversary; the terrain on which the operations are being conducted and the available resources to collect and process information. In order to adhere to their legal obligations, military forces must take a number of steps in the planning of any attack, including taking into account the IHL rules and principles of distinction, precautions and proportionality.

13.3 Fundamental Rules of the Conduct of Hostilities

Even though attacks are a subset of the more general term of military operations, the most important rules for the conduct of hostilities are those which regulate attacks. It may be said that these rules all follow from three important and interconnected principles and rules. These are distinction, precautions in attack and proportionality. The order in which these notions are discussed in this section flows logically from IHL and the way it is incorporated into predefined targeting processes. Before an attack is launched, first, a target must be identified and selected in accordance with the rules concerning distinction. Once this is done, 'constant care' must be taken to protect the civilian population through precautionary measures. When these two requirements are satisfied, IHL requires the military commander to apply the IHL proportionality rule to prevent excessive collateral civilian damage in relation to the military gain sought from the planned attack.

13.3.1 Distinction

The principle of distinction is the most central rule of the entire legal framework of IHL.[20] The specific rules that operationalise this principle make sense from the perspective of the underlying objective of IHL to regulate the means and methods of warfare, because it dictates that only the military opponent should be the object of an attack. Distinction is similarly crucial in order to shield the civilian population from the effects of hostilities, which is congruent with the other underlying objective of protecting those who are not participating in hostilities. In spite of the centrality of the rule, it was not until 1977 that civilian immunity from direct attacks was codified in unequivocal terms in treaty law.[21] Article 48 of API articulates the essence of distinction, requiring parties to the conflict to "distinguish between the civilian population and combatants and between civilian objects and military objectives and

---

[20] As Dinstein notes: "there are several cardinal principles lying at the root of the law of international armed conflict. Upon examination, none is more critical than the "principle of distinction". Dinstein 2008, p. 1.

[21] See Kalshoven 1982, p. 858. Kalshoven mentions in this regard earlier (but failed) efforts of the government of the Netherlands to include distinction in revised Hague Conventions on Land Warfare.

13 The Conduct of Hostilities

accordingly direct their operations only against military objectives". This rule is generally accepted as a rule of customary international law.[22]

The principle of distinction assists those responsible for the planning and execution of military operations to distinguish between persons protected from direct attack and those who IHL allows to be legitimately killed. In addition to medical personnel and civilians, protected persons are those placed *hors de combat* on the basis of being wounded, sick or shipwrecked, provided they refrain from any act of hostility.[23] This protection is the core of the protections provided by the Geneva Conventions since their first codification in 1864. Although the rules with regard to the protection of the wounded, sick and shipwrecked were initially designed to protect soldiers, wounded civilians are similarly protected.[24] Secondly, those who are no longer participating in the conflict because they have been detained by the adversary are also protected. This includes the elaborate rules concerning the treatment of prisoners of war as included in the Third Geneva Convention and all other persons detained in relation to the armed conflict, including civilians. With regard to objects, there are different types of specifically protected objects, including civilian objects, objects indispensable for the survival of the civilian population, medical installations, the natural environment and cultural objects. These objects do not all enjoy an identical degree of protection, even when they are used for military purposes and in situations where these objects qualify as military objectives.[25] As an example: a warehouse qualifying as a military objective may be attacked provided the rules of precautions in attack and proportionality are observed. On the other hand, attacking a hospital is prohibited even in situations in which it qualifies as a military objective because it is being used, outside its humanitarian duties, for acts harmful to the enemy, unless "after a due warning has been given, naming in all appropriate cases, a reasonable time limit, and after such warning has remained unheeded".[26] The principle of distinction furthermore includes the prohibition to use means and methods of warfare that would qualify as an indiscriminate attack.[27]

---

[22] ICRC Customary International Humanitarian Law Study, Henckaerts and Doswald-Beck 2005, p. 3: Rule 1: "The parties to the conflict must at all times distinguish between civilians and combatants. Attacks may only be directed against combatants. Attacks must not be directed against civilians." See also p. 224, Rule 71: "The use of weapons which are by their nature indiscriminate is prohibited".

[23] See Article 12 GCI, Article 12 GCII and Article 8 (a) and (b) API for international armed conflicts, and common Article 3 GC and Article 7 APII for non-international armed conflicts.

[24] See for example Article 16 GCIV.

[25] Military objectives are defined in Article 52 (1) API and rule 8 of the ICRC Customary Law Study, as well as individuals that qualify as combatants (in an international armed conflict) or those persons that have lost their protection from direct attack (in all types of armed conflicts), for example because they are directly participating in hostilities.

[26] Article 21 GCI.

[27] Dinstein 2008, p. 3: "The principle of distinction excludes not only deliberate attacks against civilians, but also indiscriminate attacks, i.e., instances in which the attacker does not target any specific military objective (due either to indifference as to whether the ensuing casualties will be civilians or combatants or, alternatively, to inability to control the effects of the attack)."

13.3.2 Precautions

Taking precautions in the context of the conduct of hostilities to protect the civilian population is an obligation for both attacking forces and defending forces. For the first category of forces, the attackers, the general principle to take constant care for the protection of the civilian population is translated in a number of specific obligations, as well as a number of more general and indirect precautions.[28]

For defending forces, specific precautions include rules against the effects of attacks, as well as more general obligations that need to be taken into account already in times of peace.[29] Examples of this latter category are the need to dislocate military installations from populated areas, because usually it is not possible that military barracks, fortified positions and defensive lines are re-located last minute away from populated areas.

The rules of precautionary measures for attacks were codified in 1977, more specifically in Article 57(2) API. These rules are partly repeating rules included elsewhere in API, such as the obligation to verify whether a planned target is indeed a military objective. The rule, which is also identified as a rule of customary IHL,[30] states that those who plan or decide upon an attack shall "do everything feasible to verify that the objectives to be attacked are neither civilians nor civilian objects and are not subject to special protection but are military objectives within the meaning of para 2 of Article 52 and that it is not prohibited by the provisions of this Protocol to attack them". This precautionary measure is closely connected to the principle of distinction, noting not only the general protection of civilians, but also acknowledging the specific protection such as cultural objects and places of worship, medical installations and works and installations containing dangerous forces.

The second precautionary measure in attack mentioned in Article 57 API relates directly to the subject of this chapter: the conduct of hostilities, emphasizing the overall goal of precautions in attack, which is to safeguard the civilian population.[31] The rule deals with the choice of means and methods of warfare, prescribing all feasible precautions to be taken with a view to avoiding, and in any event minimising collateral damage. It underlines that the default objective must be to avoid affecting the civilian population when an attack on a military objective is planned. The ICRC Customary Law Study notes that "[t]his rule must be applied independently of the simultaneous application of the principle of proportionality".[32] This latter rule, as

---

[28] See generally Corn 2015, pp. 419–466 and Van Den Boogaard and Vermeer 2019, pp. 179–194.

[29] See generally Jensen 2016, pp. 147–175.

[30] ICRC Customary International Humanitarian Law Study, Henckaerts and Doswald-Beck 2005, Rule 16, pp. 55–58.

[31] See Article 57(2)(a)(ii) API and Rule 17 (ii), in Henckaerts and Doswald-Beck: "those who plan or decide upon shall—take all feasible precautions in the choice of means and methods of attack with a view to avoiding, and in any event to minimizing, incidental loss of civilian life, injury to civilians and damage to civilian objects".

[32] ICRC Customary International Humanitarian Law Study, Henckaerts and Doswald-Beck 2005, p. 57.

noted below, deals with the situation in which it is expected that, despite taking precautionary measures, residual collateral damage is nonetheless expected to result from the planned attack. In that situation, military commanders first need to assess whether it is feasible adapting their means and methods of attack in order to minimise the collateral damage. An example of the practical application of this rule may include adjusting the timing of the attack to a moment when no or fewer civilians may be expected to be present at the location of the planned attack. Another possibility is using a smaller explosive charge or delaying the moment of the explosion of the munition until after it has penetrated the military objective to reduce fragmentation to the area around the target.

The following precautionary measure relates to the continued relevance of the precautionary obligations to protect the civilian population in all stages of military operations. It articulates that it is insufficient to merely perform a preliminary assessment of the expected collateral damage in the planning phase of an attack. Subparagraph (2)(b) of Article 57 API accordingly states that an attack must be cancelled or suspended if it becomes apparent that the objective is not a military one, is subject to special protection, or the effects of the attack are expected to be disproportionate. This obligation applies both to 'those who plan or decide upon an attack', as well as to those operators who actually execute the attack. This includes situations in which updated information indicates that initial information or assumptions regarding civilian presence were misguided, reviving the obligation to conduct a renewed proportionality assessment.

The fourth precautionary measure in attack is the duty to issue an effective advance warning to the civilian population. This is an obligation that makes sense in situations where the element of surprise is not a major component of the attack. As a result, it is more likely to require an attacking party to warn in situations where the intended target of the attack is an object, rather than persons. This is recognised in the rule, requiring the civilians to be warned "unless circumstances do not permit." This rule is generally recognised as a customary norm in both international and non-international armed conflicts.[33]

The general objective of giving advance warning to the civilian population is to allow them "the chance to protect themselves"[34] from the dangers of upcoming attacks. Warnings thus allow civilians to leave the area of hostilities, preferably with a degree of specificity of how they may safely do so. That degree of specificity ultimately determines the effectiveness of the warning. I may be that using a megaphone suffices in a practical situation, but sometimes more general warnings are conveyed through radio broadcasts, the distribution of flyers or sending out mass-text messages to mobile phones in a certain area. Attacking forces need to take this obligation into account in the planning phases of military operations, most pressingly in densely populated areas. Nonetheless, many factors may influence the ultimate safest course of action for the civilian population. Where the most intense fighting will take place

---

[33] ICRC Customary International Humanitarian Law Study, Henckaerts and Doswald-Beck 2005, Rule 20, pp. 62–65.

[34] ICRC Commentary on API, see Sandoz et al. 1987, p. 687.

is often unpredictable, since it is largely contingent on the conduct of the enemy. Creating different scenarios for warning the civilian population must therefore be contemplated in advance of an attack and included in the planning process as well as during the execution of the attack.

There is a close connection between the obligation to warn the civilian population and the IHL proportionality rule. Firstly, warning the civilian enables military commanders to implement their obligations regarding distinction and proportionality and thus assists in protecting the civilian population. An additional relationship becomes apparent when one takes into account that when civilians have evacuated an area, they no longer factor into the proportionality assessment for subsequent attacks. An effective warning may consequently place a planned attack within the confines of the law, while it would have been expected to cause excessive collateral damage in relation to the anticipated military advantage if it was not for the warning. The obligation to warn the civilian population may therefore be regarded as a "useful tool in the hands of commanders for gaining more freedom of action".[35]

The last precaution in attack mentioned specifically in Article 57 API deals with the choice between attacking targets which are expected to render similar military advantage. The rule dictates that "the objective to be selected shall be that the attack on which may be expected to cause the least danger to civilian lives and to civilian objects." It is however questionable whether there are many scenarios in which military objectives would offer a similar degree of military advantage. Nonetheless, this obligation's value is in the incentive for military commanders in situations where it is expected that collateral civilian damage will occur, to actively seek for alternatives when different targets are available that would yield a similar effect.

13.3.3 Proportionality

The IHL rule of proportionality is probably one of the most complex obligations of military commanders during the conduct of hostilities. It requires members of military forces firstly to assess the expected direct military gain of a planned attack. Subsequently, it needs to be assessed whether the planned attack may be expected to cause incidental damage to civilian objects and whether it may be expected that civilians will be harmed by the effects of the planned attack.[36] Finally, assuming the obligations in terms of precautions to minimise any incidental effects of the attack have been met, the IHL proportionality rule requires those who plan or decide on attacks to ensure that the expected incidental damage is not excessive in relation to the expected direct military advantage. This assessment is the last factor military

---

[35] Baruch and Neuman 2011, p. 373.

[36] See Articles 51 (5) (b) and 57(2) (a) (iii) and (b) of API, prohibiting "an attack which may be expected to cause incidental loss of civilian life, injury to civilians, damage to civilian objects, or a combination thereof, which would be excessive in relation to the concrete and direct military advantage anticipated".

13 The Conduct of Hostilities

commander is required to consider before launching an attack, and it must continue to be observed also during the execution phase. The IHL proportionality rule is generally recognised as a rule of customary international humanitarian law that applies in international armed conflicts as well as during non-international armed conflicts.[37]

The complexity of the IHL proportionality rule lies in the fact that even after assessing the different sides of the IHL proportionality rule, the comparison between the expected military advantage of a planned attack and the incidental effects expected from it (often called 'collateral damage') is not straightforward. Comparing these factors is different for each individual attack or series of attacks that may be assessed as a whole. This is further complicated by the extent to which the anticipated effects of the attack may be expected to turn out as calculated. An example could be that the use of a certain type of munitions may only have a fifty percent chance of attaining the intended result. Thus, the likelihood of the success of the attack in accomplishing the intended military advantage and causing collateral effects as expected is often not straightforward. This uncertainty must be factored into the proportionality assessment. Thus, while it may be clear that the intended end-result of the attack (for example, the destruction of a bridge) produces a concrete and direct military advantage, it may be uncertain how the limited likelihood the attack will be successful can be taken into account.

The IHL proportionality rule is designed to provide protection to the civilian population. It applies to all different levels of command.[38] The principle needs therefore to be applied on strategic and operational levels, where large operations are planned. This may make the obligation quite theoretical, because the outcome of the proportionality calculation regarding a large scale operation is highly dependent on the circumstances ruling at the time.[39] These circumstances may however be difficult to predict, because there are many variables that may influence the circumstances as they are expected to materialise at the exact moment the attack is planned to be launched. But it applies also on the practical level of a single unit in combat with an enemy unit. Thus, in situations where on-scene commanders, or even individual soldiers, may foresee civilian presence, or identify civilian objects which may be affected by their planned attack, they are required to make a proportionality assessment prior to firing their weapon systems.

It is important to reiterate that the application of the IHL proportionality rule is always an obligation to conduct an *ex ante*-assessment. It may be that after the practically possible has been done to acquire the relevant information to be able to conduct the proportionality assessment, crucial information is unavailable to the commander. If it turns out after the attack that is resulted in considerable collateral damage and the attack would never have been approved if that information would have been available, this often does not constitute a violation of the IHL proportionality rule. An example could be the presence of previously unknown large quantity of

---

[37] ICRC Customary International Humanitarian Law Study, Henckaerts and Doswald-Beck 2005, Rule 14, pp. 46–50.

[38] Van Den Boogaard 2015, pp. 275–277.

[39] For an assessment of the phrase 'circumstances ruling at the time', see Bill 2010, pp. 119–155.

explosive materials, causing secondary explosions that grossly exceed the munitions used in the attack causing massive collateral damage. Even though such levels of collateral damage may warrant a closer look at the available information and the precautionary measures taken in advance of it, no automatic violation of the IHL proportionality may be inferred based on the results of an attack.

13.4 Specific Prohibitions and Restrictions

The premise that the choice in the means and methods of warfare is not unlimited lies at the basis of a number of specific restrictions and prohibitions that need to be observed during the conduct of hostilities. These prohibitions and restrictions relate to both weapons (means) and methods of warfare. Some of these prohibitions and restrictions are old and developed from custom into treaty rules, such as the prohibition to use poison.[40] Other restrictions are relatively new and were emboldened by the involvement of civil society lobbying for bans on certain weapons, such as the 1997 Ottawa Convention banning antipersonnel landmines,[41] whose adoption was encouraged by the work of the International Campaign to Ban Landmines.[42]

The treaties of IHL contain rules prohibiting or restricting the use of certain types of weapons during the conduct of hostilities. Some of these obligations also attained customary status, such as the prohibition to use chemical weapons.[43] Other rules only apply to those States that ratified the treaties regulating the use of these weapons, such as anti-personnel landmines in the Ottawa Convention and cluster munitions as defined in the Convention on Cluster Munitions.[44] Furthermore, certain methods of warfare are specifically prohibited. Certain new technologies, such as the use of artificial intelligence, autonomous weapons systems, cyber operations and operations in the outer space domain, have not (yet) been subject to specific prohibitions and restrictions in treaties. Instead, their use is regulated through the basic principles and rules governing the conduct of hostilities.

With regard to methods of warfare, the principles and rules discussed above are further implemented by a number of 'rules of application'.[45] One of these specific restrictions and prohibitions in the context of the conduct of hostilities is the prohibition of terror bombing. This prohibition is a based on the principle of distinction

---

[40] Article 23 (a) Convention (IV) respecting the Laws and Customs of War on Land and its annex: Regulations concerning the Laws and Customs of War on Land, opened for signature 18 October 1907 (entered into force 26 January 2010).

[41] Convention on the Prohibition of the Use, Stockpiling, Production and Transfer of Anti-Personnel Mines and on their Destruction, opened for signature 18 September 1997, 2056 UNTS 211 (entered into force 1 March 1999) (Ottawa Convention).

[42] See generally http://www.icbl.org/en-gb/home.aspx.

[43] See Chap. 14, also authored by myself, concerning chemical weapons.

[44] Article 2 (2) Convention on Cluster Munitions, opened for signature 30 May 2008, 2688 UNTS 39 (entered into force 1 August 2010).

[45] ICRC Commentary on API, see Sandoz et al. 1987, p. 615, para 1923.

and prohibits "[a]cts or threats of violence the primary purpose of which is to spread terror among the civilian population".[46] As the ICRC Commentary clarifies, this rule is intended to cover acts of violence that offer no meaningful military advantage but are intended to terrorise the civilian population, including threats of acts to that effect. Other implementing rules include the prohibition of 'carpet-bombing';[47] the use of human shields[48] and the prohibition to use starvation of civilians as a method of warfare.[49] In addition, different rules about reprisals and protection of different objects such as hospitals, cultural property, and the natural environment further restrict the options for military forces conducting hostilities.

With joint and combined operations of sophisticated armed forces being able to act on the basis of real-time footage provided by different types of drones and other information sources, and the use of precision guided munitions, the conduct of hostilities may often be expected to be more precise. Even though from this development one may expect that the destruction resulting from contemporary warfare to become more limited, battlefields around the world tell a different tale. It seems that with the widening of the options, the reaction of opponents is to move operations into urban environments and to hide between the civilian population, including a return of underground warfare,[50] resulting in fierce house-to-house battles and extensive use of indirect fires. The devastating effects of this type of warfare are long-lasting and therefore require careful precautionary measures.[51]

13.5 Conclusion

Distinction, precautions and proportionality are three important and interconnected principles and rules of IHL governing the conduct of hostilities. It is only possible to meaningfully make a distinction between military objectives on the one hand and protected persons and objects on the other hand when feasible precautions to that effect have been taken and it has been determined, on the basis of a proportionality analysis, that the planned attack does not violate the prohibition to conduct indiscriminate attacks. Furthermore, both proportionality and distinction are listed as precautions in attack. This shows that the rules do not function in isolation, but constitute a system of interconnected obligations. To complicate matters, the notion of distinction is obscured by the fact that the application of the IHL proportionality rule is an example of an indiscriminate attack as prohibited by Article 51 (4)(c) API. (The quoted provision talks about indiscriminate attacks and not the proportionality

---

[46] Article 51 (2) API.

[47] Article 51 (5) (a) API.

[48] Article 51 (7) API.

[49] Article 54 (1) API.

[50] See for example Richemond-Barak 2018.

[51] See for example Robinson and Nohle 2016.

rule which is contained in Article 51(5)(b). This is contradictory, because a dispro-portionate attack is by definition aimed at a military objective, and thus it would necessarily already comply with the IHL rule of distinction. If this would not be the case, the attack would be illegal on the basis of the rules on distinction, thus an assessment whether the attack would comply with the IHL proportionality rule would be redundant. The wording of the interconnected rules concerning the conduct of hostilities is thus at some points confusing.

Nonetheless, the rules regulating the conduct of hostilities as captured in API and customary rules show that these are based on a limited number of fundamental prin-ciples. New means, methods and dimensions of warfare, including outer space and cyber space, are not likely to change these principles. They may however pose new challenges for the implementing these fundamental principles and require interpre-tation of existing rules in these contexts in accordance with the object and purpose of these principles.[52]

As long as there is war, escalation of the use of armed force during the conduct of hostilities could make it impossible to achieve a lasting peace after armed conflict. Even though there are regular reports of violations of the IHL principles and rules regulating the conduct of hostilities, these norms play their role in preventing this escalation. The actual application and interpretation of the rules and principles in the heat of the battle, may sometimes result in disregard of the rules, but that does not mean that the balance between military necessity and humanitarian consider-ations in these norms is inadequate. Support for IHL obligations is expressed by States, international organisations, non-governmental organisations, academics and the general public on different platforms, including social media. Whether the IHL rules concerning the conduct of hostilities will stand the test of future war where new technologies are used, is dependent on the practice of States. The adequacy of the rules, it is submitted, is contingent on their implementation, which may be improved through dissemination of knowledge of the law; thorough training and responsible leadership. Both military commanders and political leaders must be aware of the need to take their responsibility in this regard.

References

Books, (Online) Articles and Chapters in Books

Baruch PS, Neuman N (2011) Warning civilians prior to attack under international law: theory and practice. In: Pedrozo RA, Wollschlaeger DP (eds) International Law and the Changing Character of War. Naval War College International Law Studies 87:359–412.
Bill BJ (2010) The Rendulic 'Rule': military necessity, commander's knowledge, and methods of warfare. Yearbook of International Humanitarian Law 12:119–155
Boothby WH (2012) The law of targeting. Oxford University Press, Oxford

---

[52] See for example Stephens 2018.

13 The Conduct of Hostilities

Corn GS (2015) War, law, and the oft overlooked value of process as a precautionary measure. Pepperdine Law Review 42:419–466.

Corn GS, Corn GP (2012) The law of operational targeting: viewing the LOAC through an operational lens. Texas International Law Journal, 47:337–380

De Cock C (2016) Targeting in coalition operations. In: Ducheine PAL, Schmitt MN, Osinga FPB (eds) Targeting: the challenges of modern warfare. T.M.C. Asser Press, The Hague, pp 231–259

Dinstein Y (2008) Distinction and loss of civilian protection in international armed conflicts. Israel Yearbook on Human Rights 38:1–16

Ducheine PAL (2016) Non-kinetic capabilities: complementing the kinetic prevalence to targeting. In: Ducheine PAL, Schmitt MN, Osinga FPB (eds) Targeting: the challenges of modern warfare. T.M.C. Asser Press, The Hague, pp 201–230

Henckaerts J-M, Doswald-Beck L (2005) Customary international humanitarian law, volume I: Rules; Vol II: Practice. Cambridge University Press, Cambridge

Jachec-Neale A (2015) The concept of military objectives in international law and targeting practice. Routledge

Jensen ET (2016) Precautions against the effects of attacks in urban areas. International Review of the Red Cross 98:147–175.

Kalshoven F (1982) Civilian immunity and the principle of distinction: introduction. American University Law Review, 31:855–859

Kalshoven F (1984) The soldier and his golf clubs. In: Swinarski C (ed) Studies and essays on international humanitarian law and Red Cross principles. Martinus Nijhoff, pp 369–385

Pratzner PR (2016) The Current Targeting Process. In: Ducheine PAL, Schmitt MN, Osinga FPB (eds) Targeting: The Challenges of Modern Warfare. T.M.C. Asser Press, The Hague, pp 77–97

Richemond-Barak D (2018) Underground warfare. Oxford University Press, Oxford

Robinson I, Nohle E (2016) Proportionality and precautions in attack: the reverberating effects of using explosive weapons in populated areas. International Review of the Red Cross, 98 (1):107–145

Sandoz Y, Swinarski C, Zimmermann B (eds) (1987) Commentary on the additional protocols of 8 June 1977 to the Geneva Conventions of 12 August 1949. Martinus Nijhoff Publishers/International Committee of the Red Cross, Geneva

Schmitt MN et al. (eds) (2017) Tallinn Manual 2.0 on the international law applicable to cyber operations. Cambridge University Press, Cambridge

Smith H (2005) On Clausewitz, a study of military and political ideas. Palgrave Macmillan

Stephens D (2018) The international legal implications of military space operations: examining the interplay between international humanitarian law and the outer space legal regime. International Law Studies 94:75–101

Van den Boogaard JC (2015) Proportionality and Autonomous Weapons Systems. Journal of International Humanitarian Legal Studies 6:247–283

Van den Boogaard JC (2018) Knock on the roof: legitimate warning or method of warfare? Yearbook of International Humanitarian Law 19:183–209

Van den Boogaard JC, Vermeer A (2019) Precautions in attack and urban and siege warfare. Yearbook of International Humanitarian Law 20:163–198

Other Documents

Convention (IV) respecting the Laws and Customs of War on Land and its annex: Regulations concerning the Laws and Customs of War on Land, opened for signature 18 October 1907 (entered into force 26 January 2010)

Convention on Cluster Munitions, opened for signature 30 May 2008, 2688 UNTS 39 (entered into force 1 August 2010)

Convention on the Prohibition of the Use, Stockpiling, Production and Transfer of Anti-Personnel Mines and on their Destruction, opened for signature 18 September 1997, 2056 UNTS 211 (entered into force 1 March 1999) (Ottawa Convention)

Protocol Additional to the Geneva Conventions of 12 August 1949, and relating to the Protection of Victims of International Armed Conflicts (Additional Protocol I, API), opened for signature 12 December 1977, 1125 UNTS 3 (entered into force 7 December 1979)

Protocol on Prohibitions or Restrictions on the Use of Incendiary Weapons to the Convention on Prohibitions or Restrictions on the Use of Certain Conventional Weapons Which may be Deemed to be Excessively Injurious or To Have Indiscriminate Effects (Protocol III CCW), opened for signature 10 October 1980, 1342 UNTS 137 (entered into force 2 December 1983)

St. Petersburg Declaration Renouncing the Use, in Time of War, of Explosive Projectiles Under 400 Grammes Weight, opened for signature 11 December 1968, 138 CTS 297 (entered into force 11 December 1868)

Jeroen C. van den Boogaard is a senior legal counsel in international law at the Legal Department of the Ministry of Foreign Affairs of the Kingdom of the Netherlands. He is also lecturer and researcher at the University of Amsterdam. Former positions include that of assistant professor in military law at the Netherlands Defence Academy; Head of the International Humanitarian Law department of the Netherlands Red Cross and that of military lawyer in the Royal Netherlands Army. His main research interest is military law, particularly international humanitarian law.

All the usual caveats apply.

Chapter 14
Chemical Weapons

Jeroen C. van den Boogaard

Contents

14.1 Introduction 317
14.2 A Short Historic Overview of the Use of Chemical Weapons 319
14.3 Law Regulating the Use of Chemical Weapons 321
    14.3.1 IHL Principles Regulating the Use of Chemical Weapons 321
    14.3.2 Arms Control Law Regulating Chemical Weapons 328
14.4 Biological Weapons 331
14.5 Conclusion 333
References 334

Abstract There is wide agreement that using chemical weapons in warfare is abhorrent and must be prohibited. Chemical weapons have nonetheless, even recently, been used. This chapter argues that chemical weapons are prohibited on the basis of both the international humanitarian law (IHL) principles pertaining to means of warfare as well as arm control law. This is evidenced in the almost universally ratified Chemical Weapons Convention of 1993 (CWC 1993) and a corresponding rule of customary international law. Biological weapons are similarly prohibited, primarily as a result of their inherent indiscriminate character.

Keywords Chemical Weapons Convention · Chlorine · OPCW · Gas Protocol · Biological weapons

14.1 Introduction

International outrage is guaranteed whenever there is proof, or even allegations, of the use of chemical weapons such as chlorine, sarin or mustard gas. Indeed, weapons containing these substances are often referred to as weapons of mass destruction, and have played an important role in shaping the international political landscape

J. C. van den Boogaard (✉)
Ministry of Foreign Affairs, The Hague, The Netherlands
e-mail: j.c.vandenboogaard@uva.nl

University of Amsterdam, Amsterdam, The Netherlands

© T.M.C. ASSER PRESS and the authors 2022
S. Sayapin et al. (eds.), *International Conflict and Security Law*,
https://doi.org/10.1007/978-94-6265-515-7_14

in the past century. For example, the alleged possession of chemical weapons and other weapons of mass destruction was used in 2003 as a ground to invade Iraq and remove the Baath regime from power.[1] But also in more recent armed conflicts, such as the civil war in Syria, the use of chemical weapons has been confirmed and heavily criticised.[2] Chemical weapons are easy and inexpensive to manufacture. As a result, less prosperous States relied on chemical weapons as part of their deterrence strategy in the absence of their possession of nuclear weapons.[3]

Of course, chemicals come in many forms and shapes, and chemicals which may be used as weapons also have civilian usages. One example is the element of chlorine, which is commonly used to make water suitable for consumption, but is also highly toxic and has as such been used as a chemical weapon.[4]

Chemical weapons are defined in the 1993 Chemical Weapons Convention (CWC 1993) as

(a) Toxic chemicals and their precursors, except where intended for purposes not prohibited under this Convention, as long as the types and quantities are consistent with such purposes;

(b) Munitions and devices, specifically designed to cause death or other harm through the toxic properties of those toxic chemicals specified in subparagraph (a), which would be released as a result of the employment of such munitions and devices;

(c) Any equipment specifically designed for use directly in connection with the employment of munitions and devices specified in subparagraph (b).[5]

Using toxic chemicals as weapons is based on "its chemical action on life processes [causing] death, temporary incapacitation or permanent harm to humans or animals".[6] Chemical weapons may achieve their effect by working as a nerve agent, by having blistering effects, through blood-poisoning or as a choking agent. Chemical weapons may often also have a poisonous effect. Nonetheless, chemical weapons must be distinguished from poison, if only because the use of poisonous weapons has much more than chemical warfare been prohibited unequivocally since the first codifications of international humanitarian law (IHL).[7] Similarly, chemicals such as napalm and phosphorus are usually defined as incendiary weapons, and are subject to separate regulation. Defoliants and other herbicides are also chemicals. If herbicides are used as a method of warfare as defined in the CWC 1993, they are

---

[1] Spiers 2010, p. 11. For a discussion of the *ius ad bellum* aspects of the invasion of Iraq by the US and its allies, see Weller 2018, pp. 637–661.

[2] UNSC 2017.

[3] Merkin 1991, p. 175.

[4] See generally Jefferson Lab undated.

[5] Article 2(1) CWC 1993.

[6] Article 2(2) CWC 1993.

[7] See Article 23(a) Hague Regulations; Rule 72, ICRC Customary International Humanitarian Law Study, Henckaerts and Doswald-Beck 2005, pp. 251–254.

14 Chemical Weapons

covered by the regulations concerning chemical weapons.[8] Furthermore, biological weapons are regulated in both the 1925 Gas Protocol and in the 1972 Biological Weapons Convention.

This chapter discusses the rules of IHL with regard to the use of chemical weapons. To that end, a short historic overview is provided first (Sect. 14.2), followed by an overview of the response in international law to that and potential future use of chemical weapons during armed conflict (Sect. 14.3). This discussion includes aspects of both arms control law and IHL. There is considerable overlap between the regulation of chemical weapons and biological weapons, primarily due to their simultaneous regulation in the 1925 Gas Protocol. For this reason, Sect. 14.4 contains a short description of the regulation of biological weapons. Some concluding remarks regarding the adequacy of the legal framework regulating chemical weapons are offered in Sect. 14.5.

14.2 A Short Historic Overview of the Use of Chemical Weapons

The use of chemicals to defeat the enemy is nothing new. Incidental uses are recorded in antiquity, such as in the Peloponnesian War (431–404 BC); by the Romans in Spain (80 BC); and in 1456 by the defenders of Belgrade against an attacking Turkish army.[9] More modern use started by the launch of chlorine shells during the US Civil war.[10] Accounts of the use of chlorine dispersed from cylinders by the German army at Ypres in Belgium on 22 April 1915 paint a grim picture of soldiers drowning "in their own fluids".[11] A counter-use by British forces on 25 September 2015 revealed weather conditions as one of the major drawbacks from the use of gas: it is estimated that the chlorine gas caused more British than German casualties.[12] Subsequent use of other gases such as mustard gas also caused major casualties.[13] Nonetheless, the parties responded quickly and took measures with a view to reducing the effects of chemical weapons, such as the introduction of gas masks.

In the inter-war period, European States used chemical weapons in both Africa and the Middle East. Air-delivered chemical weapons were used by British forces in Iraq in 1920; by Spain and France in Morocco in 1921[14] and by Italian forces in 1935

---

[8] See generally Rule 76, ICRC Customary International Humanitarian Law Study, Henckaerts and Doswald-Beck 2005, pp. 265–267.

[9] Coleman 2005, p. 6.

[10] Coleman 2005, p. 7, see also Merkin 1991, p. 177.

[11] Coleman 2005, p. 18.

[12] Coleman 2005, pp. 22–24.

[13] For example during a German attack on Russian forces at Riga in September 1917. See Coleman 2005, p. 24.

[14] Coleman 2005, pp. 44–45.

when invading Ethiopia.[15] During World War II, the use of chemical weapons was incidental. Nonetheless, chemical weapons were used by the Japanese armed forces in China from 1937 to 1939.[16] The utility of chemical weapons was much more suitable for trench warfare, such as happened during World War I, for the purpose of "rooting out troops from trenches and fortifications".[17] Nazi Germany developed the capability to deploy nerve gas in 1936, but using this during a quickly advancing Blitzkrieg was deemed to equally affect own troops as it would affect the opponent.[18] Furthermore, fear of retaliations by the opponent and the expected horrific effects to the civilian population thereof in the cities may have played a role in the decision of all sides to refrain from widespread use of chemical weapons. Thus, despite the presence of enormous stockpiles of chemical weapons in both Germany and in Allied arsenals, both sides seemed reluctant to open Pandora's Box and be the first user of chemical weapons in the conduct of hostilities during World War II.[19]

The use of chemical weapons during armed conflicts after World War II is similarly sporadic, yet not completely absent. Chemical agents were used by American armed forces to restore order in camps for prisoners of war during the Korean War.[20] Widespread use of defoliants during the war in Vietnam was directed to the vegetation but incidentally also caused human casualties.[21] Egyptian forces used chemical weapons in North-Yemen between 1963 and 1967.[22] The last use of chemical weapons by two sides in an international armed conflict occurred during the Iran–Iraq War from 1980–1988.[23] Particularly, the use of chemical weapons in Halabja by the Iraqi government against its own nationals and Iranian troops in 1988 is a well-reported example of the horrendous effects of chemical weapons.[24]

The most recent uses in Syria, such as a sarin attack on Ghouta, a suburb of Damascus in 2013, seem to mark a regrettable return of chemical weapons to the contemporary battlefield.[25] International pressure resulted in Syria accessing to the CWC 1993 on 14 October 2013.[26] Allegations of the use of chemical weapons are not limited to the Syrian government forces. The Islamic State (Daesh) is allegedly "responsible for the use of sulphur mustard at Umm Hawsh on 15 and

---

[15] Merkin 1991, p. 181.

[16] Coleman 2005, p. 152.

[17] Coleman 2005, p. 60.

[18] Coleman 2005, p. 60.

[19] Boothby 2016, pp. 110–111; Coleman 2005, pp. 59–79; Marauhn 2016, p. 27. Chemical agents were however used on a large scale by the Nazis in their concentration camps.

[20] Coleman 2005, p. 89.

[21] Coleman 2005, pp. 90–93.

[22] Marauhn 2016, p. 27 ; Coleman 2005, pp. 101–103.

[23] Marauhn 2016, p. 27; Oygarden 2014, p. 15; Ali 2001, p. 44.

[24] Spiers 2010, pp. 104–106; Coleman 2005, pp. 110–111; Ali 2001, p. 52, See also Human Rights Watch 1993.

[25] Marauhn 2016, p. 27.

[26] See OPCW News: 14 October 2013, 'Syria's Accession to the Chemical Weapons Convention Enters into Force' https://www.opcw.org/media-centre/news/2013/10/syrias-accession-chemical-weapons-convention-enters-force.

14 Chemical Weapons 321

16 September 2016".[27] Furthermore, in the final stages of the battle in Aleppo in 2016, Syrian government forces allegedly dropped barrel-bombs filled with chemicals on numerous occasions. Also, in the beginning of 2018, air-delivered bombs containing the nerve agent sarin were allegedly dropped by Syrian government forces in Khan Sheikhoun in Idlib province.[28]

The use of chemical weapons, including merely alleged incidents, is always met with both international outrage and claims of violations of legal obligations. Given the extensive legal framework in place regulating the use of chemical weapons, this may not come as a surprise. This framework is the subject of the next section of this chapter.

14.3 Law Regulating the Use of Chemical Weapons

Weapons law consists of two components. First, arms control law, and second IHL pertaining to the conduct of hostilities. With regard to the former, there are several multilateral treaties regulating the possession, stockpile or production of certain types of weapons. Leaving nuclear weapons aside, which are regulated in a completely *sui generis* way, the framework of arms control law does generally not regulate the use, but primarily possession, production and stockpiles of weapons.[29] Secondly, principles and rules of IHL regulate the use of weapons during armed conflict. It is the intended use that matters for the assessment of the legality of a means of warfare. Obviously, with arms control law prohibiting the mere possession and manufacturing of chemical weapons, the rules with regard to their use should be redundant. Nonetheless, an essential incentive to regulate a certain weapons system in arms control law is when its use may be deemed incompatible with the principles and rules of IHL. For that reason, Sect. 14.3.1 addresses the use of chemical weapons in the context of the IHL rules and principles regulating means and methods of warfare. Section 14.3.2 subsequently addresses how chemical weapons are regulated in arms control law.

14.3.1 IHL Principles Regulating the Use of Chemical Weapons

Like all other types of weapons, the use of chemical weapons is subject to the principles underlying the specific rules of IHL. For the legality of weapons and

---

[27] UNSC 2017.

[28] Human Rights Watch 2017.

[29] Arms control law is a "branch of public international law [and] consists of the rules and principles of international law related to the control of armaments—'control' being understood as encompassing the whole range of prohibitions of armaments quantitative and qualitative arms limitations as well as obligations to disarm." Den Dekker 2008, p. 75.

their use, these principles are the principle of distinction, the prohibition to use means and methods of warfare designed to cause superfluous injury or unnecessary suffering and thirdly the protection of the environment.[30] In this context, it must be noted that on the basis of the Martens Clause, IHL governs the use of any type of weapons, including chemical weapons, also in situations where no specific applicable customary or treaty rule can be identified.[31] The International Court of Justice notes that the Martens Clause is "an effective means of addressing the rapid evolution of military technology"[32] but the practical application of the Martens Clause remains nonetheless disputed.[33] Kalshoven notes that principles are not only used for rhetorical purposes, but also "as yardsticks or guidelines".[34] Nonetheless, without general agreement that principles of IHL out of themselves are capable of prohibiting the possession or use of a specific type of weapon,[35] reference must be made to specific rules of international treaty and customary law.

As always in IHL, different law may apply during international armed conflicts as opposed to non-international armed conflicts. In terms of treaty rules applicable to non-international armed conflict, neither Common Article 3 to the Geneva Conventions nor Additional Protocol II contain explicit references to the use of specific means of warfare, including chemical weapons.[36] Instead, the protection during non-international armed conflict is deliberately much more general in treaty law regulating the conduct of hostilities until the adoption of the CWC 1993.

---

[30] See generally Boothby 2016, Chaps. 5, 6 and 7, pp. 46–91. See also Tsagourias and Morrison 2018, p. 174 and Van Den Boogaard 2018, p. 524.

[31] The Martens Clause was first included in the preamble to the 1907 Hague convention concerning land warfare and subsequently in most IHL instruments. See for example O'Connell 2013, pp. 33–34. The Martens Clause is commonly understood to mean that "[i]f an act of war is not expressly prohibited by international agreements or customary law, this does not necessarily mean that it is actually permissible."

[32] International Court of Justice Advisory Opinion, 8 July 1996, *Legality of the Threat or Use of Nuclear Weapons*, p. 257, para 78. Available here: http://www.icj-cij.org/files/case-related/95/095-19960708-ADV-01-00-EN.pdf.

[33] Cassese 2008, p. 41.

[34] Kalshoven 2007, pp. 395–396: "...as yardsticks, they should be able to support a fairly straightforward determination of the legal issue. As guidelines, they need to provide little more tha[n] a set of basic, perhaps mutually conflicting, considerations that must be weighed in arriving at such a decision."

[35] Henckaerts and Doswald-Beck 2005, p. 242 and 248. See also generally Van Den Boogaard 2013 and Zwanenburg 2008, pp. 114–119.

[36] Geneva Convention relative to the Treatment of Prisoners of War (12 August 1949) 75 UNTS 135, entered into force 21 October 1950 Common Article 3; Protocol Additional to the Geneva Conventions of 12 August 1949, and relating to the Protection of Victims of Non-International Armed Conflicts (8 June 1977) 1125 UNTS 609, entered into force 7 December 1978.

14 Chemical Weapons

14.3.1.1 The Principle of Distinction

Distinction is one of the most important principles of IHL.[37] The need to distinguish between those who are participating in the hostilities and military objectives on the one hand and on the other hand those who do not as well as protected objects is pivotal to the entire framework of IHL.[38] The basic customary rule is that weapons that are by nature indiscriminate are prohibited. According to the ICRC, these weapons "are those that cannot be directed at a military objective or whose effects cannot be limited as required by international humanitarian law."[39] Some types of weapons are designed to be used against an area. That purpose alone does not render them illegal per se: it all depends on the circumstances ruling at the time, such as the location of the attack, the type of target (which may indeed be an area), the available weapons systems and the extent to which civilians, civilian objects and other protected persons and objects are present in the vicinity of the military objective.

Chemical weapons may be delivered as gas, in liquid form or as dust. Once deployed, chemical weapons often rely primarily on the weather conditions to affect the enemy, or the civilian population. In order to be effective against a military objective, as well as in order to spare the civilian population in accordance with the IHL rules on distinction, precautions in attack and proportionality, the use of a weapon must to a certain extent be predictable. For chemical weapons that rely on the direction of the wind to have effect, this may be problematic because even meteorological experts cannot always predict this with a hundred percent certainty as a result of the fact that the atmosphere is a non-linear environment.[40] Also, chemical weapons may linger for a substantive period after their initial launch, and some types of weapons, such as for example sarin, are capable of spreading far beyond a military objective because sarin sticks to other objects, such as clothing. As a result, chemical weapons are inherently unpredictable at least to a certain extent and certainly uncontrollable after initial release. These factors lead to the conclusion that on the basis of the principle of distinction, there are reasons to maintain that the use of chemical weapons is in many circumstances problematic and perhaps many types of chemical weapons may inherently be contrary to this principle. Chemical weapons have been declared indiscriminate by different international organisations, including the World Health Organisation and the United Nations General Assembly.[41]

---

[37] As Dinstein notes: "there are several cardinal principles lying at the root of the law of international armed conflict. Upon examination, none is more critical than the principle of distinction." Dinstein 2008, p. 1.

[38] ICRC Customary International Humanitarian Law Study, Henckaerts and Doswald-Beck 2005, Rules 1-24, pp. 1–76.

[39] ICRC Customary International Humanitarian Law Study, Henckaerts and Doswald-Beck 2005, Rule 71, pp. 244–250.

[40] For a short explanation: Doswell 2015: What makes weather so unpredictable? Available online https://www.quora.com/What-makes-weather-so-unpredictable-Why-is-it-so. See also this explanation of the so-called 'butterfly effect': Wikipedia undated.

[41] See for example World Health Organisation 1970, see also UNGA undated.

14.3.1.2 The Prohibition to Use Means and Methods of Warfare of a Nature to Cause Superfluous Injury or Unnecessary Suffering

In addition to distinction, the prohibition to use means and method of warfare designed to cause superfluous injury or unnecessary suffering is the other 'cardinal' principle of IHL according to the International Court of Justice (ICJ).[42] This principle is primarily aimed to regulate the intended effects of weapons to the soldiers of the opponent. As a result, the effects of chemical weapons on the civilian population is assumed to be addressed by the principle of distinction. The prohibition to use weapons of a nature to cause superfluous injury or unnecessary suffering is grounded on the premise, as expressed in the 1868 St. Petersburg Declaration, that "the only legitimate objective which States should endeavour to accomplish during war is to weaken the military forces of the enemy; that for this purpose it is sufficient to disable the greatest possible number of men [and] that this object would be exceeded by the employment of arms which uselessly aggravate the sufferings of disabled men, or render their death inevitable."[43] It should be noted that the principle applies both to means and methods of warfare. Thus, the principle also covers attacks carried out with legitimate weapons in a manner inconsistent with the prohibition to use methods of warfare that cause superfluous injury or unnecessary suffering. As may be derived from this description, the principle is a balance between the notions of humanity and military necessity, or, in more precise terms for the purpose of this particular principle, between the effects of a means or method and its military utility.[44]

To be hit by some types of weapons simply causes more suffering than others, based on the extent to which one may recover, the wounds it causes, the pain it causes, or the psychological effect the weapon has on human beings.[45] To a certain extent, however, whether a certain injury is superfluous or suffering necessary is an inherently subjective valuation.[46] Nonetheless, this principle may also be directly relevant during combat. Thus, if a legitimate incendiary weapon, such as a white phosphorus grenade, is used with the specific intention to inflict effects against an opponent due to its (secondary) effect of releasing poisonous gases, this use would violate the principle. In addition, as Boutruche notes: "it bans the modification of weapons for the purpose of increasing or causing suffering beyond that required by military necessity."[47] Since this principle is included as a rule in both treaty law and

---

[42] International Court of Justice, *Legality of the Threat or Use of Nuclear Weapons*, Advisory Opinion, I.C.J. Reports 1996, p. 226, para 78 on p. 257.

[43] 1868 St. Petersburg Declaration Renouncing the Use, in Time of War, of Explosive Projectiles under 400 Grammes Weight, Preamble.

[44] Boutruche 2008, pp. 103–106.

[45] Aubert describes how this principle may be put into practice using the example of incendiary weapons: "[i]nstinctively, man is afraid of fire. The injuries caused by incendiary weapons (burns and lesions due to the release of toxic gases) are particularly painful and, to be treated, they require greater hospital facilities than is the case for bullet or shrapnel wounds." Aubert 1990, p. 489.

[46] Haines 2014, pp. 285–286.

[47] Boutruche 2008, p. 108.

14 Chemical Weapons

customary law, it is a clear example of how the rules pertaining to chemical weapons may be of relevance to the use of other weapons systems.

With regard to the extent to which chemical weapons may be understood to be contrary to the prohibition to causing superfluous injury or unnecessary suffering, the extreme suffering caused by chemical weapons is exemplified in many historic examples. One example is the Iran–Iraq war (1980–1988), during which extensive use of chemical weapons took place, reportedly causing 60,000 casualties among civilians and Iranian combatants.[48] Also, the argument is easily made that the type of injury caused by chemical weapons causes immense suffering. The drowning of soldiers "in their own fluids"[49] as a result of chemical gas such as chlorine is clearly a gruesome way to put the opponent *hors de combat*. Furthermore, mustard gas is very hazardous to the human eye and can sometimes cause permanent blindness.[50] Nerve agents such as sarin deprive a person of all oxygen, irreversibly affecting neurological and nervous systems.[51] Some types of chemical weapons only produce harmful effects after a certain period.[52] For example, the effects of phosgene may not be become evident until 48 hours after contact with the substance, and the resulting injuries may after this time have become largely untreatable.[53] Many of these effects are long-term effects, including life changing injuries, such as permanent disability, chronic illnesses and increased risk of cancer. It is then the question, first, to what extent chemical weapons produce militarily advantageous results and, second, the extent to which other types of weapons systems are available that produce comparable effects in terms of attaining military advantage while causing less suffering or better treatable injuries. In terms of psychological effects, attacks by chemical weapons tend to cause extreme panic and suffering among both the opponents and the civilian population.[54]

In sum, the high number of casualties caused by attacks with chemical weapons, the type of injuries and diseases, as well as the continued physical and mental suffering and need for continuous medical treatment of survivors of attacks using

---

[48] Ali 2001, p. 52.

[49] Coleman 2005, p. 18.

[50] Pechura and Rall 1993, pp. 131–145. Causing permanent blindness was also one of the major drivers for prohibiting laser weapons in Protocol IV to the Certain Conventional Weapons Convention of 1995.

[51] Uribe 2013: "Nerve agents such as sarin cause an overstimulation of the nerve cells and prevent the proper operation of glands and muscles. Symptoms can appear within seconds or even hours and include blurred vision, excess salivation, vomiting, difficulty thinking, muscle twitches, convulsions, paralysis and respiratory failure." Available at: https://www.undispatch.com/syrians-now-face-the-long-term-effects-of-exposure-to-chemical-warfare/.

[52] See for example World Health Organisation 1970.

[53] Centers for Disease Control and Prevention 2018, *'Phosgene'*. Available at: https://emergency.cdc.gov/agent/phosgene/basics/facts.asp.

[54] Jones and Greenberg 2007, pp. 727–728.

chemical weapons, show how chemical weapons may be deemed contrary to the principle that prohibits the use of means and methods of warfare that cause superfluous injury or unnecessary suffering.[55]

14.3.1.3 The Protection of the Environment

The protection of the environment is firstly codified in Article 35 (3) API, (Additional Protocol I) stating that "[i]t is prohibited to employ methods or means of warfare which are intended, or may be expected, to cause widespread, long-term and severe damage to the natural environment."[56] The use of defoliants during the Vietnam War was an incentive for the adoption of the 1976 United Nations Convention on the Prohibition of Military or Any Other Hostile Use of Environmental Modification Techniques (ENMOD Convention), prohibiting the use of the environment as a weapon.[57]

The customary rules with regard to the protection of the environment are grounded on the general principle that methods and means of warfare must be employed with due regard to the protection and preservation of the natural environment. Furthermore, in the conduct of military operations, proportionality and feasible precautions are the implementing obligations to avoid, and in any event to minimize, incidental damage to the environment. Also, mere absence of scientific certainty as to the effects on the environment of certain military operations does not absolve a party to the conflict from taking such precautions.[58] More specifically, the overall picture is that damage caused to the environment must be cumulatively severe, widespread and long-lasting before it may be deemed to be contrary to IHL.[59] This is generally understood as a high threshold.[60] Nonetheless, recent developments in the International Law Commission (ILC) have led to the adoption of draft principles with regard to the protection of the environment in relation to armed conflicts. After stressing the importance of the

---

[55] The ICRC Customary Law Study cites the military manuals of Australia, France and Germany in support of this conclusion, noting that "[t]he prohibition on the use of chemical and biological weapons in the Geneva Gas Protocol was originally motivated by this rule". ICRC Customary International Humanitarian Law Study, Henckaerts and Doswald-Beck 2005, Rule 70, p. 237.

[56] See also Article 55 (1) API: "Care shall be taken in warfare to protect the natural environment against widespread, long-term and severe damage. This protection includes a prohibition of the use of methods or means of warfare which are intended or may be expected to cause such damage to the natural environment and thereby to prejudice the health or survival of the population."

[57] This treaty however has limited relevance, since it merely prohibits the use of the environment as a weapon. Nonetheless, the ENMOD Convention has a lower threshold for effects on the natural environment, because the damage can be alternatively widespread, long-lasting *or* severe. See Article 1: "[e]ach State Party to this Convention undertakes not to engage in military or any other hostile use of environmental modification techniques having widespread, long-lasting or severe effects as the means of destruction, damage or injury to any other State Party."

[58] Rule 44, ICRC Customary International Humanitarian Law Study, Henckaerts and Doswald-Beck 2005, pp. 147–151.

[59] See for example Dinstein 2016, p. 244. See also International Law Commission undated.

[60] Dinstein notes that in his opinion, "the bar set up by API is too high". Dinstein 2016, p. 250.

14 Chemical Weapons

Martens Clause with respect to the protection of the environment in relation to armed conflict, in Draft principle 12,[61] Draft principle 13 mentions three main aspects:

1. The natural environment shall be respected and protected in accordance with applicable international law and, in particular, the law of armed conflict;
2. Care shall be taken to protect the natural environment against widespread, long-term and severe damage;
3. No part of the natural environment may be attacked, unless it has become a military objective.[62]

Although there is no mention of chemical weapons in either the treaty rules, customary law rules or the draft-ILC principles regarding the protection of the environment, the past has shown that the use of chemical weapons can have far-reaching consequences for the environment. Even leaving the question aside of whether the protection of the environment under IHL must be understood in the context of human beings or is deemed to constitute a separate protected object, many types of chemicals have the potential to lead to the pollution of the natural environment. There is no doubt about the prohibition to attack any part of the natural environment as such, unless it constitutes a military objective.[63] The widespread dumping of large stockpiles of chemical weapons in the oceans after World War II[64] may be a future threat to the environment with consequences which are presently still unknown. Nonetheless, as is noted by Rogers, it is doubtful whether the effects of chemical weapons are in fact sufficiently long-term in a given area to regard them as relevant for regulating the protection of the environment.[65] It may be added however that the interpretation of what constitutes "widespread, long-term and severe damage" to the environment in the context of chemical weapons may change and is thus not necessarily set in stone.

One of the functions of principles is that they provide a basis for legally binding rules of treaty and customary international law. Therefore, the next section of this chapter provides a short overview of rules of arms control that regulate chemical weapons.

---

[61] "In cases not covered by international agreements, the environment remains under the protection and authority of the principles of international law derived from established custom, from the principles of humanity and from the dictates of public conscience."

[62] The draft principles were adopted during the 77th Session of the ILC in Geneva in April–June 2019. See http://legal.un.org/docs/index.asp?symbol=A/CN.4/L.937.

[63] Rule 3, ICRC Customary International Humanitarian Law Study, Henckaerts and Doswald-Beck 2005, pp. 11–14.

[64] OPCW undated-a, Concerns, https://www.opcw.org/our-work/eliminating-chemical-weapons. See also Edwards 2011, "MoD investigates former chemical weapons factories for contamination" The Guardian.

[65] Rogers 2004, p. 176.

14.3.2 Arms Control Law Regulating Chemical Weapons

Chemical weapons are regulated in a number of international treaties. Chemical weapons were first regulated in the 1899 Hague Declaration (IV, 2) concerning Asphyxiating gases. However, the Declaration only prohibits the *use* of "projectiles the sole object of which is the diffusion of asphyxiating or deleterious gases", and it is only binding in situations where two of the signatories to the declaration were be at war with each other. This declaration left the possession of the gases as such unregulated. As a result, many States circumvented the prohibition of the 1899 Hague Declaration by developing as methods of warfare multi-purpose projectiles containing these gases and cylinders for releasing chemical weapons, as were used during World War I.[66]

After World War I, the need was clearly felt to further regulate chemical weapons. One early example of a disarmament treaty is the Versailles treaty adopted in 1919 prohibiting the possession of chemical weapons by Germany. More comprehensively, the 1925 Gas Protocol aimed to improve the restrictions on the use of chemical weapons. Again, unfortunately, there were significant shortcomings to the instrument that was adopted. The first is that the Gas Protocol prohibits the use of chemical weapons, not its possession or development. Another major shortcoming of the Gas Protocol is its reliance on reciprocity. Thus, the prohibition to use chemical weapons would not apply in wars between States when one of these States had not ratified the Gas Protocol.[67] Also, many States ratifying the Gas Protocol did so reserving the right to respond using chemical weapons after a first use by their opponent.[68] Also, certainly on the basis of the law at that time, a first use of chemical weapons by one State party to the Geneva Gas Protocol, even in violation of the law, could incite the other party to use chemical weapons against them as a military reprisal, provided the requirements for reprisals were met.[69] As a result, there was no incentive for States to destroy their stockpiles of chemical weapons or to stop developing new types of chemical weapons in tandem with scientific progress in the field of chemistry for industrial uses. Furthermore, because the Gas Protocol is an instrument designed for international armed conflict in response to interstate use during World War I, it is inapplicable to the use of chemical weapons against a State's own population during an internal armed conflict.[70]

As noted above, the use of chemical weapons during World War II only occurred in extremely exceptional incidents, in spite of the shortcomings of the Gas Protocol. It was not until the adoption of the CWC 1993 that the regulation of chemical weapons was significantly improved. In the meantime, the issue of the regulation of chemical

---

[66] Merkin 1991, p. 178. See also Coleman 2005, p. 151.

[67] Oeter 2013, p. 163.

[68] Raičević 2001, p. 621.

[69] Oeter 2013, p. 164.

[70] Scharf 1999, p. 481.

weapons was not completely off the agenda of States. Notably, the United Nations General Assembly adopted resolutions condemning chemical weapons.[71]

The CWC 1993 significantly extends the scope of the earlier treaty rules with regard to chemical weapons.[72] The CWC 1993 makes no distinction between situations of international or non-international armed conflicts. Article 1 of the CWC 1993 not only prohibits the use of chemical weapons, but also directly related activities such as the developing, producing, stockpiling, retaining or transferring of chemical weapons. Furthermore, the convention covers preparations envisaging the military use of chemical weapons and assisting, encouraging or inducing in actions prohibited by it. On top of that, States ratifying the treaty must eliminate all chemical weapons and the production facilities it owns or possesses, or which are under its jurisdiction or control. The CWC 1993 is widely ratified. As of 2019, 193 States are a State Party to the treaty, putting 98% of the world population under its protection. Only five States have not (yet) joined: Angola, Egypt, North Korea, South Sudan and Israel.[73] However, its most significant contribution to the regulation of chemical weapons is perhaps the fact that unlike most IHL treaties, the CWC 1993 initiated a mechanism to implement it: the Organisation for the Prohibition of Chemical Weapons (OPCW). This organisation, based in The Hague, is established "to achieve the object and purpose of [the CWC 1993], to ensure the implementation of its provisions, including those for international verification of compliance with it, and to provide a forum for consultation and cooperation among State Parties."[74] This implementation mechanism is rather unique in IHL treaties[75] and the treaty may be seen as a success story. The ban on the use, but also possession of chemical weapons is mostly observed by its members States and stockpiles have been destroyed.[76]

The high degree of ratification of the CWC 1993, but also of the Gas Protocol and the 1899 Hague Declaration (IV, 2) concerning Asphyxiating gases, provides a clear indication of State practice and *opinio juris* supporting the customary status of the prohibition to use chemical weapons during armed conflict. In addition to, and complementary to these treaty rules, provisions in the field of international criminal law may be interpreted as contributing to the acceptance of customary IHL rules. The Rome Statute for the International Criminal Court defines an international crime regarding the use of chemical weapons, but only for international armed conflicts (IACs). In Article 8(b)(xviii), the Rome Statute prohibits "[e]mploying asphyxiating, poisonous or other gases, and all analogous liquids, materials or devices." Since the Kampala amendments took effect, this crime also applies for situations

---

[71] See for example UNGA undated.

[72] For a commentary of the CWC 1993, see generally Krutzsch et al. 2014.

[73] See OPCW undated-b, https://www.opcw.org/about-us/member-states. It may be noted that Israel did sign the CWC 1993.

[74] Article VIII (1) CWC 1993.

[75] Krutzsch et al. 2014, p. 8.

[76] According to the OPCW, 97% of the chemical weapons stockpiles declared by possessor States have been verifiably destroyed. See OPCW undated-b, https://www.opcw.org/about-us/member-states. See also OPCW 2016.

of non-international armed conflicts (NIACs).[77] The customary status of the rule is acknowledged by the ICRC in the 2005 Customary Law Study during both IACs and NIACs.[78] The ICRC points *inter alia* to regional declarations[79] and military manuals[80] to support its position that the customary rule prohibiting the use of chemical weapons also applies during NIACs.Furthermore, the Appeals Chamber of the International Criminal Tribunal for the Former-Yugoslavia (ICTY) interpreted the prohibition to use chemical weapons as a rule of customary law applicable during NIACs.[81] This is confirmed by notable experts in the field of weapons law[82] and by the condemnation of "any use of chemical weapons in the Syrian Arab Republic… in violation of international law" by the United Nations Security Council in Resolution 2118 (2013), despite the fact that Syria had not yet ratified the CWC 1993 at that moment.[83]

In conclusion, the existence of a customary rule prohibiting the use of chemical weapons seems undisputed, although some debate remains with regard to the question of whether the prohibition also applies in NIACs.[84] This would however be relevant in very limited circumstances, more specifically only during NIACs in those States that have so far not ratified the CWC 1993. In light of the above, it seems that the use of chemical weapons in the conduct of hostilities is categorically prohibited during any type of armed conflict.

The use of certain chemical agents outside the context of hostilities may however not be prohibited. Some types of riot control measures, which would normally be prohibited to be used against the opponent in situations to which IHL applies, may

---

[77] For an analysis: see Akande 2013, https://www.ejiltalk.org/can-the-icc-prosecute-for-use-of-chemical-weapons-in-syria/.

[78] ICRC Customary International Humanitarian Law Study, Henckaerts and Doswald-Beck 2005, rule 74, pp. 259–263.

[79] ICRC Customary International Humanitarian Law Study, Henckaerts and Doswald-Beck 2005, Vol II, Practice, p. 1662: Mendoza Declaration on Chemical and Biological Weapons, Mendoza, 5 September 1991; Cartagena Declaration on the Renunciation of Weapons of Mass Destruction, Cartagena, 5 December 1991.

[80] ICRC Customary International Humanitarian Law Study, Henckaerts and Doswald-Beck 2005, Vol II, Practice, p. 1663. See for instance the military manuals of Australia, Bosnia and Herzegovina, Canada, Colombia, Ecuador, Germany, Italy, Kenya, South Africa, Spain and Yugoslavia.

[81] ICTY, Prosecutor v Tadic, Case No. 94-1-AR72, Decision on the defence motion for interlocutory appeal on jurisdiction, p. 124: "there undisputedly emerged a general consensus in the international community on the principle that the use of [chemical] weapons is also prohibited in internal armed conflicts"

[82] See for example Boothby 2016, p. 123: "[i]t is now clear that the prohibition of the use of chemical weapons is a rule of customary law, and therefore binds all States including those not party to the CWC [1993]." See also Oeter 2013, p. 162, Krutzsch et al. 2014, p. 3, Dinstein 2016, p. 92 and Asada 2016 p. 188.

[83] S/RES/2118(2013) Adopted by the Security Council at its 7038th meeting, on 27 September 2013, p. 2.

[84] See for example Blake and Mahmud 2013, available at: https://www.uclalawreview.org/a-legal-%E2%80%9Cred-line%E2%80%9D-syria-and-the-use-of-chemical-weapons-in-civil-conflict/ and Van Schaack 2016, available at: https://www.justsecurity.org/32309/chemical-weapons-returns-syria/.

14 Chemical Weapons

be legally used in situations of law enforcement. There is a sense of awkwardness in this: tear gas may not be used against an enemy, whereas a State can legally use it to disperse its own protesting civilian population. The continuing debate regarding the relation between IHL and International Human Rights Law as well as the dichotomy between situations of law enforcement and that of hostilities are relevant in this regard.[85] As Geiss notes: "[a]lthough it is now clear that riot control agents are prohibited as a method of warfare but that their use is allowed for law enforcement purposes, the CWC fails to clarify what precisely is meant by 'methods of warfare' or 'law enforcement purposes'."[86] Nonetheless, the CWC 1993 defines riot control agents as "any chemical not listed in a Schedule, which can produce rapidly in humans sensory irritation or disabling physical effects which disappear within a short time following termination of exposure."[87] In situations where the factual circumstances give rise to doubts as to the question of the existence of an armed conflict or when a situation of law enforcement is developing into one of hostilities, military forces may prefer the use of tear gas as a riot control means to address a certain situation, instead of opening fire. Even though this use of riot control agents may even during armed conflict be intended as a precaution to save civilian lives, it may be that the option of using riot control agents is nonetheless off the table in these situations, and its use would contravene the legal obligations of a party to the conflict. Some States, notably the United States, interpret the CCW 1993 to allow for the use of riot control agents during armed conflict in situations that could be seen as law enforcement.[88] This interpretation is however controversial, because indeed the use of teargas during armed conflict may be understood by the opposing party as a first use of chemical weapons during armed conflict, potentially triggering the use of prohibited weapons by the opposing side.[89]

14.4 Biological Weapons

Biological weapons have not been used on a large scale during contemporary armed conflicts. Nonetheless, a few early examples of biological warfare are recorded. First, when the city of Caffa on the Crimean peninsula was under siege in 1346, it seems that the Mongolian troops hurled the rotting corpses of those deceased as a result of plague into the city. Doing so, they caused a massacre among the defenders and

---

[85] See for example Melzer and Gaggioli Gasteyger 2015, pp. 63–92.

[86] Geiss 2010, p. 342.

[87] Article 2(7) CWC 1993. Pepper spray and tear gas are two types of chemicals that would fall within the scope of this article.

[88] Thus, in the view of the US, the use of riot control agents would be permitted to quell an uprising of prisoners of war; in situations in which civilians are used to provide cover for an attack; for rescue missions; to prevent prisoners from escaping and "to protect convoys from civil disturbances, terrorists and paramilitary organisations" See US Government 1975.

[89] Cathcart 2015, 447–448: "caution dictates that any uses of [riot control agents] that could be reasonably perceived as a 'method of warfare' should be avoided."

the civilian population of the city, although the plague raged so hard within their own ranks, that the Mongolian forces eventually abandoned the siege.[90] Also, it is claimed that Spanish conquistador Pizarro deliberately donated cloths or blankets belonging to smallpox patients to the Native American population. The smallpox is said to have subsequently decimated the Inca population.[91] The poisoning of water wells is a standard example of the use of poison, in addition to the application of poison on the tip of arrows. Technically speaking, poisoning a water well is however a biological weapon, because it entails the use of infectious substances.

Like chemical weapons, not only the use of biological weapons is prohibited by treaty law, but also its development, production, possession and stockpile. The 1925 Gas Protocol effectively prohibits the first use of biological weapons.[92] The 1972 Biological Weapons Convention (BWC) is adopted within the context of the United Nations disarmament mechanism, as part of the process which earlier lead to the adoption of the 1925 Gas Protocol.[93] It is confirmed that the BWC prohibits the use of biological weapons, even though this does not follow clearly from its text. States have however consistently confirmed this interpretation during the respective Review Conferences of the treaty.[94] The prohibition to use biological weapons is also generally accepted as a rule of customary international humanitarian law.[95]

Article I of the BWC provides:

"Each State Party to this Convention undertakes never in any circumstances to develop, produce, stockpile or otherwise acquire or retain:

(1)   microbial or other biological agents, or toxins whatever their origin or method of production, of types and in quantities that have no justification for prophylactic, protective or other peaceful purposes;
(2)   weapons, equipment or means of delivery designed to use such agents or toxins for hostile purposes or in armed conflict."[96]

---

[90] Wheelis 2002, pp. 971–975, Bartlema 1965, p. 476.

[91] Smith 2002, available at https://journalofethics.ama-assn.org/article/old-tactics-new-threat-what-todays-risk-smallpox/2002-09. A similar tactic seems to have been used by British Colonial troops fighting native American tribes. Bartlema 1965, p. 476.

[92] The parties to the 1929 Gas Protocol declared to "agree to extend [the prohibition of the use of chemical weapons] to the use of bacteriological methods of warfare (…)".

[93] Boothby 2016, p. 111.

[94] See for example UN General Assembly Resolution, A/RES/72/71, 4 December 2017: "Welcoming the reaffirmation made in the Final Declarations of the Fourth, Sixth, Seventh and Eighth Review Conferences that under all circumstances the use of bacteriological (biological) and toxin weapons and their development, production and stockpiling are effectively prohibited under Article I of the Convention".

[95] See Rule 73 of the ICRC Customary IHL Study, Henckaerts and Doswald-Beck 2005, pp. 256–248. See also Boothby, claiming that the customary rule extends also to the possession of such weapons.

[96] Convention on the Prohibition of the Development, Production and Stockpiling of Bacteriological (Biological) and Toxin Weapons and on Their Destruction. The treaty was opened for signature on

14 Chemical Weapons

Whereas the use of chemical weapons and poison may arguably in some instances be used discriminately, this is not the case for biological weapons. An inherent feature of biological weapons is that they cannot discriminate between those protected and those who may be attacked legitimately under IHL. When a virus is moving from one person to another, it cannot assess whether the next person to be infected belongs to the military medical services. Indeed, it is quite obvious that persons who became ill from a virus released upon them by an enemy, will be treated by the medical services. The fundamental rules protecting medical personnel is an additional rationale for prohibiting the use of biological weapons under the principle of distinction. This makes biological weapons perhaps one the most obvious inherently illegal weapons systems.

There is no OPCW (or rather OPBW) for biological weapons. Instead, the implementation and verification mechanisms for biological weapons are based on "confidence-building measures (CBM) in order to prevent or reduce the occurrence of ambiguities, doubts and suspicions and in order to improve international co-operation in the field of peaceful biological activities. The CBMs were expanded by the Third Review Conference (1991)."[97] During the Sixth Review Conference, an Implementation Support Unit (ISU) was, in order to assist States in implementing the Convention. Nonetheless, attempts to adopt a rigorous verification mechanism would be ineffective since it would simply be impossible to inspect the hundreds of thousands of laboratories worldwide where research into biotechnology is being conducted.[98]

14.5 Conclusion

Since its first use, soldiers, generals, politicians and the general public have mostly agreed that using chemical weapons in warfare is abhorrent and must be prohibited. Nonetheless, chemical weapons have on occasion, even recently, been used. The fact that these incidents were always followed by international outcry strengthens the belief that the use of chemical weapons must be prohibited in all circumstances. This is a customary rule that is now also codified in the almost universally ratified CWC 1993. The regulation of the use and possession of chemical weapons is unique in the existence of the OPCW as an implementation mechanism. If the codification of the rules regulating chemicals would leave any gaps, it may be argued that this void is filled by the customary IHL prohibition to use chemical weapons. In terms of international mechanisms, it is true that the CWC 1993 puts a strong verification system in place, but a compliance mechanism under general IHL is still lacking.[99] In the end, it may be concluded that the legal framework regulating chemical weapons is quite adequate. The implementation of this rule, as any legal rule, remains dependent

---

10 April 1972 and entered into force on 26 March 1975. As of July 2019, 182 State have ratified the treaty.

[97] See https://www.un.org/disarmament/wmd/bio/.

[98] Boothby 2016, note 64 on p. 114.

[99] Marauhn 2016, pp. 41–42.

334   J. C. van den Boogaard

on the (for the most part continued) willingness of parties to armed conflicts to refrain from using chemical weapons, as reinforced by the impressive work of the OPCW.

References

Akande D (2013) Can the ICC Prosecute for Use of Chemical Weapons in Syria? EJIL:Talk! Blog, 23 August 2013, https://www.ejiltalk.org/can-the-icc-prosecute-for-use-of-chemical-weapons-in-syria/. Accessed 15 March 2021

Ali J (2001) Chemical weapons and the Iran-Iraq War: a case study in noncompliance. The Non Proliferation Review, 8.1:43–58

Asada M (2016) A path to a comprehensive prohibition of the use of chemical weapons under international law: from The Hague to Damascus. Journal of Conflict & Security Law 21:153–207

Aubert M (1990) The International Committee of the Red Cross and the Problem of Excessively Injurious or Indiscriminate Weapons. International Review of the Red Cross 30:477–497

Bartlema HC (1965) Biologische oorlog. De Militaire Spectator, 134:451–501

Blake J, Mahmud A (2013) A legal 'red line'?: Syria and the use of chemical weapons in civil conflict, 61 UCLA Law Review, 15 October 2013, available at: https://www.uclalawreview.org/a-legal-%E2%80%9Cred-line%E2%80%9D-syria-and-the-use-of-chemical-weapons-in-civil-conflict/. Accessed 15 March 2021

Boothby WH (2016) Weapons and the law of armed conflict, 2nd edn. Oxford University Press, Oxford

Boutruche T (2008) The principle of the prohibition of superfluous injury or unnecessary suffering. In: Beruto GL (ed) Proceedings of the 30th Sanremo Round Table, the conduct of hostilities – revisiting the law of armed conflict, 100 years after the law of armed conflict, 30 years after the 1977 Additional Protocols. International Institute of Humanitarian Law, pp 102–108

Cassese A (2008) The Martens Clause: half a loaf or simply pie in the sky? In: Gaeta P, Zappalà S (eds) The human dimension of international law - Selected Papers of Antonio Cassese. Oxford University Press, Oxford, pp 39–69

Cathcart B (2015) Legal dimension of special operations and information operations. In: Gill TD, Fleck D (ed) The handbook of the international law of military operations. Oxford University Press, Oxford, pp 444–455

Centers for Disease Control and Prevention (2018) Phosgene. Available at: https://emergency.cdc.gov/agent/phosgene/basics/facts.asp. Accessed 15 March 2021

Coleman K (2005) A history of chemical warfare. Palgrave Macmillan, New York

Den Dekker G (2008) The Law of Arms Control and Depleted Uranium Weapons. In: MacDonald A, Kleffner JK, Toebes BCA (eds) Depleted uranium weapons and international law: a precautionary approach. T.M.C. Asser Press, The Hague, pp 75–97

Dinstein Y (2008) Distinction and Loss of Civilian Protection in International Armed Conflicts. Israel Yearbook on Human Rights 38:1

Dinstein Y (2016) The conduct of hostilities under the law of international armed conflict, 3rd edn. Cambridge University Press, Cambridge

Doswell C (2015) What makes weather so unpredictable? https://www.quora.com/What-makes-weather-so-unpredictable-Why-is-it-so. Accessed 15 March 2021

Edwards R (2011) "MoD investigates former chemical weapons factories for contamination". The Guardian, 24 July 2011, https://www.theguardian.com/environment/2011/jul/24/mod-chemical-weapons-factories-contamination. Accessed 15 March 2021

Geiss R (2010) Poison, Gas and Expanding Bullets: the Extension of the List of Prohibited Weapons at the Review Conference of the International Criminal Court in Kampala. Yearbook of International Humanitarian Law 13:337–352

Haines S (2014) The developing law of weapons, humanity, distinction and precautions in attack. In: Clapham A, Gaeta P (eds) The Oxford handbook of international law in armed conflict. Oxford University Press, Oxford, pp 337–352

14 Chemical Weapons

Henckaerts J-M, Doswald-Beck L (2005) Customary international humanitarian law, volume I: Rules; Vol II: Practice. Cambridge University Press, Cambridge

Human Rights Watch (1993) 'Genocide in Iraq' Human Rights Watch (July 1993), https://www.hrw.org/reports/1993/iraqanfal/. Accessed 15 March 2021

Human Rights Watch (2017) 'Death by Chemicals' Report on the Syrian Government's Widespread and Systematic Use of Chemical Weapons (1 May 2017), available https://www.hrw.org/report/2017/05/01/death-chemicals/syrian-governments-widespread-and-systematic-use-chemical-weapons. Accessed 15 March 2021

International Law Commission (ILC) (undated) Draft principles of protection of the environment, http://legal.un.org/docs/index.asp?symbol=A/CN.4/L.937. Accessed 15 March 2021

Jefferson Lab (undated) The element of chlorine, https://education.jlab.org/itselemental/ele017.html. Accessed 15 March 2021

Jones E, Greenberg N (2007) Long-term psychological consequences among chemical warfare survivors of World War I and their current relevance. Psychiatric Annals 37:724–728

Kalshoven F (2007) The Conventional Weapons Convention: functions of underlying legal principles. In: Kalshoven F (ed) Reflections on the law of war: collected essays. Martinus Nijhoff, Leiden, pp 393–397

Krutzsch W et al (2014) The Chemical Weapons Convention – objectives, principles, and implementation practice. In: Krutzsch W et al (eds) The Chemical Weapons Convention: A Commentary. Oxford University Press, Oxford

Krutzsch W et al (eds) (2014) The Chemical Weapons Convention: A Commentary. Oxford University Press, Oxford

Marauhn T (2016) The prohibition to use chemical weapons. In: Gill TD (ed) Yearbook of International Humanitarian Law 17:25–44

Melzer N, Gaggioli Gasteyger G (2015) Conceptual distinction and overlaps between law enforcement and the conduct of hostilities. In: Gill TD, Fleck D (eds) The handbook of the international law of military operations. Oxford University Press, Oxford, pp 63–92

Merkin DB (1991) The efficacy of chemical-arms treaties in the aftermath of the Iran-Iraq war. Boston University International Law Journal, 9:175–196

O'Connell ME (2013) Historic development and legal basis. In: Fleck D (ed) The handbook of international humanitarian law. Oxford University Press, Oxford, pp 1–42

Oeter S (2013) Methods and means of combat. In: Fleck D (ed) The handbook of international humanitarian law, 3rd edn. Oxford University Press, Oxford, pp 115–230

OPCW (undated-a) Concerns, https://www.opcw.org/our-work/eliminating-chemical-weapons. Accessed 15 March 2021

OPCW (undated-b) Member States, https://www.opcw.org/about-us/member-states. Accessed 15 March 2021

OPCW (2013) OPCW News: 14 October 2013, 'Syria's Accession to the Chemical Weapons Convention Enters into Force' https://www.opcw.org/media-centre/news/2013/10/syrias-accession-chemical-weapons-convention-enters-force. Accessed 15 March 2021

OPCW (2016) Report of the OPCW on the Implementation of the Convention on the Prohibition of the Development, Production, Stockpiling and Use of Chemical Weapons and on their Destruction, Twenty-First Session (2016), https://www.opcw.org/fileadmin/OPCW/CSP/C-21/en/c2104_e_.pdf. Accessed 15 March 2021

Oygarden RH (2014) Chemical Weapons and the Iran-Iraq War: A discussion of the UN Security Council's response to the use of gas in the Iran-Iraq war 1980–1988 (Universitas Bergensis 2014) http://bora.uib.no/bitstream/handle/1956/9153/128400983.pdf?sequence=1. Accessed 15 March 2021

Pechura CM, Rall DP (1993) Veterans at risk: the health effects of mustard gas and lewisite. National Academies Press, Washington, DC

Raičević N (2001) The history of prohibition of the use of chemical weapons in international humanitarian law. Facta Universitatis, Law and Politics Series, 1:613–631. Available at: http://facta.junis.ni.ac.rs/lap/lap2001/lap2001-05.pdf . Accessed 15 March 2021

Rogers APV (2004) Law on the battlefield, 2nd edn. Manchester University Press, Manchester

Scharf MP (1999) Clear and present danger: enforcing the international ban on biological and chemical weapons through sanctions, use of force, and criminalization. Michigan Journal of International Law, 20:477–521

Smith S (2002) Old tactics, new threat: what is today's risk of smallpox? Virtual Mentor. 2002;4(9): doi: https://doi.org/10.1001/virtualmentor.2002.4.9.mhst1-0209. https://journalofethics.ama-assn.org/article/old-tactics-new-threat-what-todays-risk-smallpox/2002-09. Accessed 15 March 2021

Spiers EM (2010) A History of chemical and biological weapons. Reaktion Books Ltd, London

Tsagourias NK, Morrison A (2018) International humanitarian law: cases, materials and commentary. Cambridge University Press, Cambridge

UNGA (undated) UNGA Resolution 2603 A (XXIV) Available at: https://documents-dds-ny.un.org/doc/RESOLUTION/GEN/NR0/257/37/IMG/NR025737.pdf?OpenElement. Accessed 15 March 2021

UNSC (2017) 'Seventh report of the Organisation for the Prohibition of Chemical Weapons- United Nations Joint Investigative Mechanism' S/2017/904. Available at: http://undocs.org/S/2017/904. Accessed 15 March 2021

Uribe C (2013) Syrians now Face the Long-term Effects of Exposure to Chemical Warfare (UN Dispatch) Available at: https://www.undispatch.com/syrians-now-face-the-long-term-effects-of-exposure-to-chemical-warfare/. Accessed 15 March 2021

US Government (1975) USA Executive Order No 11,850, 40 Fed. Reg. 16,187 (Apr. 8 1975): 143 Cong. Rec. S3657. https://www.archives.gov/federal-register/codification/executive-order/11850.html. Accessed 15 March 2021

Van Den Boogaard JC (2013) Fighting by the principles: Principles as a source of international humanitarian law. In: Matthee M, Toebes B, Bruss MMTA (eds) Armed conflict and international law: In search of the human face. Liber amicorum in memory of Avril McDonald. T.M.C. Asser Press, The Hague, pp 3–31

Van Den Boogaard JC (2018) New Weapons. In: Djukic D, Pons N (eds) The companion to international humanitarian law. Brill/Martinus Nijhoff, Leiden, pp 523–524

Van Schaack B (2016) Chemical weapons use return to Syria", Just Security blog, 8 August 2016. Available at: https://www.justsecurity.org/32309/chemical-weapons-returns-syria/. Accessed 15 March 2021

Weller M (2018) The Iraq War – 2003. In: Ruys T, Corten O, Hofer A (eds) The use of force in international law, a case-based approach, Oxford University Press, pp 637–661

Wheelis M (2002) Biological Warfare at the 1346 Siege of Caffa. Emerging Infectious Diseases. [author, insert name publication] 8:971–975. https://dx.doi.org/https://doi.org/10.3201/eid0809.010536

Wikipedia (undated) Butterfly effect, https://en.wikipedia.org/wiki/Butterfly_effect. Accessed 15 March 2021

World Health Organisation (WHO) (1970) 'Health Aspects of Chemical and Biological Weapons', http://apps.who.int/iris/bitstream/10665/39444/1/24039.pdf. Accessed 15 March 2021

Zwanenburg MC (2008) The use of depleted uranium and the prohibition of weapons of a nature to cause superfluous injury or unnecessary suffering. In: MacDonald A, Kleffner JK, Toebes BCA (eds) Depleted uranium weapons and international law: a precautionary approach. T.M.C. Asser Press, The Hague, pp 111–124

Jeroen C. van den Boogaard is a senior legal counsel in international law at the Legal Department of the Ministry of Foreign Affairs of the Kingdom of the Netherlands. He is also lecturer and researcher at the University of Amsterdam. Former positions include that of assistant professor in military law at the Netherlands Defence Academy; Head of the International Humanitarian Law department of the Netherlands Red Cross and that of military lawyer in the Royal Netherlands Army. His main research interest is military law, particularly international humanitarian law.

All the usual caveats apply.

Chapter 15
Nuclear Weapons

Rustam Atadjanov

Contents

15.1 Introduction 338
15.2 What is a Nuclear Weapon? 340
15.3 Existing International Legal Framework 340
    15.3.1 Use of Nuclear Weapons 341
    15.3.2 Non-proliferation of Nuclear Weapons 342
    15.3.3 Advisory Opinion of the International Court of Justice 345
15.4 Nuclear Weapons and Relevant Specific Rules and Principles of International Law 347
    15.4.1 *Jus ad bellum* 347
    15.4.2 *Jus in bello* 350
    15.4.3 International Criminal Law 354
    15.4.4 International Human Rights Law 358
15.5 Conclusion 361
References 363

Abstract The phrase "weapons of mass destruction" encompasses, among others, nuclear, atomic or radioactive weapons. This chapter deals with pertaining legal issues related to nuclear weapons. It starts with defining the main object of the review, i.e., what is meant by "nuclear weapons" followed by the discussion of the existing international and regional legal frameworks as well as applicable case law. It also looks at different areas of international law which pertain to the use and/or testing of nuclear weapons and considers relevant legal principles and rules as to their application to nuclear weapons. The main conclusion advanced by this chapter will be that the negative consequences flowing out of the potential use of nuclear arsenals outweigh any possible—real or perceived, benefits (including security considerations) of storing nuclear weapons in any state's possession.

Keywords Nuclear weapons · Weapons of mass destruction · International law · *Jus ad bellum* · *Jus in bello* · Principles of IHL · International criminal law · International human rights law

---

R. Atadjanov (✉)
KIMEP University, Almaty, Kazakhstan

© T.M.C. ASSER PRESS and the authors 2022
S. Sayapin et al. (eds.), *International Conflict and Security Law*,
https://doi.org/10.1007/978-94-6265-515-7_15

15.1 Introduction

Few issues have ever captured people's attention and entailed such heated and often controversial debates for decades in the modern human history to the same extent as have the problem of nuclear weapons' use and testing. Even after the end of the Cold War the famous phrase "weapons of mass destruction" continues to serve first of all as a reference to nuclear, atomic or radioactive weapons even though it is not limited only to this type of weapons but also covers chemical and biological weapons.[1] Despite the countless invocations of the emotionally strong and resonating term "nuclear weapons" in public discourse the effects caused by the potential detonation of nuclear weapon devices still appear to be either misunderstood, or underappreciated, or even simply ignored by politicians or other key decision makers in dealings between states as evidenced by recent developments in international politics.

Notwithstanding the fact that historically this type of weapon of mass destruction has been used in actual hostilities only once, it was enough to potently demonstrate the terrible consequences of even its one single employment. The names of Hiroshima, Nagasaki and Semipalatinsk stand for the horrors of the new technology—even if the latter name has no such resonance and has largely been forgotten compared to the first two.[2] However, the existing large stockpiles of nuclear weapons in some countries of the world indicate that the dangers associated with preserving, maintaining, testing and ultimately employing them have not yet been sufficiently understood or reckoned with.

Nuclear weapons raise fundamental issues which go to the very heart of international law. More than that, the threat of potential and/or actual use and/or testing these weapons closely involves several questions that go beyond law and remain as topical today as they had been during the second half of the 20th century after the end of the "Manhattan Project". Such issues include but are not limited to humanitarian, political and philosophical problems.

The first category is due to the grave consequences entailed by the explosion of nuclear weapons affecting human health and environment, often irreversibly, and

---

[1] While there is no treaty or customary international law that contains an authoritative definition of "weapons of mass destruction" one may be guided by the early broad definition offered in 1948 by the United Nations Commission for Conventional Armaments according to which the term includes "atomic explosive weapons, radioactive material weapons, lethal chemical and biological weapons, and any weapons developed in the future which have characteristics comparable in destructive effect to those of the atomic bomb or other weapons mentioned." Tannenwald 2003, p. 4. The phrase itself has appeared due to the existence of atomic bombs. See for the instructive analysis and review of the history of weapons of mass destruction Davis and Purcell 2006, pp. 3 *et seq.* For a discussion of chemical and biological weapons in international law and ICSL, see Chap. 14 by Van den Boogaard.

[2] Yet nowhere else in the world was there such a big concentration of nuclear explosions in one place over such a long period (40 years). The Soviet Union conducted 456 nuclear tests at Semipalatinsk from 1949 until 1989 with little regard for their effect on the local people or environment. The full impact of radiation exposure was hidden for many years by the Soviet authorities and has only come to light since the test site closed in 1991. It is believed that a total of 700,000 people were eventually affected by those explosions.

making a proper humanitarian response almost impossible.[3] The second category of problems is related to the political and security-related nature of the real or potential use of nuclear weapons: according to some authors, the fabric of the world's security politics as it has evolved since 1945 has made it very difficult to discuss nuclear weapons as weapons *per se* rather than overpowering political and security issue.[4] That includes a significant link between these weapons and five permanent members of the UN Security Council.[5] It appears to be accepted as a truism of contemporary international politics and practice that any state in possession of nuclear arsenal(s) would have a powerful leverage in its external policy dialogues and dealings with other state subjects of international law. The last, third category lies on the philosophical plane and involves, or rather invites reflection, *inter alia*, on such questions as the ability of humankind to build the most destructive types of weapons capable of annihilating the whole human race on the planet and what it says about the human nature which uses its most potent instrument, i.e., its mind, for the act of extermination instead of creation.

All of these serious issues are related to legal aspects of nuclear weapons. That first of all includes the regulation and most importantly the (universal and effective) prohibition of their use under applicable law. This chapter deals with pertaining legal issues related to nuclear weapons. It starts with defining the main object of the review, i.e., what is meant by "nuclear weapons" followed by the discussion of the existing international and regional legal frameworks as well as applicable case law. The most authoritative judicial decision to date, the famous Advisory Opinion on the Legality of the Threat or Use of Nuclear Weapons issued by the UN International Court of Justice in 1996 will briefly be discussed. The subsequent section looks at different areas of international law which pertain to the use and/or testing of nuclear weapons and considers relevant legal principles and rules as to their application to nuclear weapons.[6] The main conclusion advanced by this chapter will be that despite the existence of the claims to the effect that the very keeping of nuclear arsenals and maintaining them constitutes a necessary evil to sustain a fragile peace in today's world and avoid total war,[7] the negative consequences flowing out of their potential use outweigh any possible—real or perceived, benefits (including security considerations) of storing nuclear weapons in any state's possession.

---

[3] For a discussion of the effects of the use of nuclear weapons observed after the occurrence of actual or potential attacks especially in Hiroshima and Nagasaki, see Nystuen et al. 2014, pp. 4–8; Kristensen and McKinzie 2015, pp. 593–597; Maresca and Mitchell 2015, pp. 623–626.

[4] Nystuen et al. 2014, pp. 1–2.

[5] Ibid.

[6] These corpora of law include only those that appear as the most relevant ones for the purposes of ICSL or those that have a strong humanitarian component. This leaves out other pertaining branches (e.g., international disarmament law or international environmental law), not because their being less relevant which is certainly not the case but simply for reasons of limited space.

[7] See Ryan Woods, "Nuclear Weapons: A Necessary Evil?", 16 January 2016, available at: http://theorbital.co.uk/nuclear-weapons-a-necessary-evil/ Accessed 30 April 2019; Jay Nordlinger, "No Nukes, They Say", 30 October 2017, available at: https://www.nationalreview.com/magazine/2017/10/30/nuclear-weapons-deterrence-necessary-evil/ Accessed 15 March 2021.

15.2 What is a Nuclear Weapon?

Before proceeding to the main analysis in the chapter it makes sense first to define the main term. This is so for the purposes of clarity and the need to distinguish between nuclear weapons and other types of weapons of mass destruction. The following definition appears to serve these purposes well: nuclear weapons are devices in which most or all of the explosive energy is derived from fission (splitting of an atom into two or more parts), fusion (joining or fusing two atoms to form a heavier single atom) or a combination of the two.[8] The first type, i.e., "fission weapons" are represented by the simplest nuclear weapons often called "atomic bombs" while the second type incorporates a more sophisticated boosted or thermonuclear weapons more commonly known as "hydrogen bombs".[9]

Nuclear weapons may be distinguished from other types of weapons of mass destruction by two important characteristics. First, the amount of explosive energy and heat energy unleashed by their detonation is enormous and can exact more thorough physical damage over a wider area than any other non-nuclear weapon of comparable size. And second, the radioactivity dispersed through the detonation of nuclear weapons, causes long-term fatal illness in populations affected by the blast and poisons the attacked land for a very long period of time.[10]

15.3 Existing International Legal Framework

There is currently no comprehensive prohibition of the use of nuclear weapons in international law. It appears accurate to suggest that the current international legal regime: (1) seeks to *prevent the use and testing* of nuclear weapons, save in the very extreme circumstances of self-defence, in which the very survival of a State would be at stake, and regulates the use of nuclear technologies for peaceful purposes; (2) seeks to *prevent the proliferation* of nuclear weapons beyond a very limited circle of States which already possess them.

The next two subsections represent a general listing and brief overview of the key major (multilateral) treaties[11] which either prohibit or limit the use and/or testing of

---

[8] Davis and Purcell 2006, p. 4.

[9] Ibid.

[10] Ibid.

[11] The list is not exhaustive; it contains the existing adopted treaties between multiple state parties and excludes the draft or model instruments such as, e.g., the Convention on the Prohibition of the Development, Testing, Production, Stockpiling, Transfer, Use and Threat of Use of Nuclear Weapons and on Their Elimination (the so-called "Model Nuclear Weapons Convention"). It also does not include the existing bilateral treaties and agreements concluded between nuclear states, for example, between the United States and the Russian Federation (or the former USSR). Finally, the nuclear arms limitation treaties, for example, the Treaty on Principles Governing the Activities of States in the Exploration and Use of Outer Space, Including the Moon and Other Celestial Bodies, or Outer Space Treaty, do not figure in the overview for reasons of space or direct relevance.

15 Nuclear Weapons

nuclear weapons (Sect. 15.3.1), or aim at securing their non-proliferation, either internationally or at the regional level (Sect. 15.3.2). The last subsection in this part of the chapter deals with a key international judicial decision on nuclear weapons; without considering it no international legal discussion would be deemed comprehensive.

15.3.1 Use of Nuclear Weapons

The UN Treaty on the Prohibition of Nuclear Weapons (TPNW), adopted in 2017: the treaty includes a comprehensive set of prohibitions on participating in any nuclear weapon activities.[12] Those activities include undertakings not to develop, produce, test, acquire, possess, stockpile, use or threaten to use nuclear weapons. The instrument also prohibits the deployment of nuclear weapons on national territory and the provision of assistance to any State in the conduct of prohibited activities. States parties will be obliged to suppress and prevent any activity prohibited under the TPNW undertaken by persons or on territory under its jurisdiction or control.[13] In total fifty instruments of ratification (accession, acceptance or approval) are needed in order for the Treaty to enter into force.

Comprehensive Nuclear Test Ban Treaty (CTBT), adopted in 1996: the CTBT bans all nuclear explosions on Earth whether for military or for peaceful purposes.[14] It comprises of a preamble, 17 articles, two annexes and a Protocol with two annexes. The Treaty prohibits States Parties from carrying out any nuclear explosion. It also prohibits any encouragement of or participation in the carrying out of any nuclear explosion and establishes a Comprehensive Nuclear-Test-Ban Treaty Organization in Vienna to ensure the Treaty's implementation. It has not yet entered into force due to the absence of ratification of eight specific states.

Treaty Banning Nuclear Weapon Tests in the Atmosphere, in Outer Space and Under Water (Partial Nuclear Test Ban Treaty, or PTBT), adopted and entered into force in 1963: the PTBT prohibits nuclear weapons tests or any other nuclear explosion in the atmosphere, in outer space, and under water.[15] While not banning tests underground, the Treaty does prohibit nuclear explosions in this environment if they cause "radioactive debris to be present outside the territorial limits of the State under whose jurisdiction or control" the explosions were conducted. In accepting limitations on testing, the nuclear powers accepted as a common goal "an end to the contamination of man's environment by radioactive substances."

---

[12] See Lito 2018, pp. 347–357.

[13] Ibid.

[14] Comprehensive Nuclear-Test-Ban Treaty, opened for signature 24 September 1996, full text available at https://treaties.un.org/doc/Treaties/1997/09/19970910%2007-37%20AM/Ch_XXVI_04p.pdf. Accessed 15 March 2021.

[15] Treaty Banning Nuclear Weapon Tests in the Atmosphere, in Outer Space and Under Water, opened for signature 8 August 1963, entered into force 10 October 1963, full text available at http://disarmament.un.org/treaties/t/test_ban/text. Accessed 15 March 2021.

International Convention for the Suppression of Acts of Nuclear Terrorism (Nuclear Terrorism Convention, or NTC), adopted in 2005, entered into force in 2007: the NTC is designed to criminalise acts of nuclear terrorism and to promote police and judicial cooperation to prevent, investigate and punish those acts.[16] The Convention covers a broad range of acts and possible targets, including nuclear power plants and nuclear reactors; covers threats and attempts to commit such crimes or to participate in them, as an accomplice; stipulates that offenders shall be either extradited or prosecuted; encourages States to cooperate in preventing terrorist attacks by sharing information and assisting each other in connection with criminal investigations and extradition proceedings; and deals with both crisis situations, assisting States to solve the situations and post-crisis situations by rendering nuclear material safe through the International Atomic Energy Agency (IAEA).

Treaty on the Limitation of Underground Nuclear Weapon Tests, or Threshold Test Ban Treaty, adopted in 1976, entered into force in 1990: this treaty prohibits tests having a yield greater than 150 kilotons; this eliminates the possibility of testing new or existing weapons with a yield greater than a fraction of a megaton.[17] Its protocol sets forth the verification procedures; the States parties oblige themselves to continue negotiations towards a Comprehensive Nuclear Test Ban Treaty (see above).[18]

Even a brief look at these instruments above demonstrates that those which prohibit the use or the threat to use nuclear weapons have not yet entered into force (TPNW and CTBT but not NTC) as compared to those which ban nuclear weapons tests (PTBT and Threshold Test Ban Treaty). One may speculate as to the causes behind this state of affairs but it appears reasonable to suggest that here the political factor (problem) plays a crucial role: the nuclear weapons States are simply not ready to abandon their nukes and hence risk losing a powerful political influence that those provide in today's world dominated by the *Realpolitik*. The situation turns out quite different for various proliferation regimes established by universal AND regional treaties as can be seen below.

15.3.2 Non-proliferation of Nuclear Weapons

<u>Universal regime (not limited to a particular area or geographical region)</u>

Treaty on the Non-Proliferation of Nuclear Weapons (Nuclear Non-Proliferation Treaty, or NPT), adopted in 1968, entered into force in 1970: the NPT aims to prevent the spread of nuclear weapons and weapons technology, to foster the peaceful

---

[16] International Convention for the Suppression of Acts of Nuclear Terrorism, opened for signature 14 September 2005, 2445 U.N.T.S. 89 (entered into force 7 July 2007).

[17] Treaty Between The United States of America and The Union of Soviet Socialist Republics on the Limitation of Underground Nuclear Weapon Tests (and Protocol Thereto), signed at Moscow 3 July 1974, entered into force 11 December 1990, full text available at: https://www.state.gov/t/isn/5204.htm. Accessed 15 March 2021; Davis and Purcell 2006, p. 91.

[18] Ibid.

15 Nuclear Weapons

uses of nuclear energy, and to further the goal of disarmament.[19] The Treaty establishes a safeguards system under the responsibility of the International Atomic Energy Agency (IAEA), which also plays a central role under the Treaty in areas of technology transfer for peaceful purposes.

Regional nuclear weapon free zones

These treaties in general prohibit the manufacture, production, possession, testing, acquisition, receipt and deployment of nuclear weapons within the zone. They therefore represent an important reinforcement to the NPT. They also have an effect of barring deployment by the nuclear weapon states, therefore precluding arrangements like the one between NATO and the United States in which the US nuclear bombs are deployed in NATO countries. They, further, contribute to confidence-building and consensus in the region they cover.

Treaty for the Prohibition of Nuclear Weapons in Latin America (Tlatelolco Treaty), adopted in 1967, entered into force in 1968: under the Treaty, the states parties agree to prohibit and prevent the "testing, use, manufacture, production or acquisition by any means whatsoever of any nuclear weapons" and the "receipt, storage, installation, deployment and any form of possession of any nuclear weapons".[20] There are two additional protocols to the Treaty: Protocol I binds those overseas countries with territories in the region (the United States, the United Kingdom, France, and the Netherlands) to the terms of the Treaty. Protocol II requires the world's declared nuclear weapons states to refrain from undermining in any way the nuclear-free status of the region.

South Pacific Nuclear Free Zone Treaty (Rarotonga Treaty), adopted in 1985, entered into force in 1986: the treaty formalizes a nuclear-weapon-free zone in the South Pacific.[21] It bans the use, testing, and possession of nuclear weapons within the borders of the zone. There are three protocols to the Treaty: (1) no manufacture, stationing or testing in their territories within the Zone; (2) no use against the Parties to the Treaty, or against territories where Protocol 1 is in force, and (3) no testing within the Zone.

Southeast Asian Nuclear Weapon Free Zone Treaty (Treaty of Bangkok), adopted in 1995, entered into force in 1997: the treaty obliges its State parties not to develop,

---

[19] Treaty on the Non-Proliferation of Nuclear Weapons (NPT), opened for signature 1 July 1968, entered into force 5 March 1970, full text available at https://www.un.org/disarmament/wmd/nuc lear/npt/text. Accessed 15 March 2021.

[20] Treaty for the Prohibition of Nuclear Weapons in Latin America and the Caribbean, opened for signature 14 February 1967, entered into force 22 April 1968, full text available at http://disarm ament.un.org/treaties/t/tlatelolco/text. Accessed 15 March 2021.

[21] South Pacific Nuclear Free Zone Treaty, signed 6 August 1985, entered into force 11 December 1986, full text available at http://disarmament.un.org/treaties/t/rarotonga/text. Accessed 15 March 2021.

manufacture or otherwise acquire, possess or have control over nuclear weapons.[22] It includes a protocol that is open to signature by the five recognized nuclear-weapon states: China, France, Russia, the United Kingdom, and the United States. The protocol commits those states not to contribute to any violation of the treaty and not to use or threaten to use nuclear weapons within the zone.

African Nuclear Weapon Free Zone Treaty (Treaty of Pelindaba), adopted in 1996, entered into force in 2009: the treaty prohibits the research, development, manufacture, stockpiling, acquisition, testing, possession, control or stationing of nuclear explosive devices in the territory of parties to the Treaty and the dumping of radioactive wastes in the African zone by Treaty parties.[23] It also prohibits any attack against nuclear installations in the zone by Treaty parties and requires them to maintain the highest standards of physical protection of nuclear material, facilities and equipment, which are to be used exclusively for peaceful purposes. The instrument has three Protocols.

Treaty on a Nuclear-Weapon-Free Zone in Central Asia (CANWFZ), signed at Semipalatinsk, Kazakhstan in 2006, entered into force in 2009, with the Government of Kyrgyzstan acting as the treaty depositary: this instrument establishes a nuclear-weapon-free zone in Central Asia and represents a legally binding commitment by all five countries of the region, i.e., Kazakhstan, Kyrgyzstan, Tajikistan, Turkmenistan, and Uzbekistan not to manufacture, acquire, test, or possess nuclear weapons.[24] The treaty was adopted at a symbolic former nuclear Test Site of Semipalatinsk in Kazakhstan; it is also known as the Treaty of Semipalatinsk (or Treaty of Semey). All five states of Central Asia have ratified the instrument.

While the existence of these important instruments shows that effectively all the geographical regions of the world are covered by several active non-proliferation regimes a case-law concerning nuclear weapons is, by contrast, non-existent which is, of course, explained by the fortunate fact that there has been only one recourse to an actual employment of nuclear weapons in human history. The only exception is the famous ruling by the United Nations' main international judicial body.

---

[22] Treaty on the Southeast Asia Nuclear Weapon-Free Zone, opened for signature 8 September 2006, entered into force 21 March 2009, full text available at http://disarmament.un.org/treaties/t/canwfz/text. Accessed 15 March 2021.

[23] African Nuclear Weapon Free Zone Treaty, signed at Cairo 11 April 1996, entered into force 15 July 2009, full text available at http://disarmament.un.org/treaties/t/pelindaba/text. Accessed 15 March 2021.

[24] Treaty on a Nuclear-Weapon-Free Zone in Central Asia, opened for signature and signed 8 September 2006, entered into force 21 March 2009, full text available at http://disarmament.un.org/treaties/t/canwfz/text. Accessed 15 March 2021.

15.3.3 Advisory Opinion of the International Court of Justice

In July 1996, in response to a 1994 request from the United Nations General Assembly,[25] the International Court of Justice (ICJ) handed down an Advisory Opinion on the Legality of the Threat or Use of Nuclear Weapons[26]—the most authoritative (although somewhat controversial) judicial interpretation of the issue to date. The Court's findings can be summarised as follows:

1. A threat or use of force by means of nuclear weapons in violation of Articles 2(4) [prohibition of the threat or use of force] and 51 [the right of individual or collective self-defence] of the UN Charter is, as such, unlawful;[27]
2. Nuclear weapons should not be equated with chemical or biological weapons, which are prohibited by relevant treaties. These treaties do not contain any specific prohibition of recourse to nuclear weapons;
3. The treaties regulating the acquisition, manufacture and possession of nuclear weapons might suggest that a comprehensive prohibition of the use of nuclear weapons might be feasible in the future but these treaties do not currently constitute such a prohibition by themselves;
4. A threat or use of nuclear weapons should be compatible with the requirements of the international law applicable in armed conflict, particularly those of the principles and rules of international humanitarian law, as well as with specific obligations under treaties and other undertakings which expressly deal with nuclear weapons;
5. Since ensuring the compatibility of a threat or use of nuclear weapons with international humanitarian law would be hardly feasible as a matter of practice, such threat or use would generally be contrary to the rules of international law applicable in armed conflict, and in particular the principles and rules of humanitarian law;[28]

---

[25] The ICJ disregarded an analogous request from the World Health Organisation (WHO), having ruled that the WHO had acted *ultra vires* in submitting the request.

[26] ICJ, *Legality of the Threat or Use of Nuclear Weapons*, Advisory Opinion, 8 July 1996, I.C.J. Reports 1996 (*Nuclear Weapons Advisory Opinion*).

[27] *Nuclear Weapons Advisory Opinion*, para 105(2)(C).

[28] The President of the International Committee of the Red Cross (ICRC) Peter Maurer has highlighted the relevance of international humanitarian law with regard to nuclear weapons in his statement at http://www.icrc.org/eng/resources/documents/statement/2013/13-03-04-nuclear-weapons.htm. Accessed 15 March 2021.

6. Finally, the Court acknowledged that there existed an obligation for States to pursue in good faith and bring to a conclusion negotiations leading to nuclear disarmament in all its aspects under strict and effective international control.

This judicial decision currently represents the most authoritative and referential legal opinion on the matter to date.[29] It represents a first decision by an international tribunal that has unequivocally and clearly formulated limitations on nuclear weapons; it declared that nuclear weapons are subject to the requirements of the UN Charter as well as international law applicable to armed conflicts.[30] Moreover, the Court has reaffirmed the celebrated Martens' Clause concluding that the rules of humanitarian law were applicable to the threat or use of nuclear weapons because of the intrinsically humanitarian character of these rules which is applicable to all forms and types of warfare and weapons.[31]

However, it was not uncontroversial. Several expectations from the Court's Advisory Opinion have not been lived up to by the ICJ. First, the Opinion did not elaborate in detail on the *jus cogens* nature of humanitarian law as was hoped by international community. The judges opted to confine themselves to the conclusion that since the question of the character of humanitarian law which would apply to the use of nuclear weapons had not been raised in the General Assembly's request there was no need for the Court to pronounce on this matter.[32]

Second, the Court was further criticized for its eventual inability to definitively conclude whether the threat or use of nuclear weapons would be lawful or unlawful in an extreme circumstance of self-defence when the very survival of the State would be at stake.[33] Some believe that the Court should have concluded that ANY use of nuclear weapons is unlawful under international law, in particular under *jus in bello*.[34] One possible explanation could be that the Court was reluctant to "make new law" and pronounce it in an area which concerns the vital interests of some powerful, nuclear weapon-possessing States, choosing to stay cautious and politically pragmatic in its Opinion's reasoning.[35] In any case, no matter how prudent the Court turned out to act in this particular case, the perception of many progressive observers was that it failed to exploit this great opportunity to clarify applicable international law with respect to the most destructive type of modern weapons.

This, of course, does not undermine the significance of the impact this decision has had on the development of several important branches of international law—from

---

[29] For a useful analysis of various substantive aspects of the Advisory Opinion as well as its impact see the following legal works and pieces: Davis and Purcell 2006, pp. 109–112; Moxley et al. 2011, pp. 637–642; Nystuen et al. 2014, pp. 24–27, 32–50, 68–73, 136–140 and others; Shaw 2008, pp. 1112, 1303–1308.

[30] Aljaghoub 2006, p. 197.

[31] *Nuclear Weapons Advisory Opinion*, p. 259, para 85; Aljaghoub 2006, p. 196. See also further below in Sect. 15.4.2.

[32] *Nuclear Weapons Advisory Opinion*, p. 258, para 83.

[33] Ibid., p. 266, para 105(2)(E).

[34] Aljaghoub 2006, p. 198.

[35] Ibid.

international humanitarian law to international human rights law to international environmental law. Certainly, the measure with which to assess that impact should not be determined by the number of those branches—or by the quantity of the Court's opinions affecting them, for that matter.[36] It has to be the quality and persuasiveness of its statements in those opinions as well as of its reflections dealing with international law. In case of nuclear weapons, the Court's pronouncements are persuasive albeit still controversial.

15.4 Nuclear Weapons and Relevant Specific Rules and Principles of International Law

This section considers various areas of international law that deal with the use of nuclear weapons and briefly analyses the pertaining legal principles and rules as to their application to this category of weapons. It is important because their use involves or calls into question simultaneously multiple sets of rules and differing regimes of law. Some of them concern a direct use of nuclear weapons (*jus ad bellum, jus in bello*) while others look more closely at how such use might entail an individual criminal responsibility as a type of a crime under international law (international criminal law) or may affect people's rights and freedoms (international human rights law).

15.4.1 Jus ad bellum

As nuclear weapons represent the most destructive type of weapons invented by mankind to date, it seems only logical that the matter of prohibiting or regulating their use must fall, first of all, under the ambit of *jus ad bellum*, the body of law dealing with the lawfulness of use of force.[37] This includes the classical example of employing those weapons by states in self-defense against other states. Modern *jus ad bellum* limits the use of force in self-defense only to the situations in which an armed attack took place as established by the United Nations Charter.[38] The key

---

[36] Ibid., p. 200.

[37] For the discussion of the legal regulation of the use of force, see Chap. 6 by Bakircioglu.

[38] Charter of the United Nations, opened for signature 26 June 1945, 1 U.N.T.S. XVI (entered into force 24 October 1945), Article 51. The article states: "Nothing in the present Charter shall impair the inherent right of individual or collective self-defence if an armed attack occurs against a Member of the United Nations, until the Security Council has taken measures necessary to maintain international peace and security. Measures taken by Members in the exercise of this right of self-defence shall be immediately reported to the Security Council and shall not in any way affect the authority and responsibility of the Security Council under the present Charter to take at any time such action as it deems necessary in order to maintain or restore international peace and security." According to the interpretations in the relevant jurisprudence, the concept of "armed attack" as

principles of the law on the use of force which concern using nuclear weapons in self-defense are the principle of necessity and principle of proportionality.[39]

One might think that because of their indiscriminate nature the use of nuclear weapons can be neither necessary nor proportionate[40] hence rendering the discussion of the two principles irrelevant. But the situation is more complicated than that. This is due to the character of *jus ad bellum*—this corpus of law does not mention any types of weapons specifically, i.e., it is weapon-neutral, as well as to the fact that it does not contain an absolute prohibition of the use of force; it does authorize some limited force in the situations of self-defense provided that the necessary conditions are met.[41] Thus, whether the use of these weapons may be considered lawful under international law or not depends on the concrete circumstances and respect for the two above-said principles.[42]

According to Hayashi, the requirement to respect both principles of necessity and proportionality *ad bellum* in ANY use of force in self-defense nowadays appears uncontroversial.[43] However, the problematic aspects with applying the two principles include, inter alia, ambiguities related to their assessment (content, timing, duration) and separation between the two.[44] The commentators agree on few basic uncontroversial ideas; those include the requirement that self-defense must not be retaliatory and/or punitive and that the main aim of self-defense should be to halt and repel an attack.[45]

The principle of necessity in *jus ad bellum* denotes the requirement that there must be no reasonable alternative to using force.[46] Generally, it means that the law on the use of force, via its principle of necessity, concerns the circumstances in which the state exercising its right to self-defense may lawfully use force.[47] It is safe to maintain that necessity requires the defending state to use force only as a means of last resort.[48]

---

implied in the Charter includes the considerations of scale and effects but not the specific types of weapons used in the attack. See Nystuen et al. 2014, p. 16.

[39] Not to be confused with the principles of military necessity and proportionality that belong to the main principles of LoAC, i.e., law of armed conflict. Those are considered in the next subsection, within the context of *jus in bello*.

[40] Nystuen et al. 2014, p. 15.

[41] Ibid.; *Nuclear Weapons Advisory Opinion*, para 41.

[42] Nystuen et al. 2014, p. 15.

[43] Ibid., p. 17, citing *Nuclear Weapons Advisory Opinion*, para 41, ICJ, *Case Concerning Military and Paramilitary Activities in and against Nicaragua*, Judgment of 27 June 1986, para 195 (*Nicaragua Case*), and other relevant ICJ case-law.

[44] According to Greenwood, these difficulties mirror even larger differences with regard to *jus ad bellum*'s temporal scope of application. Greenwood 1983, pp. 221–234; Nystuen et al. 2014, p. 17.

[45] Gray 2008, p. 150; Green 2009, p. 89, both also cited in Nystuen et al. 2014, p. 17.

[46] Nystuen et al. 2014, pp. 17–18.

[47] Ibid., p. 17.

[48] For a detailed analysis of the problematic issues related to the application of the principle of necessity in *jus ad bellum* such as, e.g., imminence of attack, immediacy of force, and others, see ibid., pp. 18–21.

15 Nuclear Weapons

As for the proportionality, this principle may be summarized—in a two-fold format—as follows:[49] first, the force used in self-defense should be assessed in light of the fulfillment of defensive purposes, and second, the quantum of the former should not be obviously excessive, rather than strictly proportionate, vis-à-vis the latter.[50] Leaving aside a detailed discussion of the nature of the variables compared in the proportionality test and temporal scope of assessment,[51] this author concurs with Hayashi and other experts that the principle of proportionality in *jus ad bellum* must be subject to constant assessment[52]—as opposed to a fixed moment or retroactive assessment[53] (this is because the circumstances of self-defense may fluctuate from moderate to extreme, and hence the response to those fluctuations MUST be as much proportionate and reasonable as possible).

Now, applying these principles to the use of force by means of nuclear weapons, one may want to consult the Advisory Opinion of the ICJ for any guidance. As the reader recalls, the Court unanimously held that "a threat or use of force by means of nuclear weapons ... that fails to meet all the requirements of Article 51 [of the UN Charter] is unlawful."[54] She/he might also remember that the ICJ was unable to definitively conclude whether the threat or use of nuclear weapons would be lawful or unlawful in an extreme circumstance of self-defence when the very survival of the State would be at stake. However, aside from this principal matter, the Court has also, unfortunately, not dwelled much on the principles of necessity and proportionality. The first one is noted in the Opinion only once, and very briefly at that.[55] Regarding proportionality, the Court concluded that the principle of proportionality may not in itself exclude the use of nuclear weapons in self-defense in all circumstances.[56]

Thus, the Advisory Opinion does not bring much clarity in terms of how these principles relate to the use of nuclear weapons, in particular, to the notion of necessity and proportionality having a weapon-neutral nature as well as to the idea that the peculiarities of nuclear weapons are relevant for the *jus ad bellum* only incidentally.[57] A more preferable (as well as humanitarian and realistic) stance, however, would be that those peculiarities have to be taken into account in analyzing the appropriateness of using nuclear weapons.[58]

---

[49] This is with the understanding that such a summarization is rather simplified for reasons of space.

[50] Nystuen et al. 2014, p. 23.

[51] See ibid., pp. 21–24, for such discussion.

[52] Ibid., p. 24; Gardam 1993, p. 404; Gardam 1999, pp. 280–281; Gardam 2004, pp. 167–168; Gazzini 2005, p. 147.

[53] Dinstein 2011, p. 262.

[54] *Nuclear Weapons Advisory Opinion*, para 105(2)(C).

[55] Ibid., para 41.

[56] Ibid., paras 42–43.

[57] Nystuen et al. 2014, p. 25.

[58] See ibid., pp. 25–30, for a more detailed discussion of this position including such issues as "double necessity", extreme circumstance of self-defense, assurances of non-use and others.

It may be—disappointingly—concluded that due to the very nature of the existing *jus ad bellum* the prospect of comprehensively outlawing the use[59] of nuclear weapons appears rather limited; the reasons for this being, as suggested by Hayashi, the fact that this corpus of law concerns itself with the function of force rather than its form as well as that the possibility of nuclear weapons being used in compliance with the principles of necessity and proportionality cannot be completely ruled out under all possible foreseeable circumstances.[60] At this point, the question could be: does the situation differ with another body of law also concerning this matter, i.e., *jus in bello* (the law of armed conflict)?

15.4.2 **Jus in bello**

Another body of law directly relevant to the issue of the use of nuclear weapons is *jus in bello*, or the law of armed conflict (LoAC), also often referred to as international humanitarian law (IHL).[61] It may be defined as a set of rules which seek for humanitarian reasons to limit the negative effects of armed conflict—as formulated by the International Committee of the Red Cross (ICRC).[62] Among the most pertaining principles of IHL here would be the principles governing the conduct of hostilities: principles of distinction, proportionality as well as the principle of humanity.[63]

The first principle, distinction, may be simply expressed as follows: combatants must distinguish between military objectives and the civilian population, and attack only military objectives.[64] It carries a customary legal nature and is applicable in both types of armed conflicts—international (IAC) and non-international (NIAC)

---

[59] Again, it must be kept in mind that the brief discussion here does not include the issue of the lawfulness of the *threat* of use of nuclear weapons under the existing regime of *jus ad bellum*.

[60] Ibid., p. 30.

[61] For a review of certain significant issues of IHL, see Chaps. 6, 12, 13, 18 and 21 within the present book.

[62] For a useful working definition of IHL see ICRC 2013, p. 13, available at: https://www.icrc.org/eng/assets/files/publications/icrc-002-4028.pdf. Accessed 15 March 2021.

[63] See for a discussion of the role and interaction of the fundamental principles and rules of IHL Nystuen et al. 2014, pp. 89–147; *passim* Larsen et al. 2013; Atadjanov 2019. For reasons of space, the discussion of some other applicable principles and issues is omitted in this chapter (e.g., unnecessary suffering, precautions in attack, reprisals under IHL, threat of use of nuclear weapons under IHL). For a useful review of those, see in general Nystuen et al. 2014, pp. 91–190.

[64] Additional Protocol I to the Geneva Conventions of 1949 establishes an official formulation of this cornerstone principle under the heading of "Basic rule": "In order to ensure respect for and protection of the civilian population and civilian objects, the Parties to the conflict shall at all times distinguish between the civilian population and combatants and between civilian objects and military objectives and accordingly shall direct their operations only against military objectives." Protocol I Additional to the Geneva Conventions of 12 August 1949 and Relating to the Protection of Victims of International Armed Conflicts, opened for signature 12 December 1977, 1125 U.N.T.S. 3-434 (entered into force 7 December 1978), Article 48 (Additional Protocol I).

15 Nuclear Weapons

conflicts.[65] It is also argued that the principle of distinction represents a *jus cogens* norm from which no derogation is permitted.[66]

The principle of distinction governs all attacks in armed conflict—offensive and defensive alike.[67] Necessity to respect IHL logically implies that, as proposed by Casey-Maslen, any weapon which is incapable of distinguishing between civilian and military targets will be unlawful.[68] The ICJ affirmed the principle of distinction as one of the fundamental rules which must be observed by all states whether or not they have ratified the conventions that contain them because they constitute intransgressible principles of international customary law.[69] While it appears that the customary law nature of the prohibition of inherently indiscriminate weapons is not challenged today, this is apparently not the case for its overall scope and especially its specific application to concrete types of weapons.[70]

The issue of uncontrolled effects of the weapons is critical when trying to apply the principle of distinction to nuclear weapons.[71] Briefly, it is difficult to see how the effects of (most) nuclear weapons can be said to be controllable.[72] It was clearly stated by the ICJ that "[t]he destructive power of nuclear weapons cannot be contained in either space or time."[73] Despite the ICJ's pronouncement, the legal opinions as well as state practice rather diverged on this matter.[74] This author is of the opinion that the uncontrollable (i.e., indiscriminate) effects should form an integral part of the distinction test which flows out from a prohibition (of the use of weapons with indiscriminate effects) that constitutes a *jus cogens* principle.[75] Those effects are just too unpredictable, with powerful radiation waves and subsequent fall-out after the explosions (peculiar to precisely this type of weapons) prone to any air movement and capable of affecting much wider areas than the initial impact point.[76] Hence any statement sustaining that nuclear weapons must not be considered as inherently indiscriminate weapons and that they can be fired with high degree accuracy will not appear credible enough.

---

[65] Nystuen et al. 2014, pp. 95–96, citing multiple sources indicating towards the customary nature of the principle as well as its applicability in both IAC and NIAC.

[66] Ibid., p. 96.

[67] Additional Protocol I, Article 49(1).

[68] Nystuen et al. 2014, pp. 96–97.

[69] *Nuclear Weapons Advisory Opinion*, para 79.

[70] Nystuen et al. 2014, p. 99.

[71] Ibid., p. 104.

[72] Ibid., p. 112; affirmed in *Nuclear Weapons Advisory Opinion*, para 35.

[73] *Nuclear Weapons Advisory Opinion*, para 35.

[74] Nystuen et al. 2014, pp. 109–110, using as evidence of relevant state practice the official US and UK statements to the effect that nuclear weapons are not inherently indiscriminate and contrasting them with the statements issued by France and Russia.

[75] See also the *Separate Opinion of the ICJ President Mohammed Bedjaoui, Nuclear Weapons Advisory Opinion*, para 21.

[76] For a description of some of those effects, see BBC, "Neutron bomb: why 'clean' is deadly", 15 July 1999, available at http://news.bbc.co.uk/2/hi/science/nature/395689.stm Accessed 15 March 2021.

Concerning the principle of proportionality, it may be defined as follows: in attacking military objectives, combatants must take measures to avoid or minimize collateral civilian damage and refrain from attacks that would cause excessive civilian damage.[77] This principle was invoked by multiple states in their assessments of whether an attack with the use of nuclear weapons would violate IHL.[78] The ICJ itself affirmed the applicability of the principle of proportionality to nuclear weapons.[79] What is unfortunate, though, is the fact that in its Advisory Opinion the Court does not discuss how the principle of proportionality in attacks applies to the use of nuclear weapons at all.[80]

Two points are to be noted. One is related to the difference between military and civilian objectives and another to the difference between *jus ad bellum* and *jus in bello*. For the first one, as correctly observed by Dinstein, proportionality has nothing to do with injury to combatants or damage to military objectives.[81] This is because even where a lawful military objective is targeted by a party to an armed conflict, such an attack may still be unlawful—if it causes incidental civilian deaths, injuries, entails destruction or damage to civilian objects, or a combination of both which are excessive when compared to the anticipated military advantage.[82] The second point involves the political problem noted in the introduction to this chapter, and it consists in the following: it is irrelevant for the purposes of IHL that a use of nuclear weapons, as noted by Casey-Maslen, by one party to a conflict may quickly lead to an escalation in the use of those weapons.[83] That is definitely a crucial political as well as moral consideration; it pertains to *jus ad bellum* since it constitutes an element in determining proportionality under that legal regime. However, it is not a strictly legal consideration which could be relevant for *jus in bello*.[84]

The question to be answered as concerns the applicability of the proportionality principle to the use of nuclear weapons would be: are nuclear weapons inherently disproportionate in the harm they cause to civilians and thus violate the principle of proportionality? A realistic stance dictates that while there is a strong temptation to

---

[77] See *passim* Larsen et al. 2013; also Atadjanov 2019. The principle of proportionality in attack is codified in the Additional Protocol I as follows: "... Among others, the following types of attacks are to be considered as indiscriminate: ... an attack which may be expected to cause incidental loss of civilian life, injury to civilians, damage to civilian objects, or a combination thereof, which would be excessive in relation to the concrete and direct military advantage anticipated. ..." Additional Protocol I, Article 51(5)(b). It is repeated almost verbatim in the Protocol's Article 57(2)(a)(iii), in the context of precautions to be taken in attack.

[78] In their submissions to the ICJ in the Nuclear Weapons Case, see Henckaerts and Doswald-Beck 2005, p. 48.

[79] *Nuclear Weapons Advisory Opinion*, para 140.

[80] This is all the more surprising as the issue was raised by several states in their statements to the ICJ. See Nystuen et al. 2014, p. 117.

[81] Dinstein 2010, p. 129.

[82] Nystuen et al. 2014, p. 114.

[83] See ibid.

[84] Ibid. For a deserving analysis of the issue of nuclear weapons and separation between these two bodies of law, see ibid., pp. 59–88.

count nukes as inherently disproportionate as it is the case for their indiscriminate nature it would be more appropriate to sustain that that is not the case. This is because there are some types of nuclear weapons which represent low-yield weapons and there are some circumstances—albeit truly exceptional, where their use would not be deemed absolutely disproportionate.

It has been argued that "it is no longer the case that use of nuclear weapons would necessarily result in the horrendous human suffering and physical damage caused by the US attacks in 1945. ..., use of small-yield tactical nuclear weapons in particular circumstances might result in minimal civilian losses."[85] But, as concluded by Casey-Maslen, only low-yield tactical nukes could realistically be used in accordance with the rule of proportionality[86] and then only in very specific and highly improbable (read: exceptional) situations in an IAC between nuclear powers.[87] In any case, it is difficult to argue against ICJ's well-known statement that any use of nuclear weapons would "generally be contrary to the rules of international law applicable in armed conflict, and in particular the principles and rules of humanitarian law."[88]

Finally, out of those principles and rules, the principle of humanity must be noted. Indeed, the inhumane and indiscriminate nature of nuclear weapons as well as the immense negative humanitarian consequences their usage causes entail the question of such weapons violating the very principle of humanity whose core, or the so-called humanitarian considerations, lies at the heart of all other key principles constituting the cornerstone of IHL's content.

The principle of humanity may be defined as follows: "the requirement that each and every individual must be treated humanely and with respect under all circumstances, out of humanitarian considerations and fundamental standards of humanity".[89] This definition relies on the concept of humaneness understood as a sentiment of active good will towards mankind, via the inclusion of "humanitarian considerations". The concept of humaneness lies at the core of those considerations which inform the key principles of humanitarian law, first of all, its principle of humanity which in turn provides the balancing basis for the other key principles of LoAC: principles of distinction and proportionality—already considered above, military necessity, and prohibition of unnecessary suffering.[90]

In all these principles, the influence and role of the humanitarian considerations derived from the concept of humaneness can be more or less easily seen. But if the use of nuclear weapons is generally contrary to the rules of international law applicable in armed conflict, in particular the principles of humanitarian law, it means that it violates them including principles of distinction and proportionality, at least in the vast majority of (potential) cases. If these principles are breached then, by

---

[85] Ibid., pp. 125–126.

[86] He also believes that these weapons cannot be deemed inherently indiscriminate but on this point I disagree, see above.

[87] Nystuen et al. 2014, p. 126. A lawful use in NIAC is even harder to imagine.

[88] *Nuclear Weapons Advisory Opinion*, para 78.

[89] See *passim* Atadjanov 2019.

[90] Ibid.

extension, their parent principle of humanity is necessarily in breach, too. Their inhumane effects make nukes incompatible with humanity. A nuclear attack will not constitute a humane and respectful "treatment" of the victims; it may not be caused out of humanitarian considerations and fundamental standards of humanity. Indeed, it would be hard to imagine how *any* armed attack involving nuclear weapons may be carried out of humanitarian considerations; it is precisely the reverse. Even if their use may not be one hundred percent, or inherently, disproportionate (in some extremely rare cases), overall they will mostly remain outside the "legality of IHL", so to speak. In that, ICJ's conclusion is outright correct.

15.4.3 International Criminal Law

Unlike the case with the preceding two subsections, this part will only partially rely on or discuss the landmark Advisory Opinion of the International Court of Justice. This is related to the nature of the material part of international criminal law (or ICL). ICL represents a functional branch of international law which includes all legal norms that deal with individual criminal responsibility for crimes under international law.[91] The material part of ICL consists of four so-called core crimes, i.e., crimes which entail a direct individual responsibility for their commission: genocide, crimes against humanity, war crimes and the crime of aggression.[92] The Nuclear Weapons Advisory Opinion almost nowhere discusses the above crimes.[93] The issue of whether nuclear weapons use would qualify as one of the core crimes was not addressed by the Court.

ICL is of relevance to this chapter because absent the outright express prohibition of the use of nuclear weapons in international treaty and customary law as a matter of *jus ad bellum* or *jus in bellum*, it is tempting to try to qualify their possible employment under the existing definitions of crimes under international law and thus bring those responsible to account. Moreover, some of those crimes were considered, at least by some states, as relevant for the purposes of legal qualification of the use of nuclear weapons under international law.[94] This was the case for genocide, for example.

The modern definition of genocide is found in the Rome Statute of the ICC which is also reflective of the customary legal nature of the prohibition of genocide in international law:

---

[91] For a useful description of ICL, see Chap. 22 by Sayapin.

[92] According to some other authorities, this list also includes torture and terrorism as individual crimes in their own standing (not only as part of *corpus delicti*, or individual acts constituting some of the core crimes). See Cassese 2013, p. 3. This chapter focuses on the first three core crimes—genocide, crimes against humanity and war crimes. The use of nuclear weapons potentially qualifying as a crime of aggression (which is clearly a relevant issue) is not considered as it would constitute a voluminous discussion and is thus excluded here for reasons of space.

[93] Except for genocide: it does mention genocide in one single paragraph but not with a view to arriving at the conclusion that the use of nuclear weapons would amount to genocide. *Nuclear Weapons Advisory Opinion*, para 26.

[94] *Nuclear Weapons Advisory Opinion*, para 26.

15 Nuclear Weapons

For the purpose of this Statute, "genocide" means any of the following acts committed with intent to destroy, in whole or in part, a national, ethnical, racial or religious group, as such:

(a)   Killing members of the group;

(b)   Causing serious bodily or mental harm to members of the group;

(c)   Deliberately inflicting on the group conditions of life calculated to bring about its physical destruction in whole or in part;

(d)   Imposing measures intended to prevent births within the group;

(e)   Forcibly transferring children of the group to another group.[95]

Taking into account the specific elements of the crime, i.e., both its *actus reus* and *mens rea*, it can be concluded that the use of nuclear weapons will not automatically or necessarily constitute the crime of genocide. Indeed, according to the ICJ, it would be possible to arrive at the conclusion that the prohibition of genocide applies to such use only if the requisite element of intent towards a group of victims as such is present; at least, that is the impression when one reads its famous Advisory Opinion.[96] In other words, it is not sufficient that the grave consequences of the employment of nuclear weapons constitute or may constitute the acts expressed in points (a) to (c) of Rome Statute's Article 6—in order to qualify as the crime of genocide. The so-called contextual element of the crime must be satisfied for that, i.e., the special intent (or *dolus specialis*) to destroy a national, etc., group as such, in whole or in part. In that, the Court's reasoning is correct. Therefore, as also correctly pointed out by the main judicial body of the UN, in order to establish this element the specific circumstances of each case should be taken into due account.[97] Also, a "simple" intent to kill is not enough; it must be proven that the perpetrator intended to destroy a group.[98]

With respect to crimes against humanity, this type of crimes under international law involves the commission of inhuman acts including murder, torture, rape, persecution and other certain acts which constitute a part of widespread or systematic attack directed against civilian population.[99] Their contemporary treaty definition is formulated in the Rome Statute as follows:

… For the purpose of this Statute, "crime against humanity" means any of the following acts when committed as part of a widespread or systematic attack directed against any civilian population, with knowledge of the attack:

(a)   Murder;

(b)   Extermination;

(c)   Enslavement;

(d)   Deportation or forcible transfer of population;

---

[95] Rome Statute of the International Criminal Court, opened for signature 17 July 1998, 2187 UNTS 90 (entered into force 1 July 2002) (Rome Statute), Article 6.

[96] *Nuclear Weapons Advisory Opinion*, para 26.

[97] Ibid.

[98] Cassese 2013, p. 65; Nystuen et al. 2014, p. 197.

[99] See also Cryer et al. 2010, p. 230.

(e) Imprisonment or other severe deprivation of physical liberty in violation of fundamental rules of international law;

(f) Torture;

(g) Rape, sexual slavery, enforced prostitution, forced pregnancy, enforced sterilization, or any other form of sexual violence of comparable gravity;

(h) Persecution against any identifiable group or collectivity on political, racial, national, ethnic, cultural, religious, gender as defined in para 3, or other grounds that are universally recognized as impermissible under international law, in connection with any act referred to in this paragraph or any crime within the jurisdiction of the Court;

(i) Enforced disappearance of persons;

(j) The crime of apartheid;

(k) Other inhumane acts of a similar character intentionally causing great suffering, or serious injury to body or to mental or physical health. ...[100]

Article 7 further contains in its paras 2 and 3 the clarifications for different terms and elements of the crimes, and for the individual acts constituting these crimes ("attack directed against any civilian population", "extermination", "enslavement", "deportation", "torture", "gender" and so on).[101] Crimes against humanity are a popular subject of both legal and non-legal discussion. Their historical development, practical application, material and mental elements, individual acts noted above, their scope, role in ICL, pertinent jurisdiction and many other aspects have been analysed countless times. Elements of crimes against humanity are well established in ICL. All the more surprising fact is that their protective scope has not yet been holistically clarified in law or academia. In other words, the exact meaning of what "humanity" means in the context of crimes against humanity is left unclear.[102]

After a brief preceding conclusion regarding genocide and use of nuclear weapons, a kin observation springs to mind. It was noted that "many acts which do not constitute genocide will constitute crimes against humanity".[103] However, this should not automatically be assumed for each and every case. As with the case of any potentially qualifying act, the so-called contextual element of these crimes should be considered. The attack must be either "widespread" or "systematic" as flows out from the *chapeau* of the definition in Article 7. The first one of these characteristics is defined as encompassing the large scale nature of the attack: it has to be massive, frequent, carried out collectively and directed against multiple victims.[104] The second one denotes, in contrast, the organized nature of the acts of violence and improbability

---

[100] Rome Statute, Article 7(1).

[101] See for a detailed discussion of those and other elements: Schabas 2010, pp. 137–187; Boot 2002, pp. 468–532; Cassese et al. 2002, pp. 373–377; Triffterer 2008, p. 117.

[102] This author provides his own academic response to this question in Atadjanov 2019, arguing that the protected interest of crimes against humanity is the concept of humanness, or human status.

[103] Cryer et al. 2010, p. 203.

[104] Nystuen et al. 2014, p. 204, n. 59, citing the Third Report of the Independent International Commission of Inquiry on the Syrian Arab Republic, UN Human Rights Council, UN Doc. A/HRC/21/50, 16 August 2012, pp. 49, para 17.

15 Nuclear Weapons

of their random occurrence; it may often be expressed through patterns of crimes.[105] Thus, like for any case involving the qualification of individual acts as crimes against humanity, in case of the use of nuclear weapons a careful analysis should be undertaken, including the establishment of the contextual element, i.e., it must be proven that the nuclear attack was either widespread or systematic in nature. Helpful in such analysis may be to look at the relevant international criminal case law where elements of crimes against humanity have been reviewed.[106]

With respect to individual acts of crimes against humanity, or *actus reus*, i.e., criminal conduct, it may be said that such acts as murder and extermination would be particularly relevant for a nuclear attack.[107] According to Cassese, provided that all other conditions for a crime against humanity were met (contextual element, mental element), a nuclear attack could be qualified as a crime against humanity of extermination in cases involving, for example, use of a "dirty bomb" by a terrorist organization or armed non-state actor if it is established that a particular population was targeted.[108] The *mens rea* element to be established would include a need to prove that the perpetrator knew that his or her actions constitute part of a pattern of widespread or systematic attacks carried out against civilian population; he or she must know that these acts fit into such a pattern.[109]

The third category of crimes under international law—war crimes—is a distinct type of crimes in that they must be connected to the context of armed conflict. They are properly defined as follows: a war crime is a serious violation of IHL which entails direct individual criminal responsibility under international law.[110] As it is discussed above, the use of nuclear weapons clearly violates as a minimum some of the key principles of *jus in bello* (see Sect. 15.4.2). It is only logical to ask the question of could it qualify as a serious breach of IHL entailing individual criminal responsibility, i.e., war crime, at least in some cases.

The answer appears to be in the affirmative. As argued by Casey-Maslen, a number of possible uses of a nuclear weapon would constitute a war crime.[111] He maintains—and it is difficult to disagree, that such a conclusion may result from the characteristics of the weapon itself, in particular whether it is deemed to be inherently indiscriminate (this chapter argues in favour of such a vision as the reader recalls) or to be of a

---

[105] Ibid., para 18.

[106] See, for example, Nystuen et al. 2014, pp. 201–205, referring to various cases before the International Criminal Tribunal for the former Yugoslavia, International Criminal Tribunal for Ruanda and ICC.

[107] Ibid., pp. 204–205.

[108] Ibid., p. 205; Cassese 2013, p.110.

[109] Cassese 2013, p.115–116.

[110] Werle and Jessberger 2014, p. 392, para 1029; Cryer et al 2010, p. 267. ICC is applying in its work a long and complicated definition established in the Rome Statute's Article 8 which names as war crimes the grave breaches of the Geneva Conventions of 1949 and other serious violations of the laws and customs applicable in international armed conflict as well as serious violations of the laws and customs applicable in non-international armed conflict, with the ensuing detailed list of individual acts constituting the crimes. Rome Statute, Article 8.

[111] See for a detailed discussion in this regard his analysis in Nystuen et al. 2014, pp. 205–210.

nature to cause superfluous injury or unnecessary suffering.[112] But even if those two characteristics are not established, a particular case of a nuclear attack may still qualify as a war crime. For example, when the weapon is directed against the civilian population in which case it definitely violates the principle of distinction, as reviewed in the preceding section, or when it is used indiscriminately.[113] What remains to be said is that in the process of assessment the following two crucial underlying conditions, or elements, have to be present—as in the case of any war crime: first, the situation of armed conflict must be present be it international or non-international in nature, and second, the pertaining conduct, in this case a nuclear attack or use of a nuclear weapon, must have a sufficient connection to such an armed conflict in order to be deemed as falling under its ambit.[114]

To summarise the foregoing brief overview, it may be safely stated that international law, in particular ICL and ICSL, has by now developed sufficiently well in order to bring to liability those individuals who may employ, or give orders to employ such deadly weapons as nuclear bombs and warheads. Certainly, for each case a careful analysis of all relevant facts and circumstances will be required; as this section demonstrated, not every use may necessarily rise to the level of a core crime (e.g., genocide). This has been confirmed by ICJ itself (reference?). This observation is important even if history does not know of any other actual use of nukes in armed conflict since the 1945 Hiroshima and Nagasaki bombings; this is because the future is uncertain. The risks of real use of nuclear weapons are present judging by the constant number of nuclear weapon states and the unstable relationship between some of those states. The ICL regime thus provides avenues for imposing individual criminal responsibility for potential perpetrators in cases of employment of nukes. As for the state responsibility, the next section contains relevant albeit brief argumentation in this regard.

15.4.4 International Human Rights Law

It would be contrary to logic to maintain that nuclear weapons' use has implications only for use of force- or armed conflict-regulating legal regimes (*jus ad bellum, jus in bello*) and/or is exclusively linked to the commission of and responsibility for international crimes (ICL). There is no doubt that international human rights law (or IHRL)[115] is clearly relevant for nuclear weapons and their use.[116] It is rightly argued that the existence of international human rights enforcement mechanisms means that the adverse effects of these weapons are directly justiciable; it is impossible

---

[112] Ibid., pp. 128–147.

[113] Ibid., p. 205.

[114] Ibid. See for a more or less detailed discussion of the use of nuclear weapons as prohibited means and methods of warfare, ibid., pp. 206–210.

[115] See Chap. 11 by O'Brien for a description of IHRL within this volume.

[116] Nystuen et al. 2014, p. 435.

15 Nuclear Weapons

to consider nuclear weapons without analysing their possible effects in the light of IHRL.[117]

IHRL may be defined as a branch of public international law which sets forth the international legal norms, rules and principles for the protection of human rights and fundamental freedoms of every individual human being.[118] These norms, rules and principles establish the legally acceptable and, ideally, enforceable minimum standards of governmental conduct to protect the inherent human dignity of human beings.[119]

The relevance of this branch, so defined, to the present issue can be seen by referring to the fact that IHRL applies, or continues to apply, during both peacetime and the time of armed conflict.[120] Although ICJ in its Advisory Opinion stated that essentially only IHL counts as concerns the use of certain weapons,[121] it then appears to have reversed its conclusion in another case where it said that both branches, i.e., IHRL and IHL (as *lex specialis*) will have to be taken into consideration.[122] What is also important, in particular in terms of enforcing human rights violated in the case of nuclear attacks, is that human rights treaty bodies have sometimes made a reference to IHL—as a means to assist in the interpretation of human rights provisions, but this has always been done to reinforce human rights protection, not to restrict it.[123] IHRL applies at all times and is therefore relevant to any use of nuclear weapons as correctly concluded by Doswald-Beck.[124]

As for the most relevant human rights and freedoms which will be affected by any nuclear attack or any use of nuclear weapons, those include the following ones: the right to life, prohibition of inhuman treatment, the right to a healthy environment, and the right to the highest attainable standard of health.[125]

The UN Human Rights Committee has made it clear that "the designing, testing, manufacture, possession and deployment of nuclear weapons are among the greatest threats to the right to life which confront mankind today."[126] While worthy of being lauded in general, this statement raises questions with respect to some aspects, for example, the manufacturing, possession and testing of nuclear weapons would not

---

[117] Ibid.

[118] Condé 2004, p. 133.

[119] Ibid., p. 134.

[120] Ibid., p. 436; Doswald-Beck 2011, pp. 6–9. This is affirmed by the terms of human rights law treaties (with war and states of emergency directly mentioned in them) as well as by the multitude of various UN resolutions. Nystuen et al. 2014, p. 436.

[121] *Nuclear Weapons Advisory Opinion*, para 25.

[122] ICJ, *Legal Consequences of the Construction of a Wall in the Occupied Palestinian Territory*, Advisory Opinion of 9 July 2004, para 106.

[123] Nystuen et al. 2014, p. 438; for more detail see Doswald-Beck 2011, pp. 109–117.

[124] Nystuen et al. 2014, p. 438.

[125] For a more comprehensive and detailed analysis of these rights as affected by nuclear weapons use, see ibid., pp. 444–456.

[126] HRCte, General Comment 14 on Article 6 ICCPR, 9 November 1984, para 4. The Committee concluded that the deployment and use of nuclear weapons must be prohibited and recognized as crimes against humanity. Ibid., para 6.

always or necessarily amount to a loss of life or even damage to health (if no radioactivity is released, for example).[127] The Committee's statement goes in line with the logic of the Dissenting Opinion of ICJ Judge Weeramantry who, in quite a solemn manner, concludes that "[n]o weapons ever invented in the long history of man's inhumanity to man has so negatived the dignity and worth of the human person as has the nuclear bomb".[128] Earlier he makes a parallel between dignity and life: "when a weapon has the potential to kill between one million and one billion people, as the WHO has told the Court, *human life becomes reduced to a level of worthlessness that totally belies human dignity* as understood in any culture" [emphasis added].[129]

Concerning the prohibition of inhuman treatment, nuclear weapons' effects on survivors (of initial blast(-s)) are significant. As is well known, they cause especially extreme suffering for their victims. As described by Doswald-Beck, such effects may include blindness for the people from seeing the first blast, horrific burns— for those not killed instantly, and/or terribly painful effects of radiation poisoning, damage to the thyroid gland, later development of cancers and other serious long-term effects.[130] Inhuman treatment is defined as that which causes severe suffering, mental or physical, which is unjustifiable, in the particular situation, and which attains a minimum level of severity.[131] The assessment will depend on the circumstances of the case such as the duration of the treatment and the victim's situation.[132] The effects of nuclear weapons use are so monstrous, much worse than those of conventional weapons, that it would be difficult to imagine any human rights treaty body which considers that their use was sufficiently justified to prevent a finding of inhuman treatment.[133]

With respect to the right to a healthy environment, the ICJ very clearly and succinctly emphasized the effects of nuclear weapons on the environment: "they have the potential to destroy ... the entire ecosystem of the planet. ...".[134] According to Doswald-Beck, this right is perfectly justiciable; human rights bodies specify that economic, social and cultural rights create at least two directly relevant obligations on states: the first is the duty to respect rights (i.e., not to take measures depriving people of their resources) and the second is to protect rights, by adopting measures to

---

[127] Nystuen et al. 2014, p. 445.

[128] *Nuclear Weapons Advisory Opinion*, Dissenting Opinion of Judge Weeramantry, Section III.10.(f).

[129] Ibid.

[130] Nystuen et al. 2014, p. 452.

[131] Ibid., para 453, citing relevant case-law of the European Commission on Human Rights and European Court of Human Rights.

[132] It is also worthy of note that inhuman treatment here is not limited only to the persons in detention. Ibid.

[133] Ibid., p. 454.

[134] *Nuclear Weapons Advisory Opinion*, para 35.

protect persons from deprivation of their resources.[135] Thus, a detonation of a nuclear weapon by a state would definitely amount to a violation of these two duties.[136]

Finally, as concerns the last human right, the right to the highest attainable standard of health, it must be noted that what is of relevance here is the damage afflicted upon the natural environment by the radiation which then negatively affects human health in the long-term. The actual use of nuclear weapons would result in the release of substances evidently harmful to human health; the disruption of medical services will be much worse than in the case of conventional weapons use; emergency response capacities and any aid whatsoever will become much more difficult to provide, with more destruction, death and harm within those services themselves.[137] Under such circumstances, it would be hardly possible to maintain that the right to the high/highest attainable standard of health is not breached by nuclear weapons attack.

15.5 Conclusion

The foregoing brief overview has demonstrated that the issue of nuclear weapons, the effects of their use as well as the related legal aspects are too broad and complex to be comprehensively tackled in one short chapter. Correspondingly, the chapter focused on the most relevant points and principles the author deemed suitable for the textbook of this format. In order to provide as clear initial picture as possible those points encompassed the description of not only the most pertinent or authoritative treaty regimes and case-law but also of applicable rules and/or principles of international law which constitute important integral parts of ICSL.

Despite the absence of a universal and unequivocal prohibition of the use of nuclear weapons in international law, it becomes clear that there are at least several well-established legal principles that will be called upon when deciding on the legality or compatibility of such use with the law. While they cannot be considered as outlawing a nuclear attack they at least will carry out a restraining function limiting for the potential attacker a space in which that use may be justified as lawful. This first of all concerns the principles of distinction and proportionality in IHL. Moreover, it is hoped that existing types of legal responsibility under international law, both individual and state, would serve as deterrent for potential abusers. At least, there do exist possibilities for international adjudication of nuclear attacks which may fall under the category of crimes under international law—provided that their *actus reus* and *mens rea* satisfy all the necessary preconditions or elements of crimes (e.g., crimes against humanity and war crimes), as well as judicial enforcement of different rights violated by the use of nuclear weapons.

---

[135] Those human rights bodies include in particular the UN Human Rights Committee. Nystuen et al. 2014, pp. 454–455, referring to the pertaining commentary.

[136] Ibid., p. 455.

[137] Ibid., p. 456.

However, the existing applicable legal rules in no way can protect or act as safeguards against a unilateral use of force involving nuclear weapons. The absence of holistic prohibition of such use remains, unfortunately, a long-standing legal gap in modern international law. The general pronouncements in the ICJ's Advisory Opinion do not fill in this gap—even if it (i.e., the Opinion) is widely regarded as important and authoritative.

Moreover, there are still arguments—both legal and non-legal, against a universal prohibition of nukes coming from various actors, first of all, states which oppose a total legal prohibition and are themselves in possession of nuclear weapons. Such arguments include the following ones: a prohibition of nuclear weapons, in and of itself, will not improve international security; a nuclear ban would be ineffective but can negatively impact or limit the NATO-members nuclear weapons-related policies; the process to ban nuclear weapons is divisive and it is not based on genuine consensus; a legal prohibition of nuclear weapons is no substitute for actual weapons reduction; the pursuit of a nuclear weapons ban undermines the Nuclear Non-Proliferation Treaty (NPT), and, finally, a "progressive and pragmatic" approach to nuclear disarmament is better than efforts to impose a comprehensive ban.[138]

All these arguments are relatively easy to dispel with; they do not withstand a careful and close scrutiny. For example, there is never a perfect time to seek nuclear disarmament, or, for that matter, world peace, end of hunger, etc; no one is advocating or would advocate for the ban in isolation from global concerns including security.[139] In fact, the whole purpose of promoting the abolition *is* to ensure international peace and security. Or, contrary to what is said above about NPT, the negotiations on the total ban represent the ultimate actual implementation of the treaty, in logic with the leading case-law on the subject.[140] Indeed, it was the ICJ which highlighted the fact that the NPT requires states not only to engage in good faith negotiations for nuclear disarmament but also to conclude them (the so-called twofold obligation).[141]

But perhaps even more importantly than that, there are considerations which if thought through profoundly and taken really seriously demonstrate that the task of complete abolition is crucial. The first one is "humanitarian case": the universal abolition and elimination of nuclear weapons is an urgent *humanitarian necessity* as it is the only one hundred percent guarantee against the catastrophic consequences of their use, and suffering and death they entail as well as the impossibility of any effective humanitarian response.[142] The second is the "security case" already partly delineated above. Nuclear weapons pose a direct and constant threat to people everywhere; while it is clear that they only cause national and global insecurity some

---

[138] Cesar Jaramillo, "Six deceptive arguments against a nuclear weapons ban", 31 March 2017, available at https://www.opencanada.org/features/six-deceptive-arguments-against-nuclear-weapons-ban/ Accessed 15 March 2021.

[139] Ibid., p. 3.

[140] Ibid., p. 5.

[141] *Nuclear Weapons Advisory Opinion*, paras 99–100.

[142] ICAN, "Arguments for nuclear abolition", available at http://www.icanw.org/why-a-ban/arguments-for-a-ban/ Accessed 15 March 2021.

15 Nuclear Weapons

nations still cling to the misguided idea of "nuclear deterrence".[143] The third one is the "environmental case". According to it, nuclear weapons are the only devices invented so far which have the capability to destroy all complex forms of life on Earth; it would take only less than 0.1% of the explosive yield of the current global nuclear arsenal to bring about devastating agricultural collapse and widespread famine.[144] The fourth consideration is a so-called "economic case" which is also very simple: nuclear weapons programmes (often consuming tens of billions of dollars) divert public funds from health care, education, disaster relief and other vital services.[145] Finally, the risk of nuclear weapons falling into hands of dangerous actors such as, for example, terrorist groups justifies a total ban on manufacture, possession, transfer and use of nuclear weapons.

As noted in the introduction to this chapter, the use of nuclear weapons raises several critical questions. The third category of those questions is philosophical in nature as reader recalls. To conclude this chapter, it appears appropriate to remember this philosophical aspect once again and ask ourselves a question: can we as collectivity of human beings, i.e., humankind, continue claiming that we represent the most developed and complex life form on Earth, with unique ability to reason, if we know only one natural way of procreation but invented myriads of means and methods to end life, often in the most gruesome and inhumane manner? And the danger of the actual use of nuclear weapons, so far the most destructive type out of those means, has not diminished despite the end of the Cold War, but remains as topical as before. What does it all say about us?

That is why, out of sheer necessity, the four considerations described above must all incessantly drive the process of total uncompromising prohibition and abolition of nuclear weapons everywhere on the planet if mankind is to survive as a species on our Pale Blue Dot.

References

Aljaghoub M (2006) The advisory function of the International Court of Justice, 1946–2005. Springer, Berlin/Heidelberg

Atadjanov R (2019) Humanness as a protected legal interest of crimes against humanity: Conceptual and normative aspects. T.M.C. Asser Press, The Hague

Boot M (2002) Genocide, crimes against humanity, war crimes: Nullum crimen sine lege and the subject matter jurisdiction of the International Criminal Court. Intersentia, Antwerp/Oxford/New York

Cassese A et al (2002) The Rome Statute of the International Criminal Court: A commentary, Vol. I. Oxford University Press, Oxford

Cassese A (2013) Cassese's international criminal law, 3rd edn. Oxford University Press, Oxford/Gosport, Hampshire

---

[143] Ibid.

[144] Ibid.

[145] Ibid.

Condé V (2004) A handbook of international human rights terminology, 2nd edn. University of Nebraska Press, Lincoln/London

Cryer R et al (2010) An introduction to international criminal law and procedure, 2nd edn. Cambridge University Press, Cambridge

Davis M, Purcell A (2006) Weapons of mass destruction. Facts on File, New York

Dinstein Y (2010) The conduct of hostilities under the law of international armed conflict, 2nd edn. Cambridge University Press, Cambridge

Dinstein Y (2011) War, aggression and self-defense, 5th edn. Cambridge University Press, Cambridge/New York

Doswald-Beck L (2011) Human rights in times of conflict and terrorism. Cambridge University Press, Cambridge

Gardam J (1993) Proportionality and force in international law. 87 Am. J. Int'l Law 391–413

Gardam J (1999) Necessity and proportionality in *jus ad bellum* and *jus in bello*. In: Boisson de Chazournes L, Sands Ph (eds) International law, the International Court of Justice and nuclear weapons. Cambridge University Press, Cambridge

Gardam J (2004) Necessity, proportionality and the use of force by states. Cambridge University Press, Cambridge, New York

Gazzini T (2005) The changing rules on the use of force in international law. Manchester University Press, Manchester

Gray C (2008) International law and the use of force, 3rd edn. Oxford University Press, Oxford/New York

Green J (2009) The International Court of Justice and self-defense in international law. Hart Publishing, Oxford/ Portland, OR

Greenwood C (1983) The relationship between *jus ad bellum* and *jus in bello*. 9 Rev. Int'l Studies 221–234

Henckaerts J-M, Doswald-Beck L (2005) Customary international humanitarian law, Vol. I: Rules. Cambridge University Press/International Committee of the Red Cross, Cambridge

International Committee of the Red Cross (2013) The domestic implementation of international humanitarian law: A manual. International Committee of the Red Cross https://www.icrc.org/eng/assets/files/publications/icrc-002-4028.pdf Accessed 30 April 2019

Kristensen H, McKinzie M (2015) Nuclear arsenals: Current developments, trends and capabilities. 97(899) Int'l Rev. Red Cross 563–599

Larsen K, Cooper C, Nystuen G (2013) Searching for a 'principle of humanity' in international humanitarian law. Cambridge University Press, Cambridge

Lito M (2018) Treaty on the prohibition of nuclear weapons. 57(2) Int'l Legal Materials 347–357, doi:https://doi.org/10.1017/ilm.2018.15

Maresca L, Mitchell E (2015) The human costs and legal consequences of nuclear weapons under international humanitarian law. 97(899) Int'l Rev. Red Cross 621–645

Moxley C, Burroughs J, Granoff J (2011) Nuclear weapons and compliance with international humanitarian law and the Nuclear Non-Proliferation Treaty. 34 Fordham Int'l Law J. 595–696

Nystuen G, Casey-Maslen S, Bersagel A (2014) Nuclear weapons under international law. Cambridge University Press, Cambridge

Schabas W (2010) The International Criminal Court: A commentary on the Rome Statute. Oxford University Press, Oxford

Shaw M (2008) International law, 6th edn. Cambridge University Press, Cambridge

Tannenwald N (2003) Weapons of mass definition. 59 Vol. Atomic Scientists 4

Triffterer O (2008) Commentary on the Rome Statute of the International Criminal Court, 2nd edn. C.H. Beck, Hart/Nomos, Munich

Werle G, Jessberger F (2014) Principles of ICL, 3rd edn. Oxford University Press, Oxford

Rustam Atadjanov LLB, LLM, Dr. iur., Ph.D. is an Assistant Professor of Public and International Law at KIMEP University School of Law (Almaty, Kazakhstan) since 2019, and Director of the Bachelor in International Law Programme. He is a Graduate of the Karakalpak State University, Uzbekistan (2003), University of Connecticut School of Law, USA (2006), and University of Hamburg, Faculty of Law, Germany (2018). Rustam formerly worked as a Programme Responsible and Legal Adviser at the Regional Delegation of the International Committee of the Red Cross (ICRC) in Central Asia (2007–2014), dealing with international humanitarian law, public international law and criminal law issues. His areas of expertise and research include public international law, international human rights law, international criminal law, international humanitarian law, theory of law and state, and constitutional law. Rustam authored a monograph entitled *Humanness as a Protected Legal Interest of Crimes against Humanity: Conceptual and Normative Aspects* (T.M.C. Asser Press/Springer, 2019), and published 20 academic and publicist articles, encyclopaedic entries and book reviews in a number of European and Asian academic journals. At KIMEP University's School of Law, Rustam teaches Public Law and International Law-related courses.

Chapter 16
Blinding Laser Weapons

Evhen Tsybulenko

Contents

16.1 Introduction 368
16.2 Protocol on Blinding Laser Weapons 369
    16.2.1 General Provisions and Scope of Application of Protocol IV 369
    16.2.2 Question of Interpretation of Certain Articles of Protocol IV 371
16.3 Use of Laser Weapons with Consequences for Human Vision 374
16.4 Conclusion 375
References 376

Abstract The creation of the first lasers did not escape the attention of militaries all around the world, and consequently, a number of devices and methods varying from rangefinders to psychological laser warfare were invented. Fortunately, this development also did not escape the eye of international organisations and individual experts engaged in addressing contemporary humanitarian challenges, and the Protocol on Blinding Laser Weapons came to be in a rather timely manner, being the second international treaty in history that regulated a weapon before it was ever used in warfare. Today, this protocol may be more relevant than ever, due to recent recorded cases of blinding caused by lasers. This chapter aims to point out and analyse some problems with the Protocol that may grow more serious in the future. First, background and general provisions of the Protocol are discussed, then a section on interpretation raises two questions—one about a legitimate use of laser weapons and another about a definition of permanent blindness. After that, a question on the use of lasers with consequences for human vision will be touched upon, and the chapter will be summarised with a conclusion.

Keywords Protocol on Blinding Laser Weapons · Public International Law · International Humanitarian Law · Hague Law · Russian aggression in Ukraine

---

E. Tsybulenko (✉)
Faculty of Law, Tallinn University of Technology, Tallinn, Estonia
e-mail: evhen.tsybulenko@taltech.ee

Kyiv International University, Kyiv, Ukraine

© T.M.C. ASSER PRESS and the authors 2022
S. Sayapin et al. (eds.), *International Conflict and Security Law*,
https://doi.org/10.1007/978-94-6265-515-7_16

367

16.1 Introduction

The creation of the first lasers, laser being an acronym for Light Amplification by Stimulated Emission of Radiation, immediately attracted the attention of the militaries. Nevertheless, technological development allowed for starting to engineer combat lasers only in the 1970s. It is necessary to mention that there are a variety of methods through which lasers can be used for military purposes—burning through or sufficient overheating of the target, electromagnetic impulse that affects the target, destroying optical equipment of the enemy, temporary or permanent blinding and even potential methods of psychological warfare that would consist of projecting images in the sky to demoralise superstitious or unprepared enemies. Furthermore, it is also prudent to remember auxiliary laser devices such as rangefinders, laser designators, and so forth. Nevertheless, in accordance with Article 36 of Additional Protocol I, a High Contracting Party is under the obligation to examine whether a weapon that is being developed would fall under the prohibition imposed by the Protocol or any other rule of international law applicable to that party.[1]

A laser is an intense focused beam of photons of the same wavelength.[2] Blinding laser weapons induce blindness by causing a thermal burn to the retina with the concentrated laser beam and the rupture of blood vessels induced by a shockwave due to the extremely short duration of the laser pulse.[3] Such damage can be amplified by the use of direct view optics, as it would further focus the laser beam, adding to the focusing action of the eye itself.[4] There is no standard approach to the treatment of a laser eye injury; in some cases, where scarring or haemorrhaging occurs, surgically removing scar tissue and blood may be effective,[5] but damage to the central retina cannot be treated and will result in permanent blindness due to the loss of central vision.[6] Use of protective eyewear is only effective against lasers of known wavelength,[7] so it is more effective in preventing laser eye injuries caused in an industrial setting, rather than on the battlefield.

The distinction between blinding and non-blinding lasers is in the output wavelength: electromagnetic radiation with a wavelength between 400 and 1400 nanometres is known as the "retinal hazard region", and lasers with an output within that range are capable of causing retinal damage that results in blindness.[8] Additionally, it is important to note that the severity of the damage will depend not only on the

---

[1] Protocol Additional to the Geneva Conventions of 12 August 1949, and relating to the Protection of Victims of International Armed Conflicts (Protocol I), 8 June 1977, 1125 UNTS 3. www.ref world.org/docid/3ae6b36b4.html Accessed 19 May 2020.

[2] Strong 1996, p. 238.

[3] Human Rights Watch Arms Project 1995.

[4] Ibid.

[5] American Academy of Ophthalmology 2009.

[6] ICRC 1994.

[7] Ibid.

[8] Strong 1996, p. 239.

16 Blinding Laser Weapons 369

characteristics of the laser beam, but also on the atmospheric conditions and distance from the source.[9]

Currently, international humanitarian law only specifically regulates blinding laser weapons, whereas in the case of non-blinding lasers, general provisions are applicable. However, specific regulation of other laser weapons does not seem necessary, even on a doctrinal level, at the moment.

16.2 Protocol on Blinding Laser Weapons

16.2.1 General Provisions and Scope of Application of Protocol IV

Prohibition on the use of laser weapons that are "specifically designed, as their sole combat function or as one of their combat functions, to cause permanent blindness into un-enhanced vision, that is to the naked eye or to the eye with corrective eyesight devices" was established by the Protocol on Blinding Laser Weapons (Protocol IV) to the Convention on Prohibitions or Restrictions on the Use of Certain Conventional Weapons Which May Be Deemed to Be Excessively Injurious or to Have Indiscriminate Effects of 1980 (hereinafter the Convention on Certain Conventional Weapons) that was adopted on 13 October 1995 in Vienna at the Conference on revision of the aforementioned Convention.[10] Protocol IV had entered into force on 30 July 1998 and was ratified by 108 countries by July 2018, including China, the Russian Federation, the United States, Ukraine and Estonia.[11] It is prudent to note, that rangefinders and designators also fall within the retinal hazard region, but as blinding is not one of their intended combat functions, they do not fall under Protocol IV.[12]

In accordance with Article 1 of Protocol IV, not only the use but also the transfer of blinding laser weapons to state or non-state actors is prohibited. The Protocol obliges High Contracting Parties to take all possible measures, including training their armed forces, to avoid permanent blinding in the course of the use of permitted laser systems (Article 2 of Protocol IV). It is necessary to note that the prohibition does not cover cases where blinding is accidental or is an accompanying effect of the legitimate use of laser systems for military purposes, including the use of laser systems against optical equipment (Article 3 of Protocol IV). Protocol IV defines permanent blindness as "irreversible and uncorrectable loss of vision which is seriously disabling with no

---

[9] Ibid.

[10] Protocol on Blinding Laser Weapons (Protocol IV) Doc. CCW/CONF 1/16(Part 1) 11. www.ihl-databases.icrc.org/applic/ihl/ihl.nsf/Treaty.xsp?action=openDocument&docume ntId=70D9427BB965B7CEC12563FB0061CFB2. Accessed 6 July 2018.

[11] State Parties, Protocol on Blinding Laser Weapons(Protocol IV to the 1980 Convention), www.ihl-databases.icrc.org/applic/ihl/ihl.nsf/States.xsp?xp_viewStates=XPages_NORMSt atesParties&xp_treatySelected=570 Accessed 6 July 2018.

[12] Strong 1996, p. 242.

prospect of recovery where serious disability is equivalent to visual acuity of less than 20/200 Snellen measured using both eyes" (Article 4 of Protocol IV).[13]

During the discussion of the draft Protocol, a question as to whether blinding laser weapons should be produced had also been considered, but a number of states argued against that suggestion, as the adoption of such a norm would require control mechanisms to be developed and there was not enough time for the development of such mechanisms. Nevertheless, it was noted that such a measure might be adopted in the future.[14]

It is necessary to mention that this prohibition was adopted in a rather timely manner. In a number of countries (China,[15] United States,[16] USSR[17]) blinding laser weapons had already passed the trials and were ready for mass production and sales. Many other countries had also been carrying out active research in this area. Taking into account the tempo and the level of development of laser technology, it was reasonable to suggest that in recent years such technology could have been weaponised and most likely mass produced in immense quantities. Such production would have inevitably led to the expansion of its sphere of distribution, in addition to the use of such weapons not only by the state actors' military forces, but also by terrorist and criminal organisations that prefer light transportable weapons for obvious reasons.[18] It is indisputable that if the use of laser weapons had reached that stage, a solution to that problem would have required much larger and much more expensive efforts, which would likely have failed.

Some authors[19] and state delegations[20] stated that with the adoption of Protocol IV, for the first time in history, a certain type of weapon was prohibited before it was used in practice. This point of view seems to me somewhat inaccurate, as Protocol IV is the second such document. The first case is the prohibition of the use of "ecological weapons" in accordance with the Convention on the Prohibition of Military or Any Other Hostile Use of Environmental Modification Techniques (ENMOD) from 1976, which of course does not diminish the significance of Protocol IV.

Although only international armed conflicts initially fell within the scope of Protocol IV, a principal agreement was reached in Vienna that it should later expand its scope to non-international armed conflicts. The amendment of Article 1 of the Convention on Certain Conventional Weapons in 2001 officially solidified the application of Protocol IV to non-international armed conflicts. Moreover, currently, the prohibition of blinding laser weapons is considered a norm of customary law that

---

[13] Protocol on Blinding Laser Weapons (Protocol IV) Doc. CCW/CONF 1/16(Part 1) 11. www.ihl-databases.icrc.org/applic/ihl/ihl.nsf/Treaty.xsp?action=openDocument&documentId=70D9427BB965B7CEC12563FB0061CFB2. Accessed 6 July 2018.

[14] Doswald-Beck 1996, p. 289.

[15] Report on China North Industries Corp. (NORINCO) 1995, p. 3.

[16] Lockheed Sanders 1994.

[17] Getwar.ru 2011.

[18] Doswald-Beck 1993, pp. 13–355.

[19] McClelland 2005, p. 759.

[20] Chinese Delegation 1996, p. 1.

is applicable both to international and non-international armed conflicts.[21] In accordance with that, Eloisa Newalsing rightfully notes: "This example illustrates the fact that development of the customary law norm does not necessarily require extensive practice but can develop rather quickly."[22]

16.2.2 Question of Interpretation of Certain Articles of Protocol IV

16.2.2.1 Legitimate Use of Laser Systems

Despite the fact that Protocol IV consists of only four articles, several of them require additional clarifications. One of the more difficult questions is the legitimacy of the use of laser systems. During the drafting discussions on Article 3, the word 'legitimate' raised questions for some delegations. It was further elaborated that this word was used to point out the existence of the types of lasers that are permitted for use on the battlefield.

The main goal of the Article—to refrain from limiting the use of battle lasers that had acquired a wide area of use but were not aimed at damaging the eye—created certain difficulty. Nevertheless, blinding can be accidental when the laser is used with other intentions, including the cases where the victim uses optical equipment and a laser is used to disable such equipment. This is precisely the reason why the phrase 'including laser systems used against optical equipment' was only included during the last unofficial consultations held at Sweden's request. By that time, delegations had indicated that the version of the text proposed by the chairman satisfied them. This phrase had likely been included in order for some delegations to accept the final definition contained in Article 2.[23]

Nevertheless, in the opinion of Louise Doswald-Beck, who is one of the leading experts on that question, the interpretation of Article 3, even in its current form, is connected to certain difficulties. The problem lies, for example, in the fact that an optical surveillance system directing a laser beam into the eyes of an operator is perfectly legitimate. In that case, permanent blindness is not the goal, even though it can be a side effect for a person who accidentally gets in the way of the laser beam but was not specifically targeted. However, if the laser is to counteract devices such as binoculars, it will not have an effect on the device itself, but likely damage the vision of the person using that device. This type of blinding is hard to define as an accidental side effect, as it is purposeful and deliberate. That is the reason behind the conventional interpretation of Article 3, presupposing that the phrase "including laser

---

[21] Henckaerts and Doswald-Beck 2009, pp. 292–296.

[22] Newalsing 2008, p. 276.

[23] Doswald-Beck 1996, p. 293.

systems used against optical equipment" is not to be used for giving legitimacy to the purposeful blinding of persons using binoculars or other direct optical devices.[24]

The interpretation of those Articles by different states is a rather interesting subject. The Israeli manual on the Laws of War states the following: "in case a weapon based on laser technology is used for aims different from blinding (for example, rangefinders), the state has an obligation to take all necessary precautions in order to prevent accidental blinding".[25] In an annotated supplement to a naval handbook for the United States Navy, the following is stated: "Although blinding as accidental effect of 'legitimate military use' of laser systems of detection or targeting is not forbidden [by the Protocol IV], participating countries are to take all possible precautions to avoid such consequences".[26] The Canadian manual on the law of armed conflict proclaims: "Prohibition does not cover blinding as accidental or accompanying side-effect in the cases of legitimate use of laser systems. For example, legitimate use of a targeting laser system in a tank is legitimate even though an accompanying effect might be blinding. However, such a system cannot be purposefully used for blinding the enemy."[27] If the first two cases demonstrate the direct incorporation of the provisions of Protocol IV, the Canadian manual goes further by transforming the norms of Protocol IV. In our opinion, the phrase "however, such a system cannot be purposefully used for blinding the enemy" contains a straightforward prohibition on blinding persons, using binoculars or other optical devices.

16.2.2.2 Definition of "Permanent Blindness"

The question of defining "permanent blindness" is equally difficult. It is becoming more and more relevant, as a number of companies in different countries have started developing and issuing laser systems called laser dazzlers that cause temporary blindness. As those systems cause only temporary blindness, they do not fall within the scope of Protocol IV. Those devices can be used not only for military purposes, but also for combating piracy and for law enforcement.[28] In accordance with information acquired by CNN, the China-produced device ZM-87, which is an example of such a laser, was used, albeit unsuccessfully, by North Korea against United States' helicopters that were above the demilitarised zone.[29] Additionally, such laser systems could likely be used by police forces as their efficacy is expected to exceed that of conventional methods, such as electroshocks, water cannons or tear gas.[30] For example, the Ministry of Internal Affairs in Russia already included the "special

---

[24] Ibid., p. 294.

[25] Military Advocate General Headquarters 1998, p. 17.

[26] Oceans Law and Policy Department of the US 1997, § 9.8, footnote 45.

[27] Canada, LOAC Manual 1999, § 30, p. 5-3

[28] Burns 2011.

[29] Lister 2010.

[30] Popular Mechanics 2011.

laser flashlight "Potok"" which, in accordance with the statements of the manufacturer, affects vision without permanent damage in the range of up to 30 meters, thereby restricting the capacity of the target to actively resist.[31] It is worrisome that the minimum safe range for the use of the device should be no less than 4 meters, whereas the Russian police regularly breach the rules on the use of specialised devices. What will happen if the device is used at a shorter range and whether it may cause permanent blindness is not elaborated on.

Lasers can cause temporary blindness by inducing a dazzle or flash blindness—the former being an overload of retinal receptors by intense light and the subsequent severe depression of visual function, whereas the latter refers to the bleaching of photopigments due to the exposure of photoreceptors to an intense flash of light.[32] Both of those cases of temporary blindness can occur in the dark, but it is not possible to cause flash blindness during the daytime without causing permanent damage, and only lasers operating in visible spectrum are capable of inducing dazzle or flash blindness.[33] Additionally, as the level of energy required to cause flash blindness is close to the level of energy necessary to induce permanent blindness, the threshold between safe usage and potential injury is rather narrow.[34]

As Louise Doswald-Beck states, defining permanent blindness was one of the key issues during the discussion of Protocol IV, despite Article 4 being absent from the initial draft of Protocol IV.[35] Nevertheless, the inclusion of the definition in Article 4 was necessary, as it states that blindness does not necessarily mean a full loss of vision, which is a fact not known to the majority of non-specialists. It is important to note that despite a weaponised laser being able to cause a full loss of vision, being affected by a laser weapon can cause a partial loss of vision. The degree of damage depends on the energy level of the weapon and distance to the target. Other criteria such as "irreversible", "unalterable", and "incurable" are classified as the usual result of being affected by a laser.

The Austrian delegation suggested to define blindness and weak eyesight in accordance with the international statistical classification of illnesses and connected disorders adopted by WHO. In the estimation of WHO and in accordance with the so-called Snellen charts, "blindness and weak eyesight" is defined as visual acuity lower than 20/200—or the inability to see at a distance of 20 feet (6.1 m) what a person with normal vision would see at a distance of 200 feet (61 m).[36] The main difficulty was in the fact that acuity of vision, which became the backbone of the WHO's definition, was developed first and foremost for treating cataracts and took into account the 'clouding' of eyesight. Blinding by a laser, in turn, leads to the destruction of several sectors of the retina. Such impact leads to the loss of central vision and, therefore, leads to a full loss of vision. Therefore, a definition based on the Snellen charts is

---

[31] NPO SM 2007.

[32] Strong 1996, p. 240.

[33] Ibid.

[34] Ibid.

[35] Doswald-Beck 1996, p. 294.

[36] Strouse Watt 2003.

inapplicable to blindness caused by laser impact, which is why a leading expert on the effects of laser on vision, Professor Marshall, has persistently recommended using a functional test instead of the test based on numbers from WHO. This opinion was shared by Sir John Wilson, a specialist on determination of blindness in accordance with the WHO criteria, who represented the UN Development Programme (UNDP) at the conference. Both Sir Wilson and Professor Marshall offered to use the phrase "loss of vision that is permanent, irreversible and is a cause of serious disability". However, several delegations insisted on the use of a certain number, as, in their opinion, it is very important for determining a breach of the Protocol.[37]

As a result, the final version of Article 4 combined both approaches, as despite the Snellen charts not being fully suitable for measuring blindness caused by a laser because they do not take into account the loss of field of vision, they are the sole internationally recognised method of measuring vision loss. At the same time, it is necessary to take into account that in case more adequate methods of measuring vision loss are developed or a necessity for more suitable methods arises (for example, in the case of laser dazzler use), Protocol IV may be revised with regard to the definition of permanent blindness.

16.3 Use of Laser Weapons with Consequences for Human Vision

Before the beginning of Russian aggression in Ukraine, there was not a single case of officially confirmed blinding laser weapon use. However, during the Russian invasion of Eastern Ukraine, it was reported that laser weapons had begun being used against Ukrainian servicemen. In accordance with the information published on the official website of the Ukrainian state border service, a Ukrainian serviceman was blinded by a laser originating from the occupied territories at the control post Maryinka in March 2018.[38] The blinding occurred through binoculars. A similar case happened in July 2016 when a laser damaged the vision of three Ukrainian servicemen.[39] Anton Kekuh was one of the victims. Doctors were only able to restore his peripheral vision; however, his central vision was irreversibly lost, as the retina and central part of the nervous tissue were damaged.[40] As in all four cases vision damage occurred through direct optical devices, it does not seem possible to determine what type of laser was used—specific blinding laser or an anti-optical system—which brings us back to the previously discussed question of interpretation of Article 3.

In another case it was reported that Russian collaborators in the Lugansk district used a laser to disable OSCE surveillance cameras in October 2017, which resulted in

---

[37] Doswald-Beck 1996, pp. 294–295.

[38] Milne 2018.

[39] Ukrainian State Border Service 2018.

[40] Television News Service 2018.

16 Blinding Laser Weapons 375

said camera being out of service for five hours.[41] The situation is made more difficult by the continuous denial of the Russian Federation of its involvement in aggression against Ukraine, despite its role as aggressor and occupier being officially defined in a number of international legal documents. As a result of this denial, Russia refuses any investigation into war crimes committed by its servicemen, mercenaries and collaborationists on the territory of Ukraine.[42] Nevertheless, it is necessary to note that Russian President Vladimir Putin, in his letter to the Federal Assembly of the Russian Federation in 2018, stated: "Since last [2017] year military laser systems are being implemented in the army," however the type of laser systems that are being implemented were not specified.[43] The truthfulness of Putin's statement is doubtful. This doubt is exacerbated not only by Putin's frequent habit of misinforming the public, but also by the Vice-Minister of Defence Jury Borisov having already claimed in 2016 that: "We already introduced into service some models of laser weapons".[44]

16.4 Conclusion

Summarising all of the discussion above, the following conclusions can be drawn:

1. There is no doubt that Protocol IV is an outstanding achievement in the area of public international law. For the second time in modern history, a new type of cruel weapon was prohibited before being used in practice. This potentially saved millions of people from permanent blindness, which is a serious disability. The importance of Protocol IV was confirmed by the fact that it was ratified by all the largest potential manufacturers of laser weapons. Moreover, in a short period of time, a customary law norm prohibiting the use of similar weapons was formed.[45] The main achievement is the fact that before the start of Russian aggression in Ukraine, there was not a single officially confirmed case of the use of a blinding laser weapon. As the Russian Federation regularly, systematically and *en masse* breaches basic norms and principles both of law of international security and of international humanitarian law,[46] it can only be hoped that those breaches will stay as an exception to international practice and will not be repeated by other states. The international community will increase the pressure

---

[41] Ukraine Crisis Media Centre 2017.

[42] See, in particular, PACE 2018; OSCE Parliamentary Assembly 2017; Office of the Prosecutor of the ICC 2017; EU Delegation for OSCE Permanent Council 2016; GA UN 2017; Tsybulenko and Francis 2018, p. 127; Tsybulenko and Kelichavyi 2018, pp. 280–281; Tsybulenko and Platonova 2019, pp. 135–137.

[43] Petrov 2018.

[44] Seliverstova 2016.

[45] Joint Standing Committee On Treaties of the Australian Parliament 1997. Cited in Henckaerts and Doswald-Beck 2005, p. 1965.

[46] *Supra note* 42.

on the Russian administration in order to clear up the situation and prevent such actions.

2. Protocol IV prohibits not only the use but also the transfer of blinding laser weapons. However, the prohibition on manufacturing and accordingly the mechanisms of controls for such prohibition were not included in Protocol IV, which is undoubtedly a disadvantage of the Protocol, as it does not currently allow effective investigation into the question of which type of laser weapons manufactured in Russia were reportedly used by the Russian military to blind Ukrainian servicemen. However, there are reasons to believe that the adoption of Protocol IV even in its current form has led to the fact that no other state except Russia manufactures blinding laser weapons. Moreover, all research on similar weapons was stopped after the Protocol was adopted. For example, the United States Secretary of Defense stated: "Department [of Defense] is not going to waste money on development of [blinding laser] weapons that we are prohibited to use".[47]

3. The phrasing of Article 3 leaves some space for different interpretations of legitimate uses of laser systems against optical devices. Despite the fact that conscientious interpretation of that article does not give an opportunity to consider purposeful blinding of persons using binoculars or other direct optical devices as legitimate, in the case of active use of lasers aimed at destroying optical equipment, especially with automatic targeting, it can become a potential problem. In connection to that, it seems rational to amend Protocol IV in a way that would establish a direct prohibition on using lasers against binoculars and other direct optical devices.

4. Using laser devices causing temporary blindness (laser dazzlers) does not fall under the prohibition established by Protocol IV. Taking into consideration that laser dazzlers will be actively used in the near future, there are certain potential risks. As previously noted, the definition of "permanent blindness" adopted in Protocol IV is based on a method that is not intended to be used to measure blindness caused by laser weapons. In my opinion, there is a danger that this definition will not adequately reflect the possible vision damage caused by laser dazzlers. In connection to that, it would be rational to develop a new definition of "permanent blindness" and amend Protocol IV in order to include norms that would regulate the use of laser dazzlers in order to fully exclude the possibility of causing permanent blindness with those devices.

References

American Academy of Ophthalmology (2009) Managing retinal injuries from lasers www.aao.org/eyenet/article/managing-retinal-injuries-from-lasers Accessed 10 May 2020

---

[47] US, Letter from the Secretary of Defense to Senator Patrick Leahy, 8 May 1996. Cited in Henckaerts and Doswald-Beck 2005, p. 1970.

16 Blinding Laser Weapons

Burns C (2011) SMU 100 Laser Rifle tested by UK Police https://www.slashgear.com/smu-100-laser-rifle-tested-by-uk-police-13202089/ Accessed 29 June 2018

Chinese Delegation (1996) Statement at the First Review Conference of States Parties to the CCW (Second Session). United Nations Office at Geneva, Geneva.

Doswald-Beck L (1993) Blinding weapons. ICRC, Geneva

Doswald-Beck L (1996) New Protocol on Blinding Laser Weapons. International Review of the Red Cross, 312:272–299

EU Delegation for OSCE Permanent Council (2016) EU statement PC.DEL/1558/16 on "Russia's Ongoing Aggression against Ukraine and Illegal Occupation of Crimea" www.eeas.europa.eu/sites/eeas/files/pc_1118_eu_on_ukraine.pdf. Accessed 29 June 2018

GA UN (2017) GA UN resolution A/RES/72/190 Situation of human rights in the Autonomous Republic of Crimea and the city of Sevastopol, Ukraine, www.undocs.org/A/RES/72/190. Accessed 29 June 2018

Getwar.ru (2011) Laser weapon for self-defence of cosmonauts or laser pistol with pyrotechnic flashlight/ http://getwar.ru/lazernoe-oruzhie-individualnojj-samooborony-kosmonavtov-ili-lazernyjj-pistolet-s-pirotekhnicheskojj-lampojj-vspyshkojj-sssr.html. Accessed 6 July 2018

Henckaerts J-M, Doswald-Beck L (eds) (2005) Customary International Humanitarian Law, Volume 2 (Practice – Part 1). ICRC, Cambridge University Press, Cambridge

Henckaerts J-M, Doswald-Beck L (eds) (2009) Customary International Humanitarian Law, Volume 1 (Rules). ICRC, Cambridge University Press, Cambridge

Human Rights Watch Arms Project (1995) Blinding Laser Weapons: The Need to Ban a Cruel and Inhumane Weapon. www.hrw.org/reports/1995/General1.htm Accessed 10 May 2020

ICRC (1994) Blinding laser weapons: questions and answers www.aao.org/eyenet/article/managing-retinal-injuries-from-lasers Accessed 10 May 2020

Joint Standing Committee On Treaties of the Australian Parliament (1997) Restrictions on the Use of Blinding Laser https://www.aph.gov.au/Parliamentary_Business/Committees/Joint/Completed_Inquiries/jsct/reports/report5/contents. Accessed 26 June 2018

Lister T (2010) North Korea's military ageing but sizable www.edition.cnn.com/2010/WORLD/asiapcf/11/24/north.korea.capability. Accessed 29 June 2018

Lockheed Sanders (1994) Lockheed Sanders Fact Sheet on Laser Counter Measure System (LCMS) - AN/PLQ-5. Lockheed Sanders Inc., Nashua, NH

McClelland J (2005) Conventional weapons: a cluster of developments. International & Comparative Law Quarterly, 54(3):755–767

Military Advocate General Headquarters (1998) Manual on the Laws of War. Military School, Israel

Milne O (2018) Ukrainian border guard 'blinded after Russian soldiers fire LASER weapon into his eyes', https://www.mirror.co.uk/news/world-news/ukrainian-border-guard-blinded-after-12278912. Accessed 29 June 2018

Newalsing E (2008) Publication Review on Customary International Humanitarian Law (Henckaerts J-M, Doswald-Beck L (eds)). Leiden Journal of International Law, 21(1):255–279

NPO SM (2007) Special laser flashlight "Potok" www.npo-sm.ru/specialnye_sredstva/fonar_specialnyj_lazernyj_potok/. Accessed 29 June 2018

Oceans Law and Policy Department of the US (1997) Annotated Supplement to the Naval Handbook. US Naval War College, Newport, RI

Office of the Prosecutor of the ICC (2017) ICC Report on Preliminary Examination Activities. Ukraine. www.icc-cpi.int/itemsDocuments/2017-PE-rep/2017-otp-rep-PE_ENG.pdf. Accessed 29 June 2018

OSCE Parliamentary Assembly (2017) OSCE PA Resolution on Restoration of the Sovereignty and Territorial Integrity of Ukraine www.oscepa.org/documents/all-documents/annual-sessions/2017-minsk/declaration-25/3555-declaration-minsk-eng/file. Accessed 29 June 2018

PACE (2018) PACE Resolution 2198: Humanitarian consequences of the war in Ukraine www.assembly.coe.int/nw/xml/XRef/Xref-XML2HTML-en.asp?fileid=24432&lang=en. Accessed 29 June 2018

Petrov I (2018) President of RF: Military lasers are being implemented in the army. https://rg.ru/2018/03/01/putin-boevye-lazery-uzhe-postupaiut-na-vooruzhenie-vojsk.html. Accessed 29 June 2018

Popular Mechanics (2011) Too bright for the crowds: laser "democratisators". www.popmech.ru/weapon/12266-slishkom-yarko-dlya-tolpy-lazernye-demokratizatory/. Accessed on 29 June 2018

Report on China North Industries Corp. (NORINCO) (1995) Jane's Defence Weekly, 23(21):3

Seliverstova N (2016) Russian Army introduced into service some models of laser weapons www.ria.ru/amp/defense_safety/20160802/1473432412.html. Accessed 29 June 2018

Strong J (1996) Blinding Laser Weapons and Protocol IV: Obscuring the Humanitarian Vision. Dickinson Journal of International Law, 15(1):237–264

Strouse Watt W (2003) How Visual Acuity Is Measured. / www.mdsupport.org/library/acuity.html. Accessed 29 June 2018

Television News Service (2018) Doctors had treated eyes of the border guard who was blinded by a laser used by mercenaries www.1plus1.ua/1plus1video/tsn/den/tsn-za-20180504-likari-vryatu vali-ochi-prikordonniku-yakogo-bojoviki-zaslipili-lazerom Accessed 29 June 2018

Tsybulenko E, Francis J A (2018) Separatists or Russian Troops and Local Collaborators? Russian Aggression in Ukraine: The Problem of Definitions. In: Sayapin S, Tsybulenko E (eds) The Use of Force against Ukraine and International Law. T.M.C. Asser Press, The Hague, pp. 123–144

Tsybulenko E, Kelichavyi B (2018) International Legal Dimensions of the Russian Occupation of Crimea. In: Sayapin S, Tsybulenko E (eds) The Use of Force against Ukraine and International Law. T.M.C. Asser Press, The Hague, pp. 277–296

Tsybulenko E, Platonova A (2019) Violations of Freedom of Expression and Freedom of Religion by the Russian Federation as the Occupying Power in Crimea. Baltic Journal of European Studies, 9 (3 (28)):134–147.

Ukraine Crisis Media Centre (2017) OSCE SMM: Over 313,000 ceasefire violations recorded since January 1 www.uacrisis.org/61344-osce-68. Accessed 29 June 2018

Ukrainian State Border Service (2018) The State Border Service had once again detected signs of the use of prohibited special purpose laser weapons by Russian mercenaries in the area of operation of Join Forces. www.dpsu.gov.ua/ua/news/Rosiyski-naymanci-ymovirno-znovu-zastosuvali-laz ernu-zbroyu/. Accessed 29 June 2018

Evhen Tsybulenko is an Estonian Legal Scholar of Ukrainian descent. In 2000, he earned a Ph.D. in International Law from Kyiv National University, Ukraine, and carried out postdoctoral research at the International Human Rights Law Institute of De Paul University, USA, in 2002. In Ukraine, he worked at the International Committee of the Red Cross (ICRC) and the Kyiv International University where he is a Professor since 2009. In Estonia, he was elected as a Professor of Law (2005) and appointed Chair of International and Comparative Law Department at the Tallinn University of Technology's Law School (2005–2010). Currently he is a Senior lecturer at the same School. He was a Founder and Director of the Tallinn Law School's Human Rights Centre (2007–2014). He was also an Adjunct (Visiting) Professor and Senior Visiting Mentor at the Joint Command and General Staff Course (JCGSC) at Baltic Defence College (2007–2013). He published over 40 books and academic articles and more than 200 general interest articles, comments and interviews in 15 countries, mainly in Ukrainian or Russian, but also in English and other languages. He cooperates, as an external expert, with the ICRC, Estonian Red Cross, Estonian Integration Commission, Directorate-General for Education and Culture of the European Commission, and the Organization for Security and Co-operation in Europe (OSCE).

Chapter 17
Fuel Air Explosive Weapons

Evhen Tsybulenko

Contents

17.1 Introduction 380
17.2 Principle of Action of Fuel Air Explosive Weapons 382
17.3 Necessity of International Legal Regulation 383
    17.3.1 Indiscriminate Effect 383
    17.3.2 Superfluous Injury and Excessive Suffering 384
    17.3.3 Widespread, Long-term and Severe Damage to the Natural Environment 385
17.4 Conclusion 386
References 387

Abstract Fuel air explosive (FAE) weapons are being actively researched and introduced into service by different states in addition to having been used several times already, yet remain practically unknown to wider audience despite a promise to become one of the most cruel and inhumane weapons of the 21st century. This chapter aims to argue that it is absolutely necessary and crucial to specifically regulate FAE weapons, and if such a measure is not possible at this point of time, then a temporary measure needs to be introduced. First, some background is given on the political history behind FAE weapons and their principle of action. Then, consequences of use of FAE weapons are weighted from the point of view of Additional Protocol I of 1977 to Geneva Conventions of 12 August 1949 on protection of victims of international armed conflicts based on the criteria of indiscriminate action, superfluous injury and excessive suffering and widespread, long-term and severe damage to the natural environment, after which the chapter will be concluded with a summary of main points introduced therein.

Keywords Public International Law · International Humanitarian Law · Hague Law · Thermobaric weapons · Fuel air explosive weapons (FAEs) · Vacuum weapons · Volumetric weapons · Compression wave · Volume-detonating weapons · Indiscriminate action · Superfluous injury · Excessive suffering

---

E. Tsybulenko (✉)
Faculty of Law, Tallinn University of Technology, Tallinn, Estonia
e-mail: evhen.tsybulenko@taltech.ee

Kyiv International University, Kyiv, Ukraine

© T.M.C. ASSER PRESS and the authors 2022
S. Sayapin et al. (eds.), *International Conflict and Security Law*,
https://doi.org/10.1007/978-94-6265-515-7_17

17.1 Introduction

Relevance of the problem discussed in this chapter is based on the fact that fuel air explosive (FAE) weapons are being actively researched, introduced into service by different states and have already been used several times, despite being little-known to the wider audience. Moreover, this weapon has all the prerequisites necessary to become one of the most destructive and cruel types of weapons of the 21st century. At the same time, specific international legal regulations on the use of such weaponry are absent. As to the general restrictions imposed by norms of Hague Law, those norms are undoubtedly applicable but do not secure adequate regulation. This question has not been discussed enough on the doctrinal level and the few attempts of practical regulation of the use of FAE weapons have not been successful as of yet. In the absence of special regulation on the matter, according to the Martens Clause, "established customs, from the principles of humanity and the dictates of the public conscience" will still be applicable.[1]

Around half a century ago, at first in the specialised military press, then on the pages of magazines and newspapers, terms like "fuel air explosives (FAEs)", "vacuum weapons", "volumetric weapons", "compression wave", "volume-detonating weapons",[2] "боеприпасы объемного взрыва" (Rus.), "вакуумные бомбы" (Rus.)[3] and "les explosifs gazeux" (Fr.)[4] were introduced. We use terminology in three languages on purpose, as quite often there is not a unified terminology or adequate translation for such terminology in different languages. Some experts consider thermobaric ammunition to be fuel air explosive weapons, too. In our opinion, such an approach is incorrect, despite the shared features of those ammunition types. The operation principle of thermobaric weapons is slightly different and, as a result, a zone of residual lower atmospheric pressure is not formed after it is used.[5]

The first tests of the new weapons were carried out in the United States in 1960 and, nine years later, FAE bombs were used by the United States Air Force during the Vietnam campaign.[6] Since then, the Pentagon's arsenal has been allegedly supplemented by several models of such ammunition, which differ not by principle of action but by carrier class (it is not limited and could also be artillery or reactive ammunition or a specialised device) and the composition of the "liquid fuel" and aerosol creation technique.[7] FAE ammunition was also in service in the USSR and the Soviet

---

[1] Additional Protocol to the Geneva Conventions of 12 August 1949 on protection of victims of international armed conflicts (Protocol I). Geneva, 8 June 1977, www.ihl-databases.icrc.org/app lic/ihl/ihl.nsf/Treaty.xsp?documentId=D9E6B6264D7723C3C12563CD002D6CE4&action=ope nDocument Accessed 24 May 2020.

[2] Geisenheyner 1987, p. 280.

[3] Oselin 1986, p. 50.

[4] Brower 1987, p. 1406.

[5] Grek 2003.

[6] Geisenheyner 1987, p. 280; Human Rights Watch 2000.

[7] GlobalSecurity.org 1996b.

17 Fuel Air Explosive Weapons

army used this ammunition in Afghanistan.[8] Research on this type of a weapon has continued in the Russian Federation and the Russian Armed Forces used this ammunition during the Chechnya campaign.[9] In 2007, an FAE bomb was tested in the Russian Federation that was shown to be the most powerful non-nuclear aviation bomb, the efficacy of which was compared to nuclear weapons by the Deputy Chief of the General Staff of the Russian Federation Armed Forces, Alexander Rukshin.[10] At least three cases of the use by the Syrian Armed Forces of FAE bombs that were produced in Russia were recorded in Syria with devastating consequences for the civilian population.[11] Active research in China has been ongoing for many years as well.[12]

However, this technology can also be used for the good of humanity. In particular, new mine-clearing systems were produced for combat engineer divisions, which could be helpful in addressing the problem of antipersonnel landmines. For example, a system that is based on the "CARPET" rocket launcher can make a passage as deep as 100 m in a minefield in one minute.[13] There is also an elongated mine-clearing ammunition that consists of several FAE submunitions that are connected by cables with woven-in fuses. All submunitions are put in the same cassette and ejected from it at the minefield one by one where they are detonated at once. The ability of fuel air explosives to create a highly volatile cloud of fuel-air mist that penetrates a wide area using even the smallest openings, and the possibility of using a rocket launcher to fire FAE rounds, allows the detonation of the rounds from a safe distance. Their detonation will cause all trip wire and pressure activated mines in a given area to detonate as a result, thereby effectively clearing the given area of the field from the mines.[14]

The UN Commission on Conventional Armaments qualified FAE weapons as an "inhumane means of war that cause excessive human suffering".[15] Two proposals to prohibit this type of weapon were already submitted during the third session of the Diplomatic Conference on the Reaffirmation and Development of International Humanitarian Law Applicable in Armed Conflicts that was held from 21 April to 11 June of 1976.[16] In addition, a group of experts from Mexico, Sweden and Switzerland recommended a prohibition of FAE weapons in 1978.[17] Unfortunately, this

---

[8] Human Rights Watch 2000.

[9] Ibid.

[10] Lenta.ru. Science and Technology 2007.

[11] Human Rights Watch 2013.

[12] Silverberg 1991, p. 46, 50; Liu et al. 2008, p. 213.

[13] Defense Update 2006.

[14] United States Patent 1981.

[15] Geisenheyner 1987, p. 280.

[16] Diplomatic Conference on the Reaffirmation and Development of International Humanitarian Law Applicable in Armed Conflicts 1976, 467.

[17] UN Doc. A/CONF 95/PRSP, CONF. L.2/REV. 1. - 11 September 1978.

recommendation, just as proposals to adopt a corresponding protocol to the 1980 UN Convention on Certain Conventional Weapons, did not lead to action.[18]

17.2 Principle of Action of Fuel Air Explosive Weapons

A volumetric explosion has already long been known to man. In chemical factories, warehouses where granular materials are stored, coal mines, grain storages or elevators explosions could happen where one spark could, for example, cause the detonation of an accidentally formed cloud of coal or flour dust. The principle of action of FAEs is similar, whereby an aerosol that is sprayed over the target before being detonated is used instead of a traditional solid explosive.

The unique feature of FAE weapons is that the oxygen in the atmosphere plays the role of the oxidiser. This is the reason why those substances exceed the destructive capacity of conventional explosives several times over. It is known that conventional explosives are fuel and oxidiser at the same time. In particular, TNT (the equivalent of which is used to measure the power of an explosion) consists of only 40% incendiary elements. Therefore, the explosive power of an air-fuel mix that is formed by, for example, ethylene oxide, exceeds that of the equivalent mass of TNT by three to five times. Therefore, the effects of the shock wave on manpower, combat vehicles and different kinds of structures increases.[19] It is necessary to add that before detonation the air-fuel mix fully covers a certain area, while penetrating various, even minor, openings in different buildings and structures.[20]

Furthermore, when the air-fuel mix is detonated, the initial pressure in the epicentre of the explosion is much lower, as during an FAE explosion a quick burning of the mix rather than a detonation takes place, and the speed of the shock wave is slower than that of an equivalent mass TNT explosion. That is the reason why an FAE explosion does not have an expressive brisance and shrapnel effect. However, a shock wave from an FAE explosion lasts much longer than that of conventional explosives. After the explosion, a zone of residual lower atmospheric pressure remains. This is the reason why this type of weapon is sometimes called a vacuum bomb.[21] Nevertheless, it is necessary to understand that it cannot produce a full vacuum.

The design of FAE ammunition can be observed from one of the first models that was in the service of the US Army. When it was dropped near the target, a parachute was ejected in order to slow it down and a probe would be ejected. When the latter touched the ground, the central charge would detonate and spray fuel in the air to form a cloud of a finely dispersed mix. Then an initiation device would trigger and throw several detonators equipped with conventional explosives into that cloud, which would detonate with a slight delay. The air-fuel mix then detonated,

---

[18] McClelland 2005, pp. 766–767.

[19] Barnaby et al. 1978, p. 7.

[20] Geisenheyner 1987, p. 280.

[21] Grek 2003.

17 Fuel Air Explosive Weapons

thereby creating a shockwave with significant overpressure on the front that would be supported by the burning of the air-fuel mix in the cloud.[22]

17.3 Necessity of International Legal Regulation

17.3.1 Indiscriminate Effect

As already noted above, before detonation the air-fuel mix covers a certain area fully. It is capable of enveloping the crevices of the landscape, permeating any, even the slightest openings in fortifications, service and inhabited buildings, dugouts and long-term firing points. Moreover, the effect of such an explosion is significantly amplified in confined spaces. In other words, what is considered a safe cover from shrapnel and shock waves will be absolutely useless in the case of a detonation of an FAE bomb. Therefore, the civilian population will have no opportunity to safeguard themselves in the zone of military action in the absence of fully air-tight bunkers, which are not available in a sufficient amount anywhere.[23] This fact allows us to conclude that this is an indiscriminate weapon. We are convinced that FAE weapons are to be prohibited by international humanitarian law as a distinction cannot be drawn between civilians and combatants when those weapons are used,[24] as is required by Article 48 of the Additional Protocol I from 1977. Moreover, in accordance with Article 51 p.4 (c), an attack cannot be commenced if it employs "a method or means of combat the effects of which cannot be limited as required by this Protocol".[25]

There are certain disagreements as to the question of whether types of weapons that cannot be aimed at special military objectives or the consequences of which cannot be limited, as required by proportionality principles, really exist.[26] When the Protocol was adopted, certain delegates denied the existence of weapons that could be prohibited by this article under any circumstances. They saw here a reminder that the unlawful use of means of war depends on the circumstances. It is possible that this position was motivated by a desire to prevent Article 51(4) from being used as a reasoning behind prohibiting the use of nuclear weapons. If so, then this position was reached *ex abundante cautela* as projects of the Protocol did not aim to consolidate the norms regulating the use of nuclear, bacteriological and chemical weapons.[27]

---

[22] Oselin 1986, p. 50.

[23] GlobalSecurity.org 1996b.

[24] Tsybulenko 1997, p. 125.

[25] Additional Protocol to the Geneva Conventions of 12 August 1949 on protection of victims of international armed conflicts (Protocol I). Geneva, 8 June 1977 https://ihl-databases.icrc.org/app lic/ihl/ihl.nsf/Treaty.xsp?documentId=D9E6B6264D7723C3C12563CD002D6CE4&action=ope nDocument Accessed 3 July 2018.

[26] Blix 1988, p. 144.

[27] Ibid.

In accordance with this logic, the principle of proportionality requires that incidental impact on civilians and civilian facilities is not excessive in comparison to the expected military advantage. In accordance with that, the lawfulness of the use of such types of weapons will depend on the circumstances, and therefore it is enough to prohibit the indiscriminate use of the weapon rather than the weapon itself. In my opinion, this approach is not always justified, or there would be no need to prohibit cluster munitions or restrict the use of incendiary weapons. With regard to FAE weapons, this approach would only be possible outside of inhabited areas or other places of the accumulation of civilians. In other cases, it is not possible to use this type of weapon selectively.

17.3.2 Superfluous Injury and Excessive Suffering

The effects of detonation of FAE ammunition on humans and animals significantly differ from those of conventional explosives. As noted above, a prolonged shockwave after which an area of residual lower atmospheric pressure is formed is added to the classical destructive factors, with the exception of shrapnel in some cases.

As a result of such an abrupt change in atmospheric pressure, very heavy injuries are inflicted. Persons who find themselves in the epicentre of the explosion are completely vaporized, as even the land surface after the use of FAE weapons resembles that of the craters of the moon. Those outside of the epicentre, can sustain tears in their lungs and other internal organs, eardrum tears and serious injuries of the middle ear, heavy contusions and blindness in some cases.[28] It is important to note that many of those injuries of internal organs can be unnoticeable externally and hard to diagnose, especially in field conditions, which would make the death of the injured person inevitable.[29]

Moreover, an air-fuel mix does not always detonate. In that case, victims sustain heavy burns, including internal burns due to the possibility of inhaling burning fuel. Such ammunition is very dangerous even if detonation does not happen at all. Often, an air-fuel mix consists of ethylene oxide and propylene oxide, which are toxic enough to kill.[30] It should be noted that if the ammunition triggers incorrectly, FAE weapons can become a *de facto* incendiary or chemical weapon even though it is not the intended purpose for its use.

Alas, there are no precise criteria to determine "superfluous injury and excessive suffering". Within the framework of the "SIrUS" (superfluous injury or unnecessary suffering), the International Committee of the Red Cross offered four solutions for such criteria[31] but, unfortunately, none of them were adopted as a legally binding norm. The US Army field manual even states the following: "It is only possible to

---

[28] Central Intelligence Agency 1990; Human Rights Watch 2000.

[29] David 2012, p. 355.

[30] Defense Intelligence Agency 1993; Human Rights Watch 2000.

[31] Coupland 1997, p. 23; ICRC 1997, p. 23.

define whether a weapon inflicts "superfluous injury" on the basis of state practice with regards to the abandonment of weapons that are considered to inflict such injuries".[32] At one of the meetings of state experts in Lucerne, it was concluded that the terms "injury" and "suffering" presuppose the existence of such factors as mortality, pain caused by the wounds, severity of the wounds, number of cases of physical injuries and irreversible physical deformations.[33] Since FAE weapons do inflict superfluous injury and excessive suffering within the meaning of Article 35(2) of Additional Protocol I 1977,[34] their use even against combatants should be prohibited.

17.3.3 Widespread, Long-term and Severe Damage to the Natural Environment

In accordance with Article 35(3) of Additional Protocol I of 1977, "It is prohibited to employ methods or means of warfare which are intended, or may be expected, to cause widespread, long-term and severe damage to the natural environment." Moreover, in Article 55(1) this general prohibition is detailed further with regards to prejudice to the health or survival of the population.[35] Comparatively small aerial bombs were the first FAE weapons. They could not cause widespread, long-term or severe damage to the natural environment. During the first stages of development, it did not seem possible to increase the power of the explosion, as it would be necessary to increase the size of the aerosol cloud, which would become unstable as a consequence. Nevertheless, those issues were successfully solved with the help of new technology. Moreover, scientists and engineers went even further—now there can be several FAE submunitions in one casing that would be ejected above the target and dispersed over a certain area while descending by parachutes, thereby increasing the affected area.[36] This effect can also be achieved by using multiple rocket launchers.[37] Combined use of such technology allows the transformation of a virtually almost unlimited area into a burning desert.

According to some sources, trials that imitated an FAE bomb explosion were conducted in the ocean as deep as 450–700 m. The goal of the experiment was to

---

[32] Department of the Army 1956, §34, p. 18.

[33] Conference d'experts gouvernmentaux sur l'emploi de certaines armes conventionneles (Lucerne, 24 sept.-18 oct. 1974), Rapport. - Geneve: CICR, 1975, pp. 8–9.

[34] Additional Protocol to the Geneva Conventions of 12 August 1949 on protection of victims of international armed conflicts (Protocol I). Geneva, 8 June 1977 www.ihl-databases.icrc.org/applic/ihl/ihl.nsf/Treaty.xsp?documentId=D9E6B6264D7723C3C12563CD002D6CE4&action=openDocument Accessed 3 July 2018.

[35] Ibid.

[36] GlobalSecurity.org 1996a.

[37] Huber 2001, pp. 14–15, 17.

create super-powerful warheads for deep-water bombs and anti-submarine torpedoes. FAE explosions were also researched in the upper layers of the atmosphere.[38]

At the moment, it is not possible to predict with full certainty exactly how dangerous the upcoming types of FAE ammunition are for the natural environment. However, it is necessary to stress that Articles 35 and 55 do not only mention actions that aim to damage the natural environment. Those articles also directly regulate the means and the methods that "can be expected" to cause such damage.

17.4 Conclusion

The following conclusions can be made based on all that has been discussed above:

Development and introduction into service of FAE weapons aimed for land, air and sea warfare is being actively continued in different states. The third generation of FAE weapons under discussion are controlled by computers, which allows them to affect an almost unlimited area.[39] The explosive power of these is comparable to that of a nuclear bomb.[40] This state of affairs clearly demonstrates that the existing norms and principles of Hague Law, which regulates the means and methods of war, are not effective in regard to FAE weapons. As Lukashuk rightfully noted: "General principles of international humanitarian law are applicable to new types of weapons as well. However, general regulation cannot replace special regulation. Creation of corresponding specific norms is defined by the political will of states, formed under the influence of economic and military interest and partially ethical considerations."[41]

FAE weapons are (a) indiscriminate weapons, (b) inhumane means of war that cause superfluous injury and excessive suffering, and also (c) possibly capable of widespread, long-term and severe harm to the natural environment, especially in the case of their further developments. It seems reasonable to develop and adopt an international convention prohibiting the use, development, production, purchase, accumulation, storage and transfer of FAE ammunition, as well providing for its destruction, with an exception to be made that are used as mine-clearing means.[42] Alternatively, a new protocol to the UN Convention of 1980 on Certain Conventional Weapons could be adopted.[43] Moreover, if this question is solved from the point of view of international legal norm-creation—in other words an appropriate convention is adopted and enters in force—further implementation of those norms, including criminalisation of the breaches of this conventions on the national level, will be quite significant for increasing the effectiveness of its norm realisation mechanism.

---

[38] Oselin 1986, pp. 52–53.

[39] Silverberg 1991, pp. 46, 50; Geisenheyner 1987, p. 282.

[40] S patent No: 4,873,928. Nuclear-size explosions without radiation, 17.10.1989; Grek 2003.

[41] Lukashuk 1997, p. 288.

[42] Tsybulenko 1998, p. 113.

[43] Ibid.

17 Fuel Air Explosive Weapons

If it is not possible to prohibit FAE weapons at this stage, it would be necessary to restrict their use as a temporary measure with the help of adopting provisions analogous to those restricting the use of incendiary weapons in accordance with the "Protocol on prohibitions or restrictions on use of incendiary weapons" (Protocol III) to the UN Convention of 1980 on Certain Conventional Weapons.[44]

References

Barnaby F et al (1978) World armaments and disarmament. SIPRI Yearbook. Taylor & Francis, London/Philadelphia

Blix H (1988) Means and methods of combat, International Dimensions of Humanitarian Law. UNESCO, Paris

Brower K S (1987) Fuel-Air Explosives - A Blow To Dismounted Infantry. International Defense Review, 10:1405–1407

Central Intelligence Agency (CIA) (1990) Conventional Weapons Producing Chemical-Warfare-Agent-Like Injuries. Central Intelligence Agency, Washington

Coupland R (1997) The SIrUS project. ICRC, Geneva

David E (2012) Principles of law of armed conflict. ICRC, Geneva

Defense Intelligence Agency (1993) Fuel-Air and Enhanced-Blast Explosive Technology -Foreign. Defense Intelligence Agency, Washington

Defense Update (2006) CARPET – New Mine Breaching System Based on Fuel-Air Explosive (FAE) www.defense-update.com/20060627_carpet.html. Accessed 3 July 2018

DeGhett T R (2015) A New Kind of Bomb Is Being Used in Syria and It's a Humanitarian Nightmare www.news.vice.com/article/a-new-kind-of-bomb-is-being-used-in-syria-and-its-a-humanitarian-nightmare. Accessed 3 July 2018

Department of the Army (1956) Department of the Army field manual FM 27-10, The Law of Land Warfare. Department of the Army, Washington D. C.

Diplomatic Conference on the Reaffirmation and Development of International Humanitarian Law Applicable in Armed Conflicts (1976) Summary of the third session's work. International Review, 186:443–467

Geisenheyner S (1987) "FAE development: disturbing trends". Jane's Defence Weekly, 21 February, 7:280–282

GlobalSecurity.org (1996a) CBU-72 / BLU-73/B Fuel/Air Explosive (FAE) www.globalsecurity.org/military/systems/munitions/cbu-72.htm Accessed 3 July 2018

GlobalSecurity.org (1996b) Fuel/Air Explosive (FAE) www.globalsecurity.org/military/systems/munitions/fae.htm. Accessed 3 July 2018

Grek A (2003) Household bomb: volumetric explosion. Popular mechanics www.popmech.ru/weapon/8683-bytovaya-bomba-obemnyy-vzryv/ . Accessed 3 July 2018

Huber D (2001) Fuel-Air Explosives Mature, Armor, 2001(November-December):14–17

Human Rights Watch (2000) Backgrounder on Russian Fuel Air Explosives ("Vacuum Bombs") www.hrw.org/en/reports/2000/02/01/backgrounder-russian-fuel-air-explosives-vacuum-bombs. Accessed 3 July 2018

Human Rights Watch (2013) Syria: Fuel-Air Bombs Strike School www.hrw.org/news/2013/10/01/syria-fuel-air-bombs-strike-school. Accessed 3 July 2018

ICRC (1997) The SIrUS Project: towards a determination of which weapons cause "superfluous injury or unnecessary suffering". ICRC, Geneva.

Lenta.ru. Science and Technology (2007) The most powerful vacuum bomb was tested in Russia www.lenta.ru/news/2007/09/11/vacuum/. Accessed 3 July 2018

---

[44] Ibid.

Liu G et al (2008) Experimental Study of Fuel-air Explosive, Combustion, Explosion, and Shock Waves. [author, insert name publication] 44:213–217.

Lukashuk I I (1997) International jurisprudence. Special part. BEK, Moscow

McClelland J (2005) Conventional weapons: a cluster of developments. International & Comparative Law Quarterly, 54(3):755–767

Oselin V (1986) "FAE bomb". TM, 1986, №8, p 50.

Reuters (2007) Russia tests superstrength bomb, military says https://www.reuters.com/art icle/us-russia-bomb/russia-tests-superstrength-bomb-military-says-idUSL1155952320070912 Accessed 24 May 2020

Silverberg D (1991) China firm takes wraps off new fuel air bomb. Defense News, 24 June

Tsybulenko E (1997) FAE weapons in the light of international humanitarian law. Kiev University Newsletter. International relations, 7(II):124–128

Tsybulenko E (1998) FAE weapons in the light of international humanitarian law. Ukrainian jurisprudence, 12:109–113

Tsybulenko E, Francis J A (2018) Separatists or Russian Troops and Local Collaborators? Russian Aggression in Ukraine: The Problem of Definitions. In: Sayapin S, Tsybulenko E (eds) The Use of Force against Ukraine and International Law. T.M.C. Asser Press, The Hague, pp. 123–144

United States Patent (1981) Surface-launched fuel air explosive minefield clearing round https:// patentimages.storage.googleapis.com/c1/59/7a/af6507902500df/US4273048.pdf. Accessed 24 May 2020

Evhen Tsybulenko is an Estonian Legal Scholar of Ukrainian descent. In 2000, he earned a Ph.D. in International Law from Kyiv National University, Ukraine, and carried out postdoctoral research at the International Human Rights Law Institute of De Paul University, USA, in 2002. In Ukraine, he worked at the International Committee of the Red Cross (ICRC) and the Kyiv International University where he is a Professor since 2009. In Estonia, he was elected as a Professor of Law (2005) and appointed Chair of International and Comparative Law Department at the Tallinn University of Technology's Law School (2005–2010). Currently he is a Senior lecturer at the same School. He was a Founder and Director of the Tallinn Law School's Human Rights Centre (2007–2014). He was also an Adjunct (Visiting) Professor and Senior Visiting Mentor at the Joint Command and General Staff Course (JCGSC) at Baltic Defence College (2007–2013). He published over 40 books and academic articles and more than 200 general interest articles, comments and interviews in 15 countries, mainly in Ukrainian or Russian, but also in English and other languages. He cooperates, as an external expert, with the ICRC, Estonian Red Cross, Estonian Integration Commission, Directorate-General for Education and Culture of the European Commission, and the Organization for Security and Co-operation in Europe (OSCE).

Chapter 18
Current Issues of Hague Law

Evhen Tsybulenko and Anastassiya Platonova

Contents

18.1 Introduction 389
18.2 Depleted Uranium Ammunition 390
18.3 Dum-dum Bullets: Modern Aspects 393
References 395

Abstract It is indisputable that technological developments in the 21st century have kept up with the speed they had developed in the 20th century. No doubt that *jus in bello* needs to heed new technology very cautiously, albeit it is not always possible to predict how will it turn out in the future. This chapter aims to explore modern aspects of some weapons, which are still relevant for Hague Law. After addressing some general questions of Hague Law, the chapter discusses modern aspects of depleted uranium ammunition and dum-dum bullets.

Keywords Public international law · International humanitarian law · Hague Law · depleted uranium ammunition · dum-dum bullets

18.1 Introduction

A famous Ukrainian jurist, Vasiliy Nezabitovskiy, wrote in the middle of the 19th century: "Improved organisation of economic relations, modern system of tax and credit, high level of development of natural sciences and various technologies provide

E. Tsybulenko (✉)
Faculty of Law, Tallinn University of Technology, Tallinn, Estonia
e-mail: evhen.tsybulenko@taltech.ee

Kyiv International University, Kyiv, Ukraine

A. Platonova
Anastassiya Platonova, Tallinn University of Technology, Tallinn, Estonia

© T.M.C. ASSER PRESS and the authors 2022
S. Sayapin et al. (eds.), *International Conflict and Security Law*,
https://doi.org/10.1007/978-94-6265-515-7_18

enormous means and new weapons for war. It seems that, in a strange twist of irony, a natural law of development turns successes of humanity to the purpose of its demise".[1] These words have not lost their relevance to this day, when the number of armed conflicts is still high, despite all efforts of the international community to prevent them. The norms and principles of Hague Law play an important part in this environment.

Hague Law can be defined as a set of conventional and customary norms and principles of public international law, which regulate the rights and responsibilities of belligerents during an armed conflict (both international and non-international), and restrict the means and methods of warfare. At the very beginning of the 20th century, the renowned Estonian scientist Friedrich (Fedor) Martens rightfully noted: "[W]ar is not a denial of law but, on the contrary, it follows known laws, that were made sacred by custom and international agreements".[2]

In our opinion, the norms and principles of Hague Law provide a good basis for ensuring protection of civilians and other victims of international armed conflicts. At the same time, modernisation and creation of new types of conventional weapons are moving forward rather quickly. As a result, certain types of weapons are either unregulated or not regulated enough by Hague Law. In this chapter, we look at two types of weapons raising such questions.

18.2 Depleted Uranium Ammunition

One of the most discussed questions of Hague Law today is the legitimacy of the use of depleted uranium ammunition (where uranium consists of 99.8% of the U-238 isotope). The U-238 isotope cannot cause a chain reaction and is highly stable.[3] In this type of ammunition, depleted uranium is usually used as the material for the core of armour-piercing sub-caliber projectiles. Depleted uranium is also used as a component of armour. It has been reported that depleted uranium ammunition is produced in Great Britain, China, Pakistan, Russia, the USA and France.[4] The USA and Great Britain allegedly used such ammunition in the Iraq campaigns of 1991 and 2003, and in Kosovo.[5]

A unique feature of the depleted uranium is its high density—19.03 g/cm^3, which allows for the ammunition made from depleted uranium to be highly armour-piercing and relatively cheap at the same time, as depleted uranium is, in fact, waste from the nuclear industry, and countries with developed nuclear industries have amassed great amounts of it. The sole alternative to the use of depleted uranium that is actually employed in practice is wolfram (also known as tungsten) with a density of 19.03

---

[1] Nezabitovskiy 1884, p. 148.

[2] Martens 1904, p. 14.

[3] World Nuclear Association 2016.

[4] International Coalition to Ban Uranium Weapons 2016.

[5] Ibid.

g/cm^3, which is much more expensive and labour-intensive to process. In addition to that, wolfram, unlike depleted uranium, is not pyrophoric (ability to self-ignite in a finely crushed state without any heat present). It is because of pyrophoricity that the sprayed remains of a uranium core self-ignites after piercing the armour, which ensures considerable beyond-armour effects.[6] It also has to be taken into account that around 80% of the known wolfram reserves are situated in China, and that the reserves of wolfram in general are rather limited.[7]

To this day there is no specific regulation of depleted uranium ammunition in international humanitarian law. At the same time, the use of such weapons gives rise to questions of ecology and medicine.[8] Unused depleted uranium ammunition does not pose any danger. However, elements remaining after such ammunition was used, can pose a certain risk for human life and health. It is important to note that the main danger is not the radioactivity of depleted uranium as many mistakenly assume to be the case, but rather its high toxicity as a heavy metal, since after getting in the bloodstream, uranium is directed to and extracted through kidneys, and accumulated in various body parts—skeleton (66%), liver (16%), kidneys (8%) and other tissues (10%).[9]

However, radioactivity cannot be completely disregarded either. Despite the radioactivity of depleted uranium being quite low (40% lower than uranium ore) and mostly consisting of alpha-radiation that cannot pierce human skin, the dust of depleted uranium has the potential to harmfully affect the body if it enters the body through wounds, digestive or respiratory systems. Nevertheless, the WHO states that there is no exact scientific proof of such effects. It is considered that the rise of cancer rates among uranium mines workers is connected with radon gas rather than uranium. No rise in lung cancer was registered among uranium mine workers.[10] Other serious research also indicates such potential health risks, while specifying that a deciding factor would be the dose received.[11]

The WHO experts cite potentially dangerous doses of chemical and radiological effects for human beings, and note that a local clean-up of territory with a follow-up monitoring is to be performed where depleted uranium ammunition was used, as uranium can enter the food chain through soil and water during the next few years after the ammunition was used. Experts also acknowledge that not all consequences of the use of depleted uranium ammunition have been studied yet, and further research is required.[12] The lack of certainty with regard to potential (especially long-term) risks for human health is a cause for concern.

Moreover, this uncertainty makes the international legal regulation of depleted uranium ammunition problematic. On the one hand, there is an exceptionally effective

---

[6] Lawand 2006, pp. 931–956.

[7] Monet 2012.

[8] Zwijnenburg 2013, pp. 4–5.

[9] WHO 2001, p. 7.

[10] Ibid.

[11] The Royal Society 2001.

[12] WHO 2001.

weapon for which there is no alternative if the price is taken into account. On the other hand, almost none of the risks are clear at the moment but are considered to be highly likely although this requires further research. Alas, the governments of the states armed with depleted uranium ammunition are rather skeptical with regard to the idea of the restriction or complete prohibition of such weapons.[13] Such weapons are only prohibited by law in Belgium. The governments of Ireland, New Zealand and Costa Rica are considering the question of the prohibition of depleted uranium ammunition, but none of those countries are armed with such weapons.[14]

If we consider the criteria used by Hague law, based on which the use of weapons can be prohibited or restricted—indiscriminate action, the capacity to cause unnecessary suffering or superfluous injury, as well as the capacity to cause extensive, long-lasting and severe harm to the environment—then it will be apparent that at the immediate moment of use of depleted uranium ammunition, it does not fall under that criteria. Nevertheless, the remains of depleted uranium ammunition left after the use of such a weapon may potentially fall under that criteria, especially in the long-term perspective.

The precautionary principle gains a special meaning in such a situation.[15] Relying on that principle, a full prohibition of the use of depleted uranium ammunition is desirable. But sadly, the possibility of such a prohibition today does not seem realistic. Therefore, it seems reasonable to impose a moratorium on the use of depleted uranium ammunition at least in populated localities and other places of concentrated civilian populations as a temporary measure. In addition to that, it is necessary to oblige the states that use such weapons to organise a clean-up of the territory with follow-up monitoring of potential risks.

This approach is reflected in the decisions of influential international organisations. The UN General Assembly in its resolution A/RES/62/30 "Effects of the use of armaments and ammunitions containing depleted uranium" of 5 December 2007 recommended the Secretary General to ask for the opinions of the Member States and the relevant international organisations with regard to the effects of the use of armaments and ammunitions containing depleted uranium.[16] On 2 December 2008, the UN General Assembly adopted another resolution of the same name (A/RES/63/54), which noted "the potential harmful effects of the use of armaments and ammunitions containing depleted uranium on human health and the environment", observed that "as humankind is more aware of the need to take immediate measures to protect the environment, any event that could jeopardise such efforts requires urgent attention to implement the required measures", and called for further research.[17]

---

[13] See for example Ministry of Defence of the UK 2013.

[14] World Nuclear Association 2016.

[15] Weir 2012, p. 6.

[16] UN General Assembly, Sixty-second Session, Official Records, Agenda item 98, Resolution adopted by the General Assembly "Effects of the use of armaments and ammunitions containing depleted uranium", A/RES/62/30, 5 December 2007.

[17] UN General Assembly, Sixty-third Session, Official Records, Agenda item 89 (p), Resolution adopted by the General Assembly "Effects of the use of armaments and ammunitions containing depleted uranium", A/RES/63/54, 2 December 2008.

18 Current Issues of Hague Law

A number of resolutions on the question at hand were adopted by the European Parliament too. In particular, in resolution P6_TA(2008) 0233 from 22 May 2008, the European Parliament inter alia called to impose a moratorium on the use of depleted uranium ammunition and for the UN Security Council and Member States to take up an initiative to develop a convention on the prohibition of the development, production, accumulation, transfer, trials and use of depleted uranium ammunition as well as destroying or utilising existing reserves if there is convincing scientific proof of the damage caused by depleted uranium ammunition.[18]

The use of depleted uranium munitions pose a significant risk to humans, both soldiers on either side of a potential conflict[19] and civilians, as well as the environment. However, despite a number of recommendations from prominent international organisations to prohibit or restrict the use of depleted uranium munitions, depleted uranium weapons are not specifically regulated by international humanitarian law. Despite the applicability of customary law, the law of humanity, the law of nations and dictates of public conscience based on the Martens Clause,[20] due to the potential effect of the remains of depleted uranium ammunition on people and the environment, in the interest of caution, specific regulation is desirable.

18.3 Dum-dum Bullets: Modern Aspects

The prohibition of the use of bullets which "expand or flatten easily in the human body, such as bullets with a hard envelope which does not entirely cover the core, or is pierced with incisions", also known as "dum-dum" bullets or expanding bullets, was established as early as in 1899,[21] during the First Hague Peace Conference. Therefore, this prohibition is one of the oldest in Hague Law, only yielding to the prohibition of explosive bullets established by the Saint-Petersburg Declaration of 1868. Dum-dum bullets, just as explosive bullets earlier, were prohibited on the grounds that they, just as usual bullets, could incapacitate only one person, but caused superfluous injury and excessive suffering. Although the scope of Declaration (IV, 3) initially only included international armed conflicts, currently the prohibition is considered a customary

---

[18] "European Parliament resolution of 22 May 2008 on (depleted) uranium weapons and their effect on human health and the environment—towards a global ban on the use of such weapons", P6_TA(2008)0233, (2008) www.europarl.europa.eu/meetdocs/2009_2014/documents/sede/dv/sede061011epresolutionuraniumweapons_/sede061011epresolutionuraniumweapons_en.pdf. Accessed 30 June 2018.

[19] Franzen 2001.

[20] Convention (II) with Respect to the Laws and Customs of War on Land and its annex: Regulations concerning the Laws and Customs of War on Land. The Hague, 29 July 1899. http://www.ihl-databases.icrc.org/applic/ihl/ihl.nsf/Article.xsp?action=openDocument&documentId=9FE084CDAC63D10FC12563CD00515C4D Accessed 28 May 2020.

[21] Declaration (IV, 3) concerning Expanding Bullets. The Hague, 29 July 1899 www.icrc.org/applic/ihl/ihl.nsf/Article.xsp?action=openDocument&documentId=F5FF4D9CA7E41925C12563CD0051616B. Accessed 30 June 2018.

law norm applicable in both international and non-international armed conflicts.[22] Moreover, Article 8(2)(b)(xix) of the ICC Statute defines the use of dumdum bullets as a war crime. At the same time, dum-dum bullets are not prohibited for peacetime use, and are actively used for hunting, self-defence, and by police forces in different states. The main reason for this is that the bullet stays in the body of the criminal (a usual bullet can also injure other people if it goes through). Furthermore, police should have the opportunity to incapacitate the criminal quickly and effectively, in order to not allow him or her to detonate explosive devices or shoot hostages.[23] We consider those arguments convincing.

The prohibition of the use of dum-dum bullets during armed conflicts works rather effectively. Despite the fact that at the beginning of the 20th century there were reports whose authenticity in the majority of cases is doubtful, about the use of such bullets in colonial wars of that period and World War I,[24] there have not been any documented cases of the use of dum-dum bullets ever since.[25]

In the 1960s and 1970s, different states *en masse* started introducing into service firearms requiring small calibre bullets of 5.56 mm (the USA and NATO countries) and 5.45 mm (in the USSR and Warsaw Pact countries). Those bullets have a smaller weight but a higher launch speed in order to support stable flight and therefore higher kinetic energy. Despite that, such bullets remain less stable and as a result start to revolve and/or fragment, thereby transferring a major part of the kinetic energy to human organs.[26] The higher the kinetic energy of the bullet during that process, the worse are the injuries caused by that bullet to human organs. As a result, despite those bullets not being formally dum-dum bullets and therefore not falling under the prohibition of the use of dum-dum bullets, the consequences of their use are practically identical.[27] Arguments that such bullets should fall under the customary international law prohibition were not taken into account.[28] Therefore, a necessity arose to align the prohibition of the use of dum-dum bullets with modern requirements.

Starting from the 1970s, several attempts were made in order to solve this problem at various conferences, however, no legally binding documents were adopted.[29] However, a wide discussion of this question lead to certain positive changes. In 1981, NATO adopted a new standard for calibres of firearms. Despite 5.56 mm caliber becoming that standard, the Belgian ammunition model SS-109 with a higher coefficient of durability was taken up as the standard ammunition, instead of the American ammunition model M193 Ball. Technical tests have shown that an SS-109 bullet

---

[22] Henckaerts and Doswald-Beck 2005, p. 268.

[23] Waddington 1990, pp. 703–704.

[24] David 2012, pp. 373–374.

[25] Coupland and Loye 2003, p. 135.

[26] David 2012, pp. 361–362.

[27] Doswald-Beck and Cauderay 1990, p. 568.

[28] Prokosch 1995, pp. 412–413.

[29] Coupland and Loye 2003, p. 140; Doswald-Beck and Cauderay 1990, p. 567; Prokosch 1995, pp. 414–416.

started losing energy quickly (with intensity 50 and more (J) per cm) after it was submerged 14 cm into the body. After it was 20 cm submerged, it gave only 600 J of energy away to the tissues. For comparison, a 5.45 mm calibre bullet of the Russian assault rifle AK-74, which inflicts very heavy wounds, starts giving away energy to the body after it is only 9 cm submerged in the body, and gives 600 J away to the tissues when it is 14 cm submerged.[30]

Nevertheless, the problem in its essence was not solved, even an SS-109 bullet can inflict quite serious wounds, and much more dangerous 5.45 calibre bullets of the Russian model are being actively used. In addition, there are no guarantees that in the absence of proper regulation, new models of such ammunition will not be introduced.

Therefore, the necessity of regulation for the use of small calibre ammunition remains relevant. In our opinion, the suggestion developed by Swiss experts during preparation for the 1995 review conference on the 1980 UN Convention on Conventional Weapons could be a basis for such regulation. Based on this suggestion, weapons and ammunition with a calibre of less than 12.7 mm that at a shooting distance of 25 metres release more than 20 J of energy per each centimetre for the first 15 centimetres of the passage of the bullet into a human body, are to be prohibited. The advantage of this suggestion is that the impact of the bullet is measured by objective criteria. Thus, the prohibition will be effective regardless of the methods used to achieve such effect, even if the effect is achieved by the design of the weapon, and not the design of the bullet.[31]

References

Books, (Online) Articles and Chapters in Books

Coupland R, Loye D (2003) The 1899 Hague Declaration concerning Expanding Bullets. A treaty effective for more than 100 years faces complex contemporary issues. International Review of the Red Cross, 44:135–142
David E (2012) Principles of law of armed conflict. ICRC, Geneva
Doswald-Beck L, Cauderay GC (1990) The development of new anti-personnel weapons. International Review of the Red Cross, 30:565–577
Franzen H (2001) The Science of Silver Bullet. https://www.scientificamerican.com/article/the-sci ence-of-the-silver/ Accessed 25 May 2020
Henckaerts JM, Doswald-Beck L (eds) (2005) Customary International Humanitarian Law, Volume 1 (Rules). ICRC, Cambridge University Press, Cambridge
International Coalition to Ban Uranium Weapons (2016) Uranium Weapons: The problem www. icbuw.eu/en/the-problem/. Accessed 28 May 2020
Kajander A, Kasper A, Tsybulenko E (2020) Making the Cyber Mercenary – Autonomous Weapons Systems and Common Article 1 of the Geneva Conventions. In: Jančárková T et al. (eds) 12th

---

[30] Prokosch 1995, p. 419.

[31] Prokosch 1995, pp. 411, 419–421.

International Conference on Cyber Conflict. 20/20 Vision: The Next Decade. NATO CCDCOE Publications, Tallinn, pp. 79–95

Lawand K (2006) A Guide to the Legal Review of New Weapons, Means and Methods of Warfare: Measures to Implement Article 36 of Additional Protocol I of 1977. International Review of the Red Cross 47:931–956

Martens FF (1904) Contemporary International Law of Civilised Nations, Volume I. Publishing [H]ouse of the Railways Ministry, Saint Petersburg

Ministry of Defence of the UK (2013) Depleted uranium. The Ministry of Defence's policy on using depleted uranium in weapons and how we monitor munitions and health and environmental risk. UK Government portal: www.gov.uk/depleted-uranium. Accessed 30 June 2018

Monet P (2012) The World Is Running Low On Tungsten; Why You Should Care www.forbes.com/sites/ciocentral/2012/03/14/the-world-is-running-low-on-tungsten-why-you-should-care. Accessed 30 June 2018

Nezabitovskiy VA (1884) Collected writing. Kiev

Prokosch E (1995) The Swiss Draft Protocol on Small-Calibre Weapon Systems. Bringing the dumdum ban (1899) up to date. International Review of the Red Cross, 35:411–425

The Royal Society (2001) The health hazards of depleted uranium munitions. Part I, Report. The Royal Society, London

Waddington PAJ (1990) "Overkill" or "minimum force"? Criminal Law Review, October:695–707

Weir D (2012) Precaution in Practice: challenging the acceptability of depleted uranium weapons. International Coalition to Ban Uranium Weapons, Manchester

WHO (2001) Depleted uranium: sources, exposure and health effects. Executive summary. www.who.int/ionizing_radiation/pub_meet/en/DU_Eng.pdf. Accessed 30 June 2018

WHO (2001) WHO Guidance on Exposure to Depleted Uranium For Medical Officers and Programme Administrators. Annex: Characteristics of Depleted Uranium. WHO, Geneva

World Nuclear Association (2016) Uranium and Depleted Uranium www.world-nuclear.org/information-library/nuclear-fuel-cycle/uranium-resources/uranium-and-depleted-uranium.aspx. Accessed 30 June 2018

Zwijnenburg W (2013) In a state of uncertainty Impact and implications of the use of depleted uranium in Iraq. IKV Pax Christi, Utrecht

Other Documents

Convention (II) with Respect to the Laws and Customs of War on Land and its annex: Regulations concerning the Laws and Customs of War on Land. The Hague, 29 July 1899. ihl-databases.icrc.org/applic/ihl/ihl.nsf/Article.xsp?action=openDocument&documentId=9FE084CDAC63D10FC12563CD00515C4D. Accessed 28 May 2020

Evhen Tsybulenko is an Estonian Legal Scholar of Ukrainian descent. In 2000, he earned a Ph.D. in International Law from Kyiv National University, Ukraine, and carried out postdoctoral research at the International Human Rights Law Institute of De Paul University, USA, in 2002. In Ukraine, he worked at the International Committee of the Red Cross (ICRC) and the Kyiv International University where he is a Professor since 2009. In Estonia, he was elected as a Professor of Law (2005) and appointed Chair of International and Comparative Law Department at the Tallinn University of Technology's Law School (2005–2010). Currently he is a Senior lecturer at the same School. He was a Founder and Director of the Tallinn Law School's Human Rights Centre (2007–2014). He was also an Adjunct (Visiting) Professor and Senior Visiting Mentor at the Joint Command and General Staff Course (JCGSC) at Baltic Defence College (2007–2013). He published over 40 books and academic articles and more than 200 general interest articles, comments and interviews in 15 countries, mainly in Ukrainian or Russian, but also in English and other languages. He cooperates, as an external expert, with the ICRC, Estonian Red Cross, Estonian Integration Commission, Directorate-General for Education and Culture of the European Commission, and the Organization for Security and Co-operation in Europe (OSCE).

Anastassiya Platonova is a KYC Compliance Analyst on bribery and AML issues with MA in Law with the specialisation in Law and Technology from TalTech. She studied at TalTech, Tallinn and Luiss Guido Carli, Rome. She was also a part of the winning team of the All-European International Human Rights and Refugee Law Moot Court in autumn 2016 and a participant of the Cyber 9/12 in Geneva in 2019.

Chapter 19
Military Space Operations

Kubo Mačák

Contents

19.1 Introduction 400
19.2 Defining Military Space Operations 401
19.3 International Space Law 403
    19.3.1 No General Prohibition of Military Space Operations 404
    19.3.2 Specific Restrictions on Military Space Operations 404
    19.3.3 Interaction Between Space Law and Other Areas of International Law 406
19.4 International Law on the Use of Force 407
    19.4.1 Use of Force 407
    19.4.2 Threat to Use Force 409
    19.4.3 Armed Attack and Self-defence 410
19.5 International Humanitarian Law 411
    19.5.1 Distinction 413
    19.5.2 Proportionality 414
    19.5.3 Precautions 416
19.6 Conclusion 417
References 418

Abstract This chapter examines the international legal framework governing military space operations. In the chapter, 'military space operations' are understood as sequences of co-ordinated actions with a defined purpose, which are of a military character and have a material nexus to outer space. On the basis of this definition, the chapter then analyses issues raised by each of the principal bodies of international law that regulate military uses of outer space, starting with international space law, followed by the international law on the use of force and international humanitarian law. The chapter concludes by considering several overarching questions and the possible future development of the law in this area.

Keywords Armed conflict · international humanitarian law · military operations · outer space · satellites · space law · UN Charter · use of force

---

K. Mačák (✉)
Law School, University of Exeter, Exeter EX4 4RJ, UK
e-mail: k.macak@exeter.ac.uk

© T.M.C. ASSER PRESS and the authors 2022
S. Sayapin et al. (eds.), *International Conflict and Security Law*,
https://doi.org/10.1007/978-94-6265-515-7_19

19.1 Introduction

This chapter examines the international legal framework governing military space operations. Although States have been using space assets to further their security and military goals since the first satellite was launched in 1957, the main threshold moment in this area arguably came with the 1991 Gulf War. That conflict is sometimes called the First Space War because of the United States' extensive use of space capabilities in support of its military effort.[1] It was also a clarion call to other States, demonstrating vividly the unparalleled military potential offered by the space domain. Countries including Russia, China, India, France, and others have since made the development of effective space and counter-space capabilities a first-order military priority.

Several recent examples stand out to illustrate this trend. Perhaps most dramatically, a number of States now possess the capability to launch destructive earth-to-space attacks against satellites in orbit, with India being the latest member to join this growing club.[2] In addition, there have been reports of military satellites like the Russian *Luch* sidling close to other States' space assets in orbit, raising concerns that such manoeuvrable objects may be used to intercept communication or interfere with enemy satellites.[3] In response, France announced in 2019 that it would develop defensive space weapons, including so-called 'bodyguard' satellites, to protect its assets against such threats.[4]

All of these developments confirm the urgency of understanding the constraints that the law places on military uses of outer space. At present, there is no dedicated international legal regime for military space operations. Instead, the applicable law must be identified through the interpretation of the various relevant bodies of international law, which include international space law, the international law on the use of force, and international humanitarian law (IHL), against the backdrop of general international law.

To that end, two leading non-governmental initiatives—the McGill Manual on International Law Applicable to Military Uses of Outer Space (MILAMOS)[5] and the Woomera Manual on the International Law of Military Space Operations[6]—are presently underway. They share the aim of producing non-binding restatements of the

---

[1] Anson and Cummings 1991.

[2] Jeffrey Gettleman and Hari Kumar, 'India shot down a satellite, Modi says, shifting balance of power in Asia', New York Times (27 March 2019).

[3] Nathan Strout, 'Russian satellite creeps up to Intelsat satellite—again', C4ISRNET (3 September 2019).

[4] Florence Parly, 'Présentation de la stratégie spatiale de défense' (25 July 2019) <https://www.defense.gouv.fr/salle-de-presse/discours/discours-de-florence-parly/discours-de-florence-parly_presentation-de-la-strategie-spatiale-de-defense>. Accessed 30 September 2019.

[5] Manual on International Law Applicable to Military Uses of Outer Space (MILAMOS) <https://www.mcgill.ca/milamos/>.

[6] The Woomera Manual <https://law.adelaide.edu.au/woomera/>. Accessed 30 September 2019. The author is a core expert.

19 Military Space Operations

relevant rules, following the tradition of expert manuals for, *inter alia*, the sea,[7] air,[8] and cyber domains.[9] To the extent of their acceptance by States, such projects help foster the international rule of law by providing the rigour, nuance, and granularity needed for the effective development and interpretation of the law.[10]

This chapter presents an introduction into these issues and an overview of the main contemporary controversies concerning the application of international law to military space operations. It begins by proposing a working definition of the eponymous term, to be used in the remainder of the chapter (Sect. 19.2). It then dedicates a section to each of the principal bodies of law that regulate military uses of outer space, starting with international space law (Sect. 19.3), followed by the international law on the use of force (Sect. 19.4), and international humanitarian law (Sect. 19.5). The chapter concludes by considering overarching issues and the possible future development of the relevant law (Sect. 19.6).

19.2 Defining Military Space Operations

International law does not define the term 'military space operations'. In fact, each of the words in this phrase presents its own ambiguities and interpretation problems. Firstly, the distinction between military and non-military uses of outer space is notoriously blurry. Already in 1961, it was observed that '[v]irtually every activity in space has a possible military connotation; military and non-military uses are extraordinarily interdependent.'[11] The nature of the actors or objects involved in a specific activity also does not conclusively determine the character of that activity. To wit, some of the ongoing peaceful exploration and scientific investigation of outer space is done by military personnel—while civilian contractors operate various space assets used for exclusively military purposes. Similarly, although objects launched into outer space are subject to registration requirements,[12] these duties do not include an obligation to indicate whether the object is intended to be used for military or non-military purposes.[13] Whether or not an activity in space is considered military in character must therefore be assessed on a case-by-case basis by assessing the function and purpose of the activity in question.

---

[7] San Remo Manual 1995.

[8] AMW Manual 2013.

[9] Tallinn Manual 2017.

[10] See Stephens 2018, at 96–99.

[11] Lipson and Katzenbach 1961, at 806.

[12] See 1974 Convention on Registration of Objects Launched into Outer Space, 1023 UNTS 15 (hereinafter Registration Convention), Article II.

[13] But see text to note 127 below (suggesting that the registration of objects used exclusively for civilian purposes as such is a possible passive precaution under IHL).

Secondly, international law does not draw a clear line between air space and outer space.[14] This is in contrast with several domestic jurisdictions including Australia, Denmark or Kazakhstan, which have set the boundary at the altitude of 100 km.[15] At the international level, this issue has occupied the UN Committee on the Peaceful Uses of Outer Space (COPUOS) for decades without it reaching a generally acceptable solution.[16] Therefore, all that can be said with some degree of certainty is that the threshold at which outer space begins is located *above* the highest altitude at which an airplane can fly, but *below* the lowest perigee of a satellite in orbit.[17] With technological advancements, these two points are getting closer, which is emphasized by the opponents of exact delimitation as a key reason why setting any specific figure would be artificial and arbitrary.[18] Rather than looking for a precise altitude, it is thus preferable to ask whether a given activity has a material connection (nexus) with outer space as such, accepting that there may be borderline cases, which will remain difficult to categorize.

Thirdly, the term operations (or, more precisely, 'military operations') is known to IHL. As used in the IHL context, this term is generally understood to mean 'the movements, manoeuvres and actions of any sort, carried out by the armed forces with a view to combat'.[19] In that sense, the term is narrower in its meaning than 'hostilities' conducted during an armed conflict (of which military operations form a part), but broader than 'attacks' (which constitute a particular aspect of military operations).[20] However, this interpretation is inappropriate outside of the IHL context (i.e., in the absence of an ongoing armed conflict), where one therefore has to fall back on a more general conceptualization. In this regard, a NATO-agreed definition of an 'operation' as a 'sequence of coordinated actions with a defined purpose' stands out for its technology- and domain-neutral wording.[21] For those reasons, it will also be relied on in the following text.

On the basis of the foregoing, a working definition can be drawn up for the purposes of this chapter. Military space operations are understood here as sequences of coordinated actions with a defined purpose, which are of a military character and which

---

[14] Lyall and Larsen 2017, at 153.

[15] Australia, Space Activities Act 1998, sect. 8; Denmark, Outer Space Act 2016, sect. 4(4); Law of the Republic of Kazakhstan on Space Activities 2012, Sect. (6).

[16] See further UN COPUOS, Historical Summary on the Consideration of the Question on the Definition and Delimitation of Outer Space: Report of the Secretariat, UN Doc A/AC.105/769 (18 January 2002).

[17] See, e.g., AMW Manual 2013, rule 1(a).

[18] See, e.g., U.S. Statement, Definition and Delimitation of Outer Space and the Character and Utilization of the Geostationary Orbit (2001) <https://2009-2017.state.gov/s/l/22718.htm>. Accessed 30 September 2019.

[19] Sandoz et al 1987, para. 152.

[20] ICRC, Third Expert Meeting on the Notion of Direct Participation in Hostilities Geneva, 23–25 October 2005 Summary Report <https://www.icrc.org/eng/assets/files/other/direct_participation_in_hostilities_2005_eng.pdf> at 18–19.

[21] NATO Standard AJP-3, Allied Joint Doctrine for the Conduct of Operations (February 2019), point 1.4.

19 Military Space Operations   403

have a material nexus to outer space. This space nexus may take at least four main forms:[22] (1) military operations *in* space, such as on-orbit proximity operations;[23] (2) military operations *from* space, such as space-based ballistic missile defence interceptors;[24] (3) military operations *to* space, such as the launching of kinetic anti-satellite (ASAT) missiles;[25] and (4) military operations *through* space, such as the employment of long-range missiles that transit through outer space en route to their target.[26] The notion of material nexus to outer space also covers the use of space assets necessary to support or enable military activities on the Earth.

19.3 International Space Law

International space law is an area of public international law that regulates outer space and activities in and relating to outer space.[27] Its core is found in a framework Outer Space Treaty[28] and four additional treaties concerning, respectively, the rescue of astronauts and return of objects launched into space;[29] liability for damage caused by space objects;[30] registration of objects launched into space;[31] and State activities on the Moon and other celestial bodies.[32] In addition, over time, many rules of customary international law specifically applicable to outer space activities have crystallized, as well.[33]

Historically, international space law has evolved as a body of law almost exclusively focussed on peaceful use and exploration of outer space. This is confirmed by the preamble to the Outer Space Treaty, which notes that the adoption of the treaty reflected a shared desire on part of the States Parties 'to contribute to broad international cooperation in the scientific as well as the legal aspects of the exploration and

---

[22] cf Blake 2014, at 108–111 (adopting a similar classification in the context of space weapons).

[23] See, e.g., text to note 3 above.

[24] See, e.g., National Research Council 2012, at 37–38.

[25] See, e.g., text to note 2 above.

[26] See, e.g., Shaw 1999, at 23 (noting that 'the ICBM was the first weapon designed to travel into and through space').

[27] See, e.g., Lyall and Larsen 2017, at 2.

[28] 1967 Treaty on Principles Governing the Activities of States in the Exploration and Use of Outer Space, Including the Moon and Other Celestial Bodies, 610 UNTS 205 (hereinafter Outer Space Treaty).

[29] 1968 Agreement on the Rescue of Astronauts, the Return of Astronauts and the Return of Objects Launched Into Outer Space, 672 UNTS 119 (hereinafter Rescue and Return Agreement).

[30] 1972 Convention on International Liability for Damage Caused by Space Objects, 961 UNTS 187.

[31] Registration Convention.

[32] 1979 Agreement governing the Activities of States on the Moon and Other Celestial Bodies, 1363 UNTS 3.

[33] Diederiks-Verschoor and Kopal 2008, at 9–12.

use of outer space for peaceful purposes'. Nevertheless, there are certain aspects of international space law which do relate to the conduct of military space operations.

19.3.1 No General Prohibition of Military Space Operations

At the outset, it is important to note that in spite of its focus on peaceful uses of outer space, international space law does not prohibit space activities that are military in character. In other words, the term 'peaceful purposes' used by the Outer Space Treaty should be understood as 'non-aggressive' or 'non-hostile', but not 'non-military'.[34] That interpretation is supported by the binding provisions of that Treaty, including in particular Article III, which it is worth restating in full:

> States Parties to the Treaty shall carry on activities in the exploration and use of outer space, including the Moon and other celestial bodies, in accordance with international law, including the Charter of the United Nations, in the interest of maintaining international peace and security and promoting international cooperation and understanding.

The express reference to the UN Charter, which codifies the core rules on the use of force, confirms that the drafters of the Outer Space Treaty did not intend to exclude the resort to military means in outer space altogether.[35] Instead, Article III mandates that any activity in or related to outer space must be carried on 'in accordance with international law', to include the said rules in the UN Charter.[36] Accordingly, States are permitted to engage in space operations while exercising their right to self-defence or while acting under the authorization of the UN Security Council— both of which are decidedly military but non-aggressive in character. States may also engage in other military space operations as long as these are not prohibited by other applicable rules of international law. This interpretation is in line with decades of consistent State practice, which has featured extensive and wide-ranging use of outer space for military purposes by all main space-faring nations.[37]

19.3.2 Specific Restrictions on Military Space Operations

And yet, international space law does restrict and prohibit certain types of military space operations. The 'focal point' in this regard is Article IV of the Outer Space

---

[34] Similarly Meyer 1968, at 27; Bridge 1980, at 658; Schmitt 2006a, at 101; Stephens and Steer 2015, at 74; Tronchetti 2015, at 339; Borgen 2021, section II.B.2; contra Vlasic 1981, at 26.

[35] Tronchetti 2015, at 338–340; see also Yearbook of the United Nations 1966, at 39–40.

[36] Ramey 2000, at 127; Maogoto and Freeland 2007, at 1105; Schmitt 2006a, at 102.

[37] See, e.g., King and Blank 2019, at 125–127; but see Borgen 2021, section II.B.2 (suggesting that if 'activities in space [continue to] expand ..., an increasingly crowded and congested environment of space may, in the future, challenge the permissive reading of "peaceful purposes"').

19 Military Space Operations

Treaty.[38] This provision establishes two separate sets of obligations for States, the first of which relates to placement of weapons of mass destruction (WMDs) in outer space and the other one to the military uses of the Moon and other celestial bodies.

Firstly, under Article IV(1), States are obliged not to place in orbit around the Earth objects carrying nuclear weapons or other types of WMDs, install such weapons on celestial bodies, or station such weapons in outer space in any other manner. The Outer Space Treaty does not expressly list specific types of WMDs to which the prohibition applies, but it is not controversial that the concept includes, besides nuclear weapons, also chemical and biological weapons.[39] By contrast, the prohibition does not cover conventional weapons, which means that States are not precluded from placing in orbit, for example, conventional anti-satellite weapons.[40]

It is worth addressing the exact legal meaning of the phrase 'in orbit around the Earth' in Article IV(1). Only weeks after the adoption of the Outer Space Treaty, it was revealed that the Soviet Union had been testing the so-called 'Fractional Orbiting Bombardment System', which would see nuclear weapons placed into an orbital trajectory but re-entering before completing an orbit in order to strike distant targets on the Earth's surface.[41] The US official reaction was that the tests did not violate the Outer Space Treaty because the 'space weapons would be fired "in a fractional orbit, *not a full orbit*"'.[42] On that basis, one can infer that the agreed interpretation between the two only space-faring nations at the time was that the Article IV(1) prohibition only covered objects that would circumnavigate the Earth at least one full time.[43] On that interpretation, the placement of WMDs in a fractional orbit is not prohibited by the Outer Space Treaty[44]—but it should be noted that this view is not universally accepted.[45]

Secondly, Article IV(2) mandates that the Moon and other celestial bodies are to be used exclusively for peaceful purposes. In addition, it specifically prohibits the establishment of military bases, installations and fortifications, the testing of weapons, and the conduct of military manoeuvres on celestial bodies. Unlike other provisions of the Outer Space Treaty, Article IV(2) only refers to 'the Moon and

---

[38] Schrogl and Neumann 2009, para. 1.

[39] Strydom 2017, para. 2; Schrogl and Neumann 2009, paras. 24–25.

[40] Schrogl and Neumann 2009, para. 27.

[41] Murrey Marder, 'Orbital bomb rationalizing jolts officials', Washington Post (5 November 1967), at A14.

[42] Ibid. (emphasis added).

[43] See Ramey 2000, at 84 fn 355; see also Jasentuliyana and Lee 1979, at 14 (arguing that this interpretation reflects 'the clear intention of the drafters').

[44] See, e.g., U.S. Department of Defense, Law of War Manual (rev ed Dec 2016) (hereinafter DoD Manual), para. 14.10.3.1.

[45] See, e.g., Schrogl and Neumann 2009, para. 30 (arguing that 'in orbit' means 'in a state of being or moving in an orbit', which thus includes the placement of objects that follow only a section of a full orbit).

other celestial bodies', but not to outer space generally.[46] That means that the scope of Article IV(2) does not include the so-called 'empty space' between celestial bodies.[47] Therefore, the proscriptions contained in this provision only apply to celestial bodies, including the Moon.

19.3.3 *Interaction Between Space Law and Other Areas of International Law*

For issues that are not directly regulated by international space law, reference must be made to the other applicable areas of international law. Article III of the Outer Space Treaty, reproduced in full earlier, stipulates that all activities in outer space must be carried on in accordance with international law. In this way, the provision acts as a general incorporation clause, confirming that international law generally applies to human activities in outer space,[48] with the exception of those rules that are domain-specific, geographically constrained or otherwise incompatible with the space environment.[49] For the purposes of military space operations, the two main relevant areas are the law on the use of force and international humanitarian law, which are discussed in the following two sections.

At this junction, it is thus useful to consider the interplay between these different areas of international law, particularly in situations where rules of a different origin are in mutual tension or outright conflict.[50] It is sometimes suggested that one of these areas must in such cases always prevail over the others because it is supposedly more specifically tied to the relevant circumstances. Thus it has been said, for example, that due to the unique characteristics of the space environment, space law is 'the *lex specialis*', which prevails over other bodies of law in case of normative conflict;[51] but there is also the very different view that in the conduct of hostilities, IHL is 'the *lex specialis*', which prevails over other conflicting norms.[52]

---

[46] See Outer Space Treaty, Articles I-III, V-VII, IX-XI, XIII (using the phrase 'outer space, including the Moon and other celestial bodies'); see also ibid, Article V (using the phrase 'activities in outer space and on celestial bodies').

[47] See Yearbook of the United Nations 1966, at 39 (noting that during the drafting process of the Outer Space Treaty, a number of States 'expressed regret that, according to the draft treaty, only the celestial bodies were to be used exclusively for peaceful purposes and that this requirement was not applicable generally to outer space'); see also Christol 1982, at 20; Schrogl and Neumann 2009, para. 42.

[48] Lachs 1972, at 21; Hansen 2015, at 28; Borgen 2021, section II.B.1.

[49] See, e.g., DoD Manual, para. 14.10.2.2 (excluding rules that 'apply only in certain geographical locations (such as a State's own territory), and thus might not create obligations applicable to a State's activities in outer space').

[50] See further Stephens 2018.

[51] See, e.g., Freeland and Jakhu 2016, at 228.

[52] See, e.g., ILC, Draft Articles on the Effects of Armed Conflicts on Treaties, with Commentaries, Yearbook of the ILC, 2011, vol. II, Part Two, Article 2, commentary para. 4.

19 Military Space Operations

It is submitted that neither of these views is compelling as it is imprecise and unrealistic to label an entire area of law as 'the *lex specialis*'. A better approach is to acknowledge that *lex specialis derogat legi generali* is an interpretive principle, which must be resorted to on a rule-by-rule basis.[53] In that sense, the principle entails that if two norms from different bodies deal with the same subject matter, priority should be given to that norm which is the more specific of the two,[54] in other words, 'the one which has the larger common contact surface area with the situation'.[55] This is also the approach taken in the rest of this chapter.

19.4 International Law on the Use of Force

The cornerstone of the international law on the use of force is found in Article 2(4) of the UN Charter, which provides for a general prohibition of the threat or use of force in international relations.[56] This prohibition must be considered in light of other relevant provisions of the UN Charter,[57] which include Article 51 (recognizing the inherent right of individual and collective self-defence in response to an armed attack) and Article 42 (providing a legal basis for military enforcement measures authorized by the UN Security Council). As noted earlier, Article III of the Outer Space Treaty expressly recognizes the applicability of the UN Charter to activities in space. It thus follows that Article 2(4) and other relevant rules in the Charter cover military space operations, as well.[58] As the ICJ held in the *Nuclear Weapons* advisory opinion, these provisions 'apply to any use of force, regardless of the weapons employed'.[59] Accordingly, any use of force employing space capabilities must also comply with the law on the use of force as codified in the UN Charter.

19.4.1 Use of Force

The applicable international legal regime is organized around the notion of 'force'. Although non-forcible hostile measures in outer space may amount to violations of other rules of international law (for example, the prohibition of intervention),

---

[53] See Happold 2012, at 464; Stephens 2018, at 91; Borgen 2021, section II.B.1.

[54] Koskenniemi 2006, para. 56.

[55] Sassòli and Olson 2008, at 604 (internal quotation marks and footnote omitted).

[56] 1945 Charter of the United Nations, 1 UNTS XVI (hereinafter UN Charter), Article 2(4) ('All Members shall refrain in their international relations from the threat or use of force against the territorial integrity or political independence of any state, or in any other manner inconsistent with the Purposes of the United Nations.').

[57] See *Legality of the Threat or Use of Nuclear Weapons*, ICJ, Advisory Opinion of 8 July 1996 (hereinafter *Nuclear Weapons*), para. 38.

[58] Similarly Bridge 1980, at 659; Hansen 2015, at 48; Tronchetti 2015, at 350.

[59] *Nuclear Weapons*, para. 39.

they do not trigger the application of the law on the use of force. Any response to such violations would also have to be non-forcible in nature, with the primary legal framework provided by the law of countermeasures.[60] It follows that the threshold between forcible and non-forcible measures is of paramount importance and it is thus essential to examine what constitutes a use of force in the space environment.

In that regard, the extreme situations are well understood. Thus, the use of destructive means against a space asset, such as firing a kinetic anti-satellite weapon against a satellite in orbit belonging to another State, clearly amounts to a use of force in the Charter sense. By contrast, hacking into an adversary's satellite communication in order to clandestinely exfiltrate national security data without causing any damage or disruption to the satellite in question does not qualify as a use of force.

However, many other conceivable hostile acts in the space environment fall into the grey zone in the middle. In particular, it is unclear how to qualify acts that result in the temporary and/or reversible loss of functionality of a space object, such as optical sensor dazzling or radio frequency jamming. On the one hand, in 2008 China and Russia proposed a definition of the use of force, which would expressly include 'any hostile actions against outer space objects' aimed at 'temporarily ... disrupting their normal functioning'.[61] On the other hand, the US rejected this definition as too broad given that it included not only activities 'that result in permanent and irreversible damage, but *also hostile activities and actions that cause temporary and reversible effects*'.[62]

Since this exchange, China and Russia have abandoned the original extensive definition and replaced it with 'any action intended to inflict damage on an outer space object under the jurisdiction and/or control of other States',[63] which indicates a degree of convergence among the main space powers. To put the point at its lowest, it can probably be inferred that these States now consider at least some acts causing temporary or reversible loss of functionality of space objects—namely those that are not intended to inflict any damage—as falling below the threshold of force. But the exact criteria remain unsettled in the present state of the law.

---

[60] See UN General Assembly 2001 Draft Articles on Responsibility of States for Internationally Wrongful Acts with Commentaries, UN Doc. A/56/10 (hereinafter Articles on State Responsibility), Articles 22 and 49–54.

[61] Russia and China, Draft Treaty on Prevention of the Placement of Weapons in Outer Space and of the Threat or Use of Force against Outer Space Objects, UN Doc. CD/1839 (29 February 2008), Article I(e).

[62] United States, Analysis of a Draft "Treaty on Prevention of the Placement of Weapons in Outer Space, or the Threat or Use of Force against Outer Space Objects", UN Doc. CD/1847 (26 August 2008), para. 5(i) (emphasis original).

[63] Russia and China, Draft Treaty on the Prevention of the Placement of Weapons in Outer Space, the Threat or Use of Force against Outer Space Objects, UN Doc. CD/1985 (12 June 2014), Article I(d).

19.4.2 Threat to Use Force

International law does not only prohibit actual uses of force by States, but also the threat to use force. The notions of 'threat' and 'use' of force are interrelated in the sense that if a given use of force is unlawful under international law, then the threat to use such force is also unlawful.[64] Therefore, an unprovoked express threat by one State to deploy a kinetic anti-satellite weapon against a space object of another State would constitute a prohibited threat to use force. By contrast, a statement that a State is ready to engage in an equivalent operation in the exercise of self-defence against an armed attack by another State would not in itself be unlawful.

The threat to use force does not need to be expressly pronounced to be covered by the prohibition. In the terrestrial environment, sudden massive build-up of troops on the border with a neighbouring State may amount to an implicit threat to use force against that State, in particular if the acting State has a history of resorting to such troop movements as a precursor to invasion.[65] Analogically, consider the example of a State that, in a short span of time, repeatedly engages in unconsented-to close-proximity orbital operations, thus putting the satellites belonging to its adversary within the reach of the former State's on-board weapons. If the acting State has in the past followed up such operations with actual use of these weapons, its conduct could amount to an implicit threat to use force. By contrast, if the acting State does not have such a history, then the orbital manoeuvres would not automatically be considered as a threat of force.[66]

Although a threat need not be expressly stated, it must be communicated towards the potential victim State in some manner. In the example in the previous paragraph, that communication is implicit, but the conduct of the acting State leaves no doubt as to the target of its operations. By contrast, the mere acquisition of capabilities that can potentially be used to engage in the use of force does not constitute a threat.[67] Thus the mere placement of anti-satellite weapons in orbit unaccompanied by an either express or implied communication towards a specific third State does not qualify as a prohibited threat to use force against that State.[68] However, if the acting State issues an ultimatum to the third State that the weapons will be used against it unless certain demands are met, the former State will be in violation of Article 2(4).[69]

---

[64] *Nuclear Weapons*, para. 47.

[65] See, e.g., UN Doc. S/PV.3438 (15 October 1994), at 11 (United Kingdom)

[66] Cf. ICJ, *Case Concerning Military and Paramilitary Activities in and Against Nicaragua (Merits)*, Judgment, [1986] ICJ Rep 14 (hereinafter *Nicaragua*), para. 227 (holding that the mere existence of military manoeuvres near another State's borders does not constitute a threat of force).

[67] Tallinn Manual 2.0 2017, rule 70, commentary para. 4.

[68] But see Maogoto and Freeland 2007, at 1111 ('mere deployment of [anti-satellite] weaponry can amount to the threat of the use of force, particularly where space weaponry is hoisted to the same orbital plane as another state's space assets').

[69] Cf. Tallinn Manual 2.0 2017, rule 70, commentary para. 4.

19.4.3 Armed Attack and Self-defence

If the use of force against a victim State crosses the threshold of an armed attack, the said State is entitled to take forcible measures in the exercise of its right to self-defence.[70] In this regard, the US takes the otherwise exceptional position that any unlawful use of force automatically triggers the right to self-defence.[71] By contrast, the prevailing view in the international community corresponds to the ICJ ruling in the *Nicaragua* case that only 'the most grave forms of the use of force' constitute an armed attack.[72] However, the distinction between the most grave forms and other less grave forms of the use of force is difficult to make in practice and especially so in the space environment due to the virtual absence of relevant State practice.

To that end, the ICJ jurisprudence assesses the scale and effects of an operation in order to determine whether it should be classified as an armed attack.[73] On that approach, an isolated incident of permanently disabling another State's satellite used exclusively for commercial purposes would likely fall short of the threshold. Conversely, a large-scale operation aimed simultaneously at a constellation of an adversary's missile warning satellites would certainly constitute an armed attack. Situations falling between these two extremes are harder to classify, with the resulting grey zone demonstrating further the need to develop and clarify the law in this area.

Any measures taken by the victim State in the exercise of its right to self-defence must comply with the customary principles of necessity and proportionality.[74] In that respect, the principle of necessity requires that the use of force in self-defence is the only way to successfully repel an armed attack against the victim State; if lesser non-forcible means are available, then that State must use those means instead.[75] Consider, for instance, a massive cyber operation by State A aimed at assuming control over a constellation of State B's military remote sensing satellites and then destroying their sensors by pointing them towards the Sun. If successful, the large scale and destructive effects of the operation would justify its qualification as an armed attack. However, if State B has at its disposal non-forcible means to thwart the hostile operation (such as rapid cyber countermeasures or the ability to jam all communications with its own satellites), it would be obliged to make a reasonable

---

[70] UN Charter, Article 51.

[71] See, e.g., DoD Manual, para. 1.11.5.2.

[72] *Nicaragua*, para. 191.

[73] Ibid, para. 195; see also, e.g., ICJ, *Legal Consequences of the Construction of a Wall in the Occupied Palestinian Territory*, Advisory Opinion, [2004] ICJ Rep 136, Separate Opinion of Judge Higgins, para. 33; ICJ, *Armed Activities on the Territory of the Congo (Democratic Republic of the Congo v. Uganda)*, Judgment, [2005] ICJ Rep 168 (hereinafter *Armed Activities*), Separate Opinion of Judge Kooijmans, para. 29.

[74] *Nicaragua*, para. 176; *Nuclear Weapons*, para. 41; ICJ, *Oil Platforms (Islamic Republic of Iran v. United States of America)*, Judgment, [2003] ICJ Rep 161 (hereinafter *Oil Platforms*), para. 76; *Armed Activities*, para. 147.

[75] Cf. *Oil Platforms*, para. 73 ('the requirement of international law that measures taken avowedly in self-defence must have been necessary for that purpose is strict and objective, leaving no room for any "measure of discretion"').

attempt to resort to those alternative means before taking forcible measures against State A.[76]

Any use of force in self-defence must also be consistent with the principle of proportionality. Importantly, this principle does not require symmetry between the mode of initial attack and the mode of response; rather, the response must be limited to the minimum needed to repel the attack.[77] In the example above, if non-forcible measures proved ineffectual against the attack, State B would be permitted to engage in an amount of force proportionate to the gravity of the attack, but no more.[78] It would thus be within its rights to apply a targeted strike against a command centre on State A's territory whence the hostile cyber operations are executed. By contrast, assuming that the strike was successful and State A has ceased all hostile activity, it would be disproportionate for State B to then launch a ground invasion of State A with the aim to retaliate and deter future attacks.[79]

19.5 International Humanitarian Law

International humanitarian law (IHL), also known as the law of armed conflict, is the area of public international law that governs the conduct of belligerents during an armed conflict.[80] With respect to military space operations, a number of scholars have questioned the extent to which the rules of IHL apply in outer space.[81] In fact, for a long time, the possibility of hostilities reaching outer space had been seen as both inconceivable and too impractical to be seriously considered in the development of the law. For example, in the early years of space exploration, India argued that military aspects of terrestrial international law should be totally inapplicable to outer space, which should remain 'a kind of warless world'.[82] And during the drafting of the Additional Protocols to the Geneva Conventions over a decade later, the rapporteur of a working group on methods and means of warfare and the protection of the civilian population expressly said that 'the Working Group had at no time considered the effects of hostilities taking place in outer space'.[83]

Still, the continuing militarization of outer space and the increasing reliance on space assets by all major military powers in the 21st century underline the urgency

---

[76] Cf. Tallinn Manual 2.0 2017, rule 72, commentary para. 3.

[77] ILC, Addendum: Eighth Report on State Responsibility by Mr. Roberto Ago, Special Rapporteur, UN Doc. A/CN.4/318/Add.5-7, para. 121; *Nuclear Weapons*, Dissenting Opinion of Judge Higgins, para. 5.

[78] Cf. *Oil Platforms*, para. 77 (noting that the destruction of several naval vessels and aircraft by the US was disproportionate to the mining of a single US warship).

[79] Cf. Nolte and Randelzhofer 2012, para. 57 (noting that lawful self-defence 'must not acquire a retaliatory, deterrent, or punitive character').

[80] See, e.g., Sassòli 2019, para. 1.01.

[81] See, e.g., Vermeer 2007, at 74; Freeland 2015, at 102; Boothby 2014, at 224.

[82] UN Doc. A/AC.105/PV.3 (7 May 1962), at 63 (India).

[83] CDDH/III/SR.11, at 86, para. 9 (Baxter).

of clarifying the applicability of IHL in outer space. It is the position of this author that the scope of application of this body of law is not limited to the terrestrial environment.[84] This view is justified by reasons arising both from international space law and from IHL itself. As far as space law is concerned, as noted earlier, Article III of the Outer Space Treaty operates as a general incorporation clause, which thus confirms the general applicability of international law to activities in outer space.[85] Because IHL is a constituent part of international law, Article III thus also incorporates the rules of this body of law: *a maiori ad minus*.[86]

The same interpretive outcome also follows from the fundamental tenets of IHL itself. Specifically, States have a general obligation to respect and ensure respect for IHL 'in all circumstances', codified in Common Article 1 to the Geneva Conventions[87] and considered to reflect customary international law.[88] The phrase 'in all circumstances' is comprehensive and therefore extends to any location where an armed conflict may occur, including outer space.[89] It can thus be concluded that IHL applies to military space operations in general;[90] the major difficulties lie in the specific challenges that the space environment poses for IHL rules that have been developed in the terrestrial environment.

Accordingly, the remainder of this section examines *how* IHL governs military space operations. To that end, it specifically considers three fundamental rules on the conduct of hostilities: distinction, proportionality, and precautions. These rules were codified in Additional Protocol I and they are generally considered to reflect customary international law applicable in both international and non-international armed conflicts.[91] As such, they apply to all States, irrespective of whether they have ratified the Protocol, or not.

---

[84] See further Mačák 2018.

[85] See text to note 48 above.

[86] Similarly Stephens and Steer 2015, at 11; ICRC 2019, at 33.

[87] See also 1977 Protocol Additional to the Geneva Conventions of 12 August 1949, and relating to the Protection of Victims of International Armed Conflicts, 1125 UNTS 3 (hereinafter AP I), preamble (reaffirming that the provisions of the Conventions and of the Protocol 'must be fully applied in all circumstances') and Article 1(1) (extending the obligation to respect and to ensure respect for IHL in all circumstances to the provisions of the Protocol).

[88] ICRC Customary IHL Study 2005 (hereafter ICRC Customary IHL Study), Volume I, rule 139; *Nicaragua*, para. 220.

[89] Mačák 2018, at 15 and 21; see also Hathaway et al. 2017, at 576 (interpreting the phrase as meaning that the obligations to which it applies 'do not have a geographic or temporal threshold').

[90] See also ICRC 2019, at 33 ('IHL applies to any military operations conducted as part of an armed conflict, including those occurring in outer space').

[91] See ICRC Customary IHL Study, Volume I, in particular rules 1, 7, 14, 15, and 22.

19.5.1 Distinction

The rule on distinction requires the belligerents to distinguish at all times between the civilian population and combatants and between civilian objects and military objectives.[92] With respect to persons, IHL thus forbids the lethal targeting of civilians unless they directly participate in hostilities.[93] Conversely, members of the armed forces (with the exception of medical and religious personnel) qualify as combatants and they may therefore be attacked during an armed conflict[94] unless they are *hors de combat*.[95] Although this rule is fairly uncontroversial in the terrestrial environment, it poses a specific problem with respect to military astronauts.

Unlike IHL, space law does not distinguish between civilian and military personnel. Instead, it designates all personnel of crewed spacecraft as 'envoys of mankind' who are subject to specific protections, which include the duty of all States to render them 'all possible assistance' in time of need.[96] In this regard, space law and IHL thus seem to be at loggerheads. Supposing that there is an international armed conflict between States A and B, how can a military astronaut of State A qualify as a lawful target and, at the same time, be entitled to all possible assistance from State B?

It is proposed that this normative tension is best resolved through reference to the respective aims of the two applicable bodies of law. While space law protections for astronauts as envoys of mankind are predicated on the general goal of this body of law to facilitate peaceful uses and exploration of outer space, the category of combatants under IHL was designed to cover those persons who materially contribute to the efforts of the belligerents to prosecute an existing armed conflict.[97] Accordingly, military astronauts should maintain their space law status and protections unless and until they engage in conduct with a material nexus to an armed conflict, at which point they become targetable in accordance with the rules of IHL.[98]

As far as objects are concerned, belligerents may direct their attacks only against military objectives, which are defined as those objects that through their nature, purpose, use or location make an effective contribution to the enemy's military action and whose destruction, capture or neutralization offers a definite military advantage.[99] A key issue relates to the interpretation of the term 'military action' in this definition. In this regard, two main views have emerged in international practice and academic writings.

---

[92] AP I, Article 48.

[93] AP I, Article 51(3).

[94] AP I, Article 43.

[95] AP I, Article 41(1); see also AP I, Article 41(2) (defining persons *hors de combat* as those who are in the power of the adversary; those who clearly express an intention to surrender; and those who are unconscious or otherwise incapacitated, and thus incapable of defending themselves).

[96] Outer Space Treaty, Article V(1); see also Rescue and Return Agreement, Article 2.

[97] Mačák 2018, at 30.

[98] Ibid., at 31.

[99] AP I, Article 52(2).

According to the broad view, all objects that make a contribution to the war-sustaining capability of the enemy qualify as military objectives. Importantly, this includes economic targets or, in other words, objects that are of economic importance to the adversary, because the revenues from those targets may be used to sustain the enemy's war-fighting effort. This view has been endorsed by various actors including the US[100] and Ecuador,[101] the Ethiopia-Eritrea Claims Commission,[102] and several scholars.[103] As one of the proponents of this view admits, in outer space this means that due to their economic importance, 'satellites and their architecture can be perceived as legitimate military targets and become the object of attacks'.[104]

It is submitted that this admission in fact convincingly illustrates the excessively far-reaching nature of the broad view. An interpretation according to which any satellite providing commercial profits to the enemy would be targetable is too permissive and should be rejected, because it would render virtually meaningless the protection of civilian objects in outer space.[105] Instead, the notion of military action should be interpreted more narrowly to mean that objects are targetable only if they have a proximate nexus to the war-fighting capability of the enemy.[106] This is also the view taken by most States,[107] expert manuals,[108] and many scholars.[109] On this interpretation, military imaging and reconnaissance satellites could qualify as military objectives, whereas purely commercial satellites normally would not.

19.5.2 Proportionality

Even if an object qualifies as a military objective, it may still only be targeted if doing so is consistent with the proportionality rule. This rule requires that attacking the object must not be expected to cause incidental civilian harm that would be excessive in relation to the concrete and direct military advantage anticipated.[110] Interpreting this rule in the outer space context poses particular difficulties given that

---

[100] DoD Manual, para. 5.6.6.2.

[101] Ecuador, Naval Manual 1989, para. 8.1.1, cited in ICRC Customary IHL Study, Volume II(1), at 183.

[102] Eritrea-Ethiopia Claims Commission, Partial Award, Western Front, Aerial Bombardment and Related Claims, Eritrea's Claims 1, 3, 5, 9–13, 14, 21, 25 and 26 (2005) 26 RIAA 291, para. 121.

[103] See, e.g., Bourbonnière 2004; Watkin 2014; Goodman 2016.

[104] Bourbonnière 2004, at 61.

[105] Cf. Stephens and Steer 2015, at 92–93.

[106] Dinstein 2016, at 109.

[107] Crawford 2017, at 60 fn 49.

[108] San Remo Manual 1995, para. 60.11; AMW Manual 2013, rule 24, commentary para. 2; Tallinn Manual 2.0 2017, rule 100, commentary para. 19.

[109] See, e.g., Schmitt 2006b, at 281; Oeter 2013, at 113; Jachec-Neale 2014, at 108–109 and 254; Dinstein 2016, at 109; Boothby 2019, at 177.

[110] AP I, Articles 51(5) (b) and 57(2)(a)(iii).

the vast majority of space assets are so-called 'dual-use' objects, which means that they are being simultaneously used for both civilian and military purposes. When such objects are attacked, incidental harm is 'inevitable, and often considerable'.[111]

Consider, for example, a commercial communications satellite that carries a total of 24 individual transponders, one of which is used for military communications by State A's armed forces and the remaining ones are used to provide broadband services to civilian schools, hospitals, and disaster relief agencies in the same State. If an international armed conflict were to break out between States A and B, the satellite would qualify as a military objective because it is being presently used for military purposes.[112] However, before attacking this satellite, State B would have to weigh the anticipated military advantage against the expected incidental harm. In that sense, the loss of connectivity for schools might amount to little more than inconvenience, which does not factor in the proportionality calculus.[113] Conversely, the consequences could be significantly graver for hospitals and the disruption to disaster relief could foreseeably cause a considerable loss of civilian life.[114] If that was the case and, at the same time, the anticipated military advantage was minimal— for instance because State A's military communications are known to be very resilient and would reasonably be expected to be rerouted very quickly after the satellite was destroyed—the expected incidental harm would be excessive relative to that military advantage. Accordingly, the attack against the satellite would be prohibited by IHL.

A final issue to consider with respect to proportionality is the question of space debris. In that respect, kinetic attacks against objects in Earth orbit are particularly problematic due to the near certainty that they will generate significant amounts of persistent debris. For example, the 2007 Chinese anti-satellite test against a defunct weather satellite created more than 3,000 pieces of debris, many of which will remain in orbit for decades and thus pose danger to other space assets in low Earth orbit.[115] Even the 2019 Indian anti-satellite test, which according to India was specifically designed 'to ensure that there is no space debris',[116] still reportedly created at least 400 pieces of debris, a few of which were thrown into orbits with high apogees, resulting in an increased impact risk to the International Space Station.[117]

---

[111] Oeter 2013, at 197.

[112] AP I, Article 52(2).

[113] AMW Manual 2013, rule 1(l), commentary para. 5; Tallinn Manual 2.0 2017, rule 113, commentary para. 5.

[114] See also ICRC 2019, at 34 (noting that 'disabling the civilian functions of satellites could disrupt large segments of modern-day societies, especially if they support safety-critical civilian activities and essential civilian services on earth').

[115] Weeden 2012, at 1.

[116] India, Ministry of External Affairs, 'Frequently asked questions on Mission Shakti' (27 March 2019) <https://www.mea.gov.in/press-releases.htm?dtl/31179/Frequently_Asked_Questions_on_Mission_Shakti_Indias_AntiSatellite_Missile_test_conducted_on_27_March_2019>. Accessed 30 September 2019.

[117] Jeff Foust, 'NASA warns Indian anti-satellite test increased debris risk to ISS' Space News (2 April 2019) <https://spacenews.com/nasa-warns-indian-anti-satellite-test-increased-debris-risk-to-iss/>. Accessed 30 September 2019.

416 K. Mačák

A key question of law with respect to kinetic attacks in outer space is to what extent the debris-creation risk should be factored into the proportionality analysis. The rule on proportionality requires that all reasonably foreseeable incidental harm be taken into account by those who plan or decide upon an attack.[118] The ICRC has interpreted this to mean that commanders must also take into account the foreseeable reverberating effects of an attack.[119] However, the exact impact of an orbital collision cannot be fully foreseen and can only be expressed in probabilistic terms. There are some instances of State practice suggesting that in undertaking a proportionality evaluation, belligerents 'should consider the *risk* of unintended or cascading effects on civilians and civilian objects'.[120] Nevertheless, the exact level of probability required for the resulting incidental harm to be considered as 'expected' in the sense of the proportionality rule remains controversial.[121]

19.5.3 Precautions

Happily, the difficulties identified in the preceding section are at least to some extent alleviated by the rules on precautions in attacks (also known as active precautions). Central among them is the requirement that in the conduct of military operations, belligerents must take constant care to spare the civilian population, civilians and civilian objects.[122] To that end, military commanders must take all feasible precautions to avoid, and in any event to minimize, incidental civilian harm caused by any attack they plan or decide upon.[123] In situations where a non-debris producing alternative (e.g. a cyber operation, signal jamming, or blinding by lasers) is available for the purposes of neutralizing a military objective in outer space, the military commander is thus under an obligation to utilize that alternative in order to keep any incidental harm to a minimum.[124] This way, the commander can achieve the same military effect while avoiding the creation of debris implicit in any act of physical destruction in outer space.

Finally, IHL complements the rules on active precautions with those prescribing passive precautions. Specifically, the parties to armed conflicts must, to the maximum extent feasible, protect civilians and civilian objects against the dangers resulting

---

[118] AP I, Article 57(2)(a)(iii); ICTY, *Prosecutor v Galić*, Judgement (Trial Chamber), 5 December 2003, Case No. IT-98-29-T, para. 58.

[119] ICRC 2015, at 42, 52.

[120] Guymon 2014, at 737.

[121] Compare AMW Manual 2013, rule 14, commentary para. 6 (arguing that 'expected' means that the 'outcome is probable, i.e. more likely than not') with Robinson and Nohle 2016, at 118 (arguing that 'expected' means that the outcome 'is likely to occur rather than more likely than not').

[122] AP I, Article 57(1); ICRC Customary IHL Study, Volume I, rule 15, first sentence.

[123] AP I, Article 57(2) (a) (ii); ICRC Customary IHL Study, Volume I, rule 15, second sentence.

[124] Hansen 2015, at 58–59; Stephens and Steer 2015, at 29.

19 Military Space Operations

from military operations.[125] As noted earlier, much of the dangers that military space operations pose for civilians result from the dual-use character of many space assets. Insofar as doing so is practicable and practically possible, States should thus separate military from civilian uses of the space objects that they operate.[126] In situations where such separation is not feasible, they should in any event aim to improve the resilience of those aspects of dual-use space objects that are used for civilian purposes. Conversely, if a given satellite is exclusively dedicated to civilian purposes (e.g. water conservation and agriculture), a possible good practice consistent with these obligations would be for the launching State to mark and register the satellite accordingly, thus indicating its protected status to any potential attacker.[127]

19.6 Conclusion

With the increasing use of outer space for military purposes, understanding the international legal framework applicable to military space operations is becoming ever more important. Thus far, this body of law has not been codified in an easily accessible single source. However, as demonstrated throughout this chapter, that does not mean that military activities in outer space escape legal regulation altogether. Conversely, such activities are subject to a multitude of legal constraints established principally by international space law, international law on the use of force, and international humanitarian law.

Very few of the relevant rules of these areas of international law expressly consider military space operations as understood in this chapter. As we have seen, the cornerstone treaties of the law on the use of force and IHL were drawn up at a time when military activities in space were either science-fiction or, at best, still in their infancy. Moreover, space law treaties predominantly concentrate on the peaceful exploration and use of outer space and their coverage of military aspects is minimal. Therefore, much of the analysis presented in this chapter has focussed on the interpretation of rules developed for the terrestrial environment and their extrapolation into the space domain.

In doing so, the chapter has identified a number of areas where the law is either underdeveloped or unclear. For example, opinions differ as to whether the prohibition to place objects carrying WMDs 'in orbit around the Earth' covers such objects if they are only placed into a partial orbital trajectory.[128] Similarly, it remains unclear under what conditions does causing temporary or reversible loss of functionality of space objects qualify as a use of force.[129] And the debate around war-sustaining

---

[125] AP I, Article 58(c); ICRC Customary IHL Study, Volume I, rule 22.

[126] Cf. ICRC Customary IHL Study, Volume I, at 70-71.

[127] Cf. DoD Manual, para. 5.14.4 (considering that the use of distinctive and visible signs to identify protected objects as such is a possible passive precaution).

[128] Section 19.3.2 above.

[129] Section 19.4.1 above.

objects poses specific problems for the application on the rule of distinction in outer space.[130]

All of these examples underline the need for further clarity in this area. To that end, States should be encouraged to develop legal positions on these and related matters. Comprehensive expert manuals like those that will be produced in the scope of the MILAMOS and Woomera projects can certainly help by providing interpretations tested through inclusive deliberative processes. However, in the final analysis, States still are the primary legislators of the international legal system. It is thus the action that they take, including in response to the non-State-driven initiatives, that will shape the future legal landscape applicable to military space operations.

References

AMW Manual (2013) Manual on international law applicable to air and missile warfare (Humanitarian Policy and Conflict Research). Cambridge University Press, Cambridge

Anson P, Cummings D (1991) The First Space War: The contribution of satellites to the Gulf War. The RUSI Journal 136:45–53

Blake D (2014) Military strategic use of outer space. In: Nasu H, McLaughlin R (eds) New technologies and the law of armed conflict. T.M.C. Asser Press, The Hague, pp 97–114

Boothby W (2014) Does the law of targeting meet twenty-first-century needs? In: Harvey C, Summers J, White ND (eds) Contemporary challenges to the laws of war: Essays in honour of Professor Peter Rowe. Cambridge University Press, Cambridge, pp 216–234

Boothby B (2019) Aspects of the distinction principle under the US DoD Law of War Manual. In: Newton MN (ed) The United States Department of Defense Law of War Manual: Commentary and Critique. Cambridge University Press, Cambridge, pp 161–200

Borgen CJ (2021) The Second Space Age: The Regulation of Military Space Operations and the Role of Private Actors. In: Waxman M, Oakley TW (eds) The Future Law of Armed Conflict. Oxford University Press, Oxford (forthcoming)

Bourbonnière M (2004) Law of armed conflict (LOAC) and the neutralisation of satellites or *ius in bello satellitis*. Journal of Conflict and Security Law 9:43–69

Bridge RL (1980) International law and military activities in outer space. Akron Law Review 13:649–664

Christol CQ (1982) Modern international law of outer space. Pergamon Press, New York.

Crawford E (2017) The principle of distinction and remote warfare. In: Ohlin J (ed) Research handbook on remote warfare. Edward Elgar, Cheltenham, pp 50–78

Diederiks-Verschoor IPP, Kopal V (2008) An introduction to space law, 3rd rev edn. Kluwer Law International, The Hague

Dinstein Y (2016) The conduct of hostilities under the law of international armed conflict, 3rd edn, Cambridge University Press, Cambridge

Freeland S (2015) The laws of war in outer space. In: Schrogl KU, Hays PL, Robinson J, Moura D, Giannopapa C (eds) Handbook of space security: Policies, applications and programs. Springer, New York, pp 81–112

Freeland S, Jakhu RS (2016) The intersection between space law and international human rights law. In: Jakhu RS, Dempsey PS (eds) Routledge handbook of space law. Routledge, pp 225–238

Goodman R (2016) The Obama administration and targeting "war-sustaining" objects in noninternational armed conflict. American Journal of International Law 110:663–679

---

[130] Section 19.5.1 above.

Guymon CD (ed) (2014) Digest of United States practice in international law. Office of the Legal Adviser, United States Department of State, Washington DC

Hansen R (2015) The role of the air-space boundary in regulating military use of outer space. Annals of Air and Space Law 40:25–70

Happold M (2012) International humanitarian law and human rights law. In: Henderson C, White N (eds) Research handbook on international conflict and security law. Edward Elgar, Cheltenham, pp 444–466

Hathaway OA et al (2017) Ensuring responsibility: Common Article 1 and state responsibility for non-state actors. Texas Law Review 95:539–590

ICRC (2015) International humanitarian law and the challenges of contemporary armed conflicts (Report prepared for the 32nd International Conference of the Red Cross and Red Crescent). ICRC, Geneva

ICRC (2019) International humanitarian law and the challenges of contemporary armed conflicts (Report prepared for the 33rd International Conference of the Red Cross and Red Crescent). ICRC, Geneva

ICRC Customary IHL Study (2005) Customary international humanitarian law, volumes I, 574 II(1), and II(2). Cambridge University Press, Cambridge

Jachec-Neale A (2014) The concept of military objectives in international law and targeting practice. Routledge, Abingdon

Jasentuliyana N, Lee RS (1979) Manual on space law, volume I. Oceana Publications, Dobbs Ferry

King MT, Blank LR (2019) International law and security in outer space: Now and tomorrow. AJIL Unbound 113:125–129

Koskenniemi M (2006) Fragmentation of international law: Difficulties arising from the diversification and expansion of international law – Report of the Study Group of the International Law Commission. UN Doc A/CN.4/L.682

Lachs M (1972) The law of outer space. Martinus Nijhoff, Leiden

Lipson L, Katzenbach N (1961) The Law of outer space. In Legal problems of space exploration: A symposium. Library of Congress, Washington DC

Lyall F, Larsen PB (2017) Space law: A treatise, 2nd edn. Routledge, Abingdon

Mačák K (2018) Silent War: Applicability of the *jus in bello* to military space operations. International Law Studies 94:1–38

Maogoto JN, Freeland S (2007) Space weaponization and the United Nations Charter regime on force: A thick legal fog or a receding mist? The International Lawyer 41:1091–1119

Meyer A (1968) Interpretation of the term 'peaceful' in the light of the Space Treaty, Proceedings. Colloquium on Law of Outer Space 11:24–29

National Research Council (2012) Making sense of ballistic missile defense: An assessment of concepts and systems for U.S. boost-phase missile defense in comparison to other alternatives. National Academies Press, Washington DC

Nolte G, Randelzhofer A (2012) Article 51. In: Simma B et al (eds) The Charter of the United Nations: A commentary, 3rd edn., volume II. Oxford University Press, Oxford, pp 1397–1428

Oeter S (2013) Methods and means of combat. In: Fleck D (ed) The handbook of international humanitarian law, 3rd edn. Oxford University Press, Oxford

Ramey R (2000) Armed conflict on the final frontier: The law of war in space. Air Force Law Review 48:1–157

Robinson I, Nohle E (2016) Proportionality and precautions in attack: The reverberating effects of using explosive weapons in populated areas. International Review of the Red Cross 98:107–145

San Remo Manual (1995) San Remo Manual on International Law Applicable to Armed Conflicts at Sea. Cambridge University Press, Cambridge

Sandoz Y, Swinarski C, Zimmermann B (eds) (1987) Commentary on the Additional Protocols of 8 June 1977 to the Geneva Conventions of 12 August 1949. ICRC, Geneva

Sassòli M (2019) International humanitarian law: Rules, controversies, and solutions to problems arising in warfare. Edward Elgar, Cheltenham

Sassòli M, Olson LM (2008) The relationship between international humanitarian and human rights law where it matters: Admissible killing and internment of fighters in non-international armed conflicts. International Review of the Red Cross 90:599–627

Schmitt MN (2006a) International law and military operations in space. Max Planck Yearbook of United Nations Law 10:89–125

Schmitt MN (2006b) Fault lines in the law of attack. In: Breau S, Jachec-Neale A (eds) Testing the boundaries of international humanitarian law. BIICL, London, pp 277–307

Schrogl KU, Neumann J (2009) Article IV. In: Cologne commentary on space law, Volume 1. Carl Heymanns Verlag, Cologne, pp 70–85

Shaw JE (1999) The influence of space power upon history 1944-1998. Air Power History 46:20–29

Stephens D (2018) The international legal implications of military space operations: Examining the interplay between international humanitarian law and the outer space regime. International Law Studies 94:75–101

Stephens D, Steer C (2015) Conflicts in space: International humanitarian law and its application to space warfare. Annals of Air and Space Law 40:1–32

Strydom HA (2017) Weapons of mass destruction. In: Wolfrum R (ed) Max Planck Encyclopedia of public international law. Oxford University Press, Oxford

Tallinn Manual 2.0 (2017) Tallinn Manual 2.0 on the international law applicable to cyber operations. Cambridge University Press, Cambridge

Tronchetti F (2015) Legal aspects of the military uses of outer space. In: von der Dunk F, Tronchetti F (eds) Handbook of space law. Edward Elgar, Cheltenham

UN General Assembly (2001) Draft articles on responsibility of States for internationally wrongful acts with commentaries. UN Doc. A/56/10

Vermeer A (2007) A legal exploration of force application in outer space. Military Law and Law of War Review 46:299–340

Vlasic IA (1981) Disarmament decade, outer space and international law. Annals of Air and Space Law 26:135–206

Watkin K (2014) Targeting "Islamic state" oil facilities. International Law Studies 90:499–513

Weeden B (2012) 2007 Chinese anti-satellite test: Fact sheet, https://swfound.org/media/205391/chinese_asat_fact_sheet_updated_2012.pdf. Accessed 30 September 2019

Yearbook of the United Nations (1966) United Nations, Office of Public Information, New York. See https://www.unmultimedia.org/searchers/yearbook/page_un2.jsp?volume=1966&page=1

Dr. Kubo Mačák is an Associate Professor of Public International Law at the University of Exeter. He holds the degrees of DPhil, MPhil, and MJur from Somerville College, University of Oxford, as well as an undergraduate degree in law from Charles University in Prague. He was awarded the Diploma of the Hague Academy of International Law. He has worked at the International Criminal Tribunal for the former Yugoslavia (ICTY) and the International Criminal Tribunal for Rwanda (ICTR), and he has served as a core expert on the Woomera Manual on the International Law of Military Space Operations project. He is currently acting as the General Editor of the Cyber Law Toolkit. Since October 2019, he has been on leave from Exeter to serve as a Legal Adviser at the International Committee of the Red Cross in Geneva. His research interests span general international law, international humanitarian law, and the law of cyber security.

This chapter was entirely researched and written prior to the author's engagement in the Legal Division of the ICRC, in the context of an independent academic project. The opinions expressed herein are his own and do not necessarily correspond to those held by the ICRC or its Legal Division. The author is grateful to Ana Beduschi, Laura Grego, Agnieszka Jachec-Neale, Dale Stephens, and Wen Zhou for their helpful comments on earlier drafts of this chapter.

Chapter 20
The Protection of the Environment and Natural Resources in Armed Conflict

Tara Smith

Contents

20.1 Introduction 421
20.2 A Brief History of the Environmental Consequences of Armed Conflict 423
20.3 Relevant Treaty-based International Law 427
    20.3.1 Additional Protocol I 428
    20.3.2 The Environmental Modification Convention 429
    20.3.3 Statute of the International Criminal Court 430
    20.3.4 Common Article 3 431
    20.3.5 Additional Protocol II 432
20.4 International Jurisprudence 434
    20.4.1 International Military Tribunals at Nuremberg 434
    20.4.2 International Court of Justice 436
    20.4.3 United Nations Compensation Commission 437
20.5 Future Developments 438
20.6 Conclusion 439
References 439

Abstract The environment and natural resources play a significant role in contemporary armed conflict. This chapter first briefly traces the history of the environmental consequences of armed conflict before examining relevant treaty-based laws of armed conflict and significant jurisprudence related to the protection of the environment and natural resources in both international and non-international armed conflict.

Keywords Armed conflict · environment · international armed conflict · natural resources · non-international armed conflict · protection

20.1 Introduction

The natural environment has, without doubt, played a significant role in most armed conflicts that have taken place to date. The environment provides belligerents with the space in which armed conflict can be strategically conducted, and as such has

---

T. Smith (✉)
School of Law, Bangor University, Wales, UK
e-mail: t.smith@bangor.ac.uk

© T.M.C. ASSER PRESS and the authors 2022
S. Sayapin et al. (eds.), *International Conflict and Security Law*,
https://doi.org/10.1007/978-94-6265-515-7_20

sustained harm in almost every armed conflict that has ever taken place. However, the relationship between the natural environment and armed conflict is changing as armed conflicts are waged over control of and access to valuable natural resources. The environment in no longer a benign location for conflict. It is being used more strategically than ever before by belligerents, not only for tactical purposes in defeating the enemy, but for financial gain and political capital. Assessing protection of the environment and natural resources in times of armed conflict has therefore never been more timely.

This chapter begins with a brief history of the environmental consequences of armed conflict, focusing on significant events that have shaped the development of the laws of armed conflict in this regard. A comparison between historical events and contemporary armed conflict will highlight the changing nature of the relationship, and the strong links between conflict and natural resources in the present day will be used to ask robust questions of the laws of armed conflict that are subsequently outlined.

In evaluating the protection of the environment and natural resources in armed conflict, this review focuses on the *jus in bello*—the laws that apply as *lex specialis* for the duration of the conflict. As such, laws applicable in both international and non-international armed conflict will be discussed with the aim of determining the adequacy of this law to achieve environmental protection in contemporary armed conflict. Of course, the protection of the environment is not limited to the duration of the armed conflict—the environment may be in jeopardy during preparations for armed conflict, and also in the post-conflict phase. Indeed, the environment may be protected through fields of international law beyond the laws of armed conflict and international criminal law; international environmental law and international human rights law have an important role to play in this regard. Although this review focuses on times of armed conflict and on the laws of armed conflict, it is intended to serve as a primer on the most directly relevant laws and as a springboard into which further research on this very important topic can be conducted.

This review will conclude with a discussion of current developments and potential challenges which will play a role in shaping the relationship between armed conflict and the environment for future generations. The laws of armed conflict were largely drafted prior to the formulation of contemporary international environmental law, and before any major movement had begun to generate momentum for the need to protect the environment at all times. Questions regarding the adequacy of the laws of armed conflict in protecting the environment and natural resources may be addressed over time, and in a variety of forums. This is a dynamic issue in international law, and one in which significant changes are long overdue.

20.2 A Brief History of the Environmental Consequences of Armed Conflict

As far back as the fourth century B.C., the environment was recognised as something that ought to be shielded from harm in non-international armed conflict. Hughes recalls that

> one of the earliest calls for restraint was recorded by a scribe serving the Greek admiral, Nearkhos, exploring India in the fourth century B.C., who noted that "if there is an internal war among the Indians, it is not lawful for them to touch these land workers, nor even devastate the land itself [1]

Indeed intentional and unintentional destruction of the environment has always been a feature of war. From the scorched-earth policy employed by the Scythians in retreat from the Persians in 512 B.C. and reported accounts of the Spartans annually laying waste to Athenian fields during the Peloponnesian Wars of 431-404 B.C. to the Mongolian invasion of Mesopotamia between 1213 and 1224 and the creation of the 'Holland water line' during the Franco-Dutch War from 1672 to 1678, early evidence of the potential damage that can be caused to the environment during armed conflict were not in short supply.[2] More recently, the trench warfare that permanently altered the landscape of Europe during the First World War and the widespread and careless destruction of the dams, factories, power-stations and coal mines from aerial bombardments, not to mention the use of nuclear weapons, during the Second World War have proved that the potential for serious environmental damage to be caused during conflicts is a dangerous and evolving threat.

Over the past three decades, armed conflict and war across all continents has resulted in significant yet forgotten or disputed evidence of serious environmental damage. States are responsible for causing significant environmental damage during armed conflict. For example, during the conflict in Vietnam in the early 1970s, US forces were condemned for their widespread use of chemical defoliants, such as Agent Orange, and cloud seeding techniques which caused excessive rainfall.[3] Even more serious, in retreat from their occupation of Kuwait, the Iraqi army set more than 700 oil wells on fire across the Persian Gulf in the early 1990s, which caused extensive long-term damage across the region in little over nine months.[4] In all, over six hundred miles of sea surface and three hundred miles of coastline were covered in an oil slick.[5] All aspects of the environment were affected, from the marine pollution caused by the oil spills and well fires, to the air quality that was severely impaired by plumes of smoke that, at times, reached a distance of over one hundred kilometres from their point of origin, to the contaminated soil and contaminated groundwater.

---

[1] De Jong et al 2007, p. 18.

[2] See Ross 1992, p. 516 for more examples.

[3] See for example Schmitt 1999-2000, p. 268; Cohan 2002–2003, p. 487.

[4] Low and Hodgkinson 1994–1995, p. 411.

[5] DuBarry Huston 2002, p. 909.

Further destruction of all manner of flora and fauna from that region was evident as a result of the combined effects of the sea and air pollution.[6]

Moreover, during the NATO bombing of Kosovo in 1999, serious damage was caused when the chemical plant at Pancevo was hit and its contents were spilled. This polluted the surrounding area including the Danube, which carried the toxins and pollutants with it downstream. Not only was the natural environment affected, but the people inhabiting the immediate and surrounding areas suffered serious injury because of the damaged environment too. Equally, the use of depleted uranium at Kragujevac and an abundance of unexploded munitions in the area will continue to pose long-term health hazards to the people of Kosovo.[7]

Environmental damage was, of course, the centrepiece of the contentious case between the Democratic Republic of the Congo and Uganda, decided by the International Court of Justice in 2005.[8] Furthermore, in Sudan, the Janjaweed were responsible for implementing a government-sanctioned[9] scorched earth policy;[10] burning fields and villages, contaminating water supplies and destroying the natural environment in Darfur. During the 2006 armed conflict between Hezbollah and Israel significant and well-documented environmental damage was caused in Lebanon after the Jiyeh power plant was the target of an attack.[11] Iraq, in 1998, also used chemical weapons to repress Kurdish insurgents in Northern Iraq which resulted in environmental damage.[12] There are also reports from the ongoing armed conflict in Yemen of environmental damage being caused by Yemeni, Saudi Arabian and US bombings,[13] as well as a military operation code-named 'Operation Scorched Earth'.[14]

However, non-state actors are also responsible for causing extensive environmental damage when they engage in armed conflict. De Jong, Donovan and Abe have observed that

> Recent events in Rwanda and the former Yugoslavia underscore that the environment will suffer even in the event of a civil war. Insurgency and counter-insurgency guerrilla civil wars have a particularly devastating effect on local environments. Insurgents often use tropical forests as home bases and hiding grounds; counter-insurgency forces often respond by slashing and burning forests and by polluting rivers, viewing both as legitimate theatres of operations.[15]

For example, in the context of the non-international armed conflict in Colombia, 'rebels have waged war against the government by destroying oil pipelines in order

---

[6] Jacoby 2000, p. 298.

[7] Schwabach 2000, p. 120.

[8] Armed Activities on the Territory of the Congo (Democratic Republic of the Congo v Uganda), Judgment, ICJ Reports 2005, p. 168. This case is discussed in greater detail below.

[9] Glassborow 2007.

[10] Bloomfield and Butler 2008.

[11] Stewart 2007; Takshe 2010; Tranquillo 2007.

[12] Hulme 2004, p. 205.

[13] The Independent 2010.

[14] Von Mittelstaedt 2010.

[15] De Jong et al 2007; see also Drumbl 2000.

20 The Protection of the Environment and Natural …

to spill millions of barrels of oil into rivers—spills that, not surprisingly, killed vast numbers of fish and destroyed large areas of the ecosystem, in addition to poisoning human water supplies.'[16] It has been calculated that by '1998, the affected areas were estimated to include 2,600km of watercourses, 1,600ha of wetlands, and 6,000ha of agricultural land.'[17] In addition, 'guerrilla groups operate out of remote forest and jungle regions; some have their bases in designated national protected areas, and the numerous mines planted by army and guerrilla troops have devastating impacts on forest wildlife and people.'[18]

In order to prevent the Sudanese government from using oil revenues to purchase more weapons, large oil installations were targeted by armed Sudanese rebels in the recent conflict between these groups.[19] The environmental damage caused during the Rwandan Civil War in the early 1990s 'left national parks polluted with landmines and bodies, and agricultural land stripped to force movements of people.'[20] Land mines were placed extensively throughout national parks, which then killed a significant number of endangered mountain gorillas.[21] In Somalia, 'practices of deforestation and assaults on water purity'[22] are 'commonplace in the conflict'.[23] Forests are frequently targeted in armed conflict[24] as they provide natural cover and camouflage for non-state armed groups in addition to 'food, water, fuel, and medicine'.[25] To date, '[t]hree-quarters of Asian forests, two-thirds of African forests and one-third of Latin American forests have been affected by violent conflict.'[26] There are issues with the poaching and killing of gorillas in the Virunga National Park in the Democratic Republic of the Congo by rebel groups, including M23, hiding in the Park.[27] Indeed '[g]reat apes are particularly vulnerable in wartime...more than two-thirds of the 23 protected areas with great apes have been disturbed by military conflicts during the past 10 years.'[28] Indeed wildlife and animals are an integral part of the natural environment that often face danger in the context of non-international armed conflict at the hands of non-state armed groups.[29] However, it is not unheard of for non-state armed groups to be sympathetic to the environment and to play some part in its protection throughout the conflict.[30]

---

[16] Lawrence and Heller 2007, p. 85; see also Bruch 2000–2001.

[17] Austin and Bruch 2003, 165.

[18] Austin and Bruch 2003, 164.

[19] Austin and Bruch 2003, 166.

[20] Weinstein 2004–2005, 700.

[21] Lawrence and Heller 2007, 85.

[22] Drumbl 2000, 644.

[23] Drumbl 2000, 644.

[24] De Jong et al 2007; see also Drumbl 2000, p. 631.

[25] Austin and Bruch 2003, pp. 162–163.

[26] De Jong et al 2007, p. 1.

[27] African Wildlife Foundation 2012.

[28] Draulans and Van Krunkelsven 2002, p. 35.

[29] Dudley et al 2002.

[30] Adam 2006; see also Draulans and Van Krunkelsven 2002, pp. 36–37.

The exploitation of natural resources is often linked to both international and non-international armed conflict.[31] State and non-state actors alike have been involved in this activity to a greater or lesser degree. Natural resources have caused or financed a significant number of contemporary armed conflicts. For example, trade in timber has been linked to conflicts in the DRC, Sierra Leone, Liberia, Cambodia and the Philippines.[32] In addition, '[a]mong the longest continuous conflicts are those found in the remote hinterlands of Myanmar...[t]hese conflict regions are rich in natural resources, including rubies, jade, petroleum, and timber, as well as opium poppy.'[33] In fact, '[t]here is no shortage of long-lived resource-funded insurgencies around: examples include Afghanistan (opium), Colombia (cocaine), Myanmar (timber, opium, gems), and Cambodia (timber and gemstones).'[34] Recent empirical research suggests that

> lootable gemstones were available in 26% of all intrastate conflicts and 38% of all conflict years since 1946. Similarly, 15% of the conflicts and 21% of all conflict years occurred in areas with significant narcotics cultivation. For petroleum, the figures are 44 and 52%, respectively. The fact that a larger share of the observations (conflict years) than the conflicts include these resources tentatively indicates a positive association between local resource wealth and conflict duration.[35]

However, resource exploitation *per se* is not something that the laws of armed conflict were created to address. Opportunistic looting and exploitation of resources in the context of an armed conflict—whether carried out by a belligerent group or not—may be covered by the prohibition against pillage. However, if a specific diamond mine, for instance, is clearly linked to the funding of a non-state armed group, then that diamond mine may be a military objective. As such, the laws of armed conflict would permit the targeting of that mine, but would also regulate the amount of force that could be used, the extent of the damage that would be permitted. In light of these examples of the environmental consequences of armed conflict, the discussion now turns to an assessment of relevant treaty-based laws.

---

[31] See, for example, Humphreys 2005; Lujala 2010; Lujala et al 2005; Ross 2004; Schwartz and Singh 1999; Schwartz et al 2000; Weinstein 2005; Le Billon 2001; Binningsbo et al 2006; Collier and Hoeffler 2005; Percival and Homer-Dixon 1998.

[32] De Jong et al 2007, p. 2.

[33] Buhaug et al 2009, p. 544.

[34] Buhaug et al 2009, p. 555.

[35] Buhaug et al 2009, p. 558.

20.3 Relevant Treaty-based International Law

Explicit environmental protection in the laws of armed conflict has only existed since 1977.[36] Prior to that, no direct limitations on the nature and extent of the environmental damage that could be caused during armed conflict were to be found in international law. The decision to 'green' the laws of armed conflict most likely began in the mid-1960s, buoyed by strong public reaction to environmental damage caused during the conflict in Vietnam. The laws of armed conflict that resulted from this public reaction are featured in Additional Protocol I, and they have been reproduced in several key instruments since then including the 1998 Statute of the International Criminal Court.[37] No environmental provision was included in Additional Protocol II and so the laws of armed conflict that are applicable in non-international armed conflict do not directly prohibit environmental damage. The United Nations Environment Programme has recognised this as an inadequacy that poses 'a significant challenge to the applicability and enforcement of IHL for environmental protection'.[38]

The first attempted codification of the laws of armed conflict is recognised to be the Instructions for the Government of Armies of the United States in the Field 1863,[39] more commonly referred to as the Lieber Code. The Lieber Code was drafted to apply to Union forces during the American Civil War. The Lieber Code prohibited in Article 16,[40] 'the use of poison in any way' and 'the wanton devastation of a district'. Environmental damage could foreseeably breach Article 16. Another relevant limitation is contained in Article 44[41] of the Lieber Code, which states that 'all destruction of property not commanded by the authorized officer, all robbery, all pillage or sacking, even after taking a place by main force...are prohibited...' Pillage, as discussed below, may be a strong means of protecting certain types of environmental damage in conflict, particularly the exploitation of natural resources. Despite these prohibitions, Union troops nonetheless caused serious environmental damage in their efforts to subordinate Confederate forces, with, it seems, general impunity.[42] From the very first codification of the modern laws of armed conflict, therefore, environmental damage was an issue that needed to be addressed.

---

[36] At which time prohibitions on environmental damage were included in Additional Protocol I in articles 35(3) and 55. Protocol Additional to the Geneva Conventions of 12 August 1949, and relating to the Protection of Victims of International Armed Conflicts (Protocol I), 8 June 1977, 1125 UNTS 3.

[37] Article 8(2)(b)(iv), Rome Statute of the International Criminal Court, UN Doc. A/CONF. 183/9; 37 ILM 1002 (1998); 2187 UNTS 90.

[38] United Nations Environment Programme 2009, p. 10.

[39] US War Department, Instructions for the Government of Armies of the United States in the Field, General Orders No 100 (Apr. 24, 1863).

[40] US War Department, Instructions for the Government of Armies of the United States in the Field, General Orders No 100 (Apr. 24, 1863) Article 16.

[41] US War Department, Instructions for the Government of Armies of the United States in the Field, General Orders No 100 (Apr. 24, 1863) Article 44.

[42] Bruch 2000-2001, pp. 695–697.

Despite the serious environmental damage that was caused during the Second World War—in particular as a result of widespread aerial bombardment and from the use of nuclear weapons in Japan—and despite prosecutions for environmental damage in the International Military Tribunal at Nuremberg,[43] no prohibition against environmental damage was included in the codification of the laws of armed conflict that took place immediately after the War which resulted in the 1949 Geneva Conventions.[44] In fact, it took almost another three decades for the international community to agree to limitations on environmental damage in international armed conflict. The Vietnam War is widely regarded as being the major trigger for the inclusion of articles on environmental protection in Additional Protocol I.[45]

In the following sub-sections, relevant treaty-based rules that apply during both international and non-international armed conflict will be examined. Applicable during international armed conflict are provisions of Additional Protocol I, the Environmental Modification Treaty, and the Statute of the International Criminal Court. Though provisions which directly protect the environment in non-international armed conflict exist, some treaty-based laws of armed conflict may still indirectly prohibit environmental damage to some degree. To that end, Common Article 3 and certain provisions of Additional Protocol II are frequently raised as having the potential to protect the environment in the absence of specific rules on environmental damage,[46] and these provisions are analysed in turn below.

20.3.1 Additional Protocol I

The environmental consequences of the conflict in Vietnam in the 1970s influenced drafters at the Diplomatic Conference between 1974 and 1977 to include for the first-time environment-specific provisions in the codified laws of armed conflict. These provisions remain in force and can be found in Articles 35(3)[47] and 55[48] of Additional Protocol I. As these provisions are contained in Additional Protocol I, they only apply to international armed conflict. It should be noted that states did not want to limit their ability to exercise military force on foot of purely environmental considerations and so the content of Articles 35(3) and 55(1) of Additional Protocol

---

[43] Discussed below in the section on international jurisprudence (Sect. 20.4).

[44] See Geneva Convention for the Amelioration of the Condition of the Wounded and Sick in Armed Forces in the Field (First Geneva Convention), 12 August 1949, 75 UNTS 31; Geneva Convention for the Amelioration of the Condition of Wounded, Sick and Shipwrecked Members of Armed Forces at Sea (Second Geneva Convention), 12 August 1949, 75 UNTS 85; Geneva Convention Relative to the Treatment of Prisoners of War (Third Geneva Convention), 12 August 1949, 75 UNTS 135; Geneva Convention Relative to the Protection of Civilian Persons in Time of War (Fourth Geneva Convention), 12 August 1949, 75 UNTS 287.

[45] See, for example, Hulme 1997, p. 45; Schmitt 2000, pp. 87–88.

[46] United Nations Environment Programme 2009, p. 10.

[47] Additional Protocol I Article 35(3).

[48] Additional Protocol I Article 55.

I were deliberately drafted with thresholds of harm so high that they would in reality impose no environmental limitation on state parties engaging in hostilities.[49]

Article 35 of Additional Protocol I relates to 'basic rules' of armed conflict. It reiterates Article 22 of the 1899 and 1907 Hague Conventions in stating that means and methods of warfare are not unlimited and that means and methods of warfare, which cause superfluous injury, are prohibited. Article 35 also prohibits widespread, long-term and severe environmental damage.[50] As such, it would seem that Additional Protocol I considers the protection of the environment to be a basic rule within the laws of armed conflict. Article 35(3) states that:

> It is prohibited to employ methods or means of warfare which are intended, or may be expected, to cause widespread, long-term and severe damage to the natural environment.[51]

The second provision protecting the environment is contained in Article 55. The chapeau of Article 55 identifies it as the provision specifically designed for the 'Protection of the Natural Environment'. Article 55 states that:

> Care shall be taken in warfare to protect the natural environment against widespread, long-term and severe damage. This protection includes a prohibition of the use of methods or means of warfare which are intended or may be expected to cause such damage to the natural environment and thereby to prejudice the health or survival of the population.[52]

The specific terms of Articles 35(3) and 55 are extremely problematic. The thresholds of harm in both provisions are the same—widespread, long-term, and severe—and these have been condemned as being inherently ambiguous and too wide in scope to be of any practical relevance.[53] Meron observes that because of the high thresholds of harm, 'their usefulness for international armed conflicts is limited.'[54]

20.3.2 The Environmental Modification Convention

Around the same time as the Additional Protocols were being negotiated, States agreed to the Convention on the Prohibition of Military or Any Other Hostile Use of Environmental Modification Techniques,[55] commonly referred to as the Environmental Modification Convention, or ENMOD. This short international treaty was designed specifically to prevent the environmental modification techniques that were used in the Vietnam War. The first operative paragraph includes similar limitations on environmental damage to those in Additional Protocol I. There is but one

---

[49] Schmitt 2011.

[50] Additional Protocol I Article 35(3).

[51] Additional Protocol I Article 35(3).

[52] Additional Protocol I Article 55.

[53] Hulme 2004.

[54] Meron 1996, p. 356.

[55] Convention on the Prohibition of Military or Any Other Hostile Use of Environmental Modification Techniques, 10 December 1976, 1108 UNTS 151.

crucial difference: the Additional Protocol I requirements of long-term, widespread and severe damage are conjunctive, that is, all three criteria must be satisfied. In the ENMOD Convention, the phrase is disjunctive—the thresholds are long-lasting, widespread *or* severe[56]—so environmental damage amounting to one of the three criteria will be enough to breach the Convention.

Despite the lower threshold of harm, the ENMOD Convention does not actually result in increased environmental protection in armed conflict as it only prohibits environmental modification techniques not environmental damage in general. Indeed 'it is not always easy to see how these environmental modification techniques could actually be used as weapons of warfare and most of them have a high science-fiction calibre.'[57] While the environment is inherently implicated in these actions as weapons, it 'would not necessarily be *harmed*, or destroyed, by the use of such techniques'.[58]

20.3.3 Statute of the International Criminal Court

Despite the environmental provisions in Additional Protocol I and the ENMOD Convention, significant environmental damage has been caused in armed conflicts since these treaties were adopted in 1977. The most recent addition to international law which protects the environment in armed conflict is the inclusion of an environmental war crime in the Statute of the International Criminal Court.[59] The Rome Statute, as it is often referred to, was agreed in 1998 and came into force in 2002. However, the environmental war crime in question, Article 8(2)(b)(iv),[60] uses an almost identical provision to the problematic Article 35(3) of Additional Protocol I. It also only applies to international armed conflict: no environmental war crime was included in the Statute to apply to circumstances of non-international armed conflict. There was an option on the table at the time the Rome Statute was being negotiated, to insert a provision on environmental protection into Article 8(2)(e)[61] which relates to war crimes in non-international armed conflict, but delegates failed to agree on this issue at the Diplomatic Conference of Plenipotentiaries and so the option was dropped.

---

[56] Convention on the Prohibition of Military or Any Other Hostile Use of Environmental Modification Techniques, 10 December 1976, 1108 UNTS 151 Article 1.

[57] Koppe 2008, 263.

[58] Hulme 2007, p. 235.

[59] Rome Statute of the International Criminal Court, UN Doc. A/CONF. 183/9; 37 ILM 1002 (1998); 2187 UNTS 90.

[60] Rome Statute of the International Criminal Court, UN Doc. A/CONF. 183/9; 37 ILM 1002 (1998); 2187 UNTS 90 Article 8(2)(b)(iv).

[61] United Nations Diplomatic Conference of Plenipotentiaries on the Establishment of an International Criminal Court, Rome 15 June-17 July 1998, A/CONF.183/13 (Vol. III), Official Records Vol III–Reports and Other Documents, 20.

20 The Protection of the Environment and Natural ...

20.3.4 *Common Article 3*

Common Article 3 to the four Geneva Conventions of 1949[62] was the first provision in the laws of armed conflict to identify non-international armed conflict as a category of armed conflict in its own right.[63] It has been suggested as a means of indirectly prohibiting environmental damage in non-international armed conflict.[64] However, Common Article 3 is neither the strongest nor the most convincing provision in this regard.

Common Article 3 contains 'a set of minimum standards of humane treatment to be adhered to in all circumstances'.[65] It is focused on the bodily integrity, and therefore the protection, of civilians and persons *hors de combat*. As such, it contains prohibitions on the physical treatment of persons in armed conflict. It may be possible to interpret environmental damage as being, for instance, an outrage on personal dignity, or amounting to cruel and inhuman treatment. However, it would be stretching these concepts too far to determine that they had any foreseeable effect on the prohibition of environmental damage in non-international armed conflict.

If the environment were to benefit from any indirect protection as a result of the application of the minimum standards of humanity contained in Common Article 3, it would have to depend on the extent to which civilians and persons *hors de combat* were directly jeopardised as result of specific environmental damage. In this regard, Bruch has observed that

> certain instances of environmental warfare—for example, poison gas, landmines, and scorched earth practices—may cause "violence to life and person." This arguably would violate Article 3(l)(a), but only to the extent that the anthropomorphic standards applied, since Article 3 does not speak to general environmental damage. [66]

As Common Article 3 was drafted three decades before the Additional Protocols and in advance of any discernible global environmental movement,[67] the degree to which the environment was damaged in armed conflict may not have been of immediate concern to drafters of the 1949 Geneva Conventions, in spite of the level of environmental damage that resulted from the Second World War. Nonetheless, provisions

---

[62] Common Article 3 refers to Article 3 which is common to all four of the 1949 Geneva Conventions. See Geneva Convention for the Amelioration of the Condition of the Wounded and Sick in Armed Forces in the Field (First Geneva Convention), 12 August 1949, 75 UNTS 31, Article 3; Geneva Convention for the Amelioration of the Condition of Wounded, Sick and Shipwrecked Members of Armed Forces at Sea (Second Geneva Convention), 12 August 1949, 75 UNTS 85, Article 3; Geneva Convention Relative to the Treatment of Prisoners of War (Third Geneva Convention), 12 August 1949, 75 UNTS 135, Article 3; Geneva Convention Relative to the Protection of Civilian Persons in Time of War (Fourth Geneva Convention), 12 August 1949, 75 UNTS 287, Article 3.

[63] See for example Elder 1979; Lysaght 1983–1984; Pejic 2011.

[64] See for example Lopez 2006-2007, p. 240.

[65] Cullen 2010, p. 59.

[66] Bruch 2000-2001, p. 709–710.

[67] As the drafters of the Commentary to the Additional Protocols maintain in 1987, 'Respect for the environment, even in peacetime, has only recently become a matter of concern'—Sandoz et al 1987, p. 662.

in Common Article 3 on violence to life,[68] cruel treatment and torture,[69] outrages on personal dignity,[70] and degrading treatment[71] could be interpreted as having some kind of environmental dimension, just as their human rights law counterparts have been in recent times.

20.3.5 Additional Protocol II

Additional Protocol II is generally regarded to be 'a considerable improvement on common article 3'[72] because its provisions are more detailed and more specific. However, in comparison to the treaties that apply to international armed conflict, Additional Protocol II is 'still quite basic'.[73] Nonetheless Meron has clearly stated that certain provisions of Additional Protocol II could be broadly interpreted to provide indirect protection to the environment in non-international armed conflict.[74] Indeed, the United Nations Environment Programme have asserted that protecting the environment as *property* could result in greater protection than that achieved by the direct environmental protection provisions in Additional Protocol I.[75] Therefore provisions of Additional Protocol II prohibiting pillage, protecting objects indispensable to the survival of the civilian population, protecting works and installations containing dangerous forces, and protecting cultural objects and places of worship are relevant and will be examined in this sub-section.

Firstly, the prohibition against pillage, one of the oldest prohibitions within the laws of armed conflict, is relevant to the protection of natural resources in non-international armed conflict. Article 4(2)(g) of Additional Protocol II[76] contains the prohibition, and it can apply to certain instances of natural resource exploitation—a growing feature of contemporary non-international armed conflicts. The issue of conflict resource exploitation pervades contemporary scholarship on the relationship between the environment and non-international armed conflict, yet it does not naturally fall within the scope of protection envisaged by the laws of armed conflict

---

[68] Common Article 3(1)(a).

[69] Common Article 3(1)(a).

[70] Common Article 3(1)(c).

[71] Common Article 3(1)(c).

[72] Report of the Sub-Commission on Prevention of Discrimination and Protection of Minorities, 'Minimum Humanitarian Standards', Analytical report of the Secretary-General submitted pursuant to Commission on Human Rights resolution 1997/21, UN Doc E/CN.4/1998/87 5 January 1998, para. 77.

[73] Report of the Sub-Commission on Prevention of Discrimination and Protection of Minorities, 'Minimum Humanitarian Standards', Analytical report of the Secretary-General submitted pursuant to Commission on Human Rights resolution 1997/21, UN Doc E/CN.4/1998/87 5 January 1998 para. 77.

[74] Meron 1996, p. 357.

[75] United Nations Environment Programme 2009, p. 16.

[76] Additional Protocol II, Article 4(2)(g).

in general. However, the International Court of Justice created a specific precedent for natural resource exploitation to be considered as pillage in the 2005 Democratic Republic of the Congo v Uganda case.[77] By recognising natural resource exploitation as a property-based act of armed conflict, it can be forbidden by the prohibition on pillage in certain circumstances.[78] Indeed, the prohibition against pillage may be a 'powerful mechanism'[79] by which non-state armed groups can be held to account for the exploitation of natural resources under the fog of war.[80] However, despite its relative strength, the prohibition against pillage has its weaknesses and it remains 'important not to overly and exclusively focus on pillage as the new promise on the horizon and to be aware of its inherent limits'.[81]

Secondly, the prohibition against the destruction of objects indispensable to the survival of the civilian population is contained in Article 14 of Additional Protocol II and it specifically identifies foodstuffs, agricultural areas that produce foodstuffs, crops, livestock, drinking water installations and irrigation works as objects which cannot be directly targeted. However, Article 14 prohibits the destruction of these objects only to the extent that damaging them would result in the starvation of the civilian population. Although it is limited in scope by this qualification, Article 14 of Additional Protocol II may be the closest one can get to direct environmental protection in the laws of non-international armed conflict.

Thirdly, Article 15 of Additional Protocol II[82] prohibits attacks on works and installations containing dangerous forces in non-international armed conflict, but those works and installations are limited to dams, dykes and nuclear electrical generating stations. The environmental damage that would result from targeting these objects is not difficult to imagine, but conflicts over natural resources such as oil and gas may be more frequent than over dams or dykes in the coming decades. Indeed, the extent of the damage that can be caused by targeting petrochemical plants is evident from recent conflicts in Kosovo[83] and Lebanon.[84] Yet it has been suggested that petrochemical plants have 'been intentionally excluded' from the absolute prohibition contained in Article 15 for strategic reasons.[85] While Article 15 is not devoid of value, its limitations should be recognised.

Fourthly, though it does not describe the environment *per se*, the protection of cultural objects[86] in Article 16 of Additional Protocol II is frequently considered to

---

[77] *Armed Activities on the Territory of the Congo (Democratic Republic of the Congo v Uganda)* Judgment, ICJ Reports 2005 168. Discussed in detail below in the section on relevant international jurisprudence (Sect. 20.4).

[78] Lundberg 2007-2008, p. 502.

[79] Dam-de Jong 2009.

[80] Dam-de Jong 2009.

[81] Van den Herik and Dam-de Jong 2011, p. 273.

[82] Additional Protocol II, Article 15.

[83] Bruch and Austin 2000.

[84] Takshe et al 2010.

[85] United Nations Environment Programme 2009, p. 18.

[86] See generally Keane 2004.

prohibit some environmental damage in non-international armed conflict.[87] However, just like many aspects of indirect environmental protection, cultural property protection has 'rarely been effectively implemented or enforced'[88] and so the extent to which actual environmental protection can be achieved is unclear. Assistance in identifying environmental cultural objects that would benefit from protection under this provision can be found in UNESCO's classification of certain environmental sites as being of significant importance to world heritage, pursuant to the 1972 Convention Concerning the Protection of the World Cultural and Natural Heritage.[89] There are currently 188 sites on the UNESCO World Heritage List that have been classified as being 'natural' as opposed to man-made, and a further 29 that are a mixture of both.[90] In the context of armed conflict, UNESCO have compiled a list of world heritage sites that are in danger—of the 28 sites on the danger list, 18 are part of the natural environment.[91]

20.4 International Jurisprudence

The protection of the environment during armed conflict has been addressed by Courts and innovative precedent-setting bodies. Examples from the International Military Tribunals at Nuremberg, the International Court of Justice, and the United Nations Compensation Commission will be discussed below.

20.4.1 International Military Tribunals at Nuremberg

During the Nuremberg Trials that followed World War II, three significant prosecutions pursued instances of environmental damage through pre-1949 laws of armed conflict. These prosecutions remain the only criminal enforcement of the laws of armed conflict for environmental damage and as such they establish important jurisprudential precedents.

Firstly, charges were brought against General Lothar Rendulic pursuant to Article 23(g) of the 1907 Hague Regulations[92] for the implementation of a scorched earth

---

[87] United Nations Environment Programme 2009, p. 18.

[88] United Nations Environment Programme 2009, p. 51.

[89] Convention Concerning the Protection of the World Cultural and Natural Heritage, 1037 UNTS 151; 27 UST 37; 11 ILM 1358 (1972).

[90] 'UNESCO World Heritage List' <http://whc.unesco.org/en/list/> accessed 3 January 2013.

[91] 'UNESCO List of World Heritage in Danger' <http://whc.unesco.org/en/danger> accessed 3 January 2013.

[92] Hague Convention (IV) respecting the Laws and Customs of War on Land and its annex: Regulations concerning the Laws and Customs of War on Land. The Hague, 18 October 1907.

policy in the German retreat from the Norwegian province of Finnmark.[93] The scorched earth policy was ordered by General Rendulic as a counter-measure to perceived advancements upon German troops by a superior Russian side. Objectively, this belief was unfounded as the Russian Army did not pursue the German Army as expected. However, the Court decided that the military necessity for the scorched earth tactics had to be judged against the information held by the commander at the time. It was held that General Rendulic's sincere but mistaken beliefs represented an error in judgement but not a criminal act.[94] General Rendulic therefore acted within the parameters of military necessity and was found not guilty on that portion of the charge.[95] He was, however, found guilty on all other charges and sentenced to 20 years' imprisonment.[96]

Secondly, General Alfred Jodl was found guilty of implementing a scorched earth policy during the German Army's retreat in Norway in 1941, pursuant to the provisions of the 1907 Hague Convention mentioned above.[97] General Jodl entered a defence of superior orders, which was prohibited by the Statute of the Tribunal and so he was found guilty of this charge.[98] As result of all counts on which he was found guilty, General Jodl was sentenced to death by hanging.[99]

Thirdly, natural resource exploitation during World War II was also pursued in post-War prosecutions which took place alongside those at the main Tribunal at Nuremberg. In Polish Forestry Case No. 7150, for example, the United Nations War Crimes Commission 'determined that nine of ten German civil administrators could be considered war criminals for cutting down Polish timber'.[100]

Although these cases set important early precedents which apply the laws of armed conflict to environmental damage, 'no tribunal since Nuremberg has prosecuted individuals for war-related environmental damage'.[101] Perhaps a simple explanation could be that the environmental dimension of these prosecutions was not stressed or publicised at the time. Indeed, there is no sustained discussion of the environmental dimensions of the Nuremberg Tribunals in scholarship until the early 1990s, following the oil fires that were caused by Iraq during the Persian Gulf War.

---

[93] *Wilhelm List and Others (The Hostages Trial)* (1949) Law Reports of Trials of War Criminals Selected and Prepared by the United Nations War Crimes Committee Vol VIII 34, 45.

[94] *Wilhelm List and Others (The Hostages Trial)* (1949) Law Reports of Trials of War Criminals Selected and Prepared by the United Nations War Crimes Committee Vol VIII 34 69.

[95] *Wilhelm List and Others (The Hostages Trial)* (1949) Law Reports of Trials of War Criminals Selected and Prepared by the United Nations War Crimes Committee Vol VIII 34 67–69.

[96] *Wilhelm List and Others (The Hostages Trial)* (1949) Law Reports of Trials of War Criminals Selected and Prepared by the United Nations War Crimes Committee Vol VIII 34 76.

[97] *Trial of Alfred Jodl* (1948) Trial of the Major War Criminals before The International Military Tribunal "Blue Series" Vol XXII, 463.

[98] *Trial of Alfred Jodl* (1948) Trial of the Major War Criminals before The International Military Tribunal "Blue Series" Vol XXII, 571.

[99] *Trial of Alfred Jodl* (1948) Trial of the Major War Criminals before The International Military Tribunal "Blue Series" Vol XXII 570–571.

[100] Weinstein 2004-2005, p. 704.

[101] Weinstein 2004-2005, p. 704.

20.4.2 International Court of Justice

The pillage of natural resources was raised explicitly at the International Court of Justice (ICJ) in the case of Armed Activities on the Territory of the Congo between the Democratic Republic of the Congo (DRC) and Uganda. In this contentious case, the DRC alleged that Uganda was responsible for the pillage of natural resources in the Democratic Republic of the Congo in the context of the ongoing non-international armed conflict there.[102] The ICJ noted that the laws of armed conflict prohibit pillage and in that regard 'whenever members of the UPDF were involved in the looting, plundering and exploitation of natural resources in the territory of the DRC, they acted in violation of the *jus in bello...*'.[103] This case is important in setting a precedent for the association of pillage with the exploitation of natural resources, thereby making this a foreseeable element of the prohibition on pillage in the laws of armed conflict from now on. Though of course the ICJ previously indicated, in the Advisory Opinion on the Threat and Use of Nuclear Weapons, that '[r]espect for the environment is one of the elements that go to assessing whether an action is in conformity with the principles of necessity and proportionality'[104] during armed conflict generally. In the case between the DRC and Uganda, the ICJ concluded that Ugandan troops

> including the most high-ranking officers, were involved in the looting, plundering and exploitation of the DRC's natural resources and that the military authorities did not take any measures to put an end to these acts.[105]

As such, the ICJ held that Uganda was responsible for these acts.[106] In this regard, a state may not 'permit—or fail to prevent, or turn a blind eye to—the exploitation of resources by its armed forces for personal benefit'.[107] To the extent that Uganda was considered to be an occupying power in the Ituri district, it was held to be responsible for the actions of non-state actors for the exploitation of natural resources there also.[108] Although ground-breaking, the approach taken by the ICJ has been criticised as being 'lop-sided'[109] as 'it did not consider the extensive role played by all the parties to the Congolese conflict in the illegal exploitation of its resources.'[110]

---

[102] Okawa 2006, p. 743.

[103] *Armed Activities on the Territory of the Congo (Democratic Republic of the Congo v Uganda)* para. 245.

[104] *Legality of the Threat or Use of Nuclear Weapons, Advisory Opinion, ICJ Reports 1996 p 226*, para. 30 at p. 242.

[105] *Armed Activities on the Territory of the Congo (Democratic Republic of the Congo v Uganda)* para. 242.

[106] *Armed Activities on the Territory of the Congo (Democratic Republic of the Congo v Uganda)* para. 246.

[107] Arguments of Professor Sands in *Armed Activities on the Territory of the Congo (DRC v Uganda)*, CR 2005/9 , 18 para. 8.

[108] *Armed Activities on the Territory of the Congo (Democratic Republic of the Congo v Uganda)* para. 248.

[109] Okowa 2006, p. 752.

[110] Okowa 2006, p. 752.

20.4.3 United Nations Compensation Commission

Beyond courts, innovative mechanisms have been created to address war-time environmental damage. These include the Ethiopia Eritrea Claims Commission and the United Nations Compensation Commission (UNCC).[111] The UNCC will be discussed here as an example of the way in which these innovative mechanisms work. The UNCC was created in 1991 to process claims and pay compensation for damages and losses resulting from Iraq's unlawful invasion and occupation of Kuwait. It is a 'single-mission organisation of limited lifetime'[112] established by Security Council Resolution 687[113] under Chapter VII of the UN Charter[114] on 3 April 1991. Iraq was deemed to have violated article 2(4) of the UN Charter[115] and was as a result made liable for the damage it caused in the preceding conflict. In all, the entire conflict is thought to have caused over $300 billion[116] worth of damage to the environment, property and human life. Security Council Resolution 687 not only established Iraq's liability for the actions which brought about this damage, but also created a fund from which compensation could be claimed.[117] Environmental destruction, which had previously been considered to be an incidental and inevitable, if unfortunate, consequence of warfare was recognised as being a 'fundamental part of military strategy'[118] that was explicitly compensable in its own right.

In 1996, the United Nations Environment Programme took the view that 'compensation must make the environment "whole" through restoration, replacement of those resources that cannot be fully restored, or monetary damages if neither restoration nor replacement can be achieved.'[119] Indeed the Security Council maintained that the compensation should 'address damages so thoroughly that an observer could not discern that the Iraqi invasion of Kuwait [or indeed any conflict] ever occurred.'[120] The environmental claims were some of the most complex that the Commission had to consider and environmental claims were divided into five categories of damages.[121]

---

[111] Formally created by S.C. Res. 692, UN SCOR, 46th Sess., 2987th mtg., para. 3, U.N. Doc. S/RES/692 (1991).

[112] Klee 2005, p. 598.

[113] S.C. Res. 687, UN SCOR, 46th Sess., 2981st mtg., para. 16, U.N. Doc. S/RES/687 (1991).

[114] Pursuant to Article 39 which 'grants the Security Council the power to decide what measures to take pursuant to Articles 41 (sanctions) and Article 42 (use of force) "to maintain or restore international peace and security"—Libera 2001, p. 294.

[115] Low and Hodgkinson 1994–1995, p. 412.

[116] Klee 2005, p. 600.

[117] S.C. Res. 687, UN SCOR, 46th Sess., 2981st mtg., para. 18, U.N. Doc. S/RES/687 (1991).

[118] Low and Hodgkinson 1994–1995, p. 406.

[119] Juni 2000, p. 66.

[120] Juni 2000, p. 66.

[121] Decision taken by the Governing Council of the United Nations Compensation Commission, S/AC.26/1991/7/Rev.1, 17 March 1992–Criteria for Expedited Processing of Urgent Claims, para. 35.

In total, 109 environmental claims were successful, worth approximately $5.3 billion in compensation.[122]

20.5 Future Developments

In 1994 the International Committee of the Red Cross published guidelines on the protection of the environment in armed conflict.[123] However, four significant commentators on this subject, Bothe, Bruch, Diamond and Jensen, argue that 'these Guidelines...did not constitute any significant progress for better protection of the environment during armed conflict, and even this modest document received a somewhat hostile reception at the UN. The UN General Assembly politely buried it...'.[124] However the International Law Commission are now exploring the issue of environmental protection in armed conflict anew as part of their current programme of work.[125] Guidelines or draft principles are an expected output from this ongoing research, which considers environmental protection in pre-conflict,[126] *in bello*,[127] and post-conflict[128] circumstances, as well in situations of occupation. It is hoped that the International Law Commission's work goes further than the ICRC's guidelines given the extent to which the environment is damaged and natural resources are exploited in contemporary armed conflict.

In addition, in 2016, the Office of the Prosecutor at the International Criminal Court released a Policy Paper on Case Selection and Prioritisation, which indicates that environmental damage may be prosecuted as genocide, war crimes, crimes against humanity or aggression in the future.[129] In the absence of new law being adopted, purposeful interpretations of existing law at the International Criminal Court may help to improve environmental protection and the protection of natural resources during armed conflict going forward.

---

[122] All monetary statistics are taken from regular updates posted on the United Nations Compensation Commission website: < https://uncc.ch/home> accessed 26 September 2018.

[123] Report Submitted by the ICRC at the 48th Session of the United Nations General Assembly on the Protection of the Environment in Time of Armed Conflict, 29 July 1993 <http://www.icrc.org/eng/resources/documents/misc/5deesv.htm> accessed 2 January 2013, Annex.

[124] Bothe et al 2010, p. 573 footnotes omitted.

[125] International Law Commission, 'Protection of the Environment in Relation to Armed Conflict' <http://legal.un.org/ilc/guide/8_7.shtml> accessed 30 August 2018.

[126] International Law Commission 2014.

[127] International Law Commission 2015.

[128] International Law Commission 2016.

[129] Office of the Prosecutor at the International Criminal Court 2016, paras. 7, 40, 41.

20.6 Conclusion

In conclusion, while the environment is almost always damaged in some way during armed conflict, this has not been reflected in prohibitions on damage in the over 200 years of developments in the laws of armed conflict. In particular, the issue of prohibiting environmental damage in non-international armed conflict has been fraught with political concerns and considerations. While proposals for direct prohibitions on environmental damage in non-international armed conflict have been on the table at one time or another, states have shown a marked reluctance to adopt such measures. However, the current work of the International Law Commission, and the future jurisprudence that may emerge from the International Criminal Court may result in future developments that enhance environmental protection and the protection of natural resources in armed conflict.

References

Adam D (2006) Wildlife Expert Persuades Notorious Rebel Army to Join Fight to Save Rare White Rhino. The Guardian (London, 13 September 2006) <http://www.guardian.co.uk/environment/2006/sep/13/conservationandendangeredspecies.internationalnews> accessed 30 December 2012

African Wildlife Foundation (2012) Continued Fighting Threatens Mountain Gorillas, Staff of Virunga National Park, <http://www.awf.org/content/headline/detail/4611> accessed 30 December 2012

Austin JE, Bruch CE (2003) Legal Mechanisms for Addressing Wartime Damage to Tropical Forests. 16 Journal of Sustainable Forestry 161

Binningsbo HM, de Soysa I, Gleditsch NP (2006) Green Giant or Straw Man? Environmental Pressure and Civil Conflict, 1961-99. (47th Annual Convention of the International Studies Association, San Diego, California, 22-25 March 2006)

Bloomfield S, Butler K (2008) 'Scorched Earth' Unleashed on Darfur, Despite UN Presence, Irish Independent (Dublin, 12 March 2008) <http://www.independent.ie/world-news/africa/scorched-earth-unleashed-on-darfur-despite-un-presence-1314715.html> accessed 29 December 2012

Bothe M et al (2010) International Law Protecting the Environment During Armed Conflict: Gaps and Opportunities. 92 International Review of the Red Cross 569

Bruch CE (2000-2001) All's Not Fair in (Civil) War: Criminal Liability for Environmental Damage in Internal Armed Conflict. 25 Vermont Law Review 695

Bruch CE, Austin JE (2000) The 1999 Kosovo Conflict: Unresolved Issues in Addressing the Environmental Consequences of War. 30 Environmental Law Reporter 10069

Buhaug H, Gates S, Lujala P (2009) Geography, Rebel Capability, and the Duration of Civil Conflict. 53 Journal of Conflict Resolution 544

Cohan JA (2002–2003) Modes of Warfare and Evolving Standards of Environmental Protection Under the International Law of War. 15 Florida Journal of International Law 481

Collier P, Hoeffler A (2005) Resource Rents, Governance and Conflict. 49 Journal of Conflict Resolution 625

Cullen A (2010) The Concept of Non-International Armed Conflict in International Humanitarian Law. Cambridge University Press

Dam-de Jong D (2009) International Law and Resource Plunder: The Protection of Natural Resources during Armed Conflict. 19(1) Yearbook of International Environmental Law 27

De Jong W, Donovan D, Abe K (eds) (2007) Extreme Conflict and Tropical Forests. Springer

Draulans D, Van Krunkelsven E (2002) The Impact of War on Forest Areas in the Democratic Republic of Congo. 36 Oryx 35

Drumbl MA (2000) Waging War Against the World: The Need to Move from War Crimes to Environmental Crimes. In: Austin JE, Bruch CE (eds) The Environmental Consequences of War: Legal, Economic, and Scientific Perspectives. Cambridge University Press, 631

DuBarry Huston M (2002) Wartime Environmental Damages: Financing the Clean-up. 23 University of Pennsylvania. Journal of International Economic Law 899

Dudley JP et al (2002) Effects of War and Civil Strife on Wildlife and Wildlife Habitats. 16 Conservation Biology 319

Elder DA (1979) The Historical Background of Common Article 3 of the Geneva Convention of 1949. 11 Case Western Reserve Journal of International Law 37

Glassborow K (2007) International Court Urged to Consider Environmental Crimes in Darfur, Environment News Service (The Hague, 30 August 2007) <http://www.ens-newswire.com/ens/aug2007/2007-08-30-02.asp> accessed 29 December 2012

Hulme K (1997) Armed Conflict, Wanton Ecological Devastation and Scorched Earth Policies: How the 1990-91 Gulf Conflict Revealed the Inadequacies of the Current Laws to Ensure Effective Protection and Preservation of the Natural Environment. 2 Journal of Armed Conflict Law 45

Hulme K (2004) War Torn Environment: Interpreting the Legal Threshold. Martinus Nijhoff Publishers

Hulme K (2007) Natural Environment. In: Wilmshurst E, Breau S (eds) Perspectives on the ICRC Study on Customary International Humanitarian Law. Cambridge University Press, 235

Humphreys M (2005) Natural Resources, Conflict and Conflict Resolution. (2005) 49 Journal of Conflict Resolution 508

International Law Commission (2014) Preliminary Report on the Protection of the Environment in relation to Armed Conflicts, A/CN.4/674 <http://legal.un.org/docs/?symbol=A/CN.4/674> accessed 26 September 2018

International Law Commission (2015) Second Report on the Protection of the Environment in Relation to Armed Conflicts, Sixty-Seventh Session, A/CN.4/685, <http://legal.un.org/docs/?symbol=A/CN.4/685> accessed 26 September 2018

International Law Commission (2016) Third Report on the Protection of the Environment in Relation to Armed Conflicts, Sixty-Eighth Session A/CN.4/700, <http://legal.un.org/docs/?symbol=A/CN.4/700> accessed 26 September 2018

Jacoby JD (2000) Ecological and Natural Resource Impacts: Introduction. In: Austin JE, Bruch CE (eds) The Environmental Consequences of War: Legal, Economic and Scientific Perspectives. Cambridge University Press, 298

Juni RL (2000) The United Nations Compensation Commission as a Model for an International Environmental Court. 7 Environmental Law 53

Keane D (2004) The Failure to Protect Cultural Property in Wartime. 14 DePaul-LCA Journal of Art and Entertainment Law 1

Klee J (2005) Symposium: The International Responses to the Environmental Impacts of War - Morning Panel: Response, Assessment and Remediation of Environmental Damages. 17 Georgetown International Environmental Law Review 565

Koppe E (2008) The Use of Nuclear Weapons and the Protection of the Environment during International Armed Conflict, vol 18. Hart Publishing

Lawrence JC, Heller KJ (2007) The First Ecocentric Environmental War Crime: The Limits of Article 8(2)(b)(iv) of the Rome Statute. 20 Georgetown International Environmental Law Review 61

Le Billon P (2001) The Political Ecology of War: Natural Resources and Armed Conflicts. 20 Political Geography 561

Libera RE (2001) Divide, Conquer and Pay: Civil Compensation for Wartime Damages. 24 Boston College International & Comparative Law Review, 291

20 The Protection of the Environment and Natural …

Lopez A (2006–2007) Criminal Liability for Environmental Damage Occurring in Times of Non-International Armed Conflict: Rights and Remedies. (2006–2007) 18 Fordham Environmental Law Review 231

Low L, Hodgkinson D (1994-1995) Compensation for Wartime Environmental Damage: Challenges to International Law After the Gulf War. 35 Vanderbilt Journal of International Law 405

Lujala P (2010) The Spoils of Nature: Armed Civil Conflict and Rebel Access to Natural Resources. 47 Journal of Peace Research 15

Lujala P, Gleditsc NP, Gilmore E (2005) A Diamond Curse? Civil War and a Lootable Resource. 49 Journal of Conflict Resolution 538

Lundberg MA (2007–2008) The Plunder of Natural Resources During War: A War Crime (?). 39 Georgetown Journal of International Law 495

Lysaght C (1983–1984) The Scope of Protocol II and its Relation to Common Article 3 of the Geneva Conventions of 1949 and Other Human Rights Instruments. 33 American University Law Review 9

Meron T (1996) Chapter XX - Comment: Protection of the Environment During Non-International Armed Conflicts. In: Grunawalt RJ, King JE, McClain RS (eds) Protection of the Environment During Armed Conflict and Other Military Operations. Naval War College, 356

Office of the Prosecutor at the International Criminal Court (2016) Policy Paper on Case Selection and Prioritisation, 15 September 2016, < https://www.icc-cpi.int/itemsDocuments/20160915_OTP-Policy_Case-Selection_Eng.pdf> accessed 26 September 2018

Okawa PN (2006) Case Concerning Armed Activities on the Territory of the Congo (Democratic Republic of the Congo v Uganda). 55 International & Comparative Law Quarterly 742, 743

Pejic J (2011) The Protective Scope of Common Article 3: More than Meets the Eye. (2011) 93 International Review of the Red Cross 189

Percival V, Homer-Dixon TF (1998) Environmental Scarcity and Violent Conflict: The Case of South Africa. 35 Journal of Peace Research 279

Ross MA (1992) Environmental Warfare and the Persian Gulf War: Possible Remedies to Combat Intentional Destruction of the Environment. 10 Dickinson Journal of International Law 515

Ross ML (2004) How Do Natural Resources Influence Civil War? Evidence from Thirteen Cases. (2004) 58 International Organization 35

Sandoz Y, Swinarski C, Zimmermann B (1987) Commentary on the Additional Protocols of 8 June 1977 to the Geneva Conventions of 12 August 1949. Martinus Nijhoff Publishers

Schmitt M (2011) Keynote address: Armed Conflict, the Environment and International Law – Concern for Future Generations during Armed Conflict? Conference on the Protection of the Environment in Armed Conflict, TMC Asser Instituut, The Hague, 7 November 2011

Schmitt MN (1999-2000) Humanitarian Law and the Environment. 28 Denver Journal of International Law and Policy 265

Schmitt MN (2000) War and the Environment: Fault Lines in the Prescriptive Landscape. In: Austin JE, Bruch CE (eds) The Environmental Consequences of War: Legal, Scientific and Economic Perspectives. Cambridge University Press

Schwabach A (2000) Environmental Damage Resulting from the NATO Military Action Against Yugoslavia. 25 Columbia Journal of Environmental Law, 117

Schwartz D, Singh A (1999) Environmental Conditions, Resources, and Conflicts: An Introductory Overview and Data Collection. United Nations Environment Programme, Division of Environmental Information, Assessment & Early Warning

Schwartz DM, Deligiannis T, Homer-Dixon TF (2000) The Environment and Violent Conflict: A Response to Gleditsch's Critique and Some Suggestions for Future Research. (2000) Environmental Change & Security Project Report 77

Stewart JG (2007) The UN Commission of Inquiry on Lebanon: A Legal Appraisal. 5 Journal of International Criminal Justice 1039

Takshe AA et al (2010) Dealing with Pollution from Conflict: Analysis of Discourses Around the 2006 Lebanon Oil Spill. 91 Journal of Environmental Management 887

The Independent (2010) Charity reveals 'scorched earth' Yemen images, The Independent (London, 7 April 2010) <http://www.independent.co.uk/news/world/middle-east/charity-reveals-scorched-earth-yemen-images-1938207.html> accessed 30 December 2012

Tranquillo N (2007) Green Casualties of War: The Need for International Protection of the Environment During Armed Conflicts and the Case of the War between Israel and Lebanon in 2006. Lund University

United Nations Environment Programme (2009) Protecting the Environment During Armed Conflict: An Inventory and Analysis of International Law. UNEP Post-Conflict and Disaster Management Branch

Van den Herik L, Dam-de Jong D (2011) Revitalising the Antique War Crime of Pillage: The Potential and Pitfalls of Using International Criminal Law to Address Illegal Resource Exploitation During Armed Conflict. 22 Criminal Law Forum 237

Von Mittelstaedt J (2010) A US Hand in Yemen's Civil War. Der Spiegel (12 March 2010) <http://www.spiegel.de/international/world/operation-scorched-earth-a-us-hand-in-yemen-s-civil-war-a-732734.html> accessed 30 December 2012

Weinstein JM (2005) Resources and the Information Problem in Rebel Recruitment. 49 Journal of Conflict Resolution 598

Weinstein T (2004–2005) Prosecuting Attacks that Destroy the Environment: Environmental Crimes or Humanitarian Atrocities? 17 Georgetown International Environmental Law Review 697

Tara Smith is a Senior Lecturer in International Law and Human Rights at Bangor University, North Wales. She graduated with her Ph.D from the National University of Ireland Galway in 2013 with her thesis titled 'The Prohibition of Environmental Damage during the Conduct of Hostilities in Non-International Armed Conflict' which she completed as a Doctoral Fellow at the Irish Centre for Human Rights. Prior to this, Dr. Smith graduated from University College Dublin in 2006 with a Bachelor of Civil Law, and the National University of Ireland Galway in 2007 with an LL.M in International Human Rights Law. Dr. Smith has also qualified as an Attorney-at-Law in New York. Dr. Smith's research explores contemporary challenges in international law and policy connecting climate change, armed conflict and environmental human rights.

Chapter 21
The Protection of Cultural Property in Armed Conflict and Occupation

Marina Lostal

Contents

21.1 Introduction 444
21.2 Historical Overview 445
    21.2.1 Plunder and Destruction of Cultural Property in History 445
    21.2.2 The Intellectual Change as Introduced by Modern Legal Thinkers 446
21.3 The Legal Framework Applicable to the Protection of Cultural Heritage 448
    21.3.1 The IV 1907 Hague Regulations 448
    21.3.2 The Roerich Pact 450
    21.3.3 The 1954 Hague Convention 451
21.4 The Regime Applicable During Occupation 461
    21.4.1 1907 Hague Regulations 461
    21.4.2 1954 Hague Convention and 1999 Second Protocol 461
    21.4.3 1954 First Protocol 462
21.5 UN Security Council Resolutions 463
21.6 Conclusion 464
References 465

Abstract This chapter explains the basic provisions for the protection of cultural property in armed conflict and occupation. It first offers an overview of the history of plunder and destruction of cultural property until the time where there was a shift in attitude and this practice started to be considered unlawful. Then, it examines the legal framework currently applicable, including customary international rules enshrined in the 1907 IV Hague Regulations, the main provisions of the 1954 Hague Convention, its First Protocol, its 1999 Second Protocol, the 1977 Additional Protocols and relevant resolutions from the UN Security Council. Special emphasis is placed on individual criminal responsibility and the criminalization of offences against cultural property.

Keywords Cultural Property · 1954 Hague Convention · Armed Conflict · Occupation · 1999 Second Protocol · Criminalization

---

M. Lostal (✉)
School of Law, University of Essex, Colchester, UK
e-mail: marina.lostal@cantab.net

© T.M.C. ASSER PRESS and the authors 2022
S. Sayapin et al. (eds.), *International Conflict and Security Law*,
https://doi.org/10.1007/978-94-6265-515-7_21

21.1 Introduction

Historically, the destruction of cultural property and armed conflicts have gone hand in hand. Despite this relationship of co-dependence, the destruction of cultural heritage has not received the same level of disavowing as the one experienced today. This has been reflected in the legislative history of international cultural heritage law which development has been reactive. The adoption of legal instruments in this field has consistently been promoted in the wake of a major conflict and mainly where the damage occasioned to cultural property was vast and notorious. For example, it is no coincidence that the 1954 Hague Convention for the Protection of Cultural Property in the Event of Armed Conflict (1954 Hague Convention)[1]—the first convention covering exclusively the treatment of cultural property in armed conflict—was adopted in the aftermath of World War II; or that its 1999 Second Protocol, which aimed to improve and update the undertakings of 1954, was only drafted in the context of the Balkan war.

Currently, the world is witnessing a period where cultural property is topical again. Just in 2015, the so-called Islamic State partially destroyed the archaeological and world heritage site of Palmyra in Syria and raided the Mosul Museum in Iraq. While the images are reminiscent of the looting of the National Museum of Iraq (Baghdad), the motives behind this practice have significantly changed since 2003 and belong in part to the quest of fundamentalist groups to erase parts of history. Cultural property has been re-discovered as a tool of power which is not only coveted for its economic value but also as a direct line to peoples' identities and history. Its looting and destruction have now become a common method of warfare to cash revenue, demoralize populations, shock the international community, and control narratives of the past to shape the future to their liking.

While this chapter prefers to use the expression "cultural property" over that of "cultural heritage", it must be stressed that, although the realm of international humanitarian law refers to "cultural property" in its instruments and manuals, this term has become a bit démodé and has fallen out of grace in the cultural heritage circles, which prefer the notion of "cultural heritage" because it rids the expression from ownership connotations, and is able of encompassing the intangible side of cultural objects.[2]

---

[1] UN Educational, Scientific and Cultural Organisation (UNESCO), Convention for the Protection of Cultural Property in the Event of Armed Conflict, 14 May 1954.

[2] Prott and O' Keefe 1992, pp. 307–320.

21.2 Historical Overview

21.2.1 Plunder and Destruction of Cultural Property in History

Plunder of cultural property has been a recurrent theme in war throughout history.[3] This is because looting allowed conquerors to display their *grandeur*, accomplish nationalist interests and compensate soldiers for their service.[4] Far from being condemned, this practice was an expression of the right of winners to acquire property belonging to the defeated party.[5] However, while this line of thought towards cultural property was maintained for centuries, evidence of an intellectual reconsideration appeared at times. Notoriously, Cicero heavily condemned Gaius Verres (a governor of Sicily) for his extensive looting in the region. In his speeches for Verres' prosecution, he drew a difference between what was an acceptable war booty (*spolia*), which conquerors could freely take, and removal of artistic items and architecture, which was unlawful (*spoliatio*).[6] Similarly, Polybius denounced the extensive pillaging following Rome's siege of Syracuse between 214 and 212 BC, affirming that '[Roman soldiers] should not strip cities under the idea that the misfortunes of others are an ornament to their own country.'[7]

Despite these instances of condemnation, looting persevered and Romans evolved into avid collectors.[8] Private libraries and collections surfaced among politicians and soldiers' habitations, thriving off the acquisitions made through looting.[9] This practice reached a peak in 400 B.C., when items of artistic importance from Asia Minor, Egypt and Greece began to be displayed during processions referred to as the "Triumph",[10] which were processions of returning winners meant to glorify Rome's might.[11]

Plunder was not an exclusive roman prerogative and was carried out by many thereafter. Hydatius reports that the Goths, during the invasion of Spain in 456-7 'lost control of themselves, plundering and destroying whole roman towns.'[12] Similarly, the crusaders did not abstain from looting and destruction. During the sack of Constantinople numerous artistic works, as well the great library of Constantinople, were destroyed.[13] A reminder thereof has permeated to our days and can be

---

[3] Gerstenblith 2006, 248–59.

[4] Warner 2016, 487.

[5] Xenophon 1989, para 7.5.73.

[6] Miles 2008, p. 14; Miles 2002, p. 42.

[7] Gerstenblith 2006, pp. 248–59.

[8] Poulos 2000, p. 7.

[9] Ibid.

[10] Ibid.

[11] Guhl and Koner 1989, p. 586.

[12] Burgess 1992, p. 22.

[13] Wilson 1967, p. 57.

446   M. Lostal

admired in Venice, as the famous bronze horses that used to adorn the façade of St. Mark's Basilica—now kept inside and replaced by replicas—were taken from Constantinople's Hippodrome.[14]

Ironically, while the horses are currently located in Venice, they were once again stolen in 1797 during the loot of Venice and were only returned in 1815. This theft was one of many that took place during Napoleon's quest to render Paris the "new Rome"[15] and was joined by the looting of many other artistic items, such as the Apollo Belvedere, the Laocoon, and the Discobolus from the Vatican and Capitoline museums.[16] Napoleon justified the plunder of art on the grounds that France was the only republic among tyrannies in Europe, and therefore, its only possible custodian, a view met with great criticism by his contemporaries.[17] For example, Quatremere de Quincy was a fierce opposer of this practice, maintaining that 'the best art had a universal quality and therefore could not be possessed but ought to be held in the original context in which it was nurtured a view'.[18] This idea was later tentatively put into practice by the Duke of Wellington who, towards the end of the Napoleonic wars, compelled the French to return the artworks stolen. Nonetheless, only 55% of these were restituted to their original owners.[19]

Napoleon's custodian narrative was later displayed by the Nazi regime through the "Einsatzstab Reichsleiter Rosenberg" (ERR), the "Special Task Force" whose mission was to plunder the art of the occupied territories considered noteworthy. This eventually led to the conviction of Alfred Rosenberg at Nuremberg, charged inter alia with the plunder of cultural property.[20]

21.2.2 The Intellectual Change as Introduced by Modern Legal Thinkers

The shift in the attitude towards cultural property began with the acknowledgement that the destruction and plunder of artistic monuments, temples and all works of remarkable beauty were unnecessary for the support of one's armed forces.[21] In the words of Hugo Grotius:

> There are some things of such a nature, as to contribute, no way, to the support and prolongation of war: things which reason itself requires to be spared even during the heat and continuance of war. *Polybius* calls it brutal rage and madness to destroy things, the destruction of which does not in the least tend to impair an enemy's strength, nor to increase that of

---

[14] Choniates 1984, p. 67.

[15] Gerstenblith 2006, p. 248.

[16] Ibid.

[17] Merryman and Elsen 1998, pp. 2–5, O'Keefe 2006, p. 15.

[18] Cited in Merryman 2005, p. 11.

[19] Miles 2002, pp. 42–43.

[20] Ibid., p. 22; see also Egbert 1947, p. 282.

[21] Grotius 2009, Book III, Ch. XII, Sect. V–VII.

21 The Protection of Cultural Property in Armed Conflict … 447

the destroyer: such are Porticos, Temples, statues, and all other elegant works and monuments of art […]

What has been said of the sacred edifices of religion applies also to monuments raised in honour of the dead, unnecessarily to disturb whose ashes in their repose bespeaks a total disregard to the laws and ties of our common humanity.[22]

Nonetheless, in this same work, Grotius continued to view plunder as a permissible war practice:

According to the law of nations it is undoubtedly true, that things taken from an enemy which had been captured by him cannot be claimed by those, to whom they belonged before they were in the enemy's possession, and who had lost them in war. Because the law of nations assigned them to the enemy by the first capture, and then to the person, who took them from him by the second.[23]

Cultural heritage protection began to be given a place in legal manuals. Emerich de Vattel, an 18th century Swiss jurist and diplomat who began codifying the laws of war, observed a trend towards the progressive prohibition of the pillage and wanton destruction of cultural property and noted:

What things are to be spared: for whatever cause a country is ravaged, we ought to spare those edifices which do honour to human society, and do not contribute to increase the enemy's strength—such as temples, tombs, public buildings, and all works of remarkable beauty. What advantage is obtained by destroying them? It is declaring one's self an enemy to mankind, thus wantonly to deprive them of these monuments of art and models of taste […] We still detest those barbarians who destroyed so many wonders of art, when they overran the Roman Empire.[24]

Nevertheless, he also contended that if it was 'necessary to destroy edifices of that nature in order to carry on the operations of war, or to advance the works in a siege, [there is] an undoubted right to take such a step',[25] thus indicating that the protection of cultural property was not absolute, as continues to be the case today.

Cultural heritage began to be widely appreciated for the value it held during the *Renaissance*, when elite scholars and literary figures in the European scenario clustered in an intellectual community known as the *Republique de Lettres*. Among the founding reasons for this community was the consideration that the arts, literature and science comprised a "transnational commonwealth".[26] This thought was best articulated by Quatremere de Quincy in his work *"Lettres à Miranda sur le déplacement des monuments de l'art de l'Italie"*, where he maintained that:

[I]n Europe the arts and sciences form a republic whose members, joined by the love of and quest for truth and beauty, tend less to isolate themselves in their respective nations than to pursue their interests from the point of view of a universal fraternity. [T]he arts and sciences belong to all of Europe and are no longer the exclusive property of any nation.

---

[22] Ibid.

[23] Ibid.

[24] de Vattel 1758, Book III, Ch. IX, para. 168 (emphasis added).

[25] Ibid.

[26] O'Keefe 2006, p. 9.

448   M. Lostal

This idea, which represents an early formulation of the current notion of a "common cultural heritage of humankind"—present, e.g., in the preamble of the 1954 Hague Convention—also found a home in the jurisprudence of the era, particularly, in *The Marquis de Somerueles* (1813). This case concerned a dispute between the United States and England over the possession of Italian artworks which had been wrongly seized by an English ship. The presiding judge—Dr Croke—ruled in favour of the United States, maintaining that:

> The same law of nations, which prescribes that all property belonging to the enemy shall be liable to confiscation, has likewise its modifications and relaxations of that rule. The arts and sciences are admitted amongst all civilized nations as forming an exception to the severe rights of warfare, and as entitled to favour and protection. They are considered not as the peculium of this or that nation, but as the property of mankind at large, and as belonging to the common interests of the whole species.[27]

The prohibition against looting turned into binding instructions for the Union Forces of the United States during the American Civil War. In that context, Abraham Lincoln sanctioned the so-called "Lieber Code" which stated that 'classical works of art, libraries, scientific collections, or precious instruments […] must be secured against all avoidable injury'.[28] This effort was later reinforced by Tsar Nikolas II, who convened the First Hague Peace Conference in 1899 intending to codify the laws and customs of war, and afforded special consideration for institutions dedicated to religion, charity and education, the arts and sciences in the ensuing 1899 Annex to The Hague Convention (II) with Respect to the Laws and Customs of War on Land. The text of which was later superseded by the 1907 Hague Convention of Laws and Customs on Land and Annexed Regulations.

21.3 The Legal Framework Applicable to the Protection of Cultural Heritage

21.3.1 The IV 1907 Hague Regulations

The IV 1907 Hague Convention of Laws and Customs on Land and Annexed Regulations ("1907 IV Hague Regulations")[29] were adopted during the second Hague

---

[27] The Marquis de Somerueles (1814) Stewart's Rep. 482, Court of Vice-Admiralty, Nova Scotia, 1813. In: Stewart J, Reports of cases, argued and determined in the Court of Vice-Admiralty at Halifax, Nova Scotia, from the commencement of the war, in 1803, to the end of the year 1813 in the time of Alexander Croke, LL.D., Judge of that Court. J. Butterworth and Son, London, p. 483.

[28] Instructions for the Government of Armies of the United States in the Field (Lieber Code), Article 35 (24 April 1863) available at https://ihl-databases.icrc.org/ihl/INTRO/110 (last accessed on 27 July 2020).

[29] International Conferences (The Hague), *Hague Convention (IV) Respecting the Laws and Customs of War on Land and Its Annex: Regulations Concerning the Laws and Customs of War on Land*, 18 October 1907.

Conference to revisit the laws and customs of war laid down in 1899. They constitute the first step towards outlawing destruction and plunder of cultural property as found respectively in Articles 27 and 56:

Article 27

In sieges and bombardments all necessary steps must be taken to spare, as far as possible, buildings dedicated to religion, art, science, or charitable purposes, historic monuments, hospitals, and places where the sick and wounded are collected, provided they are not being used at the time for military purposes.

It is the duty of the besieged to indicate the presence of such buildings or places by distinctive and visible signs, which shall be notified to the enemy beforehand.

Article 56 (applicable during occupation)

The property of municipalities, that of institutions dedicated to religion, charity and education, the arts and sciences, even when State property, shall be treated as private property.

All seizure of, destruction or wilful damage done to institutions of this character, historic monuments, works of art and science, is forbidden, and should be made the subject of legal proceedings.

The International Military Tribunal of Nuremberg found that the 1907 IV Hague Regulations were declaratory of international customary law.[30] The updated reading of this customary prohibition extends to non-international armed conflicts, to methods of warfare beyond "sieges and bombardments" and may only be waived if the cultural object at hand has been turned into a military objective.[31]

The 1907 IV Hague Regulations applied during World War I where, for example, the Cathedral of Reims (France) and the university library of Louvain (Belgium) were extensively damaged. The 1907 IV Hague Regulations were considered obsolete in light of the new widespread method of warfare (*i.e.* aerial bombardments)[32] which, in the inter-war years, led to attempts by the Netherlands Archaeological Society and the *Office International des Musées* of the League of Nations to improve the protection of historic monuments and cultural objects during wartime. The only initiative that was relatively successful was the Washington Treaty of 1935—more commonly known as the Roerich Pact—named after its driving force, Nikolas Roerich (1874–1947), a Russian painter and philosopher who devoted most of his life to advocating for the immunity from seizure and destruction of cultural heritage during wartime. This work earned him several nominations for the Nobel Peace prize and eventually materialized in the very avant-garde, but now largely forgotten, "Roerich Pact".

---

[30] ICTY, *Prosecutor v. Kordić and Čerkez*, Case No. IT-95-14/2-T, Judgment (Trial Chamber), para. 362; see also UNSC, 'Report of the Secretary-General pursuant to para. 2 of UNSC Res 808' (1993) UN Doc S/25704.

[31] ICRC, 'Customary IHL Rules' Rule 38 available at https://ihl-databases.icrc.org/customary-ihl/eng/docs/v1_rul_rule38 (last accessed on 29 July 2020).

[32] O'Keefe 2006, p. 44; Poulos 2000, p. 19.

21.3.2 The Roerich Pact

The Roerich Pact (1935)[33] constituted a key development for the recognition of cultural property as a distinct group of objects deserving special protection in time of armed conflict and occupation. This is because it was the first international treaty devoted exclusively this matter. Monuments and museums, but also scientific, artistic, educational and cultural institutions were declared neutral and earned respect regardless of the means of attacks employed during hostilities (Article II). Henceforth, the distinction between bombardment and general methods of attack was abandoned and these buildings only lost their neutrality if used for military purposes.

The Roerich Pact was however relatively unsuccessful from an implementation perspective as it was adopted under the aegis of the Pan-American Union and only ten (American) states, including the United States, became parties to it.[34] This meant that it was of no relevance during World War II, rendering the 1907 IV Hague Regulations the only applicable instrument, again. Nonetheless, the change inspired by this Pact was still tangible. When the outbreak of the war was imminent, the United Kingdom and France issued the following official statement, at the request of President Franklin Roosevelt:

> The Governments of France and the United Kingdom, solemnly and publicly affirm their intention to conduct the hostilities which have been imposed upon them with the firm desire to protect the civilian populations and to preserve, with every possible measure, the monuments of human civilization.[35]

Germany obliged and recognized such a need. Even the Nazi regime—which had begun a war of cultural aggression in the rest of Europe—replied with a message similar to the one jointly issued by France and the United Kingdom.[36] Remarkably, this political pact was largely adhered to by France, the United Kingdom and Germany among themselves during the first two years and was only put a stop to when the United Kingdom air-raided the city of Lübeck, which triggered Germany's retaliation in kind against Bath, leading to the escalation of destruction.[37] Many other monuments and cities were destroyed during the war and hundreds of works of art plundered.[38]

---

[33] Washington Pact of 15 April, 1935 for the Protection of Artistic and Scientific Institutions and of Historic Monuments (Roerich Pact).

[34] Brazil, Chile, Colombia, Cuba, Dominican Republic, El Salvador, Guatemala, Mexico, United States and Venezuela; see ICRC, 'IHL Database' <https://ihl-databases.icrc.org/ihl/INTRO/325?OpenDocument> accessed 4 January 2019.

[35] Boylan 1993, pp. 33–34.

[36] Ibid.

[37] Lambourne 2001, pp. 13, 43, 51–6, 143. For example, the Cologne Cathedral (Germany) was bombed fourteen times as a consequence of the especially aggressive Allied "thousand-bomber" raid against Cologne in May 1942. This raid triggered, in turn, the bombing of Canterbury the day after.

[38] Nicholas 1994, p. 226.

The reactive law-making pattern concerning the protection of cultural property became patent after the end of World War II. The objects listed in Article 27 were deemed over-ambitious in the sense that they covered every historic monument, place of worship and so forth, and afforded them the same level of protection. For this reason, they were chided with having aimed too high and having risked getting too little.[39] Instead, 'what was wanted was a convention of narrower application, so as to render feasible a higher standard of protection'.[40] Against this backdrop, 57 states gathered in The Hague under the aegis of the recently established UNESCO, which resulted in the adoption of the 1954 Hague Convention, as well as its First Additional Protocol.[41]

21.3.3 The 1954 Hague Convention

The 1954 Hague Convention represents the first one establishing a comprehensive protective framework over cultural property in armed conflict,[42] as well as the first treaty which defined "cultural property":

Article 1

(a) [M]ovable or immovable property of great importance to the cultural heritage of every people, such as monuments of architecture, art or history, whether religious or secular; archaeological sites; groups of buildings which, as a whole, are of historical or artistic interest; works of art; manuscripts, books and other objects of artistic, historical or archaeological interest; as well as scientific collections and important collections of books or archives or of reproductions of the property defined above;

(b) buildings whose main and effective purpose is to preserve or exhibit the movable cultural property defined in sub-paragraph (a) such as museums, large libraries and depositories of archives, and refuges intended to shelter, in the event of armed conflict, the movable cultural property defined in subparagraph (a);

(c) centres containing a large amount of cultural property as defined in sub-paragraphs (a) and (b), to be known as "centres containing monuments.

---

[39] O'Keefe 2006, p. 101; UNESCO, 'Records of the 7th Session' (Paris, 2018) Doc. No. 7/PRG/7, 56.

[40] O'Keefe 2006, p. 101.

[41] UN Educational, Scientific and Cultural Organisation (UNESCO), Protocol to the Convention for the Protection of Cultural Property in the Event of Armed conflict 1954, 14 May 1954. The wording of the 1954 First Protocol suggests that states can ratify it independently of whether they are parties to the 1954 Hague Convention. Article 6 declared that "[t]he present Protocol [...] shall remain open for signature by all States *invited* to the Conference which met at The Hague from 21 April, 1954 to 14 May, 1954" (emphasis added). Indeed, according to Article 7(a), the Protocol can be ratified by signatory states in accordance with their respective constitutional procedures, meaning that any State that took part in the International Conference that led to the 1954 Hague Convention (and not necessarily that became a party to it) could sign and ratify the 1954 First Protocol.

[42] For a comprehensive article-by-article analysis of the 1954 Hague Convention, *see* Toman 1996.

452   M. Lostal

Unlike the 1907 IV Hague Regulations, this definition manages to spell out the elements that render cultural property a category, *i.e.* movable or immovable property that is of great importance to the cultural heritage of every people—understood as each nation.[43] It is therefore up to each state to decide what it wishes to categorize as cultural property for the purposes of this convention.[44] Currently, the 1954 Hague Convention has 133 State Parties, including major players in armed conflicts and occupation, such as the United States, Russia, Ukraine, Israel, Egypt, Mali, Syria, Iraq, Libya, Saudi Arabia and Yemen.[45]

21.3.3.1   Central Provisions

The Convention regulates the protection of cultural property in and out of hostilities. Article 3 obliges States Parties to adopt safeguarding measures within their territory to protect cultural property against all foreseeable effects of armed conflict. Article 7 introduces more specific obligations such as the incorporation of the 1954 Hague Convention's provisions into military manuals, and the obligation to hire specialist personnel. This requirement was notoriously put into practice by the United States which, despite ratifying the convention only in 2009—55 years after signing it—introduced specialist personnel amidst its military ranks to ensure compliance with cultural heritage obligations, as well as to avoid incidents such the infamous establishment of a military base on the ancient site of Babylon.[46]

Article 4 constitutes the epicentre of the 1954 Hague Convention as far as armed conflict is concerned. This provision outlaws several practices relating to cultural property and its surroundings. Most importantly, these rules have a heightened relevance in current warfare because they constitute the only part of the 1954 Hague Convention that applies, without a doubt,[47] to non-international armed conflicts.

---

[43] O'Keefe 1999, pp. 29-30. In addition, Forrest rightly contends that this feature of cultural property within the meaning of the 1954 Hague Convention resembles more the concept of "a *collective* heritage than a *common* heritage", see Forrest 2010, p. 85.

[44] O'Keefe 1999, p. 27. This can be inferred from the general nature of responsibility posited by the 1954 Hague Convention, which sees in Articles 3,6,10,16,17 and 26(2) the territorial State—not the opposing actor—as the entity with a primary responsibility for laying down the conditions for the Convention to be respected.

[45] The updated list of State Parties to the 1954 Hague Convention and related instruments is available at http://www.unesco.org/new/en/culture/themes/armed-conflict-and-heritage/convention-and-protocols/states-parties/.

[46] For a more comprehensive overview of strategies employed to instruct the military, see Kristoffer and Rush 2017, pp. 107–115.

[47] Article 19(1) of the 1954 Hague Convention says: "In the event of an armed conflict not of an international character occurring within the territory of one of the High Contracting Parties, each party to the conflict shall be bound to apply, as a minimum, the provisions of the present Convention which relate to respect for cultural property." The question is, what are the rules that relate to the respect of cultural property? The teleological (broad) view, represented by Forrest, argues that this would include all those clauses "that have a bearing on giving respect to cultural heritage" because the 1954 Hague Convention has the protection of cultural heritage as a general aim. By contrast,

First, under Article 4(1), acts of hostility against cultural property and surroundings are not allowed unless mandated by imperative military necessity. Similarly, the use of cultural property or its surroundings for purposes which are likely to expose it to destruction (such as military purposes) is also prohibited. This encompasses both the active and passive use of any cultural object and its surroundings, meaning that both using a fortress to shelter an army's forces within it or shield them behind it would not be allowed under this convention.

Article 4(2) provides that the prohibition to direct acts of hostility against cultural property and its surroundings or use it for purposes which may lead to its damage or destruction may be waived in cases of imperative military necessity. The concept of "imperative military necessity" was left undefined in the 1954 Hague Convention. This is because the mere inclusion of such a waiver to the rules of protection concerning use and acts of hostility were hotly debated at the conference leading to the Convention's adoption. Some delegations, such as The Netherlands, Belgium and Israel insisted in including a waiver to render the 1954 Hague Convention more realistic and acceptable to the military authorities of every country. On the other side of the spectrum, the USSR's delegation asked for such waiver to be removed, which resulted in the inclusion of this term without proper clarification. This concept was only defined in its additional 1999 Second Protocol[48] which rules are only applicable to its parties.

Second, under Article 4(3), the parties to the 1954 Hague Convention must 'prohibit, prevent and, if necessary, put a stop to any form of theft, pillage or misappropriation of, and any acts of vandalism directed against, cultural property'. Furthermore, States must also refrain from requisitioning movable cultural property situated in the territory of another party. There has been disagreement as to whether the use of the term "any" form of theft, pillage etc. encompassed the actions of any person, or only of those who are members of the armed forces.[49] This question has recently acquired a practical implication in the Syrian armed conflict.[50] For example, the archaeological city of Apamea, included on the Syrian tentative list of world heritage, has been extensively looted during the armed conflict. Satellite imaginary research indicates that some of the lootings took place while the site was under the control of the Syrian regime forces.[51] If the looting was carried out spontaneously by members of the local population, the scope of the term "any" would become crucial to ascertain

---

the literal (restrictive) view –espoused by this author—posits that "respect for cultural property" matches *verbatim* the heading of Article 4 and, although it might seem too restricted when compared to all that stated in the 1954 Hague Convention, the truth is that Article 19(1) is only looking for "minimum" standards. See Forrest 2010, p. 84.

[48] UN Educational, Scientific and Cultural Organisation (UNESCO), Second Protocol to the Hague Convention of 1954 for the Protection of Cultural Property in the Event of Armed Conflict 1999, 26 March 1999.

[49] Gerstenblith 2008-2009, p. 693.

[50] Syria has been a party to the 1954 Hague Convention since 1958 and was in the process of ratifying the 1999 Second Protocol when its armed conflict broke out.

[51] Casana and Panahipour 2014, p. 129.

454   M. Lostal

whether the State had an obligation to prevent such actions and is in part responsible for the events.

Third, Article 4(4) bans reprisals against cultural objects without exception. On 4 January 2020, Donald Trump threatened to target 52 Iranian sites important to Iranian culture in a purported attempt to retaliate against the 1979 Iranian hostage crisis where 52 American citizens were held hostage. It is this precise Article which would have qualified Donald Trump's intention to hit 52 cultural Iranian sites "very fast and very hard"[52] as a violation of international law and, as we shall see later, a war crime.

In the realm of international criminal law, only once has an International Tribunal—the International Criminal Tribunal for the Former Yugoslavia (ICTY) —found one instance where the destruction of cultural property was justified. This took place at the appeals stage of the *Prlic et al.* case—the last hearing held at the ICTY (29 November 2017)—where Slobodan Praljak was one of six persons whose trial conviction was at stake.[53] As the reader may remember, Mr Praljak committed suicide at this hearing due to the other charges he was accused of and that were confirmed, drinking cyanide after claiming that he was not a war criminal. Destruction of cultural heritage ended up being not one of such confirmed charges. At the trial stage, he had been found responsible of the destruction of the Mostar Bridge, a bridge from 1566 that connected the Eastern and Western sides of the city and allowed passage over the Neretva River. Nowadays, the reconstructed Mostar Bridge appears on the UNESCO World Heritage List.[54] Back then, during the war, the bridge played a role in the communications and the transport of provisions of the HVO army. The Appeals Chamber reversed Mr Praljak's conviction on this ground (with one dissenting opinion) arguing that the Old Bridge was a military objective at the moment of the attack, and its destruction offered a definitive military advantage.[55] While the ICTY heard a significant amount of cases containing charges of crimes against cultural property, this finding remains the exception.[56]

---

[52] See Donald Trump's original tweets at https://twitter.com/realdonaldtrump/status/121359397573 2527112?lang=en (last accessed on 28 July 2020).

[53] ICTY, *Prosecutor v. Prlić et al.*, Case No. IT-04-74, Summary of Trial Chamber Judgment, 12.

[54] The UNESCO World Heritage List describes the Old Bridge and the neighboring area as "an outstanding example of a multicultural urban settlement with its pre-Ottoman, eastern Ottoman, Mediterranean and western European architectural features." See UNESCO, World Heritage List, Bosnia and Herzegovina, Doc. No. 946rev <http://whc.unesco.org/en/list/946/> accessed 4 January 2019.

[55] ICTY, *Prosecutor v. Prlić et al.*, Case No. IT-04-74, Summary of Appeals Chamber Judgment, p. 5; *Prosecutor v. Prlić et al.*, Case No. IT-04-74, Judgment Vol. I (Appeals Chamber), para. 426.

[56] See ICTY, *Prosecutor v. Pavle Strugar*, Case No. IT-01-42-T, Judgment (Trial Chamber), paras 296, 312; *Prosecutor v. Mladen Naletilić and Vinko Martinović*, Case No. IT-98-34-T, Judgment (Trial Chamber), para. 605; *Prosecutor v. Vladimir Đorđević*, Case No. IT-05-87/1-T, Judgment (Trial Chamber), para. 1773; *Prosecutor v. Hadžihasanović and Kubura*, Case No. IT-01-47-T, Judgment (Trial Chamber), para. 59; *Prosecutor v. Martić*, Case No. IT-95-11-T, Judgment (Trial Chamber), para. 96; and *Prosecutor v. Pavle Strugar*, Case No. IT-01-42-A, Judgment (Appeals Chamber), para. 278.

21 The Protection of Cultural Property in Armed Conflict … 455

These and other obligations of the 1954 Hague Convention are backed by Article 28, which entrusts States Parties with the prosecution and punishment—within their domestic jurisdiction—of persons "of whatever nationality" who commit a breach of the Convention. This provision, however, falls short of directly establishing universal criminal jurisdiction as it does not specify whether State Parties can prosecute such crimes when committed *outside* their national territory.[57] To date, it is unclear how many State Parties had incorporated Article 28 into their domestic systems.[58] The 1999 Second Protocol expanded on issues of individual criminal responsibility and the obligation to extradite or prosecute, giving more detailed instructions to States for their implementation.

21.3.3.2 Contentious Elements

The preamble of the 1954 Hague Convention speaks to a reactive policy-making trend in this field as it begins by recognizing that 'cultural property has suffered grave damage during recent armed conflicts and […] by reason of the developments in the technique of warfare, it is in increasing danger of destruction'. In adopting said formulation, the drafters created a link between the proliferation of means of warfare and the necessity to expand this regulatory field. This solution, although leading the way towards further political and legal engagement, is nonetheless problematic as it was bound to increase fragmentation. For example, the 1999 Second Protocol was adopted to improve and update the 1954 regime, it created an additional layer of protection for certain cultural objects (the enhanced protection regime) but it did not address issues such as the protection of intangible cultural heritage or the obligations of armed non-State actors.

The identification and communication of what constitutes cultural property is another weakness of the current legal framework. State Parties to the 1954 Hague Convention are supposed to designate their cultural property, but it does not foresee the preparation or publication of national inventories. It is unclear to what extent State Parties have identified objects to this end, and makes the opposing party at any given armed conflict enter into a guessing game. Admittedly, in Article 16, the 1954 Hague Convention foresees the "blue shield", an emblem in the shape of a shield, half-blue, half-white, which is meant to be deployed on protected property. However, there are three important caveats concerning the deployment of the blue shield. One, it cannot be used on movable cultural property; second, its use is not mandatory; and, third, the emblem cannot be seen from the air, which decreases its practical meaning in modern warfare, fulfilling the omen that this field is designed to be one-step behind due to its reactive nature. This has been tackled on an *ad hoc* basis by setting up "no-strike lists" for such places as Libya or the city of Aleppo (Syria) by organizations like the

---

[57] Bassiouni 1983, p. 312; and O'Keefe 2010, pp. 361–362.

[58] The periodic reports from State Parties where they include information on the implementation of the 1954 Hague Convention and its two Protocols can be accessed here http://www.unesco.org/new/en/culture/themes/armed-conflict-and-heritage/convention-and-protocols/periodic-reporting/.

UK and US Blue Shield committees and Heritage for Peace. Some could argue, with good reasons, that identifying the location of cultural heritage may pay lip service to its protection nowadays since it would facilitate the job of those groups who vow to destroy it as a method of warfare. It is true that the "blue shield" or similar methods of identification may be turned from shield to target, but there is not much that the law can do to deter the lawless, and instead, it should focus on putting a system in place to make sure that law-abiders have a chance to honour the commitment.

In sum, the 1954 Hague Convention remains today the most important instrument for the protection of cultural property in armed conflict with 133 State parties. As far as armed conflict is concerned, the 1954 Hague Convention obliges State Parties to implement safeguarding measures during peacetime to avoid damage and destruction of cultural property. During armed conflict, it prohibits directing acts of hostility against cultural property and its immediate surroundings, and their use for purposes which may expose it to damage or destruction, unless in cases of imperative military necessity. States have an obligation to prevent and put a stop to vandalism, theft, pillage or any other type of misappropriation, and cannot direct any reprisal whatsoever against cultural property. The provisions related to occupation are dealt with in Sect. 21.4.

21.3.3.3 The 1977 Additional Protocols

Due to the slow ratification pace of the 1954 Hague Convention, the drafters of the 1977 Additional Protocols to the Four Geneva Conventions of 1949[59] pushed for the inclusion of a provision relating to the protection of cultural heritage—although not expressly using this term—in the two additional protocols, covering international armed conflicts and non-international armed conflicts, respectively. Notably, Article 53 of Additional Protocol I reads:

> Without prejudice to the provisions of The Hague Convention for the Protection of Cultural Property in the Event of Armed Conflict of 14 May 1954, and of other relevant international instruments, it is prohibited: (a) to commit any acts of hostility directed against the historic monuments, works of art or places of worship which constitute the cultural or spiritual heritage of peoples; (b) to use such objects in support of the military effort; (c) to make such objects the object of reprisals.

Article 16 of Additional Protocol II reproduces a very similar wording, save for the prohibition of reprisals. Although there is no explicit waiver for imperative military necessity, this prohibition is commonly understood to cease if the property has been transformed into a military objective. One may wonder what *additional* layer of protection cultural property has under the Additional Protocols since "plain" civilian

---

[59] International Committee of the Red Cross (ICRC), *Protocol Additional to the Geneva Conventions of 12 August 1949, and relating to the Protection of Victims of International Armed Conflicts (Protocol I)*, 8 June 1977, 1125 UNTS 3; and International Committee of the Red Cross (ICRC), *Protocol Additional to the Geneva Conventions of 12 August 1949, and relating to the Protection of Victims of Non-International Armed Conflicts (Protocol II)*, 8 June 1977, 1125 UNTS 609.

property can also be subject to attack only if it has become a military objective. It can be argued that Articles 53 and 16 of, respectively, Additional Protocols I and II, attempt underlying the importance of the previous legislative commitment highlighting the special nature of cultural objects. In this sense, these Articles from the Additional Protocols continue to play a role in those conflicts where warring factions are not bound by the 1954 Hague Convention.[60]

21.3.3.4 The 1999 Second Protocol to the 1954 Hague Convention

In 1992, the then UNESCO Director-General reported that the 1954 Hague Convention needed to be revisited because, among other things, it did not take into account current military science and was drafted based on the experience of World War II.[61] The ensuing 1999 Diplomatic Conference on the Second Protocol to the 1954 Hague Convention adopted the 1999 Second Protocol, which entered into force in 2002 and has 83 State Parties.[62]

This instrument supplements the provisions of the 1954 Convention and may only be ratified by states that are parties to the main Convention. One of its major innovations is that the Protocol applies to non-international armed conflicts that are occurring on the territory of a State party (Article 22(1)). While the 1999 Second Protocol maintains the definition of 'cultural property' provided by the 1954 Hague Convention, the changes it introduces are manifold, and include: (a) defining the waiver of imperative military necessity; (b) the establishment of the enhanced protection regime; and (c) the refinement of provisions relating to individual criminal responsibility.[63]

Imperative Military Necessity

Imperative military necessity may only be invoked when: (i) the cultural object (or surroundings) against which a party intends to direct an act of hostility has been turned into a military objective by its function; and (ii) that attack allows the attacking party to secure a definite military advantage. If the waiver is being invoked to lift the prohibition of use, there must be no choice between such use and another feasible method of obtaining a similar military advantage. In both cases, the decision to attack must come from a commander in charge of, at least, a battalion—unless circumstances do not permit, in which case he might be an officer commanding a

---

[60] Additional Protocol I counts with 174 State Parties, and Additional Protocol II 169, in contrast to the 133 of the 1954 Hague Convention (information retrieved on 28 July 2020).

[61] UNESCO, 'Report by the Director-General on the Reinforcement of UNESCO's Action for the Protection of the World Cultural and Natural Heritage', 140th Session (1992) UN Doc. No.140 EX/13, 3, 11. See also Boylan 1993.

[62] The last accession dates from 30 June 2020 and is from Ukraine (information retrieved on 28 July 2020).

[63] Mainetti 2004, pp. 344–345. For a comprehensive article-by-article analysis of the 1999 Second Protocol, *see* Toman 2009.

smaller force in size.[64] Also, an effective warning must be given in advance whenever circumstances permit.

Enhanced Protection Regime

The drafters of the 1999 Second Protocol reprised the idea—attempted, quite unsuccessfully, in the 1954 Hague Convention[65]—that some cultural property requires higher safeguarding standards, and consequently created a regime of "enhanced protection" to, once for all, achieve this goal. This regime affords protection (in quite an innovative way) to both movable and immovable cultural property, regardless of whether they are in proximity of a military objective. In order to benefit from such enhanced protection, the following cumulative conditions apply.[66] First, cultural property must be cultural heritage of value to the whole of humanity. Second, its cultural and historic value must be recognized by adequate administrative and legal measures at the domestic level. Third, it can never be utilized for military purposes and a declaration certifying that must be issued by the party exercising control over it.

Properties may lose their enhanced protection if such status is suspended or cancelled, and also "if, and for as long as, the property has, by its use, become a military objective" and, in such case, the property may only be targeted if the attack is the only feasible means of terminating the military use of the property, all feasible precautions are taken in the choice of means and methods of attack. Besides, unless circumstances do not permit, due to requirements of immediate self-defence, the attack must be ordered at the highest operational level of command, effective warning needs to be issued requiring the termination of the military use of the property and, lastly, reasonable time must be given to the opposing party to address the situation (Article 13).

As Toman argues, the 1999 Second Protocol refers to "cultural heritage" in the context of enhanced protection without defining it, making it necessary to turn to the World Heritage Convention to shed light on its meaning. He finds that the only definitional difference between "world heritage" and cultural property liable to benefit from "enhanced protection" is that the latter comprises movables as well.[67] After

---

[64] Battalions in State forces usually count ca. 500-600 soldiers, a number which armed non-State actors do not usually equal. Thus, the corresponded definition of battalion for non-State actors must be built in accordance with their command structure. See Lostal et al. 2018, p. 17.

[65] The 1954 Hague Convention created the special protection regime in Article 8 for "a limited number of refuges intended to shelter movable cultural property in the event of armed conflict, of centers containing monuments and other immovable cultural property of very great importance". Some States have cancelled the inscription of properties on the Register, except for Mexico which inscribed new properties in 2015. The International Register of Cultural Property under Special Protection, updated to 23 July 2015, can be accessed at http://www.unesco.org/new/fileadmin/MULTIMEDIA/HQ/CLT/pdf/Register2015EN.pdf.

[66] Hausler 2014, pp. 371–373.

[67] Toman 2009, p. 190.

more than 15 years in force, this enhanced protection list only contained 17 properties,[68] a number that is strikingly low in contrast with the around 900 cultural heritage sites on the well-known World Heritage List. All inscribed properties on the list of enhanced protection, except the National Central Library of Florence, are also part of the World Heritage List. Regrettably, a specific system of protection for world cultural heritage has not been worked out by, for example, proposing to amend the World Heritage Convention to include the enhanced protection regime or, at least, by creating a short-cut system to extend the enhanced protection regime to all world heritage sites for States that are parties to both instruments.

Individual Criminal Responsibility

The 1999 Second Protocol brought about two other significant changes. The first is the specification of the types of conduct over which State Parties have an obligation to establish criminal individual responsibility:

Article 15

1. Any person commits an offence within the meaning of this Protocol if that person intentionally and in violation of the Convention or this Protocol commits any of the following acts:

   a. making cultural property under enhanced protection the object of attack;
   b. using cultural property under enhanced protection or its immediate surroundings in support of military action;
   c. extensive destruction or appropriation of cultural property protected under the Convention and this Protocol;
   d. making cultural property protected under the Convention and this Protocol the object of attack;
   e. theft, pillage or misappropriation of, or acts of vandalism directed against cultural property protected under the Convention.

2. Each Party shall adopt such measures as may be necessary to establish as criminal offences under its domestic law the offences set forth in this Article and to make such offences punishable by appropriate penalties. When doing so, Parties shall comply with general principles of law and international law, including the rules extending individual criminal responsibility to persons other than those who directly commit the act.

Offences (a) to (c) give rise to universal criminal jurisdiction (Article 16(1)(c)), meaning that they can be prosecuted within a domestic jurisdiction regardless of the nationality of the offender and the place where the violation was committed. This means that Donald Trump's threat to destroy 52 Iranian cultural sites, if materialized, would have fallen under paragraph (c), that is, "extensive destruction or appropriation of cultural property protected under the [1954 Hague] Convention and this Protocol."

---

[68] 'Enhanced Protection, United Nations Educational, Scientific and Cultural Organization' (*Unesco.org*, 2019) <http://www.unesco.org/new/fileadmin/MULTIMEDIA/HQ/CLT/pdf/Enhanced-Protection-List-2019_Eng_04.pdf> accessed 28 July 2020.

However, given that the United States is not yet a party to the 1999 Second Protocol, Donald Trump would have fallen out of the scope of the duty to prosecute or extradite because, "members of the armed forces and nationals of a State which is not Party to this Protocol [...] do not incur individual criminal responsibility by virtue of this Protocol, nor does this Protocol impose an obligation to establish jurisdiction over such persons or to extradite them" (Article 16(b)).

The rest of offences, such as the use of cultural property in violation of the 1954 Hague Convention or the 1999 Second Protocol, and any illicit export, removal or transfer of ownership of cultural property from occupied territory represent a sort of "second tier" violation over which State Parties may choose between legislative, administrative or disciplinary measures to suppress them (Article 21).

The rather sophisticated provisions on offences against cultural property of the 1999 Second Protocol stand in contrast with the more rudimentary formulation of the war crime against cultural objects of the Rome Statute of the International Criminal Court.[69] Articles 8(2)(b)(ix) and 8(2)(e)(iv) of the Rome Statute which apply, respectively, in international and non-international armed conflicts, define as a war crime:

> Intentionally directing attacks against buildings dedicated to religion, education, art, science or charitable purposes, historic monuments, hospitals and places where the sick and wounded are collected, provided they are not military objectives.

This wording repeats almost *verbatim* the formulation of Article 27 of the 1907 IV Hague Regulations, and bears no resemblance whatsoever to the 1954 Hague Convention. The war crime only covers immovable cultural objects, leaving works of art and the like aside.[70] This is the only war crime relating to cultural property in the Rome Statute, which means that conduct concerning the use of such objects for military purposes, or of their theft, pillage, misappropriation and the like are not regarded as war crimes as such. While the provisions of the 1999 Second Protocol are more sophisticated, they are rarely resorted to and, to date in this author's knowledge, no domestic prosecution has been based on them. By contrast, the Rome Statute, while more basic in character, has been the legal basis for the landmark case against Ahmad Al Faqi Al Mahdi (Mr Al Mahdi), a member of a radical group known as the Ansar Dine, operative in the North of Mali. He pled guilty to the destruction of ten protected buildings in the town of Timbuktu (Mali), nine of which were world heritage sites.[71] As a result, he was sentenced to nine years' imprisonment (now reduced to seven) and his liability was set at EUR 2.7 million, an amount which will be used for the benefit of the victims of his crime. Since 2020, another accused—Al Hassan Ag Abdoul Aziz Ag Mohamed Ag Mahmoud (Mr Al Hassan)—is standing

---

[69] UN General Assembly, *Rome Statute of the International Criminal Court (last amended 2010)*, 17 July 1998, ISBN No. 92-9227-227-6.

[70] For a discussion on the different approaches towards the war crime against cultural objects, *see* Frulli 2011, pp. 203–217.

[71] ICC, Trial Chamber VIII, *Prosecutor v. Al Mahdi*, Judgment and Sentence, 27 September 2016 (ICC-01/12-01/15-171).

trial for charges which include destruction of cultural property,[72] also in connection with the destruction of mausolea and the door of a mosque in the town of Timbuktu.

21.4 The Regime Applicable During Occupation

21.4.1 1907 Hague Regulations

Article 56 of the 1907 IV Hague Regulations (which has customary status) provides that *all* seizure of, destruction or wilful damage done to institutions dedicated to religion, charity and education, the arts and sciences, historic monuments, works of art and science, is forbidden. Furthermore, under Article 43 the occupying power has the general obligation to maintain "public order and safety, while respecting, unless absolutely prevented, the laws in force in the country" insofar as the circumstances do permit. In the cultural heritage realm, this could translate, for example, into a positive obligation to assess whether a world heritage site may fall prey to acts of looting of vandalism and, if so, prevent it for the sake of maintaining public order.

21.4.2 1954 Hague Convention and 1999 Second Protocol

Under Article 5 of the 1954 Hague Convention a party in total or partial occupation of another party's territory has the positive obligation to support as far as possible 'the competent national authorities in safeguarding and preserving cultural property'. Further, Article 5(2) provides that, where cultural property is damaged by military activity in the occupied territory and the competent authorities are unable to assist, 'the Occupying Power [must], as far as possible, and in close co-operation with such authorities, take the most necessary measures of preservation.'

Article 5(3) also envisages an obligation on the side of the government considered to be legitimate by the resistance movement to inform the occupying power of its obligations under the 1954 Hague regime. The legal framework relating to occupation was expanded through (i) the First Hague Protocol of 1954, (which, despite its brevity, is entirely dedicated to this purpose); and the 1999 Second Protocol, which contains complementary provisions on the matter.

Under Article 9 of the 1999 Second Protocol, parties must prevent any illicit export, removal or transfer of cultural property.[73] In addition, they have the negative obligation of not conducting any archaeological excavation or change of use of cultural property unless circumstances so demand.

---

[72] The Prosecutor v. Al Hassan Ag Abdoul Aziz Ag Mohamed Ag Mahmoud (ICC-01/12-01/18), *see* Case Information Sheet at https://www.icc-cpi.int/CaseInformationSheets/al-hassanEng.pdf.

[73] This is in contrast with the obligation under Art. I.1 of the 1954 First Protocol to prevent *any* exportation, whether licit or illicit.

21.4.3 1954 First Protocol

The 1954 Hague Conference adopted an additional instrument to the Convention entirely devoted to occupation and devised to prevent the exportation of cultural property from occupied territories: the 1954 First Protocol.[74] This matter could not be included in the main text of the 1954 Hague Convention due to the lack of general agreement among State Parties. The form of a protocol was thus preferred to ensure greater adhesion to the main Convention.

The 1954 First Protocol regulates three different, yet related scenarios. First, in the territory of the occupied nation, the occupying power has the absolute obligation to prevent all exportation of cultural property (Article I.1). The obligation is absolute for there is no exception whatsoever: all exportations, including of those objects that have been lawfully purchased, cannot leave the occupied country.

Then, the First Hague Protocol deals with the situation in which the occupying country has failed to comply with its duties and a cultural object has left the occupied country (Articles I.2 and 3). In that case, the receiving state must seize it and take it into custody for as long as the occupation lasts. There is no time limit to this obligation and no prescription applies. This means that if an occupation lasts for 50 years, the receiving state must keep the object in its custody for 50 years and cannot acquire any title of ownership for the passage of time. When the occupation ends, the State must return the cultural object to the formerly occupied national authorities, not to the individual owner (Article I.3).[75]

Lastly, if the receiving state fails to seize the cultural object which is then consequently sold to a *bona fide* purchaser, the principle to follow is that of *nemo dat quod non habet* ("no one can give what s/he does not have"). Nonetheless, the *bona fide* purchaser is entitled to fair compensation to be paid by the occupying power, presumably, because it was the first one failing to comply with its obligation to prevent the exportation of said item(s) (Article I.4).

21.4.3.1 Problematic Elements of the 1954 First Protocol

Although the obligations under the First Protocol seem to be rather straightforward, they leave one fundamental question open: how many of the (up to) three states that can be involved in the scenarios described above need to be parties to the 1954 First Protocol? Some say all three—which would undoubtedly render the Protocol applicable. Others contend that only the occupying state needs to be a party to the 1954 First Protocol for the whole regime to apply.[76] Yet there is another possibility:

---

[74] First Protocol (1954) to the 1954 Hague Convention for the Protection of Cultural Property in the Event of Armed Conflict (adopted 14 May 1954, entered into force 7 August 1956).

[75] This Article codifies the practice followed after the Second World War where the Allied powers returned the stolen cultural objects to the several national committees that had been established for that purpose. See Nicholas 1994, pp. 409-415.

[76] See Forrest 2010, pp. 104–107.

the two states that need to be parties to the 1954 First Protocol to render its regime operative are (i) the occupied country; and (ii) the State which receives the cultural object within its borders. This option seems more likely because the 1954 First Protocol cannot be imposed on a non-party. The application would then be triggered by the occupied power, since, according to the—customary—obligation of the 1907 IV Hague Regulations, the occupying power has an obligation to respect, "unless absolutely prevented, the laws in force in the country" (Article 43).

The recent Scythian gold dispute has put under spotlight another *lacuna* in the framework applicable to occupation, namely, to who does the cultural object belong in case of state secession. The Scythian gold case concerns a dispute between Russia and Ukraine over the possession of a collection of gold artefacts, currently located at the Allard Pierson Museum (APM) in Amsterdam.[77] These items, which were displayed in the context of an exhibition named "Crimea—the Golden Island in the Black Sea", had been loaned to the APM by several Crimean Museums and the National Museum of History of Ukraine in Kyiv, to which they should have been returned in September 2014.[78]

The dispute arose when, following the secession of Crimea and annexation to the Russian Federation, the return of the artefacts was requested by both Ukraine—who holds that the items are an integral part of its *national* State Museum Fund[79]—and the Crimean Museums which are now under Russian jurisdiction, who rely on the contractual agreement entered into by the APM.[80]

The legal aspect of the issue was tentatively settled by the District Court of Amsterdam in a 2016 judgment—now on appeal—which ordered the items to be returned to Ukraine,[81] a conclusion reconcilable with the Netherlands' stance on the annexation of Crimea, as the State does not recognize it as lawful.[82]

21.5 UN Security Council Resolutions

The Security Council has been increasingly active in complementing the protection of cultural property from some countries engulfed in armed conflicts or occupation, particularly if it has found that there are ties between the sale of illicitly exported property and the funding of terrorist organizations.[83] One of the earliest examples is Resolution 1483 (2003) where the Security Council obliged member states to "take appropriate steps to facilitate the safe return to Iraqi institutions of Iraqi cultural

---

[77] Campfens 2017 p. 194.

[78] Rechtbank Amsterdam, [Amsterdam District Court] C/13/577586/HA ZA 14-1179 [ECLI:NL:RBAMS:2016:8264] (14 December 2016) para. 2.1. ('District Court Judgment').

[79] Ibid para. 2.6.

[80] Ibid para. 2.9.

[81] Ibid paras 5.1–5.15.

[82] Ibid para. 2.1.

[83] Lostal 2020.

property and other items of archaeological, historical, cultural, rare scientific, and religious importance illegally removed from the Iraq National Museum, the National Library, and other locations in Iraq since the adoption of resolution 661 (1990) of 6 August 1990" (para. 7). Resolution 2199 (2015) reinforces this obligation and extends it to Syrian cultural property removed from the country since 15 March 2011 (para. 15). Security Council Resolution 2322 (2016) reaffirmed these bans and specified concrete measures to combat the illicit trade of cultural property. Resolution 2347 (2017) is, for the first time, dedicated entirely to cultural heritage. It "[d]eplores and condemns the unlawful destruction of cultural heritage, inter alia destruction of religious sites and artefacts [...] notably by terrorist groups" (para. 1) and also emphasizes that the unlawful destruction of cultural heritage can fuel the causes of conflict, notes the link between illicit trafficking of cultural artefacts and the funding of terrorist organizations, and requests UN member states to take appropriate measures within their domestic jurisdiction and in cooperation with each other and international organizations to protect cultural heritage.[84]

Even though the Security Council has put cultural heritage on the agenda as an item of its own because, for example, protection of cultural heritage is a key means for the maintenance of international peace and security,[85] it must also be noted that the Security Council has also taken a step back in this regard. When it established the peacekeeping mission in Mali—MINUSMA—the Security Council included in its mandate assisting "the Malian authorities, as necessary and feasible, in protecting from attack the cultural and historical sites in Mali, in collaboration with UNESCO."[86] However, this part of the mandate was removed in 2018[87] without any clear explanation why, and in stark contrast with the spirit of Resolution 2347 (2017).

21.6   Conclusion

This chapter has provided an overview of the basic norms that are part of the legal framework for the protection of cultural property during armed conflict and occupation. It has shown how the practice of looting and destruction is as old as war itself, but the view that such practice was undesirable and eventually unlawful came about during the *Renaissance* and modern legal thinking. The core components of this international legal framework are the 1954 Hague Convention and its two additional protocols, from 1954 and 1999, respectively. To this, one must add customary international law such as the 1907 IV Hague Regulations, the fall-back provisions of

---

[84] For a full commentary on UN Security Council Resolutions concerning cultural heritage, *see* Hausler 2018.

[85] Ibid.

[86] UNSC Resolution 2164 (2014) para. 14(b).

[87] UNSC Resolution 2423 (2018).

the 1977 Additional Protocols and the resolutions stemming from the UN Security Council which, since 2015, has increased its attention over cultural heritage matters.

There are two key take-aways to take from the applicable framework: one is that its legislative history is reactive and thus, prone to be atomized. For example, it is apparent from the putting in contrast of Article 27 of the 1907 IV Hague Regulations, Article 4 of the 1954 Hague Convention, and Article 53 of 1977 Additional Protocol I that there is not a unitary understanding of the terms "cultural property" nor of "protection". Secondly, one thing clear about this legal framework is that the protection afforded to cultural property is not absolute. It falls within a system where exceptions owing to military logic (i.e. imperative military necessity) are granted.

While the inclusion of this waiver was the subject of hot debate during the diplomatic conference leading to the adoption of the 1954 Hague Convention, its application is not very controversial in current practice. This is because the conduct of fundamentalist groups, such as the so-called Islamic State (operative in Syria and Iraq) or the Ansar Dine (Mali) clearly fall outside the scope of the waiver. Instead, they are instances of deliberate attacks which speak to a new reality where cultural property destruction and plunder are a method of warfare which serves several purposes, from demoralization to cashing funds. In such circumstances, efforts to strengthen the legal framework should shift towards incorporating the provisions on individual responsibility stemming from customary international law, Article 28 of the 1954 Hague Convention and Article 16 of the 1999 Second Protocol in States' domestic legal systems. The recent conviction of Mr Al Mahdi before the International Criminal Court only on account of his involvement in the destruction of ten cultural and religious sites should serve as a leading example for domestic jurisdictions to follow. The *Al Mahdi* case has shown that, in general, the investigation and prosecution of such cases should not be too onerous once the right individual has been apprehended because, as part of this new method of warfare, radical groups publicize and stream on social media the destruction of cultural heritage, therefore tendering the key element of evidence to the prosecution and the judges, a factor that may have played a role in his decision to plead guilty.

References

Bassiouni MC (1983) Reflections on Criminal Jurisdiction in International Protection of Cultural Property. Syracuse J. Intl. L. Commerce 10(2):281–322.

Boylan J (1993) Review of the Convention for the Protection of Cultural Property in the Event of Armed Conflict: the Hague Convention of 1954. UNESCO Programme and Meeting Document, No. CLT.93/WS/12, https://unesdoc.unesco.org/ark:/48223/pf0000100159. Accessed 31 July 2020.

Burgess RW (1992) From Gallia Romana to Gallia Gothica: the view from Spain. In: Drinkwater J, Elton H (eds) Fifth-Century Gaul: A Crisis of Identity? Cambridge University Press, Cambridge, pp. 19–27.

Campfens E (2017) Whose Cultural Heritage? Crimean Treasures at the Crossroads of Politics, Law and Ethics. J. of Art, Antiquity and Law 22(3):193–212.

Casana J, Panahipour M (2014) Satellite-Based Monitoring of Looting and Damage to Archaeological Sites in Syria. Journal of Eastern Mediterranean Archaeology and Heritage Studies 2:128–151.

Choniates N (1984) Annals (WSUP) CXIX.

Egbert LD (1947) Judicial Decisions: International Military Tribunal (Nuremberg) Judgment and Sentences. Am. J. Intl. L. 41:172–333.

Forrest C (2010) International Law and the Protection of Cultural Heritage. Routledge, Oxon.

Frulli M (2011) The Criminalization of Offences against Cultural Heritage in Times of Armed Conflict: The Quest for Consistency. European Journal of International Law 22(1):203–2017.

Gerstenblith P (2006) From Bamiyan to Baghdad: Warfare and the Preservation of Cultural Heritage at the Beginning of the 21st Century. Geo. J. Intl. L. 37:248–59.

Gerstenblith P (2008-2009) Protecting Cultural Heritage in Armed Conflict: Looking back, Looking Forward. Cardozo Pub. L., Pol'y & Ethics J., 7:677–708.

Grotius (2009) On the Law of War and Peace. Kessinger Publishing, Whitefish.

Guhl E, Koner W (1989) Everyday Life of the Greeks and Romans. Crescent.

Hausler K (2014) The protection of cultural heritage in armed conflict. In: Casey-Maslen S (ed) The War Report. Oxford University Press, Oxford, pp. 361–387.

Hausler K (2018) Cultural Heritage and the Security Council: Why Resolution 2347 matters. Questions of International Law 48:5–19.

Kristoffer M, Rush L (2017) Integration of Cultural Property Protection into a Decisive Action Training Exercise. Military Review, November-December:106–116.

Lambourne N (2001) War Damage in Western Europe: The Destruction of Historic Monuments During the Second World War. Edinburgh University Press, Edinburgh.

Lostal M, Hausler K, Bongard P (2018), 'Culture under Fire: Armed Non-State Actors and Cultural Heritage in Wartime', Geneva Call report. https://genevacall.org/wp-content/uploads/2017/10/Cultural_Heritage_Study_Final.pdf. Accessed on 31 July 2020.

Lostal M (2020) Islamic State and the Illicit Traffic of Cultural Property. In: Jørgensen NHB (ed) The International Criminal Responsibility of War's Funders and Profiteers. Cambridge University Press, pp. 122-147.

Mainetti V (2004) De Nouvelles Perspectives Pour La Protection Des Biens Culturels En Cas De Conflit Armé: L'entrée En Vigueur Du Deuxième Protocole Relatif À La Convention De La Haye De 1954. Intl. Rev. Red Cross 86(854):337–366.

Merryman JH (2005) Cultural Property Internationalism. Intl. J. Cultural Prop. 12:11–39.

Merryman JH, Elsen A (1998) Law, Ethics and the Visual Arts, 3rd edn. Kluwer Law International, Alphen aan den Rijn.

Miles M (2002) Cicero's Prosecution of Gaius Verres: A Roman View of the Ethics of Acquisition of Art. Intl. J. Cultural Prop. 11:28–49.

Miles M (2008) Art as Plunder: The Ancient Origins of Debate about Cultural Property. Cambridge University Press, New York.

Nicholas LH (1994) The Rape of Europa: The Fate of Europe's Treasures in the Third Reich and the Second World War. Knopf, New York.

O'Keefe R (1999) The Meaning of 'Cultural Property' under the 1954 Hague Convention. Netherlands Intl. L. Rev. 46:26–56.

O'Keefe R (2006) The Protection of Cultural Property in Armed Conflict. Cambridge University Press, New York.

O'Keefe R (2010) Protection of Cultural Property under International Criminal Law. Melbourne Journal of International Law 11: 339–392.

Poulos AH (2000) The 1954 Hague Convention for the Protection of Cultural Property in the Even of Armed Conflict: An Historic Analysis. Intl. J. Legal Info. 28:1–44.

Prott L, O' Keefe R (1992) Cultural Heritage or Cultural Property? Intl. J. Cultural Prop. 1:307–320.

Toman J (1996) The Protection of Cultural Property in the Event of Armed Conflict: Commentary on the Convention for the Protection of Cultural Property in the Event of Armed Conflict and Its

Protocol, Signed on 14 May 1954 in The Hague, and on Other Instruments of International Law Concerning Such Protection. Darmouth/UNESCO, Paris.

Toman J (2009) Cultural Property in War: Improvement in Protection: Commentary on the 1999 Second Protocol to the Hague Convention of 1954 for the Protection of Cultural Property in the Event of Armed Conflict. UNESCO Publishing, Paris.

de Vattel E (1758) Le Droit Des Gens. Apud Liberos Tutior, London.

Warner M (2016) The Last Poor Plunder from a Bleeding Land: The Failure of International Law to Protect Syrian Antiquities. Brook. J. Intl. L. 42:481–523.

Wilson N (1967) The Libraries of the Byzantine World. Greek, Roman and Byzantine Studies 8:53–80.

Xenophon (1989) Cyropaedia [430-354 B.C.] (Miller W (translator)). Harvard University Press, Cambridge, volume VI.

Marina Lostal holds a PhD from the European University Institute (Italy), an LLM from the University of Cambridge (UK), and an LLB from the University of Zaragoza (Spain). She is a Senior Lecturer at the School of Law of the University of Essex, and an elected member of the International Law Association's Committee on Participation in Global Cultural Heritage Governance. She is regularly consulted on cultural heritage issues by different international organisations, including UNESCO and the International Criminal Court. Her current research interests are reparations for victims in international law and the legal protection of animals.

I am indebted to Ms Alina Carrozzini for her research assistance during the drafting of this chapter. All errors are mine.

Chapter 22
Transnational and International Criminal Law

Sergey Sayapin

Contents

22.1 Introduction	470
22.2 Multiple Definitions of Transnational and International Criminal Law	470
22.3 Substantive "Transnational" Rules of Domestic Criminal Law (*Droit Pénal International*): Principles of Transnational Criminal Jurisdiction	471
22.3.1 Territorial Jurisdiction	472
22.3.2 Active Personality Principle	472
22.3.3 Passive Personality Principle	473
22.3.4 Protective Principle	473
22.3.5 Exclusive Jurisdiction	474
22.3.6 Vicarious (Representational) Jurisdiction	474
22.3.7 Universal Jurisdiction	475
22.4 International Criminal Procedure	476
22.4.1 Principles of International Criminal Procedure	476
22.4.2 International Cooperation in Penal Matters	478
22.5 International Criminal Law *stricto sensu* (*Droit International Pénal*)	482
22.5.1 General Part of International Criminal Law	483
22.5.2 "Core Crimes" Under International Law	484
22.5.3 International Crimes, Delicts, and Infractions	488
22.5.4 Direct Enforcement of International Criminal Law	490
22.5.5 Indirect Enforcement of International Criminal Law	493
22.6 Transitional Justice	493
22.6.1 Penal Prosecutions	494
22.6.2 Amnesty	494
22.6.3 Truth and Reconciliation Commission	495
22.6.4 Compensation	495
22.6.5 Lustration	496
22.7 Conclusion	496
References	497

Abstract Transnational and international criminal law are bodies of law regulating cooperation between States, as well as between States and various institutions of international criminal justice, in the prevention, prosecution and punishment of individuals for transnational and international crimes. Ever since the Nuremberg and

---

S. Sayapin (✉)
School of Law, KIMEP University, Almaty, Kazakhstan
e-mail: s.sayapin@kimep.kz

© T.M.C. ASSER PRESS and the authors 2022
S. Sayapin et al. (eds.), *International Conflict and Security Law*,
https://doi.org/10.1007/978-94-6265-515-7_22

Tokyo trials after the Second World War, both transnational and international criminal law developed into full-scale branches of law dealing with the substantive and procedural aspects of combating such crimes as genocide, crimes against humanity, war crimes and other international and transnational crimes. The penalisation of the crime of aggression has been relatively less successful. In 2002, a permanent International Criminal Court (ICC) was established but it does not yet enjoy universal support, and alternative regional formats such as the Malabo Protocol are contemplated. With due regard to the principle of complementarity, the indirect enforcement of international criminal law and transitional justice mechanisms will remain continually significant.

Keywords Crime of aggression · crime under international law · crimes against humanity · genocide · International Criminal Court (ICC) · international criminal law · international criminal procedure · Malabo Protocol · Nuremberg trial · Tokyo trial · transitional justice · transnational criminal law · war crimes

22.1 Introduction

International and transnational criminal law contribute to the maintenance of international peace and security inasmuch as they regulate cooperation between States and various institutions of international criminal justice in the prevention, prosecution and punishment of individuals for transnational and international crimes.[1] To facilitate the attainment of these goals, States put in place normative and institutional mechanisms at the international level, and implement related substantive and procedural regulations in their domestic laws. This chapter provides an overview of customary principles of penal jurisdiction, followed by the main principles of international criminal procedure and modalities of international cooperation in penal matters, "core crimes" under international law and other international crimes, direct and indirect enforcement of international criminal law, and concludes with a section on transitional justice. The chapter is meant to be studied in conjunction with other thematic chapters dealing with the law of armed conflict (international humanitarian law), international human rights law, international institutions, and crimes under international law.

22.2 Multiple Definitions of Transnational and International Criminal Law

The concept of international criminal law (ICL) has a few meanings. In 1950, Georg Schwarzenberger offered six distinct meanings of ICL.[2] For our purpose, it will be

---

[1] See Shelley 2011; Ambos 2016, pp. 44–56.

[2] Cryer et al. 2014, p. 4; Ambos 2013, p. 54.

22 Transnational and International Criminal Law

useful to draw a distinction between transnational criminal law, international criminal procedure, and international criminal law *stricto sensu*.[3] Transnational criminal law may be defined as substantive rules of domestic criminal law (*droit pénal international*) having a bearing on crimes with a transnational element. Such an element may consist, for example, in a foreign nationality of a perpetrator of a crime or its victim, the commission of a crime abroad (with or without domestic effects of the crime), the commission of a crime affecting the interests of a foreign State, or the commission of a crime affecting the community of States as a whole. The focus of transnational criminal law is on the assertion of a State´s penal jurisdiction with respect to a transnational crime.

In turn, international criminal procedure regulates bilateral or multilateral cooperation between States in criminal matters. As a rule, international criminal procedure is based on bilateral or multilateral treaties regulating extradition, mutual legal assistance, execution of foreign penal judgments, etc., although *ad hoc* formats of inter-State cooperation in penal matters are also possible. Rules of international criminal procedure are usually implemented in domestic criminal procedure laws.[4]

Finally, international criminal law *stricto sensu* (*droit international pénal*) are rules of public international law establishing the criminality of a few "core crimes" directly under international law, and regulating the prosecution of individuals for the commission of such crimes by international or "hybrid" criminal tribunals, or within domestic legal systems.[5] International criminal law also serves as a normative foundation for States to penalise other international crimes, delicts and infractions.

22.3 Substantive "Transnational" Rules of Domestic Criminal Law (*Droit Pénal International*): Principles of Transnational Criminal Jurisdiction

Whenever a transnational crime is committed, at least two States will have jurisdiction with respect to the crime. One of the States is the so-called territorial State—that is, the State in whose territory the crime takes places—and the other one may be a State of the perpetrator´s nationality (if he or she is a foreigner), of the crime´s victim (if he or she is a foreigner), a foreign State whose interests are injured by the crime, or another State, depending on the circumstances.[6] Domestic criminal laws contain principles on whose basis States assert their penal jurisdiction with respect to transnational crimes and crimes under international law, and make practical decisions about who will prosecute the perpetrators of such crimes.

---

[3] Bassiouni 2008b; Safferling 2011, pp. 3–6.

[4] See, for example, Section 12 of the Criminal Procedure Code of the Republic of Kazakhstan ("International cooperation in the field of penal proceedings").

[5] Cryer et al. 2014, p. 6; Werle and Jessberger 2020, pp. 34–37.

[6] Ambos 2016, pp. 233–242; David 2009, pp. 273–283.

22.3.1 Territorial Jurisdiction

The main rule is the principle of territorial jurisdiction, and in most cases, the territorial State will have priority in prosecuting for a transnational crime committed in its territory.[7] On the one hand, the principle of territorial jurisdiction is a reflection of a State´s sovereignty.[8] On the other hand, the principle is very pragmatic, because it is practically easier to prosecute one where a crime in question was committed, due to evidence, witnesses, etc., being within reach. The principle means that every State may prescribe rules of penal law, which extend to all of its territory,[9] and everyone, including foreigners, must obey these rules. Hence, if a foreigner violates a rule of a State´s domestic penal law, he or she will be liable under that law, if the State chooses to prosecute (instead of extraditing or surrendering the foreigner to the State of his or her nationality).[10] Likewise, a State is entitled to use its penal law to protect a foreign victim or a crime committed on its territory, unless it chooses to extradite or surrender the perpetrator to the State of the victim´s nationality.[11] The principle of territorial penal jurisdiction may have two variations, depending on where a crime originates and is completed. If a crime originates within a State but its effects occur abroad, the State has *objective* territorial jurisdiction. If a crime originates abroad but its effects occur locally, the State has *subjective* territorial jurisdiction.[12] A scenario like this can ensue, for instance, if a transboundary river is polluted by a natural person or legal entity located in an upstream State but the effects of the pollution occur in a downstream State.

22.3.2 Active Personality Principle

When an individual travels abroad, he or she normally remains bound by the penal laws of a State of his or her nationality.[13] By extension, this principle may also apply to foreigners or stateless persons who are permanent residents of a State.[14] In practical terms, the principle means that if an individual commits a crime abroad and returns

---

[7] Ambos 2016, p. 242.

[8] Safferling 2011, p. 14; Ambos 2016, p. 206.

[9] O´Keefe 2015, pp. 6–29; David 2009, pp. 14–56.

[10] Safferling 2011, pp. 14–21; Ambos 2016, pp. 211–217.

[11] It should be noted, though, that domestic laws often prohibit the extradition or surrender of a State´s own nationals to foreign States. See, for example, Article 61(1) of the Constitution of the Russian Federation, or Article 25 of the Constitution of Ukraine. The second paragraph of Article 12 of the Criminal Code of Uzbekistan contains a qualification to the effect that "A citizen of Uzbekistan cannot be extradited for a crime committed on the territory of a foreign state, *unless otherwise provided by international treaties or agreements*" (emphasis added). See also Cryer et al. 2014, pp. 102–103.

[12] Cryer et al. 2014, pp. 52–53.

[13] Lukashuk 2008, p. 331.

[14] Ambos 2016, pp. 219–220.

home before the territorial State could exercise its territorial penal jurisdiction, he or she may be held criminally liable by the State of his or her nationality or permanent residence (subject to the principle of double criminality).[15] Complex conflicts of penal jurisdictions may occur where a perpetrator of a transnational crime holds two or more nationalities. In such cases, the genuine link between the individual and a State may help determine which State should be given priority in prosecuting the perpetrator on the basis of the active personality principle.

22.3.3 *Passive Personality Principle*

In turn, the passive personality principle offers protection to a State´s nationals, if they become victims of a crime abroad.[16] This protection is additional to the principles of territorial jurisdiction and active personality, and may apply if the territorial State or a State of the perpetrator´s nationality are unable or unwilling to prosecute. Since both the perpetrators and victims of transnational crimes may change nationalities in the course of their lifetime, the relevant moment for determining nationality for the purpose of the active or passive personality principles is the time of the offence.[17]

22.3.4 *Protective Principle*

Although most crimes affect individual interests,[18] some have a direct impact on the security of States. Such offences as espionage, currency counterfeiting, certain trans-border cybercrimes,[19] or aggression are directed against the political, economic and other dimensions of States´ national security–indeed, sometimes against their very existence. The protective principle of penal jurisdiction enables States to prosecute individuals for such crimes, irrespective of where the crimes were committed, and of the nationality of perpetrators.[20] Notably, the passive personality principle is sometimes regarded as a spin-off of the protective principle: since permanent population is an essential attribute of statehood,[21] an attack against a State´s nationals may be

---

[15] Cryer et al. 2014, p. 55, Safferling 2011, pp. 21–24; Ambos 2016, pp. 217–220; David 2009, pp. 188–203.

[16] Cryer et al. 2014, pp. 55–56; Ambos 2016, pp. 222–223; David 2009, pp. 203–217.

[17] Cryer et al. 2014, p. 56.

[18] Ormerod and Laird 2015, pp. 10–12.

[19] See Lovely 2011; David 2009, pp. 1432–1435.

[20] Cryer et al. 2014, p. 56; Safferling 2011, pp. 26–28; Ambos 2016, pp. 220–222; David 2009, pp. 237–241.

[21] Cf. Article 1 of the Montevideo Convention on the Rights and Duties of States (1926).

regarded as an attack against the State as such.[22] This adds weight to the passive personality principle, which may otherwise appear controversial.[23]

22.3.5 Exclusive Jurisdiction

As a rule, States retain exclusive jurisdiction over their diplomats and military personnel stationed abroad. Article 31(1) of the 1961 Vienna Convention on Diplomatic Relations provides explicitly that diplomatic agents enjoy immunity from the criminal jurisdiction of the receiving State. Article 32 of the Convention stipulates that the immunity from jurisdiction of diplomatic agents may be waived by the sending State but the waiver must always be express. Likewise, the Status of Forces Agreements (SOFA) include standard clauses to the effect that the host State authorises the sending State to exercise criminal jurisdiction over its own personnel while in the territory of the host State.[24] Such exclusive jurisdictional regime is a manifestation of State sovereignty inherent in the exercise of the diplomatic and military functions.[25]

22.3.6 Vicarious (Representational) Jurisdiction

There may be scenarios where a State lawfully refuses to extradite an individual to another State (for instance, on the basis of the principle of *non-refoulement*) but nonetheless assumes penal jurisdiction "on behalf" of the requesting State.[26] This jurisdictional ground enables the requested State to hold the individual who committed a crime abroad criminally liable with due regard to his or her fundamental rights (e.g. procedural rights, or the prohibition of ill-treatment). In other words, vicarious jurisdiction reduces instances of impunity in that it does not permit individuals who committed crimes to escape justice, and helps maintain the due process standards.

---

[22] Safferling 2011, pp. 24–26; Ambos 2016, pp. 222–223.

[23] Cryer et al. 2014, p. 55.

[24] Cf. Article III(2) of the Agreement between the Government of the United States of America and the Government of the Republic of Rwanda Regarding the Status of United States Forces in the Republic of Rwanda: "Rwanda recognizes the particular importance of disciplinary control by U.S. Armed Forces authorities over U.S. personnel and, therefore, authorizes the United States to exercise criminal jurisdiction over U.S. personnel while in the territory of the Republic of Rwanda". See a collection of the US Status of Forces Agreements at: https://www.state.gov/subjects/status-of-forces-agreement/ (accessed 20 February 2021).

[25] David 2009, pp. 56–136.

[26] Safferling 2011, pp. 32–33; Ambos 2016, pp. 230–233.

22.3.7 *Universal Jurisdiction*

Some crimes are so grave that they affect the international legal order as such. Habitually termed "crimes against the peace and security of mankind",[27] such crimes include the so-called "core crimes" under international law–genocide, crimes against humanity, war crimes, and the crime of aggression—and a few other crimes, which affect international peace and security, fundamental human rights, the integrity of the international system, and other values protected by international law. Although not without some controversy,[28] it is accepted that such crimes are subject to universal jurisdiction—that is, States may assert their jurisdiction with respect to such crimes irrespective of the place of their commission, the nationality of perpetrators and victims, and other customary jurisdictional links.[29]

There are two main approaches to universal jurisdiction. The "pure" universal jurisdiction enables a State to prosecute anyone for genocide, crimes against humanity, or war crimes (and, as the case may be, other crimes against the peace and security of mankind) committed anywhere in the world,[30] with no regard to immunities attendant to a perpetrator´s official position, and even *in absentia*.[31] A classic example is Belgium´s law on universal jurisdiction (1993) whose scope of application was restricted in 2003.[32] Similarly, in 2009 and 2014, Spain substantially restricted the application of its 1985 universal jurisdiction law.[33] Kazakhstan offers a more recent example: the second paragraph of Article 8(1) of its Criminal Code provides for universal jurisdiction with respect to terrorist or extremist crimes, crimes against the peace and security of mankind, or for causing grave harm to the vital interests of the Republic of Kazakhstan, unless an applicable treaty provides otherwise.[34] In turn, the "conditional" universal jurisdiction regime requires the presence of a suspect in the territory of the State asserting jurisdiction.[35] This approach is helpful, especially, in scenarios where multiple States assert universal jurisdiction with respect to the same crime.

---

[27] See Draft Code of Offences against the Peace and Security of Mankind with commentaries 1951; Draft Code of Crimes against the Peace and Security of Mankind with commentaries 1996.

[28] Cryer et al. 2014, p. 56.

[29] Cryer et al. 2014, p. 57; Safferling 2011, pp. 28–32; Ambos 2016, pp. 224–230; David 2009, pp. 242–271.

[30] Cryer et al. 2014, pp. 57–58.

[31] Cryer et al. 2014, p. 57.

[32] Cryer et al. 2014, pp. 61–62.

[33] Cryer et al. 2014, p. 63.

[34] Cf. Article 8(1) of the Criminal Code of Kazakhstan: "The provisions of this Code shall apply regardless of the place of the crime in relation to citizens of the Republic of Kazakhstan, stateless persons permanently residing in the territory of the Republic of Kazakhstan, in cases of committing a terrorist or extremist crime or a crime against the peace and security of mankind or for causing other grave harm to the vital interests of the Republic. Kazakhstan, unless otherwise established by an international treaty of the Republic of Kazakhstan".

[35] Cryer et al. 2014, pp. 57–58.

22.4 International Criminal Procedure

International criminal procedure serves the purposes of investigating, prosecuting and punishing for transnational crimes and crimes under international law. The very nature of such crimes requires States to put in place bilateral or multilateral rules to enable transfers of criminal proceedings, evidence, and persons participating in such proceedings across international borders. As a rule, such cooperation is based on treaties, although States can also provide legal assistance in penal matters unilaterally.[36] This section highlights the essential principles of international criminal procedure, and offers a brief overview of the main forms of international cooperation in penal matters.

22.4.1 Principles of International Criminal Procedure

Principles of international criminal procedures strike a pragmatic balance between State sovereignty and human rights. They enable States to cooperate in the prosecution of relevant crimes, while making sure that the rights of victims and perpetrators are upheld. Although States certainly have a common interest in combating crime, they retain broad discretionary powers in arranging the specific modalities of cooperation through the medium of treaties and domestic laws, and the provision of assistance may be refused, if an essential principle is breached.

22.4.1.1 Double Criminality

The principle of double (or dual) criminality is a standard rule in treaties on mutual legal assistance in penal matters. It means that States render each other assistance in the prosecution of alleged acts, which constitute crimes in both the requesting and the requested State already at the time of their commission, and not (only) at the time of filing a request for legal assistance.[37] The principle of double criminality is closely related with the *nullum crimen sine lege* maxim, and with the principle of reciprocity.[38] The specific modalities of applying this principle may differ. Some treaties require identical crimes, whereas others specify that legal assistance is rendered, if a crime meets a minimum threshold of gravity in both jurisdictions.[39]

---

[36] Sadoff 2016, pp. 327–329.

[37] Cryer et al. 2014, pp. 94–95.

[38] Cryer et al. 2014, p. 94.

[39] Cryer et al. 2014, p. 94.

22.4.1.2 Specialty

The rule of specialty derives from international comity,[40] and means that the pursuing State may hold a person accountable only for crimes for which he or she was extradited by the requested State, unless the requested State subsequently agrees otherwise, or the same underlying facts provide a basis for a lesser included offence.[41] Sadoff notes that [... s]pecialty is a right conferred on the transferor State, which can be invoked by diplomatic protest [...] or waived at its discretion (possibly through acquiescence".[42] The principle also applies to mutual legal assistance, for example, as far as the imposition of conditions on the use of information or evidence is concerned.[43]

22.4.1.3 Prohibition of Double Jeopardy (*ne bis in idem*)

The prohibition of double jeopardy (*ne bis in idem*) is another standard rule in extradition treaties.[44] It means that an individual may not be prosecuted or punished again for the same criminal offence where he or she has already been finally convicted for, or acquitted of, the offence. Some extradition treaties prevent double punishment, whereas others aim at preventing double prosecutions as such.[45] The rule effectively applies within one jurisdiction but it may not always prevent multiple prosecutions in different legal systems,[46] especially where an offence is criminal in one jurisdiction and administrative in another.

---

[40] Cf. Abass 2014, p. 263.

[41] Cryer et al. 2014, p. 95.

[42] Sadoff 2016, pp. 284–285, footnotes omitted.

[43] Cryer et al. 2014, p. 95.

[44] Cryer et al. 2014, pp. 95–96; Ambos 2013, pp. 396–406. Cf. Article 14(7) of the International Covenant on Civil and Political Rights (1966): "No one shall be liable to be tried or punished again for an offence for which he has already been finally convicted or acquitted in accordance with the law and penal procedure of each country".

[45] Cryer et al. 2014, p. 96.

[46] Cf. Article 10 of the Criminal Code of the People´s Republic of China: "Any person who commits a crime outside PRC territory and according to this law bear criminal responsibility may still be dealt with according to this law even if he has been tried in a foreign country; however, a person who has already received criminal punishment in a foreign country may be exempted from punishment or given a mitigated punishment". See also Article 5 of the Penal Code of Japan: "Even when a final and binding decision has been rendered by a foreign judiciary against the criminal act of a person, it shall not preclude further punishment in Japan with regard to the same act; provided, however, that when the person has already served either the whole or part of the punishment abroad, execution of the punishment shall be mitigated or remitted".

22.4.1.4 Statutory Limitations

Statutory limitations may bar cooperation (and, in particular, extradition) where the passage of time makes a prosecution unjust or impractical.[47] It should be noted, though, that statutory limitations do not apply to the "core crimes" under international law,[48] and domestic penal laws may extend this regime to other crimes against the peace and security of mankind as well as terrorism.[49]

22.4.1.5 Non-refoulement

The principle of *non-refoulement* prohibits the extradition of an individual to a State where he or she would not have a fair trial, or where there are serious grounds to believe that the individual would be subjected to torture or other inhuman or degrading treatment or punishment in the requesting State.[50] If extradition is refused based on the principle of *non-refoulement*, the requested State may exercise vicarious jurisdiction to hold the individual accountable for the crime for which his or her extradition was requested.

22.4.2 *International Cooperation in Penal Matters*

M. Cherif Bassiouni singled out eight main modalities of international cooperation in penal matters,[51] which are briefly explained in this section:

- extradition;
- legal assistance;
- execution of foreign penal sentences;
- recognition of foreign penal judgments;
- transfer of criminal proceedings;
- freezing and seizing of assets deriving from criminal conduct;
- intelligence and law enforcement information-sharing;
- regional and sub-regional "judicial spaces".

---

[47] Cryer et al. 2014, p. 95; Safferling 2011, p. 123.

[48] See Convention on the Non-Applicability of Statutory Limitations to War Crimes and Crimes Against Humanity (1968).

[49] Cf. Article 8(1) of the Criminal Code of Kazakhstan, *supra* note 34.

[50] Cryer et al. 2014, p. 97.

[51] Bassiouni 2003, pp. 347–378.

22.4.2.1 Extradition

Extradition is the earliest form of international cooperation in penal matters. It dates back to a treaty concluded between Ramses II and Hattusili III around 1268 BC,[52] which means that historically, international criminal procedure is one of the oldest areas of public international law. Extradition means the physical relocation of a person from the requested State to the requesting State for that person´s prosecution or punishment for an alleged crime, with respect to which the requesting State has penal jurisdiction.[53] As a rule, extradition is effectuated on the basis of a bilateral or multilateral treaty between the requesting and requested States. In the absence of such a treaty, alternative—more or less formal–procedural routes may be used to obtain custody of a suspect.[54]

22.4.2.2 Legal Assistance

In turn, Bassiouni explains legal assistance (or mutual legal assistance) as follows:

> This is when the courts of one state address a request to those of another state for judicial assistance in the form of taking the testimony of a witness or securing tangible evidence. The courts then transmit the oral or tangible evidence to the requesting court, certifying that the evidence has been secured in accordance with the legal requirements of the requested state [...][55]
>
> The forms of legal assistance vary widely. They include: taking of witness testimony, securing tangible evidence such as business and bank records, and conducting investigations. These forms of legal assistance can be conducted by the judicial, prosecutorial or law enforcement personnel of the requested state. Sometimes, the requested state allows a judge or prosecutor from a requesting state to conduct the investigation on its territory, but under the supervision of the requested state´s judicial authorities.[56]

It may be assumed that the best practices learned from a wider use of telecommunication technologies in the administration of justice during the COVID-19 pandemic will be used in the post-pandemic world as well, given that they reasonably expedite proceedings, and reduce associated costs.[57]

---

[52] Bassiouni 2003, p. 348; Sayapin 2014, p. 9.

[53] David 2009, pp. 436–558.

[54] Sadoff 2016, pp. 389–550.

[55] Bassiouni 2003, p. 352.

[56] Bassiouni 2003, p. 354. See also David 2009, pp. 409–431.

[57] Cf. Bassiouni 2003, p. 354.

22.4.2.3 Execution of Foreign Penal Sentences

This modality of international cooperation means that the execution of penal sentences is transferred to convicted foreigners´ countries of origin.[58] The procedure is not equivalent to the recognition of foreign penal judgments. According to Bassiouni, "executing a foreign sentence does not imply the recognition of the penal judgment that gives rise to it".[59] Instead, it "separates the execution of the sentence from the recognition of the penal judgment, which gave rise to the sentence",[60] and simply means bringing "sentenced persons physically closer to family in their countries of origin".[61] Hence, the purposes of the mechanism are chiefly "humanitarian and rehabilitative".[62] Indeed, if a person was judged abroad but serves the sentence in his or her country of origin, he or she is likely to be in a closer contact with the family than would have been the case, if the penal sentence had been executed abroad. Likewise, the rehabilitation of offenders in a foreign country is likely to be complicated by practical matters—such as a possible language barrier.

22.4.2.4 Recognition of Foreign Penal Judgments

As noted above, the execution of foreign penal sentences is different from the recognition of foreign penal judgments. As a rule, States refrain from recognising foreign penal judgments, because these are regarded as a manifestation of national sovereignty.[63] Instead, international cooperation in penal matters is based on recognising the *consequences* of a foreign penal judgment (not the judgment as such), and extradition and other forms of international cooperation in penal matters are seen as the effects of the judgment. This certainly is a legal fiction but as such it appears to be fairly dogmatic, and a matter of principle.[64]

22.4.2.5 Transfer of Criminal Proceedings

A State may choose to transfer criminal proceedings to another State, which, in Bassiouni´s words, "has more significant contacts with the parties, and is therefore a *forum conveniens*. This is in contrast to the transferring state being a *forum non conveniens*, or where some public policy interest exists that justifies the transfer of the proceedings to achieve the best interests of justice".[65] Thus, this modality is different

---

[58] David 2009, pp. 573–582.

[59] Bassiouni 2003, pp. 355–356.

[60] Bassiouni 2003, p. 356.

[61] Bassiouni 2003, p. 355.

[62] Bassiouni 2003, p. 357.

[63] Bassiouni 2003, p. 357. See also David 2009, pp. 571–572.

[64] Bassiouni 2003, p. 357.

[65] Bassiouni 2003, p. 358. See also David 2009, pp. 559–565.

22 Transnational and International Criminal Law

from the assumption of extraterritorial jurisdiction on the basis of any recognised principle (see *supra* Sect. 22.3).[66] It simply means that a State has a closer link to a case or its parties, and another State transfers proceedings to the former for pragmatic reasons, or in the interests of justice.

22.4.2.6 Freezing and Seizing of Assets Deriving from Criminal Conduct

On the one hand, the freezing and seizing of assets deriving from criminal conduct is a specific form of enforcing foreign penal judgments. On the other hand, it is specific enough to constitute a distinct modality of international cooperation in penal matters.[67] Such confiscation "is predicated on a foreign penal judgment entered in the requesting state for a criminal activity that occurred in the requesting state or over which it had jurisdiction",[68] and cooperation can be based on a regional or universal treaty addressing such criminal phenomena as the drug trafficking,[69] organised crime,[70] international terrorism,[71] or corruption.[72] Given the dual (administrative and penal) nature of measures taken by States in the framework of this modality, and the difficulties "relating to the[ir] fusion into a single control regime",[73] more efforts are required to synchronise applicable domestic laws.

22.4.2.7 Intelligence and Law-Enforcement Information-Sharing

The fundamental difference between this and other modalities of international cooperation consists in that unlike the latter, intelligence and law-enforcement information-sharing is not based on treaties.[74] Given the sensitive nature of information transmitted in the framework of this modality, "[i]ntelligence and law enforcement agencies have historically shared information outside legal and judicial supervision. This *de facto* modality of international cooperation has historically been secretive, and the laws of almost all countries seldom deal with the regulation of this type of activity, except when national legislation limits or regulates the scope and context of these agencies' domestic work".[75] In the current environment of mutual

---

[66] Bassiouni 2003, p. 359.

[67] Bassiouni 2003, p. 359.

[68] Bassiouni 2003, pp. 359–360.

[69] See the United Nations Convention against Illicit Traffic in Narcotic Drugs and Psychotropic Substances (1988).

[70] See the United Nations Convention against Transnational Organized Crime (2000).

[71] See the International Convention for the Suppression of the Financing of Terrorism (1999).

[72] See the United Nations Convention against Corruption (2003).

[73] Bassiouni 2003, p. 365.

[74] Bassiouni 2003, p. 368.

[75] Bassiouni 2003, p. 369.

distrust between some of the world´s major powers, "potential for inefficiency, error, and infringement of the general right of privacy as well as for the specific rights of individuals"[76] is likely to grow.

22.4.2.8 Regional and Sub-regional "Judicial Spaces"

Regional and sub-regional integration between States may lead to the emergence of "judicial spaces". This modality means an even closer integration than cooperation on the basis of multilateral treaties on mutual legal assistance as described above, to the extent that "within the area determined as part of the "judicial space" judicial orders shall be enforced automatically by the respective states without the need for the intermediation of a judicial order issued by the enforcing state. This would also mean that law enforcement officials from one member-state can pursue their investigations or pursue fugitives outside their national boundaries (obviously, with some coordination with local law enforcement)".[77] It appears that efficient "judicial spaces" emerge within otherwise successful integration formats with common approaches to penal policies, the rule of law, and respect for human rights. In the EU, for example, the European Arrest Warrant scheme is "generally perceived as successful, at least from a law enforcement perspective".[78] In turn, relations between member States of a "judicial space" and non-members are regulated by traditional mechanisms—that is, treaties on mutual legal assistance in penal matters.

22.5 International Criminal Law *stricto sensu* (*Droit International Pénal*)

International criminal law (ICL) are rules of public international law directly establishing the criminal responsibility of individuals for acts (more rarely, omissions), which affect the peace and security of mankind. In the 20th century, the first attempts to criminalise such acts were made after the First World War[79] but the first trials on relevant charges did not take place until after the Second World War. The Charters and jurisprudence of the Nuremberg and Tokyo Tribunals laid the foundations for the General and Special Parts of the contemporary ICL,[80] and the rules were refined during the ensuing decades. Now, ICL is enforced in two main ways–directly (by the International Criminal Court and other international and "hybrid" tribunals), and indirectly (by States, through their domestic systems of criminal justice). Given the

---

[76] Bassiouni 2003, p. 371.

[77] Bassiouni 2003, p. 378.

[78] Cryer et al. 2014, p. 100. See also Safferling 2011, pp. 341–441.

[79] Werle and Jessberger 2020, pp. 2–5; Schabas 2018.

[80] Werle and Jessberger 2020, pp. 6–11.

22 Transnational and International Criminal Law

limited capacities of international institutions, the indirect enforcement of ICL will continue gaining significance.

22.5.1 General Part of International Criminal Law

According to Werle and Jessberger, "[u]ntil the entry into force of the ICC Statute, general principles were of secondary importance in efforts to codify international criminal law".[81] Indeed, during the Nuremberg and Tokyo trials, for example, the victorious Powers held accountable the leaders of States they had defeated but not their own nationals,[82] the prohibition of retroactivity of criminal law was obviously disregarded,[83] and some rules on evidence were below the standard.[84] As the International Criminal Tribunals for the Former Yugoslavia and Rwanda were established by the Security Council of the United Nations, respectively, in 1993 and 1994, some commentators questioned the authority of the Security Council, a political organ, to establish judicial organs.[85] The drafters of the ICC Statute had to take account of such criticisms, and to consolidate the general principles of ICL for the purpose of setting a high standard of justice at the ICC.

The general principles of criminal law are codified in Part 3 of the ICC Statute (Articles 22–33), and draw mostly on the common and civil law traditions.[86] The Islamic legal tradition is, unfortunately, largely disregarded in the ICC Statute. The Statute includes the following general principles of criminal law:

- *Nullum crimen sine lege* (Article 22);[87]
- *Nulla poena sine lege* (Article 23);[88]
- Non-retroactivity *ratione personae* (Article 24);[89]
- Individual criminal responsibility (Article 25);[90]
- Exclusion of jurisdiction over persons under eighteen (Article 26);[91]

---

[81] Werle and Jessberger 2020, p. 205.

[82] Werle and Jessberger 2020, p. 9. See also Tanaka 2011 and Henderson 2011.

[83] Werle and Jessberger 2020, p. 9.

[84] Cf. Article 19 of the Nuremberg Charter (1945): "The Tribunal shall not be bound by technical rules of evidence. It shall adopt and apply to the greatest possible extent expeditious and non-technical procedure, and shall admit any evidence which it deems to have probative value". Article 13(a) of the Tokyo Charter (1946) repeated these provisions verbatim, and contains a further sentence: "All purported admissions or statements of the accused are admissible".

[85] See Waters 2018.

[86] Werle and Jessberger 2020, p. 207. On the implementation of general principles of criminal law in Kazakhstan, see Sayapin 2019a.

[87] Werle and Jessberger 2020, pp. 48–50, 212–215.

[88] Werle and Jessberger 2020, pp. 48–50; Ambos 2014, pp. 271–277.

[89] Cryer et al. 2014, pp. 84–85.

[90] Werle and Jessberger 2020, pp. 233–264; Ambos 2013, pp. 102–179.

[91] Ambos 2013, pp. 430–432.

- Irrelevance of official capacity (Article 27);[92]
- Responsibility of commanders and other superiors (Article 28);[93]
- Non-applicability of statute of limitations (Article 29);[94]
- Mental element (Article 30);[95]
- Grounds for excluding criminal responsibility (Article 31);[96]
- Mistake of fact or mistake of law (Article 32);[97]
- Superior orders and prescription of law (Article 33).[98]

Werle and Jessberger point out that "discussing the general principles of international criminal law requires freeing oneself from the ways of thinking and the doctrinal concepts of one´s own domestic law".[99] This approach is useful for at least two practical reasons. At the international level, the general principles serve as common normative guidelines for the ICC Judges and Prosecutor who represent various legal traditions of the world. Since their professional perceptions of international and criminal law are inevitably informed by their national academic and law enforcement practices, common normative guidelines are useful. At the domestic level, general principles of criminal law help maintain the appropriate standards of justice, both in the States Parties to the Rome Statute and States, which have not ratified the Statute.

22.5.2 "Core Crimes" Under International Law

The "core crimes" under international law are within the scope of "crimes against the peace and security of mankind".[100] They are "the most serious crimes of concern to the international community as a whole",[101] and therefore are within the jurisdiction of the International Criminal Court. They are also widely criminalised (with the exceptions of the crime of aggression and crimes against humanity) at the domestic level. A common feature of all "core crimes" under international law consists in the so-called "context of organised violence", in which they are committed.[102] The "core

---

[92] Werle and Jessberger 2020, pp. 311–325; Safferling 2011, pp. 121–123; Ambos 2013, pp. 406–419; O´Keefe 2015, pp. 409–458.

[93] Werle and Jessberger 2020, pp. 264–276; Ambos 2013, pp. 197–232.

[94] Cf. Article 7 of the Nuremberg Charter (1945), Article 6 of the Tokyo Charter (1946). See also Ambos 2013, pp. 427–430.

[95] Werle and Jessberger 2020, pp. 215–233; Safferling 2011, pp. 119–120; Ambos 2013, pp. 266–300; See also *passim* Badar 2015.

[96] Werle and Jessberger 2020, pp. 277–302; Ambos 2013, pp. 301–437.

[97] Werle and Jessberger 2020, pp. 287–290; Ambos 2013, pp. 366–376.

[98] Werle and Jessberger 2020, pp. 290–295; Safferling 2011, p. 121; Ambos 2013, pp 376–386

[99] Werle and Jessberger 2020, p. 206.

[100] Cf. *supra* note 27. See also O´Keefe 2015, pp. 67–84; David 2009, pp. 1190–1195.

[101] Cf. Article 5 of the ICC Statute.

[102] Werle and Jessberger 2020, p. 210.

22 Transnational and International Criminal Law

crimes" are briefly discussed below, and explained in greater detail elsewhere in this book.

22.5.2.1 Genocide

The term "genocide" was suggested by a Polish-American lawyer Raphael Lemkin (1900–1959) to designate criminal acts committed with intent to destroy, in whole or in part, a national, ethnical, racial, or religious group, as such.[103] When designing the term, Lemkin bore in mind, in particular, acts perpetrated against Armenians during the First World War,[104] and against "Jews, Poles, Slovenes and Russians" before and during the Second World War.[105] In 1948, the Convention for the Prevention and Punishment of the Crime of Genocide was adopted. As of this writing, the Convention has 152 States Parties.[106] At times, genocide is confounded with crimes against humanity, because both affect large numbers of victims as a matter of practice. The differences between the two crimes essentially consist in (1) the range of protected groups and interests, and (2) the *mens rea*. The crime of genocide is limited to four protected groups, and does not include other identifiable groups (such as political groups or groups based on the sexual orientation of their members).[107] In turn, the "genocidal intent" is aimed at the destruction of a protected group, in whole or in part, as such,[108] whereas the *mens rea* of crimes against humanity requires that "the perpetrator must be aware that a (widespread or systematic) attack on a civilian population is taking place and that his or her action is part of this attack".[109]

22.5.2.2 Crimes against Humanity

In practical terms, crimes against humanity are mass crimes against identifiable civilian groups.[110] The term was suggested by Professor Hersch Lauterpacht (1897–1960) for the purpose of the Nuremberg Charter where the concept appeared in Article

---

[103] See Lemkin 2008; Bassiouni 2003, pp. 138–139; Cryer et al. 2014, pp. 205–228, Safferling 2011, pp. 155–178; Sayapin 2009; Sneh 2011; Lippman 2008; Ambos 2014, pp. 1–45; O´Keefe 2015, pp. 145–154; Mayroz 2018; Werle and Jessberger 2020, pp. 334–372.

[104] Sands 2016, p. 143.

[105] Sands 2016, p. 178.

[106] United Nations Treaty Collection (2021) Chapter IV: Human Rights, Convention on the Prevention and Punishment of the Crime of Genocide. https://treaties.un.org/Pages/ViewDetails.aspx?src=TREATY&mtdsg_no=IV-1&chapter=4&clang=_en. Accessed 23 February 2021.

[107] For a critical view on the definition of genocide, see Bassiouni 2016, pp. 383–384.

[108] May 2010, pp. 115–154; Ambos 2014, pp. 18–45.

[109] Werle and Jessberger 2020, p. 393. For a more detailed review of the similarities and differences between genocide and crimes against humanity, see also Atadjanov 2019, pp. 280–285.

[110] Bassiouni 2003, pp. 139–141; David 2009, pp. 1239–1342; Bassiouni 2011, pp. 51–166; Cryer et al. 2014, pp. 229–263; Safferling 2011, pp. 179–211; Ambos 2014, pp. 46–116; O´Keefe 2015, pp. 137–145; Nollez-Goldbach 2018; Werle and Jessberger 2020, pp. 373–440. On enforced

6(c).[111] It later appeared, with some modifications, in the Tokyo Charter (Article 5(c)), the Control Council Law No. 10 (Article II(1)(c)), the Statutes of the International Criminal Tribunals for the Former Yugoslavia (Article 5) and Rwanda (Article 3), and in Article 7 of the Rome Statute of the International Criminal Court. There is an ongoing discussion regarding a possible adoption of a Convention on Crimes against Humanity, which, if adopted, would not only consolidate the concept but also serve as a multilateral legal basis for mutual legal assistance in the prosecution of, and punishment for, crimes against humanity.[112] Modern discussions regarding crimes against humanity emphasise, on the one hand, positivist approaches explaining the crimes as widespread or systematic violations of fundamental human rights of members of identifiable civilian groups,[113] and, on the other hand, approaches based on the natural law theory and focusing on multifaceted meanings of "humanity" as a protected *Rechtsgut*.[114]

22.5.2.3 War Crimes

War crimes are criminal violations of international humanitarian law (IHL).[115] Their legal basis is found in various treaties of IHL as well as in customary international law.[116] Like crimes against humanity, war crimes were codified in the Nuremberg (Article 6(b)) and Tokyo (Article 5(b)) Charters, the Control Council Law No. 10 (Article II(1)(b)), the Statutes of the International Criminal Tribunals for the Former Yugoslavia (Articles 2 and 3) and Rwanda (Article 4), and in Article 8 of the Rome Statute of the International Criminal Court.[117] The law of war crimes customarily follows a characteristic distinction between international and non-international armed conflicts,[118] although a gradual convergence of the two legal regimes is ongoing.[119] All war crimes, irrespective of whether they are committed in an international or non-international armed conflict, share a few common attributes: (1) they are committed in connection with the armed conflict;[120] (2) by a person or

---

disappearance, see David 2009, pp. 1381–1388. On violence against women, see David 2009, pp. 1388–1392; Grey 2018. On crimes against children, see David 2009, pp. 1401–1404.

[111] Sands 2016, pp. 108–114; Atadjanov 2019, p. 92.

[112] Sayapin 2020c, p 135.

[113] Sayapin 2020a, pp. 48–51. See also May 2005, pp. 24–60.

[114] See *passim* Atadjanov 2019. See also May 2005, pp. 80–95.

[115] Bassiouni 2003, pp. 141–142; Cryer et al. 2014, pp. 264–306; Safferling 2011, pp. 212–246; Weisbord and Reyes 2011; Ambos 2014, pp. 117–183; O´Keefe 2015, pp. 123–137; Stephens and Wooden 2018; Werle and Jessberger 2020, pp. 441–583. See also *passim* May 2007.

[116] See Sandoz 2008.

[117] David 2009, pp. 1006–1043.

[118] See Moir 2008; Ambos 2014, pp. 131–140.

[119] Quénivet and Shah-Davis 2010, pp. 5–10.

[120] Ambos 2014, pp. 140–144.

persons belonging to one side in the armed conflict;[121] (3) against persons or objects belonging to another side in the armed conflict;[122] (4) in violation of one or more treaty-based or customary rules of IHL.[123] As IHL is developing, the law of war crimes is evolving accordingly. Emerging war crimes are related, for example, to the hostile use of information technologies.[124]

22.5.2.4 Crime of Aggression

The crime of aggression is probably the most controversial of all "core crimes" under international law.[125] As the Nuremberg Charter was being drafted, expert views on the criminalisation of aggression were divided,[126] and just a few pages were devoted to crimes against peace in the Nuremberg Judgment.[127] By contrast, already in the Tokyo Judgment, crimes against peace were much more prominent.[128] After the follow-up trials under the Control Council Law No. 10,[129] there were no international or domestic prosecutions on charges of aggression until Ukraine prosecuted two Russian military servicemen,[130] and its own former President V. Yanukovych[131] on

---

[121] Ambos 2014, pp. 145–146.

[122] Ambos 2014, pp. 146–152.

[123] Ambos 2014, pp. 160–183.

[124] See Geiß and Lahmann 2021.

[125] Bassiouni 2003, pp. 136–138; Bassiouni and Ferencz 2008; Cryer et al. 2014, pp. 307–328; David 2009, pp. 1083–1097; Barriga 2011; Safferling 2011, pp. 247–267; Ambos 2014, pp. 184–221; O´Keefe 2015, pp. 154–160; Ferencz and Ferencz 2016; Richmond 2018; Werle and Jessberger 2020, pp. 584–614.

[126] See Sayapin 2014, p. 40 (footnotes omitted): "While the United Nations War Crimes Commission [...] was preparing a practical ground for the future trials and collecting evidence, the Allied leaders were planning the post-war political organization of the world and formulating policies for the criminal prosecutions of the Axis major war criminals [...] Notably, the Allies' early approaches to the prosecution were quite divergent. As Telford Taylor (1908–1998) recalled, the United Kingdom had initially favored their summary execution, because "their guilt was so black" that it was "beyond the scope of any judicial process" [...] It seems the true reason for this reluctance lay in the United Kingdom's concern that the accused would use the trial as a forum for propaganda and self-justification—a concern which ultimately proved true [...] The United States and France intended the prospective tribunal to help document the history of the Second World War, inform the world and serve as a future deterrent [...] The Soviet Union, which advocated for the International Military Tribunal from, at least, as early as 1943, for it had undoubtedly borne the heaviest human and economic burden of the war [...] did not, at the same time, miss the opportunity to use it to cover up some advantages it had taken of the non-aggression pact it had concluded with Germany in 1939, such as the invasion of Eastern Poland, Finland, and the Baltic States". See also May 2008, pp. 141–162.

[127] Sayapin 2014, pp. 149–161.

[128] Sayapin 2014, pp. 161–180.

[129] Sayapin 2014, pp. 180–190.

[130] See Sayapin 2018.

[131] See Sayapin 2020b. On the territorial integrity of Ukraine, see Sayapin 2015. For a detailed legal analysis of Russia´s use of force against Ukraine, see *passim* Sayapin and Tsybulenko 2018.

such charges. Unlike the other "core crimes", aggression is usually regarded as a "leadership crime", and is codified as such in Article 8 bis of the Rome Statute of the International Criminal Court,[132] and in some domestic penal statutes. According to this author's calculations, some forty States introduced criminal responsibility for aggression and other crimes against peace,[133] and it may be assumed that domestic prosecutions on such charges are more likely than international ones at the ICC. Once the Malabo Protocol enters into force,[134] regional prosecutions in Africa will become feasible. Potentially, the Malabo mechanism might be even more effective in preventing and punishing for aggression than the ICC mechanism has been designed to be.[135]

22.5.3 International Crimes, Delicts, and Infractions

M. Cherif Bassiouni identified 28 distinct categories of "international violations"[136] on the basis of 281 conventions.[137] Depending on their gravity and the protected values they affect, he classified such violations under the headings of (1) international crimes, (2) international delicts, and (3) international infractions. Most of them are not within the jurisdiction of the ICC, either because they are not clearly defined in international law, or because relevant treaties explicitly assign penal jurisdiction over such crimes to individual States.

22.5.3.1 International Crimes

The first category mostly includes crimes, which are part of *jus cogens*, and is "typically characterized by the fact that their commission cannot occur without state action or a state-favoring policy".[138] In addition to the four "core crimes" under international law, according to Bassiouni, international crimes include:[139]

- unlawful possession or use of emplacement of weapons;[140]

---

[132] Clark 2008b; Sayapin 2008; Ambos 2014, pp. 186–220. On a human rights perspective on the crime of aggression, see Dannenbaum 2018.

[133] Sayapin 2014, pp. 202 222; Sayapin 2010, at 169–185.

[134] The Protocol on Amendments to the Protocol on the Statute of the African Court of Justice and Human Rights (Malabo Protocol) was adopted on 27 June 2014. In accordance with its Article 15, the Protocol shall enter into force 30 days after the deposit of instruments of instruments of ratification by 15 Member States. As of this writing, the Protocol has 15 signatures and no ratifications.

[135] Sayapin 2019b, at 334–335.

[136] Bassiouni 2003, p. 121.

[137] Bassiouni 2003, p. 116; Bassiouni 2008a. See also O´Keefe 2015, pp. 61–67.

[138] Bassiouni 2003, p. 121.

[139] Bassiouni 2003, p. 121.

[140] Bassiouni 2003, pp. 142–144; Bassiouni 2008c; Leggett 2011.

22 Transnational and International Criminal Law

- theft of nuclear materials;[141]
- mercenarism;[142]
- apartheid;[143]
- slavery or slave-related practices;[144]
- torture and other forms of cruel, inhuman or degrading treatment or punishment;[145]
- unlawful human experimentation.[146]

Bassiouni notes that, in addition to individual criminal responsibility, international crimes constitute internationally wrongful conduct, and entail the responsibility of States under international law.[147]

22.5.3.2 International Delicts

According to Bassiouni, the gravity of some "international delicts" may amount to that of international crimes but as a rule, they are "committed by individuals or small groups", and cause relatively lesser harm.[148] International delicts include:[149]

- piracy;[150]
- aircraft hijacking and unlawful acts against international air safety;[151]
- unlawful acts against the safety of maritime navigation and the safety of platforms on the high seas;[152]
- threat and use of force against internationally protected persons;[153]
- crimes against United Nations and associated personnel;[154]
- taking of civilian hostages;[155]
- unlawful use of the mail;[156]

---

[141] Bassiouni 2003, p. 144; David 2009, pp. 1378–1381.

[142] Bassiouni 2003, pp. 144–145; Dickinson 2008; David 2009, pp. 1154–1169.

[143] Bassiouni 2003, p. 145; Clark 2008a; Kapstein 2011; David 2009, pp. 1342–1349.

[144] Bassiouni 2003, pp. 145–146; David 2009, pp. 1211–1227.

[145] Bassiouni 2003, pp. 146–147; Derby 2008; David 2009, pp. 1353–1378; Ambos 2014, pp. 241–245.

[146] Bassiouni 2003, pp. 147–148.

[147] Bassiouni 2003, p. 121; David 2009, pp. 1392–1394.

[148] Bassiouni 2003, p. 122.

[149] Bassiouni 2003, pp. 122–123.

[150] Bassiouni 2003, p. 159; Sundberg 2008; David 2009, pp. 1405–1414; Ambos 2014, pp. 238–241.

[151] Bassiouni 2003, pp. 149–150; Joyner and Friedlander 2008; David 2009, pp. 1424–1427.

[152] Bassiouni 2003, p. 150; Halberstam 2008; David 2009, pp. 1414–1416, 1427–1431.

[153] Bassiouni 2003, pp. 150–151; David 2009, pp. 1169–1177.

[154] Bassiouni 2003, p 151.

[155] Bassiouni 2003, p. 151; DeFeo 2008; David 2009, pp. 1349–1353.

[156] Bassiouni 2003, pp. 151–153.

- use of explosives;[157]
- financing of terrorism;[158]
- unlawful traffic in drugs and related drug offences;[159]
- organised crime;[160]
- destruction and/or theft of national treasures;[161]
- unlawful acts against certain internationally protected elements of the environment.[162]

22.5.3.3 International Infractions

In Bassiouni´s classification, international infractions are normative violations of ICL not included in the categories of international crimes or international delicts:[163]

- international traffic in obscene materials;[164]
- falsification and counterfeiting;[165]
- unlawful interference with international submarine cables;[166]
- bribery of foreign public officials.[167]

Similarly, other transnational manifestation of corruption, as defined in the United Nations Convention against Corruption,[168] should be included within this category.

22.5.4 Direct Enforcement of International Criminal Law

Historically, ICL originated as a branch of public international law enforceable directly through the medium of international criminal tribunals. The Nuremberg (1945–1946) and Tokyo (1946–1948) trials[169] were followed by the International

---

[157] Bassiouni 2003, p. 153.

[158] Bassiouni 2003, p. 153; El-Dawla 2008; David 2009, pp. 1098–1154; Newman and Clarke 2011; Ambos 2014, pp. 228–234.

[159] Bassiouni 2003, pp. 153–154; Leroy et al. 2008; Natarajan 2011; David 2009, pp. 1230–1239; Ambos 2014, pp. 234–238.

[160] Bassiouni 2003, p. 154; Schloenhardt 2008; Vlassis 2008, at 907–925; David 2009, pp. 1394–1401; Albanese 2011.

[161] Bassiouni 2003, pp. 154–155; Nafziger 2008; Mackenzie 2011; David 2009, pp. 1523–1526.

[162] Bassiouni 2003, pp. 155–156; McCaffrey 2008; White 2011; David 2009, pp. 1437–1477.

[163] Bassiouni 2003, p 123.

[164] Bassiouni 2003, p. 156; David 2009, pp. 1228–1230.

[165] Bassiouni 2003, pp. 156–157; David 2009, pp. 1097–1098.

[166] Bassiouni 2003, pp. 157–158; David 2009, pp. 1417–1419.

[167] Bassiouni 2003, p. 158; Sandgren 2008; Vlassis 2008, at 925–937.

[168] David 2009, pp. 1177–1190. See also Graycar 2011.

[169] See Ambos 2013, pp. 4–6.

Criminal Tribunal for the Former Yugoslavia (ICTY)[170] and the International Criminal Tribunal for Rwanda (ICTR),[171] both established by the Security Council of the United Nations (respectively, in 1993 and 1994).[172] The jurisdiction of these international criminal tribunals extended to specific territories and armed conflicts, and was superior to the domestic penal jurisdictions of the States concerned.[173] Likewise, the personal, temporal, and territorial jurisdiction of internationalised or "hybrid" tribunals was defined in limited terms.[174] In turn, the founders of the International Criminal Court (ICC) decided to establish the new Court on the basis of the principle of complementarity,[175] and thus to give the ICC a potentially universal reach, without formally relying on the principle of universal jurisdiction.

22.5.4.1 International Criminal Court

The Rome Statute of the International Criminal Court (ICC) was adopted on 17 July 1998,[176] and entered into force, in accordance with its Article 126(1), on 1 April 2002. The eleventh preambular paragraph of the ICC Statute states that the Court was established "to guarantee lasting respect for and the enforcement of international justice". Indeed, a major difference between the ICC and all previous international criminal tribunals consisted precisely in that the ICC was designed to be a permanent judicial institution having authority to prosecute individuals for the most serious crimes of concern to the international community as a whole (cf. the fourth preambular paragraph of the Statute).[177] Next, the ICC Statute is a potentially universal treaty but this potential universality is made possible by virtue of the principle of territorial jurisdiction and the active personality principle whose customary character is beyond dispute. As of this writing, the Rome Statute has 123 States Parties mostly representing the common and civil legal traditions.[178]

According to Article 5 of the Rome Statute, the ICC has jurisdiction with respect to the "core crimes" under international law. The Statute originally contained the definitions of genocide (Article 6), crimes against humanity (Article 7), and war crimes (Article 8) for the purpose of the ICC but the definition of the crime of aggression was left to a later date.[179] The latter crime was defined for the purpose of the ICC and included in Article 8 *bis* of the Statute at a Review Conference in

---

[170] See Ambos 2013, pp. 19–22.

[171] See Ambos 2013, pp. 22–23.

[172] See Scheffer 2016.

[173] Werle and Jessberger 2020, p. 15.

[174] Werle and Jessberger 2020, p. 158–161; Ambos 2013, pp. 40–53; David 2009, pp. 910–927; Kastner 2018

[175] Ambos 2016, pp. 266–333; O´Keefe 2015, pp. 554–563; Lafontaine and Gagné 2018

[176] In 2010, this date was proclaimed as the World Day for International Justice.

[177] See Sadat 2016; David 2009, pp. 929–1002; De Vos 2018.

[178] See Joutsen 2011; Ambos 2016, pp. 1–4.

[179] Werle and Jessberger 2020, p. 602.

Kampala (Uganda), in 2010.[180] The same Review Conference adopted provisions regulating the exercise of jurisdiction with respect to the crime of aggression by the ICC (Articles 15 *bis* and 15 *ter*). The ICC jurisdiction with respect to the crime of aggression was activated on 17 July 2018.[181]

Pursuant to Article 34 of the Statute, the ICC consists of (a) the Presidency, (b) an Appeals Division, a Trial Division and a Pre-Trial Division, (c) the Office of the Prosecutor, and (d) the Registry.[182] The Court should normally have 18 Judges (Article 36(1)) "chosen from among persons of high moral character, impartiality and integrity who possess the qualifications required in their respective States for appointment to the highest judicial offices" (Article 36(3)(a)). They should have "established competence", respectively, in criminal law and procedure (Article 36(3)(b)(i)), and "in relevant areas of international law such as international humanitarian law and the law of human rights" (Article 36(3)(b)(ii)). Judges are elected from among nationals of the States Parties to the ICC Statute. In turn, the ICC Prosecutor and Deputy Prosecutors should be "persons of high moral character, be highly competent in and have extensive practical experience in the prosecution or trial of criminal cases. They [should] have an excellent knowledge of and be fluent in at least one of the working languages of the Court" (Article 42(3)). Finally, the Registry is "responsible for the non-judicial aspects of the administration and servicing of the Court" (Article 43(1)), and is headed by a Registrar (Article 43(2)). The Registrar and the Deputy Registrar should be "persons of high moral character, be highly competent and have an excellent knowledge of and be fluent in at least one of the working languages of the Court" (Article 43(3)). Article 44(1) provides that the Prosecutor and the Registrar "appoint such qualified staff as may be required to their respective offices. In the case of the Prosecutor, this [includes] the appointment of investigators". Now, the ICC has over 900 staff members from about 100 States.[183]

Since 2002, the ICC—and more generally, international criminal justice as such—attracted notable criticism, including from some of its prominent founders.[184] The most significant grounds for criticism included unwarranted length of the ICC proceedings, and their high cost.[185] Some members of the African Union were especially vocal in voicing their disapproving viewpoints about an alleged lack of impartiality in preliminary examinations, investigations and prosecutions.[186] The functionality of the Court is considerably weakened by reluctance on the part of

---

[180] Safferling 2011, pp. 252–265.

[181] Werle and Jessberger 2020, p. 603.

[182] Safferling 2011, pp. 272–275.

[183] See International Criminal Court 2021.

[184] See *passim* Bassiouni 2016.

[185] Bassiouni 2016, pp. 374–375.

[186] See Shilaho 2018. See also Clarke 2018.

22.5.5 *Indirect Enforcement of International Criminal Law*

The indirect enforcement of ICL is essential for at least two reasons. First, States are sovereign, and the enforcement of their domestic penal laws is one of the most important manifestations of their sovereignty. Second, whereas the earlier international criminal tribunals (e.g. the Nuremberg and Tokyo Tribunals, the ICTY, or the ICTR) had primary jurisdiction, the ICC´s jurisdiction already is complementary to the domestic systems of criminal justice, in recognition of States´ primary role in prosecuting individuals for the commission of the "core crimes" under international law and other crimes against the peace and security of mankind. A few notable domestic trials for crimes under international law took place since 1945,[191] as States took measures to implement ICL in their domestic laws and practices.[192] Most importantly, the General Part of ICL and the elements of relevant crimes should be included in the domestic Criminal Codes and other penal laws, in accordance with the principle of legality.[193] Next, law enforcement officials and judges should be trained on the proper application of ICL.[194] Last but not least, States´ bilateral and multilateral cooperation in penal matters should continually improve, with a view to effectively preventing, prosecuting and punishing individuals (and, where applicable, legal entities) for transnational crimes and crimes under ICL.

22.6 Transitional Justice

In the past few decades, several societies in Asia, Europe, Africa, and Latin America have notably transitioned from dictatorship, criminal or military violence to more peaceful and constructive ways of life.[195] Transition from dictatorship to democracy, or from war to peace, is difficult and requires that workable measures be taken, in order to make sure that the transition is efficient and irreversible. In a broad sense,

---

[187] See Sayapin 2016a.

[188] See Zhu 2019.

[189] See Sayapin 2016b.

[190] See Schabas 2004.

[191] Werle and Jessberger 2020, pp. 162–179. See also Lafontaine 2016, Sellars 2016.

[192] Werle and Jessberger 2020, pp. 179–204.

[193] Werle and Jessberger 2020, pp. 48–50.

[194] Sayapin 2020a, p. 46.

[195] Werle and Vormbaum 2018, pp. 159–299. See also Parmentier and Weitekamp 2011; Esparza 2011.

all such measures are referred to as "transitional justice".[196] In a narrow sense, transitional justice means a "toolkit" of five methods, which help come to terms with the past, and construct the future on the basis of the rule of law. These methods may be used individually or in combination, and the choice of methods for a specific society in transition depends on circumstances.

22.6.1 Penal Prosecutions

Penal prosecutions of the perpetrators of atrocity crimes, which are typical of dictatorial regimes, armed conflicts and other situations of violence is the most obvious modality of transitional justice.[197] Prosecutions are required by the interests of justice in favour of thousands, if not millions, of victims of crimes like genocide, crimes against humanity, war crimes, or of organised criminal groups. Perpetrators of such crimes are likely to be powerful figures–former politicians, military or social leaders, or criminal authorities—whose prosecutions may not have been possible under a previous regime, due to their status, influence, or wealth.[198] In this sense, the willingness and ability to hold such individuals liable for their past crimes is an important indicator of the new regime´s legitimacy and efficiency.

22.6.2 Amnesty

Practical considerations sometimes may lead the authorities in power to offer amnesty to selected perpetrators of the past crimes.[199] Although such a policy appears to endorse impunity, it is included in the transitional justice "toolkit" inasmuch as it is able to contribute to social reconciliation and a lasting peace (unlike prosecutions, which can aggravate the conflict).[200] Amnesties can be general or selective.[201] In the latter case, prosecutions are reserved for the masterminds of the crimes in question, and amnesty is offered to lower-ranking perpetrators, with due regard to their subordinate roles in the criminal activities.[202]

---

[196] Safferling 2011, p. 75; Parmentier 2016; Lambourne 2018

[197] Werle and Vormbaum 2018, pp. 43–65.

[198] See *passim* Lutz and Reiger 2009.

[199] Werle and Vormbaum 2018, pp. 67–81.

[200] Werle and Vormbaum 2018, p. 67.

[201] Ambos 2013, pp. 422–427.

[202] Cf. Article 6(5) of the Second Additional Protocol (1977) to the Geneva Conventions of 12 August 1949: " At the end of hostilities, the authorities in power shall endeavour to grant the broadest possible amnesty to persons who have participated in the armed conflict, or those deprived of their liberty for reasons related to the armed conflict, whether they are interned or detained".

22 Transnational and International Criminal Law

22.6.3 *Truth and Reconciliation Commission*

Truth and reconciliation commissions are alternatives to criminal prosecutions and / or amnesties in that they seek to establish peace by means of recording personal accounts about a conflict, and making those records accessible to the public.[203] The commissions are temporary fora where former political or military enemies, or victims and their relatives, on the one hand, and offenders, on the other hand, can share their perspectives on the past events, and by doing so, create a foundation for a future peace. They can be established by laws, governmental bylaws, or peace treaties.[204] The commissions´ final reports can also make recommendations relative to compensations or future political reforms.[205]

22.6.4 *Compensation*

According to Werle and Vormbaum,[206] compensation is a way "to recognise victims´ suffering, and to contribute to letting them overcome the incurred injuries".[207] It can take a variety of forms. *Restitution* means the re-establishment of a *status quo*, which existed before a violation (for instance, by returning works of art unlawfully exported during an international armed conflict).[208] *Compensation* in a direct, or narrow, sense of the term covers the material (for instance, the cost of medical and psychological treatment after torture) and moral damage sustained by a victim of a crime.[209] *Rehabilitation* includes medical and psychological support as well as measures such as repealing unlawful judgments.[210] *Satisfaction* encompasses official apologies and the installation of memorial sites.[211] Last but not least, *guarantees of non-repetition* involve institutional reforms such as the disarmament of weapon bearers, or the repealing of discriminatory laws,[212] with a view to outlawing previously permissible hostile practices.

---

[203] Werle and Vormbaum 2018, pp. 83–103.

[204] Werle and Vormbaum 2018, p. 88.

[205] Werle and Vormbaum 2018, p. 87.

[206] Werle and Vormbaum 2018, pp. 105–120.

[207] Werle and Vormbaum 2018, p 105.

[208] Werle and Vormbaum 2018, p. 107.

[209] Werle and Vormbaum 2018, p. 108.

[210] Werle and Vormbaum 2018, p. 108.

[211] Werle and Vormbaum 2018, p. 108.

[212] Werle and Vormbaum 2018, p. 108.

22.6.5 Lustration

Also known as *vetting*, lustration is a procedure whereby officials of a former dictatorial regime are screened with the aim of determining their eligibility to hold public office after the regime change.[213] As a rule, the procedure affects officials of the former government, law enforcement officials, judges, prosecutors but may also involve university professors and other education officials.[214] The ultimate goal of lustration consists in "purifying" the political system, in order to regain popular trust,[215] and making progressive institutional reforms irreversible.

22.7 Conclusion

Transnational and international criminal law and procedure have made ample progress since 1945, and now represent significant and functional bodies of law. States have responded to emerging security challenges by concluding some 300 multilateral treaties dealing with specific crimes as well as multilateral and bilateral treaties on international cooperation in penal matters, and this process is ongoing. For instance, the prospective adoption of a Convention on Crimes against Humanity would contribute to further consolidation of the international criminal law regime, and strengthen the indirect enforcement of ICL. With due regard to the International Criminal Court´s institutional limitations and its key principle of complementarity, the indirect—and regional–enforcement of ICL will remain a priority. For this, States should continue implementing the "core crimes" under international law and other violations of ICL in their domestic penal laws, and develop international cooperation in penal matters.

The ICC should work on its institutional limitations, in order to increase its efficiency and acceptance. In particular, ways should be identified to make the ICC more appealing to Muslim States. Also, for the time being, prospects for the Court´s cooperation with some of its most potent opponents—such as China, the United States, or Russia—remain bleak. Until the ICC is able to expand its jurisdictional reach to such States, it will not be truly "international".

Now, the world is facing challenges, which were not as pressing, or did not exist at all, in 1945 when modern transnational and international criminal law emerged– international terrorism, climate change, or cybercrime are just a few examples. States should learn using transnational criminal law and ICL, in conjunction with international human rights law, international humanitarian law, and other relevant bodies of law, to respond to such modern challenges quickly and efficiently. Traditionally, ICL was used to come to terms with the past, and thus, ICL´s repressive function

---

[213] Werle and Vormbaum 2018, pp. 121–138.

[214] See Bollag 1996.

[215] Werle and Vormbaum 2018, p. 124.

was prevailing. However, law also has preventive, deterrent and educative functions, and if we use ICL well today, we can contribute to building a safer and better future.

References

Abass A (2014) International Law: Text, Cases, and Materials, 2nd edn. Oxford University Press, Oxford.

Albanese JS (2011) Transnational Organized Crime. In: Natarajan M (ed) International Crime and Justice. Cambridge University Press, Cambridge, pp 231 – 238

Ambos K (2013) Treatise on International Criminal Law, Volume I: Foundations and General Part. Oxford University Press, Oxford

Ambos K (2014) Treatise on International Criminal Law, Volume II: The Crimes and Sentencing. Oxford University Press, Oxford

Ambos K (2016) Treatise on International Criminal Law, Volume III: International Criminal Procedure. Oxford University Press, Oxford

Atadjanov R (2019) Humanness as a Protected Legal Interest of Crimes Against Humanity:Conceptual and Normative Aspects. T. M. C. Asser Press, The Hague.

Badar ME (2015) The Concept of *Mens Rea* in International Criminal Law: The Case for a Unified Approach. Hart Publishing, Oxford

Barriga S (2011) The Crime of Aggression. In: Natarajan M (ed) International Crime and Justice. Cambridge University Press, Cambridge, pp 329–334.

Bassiouni MC (2003) Introduction to International Criminal Law. Transnational Publishers, Inc., Ardsley.

Bassiouni MC (2008a) International Crimes: The Ratione Materiae of International Criminal Law. In: Bassiouni MC (ed) International Criminal Law, Volume I: Sources, Subjects and Contents, 3rd edn. Koninklijke Brill NV, Leiden, pp 129–203.

Bassiouni MC (2008b) The Discipline of International Criminal Law. In Bassiouni MC (ed) International Criminal Law Volume I: Sources, Subjects and Contents, 3rd edn. Koninklijke Brill NV, Leiden, pp 3–40.

Bassiouni MC (2008c) The Regulation, Control, and Prohibition of the Use of Certain Weapons in the Context of War. In: Bassiouni MC (ed) International Criminal Law Volume I: Sources, Subjects and Contents, 3rd edn. Koninklijke Brill NV, Leiden, pp 377 – 401

Bassiouni MC (2011) Crimes Against Humanity: Historical Evolution and Contemporary Application, Cambridge University Press, Cambridge

Bassiouni MC (2016) Challenges to International Criminal Justice and International Criminal Law. In: Schabas WA (ed) The Cambridge Companion to International Criminal Law. Cambridge University Press, Cambridge, pp 353–391.

Bassiouni MC, Ferencz B (2008) The Crime Against Peace and Aggression: From Its Origins to the ICC. In: Bassiouni MC (ed) International Criminal Law Volume I: Sources, Subjects and Contents, 3rd edn. Koninklijke Brill NV, Leiden, pp 207–242.

Bollag B (1996) Germany Restructures Universities Once Under Communist Control. https://www.chronicle.com/article/germany-restructures-universities-once-under-communist-control/. Accessed 24 February 2021.

Clark RS (2008a) Apartheid. In: Bassiouni MC (ed) International Criminal Law Volume I: Sources, Subjects and Contents, 3rd edn. Koninklijke Brill NV, Leiden, pp 599–620.

Clark RS (2008b) The Crime of Aggression and the International Criminal Court. In: Bassiouni MC (ed) International Criminal Law Volume I: Sources, Subjects and Contents, 3rd edn. Koninklijke Brill NV, Leiden, pp 243–265.

Clarke KM (2018) Rethinking liberal legality through the African Court of Justice and Human Rights: re-situating economic crimes and other enablers of violence. In: Kastner P (ed) International Criminal Law in Context. Routledge, Abington, New York, pp 170–196.

Cryer R, Friman H, Robinson D, Wilmshurst E (2014) An Introduction to International Criminal Law and Procedure, 3rd edn. Cambridge University Press, Cambridge.

Dannenbaum T (2018) The Crime of Aggression, Humanity, and the Soldier. Cambridge University Press, Cambridge.

David É (2009) Éléments de droit pénal international et europeén. Bruylant, Brussels.

DeFeo MA (2008) Hostage Taking and Kidnapping as Forms of Terror Violence. In: Bassiouni MC (ed) International Criminal Law Volume I: Sources, Subjects and Contents, 3rd edn. Koninklijke Brill NV, Leiden, pp 751–778.

Derby DH (2008) The International Prohibition of Torture. In: Bassiouni MC (ed) International Criminal Law Volume I: Sources, Subjects and Contents, 3rd edn. Koninklijke Brill NV, Leiden, pp 621–657.

De Vos CM (2018) The International Criminal Court: between law and politics. In: Kastner P (ed) International Criminal Law in Context, Routledge, Abington, New York, pp 240–259.

Dickinson LA (2008) Mercenarism and Private Military Contractors. In: Bassiouni MC (ed) International Criminal Law Volume I: Sources, Subjects and Contents, 3rd edn. Koninklijke Brill NV, Leiden, pp 355–375.

Draft Code of Crimes against the Peace and Security of Mankind with commentaries (1996) Yearbook of the International Law Commission, vol II (Part Two), pp 17–56.

Draft Code of Offences against the Peace and Security of Mankind with commentaries (1951) Yearbook of the International Law Commission, vol II, pp 133–137.

El-Dawla AS (2008) Effects of Contemporary International Obligations for Combating the Financing of Terrorism on Interstate Cooperation in Criminal Matters. In: Bassiouni MC (ed) International Criminal Law Volume I: Sources, Subjects and Contents, 3rd edn. Koninklijke Brill NV, Leiden, pp 3–40.

Esparza M (2011) The Guatemala Truth Commission: Genocide through the Lens of Transitional Justice. In: Natarajan M (ed) International Crime and Justice. Cambridge University Press, Cambridge, pp 400–408.

Ferencz BB, Ferencz DM (2016) Criminalising the Illegal Use of Force. In: Schabas WA (ed) The Cambridge Companion to International Criminal Law. Cambridge University Press, Cambridge, pp 230–252.

Geiß R, Lahmann H (2021) Protecting Societies – Anchoring a new protection dimension in international law during armed conflict: An agenda for discussion. https://www.ejiltalk.org/protecting-societies-anchoring-a-new-protection-dimension-in-international-law-during-armed-conflict-an-agenda-for-discussion/?utm_source=mailpoet&utm_medium=email&utm_campaign=ejil-talk-newsletter-post-title_2. Accessed 24 February 2021.

Graycar A (2011) Corruption. In: Natarajan M (ed) International Crime and Justice. Cambridge University Press, Cambridge, pp 215–222.

Grey R (2018) Sexual and gender-based crimes. In: Kastner P (ed) International Criminal Law in Context. Routledge, Abington, New York, pp 130–148.

Halberstam M (2008) International Maritime Navigation and Installation on the High Seas. In: Bassiouni MC (ed) International Criminal Law Volume I: Sources, Subjects and Contents, 3rd edn. Koninklijke Brill NV, Leiden, pp 815–829.

Henderson I (2011) The Firebombing of Tokyo and Other Japanese Cities. In: Tanaka Y, McCormack [author, insert initial(s)], Simpson [author, insert initial(s)] (eds) Beyond Victor´s Justice? The Tokyo War Crimes Trial Revisited. Koninklijke Brill NV, Leiden, pp 311–321.

International Criminal Court (2021) Facts and Figures. https://www.icc-cpi.int/about. Accessed 23 February 2021.

Joutsen M (2011) Legal Traditions. In: Natarajan M (ed) International Crime and Justice. Cambridge University Press, Cambridge, pp 67–74.

Joyner CC, Friedlander RA (2008) International Civil Aviation. In: Bassiouni MC (ed) International Criminal Law Volume I: Sources, Subjects and Contents, 3rd edn. Koninklijke Brill NV, Leiden, pp 831–851.

Kapstein H (2011) Apartheid. In: Natarajan M (ed) International Crime and Justice. Cambridge University Press, Cambridge, pp 314–320.

Kastner P (2018) Hybrid tribunals: institutional experiments and the potential for creativity within international criminal law. In: Kastner P (ed) International Criminal Law in Context. Routledge, Abington, New York, pp 221–239.

Lafontaine F (2016) National Jurisdictions. In: Schabas WA (ed) The Cambridge Companion to International Criminal Law. Cambridge University Press, Cambridge, pp 155–177.

Lafontaine F, Gagné S (2018) Complementarity revisited: national prosecutions of international crimes and the gaps in international law. In: Kastner P (ed) International Criminal Law in Context. Routledge, Abington, New York, pp 260–279.

Lambourne W (2018) The idea of transitional justice: international criminal justice and beyond. In: Kastner P (ed) International Criminal Law in Context. Routledge, Abington, New York, pp 46–67.

Leggett T (2011) Transnational Firearms Trafficking: Guns for Crime and Conflict. In: Natarajan M (ed) International Crime and Justice. Cambridge University Press, Cambridge, pp 133–140.

Lemkin R (2008) Axis Rule in Occupied Europe: Laws of Occupation, Analysis of Government, Proposals for Redress, 2nd edn. The Lawbook Exchange, Ltd., Clark, New Jersey.

Leroy B, Bassiouni MC, Thony JF (2008) The International Drug Control System. In: Bassiouni MC (ed) International Criminal Law Volume I: Sources, Subjects and Contents, 3rd edn. Koninklijke Brill NV, Leiden, pp 855–905.

Lippman M (2008) Genocide. In: Bassiouni MC (ed) International Criminal Law Volume I: Sources, Subjects and Contents, 3rd edn. Koninklijke Brill NV, Leiden, pp 403–435.

Lovely R (2011) Cybercrime. In: Natarajan M (ed) International Crime and Justice. Cambridge University Press, Cambridge, pp 155–161.

Lukashuk II (2008) Mezhdunarodnoye pravo: Obshaya chast [International Law: General Part]. Wolters Kluwer, Moscow.

Lutz EL, Reiger C (eds) (2009) Prosecuting Heads of State. Cambridge University Press, Cambridge.

Mackenzie S (2011) Trafficking Antiquities. In: Natarajan M (ed) International Crime and Justice. Cambridge University Press, Cambridge, pp 141–147.

May L (2005) Crimes Against Humanity: A Normative Account. Cambridge University Press, Cambridge.

May L (2007) War Crimes and Just War. Cambridge University Press, Cambridge.

May L (2008) Aggression and Crimes against Peace. Cambridge University Press, Cambridge.

May L (2010) Genocide: A Normative Account. Cambridge University Press, Cambridge.

Mayroz E (2018) Genocide: to prevent and punish ´radical evil´. In: Kastner P (ed) International Criminal Law in Context. Routledge, Abington, New York, pp 69–90.

McCaffrey SC (2008) Criminalization of Environmental Protection. In: Bassiouni MC (ed) International Criminal Law Volume I: Sources, Subjects and Contents, 3rd edn. Koninklijke Brill NV, Leiden, pp 1013–1035.

Moir L (2008) Non-International Armed Conflict and Guerrilla Warfare. In: Bassiouni MC (ed) International Criminal Law Volume I: Sources, Subjects and Contents, 3rd edn. Koninklijke Brill NV, Leiden, pp 323–354.

Nafziger JAR (2008) Protection of Cultural Property. In: Bassiouni MC (ed) International Criminal Law Volume I: Sources, Subjects and Contents, 3rd edn. Koninklijke Brill NV, Leiden, pp 977–1011.

Natarajan M (2011) Drug Trafficking. In: Natarajan M (ed) International Crime and Justice. Cambridge University Press, Cambridge, pp 109–117.

Newman GR, Clarke RV (2011) Terrorism. In Natarajan (ed), International Crime and Justice. Cambridge University Press, Cambridge, pp 290–298.

O´Keefe R (2015) International Criminal Law. Oxford University Press, Oxford.

Parmentier S (2016) Transitional Justice. In: Schabas WA (ed) The Cambridge Companion to International Criminal Law. Cambridge University Press, Cambridge, pp 52−72.

Ormerod D, Laird K (2015) Smith and Hogan´s Criminal Law, 14th edn. Oxford University Press, Oxford.

Parmentier S, Weitekamp E (2011) The Truth and Reconciliation Commission in South Africa. In: Natarajan M (ed) International Crime and Justice. Cambridge University Press, Cambridge, pp 393−399.

Nollez-Goldbach R (2018) Crimes against humanity: the concept of humanity in international law. In: Kastner P (ed) International Criminal Law in Context. Routledge, Abington, New York, pp 91−108.

Quénivet N, Shah-Davis S (2010) Confronting the Challenges of International Law and Armed Conflict in the 21st Century. In Quénivet N, Shah-Davis S (eds) International Law and Armed Conflict: Challenges in the 21st Century. T. M. C. Asser Press, The Hague, pp 3−30.

Richmond S (2018) The crime of aggression: shifting authority for international peace? In: Kastner P (ed) International Criminal Law in Context. Routledge, Abington, New York, pp 149−169.

Sadat L (2016) The International Criminal Court. In: Schabas WA (ed) The Cambridge Companion to International Criminal Law. Cambridge University Press, Cambridge, pp 137–154.

Sadoff DA (2016) Bringing International Fugitives to Justice: Extradition and Its Alternatives. Cambridge University Press, Cambridge

Safferling C (2011) Internationales Strafrecht: Strafanwendungsrecht—Völkerstrafrecht − Europäisches Strafrecht. Springer, Berlin/Heidelberg

Sandgren C (2008) Corruption of Foreign Public Officials. In: Bassiouni MC (ed) International Criminal Law Volume I: Sources, Subjects and Contents, 3rd edn. Koninklijke Brill NV, Leiden, pp 963–976.

Sandoz Y (2008) Penal Aspects of International Humanitarian Law. In: Bassiouni MC (ed) International Criminal Law Volume I: Sources, Subjects and Contents, 3rd edn. Koninklijke Brill NV, Leiden, pp 293–321

Sands Ph (2016) East West Street: On the Origins of Genocide and Crimes against Humanity. Weidenfeld & Nicolson, London.

Sayapin S (2008) A Great Unknown: the Definition of Aggression Revisited. Michigan State Journal of International Law 17:375–398.

Sayapin S (2009) Raphael Lemkin: a Tribute. EJIL 20:1157–1162.

Sayapin S (2010) The Compatibility of the Rome Statute's Draft Definition of the Crime of Aggression with National Criminal Justice Systems. Revue internationale de droit pénal 81:165–188.

Sayapin S (2014) The Crime of Aggression in International Criminal Law: Historical Development. Comparative Analysis and Present State, T. M. C. Asser Press, The Hague.

Sayapin S (2015) The United Nations General Assembly Resolution 68/262 in the Context of General International Law. Evropsky politicky a pravni diskurz 2:19–30.

Sayapin S (2016a) A "Hybrid" Tribunal for Daesh? https://www.ejiltalk.org/a-hybrid-tribunal-for-daesh/. Accessed 23 February 2021.

Sayapin S (2016b) Russia's Withdrawal of Signature from the Rome Statute Would not Shield its Nationals from Potential Prosecution at the ICC. https://www.ejiltalk.org/russias-withdrawal-of-signature-from-the-rome-statute-would-not-shield-its-nationals-from-potential-prosecution-at-the-icc/. Accessed 21 February 2021.

Sayapin S (2018) A Curious Aggression Trial in Ukraine: Some Reflections on the *Alexandrov and Yerofeyev* Case. JICJ 16:1093–1104.

Sayapin S (2019a) The General Principles of International Criminal Law in the Criminal Code of the Republic of Kazakhstan. Asian Journal of International Law 9:1–9.

Sayapin S (2019b) The Crime of Aggression in the African Court of Justice and Human and Peoples' Rights. In: Jalloh CC, Clarke KM, Nmehielle VO (eds) The African Court of Justice and Human and Peoples' Rights in Context: Development and Challenges, Cambridge University Press, Cambridge, pp 314–335.

Sayapin S (2020a) Crimes against the Peace and Security of Mankind in the Revised Edition of the Criminal Code of the Republic of Uzbekistan, RCEEL 45:36–58.

Sayapin S (2020b) The *Yanukovych* Trial in Ukraine: A Revival of the Crime of Aggression?" Israel Yearbook on Human Rights 50:63–79.

Sayapin S (2020c) Why a Crimes against Humanity Convention from a Perspective of Post-Soviet States? African Journal of International Criminal Justice 6:125–135.

Sayapin S, Tsybulenko E (2018) The Use of Force against Ukraine and International Law: Jus Ad Bellum, Jus In Bello, Jus Post Bellum. T. M. C. Asser Press, The Hague.

Schabas W (2004) United States Hostility to the International Criminal Court: It´s All About the Security Council. EJIL 15:701–720

Schabas W (2018) The Trial of the Kaiser. Oxford University Press, Oxford

Scheffer D (2016) The United Nations Security Council and International Criminal Justice. In: Schabas WA (ed) The Cambridge Companion to International Criminal Law. Cambridge University Press, Cambridge, pp 178–195.

Schloenhardt A (2008) Transnational Organized Crime and International Criminal Law. In: Bassiouni MC (ed) International Criminal Law Volume I: Sources, Subjects and Contents, 3rd edn. Koninklijke Brill NV, Leiden, pp 939–962.

Sellars K (ed) (2016) Trials for International Crimes in Asia. Cambridge University Press, Cambridge.

Shelley L (2011) The Globalization of Crime. In: Natarajan M (ed) International Crime and Justice. Cambridge University Press, Cambridge, pp 3–10.

Shilaho WK (2018) The International Criminal Court and the African Union: Is the ICC a bulwark against impunity or an imperial Trojan horse? https://www.accord.org.za/ajcr-issues/the-intern ational-criminal-court-and-the-african-union/. Accessed 23 February 2021.

Sneh I (2011) History of Genocide. In: Natarajan M (ed) International Crime and Justice. Cambridge University Press, Cambridge, pp 306–313.

Stephens D, Wooden T (2018) War crimes: increasing compliance with international humanitarian law through international criminal law? In: Kastner P (ed) International Criminal Law in Context. Routledge, Abington, New York, pp 109–129.

Sundberg JWF (2008) The Crime of Piracy. In: Bassiouni MC (ed) International Criminal Law Volume I: Sources, Subjects and Contents, 3rd edn. Koninklijke Brill NV, Leiden, pp 799–813.

Tanaka Y (2011) The Atomic Bombing, the Tokyo Tribunal and the *Shimoda* Case: Lessons for Anti-Nuclear Legal Movements. In: Tanaka Y, McCormack Tanaka Y, McCormack TLH, Simpson G (eds) Beyond Victor´s Justice? The Tokyo War Crimes Trial Revisited. Koninklijke Brill NV, Leiden, pp 293–310

Vlassis D (2008) Challenges in the Development of International Criminal Law: The Negotiations of the United Nations Convention Against Transnational Organized Crime and the United Nations Convention Against Corruption. In: Bassiouni MC (ed) International Criminal Law Volume I: Sources, Subjects and Contents, 3rd edn. Koninklijke Brill NV, Leiden, pp 907–937.

Waters TW (2018) The ad hoc tribunals: image, origins, pathways, legacies. In: Kastner P (ed) International Criminal Law in Context. Routledge, Abington, New York, pp 199–220.

Weisbord N, Reyes C (2011) War Crimes. In: Natarajan M (ed) International Crime and Justice. Cambridge University Press, Cambridge, pp 321–328

Werle G, Jessberger F (2020) Principles of International Criminal Law, 4th edn. Oxford University Press, Oxford.

Werle G, Vormbaum M (2018) Transitional Justice: Vergangenheitsbewältigung durch Recht. Springer, Berlin.

White R (2011) Transnational Environmental Crime. In: Natarajan M (ed) International Crime and Justice. Cambridge University Press, Cambridge, pp 193–199.

Zhu D (2019) China, the International Criminal Court, and Global Governance. Australian Journal of International Affairs 73:585–608.

Sergey Sayapin LLB, LLM, Dr. iur., PhD is an Associate Professor and Associate Dean at the School of Law, KIMEP University (Almaty, Kazakhstan). In 2000–2014, he held various posts at the Communication Department of the Regional Delegation of the International Committee of the Red Cross (ICRC) in Central Asia. His current research focuses on Central Asian and post-Soviet approaches to international law, international and comparative criminal law, human rights, and sociology of law. Dr. Sayapin regularly advises the Central Asian Governments as well as UNODC and the ICRC on international and criminal law, and has recently joined Chatham House´s expert pool. He is sub-editor for Central Asia of the Encyclopedia of Public International Law in Asia (Brill, 2021).

Chapter 23
International Anti-corruption Law

Thomas Kruessmann

Contents

23.1 Introduction 504
23.2 Overview of the Main Sources 505
    23.2.1 International Law 505
    23.2.2 Pledges, Commitments and "Leading by Example" 507
    23.2.3 National Law with Extraterritorial Effect 508
    23.2.4 Anti-corruption Compliance 508
23.3 Overview of Relevant Case Law 510
    23.3.1 Petty Corruption 510
    23.3.2 Corruption in the Corporate Realm 510
    23.3.3 Grand Corruption and the Proposal for an International Anti-Corruption
        Court 512
    23.3.4 Specialized National Anti-corruption Courts 512
23.4 New Developments Resulting from Current Challenges, and Possible Ways
    Forward 513
    23.4.1 Integrity and the Emphasis on Ethics 513
    23.4.2 Collective Action 514
    23.4.3 Enhancing Transparency, Publicity and Open Access to Information 516
    23.4.4 Whistleblower Protection 518
    23.4.5 Public Procurement Rules 520
    23.4.6 Infrastructure Development 521
23.5 Conclusion 523
References 524

Abstract Anti-corruption law has been on the agenda of states, international organizations and national prosecutors and regulators for several decades. It has now become an independent force, no longer relying on international law-making, but on initiatives of a variety of stakeholders and cross-stakeholder action. After giving a short introduction into the legal developments leading up to the United Nations Convention against Corruption, this chapter will focus on the concepts of integrity, collective action and compliance as "next generation" approaches to anti-corruption. Its main argument is that we are seeing anti-corruption becoming increasingly submerged into a broader sustainability approach.

T. Kruessmann (✉)
King's College London, London, UK

Global Europe Centre, University of Kent, Canterbury, UK

© T.M.C. ASSER PRESS and the authors 2022
S. Sayapin et al. (eds.), *International Conflict and Security Law*,
https://doi.org/10.1007/978-94-6265-515-7_23

Keywords Petty vs. grand corruption · Compliance · Collective action · Integrity

23.1 Introduction

The relationship between international anti-corruption law and international conflict and security law, as the overall title of this work goes, is not quite as straightforward as it might seem. Growing inequalities, massive welfare losses and the deteriorating legitimacy of ruling regimes all lead to conflict and insecurity. From this point of view, corruption is one of the root causes of the crises that we are witnessing in our days. This point is all the easier to make since the definition of corruption has been expanding over the past couple of decades, from straightforward (transactional) bribery to the abuse of entrusted power for private gain, as the most influential definition currently holds.[1] We are now seeing corruption in a number of practices that either do not meet straightforward definitions of criminal law (e.g. nepotism) or that are usually conceptualized as economic crime outside the traditional corruption context (e.g. embezzlement, fraud).

To understand the impact of corruption on international conflict and security,[2] it is worthwhile to look at it from the point of view of distinguishing petty and grand corruption. Again, while these are not legal terms, it is most often understood that petty corruption is characterized by its situational and occasional type of occurrence, with a generally low monetary value of the financial benefit involved. Petty corruption in this sense can be the *ad hoc* offering of a bribe to a police officer; it can also be the culturally accepted practice of giving gifts to doctors or teachers in recognition of their services. However, there is a slippery slope, as can be seen in many countries with high levels of corruption. Traffic police might follow the expectation that police administration is generally tolerant of police officers "milking" drivers to make up for their meagre wages, customs officers develop a "legitimate expectation" that extra money is going to be paid to facilitate their services, and hospital staff will only offer minimal services if no advance "gratification" is paid to them. In many similar scenarios, the occurrence of corruption is no longer *ad hoc* and situational, but systemic and structural. While perhaps still in the category of "petty corruption", it develops like a cancer and infects the fabric of society, creating the expectation that there is just no alternative to paying bribes.

Grand corruption, on the other hand, refers to kleptocratic regimes which are often autocratic, illegitimate (with elections, if at all, frequently manipulated) and which rely on coopting relevant parts of the business and/or security communities into their criminal schemes. There are hosts of examples for such types of governance which are repressive at heart, but pretend to be modernizing forces, guaranteeing stability

---

[1] Thanks to the work of Transparency International, this definition of corruption is currently the most widely used one. Since there is no *a priori* definition of corruption, the issue is continually in flux and has helped to sharpen our attention to the breadth of corruptive practices.

[2] For perspectives on a number of more detailed interrelationships, e.g. corruption-terrorism, please see the literature review at Ferguson 2017, pp. 1–12.

and development (albeit on a modest scale). Grand corruption in this sense is deeply structural, and even a regime change is no guarantee that the incoming elites are not likewise corrupt.

Using the distinction between petty and grand corruption, it is clear that grand corruption is a potent source of international conflict and insecurity. Petty corruption, by comparison, often acts like an extra tax on business, but it has a deeply demoralizing effect. While drowning in a sea of petty corruption, people get used to the fact that those in power are "stealing", and the "stealing" on top only gives them the moral conviction that "stealing" in their own small world is an acceptable practice. Therefore, so-called politicians are no longer held to account, but given *card blanche* to engage in the policies that stabilize their own regimes and modes of power. The result may appear to be an autocratic version of stability, but with no legitimacy and accountability. As experience shows, such supposedly "stable" regimes can swiftly deteriorate into conflict and insecurity.

When it comes to the specific role of international law in the movement against corruption, the aforementioned distinction has a direct bearing: international law describes the legal obligations primarily between states. However, a large number of states are run by kleptocratic regimes with no functioning division of powers. Those regimes might find reasons to ratify anti-corruption conventions if they are not hurting vested interests, or they might even find it useful to have a legal framework of anti-corruption offenses in place if ever the need arises to stage purges against illoyal members of the business elite or political competitors. But it is hard to imagine that kleptocratic regimes will sign up to the type of obligations that will effectively judge their own behaviour. Interestingly, while the mainstream anti-corruption conventions have been ratified even by the most corrupt regimes, a number of non-legal initiatives such as the Open Government Partnership or the Extractive Industries Transparency Initiative have shown real "teeth" and provoked a lot of contestation from regimes that do not want to follow them.

With this assumption in mind, let us turn to an overview of the main international law sources and their effects in practice. Ultimately, when it comes to international conflict and security, there are arguably more innovative ways of counteracting corruption than using law and the courts and/or regulatory action.

23.2 Overview of the Main Sources

23.2.1 International Law

When looking at the sources of what can be described as the movement towards one global anti-corruption norm,[3] international law is certainly an important pillar, but by far not the most dynamically developing one. Over the past 30 years, the United

---

[3] Gutterman and Lohaus 2018, p. 241.

States have been a very influential agenda-setter for developing a network of anti-corruption conventions in various regional fora, ultimately leading to the adoption and entry into force of the United Nations Convention against Corruption (UNCAC) in December 2005.

The 1977 U.S. Foreign Corrupt Practices Act (FCPA) stands at the beginning of this anti-corruption movement and is still driving it to a large extent. Originally adopted as a reaction to the Watergate Scandal and the realization that U.S. corporations had been using bribery both domestically and abroad with practically no limits,[4] U.S. lawmakers made it an offence for certain classes of persons and entities connected to the U.S. to make payments to foreign government officials to assist in obtaining or retaining business. This prohibition lies at the heart of the changes that rocked the legal landscape in anti-corruption during the following decades.

Following a storm of protest from U.S. companies who pointed out that bribing foreign public officials to gain government contracts abroad was a standard practice at the time, the U.S. Government vowed that it would embark on a major foreign policy initiative to establish anti-bribery norms in all relevant regional systems and also on the universal level. The first and most straightforward result of this initiative was the adoption of the so-called OECD Anti-Bribery Convention which entered into force in 1999,[5] followed by the 2009 Recommendation for Further Combating Bribery.[6] Beyond this somewhat narrow focus on bribing foreign public officials, the U.S. was instrumental in creating more broadly framed regional conventions against corruption (including, *inter alia*, bribery, but going significantly beyond), such as the Inter-American Convention against Corruption[7] adopted in 1996, the Council of Europe Criminal Law Convention against Corruption[8] and the Civil Law Convention against Corruption,[9] both adopted in 1999, and the African Union Convention on Preventing and Combating Corruption,[10] adopted in 2003. And finally, it was UNCAC that became the crowning achievement of this foreign policy agenda.

Arguably, the dynamics of this movement follow the same script: a policy agenda is rolled out that sets in train a series of diplomatic activities, negotiations, adoption and opening up for signature, finally a race to collect the required number of ratifications from states to have the convention enter into force, followed by a shift of attention to the level of domestic implementation. As it is uncommon to agree a system of sanctions for non-implementation, most of the recent conventions, particularly from the Council of Europe family, have created specific follow-up mechanisms such

---

[4] For more details, see Gorman 2015.

[5] OECD Convention on Combating Bribery of Foreign Public Officials in International Business Transactions. For details see <http://www.oecd.org/corruption/oecdantibriberyconvention.htm>. Accessed 18 June 2020.

[6] For details, see the commentary by Pieth et al. 2014.

[7] See <http://oas.org/juridico/english/corr_bg.htm>. Accessed 18 June 2020.

[8] See <https://rm.coe.int/168007f3f5>. Accessed 18 June 2020.

[9] <https://rm.coe.int/168007f3f6>.

[10] See <https://au.int/en/treaties/african-union-convention-preventing-and-combating-corruption>. Accessed 18 June 2020.

23 International Anti-Corruption Law 507

as monitoring rounds.[11] These rounds, often focusing on one or the other issue, ask states to report on their level of implementation, dispatch monitoring missions that also hear shadow reports from relevant civil society organizations, and compile reports that are again replied to by the respective state. These reporting mechanisms are important for giving civil society a voice, and they are generally built on the principle of "naming and shaming". It is perhaps overly optimistic to expect a race to the top, as states are hardly ambitious to excel in fulfilling their obligations. But by and large, the mechanism is useful in pinpointing weaknesses and creating "reminders" how to improve a situation. For kleptocratic regimes, such rounds of reporting are often uncomfortable, but compared to human rights reporting which is generally more aggressive, the anti-corruption benchmarking is an exercise that can reliably be weathered by a certain amount of window-dressing.

23.2.2 Pledges, Commitments and "Leading by Example"

To address the slow fulfilment of anti-corruption obligations under international law, in 2010 a new force entered the scene. Never before had the G8 or G20 committed themselves to anti-corruption. But when the summit in Seoul arrived, the world's leading economies were ready to throw their weight behind the topic, calling for the ratification and implementation of UNCAC, enforcement of laws against foreign bribery, international cooperation in preventing illicit flows into G20 financial markets, tracing and recovering stolen assets and for the protection of whistleblowers. The G20 Working Group on Anti-Corruption (ACWG) which had been established earlier, presented its first Anti-Corruption Action Plan to cover the years 2011–12. It was agreed that fulfilment of this action plan was to be monitored by the ACWG and that henceforth all G20 countries would annually submit their progress under the relevant action plan to the G20 summit. Since then, the ACWG has prepared a number of monitoring and accountability reports. Also, the action plans which were proposed for every two years were complemented by implementation plans to make progress in implementation measurable.[12]

While not creating new obligations under international law, the G20 summits help to produce pledges and commitments that are keenly remembered and measured up against reality by the various civil society organisations in the field. A similar effect can be noted for the London Anti-Corruption Summit in May 2016.[13] Although it

---

[11] The leading example in the Council of Europe system is the Group of States against Corruption (GRECO), see <https://www.coe.int/en/web/greco>. Accessed 18 June 2020. UNCAC, by contrast, relies on the Conference of State Parties (Article 63 UNCAC).

[12] The various documents are scattered over the various dedicated websites created for every G20 summit. A useful collection is presented by the German Federal Ministry of Justice at <https://www.bmjv.de/DE/Themen/G20/G20_node.html>. Accessed 18 June 2020.

[13] <https://www.gov.uk/government/topical-events/anti-corruption-summit-london-2016/about>. Accessed 18 June 2020.

was effectively a one-time event, the Summit helped to galvanize action in a variety of fields.[14]

23.2.3 National Law with Extraterritorial Effect

A second important pillar of the anti-corruption movement is national law. The FCPA inspired lawmakers around the world to adopt laws that go beyond what is needed to merely implement one of the international law prescriptions. Examples include the 1999 Canadian Corruption of Foreign Public Officials Act,[15] the 2010 United Kingdom Bribery Act,[16] China's 2011 and 2015 anti-bribery amendments to its Criminal Law,[17] India's 2013 Lokpal and Lokayuktas Act to combat corruption,[18] the 2014 Brazil Clean Company Act[19] and France's 2016 Act on Transparency, the Fight Against Corruption and Modernization of Economic Life, commonly called the "Sapin II" Act.[20] Following the example of the FCPA, some of these laws have a transnational effect in that they also attach to relevant conduct abroad, e.g. bribing a foreign public official, if the perpetrator is connected to the mother jurisdiction of the statute. For companies, incorporation in the relevant jurisdiction is typically not required. Instead, the statute will attach if the company decides to issue securities in the relevant jurisdiction, mostly by trading on one of the local stock exchanges.

23.2.4 Anti-corruption Compliance

A third important pillar of the anti-corruption movement rests on corporate practice. Often summarized by the term "compliance", it is a state of art in corporate governance that has been significantly pushed by the enforcement practice of the

---

[14] The Summit was also outside the regular series of International Anti-Corruption Conferences, held every two years by a broad coalition of stakeholders of the anti-corruption movement. For details, see <https://iaccseries.org/>. Accessed 18 June 2020.

[15] Corruption of Foreign Public Officials Act, S.C. 1998, c 34, see <https://laws-lois.justice.gc.ca/eng/acts/C-45.2/page-1.html>. Accessed 18 June 2020.

[16] See <https://www.legislation.gov.uk/ukpga/2010/23/contents>. Accessed 18 June 2020.

[17] Criminal Law of the People's Republic of China, pt 2, ch VIII (Crimes of Embezzlement and Bribery) (adopted at the Second Session of the Fifth National People's Congress on 1 July 1979, amended 25 February 2011); and Criminal Law of the People's Republic of China Amendment 9 (promulgated 29 Aug. 2015). But see also Tso (2018) on the lack of practical relevance.

[18] The Lokpal and Lokayuktas Act (2013) No 1 of 2014, India Code (rev 29 July 2016).

[19] Law No 12.846 (1 August 2013). The Act took effect in January 2014, and thus is commonly referred to as the 2014 Statute.

[20] See <https://www.legifrance.gouv.fr/affichTexte.do?cidTexte=JORFTEXT000033558528&categorieLien=id>. Accessed 18 June 2020.

23 International Anti-Corruption Law

FCPA, but essentially goes further and embraces many other dimensions of corporate behaviour. It intersects with the work of the UN when opening up UNCAC, placing anti-corruption among the 10 principles of the UN Global Compact[21] and also including anti-corruption in the Sustainable Development Goals.[22]

At the core of this development is the corporate governance of anti-corruption. Arguably, the enforcement practice of the FCPA is the most important driver of compliance standards in the sphere of anti-corruption. Enforcement practice in this context does not only mean the absolute number of FCPA investigations that were launched by the competent regulators, i.e. the U.S. Department of Justice and the Securities and Exchange Commission.[23] It means first and foremost the elaboration of a set of standards that companies can use to defend themselves against the accusation that they have been negligent in permitting bribery abroad to happen. Over the years, the FCPA Corporate Enforcement Policy[24] has thus created minimum standards for an anti-corruption compliance management system. Nowadays, there is an entire industry devoted to ABC ("anti-bribery and corruption"), dozens of conferences across the world are offered every month to discuss the latest practices in anti-corruption, and the FCPA Blog has established itself as the premier forum for sharing new developments.[25]

To summarize, over the past decades there has been a remarkable wave of activity addressing the issue of corruption. Starting with a rather narrow focus on prohibiting the bribery of foreign public officials, it has broadened to include prohibitions of other types of corruption and, most importantly, has shifted its focus from repression to prevention, including strengthening the role of civil society and a desire to place anti-corruption into the wider context of corporate governance.

In the public domain, adoption of UNCAC marks both a moment of achievement and of saturation. It defines a certain turning point in that a normative state of the art has been attained that plays the ball back into the court of national lawmakers who are tasked with implementing the various tools. It is probably fair to say that UNCAC has absorbed by and large all the standard features of the regional anti-corruption conventions that had been created earlier, and that it offers a substantial degree of flexibility for national lawmakers to consider the peculiarities of their national law or matters of national policy.[26] There are perhaps only two areas in which UNCAC has been posing real challenges to national legal systems: by asking states to make illicit

---

[21] "Principle 10. Businesses should work against corruption in all its forms, including extortion and bribery".

[22] "Goal 16. Promote peaceful and inclusive societies for sustainable development, provide access to justice for all and build effective, accountable and inclusive institutions at all levels".

[23] This number has been steadily increasing, with a significant jolt in 2005/2006. See <https://www.sec.gov/spotlight/fcpa/fcpa-cases.shtml>. Accessed 18 June 2020.

[24] See <https://www.justice.gov/jm/jm-9-47000-foreign-corrupt-practices-act-1977>, last amended in April 2019. Accessed 18 June 2020.

[25] <http://www.fcpablog.com/>. For a more academic, yet also highly influential blog, see the Global Anticorruption Blog at <https://globalanticorruptionblog.com/>. Both accessed 18 June 2020.

[26] See, in general, Rose et al. 2019.

enrichment a crime[27] and by calling for the criminal liability of legal persons.[28] Otherwise, the provisions are fairly standard, but still innovative in that UNCAC places a special emphasis on the idea of prevention rather than on repression and that it gives civil society significant legitimacy to involve itself in anti-corruption.

In the private, i.e. corporate, domain, the FCPA enforcement practice has created an industry that has spawned ever more standards. A leading role is currently played by the International Organization for Standardization (ISO) which has been prolific in codifying the existing state of art into coherent systems for standardization such as ISO 37001 "Anti-bribery management systems". ISO itself does not certify its own standards. Instead, there is an industry providing certification both for corporations and also for individuals desiring to become recognized as compliance officers. By and large, there are now more than a dozen different standards available on the market.

23.3 Overview of Relevant Case Law

23.3.1 Petty Corruption

In the area of petty corruption, there is generally not much litigation because cases of gift giving and gratification often go unnoticed or are dealt with below the threshold of criminal intervention (i.e. in a corporate setting a reprimand may be issued to an employee). Cases involving the bribery of public officials are more serious and regularly end up in criminal courts, but apart from evidentiary issues there is, as a rule, no legal novelty involved.

23.3.2 Corruption in the Corporate Realm

In the corporate realm, corruption cases very often do not make it into court, but for entirely different reasons. If corruption occurs between the parties of a contract (for example in fulfilling a certain obligation, a party to the contract uses an intermediary while taking kickbacks), it is first and foremost between the parties to settle the situation. The International Chamber of Commerce since 2012 offers the so-called "ICC Anti-Corruption Clause"[29] to be included into contracts which effectively makes the ICC Rules of Combating Corruption 2011 applicable to the agreement. The gist of this mechanism is that the party that has engaged in corruption is asked to undertake remedial action, otherwise there will be a right to suspend or even terminate the contract. When conflicts around incidences of corruption cannot be settled directly

---

[27] Article 20 UNCAC.

[28] Article 26 UNCAC.

[29] <https://iccwbo.org/publication/icc-anti-corruption-clause/>. Accessed 18 June 2020.

23 International Anti-Corruption Law

between the parties, they usually do not go into courts, but into arbitration. There, the allegation of corruption (among other illegal acts) poses specific problems for the arbitrators. Not only do they lack the support of law enforcement agencies and coercive measures. They must also be wary that bringing the allegation of corrupt practices can be an easy way to skirt obligations. On the other hand, if substantiated, it is difficult to find a proportionate response in light of the goodwill and investment of the parties undertaken so far.[30] The results of arbitration are, as a rule, confidential so that a wider discussion of the adopted solutions is often not possible.

If corruption cases go into court, there is a tendency in the jurisdictions influenced by Anglo-American law to use deferred or non-prosecution agreements to settle the issue by asking the perpetrator to pay a fine and accept remedial action, for instance the obligation to install a compliance management system and accept a monitoring for a certain period of time.

Very rarely do corruption cases get adjudicated. One example, and one which has had an enormous effect in the German world of compliance, was the so-called Siemens/Neubürger decision of *Landgericht München I*.[31] In the wake of the Siemens corruption scandal, the Siemens supervisory board in January 2008 claimed compensation from its former executive managers and simultaneously offered the possibility of reaching settlements. This route was taken by two former chief executive officers and seven other ex-managers. Among them, the former Chief Executive Officer Heinrich von Pierer agreed to pay 5 Mio. Euros in settlements. A settlement of 4 Mio. Euros was offered to the former Chief Financial Officer, Heinz-Joachim Neubürger. However, Neubürger refused, claiming that he did not violate any relevant duties. Siemens then sued Neubürger for 15 Mio. Euros damages and won this claim in full. As a result, Neubürger committed suicide.

In its decision, *Landgericht München*, I developed a comprehensive view of what anti-bribery compliance precautions had to be taken under German corporate law. Although due to a later settlement with the family of Neubürger the decision was not appealed and thus never made it to the *Bundesgerichtshof*, it stands out as a *de facto* precedent and wake-up call for the entire corporate world in Germany.[32] At the heart is the demand for a risk-based compliance system which fully corresponds to the international state of art.

---

[30] For guidelines, see the „Toolkit for Arbitrators", prepared by the Basel Institute on Governance and its Competence Centre Arbitration and Crime, available at <https://arbcrime.org/>. Accessed 18 June 2020.

[31] Fleischer 2014, p. 345.

[32] For a discussion, see Fleischer 2014, p. 321; Hauschka 2018, p. 159.

23.3.3 Grand Corruption and the Proposal for an International Anti-Corruption Court

Grand corruption is characterized by a large amount of impunity. While ruling regimes are in power, they reliably protect themselves from any legal challenge, and even when representatives of such regimes go into retirement they often procure the necessary provisions in the constitutions of their countries that give them indemnity. It is only in those rare moments when a kleptocratic regime gets overthrown that its representatives can be brought to justice. Most often, however, they manage to escape, find safe havens in some other countries and have their wealth so reliably channelled through offshores that it is next to impossible to reach the proceeds of their corruptive crimes.

Legally, there is no international court that could take up corruption-related charges. The International Criminal Court (ICC) in The Hague, under its Rome Statute, is not competent to hear issues of grand corruption. Recently, U.S. Federal Judge Mark L. Wolf started a campaign to create an International Anti-Corruption Court (IACC),[33] and there is quite a movement of governments, primarily from Latin America, and civil society organizations which support his campaign. Critics mostly sympathize with the idea, but consider it too far from reality. They argue that the case of the ICC has shown how contentious the idea of fighting impunity on the international level is. Even if politically there could be a relevant majority of states to create the IACC, it would be much harder to prosecute corruption allegations due to the different type of crime and the evidentiary problems related to it.[34]

23.3.4 Specialized National Anti-corruption Courts

Relevant case law may originate from specialized anti-corruption courts. So far, a number of countries have experimented with either specialized prosecution authorities and/or specialized divisions in established courts, in a few cases also creating specialized anti-corruption courts. So far, not a single "best practice" has emerged,[35] and the cases decided are invariably tied to the national context.

---

[33] Wolf 2014.

[34] See, for instance, Whiting 2018.

[35] Stephenson and Schütte 2016.

23.4 New Developments Resulting from Current Challenges, and Possible Ways Forward

23.4.1 Integrity and the Emphasis on Ethics

One recent development is to couch anti-corruption compliance in terms of an integrity paradigm.[36] In the traditionally repressive approaches to anti-corruption, there is little concern for the motivation of the culprit and only a superficial analysis why he or she has succumbed to the temptation of offering or taking bribes or engaging in other types of corruptive behaviour. The criminal law perspective on guilt is simply too limited, as it only asks about knowledge and volition.

The concept of integrity goes deeper and asks why somebody has engaged in corruptive practices. One very fruitful approach is to study conflicts of interest and to visualize (e.g., by heat-mapping) areas in which conflicts of interest are more likely to occur than in others. This is also where principal-agent-analysis comes in and the environment in which decisions are taken can be scrutinized. Even more advanced approaches adopt a behavioural perspective on the nature of man and use nudging techniques instead of prohibitions to motivate people towards the desired behaviour.

While the foundations of the integrity paradigm thus rest on the social sciences (cultural anthropology, behaviourism) and lead to a number of highly diversified proposals, there is one approach that can be considered mainstream: to advance integrity by reinforcing the concept of ethics, either in the form of business ethics or of public administration ethics.

The OECD in 2017 published a set of public integrity recommendations that represents the so far most comprehensive standard in operationalizing the idea of ethics in a public administration setting. The recommendations take a decidedly holistic perspective and postulate a coherent integrity system (commitments, responsibilities, strategy, standards), accompanied by a culture of public integrity and effective accountability.[37]

Interestingly, while research into business ethics goes back to the seminal work of Werner Sombart and Max Weber, linking the spirit of capitalism to Protestantism, Calvinism and Quakerism,[38] there is little we know about the spirit of capitalism in the 20th century from an anti-corruption perspective. From an unregulated "free for all" in the early decades of the 20th century to the post WWII notions of a social market economy where individual economic activity contributes to the public good, there appears to be the unashamed idea of (very often male) loyalty in profit-making at any cost, vaguely hidden behind the noble goals that the market economy was supposed to be serving. Arguably, beyond the early years of capitalism when markets were not so developed yet, engaging in corruptive behaviour has always

---

[36] See, for instance, Integrity Action 2015.

[37] OECD 2017a.

[38] Weber 1904/05.

been in the genetic make-up of capitalism, much like the Soviet "rational" project of central planning cannot be explained without the undercurrent of corruption. It is therefore research into rationalization strategies of persons involved in corruption that opens up fascinating views into the sense of identity that the protagonists have and how they see themselves in their social world.[39] It is also the entry point for the most important tool of counteracting such perspectives: the code of conduct.

Nowadays, there is hardly a company that does not have its own code of conduct. It is a standard practice to ask employees to sign up to such codes and to send them to workshops and e-learning trainings in which the essence of ethical behaviour is explained. It is also a standard feature to demand a "tone from the top", i.e. a commitment from the top management to the same corporate values and mission statements that employees are asked to sign up to.

Recent research[40] has shown, however, that the ethical orientation of a company (or of a public entity) is not a given and that codes of conduct are often not efficiently implemented. While marketing specialists are paid to present the value-orientation of a company in corporate brochures and on websites with generic staff pictures, employees are often routinely sent to trainings where they are taught to "tick the right boxes". Despite recognition that the "tone from the top" is an important element, too many codes of conduct come across as tools for drilling employees while not addressing executive management and/or the board of directors in an equal manner. Such lack of reach is noticed by employees immediately, and it often undermines the efficiency of the codes when it comes to preventing employees from devising their own rationalization strategies.

A second recent finding was that some messages of the codes of conduct exist in a cultural void. For example, while preaching non-harassment, companies fail to realize the goals of diversity and inclusiveness in their hiring practice.[41]

Apart from reinforcing values and counteracting rationalization strategies, codes of conduct are also important in creating an atmosphere in which whistleblowing becomes an accepted practice. The topic will be discussed below, but apart from technicalities it is obvious that only when a company's ethical foundations are clearly explained, an employee may find the courage to act on this knowledge and to go against the superiors who may materially affect his or her own well-being in the company.

23.4.2 Collective Action

Collective action is the next most important rallying cry for the anti-corruption community. It is currently promoted by the UN Global Compact under the afore-mentioned Principle 10 as a way of escaping from the prisoner's dilemma in which

---

[39] Tsang 2002.

[40] Bulgarella 2019.

[41] Ibid.

23 International Anti-Corruption Law

companies often find themselves when individually desiring to act against corruption while competing in the market place. In the UN's understanding, it is a tool to encourage companies to team up and build coalitions with the goal of

- creating a deeper understanding of corruption issues;
- consolidating knowledge and financial and technical resources to achieve greater impact;
- creating solutions that are perceived as more credible, acceptable and are more sustainable;
- helping to ensure fair competition and a level playing field for all stakeholders;
- creating a more stable and enabling business environment;
- complementing existing anti-corruption efforts in vulnerable regions and sectors, where industry or government-led regulations are not robust.[42]

In the Basel Institute on Governance's understanding, the focus of collective action is slightly different. Following the World Bank Institute's earlier definition,[43] it holds that collective action involves multi-stakeholder initiatives, bringing together the private and public sectors, civil society and international organizations.[44] The following are common types of collective action approaches:

- Anti-corruption declarations as short-term, project- or transaction-specific statements of intent to ensure compliance with anti-corruption commitments. Companies, governments and/or sub-contractors can all be signatories of an Anti-Corruption Declaration.
- Integrity Pacts are short-term, project-or transaction-specific formal agreements between a customer (usually a public entity) and a bidder (usually a company) in which the parties agree to adhere to a fair and transparent public procurement bidding process.
- Certifying Business Coalitions can be applicable to a country, region or sector. To join, a company must show a clear commitment to anti-corruption principles and adhere to ethical business standards. Regular independent audits and monitoring processes ensure compliance.

The Basel Institute on Governance is host to the B20 Collective Action Hub[45] which is the most comprehensive resource in the field of collective action.

The most visible result of collective action strategies so far is the development of a tool called High-Level Reporting Mechanism (HLRM). The idea of the HLMR is to create a multi-stakeholder alliance around the demand side of corruption, to target bribery solicitations and other unfair practices affecting business. It is designed to achieve the following aims:

---

[42] See <https://www.unglobalcompact.org/take-action/action/anti-corruption-collective-action>. Accessed 18 June 2020.

[43] World Bank Institute 2008.

[44] See <https://www.baselgovernance.org/collective-action>. Accessed 18 June 2020.

[45] See <https://www.collective-action.com/>. Accessed 18 June 2020.

- receive complaints of bribery requests or suspicious behaviour in interactions between businesses and governments, such as in the context of public procurement, issuance of commercial licences, customs clearance or tax-related issues, among many other potential applications as determined by each country;
- function as an alternative dispute resolution mechanism, with the advantage of not incurring operation costs to complainants that resort to it;
- identify systemic issues arising from recurring corruption claims and propose reforms to the government.[46]

So far, HLRMs have been created in Argentina, Colombia, Panama, Peru and Ukraine,[47] focusing mostly on situations of public procurement where there is a temptation for procuring agencies to use tender procedures to extract illegal benefits from bidders.

23.4.3 Enhancing Transparency, Publicity and Open Access to Information

As the flowers of corruption blossom in the dark, there is a common understanding that creating publicity, access to information and transparency are the most important tools in creating accountability and preventing corruption. Freedom of information legislation patterned on the U.S. Freedom of Information Act is now a common feature in many jurisdictions of the world, but the governments' instincts still tend to favour secrecy when it comes to so-called state interests, in particular in the area of national security. The so-called Tshwane Principles[48] therefore represent an important initiative to define the legal contours of national security exceptions when it comes to the right to information.

To bring together likeminded governments and push forward the idea of openness in government, in 2011 the so-called Open Government Partnership (OGP) was created.[49] It currently has 79 member states and collaborates with thousands of civil society organisations. Upon joining, a government endorses the Open Government Declaration, pledging, *inter alia*, to promote transparency, fight corruption, empower citizens, and harness the power of new technologies to make government more effective and accountable.[50] Governments will then work with civil society to co-create two-year action plans with commitments across a broad range of issues. Finally, there is an Independent Reporting Mechanism which monitors all action plans to ensure governments follow through on their commitments. Civil society and government

---

[46] OECD 2017b.

[47] Silva and Aiolfi 2018.

[48] Open Society Justice Initiative 2013.

[49] See <https://www.opengovpartnership.org/>. Accessed 18 June 2020.

[50] See <https://www.opengovpartnership.org/process/joining-ogp/open-government-declaration/>. Accessed 18 June 2020.

23 International Anti-Corruption Law

leaders use the evaluations to reflect on their own progress and determine if actions have made an impact.

In the area of anti-corruption, OGP currently focuses on the following three issues:

- beneficial ownership;
- money in politics;
- open contracting and procurement.

In comparison to OGP which covers a range of corruption-related issues, there are also a number of government-run initiatives striving to establish standards in particular sectors of the economy. The most well-known one is the Extractive Industries Transparency Initiative (EITI), describing itself as the global standard to promote the open and accountable management of extractive resources.[51] EITI currently has 52 member states; in each member state it is supported by a coalition of government, industry and civil society. At the heart of EITI is the so-called EITI Standard, now in its 2019 edition.[52] It requires information along the extractive industry value chain from the point of extraction to how the revenue makes its way through the government and its contribution to the economy. This includes how licenses and contracts are allocated and registered, who the beneficial owners of those operations are, what the fiscal and legal arrangements are, how much is produced, how much is paid, where the revenue is allocated, and its contributions to the economy, including employment. Every country goes through a quality-assurance mechanism, called validation, at least every three years. Validation serves to assess performance towards meeting the EITI Standard and promote dialogue and learning at the country level. It also safeguards the integrity of the EITI by holding all EITI implementing countries to the same global standard.

A second, slightly less well-known initiative is the Infrastructure Transparency Initiative (CoST).[53] It currently works in 14 countries; compared to EITI it has a stronger multi-stakeholder character, but again combining governments, businesses and civil society. The CoST approach is focused on four core features: disclosure, assurance, multi-stakeholder working and social accountability. At the heart of this system is the CoST Infrastructure Data Standard (CoST IDS) which is a system of 40 data points to be disclosed at key stages of an infrastructure project cycle including: identification, preparation, completion, procurement and implementation. The information thus disclosed goes into an independent review by assurance teams based within the CoST national programmes. The teams identify key issues of concern in relation to the items listed in the CoST IDS and put technical jargon into plain language. This allows social accountability stakeholders to easily understand the issues and hold decision-makers to account.

---

[51] See <https://eiti.org>. Accessed 18 June 2020.

[52] See <https://eiti.org/document/eiti-standard-2019-0>. Accessed 18 June 2020.

[53] See <http://infrastructuretransparency.org>. Accessed 18 June 2020.

23.4.4 Whistleblower Protection

Openness and transparency are values in anti-corruption which have a game-changing quality. The same values when applied to organizations (both private and public) are discussed when it comes to encouraging people to report on violations that they may have come across as staff, public servant, etc. The demand to implement whistleblower legislation has recently acquired a strong momentum, but it has also encountered a number of difficulties. We earlier mentioned that in the corporate setting and in public administration whistleblowing is tightly connected to the idea of codes of conduct and a culture of integrity. However, legislation is called upon to establish reliable systems and prevent individual organizations from arbitrarily defining their own approaches.

On the global level, both UNCAC and the G20 Action Plan against Corruption call upon states to establish legal frameworks for whistleblower protection, leading to the G20 Anti-Corruption Action Plan "Protection of Whistleblowers" adopted in 2017.[54] Earlier in the European context, the Council of Europe's Criminal Law Convention against Corruption had imposed an obligation "to provide effective and appropriate protection", but the provision lacked the necessary details.[55] Clarifications were only provided by the 2014 Committee of Ministers Recommendation (2014)7 which includes 29 Principles and an Explanatory Memorandum.[56]

Without going into the details of these different recommendations and their applicability in different cultural settings, the international discussions have recently crystallized around the European Commission's proposal to adopt a Directive "On the protection of persons reporting on breaches of Union law".[57] While limited to Union law and thus not applicable to national law governing the various public and private organizations, the proposal has elicited a large number of comments and position papers not only from the anti-corruption community, but also from labor rights representatives, employers' unions and so on.

There is one line of criticism that is particularly relevant in the given context of openness and transparency. It is the human rights perspective seen from which whistleblowing is an act of freedom of expression, protected both by Article 19 of the International Covenant on Civil and Political Rights (ICCPR) and Article 10 of the European Convention on Human Rights (ECHR). As such, any system of whistleblowing limiting or discouraging the reporting would have to be justified (provided by law and necessary, including being proportionate) in the interest of the rights and reputations of others, for the protection of national security, public order

---

[54] See <https://www.oecd.org/g20/topics/anti-corruption/48972967.pdf>. Accessed 18 June 2020.

[55] Article 22 Criminal Law Convention: "Each Party shall adopt such measures as may be necessary to provide effective and appropriate protection for: a) those who report the criminal offences established in accordance with Articles 2 to 14 or otherwise co-operate with the investigating or prosecuting authorities; b) witnesses who give testimony concerning these offences".

[56] See <https://rm.coe.int/16807096c7>. Accessed 18 June 2020.

[57] COM(2018)218 final.

23 International Anti-Corruption Law

or of public health and morals.[58] However, in the version of the Directive that went into first reading of the European Parliament on 16 April 2019, Article 3(2) is fairly rigorous in giving Member states the possibility to curtail whistleblowing with regard to national security and essential security interests.

In an earlier letter dated 5 March 2019, the UN Special Rapporteur on the promotion and protection of the right to freedom of opinion and expression, together with the OSCE Representative of Freedom of the Media, criticized[59] the Directive's lack of sensitivity in giving room to proportionality, even advocating that reporting on certain matters such as criminal offences and human rights or international humanitarian law violations, corruption, public safety and environmental harm and abuse of public office should presumptively always be in the public interest.[60] The later version of the Directive that went into first reading with the European Parliament did not follow up on this suggestion. On the contrary, in the very important area of procurement it even takes the opposite view. It mandates that the Directive shall not apply to reports on breaches of procurement rules involving defence or security aspects, "unless they are covered by the relevant instruments of the European Union".[61]

A second issue that has created lively discussions was whether the Directive would insist on requiring whistleblowers first to report internally (or to use a dedicated external channel) before going public. Public disclosure, seen as the most straightforward way of using one's freedom of expression, has raised a lot of eyebrows, and there have been many attempts to limit the Directive's protection to those whistleblowers who follow the course of internal reporting first. The compromise found in the Directive's version that went into first reading is that public disclosure while maintaining the protection of the Directive is possible only under two circumstances: either the whistleblower has exhausted internal and external reporting channels without having received an answer within three months unless there is a risk of retaliation, or the whistleblower turns to public disclosure directly, having reasonable grounds to believe that the breach may constitute an imminent or manifest danger for the public interest.[62] Needless to say, this latter version, although quite reasonably phrased, will still produce a chilling effect.

---

[58] Article 19(3) ICCPR. See also the slightly different wording of Article 10(2) ECHR.

[59] In summarizing his criticisms, the UN Special Rapporteur referred to his earlier report to the UN General Assembly in the context of whistleblowing. See UN General Assembly Doc. A/70/361 of 8 September 2015.

[60] See <https://freedex.org/wp-content/blogs.dir/2015/files/2019/03/OL-OTH-11.2019-1.pdf>. Accessed 18 June 2020.

[61] Article 3(2) Draft Directive.

[62] Article 15(1) b) Draft Directive.

23.4.5 Public Procurement Rules

In the preceding sections, we have repeatedly made references to public procurement (e.g., regarding the HLRM). Indeed, there is a significant share of GDP going every year into public procurement[63] and governments are most vulnerable to fraudulent practices and corruption. Recent initiatives like the "One Belt One Road" policy as well as the EU's Europe-Asia Connectivity scheme have shifted the attention to public procurement needed for infrastructure investment even more. So, fighting corruption in public procurement is an imperative that becomes stronger day by day.

The traditional approach in international law is expressed by Article 9 UNCAC which calls for State Parties, in accordance with fundamental principles of their legal systems, "to establish appropriate systems of procurement, based on transparency, competition and objective criteria in decision-making, that are effective, inter alia, in preventing corruption". Beyond this principled approach, Article 9(1) UNCAC contains a system of detailed prescriptions for the pre-bidding, bidding and post-bidding stage. The Article 9 UNCAC provisions are taken up by the 2015 OECD Recommendations on Public Procurement which is the most comprehensive guide on the topic to date. In addition, on its dedicated website[64] the OECD carries a wide array of best practice examples and research into different country models of procurement.

One new development that has been gathering strength over the years and is now coming to the fore is the involvement of the World Trade Organization (WTO) in anti-corruption. The United States, when implementing their anti-corruption agenda, had for a variety of reasons[65] left out trade negotiations and focused instead on the OECD and a variety of regional fora, leading to UNCAC. In trade circles, the dominant understanding was that the WTO had already been doing its share in anti-corruption by promoting transparency and efficiency in getting rid of unclear regulations and "red tape" in customs procedures. In 1996, the Singapore Ministerial Conference even commissioned a working group to conduct a study on transparency in government procurement practices, but the idea of negotiating a "Transparency in Government Procurement Agreement" (T-GPA) was put aside by WTO member states in 2003/04.

Obviously, the idea of limiting anti-corruption to transparency was not sustainable. Several years later, in re-negotiating the 1994 Government Procurement Agreement (GAP),[66] proposals were put on the table that the WTO should confront corruption head-on. The result was the 2012 (Revised) Government Procurement Agreement which entered into force in 2014. It is a plurilateral agreement, meaning that not all WTO members are parties. At present, the Agreement has 20 parties comprising (due to the EU's membership) 48 WTO members. Another 34 WTO members/observers

---

[63] According to the OECD, this is 12 % of GDP in the OECD countries. See <http://www.oecd.org/gov/public-procurement/>. Accessed 18 June 2020.

[64] Ibid.

[65] For a background, see Silveira 2019.

[66] WTO, Agreement on Government Procurement [GPA], Art. XIV (7)(b) (1994).

23 International Anti-Corruption Law 521

participate in the GPA Committee as observers. Out of these, 9 members are in the process of acceding to the Agreement.[67]

In the Revised GPA, anti-corruption is covered in two distinct provisions. On the one hand, in the Agreement's Preamble, the parties realize "the importance of transparent measures regarding government procurement, of carrying out procurement in a transparent and impartial manner and of avoiding conflicts of interest and corruptive practices, in accordance with applicable instruments such as the United Nations Convention against Corruption." On the other hand, Art. IV (4) sets out:

"A procuring entity shall conduct covered procurement in a transparent and impartial manner that:

(a) is consistent with this Agreement, using methods such as open tendering, selective tendering and limited tendering;

(b) avoids conflicts of interest; and

(c) prevents corrupt practices".

In the literature there are strong voices arguing that Art. IV (4) is not a stand-alone provision, but must be interpreted in light of the relevant provisions in the Preamble of the Agreement.[68] This would lead to including not only the explicitly mentioned UNCAC, particularly Article 9 mentioned above, but also the OECD Anti-Bribery Convention as the second most important "applicable instrument". Furthermore, it would be logical to infer that breaches of UNCAC[69] or the OECD Anti-Bribery Convention in procurement situations could be raised in the WTO dispute settlement mechanism as breaches of Art. IV (4). So far, however, there have obviously been no attempts to test this mechanism.

23.4.6 Infrastructure Development

While public procurement can be used by governments from purchasing pencils to awarding multi-billion contracts for infrastructure projects, certain additional anti-corruption features come into play when the procurement is done by multilateral development banks (MDBs). Inspired by the example of the World Bank,[70] the major MDBs in 2006 agreed a "Uniform Framework for Preventing and Combating Fraud and Corruption".[71] This Framework includes, on the hand, the creation of a Joint International Financial Institutions (IFI) Anti-Corruption Task Force to work towards

---

[67] See <https://www.wto.org/english/tratop_e/gproc_e/memobs_e.htm>. Accessed 18 June 2020.

[68] Lo 2015; Schefer 2013. See also Anderson et al. 2011.

[69] Lo 2015, p. 40.

[70] Jenkins 2016.

[71] See e.g. <https://www.adb.org/publications/uniform-framework-preventing-and-combating-fraud-and corruption>, accessed 18 June 2020. Participating institutions include the African Development Bank Group, Asian Development Bank, European Bank for Reconstruction and Development, European Investment Bank Group, International Monetary Fund, Inter-American Development Bank Group and the World Bank Group.

a consistent and harmonized approach to combatting corruption in the activities and operations of the member institutions. On the other hand, it provides for harmonized definitions of fraudulent and corrupt practices, to be used in investigations of activities financed by the member institutions. Corruption, for example, is defined as the "offering, giving, receiving, or soliciting, directly or indirectly, anything of value to influence improperly the actions of another party". The other prohibited practices are fraud, collusion and coercion. When the 2006 Uniform Framework was agreed, it was merely anticipated that the participating MDBs would implement the harmonized definitions in their relevant policies and procedures, creating in due course a coherent approach to integrity due diligence. Already in 2010, the seven participating MDBs went one step further and concluded an Agreement on Mutual Enforcement of Debarment Decisions.[72] Specifically, the parties agreed that any decision by one of them to debar an entity or individual for a minimum period of one year based on the harmonized elements of prohibited practices will be enforced by the others ("cross-debarment"). The Agreement reserves the right for each participating MDB to pursue independent debarment proceedings and does not exclude concurrent, consecutive and subsequent periods of debarment.

It could be argued that debarment is the analogue to the death penalty in development finance. With its exclusively punitive character it does not support the rehabilitation of the offender, in particular to make him act more compliantly in the future. Therefore, it has become usual practice to limit debarment to a minimum and engage in negotiated settlements instead. Similar to FCPA enforcement, the purpose is to create incentives to introduce good corporate practices. In the World Bank Group's sanctions system, there are now five types of sanctions: (1) debarment either unlimited or for a certain period of time; (2) debarment with conditional release; (3) conditional non-debarment; (4) restitution; and (5) reprimand.[73]

Interestingly, while most MDBs follow this same philosophy, there is still no agreement on harmonizing the types of sanctions below the level of debarment. Another weakness is that the major MDBs are still unable (for data privacy reasons?) or unwilling to pool their data beyond the list of cross-debarred persons or entities to create a comprehensive data warehouse that would enable tools based on big data and artificial intelligence (AI) to search for suspicious information ("red flags"). There is a strong interest among MDBs, particularly by the World Bank Group,[74] to use data mining to capture fraud and corruption risks in procurement. The recent EIB Anti-Corruption Conference that took place in December 2018 devoted an entire session to so-called Proactive Integrity Reviews (PIRs). In the EIBs own experience, PIRs are based on a so-called Fraud Risk Scoring Model that contains 30 fraud risk

---

[72] See, e.g., <https://www.adb.org/sites/default/files/institutional-document/32774/files/cross-debarment-agreement.pdf>. Accessed 18 June 2020.

[73] For details, see Dubois et al. 2018, p. 139.

[74] See the interview with Stephen Zimmermann, Senior Advisor to the Governance Global Practice Group, World Bank, at <https://www.youtube.com/watch?v=c-0CEp6_bRk&list=PLYRnhpCcnLP_7VAlWBv24_BAbj_1HMxlU&index=5> at 2:07. Accessed 18 June 2020.

factors.[75] It appears however that PIRs are more useful in the area of anti-fraud than in anti-corruption, perhaps due to the fact that fraud leaves a better paper trail while corruption can only be risk-flagged by detecting erratic or abnormal decision-making. In any case, anti-corruption will profit from PIRs, and the broadly cut definition of corruption will help in that the border lines to fraud are not acutely felt.

23.5 Conclusion

No doubt, anti-corruption has become a mature field in public policy. It has evolved over time and there is now a clear agreement that there is not a single "silver bullet" that can kill the problem. As the participants of the high-level segment of the 18th International Anti-Corruption Conference in October 2018 aptly explained, "We want to highlight that long term, systemic and comprehensive anti-corruption efforts at local, national and international levels continue to be critical for progress".[76]

Looking at the developments described in the preceding sections, it is now also obvious that anti-corruption is becoming increasingly submerged in a sustainability paradigm. Strikingly, the UN 2030 Agenda for Sustainable Development does no longer contain anti-corruption as an explicit item among the Sustainable Development Goals (SDGs). Instead, anti-corruption appears under SDG 16.5: "Substantially reduce corruption and bribery in all their forms." The same happens in other areas. The UN are now promoting a Sustainable Stock Exchanges Initiative (SSE)[77] that encourages stock exchanges to provide listed companies with guidance on reporting on environmental, social and governance issues (ESG reporting). The idea is to establish ESG reporting as a key reference for investors, with governance including also information on anti-corruption.

Anti-corruption is thus elevated to a higher level, more strategically integrated into long-term developments and more clearly established among the incentives to guide the markets. As with climate change, what is needed is not the eradication of an isolated evil, but a substantial re-thinking of the way we do business. Like the so-called peace dividend after WWII, there could be an anti-corruption dividend when imaging that huge fortunes of money and resources could be turned into profitable investments instead of disappearing into the pockets of corrupt politicians and businessmen.

---

[75] European Investment Bank 2019, p. 20.

[76] <https://iaccseries.org/wp-content/uploads/2018/10/High-Level-Joint-Statement-IACC-2018.pdf>. Accessed 18 June 2020.

[77] See <https://sseinitiative.org/>. Accessed 18 June 2020.

References

Anderson RD, Kovacic WE, Müller AC (2011) Ensuring Integrity and Competition in Public Procurement Markets: A Dual Challenge for Good Governance. In: Arrowsmith S, Anderson RD (eds) The WTO Regime on Government Procurement: Challenge and Reform. Cambridge University Press, Cambridge, pp 681–718

Bulgarella C (2019) Do Modern Codes of Conduct Help Cause and Conceal Unethical Behavior? FCPA Blog of 16 July 2019, available at <http://www.fcpablog.com/blog/2019/7/16/do-modern-codes-of-conduct-help-cause-and-conceal-unethical.html>. Accessed 18 June 2020

Dubois, PH, Fielder JD, Delonis R, Fariello F, Peters K (2018) The World Bank's Sanctions System: Using Debarment to Combat Fraud and Corruption in International Development. AIIB Yearbook of International Law 129–142

European Investment Bank (2019) Fraud Investigations. Activity Report 2018, available at <https://www.eib.org/en/publications/fraud-investigations-activity-report-2018>. Accessed 18 June 2020

Ferguson G (2017) Global Corruption: Law, Theory and Practice, 2nd edn. United Nations Office of Drugs and Crime, Vienna

Fleischer H (2014) Aktienrechtliche Compliance-Pflichten im Praxistest: Das Siemens/Neubürger-Urteil des LG München I. Neue Zeitschrift für Gesellschaftsrecht 321–329, available at <https://rsw.beck.de/zeitschriften/nzg>. Accessed 19 February 2022

Gorman T (2015) The Origins of the FCPA: Lessons for Effective Compliance and Enforcement. Securities Regulation Journal 43–66

Gutterman E, Lohaus M (2018) What is the „Anti-corruption Norm" in Global Politics? In: Kubbe I, Engelbert A (eds) Corruption and Norms, Political Corruption and Governance. Palgrave Macmillan, Cham, pp 241–268

Hauschka CE (2018) Fünf Jahre Siemens-Entscheidung des LG München I. Corporate Compliance Zeitschrift 159–162

Integrity Action (2015) Live and Work with Integrity! You Can Do It, available at <https://integrityaction.org/publication/live-and-work-integrity-you-can-do-it>. Accessed 18 June 2020

Jenkins M (2016) Multilateral Development Banks' Integrity Management Systems. U4 Query No. 5 of 14 September 2016, Chr.Michelsen Institute, Bergen

Lo C-F (2015) Making the Anti-Corruption Provisions in the New Government Procurement Agreement under the WTO Operable. Trade Law and Development VII:1, 21–41

OECD (2017a) Recommendation of the Council on Public Integrity "Public Integrity", Paris, available at <http://www.oecd.org/gov/ethics/recommendation-public-integrity/>. Accessed 18 June 2020

OECD (2017b) The High Level Reporting Mechanism. A Tool to Prevent Bribery and Related Practices, Paris, available at <http://www.oecd.org/corruption/High-Level-Reporting-Mechanism-Overview.pdf>. Accessed 18 June 2020

Open Society Justice Initiative (2013) The Global Principles on National Security and the Right to Information (The Tshwane Principles), available at <https://www.justiceinitiative.org/publications/global-principles-national-security-and-freedom-information-tshwane-principles>. Accessed 18 June 2020

Pieth M, Low LA, Bonucci N (2014) The OECD Convention on Bribery. A Commentary. Cambridge University Press, Cambridge

Rose C, Kubiciel M, Landwehr O (2019) The United Nations Convention against Corruption: A Commentary. Oxford University Press, Oxford

Silva V, Aiolfi G (2018) High Level Reporting Mechanisms. A Comparative Analysis: Argentina, Colombia, Ukraine, Panama and Peru. International Centre for Collective Action/OECD, Basel/Paris

Schefer KN (2013) Will the WTO Finally Tackle Corruption in Public Purchasing? The Revised Agreement on Government Procurement, insights 17:11 of 15 April 2013, available at <https://asil.org/insights/volume/17/issue/11/will-wto-finally-tackle-corruption-public-purchasing-revised-agreement>. Accessed 18 June 2020

Silveira L (2019) Can the WTO Bring More Teeth to the Global Anticorruption Agenda? Journal of World Trade 53,1: 129–152

Stephenson M, Schütte SA (2016) Specialized Anti-Corruption Courts: A Comparative Mapping, Chr.Michelsen Institute, U4 Issue No. 7, December 2016, available at <https://www.u4.no/public ations/specialised-anti-corruption-courts-a-comparative-mapping.pdf>. Accessed 18 June 2020

Tsang J-A (2002) Moral Rationalization and the Integration of Situational Factors and Psychological Processes in Immoral Behavior. Review of General Psychology 6:1, 25–50

Tso J (2018) It's Time for China to Show Its Foreign Bribery Law is not a Paper Tiger. Global Anti-corruption Blog of 14 May 2018, available at <https://globalanticorruptionblog.com/2018/05/14/its-time-for-china-to-show-its-foreign-bribery-law-is-not-a-paper-tiger/>. Accessed 18 June 2020

Weber M (1904/05) Die protestantische Ethik und der Geist des Kapitalismus. Archiv für Sozialwissenschaften und Sozialpolitik vol. XX and XXI

Whiting A (2018) Is an International Anti-Corruption Court a Dream or a Distraction? The Global Anticorruption Blog of 4 October 2018, available at <https://globalanticorruptionblog.com/2018/10/04/guest-post-is-an-international-anti-corruption-court-a-dream-or-a-distraction/>. Accessed 18 June 2020

Wolf Mark L (2014) The Case for an International Anti-Corruption Court. Governance Studies at Brookings, available at <https://www.brookings.edu/research/the-case-for-an-international-anti-corruption-court/>. Accessed 18 June 2020

World Bank Institute (2008) Fighting Corruption Through Collective Action: A Guide for Business. The World Bank, Washington, DC

Prof. Dr. Dr. h.c. Thomas Kruessmann LLM (King's College) is co-ordinator of the Erasmus+ Capacity Building in Higher Education Project "Modernisation of master programmes for future judges, prosecutors, investigators with respect to European standard on human rights" for Ukraine and Belarus with the University of Graz. As President of the Association of European Studies for the Caucasus, he devotes himself to European Studies in the wider Caucasus region, including by acting as series editor of the book series "European Studies in the Caucasus". Prof. Kruessmann is a German-qualified lawyer with extensive legal practice in one of Vienna's leading law firms. He is founding director of the Russian, East European and Eurasian Studies Centre at the University of Graz (2010 - 2015) and Visiting Professor at Kazan Federal University (2015 - 2016). Beyond the Caucasus, his research interests extend to issues of comparative, European and international criminal law, gender and the law as well as corruption and compliance.

Chapter 24
The Due Diligence Obligations of International Organisations Engaged in Disaster Management

Katja L. H. Samuel and Silvia Venier

Contents

24.1 Introduction 528
24.2 The Concept and Sources of Due Diligence Obligations for IOs 530
24.3 Due Diligence Obligations Related to Disaster Management Incumbent
　　　upon the UN 535
　　　24.3.1 Haiti Cholera Epidemic Outbreak 535
　　　24.3.2 Kosovo Lead Poisoning 538
　　　24.3.3 Bangladesh Tube Wells Arsenic Poisoning 539
24.4 Due Diligence Obligations of Regional Organisations and Specialised Agencies 541
24.5 Conclusions 547
References 548

Abstract Although international organisations (IOs) play a pivotal disaster management role in the global arena, this is often not accompanied by appropriate levels
of accountability, especially in circumstances when their involvement further aggravates rather than alleviates the effects of an actual or impeding disaster. This chapter
examines these important issues through the lenses of due diligence, an open-ended
and flexible concept that is generally under-utilised and has been overlooked also
in this area. Following an introductory section which establishes the context, the
second part explores the concept and sources of due diligence obligations for IOs,
which are then illustrated by three case studies involving the UN in the third part.
The chapter then examines the relevance of due diligence obligations in relation to
regional organisations (focusing on the European Union) and specialised agencies
that have responsibilities for dealing with specific types of crisis.

Keywords International Organisations · due diligence · disasters · accountability ·
Responsibility · victims · remedies · Haiti · Kosovo · Bangladesh · Fukushima ·
Ebola

K. L. H. Samuel (✉) · S. Venier
GSDM, Southampton, UK
e-mail: director@gsdm.global

S. Venier
Scuola Superiore Sant'Anna, Pisa, Italy
e-mail: silvia.venier@santannapisa.it

© T.M.C. ASSER PRESS and the authors 2022
S. Sayapin et al. (eds.), *International Conflict and Security Law*,
https://doi.org/10.1007/978-94-6265-515-7_24

24.1 Introduction

Recently published statistics by the Centre for Research on Epidemiology of Disasters estimate that in 2019 there were at least 396 disasters attributable to natural hazards, resulting in the reported deaths of 11,755 people, 95 million affected lives, and an estimated US$ 130 billion economic damages.[1] Issues relating to effective and appropriate responses to disasters are increasingly critical, with the international community devoting significant effort and resources to developing common strategies to minimise the risk and adequately prepare for such occurrences.[2] The situation in post-conflict countries may also be further negatively impacted by disaster events, with accompanying security implications.[3]

Though the ultimate responsibility for disaster management lies with States in relation to their own territories, other actors such as International Organisations (IOs), non-governmental organisations, corporations and private actors, often offer further support. This chapter focuses on one currently under-researched category, IOs, arguing that their pivotal disaster management roles are often not accompanied by adequate levels of accountability and responsibility,[4] especially in circumstances when their involvement further aggravates rather than alleviates the effects of an actual or impeding disaster. States and individuals seeking redress and reparations in such cases—which are generally due to negligent or ill-informed activities on the part of the IOs concerned—can face a number of significant hurdles. The primary challenge is establishing that a breach of an international obligation possessed by the IO has actually occurred, which can be difficult and contentious to achieve: IOs are often not parties to relevant treaties and the exact scope and reach of customary international law obligations to IOs is generally less clear than in relation to States. This means that it can be difficult to establish the existence of an international obligation that has been breached for the purposes of establishing the existence of a wrongful

---

[1] CRED 2020.

[2] A disaster is usually understood as resulting from the equation "vulnerability + natural or manmade hazard" / capacity to cope. In the absence of an internationally agreed definition of 'disaster', this term is used throughout the chapter as referring to 'a calamitous event or series of events resulting in widespread loss of life, great human suffering and distress, or large-scale material or environmental damage, thereby seriously disrupting the functioning of society', a definition provided by the International Law Commission (ILC) in its Draft Articles on the Protection of Persons in the Event of Disasters ILC 2016. The term 'disaster management' refers to all aspects of the disaster cycle, including prevention and risk mitigation, preparedness, response and recovery Farber 2014.

[3] Note, however, that the ILC explicitly excluded disasters occurring in situations of armed conflicts from the scope of its Articles. For a critique of this approach, see e.g. the Introduction in Breau and Samuel 2016, pp. 3–10.

[4] See further e.g. Proulx 2013, p. 111. In terms of understanding the distinction between these two concepts, '[p]ower entails accountability, that is the duty to account for its exercise' International Law Association (ILA) 2002 and as such includes but is not limited to legal and political processes; whereas '[i]nternational legal responsibility, by contrast, is a specific element of accountability; the notion that a violation of a pre-determined norm triggers a likewise pre-determined sanction determined in accordance with international law.' See Sari 2011, p. 260.

24 The Due Diligence Obligations of International Organisations ... 529

act under international law without which it is not possible to define secondary responsibility.

The present chapter explores how increased comprehension, as well as application, of the concept of due diligence and its accompanying principles in an institutional context may assist in establishing the existence of such primary obligations. Due diligence is a flexible, evolving and commonly under-utilised concept that appears to be an increasingly important tool in case of legal loopholes or in relation to emerging challenges (e.g. cyber attacks). Yet it is one which generally has not been taken into consideration in relation to IOs' responsibilities, including in disaster situations. Other challenges in relation to ensuring accountability of IOs in these settings, which will be touched upon briefly in the following sections, are related to attribution of an established breach to an IO in circumstances when other actors (generally states and/or other IOs) are involved,[5] as well as to overcoming the obstacles posed by institutional immunity to ensure redress for the harm caused.

This chapter is thus concerned with critiquing the potential role of due diligence in achieving increased institutional accountability and responsibility in disaster management contexts. In the second section, the concept of due diligence and the sources of due diligence obligations under international law are discussed. These principles are then examined in the institutional context of the United Nations (UN). As the IO most engaged in disaster related activities worldwide, the UN offers some of the clearest, most high-profile and readily accessible examples of institutional failings of due diligence significance. The chapter discusses three case studies related to the UN through the lenses of due diligence in order to assess whether and how due diligence may assist persons and states, whose circumstances deteriorate as a result of institutional disaster management activities, to secure appropriate remedies for harm caused. As it will be seen—which is both intriguing and concerning—discussion of due diligence obligations for the UN in relation to the selected case studies is largely noticeable by its omission in academic scholarship, professional and policy reports, as well as judicial determinations. Though the discussion centres around those legal regimes of particular relevance to the selected case studies, the resultant findings are intended to be illustrative rather than exhaustive regarding the potential reach of due diligence in disaster management contexts, including their wider reach and applicability to IOs more generally. In the last part, the chapter further discusses to what extent due diligence obligations related to disaster management are applicable to a regional organisation (i.e. the European Union (EU)) and specialized agencies (i.e. the International Atomic Energy Agency (IAEA) and World Health Organisation (WHO)) that are increasingly involved in disaster management related activities.

---

[5] Recent academic work includes e.g. the concept of shared responsibility, see Nollkaemper and Plakokefalos 2014 and 2017.

24.2 The Concept and Sources of Due Diligence Obligations for IOs

In the international sphere, the concept of due diligence has been in existence for well over a century, having been applied as early as the 1870s in the *Alabama Arbitration* case.[6] As Kulesza suggests, new threats generated by highly dangerous activities during the second half of the 1900s resulted in new standards of care being developed by international tribunals, focusing especially on the careful use of new technologies and the duty to carry out risk assessments to avoid transboundary environmental harm.[7] Due diligence is now core to many areas of international law and can be understood as one of its established general principles, accompanied by more specific standards, rules and obligations.[8] Indeed, though due diligence obligations tend to be implied rather than expressly stated in legal instruments, courts and other bodies have developed a number of associated, generally applicable legal principles and more specific obligations, including protection, prevention, investigation, punishment and ensuring redress.[9] These principles can inform the interpretation and application of other sources of law such as specific treaty regimes and general customary international law,[10] as well as exist as a supplementary source of self-standing obligations.[11]

Essentially a reasonableness standard of conduct associated with 'due, or merited, care',[12] the exact parameters of due diligence can be difficult to pin down due to its flexible and open-ended nature.[13] The degree of diligence required may indeed vary depending on different factors, including the importance of the interest requiring protection as well as subjective considerations related to the capabilities of the actor responsible for such protection. The exact requirements may differ not only between legal regimes but also within specific legal regimes, since the concept and its accompanying legal principles are not static but rather reflect new developments and understandings such as in relation to changing technology or risk.[14] As indicated by the

---

[6] Alabama claims of the United States of America against Great Britain, Award of Sept. 14, 1872, XXIX Reports of International Arbitration Awards 122, 129.

[7] Kulesza 2016, p. 4.

[8] International Law Association (ILA) 2014 and International Law Association (ILA) 2016; Koivurova 2013, para 2.

[9] For an extensive overview of these principles see, generally, Barnidge 2006.

[10] See e.g. Bassiouni 1990, p. 770; Gutteridge 1953, p. 132.

[11] Bassiouni 1990, pp. 775–776.

[12] Barnidge 2006, p. 118 citing Corino 2000, p. 120.

[13] Due diligence is described as 'a variable concept' in the International Tribunal for the Law of the Sea (ITLOS), *Responsibilities and obligations of States sponsoring persons and entities with respect to activities in the Area*, Advisory Opinion of 1 February 2011, ITLOS Reports 2011, para 117.

[14] This was recognised as early as the Alabama Arbitration case where the Tribunal stated that the resultant obligations were 'in exact proportion to the risks' (Alabama Arbitration case supra n 7 p. 129). See further ITLOS Advisory Opinion supra para 117 quoted also in ITLOS, *Request for an Advisory Opinion Submitted by the Sub-Regional Fisheries Commission (SRFC Advisory Opinion)*,

International Court of Justice (ICJ) in the *Genocide* case, due diligence calls for an assessment *in concreto*.[15] In any case, this standard is generally concerned with taking adequate measures to achieve a particular result, such as the prevention of environmental harm[16] or the protection of the right to life.[17] As one commentator has observed, '[a] breach of these [due diligence] obligations consists not of failing to achieve the desired result but failing to take the necessary, diligent steps towards that end'.[18] In other words, negligent acts or omissions may constitute a breach.[19]

Though due diligence standards have been developed to date largely through the practice of states, nevertheless they apply equally to IOs, whose international legal personality means that they have rights and duties under international law from which due diligence obligations can result.[20] In relation to the UN specifically, the ICJ has observed that it possess 'a large measure of international legal personality' meaning that it also has the capacity to bear rights and duties under international law,[21] including customary due diligence obligations.[22] That said, since IOs do not generally have the same degree of power or function compared with states, and the nature of due diligence obligations can be context specific, generally IOs will not have the same extent of obligations compared with the parallel ones of states.[23]

Advisory Opinion of 2 April 2015, para 132, calling for a more severe standard of due diligence for riskier activities. For a comment see Stephens 2015.

[15] *Case concerning the Application of the Convention on the Prevention and Punishment of the Crime of Genocide (Bosnia and Herzegovina v Serbia and Montenegro)*, Judgment of 26 February 2007, ICJ Reports 2007 para 430.

[16] *Pulp Mills on the River Uruguay (Argentina v Uruguay)*, Judgment of 20 April 2010, ICJ Reports 14, para 197. According to the ICJ, the standard expected in this case was 'not only the adoption of appropriate rules and measures, but also a certain level of vigilance in their enforcement and the exercise of administrative control', by taking 'all appropriate measures to enforce its relevant regulations'.

[17] Inter-American Court of Human Rights (IACtHR), *Velasquez Rodriguez v Honduras*, Judgement of 29 July 1988, Series C, No. 4, paras 174–175; European Court of Human Rights (ECtHR), *Öneryildiz v. Turkey* (2005) 41 EHHR 20, para 93; ECtHR, *Budayeva and others v Russia* (2014) 59 EHRR 2 para 152. Shelton and Gould 2013 p. 577 have noted that while the IACtHR has explicitly referred to 'due diligence', the ECtHR has not explicitly mentioned this term in its jurisprudence dealing with positive obligations to protect the right to life.

[18] Koivurova 2013, para 3 and paras 37–38.

[19] See e.g. *Youmans (U.S. v. Mex.)*, 4 R.I.A.A. 110 (1926) para 114; for further discussion of the case see Barnidge 2006, pp. 95–96.

[20] E.g. ICJ, *Interpretation of the Agreement of 25 March 1951 between the WHO and Egypt*, Advisory Opinion, ICJ Reports 1980, p. 73, at 89–90 para 37.

[21] See *Case Concerning the Reparation for Injuries Suffered in the Service for the United Nations*, Advisory Opinion, ICJ Reports 1949 174, para 179.

[22] See e.g. White 2012, pp. 259–61; Tzanakopoulos 2014, p. 417: 'The UN has a "large measure of international legal personality" and is thus bound by customary international obligations, especially to respect and protect human rights, that are applicable to its conduct and functions'.

[23] See e.g. Orakhelashvili 2014, p. 119, suggesting that IOs are 'dependent on member States for all of their powers, institutions and resources, as well as for formation of their will through voting and lobbying by members'. See also ILC, Third Report on the identification of customary international law, A/CN.4/682, 27 March 2015, p. 46 para 69.

Similarly, the principle of institutional speciality, which limits the scope of an IO's powers and functions, may also mean that some rules of responsibility for states do not translate fully to an institutional context.[24] Therefore, though it is necessary to consider the more developed practice in relation to states in order to discern due diligence obligations for IOs, the limitations inherent in seeking to draw parallels between states and IOs as well as analogies are fully recognised.[25]

Due diligence played a significant role in the International Law Commission's (ILC) drafting efforts related to the Articles on Responsibility of States for Internationally Wrongful Acts (ARSIWA) adopted in 2001[26] and the Draft Articles on the Responsibility of International Organizations (DARIO) adopted in 2011.[27] Due to exigencies of codification, however, it was shifted to the level of 'primary rules' and thus removed from the ILC work. DARIO represents the most comprehensive consideration of international law on institutional responsibility as it currently stands, even if these articles are generally regarded as developing rather than codifying international law principles, largely due to the paucity or absence of relevant institutional practice.[28] Similar to the ARSIWA, an internationally wrongful act of an IO is defined as an act or an omission attributable to an IO and constituting a breach of an international obligation of that organization.[29] Even if the ILC took the position of considering the exact content of due diligence as depending on specific primary rules, institutional due diligence obligations seem to be reflected in some Articles, such as in the IO's obligation to prevent its member states from carrying out a certain conduct (Article 10), the obligation to take steps to ensure the fulfilment of the obligation to make reparation (Article 40), or in relation to a serious breach of an obligation arising under a peremptory norm (Article 41).

Looking at the legal sources that may enshrine due diligence obligations for IOs, these include treaties, customary international law, principles of general international law, and an IO's own institutional rules.[30] With respect to treaty based primary obligations, the principal treaty of potential relevance will normally be the IO's

---

[24] Leckow and Plith 2013, pp. 230–233.

[25] See e.g. Ahlborn 2012; Orakhelashvili 2014; Proulx 2013, p. 113.

[26] International Law Commission (ILC), Draft Articles on Responsibility of States for Internationally Wrongful Acts, with commentaries' (2001) II(2) Yearbook of the International Law Commission.

[27] ILC, Draft articles on the responsibility of international organizations, with commentaries (2011) II(2) Yearbook of the International Law Commission.

[28] Shraga 2013, p. 201; similarly, Orakhelashvili 2014, p. 116. Even the concept of 'practice' can be controversial and unclear, and what exactly constitutes practice can differ between states and IOs. See further Roucounas 2013, p. 164; Murphy 2013, pp. 29–30; G Gaja, 'Eighth report on responsibility of international organizations' (A/CN.4/640), para 6.

[29] Commentary to Article 4 para 2. In relation to states, Stern argues that due diligence obligations arise in relation to acts of omissions by states that failed to prevent or punish the illegal conduct of private parties, see Stern 2010, p. 209.

[30] According to Article 10(1) DARIO, a breach of an international obligation occurs when an IO fails to act 'in conformity with what is required of it by that obligation, *regardless of the origin or character of the obligation concerned*' (emphasis added). The Commentary to this article suggests that this is intended to convey that the international obligation 'may be established by a customary

constituent instrument.[31] This, however, may not create clear or extensive obligations that bind the IO itself across the full remit of its often expanding roles and activities in the global arena, including those associated with disaster management. Disagreement exists too regarding the exact parameters in relation to the potential reach of customary international law obligations to IOs. There seems to be general agreement that IOs are bound by *jus cogens* norms with accompanying *erga omnes* obligations, as with any other public or private actors.[32] Some commentators suggest that an IO should be bound by those international obligations which have acquired customary international law status[33] to the extent that this is consistent with an IO's legal nature[34] and relevant to their conduct and functions.[35]

Two potentially clearer sources of institutional legal obligations for IOs, which are generally under-utilised in discussions and efforts to secure increased institutional accountability, are due diligence obligations sourced in general principles of international law and in the rules of the organisation. With respect to the former, international courts and tribunals have relied upon general rules of international law as the source of obligations, including ones of due diligence, notably also in the absence of treaty and customary international law obligations.[36] This is important since it means that a breach of due diligence obligations sourced in general principles alone may constitute a breach of an international obligation and, therefore, a wrongful act or omission for the purposes of DARIO. An additional or alternative source of obligations for an IO, including those of due diligence, are the rules of the organisation, which include 'the constituent instruments, decisions, resolutions and other acts of the international organization adopted in accordance with those instruments, and established practice of the organization'.[37] While these IO rules must create an international obligation if seeking to establish the existence of a wrongful act under DARIO, they are not required to be formally binding under Article 38(1) ICJ Statute. As the Commentary to Article 2(b) DARIO clarifies 'decisions, resolutions and other acts of the organization are relevant, *whether they are regarded as binding or not*, insofar as they give functions to organs or agents in accordance with the constituent instruments of the organization'.[38] Furthermore, Article 10(2) DARIO clearly states that these rules

---

rule of international law, by a treaty or by a general principle applicable within the international legal order'.

[31] ICJ Advisory Opinion on the Interpretation of the Agreement of 25 March 1951 between the WHO and Egypt, ICJ Reports 1980, para 37, pp. 89–90.

[32] White 2012, pp. 24–25; ILA 2016, p. 18; Tzanakopoulos 2014, p. 417; Paust 2010.

[33] Mégret and Hoffmann 2003, p. 317.

[34] Dannenbaum 2010, p. 136.

[35] Tzanakopoulos 2014, p. 417.

[36] See ICJ, Interpretation of the Agreement of 25 March 1951 between the WHO and Egypt, Advisory Opinion (above n 21). In the SRFC Advisory Opinion, ITLOS found the existence of due diligence obligations based on general rules of international law in the absence of guidance on flag state liability from other sources (notably here the UN Convention on the Law of the Sea, which codifies customary international law, and the MCA Convention).

[37] DARIO Article 2(b).

[38] DARIO Commentary p. 11 para 16 (emphasis added). See also Tzanakopoulos 2014, p. 416.

may also form the basis of breach of an international obligation in relation to an IO's membership for the purposes of DARIO.[39] That said, DARIO recognises that not all IO rules will create obligations governed by international law and, therefore, that not all breaches of IO rules will constitute breaches of international law.[40] For example 'other acts of the organization' could incorporate binding international agreements between an IO and another IO or state, whereas institutional resolutions are normally exhortatory or recommendatory in nature and are not intended to create obligations on the IO or its membership.

Of interest to the present discussion are also the specific rules covering due diligence issues adopted by the UN in relation to its peacekeeping missions, in response to recurring allegations of serious violations of international human rights law and international humanitarian law being perpetrated by inter alia UN troops on the ground.[41] It is likely that at least two of these documents—i.e. the Bulletin issued by the UN Secretary-General in 1999, and the Capstone Document 2008—have become part of the UN's customary international institutional law. This is due to such factors as the language of obligation utilised (i.e. 'ensuring', 'promoting' and 'protecting' human rights on the ground), the period of time they have been reiterated consistently, and the accompanying sense of institutional obligation regarding these serious issues. Indeed, Shraga has suggested that '[b]y the time it was articulated in the 1995 Secretary-General's report on the limitation of the UN third-party liability, the principle of UN responsibility for combat-related damage, and damage caused in the course of the operational activities of its forces, was generally accepted as a customary international law principle.'[42] The fact that particular IO rules may have acquired the status of customary international institutional law within the IO concerned can affect not only their practical importance and weight, but also point to the likelihood that such rules create international obligations on the UN and its Membership that can be breached and, therefore, constitute a wrongful act when attributable to the UN.

In the following section, the discussion turns to considering what due diligence obligations may have existed in relation to three case studies involving the UN. The final section ends by exploring due diligence obligations of regional organisations that are expected to be increasingly involved in disaster situations (the EU), as well

---

[39] This is made explicit in DARIO Commentary to Article 10 para 4 pp. 31–32.

[40] DARIO Commentary to Article 10 para 7.

[41] Observance by United Nations forces of international humanitarian law, UN Secretary-General's Bulletin ST/SGB/1999/13, 6 August 1999, reprinted in ILM, 1999, 1656. (UN Secretary-General's Bulletin); UN, United Nations Peacekeeping Operations, Principles and Guidelines (Dept of Peacekeeping Operations/Dept of Field Support 2008) (Capstone Document), https://www.un.org/ruleoflaw/blog/document/united-nations-peacekeeping-operations-principles-and-guidelines-the-capstone-doctrine/; UN, Human rights due diligence policy on United Nations support to non-United Nations security forces, Annex to Identical letters dated 25 February 2013 form the Secretary-General addressed to the President of the General Assembly and to the President of the Security Council, A/67/775-S/2013/110 dated 5 March 2013.

[42] Shraga 2013, p. 202.

as of other specialized agencies that are responsible for specific types of emergencies (the IAEA for nuclear emergencies and the WHO for epidemic outbreaks).

24.3 Due Diligence Obligations Related to Disaster Management Incumbent upon the UN

Significant breaches of due diligence by the UN have emerged in three case studies discussed in this section, namely: the 2010 cholera epidemic outbreak in Haiti that followed the devastating earthquake, triggered by the Nepalese contingent of UN peacekeeping forces; the lead poisoning of the Roma population, triggered by the UN Mission in Kosovo (UNMIK); the decision by UN Children's Fund (UNICEF), together with Bangladesh's Department of Public Health and Engineering, to sink tube wells across the country following the 1972 war which resulted in arsenic poisoning. The first two case studies are illustrative of how IOs' responses can aggravate an existing disaster situation, whereas the third demonstrates how ill-informed activities aimed at reducing risk can in fact themselves become the catalyst for a disaster.

24.3.1 Haiti Cholera Epidemic Outbreak

The spread of cholera in Haiti in October 2010 occurred a few months after a massive earthquake. It was attributed to the UN peacekeeping forces contingent (the UN Stabilization Mission in Haiti—MINUSTAH) which had arrived from Nepal, a cholera-endemic country that was experiencing a cholera outbreak at the time the contingent was sent to Haiti. The Nepalese soldiers, however, were not tested for cholera due to no exhibition of active symptoms. The spread of the disease was caused by inadequate waste management in the UN forces' camp, whereby septic tanks were emptied into a tributary of the longest Haitian river, the Artibonite, one the country's main sources of water for drinking, cooking and bathing. The country's already weak and over-burdened sanitary system exacerbated transmission of the disease among Haitians. As of July 2018, it is estimated that more than 9000 people have died, and more than 800,000 have required treatment in hospitals, as a consequence of the devastating outbreak.[43]

Despite overwhelming evidence linking the UN troops with the outbreak,[44] the UN forces denied responsibility for these allegations while their headquarters remained silent for a long time. The UN then relied upon absolute immunity against public

---

[43] PAHO and WHO 2018.

[44] Piarroux 2010; Piarroux et al. 2011.

law claims, i.e. claims related to policy or political matters.[45] This raised the issue of the conflict between immunity, which serves some important aims, and respect and protection of human rights, which are among the key objectives of the UN.[46] It has to be noted that the exclusion of public law claims in the Status of Forces Agreements (SOFA), that the UN usually signs with host countries, is however procedural in nature and subject to waiver. Nor does this impact upon the existence of substantial obligations, including due diligence ones, that are examined in the following paragraphs.

First, it can be argued that the UN has the primary obligation to prevent and remove threats to peace under Article 1(1) UN Charter, which necessarily includes a duty to adopt all feasible measures to reduce these risks in the first place. The cholera outbreak, and especially the reaction by the UN—which was more concerned with deflecting responsibility elsewhere than ascertaining its causes—resulted in protests against the peacekeeping forces, with the potential to create further social unrest in an already extremely volatile and unstable country.[47] Furthermore, considering that the Haitian governmental structures were still devastated as a consequence of the earthquake, it could be argued that MINUSTAH was performing governmental functions. As such, it was under an obligation to respect, and ensure respect of, international human rights law, which demands due diligence in, e.g., preventing risks to the right to life and health, in ensuring access to clear water, as well as access to adequate remedies in case of related violations.[48] Due diligence obligations arose due to the fact that the UN knew, or in any case should have known, that Nepal was recovering from a cholera outbreak and should have screened the Nepalese contingent,[49] and because more attention should have been devoted to ensuring a sound sanitation and waste management infrastructure within the MINUSTAH base. Furthermore, instead of being concerned with efforts to deflect responsibility elsewhere, the UN should have devoted all its efforts to ensuring an adequate international response to the outbreak. Due diligence was not shown with respect to the duty to investigate

---

[45] As a Yale report points out (see Yale Law School 2013), the UN did not respond for over a year, then relied upon a 2011 report by independent experts stating that there was no evidence of the origin of the outbreak. In February 2013, invoking the Convention on Privileges and Immunities, the UN summarily dismissed the victims' claims and refused to address the merits of the complaint or the factual question of how the epidemic started.

[46] Freedman and Lemay-Hebert 2015.

[47] Al Jazeera, 'Cholera unrest hits Haiti Capital' (Al Jazeera, 19 November 2010) https://www.alj azeera.com/news/americas/2010/11/20101118173955660861.html Accessed 15 September 2020.

[48] While for the right to life it can be argued that it has acquired customary law status, including with reference to the accompanying due diligence obligations to prevent violations and ensure remedies should these occur, other rights may still be understood as customary rights in *status nascendi*. See Toebes 2013 (on the right to health in humanitarian contexts) and Winkler 2012, p. 97 (on the right to water).

[49] As of March 2014, the UN troops were still not screened for cholera, see Murphy 2014. The UN has not revised its policies on screening and prophylaxis for cholera for UN troops, even though a recent study found that these strategies are both inexpensive and effective to reduce the probability of the outbreak. See Lewnard et al. 2016.

the outbreak's occurrence,[50] nor to ensure access to adequate remedies attributable to the UN's breaches of its obligations. It is of note that in the agreement between MINUSTAH and the Haitian government, the UN promised to create a standing commission to review third parties' claims of a private law character arising from peacekeeping operations, a promise that was never maintained however. Due to the existence of UN absolute immunity, remedies other than access to a national court or international tribunal could have been provided.[51] Finally, it would be important that the UN provides guarantees of non-repetition, by adopting and implementing adequate prevention and risk mitigation policies.

In addition to the obligations enshrined under the UN Charter, the SOFA and human rights law, due diligence is required as a basic principle of general international law and of other specific areas, such as international environmental law, which may be of relevance to this case considering the environmental implications of the contamination of the Haitian larger river. Furthermore, as a Yale University report suggests, the UN violated widely recognized humanitarian standards, including the 'do not harm' and accountability principles, a fact that is particularly troubling in consideration of the core humanitarian functions of UN peacekeeping forces.[52] As indicated in the previous section, due diligence is indeed required by the UN's own rules governing the conduct of UN peacekeeping forces that are likely to have acquired customary institutional law status.

Formal UN responsibility for the cholera outbreak was acknowledged only in 2016 by the UN Secretary General, who confirmed ongoing UN efforts to stop the outbreak and promised to provide financial support to the victims.[53] The first track of the new UN approach comprises an intensified and better-resourced effort to respond to and reduce the incidence of cholera in Haiti, by addressing issues of access to water, sanitation and health care. The second track involves the development of a package of material assistance and support to those Haitians most directly affected by cholera. The actual implementation of this new approach, however, depends on the contribution by member states to the trust fund that was established to support the approach. According to the most recently available data at the time of writing, the amount received is well below initial expectations, with some key donors recently expressing a lack of interest in continuing to contribute to the fund.[54] Therefore, due

---

[50] See the case of the Nepalese peacekeepers seeking to remove the pipes that connected the camp's latrines with the river to hide evidence. The Haitian government instead immediately asked the French embassy assistance for an outbreak investigation, which resulted in the Piarroux report mentioned above.

[51] These alternative remedies are discussed by Schrijver 2014.

[52] Yale Law School 2013, p. 44.

[53] UNSG, A new approach to cholera in Haiti. Report by the Secretary General, 25 November 2016, UN Doc A/71/620.

[54] Recent data refer to 20 million dollars received, while the strategy was expected to cover 400 million dollars, see http://mptf.undp.org/factsheet/fund/CLH00; R. Gladstone, 'After Bringing Cholera to Haiti, U.N. Can't Raise Money to Fight It' (NY Times, 13 March 2017) https://www.nyt imes.com/2017/03/19/world/americas/cholera-haiti-united-nations.html Accessed 15 September 2020.

538   K. L. H. Samuel and S. Venier

diligence issues related to ensuring adequate remedies to the victims of the Haitian cholera epidemic, and to preventing similar situations in the future, remain an open matter.

24.3.2 Kosovo Lead Poisoning

The second case study refers to similar negligence demonstrated by a UN Mission in Kosovo (UNMIK), which was mandated by the UN Security Council *inter alia* to establish 'a secure environment in which refugees and displaced persons can return home in safety'.[55] Towards the end of the armed conflict between Serbia and the Kosovo Liberation Army, there were concerns regarding the safety of Internally Displaced Persons (IDPs) of Roma, Ashkali and Egyptian (RAE) origin, in particular that they could suffer serious retaliatory violence for being regarded by some to have collaborated with Serbian forces. The camps were set up by UNMIK in the Mitrovica province near to the Trepca smelter and mining complex, which had extracted metals including lead for over sixty years and which had been known since the 1970s to be a cause of significant environmental pollution, including lead contamination. Additionally, due to squalid living conditions within the camps, such as a lack of water and poor drainage resulting in poor levels of hygiene, inadequate healthcare and access to food, many of the residents suffered from frequent sickness and there were a number of mortalities. Despite clear knowledge of excessive and grossly unacceptable levels of lead contamination present in the camps,[56] with their accompanying threats to the IDPs' health and even lives, underpinned by robust scientific and medical evidence,[57] UNMIK failed to address the root cause of the problem of the lead poisoning for approximately ten years. Nor did it inform the UN Secretary General or the IDPs living in these camps of its own findings and the associated risks of continuing to live in the camps.[58] Even the relocation of most IDPs in 2006 to the Osterode camp continued to expose them to unacceptably high blood levels of lead. In 2016, an opinion of the Human Rights Advisory Panel (HRAP), a semi-independent body created by UNMIK, delivered its findings in support of the applicants.[59]

---

[55] UNSC Res 1244 (10 June 1999) para 9(c). UNMIK was more generally mandated to provide interim-administration of Kosovo 'while establishing and overseeing the development of provisional democratic self-governing institutions', para 10.

[56] Human Rights Watch 2009, p. 23.

[57] Notably, UNMIK commissioned a report in 2000 'First Phase of Public Health Project on Lead Pollution in Mitrovica Region' which revealed high blood level of lead contamination, yet was never made public including to the UN or IDPs. There were also sporadic medical testings carried out by the WHO, as well as repeated calls by UN Special rapporteurs, NGOs of the risks and need to close the camps.

[58] The Human Rights Advisory Panel (HRAP), NM and Others v UNMIK, Case No 26/08, Opinion (26 February 2016) para 281.

[59] Ibid., pp. 4–21.

24 The Due Diligence Obligations of International Organisations …   539

There are both similarities and differences in the due diligence obligations incumbent upon the UN in the Haiti Cholera and the Kosovo Lead Poisoning cases. First, differently from MINUSTAH, UNMIK was acting as a *de facto* state in Kosovo at the time of the events. Notably, under Regulation 1999/1 it undertook an obligation 'to observe internationally recognised human rights standards in exercising its functions'.[60] As was mentioned above, human rights obligations include the duty to exercise due diligence in preventing threats to the right to life and health. Furthermore, UNMIK also breached the duty to provide adequate and timely information on these risks to the affected population, a procedural obligation inherent in the protection of the right to life and private life which has consolidated for instance as part of the ECtHR case law.[61] The duty to protect against discrimination may also be particularly relevant in this case, considering that these minorities had been identified as vulnerable and disadvantaged groups in need of special protection.[62] Furthermore, UNMIK did not show due diligence in protecting particularly vulnerable persons within these groups, such as women and children, contrary to international human rights standards.[63] Finally, as per the right to a remedy, which can be considered both as a procedural limb of the right to life and as a self-standing right, in the Kosovo case though investigations were carried out, the findings of the advisory panel can be seen as an influential opinion rather than as a binding judgment of a court.[64] Similar to MINUSTAH, it seems reasonable to argue that UNMIK was required to act with due diligence in relation to abiding to widely recognised humanitarian standards and principles, including those related to internal displacement, which apply 'to all authorities […] irrespective of their legal status'.[65]

24.3.3 Bangladesh Tube Wells Arsenic Poisoning

The last case study concerns the installation of tube wells across Bangladesh since the 1970s, intended to act as a preventative measure against disease attributable to pathogen-laden surface waters. This initiative was promoted by UNICEF in partnership with the UN Development Programme, the World Bank and the Bangladeshi Department of Public Health and Engineering. Initially, the project was regarded as

---

[60] Ibid., para 182. Note however the ambiguity of the term 'observe', which was perhaps used to signify that the extent of obligations enshrined in human rights law may be different for an international mission with respect to those incumbent upon a state, to which the tripartite typology of duties (to respect, protect and fulfil) generally applies.

[61] See e.g. *Budayeva and Others v Russia* (2014) 59 EHRR 2, para 133; *Öneryildiz v Turkey* (2005) 41 EHRR 20 para 90.

[62] The Human Rights Advisory Panel. (n 59) paras 298–299.

[63] Crocker 2016, pp. 383–405.

[64] In 2006, the complaint filed by an NGO on behalf of Roma population was declared inadmissible by the ECtHR, on the ground that the Strasbourg Court lacked jurisdiction over UNMIK-administered Kosovo.

[65] UN Doc. E/CN.4/1998/53/Add.2, see e.g. principle 2.

a big success until the mid-1980s, when the presence of arsenic started to be detected in half of the 10 million tube wells,[66] and became soon termed as 'the largest mass poisoning in history'.[67] Long-term exposure to the highly toxic, colourless, tasteless and odourless substance leads to skin lesions, cancer, cardiovascular disease and diabetes, as well as impaired cognitive function in children.

While scientists agree that arsenic is geological in origin, the likelihood of the contamination of water generally depends upon the depth of the tube wells, with lower tube wells having lower concentrations. Prior to the installation of the tube wells, according to UNICEF and other agencies extensive tests of the water were conducted but that these tests did not include arsenic. Some experts, notably geochemists, have contended instead that testing for arsenic at that time would have been both reasonable and inexpensive.[68] Doctors began to recognize the symptoms of arsenic poisoning in the mid-1980s, but concerted steps were not taken to provide alternative sources of water until the mid-1990s. Many of the benefits of earlier public awareness efforts have since faded and there is currently no infrastructure in place for ongoing monitoring of existing and new wells nor a coherent national plan in place to ensure sustainable safe water sources throughout Bangladesh.[69] A survey conducted by UNICEF in 2009 found that 13% of people were still using contaminated water, with more recent studies suggesting that an estimated 43,000 people die each year from arsenic-related illness in Bangladesh.[70]

From a due diligence perspective, it is important to mention that the motivation behind the original decision to install tube wells was aimed at mitigating the effects of an existing health crisis attributable to water-borne pathogens. The question however arises as per the level of diligence required to ensure that the potential adverse effects of the tube wells project were limited. According to the due diligence principle, what is considered to be 'reasonable measures' must be assessed by the standards prevailing at the time, including those influenced by scientific knowledge. It seems entirely reasonable to assert here that diligence was not shown adequately or at all, either on the part of international actors or the Bangladeshi authorities, because they knew, or should have known, that arsenic was present in the geological formations of Bangladesh and did not test underground water for it. Due diligence was not demonstrated when the first cases emerged in the mid-1980s and steps were not taken until late 1990s, measures that, according to Human Rights Watch (HRW), were not in line with prioritisation of needs.[71] Even today, a significant number of tube wells and people remain untested for arsenic poisoning.

---

[66] A Akbar, 'Arsenic-tainted water from Unicef wells is poisoning half of Bangladesh' (The Independent, 5 September 1998) http://www.independent.co.uk/news/arsenic-tainted-water-from-unicef-wells-is-poisoning-half-of-bangladesh-1196091.html

[67] World Health Organisation (WHO), 'Arsenic. Mass Poisoning of an unprecedented scale' (WHO, March 2002). http://www.who.int/features/archives/feature206/en/

[68] Kornhauser 2015, p. 145.

[69] Flanagan et al. 2012, p. 841.

[70] Ibid., p. 840.

[71] Human Rights Watch 2016.

As Kornhauser points out, the arsenic poisoning case in Bangladesh raises complex issues in terms of establishing responsibility for a complicate project in which a multitude of actors intervened. Although the Bangladeshi government bears the primary responsibility for providing the country with access to clean water, international donors promoted and facilitated the tube wells project and commissioned feasibility studies to foreign engineers and public health experts. Kornhauser suggests that, in the scope of these studies, tests should have been carried out by those responsible once they had or at least should have become aware that there was some chance that the groundwater in Bangladesh was contaminated, i.e. at least since the first arsenic poisoning cases emerged from the early to mid 1980s onwards. The same author further considers both the financial harm—which includes the cost of remediation and should be shared between responsible actors according to the degree of causation between the omission and the harm caused—and irreparable harm—including in terms of deaths and disabilities, as well as damage to the local ecosystem, which were preventable but not compensable.[72] Also in this case, victims have not received any apologies from the part of responsible actors or any compensation for the harm suffered.

The three case studies clearly demonstrate that due diligence should and indeed does have an important role to play in understanding issues of institutional responsibility in disaster situations. Due diligence obligations may be enshrined in different instruments, including the IOs' own rules, and can be understood as a general principle of international law, being therefore key to interpret obligations in specific contexts. From a due diligence perspective, it is important to put emphasis on the standard of care required in a specific circumstance, which can be identified as having regard to the level of knowledge of particular risks, the interest requiring protection (which in these cases are very important, i.e. the right to life and health accompanied by environmental protection), as well as the capabilities of the responsible actors to ensure such protection. More detailed obligations can then be established depending on the circumstances of the case, but with the general principles of prevention, mitigation, investigation and accountability for the harm caused being common and recurring themes of the three case studies.

The next section explores the relevance of due diligence obligations related to disaster management as being incumbent upon regional organisations and specialised agencies that have responsibilities to deal with specific types of crisis.

24.4 Due Diligence Obligations of Regional Organisations and Specialised Agencies

At the regional level, Europe currently provides the largest share of official international humanitarian aid collectively, i.e. comprising both EU and EU Member

---

[72] Ibid., p. 150.

State bilateral contributions. The EU has been endowed with new shared competences on humanitarian aid by the Lisbon Treaty.[73] Article 214 of the Treaty of the Functioning of the European Union 2007 (TFEU), which reinforces humanitarian aid as a separate external policy, not only codifies the EU's competence to act in this field, but also underlines the importance of respect for the key principles derived from international humanitarian law as a crucial precondition for the implementation of the EU's humanitarian activities. Furthermore, pursuant to Article 21 TFEU the Union's external action shall by guided by, amongst other things, 'respect for human dignity, the principles of equality and solidarity and respect for the principles of the United Nations Charter and international law'. Of especial note is the fact that the EU Charter of Fundamental Rights, now legally binding upon EU institutions and Member States when implementing EU law, introduces a new standard so far as it explicitly requires a supranational organisation to provide for human rights protection against its own conduct under Article 6. This includes the obligation to accede to the European Convention on Human Rights (para 2), further establishing that human rights should be interpreted as guiding principles of EU law (para 3). With this in mind, it is interesting to explore to what extent due diligence obligations are currently taken into account within EU policy instruments devoted to protection from serious emergencies.

The new legal basis introduced under Article 214 complements the Council Regulation 1257/1996[74] and the European Consensus on Humanitarian Aid adopted in 2007,[75] which form the key political reference documents on the EU's approach to humanitarian action. The European Consensus suggests that 'the EU has both the experience and the duty to ensure that its overall contribution to the humanitarian response is effective and appropriate, underpins the international humanitarian effort to deliver aid to people in need, and addresses adequately the challenges facing humanitarian actors today' (para 5). It also includes references to quality, effectiveness and accountability of humanitarian action (paras 40–47), mentioning the need to adhere to internationally recognised humanitarian standards and, in particular, to the 'do not harm' principle which inter alia 'means that environmental and other longer-term considerations must be taken into account from the outset even in short-term emergency interventions' (para 42). The same provision clarifies that 'accountability to people assisted commits the aid provider to work within a framework of quality standards, principles, policies and guidelines, and promotes training and capacity building activities'.

Following the adoption of the European Consensus, the European Commission has presented Action Plans in 2008 and 2015 outlining practical measures to implement the provisions of the European Consensus. The three priorities identified in the more recently adopted Action Plan include to 'uphold humanitarian principles', and foresee

---

[73] Treaty on the Functioning of the European Union (2012) OJ C 326/1.

[74] Regulation 1257/96 concerning humanitarian aid, [1996] OJ L163/1.

[75] Joint Statement by the Council and the Representatives of the Governments of the Member States meeting within the Council, the European Parliament and the European Commission, The European Consensus on Humanitarian Aid, OJ 2008 C25/01.

24 The Due Diligence Obligations of International Organisations … 543

the identification of a case study to explore to what extent this priority is implemented in practice.[76] The European Commission has also developed a set of thematic reports including one on 'humanitarian protection', which recognises that '[i]t is fundamental that humanitarian actors are fully familiar with human rights and respect them, and in any case never consciously violate them or do so due to negligence and lack of accountability.'[77] In the context of humanitarian aid, accountability is understood at the EU level as encompassing both accountability to European citizens on the good use of public funds and accountability to those in need in the countries facing humanitarian crisis.

It seems thus that the EU approach to humanitarian aid, which has existed since the 1960s and has expanded progressively during recent decades, is moving towards a more principled and accountable approach. It remains to be seen, however, to what extent these principles are implemented in practice. An evaluation of the implementation of the European Consensus carried out in 2014 found, for instance, that the declaration was not well-known or influential in shaping humanitarian aid policies of EU member states.[78] With reference to the principles relating to the quality of aid, the study further suggests that EU Institutions and Member States are committed at the policy level to upholding and promoting fundamental humanitarian principles, but that different approaches and positions have appeared in applying these principles in specific situations.[79] It is also crucial to mention that the EU does not generally operate in the field, but rather that it finances and coordinates projects implemented by other actors. The relationships between the EU and humanitarian aid partners, such as specialised international organisations and NGOs, are governed by Framework Partnership Agreements (FPAs), which are based on the respect of humanitarian principles as mentioned above together with clear performance indicators. Article 2 of the model FPA clarifies that '[o]wnership of humanitarian aid actions is vested in the humanitarian organisation which implements them, preserving its freedom and independence, and assuming its responsibilities.'[80] That said, the European Commission remains responsible for exercising diligent control of these actions carried out on its behalf during all of their phases.

Turning our attention now to international actors that have responsibilities to mitigate the risk and consequences of particular types of crisis, it is important to discuss the role of the WHO in relation to public health emergencies of international concern (PHEIC), as well as the IAEA with reference to nuclear and radiological emergencies. Recent case studies, including the 2014 Ebola outbreak in West Africa and the 2011 Fukushima Nuclear Power Plant (NPP) disaster, have pointed out a number of shortcomings in the applicable legal frameworks at the international level, including with reference to the role of IOs. The next paragraphs explore what due

---

[76] European Commission 2015, p. 3.

[77] Directorate General European Civil Protection and Humanitarian Operations (DG ECHO) 2016, p. 8.

[78] Analysis for Economic Decisions (ADE) and Kings College London (KCL) 2014, p. 21.

[79] Analysis for Economic Decisions (ADE) and Kings College London (KCL) 2014, pp. 86–88.

[80] See a model FPA at http://dgecho-partners-helpdesk.eu/reference_documents/start.

diligence obligations may have existed at the time of the emergency and whether the IO breached these obligations.

Among the different types of emergencies, nuclear disasters are particularly challenging due to their potential transboundary implications and their long-term consequences. Therefore, it comes as no surprise that the international community has devoted significant attention to regulating the safety of nuclear installations as well as to establishing rules for emergency preparedness and response. Due diligence plays an important role in international nuclear law, which establishes that the primary responsibility of national authorities is to adopt adequate protection measures.[81]

Under the IAEA Statute, the agency is tasked with establishing standards for nuclear safety which, albeit formally non-binding, represent the starting point for determining what represents appropriate steps for ensuring nuclear safety with regard to safety control as is required by the Convention on Nuclear Safety.[82] It may be argued, therefore, that the Agency exercises due diligence in determining and reviewing the international consensus on nuclear safety standards, which represent the guidelines upon which the due diligence of States can be assessed. The standards are not mandatory, however, meaning that they lack appropriate enforcement mechanisms. International oversight on nuclear safety is mainly based on voluntary instruments, such as the assistance and peer review missions organised by the IAEA in partnership with national governments, and on mandatory ones, such as the peer review of national reports as is required by the Convention on Nuclear Safety, on which the IAEA does not take an active role.

The Fukushima disaster highlighted that these peer review mechanisms on nuclear safety need to be strengthened.[83] For instance, an issue that emerged from the Fukushima NPP disaster, and that would benefit from increased international oversight and scrutiny, was the absence of separation of powers between the promotion of nuclear energy and safety protection. The Japanese Independent Commission emphasised that the Fukushima accident 'was the result of collusion between the government, the regulators and TEPCO [the NPP owner], and the lack of governance by said parties' who 'effectively betrayed the nation's right to be safe from nuclear accidents'.[84] In Farber's words, '[t]he cosy relationship between the industry and regulators may have contributed to complacency and overconfidence about the future and the corresponding failure to anticipate the severity of future disaster risks.'[85] For the purposes of the present discussion, it is of especial note that the Integrated Regulatory Service (IRSS) of the IAEA had indeed raised this concern in 2007, as part of the assistance and peer review services it provides to Member States, and made several recommendations to the Japanese government that did not result in specific

---

[81] Convention on Nuclear Safety (adopted 17 June 1994, entered into force 24 October 1996) 1963 UNTS 317, see in particular Article 7 (Legislative and Regulatory Framework) and Article 18 (Design and Construction).

[82] Ibid.

[83] IAEA 2011, p. 1.

[84] National Diet of Japan 2012, p. 16.

[85] Farber 2012, p. 7.

24 The Due Diligence Obligations of International Organisations ... 545

actions from the part of the government.[86] This seems to suggests that in the nuclear safety field even if the responsible international actor acts diligently—by determining and reviewing internationally accepted standards, and by assisting states in meeting them—it does not have the accompanying mandate to ensure that these are actually enforced. It is important to mention too that the same concern regarding the separation of powers can be identified also at the international level, with the IAEA being tasked with both promoting nuclear energy and ensuring the safety of nuclear installations.

The second aspect of the IAEA's role in a nuclear emergency relates to the acute response phase, which is governed by the Early Notification and the Assistance Conventions.[87] In the aftermath of Fukushima, the IAEA was blamed for long delays in issuing information which may have contributed to confusion and fear in the immediate aftermath of the tragedy. In particular, it has been pointed out that 'the agency has been reluctant to deviate even slightly from information delivered by the Japanese government' on the situation at the reactors.[88] In its report on the NPP disaster, the Agency acknowledged that 'communication with the official contact point in Japan in the early phase of the emergency was difficult'[89] and noted the differences among States in the advice given to their nationals who found themselves in Japan at the moment of the disaster, which caused additional concern.[90] The problem is that under the Early Notification Convention the Agency is tasked with distributing information provided by national authorities (Article 4) and thus needs to verify information with the domestic government before disclosing it. In discussing the limitations of the emergency response at Fukushima, Cavoski pointed out that the lack of adequate information provided by the Japanese government to other States could be considered to constitute a breach of the Early Notification Convention though, as she further noted, so far no State has raised the question of Japan's responsibility on these issues.[91] In its own assessment of the accident, the IAEA noted that the international framework on nuclear early warning and response should be strengthened by pointing out that 'awareness of international arrangements for notification and assistance in a nuclear or radiological emergency, as well as existing operational mechanisms, needs to be increased'.[92] It further observed that 'there is a need for enhanced training and exercises on the operational aspects of the

---

[86] Japanese Ministry of Economy, Trade and Industry 2012, p. 27. See also Cavoski 2013, p. 376.

[87] Convention on Early Notification of a Nuclear Accident (adopted 26 September 1986, entered into force 27 October 1986) 1457 UNTS 133; Convention on Assistance in the Case of a Nuclear Accident or Radiological Emergency (adopted 26 September 1986, entered into force 26 February 1987) 1457 UNTS 133.

[88] Nature Editorial 2011, p. 389.

[89] IAEA 2015, pp. 94–96.

[90] Ibid.

[91] Cavoski 2013, pp. 385–386.

[92] IAEA 2015, pp. 98–99.

Early Notification Convention and the Assistance Convention', as well as 'to consult and share information on protective measures and their technical basis'.[93]

Turning now to global public health, in 2005 the World Health Assembly adopted the revised International Health Regulations (IHR), under which the WHO is granted an enhanced role, inter alia by having the authority to declare a Public Health Emergency of International Concern (Article 12). WHO authority is also strengthened by the possibility to take into account 'unofficial reports' (Article 9.1), i.e. reports by non-state actors which may complement official information provided by public authorities, even if the same provision clarifies that '[b]efore taking any action based on such reports, WHO shall consult with and attempt to obtain verification from the State Party in whose territory the event is allegedly occurring' (Article 9.1 and Article 10 on Verification). In the determination of a PHEIC, the WHO is supported by a Roster of Experts (Article 47) and by an Emergency Committee (Articles 48-49).

The Ebola crisis that began in West Africa in December 2013 provided an occasion to test how the IHR work in practice, including with reference to the role of the WHO. Ebola occurred in three of the world's poorest countries, in post-conflict situations and with weak public health infrastructures. In the early phases of the emergency, the WHO was reluctant to mobilise global assistance and to declare a PHEIC, probably fearing States' overreactions and general panic as had occurred after the H1N1 flu declaration in 2011. In a 2015 report on the Ebola outbreak, Médicins Sans Frontières (MSF) claims to have publicly declared the outbreak as 'unprecedented' due to the geographic spread of the cases on 31 March 2014, but to have been downplayed as exaggerated and alarmist by many, including the WHO.[94] Instead, the WHO's declaration of Ebola as a PHEIC was not delivered until 7 August 2014, more than 4 months after the MSF warning. As Garret has noted, throughout the Ebola crisis 'the WHO has struggled to remain credible, as its financial resources have shrunk, tensions have grown between its Geneva headquarters and its regional offices, and rival multilateral organizations have taken control over much of the global health action and agenda'.[95] The WHO's delayed and fragmented response, coupled with the already terrible conditions of impoverished post-conflict countries, left a leadership vacuum that resulted in a plea for military assets to be sent by high-income countries. It further led to the adoption of Security Council Resolution 2177 (2014), co-sponsored by some 130 states (the highest number in the history of the Security Council) which, for the first time, referred to a public health emergency as constituting 'a threat to international peace and security'.[96]

The subsequent report of the Ebola Interim Assessment Panel (EIAP), commissioned by the WHO, pointed out that the 'WHO was incapable of responding to emergencies in a timely fashion and lacked the credibility to enforce the IHR, its own instrument'.[97] The Panel further concluded that '[t]he Ebola crisis not only

---

[93] IAEA 2015, pp. 98–99.

[94] Médicins Sans Frontières 2015, p. 6.

[95] Garret 2015, p. 85.

[96] UN SC Resolution 2177 (2014) preamble.

[97] EIAP 2015 p. 103.

24 The Due Diligence Obligations of International Organisations ... 547

exposed organizational failings in the functioning of WHO, but it also demonstrated shortcomings in the International Health Regulations (2005).' (p. 5). The panel also found that had the 2011 recommendations (released by the IHR review panel with reference to the response to the H1N1 flu pandemic) been fully implemented, the WHO would have been in a better position to respond to the Ebola crisis. This raises an additional issue as to what extent these review panels are useful if their findings are not subsequently (effectively or at all) implemented (Ibid.).

To conclude, with reference to particular types of crisis including nuclear and public health emergencies, IOs are tasked with specific responsibilities that may entail due diligence obligations, such as verifying official information provided by national authorities or taking adequate steps to support the response efforts and mobilise international assistance. Recent case studies have pointed out that there are some significant shortcomings in the legal instruments applicable to these emergencies or in their actual implementation, including with reference to the role of these IOs. There is thus some room to further improve the contribution of IOs to such disaster scenarios, including from a due diligence perspective.

24.5 Conclusions

This chapter has explored what role due diligence may play in terms of ensuring higher levels of institutional accountability and responsibility in disaster management contexts. It has been argued that looking at previous case studies through the lenses of due diligence allows for a more comprehensive examination of the obligations incumbent upon IOs under international law to be undertaken, especially to address current perceived gaps. Considering the difficulties in establishing treaty-based and customary law obligations with reference to IOs, one notable advantage associated with adopting a due diligence approach is that it can also be understood as a general principle of international law which may increasingly influence IOs' own rules of conduct.

Probably due to its flexible and open-ended nature, however, due diligence obligations have not been explored adequately by the academic community, especially with reference to IOs' conduct in disaster settings; nor have State or institutional actors been keen to engage more fully with its associated principles since these can assist in the establishment of primary obligations (acts or omissions) for which they may in turn be liable to provide remedies in the event of their breach, denying affected victims of basic human rights protections in the process. This chapter aimed to begin to address this gap by identifying such issues, illustrated through the analysis of three case studies representing significant due diligence failings from the part of the UN, together with an examination as to how due diligence can and should be reflected within the activities of other specialized agencies (IAEA and WHO) and regional organisations (EU).

It has been shown how due diligence is a multifaceted concept that adapts to specific circumstances, i.e. according to the functions and responsibilities of an IO, to the type of emergency under consideration, or to the level of knowledge of risk that can be reasonably expected. Generally speaking, due diligence is implied in primary obligations related to the protection of the most important interests (e.g. the right to life) and to granting redress for violations and refers to the duty to take all necessary steps to ensure that these interests are protected. This is particularly relevant to actions carried out by the UN, whose founding instrument enshrines the obligations to ensure maintenance of peace and security and to respect and protect human rights. Due diligence also may be understood as complementing more specific disaster response obligations as enshrined in relevant treaties and incumbent upon specialised agencies (such as the IAEA and the WHO), which have acquired important functions in the prevention and response to specific emergencies, such as nuclear accidents or pandemic outbreaks. Due diligence is finally a key constitutive element of the obligation to exercise control over third parties' humanitarian operations, as demonstrated by the European Commission's approach to humanitarian aid.

Better comprehension of the breadth of IOs' institutional obligations through the broader and more adaptable lens of due diligence may go some way to applying further legal and moral pressure upon the UN and other IOs to exercise more care in their disaster related activities. This is of special importance, where institutional immunity shields are not waived, to ensure that particularly victims of their periodic seismic failings are not denied basic justice, including in the form of the carrying out of a credible investigation as to why harm occurred and the provision of adequate and appropriate reparation. Certainly, understanding and respecting due diligence obligations would go some way to assisting organisations such as the UN, IAEA and WHO to regain any lost ground in terms of their credibility as effective international legal actors in disaster situations.

References

Analysis for Economic Decisions (ADE) and Kings College London (KCL) (2014) Evaluation of the implementation of the European Consensus on Humanitarian Aid. http://ec.europa.eu/echo/files/evaluation/2014/european_consensus_main_en.pdf. Accessed 15 September 2020

Ahlborn C (2012) The Use of Analogies in Drafting the Articles on the Responsibility of International Organizations. An Appraisal of the 'Copy-Paste' Approach. International Organisations Law Review 9:53–66

Barnidge RP (2006) The Due Diligence Principle under International Law. International Community Law Review 8:81–121

Bassiouni MC (1990) Functional Approach to 'General Principles'. Michigan Journal of International Law 11: 768–818

Breau SC, Samuel KLH (2016) Research Handbook on Disasters and International Law. Edward Elgar

Cavoski A (2013) Revisiting the Convention on Nuclear Safety: Lessons Learned from the Fukushima Accident. Asian Journal International Law 3:365–391

Centre for Research on Epidemiology of Disasters (2020) Disaster* Year in Review 2019. Cred Crunch 58

Corino C (2000) Environmental Due Diligence. European Energy and Environmental Law Review 9(4):120–124

Crocker M (2016) The Protection of Vulnerable Groups. In: Breau SC, Samuel KLH (eds) The Research Handbook on Disasters and International Law. Edward Elgar.

Dannenbaum T (2010) Translating the Standard of Effective Control into a System of Effective Accountability. How Liability Should be Apportioned for Violations of Human Rights by Member State Troop Contingents Serving as United Nations Peacekeepers. Harvard International Law Journal Online 51:113–192

Directorate General European Civil Protection and Humanitarian Operations (DG ECHO) (2016) Humanitarian Protection. Improving protection outcomes to reduce risks for people in humanitarian crisis. DG ECHO Thematic Policy Report 8

European Commission (2015) Implementation Plan of the European Consensus on Humanitarian Aid. SWD(2015) 269 final

Farber DA (2012) Legal Scholarship, the Disaster Cycle, and the Fukushima Accident. Duke Environmental Law and Policy Forum 23:1–21

Farber DA (2014) International Law and the Disaster Cycle. In: Caron DD et al (ed) The International Law of Disaster Relief. Cambridge University Press, New York

Flanagan SV et al (2012) Arsenic in tube well water in Bangladesh: health and economic impacts and implications for arsenic mitigation. Bulletin of the World Health Organization 90:839–846. doi: https://doi.org/10.2471/BLT.11.101253

Freedman R, Leemay-Hebert N (2015) Towards an alternative interpretation of UN immunity: A human rights-based approach to the Haiti Cholera Case. QIL-Zoom In 19:5–18

Garret L (2015) Ebola's Lessons. How the WHO mishandled the crisis. Foreign Affairs 94(5):80–107

Gutteridge HC (1953) The Meaning and Scope of Article 38(1)(c) of the Statute of the International Court of Justice. Grotius Society Transactions for the Year 1952 38:125–134

Human Rights Watch (2009) Poisoned by Lead, a Health and Human Rights Crisis in Mitrovica's Roma Camps. https://www.hrw.org/report/2009/06/23/kosovo-poisoned-lead/health-and-human-rights-crisis-mitrovicas-roma-camps Accessed 15 September 2020

Human Rights Watch (2016) Nepotism and Neglect. The Failing Response to Arsenic in the Drinking Water of Bangladesh's Rural Poor. https://www.hrw.org/report/2016/04/06/nepotism-and-neglect/failing-response-arsenic-drinking-water-bangladeshs-rural Accessed 15 September 2020

International Atomic Energy Agency (2011) IAEA Action Plan on Nuclear Safety. https://www.iaea.org/sites/default/files/actionplanns.pdf Accessed 15 September 2020

International Atomic Energy Agency (2015) The Fukushima Daiichi Accident. Report by the Director General. IAEA, GC 59/14

International Law Association (ILA) (2002) Committee to Accountability of International Organisations, Third Report Consolidated, Revised and Enlarged Version of Recommended Rules and Practices.

International Law Association (2014) ILA Study Group in Due Diligence in International Law. First Report. Available at http://www.ila-hq.org/index.php/study-groups Accessed 15 September 2020

International Law Association (2016) ILA Study Group in Due Diligence in International Law. Second Report. Available at http://www.ila-hq.org/index.php/study-groups Accessed 15 September 2020

Japanese Ministry of Economy, Trade and Industry (2012) Convention on Nuclear Safety-National Report of Japan for the Second Extraordinary Meeting

Koivurova T (2013) Due Diligence in International Law. Max Planck Encyclopaedia of Public International Law. Heidelberg and Oxford University Press

Kornhauser LA (2015) Incentives, Compensation, and Irreparable Harm. In: Nollkaemper A, Jacobs D (eds) Distribution of Responsibilities in International Law. Cambridge University Press, Cambridge, pp. 120–155

Kulesza J (2016) Due diligence in international law. Brill

Leckow R, Plith E (2013) Codification, Progressive Development or Innovation? Some Reflections on the ILC Articles on the Responsibility of International Organizations. In: Ragazzi M (ed) Responsibility of International Organizations: Essays in Memory of Sir Ian Brownlie. Martinus Nijhoff, Leiden

Lewnard JA et al (2016) Strategies to Prevent Cholera Introduction during International Personnel Deployments: A Computational Modeling Analysis Based on the 2010 Haiti Outbreak. PLoS Med 13(1). doi:https://doi.org/10.1371/journal. pmed.1001947

Médicins Sans Frontières (2015) Pushed to the Limits and Beyond. A year into the largest ever Ebola outbreak https://www.msf.org/ebola-pushed-limit-and-beyond Accessed 15 September 2020

Mégret F, Hoffmann F (2003) The UN as a Human Rights Violator? Some Reflections on the United Nations Changing Human Rights Responsibilities. Human Rights Quarterly 25:314–342

Murphy SE (2013) The Art of Packaging the ILC's Work Product. In: Ragazzi M (ed) Responsibility of International Organizations: Essays in Memory of Sir Ian Brownlie. Martinus Nijhoff, Leiden

Murphy T (2014) UN Peacekeepers still not screened for cholera despite causing outbreak http://www.humanosphere.org/global-health/2014/01/un-peacekeepers-still-screened-cholera-three-years-since-haiti-outbreak/ Accessed 15 September 2020

Nature Editorial (2011) A watchdog with bite. Nature 472:389–390

Nollkaemper A, Plakokefalos I (eds) (2014) Principles of Shared Responsibility in International Law: An Appraisal of the State of the Art. Cambridge University Press

Nollkaemper A and Plakokefalos I (eds) (2017) The Practice of Shared Responsibility: A Framework for Analysis. Cambridge University Press

Orakhelashvili A (2014) Responsibility and Immunities: Similarities and Differences between International Organizations and States. International Organisations Law Review 11:114–171

Pan American Health Organization and World Health Organization (2018) Epidemiological Update: Cholera. Washington, D.C. https://reliefweb.int/sites/reliefweb.int/files/resources/2018-aug-6-phe-epi-update-cholera.pdf Accessed 15 September 2020

Paust JJ (2010) The U.N. Is Bound By Human Rights: Understanding the Full Reach of Human Rights, Remedies, and Nonimmunity. Harvard International Law Journal Online 51:1–12

Piarroux R (2010) Rapport de mission sur l'épidémie de choléra en Haïti. http://www.ph.ucla.edu/epi/snow/piarrouxcholerareport_french.pdf Accessed 15 September 2020

Piarroux R et al (2011) Understanding the Cholera Epidemic, Haiti. Emerging Infectious Diseases 17(7):1161–1168

Proulx VJ (2013) An Uneasy Transition? Linkages between the Law of State Responsibility and the Law Governing the Responsibility of International Organizations. In: Ragazzi M (ed) Responsibility of International Organizations: Essays in Memory of Sir Ian Brownlie. Martinus Nijhoff, Leiden

Roucounas E (2013) Practice as a Relevant Factor for the Responsibility of International Organizations. In: Ragazzi M (ed) Responsibility of International Organizations: Essays in Memory of Sir Ian Brownlie. Martinus Nijhoff, Leiden

Sari A (2011) Autonomy, attribution and accountability: reflections on the Behrami case. In: Collins R, White ND (eds) International Organizations and the Idea of Autonomy. Institutional Independence in the International Legal Order. Routledge, London

Schrijver N (2014) Beyond Srebrenica and Haiti: Exploring Alternative Remedies against the United Nations. International Organisations Law Review 10:588–600

Shraga D (2013) The Interplay between the Practice and the Rule. In: Ragazzi M (ed) Responsibility of International Organizations: Essays in Memory of Sir Ian Brownlie. Martinus Nijhoff, Leiden

Stephens T (2015) ITLOS Advisory Opinion: Coastal and Flag State Duties to Ensure Sustainable Fisheries Management'. ASIL Insights 19. https://www.asil.org/insights/volume/19/issue/8/itlos-advisory-opinion-coastal-and-flag-state-duties-ensure Accessed 15 September 2020

Stern B (2010) The Elements of an Internationally Wrongful Act. In: Crawford J, Pellet A, Olleson S (eds) The Law of International Responsibility. Oxford University Press

The National Diet of Japan (2012) The official report of the Fukushima Nuclear Accident Independent Investigative Commission. Executive Summary. The National Diet of Japan

24 The Due Diligence Obligations of International Organisations …

Toebes B (2013) Health and Humanitarian Assistance: Towards and Integrated Norm under International Law. Tilburg Law Review 18(2): 133–151. doi:https://doi.org/10.1163/22112596-018 02006

Tzanakopoulos A (2014) Strengthening Security Council Accountability for Sanctions: The Role of International Responsibility. Journal of Conflict and Security Law 19:409–426

White ND (2012) Due diligence obligations of conduct: developing a responsibility regime for PMSCs. Criminal Justice Ethics 31:233–61

WHO EIAP (2015) Report of the Ebola Interim Assessment Panel http://www.who.int/csr/resour ces/publications/ebola/report-by-panel.pdf?ua=1 Accessed 15 September 2020

Winkler I (2012) The Human Right to Water. Significance, Legal Status and Implications for Water Allocation. Hart Publishing

Yale Law School (2013) Peacekeeping without accountability. The United Nations' responsibility for the Haitian Cholera Outbreak. https://law.yale.edu/sites/default/files/documents/pdf/Clinics/ Haiti_TDC_Final_Report.pdf Accessed 15 September 2020

Katja L. H. Samuel is a GSDM Founding Director. She is a professional, strategically minded, resourceful lawyer with multinational, multidisciplinary, academic, practitioner, military, and civil society experience. Katja served in the UK's Royal Navy for 12 years as a sea-going logistics officer, as well as naval barrister advising on criminal, military and international law matters. After leaving the Royal Navy in 2004, Katja worked mainly within the academic sector at a number of leading UK universities, including as an award-winning researcher and author.

Silvia Venier PhD is postdoctoral researcher at the Scuola Superiore Sant'Anna, Institute of Law, Politics, Development, in Pisa (Italy) and Associate at GSDM (UK). Silvia's main area of expertise is international disaster law, with a particular focus on human rights and emergency management. She is currently involved in a research project dealing with International Obligations related to CBRN risks and status of their implementation in Italy (http://www.cbrn-italy. it/en). Silvia has a ten-year experience in contributing to research projects funded by the European Union and focusing on new technologies for security and emergency management. She has been visiting research fellow at the Centre for International Law, Conflict and Crisis of the Copenhagen University, and at the Human Rights Centre at Essex University.

Part III
Institutions

Chapter 25
Organization for Security and Co-operation in Europe (OSCE)

Ioannis P. Tzivaras

Contents

25.1 Introduction 556
25.2 Historical Evolution of the OSCE 557
25.3 Purpose of the OSCE 559
25.4 OSCE's Institutions and Activities on International Security and Co-operation 561
25.5 OSCE's Legal Framework through International Security 567
25.6 Conclusion 568
References 569

Abstract The Organization for Security and Co-operation in Europe (OSCE) was founded as a forum on inter-state cooperation during the recession of the Cold War. It concerns the Conference on Security and Co-operation in Europe (CSCE), the creation of which was made possible by the normalization of relations between the East and West. The fundamental document of the CSCE was the Helsinki Final Act of 1975, following biannual negotiations between 35 European States along with the United States and Canada. On this basis, the CSCE gradually adopted a broad concept of security, a precursor to the later concept of human security, not only limited to the traditional aspects of civilian and military affairs, but also to cooperation on economic and environmental matters, alongside the protection of human rights. The end of the Cold War marked a new era for the CSCE. The gradual establishment of permanent institutions led, in 1994, to the decision to rename the CSCE as OSCE, replacing the term "Conference" with that of "Organization". The permanent power of the organization is clearly reflected in its role in the modern international environment. The organization's priorities were strengthened through the implementation of objectives and strategies related to security, democratization, stability and the protection of human rights. Through OSCE's three expanded dimensions, the 57 participating states and partners of the organization co-operate and strengthen dialogue between themselves, preventing any conflicts and reaching settlement of disputes by peaceful means.

I. P. Tzivaras (✉)
Department of Economics and Management, Open University of Cyprus (OUC), Nicosia, Cyprus
e-mail: ioannis.tzivaras@ouc.ac.cy

© T.M.C. ASSER PRESS and the authors 2022
S. Sayapin et al. (eds.), *International Conflict and Security Law*,
https://doi.org/10.1007/978-94-6265-515-7_25

Keywords Organization for Security and Co-operation in Europe · Conference for Security and Co-operation in Europe · Organization · International Organization · Security · Co-operation · Human Rights · Military · Security Concept

25.1 Introduction

The stabilization of countries is important in order to guarantee security and peace, both at the national and international levels. In the wake of the Cold War, achieving interstate stability has become more important. In this respect, democracies and rule of law have been the catalyst behind the states' integration into international peace and security architecture. Within the ongoing transformation process, OSCE plays a key role in laying the normative foundations for the international community's security norms.

With emphasis on the principles of co-operative and comprehensive security and a strong emphasis on dialogue, the OSCE is the world's largest regional security arrangement. It is a unique platform for open dialogue, joint action, mutual understanding, fostering cooperation and inclusive security among the participating states. OSCE's region has faced many security challenges from its beginning till now, including *inter alia*; armed conflicts; human, drugs and arms trafficking; manifestations of intolerance; extremism; nationalist rhetoric; xenophobia; radicalization; hate speech and hate crimes; cybercrime; in general, rapidly growing divisions in the OSCE area that undermine the common security and co-operation. This paper examines how OSCE's structure faced problems, challenges, contexts and cases in the past and still faces them at present due to the increasing security challenges in the world, as well as how the OSCE contributes to the solution of those international challenges. Furthermore, it gives an analytical and specific overview of the work of the OSCE and what it has to offer to solve current difficult situations involving peace, security, human rights, etc.

Generally, dialogue is a major *modus operandi* of the OSCE, and relevant opportunities help the OSCE to find positive ways to move to constructive co-operation. Methods such as the Structured Dialogue initiative or the sixteen OSCE Cyber-ICT confidence-building measures progressed towards the implementation of the organization's goals of comprehensive security and co-operation.[1] In addition, the sixteen field operations, OSCE's institutions, the Parliamentary Assembly, the Permanent Council, the Forum for Security Co-operation, as well as the specialized departments in the Secretariat, help to promote stability, the rule of law, and the respect for human rights in the organization's region.

In the framework of international security, OSCE has dealt with many transnational developments in the recent past. The OSCE's support in Central Asian governments on good governance and economic connectivity, the Prespa Agreement between Greece and North Macedonia and the settlement of the name dispute, the Armenia Co-operation Programme, OSCE's Special Monitoring Mission to

---

[1] Adler 1998, pp. 132–160.

25 Organization for Security and Co-operation in Europe (OSCE)   557

Ukraine, the situation in South Caucasus, the Minsk Process, and the Transdniestrian Settlement Process are a few of the paradigms of the OSCE's responsiveness and effectiveness when it comes to the protection of the international community's values.

25.2 Historical Evolution of the OSCE

The OSCE started as a cooperation forum during the Cold War's recession.[2] OSCE's predecessor, Conference on Security and Co-operation in Europe (CSCE) had its roots in 1930, when the idea of a collective intrastate security system in Europe[3] was formulated for the first time. In 1966, the Warsaw Pact stressed that the meeting of European heads of state or government was necessary for the definition of territorial *status quo* and the cooperation between the East and West.[4] CSCE's first meeting was held in September 1973 in Helsinki with the major participation of all European states. The meeting adopted the Helsinki Multilateral Consultations, also known as the 'Blue Book', containing CSCE's procedural directives where the participating states had found a common normative ground.[5]

Following negotiations during the Helsinki Process and the signature of the Helsinki Final Act, the 35 participating states[6] agreed to strengthen international security matters, state relations and a series of basic principles of rational behaviour among them.[7] As a method by which the post-War European territorial settlement would be finally accepted, the states divided CSCE's areas of activities into three dimensions (baskets).[8] CSCE's conferences in Belgrade (1977–1978),[9] Madrid (1980–1983), Vienna (1986–1989) and Bonn (1990) highlighted the progress made in the fields of human rights protection, military security, information, environment, peaceful resolution of disputes, cultural heritage, minorities, economic cooperation

---

[2] Bortloff 1996, pp. 327–330; Wegner and Mastny 2008, pp. 3–17; Birnbaum and Peters 1990, pp. 305–319; Biscop 2005.

[3] Flynn and Farrell 1999, pp. 505–536.

[4] Shaw 2017, pp. 372–378; Ghebali 1989, pp. 23–78; Bekes 2009, pp. 201–219; Alcock 2000, p. 182.

[5] Holsti 1982, pp. 159–170.

[6] Bloed 1994, pp. 12–28; Maresca 1985.

[7] Wohlfeld 2008, pp. 643–644.

[8] In particular, the first dimension on "Questions relating to Security in Europe" covers ten basic principles on political and military aspects of security between the States, involving, also, confidence-building measures and aspects of security and disarmament. The second dimension comprises matters on co-operation in the fields of economics, of science and technology and of the environment while the third dimension involves aspects relating to security and co-operation in humanitarian aspects and other fields. Furthermore, *see* CSCE 1975, Helsinki Final Act. https://www.osce.org/helsinki-final-act?download=true. Accessed 16 August 2020. Shaw 2017, pp. 1179–1182.

[9] Romano 2012, pp. 205–224.

558   I. P. Tzivaras

and democratic institutions.[10] Subsequently, the 1990 CSCE Copenhagen Meeting on Human Dimension outlined a number of human rights and fundamental freedoms, outlined provisions regarding national minorities, and broadened human rights matters to include election commitments.[11]

Given the changes that took place in Central and Eastern Europe and the new challenges of the disintegration of the Soviet Union and Yugoslavia, the CSCE Summit in Paris (1990) laid the foundations for a turning point in the history of CSCE in the post-Cold War era.[12] The participating states signed the Charter of Paris for a New Europe, which was of significant importance to the accelerated institutionalization process, adding a new, more active structure to the CSCE's role as an important factor for dialogue and negotiation.[13]

Specifically, the Charter of Paris emphasized the need for the creation of a new era of democracy, peace and unity in Europe. It also emphasized the issue of the protection of human rights, the promotion of economic cooperation and friendly relations, the empowerment of security and unity in Europe, and the definition of CSCE's new institutional structure—parameters that had also been discussed in CSCE's Meeting in Valletta, Madrid and Berlin (1991).[14]

On the 30th and 31st of January 1992, the Council of the CSCE held its Second Meeting in Prague, where they had consultations on the transformation in Europe, the role of the CSCE and the issue of the institutional contributions to the strengthening of CSCE institutions and orientations for the Helsinki follow-up meeting. As a result, this meeting adopted the Prague Document of the further development of the CSCE institutions and structures.[15] In July 1992, heads of states or government held the Second Helsinki Summit, known as Helsinki II, which completed the process of setting up the CSCE. Furthermore, the CSCE to be a regional arrangement in the sense of Chapter IX of the United Nations Charter.[16] Helsinki II recognized the "CSCE Helsinki Summit Document 1992: The Challenges of Change" and made official the creation of the institutions of the High Commissioner on National Minorities, the Economic Forum and the Forum for Security Co-operation.[17]

Following up at the Summit of Budapest in December 1994, heads of state or government agreed, primarily, to rename CSCE to OSCE for the purpose of reflecting its work and strengthening a number of its bodies and institutions.[18] Given that the new Organization had been operational since 1 January 1995 and new challenges

---

[10] CSCE 1990b; Tretter 1989, pp. 257–261; Bloed 1990; Lehne 1991.

[11] CSCE 1990c; Roukounas 1993, pp. 88–91; Buergenthal 1990, pp. 217–221; Glover 1995, pp. 31–39; Bloed 1991, pp. 55–91.

[12] Lucas 1990, 1993; Flynn and Farrell 1999, pp. 507–509.

[13] CSCE 1990a.

[14] CSCE 1991e, 1991f, 1991b, 1991a; Buergenthal 1991, pp. 375–381; Roth 1991, pp. 330–334; Johannsen and Hvenegaard-Lassen 1992, pp. 11–12; Raday 2002, pp. 453–455.

[15] CSCE 1992b.

[16] Heraclides 1993b.

[17] CSCE 1992a.

[18] Decaux 1994a, pp. 18–26; Sapiro 1995, pp. 631–637; Nesi 1994, pp. 736–757.

25 Organization for Security and Co-operation in Europe (OSCE)

were shortly ahead, the Budapest Document "Towards a Genuine Partnership in a New Era", reinforced the role of organization's institutions, such as the Chairman-in-Office, the Secretary General, the Secretariat, the High Commissioner on National Minorities and the Office for Democratic Institutions and Human Rights.[19]

Furthermore, given that co-operative security became the underlying principle of the new organization at the OSCE Summit in Lisbon in 1996, the organization adopted the Lisbon Declaration on a Common and Comprehensive Security Model for Europe for the 21st Century.[20] This Declaration stressed both security challenges and possibilities for co-operative approaches between the participating states.[21] Subsequently,[22] the Sixth OSCE Summit of Heads of State or Government was held in Istanbul in 1999. It adopted, in total, three important documents, which are the Charter for European Security, Istanbul Summit Declaration and the Agreement on Adaption of the Treaty on Conventional Armed Forces in Europe, documents which aim to strengthen organization's ability on the prevention of conflicts, peace keeping operations and the rehabilitation of European societies ravaged by them.[23]

Through cooperation with other international bodies, the Istanbul Summit proceeded to the establishment of the Platform for Co-operative Security and reaffirmed the Human Dimension as one of the main basic areas of responsibility for the Organization.[24] In 2010, the OSCE Summit was held in Astana. There, the heads of state or government adopted the Astana Commemorative Declaration, reconfirmed the organization's approach to vital security, and main principles based on transparency and trust respecting the norms of International Law enshrined in the United Nations Charter and the Helsinki Final Act.[25]

25.3 Purpose of the OSCE

The original purpose of the CSCE as it was in the three dimensions of Helsinki's Final Act of 1975 has been widened. The CSCE has played a significant role in developing cooperation in Europe on security issues, the promotion of democratic institutions, human rights and other freedoms.[26] In accordance with the basic principles of the Helsinki Final Act, it has strengthened the means to avoid conflicts between states

---

[19] CSCE 1994, CSCE Budapest Document 1994: Towards a Genuine Partnership in a New Era. https://www.osce.org/mc/39554?download=true. Accessed 20 August 2020; Ghebali 1996.

[20] Pentikainen 1997, pp. 5–11.

[21] OSCE 1996 Lisbon Document 1996. https://www.osce.org/mc/39539?download=true. Accessed 16 August 2020.

[22] Pentikainen 1998, pp. 18–37.

[23] Mosser 2015, pp. 579–599.

[24] OSCE 1999, Istanbul Document 1999. https://www.osce.org/mc/39569?download=true. Accessed 11 August 2020; Heraclides 1993a.

[25] OSCE 2010, Astana Commemorative Declaration towards a Security Community. https://www.osce.org/cio/74985?download=true. Accessed 16 August 2020.

[26] Schweisfurth 1976, pp. 681–725; Sneek 1994, pp. 1–33.

and to establish peace, security and prosperity in Europe.[27] Now, the OSCE's main priorities start from the assumption that security is indivisible, and that cooperation among states is required to guarantee peace, security and stability. These results can be achieved through a collective effort from participating states to create democratic societies based on the rule of law, the prevention of hostilities, the establishment of stability, and close cooperation on security issues to overcome social, political and economic disputes through a wide range of specific security-related concerns.

Based on the above, the OSCE's participating states' comprehensive approach to security is illustrated by the organization's wide geographical scope, the broad understanding of security, the organization's involvement in all phases of a conflict cycle (i.e., early warning, prevention, crisis management and post-conflict peace-building), as well as its operation as a regional organization under Chapter VIII of the UN Charter. In general, the OSCE deals directly with issues that concern a common regional security based on the organization's three dimensions—politico-military, economic-environmental and the human dimension—and covers arms control and cross-border threats, along with transnational crimes, such as organized crime, terrorism and trafficking in human beings, weapons and drugs. The OSCE's issues also include economic progress, environmental issues, good governance and democratization, the protection of human rights, fundamental freedoms and energy security.

Since its inception, the OSCE has achieved a high level of legitimacy. After 1990 and the adoption of the Paris Charter, the participating states paved the way for the recognition of democracy as the only legitimate principle of governance within the organization's area, directly linked to the interstate ability to organize internal sovereignty along democratic lines. In this context, with 57 participating states in Europe, Asia and North America, the OSCE is the world's largest regional security organization.[28] Beyond its participants, OSCE has maintained relations with 11 Asian and Mediterranean partners for co-operation, strengthening through dialogue and sharing commitments and expertise to address security issues.[29]

---

[27] Sadigbayli 2014, pp. 392–417.

[28] OSCE's participating States are: Albania, Andorra, Armenia, Austria, Azerbaijan, Belarus, Belgium, Bosnia and Herzegovina, Bulgaria, Canada, Croatia, Cyprus Republic, Czech Republic, Denmark, Estonia, Finland, France, Georgia, Germany, Greece, Holy See, Hungary, Iceland, Ireland, Italy, Kazakhstan, Kyrgyzstan, Latvia, Liechtenstein, Lithuania, Luxembourg, Malta, Moldova, Monaco, Mongolia, Montenegro, Netherlands, Norway, Poland, Portugal, Romania, Russian Federation, San Marino, Serbia, Slovakia, Slovenia, Spain, Sweden, Switzerland, Tajikistan, former Yugoslav Republic of Macedonia, Turkey, Turkmenistan, Ukraine, United Kingdom, United States of America and Uzbekistan.

[29] OSCE's Asian partners are: Afghanistan, Australia, Japan, Republic of Korea and Thailand. OSCE's Mediterranean partners for co-operation are: Algeria, Egypt, Israel, Jordan, Morocco and Tunisia.

25.4 OSCE's Institutions and Activities on International Security and Co-operation

Since 1975, the OSCE has been following a continuous and evolving path, displaying, after the Charter of Paris in 1990, features of an international organization.[30] In the final text adopted at the Helsinki Summit in July 1992, the participating states nominated the OSCE to a regional organization and, in particular, to a regional agreement in accordance with Chapter VIII of the Charter of the United Nations.

Like other security organizations, the OSCE has been determined to adapt to the new political situation that has prevailed since 1989[31] as a major factor in European democracy promotion policies.[32] Since the signing of the Helsinki Final Act, more than 30 years have passed, during which Europe has radically transformed. The division into two coalitions, the confrontation between two opposing systems, and the differences around ideologies now belong to the past. Now, inspired by the shared values of democracy, collective security, the protection of human rights, the rule of law, economic freedom, social justice and environmental protection, Europe has taken the road of cooperation.[33]

The OSCE has played an important role in this process. By initiating a forum for dialogue and creating rules of conduct that apply both to relations between states and to the behaviour of states towards their citizens, it delimits areas where cooperation has been imposed on any confrontation.[34] Today, the organization fulfils four missions in total. First, it is a community of values that prioritizes democracy, human rights, fundamental freedoms and the rule of law. Second, the OSCE is a permanent forum for dialogue on security-related issues in Europe. Each participating state can at any time express its concerns about events occurring in the areas for which the organization has competence, a process that contributes to transparency, represents a measure of confidence and reflects a sense of collective security. Third, the OSCE is a step towards controlling armaments and disarmament. The confidence and security-of-confidence measures contained in the 1994 Vienna Document have been negotiated under the auspices of the organization, which also monitored the implementation of the provisions of the Vienna Document (CSCE 1990b). Beyond the Treaty on Conventional Armed Forces in Europe, the OSCE continuously processes the arms control framework to cover the entire area for which the organization has jurisdiction. Alongside these goals, arms control agreements at the regional and subregional levels can be negotiated within the framework of the OSCE, as in the case of the former Yugoslavia and Bosnia and Herzegovina.[35] Fourth, the OSCE is equipped with all the means needed to intervene in conflict areas, which has already become

---

[30] Schlager 1991, pp. 221–222.

[31] Kokkinides 1995, pp. 89–99.

[32] Gawrich 2017, pp. 527–528; Graeger and Novosseloff 2003, pp. 75–94; Merlingen and Ostrauskaite 2005, pp. 341–357.

[33] Bothe et al. 1997, pp. 14–19.

[34] Kropatcheva 2012, pp. 370–378.

[35] Du Pont 2000, pp. 7–18.

evident from the growing collisions since the end of the Cold War. Already, since the end of armed conflict in former Yugoslavia, the organization undertook a new activity of post-conflict rehabilitation. In addition, since 1992, the organization has publicly requested to be given the authority to carry out its own peacekeeping operations whenever it is needed, even though this possibility has not yet been implemented.[36]

The OSCE performs its complex work on security and cooperation with a fairly significant number of institutions and structures. Its basic structure includes decision-making and negotiating bodies, as well as structures, institutions, and summits in order to set the organization's priorities and directions at the highest political level. Several sections of the organization are responsible for ensuring that the organization's activities are relevant to its objectives. Namely, these are: the Permanent Council, which is the principal regular decision-making body and has one committee for each of the three OSCE's dimensions (security, economic and environmental, human); the Forum for Security Co-operation, which has jurisdiction on the strengthening of politico-military security in Europe focusing on certain tasks, including negotiations and consultations on confidence and security-building measures, intensive cooperation on military matters, agreed-upon measures and reduction of conflict risks;[37] and the Ministerial Council as the central, decisive and governing body of the OSCE.

As for the OSCE's structures and institutions, the organization, in order to comply with the decisions of the organization's participating states, operates by the Chairman-in-Office, the Parliamentary Assembly, the Office for Democratic Institutions and Human Rights,[38] the High Commissioner on National Minorities, the Representative on Freedom of the Media, the Court of Conciliation and Arbitration, the OSCE Minsk Group[39] and the Secretariat. Moreover, the OSCE-related bodies included in the organization are the Joint Consultative Group (which is a body that deals with the implementation of the provisions of the Treaty on Conventional Armed Forces in Europe of 1990, negotiated by the Warsaw Treaty Organization), NATO, and the Open Skies Consultative Commission as the implementing body of the Treaty on Open Skies of 1992, which established a regime of unarmed flight and flying details over the territories of 34 participating states.[40]

The OSCE Parliamentary Assembly promotes parliamentary engagement on issues of international concern, and deepens its relations with other institutions and partnerships with other international organizations, including through bilateral diplomacy on such matters as Turkey's military operation in north-eastern Syria in October 2019, the preparation of Albanian OSCE Chairmanship, the challenges facing the Arctic region, environmental risks, conflict resolutions in Eastern Ukraine, Mediterranean affairs, etc. Beyond those, the Parliamentary Assembly faced many other international issues, such as counter-terrorism cooperation in accordance with UN

---

[36] Ackermann 2012, pp. 11–18; Bakker 2004, pp. 393–413.

[37] Ackermann 2007.

[38] Glover 1997, pp. 166–168; Galbreath 2009, pp. 161–162.

[39] Haug 2016, pp. 342–357.

[40] Barberini 1998, pp. 12–22; Caruso 2007.

25 Organization for Security and Co-operation in Europe (OSCE)

SC Resolutions, migrant policies and the returning of minors from conflict zones with the support of IOM as well as the promotion of sustainable development and political experience to OSCE Election Observation.

The Secretariat, led by the OSCE's Secretary General, supports the organization's field activities and maintains strong relations with international, regional and non-governmental organizations in order to ensure implementation of the organization's political decisions and the empowerment of political dialogue and negotiation among the participating states. Within Secretariat, OSCE's Conflict Prevention Centre (CPC) supports OSCE's response in crisis situations and works in the politico-military dimension.[41] In terms of international security, CPC continues to focus on the crisis in and around Ukraine by supporting efforts to stabilize the security situation and implementation of the Minsk Agreements by the OSCE's Special Monitoring Mission in Ukraine (SMM), the Project Coordinator, and the Observer Mission at the Russian Checkpoints at Gukovo and Donetsk.

What's more, the OSCE's CPC supported the Transdniestrian process in Moldova in close cooperation with both the OSCE Mission to Moldova, as well as a Special Representative of the OSCE Chairperson-in-Office for the Transdniestrian Settlement Process, in order to reach an agreement on a list of measures agreed upon by both sides by the beginning of 2017. Beyond that, CPC supported a Special Representative of the OSCE Chairperson-in-Office for the South Caucasus and the OSCE Minsk Group Co-Chairs, the High-Level Planning Group and the Personal Representative of the Chairperson-in-Office on the conflict dealt within the OSCE Minsk Conference. In terms of international security and cooperation, CPC's activities include those in south-eastern Europe by assisting in political developments and joint efforts with the Member States, as well as activities in Central Asia and, especially, the OSCE Academy in Bishkek and the Border Management Staff College in Dushanbe.

In collaboration with other OSCE instruments, the Organization's Transnational Threats Department (TNTD) tried to address a series of transnational threats by providing assistance and sustainable activities, such as sharing information and best practices, convening joint expert meetings and coordinating on the implementation of similar projects. In particular, TNTD—through the Action against Terrorism Unit, the Strategic Police Matters Unit and the Border Security and Management Unit— tried to deal with many threats that have appeared in recent years. On the issue of combating cyber security and terrorism, violent extremism and radicalization, TNDT trained facilitators of the Leaders against Intolerance and Violent Extremism Initiative (LIVE) in close cooperation with INTERPOL and the UN and especially the UN Counterterrorism Executive Directorate (UNCTED) and CPC's activities, the UN Office on Drugs and Crime (UNODC).

In accordance with the above mentioned, OSCE addressed the threat posed by returning foreign terrorist fighters and capacity-building support to establish passenger data systems through the drafting of certain roadmaps within the support of the OSCE PolIS system and the TNDT-led Gender Equality Platform. Beyond

---

[41] De Graaf and Verstichel 2008, pp. 255–276.

those, the organization provided police assistance to participating states, both in countering threats posed by criminal activities and police development and reform, and especially by the implementation of the Annual Meetings on Artificial Intelligence and Law Enforcement and the Organization's Anti-drug Conference on Tackling Trafficking in Synthetic Drugs. In that situation, TNDT assisted law enforcement experts from the participating states and partners, including Russia, Bulgaria, Hungary, Romania, Georgia, Armenia and Azerbaijan.

The Organization is able to send missions to various participating states, with their consent, as part of crisis management and conflict prevention. It must be said that the OSCE has established a number of missions in order to help mitigate conflicts. Of particular importance were the Minsk Process, and the adoption, in 1992, of the Treaty on Open Skies and the Convention on Conciliation and Arbitration within the CSCE.

By the beginning of 2020, through the development of its institutional mechanisms, the OSCE ran various field operations and field activities in participating states that were structured to correspond to the three primary stages of the conflict-cycle—especially, unstable peace, crisis and conflict, as well as post-conflict rehabilitation. OSCE's Missions of Long Duration in Kosovo, Sandjak and Vojvodina (September 1992–July 1993) promoted dialogue between communities of those three regions and collected information on aspects relevant to human rights and fundamental freedoms violations, while also assisting in providing information on legislations on the protection of minorities, free media and democratic elections.[42] OSCE's Mission to Georgia (November 1992–December 2008), assisted the Georgian Government with democratization, conflict settlement, and protection of human rights. Mission to Estonia (February 1993–December 2001) established contacts with competent authorities on both the national and the local levels and non-governmental institutions and organizations, including political parties, trade unions and mass media organizations in order to re-create a civil society and facilitate dialogue.

Furthermore, the OSCE Mission to Latvia (November 1993–December 2001) addressed citizenship issues and was at the disposal of the Latvian Government, while the OSCE Mission to Ukraine (November 1994–April 1999), and its successor, the OSCE Project Co-ordinator in Ukraine, established the main task of supporting the work of experts on constitutional and economic matters to Ukraine and, especially, Crimea. Finally, the OSCE Mission to Croatia (July 1996–December 2007), which was replaced by the OSCE Office in Zagreb, provided, in cooperation with OSCE High Commissioner on National Minorities, the Office for Democratic Institutions and Human Rights and UN Transitional Authority in Eastern Slavonia, Baranja and Western Sirmium (UNTAES), assistance to Croatian authorities and individuals on the protection of human rights of national minorities and assisted with the full implementation of legislation and the functioning of democratic institutions and mechanisms.

Moreover, the OSCE Kosovo Verification Mission (October 1998–June 1999), which was replaced by the OSCE Mission in Kosovo, verified compliance by all

---

[42] Bellamy and Griffin 2002, pp. 1–26.

parties in Kosovo with UN SC Resolution 1199, maintained liaison with Federal Republic of Yugoslavia, Serbian and Kosovo authorities, supervised free elections in Kosovo, and reported recommendations to the OSCE Permanent Council. In 2019, OSCE ran fifteen field operations in eastern and south-eastern Europe, as well as in Asia—activities which vary with the context of the field operation and host country and governed by the mandate of each operation. Those operations enabled OSCE to play a key role in crisis management and contribute to early warning and conflict prevention.

While maintaining a catalytic presence even in the most dangerous situations, the OSCE is in the position to act as a neutral third party. More specifically, the OSCE has field operations in eastern and south-eastern Europe, central Asia and south Caucasus, established with the agreement of the host country and by consensus of the participating states. Putting commitments into practice, the organization's main activities have to do with the rule of law, democracy, legislative reform and law enforcement, the promotion of non-discrimination, minority rights, and media freedom.

This method of cooperation is the cornerstone of long-term missions, as it is inspired by the establishment of lasting confidence among the participating states. Moreover, depending on the circumstances and the situation prevailing in the region, several field operations and missions have a specific mandate that concerns, especially, early warning and conflict prevention, as well as developments on the ground and managing post-conflict crises. Given the responsibility of the OSCE's Conflict Prevention Centre for planning the establishment of and the closure of field operations, these operations maintain partnerships with national authorities, civil societies, institutions, NGOs and other International Organizations, in the interest of achieving the desired result.

Based on the above principles and aspirations, missions have been undertaken in Albania, Armenia, Azerbaijan, Bosnia and Herzegovina, Kazakhstan, Kyrgyzstan, Kosovo, Belarus, Uzbekistan, Russia Federation, Serbia and Montenegro, Turkmenistan, Estonia, Latvia, Georgia, Tajikistan, former Yugoslav Republic of Macedonia, Croatia, Ukraine, South Caucasus and Moldova. The OSCE and the High Commissioner on National Minorities Mission to Ukraine were particularly successful, which contributed significantly to resolving the country's constitutional crisis. Georgia and Moldova have also made significant progress towards a political solution to the conflict.

The OSCE has recently intervened in the crisis of Ukraine at the invitation of the government to facilitate political dialogue with the aim of resolving the conflict and finding a solution. The strategic discussions that took place during Security Dialogues in 2019 indicated the major importance of the Forums for Security and Co-operation as a unique platform for dialogue on security issues. Even though the situation in Ukraine remained the dominant issue, the Forum nonetheless discussed matters related to military and defence co-operation, such as aspects of the field of small arms and light weapons, stockpiles of conventional ammunition, politico-military aspects of security and the implementation of Security Council Resolution 1540, the implementation of women, peace and security agenda, confidence and security-building measures as well as aspects of modern warfare. More specifically, in order to promote stability and cooperative security, the OSCE empowered dialogue on subregional military defence cooperation using an approach of transparency and confidence, especially in the Visegrad Group, regional organizations in Central Asia, as well as the Collective Security Treaty Organization (CSTO).

The Office for Democratic Institutions and Human Rights (ODIHR), as the OSCE's primary institution for focusing on the human dimension of security, promotes assistance to participating states to promote and strengthen the rule of law, the respect of human rights, democracy and non-discrimination. In 2019, ODIHR observed 15 elections and electoral processes and supported 13 participating states by providing technical expertise and recommendations on the electoral legislation and process. Also, ODIHR continued to support the participating states in strengthening their judicial accountability and independence as well as the promotion of openness in law-making processes and the protection of human rights and fundamental values.

The OSCE High Commissioner on National Minorities (HCNM) supported many programmes centred on tolerance, diversity and education in Central Asia and Balkans and through regional partnerships, contributing to early warning, conflict prevention and crisis management. Also, the OSCE Representative on Freedom of the Media observed media developments among the participating states in respect to free media and freedom of expression as well as the safety of journalists through various conferences and meetings.

The Office of the Co-ordinator of OSCE Economic and Environmental Activities (OCEEA) also supported the participating states in the implementation of their commitments to environmental and economic progress and security with the aim of strengthening stability and security and preventing conflicts in the organization's area. More specifically, OCEEA supported states in meeting objectives set up by transnational frameworks, such as good economic governance and the fight against corruption in Ukraine and Armenia, via establishing integrity systems at the municipal level and an anti-corruption strategy. From the scope of environmental co-operation, OCEEA, continued to focus on transboundary water cooperation and recently implemented the Dniester River Basin Commission and Water Diplomacy Workshops in order to enhance water cooperation among the participating states and promote good environmental governance.

In addition, from that point of view, the OSCE's Office of the Special Representative and Co-ordinator for Combating Human Trafficking in Human Beings (CTHB) is extremely important for preventing human trafficking, prosecuting perpetrators and supporting victims. The Office dealt with the usage of technology to combat trafficking in human beings along migration routes and the building of new partnerships in order to minimize the related crimes through the OSCE area and identify victims, especially in Serbia, Croatia, Austria, Georgia, Romania, Iceland, Turkmenistan and Tajikistan.

25.5 OSCE's Legal Framework through International Security

The OSCE undoubtedly possesses rights and duties under international law,[43] despite the fact that there is no formal founding treaty, which is not an insurmountable obstacle to the establishment of the organization and all of its legal documents were adopted by the heads of the executive power of each of the participating states.[44] The daily decisions of the organization are taken by the Ministers of Foreign Affairs or their representatives, who are permanently accredited to the organization and form the OSCE Permanent Council. The management of issues relevant to the organization's activities at the national level is carried out by the relevant governmental bodies under the coordination of the Ministries of Foreign Affairs.

The OSCE plays a major role in strengthening and developing the foundation of Europe's security architecture and in assisting countries in transition.[45] This state partnership, which is the OSCE's root cause, has a permanent character and not just a framework for meetings and consultations between the participating states.[46] This was already revealed by the recommendation of the CSCE, which was not set up with a limited duration or a specific purpose that it should fulfil and then ceased to exist but as a permanent framework for co-operation. This permanence of the character and the competences of the organization derive from the subsequent creation and operation of a stable structure with permanent functional structure, which is implemented with the traditional form for all the International Organizations with decisive, executive and administrative institutions.

The organization sets a specific aim for objectives that are in the agreed texts and documents that provide for the three dimensions of security cooperation in the participating states and constitute the outline of the competences of the OSCE institutions. All of the organization's activities are aimed at achieving these objectives while ensuring the equal and consistent security of all participating states. Thus, the OSCE as an international actor has legal personality which derives from the interaction of the participating states in the organization itself.[47] A strong criterion for establishing the organization's legal personality is also the fact that the existence and activation of the institutions that make up the organization is a necessary prerequisite for the status of the OSCE as an International Organization which certifies, as a matter of substance, the autonomy of the Organization against of its members.[48]

What needs to be also stressed is that the existence of an International Organization requires an internal autonomy of the organization itself. This, practically, means that the organization is governed by an institutional framework that does not fall within

---

[43] Akande 2018, pp. 281–283.

[44] Bredimas 2018, pp. 75–80.

[45] Cottey 2001, pp. 43–61.

[46] Crawford 2012, pp. 687–689.

[47] McGoldrick 1993, pp. 135–182.

[48] Cassese 1990, pp. 210–231.

the internal legal order of a participating state or of another subject of international law, but is developed within the framework set forth by International Law itself. Since its inception, the CSCE has been placed within the international legal order by the decision of the participating states to distribute the Helsinki Final Act as a document of the United Nations decision, which was also repeated on the Paris Charter for a New Europe.[49] The integration into the legal order confirms the practice of the participating states and the OSCE institutions, as well as third parties, which have an institutionalized relationship with the organization.[50]

Within the framework of international law, the OSCE has developed a sophisticated legal and administrative system, distinct from any participating state, which allows the organization to fulfil its objectives.[51] The organization shall be financed by a budget adopted by the OSCE Permanent Council with contributions from the participating States, calculated on the basis of the criteria adopted by all International Organizations. There is also the possibility of voluntary contributions, which are used to implement specific programs in the three dimensions of security. The financial management of the organization follows the procedures adopted by its institutions. Finally, the OSCE enjoys the same autonomy in terms of personnel and staffing, which are regulated by the Organization's Staff Regulations.[52]

25.6 Conclusion

The OSCE, formerly the CSCE, is the broadest international structure and the largest regional organization in the Euro-Atlantic area, and includes member states from European countries, non-European former Soviet republics, the United States, Canada and Asian states.[53] Going back to the Cold War, the CSCE's constituting document, the Helsinki Final Act, was signed on 1 August 1975, playing an important role as it brought the two sides in the conflict closer under conditions of uncertainty.[54] Since the creation of the Organization, it has been clear that its purpose was to establish and empower transnational security through cooperation and dialogue among the participating states.

The CSCE, as said, concentrated on the establishment of a collective security system through agreements, dialogue and political cooperation on the basic principles of international relations between the participating states. As a mechanism on cooperative security, through its three dimensions, the CSCE directly linked to the establishment of major changes in the institutional democratization in European states, based on respect for human rights and fundamental freedoms. Used to being

---

[49] Schermers and Blokker 2011, pp. 1196–1997.

[50] Merini 1996, pp. 21–34.

[51] Di Stasi 1999, pp. 237–270.

[52] Decaux 1994b, pp. 271–273.

[53] Zieba 2018, pp. 214–222.

[54] Kropatcheva 2015, pp. 10–11.

25 Organization for Security and Co-operation in Europe (OSCE)

at the heart of the European security dialogue,[55] it is significant to note that the concept of security from CSCE to OSCE has rapidly changed, with many transformations along with social and political changes in the organization's area.

As a regional international organization, with political, human, economic and ecological dimensions, with a military dimension and mechanisms on collective security for observing its provisions, the OSCE has a major role as a European security mechanism,[56] through the rise of international norms and standards, the promotion of democratic values, the establishment of peace, the resolving of crises and disputes, and the establishment of military order and disarmament. Given the particularity of the OSCE's peace-building instruments and the co-operative approach,[57] the organization, among others, is a forum for the promotion of democratization in Europe. It is assumed that the OSCE's purpose is to address challenges in a co-operative and comprehensive security community through the cooperation, stability and security in the organization's area. As a modern security organization, the OSCE's goal is to create and promote an inter-state community of security.

Beyond that, the OSCE follows an institutional approach: the participating states should devote more attention to strengthening the organization and operational management should be reinforced in order to focus the OSCE's continuity on tackling the major issues that it is dealing with. The organization's approach towards establishing democratic structures is a prerequisite for the long-term goal of building a safe and operational area of democratization, stability and peace. Given its pivotal role in the preventive diplomacy, since its beginning the OSCE has promoted the development of a security community through the redefinition of security and the development of mutual trust among the participating states.

The functioning of the OSCE suggests the neoliberal argument that such international institutions matter in the context of the coordination of states and security-building institutions are mobilizing materials and normative resources for the development of a transnational collective identity.

References

Ackermann A (2007) Forward to Peace and Security in the Postmodern World: The OSCE and Conflict Resolution. Routledge, New York

Ackermann A (2012) Strengthening the OSCE's Capacities in Conflict Prevention, Crisis Management and Conflict Resolution. Security and Human Rights 1: 11–18

Adler M (1998) Seeds of Peaceful Change: The OSCE's Security Community Building Model. In: Adler M, Barnett M (eds) Security Communities. Cambridge University Press, Cambridge, pp 132–160

Akande D (2018) International Organizations. In: Evans D M (ed) International Law, 5th edn. Oxford University Press, Oxford, pp 248–279

---

[55] Simakova 2016, p. 3.

[56] Larive 2014, pp. 173–175.

[57] Biscop 2006, pp. 25–29.

Alcock A (2000) A History of the Protection of Regional Cultural Minorities in Europe. From the Edict of Nantes to the Present Day. Palgrave Macmillan, London

Bakker E (2004) A Culture of Conflict Prevention: OSCE Experiences and Cooperation with the EU. In: Kronenberger V, Wouters J (eds) The European Union and Conflict Prevention. Policy and Legal Aspects. TMC Asser Press, The Hague, pp 393–413

Barberini G (1998) Sicurezza e Cooperazione da Vancouver a Vladivostock: Introduzione allo Studio dell' Organizzazione per la Sicurezza e la Cooperazione in Europa (OSCE). Giappichelli, Turin

Bekes L (2009) The Warsaw Pact and the 1991 Process from 1965 to 1970. In: Loth W, Soutou G H (eds) Making of Détente: Eastern and Western Europe in the Cold War. Routledge, Arlington, pp 201–220

Bellamy J A, Griffin S (2002) OSCE Peacekeeping: Lessons from the Kosovo Verification Mission. European Security 11(1): 1–26

Birnbaum E K, Peters I (1990) The CSCE: A Reassessment of its Role in the 1980's. Review of International Studies 16(4): 305–319

Biscop S (2005) The European Security Strategy: A Global Agenda for Positive Power. Ashgate Publishing, Aldershot

Biscop S (2006) The EU, the OSCE and the European Security Architecture: Network or Labyrinth? Asia Europe Journal 4(1): 25–29

Bloed A (1990) From Helsinki to Vienna: Basic Documents of the Helsinki Process. Martinus Nijhoff Publishers, Dordrecht/London

Bloed A (1991) Monitoring the Human Dimension of the CSCE: In Search of its Effectiveness. In: Bloed A et al (eds) Monitoring Human Rights in Europe: Comparing International Procedures and Mechanisms. Martinus Nijhoff Publishers, Dordrecht/Boston/London

Bloed A (1994) The Challenges of Change: The Helsinki Summit of the CSCE and its Aftermath. Martinus Nijhoff Publishers, Dordrecht

Bortloff J (1996) Die Organisation fur Sicherheit und Zusammenarbeit in Europa: Eine Volkerrechtliche Bestandsaufnahme. Duncker und Humblot, Berlin

Bothe M et al. (1997) The OSCE in the Maintenance of Peace and Security, Conflict Prevention, Crisis Management and Peaceful Settlement of Disputes. Kluwer Law International, The Hague/London/Boston

Bredimas A (2018) Le Phenomene de la Secession dans le Cadre de l'Organization de Securite et de Cooperation en Europe (OSCE/CSCE): Aspects Juridiques et Autres. In: Samara-Krispi A (ed) Dignatio Rerum Professor Elias Krispis. Melanges a la Mémoire du Professeur Elias Krispis. Sakkoulas Publications, Athens/Thessaloniki

Buergenthal T (1990) The Copenhagen CSCE Meeting: A New Public Order for Europe. Human Rights Law Journal 11(1–2): 217–232

Buergenthal T (1991) The CSCE Rights System. George Washington Journal of International Law and Economics 25(2): 333–378

Caruso U (2007) Interplay between the Council of Europe, OSCE, EU and NATO. European Academy, Bozen

Cassese A (1990) Remarks on Scelle's Theory of "Role Splitting" (Dedoublement Fonctionnet) in International Law. European Journal of International Law 1: 210–231

Crawford J (2012) Brownlie's Principles of Public International Law, 8th edn. Cambridge University Press, Cambridge

Cottey A (2001) The OSCE: Crowning Jewel or Talking Shop? In: Smith M A, Timmins G (eds) Uncertain Europe: Building a New European Security Order? Routledge, London, pp 43–61

CSCE (1975) Helsinki Final Act. https://www.osce.org/helsinki-final-act?download=true. Accessed 16 August 2020

CSCE (1990a) Charter of Paris for a New Europe. https://www.osce.org/mc/39516?download=true. Accessed 12 August 2020

CSCE (1990b) Document of the Bonn Conference on Economic Co-operation in Europe Convened in Accordance with the Relevant Provisions of the Concluding Document of the Vienna Meeting

25 Organization for Security and Co-operation in Europe (OSCE)

of the Conference on Security and Co-operation in Europe. https://www.osce.org/eea/14081?download=true. Accessed 18 August 2020

CSCE (1990c) Document of the Copenhagen Meeting of the Conference on the Human Dimension of the CSCE. https://www.osce.org/odihr/elections/14304?download=true. Accessed 11 August 2020

CSCE (1991a) Berlin Meeting of the CSCE Council, 19–20 June 1991. https://www.osce.org/mc/40234?download=true. Accessed 5 August 2020

CSCE (1991b) Document of the Cracow Symposium on the Cultural Heritage of the CSCE Participating States. https://www.osce.org/library/24396?download=true. Accessed 3 July 2020

CSCE (1991d) Report of the CSCE Meeting of Experts on National Minorities, Geneva 1991. https://www.osce.org/hcnm/14588?download=true. Accessed 19 August 2020

CSCE (1991e) Report of the CSCE Meeting of Experts on Peaceful Settlement of Disputes, Valletta 1991. https://www.osce.org/secretariat/30115?download=true. Accessed 10 August 2020

CSCE (1991f) The Madrid Document. https://www.osce.org/pa/40791?download=true. Accessed 14 August 2020

CSCE (1992a) Concluding Act of the Negotiation on Personnel Strength of Conventional Armed Forces in Europe. https://www.osce.org/library/14093?download=true. Accessed 11 July 2020

CSCE (1992b) CSCE Helsinki Document 1992: The Challenges of Change. https://www.osce.org/mc/39530?download=true. Accessed 19 August 2020

CSCE (1992c) Second Meeting of the Council. Summary of Conclusions. Prague Document on Further Development of CSCE Institutions and Structures. Declaration on Non-Proliferation and Arms Transfers. Prague 1992. https://www.osce.org/mc/40270?download=true. Accessed 21 August 2020

CSCE (1992?) Treaty on Open Skies. https://www.osce.org/library/14127?download=true. Accessed 4 September 2020

CSCE (1994) CSCE Budapest Document 1994: Towards a Genuine Partnership in a New Era. https://www.osce.org/mc/39554?download=true. Accessed 20 August 2020

Decaux E (1994a) CSCE Institutional Issues at the Budapest Conference. Helsinki Monitor 5(3): 18–26

Decaux E (1994b) La CSCE au Lendemain du Conseil de Rome: Un Bilan de Transition Institutionnelle. European Journal of International Law 5(2): 267–284

De Graaf V, Verstichel A (2008) OSCE Crisis Management and OSCE-EU Relations. In: Blockmans S (ed) The European Union and Crisis Management. TMC Asser Press, The Hague, pp 255–276

Di Stasi A (1999) La OSCE: Effettivita Instituzionale e 'Processo Normativo'. La Comunita Internazionale: 237–270

Du Pont Y (2000) Democratization through Supporting Civil Society in Bosnia and Herzegovina. Helsinki Monitor 11(4): 7–18

Flynn G, Farrell H (1999) Piecing Together the Democratic Peace: The CSCE Norms and the 'Construction' of Security in Post-Cold War Europe. International Organizations 53(3): 505–536

Galbreath D (2009) Putting the Colour into Revolutions? The OSCE and Civil Society in the Post-Soviet Region. Journal of Communist Studies and Transition Politics 25: 161–180

Gawrich A (2017) Inter-Organizational Relations in the Field of Democratisation: Cooperation or Delegation? The European Union, the OSCE and the Council of Europe. In: Biermann R, Koops A J (eds) Palgrave Handbook of Inter-Organizational Relations in World Politics. Palgrave Macmillan, London, pp 526–546

Ghebali V Y (1989) La Diplomatie de la Détente: La CSCE, d'Helsinki a Vienne (1973–1989). Bruylant, Brussels

Ghebali V Y (1996) L'OSCE dans l'Europe Post-Communiste: 1990–1996. Vers une Identite Paneuropeenne de Securite. Bruylant, Brussels

Glover F A (1995) The Human Dimension of the OSCE: From Standard-Setting to Implementation. Helsinki Monitor 6(3): 31–39

Glover F A (1997) The Human Dimension of the OSCE: The ODIHR in Warsaw. In: von Bredow W et al. (eds) European Security. Palgrave Macmillan, London, pp 166–179

Graeger N, Novosseloff A (2003) The Role of the OSCE and the EU. In: Pugh M C, Sidh W P S (eds) The United Nations and Regional Security: Europe and beyond. Lynne Rienner, Boulder, pp 75–94

Haug H (2016) The Minsk Agreements and the OSCE Special Monitoring Mission. Security and Human Rights 27(3–4): 342–357

Heraclides A (1993a) Helsinki-II and its Aftermath: The Making of the OSCE into an International Organization. Pinter, London

Heraclides A (1993b) Security and Co-operation in Europe: The Human Dimension. Frank Cass, London

Holsti K J (1982) Bargaining Theory and Diplomatic Reality: The CSCE Negotiations. Review of International Studies 8(3): 159–170

Johannsen V L, Hvenegaard-Lassen K (1992) Minority Rights in Europe: Progress in the OSCE. Danish Center for Human Rights, Copenhagen

Kokkinides T (1995) L'OSCE: Une Opportunité Perdu pour la Sécurité Européenne? Relations Internationales et Stratégiques 18: 89–99

Kropatcheva E (2012) Russia and the Role of the OSCE in European Security: A 'Forum' for Dialogue or a 'Battlefield' of Interests? European Security 21(3): 370–394

Kropatcheva E (2015) The Evolution of Russia's OSCE Policy: From the Promises of the Helsinki Final Act to the Ukrainian Crisis. Journal of Contemporary European Studies 23(1): 6–24

Larive M (2014) The European Architecture: OSCE, NATO and the EU. In: Dominguez R (ed) The OSCE: Soft Security for a Hard World. Peter Lang, Brussels, pp 157–178

Lehne S (1991) The Vienna Meeting of the Conference on Security and Cooperation in Europe, 1986–1989: A Turning Point in East-West Relations. Westview Press, Boulder

Lucas R M (1990) The Conference on Security and Cooperation in Europe and the Post-Cold War Era. Institut fur Friedensforschung und Sicherheitspolitik, Hamburg

Lucas R M (1993) The CSCE in the 1990s: Constructing European Security and Cooperation. Nomos, Baden-Baden

Maresca J J (1985) To Helsinki: The Conference on Security and Cooperation in Europe, 1973–1975. Duke University Press, Durham

McGoldrick D (1993) The Development of the Conference on Security and Co-operation in Europe: From Process to Institution. In: Jackson B, McGoldrick D (eds) Legal Visions of a New Europe. Graham & Trotman, London, pp. 173–182

Merini C (1996) Le Partenariat: Instrument Juridique et/ou Politique: Le Cas de l'OSCE. Revue Quebecoise de Droit International 9: 21–34

Merlinger M, Ostrauskaite R (2005) A Dense Policy Space? The Police Aid of the OSCE and the EU. In: Institute for Peace Research and Security Policy (ed) OSCE Yearbook 2004, Volume 10. Nomos, Baden-Baden, pp 341–357

Mosser M W (2015) Embracing 'Embedded Security': The OSCE's Understated but Significant Role in the European Security Architecture. European Security 24(4): 579–599

Nesi G (1994) Dalla CSCE all' OSCE: La Conferenza di Riesame di Budapest. La Comunita Internazionale: 736–742

OSCE (1996) Lisbon Document 1996. https://www.osce.org/mc/39539?download=true. Accessed 16 August 2020

OSCE (1999) Istanbul Document 1999. https://www.osce.org/mc/39569?download=true. Accessed 11 August 2020

OSCE (2010) Astana Commemorative Declaration towards a Security Community. https://www.osce.org/cio/74985?download=true. Accessed 16 August 2020

Pentikainen M (1997) The Human Dimension of the OSCE in the 1996 Vienna Review Meeting. Helsinki Monitor 1: 5–11

Pentikainen M (1998) The 1997 Implementation Meeting on Human Dimension Issues of the OSCE. Helsinki Monitor 9(2): 18–37

Raday F (2002) Self-determination and Minority Rights. Fordham International Law Journal 26(3): 453–499

Romano A (2012) The European Community and the Belgrade CSCE. In: Bilandzic V et al (eds) From Helsinki to Belgrade. The First CSCE Follow-up Meeting and the Crisis of Détente. Bonn University Press, Gottingen, pp 205–224

Roth S (1991) Comments on the CSCE Meeting of Experts on National Minorities and its Concluding Document. Human Rights Law Journal 12: 330–331

Roukounas E (1993) Remarques sur la Portée Juridiques des Engagement CSCE Concernant la Dimension Humaine. In: Decaux E, Sicilianos L A (eds) La CSCE Dimension Humaine et Règlement des Différends. Montchrestien, Paris, pp 89–95

Sadigbayli V R (2014) Codification of the Inviolability of Frontier Principle in the Helsinki Final Act: Its Purpose and Implication for Conflict Resolution. Security and Human Rights 24(3–4): 392–417

Sapiro M (1995) Changing the CSCE into the OSCE: Legal Aspects of a Political Transformation. American Journal of International Law 89(3): 631–637

Schermers G H, Blokker M N (2011) International Institutional Law, 5th edn. Martinus Nijhoff Publishers, The Hague

Schlager S (1991) The Procedural Framework of the CSCE: From the Helsinki Consultations to the Paris Charter 1972–1990. Human Rights Law Journal 12: 221–229

Schweisfurth T (1976) Zur Frage der Rechtsnatur, Verbindlichkeit und Völkerrechtlichen Relevanz der KSZE Schulbauten. Zeitschrift für Ausländisches Öffentliches Recht und Völkerrecht 36: 681–689

Shaw M (2017) International Law, 8th edn. Cambridge University Press, Cambridge

Simakova A M (2016) The European Union in the OSCE in the Light of the Ukrainian Crisis: Trading Actorness for Effectiveness? EU Diplomacy Paper 3: 3–7

Sneek T (1994) The CSCE in the New Europe: From Process to Regional Arrangement. Indiana International and Comparative Law Review 5(1): 1–33

Tretter H (1989) Human Rights in the Concluding Documents of the Vienna Follow-Up Meeting of the Conference on Security and Co-operation in Europe of January 15, 1989: An Introduction. Human Rights Law Journal 1–2: 257–270

Wegner W, Mastny V (2008) New Perspectives on the Origins of the CSCE Process. In: Wegner W et al. (eds) Origins of the European Security System: The Helsinki Process Revisited, 1965–75. Routledge, London, pp 3–22

Wohlfeld M (2008) Reconceptualization of Security in the CSCE and OSCE. In: Brauch H G et al. (eds) Globalization and Environmental Challenges. Springer, Berlin/Heidelberg, pp 643–650

Zieba R (2018) The Euro-Atlantic Security System in the 21st Century, From Cooperation to Crisis. Springer, Berlin/Heidelberg

Ioannis P. Tzivaras earned the LLM and PhD degrees from the Faculty of Law at Democritus University of Thrace (Greece). He is a Tutor at the Open University of Cyprus' Department of Economics and Management.

Chapter 26
European Union (EU): Security, Conflict and Migration

Lehte Roots

Contents

26.1 Introduction 576
26.2 Historical Overview 577
26.3 Treaty Provisions for the CSDP and CFSP 580
    26.3.1 The Common Security and Defence Policy 581
    26.3.2 The Strategy of European Security 582
    26.3.3 The European Agenda on Security 583
26.4 Court Jurisdiction 584
26.5 Security and Conflict in Process of Change and Migration Management 586
    26.5.1 The Response of the European Union to the Migrant Crisis 587
26.6 Conclusion 589
References 593

Abstract This chapter discusses EU security and conflict resolution measures. The idea to maintain peace and security in the European continent was the trigger to start integrating European countries under one umbrella. In the European integration process, the security issues have taken a secondary place after the economic integration. Recent developments in the world and the massive movements of persons towards Europe have made EU countries revaluate their approach to migration and security. Terrorist attacks and massive flow of irregular migrants on the shores of Europe has made the European Union set up more instruments to tackle these issues at the European level. Security and migration management is not seen any longer as a sovereign issue of each member state. The chapter provides a short analysis of EU migration policy and legislation in the context of security. Also, the author discusses the role of the European Court of Justice in the issues of security and how the cases have been handled in the situation where the court does not have full competence. Finally, the problematics of internal and external security policy are discussed in the context of security.

Keywords EU security policy · EU defence policy · EU migration law · CFSP · CSDF · EU migration policy · European integration

---

L. Roots (✉)
School of Law, Governance and Society, Tallinn University, Tallinn, Estonia
e-mail: lehte.roots@tlu.ee

© T.M.C. ASSER PRESS and the authors 2022
S. Sayapin et al. (eds.), *International Conflict and Security Law*,
https://doi.org/10.1007/978-94-6265-515-7_26

26.1 Introduction

Security and defence have played a crucial role in European integration. As Craig and De Burca state: "During the war, the resistance movement had strongly supported the idea of a united Europe, to replace the destructive forces of national chauvinism".[1] When Europe started to reunite and the first steps to create a community between national states were initiated, the aim was to bring peace to the European continent. There have been several initiatives that attempted to start coordinating the security issues under one umbrella but it has always been and is still in the form of cooperation. The European Union cannot be compared with federal states like the United States, as the European Union is a special type of union where its member states have maintained their sovereignty in many fields. The first evidence of cooperation in defence between countries situated at the European continents dates back to 1948 when the Brussels Treaty between France, the United Kingdom and the three Benelux countries were signed. The Western European Union was created in 1954. Also, the NATO agreement of 1949 played a role in further cooperation between states in Europe.

Proposals for a political union were discussed in 1948 in the Hague at the Congress of Europe, but it was easier to continue cooperation at the economic level than in the field of security. Even now, the European Union does not have its own army, but it does have a Common Security and Defence Policy. Article 2 point 4 of the Treaty on the Functioning of the European Union (TFEU) states that "The Union shall have competence, in accordance with the provisions of the Treaty on European Union, to define and implement a common foreign and security policy, including the progressive framing of common defence policy." Nevertheless, it cannot be compared to NATO cooperation, which has troops that can physically react in situations when it is needed and decided. Therefore, the reaction of the European Union to conflicts and conflict resolution might not be what is expected by the EU citizens to whom this security policy is dedicated. It is TFEU Article 67 that provides us the Union that "shall constitute an area of freedom, security and justice with respect for fundamental rights and the different legal systems and traditions of the Member States".

In the case of internal security, according to Article 67 point 3 "The Union shall endeavour to ensure a high level of security through measures to prevent and combat crime, racism and xenophobia, and through measures for coordination and cooperation between police and judicial authorities and other competent authorities, as well as through the mutual recognition of judgments in criminal matters and, if necessary, through the approximation of criminal laws". Therefore, it is not only the task of EU member states to keep up security, but also the responsibility of the whole European Union as an institution. It is the obligation of the European Council to define the strategic guidelines for legislative and operational planning within the area of freedom, security and justice.[2]

---

[1] Craig and De Burca 2011, p. 4.

[2] Article 68, TFEU.

26 European Union (EU): Security, Conflict and Migration 577

The efforts of the EU to respond to both the old and the new security threats involves the concept of human security.[3] To analyse the concept, external policies of the EU have to be taken into account: the Common Foreign and Security Policy (CFSP) and the Common Security and Defence Policy (CSDP). These policies have been functioning as one of the main policy instruments for the EU in the field of safety and security. They promote and maintain both external and internal stability. The European Security Strategy (ESS) will be analysed as it outlines a common focus for the EU in the field of safety of the EU citizens. To conclude, there will be an analysis of the European Agenda on Security, which will cover five years, from 2015 to 2020. While the EU has taken a leading role in promoting peace and security, there is criticism about the lack of political strength in the EU's actions regarding the high expectations set out in the ESS.

This chapter will discuss the Security and Defence Policy and respective actions of the EU at the international level. The purpose of the chapter is to analyse the concept of human security and its promotion and visibility in the EU's foreign and security policies while dealing with the current migrant crisis in the EU. Additionally, it should be mentioned that the EU is also paying close attention to internal security concerns that will be discussed in this chapter as well.

26.2 Historical Overview

It was Robert Schuman who proposed coal and steel cooperation under a single High Authority, with the option for other European states to participate in it. The plan was drafted by Jean Monnet and it attempted to stabilize French and German relations after the war. The ECSC was set up for fifty years and expired in 2002. This was the first significant step towards European integration and stabilization of security. The ECSC Treaty was signed in 1951 by France, Germany, Italy and the Benelux countries. In 1950, France proposed the Pleven plan, the setting up of a European Defence Community (EDC) with a European army, a common budget, and joint institutions. The EDC Treaty was signed in 1952 by the six ECSC states. It was argued that if there was to be a European army, a common European foreign policy would also be needed. In 1953, a draft was presented for the European Political Community that was an effort to design a European federation, including a coordinated foreign policy. Developments of federalization were stopped by France where the National Assembly did not ratify the EDC Treaty. Only in 1992 was the Maastricht Treaty signed, which established the European Union.[4] However, the common Security and Defence Policy remained in the framework of cooperation.

After the Cold War, the EU shifted its focus from mainly economic issues towards a global political entity, which is a part of not only securing the safety of Europe but also a part of the global security agenda. The Common Foreign and Security Policy

---

[3] For more about human security, see United Nations Trust Fund for Human Security 2020.

[4] Craig and De Burca 2011, p. 5.

(CFSP), established in the Treaty of Maastricht in 1992, enables the EU to speak and act as one entity in global affairs. The EU's Foreign and Security Policy seeks to "preserve peace and strengthen international security; promote international cooperation; develop and consolidate: democracy, rule of law and respect for human rights and fundamental freedoms".[5] The establishment of the CFSP added a new framework to the EU's external policies, giving more room for a common involvement. The objectives of the CFSP[6] include safeguarding the EU's values, fundamental interests, security, independence and integrity. Preserving peace and preventing conflict in order to strengthen international security is done in accordance with the purposes and principles of the UN Charter. The EU promotes supporting the human rights and principles of international law.[7]

Significant changes were introduced by the Lisbon Treaty in 2009. It abolished the three-pillar system of the European Union and the European Community.[8] Furthermore, the CFSP rules remained distinct and executive authority continues to reside principally with the European Council and the Council.[9] Article 2(4) of the TFEU gives the following guidance: "The Union shall have competence, in accordance with the provisions of the Treaty on European Union, to define and implement a common foreign and security policy, including the progressive framing of a common defence policy". Title V of TEU is setting up the rules for common foreign and security policy and it derives from it that the decision making in this area continues to be more intergovernmental and less supranational compared to other areas of Union competence. Also, the fact that the European Council and the Council have dominance in decision making, the instruments used for CFSP are different compared to other policies, give us an understanding that CFSP holds a special position within EU. As the common security and defence policy is not listed in part 3 of the TFEU, it is clear that it is not exclusive the competence of the European Union nor is it mentioned in article 6 of TFEU which sets supporting, coordinating and supplementing member state action. One can find the guidelines for European foreign and security policy in declarations 13 and 14 attached to the treaty.

From these declarations we learn that there is an "office of High Representative of the Union for Foreign Affairs and Security Policy and the establishment of an External Action Service and it should not "affect the responsibilities of the Member States, as they currently exist, for the formulation and conduct of their foreign policy nor of their national representation in third countries and international organisations".[10]

States have also maintained their direct obligations to the United Nations and its Security Council and Common Defence policy of EU "do not prejudice the specific character"[11] and "will not affect the existing legal basis, responsibilities, and powers

---

[5] EU undated.

[6] Article 21.2 TEU Treaty of European Union

[7] EUISS 2016.

[8] Roots 2009.

[9] Article 22, 24 TEU.

[10] Declaration 13 on the common foreign and security policy.

[11] Declaration 13 on the common foreign and security policy.

26 European Union (EU): Security, Conflict and Migration

of each Member State in relation to the formulation and conduct of its foreign policy, its national diplomatic service, relations with third countries and participation in international organisations"[12] of member state policies. It is also very clearly stated in the declaration that "Common Foreign and Security Policy do not give new powers to the Commission to initiate decisions, nor do they increase the role of the European Parliament".[13]

In June 1999, Cologne European Council discussion was improved about The European Security and Defence Policy (ESDP). Prior to that, one can observe a British-French declaration on developing Europe's ability to take action in this field issued in Saint-Malo in 1998. The EU heads of state and government adopted a "Declaration on strengthening the common European policy on security and defence", which stated the fundamental objective of the European Security and Defence Policy. Europe has to conduct international crisis management operations and establish the necessary structures and the required civilian and military capabilities.[14] The 1999 Helsinki European Council stated: "The European Council underlines its determination to develop an autonomous capacity to take decisions and, where NATO as a whole is not engaged, to launch and conduct EU-led military operations in response to international crises."[15] The Council also arranged to build up the military capabilities essential for such operations by 2003, also known as the 'Helsinki Headline Goal'.

The required structural decisions for Common Security policy implementation were made at the Nice European Council in 2000. The most important bodies that were created are:

Firstly, the Political and Security Committee (PSC) that includes ambassadors from the 28 EU member states who deal with all Common Foreign and Security Policy issues. It exercises political control and strategic direction of crisis management operations on behalf of the Council.

Secondly, the Military Committee of the EU (EUMC) that is made up of the member states' Chiefs of General Staff or their representatives. The Military Committee advises the PSC on military crisis management issues and the development of military capabilities. The Chair of the Military Committee also acts as an advisor to the Secretary-General/High Representative on all military issues. The Military Staff, part of the EU-Council Secretariat, does the preparatory work for the Military Committee.

Thirdly, the Committee for Civilian Aspects of Crisis Management (CIVCOM) that involves diplomats and civilian crisis management specialists and advises the PSC on all issues of civilian crisis management.

---

[12] Declaration 14 on the common foreign and security policy.

[13] Declaration 14 on the common foreign and security policy.

[14] Cologne European Council 3–4 June 1999: Conclusions of the Presidency. Available at https://www.europarl.europa.eu/summits/kol1_en.htm.

[15] Helsinki European Council 10–11 December 1999: Conclusions of the Presidency. Available at https://www.europarl.europa.eu/summits/hel1_en.htm.

The ESDP is an integral part of the CFSP and functions according to the traditional rules of intergovernmental cooperation. Decisions must be unanimous and are usually made by the General Affairs and External Relations Council (GAERC). Since 2004 the defence ministers of Member States meet in GAERC format. They can make decisions regarding the European Defence Agency and military capabilities. To be able to carry out crisis management operations, the EU had to create the relevant structures and develop the necessary procedures.

The 2014 Annual report from the High Representative of the European Union for Foreign Affairs and Security Policy to the European Parliament on the main aspects and basic choices of the CFSP addressed issues concerning migration, multilateral order and support to democracy, human rights, international humanitarian law and the rule of law. The report was endorsed by the Council on June 20, 2015. It acknowledges that there is a need to further improve the links between the EU's internal and external policies and migration policy needs to be a much stronger part of the Union's external policy. The EU tries to place migration on its political, economic and social agendas in cooperation with its neighbouring countries. Migration is seen as a global, complex and multilateral phenomenon that requires comprehensive, coherent and long-term responses from the EU.

In 2014, the European Union Institute for Security Studies was established to provide research and analysis on international issues and to help the EU develop its foreign and security policy.[16] Through this Council decision, the European Union (EU) has decided to provide research and analysis on international issues for the EU's common foreign and security policy (CFSP). The EUISS was originally set up in January 2002. It is based in Paris and has a liaison office in Brussels.[17]

The Common Security and Defence Policy (CSDP) sets the framework for EU political and military structures and military and civilian missions and operations abroad. The 2016 EU Global Strategy lays out the strategy for the CSDP, while the Lisbon Treaty clarifies the institutional aspects and strengthens the role of the EP. The CSDP has recently undergone major strategic and operational changes. It is continuing to evolve to meet security challenges and popular demand for increased EU responses.

26.3 Treaty Provisions for the CSDP and CFSP

The Common Security and Defence Policy (CSDP) is an integral part of the Union's Common Foreign and Security Policy (CFSP). The CSDP is framed by the Treaty on European Union (TEU). Article 41 outlines the funding of the CFSP and CSDP, and the policy is further described in Articles 42 to 46, in Chapter 2, Section 2 of Title V

---

[16] Council Decision 2014/75/CFSP of 10 February 2014 on the European Union Institute for Security Studies; OJ L 41 of 12 February 2014;

[17] https://www.auswaertiges-amt.de/blob/1337496/ed8676e37515e39486ba8fe1f562c2b3/the-eur opean-security-and-defense-policy-data.pdf; accessed 7 May 2018.

('Provisions on the Common Security and Defence Policy'), and in Protocols 1, 10 and 11 and Declarations 13 and 14. The particular role of the European Parliament in the CFSP and CSDP is described in Article 36 of the TEU.

Decisions relating to the CSDP are taken by the European Council and the Council of the European Union (Article 42 TEU). They are taken by unanimity, with some notable exceptions relating to the European Defence Agency (EDA, Article 45 TEU) and permanent structured cooperation (PESCO, Article 46 TEU), to which majority voting applies. Proposals for decisions are normally made by the High Representative of the Union for Foreign Affairs and Security Policy, who also acts as Vice-President of the European Commission.

The Lisbon Treaty introduced the notion of European capabilities and armaments policy (Article 42(3) TEU), though this has yet to be framed. It also established a link between the CSDP and other Union policies by requiring that the EDA and the Commission work in liaison when necessary (Article 45(2) TEU). This concerns, in particular, the Union's research, industrial and space policies, for which Parliament was empowered to seek to develop a much stronger role regarding the CSDP than it had in the past.

The foreign and security policy of the European Union aims to enable the 28 member countries to carry more weight on the world stage than if they were to act alone. As well as preserving peace and bolstering international security, the policy seeks to promote democracy, the rule of law and respect for human rights and freedoms around the world. The 2009 Lisbon Treaty established the EU's diplomatic arm, the European External Action Service (EEAS) under the authority of the High Representative of the Union for Foreign Affairs & Security Policy. However, one should not forget the role of the Court of Justice of the European Union as its decisions are influencing the policy implementation and further policy development.

In the EU the security, defence and foreign policy are divided because of the different competence the EU has in it. Within the Common Foreign and Security Policy, the EU has established certain ethical values as its core principles. Therefore, it needs to be assessed how these are conducted in its security policies and can it fulfil objectives and to what extent the international law and the internal law of the EU function together? In the EU the security, economic, political and social dimensions are integrated, and all of these are threatened at the present time with the mass influx of immigrants that were not expected to come. This development has a human rights dimension, which leads to the question of how to deal with the immigration crisis, which is affecting the internal and external dimensions of the EU.

26.3.1 *The Common Security and Defence Policy*

The CFSP has a close link with the Common Security and Defence Policy (CSDP), as it is part of the CFSP. The CSDP is a coherent and comprehensive political, diplomatic, economic, humanitarian, civil and military instrument.[18] With the former name, the European Security and Defence Policy, the CFSP were given a new dimension in the Lisbon Treaty which entered into force in 2009. It aims to provide the EU with an operational capacity for missions of peacekeeping, conflict prevention and strengthening international security in accordance with the principles of the UN Charter. The CSDP is an operational framework to address security issues and it creates an important aspect in the EU's security policies and thus, it cannot be left ignored when assessing the human security approach. The CSDP has both civilian and military operations across the globe. The civilian missions include strengthening missions, monitoring missions and executive missions. These include capacity-building, third-party observation and implementation of an agreement.[19]

The military operations range from executive missions with training to capacity building activities. They are implemented by the council decision and with either invitation of a host state or by the UN Security Council resolution under Chapter VII. For example, in 2015, there were two military operations created, one placed in the Central African Republic and the other in the Southern Mediterranean Sea (EUNAVFOR MED).[20] The operation in the Southern Mediterranean was launched on the 22nd of June to prevent further losses of lives at sea, to tackle the root causes of the humanitarian emergency in cooperation with the countries of origin and transit, and also to fight against the human smugglers. The main actions taken under this operation have been to identify, capture and dispose of vessels of the smugglers and traffickers.[21] Military operations can be sometimes justified when it is needed to ensure and return human security. However, the CSDP has been used in targeting the migrant smugglers which of course saves lives at the sea in a preventive manner, but in the end, has little to do with ensuring the secure transit of the migrants.

26.3.2 The Strategy of European Security

In 2003, the human security concept was taken as part of its security strategy. The European Security Strategy (ESS), adopted by the European Council on 12–13 December 2003, provided the framework for the Common Foreign and Security Policy (CFSP) and the Common Security and Defence Policy (CSDP). The strategy that was titled "A Secure Europe in a Better World" analyses and defines for the first time the EU's security environment, key security challenges and political implications. The ESS framed out five key threats that the EU is dealing with: terrorism, the proliferation of weapons of mass destruction (WMD), regional conflicts, State failure, and organized crime.

---

[18] Glume and Rehrl 2015, p. 68.
[19] EUISS 2016.
[20] Ibid.
[21] EEAS undated.

26 European Union (EU): Security, Conflict and Migration   583

It was recognized after the conflict of 2003 in Iraq, which split the EU member states into different directions, that a common strategic vision was needed at the EU level. The ESS addressed the interdependence of global security challenges by linking security and development issues and emphasizing the key threats interlinking these. Notably, "[p]reventive engagement to crisis management and improving the neighbouring region's security (Balkans, the Mediterranean, and Southern Caucasus) was seen as an important aspect of the security. The demands of the EU's more active, coherent and capable role in the changed security environment emphasized cooperation because none of the threats could be solved by the EU alone".[22]

The "Report of the Implementation of the European Security Strategy: Providing Security in a Changing World" was released in 2008 to reinforce the ESS. The following report of 2010, "Internal Security Strategy in Action—Five Steps Towards a More Secure Europe", posed five strategic objectives to better security in Europe. These were organized crime, terrorism, cybercrime, border security, and disaster response. As one can see, there are new issues like cybercrime, border security and disaster response added to the objectives that were not in place at the 2003 strategy plan.

The following report of 2015 "Fighting terrorism at EU level", gives an overview of Commission's actions, measures and initiatives which covers the years 2015–2020, and focuses on issues such as: creating a legal framework for cooperation; developing common systems such as the Schengen Information System (SIS); and financing member states in the field of internal security through the Internal security fund.[23] European Strategy plans and reinforcing reports put global security as a centrepiece of a European security strategy.

26.3.3 The European Agenda on Security

In May 2015, the European Agenda on Security that replaced the previous Internal Security Strategy (2010–2014), set out how the EU can bring added value in order to support the Members States to ensure security.[24] The Security Agenda covered the years from 2015 to 2020 and highlighted the fact of how Europeans can live in an area of freedom, security and justice, without internal frontiers. This shared agenda between the EU and the Member States was supposed to lead "an EU area of internal security where individuals are protected in full compliance with fundamental rights".[25] It recognised that many of today's security threats are caused by instability in the EU's neighbourhood, such as radicalization, violence and terrorism, which are international threats and thus, stretch out national borders. To tackle these threats, the EU needs a more effective and coordinated response at the Union level. Even

---

[22] EC 2009.
[23] LSE 2004.
[24] EC 2015b.
[25] Ibid.

though each member state holds the prior responsibility for their security, it is clear that they can no longer act successfully on their own. This is also an issue of EU competence as the EU cannot have full competence in the security or in the foreign policy area and it has to function based on limitations given in the treaties.

The European Agenda of Security sets out three priorities: terrorism, organized crime and cybercrime, and actions taken by the EU to address these priorities. We can see the decrease from five priorities to three; border security and disaster response are missing from the list. It does not mean that these two are not important, but the EU has shown weakness and incapacity in these fields and southern EU member states have been left slightly alone with border and disaster management issues in the case of immigration influx.

The Agenda itself is set on European core values and thus all actors need to work together based on five key principles. First, to ensure compliance with fundamental rights; second, to guarantee more transparency, accountability and democratic control; third, to ensure better application and implementation of existing EU legal instruments; fourth, to provide more joined-up inter-agency and a cross-sectorial approach; fifth, to bring together all internal and external dimensions of security.[26] The fifth principle acknowledges the fact that these threats are not limited only to the outside or inside of the EU borders, they are cross-border and thus the internal security of the EU and global security are dependent and interlinked. The success of the EU is dependent on cooperation with international partners and preventive engagement with third world countries is needed in order to respond to the causes of these security issues. The Agenda on Security stresses the importance of using the already existing policies on security such as the Common Security and Defence policy and enforcing EU's relations with international organizations such as the UN. Jones, for example, has been very critical about the priorities by saying that, "even though the Agenda priorities notions of fundamental rights, transparency and democratic control, towards the end the main focus, however, is on the EU's internal security policies. The achievement of full compliance with fundamental rights can be seen as not achieved. The objective concerning the current migrant crisis and the Agenda looks more like legitimizing oppressive laws and policies in both the EU and national level".[27]

26.4 Court Jurisdiction

The court jurisdiction seems to be very clear, as Article 275 of the TFEU is says: "The Court of Justice of the European Union shall not have jurisdiction with respect to the provisions relating to the common foreign and security policy nor with respect to acts adopted based on those provisions." The issue of controlling legality though is resolved by the second sentence of the same article, "However, the Court shall

---

[26] EC 2015b.

[27] Jones 2015.

26 European Union (EU): Security, Conflict and Migration

have jurisdiction to monitor compliance with Article 40 of the Treaty on European Union and to rule on proceedings, brought in accordance with the conditions laid down in the fourth paragraph of Article 263 of this Treaty, reviewing the legality of decisions providing for restrictive measures against natural or legal persons adopted by the Council on the basis of Chapter 2 of Title V of the Treaty on European Union."

The Court has jurisdiction in migration matters and will cover security issues in the third country nationals visa applications, who are covered by EU secondary legislation (like students from third countries) as it is reflected in most recent developments, namely the decision of the European Court of Justice (CJEU) in Fahimian.[28] It will also comparatively refer to the grounds of public security as they appear in other EU external relations instruments. The main focus will be the extent of discretion left to the member states. Public security cannot be regarded as a general and self-standing recourse for the member states when they, even for a good security reason, do not intend to apply the EU law in full. The CJEU made it clear that any justification on public security grounds must strictly rest on an individual legal basis.[29]

The EU provisions on four freedoms do not define public security, and any details or directions to the member states as to how to use it in their legislation and interpret it in national disputes are left to the interpretation of the CJEU.[30]

The basic principles were set up in cases delivered in relation to the free movement of goods. Accordingly, public security exception covers goods of fundamental importance for a country's existence which are crucial not only for its economy but especially for its institutions, essential public services and even the survival of its inhabitants.[31] Any restrictions based on public security cannot be used for economic ends[32] and a country cannot implore economic difficulties. The public security covers both a Member State's internal and external security.[33] The jurisdiction becomes even more complicated regarding security in the migration field as EU Court in the past did not have jurisdiction to rule in migration cases and it was considered a sovereign issue of each EU member state.[34]

The strict reading was also confirmed in the external dimension of trade and the CJEU refused that the concept of public security would be different and would allow a broader discretion of Member States. Consequently, the CJEU ruled in favour of parallelism in this regard.[35]

---

[28] C-544/15 Fahimian, ECLI:EU:C:2017:255.

[29] 222/84 Johnston v Chief Constable of the Royal Ulster Constabulary, ECLI:EU:C:1986:206, point 26.

[30] See more discussion in Roots 2014a.

[31] See Article 36 TFEU, C-398/98 Commission of the European Communities v Hellenic Republic, ECLI:EU:C:2001:565, points 30–31, C-72/83 Campus Oil, ECLI:EU:C:1984:256, pp. 34–35.

[32] See also Article 6, para 2 of Directive 2003/109/EC of 25 November 2003 concerning the status of third-country nationals who are long-term residents, OJ L 16, 23.1.2004, pp. 44–53.

[33] C-367/89 Richardt, ECLI:EU:C:1991:376, p. 22.

[34] See more discussion in Roots 2014b.

[35] C-70/94 Werner v Bundesrepublik Deutschland, ECLI:EU:C:1995:328, point 25.

26.5 Security and Conflict in Process of Change and Migration Management

As the security environment and the concept of states' sovereignty has changed, the concept of the conflict itself has also transformed. The traditional interstate wars have been replaced with intrastate conflicts, which has created a problem of forcibly displaced people due to humanitarian crises—for example in the Middle East and Africa—that cannot be ignored by the international actors. To tackle these new issues, the concept of human security was adopted in 1994 when it was introduced in the Human Development Report by the United Nations Development Programme (UNDP). Traditional security concepts are no longer enough to address both the old and new threats to human lives. Human security means the protection of fundamental freedoms of people, including aspects of development and national security while moving away from the state-centric conceptions towards the security of individuals. As stated before, the EU adopted the human security concept to be part of the ESS in 2003.[36]

While the European Commission (EC) has proposed agendas in order to help the crisis, the main difficulty has been the implementation by the individual member states. The discussion of migration has shifted from a human security issue to a national security issue, jeopardizing the founding principles of the EU and constitutional principles of many member states of EU. Therefore, the research questions are how the human security concept is visible in the EU's policies and how has it been implemented to tackle the migrant crisis? As mentioned, human security works as an adequate concept to address new security issues and while the EU has taken the concept to its use, it is important to analyse how it is used and how successful it has been.

The migrant crisis, which started in 2014, has created one of the biggest migration movements since the Second World War. In this context, the term 'migrant' is used as an umbrella term for all three groups: migrants, refugees and asylum seekers, while all refugees are considered migrants but not all migrants are considered refugees. Migrants and refugees who are fleeing into Europe from Africa, the Middle East and South Asia have caused the greatest challenge for European leaders and policymakers since the 2008 financial crisis.[37]

According to the International Organization for Migration (IOM), Europe and, more importantly, the Mediterranean have become the most dangerous destinations and border crossings. Also, according to the United Nations High Commissioner for Refugees (UNHCR), the current migrant crisis is the most severe since the end of the World War II, with more than 60 million refugees worldwide. With no end in sight, migration might turn into the norm, because the push and pull factors for migration have and will continue to multiply. The push factors include political crises, civil wars, ethnic and religious cleansing mainly done by extremist organizations due to

---

[36] European Commission, European Security Strategy (ESS) adopted in 2003.

[37] Roots 2012a, 2015a; Park 2015.

lack of economic prospects. The EU has a duty to take in migrants, especially those who are in need of international protection. In 2015, more than a million irregular migrants crossed EU's external borders, creating a need for the EU to assess their migration policies and their effects.[38]

The 1951 Convention defines a refugee and their rights, as well as which states should accept refugees. The core principle in international law is that refugees should not be expelled or returned to countries and situations where their life and right to freedom could be under threat.[39] If the refugee status is not approved they can be sent back to their countries of origin.[40] The problem arises when both the migrants and the refugees are fleeing to Europe through the same routes, causing difficulties for border control as well as for the assessment of their status. Greece and Italy, countries which also suffered most from the economic crisis, have served as a route to Europe. Countries, for example Hungary, have also been exposed to difficulties with migrant flows situated in the EU's eastern border. All EU member states are bound by the Regulation (EU) No 604/2013, called the Dublin Regulation, which poses the responsibility to examine migrants' asylum applications. This EU regulation "establishes the principle that only one Member State is responsible for examining an asylum application. The objective is to avoid asylum seekers from being sent from one country to another, and also to prevent abuse of the system by the submission of several applications for asylum by one person. The objective and hierarchical criteria are therefore defined in order to identify the Member State responsible for each asylum application".[41] All these insecurities and long asylum application process times lead people to stress that increases security issues and mental suffering; they also lead to tensions, which are good fuel for terrorism and conflicts. Therefore, the discussion in Europe has shifted from protecting the rights of the migrants to concerns of national security, because of the fears that irregular migrants pose a threat to states and societies.

26.5.1 The Response of the European Union to the Migrant Crisis

To tackle the migrant crisis within the EU borders, the EC created two documents prioritizing the fight against migrant smuggling. The European Agenda on Security in April 2015 and the European Agenda on Migration in May 2015. The European Agenda on Security enhanced cooperation against the smuggling within the EU and with third world countries and set it as a priority. The European Agenda on Migration identifies fight against migrant smuggling as a first priority in order to "prevent the exploitation of migrants by criminal networks and reduce incentives for irregular

---

[38] See more on www.unhcr.org.

[39] Roots 2012b, 2015b, 2017, Edwards 2015.

[40] See more in Roots 2017, 2012b.

[41] Regulation (EU) No 604/2013 further as Dublin regulation, see more in Roots 2017.

migration".[42] Leaning on these two frameworks, the EC presented in May 2015 an Action Plan to create an operationalized response against migrant smuggling.[43] The Action Plan from 2015 to 2020 created a comprehensive approach, which included all relevant actors, including stakeholders and institutions at different levels. One of the key issues in the migrant crisis has been the migrant smuggling, which has caused the death of more than 300 people in the first two months of this year alone.[44] It has become clear that no member state can tackle the migrant crisis alone – it jeopardizes the security of its own nationals as well as the migrants. With the European Agenda on Migration, the EU aims to create better tools to manage migration in the medium and long-term. The migrant crisis is not only a shared problem but also a shared responsibility among the member states, transit and origin countries. This agenda combines both internal and external policies with a new comprehensive approach based on mutual trust and solidarity. The Agenda on Migration proposed by the EC set a framework for a common European response combining both internal and external policies while cooperating with different stakeholders; international organizations, civil society, regional and national agencies outside the EU.[45] The Agenda on Migration is based on four pillars: first, reducing the incentives for irregular migration: addressing the primary causes of irregular migration, defining actions for better application of return policies; second, saving lives and securing external borders: better management of external borders, and solidarity towards the Member States located there; third, strengthening the common asylum policy: the EU's asylum policies need to be based on solidarity towards those needing international protection as well as among the member states, whose full application of the common rules must be ensured through systematic monitoring; fourth, a new policy on legal migration: focus on keeping Europe attractive to workers that the EU economy needs.[46]

Global poverty and conflicts do not obey the national frontiers and thus, the EU cannot solve the migrant crisis by itself. However, based on the founding principle of the EU, Europe should be a safe haven for people in need. The human security concept was introduced to a wider audience in the 1994 UNDP Human Development Report and since then it has remained a relevant concept to address the current security issues in the world. Many of the Western countries, including the EU, included this narrow definition of human security: freedom from violent threats to individuals and communities, to their foreign and security policies. Officially the EU added the human security concept to their policies in 2003. Since then, notions of human security have been part of many of the EU's foreign policy agendas. When addressing the human security concept in the EU's actions in the migrant crisis, one needs to bear in mind that in the new global context the EU's security policies should change more from concentrating on states' security to human security. In the post-Cold War security environment, current security capabilities which consist mainly of military

---

[42] EC 2015a.

[43] Carrera and Guild 2016.

[44] IOM 2016.

[45] EC 2015b.

[46] EC 2015b.

forces, cannot address the actual security needs in the world. The human security concept takes into consideration the current security issues to human beings and the acknowledgement of this is visible in the ESS. The seven key threats laid out in the ESS cannot be handled by purely military means because none of them is purely a military issue. Also, these threats are not reality only for Europe, but they are global. As mentioned before, population displacement is a typical feature of the so-called "new wars" and one of the contributors creating threats such as migration are authoritarian states and this is visible when considering the origin countries of the migrants: Syria, Iraq, and Afghanistan.

The rights to food, healthcare and housing are part of the human security concept—however, their legal status is less elevated.[47] The situation in the origin countries of many migrants is inhumane. The human security approach as a part of the EU's foreign and security policy means that it should contribute to the protection of each individual in need and not only focus on the military state defence of nation states and the EU's borders. This is something that has happened in the aftermath of the migrant crisis when public pressure has overruled humane actions. After all, Europe needs to act in a way that respects its international commitments and values, while securing its borders. The EU should promote the human security concept more, as the EU is a promoter of democratic values and the rule of law should also promote common humanity. Protection of human security should be based on morality and all human lives should be equal in worth and not lose their value in situations of crisis, which has happened at least at the level of discussion in the EU. As all member states of the EU have signed and ratified the UN's Universal Declaration of Human Rights, they have also a legal obligation to protect these rights and the life of Europeans is not secure before lives of others are.[48] So there are several reasons why Europe should be interested in keeping peace and security in the world and can play a bigger role in the maintenance of these values.

26.6 Conclusion

After assessing the human security concept in the EU's foreign and security policies by going through the CFSP, the CSDP, the ESS and the European Agenda on Security it can be seen that the notions of promoting the values such as human rights and fundamental freedom are the keywords and they are repeated in all policy papers. However, a further increase of links between internal and external policies needs to be promoted in CFSP. This might help the EU be able to adjust to more human security-based policies and the CSDP offers an operational framework to achieve better results.

One of the issues when addressing the migrant crisis, which is connected to universal human rights, is that the EU places promotion and respect of human rights

---

[47] LSE 2004.
[48] LSE 2004.

more to the external policies of the EU rather than internal. This makes it problematic to deal with the migrant crisis when it affects both EU's internal and external policies. Also, even though the CFSP created a common framework for the EU's foreign policy, the member states still hold their sovereignty and thus the CFSP is not as effective as it should. The European Agenda on Migration and the Action Plan, which implements both the European Agenda on Migration as well as the European Agenda on Security, were created to tackle the migrant crisis. It is clear that the EC has created a common framework to tackle the crisis at the EU level, even though it has mainly been addressing it as a migrant smuggling issue. It is clear that Europe must invest in human security in order to have security themselves. This has been noticed by the EC, however, the role of national parliaments in the area of freedom, security and justice can be argued to be too dominating and might end up causing damage to the EC's work.[49] When dealing with the migrant crisis the national governments have taken a leading role, and while some of the countries have contributed more than others, no government should act unilaterally. It can be seen as a failure of the EU for not being able to create a common response to the migrant crisis. Lack of cooperation reflects the absence of shared values and principles upon which the EU has been built.[50] Before, the security of others outside own national borders were considered more as an ethical human rights and development issue without linkage to the security of Europeans.[51] The connection between migration and security was acknowledged in the 5 years Programme for EU Justice and Home Affairs law and policy by the European Council in 2004, called the Hague Programme.[52] While every sovereign state has its rights to control its borders, it also has a responsibility to irregular asylum seekers and refugees, who are in need and have a right to seek protection.

Currently, the irregular flows of migrants pose challenges to the member states concerning the controlling and managing of the migrants, as well as ensuring their safety and fundamental rights. Europeans need to see migrants as victims of the threats to human security, such as political, economic and personal situations due to which they decide to migrate—unfortunately, some through the wrong channels. Hence, leaning on these reasons, the EU should adapt and adjust a human rights-based migration policy, which would be based on the same principles when dealing with a humanitarian crisis outside the EU borders. The member states need to continue their work in saving lives at sea; responding the high numbers of arrivals; targeting criminal smuggling networks; granting protection for migrants through resettlements and long-term political action to tackle the reasons driving for irregular migration. Collective legal action from the EU is needed in order to protect the rights of the people in need of protection whether as a refugee or as an asylum seeker. The actions taken by some of the member states today, such as building fences, using tear gas or setting up detention camps is not a solution, nor will it prevent migrants reaching

---

[49] EC 2015b.

[50] Khalaf 2016.

[51] Ibid., p. 28.

[52] Mitsilegas 2015, p. 29.

26 European Union (EU): Security, Conflict and Migration 591

Europe. The rise of right-wing parties, as well as public, media and political hate talk about migrants, should not become a norm in the discussion of migration.

An adequate conceptualization of human security for the EU would be to link human security with national security, not one over another. The member states need to acknowledge that the EU will not be safe until the neighbourhood of Europe is. Currently, the lack of will is also causing the lack of cooperation that is connected to the scale that this crisis has taken. While the human security approach highlights the preventive actions, it is clear that neither the international community nor the EU has been acting in that way in the origin countries of the migrants such as Iraq and Syria. The migration crisis is not ending in the near future and the EC has been addressing it through the human security approach; ensuring the safety of the migrants as well as taking into consideration the security of the EU. However, the lack of common approach at the member state level makes it difficult to address these policies in action. Even though the EU is not to blame for causing the crisis in the first place, it has not been acting in a preventive manner. Before the migrant crisis, many of the EU policymakers thought of migration as a human security issue, but now the discussion, as well as the implementation of new policies, has turned to see migration as a national security issue. As Khalid Kosher states "the risk of securitizing migration is that you risk legitimizing extraordinary responses."[53]

What the EU needs is a permanent system for dealing with migrants and shared responsibility amongst the member states.[54] The EU need not only relocate migrants who have already reached the EU soil, but also protect and help the people in need of international protection in third countries too. To achieve this, the EU needs to work more closely with the international community, such as the UNHCR. The duty of the international community is to recognize people in need and ensure their safe journey to Europe. The EC has started a process of developing risk assessments and mapping guidelines for disaster management, as well as guidelines assessing member states' risk management capability. By cooperation, a coherent European response could be created during crisis situations which would be more effective, efficient and would not cause double efforts within the EU and create situations like this again.[55]

In the EU's policies, as well as in public and political talks, it is important to separate the current migrant crisis from the broader debate on irregular migration. Even though in the current migrant crisis some of the asylum seekers and refugees have been taken into Europe by migrant smugglers, it is important that they do not lose their protection rights because they have not come through official asylum channels. Under Article 14 of the Universal Declaration of Human Rights "Everyone has the right to seek and to enjoy asylum from persecution in other countries". Both the member states and the Union have a duty to respond and act under international law. However, a failing EU policy response to the migrant crisis can be seen. The EU is lacking both will and unity in addressing the migrant crisis, which has split the member states. The European Commission Agenda on Migration highlighted the

---

[53] Park 2015.

[54] Roots 2017.

[55] EC 2015b, p. 9.

duty to protect people in need, but so far the EU is assessing the migration crisis through the security of Europe, not the security of all human beings. At first, the scale of the migrant crisis surprised the policy leaders, however it has continued for over two years and thus the scale and the speed of people arriving should be known.

As stated before, the EU included the human security concept in its security policy agenda in the 2003 ESS by linking the security and development issues and giving a framework for the CFSP and CSDP. When assessing the visibility of the human security in the EU's policies it can be noticed that it is included in many working documents, policies and agendas that the EC has produced. The human security concept works as an adequate framework to address current security issues in the world, which goes beyond traditional security notions towards the security of the individuals. The EU works as a promoter of universal human rights, democracy and the rule of law and thus they are part of its founding principles.

The EU should promote the human security concept.[56] Firstly, as a promoter of democratic values it should promote common humanity; secondly, all member states have ratified the UN's Universal Declaration of Human Rights and thus have a legal obligation to promote these values, thirdly, the lives of Europeans will not be secure before the lives of the others. All human lives should be equal in worth, both the Europeans as well as the migrants. Also, human lives should not lose their value in the situation of crisis, and this is something that has happened in the outcome of the migrant crisis. Before, the migration was linked with human security issues but now it has become more and more about national security. Closing borders and detaining migrants into inhumane circumstances is crumbling the founding principles of the EU.

When it comes to the migrant crisis, the EU has mainly been addressing the irregular smuggling of migrants into Europe as one of the main problems and has concentrated its efforts on targeting the smugglers of migrants in the Mediterranean. This indicates both the urgent need of saving the lives of the refugees but also a way to prevent irregular migration inside the EU. This is evident in the European Agenda on Migration and The EU Action Plan. Europe needs to act in a way that respects its international commitments and values while securing the borders. To achieve this, the EU needs to act in a consistent and clear way through common policy. Both the EU and the member states need to act in a way that respects the international and ethical obligations, solidarity and shared responsibility. Migration management should be part of both the external and internal security policies of the EU.

The objective of this chapter was to analyse the visibility and impact of the human security concept in the EU's policies using as a case study the current migrant crisis. As stated, the human security concept has been part of the ESS since 2003 and is part of the policies that the EC has been producing when tackling the migrant crisis. To answer the research questions, it can be concluded that the human security concept is visible in the EU's policies and has been used when tackling the migrant crisis. However, lack of implementation, will, and legislations are causing its failure and, in many cases, the internal aspects overcome the external ones. The EC has

---

[56] United Nations Trust Fund for Human Security 2020

26 European Union (EU): Security, Conflict and Migration

been trying to gather all the member states under one framework in addressing the migrant crisis but so far it has not succeeded, and many member states have taken a different approach towards migration. Europe should act as a uniting (*or united?*) community to achieve the best outcome for both the EU and the security of human beings. The human security concept could work as an adequate framework for the EU, emphasizing both the security of the individuals as well as the security of the member states.

References

Carrera S, Guild E (2016) Irregular Migration, Trafficking and Smuggling of Human Beings. Centre for European Policy Studies

Craig P, De Burca G (2011) EU Law Text, Cases and Materials, 5th edn. Oxford University Press

Edwards A (2015) Refugee or migrant - Which is right? United Nations High Commissioner for Refugees, 27 August 2015. http://www.unhcr.org/55df0e556.html, accessed 2 May 2018

European Commission (EC) (2003) The European Security Strategy. https://www.consilium.eur opa.eu/uedocs/cmsUpload/78367.pdf, accessed 2 April 2018

European Commission (EC) (2009) European Security Strategy - A secure Europe in a better world (2003). Council of the European Union, Brussels https://www.consilium.europa.eu/en/docume nts-publications/publications/european-security-strategy-secure-europe-better-world/ accessed 2 May 2018

European Commission (EC) (2015a) EU Action Plan against migrant smuggling (2015–2020). European Commission, 27 May 2015 http://ec.europa.eu/dgs/home-affairs/elibrary/docume nts/policies/asylum/general/docs/eu_action_plan_against_migrant_suggling_en.pdf, accessed 2 May 2018

European Commission (EC) (2015b) European Agenda on Migration: Why a new European Agenda on Migration?

European External Action Service (EEAS) (undated) http://www.eeas.europa.eu/csdp/missions-and-operations/eunavfor-med/index_en.htm accessed 3 May 2018

European Commission EC (2015d) The European Agenda on Security. European Commission, Strasbourg, http://ec.europa.eu/dgs/home-affairs/what-we-do/policies/european-agendasecurity/index_en.htm, accessed 3 May 2018

European Union (EU) (undated) Foreign & Security Policy s.a. European Union http://europa.eu/pol/cfsp/index_en.htm, accessed 5 September 2018

European Union Institute for Security Studies (EUISS) (2016) EUISS Yearbook of European Security http://www.iss.europa.eu/publications/detail/article/euiss-yearbook-ofeuropean-security-2016/, accessed 3 May 2018

Glume G, Rehrl J (2015) Handbook on CSDP Missions and Operations – The Common Security and Defence Policy of the European Union. Armed Forces Printing Centre, Vienna. http://eeas.europa.eu/csdp/structures-instruments-agencies/european-securitydefence-college/pdf/handbook/final_-_handbook_on_csdp_missions_and_operations.pdf, accessed 3 May 2018

International Organization for Immigration (IOM) (2016) Mediterranean Update – Migration Flows Europe: Arrivals and Fatalities. Available http://missingmigrants.iom.int, accessed 2 May 2018

Jones C (2015) Full compliance: the EU's new security agenda, Statewatch http://statewatch.org/analyses/no-268-eu-security-agenda.pdf, accessed 3 May 2018

Khalaf R (2016) How has the EU mismanaged the migrant crisis? Financial Times, 12 March 2016 http://www.ft.com/intl/cms/s/0/a3d7f394-e6dd-11e5-a09b-1f8b0d268c39.html#axz z47aoNM12n , accessed 3 May 2018

LSE (2004) A Human Security Doctrine for Europe – The Barcelona Report of the Study Group on Europe's Security Capabilities (2004). Barcelona. http://www.lse.ac.uk/internationalDevelopment/research/CSHS/humanSecurity/barcelonaReport.pdf, accessed 3 May 2018

Mitsilegas V (2015) The Criminalisation of Migration in Europe – Challenges for Human Rights and the Rule of Law. Springer International Publishing

Park J (2015) Europe's Migration Crisis. Council on Foreign Relations, 23 September. http://www.cfr.org/migration/europes-migration-crisis/p32874, accessed 2 May 2018

Roots L (2009) The impact of the Lisbon Treaty on the development of EU immigration legislation. Croatian Yearbook of European Law & Policy, 261–281.

Roots L (2012a) Irregular migration in European Union after Lisbon. L'Europe unie/United Europe, 6, 99–112

Roots L (2012b) Sharing Refugees after Lisbon - solution for small states? The Romanian Journal of International Relations and European Studies, 1 (2), 5–19

Roots L (2014a) Balance between national interests and EU citizenship. In: Flaga-Gieruszyńska KE, Wacinkiewicz C, Wacinkiewicz D (eds) Citizen, state, international community. A collection of studies. C. H. Beck, Munich, 543–556

Roots L (2014b) European court of asylum – does it exist? In: Kerikmäe T (ed) Protecting Human Rights in EU: Controversies and Challenges of the Charter of Fundamental Rights (129–143). Springer Verlag, Heidelberg

Roots L (2015a) La futura Política de migración. In: Ramiro Troitino D, Kerikmäe T (eds) Pasado, presente y futuro de la Unión Europea (169–174). McGraw-Hill Publishers

Roots L (2015b) The New Eurodac Regulation: Fingerprints as Source of Informal Discrimination. Baltic Journal of European Studies, 5 (2), 108–129

Roots L (2017) Burden Sharing and Dublin Rules – Challenges of Relocation of Asylum Seekers. In: Frenkel DA (ed) Role of law, human rights and social justice, justice systems, commerce, and law curriculum selected issues (47–62). Athens Institute for Education and Research, Athens, Greece

United Nations Trust Fund for Human Security (2020) https://www.un.org/humansecurity/what-is-human-security/, accessed 24 July 2020

Lehte Roots is a Visiting Professor of International Law in Tallinn University. She has obtained her PhD from the European University Institute, Florence, Italy and Master Degree in Public Management from Potsdam University, Germany. Professor Roots has published book chapters and articles in the field of EU law, migration, asylum, e-governance, security and public administration. Recently she was Research Fellow of Fulbright in Miami University, USA. She is Member of Editorial Committee Athens Journal of Mediterranean Studies, Member of the Scientific Committee, Administrative Law Review and the Journal, Studii Europene, Center of European Studies. She has provided expertise for European Commission, European Parliament.

Chapter 27
Association of Southeast Asian Nations (ASEAN)

Jozef Valuch and Ondrej Hamuľák

Contents

27.1 Introduction 596
27.2 The Creation and Evolution of ASEAN 596
27.3 ASEAN and International / Regional Security 600
27.4 Conclusion 606
References 607

Abstract One of the most prominent manifestations of cooperation between states as traditional subjects of international law is the creation and activities of international organizations (IOs). There are several criteria of classification of IOs. From a territorial point of view, we could distinguish the organisations with the universal scope and operability and organisations active at a regional level. The significance and position of a particular IO within the international community depends on several factors such as the number, economic or military power of its member states, the capacity and operability, competencies and the level of participation in the life of the international community. The Association of Southeast Asian Nations (ASEAN) serves as a typical regional IO, which plays the key role in international cooperation within the region of Southeast Asia. This chapter analyses the foundations, activities, actions and positions of ASEAN with specific emphasis on the questions of regional security management. In particular examples we deal with the real problems and the practical role of ASEAN in the field of regional cooperation and security. After more than half a century of its existence there is not only enough data to evaluate its outcomes but also to define the challenges which lie ahead of the region and cooperation within it.

J. Valuch (✉)
Faculty of Law, Comenius University, Bratislava, Slovakia
e-mail: jozef.valuch@flaw.uniba.sk

O. Hamuľák
Faculty of Law, Palacký University Olomouc, Olomouc, Czech Republic
e-mail: ondrej.hamulak@upol.cz

TalTech Law School, Tallinn, Estonia

© T.M.C. ASSER PRESS and the authors 2022
S. Sayapin et al. (eds.), *International Conflict and Security Law*,
https://doi.org/10.1007/978-94-6265-515-7_27

Keywords Southeast Asia · ASEAN · international organization · regional cooperation · regional security

27.1 Introduction

The term ASEAN presents the abbreviation and common name of an international organization operating in the region of Southeast Asia. The full name of this organization is the Association of Southeast Asian Nations. It is the informal successor of the former Association of South East Asia (ASA), originally formed by the Philippines, Thailand, and the Federation of Malaysia (now part of Malaysia) dating back to 1961.[1] In fact, it associates 10 countries from the region. Even though ASEAN is a typical regional international organisation, it has a huge potential to play a crucial role in broader international relations (business and security), and it is worth saying, that it is becoming an important global player.

There are several factors influencing the growing importance and potential of the ASEAN. Besides the accelerated development of its individual member states, there is the big economic potential of the whole region, which belongs to the major world economies (aggregated market GDP of 2.6 trillion US $).[2] It is one of the most populated regions, with a rich ethnic and religious variety (over 600 million inhabitants); it has a large geographical area (a total area of 1.7 million square miles = 4.5 million square kilometres)[3] and it has a strong geo-political importance (location between India, China, Korea, Japan and Australia). It is no wonder, therefore, that it is a very important player not only in that region. All these facts make ASEAN an important player and offer it a key position in maintaining security within the region.

27.2 The Creation and Evolution of ASEAN

ASEAN was founded by the ASEAN Declaration (known as the Bangkok Declaration) of 8 August 1967, signed by representatives of

- Indonesia
- Malaysia
- Philippines
- Singapore and
- Thailand.[4]

---

[1] See further Moon 2018.

[2] See ASEAN undated-a.

[3] See further Moon 2018.

[4] Grant and Barker 2009, p. 46.

27 Association of Southeast Asian Nations (ASEAN)

The constituent charter is a very brief and general document. Originally the founding document contained only five articles, in which it outlined the following aims and purposes of the Association:

- to accelerate economic growth, social progress and cultural development in the region through joint endeavours in the spirit of equality and partnership in order to strengthen the foundations for a prosperous and peaceful community among South-East Asian Nations;
- to promote regional peace and stability through abiding respect for justice and the rule of law in the relationship among countries of the region and adherence to the principles of the United Nations Charter;
- to promote active collaboration and mutual assistance on matters of common interest in the economic, social, cultural, technical, scientific and administrative fields;
- to provide assistance to each other in the form of training and research facilities in the educational, professional, technical and administrative spheres;
- to collaborate more effectively for the greater utilization of their agriculture and industries, the expansion of their trade, including the study of the problems of international commodity trade, the improvement of their transportation and communications facilities and the raising of the living standards of their peoples;
- to promote South-East Asian studies;
- to maintain close and beneficial cooperation with existing international and regional organizations with similar aims and purposes, and explore all avenues for an even closer cooperation among themselves.[5]

At the same time, it stated that the Association would be open to the participation of all states from the Southeast Asian region subscribing to its objectives, principles and purposes.[6] In the following periods the mission of ASEAN and its activities attracted the interest of other states from the region and the Association was enlarged by several accessions:

- Brunei (1984)
- Vietnam (1995)
- Laos and Myanmar (1997)
- Cambodia (1999).

In 1976, the Member States established the basic principles of their cooperation and mutual relations. These principles were included into the Treaty of Amity and Cooperation in Southeast Asia, which in particular governs the forthcoming questions as key factors of cooperation within the ASEAN:

(a) Mutual respect for the independence, sovereignty, equality, territorial integrity and national identity of all nations;

(b) The right of every state to lead its national existence free from external interference, subversion or coercion;

---

[5] The Asean Declaration 1967.

[6] ASEAN undated-c.

(c) non-interference in the internal affairs of one another;
(d) Settlement of differences or disputes by peaceful means;
(e) Renunciation of the threat or use of force;
(f) Effective cooperation among themselves.[7]

Each of these principles is related to the organization's basic goals, above all to maintaining peace and stability in the region. This goal forms an integral part of the DNA of ASEAN, as its establishment served as an expression of the desire of the five original founding members to create (beside other things) the efficient mechanism for the prevention of war and for conflict management.[8]

The biggest shift in evolution of integration in Southeast Asia came in 2003. The representatives of the Member States agreed to establish an ASEAN Community comprising of three pillars[9] which are currently:

- The ASEAN Political-Security Community (APSC): responsible for the establishment and providing of peaceful processes in the settlement of intra-regional differences. The main instruments and components to follow this objective are the following: political development; shaping and sharing of norms; conflict prevention; conflict resolution; post-conflict peace building; and implementing mechanisms. The aim of APSC is to ensure the peaceful coexistence of the countries in the region and their peaceful participation in the world order, as well as a fair, democratic and harmonious environment for their development and cooperation. Members rely on peace processes to address regional disparities, considering their security to be mutually interconnected and associated to their geographical links, shared visions and goals.[10]
- The ASEAN Economic Community (AEC): with a goal of creating a stable, prosperous and highly competitive economic region with a common market logic, where a free movement of goods, services and capital is protected; to secure the fair economic development and the reduction of poverty and socio-economic disparities.[11] Its establishment in 2015 is an important milestone in the regional economic integration agenda, which offers opportunities in the form of a huge market.[12]
- ASEAN Socio-Cultural Community (ASCC): it represents an effort to improve the quality of life of its inhabitants through human-oriented activities based on a common regional identity, with an emphasis on social development, raising living standards, including the disadvantaged groups and the rural population. Efforts

---

[7] Treaty of Amity and Cooperation in Southeast Asia Indonesia 1976, Article 2.

[8] "The idea of ASEAN itself was conceived in the course of intra-regional negotiations leading to the end of confrontation between Indonesia and Malaysia." Acharya 2001, p. 48.

[9] Grant and Barker 2009, p. 47.

[10] See further ASEAN undated-b.

[11] Wahyuningrum 2009.

[12] See further ASEAN undated-a.

27 Association of Southeast Asian Nations (ASEAN)

are also being made to actively involve all the components of society, especially women, youth and local communities.[13]

All three pillars are interconnected and should promote the mutual goals. There is a plan of gradual development and interconnection of all three communities in one strategic movement.[14] Another extremely important document which was developed by the ASEAN itself and deepened the forms of regional integration is the ASEAN Charter, which came into force in December 2008. According to this Charter, the ASEAN gained a status of an intergovernmental organization that has been given a legal personality. It represents the legal framework of ASEAN, sets out its principles, operating rules and institutional background, and it is binding upon all Member States.[15]

ASEAN's internal functioning mechanism is based on the regular meetings of the Heads of State and Government (called Summits), Foreign Ministers' Meetings and Sectoral Meetings at a ministerial level. Decisions are adopted on the basis of unanimity and consensus.[16] The work of numerous committees of senior officials and technical working groups is also significant.[17] The administrative and technical functions are carried out by a secretariat based in Jakarta (Indonesia) headed by the Secretary-General. This function has been extended to all summits and ministerial meetings, thus replacing the role originally exercised by national secretariats.[18]

ASEAN also develops relations with third countries, collaborating in the form of Partnership dialogues with the European Union, Australia and New Zealand,[19] Canada, Russia and others. Since 1997 it has been working closely with the Republic of South Korea, China and Japan in the ASEAN Plus Three format.[20] Other forms of cooperation are known as ASEAN Plus Six, which includes ASEAN Plus Three and Australia, India, and New Zealand, or the East Asia Summit, and ASEAN Plus Six and Russia and the United States.[21]

---

[13] Wahyuningrum 2009.

[14] As provided by the AEC Blueprint 2025, ASEAN Community Vision 2025, APSC Blueprint 2025 and the ASCC Blueprint 2025, forming the parts of ASEAN 2025: Forging Ahead Together strategy. See further ASEAN undated-a.

[15] Valuch et al. 2001, p. 288.

[16] See in detail Hernandez 2007.

[17] Grant and Barker 2009, p. 46–47.

[18] Ibid., p. 47.

[19] The mutual relations with Australia and New Zealand are the most developed example of external activities of ASEAN. In 2012 the ASEAN Australia New Zealand Free Trade Area (AANZFTA) established as the very first comprehensive free trade area on which ASEAN Participates.

[20] Valuch et al. 2001, p. 289.

[21] See further Moon 2018.

27.3 ASEAN and International / Regional Security

The gradual transformation of the security environment in the sixties and seventies of the last century has given rise to a new approach and new strategies for security issues. It led to a significant shift away from the military perspective on the issue of the security of states. The main emphasis is given to research on non-military threats. The whole concept has been moving from the originally realistic concept of "national security" to the concept of "international security",[22] i.e. the preservation of the condition of international relations where neither the interests of national security nor the international peace are compromised. One of the basic prerequisites for international security is the maintenance of reciprocity in the behaviour of states, especially in connection to nuclear powers.[23] This phenomenon was accentuated also by ASEAN Member States, which have concluded the Nuclear-Weapon-Free Zone Treaty, which entered into force in 1997. Under this Treaty (Article 3 para 2), Member States undertake not to develop, manufacture or otherwise acquire, possess or control nuclear weapons. They also accepted other obligations related to radioactive waste, the transport and proliferation of nuclear weapons, and the peaceful use of nuclear energy.[24]

The international security law itself presents a system of principles and norms governing the military and political relations between the states and the relevant provisions of the statutes of international organizations, which deals with security matters. All these regulations together concern the maintenance of international peace and security in order to prevent the use of force in international relations, as well as securing the limitation and the reduction of amounts of weapons in use.[25] According to some other views, the international security law could be characterized as a set of standards designed to ensure the peaceful relations between the states, in particular the protection of their territorial integrity and political independence in accordance with the UN Charter, and to create basic legal conditions for peaceful coexistence, which presupposes extensive and equitable international cooperation.[26] One of the most prominent expressions of this form of cooperation is the work of international organizations, and thus also the activities of ASEAN.

International/regional security issues are undoubtedly within the sphere of interest of ASEAN. Several different fora were established to promote and develop this policy field. We could mention, for example:

---

[22] Novotný 2011, p. 204.

[23] Ondřej 2008, p. 11.

[24] Severino 2012.

[25] Poredoš 2007, p. 98.

[26] Ondřej 2004, p. 231.

27 Association of Southeast Asian Nations (ASEAN)

- The ASEAN Regional Forum (ARF): its beginnings date back to 1993. It represents a twenty-seven-member multilateral grouping[27] aimed at facilitating cooperation on political and security issues and contributing to regional confidence-building and preventive diplomacy. It is a pan-regional forum with a wide range of participants including, among others, ASEAN, its dialogue partners, North Korea and Pakistan. Even though this forum is often mired in geopolitical disputes that limit its effectiveness,[28] its impact and significance lays in a point that it represents the only regional multilateral mechanism where North Korea is a member and regularly participates in its meetings. This fact further enhances the potential of ASEAN in providing a cooperative platform to engage North Korea.[29]
- ASEAN Plus Three: It is an advisory group set up in 1997. It brings together the ten members of ASEAN, China, Japan, and South Korea. Some authors referred to it as the most coherent pan-Asian grouping.
- The East Asia Summit (EAS): first held in 2005. The aim is to promote security and prosperity in the region. It is usually attended by heads of ASEAN, Australia, China, India, Japan, New Zealand, Russia, South Korea and the United States. ASEAN plays a central role in drafting its agenda. According to some authors, this is a unique forum where the President of the United States can collectively involve his Asia-Pacific counterparts on the main political and security issues.[30]

ASEAN, or better said the region itself, also face a number of security challenges, including cross-border terrorism, trafficking in human beings, natural and man-made disasters, as well as the different views of individual members on particular international threats and tensions, like border disputes or other conflict situations. The capability to deal with these conflicts (like some hot border-line issues between Vietnam and some other members of ASEAN, notably Malaysia and Indonesia) could serve as a testing tool for intra-mural peace.[31]

The most sensitive and politically important issues related to this region are related to the unclear situation of state borders and territorial disputes associated with them. These problems influence the security and overall stability of the region of Southeast Asia.

One of the most substantial problems deals with a long-lasting dispute in the South China Sea. This is an area with more than 200 islands, cliffs and sea rocks with a considerable strategic importance. The primary source of interest for all parties of the dispute are the mineral resources at the bottom of the South China Sea, especially oil and natural gas. Next to this, the region is significant for shipping because of the many important shipping routes crossing it. Several authors also emphasize the

---

[27] Australia, Bangladesh, Brunei Darussalam, Cambodia, Canada, China, the European Union, India, Indonesia, Japan, the Democratic Peoples' Republic of Korea, the Republic of Korea, Laos, Malaysia, Myanmar, Mongolia, New Zealand, Pakistan, Papua New Guinea, the Philippines, the Russian Federation, Singapore, Sri Lanka, Thailand, Timor Leste, the United States, and Vietnam.

[28] Albert 2017.

[29] Chiew-Ping 2018.

[30] Albert 2017.

[31] Acharya 2001, p. 130.

importance of fishing, which is an extremely vital source of food for countries with rapidly growing populations and limited agricultural opportunities (especially China and Vietnam).[32] Of the 200 islands, cliffs and rocks mentioned most are two larger archipelagos: the Spratly Islands and the Paracel Islands, which are the subject of major territorial disputes including a multitude of parties. Both archipelagos, along with a significant part of the South China Sea, are being claimed mostly by China, Vietnam and Taiwan. The Philippines and Malaysia claim the parts of the Spratly Islands and adjacent areas of the South China Sea, and Brunei also claims one reef and the surrounding water areas. Indonesia, in turn, claims part of the South China Sea within its exclusive economic zone, which does not extend to any of these archipelagos. Most parties to the disputes justify their claims and demands by using historical arguments (China, Taiwan, Vietnam, and the Philippines), another claims the UN Convention on the Law of the Sea from 1982 (Malaysia, Brunei, Indonesia) and some claim both arguments (Philippines, Vietnam). Some of the actors have already built naval bases on certain islands and reefs, particularly (according to available data) Vietnam, which occupied 21, the Philippines 9, China 7, Malaysia 5 and Taiwan 1 of these maritime features.[33]

The overlapping territorial demands of all the mentioned states have already given rise to some armed incidents in the area, which significantly impacts the overall stability and security of the region. Here ASEAN plays an important conciliatory role, as most of the countries (except China and Taiwan) involved in the disputes are members of the association. A joint report by ASEAN and the Institute for Science and International Security has even stated that territorial disputes over the Spratly Islands are the greatest threat to the stability of the region. Gradually, several important documents were adopted, including the ASEAN Declaration on the South China Sea of 1992, which emphasizes the need to resolve all issues of sovereignty and jurisdiction in the South China Sea by peaceful means.[34] Another noteworthy document is the 2002 Declaration of Conduct of Parties in the South China Sea, adopted by the ASEAN Member States together with China. In this declaration all parties reaffirmed, inter alia, their commitment to the purposes and principles of the Charter of the United Nations, the 1982 UN Convention on the Law of the Sea and other universally recognized principles of international law which shall serve as the basic norms governing state-to-state relations.[35] This topic also appears regularly in various declarations, joint declarations and reports of the ASEAN Regional Forum and other partner countries, etc.[36]

The territorial tensions in the South China Sea have given rise to an important decision of the Permanent Court of Arbitration in the dispute between the Philippines and China in 2016. In 2013 the Philippines challenged China's claims to territories in the South China Sea. However, China had announced in advance that it would

---

[32] See further Suchánek 2010, pp. 87–89.

[33] Nosál 2012, compare to BBC 2016.

[34] ASEAN Declaration on the South China Sea, 1992, p. 1.

[35] Declaration on the Conduct of Parties in the South China Sea, 2002, p. 1.

[36] Nosál 2012.

not actively participate in the dispute and would not accept any verdict. Even though the PCA did not rule on the issue of the territorial claims of the disputing parties themselves, nor on the question of sovereignty or on the demarcation of maritime borders, its award is of significant importance for the developments of the status of the South China Sea maritime features and adjacent waters. In particular, its task was to assess the legality of China's historical rights, the nature of maritime features and their capability to generate claims to the surrounding sea waters, and the legality of China's conduct in relation to Philippine territorial claims.[37] The PCA decided in favour of the Philippines on almost all points of the arbitration. It rejected the legality of China's historical claims, in particular stating that none of the Spratly Islands could be considered as a geographic feature generating any claims on the surrounding seas and also alleged a violation of the rights of the Philippines by China.[38] As we mentioned above, China refused to recognise the decision of the PCA *ab initio* and it continues with its policy in the territories of the South China Sea, which opens up other international tensions from a global perspective.[39] Despite visible efforts,[40] the role of the ASEAN in managing these long-lasting tensions is not satisfactory. The ASEAN is not able to come up with any acceptable solution to the multilateral conflict mostly because of inconsistent views and different interests of the particular Member States.

When dealing with the international security issues and the role of ASEAN, we must mention the special policy approach called the "ASEAN Way". This special doctrine is based on the policy of non-intervention in domestic affairs and its implementation in practice significantly affects (one should say weakens) the position of the organisation as a security actor in the region of Southeast Asia. This specific approach is based on the deep respect for national sovereignty and specifics (including cultural) of the region. Its core is determined directly in the ASEAN Charter. Article 2 thereof proclaims the main principles, among others as the "respect for the independence, sovereignty, equality, territorial integrity and national identity of all member states; non-interference in the internal affairs of member states; respect for the right of every member state to lead its national existence free from external interference, subversion and coercion or also enhance consultations on matters seriously affecting the common interest of ASEAN."[41] Also article 20 of the ASEAN Charter confirms as a basic principle that decision-making in ASEAN shall be based on consultation and consensus.[42] This specific way of decision-making requires a lot of debates and consultations on multilateral fora. It emphasises the equality of all ASEAN Member States and the importance of cooperation, but on the other side it requires

---

[37] See further The South China Sea Arbitration (The Republic of Philippines v. The People's Republic of China).

[38] See further PCA Case N° 2013-19 2016, In the Matter of the South China Sea Arbitration (The Republic of the Philippines v. The People's Republic of China.

[39] See e.g. Stilwell 2020.

[40] See Cheeppensook 2020.

[41] Charter of the Association of Southeast Asian Nation 2007, Article 2.

[42] Ibid., Article 20.

a lot of time for the searching for a consensus, leads to minimal solutions and a lack of efficiency. The main features of the approach, in relation to security matters in particular, are non-interference, the non-use of force, quiet diplomacy and the consensus approach.[43] The "ASEAN Way" approach opens up some controversies. According to its proponents this approach forms the basis of the ASEAN's integrational successes as it helps to keep the peace in the region based on the mutual respect between the Member States. On the other side it is criticised as the reason of ASEAN's low success rate in the resolution of complex disputes (like in the South China Sea) and the lack of overt results.[44]

To illustrate the practical application of this approach, we could use the example of the situation in Myanmar in the 1980s and 1990s. At a time when Western countries were openly criticizing human rights abuses in this country, ASEAN was adhering to non-interference in internal affairs and in 1997 accepted the country as a Member state. ASEAN has received considerable criticism from the international community (not only in this case) for this type of approach and policy. The "ASEAN Way" protects each country from others interfering in their domestic affairs while maintaining cooperation and good relations with other Members and neighbouring countries. Following these aims, it sacrifices even very serious questions, e.g. human rights violations or trafficking in human beings, which are considered domestic issues.[45]

The evolution and operation of ASEAN throughout the decades in the field of international security reflects regional as well as global events. The changes in the balance of powers after the end of Vietnam War as well as the subsequent economic growth of the whole region has had a significant impact on cohesion within this organisation and increased its role in maintaining security within the region. The impacts in this field could be seen in its active role in the resolution of clashes between Chinese-dominated Singapore and its Malay-Muslim neighbours (Singapore–Malaysia or Singapore–Indonesia mistrust and tensions)[46] and noticeably ASEAN's united response to the invasion and subsequent occupation of Cambodia by Vietnamese forces in 1978/1979. This invasion has presented one of the most serious security challenges with which ASEAN had to deal. This conflict was a real test for relations within the ASEAN group. Even ASEAN itself perceived Vietnam's action as an obvious violation of its norms and a threat to the emerging culture of unity and consensus in the region.[47] ASEAN's own role in the Cambodian conflict has been shaped by two main objectives: the attempt to punish Vietnam for violating the regional peace and security standards and the desire for a peaceful settlement of the conflict without the significant involvement of external powers. ASEAN thus sought to maintain its own norms of non-use of force and to maintain its own norms of the regional settlement of regional conflicts.[48] The peace agreement

---

[43] Compare to Katsumata 2003, pp. 104–121.

[44] Tekunan 2014, p. 144.

[45] Ibid., p. 145.

[46] Acharya 2001, p. 48.

[47] Ibid., p. 80 etc.

[48] Ibid., s. 90.

ending the conflict in Cambodia was only concluded in 1991 at the Paris Conference on Cambodia.

An important step to the further increasing of ASEAN's role is connected with the end of the Cold War, which allowed the ASEAN countries to exercise greater political independence in the region and globally. Subsequently, in the 1990s ASEAN emerged as a leading voice on regional trade and security issues.[49] But despite the developments in internal cohesion and the establishment of different forums of cooperation within the organisation (which had definitely promoted the growing importance of ASEAN as a whole), there are still intriguing risks and challenges. Most of them stem from the different views on security issues and serve as a perpetual threat to the unity of this organization. One of the biggest challenges is to find a united response to the rise of China's power and influence. The re-establishment of China to the position of the main power in the East Asian region is most likely not only to change relations between Southeast Asia and China, but also relations within the ASEAN itself. One particular challenge is connected to the maritime disputes in the South China Sea, which have been the biggest irritant among some ASEAN members. Several ASEAN members (Brunei, Malaysia, the Philippines and Vietnam) share overlapping claims to features in contested waters with China. For these countries, China's moves to recover land and to construct artificial islands are threatening and seen as violations of their national sovereignty. On the other hand, for some other members (like Cambodia) these territorial tensions are geographically very distant and therefore irrelevant. In any case, without a consensus all efforts to make the Declaration of Conduct of Parties in the South China Sea between ASEAN and Beijing into a binding code of conduct, would be ineffective. In response to the growing pressure from China, several states are keen to start cooperation and accept support from the USA. As a result, US military cooperation with ASEAN members such as the Philippines and Vietnam was stepped up. It has led to the modernization of the ASEAN member states' armies with support from the USA as well as to increased maritime presence of the USA, with the declared objective of promoting freedom of navigation in international waters. The influence of China on one side and the cooperation with the USA on the other has introduced important differences between the ASEAN members. The fact is that the developing region needs significant investments, trade relations, and above all infrastructure development. In some views, all these needs could be satisfied by the action of China. On the other hand, however, some ASEAN members are worried that they will become too dependent on China and turn their interests more to the United States.[50]

The important challenge and potential for the improvement of the international security role of ASEAN is connected to the developments on the Korean peninsula. ASEAN could serve as a platform for the inter-Korean peace process (this role has already been played by Singapore in providing a neutral and safe place to facilitate communication between the key parties to the Korean hostilities). Another important role could also be played within the process of the North Korean denuclearisation

---

[49] See further Moon 2018.

[50] Albert 2017.

issue, which would give ASEAN a significant chance to play a key role in one of the major regional security issues which has global implications.[51]

27.4 Conclusion

ASEAN, as an intergovernmental organization founded in 1967, has gone through major developments which have verified the coherence of this grouping and the relations between its members. It has adopted several important documents of a different legal force and faced several security challenges.

After a brief analysis of the developments in this region, we could state that the most sensitive and risky question that threatens the stability and security thereof, is the unclear delimitation of state borders and related territorial disputes. A specific feature of ASEAN in the field of international security is its policy called the "ASEAN Way". This approach is based on the soft instruments for the resolution of conflicting situations, e.g. consensus and consultations. Its main feature is a doctrine of non-interference into internal affairs, which has been criticized by Western countries.

In spite of the common goals and the declared noble principles of mutual co-existence, however, the different views of individual members on security issues may still be considered a warning for the unity of this organization. One cannot ignore the fact underlined by Acharya, according to which 'During the Cold War and immediately thereafter, ASEAN was able to develop a common response to the major powers. In the new and uncertain geo-political environment that we are venturing into, can we be sure that ASEAN members will not be pulled in different directions by different powers?,[52] The differences among several ASEAN Members in their position towards and ways of cooperation with China and the United States, serve as a vivid example thereof.

On the other hand, it is an undeniable fact that the activity of this organisation has made a visible impact and has had some successes. Among other things, one may consider ASEAN's adoption of a declaration to resolve disputes in the South China Sea; the establishment of the ASEAN Regional Forum; activities related to the resolution of the conflict in East Timor, calming down the tensions between members; and its significant role in solving the Vietnam-Cambodia conflict. Over the last half a century, this organisation can be said to be becoming a major player in the field of regional co-operation and security.

---

[51] Chiew-Ping 2018.

[52] Acharya 2001, p. 185.

References

Books, (Online) Articles and Chapters in Books

Acharya A (2001) Constructing a security Community in Southeast Asia: ASEAN and the problem of Regional order. Routledge, London.

Albert E (2017) ASEAN: The Association of Southeast Asian Nations. In: Council on Foreign Relations (backgrounder). https://www.cfr.org/backgrounder/asean-association-southeast-asian-nations. Accessed 6 August 2019.

ASEAN (undated-a) ASEAN Economic Community. http://asean.org/asean-economic-community/. Accessed 11 August 2019.

ASEAN (undated-b) ASEAN Political-Security Community. http://asean.org/asean-political-security-community/. Accessed 13 August 2019.

ASEAN (undated-c) History, The Founding of ASEAN. http://asean.org/asean/about-asean/history/. Accessed 11 August 2019.

BBC (2016) Why is the South China Sea contentious? https://www.bbc.com/news/world-asia-pacific-13748349?utm_source=valka_cz&utm_medium=article&utm_campaign=linkthru. Accessed 20 September 2019.

Cheeppensook K (2020) ASEAN in the South China Sea conflict, 2012–2018: A lesson in conflict transformation from normative power Europe. Int Econ Econ Policy 17 (3). https://doi.org/10.1007/s10368-020-00477-z.

Chiew-Ping H (2018) Asean as an interlocutor for peace on Korean peninsula? In: Khmer Times, 7/25/2018; https://www.academia.edu/37130952/ASEAN_as_an_interlocutor_for_peace_on_Korean_peninsula, Accessed 13. August 2018; https://www.khmertimeskh.com/50514829/asean-as-an-interlocutor-for-peace-on-korean-peninsula. Accessed 13. August 2019.

Grant J P, Barker J C (2009) Parry & Grant Encyclopaedic Dictionary of International Law, 3rd edn. Oxford University Press, Oxford.

Hernandez C G (2007) Institution Building through an ASEAN Charter. https://www.kas.de/c/document_library/get_file?uuid=c81cf9d9-b4d1-107b-6692 86b73e575ce8&groupId=252038. Accessed 30 July 2020.

Katsumata H (2003) Reconstruction of Diplomatic Norms in Southeast Asia: The Case for Strict Adherence to the "ASEAN Way". Contemporary Southeast Asia (A Journal of International and Strategic Affairs) 25 (1): 104–121.

Moon Ch (2018) ASEAN International Organization. In ENCYCLOPÆDIA BRITANNICA, https://www.britannica.com/topic/ASEAN. Accessed 13 August 2019.

Nosál J (2012) Region Jihočínského moře jako bezpečnostní komplex. https://www.valka.cz/14665-Region-Jihocinskeho-more-jako-bezpecnostni-komplex#p14665 _ 10. Accessed 5 August 2019.

Novotný A (2011) Teorie a praxe mezinárodních vztahů, 3. vydání. Eurokódex, s.r.o., Bratislava.

Ondřej J (2004) Mezinárodní právo veřejné, soukromé, obchodní. Aleš Čeněk, s.r.o., Plzeň.

Ondřej J (2008) Odzbrojení, prostředek zajištění mezinárodní bezpečnosti, 2. rozšířené vydání. Aleš Čeněk, s.r.o., Plzeň.

PCA Case N° 2013-19 (2016) In the Matter of the South China Sea Arbitration (The Republic of the Philippines v. The People's Republic of China. https://docs.pca-cpa.org/2016/07/PH-CN-20160712-Award.pdf. Accessed 10 September 2019.

Poredoš F (2007) K niektorým otázkam práva medzinárodnej bezpečnosti. In: Aktuálne problémy medzinárodného práva. VO PraF UK, Bratislava.

Severino R C (2012) The Asean Way and The Rule of Law. https://asean.org/?static_post=the-asean-way-and-the-rule-of-law. Accessed 6 August 2019.

Stilwell R D (2020) The South China Sea, Southeast Asia's Patrimony, and Everybody's Own Backyard. Report. Bureau of East Asian and Pacific Affairs, U.S. Department of State. https://www.state.gov/the-south-china-sea-southeast-asias-patrimony-and-everybodys-own-backyard/. Accessed 3 August 2020.

Suchánek J (2010) Surovinový konflikt v Jihočínském moři, In Šmíd T (ed. 2011): Vybrané konflikty o zdroje a suroviny. Mezinárodní politologický ústav, Brno, pp. 85–103.

Tekunan S (2014) The Asean Way: The Way To Regional Peace? Jurnal Hubungan Internasional, Vol. 3, No. 2, pp. 142–147.

Valuch J et al (2001) Právo medzinárodných organizácií. C. H. Beck, Prague.

Wahyuningrum Y (2009) Understanding ASEAN: Its Systems & Structures. Oxfam International. http://www.burmapartnership.org/2009/12/understanding-asean-its-systems-and-structures/. Accessed 6 August 2019.

Other Documents

ASEAN Declaration (Bangkok Declaration) Bangkok, 8 August 1967.

ASEAN Declaration on the South China Sea, 1992.

Charter of the Association of Southeast Asian Nation (2007).

Declaration on the Conduct of Parties in the South China Sea, 2002.

Treaty of Amity and Cooperation in Southeast Asia Indonesia, 24 February 1976.

Jozef Valuch JUDr., PhD is an Associate Professor of International Law at Faculty of Law, Comenius University in Bratislava (Slovakia). He is the head of the group of authors of several textbooks in the field of public international law. In his research, he focuses on the international security, the diplomatic and consular law, the international legal personality and human rights. He took part in several research stays abroad (Austria, Japan, Israel, Taiwan). He is a member of the Slovak Society of International Law.

JUDr. Ondrej Hamuľák PhD (adj. prof. TalTech) is a senior lecturer and vice-dean for science and research at the Faculty of Law, Palacký University Olomouc (CZE), adjunct professor in EU Strategic Legal Affairs, TalTech Law School (EST) and senior researcher at the Jean Monnet Centre of Excellence in EU law, Comenius University in Bratislava (SVK). In his research he focuses on interactions between EU law and national law, impacts of the membership in the EU on the state sovereignty, the legitimacy and rule of law within the EU. Ondrej is an editor-in-chief of *International and Comparative Law Review*, the Scopus indexed journal published by Palacký University Olomouc (CZE) in cooperation with Johannes Kepler Universität in Linz and Karl-Franzens Universität in Graz (AUT). (https://content.sciendo.com/view/journals/iclr/iclr-overview. xml). The detailed information about his research is available at personal profile https://www.researchgate.net/profile/Ondrej_Hamulak.

Chapter 28
Collective Security Treaty Organization (CSTO)

Sultan Sakhariyev

Contents

28.1 Introduction 609
    28.1.1 History, Nature, and Idea of Collective Security 609
28.2 Historical Background of Collective Security Treaty Organization 611
28.3 Legal Framework and Legal Structure of the Collective Security Treaty
    Organization 612
28.4 Activities of Collective Security Treaty Organization 615
28.5 Conclusion 616
References 617

Abstract This chapter aims to analyze the legal framework of Collective Security Treaty Organization (CSTO), its legal standing, history, efficiency, and challenges. The first part of the chapter provides a brief historical background of the idea of collective security, and of the CSTO. The second part is devoted to the legal background of the CSTO, its legal structure, and regulatory documents. The third part analyses selected case studies and challenges faced by the CSTO.

Keywords collective security · Collective Security Treaty Organization · CSTO · post-Soviet Union · Central Asia · CIS · Commonwealth of Independent States

28.1 Introduction

28.1.1 History, Nature, and Idea of Collective Security

International relations and international politics being interdisciplinary fields consist of various disciplines regulating, studying, and explaining international cooperation and international conflicts. Yet, simplifying the nature of international relations, it may be narrowed down to two major parts: international trade and international security.

S. Sakhariyev (✉)
KIMEP University School of Law, Almaty, Kazakhstan

© T.M.C. ASSER PRESS and the authors 2022
S. Sayapin et al. (eds.), *International Conflict and Security Law*,
https://doi.org/10.1007/978-94-6265-515-7_28

International peace and security have always been one of the major concerns of global society. In the 19th and early 20th century, international peace and security were maintained by the balance of powers, known as the Concert of Europe.[1] After World War I, the newly established League of Nations was the first global formalized attempt to regulate and protect international peace and security by a joint global effort.[2] In addition to other methods of maintaining international peace and security, such as reduction of national armaments,[3] provision of forums for international dispute settlement[4] and negotiations, the League of Nations has introduced the idea of collective security.[5] Thus, under Article 16 of the Covenant of the League of Nations, the contracting parties have undertaken a very serious obligation to consider any act of war by a member state as an act of war against all other members of the League of Nations[6] The Covenant, however, entitled the League of Nations only to a limited right to advise member states on the types and extent of military forces to be used.[7]

The successor of the League of Nations, the United Nations, has further developed the idea and concept of collective security. Chapter VII of the UN Charter provides for detailed powers of the United Nations in terms of measures to be taken with respect to the maintenance of international peace and security. While Chapter VII does not use the term "collective security", it recognizes states' inherent right to individual or collective self-defense.[8] The UN Charter also authorizes the Security Council to utilize such regional arrangements or agencies for enforcement action under its authority.[9] In other words, for the purpose of maintaining international peace and security, the UN may call for regional international organizations to act respectively.

Summing up the above, let us define the concept: collective security means a system, regional or global, in which each state in the system accepts that the security of one is the concern of all, and agrees to join in a collective response to threats to, and breaches of, the peace.[10] Such systems may exist at the global or regional levels. The examples of regional collective security arrangements may be the North Atlantic Treaty Organization (NATO), and the Collective Security Treaty Organization (CSTO). The following sections will analyze the legal framework of the CSTO, focusing on its founding treaty and other applicable sources, and provide a brief overview of its action.

---

[1] De Wet and Wood 2013, para 6.

[2] Covenant of the League of Nations, Preamble.

[3] Ibid., Article 8.

[4] Ibid., Articles 12–15.

[5] Ibid., Article 16.

[6] Ibid.

[7] Ibid.

[8] UN Charter, Article 51.

[9] Ibid., Article 53.

[10] Lowe et al. 2008, p. 13.

28.2 Historical Background of Collective Security Treaty Organization

After the collapse of the Soviet Union, former Soviet states, in order to maintain international cooperation, have established the Commonwealth of Independent States (CIS).[11] The main goals of the CIS include cooperation in the sphere of protection of international peace and security.[12] To achieve this goal, the CIS member states signed the Collective Security Treaty on 15 May 1992.[13] The Treaty was signed in Tashkent by Armenia, Kazakhstan, Kyrgyzstan, Russia, Tajikistan, and Uzbekistan. The initial term of the Treaty was five years.[14] The Treaty became effective on 20 April 1994, and was prolonged in 1999.[15] The Treaty was subsequently transformed into the Collective Security Treaty Organization (CSTO), and its Charter was adopted on 7 October 2002. As of 1 January 2020, the following states are members of the CSTO: the Republic of Armenia, the Republic of Belarus, the Republic of Kazakhstan, the Kyrgyz Republic, the Russian Federation and the Republic of Tajikistan.

In accordance with Article 10 of the Treaty, the Treaty is open for accession by all interested states sharing its goals and principles.[16] Such a qualification requirement for a membership leaves a great room for interpretation, as the Treaty itself does not directly define its principles and specific goals. Therefore, it appears that a decision on a membership of a potential new member will be decided *ad hoc*, based on how the current member states understand the Treaty's current goals and principles. In turn, the termination of membership in the Organization requires a one-month notification prior to the termination.[17] While this does not contradict the law of treaties, such notification requirements could be problematic in circumstances where an urgent termination were preferable, considering the nature and the sphere of the Treaty. However, the provisions of the 1969 Vienna Convention on the Law of Treaties of on termination of a treaty in the case of its breach,[18] or a fundamental change of circumstances[19] may solve such potential issues.

---

[11] Charter of the Commonwealth of Independent States, Preamble.

[12] Ibid., Article 2.

[13] Collective Security Treaty, Preamble.

[14] Ibid., Article 11.

[15] Protocol on Prolongation of Collective Security Treaty, Article 1.

[16] Supra note 13, Article 10.

[17] Ibid., Article 11.

[18] Vienna Convention on the Law of Treaties (adopted on 23 May 1969), Article 60.

[19] Ibid., Article 62.

28.3 Legal Framework and Legal Structure of the Collective Security Treaty Organization

The fundamental documents of the CSTO Security Treaty Organization are the Collective Security Treaty of 1992, the Charter of the Collective Security Treaty Organization dated 7 October 2002, and the Agreement on Legal Status of the Collective Security Treaty Organization dated 7 October 2002.

The Collective Security Treaty of 1992 was aimed at regulating any relations of the state parties dealing with collective security issues. As such, the state parties agreed to refrain from entering into any military alliances, and from joining any collective security arrangements without prior consultations with each other. On 10 December 2010, the Collective Security Treaty was amended by the Protocol on Introduction of Amendments to the Collective Security Treaty. This Protocol among other things has introduced amendments to Article 4 of the Treaty defining the concept of collective security. The amended Article 4 states:

> If an aggression is committed against one of the States Parties by any state or a group of states, it will be considered as an aggression against all the States Parties to this Treaty.
>
> In case an act of aggression is committed against any of the States Parties, all the other States Parties will render it necessary assistance, including military one, as well as provide support with the means at their disposal through an exercise of the right to collective defense in accordance with Article 51 of the UN Charter.
>
> The States Parties will immediately inform the United Nations Security Council of the measures taken in accordance with this Article. While taking these measures, the States Parties will abide by the relevant provisions of the UN Charter.

The amended Article 4 fully complies with the aforementioned provisions of the UN Charter on collective self-defense.

State parties to the Treaty also adopted the Protocol on the Mechanism of Providing Military Technical Assistance to the Member States of the Collective Security Treaty Organization in Cases of Threats of Aggression and Committed Acts of Aggression on 6 October 2007 in Dushanbe, Tajikistan. This Protocol regulates actions of member states of the CSTO not only in response to actual acts of aggression under *jus ad bellum*, but also in cases of preparation for planned aggression revealed in advance, and other external threats to security, sovereignty, and territorial integrity.[20] Therefore, the CSTO recognizes and applies the practice of preventive self-defense.

On 7 October 2002, the state parties to the Collective Security Treaty adopted the Charter of the Collective Security Treaty Organization. This document transformed the Collective Security Treaty into a regional international organization, recognized and registered within the UN.[21] The Charter of the CSTO provides that the goals

---

[20] Protocol on the Mechanism of Providing Military Technical Assistance to the Member States of the Collective Security Treaty Organization in Cases of Threats of Aggression and Committed Acts of Aggression, Article 2.

[21] Charter of the Collective Security Treaty Organization, Article 1, Article 29.

28 Collective Security Treaty Organization (CSTO)

of the organization are the enforcement of peace, regional and international security and stability, collective protection of the independence, sovereignty and territorial integrity of the member-states.[22] For the purpose of achieving the goals of the organization, member states may apply various collective security measures, including, but not limited to, creation of collective military forces, regional groupings of forces, peacekeeping forces, military infrastructure, joint trainings, and more.[23]

The three major directions of activities of the Collective Security Treaty Organization are the following:

(a) coordination of efforts in combating international terrorism, drug trafficking, transnational crimes and illegal migration;[24]

(b) coordination of foreign policy positions regarding international and regional security problems;[25] and

(c) development of the legal basis governing the collective security system, and harmonization of national legislations of member-states.[26]

The supreme governing body of the Collective Security Treaty Organization is the Collective Security Council.[27] It consists of the heads of states of the member states,[28] and is authorized to consider the main questions concerning the activities of the organization, to make decisions aimed at achieving its goals and purposes, to coordinate joint actions between member states.[29] The Collective Security Council is also authorized to establish subsidiary governing bodies.[30] Its decisions are binding for all member states, and are made by consensus.[31]

There are three advisory and executive bodies of the organization:

(a) the Council of Ministers for Foreign Affairs for the issues of coordination in foreign policy;[32]

(b) the Council of Ministers of Defense for the issues of coordination in military policy, military structures and cooperation in military technology;[33] and

(c) the Committee of Secretaries of the Security Councils for the issues of coordination in the provision of member states' national security.[34]

---

[22] Ibid., Article 3.

[23] Ibid., Article 7.

[24] Ibid., Article 8.

[25] Ibid., Article 9.

[26] Ibid., Article 10.

[27] Ibid., Article 13.

[28] Ibid.

[29] Ibid.

[30] Ibid.

[31] Ibid., Article 12.

[32] Ibid., Article 14.

[33] Ibid., Article 15.

[34] Ibid., Article 16.

There is also a permanent executive body of the organization—the Secretariat—that provides organizational, information, analytical and advisory services for the activities of the organs of the Organization.[35]

There are multiple other documents defining the procedure, politics and strategies of the CSTO. On 10 February 1995, the Collective Security Council adopted the Collective Security Concept for Member States of the Collective Security Treaty Organization. This Concept *inter alia* defines main sources of military threats starting with territorial claims of other states.[36] Some other important legal documents include the Collective Security Treaty Organization Peacekeeping Agreement dated 6 October 2007, and Agreement on the Status of the Collective Security System Forces of the Collective Security Treaty Organization dated 10 December 2010.

The Collective Security Treaty Organization Peacekeeping Agreement dated 6 October 2007 provided for the establishment of the CSTO peacekeeping forces, which constitute the joint forces of the member states and are trained and equipped according to unified programs.[37] The peacekeeping activities are to be conducted according to a decision of the Collective Security Council based on a request of a member state (if the peacekeeping activities are to be carried out on the territory of such member state) or based on the resolution of the UN Security Council (if the peacekeeping activities are to be carried out on the territory of a non-member state). Therefore, a request to conduct a peacekeeping operation, i.e. the call for help, of a CSTO member state is not enough for the Organization to act *per se*. The decision of the Organization on conducting the peacekeeping activities must be based on the recommendations of the Council of Ministers for Foreign Affairs, the Council of Ministers of Defense, and the Committee of Secretaries of the Security Councils.

With due regard to modern challenges, the CSTO pays close attention to information security and cyberwarfare. According to Article 8 of the Charter of the CSTO, the member states co-operate, *inter alia*, in the spheres of information exchange and information security.[38] This expands the scope of application of the Collective Security Treaty to cyberspace. The CSTO member states adopted the Agreement on Cooperation in the Provision of Information Security on 30 November 2017,[39] which provides for a detailed description of factors posing threats to information security of the member states. The Agreement defines the directions of cooperation between member states in the area of information security, including the following:

(1) Development of joint legal bases;
(2) Formation of practical mechanisms for joint reaction to threats to information security;
(3) Trust enforcement measures;

---

[35] Ibid., Article 17.

[36] Collective Security Concept for Member States of the Collective Security Treaty Organization, para 11.

[37] Collective Security Treaty Organization Peacekeeping Agreement (adopted on 6 October 2007), Article 2.

[38] Supra note 26, Article 8.

[39] Elamiryan and Bolgov 2018, p. 6.

28 Collective Security Treaty Organization (CSTO)

(4)   Modernization of technological basis of information security;
(5)   Establishment of the necessary conditions for the development of inter-institutional cooperation of the member-states.[40]

While the Agreement contains detailed descriptions of necessary actions in each of the aforementioned directions,[41] the CSTO action in the area of information security is now focused on coordinating the efforts of member states rather than on active collective operations in cyberspace.[42]

28.4   Activities of Collective Security Treaty Organization

On 14 June 2009, the CSTO member states adopted the Agreement on the Collective Rapid Reaction Force—a military contingent and special forces provided by member states for the purpose of responding to collective security issues.[43] The main purpose of the Collective Rapid Reaction Force is to respond to threats of military aggression, international terrorism, drug trafficking, transnational crimes, emergency situations, and more.[44] The composition of the Collective Rapid Reaction Force is decided by the Collective Security Council.[45] The Collective Rapid Reaction Force has conducted multiple successful joint military trainings. The control over the Collective Rapid Reaction Force in the framework of a particular operation is carried out by the Command specifically authorized by the Collective Security Council.[46]

In recent years, the CSTO faced multiple regional security threats. The most intense cases were the armed conflict in Georgia in 2008, violence in Kyrgyzstan in 2010, the armed conflict in Ukraine since 2014, and in Nagorno-Karabakh in 2020. As regards the conflict in Georgia in 2008, the CSTO forces did not take part in hostilities. The Ministers of Foreign Affairs of the CSTO member states issued a statement whereby they expressed deep concern about the "military actions taken by Georgia", and support for "Russia's active role in related peacekeeping activities".[47] In addition, on 5 September 2008, the Collective Security Council issued a Declaration, which called upon NATO "to weigh all the possible consequences of expanding the Alliance to the east" to the borders of the CSTO member states.[48]

---

[40] Ibid., p. 8.

[41] Ibid., p. 8.

[42] Ibid., p. 10.

[43] Agreement on the Collective Rapid Reaction Force (adopted on 14 June 2009), Article 1.

[44] Ibid., Article 2.

[45] Ibid., Article 4.

[46] Ibid., Article 7.

[47] Statement by the Ministers of Foreign Affairs of the Member States of the Collective Security Treaty Organization in connection with the events in South Ossetia 2008, para 1–3.

[48] Declaration of the Moscow Session of the Collective Security Council of the Collective Security Treaty Organization 2008, para 3.

In 2010, in the context of an "unconstitutional change of government" in Kyrgyzstan, the CSTO again decided to refrain from the use of military force. In their statement, the CSTO member states defined the situation in Kyrgyzstan as "the Kyrgyz Republic's internal affairs".[49]

The armed conflict in Ukraine since 2014 became one of the CSTO's major concerns. In August 2014, the CSTO Secretary General Nikolai Bordyuzha made an unclear statement implying that the CSTO peacekeeping forces are prepared for any external operations, subject to the consensus of the CSTO member states.[50] Although the CSTO had to clarify that such a decision was not under consideration,[51] some member states were disturbed by the possibility of getting involved in the Ukrainian conflict.[52] The CSTO had to reply assuring its member states that any military actions would be subject to consensus.[53] While involvement in the Ukraine conflict is not an obligation for the CSTO member states, it remains unclear whether the CSTO members would comply with their collective security obligation in the case of Ukraine's military attempt to reclaim Crimea, which Russia now considers its sovereign territory.[54]

28.5 Conclusion

Although the Collective Security Treaty has been directing the activities and international obligations of the CSTO member states in the area of international peace and security for more than 25 years now, and despite the fact there have been multiple occasions when collective security efforts could be deemed necessary, the CSTO did not carry out any proper collective security operations. Nevertheless, one cannot fail to note the CSTO's ability to pragmatically assess, and its organizational, technical and regulatory readiness to respond to, a variety of challenges to international peace and security.

---

[49] Statement by the Heads of Member States of the Collective Security Treaty Organization—the Republic of Armenia, the Republic of Belarus, the Republic of Kazakhstan, the Russian Federation, the Republic of Tajikistan, the Republic of Uzbekistan on the situation in the Kyrgyz Republic 2010, para 1.

[50] Sputnik International 2014, para 1.

[51] Senyuk 2014, para 1.

[52] Abdyraeva 2014, para 3.

[53] Kucera 2014, para 4.

[54] Ibid., para 5.

References

Books, (Online) Articles and Chapters in Books

Abdyraeva A (2014) Supreme Council Believes that the CSTO Agreement on Collective Security Can Drag Kyrgyzstan into the War between Russia and Ukraine. https://knews.kg/2014/03/24/v-jogorku-keneshe-schitayut-chto-soglashenie-o-kollektivnyih-silah-odkb-mojet-vtyanut-kr-v-voynu-mejdu-rf-i-ukrainoy. Accessed 6 may 2020
de Wet E, Wood M (2013) Collective Security. https://opil.ouplaw.com/view/https://doi.org/10.1093/law:epil/9780199231690/law-9780199231690-e270. Accessed 6 May 2020
Elamiryan R, Bolgov R (2018) Comparing Cybersecurity in NATO and CSTO: Legal and Political Aspects (15 November 2018). GigaNet: Global Internet Governance Academic Network, Annual Symposium 2018. https://doi.org/10.2139/ssrn.3490191
Kucera J (2014) Moscow Assures Allies: You Won't Have To Fight In Ukraine. https://eurasianet.org/moscow-assures-allies-you-wont-have-to-fight-in-ukraine. Accessed 6 May 2020
Lowe V et al. (2008) The United Nations Security Council and War: The Evolution of Thought and Practice since 1945. Oxford University Press, Oxford, UK
Senyuk E (2014) CSTO secretariat: "CSTO peacekeeping forces are not going to Ukraine". https://news.tut.by/politics/413308.html. Accessed 6 May 2020
Sputnik International (2014) CSTO Says Ready for Peacekeeping Operations in Ukraine, Decision Up to Members. https://sputniknews.com/world/20140829192451895-CSTO-Says-Ready-for-Peacekeeping-Operations-in-Ukraine-Decision. Accessed 6 May 2020

Other Documents

Agreement on the Collective Rapid Reaction Force (adopted on 14 June 2009)
Agreement on Cooperation in the Provision of Information Security (adopted on 30 November 2017)
Agreement on the Status of the Collective Security Forces of the Collective Security Treaty Organization (adopted on 10 December 2010)
Charter of the Collective Security Treaty Organization (adopted on 7 October 2002)
Charter of the Commonwealth of Independent States (adopted on 22 January 1993, entered into force on 22 January 1994)
Charter of the United Nations (adopted on 26 June 1945, entered into force on 24 October 1945)
Collective Security Treaty (adopted on 15 May 1992, entered into force on 20 April 1994)
Collective Security Treaty Organization Peacekeeping Agreement (adopted on 6 October 2007)
Collective Security Treaty Organization, From the Treaty to the Organization. https://en.odkb-csto.org/25years/index.php. Accessed on 6 May 2020
Collective Security Concept for Member States of the Collective Security Treaty Organization (adopted on 10 February 1995)
Covenant of the League of Nations (adopted on 28 June 1919, entered into force on 10 January 1920)
Declaration of the Moscow Session of the Collective Security Council of the Collective Security Treaty Organization (2008). https://odkb-csto.org/documents/statements/deklaratsiya-moskovskoy-sessii-soveta-kollektivnoy-bezopasnosti-organizatsii-dogovora-o-kollektivnoy. Accessed 6 May 2020
Protocol on the Introduction of Amendments to the Collective Security Treaty (adopted on 10 December 2010)

Protocol on the Mechanism of Providing Military Technical Assistance to the Member States of the Collective Security Treaty Organization in Cases of Threats of Aggression and Committed Acts of Aggression (adopted on 6 October 2007)

Protocol on Prolongation of Collective Security Treaty (adopted on 2 April 1999)

Statement by the Heads of Member States of the Collective Security Treaty Organization - the Republic of Armenia, the Republic of Belarus, the Republic of Kazakhstan, the Russian Federation, the Republic of Tajikistan, the Republic of Uzbekistan on the situation in the Kyrgyz Republic (2010), https://odkb-csto.org/documents/statements/zayavlenie-glav-gosudarstv-chlenov-organi zatsii-dogovora-o-kollektivnoy-bezopasnosti-respubliki-arme. Accessed 6 May 2020

Statement by the Ministers of Foreign Affairs of the Member States of the Collective Security Treaty Organization in connection with the events in South Ossetia (2008), https://odkb-csto.org/documents/statements/zayavlenie-ministrov-inostrannykh. Accessed 6 May 2020

Vienna Convention on the Law of Treaties (adopted on 23 May 1969)

Sultan Sakhariyev is a Senior Lecturer at KIMEP University School of Law, Almaty, Kazakhstan.

Chapter 29
The Extraordinary Chambers in the Courts of Cambodia

Olivier Beauvallet and Jeanne-Thérèse Schmit

Contents

29.1 The Long Way to Transitional Justice 620
    29.1.1 An Incapacitating Post-Conflict Situation 620
    29.1.2 One Step Forward and Two Steps Back Negotiation Process 621
29.2 A Limited Jurisdiction 623
    29.2.1 Temporal Jurisdiction 623
    29.2.2 Territorial Jurisdiction 624
    29.2.3 Subject-Matter Jurisdiction 624
    29.2.4 Personal Jurisdiction 625
29.3 A Hybrid Jurisdiction of Extraordinary Nature 625
    29.3.1 A Hybrid Structure... 625
    29.3.2 ... Inserted Into the National Judicial System 626
29.4 A Review of the ECCC Caseload 627
    29.4.1 Case 001 628
    29.4.2 Case 002/01 and Case 002/02 628
    29.4.3 Other Cases 629
29.5 A Potential Legacy for an Extraordinary Set-up? 631
References 631

Abstract From 17 April 1975 until 7 January 1979, Cambodia was ruled by the brutal Khmer Rouge (KR) regime. Almost twenty years later, negotiations started between the Cambodian Government and the United Nations (UN) for assisting in the trials of the senior leaders and those most responsible for the atrocities committed. In June 2003, an agreement was reached after eight years of negotiations. This unique judiciary mechanism is called the Extraordinary Chambers in the Courts of Cambodia for the Prosecution of Crimes Committed during the Period of Democratic Kampuchea (ECCC). Decades after the commission of the atrocious crimes, this chapter exposes the contextual reasons that lead to such a delay, and presents the *sui generis* framework based on a delimited jurisdiction, and a hybrid judicial

---

O. Beauvallet (✉)
Extraordinary Chambers in the Courts of Cambodia, Phnom Penh, Cambodia
e-mail: beauvallet@un.org

J.-T. Schmit
Paris Bar, France

© T.M.C. ASSER PRESS and the authors 2022
S. Sayapin et al. (eds.), *International Conflict and Security Law*,
https://doi.org/10.1007/978-94-6265-515-7_29

set-up. A caseload overview is then provided, and some perspectives are attempted (V).

Keywords Cambodia · Khmer Rouge · civil and common law · hybrid justice

29.1 The Long Way to Transitional Justice

The specificity of the ECCC is deeply linked to the historical context of Cambodia and cannot be understood without a consideration of the events of the overthrow of the Khmer Rouge (KR) from 1979 to the 1990s.

29.1.1 An Incapacitating Post-Conflict Situation

When the Democratic Kampuchea (DK) regime collapsed in Phnom Penh on 7 January 1979, it left behind a country stung with the loss of more than 1.7 million individuals and a range of cruelties unmet since World War II.

Domestically, the survivors had to move "from violent reprisal to the legitimate realm of procedural justice".[1] The state of war between the emerging People's Republic of Kampuchea (PRK) and KR forces was encouraged by Pol Pot. The poorly functioning state security was also a legacy of the Angkar (the war name of the communist party of Kampuchea that ruled the country from 1975 to 1979), which led to a policy of disintegration of the institutions of previous regimes.[2] The ordinary political structures, in particular the courts, had disappeared four years ago and no magistrates were available.

However, this troubled period saw the beginnings of transitional justice, consisting of the implementation of two measures by the PRK. First, the People's Revolutionary Tribunal was set up in Phnom Penh[3] to try the acts of genocide committed by the Pol Pot-Ieng Sary Clique. After five days of hearings, Pol Pot and Ieng Sary were found guilty of genocide and sentenced to death *in absentia*. Second, the Raknase campaign[4] was undertaken in the early 1980s, consisting of the filing of 1,898 petitions against the KR's crimes.[5]

Pursuant to a Decree—Law No. 02 K.C (15/5/1980) "On the Penalty of Revolution's Betrayal and Some Penalties of the Other Betrayals"—the People's Revolutionary Council decided to identify urgently with a firm and fair trial for those who

---

[1] Sok-Kheang 2017, p. 60.

[2] Lavergne 2017, p. 145.

[3] Decree Law No.1: Establishment of People's Revolutionary Tribunal at Phnom Penh to Try the POL Pot-IENG Sary Clique for the Crime of Genocide, Article 1, 15 July 1979.

[4] Sok-Kheang 2017, p. 61.

[5] See https://english.cambodiadaily.com/features/healing-a-nation-128377/. Accessed 28 July 2020.

29 The Extraordinary Chambers in the Courts of Cambodia   621

had massacred millions of persons and forced the entire Kampuchean people to live in genocidal conditions (Article 1).

Although instigated by the Vietnamese and led by a non-internationally recognized government, these experiments were a milestone for the country and have been considered important precedents to the ECCC.[6]

Internationally, the context of the Cold War also hampered the organization of trials. Hostile to the Vietnamese occupation of the country,[7] the UN refused to support the new PRK but recognized the exiled KR regime as the legitimate government, allowing it to occupy Cambodia's seat until 1992.[8]

The violence gradually ceased in the late 1990s thanks to some key events. On 26 September 1989, the last Vietnamese troops officially left Cambodia. The signing of the Paris Agreements on 23 October 1991 enabled a peace process under the aegis of the UN, but the Khmer Rouge continued their guerrilla warfare. On 8 August 1996, Ieng Sary joined the regime along with several thousand supporters and was offered amnesty by King Norodom Sihanouk. Pol Pot was captured in June 1997 by Ta Mok and detained until his passing. Finally, a series of KR rallied the regime after the fall of the last stronghold in March 1998.[9]

29.1.2 *One Step Forward and Two Steps Back Negotiation Process*

The idea of bringing KR cadres to trial was not unanimously shared within Cambodian society. Some feared the revival of violence outside the courtroom. Buddhist followers sometimes also considered the trial a vindictive act.[10] The opponents of a judicial process stressed the preponderance of peace over the quest for truth, while the proponents considered the trial crucial for the sake of reconciliation.[11] It is important to underline that the Paris Agreement made no mention of a trial.[12]

The administration of justice then formed part of a more global policy conducted in the context of civil war. Justice was rather presented as a promise of the repression of new crimes by the still active guerrillas than the sanctioning of past massive criminal policies.[13]

---

[6] Gidley 2019, p. 53, 59.

[7] Poissonnier 2007, p. 235.

[8] Lavergne 2017, p. 145; Widyono 2019.

[9] «Le Cambodge à l'entrée du 21e siècle», Rapport de groupe interparlementaire d'amitié n° 75 (2006–2007), 10 juillet 2007, French Senate. available at: https://www.senat.fr/ga/ga75/ga75_mono.html. Accessed 28 July 2020.

[10] Ly Sok-Kheang, Reconciliation process in Cambodia: 1970–2007, Before the Khmer Rouge Tribunal, op. cit., p. 172.

[11] Lemonde 2011, p. 597.

[12] Gidley 2019, op. cit., p. 65.

[13] An example of that approach is provided by the "Law on the Outlawing of the Democratic Kampuchea Group", Royal Kram No. 01. NS.94, 15 July 1994, whom article 5 reads: "This Law

For international observers, the need for a judicial process became more pressing after Ieng Sary's royal pardon on 14 September 1996 and Pol Pot's death on 15 April 1998, since these events heightened fears that the KR leaders would not be brought to a proper trial. Furthermore, this decade had seen the development of international jurisdictions such as the International Criminal Tribunal for the former Yugoslavia and the International Criminal Tribunal for Rwanda, contrasting with the situation in Cambodia.

The call for a trial surprisingly arose from the Cambodian Government. On 21 June 1997, Co-Prime Ministers Prince Norodom Rannariddh and Hun Sen requested the "assistance of the UN and the international community in bringing to justice those persons responsible for the genocide and crimes against humanity during the rule of the KR from 1975 to 1979".[14] The sharing of the executive power back then, a pattern to be repeated in the ECCC design, does not bring much clarity to modern interpretations of the real intention supporting that initiative.

In response, a group of experts was appointed by the Secretary General, upon the request of the general assembly.[15] It recommended the establishment of an *ad hoc* international tribunal, which was due to the weakness of the Cambodian judicial system that had been unable to meet minimal international standards of justice.[16] The Cambodian government objected to this recommendation on the grounds of the principle of sovereignty. An extensive negotiation process ensued. In July 2001, the National Assembly unilaterally adopted the Law on the Establishment of the Extraordinary Chambers in the Courts of Cambodia for the Prosecution of Crimes Committed during the Period of Democratic Kampuchea (ECCC Law).[17] An agreement drawing up the structure of the court operation was finally reached on 6 June

---

shall grant a stay of six months after coming into effect to permit people who are members of the political organization of military forces of the "Democratic Kampuchea" group to return to live under the control of the Royal Government in the Kingdom of Cambodia without facing punishment for crimes which they have committed".

[14] Letter dated 21 June 1997 from the First and Second Prime Ministers of Cambodia addressed to the Secretary General, attached to Identical letters dated 23 June 1997 from the Secretary-General addressed to the President of the General Assembly and to the President of the Security Council, available at: https://www.un.org/ga/search/view_doc.asp?symbol=A/51/930. Accessed 28 July 2020.

[15] A/RES/52/135, 12 December 1997, available at: https://undocs.org/en/A/RES/52/135. Accessed 28 July 2020.

[16] Report of the Group of Experts for Cambodia established pursuant to General Assembly resolution 52/135, 18 February 1999, available at: https://undocs.org/A/53/850. Accessed 28 July 2020.

[17] Agreement between the United Nations and the Royal Government of Cambodia concerning the prosecution under Cambodian law of crimes committed during the period of Democratic Kampuchea, Phnom Penh, 6 June 2003, available at: https://treaties.un.org/doc/Publication/UNTS/Volume%202329/Part/volume-2329-I-41723.pdf. Accessed 28 July 2020.

29 The Extraordinary Chambers in the Courts of Cambodia 623

2003 (Agreement)[18] and ratified by the National Assembly on 4 October 2004.[19] As a UN requirement for the functioning of the court, the financial guarantee for starting its operations was secured on 28 April 2005.[20] The last step of this complex creation process—the writing of the internal dispositions—was fulfilled on 12 June 2007 by the adoption of the Internal Rules,[21] which were complemented by national Cambodian law and international law.

29.2 A Limited Jurisdiction

Pursuant to Article 1 of the Agreement and Articles 1 and 2 (new) of the ECCC Law, the purpose of these chambers was "to bring to trial senior leaders of Democratic Kampuchea and those who were most responsible for the crimes and serious violations of Cambodian laws related to crimes, international humanitarian law and custom, and international conventions recognized by Cambodia, that were committed during the period from 17 April 1975 to 6 January 1979".

In recognizing[22] the scope of jurisdiction set out in the ECCC Law, the negotiators agreed to contain prosecutions, given the complexity of the conflict, within necessary precise geographical and temporal limits.

29.2.1 Temporal Jurisdiction

According to the abovementioned articles, the Extraordinary Chambers had the competence to judge crimes committed in the period between the KR's seizure of power and their defection from the Vietnamese Army. As a consequence, the tribunal had no jurisdiction on crimes committed by the KR before the fall of Phnom Penh, nor on those committed during the fighting that pitted the KR guerrilla against the government from 1979 to the end of the 1990s. This limitation also excluded any

---

[18] *See* https://www.eccc.gov.kh/sites/default/files/legal-documents/KR_Law_as_ame nded_27_Oct_2004_Eng.pdf. Accessed 28 July 2020.

[19] By adopting the "Law to Amend the 2001 Law on the ECCC on 27 October 2004"; *see* https://www.eccc.gov.kh/sites/default/files/legal-documents/KR_Law_as_amended_27_Oct_ 2004_Eng.pdf.

[20] Rebecca Gidley, Illiberal Transitional Justice and the Extraordinary Chambers in the Courts of Cambodia, op. cit., pages 120–122. *See also* Chronology of Establishment of the ECCC: https://www.eccc.gov.kh/en/chronlologies/letter-kofi-annan-secretary-general-united-nations-samdech-hun-sen-prime-minister-info. Accessed 28 July 2020.

[21] *See* https://www.eccc.gov.kh/sites/default/files/legal-documents/Internal_Rules_Rev_9_Eng. pdf. Accessed 28 July 2020.

[22] Agreement, Article 2(1).

consideration of the diplomatic and military policies of states that had played a determining role in the region, before and after the DK regime, namely during the Vietnam war.

29.2.2 Territorial Jurisdiction

The aforementioned articles do not precisely explain whether crimes and offences must have been committed in Cambodian territory. However, it has been interpreted as referring only to atrocities committed on Cambodian soil or waters.

When the court was established, the question arose whether the ECCC would be competent to try nationals of other states who committed crimes and breaches within Cambodia. In the same way, it was not certain that the court would not examine crimes and offences committed by the KR outside the country. But the Extraordinary Chambers have maintained a strict understanding of their jurisdiction.[23]

29.2.3 Subject-Matter Jurisdiction

The ECCC has jurisdiction over genocide,[24] crimes against humanity,[25] grave breaches of the Geneva Conventions[26] and an array of domestic crimes.[27] In addition, they have jurisdiction over destruction of cultural property during an armed conflict[28] and crimes against internationally protected persons,[29] but these crimes have not been prosecuted.

Since the KR leaders had exterminated part of their own people, it was questioned whether genocide would be a suitable characterization for the destruction of its own Khmer people by the KR rulers. The Extraordinary Chambers' creativity and boldness in the delimitation of their material competence is noteworthy. Faced with the specificity of the Khmer Rouge's policy regulating marriage and the inadequacy of the enumerated categories of crimes against humanity, the Trial Chamber recognized

---

[23] Poissonnier 2007, op. cit., p. 235.

[24] ECCC law, Article 4.

[25] ECCC law, Article 5, including forced marriage (ECCC, Case File No. 002/19-09-2007/ECCC/TC, 16 November 2018, Case 002/02 Judgment, Doc. No. E465, §§3688–3694) and enforced disappearances as other inhumane acts.

[26] ECCC law, Article 6.

[27] ECCC law, Article 3.

[28] ECCC law, Article 7, referring to the 1954 Hague Convention.

[29] ECCC law, Article 8, referring to the 1961 Vienna Convention.

29 The Extraordinary Chambers in the Courts of Cambodia

indeed that "the crime against humanity of other inhumane acts through conduct characterized as forced marriage and rape in the context of forced marriage was committed".[30] In the same vein, the Trial Chamber found that enforced disappearances fall under the qualification of "other inhumane acts".[31]

29.2.4 *Personal Jurisdiction*

Personal jurisdiction was limited to two categories of Cambodian citizens, namely senior leaders of the KR who were among the most responsible, as well as non-senior leaders of the KR who were also among the most responsible. Both categories must be KR officials and among the most responsible. The criteria were thus cumulative, not disjunctive.[32] The identification of those who were amongst the "most responsible" entailed the assessment of both the gravity of the crimes alleged or charged and the level of responsibility of the suspect.[33] As specified below, whether a suspect was subject to personal jurisdiction was a recurrent point of cleavage, especially between the Co-Investigating Judges.

29.3 A Hybrid Jurisdiction of Extraordinary Nature

29.3.1 *A Hybrid Structure…*

Every office or chamber of the ECCC is bifurcated by nature (Cambodian and international). Two co-prosecutors are jointly responsible for preliminary investigations and the prosecution of cases.[34] When they have reason to believe that crimes falling

---

[30] ECCC, Case File No. 002/19-09-2007/ECCC/TC, 16 November 2018, Case 002/02 Judgment, Doc. No. E465, §§3688–3694. In doing so, the Trial Chamber was taking the path opened up by the Appeals Chamber of the Special Court for Sierra Leone (SCSL), which hold in 2008 forced marriage to be a distinct category of crimes against humanity (*see* Neha Jain, "Forced Marriage as Crime against Humanity: Problems of Definition and Prosecution", *Journal of International Criminal Justice,* Volume 6, Issue 5, November 2008, pp. 1013–1032 (https://doi.org/10.1093/jicj/mqn064), *referring to* SCSL, Case No. SCSL-2004-16-A, 22 February 2008, *Prosecutor v. Brima, Kamara, and Kanu,* §§175–203).

[31] ECCC, Case File No. 002/19-09-2007/ECCC/TC, 7 August 2014, Case 002/01 Judgement, Doc. No. E313, §§ 441–448.

[32] ECCC, Case File No. 001/18-07-2007-ECCC/SC, 3 February 2012, Appeal Judgement, Doc. No. F28, §61.

[33] ECCC, Case File No. 001/18-07-2007/ECCC/TC, 26 July 2010, Judgement, Doc. No. E188, §22; ECCC, Case File No. 004/01/07-09-2009-ECCC/OCIJ (PTC50), 28 June 2018, Considerations on the International Co-Prosecutor's Appeal of Closing Order (Reasons), Doc. No. D308/3/1/20, §321.

[34] Agreement, Article 6(1).

under the ECCC jurisdiction have been committed, they may open a judicial investigation.[35] From that time on, two co-investigating judges are responsible for the conduct of the investigation[36] until they issue a closing order, either dismissing the case or indicting the charged persons.

A Pre-Trial Chamber has been created to sort out disagreements between co-prosecutors[37] or co-investigating judges.[38] That chamber (composed of five judges—three nationals, two internationals) is also in charge of different other proceedings,[39] including appeals[40] and annulments.[41] The latter requires a procedural defect and an infringement of rights to strike from the defective record files. The Trial Chamber is composed of five judges (three nationals, two internationals)[42] and the Supreme Court Chamber of seven (four nationals, three internationals).[43]

The judges shall attempt to achieve unanimity in their decisions.[44] If this is not possible, a decision by the Pre-Trial Chamber[45] or the Trial Chamber[46] shall require the affirmative vote of at least four judges, while the vote of at least five is required for a decision by the Supreme Court Chamber.[47] That rule is known as the "super majority vote" that requires at least one international judge to approve any decision. It also requires the majority of the national judges. It is completed by a set of presumptions known as the "default position". When there is no unanimity, the decision shall contain the views of the majority and the minority. At the pre-trial stage, if the required majority is not attained, the investigation or prosecution shall proceed,[48] while at the trial stage, the default decision shall be that the accused is acquitted.[49]

29.3.2 ... Inserted Into the National Judicial System

All the judges and prosecutors of the ECCC are appointed by royal decree following a decision by the Supreme Judicial Council of Cambodia, including international judges who are selected from a list of candidates proposed by the Secretary-General

---

[35] ECCC Law, Article 16.

[36] ECCC Law, Article 23 new.

[37] Internal Rule 71.

[38] Internal Rule 72.

[39] Beauvallet and Baik 2021.

[40] Internal Rule 74.

[41] Internal Rule 76.

[42] Agreement, Article 2(3)(a); ECCC Law, Article 9(1).

[43] Agreement, Article 2(3)(b); ECCC Law, Article 9(2).

[44] Agreement, Article 4; ECCC Law, Article 14.

[45] Agreement, Article 7.

[46] Agreement, Article 4(1)(a); ECCC law, Article 14(1)(a).

[47] Agreement, Article 4(1)(b); ECCC law, Article 14(1)(b).

[48] Agreement, Article 7(4); ECCC law, Article 23(6).

[49] Internal rule 98 (4).

of the UN.[50] The Extraordinary Chambers established in the Trial Chamber and the Supreme Court Chamber shall be located in Phnom Penh.[51] All judges under this law shall enjoy equal status and conditions of service according to each level of the ECCC.[52]

The official language of the Extraordinary Chambers and the Pre-Trial Chamber is Khmer, but the official working languages of the Extraordinary Chambers and the Pre-Trial Chamber shall be Khmer, English and French.[53]

The proceedings were mostly inspired by the inquisitorial system and civil law. During the activity of the ECCC, the legal system of Cambodia confirmed its attachment to that system through the enactment in 2007 of a Code of Criminal Proceedings and in 2009 of a new Penal Code.

The procedure applicable before the ECCC is governed by Cambodian law, which can be silent on one particular point or discordant with international standards. Internal Rules have consequently been enacted to ensure the consistency of the applicable law and bridge some gaps left after the ECCC Law was adopted. Thus, the provisions of the Cambodian Code of Criminal Proceedings do apply only when an issue is raised that is not covered in the rules of procedure.[54] But they cannot be avoided.[55] Indeed the Cambodian Code of Criminal Proceedings "aims at defining the rules to be strictly followed and applied in order to clearly determine the existence of a criminal offense" (Article 1).

29.4 A Review of the ECCC Caseload

On 18 July 2007, the Co-Prosecutors filed the first Introductory Submission against Nuon Chea, Ieng Sary, Khieu Samphan, Ieng Thirith and Kaing Guek Eav (alias Duch). On 19 September 2007, the Co-Investigating Judges ordered the severance of the charges into Case 001 and Case 002.

---

[50] Agreement, Article 3.

[51] ECCC Law, Article 43 new.

[52] ECCC Law, Article 12.

[53] Agreement, Article 19; ECCC Law, Article 45.

[54] ECCC, Case File No. 002/19-09-2007/ECCC/OCIJ (PTC06), 26 August 2008, Decision on NUON Chea's Appeal against Order Refusing Request for Annulment, Doc. No. D55/I/8, §§14–15.

[55] ECCC, Case File No. 004/2/07-09-2009-ECCC/OCIJ (PTC60), 19 December 2019, Considerations on Appeals against Closing Orders, Docs. Nos. D359/24 and D360/3, §95.

29.4.1 Case 001

Duch was in charge of the S-21 security centre, located in Phnom Penh, from 15 August 1975 through the collapse of the DK regime. S-21 was tasked with interrogating and executing perceived opponents of the regime and included a detention centre (Tuol Sleng) as well as an execution camp (Choeung Ek) and re-education camp (S-24) on the outskirts of the city.

On 26 July 2010, the Trial Chamber found that Duch "managed and refined a system over the course of three years that resulted in the execution of no fewer than 12,272 victims, the majority of whom were also systematically tortured" and sentenced him to 35 years of imprisonment.[56] On 3 February 2012, the Supreme Court Chamber increased this sentence to life imprisonment.[57]

29.4.2 Case 002/01 and Case 002/02

On 15 September 2010, the Co-Investigating Judges indicted Nuon Chea,[58] Ieng Sary,[59] Khieu Samphan[60] and Ieng Thirith.[61] The latter was found unfit to trial and passed away in August 2015.[62] Her husband Ieng Sary died in March 2013, so the proceedings against him were terminated.[63]

The Trial Chamber ordered the severance of the case into Cases 002/01 and 002/02. Case 002/01 focused on alleged crimes against humanity related to the forced movements of the population from Phnom Penh in April 1975 and later from other regions, and to the execution of Khmer Republic soldiers at the Toul Po Chrey execution site following the KR takeover. On 7 August 2014, the Trial Chamber found Nuon Chea and Khieu Samphan guilty and sentenced them to life imprisonment.[64] On 23 November 2016, the Supreme Court Chamber widely upheld these sentences.[65]

---

[56] ECCC, Case File No. 001/18-07-2007/ECCC/TC, 26 July 2010, Judgement, Doc. No. E188.

[57] ECCC, Case File No. 001/18-07-2007/ECCC/SC, 3 February 2012, Appeal Judgement, Doc. No. F28.

[58] Chairman of the Democratic Kampuchea National Assembly and Deputy Secretary of the Communist Party of Kampuchea.

[59] Deputy Prime Minister for Foreign Affairs.

[60] Head of State of the Democratic Kampuchea.

[61] Minister of Social Affairs in Democratic Kampuchea.

[62] ECCC, Case File No. 002/19-09-2007/ECCC/TC, 27 August 2015, Termination of the Proceedings against the Accused IENG Tirith, Doc. No. E359/1.

[63] ECCC, Case File No. 002/19-09-2007/ECCC/TC, 14 March 2013, Termination of the Proceedings against the Accused IENG Sary, Doc. No. E270/1.

[64] ECCC, Case File No. 002/19-09-2007/ECCC/TC, 7 August 2014, Case 002/01 Judgement, Doc. No. E313.

[65] ECCC, Case File No. 002/19-09-2007/ECCC/SC, 23 November 2016, Appeal Judgement, Doc. No. F36.

29 The Extraordinary Chambers in the Courts of Cambodia

Case 002/02 relates to genocide against the Cham and the Vietnamese, forced marriages and rape, internal purges, treatment of Buddhists, three worksites, four security centres and one cooperative. On 28 March 2019, the Trial Chamber notified its judgement finding Nuon Chea and Khieu Samphan guilty and sentencing them to life imprisonment.[66] In July 2019, both accused filed their notices of appeal against the trial judgement. Nuon Chea passed away on 9 August 2019, and the case was consequently terminated.[67] The appeal of Khieu Samphan is still pending before the Supreme Court Chamber.

Pursuant to Internal Rule 89 *quater*,[68] the remaining charges in Case 002/03 that were not addressed at the main trial were dismissed in February 2017.[69]

29.4.3 Other Cases

On 7 September 2009, the International Co-Prosecutor initiated two more investigations involving five additional suspected persons.

29.4.3.1 Case 003

Case 003 deals with crimes committed by and within the Kampuchea Revolutionary Army. This case initially involved two suspects, SOU MET and Meas Muth.

Sou Met was Brigade 512 commander and an Air Force commander. The investigation against him was terminated in June 2015 due to his death in 2013.[70]

On 3 March 2015, Meas Muth was charged *in absentia*. At his first appearance on 14 December 2015, he was charged with genocide, crimes against humanity, graves breaches of the Geneva Conventions and assassination as a domestic crime, committed as a former member of the Military General Staff, as well as the former Commander of Division 164, which included the DK Navy and as the former highest civilian authority of the Kampong Som Autonomous Sector. Interestingly enough,

---

[66] ECCC, Case File No. 002/19-09-2007/ECCC/TC, 16 November 2018, Case 002/02 Judgement, Doc. No. E465. The findings and the disposition were announced in a summary on 16 November 2018.

[67] ECCC, Case File No. 002/19-09-2007/ECCC/SC, 13 August 2019, Decision to Terminate Proceedings against NUON Chea, Doc. No. F46/3.

[68] IR 89 *quater* (1) reads: "In order to ensure a fair, meaningful and expeditious judicial process, in consideration of the specific requirements of the proceedings before the ECCC, the Trial Chamber may decide to reduce the scope of the trial by excluding certain facts set out in the Indictment. The Trial Chamber shall ensure that the remaining facts are representative of the scope of the Indictment".

[69] ECCC, Case File No. 002/19-09-2007/ECCC/TC, 27 February 2017, Decision on Reduction of the Scope of Case 002, Doc. No. E439/5.

[70] ECCC, Case File No. 003/07-09-2009/ECCC/OCIJ, 2 June 2015, Dismissal of Allegations Against SOU Met, Doc. No. D86/3.

on 28 November 2018, the International Co-Investigating Judge issued a closing order indicting Meas Muth,[71] while the National Co-Investigating Judge issued a dismissal order.[72] The disagreement is about whether Meas Muth is subject to the ECCC's personal jurisdiction. The case is currently pending before the Pre-Trial Chamber.

29.4.3.2 Cases 004, 004/01, 004/02

Case 004 focuses on purges in different zones and has been divided into three different prosecutions. Case 004/01 alleged various criminal charges against Im Chaem.[73] The Co-Investigating Judges dismissed this case in February 2017, Im Chaem being allegedly neither a senior leader nor a most responsible of the crimes committed during the DK time.[74] While the case stopped at the ECCC for a lack of personal jurisdiction, no domestic prosecution was started after the Pre-Trial Chamber issued its appeal considerations on 28 June 2018.[75]

On 27 March 2015, AO An was charged in Case 004/02 with the crimes of genocide of the Cham, crimes against humanity and assassination in Southwest zone and Central Zone. On 16 August 2018, the Co-Investigating Judges issued simultaneously conflicting closing orders about whether the accused was subject to the ECCC's personal jurisdiction.[76] On appeal, the Pre-Trial Chamber found such a practice was unlawful under ECCC law and had not reached the supermajority vote to reverse the International Co-Investigating Judge's Closing Order (Indictment).[77] Interpretation of Internal Rule 77(13) would be a cause of confusion. As some commentators put it, it then appeared that the default position was caught in default.

On 9 December 2015, the International Co-Investigating Judge charged Yim Tith in Case 004 with the genocide of the Khmer Krom, crimes against humanity, graves breaches of the Geneva Conventions of 1949, and premeditated homicide. Again,

---

[71] ECCC, Case File No. 003/07-09-2009/ECCC/OCIJ, 28 November 2018, Closing Order, Doc. No. D267.

[72] ECCC, Case File No. 003/07-09-2009/ECCC/OCIJ, 28 November 2018, Order Dismissing the Case against MEAS Muth, Doc. No. D266.

[73] A District Secretary in different locations of Cambodia and a Member of Parliament.

[74] ECCC, Case File No. 004/1/07-09-2009/ECCC/OCIJ, 22 February 2017, Closing Order (Disposition), Doc. No. D308; ECCC, Case File No. 004/1/07-09-2009/ECCC/OCIJ, 10 July 2017, Closing Order (Reasons), Doc. No. D308/3.

[75] ECCC, Case File No. 004/1/07-09-2009/ECCC/OCIJ (PTC50), 28 June 2018, Considerations on the International Co-Prosecutor's Appeal of Closing Order (Reasons), Doc. No. D308/3/1/20.

[76] ECCC, Case File No. 004/2/07-09-2009/ECCC/OCIJ, 16 August 2018, Order Dismissing the Case against AO An, Doc. No. D359; ECCC, Case File No. 004/2/07-09-2009/ECCC/OCIJ, 16 August 2018, Closing Order (Indictment), Doc. No. D360.

[77] ECCC, Case File No. 004/2/07-09-2009/ECCC/OCIJ (PTC60), 19 December 2019, Considerations on Appeals against Closing Orders, Docs. Nos. D359/24 and D360/33.

29 The Extraordinary Chambers in the Courts of Cambodia

the Co-Investigating Judges disagreed concerning the ECCC's personal jurisdiction and issued conflicting closing orders.[78]

29.5 A Potential Legacy for an Extraordinary Set-up?

While many did not believe in the viability of the ECCC and criticisms persist,[79] they have performed a good deal of work as long as the hybridism was accepted by the stakeholders and the protagonists of those prosecutions. On the one hand, many readings expose the weakness and such drawbacks that, in their view, this experience is rather unsuccessful and not to be repeated. Others stress that the ECCC, despite all their complexity, has shown that they are capable of functioning and rendering court decisions in the same country where the crimes were committed, which made it possible to give the trials more resonance.[80]

The ECCC experience seems indeed to have left a contrasted balance sheet that perhaps is not all related to the legal structure. Most of the issues are known and were even identified at the time the creation of the ECCC was decided.[81] If the conditions are set, besides the UN *ad hoc* courts and ICC, the ECCC may well be a source of inspiration for the next generation of international criminal courts, especially when sharing the same legal tradition as the African Extraordinary Chambers or the Special Criminal Court.

In the positive scale of the balance, it must be remembered that the ECCC has filled an essential vacuum. The ECCC came right on time to be transferred the case of Duch—already detained by the Cambodian Military Court—and a bit too late for many others including Ta Mok—also detained by that jurisdiction. The ECCC has been indeed the only court able to investigate, prosecute and judge with the highest standards some crimes committed by KR criminals. Their work and legacy are no comparison to the June 1979 show process. No national criminal prosecution was ever entertained in Cambodia against a KR leader for crimes committed during that era. International assistance in that sense was instrumental.

References

Beauvallet O, Baik KJ (eds) (2021) Jurisprudence of the Pre-Trial Chamber of the Extraordinary Chambers in the Courts of Cambodia, 1st edn. Phnom Penh

---

[78] ECCC, Case File No. 004/07-09-2009/ECCC/OCIJ, 28 June 2019, Order Dismissing the Case against YIM Tith, Doc. No. D381; ECCC, Case File No. 004/07-09-2009/ECCC/OCIJ, 28 June 2019, Closing Order, Doc. No. D382.

[79] Etcheson 2019; Gidley 2019, op. cit.

[80] Lavergne 2017, op. cit.

[81] Orentlicher 2020.

Ciorcari J, Heindel A (2014), Hybrid Justice: the Extraordinary Chambers in the Court of Cambodia. The University Press of Michigan

Etcheson C (2019) Extraordinary Justice: Law, Politics, and the Khmer Rouge Tribunals. Columbia University Press

French Senate (2007) Le Cambodge à l'entrée du 21e siècle, Rapport de groupe interparlementaire d'amitié n° 75 (2006–2007), available at: https://www.senat.fr/ga/ga75/ga75_mono.html

Gidley R (2019) Illiberal Transitional Justice and the Extraordinary Chambers in the Courts of Cambodia. Palgrave Studies in the History of Genocide, Palgrave Macmillan

Jain N (2008) Forced Marriage as Crime against Humanity: Problems of Definition and Prosecution. Journal of International Criminal Justice, Volume 6, Issue 5, November 2008, pages 1013–1032, available at: https://doi.org/10.1093/jicj/mqn064

Lavergne J-M (2017) Chambres extraordinaires au sein des tribunaux cambodgiens (création et structure). In: Dictionnaire encyclopédique de la justice pénale internationale. Berger-Levrault

Lemonde M (2011) Quelles leçons tirer du procès des Khmers rouges ? RSC, Dalloz

Orentlicher D (2020) 'Worth the Effort'?: Assessing the Khmer Rouge Tribunal. Social Science Research Network, available at: https://ssrn.com/abstract=3539204

Poissonnier G (2007) La mise en place des Chambres extraordinaires au sein des tribunaux cambodgiens. RSC, Dalloz

Sok-Kheang L (2017) Reconciliation process in Cambodia: 1970–2007, Before the Khmer Rouge Tribunal. Documentation Series No. 24, Document Center of Cambodia

Widyono B (2019) The Spectre of the Khmer Rouge over Cambodia. UN Chronicle, available at: https://www.un.org/en/chronicle/article/spectre-khmer-rouge-over-cambodia

Olivier Beauvallet is currently an international judge at the Pre-trial Chamber of the Extraordinary Chambers in the Cambodia Courts (ECCC). An investigative judge by background, he has also served as Special prosecutor in EULEX and the SITF. He holds a doctorate in law (EHESS Paris), and has authored various books and article on criminal and international criminal law. He participated in various international projects in Europe especially in the Balkans, Africa and Central Asia.

Jeanne-Thérèse Schmit is a lawyer at the Paris Bar. She is a graduate of Paris I Panthéon-Sorbonne University and Paris II Panthéon-Assas University, specialised in public and criminal law. During her studies, she enjoyed discovering international law and human rights. For her thesis, she focused on the constitutional ideas of the French philosopher and political scientist Raymond Aron who was very committed to the defence of democracy and freedom. Her recent experience in the Extraordinary Chambers in the Courts of Cambodia (ECCC) was an enriching opportunity to learn about this specific jurisdiction, as an insider.

The views expressed in this chapter do not necessarily reflect the opinion of any institutions the authors are or have been working for.

Chapter 30
Other "Hybrid" Tribunals

Michail Vagias

Contents

30.1 Introduction 634
30.2 Hybrid Tribunals: Definition 634
30.3 Hybrid Tribunals: Reasons for Their Creation 635
30.4 Critique on the Establishment of Hybrid Tribunals 636
30.5 The Worldwide and Continuous Allure of Hybrid Courts and Their Relationship
     with the ICC 637
    30.5.1 Special Panels for Serious Crimes in Timor-Leste 1999–2005 638
    30.5.2 The Special Court for Sierra Leone 2002–2013 640
    30.5.3 The Special Tribunal for Lebanon 641
    30.5.4 The Extraordinary African Chambers of the Courts of Senegal 644
30.6 Conclusion 646
References 646

Abstract The term 'hybrid tribunals' denotes judicial mechanisms for the administration of justice whose organizational set up combines international and domestic features. In this chapter, the emphasis is on hybrid tribunals established to prosecute international and transnational crimes, such as the Special Panels for Serious Crimes in East Timor, the Special Court for Sierra Leone and the Special Tribunal for Lebanon. The chapter discusses the definition of hybrid tribunals, the reasons put forward to justify their creation and the most frequent criticisms against them. Following this *tour d'horizon*, it explains that hybrid tribunals retain their attraction as a constant feature of the post-conflict peace-building toolbox, even after the establishment of the ICC. It presents four examples of hybrid courts (East Timor, Sierra Leone, Lebanon and Chad) which operated after the adoption of the 1998 ICC Statute. In conclusion, the chapter highlights that hybrid courts come in many different shapes and sizes; this versatility may constitute their most attractive feature for post-conflict justice, as well as their utmost vulnerability to claims of politicisation and 'victor's justice'.

Keywords hybrid tribunals · internationalised courts · Sierra Leone · Lebanon · Kosovo

---

M. Vagias (✉)
The Hague University of Applied Sciences, The Hague, The Netherlands
e-mail: m.vagias@hhs.nl

© T.M.C. ASSER PRESS and the authors 2022
S. Sayapin et al. (eds.), *International Conflict and Security Law*,
https://doi.org/10.1007/978-94-6265-515-7_30

30.1 Introduction

After the creation of the ICTY and the ICTR, the question soon emerged whether international tribunals should be established for other conflicts plaguing the world at the time. UN organs and commentators were aware of the resource-intensive and time-consuming nature of the Yugoslav and Rwandan tribunals. This led to a search for tribunals that would administer justice in post-conflict societies with less cost and more speed. The result of this process was the creation of 'hybrid tribunals'.

30.2 Hybrid Tribunals: Definition

The term 'hybrid tribunals' denotes in this chapter the criminal courts and tribunals that combine national and international elements in their institutional make-up. In international literature the term is often used inter-changeably with the synonyms 'mixed courts' or 'internationalised courts'.[1]

Two key characteristics may be said to apply across the board to hybrid tribunals and distinguish them from other courts. First, hybrid courts typically include a combination of domestic and international elements in their institutional design. This mix-up has been labelled as their 'hybridity' and may extend to mixing of domestic and international crimes or judges of different nationalities.[2] Second, hybrid courts are typically created as a reaction to a conflict; they are not 'free standing judicial bodies' but rather ad hoc mechanisms.[3]

In the literature, additional criteria have been proposed for the identification of hybrid courts. The judicial function of the institution, the participation of international personnel, its seat in another state, the involvement of international actors and/or instruments in its creation, are some indicative features.[4] However, the list is not exhaustive and does not appear to be always capable of general application. For example, while some hybrid courts seat within the relevant state (e.g. the Cambodia Extraordinary Chambers sitting in Cambodia or the Special Chambers for East Timor sitting in Dili), others have their seat in other states (e.g. the Special Tribunal for Lebanon has its seat in The Hague). Therefore, the combination of domestic and international elements as well as their *ad hoc* nature as courts created in response to specific needs arising from a certain conflict appear to be the two most reliable characteristics distinguishing hybrid courts as a class.

---

[1] Williams 2009, at 445–446.

[2] Nouwen 2006, at 203.

[3] Fichtelberg 2015, at 1.

[4] Williams 2012, at 201–212.

30.3 Hybrid Tribunals: Reasons for Their Creation

Many justifications for the creation of hybrid courts have been presented over the years. Typically, they revolve around themes of legitimacy, effectiveness, efficiency and capacity-building. In sum, the argument is that hybrid courts are better than either purely national or purely international courts because they combine the 'best of both worlds'[5] in unique institutional mixes tailored to the post-conflict justice needs of each situation.[6] Accordingly, hybrid courts are said to represent the next step in the administration of justice for international crimes after Nuremberg and the ad hoc tribunals; 'international criminal justice 3.0'.[7]

First, 'hybrid courts' are justified as a more legitimate option to either fully domestic or fully international prosecutions. Whereas domestic trials run a high risk of politicisation, international trials are perceived as 'foreign justice'. Hybrid courts are considered a better alternative, because they are said to spur domestic ownership of the judicial process while at the same time they appear to provide the necessary conditions of a fair trial, such as an independent and impartial judiciary.[8]

Second, hybrid tribunals are expected to be more effective than domestic institutions in the prosecution of international crimes. This is probably self-evident, considering that domestic judicial infrastructure is usually in shambles in the immediate aftermath of an armed conflict. In these circumstances, domestic courts find themselves unable to perform their judicial function. Hybrid courts are specifically designed to fill in this gap. They come with a full panoply of external support in terms of funding, personnel and human rights guarantees for the judiciary and the accused. As such, they make possible fair trials that would otherwise remain beyond the reach of justice, notwithstanding rare instances of universal jurisdiction by third states.[9]

In that light, hybrid courts are also portrayed as agents of capacity building and systemic change. Building domestic justice systems in the aftermath of an armed conflict has been put forward by the UN as a key justification for the creation of hybrid courts.[10] However, this 'reconstruction' is not only physical; it may also hold other transformative effects upon a domestic judicial and political system, such as the introduction of new rules in domestic substantive and procedural law. This has been called 'norm penetration' and is one of the main arguments in favour of hybrid courts.[11] In the best-case scenario, a hybrid court would facilitate the adoption of new domestic laws consistently with international standards; improve the administration of justice by domestic courts through the use of new technology and ethical standards;

---

[5] Dickinson 2003, at 296.

[6] Cassese 2010, at 433, 437.

[7] Koh 2013, at 531.

[8] Nouwen 2006, at 191.

[9] Hobbs 2016, at 489.

[10] Report of the Secretary General 2004, at 1.

[11] Dickinson 2003, at 296.

636   M. Vagias

while at the same time it would restore public trust to the rule of law through the
effective and fair administration of justice.

30.4 Critique on the Establishment of Hybrid Tribunals

At the same time, however, hybrid courts are subjected to considerable criticism.

To begin with, hybrid courts suffer from 'a problem of goals'.[12] Specifically, they
are burdened with too many goals stretching in too many directions. The list is long;
capacity-building, national reconciliation, retribution, deterrence, education and the
establishment of a credible historical record are only some of the most widely held
expectations.[13] This overabundance of expectations has two principal consequences.
It makes the successful performance of their mission impossible, which inevitably
leads to disappointment over their operation.[14] Moreover, it creates a widely-held
illusion that post-conflict reconciliation and justice may be achieved best or only
through the advent of judicial mechanisms. As such, it leads to the disregard of other
possibilities, such as truth commissions or traditional accountability mechanisms.[15]

Beyond the 'problem of goals', however, a key point of criticism is the vulnerability of hybrid courts to external pressure. The tension between law and politics
permeates to one degree or another the design of all international criminal tribunals.[16]
However, this tension has manifested with particular force to the detriment of the
reputation of hybrid institutions. Indicatively, in the case of the Extraordinary African
Chambers instituted in Senegal to prosecute the formed Chadian leader Hissène
Habré, when the prosecutors expressed their willingness to investigate allegations
and bring cases against members of the incumbent Government of Chad, the Chambers were told in no uncertain terms that doing so would lead to their demise.[17] In the
case of Cambodia, in response to an international prosecutor's statements concerning
his intention to proceed with cases 003 and 004, the Information Minister publicly
stated "[i]f they want to go into case 003 or 004, they should just pack their bags and
return home."[18] To date, the work of the ECCC has been delayed by the disagreement
of the domestic and international prosecutor whether cases 003 and 004 are significant enough that deserve to be tried. This, among other factors, has led commentators
to suggest that the ECCC is a model not to be followed in the future.[19]

Beyond explicit political influence, the greatest design flaw that affects the operation of hybrid courts is arguably their financial weakness. As *ad hoc* institutions,

---

[12] Damaška 2008, at 331–332.

[13] OHCHR 2008, at 4; De Hoon 2017, at 601–604.

[14] De Hoon 2017, at 601.

[15] Nouwen and Werner 2015.

[16] Hamilton and Ramsden 2014, at 117.

[17] Carlson 2018, at 243.

[18] Herman 2013, at 217.

[19] Jørgensen 2018, at 359.

hybrid courts usually suffer from in-built financial vulnerability; the financing of their creation and continuous operation depends more often than not on voluntary donations from international donors and does not form part of the regular budget of the UN, for example.[20] The main reason for state preference for voluntary contributions is usually the perceived disproportion between the growth of their budget and the progress of their proceedings. The argument was that the increased cost of the function of tribunals was not justified by the progress of the investigations.[21] This is such an important issue, that the UN made clear at least in two cases that it would not agree to internationalized prosecutions, until the Secretary General was satisfied that there is sufficient funding for the court's establishment and the first three years of its operation.[22] In a world of voluntary contributions, it becomes evident that fluctuation in financial commitment may implicitly yet effectively influence the operation of a hybrid court. For example, in the case of the Special Court for Sierra Leone, one of the last prosecutors publicly acknowledged that uncertainty over the financial viability of the institution precluded the possibility of opening one more case.[23] In the case of the ECCC, the Chambers themselves issued a decision acknowledging that absence of financial support could render a trial unfair and thus lead to its definite suspension.[24]

In closing, in addition to difficulties emerging from the lack of funding, the distribution of the funding within a hybrid court has also been a serious source of tension. Hybrid court recruitment history evidences significant discrepancies in the remuneration of domestic and international staff. For example, in the 2001 Special Panels of Timor-Leste, international staff was paid 32 times more than domestic staff per month, whereas in the Special Court for Sierra Leone living allowances for domestic judges were considerably lower than those for international judges.[25]

30.5 The Worldwide and Continuous Allure of Hybrid Courts and Their Relationship with the ICC

In spite of the criticisms levelled against hybrid courts, they have become a standard feature of the transitional justice toolbox. While their creation and operation have been met with a measure of skepticism, they remain to this day a viable option for the administration of post-conflict justice.

---

[20] Ciorciari and Hendel 2014 at. 7–8; Naughton 2018, at 93 mentions the Special Tribunal for Lebanon and the Timor-Leste Panels as two exceptions that received some scaled contributions.

[21] Tortora 2013, at 94.

[22] Linton 2001, at 215.

[23] Rapp 2014, at 25.

[24] Yim Tith Budgetary Situation Decision 2017, paras 22–23.

[25] Naughton 2018, at 77.

It is particularly striking that their appeal did not fade following the adoption of the Rome Statute of the International Criminal Court on 17 July 1998. The co-existence of hybrid courts and the ICC has not been a serious issue until recently, when the issue emerged in the quest for justice in the Central African Republic (CAR). The latter is a state party to the ICC Statute plagued by years of internal violence that led the ICC Prosecutor to open so far two separate investigations.[26] At the same time, the Government of CAR in co-operation with international donors has recently adopted a law, by virtue of which a Special Criminal Court is established with jurisdiction over serious international crimes committed on its territory.[27] The Court's Statute provides explicitly that the ICC has primacy in case of conflict.[28] However, this does not appear to have assuaged concerns in the literature about the legality of this provision and the division of labour between the ICC and the SCC.[29] These concerns in the literature may prove groundless, as the ICC Prosecutor has taken a co-operative approach, for example by training SCC prosecutors on the modalities of prosecuting international crimes. The debate surrounding the future of the relationship between the International Criminal Court—a court of 'last resort'—and hybrid tribunals is likely to continue in the future. This is particularly the case due to the broad geographical and inter-temporal appeal of hybrid courts over the last 20 years. From East Timor to Sierra Leone, from Cambodia to Kosovo and from Lebanon to Chad, hybrid courts are continuously created to address situations of impunity. Below, a few selected courts are discussed as examples.

30.5.1 Special Panels for Serious Crimes in Timor-Leste 1999–2005

The Special Panels for Serious Crimes (SPSC) in Timor-Leste were the first fixed hybrid panels within national courts mandated with the adjudication of cases involving serious violations of international law.[30] They have called the first 'experiment' in hybrid courts, insofar as they operated within the country and included domestic staff and judges.[31]

By virtue of Resolution 1272/1999, the UN Security Council established the UN Transitional Authority for East Timor (UNTAET). The Authority was responsible for the administration of East Timor and had all legislative and executive authority vested in it.[32] The Authority created the SPSC within the District Court of Dili by means of Regulation 15/2000. They were mandated to administer justice for serious

---

[26] Tredici and Galand 2018, at 4–6.

[27] Loi Organique No 15-003.

[28] Ibid., Article 37.

[29] In favour Tredici and Galand 2018, at 17–18, against Labuda 2018, p. 193.

[30] Donlon 2013, at 86.

[31] Cohen 2009, at 126.

[32] UN SC Res 1272/1999.

30 Other "Hybrid" Tribunals

crimes allegedly committed during the East Timor struggle for independence in 1999.[33] They had jurisdiction to try cases of genocide, war crimes, crimes against humanity, murder, sexual offences and torture,[34] committed between 1 January and 25 October 1999.[35] The applicable law was a mix of Indonesian criminal law and applicable international treaty and customary law.[36] The chambers were placed within the District Court of Dili and the Court of Appeals. The Panels in the District Court and the Court of Appeals would be composed of 2 international judges and 1 national judge.[37] Exceptionally, the Court of Appeals could be composed of 3 international judges and 2 national judges in cases of exceptional importance.[38]

The prosecution of cases before the Special Chambers was entrusted to the hybrid Serious Crimes Unit established by means of UNTAET Regulation 16/2000, it was situated in Dili and formed part of the East Timor Public Prosecution Service. The Serious Crimes Unit had exclusive authority to investigate and prosecute crimes committed in East Timor in 1999 and all cases presented before the Panels were presented by the Unit.[39]

The UN Security Council extended the Panel's mandate for a final period of six months until 20 May 2005.[40] This meant the conclusion of the Panels' work. As of May 2004, the UN Secretary General reported that 82 indictments had been filed against 369 suspects and from the 52 judgments delivered, 50 involved some sort of conviction and 2 led to acquittals.[41]

The Special Panels were the first fixed hybrid court to open and close down. As such, academic autopsies of their work emerged rather quickly.

The criticism is rather overwhelming. The first point is that numerous indictees who fled to Indonesia escaped trial. As the Chief Justice of the Special Panels wrote, "the statistics tell the tale: Of the 440 defendants who were indicted in East Timor, over 300 remain outside the country, presumably in Indonesia. Of the 87 defendants who stood trial before the Special Panels, all were Timorese nationals."[42] This situation caused dissatisfaction that was duly reflected in the report of the committee of experts set up by the Secretary General to evaluate the prosecutions before the Panels.[43]

---

[33] Cohen 2009, 105–106.

[34] Section 1.3 of Regulation 15.

[35] Section 2.3 of Regulation 15.

[36] Sections 3.1. and 3.2 of Regulation 15.

[37] Section 22.1 and 22.2 of Regulation 15.

[38] Section 22.2 of Regulation 15.

[39] Donlon 2013, at 87.

[40] UNSC 1573/2004.

[41] Report of the Secretary-General 2004, at 17.

[42] Rapoza 2006, at 525–526.

[43] Commission of Experts 2005, para 126.

Finally, judges of the Panels themselves went on the record to deplore practices that excluded either the parties' opportunity to make submissions on issues, or non-Portuguese speaking judges from aspects of the judicial process.[44] These accounts shed a rather negative light on the legacy of the Special Panels.

30.5.2 The Special Court for Sierra Leone 2002–2013

The Special Court for Sierra Leone (SCSL) was established by means of an agreement between the UN and the Government of Sierra Leone,[45] which was subsequently incorporated into Sierra Leone's domestic law. It has been called a "radically innovative institution and an unprecedented experiment", as it was the first tribunal established by means of a bilateral agreement between the UN and the interested state, as well as the first to envisage substantial involvement of domestic judges, prosecutors and personnel in its operation.[46] The UN Secretary General classified the SCSL as a 'treaty-based sui generis court of mixed jurisdiction and composition'.[47] The SCSL was established, in order to prosecute persons who bore the greatest responsibility for serious violations of international humanitarian law and Sierra Leonean law committed in the territory of Sierra Leone since 30 November 1996.[48] Its subject-matter jurisdiction covered not only war crimes and crimes against humanity under international law, but also domestic law concerning cruelty to children and malicious damage.[49] The Court had its own Trial and Appeals Chambers, as well as its own Registry and Office of the Prosecutor. The trial chamber had three judges (2 international, one national) and the Appeals Chamber five judges (3 international, two national), whereas the Prosecutor was appointed by the Secretary General and the Deputy Prosecutor by the Sierra Leone Government.[50] The SCSL tried 4 main cases—three cases involving the most responsible persons of each warring group (CDR, RUF, AFRC) and the Charles Taylor case.

The legal nature of the Chambers as a hybrid or international court came to the forefront in the Charles Taylor litigation. Taylor was the former President of Liberia. After a legal-political debacle that lasted many years, he was eventually arrested and brought to Freetown to face justice for his multi-faceted role in the civil war in neighboring Sierra Leone. Taylor sought to invoke his immunity as the head of state of Liberia at the time of commission. The SCSL rejected this plea. It held that the

---

[44] Cohen 2009, 126–217.

[45] SCSL Agreement 2002.

[46] Tortora 2013, at 96–97.

[47] Report of the Secretary-General 2000, para 39.

[48] Article 1 of the SCSL Agreement 2002.

[49] Ibid., Articles 2–5 of the Agreement.

[50] Ibid., Articles 12–15 of the Agreement.

SCSL was an international court and therefore his prosecution could not be barred due to his immunity.[51]

The SCSL concluded its operation in 2013. It is succeeded by the Residual SCSL, which is responsible for handling a number of residual functions, such as the review of judgments, the protection and support of witnesses, the preservation and management of the archive and the supervision of the enforcement of sentences.[52] The creation of the Residual Special Court—a new and independent institution with a specific mandate and organs—makes clear that, while hybrid courts may be temporary in nature, the obligations stemming from their mandate have longer term implications.[53]

In many important ways, the SCSL is arguably the most successful hybrid tribunal to date. It proved efficient and effective; the indictments were filed less than a year after the Prosecutor arrived in Freetown and trials started within two years of the Court's establishment. In the ten years of its operation, the SCSL completed its work on a "shoe-string budget" totaling 250 million USD, while at the same it developed an outreach program that became a model for other international criminal tribunals.[54] The outreach program was considered successful because it raised awareness among the local population about the existence and function of the Special Court, using innovative techniques tailored to the circumstances prevailing on the ground.[55]

Additionally, the SCSL left an important legacy in the realm of substantive criminal law. Among its many contributions, it is credited for certain landmark judicial pronouncements. For example, it made a significant determination that amnesties are not applicable for international crimes.[56] Its jurisprudence also paid particular attention to sexual offences and gender-based violence.[57]

30.5.3 The Special Tribunal for Lebanon

The Special Tribunal for Lebanon was established by Security Council Resolution 1757/2007 adopted under Chapter VII of the UN Charter. However, the Statute of the Tribunal annexed to that resolution was not the result of unilateral UN action. The statute of the tribunal was negotiated extensively between the UN Secretary General and the Lebanese government and culminated to an agreement.[58] However, due to internal political difficulties, the Lebanese parliament did not ratify the agreement. As a result, the Prime Minister wrote a letter to the Security Council, explaining that

---

[51] SCSL Appeals Chamber 2004, para 6.

[52] RSCSL Agreement 2010, Article 1.

[53] Donlon 2013, at 873.

[54] Tortora 2013, at 101–102.

[55] Clark 2009, at 109–110, Ford 2014, at 512–513.

[56] Lomé Amnesty Decision 2004.

[57] Oosterveld 2014, at 234–235.

[58] Wetzel and Mitri 2008, at 85–86.

the "domestic route had reached a dead end" and asking for the help of the Security Council in the establishment of the Tribunal.[59]

Under Article 1 of the Tribunal's Statute, its mission is to administer justice for the attack of 14 February 2005, which resulted to the death of former Lebanese Prime Minister Refik Hariri and the death or injury of others. To achieve this objective, the Tribunal is vested with jurisdiction over persons responsible for preparatory acts or other connected acts, provided they took place between 1 October 2004 and 12 December 2005. The tribunals seats in The Hague in The Netherlands and its budget is covered by the Lebanese Government (51%) and voluntary contributions (49%).[60]

The background of the Tribunal's creation makes clear that this Tribunal was tasked with the prosecution of a terrorist bombing that resulted in the death of an incumbent Prime Minister. However, terrorism does not form part of the subject-matter jurisdiction of the International Criminal Court, unless it manifests as a crime against humanity, war crime or genocide. Therefore, the Special Tribunal for Lebanon was specifically mandated with the prosecution of individuals involved in the attack and the prosecution of the crime of terrorism.[61] Specifically, the Tribunal's subject-matter jurisdiction extends to the following crimes codified in the Criminal Code of Lebanon; acts of terrorism, crimes and offences against life and personal integrity, illicit associations and failure to report crimes and offences, as well as specific provisions of the 1958 Lebanese law on increasing penalties for sedition, civil war and interfaith struggle.[62] The Tribunal enjoys primacy over domestic courts in the prosecution of its cases; this means that in the event that the same case is pending between the Tribunal and national courts, the Tribunal takes priority.[63]

The Special Tribunal of Lebanon has made headlines internationally due to its important contribution to certain significant issues in substantive and procedural international criminal law. As regards substantive law, the Lebanon Tribunal is the first international tribunal with jurisdiction over the crime of terrorism without requiring its connection to an armed conflict. In procedural law, the Statute of the Lebanon tribunal allows for trials in absentia for the first time since the Nuremberg trials; it provides for a separate procedural role for victims; it featured an independent defence office, on an equal footing with the other branches of the Tribunal; and finally, it vests in a single Pre-Trial judge an active role in the confirmation of the indictment and the preparation of the cases for an efficient trial.[64]

Notwithstanding the significance of its procedural practice, the STL's jurisprudence on the crime of terrorism takes pride of place in any contemporary debate on point. The words 'STL' and 'definition of terrorism' became inextricably intertwined in the minds of international lawyers following the 2011 landmark ruling of the Appeals Chamber on the definition of terrorism. Specifically, on 16 February 2011,

---

[59] UN Secretary General 2007, at 2.

[60] Report of the Secretary General 2006, para 25.

[61] Nsereko 2017, at 440.

[62] Article 2 STL Statute.

[63] Ibid., Article 4 STL Statute.

[64] Nsereko 2017, at 444–445.

30 Other "Hybrid" Tribunals

the Appeals Chamber issued its Interlocutory Decision on the Applicable Law.[65] The Appeals Chamber decided that under customary international law, there is a crime of terrorism committed in times of peace, which the Tribunal should consider in its interpretation of the crime of terrorism under Lebanese criminal law. The Appeals Chamber ruled as follows:

> a number of treaties, UN resolutions, and the legislative and judicial practice of States evince the formation of a general *opinio juris* in the international community, accompanied by a practice consistent with such *opinio*, to the effect that a customary rule of international law regarding the international crime of terrorism, at least in lime of peace, has indeed emerged. This customary rule requires the following three key elements: (i) the perpetration of a criminal act (such as murder, kidnapping, hostage-taking, arson, and so on), or threatening such an act; (ii) the intent to spread fear among the population (which would generally entail the creation of public danger) or directly or indirectly coerce a national or international authority to take some action, or to refrain from taking it; (iii) when the act involves a transnational element[66]

This decision caused considerable debate as regards the existence of terrorism in customary law, as well as the transnational element.[67] The Special Tribunal for Lebanon was criticized on the grounds that it created *ex post facto* a crime in customary law by overlooking the substantial differences between international instruments defining international terrorism following a '*laissez-faire* attitude both to criminal liability and custom formation'.[68] The judgment was further criticised as a form of judicial law-making, insofar as the Appeals Chamber deduced the definition from a teleological interpretation of the Statute, even though there was no legislative lacuna that needed to be filled through such form of interpretation.[69] At the same time, others seek to defend the decision by explaining that the STL did not simply "extrapolate national criminal terrorism definitions and transform them into an international crime" but rather reaching this decision after a carefully reasoned analysis of state practice and opinio juris.[70] For all its faults, the STL's decision created a starting point for contemporary discussion on the definition of terrorism in international criminal law.[71] In the absence of a generally-accepted definition endorsed by the UN General Assembly, the STL decision provides an urgently needed "practical interim measure" for the criminal prosecution of terrorism as an international crime.[72]

---

[65] STL Decision on Definition of Terrorism.

[66] Ibid., para 85.

[67] Ventura 2011, at 1027–1029.

[68] Saul 2011, at 678–679.

[69] Ambos 2011, at 658.

[70] Ventura 2011, at 1028–1029.

[71] Margariti 2017, at 159.

[72] Baragwanath 2018, at 33.

30.5.4 The Extraordinary African Chambers of the Courts of Senegal

A National Committee of Inquiry established in the Republic of Chad in the early 1990s made certain extraordinary findings; it concluded that the regime of the previous ruler Hissène Habré was responsible for a campaign of repression against its political opposition, which resulted to the estimated death of over 40,000 people.[73] For the next 20 years, regional stakeholders and the international community engaged in a legal-political tug-of-war over Habré's fate, which involved many African states and at least two international judicial instances, the International Court of Justice and the ECOWAS Court of Justice.[74] Eventually, in 2012 the African Union and the Government of Senegal signed an agreement to create a tribunal for the prosecution of serious international crimes committed in Chad in the 1980s.[75] Following negotiations, the Statute of the Extraordinary African Chambers within the Courts of Senegal was adopted in January 2013 and the Chambers started functioning in February 2013.[76]

According to article 3 of the Statute, "[t]he Extraordinary African Chambers shall have the power to prosecute and try the person or persons most responsible for crimes and serious violations of international law, customary international law and international conventions ratified by Chad, committed in the territory of Chad during the period from 7 June 1982 to 1 December 1990."[77]

In spite of the more open-ended formulation in the Statute, it became clear that the EAC were established exclusively in order to try Hissène Habré, the former ruler of Chad. They were thus described "as a political compromise to address a particular situation of impunity, such as in this case the need to secure accountability for one individual (Habré)."[78] Efforts to prosecute other individuals proved futile due to political resistance.[79]

The Chambers' had jurisdiction to try cases of genocide, war crimes, crimes against humanity and torture.[80] For cases not provided in the Statute, the Chambers were empowered to use Senegalese law.[81] The Chambers were established in Dakar, Senegal and comprised of separate Indictment Chamber, Trial Chamber and Appeals Chamber. The Presidents of the Trial Chamber and the Appeals Chambers were non-Senegalese judges appointed by another African Union member state. The

---

[73] National Commission of Inquiry 1991, at 91; Fall 2014, at 117–118.

[74] Adjovi 2011–2012, at 375; Naldi and Magliveras 2013, at 84–89; Spiga 2011, at 7–11.

[75] AU-Senegal Agreement, Statute of the Extraordinary African Chambers within the Courts of Senegal 2012.

[76] EAC Statute 2013.

[77] Ibid., Article 3 of the EAC Statute.

[78] Williams 2013, at 1147.

[79] Carlson 2018, at 342–343, Brody 2015, at 214.

[80] Article 4 EAC Statute.

[81] Article 16(2) of the Statute.

30 Other "Hybrid" Tribunals

prosecution was undertaken by a team of 4 Senegalese prosecutors. Victims had procedural standing and were allowed to participate in the process.[82]

The Chambers concluded the Habré trial within 8 months; the judgment was handed down on 30 May 2016; it found the accused guilty of crimes against humanity, war crimes and torture and sentenced him to life imprisonment.[83] The Trial Chamber found the accused guilty of organizing a system of repression against his political opponents and participating through that group to the commission of murders, summary executions, torture, enforced disappearances and inhumane acts against his political opponents.[84] The Trial Chamber issued an order of reparations. It awarded considerable financial reparations to the 7396 victims that appeared in the process, but in the absence of sufficient financial resources of the accused and lack of support by the Government of Chad in its implementation, the award of reparations remained largely symbolic.[85] On 27 April 2017 the Appeals Chamber upheld the conviction for most of the charges, as well as the sentence. Following Habré's conviction the Chambers concluded their operation.

The legacy of the Extraordinary African Chambers has been mixed. Some authors have applauded their efficient function; they managed to conclude a very complicated trial within 8 months, whereas the appellate process lasted less than a year. Compared to the first trial held before the International Criminal Court, the Extraordinary African Chambers proved very efficient.[86] At the same time, however, critics have taken issue with the extremely limited focus of prosecution and the political obstacles that prevented the prosecution of other cases[87] as well as the non-implementation of the reparations order.[88] Regardless, the Habré case is one of the clearest cases where a hybrid court was established by a regional organization in co-operation with a prosecuting state's authorities. Together with the EU-supported Kosovo Chambers, they are arguably some of the best examples of a relatively new trend in the administration of hybrid justice; the 'regionalisation' of international criminal justice. While regionally-supported (as opposed to UN-supported) hybrid courts are not without their own complications, keeping things local may hold significant benefits for strengthening the perception of legitimacy of the administration of justice in the eyes of the affected communities.[89]

---

[82] Article 14 of the Statute.

[83] Habré Trial Judgment.

[84] Dubler and Kalyk 2018, at 294–295.

[85] Stahn 2018, at 405.

[86] Dubler and Kalyk 2018, at 295.

[87] Carlson 2018, at 343.

[88] Stahn 2018, at 405.

[89] Mninde-Silungwe 2017, at 32–33.

30.6 Conclusion

This chapter provided a short introduction to the existence and operation of hybrid tribunals in the realm of international criminal justice. Following a few opening words concerning the difficulties surrounding the definition of hybrid tribunals, it discussed some among the most well-versed arguments in favour and against their creation. Ultimately, the chapter has explained that notwithstanding a measure of fluctuation in their popularity during the mid-2000s, the administration of hybrid justice seems to have become entrenched as a standard feature of the post-conflict peace-building toolbox. This trend may well continue, if the regionalisation of hybrid justice comes together with much-needed financial stability.

Regardless of the international or regional support for their establishment, however, hybrid courts continue to exist, as versatile and adaptable as ever. This appears to be their defining endearing quality; the provision of tailor-made justice. At the same time, however, it is precisely this pliability that renders them vulnerable to manipulation by the political forces prevailing at the time of their creation; as such, it may also continue to provide fertile ground for criticism.

References

Books, (Online) Articles and Chapters in Books

Adjovi R (2011–2012) Une Saga Judiciaire Autour d'un (Ex-) Chef d'Etat Africain, Hissene Habré. African Yearbook of International Law 19:375

Ambos K (2011) Judicial Creativity at the Special Tribunal for Lebanon: Is There a Crime of Terrorism under International Law? Leiden J Int'l L 24: 655–675

AU-Senegal Agreement (2012) Agreement between the Government of the Republic of Senegal and the African Union on the Establishment of the Extraordinary African Chambers within the Courts of Senegal, 22 August 2012. African Yearbook of International Law (2011–2012) 19:437

Baragwanath D (2018) Responding to Terrorism: Definition and other Actions. Nigerian Yearbook of International Law 2017, 17–49

Brody R (2015) Bringing a dictator to justice; the case of Hissène Habré. Journal of International Criminal Justice 13:209

Carlson K (2018) Trying Hissène Habré 'On Behalf of Africa': Remaking Hybrid International Criminal Justice at the Chambres Extraordinaires Africaines. In: Nicholson J, Bailliet CM (eds) Strengthening the Validity of International Criminal Tribunals. Brill, The Hague

Cassese A (2010) Reflections on the Current Prospects for International Criminal Justice. In: Arsanjani MH, Cogan J, Sloane R, Wiessner S (eds) Looking to the Future: Essays on International Law in Honor of W. Michael Reisman. Brill, The Hague

Ciorciari J D, Heindel A (2014) Hybrid Justice: The Extraordinary Chambers of the Courts of Cambodia. The University of Michigan Press, Ann Arbor

Clark J N (2009) International War Crimes Tribunals and the Challenge of Outreach. International Criminal Law Review 9:99

Cohen D (2009) Accountability in the balance: trials before the Special Panels for Serious Crimes in East Timor 1999–2005. Law in Context 27:103

Damaška M (2008) What Is the Point of International Criminal Justice? Chicago Kent Law Review 83:329–368

De Hoon M (2017) The Future of the International Criminal Court: On Critique, Legalism and Strengthening the ICC's Legitimacy. International Criminal Law Review 17:591

Dickinson L (2003) The Promise of Hybrid Courts. American Journal of International Law, 97:295–310

Donlon F (2013) The Transition of Responsibilities from the Special Court to the Residual Special Court for Sierra Leone: Challenges and Lessons Learned for Other International Tribunals. Journal of International Criminal Justice 11:857

Dubler R, Kalyk M (2018) Crimes Against Humanity in the 21st Century – Law, Practice and Threats to International Peace and Security. Brill, Boston

EAC Statute (2013) Statute of the Extraordinary African Chambers within the Courts of Senegal created to prosecute international crimes committed in Chad between 7 June 1982 and 1 December 1990, 2 September 2013. African Yearbook of International Law (2011–2012) 19:443

Fall M (2014) The Extraordinary African Chambers: The Case of Hissène Habré. In: Werle G, Fernandez L, Vormbaum M (eds) Africa and the International Criminal Court. T.M.C. Asser Press, The Hague, pp. 117–131

Fichtelberg A (2015) Hybrid Tribunals – A Comparative Examination. Springer

Fletcher L E, Weinstein H M (2002) Violence and Social Repair: Rethinking the Contribution of Justice to Reconciliation. Human Rights Quarterly 24:573–639

Ford S (2014) How Special is the Special Court's Outreach Section? In: Jalloh C C (ed) The Sierra Leone Special Court and its Legacy. Cambridge University Press, Cambridge

Hamilton T, Ramsden M (2014) The Politicisation of Hybrid Courts: Observations from the Extraordinary Chambers in the Courts of Cambodia. International Criminal Law Review 14:115

Herman J (2013) A Necessary Compromise or Compromised Justice? The Extraordinary Chambers of the Courts of Cambodia. In: Carey HF, Mitchell SM (eds) Trials and Tribulations of International Prosecution. Lexington Books, Lanham

Hobbs H (2016) Hybrid Tribunals and the Composition of the Court: In Search of Sociological Legitimacy. Chicago Journal of International Law 16: 482

Jørgensen N B (2018) The Elgar Companion to the Extraordinary Chambers of the Courts of Cambodia. Edward Elgar Publishers, Cheltenham

Koh H H (2013) International Criminal Justice 5.0. Yale Law Journal 38:525

Labuda P (2018) The Special Criminal Court in the Central African Republic: Failure or Vindication of Complementarity? 15:175–206

Linton S (2001) Cambodia, East Timor and Sierra Leone: Experiments in International Justice. Criminal Law Forum 12:185

Margariti S (2017) Defining International Terrorism: Between State Sovereignty and Cosmopolitanism. T.M.C. Asser Press, The Hague

Mninde-Silungwe F (2017) The Regionalisation of International Criminal Justice in Africa. Ph.D. Thesis, University of Western Cape, South Africa

Naldi G, Magliveras K (2013) The Ever Difficult Symbiosis of Africa with the International Criminal Court. Revue héllenique de Droit International 66:59

Naughton E (2018) Committing to Justice for Serious Human Rights Violations – Lessons from Hybrid Tribunals. International Center for Transitional Justice, available at <https://www.ictj.org/sites/default/files/ICTJ_Report_Hybrid_Tribunals.pdf>

Nouwen S, Werner W (2015) Monopolizing Global Justice; International Criminal Law as Challenge to Human Diversity. Journal of International Criminal Justice 13:157–176

Nouwen S M H (2006) 'Hybrid Courts' - The hybrid category of a new type of international crimes courts. Utrecht Law Review 2:190–214

Nsereko DDN (2017) The Special Tribunal for Lebanon and the Global Response to Terrorism. In: Acconci P, Donat Cattin D, Marchesi A, Palmisano G, Santori V (eds) International law and the protection of humanity: Essays in honor of Flavia Lattanzi. Brill, Leiden/The Hague, pp. 438–452

Office of the UN High Commissioner for Human Rights (OHCHR) (2008) Rule of Law tools for post-conflict states: Maximising the legacy of hybrid courts. UN, New York/Geneva

Oosterveld V (2014) Evaluating the Special Court for Sierra Leone's Gender Jurisprudence. In: Jalloh C C (ed) The Sierra Leone Special Court and its Legacy. Cambridge University Press, Cambridge

Rapoza Ph (2006) Hybrid Criminal Tribunals and the Concept of Ownership: Who Owns the Process, American University International Law Review 21:525

Rapp S J (2014) The Challenge of Choice in the Investigation and Prosecution of International Crimes in Post-Conflict Sierra Leone. In: Jalloh C C (ed) The Sierra Leone Special Court and Its Legacy: The Impact for Africa and International Criminal Law. Cambridge University Press, Cambridge

Report of the Secretary General on the Establishment of a Special Court for Sierra Leone (2000) UN Doc. S/2000/915

Report of the Secretary-General (2004) Report of the Secretary-General on the United Nations Mission of Support in East Timor (S/2004/333)

Report of the Secretary General (2006) Report of the Secretary-General on the establishment of a special tribunal for Lebanon to the Security Council of 15 November 2006 (UN Doc. S/2006/893)

Saul B (2011) Legislating from a Radical Hague: The United Nations Special Tribunal for Lebanon Invents an International Crime of Transnational Terrorism. Leiden Journal of International Law 24: 677–700

Spiga V (2011) Non-retroactivity of Criminal Law: A New Chapter in the Hissène Habré Saga. Journal of International Criminal Justice (2011), 9:5

Stahn C (2018) A Critical Introduction to International Criminal Law. Cambridge University Press, Cambridge

Tortora G (2013) The Financing of the Special Tribunals for Sierra Leone, Cambodia and Lebanon. International Criminal Law Review 13:93

Tredici I, Galand R (2018) Holding to Account the Commission of International Crimes in the Central African Republic: The Establishment of the Special Criminal Court. Max Planck Yearbook of United Nations Law, 21:3–35

UN Secretary General (2007) Letter dated 15 May 2007 from the Secretary General to the President of the Security Council, 16 May 2007, S/2007/281

Ventura M J (2011) Terrorism According to the STL's Interlocutory Decision on the Applicable Law: A Defining Moment or a Moment of Defining. Journal of International Criminal Justice 9:1021–1042

Wetzel J E, Mitri Y (2008) The Special Tribunal for Lebanon: A Court "off the shelf" for a Divided Country. The Law and Practice of International Courts and Tribunals 7:81

Williams S (2009) Internationalised Tribunals: A Search for their Legal Bases. In: Kaikobad KH, Bohlander M (eds) International Law and Power: Perspectives on Legal Order and Justice, Essays in honour of Colin Warbrick. Martinus Nijhoff, Leiden

Williams S (2012) Hybrid and Internationalised Criminal Tribunals – Selected Jurisdictional Issues. Hart Publishing, Oxford

Williams S (2013) The Extraordinary African Chambers in the Senegalese Courts: An African Solution to an African Problem? Journal of International Criminal Justice 11:1139

Agreements, Decisions and Other Documents

Bensouda F (2018) Statement by the Prosecutor of the International Criminal Court, Fatou Bensouda, at the conclusion of her visit to the Central African Republic on Friday, 23 March: collaboration is key to closing the impunity gap, 27 March 2018, available at https://www.icc-cpi.int/Pages/item.aspx?name=180327-otp-stat-car, last accessed 10 January 2019

Commission of Experts (2005) Report to the Secretary-General of the Commission of Experts to Review the Prosecution of Serious Violations of Human Rights in Timor-Leste (the then East Timor) in 1999, Annex II UN Doc S/2005/458 (26 May 2005)

Lomé Amnesty Decision (2004) Prosecutor v Kallon and Kamara, Decision on Challenge to Jurisdiction: Lomé Accord Amnesty, SCSL Appeals Chamber, Case no. SCSL-2004-15-AR72(E)) and Case no. SCSL-2004-16-AR72(E), 13 March 2004

National Commission of Inquiry (1991) Report of the National Commission of Inquiry of Chad. Republic of Chad

Peace Agreement (1999) Peace Agreement Between the Government of Sierra Leone and the Revolutionary United Front of Sierra Leone, Lome (Togo, 18 May 1999), U.N. Doc. S/1999/777

RSCSL Agreement (2010) Agreement between the United Nations and the Government of Sierra Leone on the Establishment of a Special Court for Sierra Leone, UN Doc. S/2002/246, 16 January 2002, Appendix II

SCSL Agreement (2002) Agreement between the United Nations and the Government of Sierra Leone on the Establishment of a Special Court for Sierra Leone, 16 January 2002, available at http://www.rscsl.org/Documents/scsl-agreement.pdf, last accessed 4 January 2019

SCSL Appeals Chamber (2004) Prosecutor v Charles Ghankay Taylor (SCSL 2003-1-I), Decision on Immunity from Prosecution

STL Decision on Definition of Terrorism (2011) Special Tribunal for Lebanon, Appeals Chamber, Interlocutory Decision on the Applicable Law: Terrorism, Conspiracy, Homicide, Perpetration, Cumulative Charging, STL-11-01/I

Yim Tith Budgetary Situation Decision (2017) Co-Investigating Judges, Combined Decision on the Impact of the Budgetary Situation on Cases 003, 004 and 004/2 and related submissions by the defence for Yim Tith, 11 August 2017

Michail Vagias holds a Ph.D. in International Law (Leiden), an LL.M. (Adv.) (hons.) (Leiden) and an LL.B. in Law (Greece, Democritus University). He is currently a Senior Lecturer in Law and Program Manager for the Judicial Training Program of the Constitutional Court of Indonesia at the Hague University of Applied Sciences. His research interests revolve around jurisdiction and admissibility in international proceedings, migration, as well as questions of amnesties and transitional justice. In addition to his academic function, Michail has acted as legal counsel before the International Court of Justice (*Djibouti v. France*), the European Court of Human Rights, as well as an expert on mission for international organisations on migration.

Chapter 31
Post-conflict Justice Mechanisms

Alison Bisset

Contents

31.1 Introduction 652
31.2 Seeking Justice in Transition 653
31.3 The Legal Framework of Transitional Justice 654
    31.3.1 The Right to Justice 655
    31.3.2 The Right to Truth 658
    31.3.3 The Right to Reparation 659
    31.3.4 Guarantees of Non-recurrence 660
31.4 The Practice of Transitional Justice 661
    31.4.1 Trials 661
    31.4.2 Truth Commissions 663
    31.4.3 Reparations 666
    31.4.4 Reform 667
31.5 Conclusion 668
References 669

Abstract In the aftermath of conflict, four key approaches have emerged for responding to past violence and violations of human rights. Together, trials, truth seeking, reparation and reform—the so-called four pillars of transitional justice— are considered to provide post-conflict states with the best possibilities for healing, repair and sustainable peace. In practice, post-conflict landscapes are notoriously complex to operate within and delivering truth, justice, reparation and reform is challenging. This chapter examines the legal foundations and operation of these key mechanisms of post-conflict justice and considers their merits, shortcomings and possibilities going forward.

Keywords Post-conflict justice · transition · trials · truth commissions · reparation · reform

---

A. Bisset (✉)
Faculty of Law, University of Reading, Reading, UK
e-mail: a.j.bisset@reading.ac.uk

© T.M.C. ASSER PRESS and the authors 2022
S. Sayapin et al. (eds.), *International Conflict and Security Law*,
https://doi.org/10.1007/978-94-6265-515-7_31

652   A. Bisset

31.1 Introduction

The consequences of armed conflict are devastating for the states involved. From the massive human rights violations committed against civilian populations to the destruction of state infrastructure and institutions, post-conflict states face a myriad of challenges in restoring order, maintaining peace, reconstructing state and social institutions and establishing sustainable governance mechanisms. While the temptation may be only to look forwards, it is widely believed that without addressing the violence of the past, states will be unable to create a durable peace and will relapse into conflict. Indeed, between 2000 and 2011, 90% of states that had experienced national conflict, relapsed at least once.[1]

How best to address past abuses and injustice is the subject of the relatively recent field of transitional justice.[2] Transitional justice is concerned with the strategies employed to deal with past human rights abuses in countries moving from conflict or repressive regime to democratic rule in order to ensure accountability, serve justice and achieve reconciliation".[3] Advocates of transitional justice argue that dealing with the past is essential to long-term peacebuilding. Failure to pursue accountability, it is claimed, undermines the rule of law,[4] the rights and needs of victims,[5] and perpetuates cycles of violence.[6] The transitional justice framework traditionally utilises prosecutions, truth commissions, reparations and reforms, among other measures,[7] to meet the diverse needs of transitional states, contribute to a sustainable peace, and bring about healing, repair and reconciliation.[8]

The purpose of this chapter is to consider the principal mechanisms established to date to address past human rights violations. The chapter will begin by explaining the international legal framework that underpins post-conflict, transitional justice. It will then examine the pursuit of criminal justice at both national and international levels, the establishment of national truth seeking initiatives, the role of reparations and domestic efforts to deliver reform, and will highlight the challenges faced in recent practice.

---

[1] International Center for Transitional Justice, 'About Us', https://www.ictj.org/about Accessed 8 November 2018.

[2] Teitel 2000.

[3] The Rule of Law and Transitional Justice in Conflict and Post Conflict Societies (2004) UN Doc. S/2004/616, para 8.

[4] Huyse 2001, p. 325.

[5] Hayner 2001, p. 28.

[6] The Rule of Law and Transitional Justice in Conflict and Post Conflict Societies (2004) UN Doc. S/2004/616, para 2.

[7] Ibid., para 8.

[8] Villa-Vicencio and Doxtader 2004, p. 72.

31.2 Seeking Justice in Transition

Transitional justice is a multidisciplinary field of study and practice, which "comprises the full range of processes and mechanisms associated with a society's attempts to come to terms with a legacy of large-scale past abuses, in order to ensure accountability, serve justice and achieve reconciliation".[9] The term "transitional justice" is in many ways misleading. It refers to "justice during transition" rather than to any particular theory or form of modified or altered justice.[10] "Justice" must be understood broadly and, in this context, has been described as,

> an ideal of accountability and fairness in the protection and vindication of rights and the prevention and punishment of wrongs. Justice implies regard for the rights of the accused, for the interests of victims and for the well-being of society at large. It is a concept rooted in all national cultures and traditions, and while its administration usually implies formal judicial mechanisms, traditional dispute resolution mechanisms are equally relevant.[11]

Prosecution can form an important element of transitional justice, but "justice" as conceived here, extends beyond retributive criminal justice, delivered through trials,[12] and encompasses a theory of restorative justice.[13] The focus in transitional justice is on repairing past harm and the aim is to involve and bring about reconciliation among those most affected by that harm.[14] The transitional justice framework therefore utilises prosecutions, truth commissions, reparations, reform and many other measures to fulfil its objectives.

The logic of addressing the past in order to maximize possibilities for a secure future is apparent. Yet, in reality, it can be extremely challenging due to the fragile peace and contested politics of post conflict states. There is frequently tension between the demands of victims groups for criminal prosecutions and the resistance of political elites to see current and/or former military, security and political leaders stand trial. International legal frameworks may stipulate the need for criminal investigations, while national amnesty laws absolving penal responsibility are passed at the domestic level. Arguments that the pursuit of criminal justice threatens peace are typical. Truth seeking may be seen as a 'softer' option and indeed will be if truth commissions are not endowed with robust mandates and powers to access information and evidence. Victims may seek reparations while states debate the availability of the resources needed to provide them. Likewise, the need to reform the corrupt laws and institutions that enabled the perpetration of human rights violations and descent

---

[9] Ibid. See also Bickford 2004, p. 1045.

[10] Ibid.

[11] The Rule of Law and Transitional Justice in Conflict and Post Conflict Societies (2004) UN Doc. S/2004/616, at para 7.

[12] Under retributive theory, the aim of prosecution is to apportion blame and ensure that the wrongdoer is punished in proportion to the harm they have inflicted upon the victim. See Hart 1968, p. 8–9; Kant 1972, p. 104.

[13] Villa-Vicencio and Doxtader 2004, p. 68; Ambos 2009, p. 23.

[14] Van Ness 1996, p. 23.

654   A. Bisset

into violence is often overlooked as economic growth and infrastructure development is pursued and prioritized. It is within this complex and contested landscape that transitional justice mechanisms are established and against this backdrop that they work to meet the rights and needs of victims and pave the way for stability.[15]

31.3 The Legal Framework of Transitional Justice

Whatever the politics, in post-conflict contexts that have involved serious violations of human rights, international human rights law, in conjunction with international humanitarian law and international criminal law, stipulates that victims have rights to justice, truth, reparation and non-recurrence, and places corresponding obligations upon states. These rights and obligations relate to the principal mechanisms—the four pillars—of transitional justice. Trials enable states to fulfil their obligation to investigate and punish the perpetrators of human rights violations and provide victims with their right to justice and an effective remedy. Fact-finding investigations are a means by which states implement their duty to investigate and identify perpetrators and thereby provide victims, their families and the wider society with the right to know or the right to truth. Through reparations states fulfil their obligation to provide restitution and compensation to victims and provide them with their right to reparation. Finally, justice reforms allow a state to implement its duty to take effective measures to prevent future violations and thereby guarantee the right of non-repetition.[16]

While these rights and obligations are separate and distinct,[17] the interconnectedness and overlapping contributions made by the different mechanisms should not be overlooked. For example, in investigating and adjudicating upon specific cases, trials will uncover and record much of the "truth" surrounding the commission of past abuses. Truth commissions may contribute to justice through their acknowledgement of the suffering of victims, assignation of institutional responsibility and formulation of recommendations for reform and the payment of reparations.[18] Equally, the recommendations for legal and institutional reforms frequently made by truth commissions may provide the foundation for the judicial reforms necessary for states to fulfil their obligations to take effective measures to prevent future violations. A programme of reforms cannot be compiled until the deficiencies of the old system are understood.

---

[15] Roht-Arriaza and Marriez-Currena 2006.

[16] See Joinet L (1997) Set of Principles for the Protection and Promotion of Human Rights Through Action to Combat Impunity, UN Doc. E/CN.4/Sub.2/1997/20/Rev.1 (Joinet Principles), updated by Orentlicher D (2005) Updated Set of Principles for the Protection and Promotion of Human Rights Through Action to Combat Impunity, UN Doc. E/CN.4/2005/102.Add.1 (Updated Principles); and Basic Principles and Guidelines on the Right to a Remedy and Reparation for Victims of Gross Violations of International Human Rights and Serious Violations of International Humanitarian Law (2005) GA Res. 60/147, Annex (Bassiouni Principles).

[17] Ibid. p. 263.

[18] Hayner 2010, p. 20.

31 Post-conflict Justice Mechanisms

In addition, both the findings of trials and the recommendations and conclusions of truth commissions may inform the design of reparation packages for victims. Again, before reparations are made, it must be determined who is to be compensated and for what. Trials and truth seeking themselves may have a reparative impact through their acknowledgement of the wrongs committed against victims and their commitment to addressing impunity. Thus, while it can be said that states possess four distinct duties in responding to past human rights violations, and victims four corresponding rights, the measures implemented to discharge particular duties may, in practice, contribute to the fulfilment of other transitional justice objectives.[19]

Nonetheless, for ease of explanation, this chapter will consider the different rights and obligations and relevant mechanisms in turn.

31.3.1 The Right to Justice

The right to justice has been confirmed in the jurisprudence of human rights courts, findings of supervisory bodies and UN sponsored studies. Although it has been argued that the right to justice does not necessarily require criminal prosecution,[20] international law, national practice and the demands of victims, suggest that trials are a key component of the response to serious human rights violations. Within the transitional justice framework, criminal trials are considered to make an important contribution to overall restoration.[21]

---

[19] On the interconnectedness of the rights of victims see UN Human Rights Council, *Right to Truth, Report of the Office of the High Commissioner for Human Rights*, A/HRC/5/7, 7 June 2007, para 81–86.

[20] Ambos 2009, p 30; Schlunk 2000, pp. 44–45.

[21] Duff 2003; Drumbl 2000, p 1263–4; Malmud-Goti 1990, pp. 14–15.

656 A. Bisset

A number of international treaties make specific provision for the delivery of criminal justice for human rights violations through the imposition of an explicit obligation to prosecute upon state parties. The Genocide Convention,[22] the Geneva Conventions,[23] the Apartheid Convention,[24] the Convention Against Torture,[25] the International Convention on Enforced Disappearance[26] and the Inter-American Convention on the Forced Disappearance of Persons[27] are all examples. For states parties to the ICC Statute, prosecution must be pursued at the national level in order to avoid intervention by the ICC.[28]

In other instruments, an obligation to provide justice in the form of prosecution has been developed through the jurisprudence of courts and monitoring bodies. The Inter-American Court has stated that the rights of victims to an effective remedy and judicial protection, under Articles 1(1) and 25 of the American Convention on Human Rights, impose obligations upon state parties to investigate, prosecute and sanction perpetrators of human rights violations.[29] It has also found that Article 8

---

[22] UN Convention on the Prevention and Punishment of the Crime of Genocide, 9 December 1948, 78 UNTS 227, Article 6.

[23] Geneva Convention I for the Amelioration of the Condition of the Wounded and Sick in Armed Forces in the Field, 12 August 1949, 75 UNTS 31, Article 49; Geneva Convention II for the Amelioration of the Condition of Wounded, Sick and Shipwrecked Members of Armed Forces at Sea, 12 August 1949, 75 UNTS 85, Article 50; Geneva Convention III Relative to the Treatment of Prisoners of War, 12 August 1949, 75 UNTS 135, Article 129; Geneva Convention IV Relative to the Protection of Civilian Persons in Time of War, 12 August 1949, 75 UNTS 287, Article 146.

[24] International Convention on the Suppression and Punishment of the Crime of Apartheid, 30 November 1973, 1015 UNTS 243, Article 4(b).

[25] UN Convention Against Torture and Other Cruel, Inhuman or Degrading Treatment or Punishment, 10 December 1984, 1465 UNTS 85, Articles 4(2) and 7.

[26] International Convention for the Protection of All Persons from Enforced Disappearance, New York, 20 December 2006, General Assembly Resolution 61/177.

[27] Inter-American Convention on the Forced Disappearance of Persons, Belém, Brazil, 9 June 1994, (1994) 33 ILM 1529.

[28] ICC Statute, Article 17.

[29] *Carpio Nicolle et al.* v. *Guatemala*, (Merits, Reparations and Costs), Inter-American Court of Human Rights, Series C, No. 117, 22 November 2004, para 128; *Moiwana Community* v. *Suriname*, (Preliminary Objections, Merits, Reparations and Costs), Inter-American Court of Human Rights, Series C, No. 124, 15 June 2005, para 204; *"Mapiripan Massacre"* v. *Colombia*, (Merits, Reparations and Costs), Inter-American Court of Human Rights, Series C, No. 134, 15 September 2005, para 295; *Blanco-Romero et al.* v. *Venezuela*, (Merits, Reparations and Costs), Inter-American Court of Human Rights, Series C, No. 138, 28 November 2005, para 95; *Pueblo Bello Massacre* v. *Colombia*, (Merits), Inter-American Court of Human Rights, Series C, No. 140, 31 January 2006, para 266; *Lopez-Alvarez* v. *Honduras*, (Merits, Reparations and Costs), Inter-American Court of Human Rights, Series C, No. 141, 1 February 2006, para 207; *Ximenes-Lopes* v. *Brazil*, (Merits, Reparations and Costs), Inter-American Court of Human Rights, Series C, No. 149, 4 July 2006, para 245; *Goiburú et al..* v. *Paraguay*, (Merits, Reparations and Costs), Inter-American Court of Human Rights, Series C, No. 153, 22 September 2006, para 164; *Vargas-Areco* v. *Paraguay*, (Merits, Reparations and Costs), Inter-American Court of Human Rights), Series C, No. 155, 26 September 2006, para 153; *Almonacid Arellano et al.* v. *Chile*, (Preliminary Objections, Merits, Reparations and Costs), Inter-American Court of Human Rights, Series C, No. 154, 26 September 2006, para 1110.

of the Convention, which outlines the right to be heard, includes the right of victims to have the crime investigated and to have those responsible prosecuted and where, appropriate, punished.[30] The European Court of Human Rights has stated that the duty on states to secure the rights within the ECHR gives rise to positive state obligations to carry out thorough and effective investigations.[31] Similarly, the United Nations Human Rights Committee (HRCe) has interpreted Article 2(3) of the ICCPR, the right to an effective remedy, as requiring states to conduct a criminal investigation that brings to justice those responsible in cases involving arbitrary detentions, forced disappearances, torture and extra-judicial executions.[32] The Joinet principles interpret the right of victims to justice as including the trial of their oppressors. In addition, they articulate obligations for the state to investigate, prosecute and punish those responsible.[33] The Bassiouni principles also make clear that a victim's right to access justice includes the state's duty to prosecute those responsible for human rights violations.[34] These principles, although non-binding, have been described as constituting the most comprehensive and widely accepted description of a state's human rights obligations and an individual's human rights.[35] The result of this discourse is that the victim's right to justice has become interwoven with the prosecution of those who commit serious human rights violations. While the existence of a customary international law duty to prosecute human rights crimes remains contested,[36] the commission of the most serious violations is likely to result in international pressure to prosecute through some means.

---

[30] *Paniagua Morales* v. *Guatemala*, (Merits), Inter-American Court of Human Rights, Series C, No. 37, 8 March 1998.

[31] *Aksoy* v. *Turkey*, (Application. No. 21987/93), Judgment of 18 December 1996, (1997) 23 EHRR 553, para 98; *M.C.* v. *Bulgaria*, (Application. No. 39272/98), Judgment of 4 December 2003, (2005) 40 EHRR 20, paras 150–151; *Kurt* v. *Turkey*, (Application No. 24276/94), Judgment of 25 May 1998, (1999) 27 EHRR 373, para 140; *Hugh Jordan* v. *UK*, (Application. No. 24746/94), Judgment of 4 May 2001, [2001] ECHR 327, para 105.

[32] *Vincente et al.* v. *Colombia*, UN Human Rights Committee, Communication No. 612/1995, UN Doc. CCPR/C/60/D/612/1995, 14 June 1994; *Rodriguez* v. *Uruguay*, UN Human Rights Committee, Communication No. 322/1998, UN Doc. CCPR/C/51/D/322/1988, 9 August 1994.; *Tshiongo* v. *Zaire*, UN Human Rights Committee, Communication No. 366/1989, UN Doc. CCPR/C/49/D/366/1989, 8 November 1993; *Bautista de Arellana* v *Colombia*, UN Human Rights Committee, Communication No. 563/1993, UN Doc. CCPR/C/55/D/563/1993, 27 October 1995; General Comment No. 31 on Article 2 of the Covenant: The Nature of the General Legal Obligation Imposed on State Parties to the Covenant, UN GAOR, Human Rights Committee, 80th Sess., UN Doc. CCPR/C/74/CRP.4/Rev.6, para 18 (2004).

[33] Joinet Principles, paras 26–27; Updated Principles, 'Summary'.

[34] Bassiouni Principles, Principles 4 and 22(f).

[35] Updated Principles, 'Summary'.

[36] Some commentators have argued strongly in favour of a customary duty to prosecute serious human rights violations. See Bassiouni 1996, p. 67; Jackson 2007. Others, however, are dubious of the existence of such an obligation and point to the lack of uniformity in state practice as regards prosecution. See Seibert-Fohr 2009; Cryer 2005.

31.3.2 *The Right to Truth*

The right to truth is not explicitly stated in any human rights treaty. Its roots can be traced to Articles 32 and 33 of the 1977 First Additional Protocol to the Geneva Conventions of 1949.[37] These provide respectively for the right of families to know the fate of their relatives and oblige states parties to search for those reported missing. The closest enunciation of a right to truth is found in Article 24(2) of the International Convention for the Protection of All Persons from Enforced Disappearance, which states "each victim has the right to know the truth regarding the circumstances of the enforced disappearance, the progress and results of the investigation and the fate of the disappeared person".[38] Primarily, the right to truth has been inferred from other rights under human rights treaties.[39] The HRCe has interpreted the right to the truth as forming part of the right to be free from torture under the ICCPR, interpreting it as a means to end or prevent the psychological torture of families of victims of forced disappearances[40] and clandestine executions.[41] The European Court of Human Rights has interpreted the right to be free from torture as encompassing a right to truth through the requirement that violations be effectively investigated and those involved promptly informed of the results.[42] The Inter-American Court of Human Rights has held that victims and their next of kin have a right to clarification of the facts surrounding serious human rights violations under the rights to a hearing and to an effective remedy and judicial protection in the American Convention.[43] Similarly, the African Commission on Human and Peoples' Rights has found the right to the truth to form part of the right to an effective remedy under its Principles and Guidelines on the Right to a Fair Trial and Legal Assistance in Africa.[44]

---

[37] Protocol I Additional to the Geneva Conventions on 12 August 1949 relating to the Protection of Victims of International Armed Conflict, 1125 UNTS 3.

[38] Inter-American Convention on the Forced Disappearance of Persons, Belém, Brazil, 9 June 1994, (1994) 33 ILM 1529.

[39] For a discussion of this, see Antkowiak 2002.

[40] See the explanation by Bertil Wennergren, member of the Human Rights Committee, in his opinion in the cases: *R. A. V. N. et al.* v *Argentina*, UN Human Rights Committee, Communication Nos. 343, 344 and 345/1988, UN Doc. CCPR/C/38/D/344/1988, 5 April 1990, (Appendix); *S.E.* v. *Argentina*, UN Human Rights Committee, Communication No. 275/1988, UN Doc. CCPR/C/38/D/275/1988, 4 April 1990 (Appendix). See *Sarma* v. *Sri Lanka*, UN Human Rights Committee, Communication No 950/2000, UN Doc. CCPR/C/78/D/950/2000, 31 July 2003, para 9.5.

[41] *Lyashkevich* v. *Belarus*, UN Human Rights Committee, Communication No 887/1999, UN Doc. CCPR/C/77/D/887/1999, 24 April 2003, para 9.2.

[42] *Kurt* v. *Turkey*, paras 130–134; *Tas* v. *Turkey*, (Application No. 24396/94), Judgment of 14 November 2000, (2001) 33 EHRR 15, paras 77–80; *Cyprus* v. *Turkey*, (Application No. 25781/94), Judgment of 10 May 2001, (2002) 35 EHRR 30, paras 136 and 157.

[43] *Bamaca Velasquez* v. *Guatemala*, (Merits), Inter-American Court of Human Rights, Series C, No. 70, Judgment of 25 November 2000, paras 159–166.

[44] African Union Doc. DOC/0S(XXX)247, 2001, Principle C which provides for the right to an effective remedy states in para (b)(iii) that the right to an effective remedy includes access to the factual information concerning the violations. See Naqvi 2006, p. 257.

31 Post-conflict Justice Mechanisms

Numerous UN Resolutions have acknowledged the right to truth[45] and the importance of uncovering and delivering the truth in order to end impunity and contribute to the attainment of peace.[46] In 2005, the UN Commission on Human Rights affirmed the right to truth and commissioned a study to determine its scope and content.[47] The study found that the right to the truth regarding gross human rights violations, violations of international humanitarian law and international crimes is an inalienable, autonomous and non-derogable right, possessed by victims, their relatives and wider society.[48] It implies knowing the full and complete truth as to the events that transpired, their specific circumstances, and who participated in them, including knowing the circumstances in which the violations took place, as well as the reasons for them.[49] The study supports the argument that the right to truth is a fundamental, emerging principle of international human rights law and a central means of addressing a legacy of abuse.[50]

31.3.3 The Right to Reparation

Reparations have long been established as a means of settling breaches of international law,[51] although traditionally, this was conceptualized as a matter between

---

[45] UN Human Rights Council Resolution 9/11, Right to Truth, 24 September 2008; UN Human Rights Council Resolution 12/12, Right to the Truth, 1 October 2009; UN Human Rights Council Resolution 14/7, Proclamation of 24 March as the International Day for the Right to the Truth Concerning Gross Human Rights Violations and for the Dignity of Victims, 17 June 2010; UN General Assembly Resolution 68/165, Right to the Truth, 21 January 2014. See too Joinet Principles, Principle 1, Updated Principles, Principle 2; Bassiouni Principles, Principle 22.

[46] UN Security Council Resolution 1606 (2005), UN Doc. S/RES/1606 (2005), 20 June 2005, Preamble, paras 2 and 7, on the peace process in Burundi; UN Security Council Resolution 1593 (2005), UN Doc. S/RES/ 1593 (2005), 31 March 2005, para 5, on the situation in Darfur; UN General Assembly Resolution 57/105 (2003), Assistance for Humanitarian Relief, Rehabilitation and Development for Timor-Leste, UN Doc. A/RES/57/105 (2003), 13 February 2003, para 12; UN General Assembly Resolution 57/161 (2003), United Nations Verification Mission in Guatemala, UN Doc. A/RES/57/161 (2003), 28 January 2003, para 17; UN General Assembly Resolution 48/149 (1994), Situation of Human Rights in El Salvador, UN Doc. A/RES/48/149 (1994), 7 March 1994, para 4; UN General Assembly Resolution 42/147 (1987), Situation of Human Rights and Fundamental Freedoms in Chile, UN Doc. A/RES/42/147 (1987), 7 December 1987, paras 10(d) and (e); UN General Assembly Resolution 40/145 (1985), Situation of Human Rights and Fundamental Freedoms in Chile, UN Doc. A/RES/40/145 (1985), 13 December 1985, para 6(b).

[47] UN Commission for Human Rights, Right to Truth: Human Rights Resolution 2005/66, E/CN.4/RES/2005/66, 20 April 2005, para 6.

[48] UN Commission on Human Rights, *Study on the Right to Truth, Report of the Office of the United Nations High Commissioner for Human Rights*, 8 February 2006, E/CN.4/2006/91, paras 58–60.

[49] Ibid., para 59.

[50] Naqvi 2006.

[51] Germany v Poland, The Factory at Chorzów (Claim for Indemnity) (The Merits), Permanent Court of International Justice, File E. c. XIII. Docket XIV:I Judgment No. 13, 13 September 1928, para 125.

states. Alongside the development of international human rights law, the obligation to make reparation has extended beyond the inter-state model to a position where breaches of international norms result in duties of redress and reparation to wronged groups and individuals. Like the right to truth, the right to reparation is not explicitly referred to in any human rights treaty. It too has been inferred from the right to a remedy,[52] which is found across a host of international[53] and regional[54] human rights instruments, as well as within international humanitarian law[55] and international criminal law.[56] It has been confirmed within the jurisprudence of international and regional human rights courts and monitoring bodies[57] and emphasized by UN institutions.[58] The UN Basic Principles and Guidelines on the Right to a Remedy and Reparation for Victims of Violations of International Human Rights and Humanitarian Law consider that full and effective reparation includes restitution, compensation, rehabilitation, satisfaction and guarantees of non-repetition.[59] These will be discussed further below.

31.3.4 Guarantees of Non-recurrence

Guarantees of non-recurrence were previously argued to be a means of making reparation.[60] Recent studies of these obligations draw distinction between the two.[61] The obligation to ensure non-recurrence of violations has its roots in the international legal obligation to 'ensure' human rights,[62] which encompasses a general duty to

---

[52] On these points see Haldemann 2018, at 338–9.

[53] Universal Declaration of Human Rights, 1948, Article 8; International Covenant on Civil and Political Rights, Article 2; International Convention on the Elimination of All Forms of Racial Discrimination, Article 6; Convention against Torture and other Cruel, Inhuman or Degrading Treatment or Punishment, Article 14; Convention on the Rights of the Child, Article 39.

[54] African Charter on Human and Peoples' Rights, At 7; American Convention on Human Rights, Article 25; Convention for the Protection of Human Rights and Fundamental Freedoms, Article 13.

[55] Hague Convention respecting the Laws and Customs of War on Land, Article 3; Protocol Additional to the Geneva Conventions Relating to the Protection of Victims of International Armed Conflicts, Article 91.

[56] Rome Statute of the International Criminal Court, Articles 86 and 75.

[57] Human Rights Committee, General Comment No. 31, The Nature of the General Legal Obligation Imposed on States Parties to the Covenant, CCPR/C/21/Rev.1/Add. 1326 May 2004, paras 15–16. Human Rights Committee, Il Khwildy v. Libya, Case 1804/2008 (1 November 2012), para 9; Committee Against Torture, General Comment No. 3, Implementation of Article 14 by States Parties, CAT/C/GC/3 (19 November 2012), para 2.

[58] General Assembly, Declaration of Basic Principles of Justice for Victims of Crime and Abuse of Power, A/RES/40/43, 29 November 1985.

[59] Bassiouni Principles, paras 19–23.

[60] Joinet Principles, Principles 37–42.

[61] Mayer-Rieckh and Duthie 2018a, p. 385.

[62] ICCPR, Article 2(1) 999 UNTS I-4668; Velasquez-Rodriguez v Honduras (judgment) IACtHR Series C no. 4 (29 July 1988), para 166.

prevent future violations of human rights as well as a specific obligation to prevent the recurrence of violations that have taken place.[63] The obligation is 'part of the overall obligation to conform to a norm of international law'.[64] Guarantees of non-recurrence is the least developed of the transitional justice mechanisms designed to respond to past human rights violations. The UN Principles to Combat Impunity outline the key measures to ensure non-recurrence as: institutional and legislative reform, disbandment of para-statal armed groups and the demobilization and reintegration of children involved in armed conflict into society.[65] The 2015 report of the Special Rapporteur on the promotion of truth, justice, reparation and guarantees of non-recurrence takes this slightly further, explaining that policies aimed at ensuring non-recurrence should include a number of elements, including institutional interventions, societal interventions and interventions in the cultural and individual spheres.[66] How these have been incorporated in practice will be considered below.

31.4 The Practice of Transitional Justice

31.4.1 Trials

Prosecution remains a key response to the commission of serious human rights violations. Criminal justice is considered essential to provide redress, assist with healing and halt the impunity that threatens sustainable peace. Prosecutions have taken place in a range of fora. Prosecution at the domestic level holds many advantages in terms of availability of evidence and witnesses and accessibility to victim populations. However, in post conflict contexts, fragile politics, failed infrastructure, weak institutions, judicial partiality and a lack of security can make national trials impossible, although it must be acknowledged that a number of domestic trials for international crimes have successfully been carried out.[67]

The practice of creating international criminal tribunals began in Nuremberg and Tokyo at the end of the Second World War.[68] More modern practice, however, gained impetus following the establishment of the *ad hoc* tribunals by the UN, under Chapter

---

[63] UN Human Rights Committee, General Comment No. 31, The Nature of the General Obligation Imposed on State Parties to the Covenant, UN Doc. CCPR/C/21/Rev.1/Add.13 (26 May 2004), para 17; Committee Against Torture, General Comment No. 3, Implementation of Article 14 by States Parties, UN Doc CAT/C/GC/3 (13 December 2012), para 18.

[64] Mayer-Rieckh and Duthie 2018a, p. 385.

[65] Principle 35.

[66] UN, Report of Special Rapporteur on the promotion of truth, justice, reparation and guarantees of non-recurrence, Pablo de Greiff, UN Doc A/HRC/30/2, 7 September 2015.

[67] Hola et al. 2019.

[68] Clark 1997.

VII, following the conflicts of the 1990s in the former Yugoslavia[69] and Rwanda.[70] The ad hoc tribunals have been enormously significant in the development of modern international criminal law and have prosecuted almost all of those indicted for the most serious crimes committed in the Balkans and Rwanda in the 1990s. They also experienced a number of difficulties, particularly in their early operation, related to cost of investigations and prosecutions, length of proceedings, cooperation from states and disconnect from affected populations; the ICTY having been established in the Hague, the Netherlands, and the ICTR in Arusha, Tanzania.[71]

The experiences of the ICTY and ICTR gave rise to a new model in the 2000s: hybrid courts (considered by Beauvallet and Schmit and Vagias in this volume). These internationalized institutions were created by temporary UN Administrations in Kosovo, Bosnia and Herzegovina and Timor Leste, and through agreements between national governments and the UN for Sierra Leone, Lebanon and Cambodia.[72] Hybrid courts were intended to combat many of the problems associated with international tribunals through their situation within the country concerned and their capacity to build and develop domestic legal systems by trying national as well as international crimes and involving a blend of national and international personnel. Yet despite some notable achievements, hybrid courts have also suffered from problems associated with haphazard and inadequate funding, a lack of powers to compel the provision of evidence and surrender of suspects and, in some instances, tension between national and international judges and prosecutors.[73]

Perhaps most notable in the field of prosecution for international crimes is the creation of the International Criminal Court (ICC). The Rome Statute of the International Criminal Court[74] was adopted in 1998 and entered into force in 2002. It created the first permanent, international criminal court with prospective powers to prosecute individuals, aged over 18 at the time of the alleged offence,[75] for genocide, crimes against humanity, war crimes and aggression.[76] Unlike the tribunals established for the former Yugoslavia and Rwanda, the ICC is a treaty institution and its regime is binding only on its states parties. That said, non-states parties can accept the jurisdiction of the ICC with respect to particular situations,[77] as has been the case for Cote d'Ivoire.[78]

---

[69] The International Criminal Tribunal for the Former Yugoslavia was established pursuant to Security Council Resolution 827 (1993), UN Doc S/Res/827 (1993).

[70] The International Criminal Tribunal for Rwanda was established pursuant to Security Council Resolution 955 (1994), UN Doc. S/Res/955 (1994), 8 November 1994.

[71] See, for example, McDonald 2004.

[72] Dickinson 2003.

[73] Fichtelberg 2015.

[74] Rome Statute of the International Criminal Court, A/Conf.183/9, 17 July 1998, (1998) 37 *International Legal Materials* 1002.

[75] Article 26.

[76] Article 5.

[77] Article 12(3).

[78] ICC Press Release, "Registrar confirms that the Republic of Cote d'Ivoire has accepted the jurisdiction of the Court", 15 February 2005.

31 Post-conflict Justice Mechanisms

The ICC's jurisdiction can be triggered by reference by a states party, reference by the UN Security Council, as in the cases of Sudan and Libya, or by the initiation of an investigation by the prosecutor.[79] The ICC's jurisdiction is complementary to that of national courts and ensures that primary responsibility for the prosecution of ICC crimes remains with states.[80] The ICC must declare a case inadmissible where it is being or has been investigated or prosecuted by a state with jurisdiction and a decision has been made not to prosecute.[81] Only where states are unable or unwilling genuinely to carry out the investigation or prosecution, criteria assessed by the Court itself, does jurisdiction fall to the ICC.[82]

Although the establishment of the ICC is undoubtedly a significant achievement in the effort to end impunity for those responsible for international crimes, the Court has been strongly criticized in its early practice. Concerns have been raised about the slow pace of cases, selectivity in the situations investigated[83] and the perception that the Court might be "anti-Africa".[84] It has been argued that the Court is a politicized institution because of its relationship with the UN Security Council.[85] It has struggled to gain cooperation from states and custody of a number of high profile indictees[86] and has now acquitted more people than it has convicted. The Office of the Prosecutor has been criticized for the ways in which it has collected and presented evidence and the types of evidence it relies upon.[87] Perhaps expectations of the Court are unrealistic and too readily overlook the complexity of prosecuting the most serious crimes, as well as the realities of the international political environment in which the Court operates. Nevertheless, the Court has considerable work to do if it is to be perceived as a credible means of ending impunity.

31.4.2 Truth Commissions

Truth commissions emerged in the early 1980s, as a number of states undertook the transition from authoritarian regime to democratic rule, often in the aftermath of violent internal conflicts. As these regimes fell, or voluntarily relinquished power, evidence of the systematic human rights violations committed under their rule came to light. As a concession that provided a means of investigating and acknowledging the past, while avoiding the political difficulties associated with trials, some states

---

[79] Article 13.

[80] Articles 1 and 17.

[81] Article 17(1)(a) and (b).

[82] Article 17.

[83] Schabas 2008.

[84] Chadwick Austin and Thieme 2016.

[85] Tiemessen 2014.

[86] Sluiter 2018.

[87] De Vos 2013.

established truth commissions.[88] Their primary purpose is to compile a historical record, but the focus on victims and generation of public discussion on accountability and social reform can build capacity for active citizenship and democratic process. The historical record is used to inform the development of recommendations for reform, thereby making a valuable contribution to strengthening the rule of law.[89]

There is no such thing as a typical truth commission; each operates within a specific context and under its own mandate, which specifies length of operation, geographic scope, subject matter, primary objectives and any investigative powers. However, truth commissions typically have five key characteristics.[90] They are: focused on past events; investigate a pattern of events over a period of time; engage directly and broadly with the affected population; are temporary bodies that aim to conclude with a final report; and are authorized by the state under review.[91] Based on this broad definition, it is agreed that there have been approximately forty truth commissions worldwide, with a propensity in sub-Saharan Africa and South America.

All commissions share two interrelated primary aims: the investigation and clarification of past human rights violations and the prevention of similar violations in the future through the formulation of recommendations for reform.[92] However, wide variation can be seen in truth commission mandates and, accordingly, their operation. Past commissions have taken from nine months to nine years to complete their work[93] and while most have concentrated on violations committed within their own state, the geographic scope of others has extended beyond the territory of the country in question.[94] Specificity and subject matter have also differed. Some early commissions were permitted only to investigate disappearances, excluding a large number of other violations from investigation and distorting the final account of the types and numbers of abuses committed.[95] More recent commissions have been given broad mandates to investigate all types of violations, with a particular focus on those which involve physical violence or repression and have been committed on a systematic scale.[96] In order to fulfil their mandates many truth commissions have been endowed with investigative powers,[97] such as subpoena,[98] search and seizure,[99]

---

[88] Tepperman 2002.

[89] De Grieff 2006.

[90] Freeman 2006, pp. 27–28.

[91] Ibid., pp. 11–12.

[92] Ibid., 33.

[93] Ibid., Appendix 1, Table A.1: Truth Commissions and Their Key Powers.

[94] Promotion of National Unity and Reconciliation Act 1995, No. 34 of 1995, Preamble; Truth and Reconciliation Commission Act 2000, Article 6(2)(a)(i).

[95] Freeman 2006, Appendix 1, Table A.1: Truth Commissions and Their Key Powers; Schey et al. 1997, p. 332.

[96] Hayner 2001 pp. 316–319.

[97] Freeman 2006, Appendix 1, Table A.1: Truth Commissions and Their Key Powers.

[98] Promotion of National Unity and Reconciliation Act, 1995, ss. 29 and 31.

[99] Ibid., s.32.

witness protection,[100] as well as the capabilities to conduct questioning under oath[101] grant confidentiality to those who offer testimony[102] and to hold public hearings.[103] While these powers can be an important means of empowering truth commissions and facilitating their establishment of the most accurate version of the past, they also have the potential to create tension with prosecutorial institutions investigating the same crimes.[104]

Some commissions have been given ambitious, and perhaps unrealistic, objectives, such as the promotion of national reconciliation,[105] restoring the dignity of victims,[106] and reintegration of low-level perpetrators.[107] While the work of truth commissions has the capacity to contribute to these objectives, such aims will not be fulfilled simply through truth commission operation. Some commissions have fulfilled adjudicative functions. The South African TRC was given the authority to grant amnesty,[108] the CAVR of Timor Leste drew up community service agreements between perpetrators and their communities[109] and the Moroccan commission had the power to make financial compensation to victims.[110]

While it seems that there is something inherently appealing about truth commissions—perhaps due to their focus upon the experiences of victims—they have also attracted criticism. Some states continue to use them as a means of avoiding criminal trials and, as bodies established by the government, they are prone to political interference.[111] Many commissions have struggled to engage with perpetrators in building accounts of the past, and more work needs to be done on addressing economic and

---

[100] Ibid., s.35.

[101] Ibid., s29(1)(c).

[102] In some cases the truth commission's mandate has stipulated that proceedings be conducted on a confidential basis. See Agreement on the establishment of the Commission to clarify past human rights violations and acts of violence that have caused the Guatemalan Population to Suffer, Oslo, 23 June 1994; Supreme Decree No. 065-2001-PCM, Article 7 on the establishment of the Peruvian TRC and Mexico Peace Agreements, Mexico City, 27 April 1991, Article 7 on the establishment of the Commission on the Truth for El Salvador. Other commissions have had discretion to grant confidentiality. See Sierra Leone, Truth and Reconciliation Commission Act 2000, s.7(3); East Timor, UNTAET Regulation No. 2001/10, s. 44.2.

[103] Promotion of National Unity and Reconciliation Act, 1995, s.33.

[104] Bisset 2009.

[105] For example the Chilean TRC, Supreme Decree No. 355, Creation of the Commission on Truth and Reconciliation, 25 April 1990, Santiago, Preamble, para 2; South African TRC, Promotion of National Unity and Reconciliation Act, 1995, Preamble.

[106] For example the East Timorese CAVR, UN Transitional Administration in East Timor Regulation No. 2001/10 on the Establishment of a Commission for Reception, Truth and Reconciliation in East Timor, UN Doc. UNTEAT/REG/2001/10, 13 July 2001, s.3.1(f); Sierra Leonean TRC, Truth and Reconciliation Commission Act 2000, s. 6(2)(b).

[107] This was also an objective of the East Timorese CAVR. See ibid., s. 3.1(h).

[108] Promotion of National Unity and Reconciliation Act, 1995, Ch. Four.

[109] UNTAET Regulation 2001/10, ss. 22–32.

[110] Freeman 2006, p. 35.

[111] Lynch 2018.

social rights violations, as well as those suffered by vulnerable groups.[112] The long-term impact of their operation is dubious, although some studies have shown that the prospects for long term peace and democracy are enhanced where truth commissions have operated alongside other mechanisms.[113] Nonetheless, truth commissions remain the most commonly established institutions to respond to past violations.

31.4.3 Reparations

Reparations also play an important role in addressing the violations of the past and charting a way forward to a peaceful future. Reparations acknowledge the violations committed against victims, seek to establish their equal citizenship within society and aim to rebuild trust among citizens as well as between citizens and public institutions.[114] They do so by demonstrating that the government is committed to making a contribution to the survivors' quality of life[115] and signalling that past modes of operation will not be tolerated in a society based on rights, rather than violence.[116]

Since the end of the Second World War, reparations for historic injustices have been claimed in a variety of national settings and regional human rights courts.[117] The ad hoc tribunals did not have powers to order reparations and neither have the hybrid courts established to date. The International Criminal Court has powers to provide redress in relation to the harm suffered by victims of core crimes under the Statute,[118] although its jurisprudence on the issue is, as yet, limited.[119] In the aftermath of mass atrocity, reparations are challenging, involving difficult questions on who should qualify as a victim,[120] whether conventional court proceedings are an appropriate avenue for resolution and what sorts of reparations should be used to remedy and redress past harm.[121] Reparations can be individual or collective, aimed, for example at a community, or involve a mixture of both. As discussed above, reparation is considered to encompass restitution, compensation, rehabilitation, satisfaction and guarantees of non-repetition.[122]

It is seldom possible to restore victims to their original situation or to provide compensation calculated on loss in cases of gross violations of human rights. As a result, many reparations programmes have been conducted as administrative, rather

---

[112] Ochoa-Sanchez 2019

[113] Olsen et al. 2010.

[114] Maggarell 2007.

[115] Mazurana and Carlson 2009.

[116] Aptel and Ladisch 2011, p 26–27.

[117] Torpey 2001.

[118] ICC Statute, Part 7 and Article 79.

[119] Moffet 2017.

[120] Sandoval 2009, p. 249.

[121] Haldemann 2018.

[122] Bassiouni Principles, paras 19–23.

31 Post-conflict Justice Mechanisms

than judicial, processes and have provided general compensation, without making distinctions between different victims.[123] For example, in South Africa, victims of apartheid received payment of approximately \$4000. In Chile, victims received a monthly pension of \$537 and in Argentina, \$224,000 was paid in each case.[124] In terms of rehabilitation, access to medical and related services is considered crucial[125] and has formed part of the reparations packages in Chile, Peru and Morocco.[126] Satisfaction can involve a range of measures, including disclosure of truth, access to information, recovery of bodies, public apology, sanctioning of perpetrators, commemoration and granting access to land or to education. Sometimes, reparations are made to victims' family members, often children, as a way to overcome the enduring consequences of past violations.[127]

The practice around reparation lags far behind the law and scholarship. In transitional states, resources are often scarce. There is competition for funding, and reparations programmes are seldom a government priority, particularly as many victims remain marginalized even after conflict. Although it is considered best practice to consult victims in designing reparations packages, they are frequently overlooked, with issues around gender, culture and other vulnerabilities unheeded. Outreach campaigns, while essential in effective reparations programmes, are often inadequate[128] and practical impediments around access to the information needed to make claims can make it difficult for many victims to realise their right to reparation.[129] Studies show that victims are frequently disappointed by reparations programmes, despite the central role that they ought to play in building sustainable peace.[130]

31.4.4 Reform

The final component of transitional justice is guarantees of non-recurrence. While there is wide agreement on the importance of preventing recurrence, it has been argued that there is limited understanding of what it entails and how best to achieve it.[131]

---

[123] Letschert et al. 2011.

[124] Office of the United Nations High Commissioner for Human Rights (OHCHR) (2008) Rule of Law Tools for Post Conflict States. Reparation Programmes. 30.

[125] Grosman 2018, p. 373.

[126] Rule of Law Tools, Reparations, 24.

[127] Ibid.

[128] Principle 33, Impunity Principles; Declaration of International Law Principles on Reparation for Victims of Armed Conflict adopted on 20 August 2010, at the ILA Hague Conference, Article 6, Res 2/2010, International Law Association.

[129] Maggarell 2007.

[130] Ibid.

[131] Mayer-Rieckh and Duthie 2018a, p. 383.

Disarmament, demobilization and reintegration schemes, whereby former combatants are removed from military structures and assisted in the process of social and economic reintegration to society, are a common feature of post-conflict justice efforts.[132] Considerable attention has also been focused on reform of state institutions so that they are accountable, operate in accordance with and preserve the rule of law and respect human rights. The measures taken to achieve this vary. Many states, including El Salvador, Bosnia and Herzegovina, Liberia and Kenya have instituted vetting processes, whereby individuals responsible for past abuses are removed from police forces, prison services, the military and the judiciary.[133] Legislative reform is also common. Some states have enacted new constitutions, such as in Kenya and Tunisia. Some have ratified international human rights treaties or incorporated international human rights standards into domestic law. Others have reformed national law to ensure the compatibility of emergency, anti-terror and security legislation with human rights standards and have removed discriminatory provisions to ensure the equal rights of all citizens.[134] Legislative reform has been undertaken to reform corrupt institutions and to ensure their accountability in the longer term through the creation of independent, civilian oversight mechanisms. It has been noted, however, that the enactment of new legislation and reform of existing provisions must be accompanied by measures of implementation, including adequate funding and strategic planning, in order to realize change.[135]

Reform is required not just at institutional levels but in cultural and individual spheres too. Cultural sphere reforms can include the creation of education programmes, access to archives, museum exhibitions, and the consideration of past oppression—and departure from it—in media broadcasts, books, plays, art, photography and music. Change in these spheres is complex and is not something that can be implemented directly by the state. It is likely to occur over time. Understanding of change of this nature is less studied and, therefore, less understood, than institutional reform. However, the studies that have been undertaken suggest that the involvement and engagement of the public, as a body and as individuals, in the processes of transition ultimately determine its impact and durability.[136]

31.5 Conclusion

Trials, truth seeking, reparations and reform have come to be recognized as the four pillars of transitional justice. The complex and difficult circumstances in which they

---

[132] Muggah 2009.

[133] Mayer-Rieckh and Duthiea 2018b, p. 396.

[134] For an overview, see Duthie and Mayer-Rieckh 2018.

[135] The rule of law and transitional justice in conflict and post-conflict societies, Report of the Secretary General, UN Doc. S/2011/634, 12 October 2011, 12–13.

[136] Ramirez-Barat 2014.

31 Post-conflict Justice Mechanisms

are established means that their operation is likely to be imperfect, with many challenges and hurdles to be overcome. However, each has the capacity to deliver distinct benefits to transitional states in the aftermath of serious human rights violations and together they can lay foundations for a peaceful and stable future.

There is no one-size-fits-all formula to deal with the past. The needs and priorities of each transitional state are different and will require different approaches. While the four pillars should not be understood as alternatives, the emphasis placed upon each one, their timing and sequencing may vary between states. Alongside the four pillars, there is space to accommodate a host of other measures, including traditional resolution methods, in order to respond to the particularities of each state. The challenge for transitional justice is to continue to provide redress for victims and reform through robust mechanisms while maintaining sufficient flexibility to evolve as new situations present themselves and lessons are learned from practice.

References

Ambos K (2009) The Legal Framework of Transitional Justice: A Systematic Study with a Special Focus on the ICC. In: Ambos K et al. (eds) Building a Future on Peace and Justice: Studies on Transitional Justice, Peace and Development. Springer-Verlag, Heidelberg/Berlin, pp 19–105

Antkowiak TM (2002) Truth as Right and Remedy in International Human Rights Experience. Michigan Journal of International Law 23:977–1013

Aptel C, Ladisch V (2011) Through a New Lens: A Child –Sensitive Approach to Transitional Justice. International Center for Transitional Justice, New York

Bassiouni MC (1996) International Crimes: Jus Cogens and Obligatio Erga Omnes. Law and Contemporary Problems 59:63–74

Bickford L (2004) The Encyclopedia of Genocide and Crimes Against Humanity, Vol 3. Macmillan Reference, New York

Bisset A (2009) Rethinking the Powers of Truth Commissions in Light of the ICC Statute. Journal of International Criminal Justice 7:963–982

Chadwick Austin W, Thieme M (2016) Is the International Criminal Court Anti-African? Peace Review: A Journal of Social Justice 28:342–350

Clark RS (1997) Nuremberg and Tokyo in Contemporary Perspective. In: McCormack T, Simpson GJ (eds) The Law of War Crimes – National and International Approaches. Kluwer Law International, The Hague/London/Boston, pp 171–89

Cryer R (2005) Prosecuting International Crimes: Selectivity and the International Criminal Law Regime. Cambridge University Press, Cambridge

De Vos C (2013) Investigating from Afar: The ICC's Evidence Problem. Leiden Journal of International Law 26:1009–1024

De Grieff P (2006) Truth Telling and the Rule of Law. In: Borer A (ed) Telling the Truths: Truth-Telling and Peace Building in Post-Conflict Societies. University of Notre Dame Press, Notre Dame, pp 188–206

Dickinson LS (2003) The Promise of Hybrid Courts. American Journal of International Law 97:295–310.

Drumbl MA (2000) Punishment Post-genocide: From Guilt to Shame to *Civis* in Rwanda. New York University Law Review 75:1221–1326

Duff A (2003) Restoration and Retribution. In: Von Hirsch A, Roberts J (eds) Restorative Justice and Criminal Justice: Competing or Reconcilable Paradigms. Hart Publishing, Oxford, pp 43–61

Duthie R, Mayer-Rieckh A (2018) Principle 38: Reform of Law and Institutions Contributing to Impunity. In: Haldemann F, Unger T (eds) The United Nations Principles to Combat Impunity: A Commentary. Oxford University Press, Oxford/New York, pp 406–412

Fichtelberg A (2015) Hybrid Tribunals: A Comparative Examination. Springer, New York

Freeman M (2006) Truth Commissions and Procedural Fairness. Cambridge University Press, Cambridge

Grosman LS (2018) Principle 34: Scope of the Right to Reparation. In: Haldemann F, Unger T (eds) The United Nations Principles to Combat Impunity: A Commentary. Oxford University Press, Oxford/New York, pp 369–379

Haldemann F (2018) Principle 31: Rights and Duties Arising out of the Obligation to Make Reparation. In: Haldemann F, Unger T (eds) The United Nations Principles to Combat Impunity: A Commentary. Oxford University Press, Oxford/New York, pp 335–348

Hart HLA (1968) Punishment and Responsibility. Clarendon Press, Oxford

Hayner PB (2001) Unspeakable Truths: Confronting State Terror and Atrocity. Routledge, London/New York

Hayner PB (2010) Unspeakable Truths: Transitional Justice and the Challenge of Truth Commissions, 2nd edn. Routledge, New York/London

Hola B, Mulgew R, van Wijk J (eds) (2019) Special Issue: National Prosecutions of International Crimes: Sentencing Practices and (Negotiated) Punishments. International Criminal Law Review 19:1–190

Huyse L (2001) Amnesty, Truth or Prosecution? In: Reychler L, Paffenholz T (eds) Peace-Building. A Field Guide. Lynne Rienner Publishers, Boulder, pp 325

Jackson MM (2007) The Customary International Law Duty to Prosecute Crimes Against Humanity: A New Framework. Tulane Journal of International and Comparative Law 16:117–135

Kant I (1972) (translated by Hastie W) Justice and Punishment. In: Ezorsky G (ed) Philosophical Perspectives on Punishment. State University of New York Press, Albany

Letschert, RM, De Brouwer A, Pemberton A (eds) (2011) Victimological Approaches to International Crimes. Intersentia, Cambridge

Lynch G (2018) Performances of Injustice: The Politics of Truth, Justice and Reconciliation in Kenya. Cambridge University Press, Cambridge

Maggarell L (2007) Reparations in Theory and Practice. International Center for Transitional Justice, New York

Malmud-Goti J (1990) Transitional Governments in the Breach: Why Punish State Criminals? Human Rights Quarterly 12:1–16

Mayer-Rieckh A, Duthie R (2018a) Principle 35. General Principles. In: Haldemann F, Unger T (eds) The United Nations Principles to Combat Impunity: A Commentary. Oxford University Press, Oxford/New York, pp 383–391

Mayer-Rieckh A, Duthie R (2018b) Principle 36: Reform of State Institutions. In: Haldemann F, Unger T (eds) The United Nations Principles to Combat Impunity: A Commentary. Oxford University Press, Oxford/New York, pp 392–398

Mazurana D, Carlson K (2009) Reparations as a Means for Recognizing and Addressing Crimes and Grave Rights Violations against Girls and Boys during Situations of Armed Conflict and under Authoritarian and Dictatorial Regimes. In: Rubio-Marin R (ed) The Gender of Reparations: Unsettling Sexual Hierarchies while Redressing Human Rights Violations. Cambridge University Press, Cambridge, pp 162–214

McDonald GK (2004) Problems, Obstacles and Achievements of the ICTY. Journal of International Criminal Justice 2:558–571

Moffet L (2017) Reparations for Victims at the International Criminal Court: A New Way Forward. International Journal of Human Rights 21:1204–1222

Muggah R (ed) (2009) Security and Post-Conflict Reconstruction: Dealing with Fighters in the Aftermath of War. Routledge, Abingdon

Naqvi Y (2006) The Right to Truth in International Law: Fact or Fiction? International Review of the Red Cross 88:245–274

Ochoa-Sanchez JC (2019) Economic and Social Rights and Truth Commissions. International Journal of Human Rights 23:1470–1493

Olsen TD, Payne LA, Reitger A (2010) Transitional Justice in Balance: Comparing Processes, Weighing Efficacy. United States Institute of Peace, Washington

Ramirez-Barat C (ed) (2014) Transitional Justice, Culture and Society. Beyond Outreach. International Center for Transitional Justice, New York

Roht-Arriaza A, Marriez-Currena J (eds) (2006) Transitional Justice in the Twenty-First Century: Beyond Truth versus Justice. Cambridge University Press, Cambridge

Sandoval C (2009) The Concept of the "Injured Party" and "Victim" of Gross Human Rights Violations in the Jurisprudence of the Inter-American Court of Human Rights: A Commentary on their Implications for Reparations. In: Ferstman C et al. (eds) Reparations for Victims of Genocide, War Crimes and Crimes Against Humanity: Systems in Place and Systems in the Making. Martinus Nijhoff, Leiden, pp 243–282

Schabas WA (2008) Prosecutorial Discretion v. Judicial Activism at the International Criminal Court. Journal of International Criminal Justice 6:731–76

Schey P, Shelton D, Roht-Arriaza N (1997) Addressing Human Rights Abuses: Truth Commissions and the Value of Amnesty. Whittier Law Review 19:325–344

Schlunk A (2000) Amnesty versus Accountability: Third Party Intervention Dealing with Gross Human Rights Violations in Internal and International Conflicts. Berlin Verlag Spitz, Berlin

Seibert-Fohr A (2009) Prosecuting Serious Human Rights Violations. Oxford University Press, Oxford

Sluiter G (2018) Enforcing Cooperation: Did the Drafters Approach it the Wrong Way? Journal of International Criminal Justice 16:383–402

Teitel R (2000) Transitional Justice, Oxford University Press, Oxford

Tepperman JD (2002) Truth and Consequences. Foreign Affairs 81:131–138

Tiemessen A (2014) The International Criminal Court and the Politics of Prosecutions. The International Journal of Human Rights 18:444–461

Torpey J (2001) "Making Whole What Has Been Smashed": On Reparations Politics. Journal of Modern History 73:333–358

Van Ness D (1996) Restorative Justice and International Human Rights. In: Galaway B, Hudson J (eds) Restorative Justice: International Perspectives. Criminal Justice Press, New York, pp 17–36

Villa-Vicencio C, Doxtader E (2004) Pieces of the Puzzle: Keywords on Reconciliation and Transitional Justice. Institute for Justice and Reconciliation, South Africa

Alison Bisset is Associate Professor in International Human Rights Law at the University of Reading. She specialises in transitional justice, with a focus on the relationship between truth commissions and prosecutorial institutions. Her monograph, *Truth Commissions and Criminal Courts* (2012, CUP), undertakes the first multi-level analysis of their relationship. Alison has provided training on international criminal law and transitional justice for the British Army, the United States Africa Command, the Commonwealth Secretariat and the International Institute for Humanitarian Law, and worked as an expert with the Bingham Centre for the Rule of Law on transitional justice in Nepal. Alison is the editor of Blackstone's International Human Rights Law Documents, published by OUP.

Chapter 32
INTERPOL

Evhen Tsybulenko and Sebastian Suarez

Contents

32.1 The History of INTERPOL's Foundation 674
    32.1.1 Origins and Nazi Takeover 674
    32.1.2 Revival 675
32.2 Challenges to INTERPOL's Legal Status 677
    32.2.1 The Nature of INTERPOL's Constitution 677
    32.2.2 The Capacity of INTERPOL's Founders 678
    32.2.3 The Member States Express Consent 678
    32.2.4 A Problem Solved 679
32.3 Governance of INTERPOL 680
    32.3.1 The Documentary Foundation 680
    32.3.2 The Deliberative Entities 682
32.4 Instruments of International Police Cooperation 684
    32.4.1 Aims and Purposes 684
    32.4.2 The Notice System 685
    32.4.3 Criticism 688
32.5 Conclusion 689
References 690

Abstract INTERPOL has always been difficult to define: a legal curiosity by virtue of its unconventional creation, a politically neutral international police organization that lacks powers of arrest, seizure, and investigation, but has control over perhaps the greatest criminal and crimes databases in existence today—this has somehow been difficult for many people to understand. Again, and again, for decades, questions have been asked: What is it? What does it do? What has it accomplished? Clearly, any detailed study of INTERPOL will reveal that the organization presents some contradictory aspects, but this is due to the nature of the beast. INTERPOL has gone through many alterations and unexpected developments since its founding in 1923

E. Tsybulenko (✉)
Faculty of Law, Tallinn University of Technology, Tallinn, Estonia
e-mail: evhen.tsybulenko@taltech.ee

Kyiv International University, Kyiv, Ukraine

S. Suarez
Equinord—International Law Counsellors, Tallinn, Estonia
e-mail: s.suarez@equinordlaw.com

© T.M.C. ASSER PRESS and the authors 2022
S. Sayapin et al. (eds.), *International Conflict and Security Law*,
https://doi.org/10.1007/978-94-6265-515-7_32

and is still changing today. This chapter will explore the organization's past, briefly touch upon the controversy surrounding its legal status, and elaborate on the different mechanisms for international police cooperation within INTERPOL's framework.

Keywords INTERPOL · International Organization · International Police Cooperation · Red Notice · Transnational Criminal Cooperation

32.1 The History of INTERPOL's Foundation

32.1.1 Origins and Nazi Takeover

The founding of the international organization most commonly known as INTERPOL can be traced to 1914, most precisely in the month of April, when under the auspices of Prince Albert I of Monaco, police and other criminal justice officials representing 24 countries convened at the first International Criminal Police Congress to reflect and share best practices on a series of common problems, such as arrest procedures, identification techniques, and extradition proceedings. During the course of the Congress, the members developed what was a novel idea at the time: the centralization of criminal records. Thus, over the next few days, the founders framed the preliminary design for an international police organization that would be entrusted with criminal records of its member states, resolving to meet again in two years to establish such organization.[1]

However, the Second International Criminal Police Congress reconvened only after World War I was over, more precisely in September 1923, in Austria. Chaired by Dr. Johann Schober, head of Vienna's police services, the second Congress was attended by 131 representatives from 20 countries, most European, but some from distant jurisdictions such as Argentina, China, Japan, and the United States. Over the next five days, the attendants to the Second International Criminal Police Congress designed a functional international organization—the International Criminal Police Commission (ICPC)—with its constitution, officers, headquarters, and procedures. At the time, the Austrian government agreed to provide the organization with financial help, headquarters, and staff, and thus Vienna was chosen as the headquarters, and Dr. Schober became the first president of the ICPC.[2]

From 1923, meetings of the organization's General Assembly were held annually, and the ICPC's membership grew exponentially. In fact, just within a few years, the ICPC had specialized departments for passport forgeries, fingerprinting, criminal records, and counterfeiting, and was publishing a monthly journal, rapidly reducing its dependence on the Austrian government. Just seven years after its foundation, the General Assembly decided at the 1930 Assembly in Antwerp (Belgium) to shy away from its previous arrangement with Austria, by which its officers were appointed

---

[1] Népote 1978, p. 128.

[2] Népote 1977, p. 285–287.

32 INTERPOL

from the Austrian police, and to elect them by majority vote from its member states.[3] This independence from Austria was short-lived. In fact, German Nazis had been manoeuvring for control of the organization for some years, and to counter the Nazi takeover, the representatives who attended the General Assembly that took place in Vienna in 1934 resolved a return to its original Austrian dependency, declaring that the head of the Vienna police would automatically become the head of the ICPC. The General Assembly further confirmed this decision in London in 1937.

This safeguard, however, backfired in 1938, when Germany invaded and annexed Austria, taking control of the ICPC headquarters in Vienna and replacing non-Nazi officials with those loyal to the party. Not long afterward, the Vienna police were absorbed into the Third Reich police, and the chief of Germany's police, Reinhard Heydrich, became the titular head of the Vienna forces. Backed by the 1934 and 1937 General Assembly resolutions, which designated the chief of the Vienna police as president of the Commission, Heydrich became the president of the ICPC.

By 1942, the ICPC headquarters had been relocated by the Nazis to Berlin, and although it maintained a semblance of normality, most countries stopped their participation. Given that Germany itself treated the ICPC as an extension of their police operations, in the mainstream of INTERPOL history, World War II is considered a period in which the ICPC effectively ceased to exist as an international organization.

32.1.2 Revival

The first post-war meeting of the ICPC took place in Belgium in 1946, which was attended by delegates from 17 countries. These delegates wrote a new Constitution and, with France accepting the financial and other obligations as the host country, agreed to establish the new headquarters in Saint-Cloud, Paris, where it remained until 1989 when it moved to their present location in Lyon.

Under French leadership, the organization grew steadily. In 1949, the UN granted INTERPOL consultative status as a non-governmental organization under the wing of the UN's Economic and Social Council (ECOSOC). By 1955, the organization had expanded from its original 17 member countries to 50. In 1956, the organization's Constitution was modernized, making the National Central Bureaus (NCBs) an integral element of the organization's structure, and changing its name from International Criminal Police Commission to International Criminal Police Organization, or just "INTERPOL." In 1971 when the ECOSOC acknowledged the organization's status by a Special Arrangement, INTERPOL's efforts were recognized by the UN as equivalent to that of an intergovernmental organization.[4] Meanwhile, INTERPOL

---

[3] Fooner 1989, p. 48.

[4] United Nations Economic and Social Council Resolution E/RES/1579(L), Special Arrangement between the International Criminal Police Organization and the Economic and Social Council, 20 May and 3 June 1971.

concluded cooperation agreements with other international actors, such as the Organization of American States, the Council of Europe, and the International Criminal Court.[5]

As of 2018, INTERPOL's membership is made up of 192 countries; its aim is "ensuring and promoting the widest possible mutual assistance between all criminal police authorities",[6] and its work is focused primarily on battling transnational crimes. It should be noted, however, that INTERPOL does not reduce its activities to transnational criminality (i.e., interstate crimes) or genuinely international crimes (i.e., crimes against humanity). Indeed, while the organization is concerned with both phenomena, through its novel alert and notifications system, INTERPOL implicates itself in fighting domestic crime in those cases where individuals whose alleged crimes may have been committed entirely within one state's borders have subsequently left that state. Thus, the organization has focused its mandate on the facilitation of domestic law enforcement practices and processes by seeking to facilitate both the tracking and capture of international fugitives and coordinating cooperation in crime investigation. In this task, INTERPOL's role is mostly facilitative, thus allowing for fast contact between police officers of different jurisdictions and providing the infrastructure required for sharing information between member police forces conducive to international police cooperation, such as a global communication system, compilation of databases and distribution of notifications. However, the organization does not conduct its investigations or intervene in cases on its own.

Having by now moved away from Austrian or French dependency, the organization's staff reflects the diversity of its membership, ensuring that INTERPOL can provide enhanced support wherever and whenever it may be needed. The staff works in any of the organization's four official languages (Arabic, English, French, and Spanish), helping member countries fight a wide range of criminal activities and encouraging communication and cooperation between NCBs.

In addition to the headquarters in Lyon, France, and the local National Central Bureaus in each of the organization's member countries, INTERPOL maintains regional bureaus in Buenos Aires (Argentina), San Salvador (El Salvador), Yaoundé (Cameroon), Abidjan (Côte d'Ivoire), Nairobi (Kenya), Harare (Zimbabwe), and Bangkok (Thailand). The organization further has liaison offices at the United Nations in New York (United States), the European Union in Brussels (Belgium), and Europol in Den Haag (Netherlands).[7] Furthermore, INTERPOL possesses three Command and Coordination Centres, the original in Lyon, a second in Buenos Aires, and a third in Singapore. These Command and Coordination Centres offer 24 hours a day, 365 days a year point of contact for national police forces seeking critical information or facing a crisis.[8] Finally, the organization also has a Global Complex for Innovation

---

[5] Martha 2010, p. 143–144.

[6] Constitution of the International Criminal Police Organization—Interpol 2017, Article 2.

[7] Interpol 2013, Annual Report, 82nd General Assembly, Cartagena, Colombia, p. 32.

[8] Interpol General Secretariat 2018, Fact Sheet: Command and Coordination Centre, Lyon, France, pp. 1–2.

32 INTERPOL

(IGCI) in Singapore, which was officially opened in April 2015, to act as its research and development facility, and a place of cooperation on digital crimes investigations.

32.2 Challenges to INTERPOL's Legal Status

Although there are no doubts that INTERPOL is an international organization, there was a long period when its legal status was dubious. Past efforts to define the organization's legal status have led to interesting discussions, and it is therefore useful, even necessary, to re-examine the issue. Questions concerning INTERPOL's status as an international organization are fundamentally linked to the irregular nature of the Constitution,[9] the capacity of its founders,[10] and the consent given by Member States.

For the analysis of INTERPOL's status as an international organization, we shall use the definition of international organization that defines them as legal entities of a certain permanency created by the will of states expressed in an instrument binding under international law, and endowed with a minimum of organs able to express a will distinct from that of its members, possessing its own international legal personality and entrusted to fulfil some common, usually public task.[11] This concept closely follows the one prepared by the Working Group of the United Nations International Law Commission, which refers to international organizations as "an organisation established by a treaty or other instrument of international law and possessing its own international legal personality distinct from that of its members".[12]

Thus, two appear to be the crucial elements for the qualification of an entity as an international organization. The first element is that membership should be made of states (or other subjects of international law) willing to create a subject of international law. The second element is the need for the establishing act to be a treaty or other international instrument. These two criteria help to distinguish international organizations from other entities operating internationally, such as NGOs or transnational corporations.

32.2.1 The Nature of INTERPOL's Constitution

Whether INTERPOL is an intergovernmental organization depends on its Constitution being considered an international agreement. Moreover, in principle, any legally

---

[9] Savino 2012, p. 125.

[10] Stalcup 2013, p. 235.

[11] Sands and Klein 2001, p. 16.

[12] United Nations General Assembly 2003, Report of the International Law Commission on the Work of its 55th Session, New York, United Nations, p. 32.

valid agreement under international law,[13] by whatever denomination, may be a treaty in the sense given by the Vienna Convention of the Law of the Treaties,[14] as long as it can be interpreted as an expression of will to create an international organization. The question, then, is whether the INTERPOL Constitution seeks to create an international organization.

Given that the express or intended heart of a constituent instrument is the formation of an organization, and given that, in the case of INTERPOL, its Constitution clearly points towards the catalogue of capacities required to obtain international personality,[15] it can be safely said that the Constitution does assemble the elements most usually associated with the creation of intergovernmental agreements constituent of international organizations.

32.2.2 The Capacity of INTERPOL's Founders

Whether INTERPOL qualifies as an intergovernmental international organization or merely as a non-governmental organization turns partly on the question of the capacity in which those who created INTERPOL acted. Was the organization created by states or by private citizens?

Considering that the rule for attribution of conduct applies to the law of the treaties and other international agreements, or, as the International Court of Justice has said, "the conduct of any organ of the State must be regarded as an act of that State",[16] and considering that no delegation but the Argentine argued lack of governmental instruction when adopting INTERPOL's Constitution in 1956,[17] there should be no objection to consider the Constitution as reflecting a consensus between governments.

32.2.3 The Member States Express Consent

However, consensus with respect to INTERPOL's Constitution is not sufficient; governments must also have expressed their "consent to be bound". In fact, the International Court of Justice has said that agreements entered into by officials who are not regularly representing the State (such as police officers), 'not approved by

---

[13] Schermers and Blokker 2003, p. 27.

[14] Vienna Convention on the Law of Treaties 1969, 1155 UNTS 331.

[15] Martha 2010, p. 49.

[16] Difference Relating to the Immunity from Legal Process of a Special Rapporteur of the Commission on Human Rights (Advisory Opinion) [1999] ICJ Rep 87–88, para 62.

[17] Martha 2010, p. 154.

the competent authorities of each Party, do not have the binding force of a convention'.[18] In this sense, an often-heard issue is the allegation that the organization's Constitution was never submitted for governmental ratification.[19]

However, this assertion seems to be groundless, given that Article 45 of INTERPOL's Constitution stipulated that the member countries listed in its Appendix I would be considered members "unless they declare through the appropriate governmental authority that they cannot accept the Constitution." It meant that if any member country remained silent, they would be deemed to have consented. Tacit expression of consent is not excluded under general international law,[20] and as a matter of international law, where the law prescribes no form, parties are free to choose whichever form they please, provided their intentions are clear.[21] In fact, this 'opting out' technique has been used regularly,[22] and the same principle can be found in other organizations.[23] Thus, considering the subsequent "post-signature" behaviour on the part of the member countries, the assertion that the INTERPOL Constitution was never submitted for governmental ratification should be refuted.

32.2.4 A Problem Solved

Today, it would be difficult to doubt INTERPOL's status as an international organization: it has manifested its international personality through acceding to treaties and signing agreements with multiple other international actors,[24] such as cooperation agreements with the UN, Universal Postal Union, the International Atomic Energy Agency, World Customs Organization, the Special Tribunal for Lebanon, and the European Central Bank, and in 2000, the Organization acceded to the Vienna Convention on the Law of Treaties between States and International Organizations or between International Organizations. Furthermore, to cement its status, in 2011, INTERPOL submitted its Constitution for registration with the UN in accordance

---

[18] Frontier Dispute (Burkina Faso/Republic of Mali) [1984] ICJ Rep 623, para 147 and Land, Island and Maritime Frontier Dispute (El Salvador/Honduras: Nicaragua intervening) (Judgment) [1992] ICJ Rep 514, para 261.

[19] Toksanbaev AB, The Peculiarities of the Legal Status of INTERPOL as an Intergovernmental Organisation, available at: http://www.kisi.kz/en/categories/geopolitics-and-international-affairs/posts/the-peculiarities-of-the-legal-status-of-interpol-as-an

[20] Giuliano et al. 1991, p. 296.

[21] Case concerning the Temple of Preah Vihear (Cambodia v Thailand) (Preliminary Objections, Judgment) [1961] ICJ Rep 31.

[22] Fitzmaurice 1998, p. 66–70.

[23] See: The Constitution of the World Health Organization; the Chicago Convention on International Civil Aviation; the Convention on the International Maritime Organization; the Convention on the Prevention of Maritime Pollution by Dumping of Wastes and Other Matter, and the Convention to Regulate International Trade in Endangered Species of Flora and Fauna.

[24] Stalcup 2013, p. 235.

with Article 102 of the UN Charter.[25] However, this is not to say that such registration retrospectively alters the nature of the Constitution, but rather would clarify the intergovernmental status of INTERPOL as an organization.[26]

32.3 Governance of INTERPOL

INTERPOL's unconventional origins and history are matched by an organizational structure that is unlike those of any other international organization, not in small part due to the organization's inherent challenge: in being a conduit to law-enforcement cooperation, the organization must balance the needs, goals, and practices of a diversity of countries worldwide.

32.3.1 The Documentary Foundation

The organization is said to be governed by four documents: the Constitution, the General Regulations, the National Central Bureau Policy, and the Rules on International Police Cooperation and on the Internal Control of Interpol Archives.

The Constitution establishes the legal framework and mechanisms for international police cooperation, and as such, it is of paramount importance to the organization. The original charter of 1923 comprised just ten articles, reflecting the founders' relatively simplistic view of their tasks. The 1946 revision, after World War II, added, among others, an Executive Committee made of five members, and although it retained the idea of preference for a citizen of the headquarters country as secretary general, opened the presidency to all members.

The Constitution's revision of 1956 was of landmark significance. It established National Central Bureaus (NCBs) as integral to INTERPOL's structure, severed the organization's financial dependence on the French Government,[27] and, attempting to establish a legal recognition of its status, and the sense of permanence required, changed its name, substituting the word "Organization" for "Commission". It was at this time, too, that the word INTERPOL was added to the name.[28] As previously stated, Article 45 of the revised Constitution listed all the countries that at that time were members and deemed that they would continue to be considered as members unless, within six months, they declared that they could not accept the Constitution. None of the listed members, however, filed a rejection.

Moreover, the bulk of INTERPOL's Constitution is devoted to the institutional elements that establish its deliberative functions and its organizational structure:

---

[25] Stalcup 2013, p. 237.

[26] Martha 2010, p. 196.

[27] Constitution of the ICPO—Interpol 2017, Article 38.

[28] Fooner 1973, p. 26–27.

Articles 6 to 14 pertain to the General Assembly; Articles 15 to 24, to the Executive Committee; Articles 25 to 30 to the General Secretariat; Articles 31 to 33, to the National Central Bureaus; and Articles 34 to 37, to the Advisers.

The General Regulations are considered INTERPOL's second pillar in the organization's governance, comprising additional articles relating to rules on how the various affairs of the organization (such as meetings, agendas, voting, budgets, etc.) are to be conducted. Among the most important provisions, the General Regulations contain those that control the election of officers and officials below the rank of president, and the policies that will ensure that all geographical sectors of the globe are truly represented. Elected positions must therefore rotate, and attention must be paid to keep the balances.

The third leg in INTERPOL's governance is the National Central Bureau Policy, which sets forth the provisions of the NCB system. Besides constituting a fundamental piece in the multinational police cooperation framework, the NCB system also provides the mechanism for bypassing the obstacles that might otherwise be imposed by the principles of national sovereignty and the procedures of diplomatic channels, allowing overcoming language and cultural barriers, and to resolve the differences among the nations in legal codes, police powers, and criminal justice systems.[29] The idea of having central police offices in each country communicating and cooperating is relatively new, evolving from an initial concept to practical mechanism in a half of the organization's lifespan: it started as a suggestion at the 1925 General Assembly, and then it was formalized in the 1956 Constitutional reform with the introduction of NCBs. Albeit the concept of NCBs might be shocking to the professional police world, where autonomy and authority within one's own jurisdiction—whether a geographical area or a category of criminal activity—are treated as unchangeable,[30] the NCB system, acting as point of contact for international cooperation, allows for a bridge between police forces with different views on laws, police powers, procedures, and law-enforcement structures.

The basis of any type of international police cooperation requires the centralization and circulation of different types of information. Thus, INTERPOL's fourth text in its documentary foundation is concerned with the control and oversight of its files. However, it was not until 1982 that information dissemination became subject to rules and supervision originating outside the organization. By an Exchange of Letters between INTERPOL and the French government in that year, the organization agreed to be bound by the Rules on International Police Cooperation and on the Internal Control of INTERPOL's Archives.[31] This agreement between INTERPOL and the French government contemplated the removal of the organization's files and records from the jurisdiction of French national privacy laws, created a new set of rules for the exchange of police information within the organization, and established a Supervisory Board that would have oversight of the records management systems.[32]

---

[29] Constitution of the ICPO—Interpol 2017, Articles 31–33.

[30] Fooner 1989, p. 71.

[31] Népote 1975, p. 182–184.

[32] Martha 2010, p. 95.

The new Headquarters Agreement between INTERPOL and France, which entered into force on 1 September 2009, provided for the control of INTERPOL's files by an independent body rather than a Supervisory Board. Thus, the Commission for the Control of INTERPOL's Files (the CCF) became one of the bodies of the Organization, currently tasked with a supervisory and advisory role, and vested with responsibility for processing requests for access to and correction and / or deletion of data in the INTERPOL Information System.

32.3.2 The Deliberative Entities

Four deliberative bodies—the General Assembly, the Executive Committee, the NCBs, and the Commission for the Control of INTERPOL's Files—constitute the organization's skeleton and define how it functions.

INTERPOL's Constitution establishes quite clearly in Article 6 that the General Assembly is the organization's highest governing body, composed of representatives appointed by the members of the organization who meet in ordinary sessions annually to carry out the duties laid down in the Constitution, determine principles and lay down the general measures suitable for attaining the objectives of the Organization, examine and approve the activities prepared by the General Secretariat for the coming year, determine any regulation deemed necessary, elect persons to perform the functions mentioned in the Constitution, adopt resolutions and make recommendations to members, determine the financial policy of the organization, and examine and approve any agreements to be made with other organizations.[33] Although the General Assembly is supreme in all matters related to INTERPOL, it has no actual power over the activities of the law enforcement agencies of the member countries, limiting itself solely to recommendations on matters of police business, policy, and suggestions on particular actions.

According to Article 22 of the INTERPOL Constitution, the Executive Committee, headed by the organization's president, is the organ tasked with supervising the execution of General Assembly decisions, the administration and work of the Secretary General, and exercising all the powers delegated to it by the Assembly. The Executive Committee is composed of the president of the organization, the three vice-presidents, and nine delegates. In order to preserve geographical diversity, the Constitution ensures that there shall never be two persons belonging to the same country holding a post in the Executive Committee at the same time, and at all times all four continents should be represented.[34]

The predecessor to INTERPOL's current General Secretariat was the ICPC International Bureau created in Article 1(1) of the 1946 ICPC Constitution, which entrusted France with the *de facto* secretariat. It was only with the 1956 Constitution

---

[33] Constitution of the ICPO—Interpol 2017, Articles 6–14.

[34] Constitution of the ICPO—Interpol 2017, Articles 15–29.

revision that the organization moved away from this idea and established the international character of its General Secretariat. In serving as an international centre in the fight against ordinary crime, serving as technical and information centre, ensuring the efficient administration of the organization, maintaining contact with national and international authorities, and producing any publication which may be considered useful, the General Secretariat, located in Lyon, is responsible for the implementation of the decisions of INTERPOL's governing bodies and the administration of the organization. The Secretariat is constituted by the permanent departments of the organization, including the directorates and offices at headquarters, the regional offices (Argentina, El Salvador, Cameroon, Côte d'Ivoire, Kenya, Zimbabwe, and Thailand), and three liaison offices outside France (United States, Belgium, and the Netherlands).

Furthermore, each member must appoint a National Central Bureau, which acts as a liaison between the Secretariat and domestic government departments. The National Central Bureaus is a unique concept of international police cooperation, developed to ensure active cooperation among member countries and the organization, ensuring rapid contact with the various police enforcement bodies in the country, other National Central Bureaus, and the General Secretariat. Thus, in the fight against transnational crime, each member nation of INTERPOL establishes and controls its own National Central Bureau, in effect, a point of contact among member countries for coordination of international investigations, transmitting assistance requests, exchanging information, or facilitating investigations.[35] Moreover, the legal status of the NCB is a subject of debate. While NCBs are mentioned in Article 5 of the Constitution as being part of the organization's structure, they are designated, staffed, and equipped by national governments, leading most scholars, and case law, to consider NCBs as not part of the organization.

Article 5 of the Constitution deems advisors as part of the organization. These advisors, according to Article 34, are appointed to be available for consultation on scientific matters. Article 35 of the Constitution deems that these Advisors shall be appointed for three years by the Executive Committee, and their appointment is definite only after notification by the General Assembly. Advisors, who must be chosen from among those who have a world-wide reputation, may be requested to submit reports, may be consulted individually or collectively, and may attend meetings of the General Assembly and may partake in discussions, but are not able to vote.

Contained in Article 5 of the Constitution as part of the organization, the Commission for the Control of INTERPOL's Files (CCF) was introduced in 2008 by amendment as the organization's response to the need for internal modes of dispute settlement.[36] The CCF is an independent body tasked with ensuring that the processing of personal information by the organization is in compliance with the regulations of the organization, advising the organization about any project, operation, set of rules or other matter involving the processing of personal information, and processing

---

[35] Constitution of the ICPO—Interpol 2017, Articles 31–33.
[36] Wellens 2002, p. 209–212.

requests concerning the information contained in the organization's files. To better accomplish the constitutional tasks, the CCF consists of two chambers: the Supervisory and Advisory Chamber, which ensures that the processing of personal data is done in compliance with the organization's internal rules, and provides the organization with advice about projects involving the processing of personal data; the Requests Chamber, which examines and decides on requests for access to data, and/or for the correction or deletion of data processed in the INTERPOL Information System. If the Requests Chamber finds that data has not been processed in accordance with the organization's rules, its decision on the corrective actions to be taken with regard to such data and other remedies is final and binding for the organization and the applicant.

32.4 Instruments of International Police Cooperation

32.4.1 Aims and Purposes

INTERPOL's main objective is to promote international police cooperation within the laws of the different member countries and establish and develop institutions likely to contribute effectively to combating crime. The two legs of the organization's aim and purposes rest on Articles 2 and 3 of its Constitution.

Article 2 of INTERPOL's Constitution expressly incorporates the principle of the rule of law, stating that the organization aims to "ensure and promote the widest possible mutual assistance between all criminal police authorities within the limits of the laws existing in the different countries and in the spirit of the "Universal Declaration of Human Rights."" Furthermore, Article 3 proscribes political and ideological neutrality and prohibits the organization from interfering in any matter of a political, religious, or racial character, stating that "It is strictly forbidden for the organization to undertake any intervention or activities of a political, military, religious or racial character."

These articles reflect the view that international police cooperation through INTERPOL's channels will be legitimate only if the organization observes the rule of law, and therefore, it is up to the General Secretariat to monitor and check that any request made by National Central Bureaus does not violate these articles.

The organization has four core functions: (i) Secure Global police communications services, (ii) operational data services and databases for police, (iii) operational police support services, and (iv) training.[37]

From its inception, one of the organizations' core functions has been to secure police communications, enabling law enforcement agencies to exchange information securely and rapidly. INTERPOL's current internet-based global communication

---

[37] Kersten 2005, pp 40–50.

system is known as I-24/7, and it connects member countries, allowing for fast and secure access to databases.

The organization's role operating databases can be traced back to Article 1(b) of the 1939 Constitution, and the current Article 26(b) and (c) of the Constitution, which states that the General Secretariat shall serve as an international centre in the fight against ordinary crime, and as a technical and information centre. Thus, the organization maintains a range of global databases, covering data such as names of individuals, wanted persons, fingerprints, photographs, DNA, stolen and lost travel documents, INTERPOL notices, etc.

The third core function of the organization is the circulation of information about wanted persons, persons with criminal records and dangerous people, and request Members' assistance for their apprehension via INTERPOL notices. Notices concern individuals wanted for serious crimes, missing persons, unidentified bodies, possible threats and criminals' modus operandi, stolen property notices, summary reports, and technical brochures. These notices are single color-coded sheets summarizing the identity particulars and legal information of international fugitives and suspects.

INTERPOL's fourth core function, to promote training and development to combat modern criminality, is fulfilled through the International Anti-corruption Academy, based in Luxemburg, Austria, and initiated by the United Nations Office on Drugs and Crime, INTERPOL, the European Anti-Fraud Office (OLAF), the Republic of Austria, and other stakeholders.

32.4.2 The Notice System

The unique wanted notice system[38] is perhaps the organization's most important feature, and it has become an essential instrument of international police cooperation, reflecting the organization's pragmatic approach to law enforcement cooperation. The notice system offers a simple method by which a police officer can reach beyond the borders of their jurisdiction, and it seems economical in terms of time and energy, given that any of these notices trigger the obligation under Article 31 of the Constitution for the active cooperation of all other member nations in the apprehension and extradition of the wanted subject.

The Red Notice is the organization's most sensitive notice, requesting member countries for either detention or arrest of a wanted person with a view of extradition based on an arrest warrant. The idea is that, upon the specific request of a member NCB, the General Secretariat will issue a red notice if certain criteria are met.[39] First, the offender must be described sufficiently to permit his identification, with identity details such as name, aliases, place and date of birth, physical description, fingerprints, photograph, and other relevant information, such as languages spoken,

---

[38] The notice system has been codified in Interpol's Rules on the Processing of data (III/IRPD/GA/2011).

[39] INTERPOL's Rules on the Processing of data, (III/IRPD/GA/2011), Article 83.

identity document number, etc. Second, the request must be accompanied with judicial information covering the offence, or investigation relating to the request, law under which the charge is made, or conviction was obtained, the penalty, and an arrest warrant issued by the corresponding authority. There must also be a commitment from the requesting NCB to request extradition of the wanted person as soon as the person is detained.

Issuing Red Notices is an exclusive power of the General Secretariat, which distributes such notices to all member NCBs, and thus the General Secretariat must ensure that all the criteria are satisfied. If there is a disagreement on this point, the Secretary General must take steps to resolve the problem. In any event, while many member countries acknowledge a Red Notice as a valid request for provisional arrest, acting on a wanted notice is wholly within the discretionary power of each member country, and they are not obliged to detain, arrest, or extradite anyone unless they wish to.

Another important notice diffused via INTERPOL's channels is the Blue Notice. The purpose of this notice is to obtain additional police information about a person, for example, to check his identity, obtain a more complete list of his convictions, or to discover his recent location or destination. The General Secretariat issues these inquiries without seeking arrest or any other action.

INTERPOL's General Secretariat also circulates Green Notices. A Green Notice is published to warn about a person's criminal activities. Green Notices may only be published under a specific series of conditions: the person must be considered to be a threat to public safety, as assessed by a national law enforcement authority or an international entity, based on the person's previous criminal conviction(s), and sufficient data concerning the threat is provided for the warning to be relevant. A Green Notice may only be published if the NCB provides sufficient identifiers, such as either family name, forename, sex, date of birth, physical description, DNA profile, fingerprints or data contained in identity documents, or a photograph of good quality, along with at least one identifier such as an alias, the name of the parents, or a specific physical characteristic.

INTERPOL circulates Yellow Notices to locate a missing person or to identify a person unable to identify himself, when the person's disappearance or discovery has been reported, and sufficient data is provided for his identification. Identifiers required for the publication of a yellow notice include: the family name, forename, sex, date of birth, and physical description, a photograph, DNA profile or fingerprints.

The General Secretariat publishes Black Notices to help in the identification of dead bodies. Publication and diffusion of a black notice must comply with a series of conditions: the discovery of the dead body has been recorded by police, the body has not been identified, and enough data on this body is provided for positive identification. Black notices are published if the NCB provides sufficient identifiers, such as a photograph, fingerprints, and/or DNA profile.

INTERPOL also circulates Purple Notices, published to warm about *modus operandi*, objects, devices or concealment methods used by offenders, and/or to request information on offences to resolve them or assist in their investigation. If the facts are no longer under investigation, a purple notice may be published: if the modus operandi is known in detail, is complex or different from other identified modus operandi for similar offences, the publication of the notice is intended to prevent these offences from being repeated, the request includes enough data on the modus operandi, objects, equipment or hiding places used by perpetrators to allow effective prevention, and the request provides sufficient identifiers for matches to be made with similar offences. If the facts are still under investigation, a purple notice may be published if they are serious offences, the offences draw the attention of the organization's members to a specific modus operandi, object, device or concealment method, and the request includes enough data on this modus operandi, and these objects, equipment or hiding places for matches to be made.

Orange Notices are published by INTERPOL to notify its members about events, persons, objects, processes or modus operandi that represent an imminent threat to public safety involving damage to property or injury to persons. In the case of a person, an orange notice is published if the persons are considered to represent an imminent threat to public safety or are preparing to commit a particularly serious ordinary-law crime, based on the assessment made by a national law enforcement agency or an international entity. Orange notices are published for objects, events, or modus operandi when they are considered an imminent threat to public safety, based on the assessment made by national law enforcement agencies. Moreover, measures taken by NCBs that receive these orange notices are entirely discretionary.

Stolen works of article notices are published by the General Secretariat to help in the location of stolen works of article or items of cultural value, or in their identification upon discovery. This notice may only be published if the work of article or item of cultural value is of interest in a criminal investigation, and the work of article or item of cultural value has some unique characteristic and/or commercial value. The General Secretariat may publish special notices related to requests made by the United Nations and other private entities with whom it cooperates in data-processing matters, insofar as these notices are relevant to the accomplishment of INTERPOL's aims and activities.

INTERPOL members can also distribute information about suspects, or request cooperation of one kind or another, by issuing diffusions. The organization's diffusion system provides NCBs with standardized requests for cooperation that can be distributed to either a limited number of members or as many countries as the issuing country wishes, and the criteria the General Secretariat establishes for notices need not be met. In general, NCBs issue diffusions as an interim step: to distribute a request and to obtain international cooperation from other members quickly, or if it is unable to submit to the General Secretariat all the information that is required for the publication of a notice. As such, the diffusion system has been used by certain members to harass individuals for whom the General Secretariat has rejected the issuance of a notice, which has been met with disapproval by human rights watchdogs.

32.4.3 Criticism

As the longest-running international organization dedicated to international police cooperation among a plethora of member countries, INTERPOL is not beyond reproach. In 2011, the International Consortium of Investigative Journalists indicated that at least 17 countries, including China, Iran, Pakistan and Venezuela, used Red Notices to restrain political opponents, economic targets or environmental activists.[40] Recently, China, Russia and Turkey have been criticized for using INTERPOL to pursue their critics abroad.[41] And while democratic governments are unwilling to extradite individuals to countries where torture is widely practiced, the publication of a Red Notice can have devastating effects on individuals, making it difficult for them to open a bank account, find employment, or travel.

Two main problems exist with the Red Notice system. The first one is an administrative problem in how INTERPOL deals with the arrest warrants that are required to publish a Red Notice. The organization simply does not have the manpower to adequately review each application made by requesting governments before issuing a Red Notice. This is not to say checks and balances do not exist—they do, but the process is largely based on faith in the good intentions of the requesting NCB. The system, created to fight against transnational crime and geared towards maintaining police cooperation, is weighted in favour of law enforcement.[42] With its entire operations based on the presumption that NCBs are responsible for the quality of the data they record[43] and transmit in the INTERPOL Information System, and that the data recorded is accurate and relevant,[44] there is very little by way of protection to keep states from misusing the process.

Second, INTERPOL has not established a sufficient appeal system through which the subject of a Notice can challenge the charges against them. Even though the Commission for the Control of Interpol's Files (CCF) has recently undergone important changes in its effort to modernize itself, it remains opaque, overburdened and slow. Removing a Red Notice subject name from the INTERPOL Information System is a long and arduous process. On the one hand, this is because the CCF only meets four times per year to deal with possibly dozens of challenges over five days. On the other, it is because the CCF is not empowered to conduct an investigation, to weigh evidence, or to make a determination on the merits of a case. This is a major flaw of the Commission because the submission of evidence that would support a contrary account to the one offered by the NCB would require the Commission to

---

[40] Sandoval Palos R, Interpol reacts to ICIJ story. International Consortium of Investigative Journalists. 20 July 2011, available at: https://www.icij.org/investigations/interpols-red-flag/interpol-reacts-icij-story/ Accessed 5 August 2020.

[41] Editorial Board. Interpol is now a crime victim. 21 March 2018, available at: https://www.bloomberg.com/view/articles/2018-03-21/russia-spy-poisoning-interpol-is-also-a-crime-victim Accessed 5 August 2020.

[42] Stalcup 2013, p. 241.

[43] Interpol's Rules on the Processing of data, (III/IRPD/GA/2011), Article 12(2).

[44] Interpol's Rules on the Processing of data, (III/IRPD/GA/2011), Article 12(1).

32 INTERPOL

689

evaluate the reliability of the evidence in a manner which, by its own admission, is not permitted. But that is not all—the Statute is unclear as to the process to obtain interim measures, and having a Red Notice suspended while the Commission investigates the substance of the claim is as difficult, if not more, than to actually request the deletion of said Notice.

While INTERPOL does have measures to protect the rights of individuals, and the CCF does identify and address requests, its limits and its lack of transparency are clear. The question is, then, how long before its effectiveness is successfully challenged in domestic courts—a blow that would endanger the very existence of the organization.

32.5 Conclusion

Transnational crimes affect many aspects of society, and there is no doubt they have an important impact on economic development and national security: drug trafficking, arms trafficking and money laundering are often considered the scourges of the modern world. Moreover, when addressing the fight against transnational crimes, governments have often been reluctant to cooperate, with various countries turning a blind eye, condoning or even sponsoring activities involving them.

Although INTERPOL's foundation differs from the more traditional international organizations, INTERPOL has been recognized by the United Nations and by states such as the United States and France (where the organization has its headquarters). The police organization still faces many criticisms, with some focusing on its unique legal basis, some on the adequacy of its independent control mechanisms, and others pointing towards the dangers that its police cooperation framework can be misused for political purposes.

What is distinctive in INTERPOL's experience is its approach to transnational crime, putting an emphasis on international cooperation in the exchange of information concerning the crime and its perpetrators. In this, the organization's success is beyond doubts: it is a police organization without the typical police powers associated with it (i.e., arrest, investigation, search, or seizure), and yet, INTERPOL has successfully utilized its power to build databases and share data to help member nations fight transnational crimes effectively. As a result, in recent years, INTERPOL has expanded its scope of activities to include criminal intelligence analysis, coordination of international police operations, and police training and professional development.

INTERPOL's crown jewel, obviously, is the notice system that helps police agencies fight crimes and criminals not excluded by Article 3 of the organization's Constitution. In addition to the red notice, a provisional arrest requests, NCBs may also employ blue notices to request additional information about a person's identity or illegal activities, or green notices to warn other NCBs about criminals who are likely to commit similar crimes in other countries.

Valid criticisms aside, member states seem to be satisfied with INTERPOL and its role in the fight against transnational crime, a circumstance that seems to be strengthened by the fact that the number of notices published each year has grown exponentially over the past years.

References

Fitzmaurice M (1998) Expression of Consent to be Bound by a Treaty as Developed in Certain Environmental Treaties. In: Klabbers J, Lefeber R (eds) Essays on the Law of Treaties – A Collection of Essays in Honour of Bert Vierdag. Martinus Nijhoff Publishers, The Hague, pp. 59-80

Fooner M (1973) Interpol: The Inside Story of the International Crime-Fighting Organization. Henry Regnery Co., Chicago

Fooner M (1989) INTERPOL. Issues in World Crime and International Criminal Justice. Plenum Press, New York

Giuliano M, Scovazzi T, Treves T (1991) Diritto internazionale. Giuffré, Milan

Interpol General Secretariat (2013) Annual Report. 82nd Interpol General Assembly, Cartagena, Colombia

Interpol General Secretariat (2018) Fact Sheet: Command and Coordination Centre. Lyon, France

Kersten U (2005) Enhancing International Law Enforcement Co-operation: A Global Overview by INTERPOL. In: Aromaa K, Viljanen T (eds) Enhancing International Law Enforcement Co-operation including Extradition Measures. Criminal Justice Press, Monsey, NY, pp. 40–50

Martha R S J (2010) The legal foundations of Interpol. Hart Publishing, Oxford/Portland, OR

Népote J (1975) The Future of International Police Cooperation: A Project and an Idea. International Criminal Police Review 293

Népote J (1977) Interpol: The Development of International Policing. In: Stead PJ (ed) Pioneers in Policing. Patterson Smith, Montclair, NJ

Népote J (1978) International Crime, International Police Cooperation and Interpol. Police Journal 21.2:125–135

Sands Ph, Klein P (eds) (2001) Bowett's Law of International Institutions, 5th edn. Sweet & Maxwell, London

Savino M (2012) Due Process for "Soft" Global Administrative Powers? The Case of Interpol Red Notices. In: Carotti B, Casini L, Cassese S, Cavalieri E, MacDonald E (eds) The Gal Casebook, 3rd edn., pp. 125–132

Schermers HG, Blokker NM (2003) International Institutional Law: Unity within Diversity. Martinus Nijhoff Publishers, Boston

Stalcup M (2013) Interpol and the Emergence of Global Policing. In: Garriot W (ed) Policing and Contemporary Governance: The Anthropology of Police in Practice. Palgrave MacMillan, New York, pp. 231–261

United Nations General Assembly (2003) Report of the International Law Commission on the Work of its 55th Session. United Nations, New York

Wellens K (2002) Remedies Against International Organisations. Cambridge University Press, Cambridge

Evhen Tsybulenko is an Estonian Legal Scholar of Ukrainian descent. In 2000, he earned a Ph.D. in International Law from Kyiv National University, Ukraine, and carried out postdoctoral research at the International Human Rights Law Institute of De Paul University, USA, in 2002. In Ukraine, he worked at the International Committee of the Red Cross (ICRC) and the Kyiv International University where he is a Professor since 2009. In Estonia, he was elected as a Professor of Law (2005) and appointed Chair of International and Comparative Law Department at the Tallinn University of Technology's Law School (2005–2010). Currently he is a Senior lecturer at the same School. He was a Founder and Director of the Tallinn Law School's Human Rights Centre (2007–2014). He was also an Adjunct (Visiting) Professor and Senior Visiting Mentor at the Joint Command and General Staff Course (JCGSC) at Baltic Defence College (2007–2013). He published over 40 books and academic articles and more than 200 general interest articles, comments and interviews in 15 countries, mainly in Ukrainian or Russian, but also in English and other languages. He cooperates, as an external expert, with the ICRC, Estonian Red Cross, Estonian Integration Commission, Directorate-General for Education and Culture of the European Commission, and the Organization for Security and Co-operation in Europe (OSCE).

Sebastian Suarez is an Argentinian lawyer holding a Master in International and Comparative Law (Estonia), and founder of Equinord—International Law Counsellors, a law firm dedicated exclusively to assist private individuals and States in challenging the INTERPOL Notices system.

Chapter 33
United Nations Educational, Scientific and Cultural Organization (UNESCO)

Umesh Kadam

> *...since wars begin in the minds of men, it is in the minds of men that the defences of peace must be constructed...*
> *Preamble, UNESCO Constitution*

Contents

33.1 UNESCO as an Intergovernmental Organization 694
    33.1.1 Historical Background 694
    33.1.2 Purposes 695
    33.1.3 Structure 696
33.2 UNESCO—Peace, Security and Conflict 699
    33.2.1 Education, Peace and Conflict 701
    33.2.2 Initiatives to Minimize Threats to Peace 705
33.3 Protection of Cultural Property During Armed Conflicts 708
33.4 Advances in Science for Peace 709
33.5 New Weapons Technologies 710
33.6 UNESCO and International Politics—Impact on Peace and Security 712
33.7 Conclusion 714
References 715

Abstract UNESCO was created as a part of the United Nations system against the background of World War II with a view to contributing to the overall efforts of the United Nations to avert future wars by promoting peace and security through the advancement and application of education, science and culture to international understanding and human welfare. After having explained the background, structure and purposes of UNESCO, this chapter proceeds to examine its mission and activities that directly and indirectly contribute to the realization of its primary objective of promotion of peace. It also looks at how UNESCO has evolved over a period of more than seven decades of its existence. Given the structure, membership and voting system of UNESCO, the Organization is bound to be affected by international political and economic undercurrents that prevail at any given time. Immediately after its creation, it became clear that the Organization's mandate can be used to pursue

U. Kadam (✉)
Independent Consultant, Pune, India

© T.M.C. ASSER PRESS and the authors 2022
S. Sayapin et al. (eds.), *International Conflict and Security Law*,
https://doi.org/10.1007/978-94-6265-515-7_33

political interests of groups of States. The chapter outlines some of the major political factors that have influenced policy and decision making in UNESCO: - the Cold War, decolonization and the consequent third-world majoritarianism, the Middle East imbroglio and international trade. It also gives an overview of some of the controversies with which it got entangled. Finally, it makes a critical assessment of UNESCO's contribution to peace, security and conflict prevention.

Keywords UNESCO · Education · Science · Technology · Culture · Peace · Conflict · Security · World Heritage

33.1 UNESCO as an Intergovernmental Organization

33.1.1 Historical Background

The United Nations Educational, Scientific and Cultural Organization (UNESCO) was established in November 1946 as a specialized agency of the United Nations to function under the auspices of the Economic and Social Council.[1] The idea of establishing a body to promote international cooperation in the field of education can be traced back to the League of Nations that set up the International Commission on Intellectual Cooperation in January 1922, as a consultative organ composed of individuals elected based on their personal qualifications.[2] The International Institute for Intellectual Cooperation was then created in Paris on 9 August 1925, to act as the executing agency for the Commission.[3] To begin with, an International Bureau of Education was set up in December 1925.[4] Eventually, the outbreak of World War II hampered its functioning.[5] When serious negotiations to set up the United Nations started, the idea of facilitating socio-economic cooperation at the international level was revived and a Conference of Allied Ministers of Education was constituted in November 1942.[6] Following a strong and serious commitment of leaders of Allied Powers to establish the United Nations, the Conference of Allied Ministers of Education continued to discuss the possibility of creation of an international agency to facilitate cooperation in the field of education.[7] This was endorsed by the United Nations Conference on International Organization, held in San Francisco from April to June 1945, and recommended to organize a United Nations Conference

---

[1] United Nations Charter, Article 57 and Article 63.

[2] UNESCO, https://atom.archives.unesco.org/international-institute-of-intellectual-co-operation. Accessed 10 February 2022.

[3] Ibid.

[4] Ibid.

[5] Ibid., p. 2.

[6] Ibid.

[7] Ibid.

33 United Nations Educational, Scientific and Cultural … 695

for the establishment of an educational and cultural organization.[8] This Conference took place in London in November 1945 in which 44 governments participated.[9] The Conference approved the Constitution of proposed UNESCO that came into force in November 1946 when it received the required twentieth ratification.[10]

33.1.2 Purposes

All the major restructuring of international relations and the new world order that was discussed and debated since the early days of World War II, or even earlier, revolves around ensuring peace and security as the paramount goal of the proposed institutional arrangements for the world in twentieth century.[11] In keeping with this and the broader objectives of the United Nations to achieve international cooperation by addressing socio-economic and cultural challenges, UNESCO's main purpose is 'to contribute to peace and security by promoting collaboration among the nations through education, science and culture' with a view to promote universal respect for justice, for the rule of law and for the human rights and fundamental freedoms for all without adverse distinction on the basis of race, sex, language or religion.[12]

UNESCO is expected to realize its purpose by undertaking a number of activities and initiatives. First, it is supposed to collaborate in the work of advancing the mutual knowledge and understanding of peoples.[13] To this end, it may explore various means of mass communication and recommend necessary international agreements to promote the free flow of ideas.[14] Secondly, it may give fresh impulse to popular education and to the spread of culture through the development of educational activities; advancement of the ideal of equality of educational opportunity without any discrimination on the basis of race or sex and without socio-economic distinctions, and by suggesting educational methods best suited to prepare the children of the world for the responsibilities of freedom.[15] Finally, it is expected to maintain, increase and diffuse knowledge through facilitating conservation and protection of the world's inheritance of books, works of article and monuments of history and science.[16] For this purpose, it may recommend conclusion of necessary international conventions and encourage co-operation among the nations in all branches of intellectual activity.[17] There is a strong emphasis on international exchange of persons active in

---

[8] Ibid.

[9] Ibid.

[10] See, generally, UNESCO 1946.

[11] Amrith and Sluga 2008, p. 254.

[12] UNESCO Constitution, Article I.1.

[13] Ibid., Article I.2(a).

[14] Ibid.

[15] Ibid., Article I.2(b).

[16] Ibid., Article 1.2(c).

[17] Ibid.

the fields of education, science and culture, the exchange of publications, objects of artistic and scientific interest and other materials of information.[18] One way in which expansion and diffusion of knowledge can be achieved is through granting access to the printed and published materials produced by any of the States to people around the world.[19]

33.1.3 Structure

UNESCO is an autonomous specialized agency of the United Nations that is affiliated with the latter through a relationship agreement that came into force on 14th December 1946. All members of the United Nations have a right to become a member of UNESCO, they are not automatically its members. A State can become a member by depositing an instrument of acceptance of the Constitution.[20] States that are not members of the United Nations may be admitted by the General Conference by a two thirds majority vote upon recommendation of the Executive Board.[21] Non self-governing territories may also be admitted as Associate Members by the General Conference with a two thirds majority vote.[22] UNESCO has three principal organs: the General Conference, the Executive Board, and the Secretariat that is headed by a Director-General.

The General Conference is the plenary body in which all members are represented. Each member can appoint five delegates.[23] It is the main policy-making body that decides main areas of work of UNESCO. It takes decisions on programmes submitted to it by the Executive Board. It has authority to convene international governmental or non-governmental conferences on issues falling within the purview of UNESCO.[24] It can adopt recommendations with a majority vote and approve international conventions with a two-thirds majority.[25] Members are expected to submit recommendations or conventions to domestic legislative or similar bodies within one year from the close of the session during which they were adopted or approved. They are also expected to submit reports on action taken upon the recommendations and conventions to the General Conference.[26] It also acts as an advisory body to the United Nations on issues concerning education, science and culture.[27] Its decisions are taken by a

---

[18] Ibid.

[19] Ibid.

[20] Ibid., Article XV.1.

[21] Ibid., Article II.2.

[22] Ibid., Article II.3.

[23] Ibid., Article IV.A.1.

[24] Ibid., Article IV.B.3.

[25] Ibid., Article IV.B.6.

[26] Ibid., Article VIII.

[27] Ibid., Article IV.B.5.

simple majority vote except on certain issues where the Constitution requires two-thirds majority. It meets twice a year in ordinary sessions, though extraordinary sessions can be convened at its own initiative or at the suggestion of the Executive Board or one-third of members. It can allow public access to its meeting and participation of observers after following certain procedural formalities.[28]

The Executive Board consisting of fifty-eight Member States is elected by the General Conference taking into account diversity of cultures and geographic distribution.[29] The President of the General Conference acts as an advisor of the Board.[30] Each Member of the Board is represented by only one representative.[31] They are expected to be experts and experienced in one or more fields of competence of UNESCO.[32] Until 1993, members of the Board were not individuals representing member states, but persons appointed in their personal capacity on the basis of their expertise in the arts, the humanities, the sciences, education and the diffusion of ideas. The amended Constitution strikes a balance between the need to ensure representative character of the Board and competence of its members in one or more areas of UNESCO's work. Their term of office starts at the end of the session of General Conference which elected them until the close of the second ordinary session of the Conference following that election.[33]

The Board prepares the agenda for the General Conference, it examines the programme of work for the Organization and corresponding budget estimates and submits them to the General Conference with its recommendations.[34] As the title indicates, it is the executive body of UNESCO that implements the programme adopted by the Conference.[35] It is responsible for taking necessary measures to ensure the effective and rational execution of the programme by the Director General, with due regard to circumstances arising between two ordinary sessions.[36] When the General Conference is not in session, it takes over the advisory function of the Conference.[37] It recommends to the General Conference the admission of new Members to the Organization.[38] It meets in regular session at least four times during a biennium and may meet in special session if summoned by the Chairman on his initiative or upon the request of six Board members.[39] Report of the activities of UNESCO prepared by the Director-General is presented to the Conference by the Board's

---

[28] Ibid., Article IV.D.12.

[29] Ibid., Article V.A.1(a) and Article V.A.3.

[30] Ibid., Article V.A.1(a).

[31] Ibid., Article V.A.2.

[32] Ibid., Article V.A.2(b).

[33] Ibid.

[34] Ibid., Article V.B.6(a).

[35] Ibid., Article V.B.6(b).

[36] Ibid.

[37] Ibid., Article V.B.6(c).

[38] Ibid., Article V.B.7.

[39] Ibid., Article V.B.9.

698 U. Kadam

Chairman with comments, if any.[40] The Board functions as a representative body of the General Conference when the latter is not in session and, as such, the Conference may delegate some of its powers to the Board.[41]

The Secretariat consists of a Director General and necessary administrative staff.[42] The Director General, who is the chief administrative officer of the Organization, is appointed for a term of six years by the General Conference upon nomination by the Executive Board.[43] He or she can be reappointed for a maximum one more term.[44] The Director General is entitled to participate in all meetings of the General Conference, of the Executive Board, and of the Committees of the Organization.[45] It is his or her responsibility to formulate proposals for appropriate action by the Conference and the Board, prepare for submission to the Board a draft programme of work for the Organization with budget estimates, prepare periodical reports on the activities of the Organization and send them to Member States and to the Executive Board.[46]

The Director General is also responsible for appointing the staff of the Secretariat taking into account requirements of highest standards of integrity, efficiency, technical competence and geographic representation.[47] All staff of the Secretariat including the Director General are expected to function as international civil servants, and not as representatives of the States to which they belong, in the best interest of the Organization.[48]

UNESCO's headquarters is in Paris. It has 193 Members and 11 Associate Members.[49] It has 53 field offices in different regions of the world.[50] With a view to facilitating the implementation of UNESCO's agenda at the national level, the Constitution recommends setting up of National Commissions comprising of representations from main national entities devoted to education, science and culture. So far, 199 Members have established National Commissions.[51] They serve as a link between UNESCO and public at large and advise their governments and the delegations that attend UNESCO General Conference on issues under its consideration.[52]

---

[40] Ibid., Article V.B.10.

[41] Ibid., Article V.B.13.

[42] Ibid., Article VI.1.

[43] Ibid., Article VI.2.

[44] Ibid.

[45] Ibid., Article VI.3(a).

[46] Ibid.

[47] Ibid., Article VI.4.

[48] Ibid., Article VI.5.

[49] UNESCO, Member States, https://en.unesco.org/countries/member-states. Accessed 23 July 2020.

[50] UNESCO, Field Offices, https://en.unesco.org/countries/field-offices. Accessed 23 July 2020.

[51] UNESCO, National Commissions, https://en.unesco.org/countries/national-commissions. Accessed 23 July 2020.

[52] UNESCO Constitution, Article VII.2.

UNESCO's Constitution enables it to consult and co-operate with international non-governmental organizations devoted to main areas of work of the Organization.[53] They can be invited to undertake specific tasks in their area of work that is likely to contribute to realization of overall objectives of the Organization.[54]

33.2 UNESCO—Peace, Security and Conflict

In keeping with the fundamental objectives of the United Nations, the UNESCO Constitution commences with an affirmation that wars begin in the minds of men and the defences of peace must be constructed in the minds of men.[55] To elaborate this affirmation, the Preamble further stresses that a peace based purely upon the political and economic arrangements of governments would not be a sustainable peace. Only the peace founded upon the intellectual and moral solidarity of mankind would be the lasting peace.[56] Acknowledging that propagation of racial inequality through ignorance and prejudice was one of the causes of World War II, it insists on the importance of wide diffusion of culture, promotion of education of humanity for justice and liberty and peace to ensure human dignity and equality. As we go deeper into UNESCO's purposes, policies and programmes adopted and implemented by it ever since its inception, it becomes apparent that the Organization's agenda is a part of a broader global campaign for promoting peace.[57] For UNESCO, peace is not a mere absence of hostilities; it presupposes existence of solidarity, concord and a concerted effort by all to achieve security and happiness, with a view to making war impossible by securing humane order in the relationship among all peoples of the world and to vanquishing causes of war through the social, material and moral progress of mankind.[58] As noted earlier, the very first purpose of UNESCO is

[t]o contribute to peace and security by promoting collaboration among the nations through education, science and culture in order to further universal respect for justice, for the rule of law and for the human rights and fundamental freedoms which are affirmed for the peoples of the world, without distinction of race, sex, language or religion, by the Charter of the United Nations.[59]

Thus, UNESCO was created to promote peace and security through the promotion and application of education, science and culture to international understanding and human welfare.[60] To this end, UNESCO has been mobilizing peace initiatives

---

[53] Ibid., Article XI.4.

[54] Ibid.

[55] Ibid., Preamble.

[56] Ibid.

[57] For a concise explanation of agendas of United Nations organs and bodies, see Ilcan and Phillips 2006, pp. 62–63.

[58] Valderrama 1995, p. 30.

[59] UNESCO Constitution, Article I.1.

[60] Valderrama 1995, p. 25.

and fostering security that aim to shape the future conduct of individuals, groups and populations.[61] Here the concept of security is much broader and goes beyond disarmament, pacific settlement of international disputes or peace-keeping initiatives that are State-centric. The UNESCO's Culture of Peace programme governs peace through rationalities or ways of thinking that are developed, disseminated and embodied in a diverse range of activities across the globe, including programmes of action, training and capacity-building and the dispersion of information with a focus on the individual rather than the State.[62] The Culture of Peace programme has evolved over the past several decades, especially after the 1990s. Today its scope has broadened to encompass all initiatives towards peace-building, mediation, conflict prevention and resolution, peace education, human rights education, education for non-violence, tolerance, acceptance, social cohesion, mutual respect, intercultural and interfaith dialogue and reconciliation, together with development considerations.[63] In view of UNESCO's commitment and work, it has been designated by the United Nations General Assembly as lead agency for the implementation of all resolutions related to the 'Culture of Peace'.[64] The United Nations General Assembly has defined the concept of culture of peace as consisting of

> (v)alues, attitudes and behaviours that reflect and inspire social interaction and sharing based on the principles of freedom, justice and democracy, all human rights, tolerance and solidarity, that reject violence and endeavour to prevent conflicts by tackling their root causes to solve problems through dialogue and negotiation and that guarantee the full exercise of all rights and the means to participate fully in the development process of their society.[65]

With a view to translating the concept of culture of peace and non-violence into action, UNESCO has launched a number of projects around the world that are organized into five thematic clusters.[66] These are:

i. Strengthening peace and non-violence through formal and non-formal education to achieve intercultural skills such as empathy, spontaneous solidarity and hospitality reflecting the diversity of contemporary societies in an active, honest and lasting dialogue;

ii. Fostering social cohesion and inclusion, pluralist and democratic participation and human rights, notably through the empowerment of women and youth;

iii. Harnessing the media and information and communication technologies to promote peace, non-violence, tolerance and intercultural dialogue;

iv. Promoting heritage and contemporary creativity as resilience tools for building harmonious interactions through dialogue;

---

[61] Ilcan and Phillips 2006, p. 60.

[62] Ibid., p. 69.

[63] UNESCO 2013, p. 6.

[64] Ibid.

[65] UNGA Res. A/RES/53/243.

[66] UNESCO 2013, p. 17.

v. Reinforcing the role of education, the sciences, culture, communication and information in their capacity to create sustainable and inclusive knowledge societies in all the regions of the world.[67]

33.2.1 Education, Peace and Conflict

33.2.1.1 Education for Peace

Since early days of its existence, UNESCO has insisted that the then existing inequality between nations constitutes a threat to world peace.[68] It placed emphasis on adult education in the field of culture, health and civic instruction, and making available didactic material.[69] It also undertook a thorough review of textbooks to expunge references to unpleasant historical past that promoted rift between peoples and societies and posed a threat to peace.[70] Eventually UNESCO emerged as the only United Nations agency with a mandate to cover all aspects of education. It provides global and regional leadership in education, strengthens education systems worldwide and responds to contemporary global challenges through education with gender equality as underlying principle.[71] It has been entrusted to lead the Global Education 2030 Agenda through Sustainable Development Goal 4. It has adopted the 'Education 2030 Framework for Action' that serves as a roadmap to achieve this goal.[72]

Lack of adequate education contributes to fuelling conflicts in many ways. For example, when large numbers of young people are denied access to a good quality education, the resulting poverty, unemployment and hopelessness can have catalytic effect on tempting such young persons to join armed militia.[73] An analysis of 120 countries over 30 years found that countries with large numbers of young men were less likely to experience violent conflict if their populations had higher levels of education.[74] Another contributory factor is inequality in education. Combined with wider disparity, it heightens the risk of conflict.[75] A study concluded in 2015 that drew on data from 100 countries over 50 years found that countries with higher levels of inequality in schooling due to ethnic and religious differences were much more

---

[67] For an elaborate explanation of each of these thematic areas, see UNESCO 2013, pp. 19–24.

[68] Valderrama 1995, p. 30.

[69] Ibid.

[70] Ibid., pp. 30–31.

[71] UNESCO, Education Transforms Lives, https://en.unesco.org/themes/education. Accessed 23 July 2020.

[72] Ibid.

[73] UNESCO 2017, p. 9.

[74] Ibid.

[75] Ibid.

likely to experience conflict.[76] Therefore, along with ensuring access to education, UNESCO also endeavours to ensure equality in education.

UNESCO's 'Framework for Action for Education 2030' reiterates its commitment to ensure that all learners acquire the knowledge and skills needed to promote sustainable development, including, among others, through promotion of a culture of peace and non-violence.[77] However, this is not new to UNESCO. At the Special Session of the United Nations General Assembly on disarmament held in 1978, the members urged UNESCO to step up its programme aimed at the development of disarmament education as a distinct field of study.[78] Following this, since early 1980s, UNESCO took an initiative to develop disarmament education as a distinct academic discipline and as a tool for mobilizing knowledgeable public opinion on questions of peace and war.[79] It was convinced that in addition to political will, the involvement in the decision-making process of well-informed and enlightened public opinion is equally important.[80] Since then, the Organization has consistently promoted disarmament education as a part of its larger agenda of 'education for peace' at various levels of study.

However, UNESCO's education for peace agenda programme is not free of controversies. It is linked to 'Education for All' (EFA) programme since objectives of peace agenda are integrated into the EFA programme. It is looked upon with suspicion since some US commentators claim that it promotes socialist agenda.

> Spearheaded by UNESCO, the EFA calls for a multi-billion dollar, ongoing program ostensibly to educate poor children worldwide. This is an enormous socialist ploy to transfer enormous sums of money to UN bureaucrats and brutal dictators, while building UNESCO into a global school board, with unprecedented resources and authority. UNESCO is now more dangerous than ever. President Bill Clinton tried to take the U.S. back into UNESCO in 1994, but conservatives blocked that effort.[81]

It is also claimed that UNESCO acts as a conduit for blatant Communist propaganda, a forum for virulent anti-Americanism, and an aggressive advocate for radical social engineering and that it acts as a daily forum for hate, recrimination, psychological warfare against freedom, and unrelenting moral aggression against peace.[82] As will be seen later, the United States has had a troubled relationship with UNESCO for many reasons since early 1980s. Needless to mention, UNESCO's objectives in promoting international peace and security through education can succeed only if there is a strong political will and necessary funding to realise them. Any such programme can succeed after years of concerted efforts. The results of such programmes are not immediately visible.

---

[76] Ibid.

[77] UNESCO 2015b, p. 21.

[78] Thee 1981, p. 328.

[79] Ibid., p. 12.

[80] Ibid.

[81] Jasper 2003.

[82] Ibid.

33.2.1.2 Protection of Education During Emergencies

In most situations of armed conflicts and violence, education is a major casualty. Deliberate or unintentional attacks on schools, killing and injuring teachers, insecure atmosphere leading to closure of schools invariably keep millions of children away from education. Depriving school-going children the right to education is a serious impairment of a vital human right of the new generation. Since UNESCO is the global coordinator of 'Education for All' programme, it has a mandate to promote full and equal opportunities for education for all, and this includes those whose access to education is hampered by situations of violence or armed conflict. In keeping with this broad objective, in times of emergencies, UNESCO helps strengthen education systems to ensure life-saving messages reach children and their families; protects children and youth from attack, abuse, and exploitation; supports peace-building; and provides physical and psychological safety to children.[83] It believes that investing in education in times of crises builds resilience and social cohesion across communities, and is fundamental to sustained recovery.[84]

During the recent past, UNESCO has taken a number of concrete steps to protect education from attack. In 2007, it commissioned a study to document in detail the incidence of attacks on schools, teachers and students and to draw attention to the need for concerted action to stop them.[85] Following this, in 2010 it published 'Protecting Education from Attack: A State-of-the-Article Review' with a view to enhancing global understanding of the nature, scope, motives and impact of attacks on education and of the work that is being done by communities, organizations and governments to prevent and respond to such violence.[86] Its concerted efforts on this front led to the creation of the inter-agency 'Global Coalition to Protect Education from Attack' (GCPCA). In December 2014, the Coalition adopted Guidelines for Protecting Schools and Universities from Military Use during Armed Conflict.[87]

In times of armed conflict, sometimes schools are deliberately targeted or they are destroyed in the course of attacks on military targets. Under international humanitarian law (IHL), deliberate attacks on civilian targets amount to serious war crimes.[88] An attack on buildings dedicated to education is a specific war crime under the Rome Statute of International Criminal Court.[89] However, when armed forces take shelter in abandoned or forcibly evicted schools in support of their military operations, the protection accorded to schools by IHL as civilian targets is lost and they can be

---

[83] UNESCO, Education in emergencies, https://en.unesco.org/themes/education-emergencies. Accessed 23 July 2020.

[84] Ibid.

[85] UNESCO, Protecting Education from Attack, https://en.unesco.org/themes/protecting-attack?language=en. Accessed 23 July 2020.

[86] Ibid. and UNESCO 2010, p. 3.

[87] GCPCA, http://www.protectingeducation.org/. Accessed 23 July 2020.

[88] ICRC, Customary IHL Database, Rule 156, https://ihl-databases.icrc.org/customary-ihl/eng/docs/v1_rul_rule156. Accessed 23 July 2020. Also see, Rome Statute of International Criminal Court, Article 8(2) (b) (ii).

[89] Article 8(2) (e) (iv).

lawfully attacked by the other party to the conflict. According to the GCPCA, fighting forces have used schools and universities for military purposes such as bases, firing positions, armouries, and detention centres in conflicts in at least 25 countries over the past decade because they are attracted by their often central location and ready for use infrastructure such as solid rooms, toilets, kitchens, and other facilities.[90]

The Guidelines for Protecting Schools and Universities from Military Use during Armed Conflict are addressed to States as well as non-state armed groups engaged in armed conflict. They provide a practical tool for preventing schools from becoming part of the front lines during war by promoting responsible practice by commanders and their troops to preserve schools for learning, the guidelines can help minimize the devastating impact of armed conflict on students.[91] The Guidelines are expected to be integrated into military doctrines and practices of parties to an armed conflict.[92]

UNESCO also addresses challenges associated with other emergencies such as natural disasters and pandemics. It helps to strengthen the capacities of its Member States to provide access to quality educational opportunities for all in times of such crises.[93] In all types of emergency situations, UNESCO engages with Ministries of Education to establish preparedness measures and its field offices located in different regions of the world strive to respond quickly in close partnership with local authorities to address threats to the education system and lead in the response and recovery efforts.[94]

The work of UNESCO in protecting education in all types of emergencies contributes to strengthening peace and security at the international, regional and national levels. However, this requires a strong commitment on the part of local partners—be they governmental or non-governmental—to support the Organization's efforts. In situations of non-international armed conflict, this presupposes convincing non-state armed group or groups to collaborate with the Organization and agree to follow its suggestions—a process that is fraught with many challenges. In many of such situations, non-state armed groups have a hostile attitude towards international agencies. Deliberate attacks on their staff, looting of their assets, hostage taking and blocking their access to affected areas is not uncommon. Some agencies like the International Committee of the Red Cross or the non-governmental organization Geneva Call are committed to convince non-state armed groups to respect IHL. A concerted effort in partnership between all such agencies and UNESCO will enable it to realise its objective of protecting education from attacks.

---

[90] GCPCA, http://www.protectingeducation.org/. Accessed 23 July 2020.

[91] Ibid.

[92] Guideline 6, GCPCA, http://protectingeducation.org/wp-content/uploads/documents/docume nts_guidelines_en.pdf. Accessed 23 July 2020.

[93] UNESCO, Protecting Education from Attack, https://en.unesco.org/themes/protecting-attack? language=en). Accessed 23 July 2020.

[94] Ibid.

33.2.2 Initiatives to Minimize Threats to Peace

33.2.2.1 Strengthening Human Security

In view of the fact that UNESCO's principal purpose is to 'contribute to peace and security by promoting collaboration among the nations through education, science and culture in order to further universal respect for justice, for the rule of law and for human rights and fundamental freedoms which are affirmed for the peoples of the world, without distinction of race, sex, language or religion', the Organization claims that human security is an integral part of its mission.[95] By human security in this sense we mean security from violence and crime as well as the security of people's livelihoods that would encompass economic security, food security, environmental security and health security.[96] UNESCO attempts to strengthen human security in three ways. First, its work in the fields of education, culture, sciences and communication and information is complementary to strengthening human security.[97] Second, it promotes national and local policies aimed at countering threats to human security.[98] Finally, it attempts to mobilize all relevant stakeholders, such as regional organizations, research institutions, civil society and non-governmental organizations to engage in long-term and integrated action targeting the needs of the most vulnerable segments of the population.[99] Thus, UNESCO's work in aforementioned areas is in conformity with other United Nations agencies, such as the UNDP,[100] to fortify human security at the local and national levels that would reduce global insecurity in terms of violence and conflict.

33.2.2.2 Combating Violent Extremism

In response to the attacks of September 11, 2001, UNESCO's General Conference adopted Resolution 39, in which it expressed 'its firm conviction that, based upon its mandate and within its areas of competence—education, science, culture and communication—UNESCO has a duty to contribute to the eradication of terrorism, drawing on its character as an intellectual and ethical organization,' and invited the Director-General to take appropriate action through UNESCO programmes and studies.[101] Thereafter UNESCO took some specific steps to contribute to the global counterterrorism measures. It has focused on sensitizing policymakers and civil society representatives to the importance of effective dialogue and constructive pluralism, such as dialogue among civilizations, cultures, and peoples, through its educational

---

[95] UNESCO 2008a, p. 5.

[96] Gomez and Gasper 2016, pp. 1–2.

[97] UNESCO 2008b, p 5.

[98] Ibid.

[99] Ibid.

[100] See also Chap. 36 by Homem de Siqueira et al.

[101] Chowdhury Fink 2012, p. 118.

programmes and intellectual activities.[102] These efforts of UNESCO are preventive in nature and ought to continue for a long term with a view to bring about transformation in the mind-set of people belonging to different cultures and faiths and imbibe a spirit of tolerance and mutual respect in the younger generation.

In July 2016, the United Nations General Assembly recognized the importance of preventing violent extremism as and when conducive to terrorism and, recommended that Member States consider the implementation of relevant recommendations of the Secretary-General's Plan of Action to Prevent Violent Extremism, as applicable to the national context.[103] In response to this initiative and recognizing that distorted interpretations of culture, hatred, and ignorance fuel extremism, UNESCO Member States decided to enhance its capacity to provide assistance to States as they craft sharper strategies to prevent violent extremism.[104] It decided to contribute to the Secretary-General's Plan of Action, with a focus on priorities of direct relevance to UNESCO's work.[105] Concretely speaking, UNESCO intends to work in four areas of particular interest to the Organization:

(a) Education as a tool to prevent violent extremism: UNESCO seeks to assist countries to deliver education programmes that build young people's resilience to violent extremist messaging and foster a positive sense of identity and belonging. This work is being undertaken within the framework of Global Citizenship Education.

(b) Youth participation and empowerment: The UNESCO Youth team focuses on creating an enabling environment for the empowerment and democratic participation of youth, in order to ensure that young women and men have the opportunities to become active global citizens.

(c) Media and online coalitions for preventing violent extremism: UNESCO is mobilizing stakeholders—particularly youth, policy-makers, researchers and media actors- to take effective actions, both online and offline, to prevent and respond to violent extremism and radicalization on the Internet.

(d) Celebrating cultural diversity: UNESCO is engaging youth in the protection of all forms of heritage and the promotion of cultural diversity to foster more fair, inclusive and peaceful societies, through the 'Unite for Heritage' campaign and 'Educational Programmes on Heritage and Creativity'.[106]

These initiatives, like UNESCO's education for peace programme, are long term initiatives that can bring about incremental change. However, one precondition for the success of such initiatives is existence of a strong sense of solidarity among its membership. Unfortunately, this is not the case, as will be seen later.

---

[102] Ibid., p. 119.

[103] UNGA Res. A/RES/70/291.

[104] UNESCO, Preventing Violent Extremism, https://en.unesco.org/preventing-violent-extremism. Accessed 23 July 2020.

[105] Ibid.

[106] Ibid.

33.2.2.3 Climate Change and Conflict

Today it is universally acknowledged that climate change is a serious threat to international peace and security.[107] The United Nations Secretary-General's 2009 Report *Climate Change and its Possible Security Implications* outlines key issues that establish a nexus between climate change and security.[108] UNESCO, on its part, has used its potential in the fields of science and education to facilitate exchange of data and ideas, create public awareness, addressing water security and promoting development of ocean sciences.[109] These are ultimately aimed at mitigation and adaptation solutions.[110]

33.2.2.4 Peace, Security and Culture

One of the purposes of UNESCO is to contribute to peace and security by promoting collaboration among the nations through culture. After having seen the devastating effects of the two World Wars, the international community realized the importance of protection of world cultural heritage as a powerful factor favourable to the peace between the people and intercultural societies.[111] To this end, UNESCO is spreading cultural values amongst its members by adopting international conventions and declarations on various aspects of protection of cultural heritage.[112]

Although these steps were taken to build international solidarity, the organization has faced many challenges and obstacles due to politicization of cultural collaboration. Developed countries have capably managed to comply with requirements of the elaborate and demanding UNESCO process of inscription of World Heritage list that requires many competencies in comparison with countries in a developmental stage.[113] As will be seen later, the UNESCO resolution on Jerusalem's holy sites has drawn heavy criticism from the United States and Israel. Some Western countries do not acknowledge the recognition of cultural diversity by favouring universality of culture.[114] Another instance of politicization of cultural collaboration is apparent in

---

[107] See generally Schorlemer and Maus 2014.

[108] UN GA Res. A/64/350.

[109] UNESCO 2015a, pp. 2–3.

[110] Ibid., p. 1.

[111] Brianso 2010, p. 169.

[112] The specific issues on which such instruments have been adopted so far include: importation of cultural materials, copyright protection, protection of cultural property during armed conflict, archaeological excavations, free access to museums, safeguarding the beauty and character of landscapes and sites, illicit trade in cultural property, international cultural cooperation, protection of world cultural heritage, avoidance of taxation of copyright royalties, cultural diversity, prevention of intentional destruction of cultural heritage, safeguarding of intangible cultural heritage, protection and promotion of diverse cultural expressions, underwater cultural heritage, performing arts, literature, etc.

[113] Brianso 2010, p. 167.

[114] Feigenbaum 2010, pp. 78–79.

the debate on 'trade and culture', especially in connection with the Convention on the Protection and Promotion of the Diversity of Cultural Expressions. It is unfortunate that national trade interests assume primacy over cultural collaboration.[115]

33.2.2.5 Communication and Conflict Prevention

UNESCO has a specific mandate to promote "the free flow of ideas by word and image" with a view to foster free, independent and pluralistic media in print, broadcast and online.[116] This is expected to enhance freedom of expression and contribute to peace, sustainability, poverty eradication and human rights.[117] From its early days, UNESCO has placed a strong emphasis on using and facilitating all means of communication in furtherance of attaining its core objectives. More specifically, UNESCO addressed the challenges posed by war propaganda since the early days of its existence pursuant to a resolution of the United Nations General Assembly of 8 November 1948 against war propaganda.[118] It went to the extent of claiming that war propaganda is a crime against humanity.[119] The initial responses of UNESCO were influenced by the events that led to the World War II. It reshaped its communication policy taking into account the changing security landscape at the international level and threats to peace that existed at any given time. In connection with recent developments concerning violent extremism, as noted earlier, UNESCO is now encouraging media and online coalitions to take effective actions, both online and offline, to prevent and respond to violent extremism and radicalization on the Internet.[120]

33.3 Protection of Cultural Property During Armed Conflicts

Wars and armed conflict invariably result in killing, injuring and displacing people as well as damaging and destroying property. Property that is damaged or destroyed during such situations often includes irreplaceable cultural heritage. Attacks on cultural property are attacks on the identity, memory, dignity and future of entire

---

[115] Rostam Neuwirth has elaborately demonstrated the impact of this debate, see, generally, Neuwirth 2006.

[116] UNESCO, Fostering Freedom of Expression. https://en.unesco.org/themes/fostering-freedom-expression. Accessed 23 July 2020.

[117] Ibid.

[118] Valderrama 1995, p. 45.

[119] Ibid., p. 137.

[120] UNESCO, Preventing Violent Extremism, https://en.unesco.org/preventing-violent-extremism. Accessed 23 July 2020.

populations.[121] Recognizing this major threat to the process of preservation and protection of cultural property, UNESCO took the initiative in the early 1950s that led to the adoption of binding legal norms for the protection of cultural property in the event of an armed conflict. This subject matter is specifically addressed in this book elsewhere.[122]

33.4 Advances in Science for Peace

One of the main purposes of UNESCO is to contribute to peace and security by promoting collaboration among the nations through science.[123] Since its establishment, the organization has taken a number of steps to facilitate such collaboration to foster a culture of peace. Its Medium Term Strategy for 2014–2021 acknowledges that peace and security remain key challenges.[124] It takes into account various challenges that pose a serious threat to global peace, such as the adverse impact of conflicts on development; needs of countries undergoing transition towards democracy, those that are in the process of recovery from the impact of conflicts, and those that are struggling for access to resources, including freshwater, socioeconomic inequalities and various forms of violence.[125] UNESCO highlights the need to build capacities of such countries in and through education, culture and the sciences for conflict prevention and for promoting a culture of peace and non-violence.[126] Its Medium-Term Strategy for 2014–2021 has a long background. In 1995, it launched the organization of International Symposia and Forums on Science for Peace to encourage scientists as part of their academic training to realize their responsibility to the protection of the human race and the environment, and to contribute to the improvement of the quality of life internationally and to the sharing of the benefits of scientific developments by everyone.[127]

In December 1997, UNESCO established the International School of Science for Peace at Como in Italy as the hub of research and training in scientific and technological aspects of international security concerns, in environmental and resource issues and in other critical issues where science and technology can enhance the culture of peace.[128] Its objective is to provide an updated and critical analysis on the most pressing global threats to a sustainable and lasting development after the Cold War

---

[121] International Committee of the Red Cross, Protection of Cultural Property: Questions and Answers. https://www.icrc.org/en/document/protection-cultural-property-questions-and-answers. Accessed 23 July 2020.

[122] See Chap. 21 by Lostal.

[123] UNESCO Constitution, Article I.1.

[124] UNESCO 2014, p. 9.

[125] Ibid.

[126] Ibid.

[127] UNESCO 1999, p. 17.

[128] Ibid. p. 7.

710   U. Kadam

and to stress the role of science as a powerful antidote to intolerance and ideological and racial barriers.[129]

33.5   New Weapons Technologies

In July 1932, Albert Einstein wrote a letter to Sigmund Freud and posed a question: *'Is there any way of delivering mankind from the menace of war? It is common knowledge that, with the advance of modern science, this issue has come to mean a matter of life and death for the civilization as we know it; nevertheless, for all the zeal displayed, every attempt at its solution has ended in a lamentable breakdown.'* In his elaborate response to Einstein, Freud explains the psychological phenomena at the root of aggressive behaviour and expresses a hope in all efforts directed at turning more and more people to pacifism and put an end to war.[130]

The apprehensions mentioned by both the stalwarts in their respective fields continue even today. In the meantime, the mankind experienced horrors of World War II and many other armed conflicts of varying degree that continued to bring annihilation and ruthless killing and destruction. Much of it was possible because of advances in science and technology. However, the community of nations has tried to rein in the destructive impact of exotic weapons by developing legal controls in the form of international conventions. This process continues even today as new technologies lure nations to develop newer weapons that are outside the regulatory regime of international law. For instance, new means of destruction through cyber operations or by developing autonomous weapons systems still remain largely outside the realm of legal controls.

UNESCO, *per se*, is not an organization that has a mandate to propose legal controls on new means of warfare. However, the organization has, since its inception, seized every opportunity to draw the world's attention to dangers of new means of warfare by relying on its mandate to address issues associated with developments in science and its commitment to ensure that scientific and technological advances are used in accordance with ethical principles. As regards all scientific developments, UNESCO as the primary UN agency with a specialized mandate in the social and human sciences, has always underscored the need to establish and promote common norms and values, promote ethical principles and standards to guide scientific progress and technological development.[131] Although its involvement in promoting international reflections on the ethics of the life sciences commenced in the 1970s, it created the Organization's Programme on Ethics of Science and Technology in the 1990s.[132] However, even during early days of UNESCO, the Organization stressed the need to facilitate international cooperation to ensure that

---

[129] Ibid.

[130] For the correspondence between Einstein and Freud, see Einstein and Freud 1976, pp. 25–26.

[131] UNESCO 2008a, p. 1.

[132] Ibid.

developments in nuclear sciences ought to be used for constructive, beneficial and peaceful purposes.[133]

Since 1955, UNESCO has advocated educating new generation and public at large to seek support for uses of nuclear energy exclusively for peaceful purposes.[134] In 1957, UNESCO established the European Organization for Nuclear Research (CERN) near Geneva in Switzerland to facilitate research on peaceful applications of nuclear energy.[135] It has also advocated for nuclear disarmament and safe disposal of nuclear material through its various fora working on ensuring use of science for peace.[136]

UNESCO has also highlighted challenges associated with other weapons of mass destruction. In the 1990s, the Organization placed a strong emphasis on advances in biotechnology and biological sciences with a view to generating debate and discussion on catastrophic effects of biological weapons. It continued to do so despite the fact that the Convention on the Prohibition of the Development, Production and Stockpiling of Bacteriological (Biological) and Toxin Weapons and on their Destruction which bans the development, production, acquisition, stockpiling and retention of biological (toxin) weapons, entered into force on 26 March 1975. UNESCO's concern was that the treaty lacks the means to verify compliance or to detect non-compliance and that this is a weakness in the treaty.[137]

As regards chemical weapons, UNESCO facilitated debates and discussion on allegations of their use in specific contexts.[138] Since the adoption of the Chemical Weapons Convention in 1993, UNESCO did not raise the issue of chemical weapons vociferously, probably because under the Chemical Weapons Convention a specialized body to oversee the promotion and implementation of the Convention—the Organization for Prohibition of Chemical Weapons—was established to undertake this task.[139]

UNESCO is also drawing attention of policy makers to the risks involved in using advances in robotics for developing autonomous weapons. In September 2017, it published a report on robotics ethics drawn up by the World Commission on the Ethics of Scientific Knowledge and Technology (WCESKT).[140] Among other things, the report highlights ethical as well as legal issues associated with use of unmanned aerial vehicles—drones—for military applications, autonomous weapons systems

---

[133] IAEA 1958. Also see Wendt 1955, p. 3.

[134] Wendt 1955, p. 71.

[135] CERN, About CERN, https://home.cern/about. Accessed 23 July 2020.

[136] UNESCO, Nuclear disarmament, safe disposal of nuclear materials or new weapons developments? Forum of the UNESCO International School of Science for Peace, at www.unesco.org/science/wcs/meetings/eur_cernobio_como_98.htm. Accessed 23 July 2020.

[137] UNESCO 1997.

[138] For example, the 1988 proposal of Iran to include the issue of alleged use of chemical weapons by Iraq in the agenda of the UNESCO to generate a debate. Proceedings of 129th Session of Executive Board of UNESCO.

[139] Chemical Weapons Convention, Article VIII.

[140] See, generally, WCESKT 2017.

and surveillance systems.[141] Already some of these issues are being discussed within the framework of the United Nations Conference on Disarmament, in particular, the review conferences of the Convention on Certain Conventional Weapons of 1980.[142] UNESCO's work is complementary to that process in as much as it underscores implications of these new technologies for maintenance of international peace and security.

Today using cyberspace as a new theatre of war is a reality. It is possible to engage in cyber operations that can cause injury or death to persons or damage to or destruction of objects with a hostile intent. Alarmed by the reality that advances in cyber technology can be manipulated for hostile purposes, the international community has been looking at ways and means of regulating what is now called as 'cyber warfare'.[143] From the perspectives of peace, conflict and security, UNESCO has so far focused its attention on use of cyber technology for addressing challenges associated with weapons trafficking, its use by terrorist and extremist groups promoting racism, hatred and violent extremism, etc.[144] It is not yet involved in any debate and discussion on regulation of cyber operations leading to attacks causing death, injury or destruction of property. It is possible to take up this issue under its broad framework of ethics and new technology.

33.6 UNESCO and International Politics—Impact on Peace and Security

Given the structure, membership and voting system in UNESCO, the organization is bound to be affected by international political and economic currents that prevail at any given time. Immediately after its creation, it became clear that the Organization's mandate can be used to pursue political interests of groups of States. Some of the major political factors that have influenced policy and decision making in UNESCO are the Cold War, decolonization and the consequent third-world majoritarian influence, and the Middle East and international trade.

The United States has had a troubled relationship with UNESCO since early 1980s. It decided to withdraw from the organization in 1984. This was a time when the Cold War tensions had reached their apogee. The United States under the Reagan administration cited corruption and what it considered an ideological tilt toward the Soviet Union against the West as the main reason for withdrawal.[145] After the

---

[141] Ibid., pp. 21–28.

[142] United Nations Office at Geneva, Lethal Autonomous Weapons Systems, https://www.unog.ch/80256EE600585943/F027DAA4966EB9C7C12580CD0039D7B5?OpenDocument. Accessed 23 July 2020.

[143] Schmitt 2017, p 1.

[144] UNESCO, Expert Meeting on DarkNet, https://en.unesco.org/news/expert-meeting-paris-explores-new-societal-technological-and-ethical-challenges-darknet. Accessed 23 July 2020.

[145] Lynch 2017.

end of the Cold War, the United States rejoined UNESCO in 2002, claiming that the Organization had changed its policy and that it had discarded anti-Western and anti-Israel biases.[146] However, in 2011, the United States decided to suspend its financial contributions to UNESCO following the formal recognition of the Palestinian Authority as a full member of UNESCO.[147] Again, in November 2017, expressing strong resentment to the UNESCO World Heritage Committee's decision to designate the site of Hebron and Al-Khalil Old Town in the West Bank as a World Heritage site, it decided to withdraw from the Organization.[148] Later, in December 2017, the UNESCO Director-General announced that Israel had also notified the Organization of its decision to withdraw.[149]

There were some other controversial issues in which UNESCO became embroiled from time to time. For instance, in the early 1960s, it came under heavy attack for its statement about biological aspects of race.[150] In connection with the international drive for liberalization of global trade, there was a debate on culture versus commercial interests involving UNESCO and GATT/WTO over national cultural industries, such as films and television.[151] The New World Information and Communication Order launched by UNESCO in 1976 at the insistence of its members from the developing world that questioned developed world's media's proclivity to one-way flow of negative news and images from the developing world was challenged by some states.[152] More recently, in February 2012, WikiLeaks strongly criticized UNESCO for not inviting it to a conference titled "The Media World after WikiLeaks and News of the World", organized by it.[153] The 2013 decision of UNESCO to make the collection "The Life and Works of Ernesto Che Guevara" a part of the Memory of the World Register received condemnation from some quarters.[154]

Such differences of opinion and discord within the membership of UNESCO is a major blow to its agenda to foster international peace and security through education and cultural cooperation. A rift among the membership on one count may have drastic impact on the entire agenda of the organization, including the one for peace and security. When members withdraw from the Organization or suspend their contributions, the financial implications for running major programmes have far-reaching consequences.

---

[146] Ibid.

[147] Coningham 2017.

[148] Lynch 2017.

[149] Declaration by the UNESCO Director-General, 29 December 2017. https://en.unesco.org/news/declaration-unesco-director-general-audrey-azoulay-withdrawal-israel-organization. Accessed 23 July 2020.

[150] Amrith and Sluga 2008, pp. 257–258.

[151] Balassa 2010, p. 85.

[152] Singh 2010, p. 14.

[153] WikiLeaks Press Release, 15 February 2012, https://wikileaks.org/WikiLeaks-denounces-UNESCO-after.html. Accessed 23 July 2020.

[154] 'Ileana Ros-Lehtinen Blasts UN for Preserving Che Guevara's Memory' https://www.miaminewtimes.com/news/ileana-ros-lehtinen-blasts-un-for-preserving-che-guevaras-memory-6549781. Accessed 23 July 2020.

714   U. Kadam

However, viewed from the perspective of majoritarian decision making in international intergovernmental organizations and contemporary political climate, such a rift among the membership of UNESCO is inevitable. Writing in 2006, noted modern philosopher and cultural theorist Kwame Anthony Appiah remarked, 'UNESCO, like all UN bodies, is the creature of the system of nations; while it speaks of World Heritage Sites, it is nevertheless bound to conceive them as ultimately at the disposal of nations.'[155] Thus, UNESCO is not insulated from political undercurrents of international relations at a given time. This is bound to continue as long as the organization does not change its constitutional framework, which is highly unlikely in the near future.

33.7 Conclusion

Despite many challenges, UNESCO has made a significant impact in improving the quality of education in many parts of the world through curriculum revision, elimination of discrimination in education, strengthening the status of teachers and improvements in the planning and management of education systems. Its educational endeavours focused on issues of contemporary importance such as, sustainable development, respect for human rights, improving health and livelihoods, vocational training as well as combating violent extremism.

One of the most successful and well-known activities of UNESCO has been in the field of recognition and protection of world cultural heritage sites. In addition, UNESCO's work concerning the safeguarding of intangible cultural heritage, the fight against the illicit trade in cultural goods, the promotion of cultural diversity or the preservation of cultural heritage under water is equally significant.

In the field of natural sciences, UNESCO has facilitated intergovernmental co-operation in oceanography, hydrology, geology and the life sciences with a view to preserving the biological diversity and drinking water resources. It has also drawn the attention of international community to the importance of using advancements in science and technology for peaceful purposes, especially by highlighting dangers in development of exotic weapons that may counter internationally agreed standards and legal norms regarding means of warfare.

UNESCO has vehemently advocated for press freedom, free access to information, the safety of journalists and the development of free and pluralistic media in developing countries. Of late, it has focused its attention on internet and unforeseen opportunities brought about by innovation in the field of information and communication technology. Its emphasis has been on using these remarkable advances in the interest of mankind, and preventing its misuse for pernicious applications and activities including those that endanger peace and security.

UNESCO has succeeded in setting international standards on issues coming within its competence. Its role in adoption of binding and non-binding standard setting

---

[155] Appiah 2006, p. 11.

instruments such as conventions, recommendations and declarations in the fields of education, natural sciences, social and human sciences, culture, communication and information is undoubtedly admirable.[156]

Since the decision making process in UNSCO is a political phenomenon, the changes occurring outside UNESCO are bound to influence the Organization's policy-making process. Ever since its creation, it has witnessed major developments in the field of international relations, trade, information and communication revolution, peace and security, and so on and so forth. These changes are bound to influence the functioning of UNESCO and its policy. Admission of Palestine as a member, decisions on inscription of world heritage sites, the UNESCO-United States relationship and the Organization's focus on developing countries are some examples that reflect these political undercurrents.

In connection with UNESCO's contribution in furtherance of international conflict and security law, a question arises: how far and to what extent UNESCO has contributed to prevention of conflict and preservation of security? If we look at the mandate of UNESCO, its work in its main areas of activity, namely, education, science and culture, is supposed to be complementary to the broader efforts of the United Nations for maintenance of international peace and security. Its work in the field of promotion of peace and security is preventive in nature. Through calculated efforts on peace education, promotion of cultural harmony, facilitation of dialogue between civilizations, enhancing human security, promotion of sustainable development and combating violent extremism, the organization is strengthening and complementing other more concrete multilateral political efforts. It is more inclined to developmental work. Needless to say, through its commitment to global peace, security and conflict prevention, UNESCO has undoubtedly propagated a culture of global peace and fought for strengthening international security.

References

Amrith S, Sluga G (2008) New Histories of the United Nations. Journal of World History, 19: 251–274.

Appiah K (2006) Whose Culture Is It? The New Yorker Review of Books, 53:1–15.

Balassa C (2010) An "Economic" Approach Towards the Trade and Culture Debate: The US Position. In: Singh J (ed) International Cultural Policies and Power. Palgrave Macmillan, pp 84–100.

Brianso I (2010) Valorization of World Cultural Heritage in Time of Globalization, Bridges Between Nations and Cultural Power. In: Singh J (ed) International Cultural Policies and Power. Palgrave Macmillan, pp. 169–180.

Chowdhury Fink N (2012) Meeting the Challenge: A Guide to United Nations Counterterrorism Activities. International Peace Institute.

---

[156] As of today, UNESCO has adopted 32 conventions, 9 protocols, 35 recommendations and 14 declarations. UNESCO, Legal Instruments, http://portal.unesco.org/en/ev.php-URL_ID=12024&URL_DO=DO_TOPIC&URL_SECTION=201.html. Accessed 23 July 2020.

Coningham R (2017) Why the US withdrawal from UNESCO is a step backward for global cultural cooperation. The Conversation. https://theconversation.com/why-the-us-withdrawal-from-unesco-is-a-step-backwards-for-global-cultural-cooperation-85692. Accessed 23 July 2020.

Einstein A, Freud S (1976) Correspondence on War. Impact of Science on Society. UNESCO, 26:25–26.

Feigenbaum H (2010) The Political Economy of Cultural Diversity in Film and Television. In: Singh J (ed) International Cultural Policies and Power. Palgrave Macmillan, pp 77–83.

GCPCA (2014) Guidelines for Protecting Schools and Universities from Military Use during Armed Conflict. http://www.protectingeducation.org/. Accessed 23 July 2020.

Gomez O, Gasper D (2016) Human Security: A Guidance Note, UNDP. http://hdr.undp.org/en/content/human-security-guidance-note. Accessed 23 July 2020.

IAEA (1958) UNESCO and Atomic Energy, https://www.iaea.org/es/publications/magazines/bulletin/2-1/unesco-and-atomic-energy. Accessed 23 July 2020.

Ilcan S, Phillips L (2006) Governing Peace: Global Rationalities of Security and UNESCO's Culture of Peace Campaign. Anthropologica, 48:62–63.

International Committee of the Red Cross (2017) Protection of Cultural Property: Questions and Answers. https://www.icrc.org/en/document/protection-cultural-property-questions-and-answers. Accessed 23 July 2020.

Jasper W (2003) UNESCO's rotten track record. The New American, https://www.thenewamerican.com/world-news/item/13845-unesco%E2%80%99s-rotten-track-record. Accessed 23 July 2020.

Lynch C (2017) US to pull out of UNESCO, again. Foreign Policy. http://foreignpolicy.com/2017/10/11/u-s-to-pull-out-of-unesco-again/. Accessed 23 July 2020.

Neuwirth R (2006) "United in Divergency": A Commentary on the UNESCO Convention on the Protection and Promotion of the Diversity of Cultural Expressions. ZaöRV, 66:819–862.

Schmitt M (2017) Tallinn Manual 2.0 on the International Law Applicable to Cyber Operations. Cambridge University Press, Cambridge.

Schorlemer S, Maus S (eds) (2014) Climate Change as a Threat to Peace. University of Dresden.

Singh J (2010) Global Cultural Policies and Power. In: Singh J (ed) International Cultural Policies and Power. Palgrave Macmillan, pp. 1–15

Thee M (Ed) (1981) Armaments, Arms control and disarmament: An UNESCO Reader for Disarmament Education. UNESCO.

UNESCO (1946) United Nations Conference for the Establishment of an Educational and Cultural Organisation, London, 1 to 16 November 1945. ECO/Conf./29.UNESCO (1987) A Chronology of UNESCO 1945–1987.

UNESCO (1997) Possible Consequences of the Misuse of Biological Sciences, Conclusions and Recommendations of the First Forum of the UNESCO International School of Science for Peace. www.unesco.org/science/wcs/meetings/eur_como_97.htm. Accessed 23 July 2020.

UNESCO (1998) Nuclear disarmament, safe disposal of nuclear materials or new weapons developments? Forum of the UNESCO International School of Science for Peace. www.unesco.org/science/wcs/meetings/ eur_ cernobio_como_98.htm. Accessed 23 July 2020.

UNESCO (1999) Possible Consequences of the Misuse of Biological Sciences, Report of the First Forum of the UNESCO International School of Science for Peace, Science for Peace Series, 6:1–41.

UNESCO (2008a) Ethics of Science and Technology at UNESCO.

UNESCO (2008b) Human Security: Approaches and Challenges, 2008.

UNESCO (2010) Protecting Education from Attack: A State-of-the-Art Review.

UNESCO (2013) UNESCO's Programme of Action Culture of Peace and Non-violence: A Vision in Action, Concept Paper.

UNESCO (2014) Medium-Term Strategy for 2014–2021.

UNESCO (2015a) Climate Change and COP 21. UNESCO.

UNESCO (2015b) Education 2030: Incheon Declaration and SDG4 – Education 2030 Framework for Action.

UNESCO (2017) Building Sustainable Peace and Global Citizenship Through Education', http://unesdoc.unesco.org/images/0024/002474/247430E.pdf. Accessed 23 July 2020.

United Nations (UN) (2009) Climate Change and its Possible Security Implications. Report of the Secretary-General, A/64/350.

Valderrama F (1995) A History of UNESCO. UNESCO.

Wendt G (1955) Nuclear Energy and its Uses in Peace. UNESCO.

World Commission on Ethics of Scientific Knowledge and Technology (WCESKT) (2017) Report of COMEST on Robotics Ethics, UNESCO.

Umesh Kadam holds a LL.M., M.Phil (Education) and a Ph.D. in International Law from Shivali University, Kolhapur, India and a LL.M. in International Law from University of London. From 1980 to 1998 he taught international law in various Indian law schools. From 1998 until 2008, he worked for the International Committee of the Red Cross (ICRC) as a Regional Legal Adviser for the promotion and implementation of International Humanitarian Law in South Asia, Southeast and East Asia and East Africa. Currently he works as a Visiting Professor in several Indian law schools. His areas of interest include international humanitarian law, international criminal law and international migration law.

Chapter 34
United Nations International Children's Emergency Fund (UNICEF)

Nataliia Hendel

Contents

34.1 Introduction 719
34.2 History of UNICEF 721
34.3 UNICEF's Principles 722
34.4 UNICEF's Activities and Missions 725
34.5 UNICEF's Response to COVID-19 727
34.6 Conclusion 729
References 730

Abstract The present chapter examines the history of the establishment of the United Nations International Children's Emergency Fund (UNICEF) after World War II and the extension of its mandate after the Convention on the Rights of the Child was adopted. The role of the United Nations' cluster approach aimed to address gaps in emergency response is reassessed with respect to UNICEF. Special attention is paid to the fulfilment of the Sustainable Development Goals (SDGs) under the UNICEF mandate, and the UNICEF activities in emergencies are analysed. The chapter also addresses UNICEF's actions in response to the COVID-19 pandemic.

Keywords United Nations International Children's Emergency Fund · United Nations · Crisis and emergencies · Armed conflict · Universal declaration of human rights · Convention on the Rights of the Child · Sustainable Development Goals

34.1 Introduction

Childhood is supposed to be the happiest period in one's life and quite often various devastating factors threaten it. An armed conflict, an emergency, or any domestic abuse may deprive people of a decent childhood. Children are generally viewed as the most vulnerable people. Everything one loves may be ruined in a moment. After the horrors of the World War II, the international community agreed to create a special

---

N. Hendel (✉)
International Law and Comparative Law Department, International Humanitarian University, Odessa, Ukraine

© T.M.C. ASSER PRESS and the authors 2022
S. Sayapin et al. (eds.), *International Conflict and Security Law*,
https://doi.org/10.1007/978-94-6265-515-7_34

agency focused on child protection in emergencies. On 11 December 1946, the United Nations International Children's Emergency Fund (UNICEF) was established. From the very beginning, the governments of the United States and Canada made significant contributions to fund the organization and, later. 46 other states adhered to the idea of supporting the fund. In 1953, UNICEF became a permanent part of the United Nations system.

The necessity to ensure that every child's rights are fully protected was called for in the Millennium Development Goals (MDGs) and later in the Sustainable Development Goals (SDGs). The main approach of UNICEF is to provide assistance for children from early childhood through adolescence who may suffer from the consequences of armed conflict, emergencies, or the spread of infectious and non-communicable diseases. Major challenges in UNICEF's operation include violence, discrimination, abuse, exploitation, poverty, lack of access to proper education and adequate health care, hunger, effects of the global climate change on children's lives, gender inequality, etc. It is worth mentioning that UNICEF's Agenda for action for refugee and migrant children is the priority of the organization. Since 2016, the organization has been closely monitoring the situation in that area. The chapter focuses on the achievement of the Sustainable Development Goals (SDGs) within the UNICEF mandate.

UNICEF is currently active in more than 190 countries and territories through state programs and National Committees.[1] UNICEF operates in these states based on a bilateral agreement between said state and the organization, with due regard to prioritizing children's rights as defined by a nation. Throughout the history of UNICEF, the main goal has always been to ensure the inalienable rights of children to a safe and healthy childhood.

UNICEF's mission is to advocate for the protection of children's rights in various areas of life: mental and physical health, access to education, legal safeguards and social protection, safe and clean water, food, sanitation and hygiene, and child's safety in emergencies, migration and armed conflicts. The role of the United Nations' cluster approach in filling gaps in response to emergencies is reassessed with respect to UNICEF in this chapter.

UNICEF provides assistance to children without any distinction as to race, religion, nationality, or economic or social situation. The sole condition made by Maurice Pate upon his appointment as the organization's first Executive Director was "that it includes all children' from both Allied and 'ex-enemy countries".[2] Former Executive Director of UNICEF, Anthony Lake, stated: "The next steps of our journey will depend on our willingness to adapt to the changing world around us ... to infuse equity throughout our programs...".[3] Hence, the major objectives of UNICEF are to prevent discrimination and ensure the rights of every child. The chapter analyses UNICEF in emergencies, and its functions are analysed on a case basis. Furthermore, the chapter addresses UNICEF's actions in response to the COVID-19 pandemic.

---

[1] UNICEF 2020a.

[2] UNICEF 2016.

[3] Ibid.

34.2 History of UNICEF

Protection and promotion of the rights of children had been an issue of international concern far before the UN was created. The first international legal instrument on the protection of children's rights was drafted at the 3rd session of The Hague Conference on International Law. The Convention of 1902 relating to the settlement of guardianship of minors was the first effort at addressing international family law.[4] In 1923, the International Save the Children Union (L'Union Internationale de Secours aux Enfants) was established, which gave rise to the Declaration of the Rights of the Child of 1924 (generally known as the Geneva Declaration of the Rights of the Child), which incorporated five major principles. The Geneva Declaration of 1924 had an essential mission of creating conditions that could ensure the normal physical and mental development of the child, as well as the child's right to assistance, proper education, and protection against threats. The Geneva Declaration of 1924 was a purely protective legal act by its nature. World War I put millions of kids in extremely difficult conditions. In 1920, Eglantyne Jebb, President of the Save the Children Fund and the International Committee of the Red Cross, successfully attempted to set up an international movement for children: International Save the Children Union. Acknowledging the existing harsh conditions, numerous branches of this international organization in many countries began to actively support children affected by the war.[5] The Declaration of the Rights of the Child adopted in an extended form by the UN in 1959 and the Convention on the Rights of the Child of 1989 reaffirmed the importance and role of the Geneva Declaration of the Rights of the Child in the children's rights evolution. The International Union for the Protection of Children became the first organization to protect the rights of children and is currently one of the UNICEF cornerstones.

The establishment of the UN inspired hope, gave people aspiration for peace and security and, more importantly, for a rapid recovery after World War II. In December 1946, the UN General Assembly announced the creation of a new organization, the International Children's Emergency Fund. The prerequisite for UNICEF's creation was an ongoing deteriorating humanitarian situation in Europe after World War II and the terrible human rights violation cases involving children. The establishment of this organization was carried out via the adoption of United Nations General Assembly Resolution 57(I) of 11 December 1946. It is worth noting that the establishment of UNICEF was the first large-scale international effort to help children affected by World War II all around the globe.

In conformity with Resolution 57(I) of 11 December 1946,

Provision shall be made for equitable and efficient… distribution of all supplies, based on need, without discrimination because of race, creed, nationality status, or political belief.[6]

---

[4] Balakiryeva and Bondar 2012, p. 100.

[5] Levchenko 2009.

[6] UNGA 1946.

The organization had a semi-autonomous status with its administrative organ and the Secretariat. The Executive Board was composed of 25 governments with a gradual increase to 30.

On 1 December 1950, the General Assembly, recalling the importance of UNICEF, extended its mandate for a further three years' period, entitling it to manage and supervise the long-term goals and needs of children. This action was undertaken to strengthen national child health and welfare systems, especially in developing countries.[7]

During 1951, the Fund developed its main lines of work with the vision of how activities should be carried out. The UNICEF Executive Board decided that its functions would be centred on humanitarian assistance, training childcare staff, campaigns to combat diseases that threaten children (tuberculosis, malaria, diphtheria, measles), and child nutrition. The same year, UNICEF opened its offices in Africa and Latin America.

On 6 October 1953, the General Assembly, considering the role that UNICEF played 'in the whole international program for the protection of the child' and in creating 'favourable conditions for the development of the long-range economic and social programs of the United Nations and the specialized agencies', decided to make the organization permanent. It was renamed the United Nations Children's Fund while retaining its already familiar acronym of UNICEF.[8]

UNICEF is a permanent agency in the United Nations system.[9] It has a special mandate to develop mechanisms and implement programs, strategies, and campaigns for the protection of children's rights. The primary objectives of UNICEF are to provide accessible health care, education, nutrition, sanitation, and protection of both children and youth. UNICEF's operation is aimed at enabling children to exercise their right to life and allow them to develop and reach their full potential for sustainable growth and stability. UNICEF cooperates with international governmental and non-governmental organizations, states, and world communities to help and protect children and adolescents.[10]

34.3 UNICEF's Principles

According to UN GA Resolution 57(I) of 11 December 1946, the establishment of an International Children's Emergency Fund 'is to be utilized for the benefit of children and adolescents of countries which were the victims of aggression'.[11]

The Declaration of the Rights of the Child proclaimed by General Assembly resolution 1386 (XIV) of 20 November 1959, in Principle 2, stated:

---

[7] UNICEF 2016.

[8] UNICEF 2020c.

[9] UNICEF 2016.

[10] UNICEF undated-a.

[11] UNGA 1946.

34 United Nations International Children's Emergency Fund (UNICEF)

The child shall enjoy special protection, and shall be given opportunities and facilities, by law and by other means, to enable him to develop physically, mentally, morally, spiritually and socially in a healthy and normal manner and in conditions of freedom and dignity. In the enactment of laws for this purpose, the best interests of the child shall be the paramount consideration.[12]

In emergencies, UNICEF seeks to provide special protection and create supportive conditions for children and adolescents and their families. Principle 8 of the Declaration of the Rights of the Child guarantees priority in the provision of protection and assistance, as follows:

The child shall in all circumstances be among the first to receive protection and relief.[13]

The United Nations Convention on the Rights of the Child (UNCRC) was adopted in 1989 and came into force a year later. The adoption of the Convention had significant outcomes for UNICEF's work in emergencies; it facilitated the protection of children from violence, abuse, and exploitation as an integral part of the crisis response. The Convention on the Rights of the Child enshrined the basic rights of the child that UNICEF strives to achieve for the benefit of children. They encompass the following rights: inherent right to life (Article 6); the protection of the child from all forms of physical or mental violence, injury or abuse, neglect or negligent treatment, maltreatment or exploitation (Article 19); the right of the child to the enjoyment of the highest attainable standard of health and to facilities for the treatment of illness and rehabilitation of health (Article 24); the right of every child to a standard of living adequate for the child's physical, mental, spiritual, moral and social development (Article 27); the right of the child to education (Article 28); the right of the child to be protected from economic exploitation and from performing any work that is likely to be hazardous or to interfere with the child's education, or to be harmful to the child's health or physical, mental, spiritual, moral or social development (Article 32); the right to protection of the child from all forms of sexual exploitation and sexual abuse (Article 34); the right to the protection of the child from all forms of exploitation prejudicial to any aspect of the child's welfare (Article 36) and others.[14]

Article 38 of the Convention on the Rights of the Child provides that states undertake to respect and to ensure respect for rules of international humanitarian law applicable to them in armed conflicts that are relevant to the child. In 2000, the Optional Protocol to the Convention on the Rights of the Child on the Involvement of Children in Armed Conflict was adopted.[15] State Parties agreed to cooperate in the implementation of the protocol, including in the prevention of any activity contrary to the protocol and in the rehabilitation and social reintegration of persons who are victims of acts contrary to this protocol, including through technical cooperation

---

[12] UN 1959.

[13] Ibid.

[14] UNGA 1989.

[15] Optional Protocol 2000.

and financial assistance. Such assistance and cooperation should be undertaken in consultation with concerned state parties and relevant international organizations.[16]

UNICEF activities are primarily guided by sustainable ethical principles, which are enshrined in the Convention on the Rights of the Child and other international standards of children's rights.[17] Additionally, UNICEF is guided by the principles of non-discrimination, the best interests of the child, the right to life, survival and development, and the right of children to express their views freely and to be heard.[18] UNICEF takes equity and gender equality into account in developing its programs of work.[19] UNICEF operates on the basis of the principles of equality and cooperation to achieve its goal.[20] It is the principle of cooperation that is the basis for the implementation of everyday tasks in protecting the rights of children and adolescents.

The goals of sustainable development correspond to the priorities of humanity in the future. UNICEF is also working to achieve Sustainable Development Goals. The UNICEF mandate includes Objectives 1, 2, 3, 4, 5, 6, 11, and 16. Goal 1 focuses on poverty alleviation in all its forms and in all states. As specified in para 1.2, through 2030, it is endeavoured to reduce the number of men, women, and children of all ages living in poverty by at least half, bearing in mind the peculiarities of each state. Goal 2 is aimed at ending hunger, achieving food security and improved nutrition, and promoting sustainable agriculture. According to its para 2.2, the goal is to end hunger and ensure access by all people, in particular, the poor and people in vulnerable situations, including infants, to safe, nutritious, and sufficient food all year round by 2030.[21]

The SDGs have the task of achieving internationally agreed-upon levels for tackling growth retardation and depletion in children under the age of five, as well as meeting the nutritional needs of adolescent girls, pregnant women, and nursing mothers. Food security and the widespread hunger issue have been both on the UN and Specialized Agencies' agenda's major priorities. The food crisis makes the consequences of armed conflict, emergencies, and the coronavirus pandemic tougher. Two factors combined make children and adolescents even more vulnerable, and malnutrition can have the most negative impact on children's health and development. Goal 3 elaborates on the meaning of health and well-being for all people at all ages. Paragraph 3.2 is devoted to children and outlines the next task: to end preventable deaths of newborns and children under 5 years of age, with all countries aiming to reduce neonatal mortality to at least as low as 12 per 1000 live births by 2030.[22]

Infant and neonatal mortality has been recognized as a global health issue by the WHO. Only after the leading health organizations (WHO, UNICEF, Doctors Without Borders, etc.) join their efforts may the issue be eliminated (e.g., through vaccination

---

[16] Optional Protocol 2000, para 1, Article 7.

[17] UNICEF undated-a.

[18] UNICEF 2019.

[19] Ibid.

[20] UNICEF 2020c, 2016.

[21] UN 2015a.

[22] UN 2015b.

companies, reshaping of national health systems). Effective national health systems that can identify and respond to public health threats are also capable of ensuring the epidemiological security of the state, which directly affects global epidemiological security in the era of constant development.

Goal 4 is also dedicated to children in the following way: "By 2030 it is aimed to ensure that all girls and boys have access to quality early childhood development, care and pre-primary education so that they are ready for primary education".[23] The goal is by 2030 to eliminate gender disparities in education and ensure equal access to all levels of education and vocational training for the vulnerable, including persons with disabilities, indigenous peoples and children in vulnerable situations.[24] There is also a need to improve educational institutions that take into account the interests of children, the special needs of persons with disabilities, and gender aspects. The main feature should be safety; schools should be free from violence and social barriers.[25] The goal is to make progressively safe, free primary and secondary education for all boys and girls, and affordable vocational training available to everyone, regardless of gender or household wealth.[26] Education and inculcation play a great role when forming the ideals of democratic values and respect for human rights that contribute to security.

Goal 5 addresses the promotion of gender equality and the empowerment of all women and girls. UNICEF's mandate is also aimed at achieving this goal, especially in countries that experience emergencies, armed conflicts, as well as post-conflict and crisis recovery periods. Goal 6 is also directly linked to UNICEF's work, as it urges states to ensure the availability and management of water and sanitation for all. Goal 11 aspires to make cities and human settlements inclusive, safe, resilient, and sustainable. Goal 16 is dedicated to promoting a peaceful and inclusive society for sustainable development, providing access to justice for all, and building effective, accountable, and inclusive institutions at all levels. Thus, UNICEF's work is aimed at protecting and helping children, which are the foundation of a healthy civil society and the future of states and the international community as a whole. Through its activities, UNICEF demonstrates that the Sustainable Development Goals are not an abstract statement; they can be exercised by people and can be achieved.

34.4 UNICEF's Activities and Missions

The difference in legal status and mandate of organizations has created difficulties in coordinating humanitarian assistance during emergencies and crises. These factors necessitated a humanitarian reform in the UN system. To advance the service of timely and effective humanitarian assistance and to ensure synergies at the universal

---

[23] Sustainable Development Goals, para 4.2.

[24] Sustainable Development Goals, para 4.5.

[25] UN 2015c.

[26] UNICEF 2016.

level, the international community applied the cluster approach. It was suggested as part of the UN's humanitarian reform in 2005.

The outcome of humanitarian reform was the identification of eleven main clusters. But what is a cluster? A cluster is a group of institutions, organizations or both that function interdependently within the limits prescribed by their mandates and cooperate to achieve common goals. The cluster approach aims to strengthen the service availability and technical capacity of the entire UN system to respond to emergencies by the clear distribution of powers and responsibilities among international governmental organizations. Additionally, the idea was to improve accountability and transparency. Looking closer at how UNICEF applies the cluster approach with other international governmental and non-governmental organizations during an emergency or armed conflict, it becomes evident that UNICEF is responsible for education, nutrition, water, sanitation, and protection. In cooperation with the United Nations Population Fund (UNFPA), the organization prevents and responds to gender-based violence.

Children are the most vulnerable subjects during emergencies, humanitarian crises, and armed conflicts. Indeed, often these circumstances deprive them of childhood, the happiest and shortest period in one's life. This is not to mention the risks to life, health, exploitation and others. The right to a decent childhood is one of the rights of the child, which is very often breached. UNICEF is trying to help children and their families in the harshest circumstances.

UNICEF is mandated by the United Nations to provide the world with humanitarian assistance in emergencies and armed conflicts.[27] It is worth highlighting that the organization also prepares communities for crises when conflicts are inevitable; this planning is referred to as 'build back better'.[28] The action plan 'build back better' was designed for a long-term perspective; not only does it improve the humanitarian situation in the states or territories, but it also promotes security through the spread of democratic values, as well as the realization of the rights of children and adolescents, including gender equality. Teaching respect and making others aware of children's rights is the foundation of observance of children's human rights in the future. This is the most reasonable way, as it goes through faith in law and democratic values. In the 1980s, UNICEF, in cooperation with international governmental and non-governmental organizations, led a global campaign to reduce child mortality.[29]

UNICEF dispenses humanitarian assistance to children and implements the Sustainable Development Goals by suggesting that governments incorporate these goals into their domestic legal systems. Children and their families receive UNICEF assistance in times of, during, and after crises.

UNICEF learned how to lead humanitarian activities during the armed conflict in Nigeria—the Nigerian-Biafran War.[30] When assisting, UNICEF stuck to a strict policy of political neutrality, which has allowed it to perform humanitarian functions

---

[27] UNGA 1989, Articles 22, 38, 45(a).

[28] UNICEF 2016.

[29] Grant 2000.

[30] UNICEF 2016, 1986.

34 United Nations International Children's Emergency Fund (UNICEF)

in the best interest of both sides. One should keep in mind that other humanitarian organizations have been restricted from accessing the conflict-affected area.

UNICEF also carried out life-changing humanitarian activities on the Thai-Cambodian border in 1979, providing the necessary assistance to children and their families.[31] UNICEF follows its principles and provided humanitarian assistance to children in need during armed conflicts in Afghanistan, Rwanda, Sudan, Chechnya (Russian Federation), Sri Lanka, Angola, and Ukraine.

In the new millennium, UNICEF took advantage of a long-overdue, if fleeting, peace in Afghanistan to emphasize the importance of education in times of emergency. When the fall of the Taliban in 2001 allowed many children to resume their education, UNICEF supplied materials for 93% of the country's 3000 schools.[32] This meant that 3 million children were able to enroll.[33] One-third of those students were girls, a major achievement in a country where, in the 1990s, only 5% of primary-school-aged girls attended school.[34] Gender equality is one of the priorities of UNICEF.

After World War II, the first recipients of the UNICEF assistance were the children of Yugoslavia.[35] UNICEF also promotes post-conflict settlement and facilitates this process for the population. It is important to emphasize that the organization provides psychological assistance to children who suffer from armed conflicts. UNICEF played a crucial role in the recovery of children of Yugoslavia and their health advancement.

34.5 UNICEF's Response to COVID-19

The COVID-19 pandemic has severely affected children and their families. The rapidly developing virus put a heavy burden on national health systems, which in turn has jeopardized vaccination campaigns in several states. Unfortunately, vaccination against diphtheria and measles became inaccessible for some time; schools were closed for quarantine, which created a significant barrier to exercise the right to education. Not all countries have the opportunity to maintain online education and not all students have the opportunity to receive it. The lockdown of schools faces another significant problem: hunger issues, as for many children school lunches are the only source of food. The closure of enterprises and the reduction of jobs affected the economic situation of families and consequently led to some ramifications related to the well-being of children. Moreover, domestic violence has been gradually increasing since the quarantine started.

---

[31] UNICEF 2016.

[32] UNICEF 2016.

[33] UNICEF 2016.

[34] UNICEF 2016.

[35] UNICEF 2020c, 2016, 1986.

The coronavirus has caused an enormous disinformation campaign that encouraged discrimination and stigma. The United Nations and its agencies have repeatedly called on states and NGOs to tackle coronavirus misinformation, discrimination and stigma, which have intensified with the spread of COVID-19 and violence. UNICEF collaborates with healthcare experts to free people from fear, substantiate new rules and make recommendations[36] to parents, nurses and teachers.[37]

The possible social and economic impact of the pandemic on children is described in the UNICEF report 'Supporting Families and Children beyond COVID-19'. The report 'Supporting Families and Children beyond COVID-19' indicates that in connection with the coronavirus pandemic, infant mortality will rise to levels that the world has not known for at least five years.[38] According to UNICEF, in the first wave of the epidemic, about a third of the OECD and EU countries did not take any special measures aimed at supporting children.[39] It is for this reason that UNICEF demands to prevent the emergence of a "lost generation".[40] States have obligations under the Convention on the Rights of the Child to ensure the best interests of the child.[41] Even in the midst of the coronavirus pandemic, states must not forget their obligations under international law to protect children.

Vaccination is a proven way to fight infectious diseases. International cooperation is an effective mechanism to combat the spread of infectious diseases. UNICEF has excellent experience with vaccination campaigns.[42] For example, the World Health Organization, UNICEF, the International Federation of Red Cross and Red Crescent Societies, and Médecins Sans Frontières have been able to stockpile the pharmaceutical company Merck's Ebola vaccine.[43] In 2021, UNICEF could potentially transport up to 850 tons of COVID-19 vaccines every month.[44] UNICEF is responsible for delivering COVID-19 vaccines to 92 low- and lower-middle-income countries.[45] UNICEF technical assistance in the fight against coronavirus could be crucial and vital for many states.

Coordination between the UN, its agencies and states in the present crisis is the only key to combatting coronavirus. In addition to implementing a cluster approach to humanitarian action, international organizations need to get used to and efficiently respond to new global threats. Almost all states have found themselves in a *zugzwang* (a disadvantageous compulsion to move) during the pandemic, given the need to respond to emergencies while demands and expectations of international organizations have also increased. The pandemic did not ceasefire or terminate armed

---

[36] UNICEF 2020b.

[37] UNICEF 2020d.

[38] Richardson et al 2020.

[39] UNICEF undated-c.

[40] UNICEF 2020.

[41] UNGA 1989, para 1, Article 3.

[42] UNICEF undated-b.

[43] UN 2021.

[44] UNICEF 2020d.

[45] Ibid.

34 United Nations International Children's Emergency Fund (UNICEF)

conflicts, crises related to famine, sanitation, global warming, human trafficking, or child exploitation; on the contrary, it made modern issues even more complicated. Only the united efforts of the international community, supported by international governmental organizations, can effectively 'conquer' the pandemic and other concerning issues and threats that become barriers to exercise the right to a happy and healthy childhood.

34.6 Conclusion

Despite the fact that UNICEF was created to help children after World War II, its effectiveness and the gradually increasing number of conflicts demanded an international authority in the field of children's life, health, and rights protection. Thus, next year humankind will commemorate the 75th anniversary of the United Nations International Children's Emergency Fund.

UNICEF protects the rights of children in the most severe cases. Sometimes this organization remains the only opportunity for a child to receive medication, access to education, nutrition, and protection.

The adoption of the Convention on the Rights of the Child and its protocols extended UNICEF's mandate and enhanced the level of protection of children and adolescents in crises and armed conflict. The Convention on the Rights of the Child and its protocols are 'constitutional documents' for UNICEF.

UNICEF functions to meet and respond to modern threats. Main objectives are divided into Sustainable Development Goals,[46] *id est*: Goal 1—End poverty in all its forms and in all states; Goal 2—End hunger, achieve food security and improved nutrition and promote sustainable agriculture; Goal 3—Ensure healthy lives and promote well-being for all at all ages; Goal 4—Ensure inclusive and equitable quality education and promote lifelong learning opportunities for all; Goal 5—Achieve gender equality and empower all women and girls; Goal 6—Ensure availability and sustainable management of water and sanitation for all; Goal 11—Make cities and human settlements inclusive, safe, resilient and sustainable; Goal 16—Promote peaceful and inclusive society for sustainable development, provide access to justice for all and build effective, accountable and inclusive institutions at all levels.

UNICEF's implementation of the Sustainable Development Goals has a long-term perspective and is focused on achieving peace and security. Nurturing democratic values and respect for human rights among children and adolescents is a strategic priority of UNICEF. UNICEF is an essential modern organization that advocates values we all cherish and makes a positive impact on the future of humanity. The pandemic taught the whole world a valuable lesson—do not procrastinate; react to the threats imminently.

---

[46] UN 2015d.

References

Balakiryeva O, Bondar T (2012) Instruktyvno-metodychni materialy shchodo roboty tsentriv sotsialnykh sluzhb dlya simyi, ditey i molodi z ditmy ta moloddyu hrup ryzyku. [Instructional and methodical materials on the work of centres of social services for families, children and youth with children and youth at risk.] USAID // Proekt rozvytku VIL/SNID-servisu v Ukrayini, Kiev

Grant J E (2000) The State of the World's Children 1980-81, https://www.unicef.org/media/84521/file/SOWC-1980-81.pdf Accessed 30 January 2021

Levchenko K (2009) 20 Years of the UN Convention on the Rights of the Child. http://khpg.org/index.php?id=1258983351. Accessed 7 August 2020

Optional Protocol to the Convention on the Rights of the Child on the involvement of children in armed conflict (2000)

Richardson D, Carraro A, Cebotari V, Gromada A (2020) Supporting Families and Children Beyond COVID-19: Social protection in high-income countries, Innocenti Research Report/UNICEF

https://www.unicef-irc.org/publications/1165-supporting-families-and-children-beyond-covid-19-social-protection-in-high-income-countries.html Accessed 30 January 2021

UN (1959) Declaration of the Rights of the Child 1959 http://www.cirp.org/library/ethics/UN-declaration/ Accessed 11 August 2020

UN (2015a) Goal 2: Zero Hunger, https://www.un.org/sustainabledevelopment/hunger/ Accessed 30 January 2021

UN (2015b) Goal 3: Ensure healthy lives and promote well-being for all at all ages, https://www.un.org/sustainabledevelopment/health/ Accessed 30 January 2021

UN (2015c) Goal 5: Quality Education, https://www.un.org/sustainabledevelopment/education/ Accessed 30 January 2021.

UN (2015d) UN 2030 Agenda for Sustainable Development, https://sustainabledevelopment.un.org/content/documents/21252030%20Agenda%20for%20Sustainable%20Development%20web.pdf Accessed 14 August 2020

UN (2021) UN agencies and partners establish global Ebola vaccine stockpile, https://news.un.org/en/story/2021/01/1081862. Accessed 30 January 2021

UNGA (1946) UN GA Resolution 57 (I) of 11 December 1946. https://undocs.org/ru/A/64/Add.1. Accessed 10 August 2020

UNGA (1989) Convention the Rights of a Child adopted by the GA Resolution 44/25 of 20 November 1989 https://www.ohchr.org/en/professionalinterest/pages/crc.aspx Accessed 14 August 2020

UNICEF (1986) UNICEF at 40, https://www.unicef.org/media/85536/file/UNICEF-at-40.pdf Accessed 30 January 2021

UNICEF (2016) For Every Child, Hope www.unicef.org/publications/files/UNICEF_For_Every_Child_Hope_1946-2016_WEB.pdf Accessed 10 August 2020

UNICEF (2019) For every child, every right. The Convention on the Rights of the Child at a crossroads, https://www.unicef.org/media/61941/file/Convention-rights-child-at-crossroads-2019.pdf Accessed 30 January 2021

UNICEF (2020a) About UNICEF www.unicef.org/about/who/index_introduction.html Accessed 14 August 2020

UNICEF (2020b) Tips and Guidance for Families https://www.unicef.org/coronavirus/covid-19#COVID-19-explainers Accessed 8 August 2020

UNICEF (2020c) UNICEF Executive Board: An Informal Guide 2020 https://www.unicef.org/about/execboard/files/EB-Informal_Guide-2020-EN-2019.11.07.pdf Accessed 12 August 2020

UNICEF (2020d) UNICEF outlining plans to transport up to 850 tonnes of COVID-19 vaccines per month on behalf of COVAX, in 'mammoth and historic' logistics, https://www.unicef.org/ukraine/en/press-releases/unicef-outlining-plans-transport-850-tonnes-covid-19-vaccines-month-behalf-covax#:~:text=UNICEF%20could%20potentially%20transport%20up,vaccines%20UNICEF%20transports%20every%20month Accessed 30 January 2021

UNICEF (2020) UNICEF issues record US$6.4 billion emergency funding appeal to reach more than 190 million children impacted by humanitarian crises and the COVID-19 pandemic, https://www.unicef.org/rosa/press-releases/unicef-issues-record-us64-billion-emergency-funding-appeal-reach-more-190-million Accessed 30 January 2021

UNICEF (undated-a) UNICEF mission statement, https://www.unicef.org/about-us/mission-statement Accessed 30 January 2021.

UNICEF (undated-b) Immunization programme, https://www.unicef.org/immunization Accessed 30 January 2021

UNICEF (undated-c) Child poverty set to remain above pre-pandemic levels for at least five years in high-income countries – UNICEF, https://www.unicef.org.uk/press-releases/child-poverty-set-to-remain-above-pre-pandemic-levels-for-at-least-five-years-in-high-income-countries-unicef/ Accessed 30 January 2021

Nataliia Hendel holds a PhD in International Law, and is Professor of the International Law and Comparative Law Department at the International Humanitarian University, Ukraine.

Chapter 35
World Health Organization (WHO)

Nataliia Hendel

Contents

35.1 Introduction 734
35.2 History of the WHO 734
35.3 The WHO—A Specialized Agency of the United Nations 735
35.4 Legal Personality 736
35.5 Organizational Structure 738
35.6 The WHO Functions 741
35.7 WHO Rule-Making Function 745
35.8 State Responsibilities in Combatting the COVID-19 Pandemic 754
35.9 Conclusion 756
References 757

Abstract The World Health Organization (WHO) works worldwide to promote health and keep the world safe. The Organization coordinates the efforts of multiple sectors of the government and international offices, NGOs and research groups in order to attain the highest possible level of health for all peoples. This chapter discusses evolution of the WHO, its structure and legal personality. Special attention is paid to the WHO regional offices and decentralization of the WHO functions. The author analyses adoption of the 'COVID-19 Response' Resolution and highlights the existing responsibility of national authorities to adopt and implement appropriate measures to combat the COVID-19 pandemic. The chapter highlights that due notice should be given to the specifics of the national health care systems and other factors. The research is relevant due to the rapid spread of the COVID-19 pandemic and it urges to assess the effectiveness of the IHR mechanism for preventing the spread of infectious diseases.

Keywords COVID-19 · World Health Organization · IHR · World Health Assembly · WHO Executive Board · United Nations Economic and Social Council · League of Nations Health Organization

---

N. Hendel (✉)
International Law and Comparative Law Department, International Humanitarian University, Odessa, Ukraine

© T.M.C. ASSER PRESS and the authors 2022
S. Sayapin et al. (eds.), *International Conflict and Security Law*,
https://doi.org/10.1007/978-94-6265-515-7_35

35.1 Introduction

The establishment of the WHO heralded a new dawn in the strengthening of international cooperation in the field of health care and led to the emergence of its modern legal framework. The WHO continues the good work of its predecessors: the International Office of Public Hygiene and the League of Nations Health Organization. The Organization develops standards for sanitary and medical statistics, medication and medical supplies; ensures global epidemiological supervision.

35.2 History of the WHO

When establishing the UN, it was highlighted that the UN members should secure comprehensive cooperation in all fields within their competence.[1] The San Francisco Conference took into account the suggestions of some delegations and recognized the relevance of cooperation in the field of healthcare, with a view to creating conditions of 'stability and well-being'.[2] Health and related matters fell within the competence of the Economic and Social Council (ECOSOC), according to the UN Charter (Article 62). The first session of the ECOSOC commenced in February 1946 and culminated in the adoption of Resolution E/9 on calling for an international conference to consider the range of tasks and issues of international cooperation in healthcare and proposals for establishment of the Universal Healthcare Organization.[3] The resolution also envisaged the set-up of a technical preparatory committee to develop an agenda for International Health Conference.

The preparatory committee held its sessions in Paris from 18 March to 5 April 1946. The composition of the committee was the following: experts in healthcare, representatives of the International Bureau of Public Hygiene, the League of Nations Health Organization and the Health Committee, which had an advisory vote. Throughout the meetings, delegates from France, the United Kingdom, the United States and Yugoslavia drafted a memorandum, which was later submitted to the UN Economic and Social Council. This memorandum clearly outlined that the main freedoms of a human being may be achieved and adhered to only when people are healthy, well-nourished and protected from any diseases.[4] June 1946 was marked with the launch of the International Conference on Health, which consolidated the forces of 64 states, observers from the control authorities of the occupation zones of Germany, Japan, Korea, and 10 international organizations. The meeting's interactive format led to fruitful results—adoption of three international treaties dated 22 July 1946, including the WHO Charter (entered into force in 1948); Protocol on the Liquidation of the International Bureau of Public Hygiene; and finally, the agreement that the

---

[1] Mileikovskiy 1962, p. 531.

[2] Mikhaylov 1984, p. 30.

[3] Ibid.

[4] WHO 1958.

35 World Health Organization (WHO)

Interim Commission would perform international cooperation functions in the field of healthcare pending the day the WHO Charter came into force. The Conference participants also confirmed that 1926 International Sanitary Convention with amendments of 1938, 1944 and 1946 and 1933 International Sanitary and Air Convention with amendments of 1944 and 1946 both remained in force.[5]

The World Health Organization Interim Commission was established on 19 June 1946. From 1 December 1946, the Interim Commission was entrusted with functions to conduct international projects for healthcare; previously, during the war, these obligations were performed by the United Nations Relief and Rehabilitation Administration Health Committee.[6] By 7 April 1948, the Charter of the WHO had already been ratified by 26 UN Member States, and on 24 June 1948, the Palace of Geneva eagerly welcomed delegates to the First World Health Assembly. The Interim Commission was dissolved on 1 September 1948 and all the international health cooperation functions were incorporated by the WHO.

35.3 The WHO—A Specialized Agency of the United Nations

The founding States stipulated in the Preamble of the Constitution that the WHO was 'established hereby as a specialized agency of the United Nations'. At the second session of the World Health Assembly, a qualified majority adopted the agreement between the WHO and the UN that became effective on 10 July 1948. Henceforth, the WHO was officially recognized as a specialized agency of the United Nations.[7]

Acting in the capacity of a specialized agency of the United Nations in the field of health[8] means to operate as a governing and coordinating body for international health cooperation. In order to achieve its aspirations, the organization established and maintains cooperation with the United Nations, its specialized agencies, governmental health institutions, professional and experts, international non-governmental organizations, etc.

In conformity with the Preamble of the WHO Constitution, the organization aims at achieving the highest attainable standard of health by all peoples, tackling global health problems, and setting rules and standards that ensure the highest attainable level of health.[9] The WHO keeps watch on the member states' compliance with the provisions of its Constitution. Under Article 62 of the Constitution, each member shall report annually on the action taken with respect to recommendations made to it by the Organization and with respect to conventions, agreements and regulations. The

---

[5] Korovin 1951, p. 464.

[6] Rozanov 1972, p. 40.

[7] UN and WHO 1948.

[8] The WHO was the first organization to be granted the UN specialized agency status.

[9] WHO 1946.

requirements on reports are set forth in Chapter XIV of the Constitution and encompass statistical and epidemiological reports, as well as information on the implementation of WHO recommendations.[10] In turn, the WHO, as a specialized agency of the United Nations, submits reports on progress towards achieving compliance with the provisions of the International Covenant on Economic, Social and Cultural Rights of 1966 relating to health to the UN Economic and Social Council.[11] Having considered reports submitted by member states, the WHO, as a specialized UN agency, reports to the Economic and Social Council on progress in the field of health, taking into account compliance with the provisions of the International Covenant on Economic, Social and Cultural Rights of 1966.[12]

35.4 Legal Personality

The legal personality of the WHO is determined in the following international instruments: the UN Charter, the WHO Constitution,[13] bilateral WHO-UN agreements and treaties relating to the law and operation of international organizations (e.g., the Convention on the Privileges and Immunities of UN Special Agencies, 1947).[14]

Ian Brownlie describes three criteria which determine the existence of international legal personality: "1) a permanent association of States equipped with organs, that act on permanent basis and pursue statutory goals; 2) a distinction in terms of legal powers and purposes between the organization and its member states; 3) the existence of legal powers exercisable on the international plane, not limited to legal system of one or more states".[15]

Having considered separate provisions of the treaty, the WHO Constitution incorporated features of an international organization, as follows:

(1) The right to establish effective relations and co-operate with Member-States, non-Member-States and any other inter-governmental organizations as may be desirable;[16]

(2) Membership in the Organization shall be open to all States;[17]

(3) The authority to adopt conventions or agreements with respect to any matter within the competence of the Organization;[18]

---

[10] WHO 1946, Articles 61–65.

[11] International Covenant on Economic, Social and Cultural Rights 1966, Article 18.

[12] Ibid.

[13] The WHO Constitution is a constituent document. The WHO Constitution was adopted by the International Health Conference held in New York from 19 June to 22 July 1946, signed on 22 July 1946 by the representatives of 61 States, entered into force on 7 April 1948. See WHO 1946.

[14] Shibaeva 1986, p. 32.

[15] Brownlie 1977, p. 410.

[16] WHO 1946, Articles 3–8 with Articles 69–72.

[17] Ibid., Article 3.

[18] Ibid., Articles 19–21.

35 World Health Organization (WHO)

(4) The Organization enjoys in the territory of each Member such privileges and immunities as may be necessary for the fulfilment of its objective and for the exercise of its functions;[19]

(5) Representatives of Members, persons designated to serve on the Board and technical and administrative personnel of the Organization shall similarly enjoy such privileges and immunities as are necessary for the independent exercise of their functions in connection with the Organization;[20]

(6) When a Member fails to meet its financial obligations to the Organization or in other exceptional circumstances, the Health Assembly may, on such conditions as it thinks proper, suspend the voting privileges and services to which a Member is entitled;[21]

(7) Under Article 96 of the UN Charter and Article 76 of the WHO Constitution, the Organization may seek the advisory opinion of the International Court of Justice on any legal matter arising within its jurisdiction.

Legal status of the WHO as one of the specialized agencies of the UN is referred to in the Agreement between the UN and the WHO of 1948. The United Nations recognizes the World Health Organization as the specialized agency responsible for taking such action as may be appropriate under its Constitution for the accomplishment of the objectives set forth hereunder:

(1) Representatives of the World Health Organization shall be invited to attend meetings of the main committees of the General Assembly when matters within the scope of its competence are under discussion, and to participate, without vote, in such discussions. Representatives of the United Nations shall be invited to attend the meetings of the World Health Assembly and its committees, at the same time representatives of the WHO shall be invited to attend meetings of the General Assembly for purposes of consultation on matters within the scope of its competence. Representatives of the WHO shall be invited to attend the meetings of the Economic and Social Council of the United Nations and Trusteeship Council and of its commissions and committees, and to participate, without vote, in the deliberations of these bodies with respect to items on their agenda relating to health matters.[22]

(2) The organization shall include on the agenda of the Health Assembly or Executive Board, as appropriate, items proposed to it by the United Nations.[23]

(3) The WHO regards the obligation of the UN to make recommendations concerning these matters to the specialized agencies concerned.[24]

(4) Exchange of information and documentation between the UN and the WHO.[25]

---

[19] Ibid., Article 67(a).

[20] Ibid., Article 67(b).

[21] Ibid., Article 7.

[22] UN and WHO 1948, Article II.

[23] Ibid., Article III.

[24] Ibid., Article IV.

[25] Ibid., Article V.

738 N. Hendel

(5) Agreement to co-operate with the Security Council and the Trusteeship Council.[26]

(6) The World Health Organization agrees to furnish any information which may be requested by the International Court of Justice in pursuance of Article 34 of the Statute of the Court.[27]

7) All regional or branch offices of the WHO shall co-operate with respective UN regional offices.[28]

(8) The WHO and the UN work in the interest of administrative and budgetary uniformity and of the most efficient use of personnel and resources, of avoiding, whenever possible, the establishment and operation of competitive or overlapping facilities.[29]

(9) Exchange of information and documentation between the UN and the WHO.[30]

A.I. Dmytriev distinguishes four features of a specialized UN agency: the intergovernmental nature of its statutory instruments; overall international liability incorporated by the statute; fulfilment of social and economic, humanitarian functions; UN recognition. These enlisted criteria are all attributable to the WHO.[31]

35.5 Organizational Structure

The organizational and legal structure of the WHO was set based on the purposes and objectives of the Organization. Under Article 9 of the WHO Constitution, the work shall be carried out by three main WHO organs, namely the World Health Assembly, the Executive Board, and the Secretariat.

The highest body of the WHO is the World Health Assembly. It consists of delegates from WHO member states. Each WHO member state is represented by no more than three delegates, one of whom heads the delegation of that country. Its annual sessions are held in May in Geneva with delegations from all 194 WHO member states. The functions of the World Health Assembly are enshrined in Article 18 of the WHO Constitution. The Assembly shall establish its own rules of procedure in accordance with Article 17 of the WHO Constitution.

The Executive Board consists of 34 members who are qualified in the field of health care. The members of the Executive Board are elected for a term of three years. The main functions of the Executive Board are to implement the decisions and policies of the Assembly, to provide it with advisory assistance.

The Secretariat operates on an ongoing basis. The Secretariat consists of technical and administrative staff headed by the Director-General.

---

[26] Ibid., Article VII with Article VIII.

[27] Ibid., Article X.

[28] Ibid., Article XI.

[29] Ibid., Article XIV with Articles XV and XVI.

[30] Ibid., Article V with Article VI.

[31] Dmytriev and Butler 2013, p. 160

35 World Health Organization (WHO)

The structure of any international organization is attributable to its objective and purposes. In order to achieve the highest attainable standard of health by all peoples, the WHO, in comparison to other international organization operates through its network of regional offices. Therefore, in terms of structure the distinctive element of the WHO is the regionalization of its performance, which combines the decentralization of powers and the centralization of management. The tasks of the organization are carried out by its central organs and six regional offices (Regional Office for Africa, Regional Office for the Americas, Regional Office for South-East Asia, Regional Office for Europe, Regional Office for the Eastern Mediterranean, Regional Office for Western Pacific). Such decentralization makes it possible to achieve statutory goals, taking into account the national, geographical, climatic, economic and environmental characteristics of different states. What is essential is that it helps to reflect regional priorities and challenges.

At the time when the WHO had been just recently establishment, there was only one intergovernmental organization of regional scope—the Pan-American Sanitary Bureau.[32] The Pan-Arab Regional Bureau of Health was in the process of being created. The International Health Conference (New York Conference, 1946) suggested two options for integrating regional health organizations into the WHO structure: via their transformation into regional offices or by signing an agreement to use the administrative bodies and centres of these organizations as regional offices. When drafting the WHO Constitution, it was agreed upon that all inter-governmental regional health organizations in existence prior to the date of signature of this Constitution, shall in due course be integrated with the Organization.[33]

The main goal of the WHO is to provide operational assistance to national health systems. The legal form of this cooperation is manifested in special agreements concluded between the governments concerned and the WHO regional office, as well as the central bodies of the Organization. Thus, the WHO regional offices have legal personality that derives from their contractual basis.

Pursuant to Article 44 of the WHO Constitution, the Health Assembly shall from time to time define the geographical areas in which it is desirable to establish a regional organization. The Health Assembly may, with the consent of a majority of the members situated within each area so defined, establish a regional organization to meet the special needs of such area. There should not be more than one regional organization in each area.

Regional offices are an integral part of the Organization, which is a stress on the administrative centralization. The scope of rights and responsibilities of regional organizations is established by the WHO Assembly. It is enshrined in sufficient detail in agreements between the WHO and the regional offices. Each regional organization is composed of a regional committee and a regional office.

The regional organization is funded from the general budget of the WHO, but if necessary, the regional committee may submit to central authorities a request to

---

[32] By decision of the XV Pan-American Conference, held in September-October 1958, this organization was integrated into the 'Pan-American Health Organization'. See WHO 1946.

[33] WHO 1946, Article 54.

increase the budget at the expense of the member states of some region. According to V.V. Rozanov,[34] financial control is the most effective tool to maintain the centralization of the organization. In addition, the supervision of central bodies over regional offices is perceptible through regular reports on the implementation of programs.[35]

The regional committees are composed of representatives of WHO member states and associate members of the region. The frequency of meetings and the agenda are set independently by the committees, which have the right to draft and adopt their own regulations and rules of procedure. Article 50 of the Constitution empowers regional committees with the following functions: to formulate policies governing matters of an exclusively regional character; to supervise the activities of the regional office; to co-operate with the respective regional committees of the United Nations and with those of other specialized agencies and with other regional international organizations having interests in common with the Organization. Deriving from this provision, in issues of a regional nature, the WHO Constitution entitles regional committees with broad autonomy.

Indeed, the tasks before member states in terms of health cooperation during the establishment of the WHO and the current challenges are very similar, although they have been transformed with due notice to modern peculiarities. The new historical era, which is characterized by the decolonization and disintegration of the world colonial system after World War II, led to the emergence of a number of newly independent states that needed to main their healthcare systems. Some of them had not had any previous experience. For this reason, the main purpose of the regionalization of the organization during its creation was the need to take urgent measures to establish and strengthen health authorities and systems in states that have gained independence from the colonial regime.

The economic and social conditions of the newly independent states of the African and Asian regions still requires assistance from developed states. It includes scientific, technical and professional assistance with a sole aim to improve the health system. Throughout time, the fields of international cooperation in the WHO regional offices have been modified to reflect today's challenges: the fight against maternal mortality and child death; the fight against infection (malaria, HIV/AIDS, new strains of influenza, Ebola, COVID-19) and non-communicable diseases (smoking, obesity and other 'diseases of globalized world'); access to necessary medicines; healthy environment, etc.

---

[34] Rozanov 1972, p. 46

[35] WHO 2010.

35.6 The WHO Functions

In order to achieve its objectives, the WHO performs the following main functions: scientific cooperation; education and dissemination of information; technical cooperation; vertical programs; cooperation with other international organizations (based on the list of functions in Article 2 of the Constitution).

The Organization is under obligation to establish and maintain the necessary statistical and epidemiological services, an international nomenclature of diseases, causes of death and public health practices. The organization is also working to set standards for diagnostics, requirements for food, biological, pharmaceutical and other similar products. This sphere of operation requires substantial amounts of data. In order to facilitate the process of report submissions, each Member is required to provide statistical and epidemiological reports in a manner to be determined by the Health Assembly (Article 64 of the WHO Constitution).

Among all functions of the WHO, special attention is paid to the promotion of cooperation among scientific and professional groups.[36] As a result, international conferences, symposia and congresses are regularly held. Promotion and research in the field of health acquired a high degree of institutionalization due to experts' involvement.[37] Within the WHO structure, representatives of various states compose Expert Panels and Committees. Their powers are laid down in the Regulations for expert advisory panels and committees. The Director-General composes the list of experts from among recognized professionals on as wide a geographical basis as possible. The lists of experts are compiled on the basis of the following areas: viral diseases, cardiovascular diseases, the International Pharmacopoeia and Pharmaceuticals, mental health and occupational hygiene.[38]

In developing and implementing its programmes, the WHO applies the results of research provided by scientific groups, takes into account suggestions from centres and national institutions cooperating with the WHO, as well as international intergovernmental organizations that recognized by the WHO.[39] The operation of researchers and scientific groups is similar to the agenda of the expert committees. On behalf of the WHO, scientific groups review and analyse tests conducted in various fields of medicine and health. The reason is to identify new priorities; they submit reports to the organization on specific issues and make recommendations on health matters that are under development at the WHO, etc.

The centres that work under the aegis of the WHO as permanent agencies make a major contribution to the development of programs at both the global and regional levels. An institution defined by a state is later regarded as a 'WHO recognized institution'. An agreement between the WHO and an institution sets out rights and obligations of both parties. They work jointly with the WHO in the following fields:

---

[36] WHO 1946, para J(n) of Article 2.

[37] WHO 1950.

[38] WHO 2000.

[39] WHO 2020.

nursing, occupational hygiene, infectious diseases, mental health, chronic diseases and technologies to protect health.[40]

The International Agency for Research on Cancer (IARC) is the specialized cancer research agency of the WHO. This agency has a special status in the WHO structure and was established on 20 May 1965 by the decision of the World Health Assembly.[41] The legal status of the IARC was enacted by its Statute.[42] The aim of the IARC is to promote international cooperation in the field of cancer research IARC's founding members were the Federal Republic of Germany, France, Italy, the United Kingdom, and the United States of America. Today, IARC's membership has grown to 27 countries.[43] The International Agency for Research on Cancer keeps its statutory budget that is composed of the contributions of member states. Only WHO member states are entitled to participate in the operation of the International Agency for Research on Cancer. Hence, the institutional component of the WHO that develops means of research includes committees of experts, national centres for health research—previously referred to as '*WHO recognized institutions*'—and, importantly, the International Agency for Research on Cancer has the status of an independent specialized international institution. Among all WHO functions, an extremely valuable and promising attitude is given to research in the field of health. Its legal framework is based on the provisions of the WHO Constitution and agreements with other international organizations and the instruments developed by the WHO. A crucial role is to coordinate these functions with the operation of national research institutions.

WHO education programs are primarily aimed at helping states to build effective national healthcare structures. The WHO has repeatedly assisted states in establishing medical schools or improving the quality of teaching of medical disciplines in existing facilities. For that reason, the WHO arranges visits of teaching groups to states that lack expertise and paid scholarships. WHO conferences and symposia also contribute to the professional development of health specialists.

WHO education missions are the result of successful implementation of the WHO goal of dissemination of information about health. To lead its projects, the WHO accumulates a huge amount of information from various areas of healthcare, including on the epidemiological situation in the world, medical technologies, pharmaceuticals, processes of planning and administration of national healthcare systems, and national healthcare laws. A vast number of collections, brochures and journals under the auspices of the WHO are published annually with a focus on specific health

---

[40] WHO 2021.

[41] In 1963 the President of the French Republic, General Charles de Gaulle declared the initiative of a group of French students, they called the powers of the vision of 0.5% of the national budget to fight against the 'common issue'—cancer. See IARC 2015.

[42] WHO 1983, p. 196.

[43] The IARC was later joined by Australia, Austria, Belgium, Brazil, Canada, Denmark, Finland, India, Iran, Ireland, Japan, Morocco, Norway, the Netherlands, Qatar, the Republic of Thailand, Korea, the Russian Federation, Spain, Switzerland. See International Agency for Research on Cancer. Membership: www.iarc.fr/en/about/membership.php. Accessed 7 January 2021.

issues. Due to the successful dissemination of knowledge and the latest developments, WHO-produced information assists national health systems, and contributes to making them more effective and sophisticated.

According to para C of Article 2 of the WHO Constitution, the organization assists governments, upon request, in strengthening health services. This assistance is aimed at developing national health systems, expanding the list of medical services provided, conducting emergency response operations, and promoting the elimination of epidemic and endemic infectious diseases. In order to exercise these, the organization also develops and implements various programs. The pivotal role is taken by the principle of non-interference in the internal affairs of the state, enshrined in the UN Charter and the Declaration of Principles of International Law relating to friendly relations and cooperation between states.

The peculiar issue of technical cooperation is that the states must pay to receive assistance. Cooperation also includes advising states on any health issue. The legal background of this assistance is based on the provisions of the WHO Statute and agreement with a particular member state.

The separate line of work of the WHO is management of health vertical programmes, which constitute adopted plans of actions implemented by special purpose bodies aimed to achieve a specific task regarding a disease. The WHO system defines one universal system of program regulation. B.V. Babin distinguishes two types of WHO programmes: those that fulfil mandate functions (e.g., *Global Strategy on Diet*, Physical Activity and Health, 2004) and those that represent internal programmes (e.g., WHO Eleventh General Program).[44]

The programme is managed by the WHO Executive Board, which makes all financial, personnel and technical decisions. The programme is implemented in countries that are part of a region, which are included in the structure of the WHO Regional Office.

Cooperation between the WHO and other international organizations is a key prerequisite to achieve the statutory goals and objectives. In accordance with Article 71 of the WHO Constitution, the organization may, on matters within its competence, make suitable arrangements for consultation and cooperation with non-governmental international organizations and, with the consent of the government concerned, with national organizations, governmental or non-governmental. Treaties usually enshrine matters and forms of cooperation, representation of parties at sessions of governing organs, exchange of information and statistics, joint research, funding of joint programs, administrative and technical cooperation, etc.

Effective relations and close cooperation with other inter-governmental organizations is an obligation of the WHO according to its Constitution (Article 70 of the WHO Constitution). Paragraph (b) of Article 2 of the Constitution codified the necessity to establish and maintain effective collaboration with the United Nations, specialized agencies, governmental health administrations, professional groups and such other organizations as may be deemed appropriate.

---

[44] Babin 2012, p. 275.

The WHO collaborates with international organizations on the basis of bilateral agreements. All agreements contain standard provisions on cooperation, exchange of information and exchange of representatives. The treaties with FAO, ILO, UNESCO and UNIDO provide for the option of setting up joint commissions to consider any issue of common interest to both High Parties. These commissions function on the basis of independently adopted regulations. The agreements with the UNESCO, the IAEA and IFAD contain terms which make it possible to split the powers of these institutions on related issues.

Special attention should be paid to inter-organizational programs, set out on the basis of the agreements between organizations. In order to achieve abovementioned, specialized institutions are established as executive bodies. To our view, this is a progressive form of inter-organizational coordination, which makes possible an amalgamation of various international organizations into a single global system.

The majority of programmes are implemented jointly by two or more organizations:

- UNAIDS collects the efforts of the WHO, ILO, UNICEF, UNESCO, UNDP, WFP, UNFPA, UNODC and the World Bank;
- WHO and UNESCO work side-by-side to implement a program, called 'the Basic School Education and Health Program';
- Joint commissions of the WHO and ILO focus on occupational health issues and the health of people who work at marine;
- Joint expert commission of WHO and FAO studies the effects of various food impurities on human beings;
- The WHO and the World Bank cooperate in professional development field and research in the sphere of tropical diseases, the struggle against cancer and harsh respiratory diseases, etc.;
- The WHO and the IAEA established a Joint Cancer Program aimed at strengthening and accelerating efforts to combat cancer in developing countries by signing the agreement dated 26 May, 2009.[45,46]

The WHO acts jointly with the United Nations Development Program on many issues. The UNDP provides funds to the WHO projects to prevent blindness, ensure access to fresh drinking water and food safety, as well as the health of the elderly and the development of new vaccines, etc.

The WHO exercises its functions on three levels—global, regional and national. Reasonably, its structure of cooperation is divided based on the universal, regional and national levels. Having obtained the expressed consent of the state, the WHO may cooperate with its governmental entities and NGOs. Cooperation with regional

---

[45] Development of the joint WHO-IAEA programme commenced in May 2005 when the WHA of the WHO adopted Resolution 58.22. In 2020, the IAEA developed a Program of Action on Cancer Therapy (PDTR) to help build capacity for radiotherapy in developing countries and to strengthen cooperation to address the huge inequalities that exist in cancer services.

[46] Karkishchenko 2007, p. 30–40.

intergovernmental organizations is led mainly through regional offices of the WHO on the terms set in the respective agreements.

In late 1968, the WHO cooperated with 78 international NGOs,[47] and as of 4 February 2020, it maintains work with 217 organizations[48] that have the right to participate in meetings of the Executive Board and the World Health Assembly, but do not have the right to vote. The WHO Executive Board reviews submissions of the organizations endeavouring to enter into relations with WHO and undertakes the decision, which is communicated to the organization through the Director-General. The criteria for the organizations to enter into official relations with the WHO are as follows: the scope of functions should be related to the competence of the WHO, entity's goals and objectives should be consistent with the spirit, goals, principles of the WHO Constitution. International NGOs regularly perform advisory functions and make proposals on certain WHO programs. The legal framework for the WHO-NGOs relations is limited to resolutions of the UN General Assembly and ECOSOC.

To recapitulate, the global system of healthcare was established under the aegis of the WHO; it is based on the international agreements as well as soft law, including programme regulation. Not only the WHO functions as a single body, it became a centre to global institutionalized health system at the core of which are international organizations of global purpose, specialized universal organizations, and regional international NGOs which possess legal personality.

Last but not least, specialized committees of experts and national research centres are at the forefront of healthcare. Those are the so-called 'WHO-recognized institutions' and they do not have an international legal personality. At the universal level, the WHO successfully fulfils a coordinating function over international organizations in the field of health, and at the regional level over the WHO regional offices. The cornerstone of such cooperation is the realization of the WHO goal 'achieving the highest attainable standard of health by all people'. The WHO operates to achieve its fundamental treaty objectives, some of which have already made progress (scientific programs, education and dissemination of information, cooperation with other organizations), whilst others remain core gaps (law making process, fulfilment of the vertical projects, technical co-operation).

35.7 WHO Rule-Making Function

The law-making function is of particular importance to an international intergovernmental organization to achieving its statutory objective. This function includes development of international legal instruments and recommendations, adoption of rules governing the operation of the Organization as well as soft law. The law-making function of the WHO is not an exception; however, it has some peculiarities. The

---

[47] Rozanov 1972, p. 89.
[48] WHO 2021.

function is enshrined in Article 2, para (k) of the WHO Constitution. Article 19 elaborates on this provision:

the Health Assembly shall have authority to adopt conventions or agreements with respect to any matter within the competence of the Organization.

In lieu of the other WHO organs, the World Health Assembly is the body that determines the policies of the organization and adopts its main documents within the powers prescribed by the Constitution. Conventions or agreements adopted by a two-thirds vote of the Health Assembly have the supreme legal force according to Article 19 of the Constitution. In conformity with Article 102, para 1 of the UN Charter and the Resolution 91 (1) of the UN General Assembly, every treaty comes into force as soon as it is registered with the Secretariat. The WHO conventions or agreements may take effect for any WHO Member State only after they have been adopted (ratified) by respective national authorities with respect to its Constitutional procedure.

An important provision contains Article 20 of the Constitution, which sets an eighteen-month acceptance period after the adoption by the Health Assembly of a convention or agreement. Each member shall notify the Director-General of the action taken, and if each member does not accept such convention or agreement within the time limit, it will furnish a statement of the reasons for non-acceptance.

The Health Assembly is also empowered to adopt regulations concerning: sanitary and quarantine requirements and other procedures designed to prevent the international spread of disease; nomenclatures with respect to diseases, causes of death and public health practices; standards with respect to diagnostic procedures for international use; standards with respect to the safety, purity and potency of biological, pharmaceutical and similar products moving in international commerce; advertising and labelling of biological, pharmaceutical and similar products moving in international commerce.[49]

The concept of letting an organization have the authority to adopt regulations is brand new in the history of health international organizations and it significantly enhances the WHO's competence compared to its predecessors. *Obiter dictum*, the described authority is not generally accepted in international law. Neither a formal agreement nor ratification is required for the rules to enter into force. However, the WHO member states are bound to comply with the rules adopted by the World Health Assembly in in accordance with the commitments made in ratifying the Constitution. Undoubtedly, there are following exceptions to the binding nature of the provisions, namely when the state rejected or communicated its waiver or made reservations about certain provisions of the rules. All such reservations are subject to consideration by the Assembly, which shall either accept or reject them on the condition it finds that the reservations are contrary to the spirit, content or purpose of the act. If the Assembly has not accepted the reservation, the State which has made the reservation shall not be considered a party to an agreement. Furthermore,

---

[49] WHO 1946, Article 21.

35 World Health Organization (WHO) 747

the adopted rules become binding on new members when they sign and accept the WHO Constitution.[50]

By legal nature, rules are not of a 'conventional' international treaty; this is substantiated by a *sui generis* adoption procedure. States have expressed their acceptance by signing the WHO Constitution, but more importantly they expressed acquiescence by silence (unless states have stated otherwise, acquiescence by silence applies). Moreover, the will of the state is clearly expressed when voting for the adoption of rules in the Assembly. Pursuant to the commentary of the Vienna Convention on the Law of Treaties (1969), an international treaty may have a particular designation that will distinguish it from others, but this fact will neither affect its legal nature nor its regulation by international law.[51]

Via this procedure, the International Health Regulations (IHR) were adopted in 1951 with subsequent amendments in 1955, 1956, 1960, 1963 and 1965. The rules evolved, and the next version of the IHR was developed in 1969; it was amended in 1973 and 1981. The latest version of the IHR was drafted by 2005 and entered into force on 15 June 2007. The IHR is a 'non-classic' international treaty binding 196 states. IHR dated 2005 outlined the objective as preventing the most serious cross-border health risks. The adoption of IHR in 2005 has led to the unification of numerous international sanitary conventions.[52]

The IHR incorporate binding standards and measures aimed to prevent the spread of diseases in international ports, airports, and all means of transport. The 2005 Edition established several measures to be taken in emergent situations. It is worth mentioning that the IHR contains a provision that prohibits discrimination and unjustified extension of quarantine, demonstrating that human rights are a number one priority. Before, these provisions were not reflected in the sanitary conventions. The Committee on International Quarantine monitors compliance with the rules.

The next crucial fact is that among traditional and primary WHO functions there has always been the fight against the spread of infectious diseases. WHO is a leading international healthcare subject that confronts epidemics and pandemics from various perspectives: professional (scientific-medical), legal, informational and coordinative. Bearing in mind the current realities in the world, there are definitely new threats to global health, unknown before, and responding to them is a function of the WHO. Whether the organization adjusts to new environment is subject to analysis.

Globalization has one severe drawback, so let us review it in more detail. Speed of spreading and the emergence of new ways of spreading are modern features of

---

[50] Ibid., Article 22.

[51] Talalaev 1997, p. 10.

[52] International Sanitary Convention, signed in Paris on 21 June 1926; the International Sanitary Convention for Aerial Navigation, signed in the Hague on 12 April 1933; Convention that amended the International Sanitary Convention dated 21 June 1926 p.; Washington Protocol dated 23 April 1946 on the prolongation of the International Sanitary Convention of 1944; Washington Protocol dated April 23, 1946 on the prolongation of the International Sanitary Convention on the dated 1944; International sanitary rules 1951 and additional rules 1955, 1956, 1960, 1963 i 1965 p.; International medical and sanitary rules 1969 p. and amendments made in 1973 and 1981.

pandemics.[53] The spread of pandemics does not affect the health of a single person only, but does lead to health issues on a mass scale. Despite obvious progress in medicine manufacturing, pandemics became a serious threat both to individual states, groups of states and to humanity as a whole. This was already marked during the outbreaks of cholera (2000–2008);[54] SARS (2003);[55] avian influenza (2003–2004,[56] 2006–2007, 2012,[57] 2013);[58] H1N1 influenza (2009,[59] 2010);[60] Zika virus (1952, 1960-1980, 2007, 2013, 2015);[61] Ebola (1995, 2000, 2002, 2007, 2014–2016);[62] COVID-19 (2019[63]–present). Unfortunately, the issue of the spread of HIV and AIDS remains.[64]

The mere existence of threats to health creates obstacles to exercising the right to health. One eminent epidemiologist, Nobel Laureate Charles Nicole, when speaking about the changes in infectious diseases stressed: '[The] Future will give birth to

---

[53] The initial local rules were developed during the Middle Ages. One of the provisions was prohibition of free movement in times of disease and limited right to property. Thus, the restriction of various individual human rights and the control of infectious diseases were the first mechanisms of health care. The right to health has a public character, which received international legal recognition earlier than the individual right to health (after the Second World War).

[54] The annual number of infected in the world in 2000–2008 is stable and reaches approximately 2.8 million cases per year. See Ali et al. 2012, p. 209.

[55] The first new disease of the twenty-first century, first discovered in southern China and spread globally within a few months, affecting 33 countries. The total number of patients reached 8437, 916 of them died (mortality 11%). See Kutierev 2008.

[56] According to the WHO, cases have been reported in 63 countries, see FAO 2012.

[57] The Indonesian Ministry of Health in 2012 notified the WHO of a new case of human infection with avian influenza A (H5N1) virus. Avian influenza—situation in Indonesia—update, see WHO 2012.

[58] As of 9 May 2013, 130 laboratory-confirmed cases of A (H7N9) virus infection were reported (including 32 fatalities). They were registered in eight provinces (Anhui, Fujian, Hunan, Henan, Jiangxi, Jiangsu, Zhejiang, Shandong) and two municipalities (Beijing and Shanghai) of China. In addition, one case was reported by the Taipei Centers for Disease Control. See the press release: http://www.euro.who.int/ru/what-we-do/health-topics/communicable-diseases/influenza/news/news/2013/05/human-infections-with-avian-influenza-ah7n9-virus-in-china-update-3. Accessed 7 January 2021.

[59] WHO 2011, para 13.2.

[60] Official reports of laboratory-confirmed cases of pandemic H1N1 flu have come from 213 countries and marine areas or local communities. See the press release: http://www.who.int/dg/speeches/2010/ihr_20100412/ru/index.html. Accessed 7 January 2021.

[61] See the press release on Zika virus: https://www.who.int/news-room/fact-sheets/detail/zika-virus#:~:text=Zika%20virus%20is%20a%20mosquito,Americas%2C%20Asia%20and%20the%20Pacific. Accessed 7 January 2021.

[62] Mercy Corps 2019.

[63] See the press release on coronavirus (COVID-19) https://www.who.int/emergencies/diseases/novel-coronavirus-2019. Accessed 7 January 2021.

[64] According to UN reports dated from 2007 to 2010, the development of HIV/AIDS is a source of global insecurity and a barrier to the realization of the right to health.

35 World Health Organization (WHO)

new infectious diseases while some old ones will slowly disappear, and those that succeeded to survive will not have the same forms we are used to'.[65]

The bottom line here is that the 'globalization' of the threat requires the 'globalization' of countermeasures. Traditional forms of state cooperation in the field of health are obsolete and do not correspond to the peculiarities of the spread of pandemics. Affirming progresses of globalization, the only means of tackling modern challenges and threats is international legal cooperation, but it requires high-level efficiency of legal regulation in the field of health.

The WHO legal action in the struggle against infectious viruses is not limited to IHR. Numerous resolutions of the organization, which contain provisions that supplement certain articles, sections and paragraphs of the rules clarifying their content and disclosing the mechanism of their implementation, are reliable tools in a battle against pandemics.

The general responsibility for the fulfilment of IHR provisions 2005 was undertaken by States' Parties and the WHO. To be able to communicate on updates or take appropriate measures on public health risks or emergencies, States' Parties must have the authority to detect such cases through a well-organized national surveillance infrastructure and appropriate measures. States' Parties are encouraged to work jointly altogether, including the WHO to accumulate financial resources to follow their IHR 2005 commitments. Based on the received requests, WHO will assist developing countries in mobilizing financial assets and providing the necessary technical support to create, strengthen and support the capacity required by IHR 2005 for such states.

One of the tools used to confront diseases within the WHO is the Global Outbreak Alert and Response Network. It was created for the international implementation of IHR 2005 based on the Guidelines for International Outbreak Alert and Response Network. The global network is a foundation of technical cooperation of institutes and networks that combine human and technical resources to quickly identify and confirm outbreaks of diseases of international importance and respond to them.[66] The Guiding Principles for International Outbreak Alert and Response aim to improve the delivery of international assistance in support of local efforts by partners in the Global Outbreak Alert and Response Network and seek to promote the highest standards of professional performance in the field.[67]

The WHO coordinates international efforts to response disease outbreaks using network resources. The WHO also provides secretarial support to the network as part of the Epidemic Alert and Response in Emergencies system. To improve coordination between partners, protocols governing network structure, operations and communication have been drafted and adopted.[68]

---

[65] Kutiriev 2008.

[66] See WHO 2005.

[67] See WHO 2018.

[68] Ibid.

The Global Outbreak Alert and Response Network heavily relies on technical and operational resources of research institutes in member states, regional technical networks, laboratory networks, UN agencies (e.g., UNICEF, UNHCR), the International Red Cross Red Crescent Movement (International Committee of the Red Cross, International Federation of the Red Cross and Red Crescent Societies (IFRC) and national Red Cross and Red Crescent Societies) together with international humanitarian NGOs (e.g., Doctors Without Borders (MSF), International Rescue Committee, etc.).[69]

For a long time, the only convention adopted within the WHO framework was the WHO Framework Convention on Tobacco Control 2003 (WHO FCTC), and in 2012 the Protocol to Eliminate Illicit Trade in Tobacco Products was adopted by consensus. The adoption of the WHO FCTC significantly influences the international legal regulation in the field of health and the development of international health regulations. First, the WHO used its law-making function for the first time; second, the WHO FCTC drafting and adoption is a joint work of international governmental and non-governmental organizations (WTO, ILO, FAO, International Union against Cancer, International Union against Tuberculosis and Lung Disease); third, the floor is free to discuss the efficiency of the WHO FCTC and the 2012 Protocol.

The issue of smoking and its implications, at first glance, usually affects only the health of the smoker. However, this problem had gradually turned into an epidemic, and its social consequences became global. The documents reiterate the global tobacco epidemic. The reason behind it is the liberalization of trade in tobacco products, global marketing and cigarette smuggling. Roughly six million people die each year from tobacco-related diseases[70] (in contrast, in the twentieth century, according to the WHO, more than 100 million people died from tobacco).[71] By 2030, this figure could rise to 10 million, with the highest death toll in developing countries. According to researchers at the University of Edinburgh, if tobacco consumption does not decrease, in the twenty-first century about one billion people will die from the effects of smoking.[72] 650,000 Europeans pass away each year due to smoking effects.[73] This boosts the need for international cooperation in the struggle against tobacco-related issues.[74]

Undoubtedly, the problem has deep roots as the tobacco industry usually involves multinational companies with significant opportunities to influence states' policies. Therefore, only international cooperation can ensure the effectiveness of the confrontation with TNCs. The abovementioned grounds became causes for the adoption of the WHO FCTC in 2003—the first international treaty to be adopted under the auspices of the WHO. The Convention was adopted by the WHO on 21 May 2003

---

[69] See WHO 2007.

[70] WHO 2013.

[71] See Prikhodko 2003.

[72] Matveev 2011, p. 29.

[73] WHO 2005.

[74] Ibid.

and entered into force on 27 February 2005. Despite only 18 years having passed since its adoption, there are already 182 parties.[75]

The objective of the WHO FCTC and its protocols is to protect current and future generations of people from the negative medical, social, environmental, economic consequences of tobacco and tobacco smoke as well as to eliminate devastating effects on human health by providing an appropriate framework for tobacco control measures that are subject to implementation by Parties at the national, regional and international levels. The States Parties shall be guided by the principles set out in Article 4 of the Convention to implement the provisions of the 2003 Convention and the WHO FCTC.

The general obligations under the WHO FCTC are incorporated in Article 5. These include, *inter alia*, the development, implementation and updating of comprehensive multisectoral national tobacco control strategies, plans and programs; establishment of a national coordination mechanism or a coordinating organ for tobacco control; undertaking adequate legislative, executive, and administrative measures to develop policies aimed to prevent and reduce tobacco consumption, nicotine dependence, and exposure to tobacco smoke. The second session of the Conference of the Parties held in July 2007 decided to establish an Intergovernmental Negotiating Body (FCTC/COP2 (12)), open to all parties, to prepare a draft and negotiate a Protocol on the Illicit Trade in Tobacco Products to supplement Article 15 of the WHO Framework Convention on Tobacco Control.[76] The fourth session of the FCTC Intergovernmental Negotiating Body negotiating the Protocol on Illicit Trade in Tobacco Products was held in Geneva during 14–21 March 2010. The session decided to recommend to the Conference of the Parties to consider a draft Protocol on the Illicit Trade in Tobacco Products on its 4th session.[77] On 10 January 2013, the Protocol on the Elimination of Illicit Trade in Tobacco Products was opened for signature.[78] It was adopted by the Parties to the WHO FCTC in November 2012.[79]

The WHO FCTC is a framework convention. In conformity with Article 3, the purpose of the Convention is 'to provide a framework for tobacco control measures to be implemented by the Parties at the national, regional and international levels to reduce continually and substantially the prevalence of tobacco use and exposure to tobacco smoke'. According to para 2 of Article 6, 'Each Party shall take account of its national health objectives concerning tobacco and adopt and maintain measures that may include establishment of tax policies or sales prohibition'. Framework conventions usually contain blanket rules that indicate the general course of action of

---

[75] WHO 2021.

[76] WHO 2021.

[77] The document is compiled in FCTC/COP/INB-IT/4/7 in accordance with decisions FCTC/COP2 (12) and FCTC/COP3 (6).

[78] Representatives of 12 states immediately signed the protocol, in particular: Gabon, China, Libya, Myanmar, Nicaragua, Panama, the Republic of Korea, the Syrian Arab Republic, Turkey, Uruguay, France and South Africa.

[79] Protocol to Eliminate Illicit Trade in Tobacco Products entered into force on 25 September 2018.

the state, but do not contain guidelines to adopt any specific rules of legal regulation.[80] Affirming the nature of the FCTC framework, the WHO provides references to the guidelines proposed by the Conference of the Parties for the implementation of the provisions of the articles of the 2003 Convention (namely, Articles 6, 7, 9). But the 2003 Convention does not make them binding. These principles are soft law. They are recommendations and they do not create legal obligations for any member states. At the same time, nothing prevents the state from considering them as such or taking them seriously. Recommendations for the implementation of the provisions of Article 8 were adopted by the Second Conference of the Parties to the Convention in Bangkok in 2007.

A distinctive feature of this convention is presence of protocols. As mentioned above, in Article 2, the WHO FCTC refers to the Convention and its Protocols as a whole. The 4th Session of the Conference of the Parties to the WHO FCTC was held from 15 to 20 November 2010 in Punta del Este, Uruguay. The participating countries considered the Protocol to Combat the Illicit Traffic in Tobacco Products and the Guidelines for the Implementation of Article 9 of the 2003 Convention—'Regulation of the contents of tobacco products'; Article 12—'Education, communication, training and public awareness'; Article—14 'Demand reduction measures concerning tobacco dependence and cessation'.[81]

It is noteworthy that throughout the WHO operation, its cornerstone policy was to cooperate with states rather than apply administrative measures,[82] which also affected the Organization's rule-making activities—namely the development and adoption of only three universal agreements in the field of health. In particular, the WHO uses its rule-making function by adopting a number of recommendations that allow states to implement their provisions in domestic legal systems depending on the development of medical science,[83] technology and the state of national health systems, without establishing severe challenges.

A special feature of the WHO rule-making process is the adoption of mostly soft law instruments, particularly regulations and recommendations, which are guidelines that are not legally binding.[84] It is worth stressing that recommendations of the Assembly are adopted by a simple majority vote of the delegations present (abstentions are not considered).[85]

---

[80] Strishchenko 2011.

[81] Melnichuk 2010.

[82] Beliakov 2009.

[83] Ibid.

[84] WHO 1946, Article 23.

[85] Rules of Procedure of the World Health Assembly, Article 69.

35 World Health Organization (WHO)

The adoption of 'Global Strategies' is a new phenomenon in international legal cooperation, which marks the transition from classical programs aimed at combating certain diseases, providing technical equipment and providing effective and affordable health care. Global strategies were adopted by a resolution of the Assembly.[86] A reflection of the global approach to public health is the strategy 'Health for All in the 21st century', adopted by the WHO in 1998. This strategy developed for the first two decades of the twenty-first century contains global priorities and challenges that should provide the opportunity to achieve the highest attainable standard of health by all peoples.

In addition, the law-making function of the WHO is used to produce 'institutional law' for the WHO. The Assembly does not adopt recommendations for member states, but it does for other WHO bodies (Executive Board, Director-General, Regional Offices, Committees of Experts, etc.). Legal force of those for states and organs is different. The WHO Assembly is the top organ in the hierarchy; its recommendations are binding on subordinate bodies. The WHO also adopts resolutions regulating the internal affairs of the organization, e.g., to approve the budget, rules of procedure, elections, etc.

Acts developed by the WHO regional offices should be examined in detail. They are similar to acts of central bodies; however, they maintain their regional nature. They should not contradict the general policy of the WHO and the rules issues by central authorities. The WHO regional offices may enter into agreements with regional bodies of other international organizations, with regional organizations, with member states of their organization, and may adopt recommendations, etc.[87] They may also adopt health regulations necessary for their respective region. For example, the Pan American Health Organization in its operation is governed by the

---

[86] The WHO has numerous strategies: *the Global Strategy* for *Infant* and Young *Child* Feeding 2002, https://apps.who.int/iris/bitstream/handle/10665/42590/9241562218.pdf. Accessed 7 January 2021; the Global Strategy for the Healthcare Sector for HIV/AIDS 2003–2007, https://apps.who.int/iris/handle/10665/42736. Accessed 7 January 2021; Strategy 'Stop tuberculosis' 2006–2015, https://www.who.int/tb/features_archive/global_plan_to_stop_tb/en/. Accessed 7 January 2021; regional strategies and plans, e.g. 'To tackle tuberculosis in 18 most priority regions of the European region' 2007–2015, https://www.euro.who.int/en/publications/abstracts/plan-to-stop-tb-in-18-high-priority-countries-in-the-who-european-region,-20072015. Accessed 7 January 2021, Chronic Disease Prevention Strategy in Europe 2005, https://www.euro.who.int/__data/assets/pdf_file/0008/96632/E93736.pdf. Accessed 7 January 2021, European Basic Strategy for Reducing the Burden of TB/HIV 2003, https://www.euro.who.int/__data/assets/pdf_file/0005/98294/e81794.pdf. Accessed 7 January 2021.

[87] For example, on 10 December 2012, the Health Cooperation Agreement between the WHO European office and the Eurasian Economic Community; Cooperation Agreement between the WHO/Europe and the Government of the Republic of Tajikistan for a two-year period 2010–2011; Cooperation Agreement between the WHO/Europe and the Ministry of Health of the Republic of Armenia for a two-year period 2010–2011; Cooperation Agreement between the WHO/Europe and the Ministry of Health of Ukraine for the biennium 2012–2013; Cooperation Agreement between the WHO/Europe and the Ministry of Health of Latvia for the biennium 2012–2013; cooperation agreement between the WHO/Europe and the Ministry of Health of the Czech Republic for the biennium 2012–2013, etc.

Pan American Sanitary Code of 1924, but is still recognized by member states of the Pan American Health Organization.

In the contemporary globalized world, health care has ceased to be exclusively a matter of domestic laws due to obstructive conditions and patterns. Aiming to solve the global issues of humankind in the field of health, the rule-making function of the WHO as a specialized UN organization should be intensified, bearing in mind its international absolute advantage in global healthcare.

35.8 State Responsibilities in Combatting the COVID-19 Pandemic

In the context of the COVID-19 pandemic, the chain of actions to be undertaken by China was set in the IHR 2005: Article 6 'Notification' and Article 7 'Information-sharing during unexpected or unusual public health events'. The WHO Assembly adopted a resolution on coronavirus[88] at the 73rd session of the WHO World Health Assembly in May 2019. On the eve of the 73rd session of the World Health Assembly, 122 states called on the WHO and the international community to investigate the source and spread of COVID-19. The 73rd session of the World Health Assembly was held on 18-19 May 2020 in the form of an online conference. The World Health Assembly pursuant to para (a) of Article 21 of the WHO Constitution of 1946, has authority to adopt regulations concerning sanitary and quarantine requirements and other procedures designed to prevent the international spread of disease. On 19 May 2020, the 73rd session of the WHO World Health Assembly adopted by consensus a resolution on combating COVID-19, which was supported by 140 states.

The 'COVID-19 Response' Resolution was submitted for consideration due to the efforts of more than 110 states, including Australia, 27 EU member states, Ukraine, Japan, the United Kingdom, Canada and 54 African states that joined later. None of the 194 WHO member states opposed the drafted COVID-19 Resolution, including the United States and China.

The text of the resolution 'COVID-19 Response' commences with consequences of COVID-19, namely death toll and adverse effects on physical and mental health and well-being. The body of the Resolution discusses ramifications for the economy and society together with aggravation of inequality both in states and among states.

The 'COVID-19 Response' Resolution highlights existing liability of national authorities to adopt and implement appropriate measures to combat the COVID-19 pandemic, with due notice to the specifics of the national health care system and other factors. 194 WHO Member States are bound by the provisions of the WHO Constitution and should comply with International Health Regulations.

The Resolution recalls:

the constitutional mandate of WHO to act, inter alia, as the directing and coordinating authority on international health work and recognizing its key leadership role within the

---

[88] WHO A73/CONF./1 2020.

broader United Nations response and the importance of strengthened multilateral cooperation in addressing the COVID-19 pandemic and its extensive negative impacts'.[89]

Pedro A. Villarreal elaborates that the 'COVID-19 Response' Resolution demands to assess the effectiveness of the WHO itself, excluding liabilities of China.[90] Indeed, the WHO is the main and coordinating international governmental organization in the field of health. However, one should acknowledge that its effectiveness depends on member states actions and fulfilment of obligations under the WHO Constitution and the 2005 International Health Regulations.[91] As noted by Sergey Sayapin, "in case an international organization is to blame for inefficiency, the reason should be sought either in the inadequate functions, initially laid down by its founding states in the statutory documents, or through the pattern of an influential state that hinders its effectiveness. Incompetence of a particular international official inevitably leads to institutional failures".[92]

The Resolution induces a review of the effectiveness of the International Health Regulations of 2005 through an analysis of the implementation of the obligations of member states, including the actions of China under Article 6 'Notification' and Article 7 'Information-sharing during unexpected or unusual public health events'. One more question arises: to what extent are the rules effective and able to be followed to prevent the spread of a virus as has happened in the COVID-19 case? The UN should determine application of legal regulations by states during an outbreak of an epidemic that could threaten all humankind. The UN as a universal organization responsible for the security of the entire international community and the WHO as a coordinating organization for health should verify whether their member states faithfully fulfil their obligations under the WHO Constitution and IHR.

It is worth highlighting that according to the 'COVID-19 Response' Resolution, investigation to assess due diligence with IHR and adaptability of these rules to the modern pandemic is the obligation of the WHO. As Villarreal stated, "within the WHO structure, actions of WHO and Member States may be assessed either by the Independent Oversight and Advisory Committee for the WHO Emergency Program or the IHR Review Committee 2005". This is provided for in Article 50 of the IHR 2005, with preference given to the IHR Review Committee 2005 adding that it will have operational and political advantages.[93]

Therefore, the process of the 'COVID-19 Response' Resolution adoption has *per aspera ad astra,* from political ultimatums to holding an online session for the first time in the history of the WHO. No barriers have prevented the adoption of this

---

[89] PP4 of the Resolution.

[90] Ibid.

[91] See the press release 'Role of Kazakhstan in the struggle against pandemics', https://365info.kz/2020/04/rol-kazahstana-v-borbe-s-pandemiej-kvi-i-mezhdunarodnoe-pravo. Accessed 7 January 2021.

[92] See the press release 'Role of Kazakhstan in the struggle against pandemics', https://365info.kz/2020/04/rol-kazahstana-v-borbe-s-pandemiej-kvi-i-mezhdunarodnoe-pravo. Accessed 7 January 2021.

[93] See Villarreal 2020.

remarkable—even if political—resolution; a document that demonstrated the unity of the international community in the fight against coronavirus. Priorities are set out in the resolution for both the WHO and states. The key to the recovery of the entire planet is simultaneously simple and comprehensive: cooperation among all. Clearly, the investigation of actions of the states and their effect on the spread of COVID-19 as well as international organizations, e.g., the WHO, is still ahead. However, international cooperation is the only way to combat the spread of the greatest threat of today—the COVID-19 pandemic and the SARS-COV-2 causing it.

35.9 Conclusion

International cooperation in the field of health on the universal level is divided between three main WHO organs, within their respective functions, and regional organizations that secure the interests of regions. The object 'to achieve the highest attainable level of health for all peoples' is at the core of such universal cooperation. The WHO operates to achieve its fundamental 'treaty' objects, some of which have already made progress (scientific programmes, education and dissemination of information, cooperation with other organizations), whilst others are whitespace areas (law making process, fulfilment of the vertical projects, technical co-operation).

The IHR 2005 is a 'non-classic' international treaty developed by the WHO that is binding on all member states that have not made respective reservations. The document codified a list of mandatory sanitary standards and measures to prevent the spread of disease in international seaports, airports, and all means of transportation. These measures are the top rules that set *de minimis* requirement for a state to protect its territory from the spread of diseases, including quarantine. It is worth noting that the IHR 2005, for the first time in the history of the adoption of international sanitary treaties, took into consideration both states' interests and, more importantly, human rights. This was achieved via prohibition of discrimination and unjustified extension of quarantine. The rapid spread of the COVID-19 pandemic served as an alarm to verify the effectiveness of the IHR mechanism for preventing the spread of infectious diseases.

One of the substantive areas of WHO work is to tackle the global tobacco epidemic. The WHO FCTC was developed to respond to the threats of the globalized tobacco epidemic. It is the first treaty concluded by member states of the World Health Organization using their mandates under the WHO Constitution. This instrument is a decisive tool for global tobacco control that contains legal obligations for contracting parties; it sets a reasonable level for reducing both tobacco demand and supply. Moreover, it provides comprehensive guidance for implementing tobacco control policies in all countries on different levels.

The WHO regionalization is inevitably characterized by its decentralization. This may be traced in the following way: powers previously assigned only to the central office were put on regional offices to carry out their functions. The win-win strategy was to let regional offices independently develop regional health policy and compile

35 World Health Organization (WHO)

their list of their own priorities, tasks and programs. Consequently, the WHO constitutional organs are no longer involved in the development of regional projects, their implementation and most importantly, evaluation of their effectiveness. Each body became liable only for functions assigned to it.

In conformity with the WHO Constitution, regional offices are empowered to settle issues of 'exclusively regional nature', while the World Health Assembly defines main lines of work of the organization. Such separation of powers points towards the WHO's desire to create a centralized organization that accumulates administrative, financial and policy-making functions. To be more precise, regional organizations have gradually succeeded to achieve broader independence than was expected when established. This idea is supported by the most effective results among other regional institutions of specialized UN agencies.

Taking a closer look at the WHO functions, two main categories arise: permanent technical maintenance of a global value (international quarantine measures, biological standardization, coordination of medical research, etc.) and provision of information, counsel and assistance in the field of health to governments. The difference between the two is the following: the first is carried out at the universal level, while the second is carried out at the regional level. This division of powers was undertaken to secure flexible local needs of particular regions by their respective regional offices. Neither standards nor model rules of procedure for the WHO regional offices have been developed with a view to achieving highest possible level of health by all peoples.

References

Ali M, Lopez A L,You Y A, Kim Y E, Sah B, Maskerya B, Clemens J (2012) The global burden of cholera. Bulletin World Health Organization. 90

Babin B (2012) Programme rehulyuvannya u suchasnomu mizhnarodnomu pravi: evolyutsiya, formy ta mekhanizmy realizatsiyi [Program regulation in modern international law: evolution, forms and mechanisms of implementation]. Phoenix. Odesa

Beliakov A (2009) Vsemirnaya organizatsiya zdravookhraneniya kak tsentral'nyy organ obespecheniya prava cheloveka na zdorov'ye [The World Health Organization as the Central Authority for Ensuring the Human Right to Health]. Russian Justice. 2009. No. 8

Brownlie I (1977) International law, 2nd edn. Progress. Moscow

Dmytriev A, Butler U (2013) Istoriya mezhdunarodnogo prava [History of International Law]. Phoenix. Odesa

FAO (2012) H5N1 Highly Pathogenic Avian Influenza Global overview. April-June 2012. Issue no. 32. http://www.fao.org/3/ap387e/ap387e.pdf. Accessed 7 January 2021

IARC (2015) The First 50. 1965–2015. https://www.iarc.fr/wp-content/uploads/2018/07/IARC_50-years.pdf. Accessed 7 January 2021

Karkishchenko E (2007) Global'noye upravleniye v oblasti mezhdunarodnogo zdravookhraneniya [Global governance in the field of international health]. MGIMO – University. Moscow

Korotkiy T, Sazhienko N. (2012) Vnutrigosudarstvennaya implementatsiya Ramochnoy Konventsii VOZ po bor'be protiv tabaka [Domestic implementation of the WHO Framework Convention on Tobacco Control 2003: the experience of Ukraine]. International law and international organizations. 2012. No. 1

Korovin E (1951) Mezhdunarodnoye pravo [International law]. State Publishing House of Legal Literature. Moscow

Kutierev V (2008) Aktual'nyye problemy osobo opasnykh infektsionnykh bolezney i sanitarnaya okhrana territoriy v sovremennykh usloviyakh [Relative issues of extremely dangerous infectious diseases and sanitary protection of territories in modern conditions]. Journal of Microbiology. 2008

Matveev V (2011) Prevrashcheniye zdorov'ya v dym [Turning health into smoke]. 2000. 29.1V. 2011

Melnichuk E (2010) Ne stoit putat' rekomendatsii s obyazatel'stvami, [Recommendations should not be confused with commitments], see the article http://www.zn.ua/2000/2675/70627/. Accessed 7 January 2021

Mercy Corps (2019) Mercy Corps, Chapter 2: Major Ebola outbreaks in Africa (2019). https://www.mercycorps.org/blog/ebola-outbreaks-africa-guide/chapter-2#:~:text=The%20Ebola%20outbreak%20from%202014,Kingdom%20and%20the%20United%20States. Accessed 7 January 2021

Mikhaylov V (1984) Istoriya mezhdunarodnogo zdravookhranitel'nogo prava [History of international health law]. Far Eastern University Publishing House. Vladivostok

Mileikovskiy A (1962) Mezhdunarodnyye otnosheniya posle vtoroy mirovoy voyny voiny (1945-1949) [International relations after the Second World War (1945-1949)], Gosudarstvennoye izdatel'stvo politicheskoy literatury. State publishing house of political literature. Moscow

Prikhodko O (2003) Cigarette Non grata, https://zn.ua/HEALTH/sigareta_non_grata.html. Accessed 7 January 2021

Rozanov V (1972) Sotsial'no-ekonomicheskiye i politicheskiye aspekty deyatel'nosti Vsemirnoy organizatsii zdravookhraneniya [Social, economic and political aspects of the functions of the World Health Organization]. Publishing house "Science". Moscow

Shibayeva E (1986) Pravo mezhdunarodnykh organizatsiy [Law of international organizations]. International relationships. Moscow

Strishchenko (2011) Smoking the ideals, see the article http://zn.ua/articles/81336. Accessed 7 January 2021

Talalaev A (1997) Commentary to the Vienna Convention on Law of Treaties. Legal Literature. Moscow

Tobes B (2001) Pravo na zdorov'ye: teoriya i praktika [The right to health: theory and practice] http://yakov.works/libr_min/19_t/ob/es_00.htm_01.htm. Accessed 7 January 2021

UN/WHO (1948) Agreement between the United Nations and the World Health Organization

Villarreal P (2020) Pandemic Intrigue in Geneva: COVID-19 and the 73rd World Health Assembly. www.ejiltalk.org/pandemic-intrigue-in-geneva-covid-19-and-the-73rd-world-health-assembly/?utm_source=mailpoet&utm_medium=email&utm_campaign=ejil-talk-newsletter-post-title_2. Accessed 7 January 2021

WHO (1946) WHO Constitution, https://www.who.int/governance/eb/who_constitution_en.pdf?ua=1. Accessed 7 January 2021

WHO (1950) Regulations for expert advisory panels and committees. https://apps.who.int/iris/handle/10665/86631. Accessed 17 November 2021

WHO (1958) WHO official press, 'The First ten years of the WHO' (1958). https://apps.who.int/iris/bitstream/handle/10665/37089/a38153_eng_LR_part1.pdf?sequence=14&isAllowed=y. Accessed 7 January 2021

WHO (1983) WHO primary documents

WHO (2000) EB 107/24 Add. 1, (2000) https://apps.who.int/gb/archive/pdf_files/EB107/re24a1.pdf. Accessed 7 January 2021

WHO (2005) WHO Framework Convention on Tobacco Control (2005)

WHO (2005) WHO Guiding Principles for International Outbreak Alert and Response http://www.who.int/csr/outbreaknetwork/guidingprinciples/en/index.html. Accessed 7 January 2021

WHO (2007) GAR. http://www.who.int/csr/outbreaknetwork/ru/. Accessed 7 January 2021

35 World Health Organization (WHO)

WHO (2010) WHO Medium-term strategic plan 2008–2013 and Proposed programme budget 2012–2013/A64/7, 4 April 2011. http://apps.who.int/gb/ebwha/pdf_files/WHA64/A64_7-en.pdf, Accessed 7 January 2021

WHO (2011) WHA64.1 (2011) www.apps.who.int/gb/ebwha/pdf_files/WHA64/A64_R1-ru.pdf. Accessed 7 January 2021

WHO (2012) Avian influenza – situation in Indonesia – update. https://www.who.int/csr/don/2012_08_10b/en/. Accessed 7 January 2021

WHO (2013) WHO Protocol to Eliminate Illicit Trade in Tobacco Products

WHO (2018) Global Outbreak Alert and Response Network-GOARN. Partnership in Outbreak Response. http://www.who.int/csr/outbreaknetwork/goarnenglish.pdf. Accessed 7 January 2021

WHO (2020) 'COVID-19 Response' Resolution, WHO A73/CONF./1. https://apps.who.int/gb/ebwha/pdf_files/WHA73/A73_CONF1Rev1-en.pdf. Accessed 7 January 2021

WHO (2020) Regulations for Study and Scientific Groups, Collaborating Institutions and Other Mechanisms of Collaboration. https://apps.who.int/gb/bd/pdf_files/BD_49th-en.pdf#page=170. Accessed 17 November 2021

WHO (2021) Intergovernmental Negotiating Body for the Protocol on Illicit Trade in Tobacco Products. www.who.int/fctc/inb/ru/. Accessed 7 January 2021

WHO (2021) WHO collaborating agencies list. www.who.int/collaboratingcentres/ru/index.html. Accessed 7 January 2021

WHO (2021) WHO in relations with other subjects, official list. https://www.who.int/publications/m/item/non-state-actors-in-official-relations-with-who. Accessed 7 January 2021

WHO (2021) List of the Member States of the WHO Framework Convention on Tobacco Control, www.who.int/fctc/signatories_parties/ru/index.html. Accessed 17 November 2021

Nataliia Hendel holds a PhD in International Law, and is Professor of the International Law and Comparative Law Department at the International Humanitarian University, Ukraine.

Chapter 36
United Nations Development Programme (UNDP)

Julio Homem de Siqueira, Andrew G. Mtewa and Daury César Fabriz

Contents

36.1 Preliminary Remarks 762
36.2 The UNDP and the Right to Development as a Human Right 762
36.3 The UNDP in a Nutshell 766
36.4 The UNDP: Roles, Challenges and Critique 769
36.5 Final Remarks 775
References 775

Abstract The United Nations Development Program (UNDP) is mandated to facilitate human development. States are free to associate with the agency in one way or another within the dictates of the law. Thus far, the UNDP has been instrumental in the development of most countries and continues to do so amidst political and religious pressure to operate (or not to operate) in a particular way, limiting its implementation of mandate and duties. Over the years, the UNDP has been praised by many for most of its achievements and scorned as well due to isolated and general observable conducts below expectations. Surveys are limited to exploiting the extent of operation of the agency by non-state actors on the ground in direly needy countries, including post-war and conflict zones, where citizens can give their say on the UNDP's intervention. However, remaining nonpartisan in a country's party politics is key to the relevance of the UNDP's mandate.

Keywords International Conflict and Security Law · United Nations Development Program · Sustainable Development Goals · Development

---

J. H. de Siqueira (✉)
Institute of Criminal Law Studies Alimena, University of Calabria, Rende, Italy

A. G. Mtewa
Malawi University of Science and Technology, Thyolo, Malawi
e-mail: amtewa@must.ac.mw

D. C. Fabriz
Vitoria Law School, Vitoria, Brazil
e-mail: daury@terra.com.br

Brazilian Academy of Human Rights, Vitoria, Brazil

© T.M.C. ASSER PRESS and the authors 2022
S. Sayapin et al. (eds.), *International Conflict and Security Law*,
https://doi.org/10.1007/978-94-6265-515-7_36

36.1 Preliminary Remarks

Peace and tranquillity are some of the major catalysts for sustainable development in any country. The hard-earned development can easily crumble within minutes of instabilities at some levels of state governance. There are many actors in the business of fostering and sustaining development. One of them is the United Nations Development Program (UNDP), which enjoys a unanimous UN mandate. UNDP has virtually been all over with impact on peaceful, warring and post-war countries, with each category having its own story to tell about the extent of support that the UNDP has offered and/or is offering. Obviously, due to differences in conditions, no one expects the UNDP to perform in the same way all over.

This chapter discusses the theoretical aspects of the relationship between the UNDP and the protection of human rights in armed conflict zones, the analytical evaluation of the roles and reported performance of the UNDP over the years, and how the relevance of the agency can be maintained in the ever-growing politically compromised world.

36.2 The UNDP and the Right to Development as a Human Right

Conceptually, human rights only reached visibility during the eighteenth century, with the American Declaration of Independence and the French Declaration of the Rights of Man and Citizen both as products of revolutions. However, a century earlier, during the British revolutions, a Bill of Rights was proclaimed—a Bill that affirmed the idea of human rights as a historical quest of humankind.

Two uncontroversial generations of human rights, the *earlier generations,* were then recognized. The human rights of the first generation were *potestative rights*, covering the *freedoms in, from* and *against* and the *rights to abstention,* such as free doms of conscience, opinion, religion, expression, movement, assembly, profession, private communication and press, as well as property rights. The human rights of the second generation were conceived in a positive dimension; they are *reivindicatory rights*, covering rights pertaining to health, education, decent work, culture, social security, social assistance, and sanitation. The third generation of human rights is the controversial generation.

There is no other dimension beyond negatives and positives. A situation that makes scholars experience some difficulties is where to allocate the new rights, listing so many generations that it seems to have one for each new recognized right. In this plan, then, there can be found third, fourth, fifth, sixth and even seventh generations of rights in various literature sources. In this catalogue are included, for example, the rights to peace, internet, clean energy, life below water, life in land, ecological balance, genetic facilities and development. It can be noted that these rights, as with many others, tend to support a collective perspective of the negative and the positive rights mentioned above, and they do not pertain to an individualistic tradition as does the first generation nor to a socialist one as does the second.[1] However, even if some scholars put such profusion of rights in a list and call it the third generation, it does not seem clear that these are all *human rights*. That is to say, some of these seem to be akin to duties rather than rights, since solidarity or fraternity are prerequisites to realizing them. The right to development is a good case in point.

The right to development was first recognised by the UN General Assembly in 1986 when the Declaration on the Right to Development (UNDRD) was adopted. However, before that, the notion was mentioned at least four times: in 1944, by President Franklin D. Roosevelt in his State of the Union Address; in 1945, when the UN Charter came into force, recognising the need to promote economic and social progress and development; in 1947, when Eleanor Roosevelt described it as "a right to the opportunity for development"; and in 1972, when Kéba Mbaye firstly employed the expression "right to development".[2] It might therefore be concluded that the right to development appeared and started to be discussed in the post-World War II years, but was only recognised under international law by the end of the century.

The concern about development after World War II is not as original as one might think. In the 17th century, some economists already had such preoccupation on development economics.[3] The discussions that culminated in the UNDRD were a kind of retake on such economic concern or a rediscovery.[4] To declare the existence of a right does not mean such a right is a new one, but that it is time to recognise it as part of the human person statute, or, as was established in the 1993 World Conference on Human Rights in Vienna, that the right to development is universal and inalienable.[5] These characteristics mean that every human being has the right to participate in the public policies of development and their outcomes, that is, standing chances and also enjoying opportunities for exercising liberties and rights. To talk about development, no matter what kind, means to enhance living conditions and quality of life,[6] including that of people in armed conflict contexts.

A better life for all is the goal of the right to development. This is also one of the overarching aims of the sustainable development goals (SDGs) and former Millennium Development Goals (MDGs) since the UN Conference on Sustainable Development in 2012. On 25 September 2015, the Conference adopted a set of 17 goals to end poverty, protect the planet, and ensure prosperity for all. As can be seen in the list of seventeen items, the UNDP seems to adopt the perspective of humanitarian duties—an approach founded in cooperation.[7] Its purpose is to understand which arrangements are possible when cooperation is practised and how the earnings they

---

[1] Marks 1981.

[2] Sengupta 2000.

[3] Sen 1988.

[4] Meier 2001.

[5] Sengupta 2000.

[6] Sen 1988.

[7] Sousa Santos 2007; Siqueira 2016.

produce can be used.[8] The possibilities detach the egoistic (an accomplishment of duties for receiving compensation in terms of rights) and altruistic (accomplishment of duties for generating opportunities and empowerment to other people too) types of cooperation. The UNDP adopts the perspective of altruistic cooperation, which includes a virtuous cycle of development for all.

The approach can be better expressed when the list of 17 SDGs is known, as follows:

(1) *end poverty* in all its forms, since the lack of income and resources has as its consequences hunger, malnutrition, limited access to basic services, social discrimination and exclusion, and lack of participation in democratic decision-making;

(2) *end hunger*, achieving food security, improving nutrition and promoting sustainable agriculture, forestry and fishery, generating also decent incomes and environmental protection;

(3) *ensure healthy lives and well-being* for everyone at all ages, reducing common killers, especially child, elderly and maternal diseases;

(4) *ensure inclusive and quality education* for all, increasing access to education and enrolment rates in schools at all levels;

(5) *achieve gender equality* with the empowerment of women and girls in all development fields (education, health care, decent work, participation in democratic decision-making, political representation, etc.);

(6) *ensure access to clean water and sanitation* for all, which includes ameliorating the infrastructure and reducing diseases associated with inadequate water supplies, sanitation, and hygiene;

(7) *ensure access to affordable, reliable, sustainable, modern and clean energy* for all;

(8) *promote decent work opportunities and economic growth* for all, stimulating the economy and helping to protect the environment;

(9) *invest in resilient infrastructure*, achieving sustainable industrialization, as well as fostering innovation, generating income and increasing living standards for all;

(10) *reduce inequalities*, reducing the disparities within and among countries;

(11) *construct and make cities and communities inclusive, safe, resilient and sustainable*, allowing or contributing to the development of ideas, commerce, culture, science, productivity, education, health care, social-economic development and more;

(12) *ensure responsible consumption and production*, promoting sustainability in a wide range of areas such as energy efficiency, infrastructure, access to basic services, decent jobs, better quality of life and more;

(13) *take urgent actions to combat climate change and its impacts*, avoiding the disruption of economies and the promotion of the worsening of life's quality;

(14) *conserve life below water*, since the sustainable use of the oceans, seas, lakes and marine resources influences life above water;

---

[8] Sen 2012.

36 United Nations Development Programme (UNDP)

(15) *conserve life on land*, avoiding human actions that tend to cause deforestation and desertification, reversing land degradations, halting biodiversity losses, and managing better forests and other biomes;

(16) *promote peace, justice and strong institutions and societies*, providing access to justice for all, giving everyone means of participating in the decision-making processes and more; and

(17) *revitalize global partnership for achieving all goals* and, of course, sustainable development for all.

The analysis of each goal individually and then of all the goals collectively shows that they maintain an interconnection and require altruistic cooperation among governments, international organizations, world leaders, and every single person and group, as taught by the Chinese proverb: *"the loftiest towers rise from the ground"*. This means that everyone must contribute and cooperate, to the extent of their capabilities, in achieving sustainable development for all, which includes the fulfilment of all 17 SDGs described above. Obviously, every person, institution, government and organization must make their own effort and assume their responsibilities to contribute to the desired difference.

The usual imagined means for realizing the SDG's purposes are the implementation of public policies and national and international aid for needy people, not only those in miserable conditions, but also people living in armed conflict zones. However, as UNDP described in a 2016 Report—'From the MDGs to Sustainable Development for All: Lessons from 15 Years of Practice'—there are many other means for achieving those goals, for example, establishing agenda and agreements with countries and stakeholders. The report can be employed too as a kind of guideline to suggest how the SDGs can concretely transform societies, as they can be exemplified:

(1) *no one can be left behind*, so early actions must be taken, with strong and visionary initiatives;

(2) *every opportunity* resulting from each effort must be pursued under the same proposal;

(3) *local* change agents must be *empowered*, helping then to build better consensus on priorities and to pursue progressive development;

(4) the targets must reflect *people's priorities*, considering each context;

(5) everyone must know about the actions, so everyone can contribute, enlarging the *mobilization* by means of *synergies* instead of trade-offs;

(6) *institutionalize participatory processes* such as consultations, dialogues and feedbacks to improve robust progress;

(7) *subnational strategies* must be taken, so the local needs can be better known and the inequalities can be better addressed;

(8) *prioritize policy accelerators* for goals that reach multiple objectives, boosting progress on targets that were deemed a priority;

(9) *develop and strength adaptive capacities* by means of repurposing and reallocating;

(10) leave coach empiricism behind and *build a big tent to face real-life problems*;

(11) *establish international partnerships* for boosting specific goals (rights, values, interests), focusing specially on development effectiveness, ensuring more impacting improvements;

(12) use SDGs reports *to engage public and private sectors*, diverse institutions, profitable or not, and individuals, and make reliable and quality data accessible to everyone.

All SDGs are linked to a general development purpose for everyone. Obviously, there are no formulae for *making* development happen, but as the former chief economist of the World Bank once observed, there are strategies for improving development, and they must rely on the transfer and transformation of knowledge, that is, good ideas that can be transformed in efforts and actions.[9] A much more adequate approach to identifying sustainable standards of life depends on the identification of what is lacking and in the aggregation of what can be done by means of criteria that meet individual basic needs within specific conditions of space and time in terms of people's capabilities to employ and use the available goods and opportunities (*rights*).[10]

The availability of goods usually comes from donations and natural resources, but opportunities come from development purposes based on the fulfilment of a specific prerequisite: solidarity. Some scholars have identified the mania of turning everything into rights,[11] so the hidden proposal of the UNDP is to leave behind such obsessions, replacing them with a perspective of altruistic cooperation, based on human duties. This means that the SDGs establish aims of fraternal/altruistic human cooperation concentrated on an end point, development, which is reached through empowerment. And development is, in turn, a right that establishes a starting point of a better life full of social commitment, opportunities, and liberties. Thus, theoretically, the UNDP and the SDGs play an important role for development purposes. But what can be said in practical terms?

36.3 The UNDP in a Nutshell

The UNDP plays a critical role in helping countries achieve the SDGs. There are many legal documents regulating its actions, as well as programmes and modalities that aim to contribute to the achievement of the SDG. Before describing them, it is necessary to present the structure of UNDP. The UNDP administrator is advised by an associate administrator, as well as by an executive office chief of staff. The administrator coordinates nine bureaus, divided into two groups: one composed of five regional bureaus, representing countries in Africa, Asia and the Pacific, Arab States, Europe and the CIS, and Latin America and the Caribbean; the other consisting of four bureaus of support, namely external relations and advocacy, management services,

---

[9] Summers 1991.

[10] Sen 1976, 1979, 1983.

[11] Baxi 2001.

policy and programme support, and crisis support. There are also eight offices, which are within the UNDP structure, but part of the administrative hierarchy, namely the ombudsman, human development report, independent evolution, audit and investigations, ethics, and South-South cooperation. In the same vein, one can also note the work administrated by the UN volunteers and the UN capital development fund.

The overview of the UNDP structure shows that the main scope of this UN organ is to provide support and assistance to governments to achieve the SDGs and deliver on the 2030 Agenda for Sustainable Development. As such, the 2030 Agenda can be seen as the main global programme for achieving development in sustainable means. The Agenda contains a world-wide commitment with 17 goals (SDGs) and 169 targets, integrating into an unprecedented and balanced manner the environmental, economic and social dimensions of sustainable development. The analysis of the 17 SDGs (see Sect. 36.2) reveals that they are integrated and must be fulfilled as a whole, being based on cooperation, such as global partnerships and comprehensive mobilisation. These are also complemented by the Addis Ababa Action Agenda (financing for development).

A very important document of the UNDP is its four-year Strategic Plan. At present we have the Strategic Plan 2018–2021, which is anchored in the 2030 Agenda. Its scope can be summarized with reference to the slogan "*leaving no one behind*". The UNDP vision is telling: It "is to help countries achieve sustainable development by eradicating poverty in all its forms and dimensions, accelerating structural transformations for sustainable development and building resilience to crises and shocks".[12] To better respond to these three development settings and focus resources and expertise, the UNDP identified six Signature Solutions, each being "built on a theory of change with a mix of interventions designed to achieve significant progress towards key Sustainable Development Goals and targets".[13] They are listed by the UNDP Strategic Plan as follows: (1) keeping people *out of poverty*; (2) strengthening effective, inclusive and accountable *governance* for inclusive, peaceful and just societies; (3) enhancing the prevention of crisis and recovery capacities to increase *resilience* in *societies*; (4) promoting *nature-based solutions* for a sustainable planet; (5) closing the *energy gap*; (6) strengthening *gender equality* and the empowerment of women and girls.[14]

A document that focuses on key development issues is the Human Development Report (HDR), which is commissioned by the UNDP. The most recent is the HDR 2020—*The Next Frontier: Human Development and the Anthropocene*.[15] It was produced in a year marked by the COVID-19 pandemic. As acknowledged by the report team, it documents the unfolding of the devastating impact of the pandemic on human development,[16] and marks the effective existence of the new Earth geological epoch, popularised by Paul Crutzen as the Anthropocene, or the age of humans.

---

[12] UNDP 2017, 1.

[13] UNDP 2017, 12.

[14] UNDP 2017, 13–15.

[15] UNDP 2020.

[16] UNDP 2020, iv.

According to the HDR 2020, whether "the Anthropocene implies enormous uncertainty for people and societies", some trends can be identified, as it "is starting to have deep development impacts, disturbing societies at large and threatening development reversals".[17] Many indicators that once revealed that in the pre-pandemic years the SDGs were being achieved now show the contrary. Some pointers help to explain this: (1) climate change is systematically affecting economic development and increasing inequality; (2) the number of undernourished people (affect by hunger) is increasing since 2014; (3) natural hazards have become more common and their effects more dramatic, impacting environmental, economic and social issues; and (4) the COVID-19 pandemic erased decades of progress in the female labour force rate.[18] The HDR 2020 sheds light on this situation and forecasts that difficult times are coming. The conflict zones will remain. Associated herewith, and with more vigour are internal problems for basic human needs. The COVID-19 pandemic erased years of development and progress.

This picture demonstrates how far the SDGs have gone with the 2030 Agenda and UNDP Strategic Plan 2018–2021, while the HDR 2020 shows how far the sustainable development indicators have regressed. It shows that the UNDP will have to review its quadrennial strategic plan to recover for the Strategic Plan 2022–2025. Importantly, the 2030 Agenda must be resized. The actuation of the UNDP administrator will be more fundamental than ever, especially considering that (s)he is also the Vice-Chair of the UN Sustainable Development Group (UNSDG), which is formed by all the funds, programmes, and organs of the UN Development System (UNDS) that play a role in sustainable development, what characterises it as the main UNDS internal coordination mechanism at the global level or as a high-level forum for cooperation on policies and decision-making about sustainable development; and that (s)he convenes the UNSDG Core Group. Besides that, it is important to underline that UNDP administers the UN Volunteers (UNV) and also the UN Capital Development Fund (UNCDF), an autonomous and voluntarily funder UN organization that pursues financing solutions for sustainable development by means of grants and loans.

Both UNV and the UNCDF provide capital for the actions of UNDP. They can be seen, if analysed together as they must be, as one of the fundamental programmes that the UNDP undertakes of provisioning aid to member states that are in need. Such aid comes in various forms, such as monetary, professional, and intellectual/conceptual, that would help shape policies. In the wake of various observations and experiences with member states over the years, the UNDP sought to streamline aid that member states receive. This is achieved through the harmonization of all aid member states receive at a specific time from various partners. This helps to avoid unnecessary duplication of aid, which usually derails the development process by unintentionally ignoring some sectors and putting much focus on a few other. Another approach employed by the UNDP is to align all aid to member states' national priorities and policies. This helps members have a sense of ownership of interventions that the UNDP brings forward to the table. This is unlike the past, where it could be perceived

---

[17] UNDP 2020, 56.

[18] UNDP 2020, 56–63.

that the UNDP was forcing particular aid packages on states that did not even need such aid. These two approaches have helped the UNDP successfully improve its efficiency in its assistance modalities, namely, General Budget Support (GBS) and Sector Wide Approaches (SWAp).

The GBS is a modality through which finances are directly injected into the budgetary pipeline of a member state to support the budgetary needs that the member has. This makes sure that members align the aid to particular needs that they feel pressing and are not forced to pull resources to other areas. The challenge with this modality, in our view, is that resources could easily be abused if no serious and effective monitoring and audit systems are in place. They can end up being fuel for corrupt systems and not reaching the intended goals that the UNDP has for its member states. Despite being aid, it is important for the UNDP to have sound systems that can make governments accountable for how they make use of the aid. The other modality is the SWAp, which provides unbound budgetary support that focuses on particular sectors of member state governments, such as education, agriculture, legal systems, technology and health, among others. This modality helps avoid an abundance of off-budget resources that could be prone to abuse and unaccountability. Another modality apart from these two is common basket funding, where donor partners are urged to pull their resources together when focusing assistance to particular member states. This approach also helps in reducing duplication of aid that risks other areas being ignored in the process.

36.4 The UNDP: Roles, Challenges and Critique

The UNDP is considered the largest actor in the field of development by working with developing countries to achieve solutions to local, national and world challenges.[19] Its mandate is to foster human development in all signatory states. It is involved in both peaceful and conflicted regions in the process of good governance and rule of law. It is instrumental in laying down operational frameworks to assist local people in establishing their own government. One aspect that is not easy to come by is that of having the local population trust in their own newly established government. Questions that arise in people's minds are not limited to the following: Whose government is this? Who is giving us the government? Who is positioning the leaders? Who is supported by the international community and why? Answers to these questions and how best the answers are being delivered to the people are what determines the level of trust and how much the people own and embrace the new administration. The UNDP makes sure that it maintains a position of no partiality in all its operations. Challenges may arise when personal matters affecting UNDP decision makers affect their judgment and ultimately compromise their decisions. Examples could be kidnappings of family members, attacks on personal properties from presumably one group of the warring sides, and other direct experiences of

---

[19] SMFA 2008.

traumatic events like shootings, bombings and their aftermaths. These are likely to affect the impartiality of UNDP officers and when it comes to that, it is better to declare how much such experiences are affecting one's job. This will help maintain the legitimacy of the agency in both parties and the local populations. To avoid putting agency members in such positions (especially if corruption is added to the equation), the agency must make sure that its staff are fully covered with all basic needs, as well as security, as much as possible. This requires a resounding budget line that should not be exhausted within the duration of the mission.

Not all situations of post-conflict governments require transitional administrations. However, there are other cases where the population has lost trust in the previous government or the previous government's continued administration risks further conflicts in future (unresolved political pendulum). Where there is no trust in the current government in the post-conflict era, a special committee is set up to see through the transition from the conflict to a new government. The new government may be carefully selected by the committee, or the committee can take the process to a situation where the civilian population shall choose a political leadership for themselves through an election of some kind. All the setting up and the running of affairs by this committee are overseen by the international community, of which the UNDP is an instrumental part. Research shows that for a trusted administration in the post-conflict era, an election setting is a key benchmark of satisfaction if selecting a political future rather than imposition of a future on the population. This is usually a way to offer legitimacy and an exit strategy from the transitioning committee. For instance, post-conflict elections were taunted as a success in the DRC in 2006 from a combination of various approaches employed by the UNDP.[20]

The first year of peace is the most stable testing period, which checks whether the policies as well as security strategies put in place are working. There is reported to be about a 40% chance in post-conflict zones for situations to slide back into conflict.[21] Largely, the risk of conflict in this period is due to the proliferation of arms, among other factors.[22] It is therefore reasonable enough in these zones to include amongst major objectives the demilitarization of individuals and groups, as well as controlling the proliferation of arms. Even formal and organized demilitarization of individuals is not easy, as armed civilians feel more secured from random robberies and other forms of armed attacks. However, mutual understanding and systematic approaches that encourage a wilful contribution to peace work effectively.

The UNDP is reported to have successfully managed to disarm several post-conflict zones, including the Ituri district of the DRC. They employed an early recovery model of integration strategies of local governance and security reforms, which saw almost a unilateral agreement from several parties involved.[23] However, the same approach failed to pick up in the Kivu region, which broke down two years after the successful general elections. Failures were also noted in Libya, Ukraine,

---

[20] Dix et al. 2010.

[21] Bigombe et al. 2000.

[22] Davies 2008; Del-Castillo 2008.

[23] Dix et al. 2010.

36 United Nations Development Programme (UNDP)

Mozambique and Uganda (among others), which still pose a risk of uncontrolled arms use if governance lapses in one way or another.

Economics and health in post-conflict zones are aid-dependent and there is no consensus amongst researchers on whether aid in post-conflict zones has an ultimate positive impact in stabilizing the zones in development or a negative impact in being a recipe for newer conflicts.[24] One school of thought is that economic development from aid is just a myth and should be discontinued, as it produces no good impact at all. Indeed, it can be said that it is making aid-dependent communities poorer.[25] Others observe that aid is effective in raising human development in post-conflict zones if one follows the European post-World War II example.[26] Despite the debate, one thing is clear: there is no universal outcome from aid in post-conflict zones, as would be almost expected with regular development aid with no conflict associations.[27] Some researchers stress the point that if any aid is to be provided in post-conflict zones, then it must be much more than optimal in terms of both policy and financing, as otherwise it could end up in failures observed in Afghanistan and Iraq.[28] On the other hand, economic development is largely impeded by corrupt practices. Countries may have the best programme and policy documents but corruption running its course will always keep the local populace miserable and begging.

The UNDP has for a long time been advocating for poverty eradication and human development, which are founded on essential values made clear in the MDGs' specific targets. At every level, the targets overlap with the UNDP's vision of promoting human development. The structure at the UN makes it easier to coordinate development under the MDGs and the SDGs, as the humanitarian coordination responsibility is entrusted with the UNDP's resident representative in a UN country team and the deputy special representative of the UN secretary general in the context of a post-conflict country.[29]

Although the structure is as clear as this, the UNDP is still operating under the mercy of most host nations and needs to abide by their sovereignty. This weakens the position that the agency has, being left more than a spectator with records, but powerless or almost powerless to do anything much about the records. However, it has had good performance in managing post-conflict governance and it remains relevant, only requiring more power to act. To use the DRC example again, it can be noted that governance strategies and operations facilitated by the UNDP, as appraised by independent consultants[30] were reported to be successful from the period leading to elections to the acceptance of election results by the international community.

Post-conflict zones are those communities that remain after a period of conflict(s). The relative size of the communities varies and could be as small as a suburb or as large

---

[24] Collier and Hoeffler 2002; Duponchel 2008.

[25] Moyo 2009.

[26] Collier 2007.

[27] Demekas et al. 2002.

[28] Del-Castillo 2008.

[29] Dix et al. 2010.

[30] Dix et al. 2010.

as a region comprising more than one country. Conflicts can never be underestimated. They usually begin as relatively trivial and then, due to compounding events, rhetoric and propaganda, evolve to armed conflicts involving weaponry of various grades. Some of the causational or contributing items to conflicts are differences in political ideologies, culture, religious beliefs, unresolved or mal-resolved historical fault lines, imbalance in resources of economic value, and general misunderstanding. One of the roles and mandates of the UNDP is to assist in the reestablishment of a functional government. There are areas that the UNDP has done exceptionally well in, rebuilding nations and systems to see that post-conflict zones are once again thriving—and sometimes even doing better than before the conflict. Evidence is available in most of the annual human development indices that the organisation publishes for every country and for various regions. This section of the chapter, though not as exhaustive as it could be, tries to highlight some of the areas that the UNDP still has a great opportunity to improve in a way that assists in its monitoring and evaluation exercises.

Usually, governments are either weak or completely non-functional (almost absent) in post-conflict zones. This is evident in Libya and Somalia post-conflict. The political structure and its composition are crucial in restoring the trust of the local civilian population, as well as of development partners from all over. It should include inclusiveness, as well as respect for justice systems and forgiveness (in some form) for the sake of national reconciliation, if that is what the civilian population wants for their future. The latter has been seen to work well in post-civil war Rwanda. However, the political structure in most, if not all, post-conflict zones tends to be dominated by individuals who took part in peace agreements, which still see less of a difference from warring ideologies. This approach forces the restoration system to compromise by appeasing those who appear to be potential future troublemakers. For example, in Tajikistan, the DRC, and Afghanistan, the political structures co-opted former commanders and their militias into the 'newly' established political process and armed forces, not from any 'forgiveness and healing programmes'. To maintain this kind of government, they still take a 'top-down' governance and political approach where only those at the top dictate what should become of the new state of affairs, and the rest at the bottom should just listen to only those who understand the peace agreement details. This in itself is against good governance that the UNDP champions, allowing the local populace to have the power to contribute to critical matters of their governments.

Governance of these new-era administrations usually dives deeper downwards, so the political structure tends to be centralized, leaving rural areas with administrative vacuums and capacity deficits. This weakens the central system more, as other power-hungry insurgences arise and cover what the central administration is failing to provide. Consequently, earning trust in the local 'peripheral' civilian communities occurs either through morally approved means like provision of basic needs, food items, security and temporary occupations, or through deception and force, propaganda, siege, and human trafficking, among others. This loosens all ties that the central government had or should have had with the rural peripheral communities and puts their fate into the hands of insurgent groups. A case in point is post-conflict

Libya, which has been hit by several peripheral governments differing sharply in ideologies and conduct from the central government.

Reconstruction approaches in post-conflict zones are mostly concerned with stability, which, on its own, is a good thing. However, when focusing on stability causes agencies and governments to ignore equally important aspects like justice and human rights, the system needs a quick redress. Looking at political processes like the one mentioned earlier regarding the co-opting in the DRC, Tajikistan, and Afghanistan of former militias and their commanders into the government (the official political structure) and military ranks already makes clear the decision of the new government system to not even consider subjecting anyone in those ranks to accountability for war crimes, or it could hardly achieve anything tangible. On this statement, it should be noted that war crimes are not only committed by militias and their commanders, but also official government ranks and sometimes opportunistic individual civilians in communities. Such stability imperatives are short-term, and any small mistrust can potentially break the peace agreement and, unfortunately, spark new conflicts.

It appears that the UNDP, in multilateral operations with other responsible agencies, gets so comfortable with such arrangements that score keeping and a feeling of achievement are recorded, for a moment disregarding the culture of impunity being cultivated in the new governance system and political structure that will sooner or later undermine all the costly efforts and the newly established security and political institutions. The tricky and complicated political decisions that the UNDP makes are well understood, but more can be done to keep the civilian community's trust for longer in the newer establishments.

The dependency of a government undergoing post-conflict recovery on donor funds is almost inevitable. Circulation of money and distribution of resources is in its infancy, which reasonably translates into a very poor and unstable economy. One of the primary factors to be handled by a transitional administration or one taking on a population from a conflict era is the budget. Usually, when development partners come in, including the UNDP, the economic focus is almost entirely on macroeconomic development. Obviously, this leaves the civilian community with a sense of continued economic insecurity. They understand that public service delivery will almost not be available, and civil servant salaries and other amenities will not be easy to come by in the foreseeable future. This feeling can lead to a loss of trust in the newly established government, and its legitimacy is likely to be undermined from time to time. If left unchecked, the situation can also lead to anarchy, public dissatisfaction and disorder, and a heavy insecure response from the state. If possible, a relatively smaller but reasonable budget line should be drawn from donations or other funds to keep a temporally microeconomic life alive in randomly selected strategic areas.

In most post-conflict zones, the reestablishment of stable law and order is one of the primary objectives both the national and the international community look forward to achieving. The UNDP is found to work cohesively on a multilateral mission with other international agencies to increase efficiency and effectiveness. This includes working hand in hand with UN peacekeeping forces, particularly bearing in mind that human development can never be achieved without peace and security.

Realizing that the military in the combat contingent of a peacekeeping mission does not give any guarantees to the local civilian population, restructuring or reorienting of missions to more civilian security, rather than emphasizing defeating combatants, at the same time, cooperating with development agencies like the UNDP towards a concerted effort in human development, is considered one of the best approaches to achieve development in post-conflict zones.[31] However, this multilateral approach to development has been met with challenges mainly in terms of the sustainability of law and order in efforts to develop stable governments. For example, after the Taliban fell in Afghanistan, this multilateral approach had a glitch in being able to deploy international security contingents outside of Kabul, which resulted in power remaining in the hands of former military commanders and an increase in internationally supported insurgency. Similar problems were also noted in the eastern parts of the Democratic Republic of the Congo and for civilian community security in Haitian communities in the control of illegal armed insurgencies.

It is important to note that, probably due to local differences in the playing fields, the success rates of the UNDP in preventing conflicts are mixed. Perhaps the 2006 mixed-strategy approach is being employed with less customization to suit particular regions. The volatile Great Lakes region in Africa has been calm for some years, but pockets of violence and potential conflicts are still present. Rwanda, adjacent to the Great Lakes region and politically part of the East African region, has been calm and relatively stable after the conflict of the 1990s. While some observers praise the work of the UNDP and other peacekeeping agencies, most of the local people as well as others suggest that it is the reconciliatory spirit of the people of Rwanda that should be credited. The same is said, though not to the same extent, of the Central African Republic's post-conflict stability. The argument goes further to post-conflict Libyan, Syrian, DRC, the FARC and Yemeni regions, questioning the impact of the UNDP with all the resources and cooperation with other equally powerful agencies. MDGs seem to be completely disconnected from governance performance and not based on their originally intended purposes.

The UNDP has been seen to be passive or to lack objectivity in dealing with the mismanagement of elections in various member states. The most recent case was the 2019 elections in Malawi, which were allegedly marred with fraud and serious irregularities. The international observer missions approved the election results and the process as free and fair, clearly without rigorous investigation, as was later openly proven in Malawi's high court and supreme court of appeal. It transpired that the elections were a fraud that had to be redone. In the future, it is important for the UNDP to maintain its integrity by closely monitoring and having an objective position; this is to avoid casting doubts on the integrity of the organization.

---

[31] EU 2004.

36.5   Final Remarks

The work of the UNDP is fundamental to assuring people of a hope that they can grasp in the future and the confidence of living in continued development, peace, dignity and harmony. The development agenda that the UNDP has set is still seen as an evident living profile that can be modified from time to time, helping nations to shape their development agenda. Various interventions that have been made in various nations over many years have given the UNDP (together with individual member states) experiences and lessons to make development and security better. There have been challenges that the UNDP has been progressing well on, but some remain outstanding. These include corruption in member states and the alleged status of the UNDP as being passive or partisan at times in various interventions, such as war recovery and election management or mismanagement in member states. We recommend that the UNDP remain fully focused on the development agenda they roll out in various states, but make sure at the same time that governments who get to be beneficiaries of aid must be fully accountable for the expenditure or use of any assistance rendered to them from the UNDP. Appropriate legal frameworks must be put in place and enforced to help check any mismanagement that could be evident. The UNDP is also urged to remain apolitical, or at least look apolitical, as this is key to being relevant in a politically complicated world. Care needs to be taken regarding the amalgamation of governance and appeasement of seemingly powerful political figures who do not care anything about good governance, but make sure they are pursuing their own interests. If need be, based on ground intelligence, the UNDP should without bias and in a timely manner liaise with appropriate organs of the UN and other agencies to intervene without involving itself with political drama. Lastly, the disparities in the levels of development between classes of developed and developing countries can be overcome through interventions that could see more sector-wide modalities. However, if technologies and industries are also included in the aid modalities for the countries in the form of directly always investing in machinery and equipment rather than money, this could further accelerate some development—particularly in industry and trade, even in developing countries.

References

Baxi U (2001) Too many, or too few, human rights? Human Rights Law Review, doi: https://doi.org/10.1093/hrlr/1.1.1.

Bigombe B, Collier P, Sambanis N (2000) Policies for Building Post-Conflict Peace. Journal of African Economics, doi: https://doi.org/10.1093/jae/9.3.323.

Collier P (2007) The Bottom Billion: Why the Poorest Countries are Failing and What Can be Done About It. Oxford University Press, Oxford.

Collier P, Hoeffler A (2002) Aid, policy and peace: reducing the risks of civil conflict. Defence and Peace Economics, doi: https://doi.org/10.1080/10242690214335.

Davies V A B (2008) The Macroeconomics of Post-Conflict Economic Recovery. Background Paper for Post-Conflict Economic Recovery: Enabling Local Ingenuity. UNDP, Bureau for Crisis Prevention and Recovery, New York.

Del-Castillo G (2008) Rebuilding War-Torn States: The Challenge of Post-Conflict Economic Reconstruction. Oxford University Press, New York.

Demekas D, McHugh J, Kosma T (2002) The Economics of Post Conflict Aid. International Monetary Fund Working Paper. https://www.imf.org/en/Publications/WP/Issues/2016/12/30/The-Economics-of-Post-Conflict-Aid-16180. Accessed 1 October 2018.

Dix S, Miranda D, Norchi C H (2010) Innovations for Post-Conflict Transitions: The United Nations Development Program in the Democratic Republic of Congo. Ash Center for Democratic Governance and Innovation, Harvard Kennedy School. https://ash.harvard.edu/files/innovations_as_postconflict.pdf. Accessed 1 October 2018.

Duponchel M (2008) Can Aid Break the Conflict Trap? Conference paper. http://www.csae.ox.ac.uk/conferences/2008EDiA/papers/316-Duponchel.pdf. Accessed 1 October 2018.

EU (2004) A Human Security Doctrine for Europe: the Barcelona Report of the Study Group on Europe's Security Capabilities. http://www.lse.ac.uk/Depts/global/researchhumansecurity.htm. Accessed 1 October 2018.

Marks S P (1981) Emerging human rights: a new generation for the 1980s? Rutgers Law Review. https://heinonline.org/HOL/LandingPage?handle=hein.journals/rutlr33&div=23&id=&page=. Accessed 1 October 2018.

Meier G M (2001) The old generation of development economists. In: Meier GM, Stiglitz JE (eds) Frontiers of development economics: the future in perspective. The World Bank/Oxford University Press, Washington/New York. https://trove.nla.gov.au/version/46552350. Accessed 1 October 2018.

Moyo D (2009) Dead Aid: Why Aid is not Working and How there is Another Way for Africa. Penguin Books, London.

Sano H-O (2000) Development and human rights: the necessary, but partial integration of human rights and development. Human Rights Quarterly, doi: https://doi.org/10.1353/hrq.2000.0037.

Sen A (1976) Poverty: an ordinal approach to measurement. Econometrica, doi: https://doi.org/10.2307/1912718.

Sen A (1979) Issues in the measurement of poverty. The Scandinavian Journal of Economics, doi: https://doi.org/10.2307/3439966.

Sen A (1983) Poor, relatively speaking. Oxford Economic Papers, doi: https://doi.org/10.1093/oxfordjournals.oep.a041587.

Sen A (1988) The concept of development. In: Chenery H, Srinivasan TN (eds) Handbook of Development Economics, vol. 1, doi: https://doi.org/10.1016/S1573-4471(88)01004-6

Sen A (2012) How to judge globalisation. In: Lechner FJ, Boli J (eds) The globalization reader. Wiley-Blackwell, Oxford, 16–21.

Sengupta A (2000) Realizing the right to development. Development and Change, doi: https://doi.org/10.1111/1467-7660.00167.

Siqueira J H (2016) Elementos para uma teoria dos deveres fundamentais: uma perspectiva jurídica. Revista de Direito Constitucional e Internacional, 95, 125–159. http://www.mpsp.mp.br/portal/page/portal/documentacao_e_divulgacao/doc_biblioteca/bibli_servicos_produtos/bibli_boletim/bibli_bol_2006/RDConsInter_n.95.06.PDF. Accessed 1 October 2018.

SMFA (2008) The United Nations Development Programme (I. a. C. D. Press (translator)). Swedish Assessment of Multilateral Organisations.

Sousa Santos B (2007). A discourse on the sciences. In: Cognitive justice in a global world: prudent knowledges for a decent life. Lexington Books, Plymouth, 13–48.

Summers L (1991) Research challenges for development economists. Finance & Development. https://asean.elibrary.imf.org/doc/IMF022/14114-9781451952087/14114-9781451952087/Other_formats/Source_PDF/14114-9781463935733.pdf. Accessed 1 October 2018.

UNDP (2016) From the MDGs to sustainable development for all: lessons from 15 years of practice. http://www.globalamalen.se/wp-content/uploads/2016/05/From-MDGs-to-SDGs-Lessons-of-15-years-of-practice.pdf. Accessed 1 October 2018.

UNDP (2017) UNDP Strategic Plan, 2018–2021. http://undocs.org/DP/2017/38. Accessed 28 February 2021.

UNDP (2020) The 2020 Human Development Report. http://hdr.undp.org/sites/default/files/hdr 2020.pdf. Accessed 28 February 2021.

Julio Homem de Siqueira is a Junior Researcher at the Institute of Criminal Law Studies "Alimena", University of Calabria—Italy (2021–2022); Researcher in Public Law at Federal University of Rio Grande do Norte (UFRN, Brazil), State University of Minas Gerais (UEMG, Brazil) and Vitoria Law School (FDV, Brazil); LL.M at FDV; Member of the Centre of Intelligence for Preventing Repetitive Demands at Rio de Janeiro Federal Justice; Law Clerk at Rio de Janeiro Federal Justice.

Andrew G. Mtewa is a pharmaceutical chemistry researcher in drug designing and development. He studies the roles of chemistry and pharmacology in armed conflicts, weaponry, antidotes. He teaches Chemistry at the Malawi University of Science and Technology, Malawi. His PhD area is drug development and designing against cancers, other cell degenerative diseases, neuro-depression and related disorders under the Pharmbiotrac project at Mbarara University of Science and Technology in Uganda. Andrew has contributed book chapters in drug discovery, has published books on Quality Assurance for developing countries and Battle tactics for military operations.

Daury César Fabriz is an Associate Professor of Laws at Espirito Santo Federal University (UFES, Brazil); Full Professor at Vitoria Law School (FDV, Brazil); Lead Researcher at State, Constitutional Democracy and Fundamental Rights Research Group (FDV); Member of Latin American Net for Democratic Constitutionalism; Lawyer at Fabriz Lawyers; Sociologist.

Chapter 37
The International Red Cross and Red Crescent Movement

Heike Spieker

Contents

37.1 Origin 780
37.2 Mission and Structure of the Movement 782
37.3 National Red Cross and Red Crescent Societies 788
    37.3.1 Recognition of National Societies 788
    37.3.2 Mandate, Role and Tasks 791
    37.3.3 Auxiliarity 792
37.4 The International Committee of the Red Cross—ICRC 793
    37.4.1 Origin 793
    37.4.2 Legal Basis and Mandate 794
    37.4.3 Functions and Role 797
    37.4.4 Tasks and Operations 799
37.5 The International Federation of Red Cross and Red Crescent Societies 801
37.6 Fundamental Principles of the International Red Cross and Red Crescent
    Movement 803
37.7 Conclusion 806
References 808

Abstract The International Red Cross and Red Crescent Movement is summarized with the slogan "Three Components – One Movement". From its very beginning, it has been characterized by a double focus: Striving to alleviate the situation of the most vulnerable, domestic activities of National Societies have constituted an essential element of developing institutionalized public welfare while international activities of both the International Committee of the Red Cross and National Societies have been reflected in evolving international humanitarian law. What started as measures by individuals and relatively small groups who were motivated by feelings of humanity has become the major actor in today's sector of humanitarian action. Sanctioned and confirmed by the international community, all Movement components have a role in further developing and, these days maybe even more importantly, ensuring respect for international humanitarian law. It is the Movement and its components who have the possibility, but also the responsibility to support States in their endeavor to experience the helpfulness of legal regulation in times of crises.

H. Spieker (✉)
German Red Cross, Berlin, Germany
e-mail: spiekerh@drk.de

© T.M.C. ASSER PRESS and the authors 2022
S. Sayapin et al. (eds.), *International Conflict and Security Law*,
https://doi.org/10.1007/978-94-6265-515-7_37

779

Keywords Auxiliarity · Fundamental Principles · Humanitarian Principles · International Conference of the Red Cross and Red Crescent · International Committee of the Red Cross · International Federation of Red Cross and Red Crescent Societies · International Humanitarian Law · International Red Cross and Red Crescent Movement · National Red Cross Societies · National Red Crescent Societies

37.1 Origin

The International Red Cross and Red Crescent Movement consists of three components: Presently 192 National Red Cross and Red Crescent Societies (NSs), the International Committee of the Red Cross (ICRC) and the International Federation of Red Cross and Red Crescent Societies (IFRC).[1] The Movement is operating worldwide. Its mission is "to prevent and alleviate human suffering wherever it may be found, to protect life and health and ensure respect for the human being, in particular in times of armed conflict and other emergencies, to work for the prevention of disease and for the promotion of health and social welfare, to encourage voluntary service and a constant readiness to give help by the members of the Movement, and a universal sense of solidarity towards all those in need of its protection and assistance".[2] The Movement and all its components are legally bound to be guided by seven Fundamental Principles, i.e. humanity, impartiality, neutrality, independence, voluntary service, unity and universality.[3]

The International Red Cross and Red Crescent Movement is based on a vision developed by the Swiss businessman Henry Dunant in 1862. Due to his personal experiences from the battle of Solferino between Austria and France on 24 June 1859 which he witnessed when travelling in northern Italy, he elaborated two groundbreaking ideas: he initiated the development of modern international humanitarian law and conceptualized specific civilian organisations performing specific tasks in war time. In his published book *A Memory of Solferino*[4] he asked the question whether "it [would] not be desirable that [authorities of different States] should (…) formulate some international principle, sanctioned by a Convention inviolate in character, which, once agreed upon and ratified, might constitute the basis for societies for the relief of the wounded in the different European countries?" and asserted that "[I]t is the more important to reach an agreement and concert measures in advance, because when hostilities once begin, the belligerents are already ill-disposed to each other, and thenceforth regard all questions from the one limited

---

[1] Cf. Article 1 para 1 Statutes of the International Red Cross and Red Crescent Movement [Movement Statutes] (2006) https://standcom.ch/download/stat/Statutes-EN-A5.pdf. Accessed 1 August 2020.

[2] PP 1 Movement Statutes.

[3] PP 2 Movement Statutes.

[4] Haug 1986, p. 129.

37 The International Red Cross and Red Crescent Movement

standpoint of their own subjects."[5] Dunant thus suggested the first multilateral treaty of modern international humanitarian law. At the same time, Henry Dunant elaborated the mandate and constitution of National Societies[6] and thereby envisioned the first component of three of the International Red Cross and Red Crescent Movement. He formulated the idea and concept of such Societies and linked this concept to his vision of a legal framework providing for a minimum humanitarian standard on the battlefield. Dunant's proposal that societies of trained volunteers be organized in all countries pursued the purpose of helping to care for wounded combatants in time of war. This was the first—and at that time sole—object of such societies which later became National Red Cross and Red Crescent Societies. The first society was established in the German State of Württemberg in November 1863.[7]

An international conference recommended in 1863 that national relief societies be set up[8] and asked governments to give them their protection and support. The conference further recommended that parties to an armed conflict declare ambulances and military hospitals neutral, that protection be granted to both army medical staff and voluntary relief workers[9] and a distinctive sign to be determined in order to mark persons and objects endowed with protection.[10] One year later, 16 States adopted the 1864 Convention for the Amelioration of the Condition of the Wounded in Armies in the Field with today 57 State Parties. The Convention contains provisions on care for the wounded without distinction in respect to nationality (Article 6) as well as

---

[5] Dunant 1862, p. 126.

[6] "For work of this kind, paid help is not what is wanted. (...) There is need, therefore, for voluntary orderlies and volunteer nurses, zealous, trained and experienced, whose position would be recognized by the commanders or armies in the field and their mission facilitated and supported. (...) Humanity and civilization call imperiously for such an organization as is here suggested. (...) Is there in the world a prince or a monarch who would decline to support the proposed societies, happy to be able to give full assurance to his soldiers that they will be at once properly cared for if they should be wounded? Is there any Government that would hesitate to give its patronage to a group endeavouring in this manner to preserve the lives of useful citizens, for assuredly the soldier who receives a bullet in the defense of this country deserves all that country's solicitude? Is there a single officer, a single general, considering his troops as 'his boys', who would not be anxious to facilitate the work of volunteer helpers? Is there a military commissary, or a military doctor, who would not be grateful for the assistance of a detachment of intelligent people, wisely and properly commanded and tactful in their work?", Dunant 1862, pp. 124, 126 f.

[7] Further societies were founded in the Grand Duchy of Oldenburg, Belgium and Prussia, followed by Denmark, France, Italy, Mecklenburg-Schwerin, Spain, Hamburg and Hesse; ICRC 2004.

[8] "Each country shall have a committee whose duty it shall be, in time of war and if the need arises, to assist the Army Medical Services by every means in its power. (...)", Geneva International Conference (1863) Resolutions, Article 1.

[9] "(...) that in time of war the belligerent nations should proclaim the neutrality of ambulances and military hospitals, and that neutrality should likewise be recognized, fully and absolutely, in respect of official medical personnel, voluntary medical personnel, inhabitants of the country who go to the relief of the wounded, and the wounded themselves", Geneva International Conference (1863) Resolutions, Recommendation (b).

[10] "(...) that a uniform distinctive sign be recognized for the Medical Corps of all armies, or at least for all persons of the same army belonging to this Service; and, that a uniform flag also be adopted in all countries for ambulances and hospitals", Geneva International Conference (1863) Resolutions, Recommendation (c).

on neutrality or inviolability of medical personnel and medical establishments and units (in particular Articles 1–5), and introduces the distinctive sign of the red cross on a white ground (Article 7).

37.2 Mission and Structure of the Movement

The International Red Cross and Red Crescent Movement is the largest humanitarian network in the world. The central purpose of the Movement and its components is to help without discrimination those who suffer. By its humanitarian work and the dissemination of its ideals, it promotes a lasting peace as a "dynamic process of cooperation among all States and peoples, cooperation founded on respect for freedom, independence, national sovereignty, equality, human rights, as well as on a fair and equitable distribution of resources to meet the needs of peoples".[11]

Its mission is "to prevent and alleviate human suffering wherever it may be found, to protect life and health and ensure respect for the human being, in particular in times of armed conflict and other emergencies, to work for the prevention of disease and for the promotion of health and social welfare, to encourage voluntary service and a constant readiness to give help by the members of the Movement, and a universal sense of solidarity towards all those in need of its protection and assistance".[12] The Movement is composed of three components, National Red Cross and Red Crescent Societies, the International Committee of the Red Cross (ICRC) and the International Federation of Red Cross and Red Crescent Societies.[13]

All three components are legally bound to observe the seven so-called Fundamental Principles of the International Red Cross and Red Crescent Movement in all their actions and behavior.[14] The Statutes of the International Red Cross and Red Crescent Movement[15] form the Movement's specific legal base, and within its limits the components act independently from each other.[16] The Statutes have been adopted by the 25th International Conference of the Red Cross in 1986 and amended in 1995 and 2006, i.e. adopted by the States Parties to the Geneva Conventions of 1949 and the three components of the Movement. The Rules of Procedure of the International

---

[11] PP 4 Movement Statutes.

[12] PP 1 Movement Statutes.

[13] Article 1 para 1 Movement Statutes.

[14] PP 2 and Article 1 para 2 Movement Statutes.

[15] International Conference (2006) Statutes of the International Red Cross and Red Crescent Movement and Rules of Procedure. https://standcom.ch/download/stat/Statutes-EN-A5.pdf. Accessed 1 August 2020.

[16] Article 1 para 2 Movement Statutes.

37 The International Red Cross and Red Crescent Movement

Red Cross and Red Crescent Movement[17] aim at ensuring the implementation of the Statutes and at regulating the work of the Movement's statutory bodies.[18]

Representatives of all three components discuss matters which concern the Movement as a whole within the framework of the Council of Delegates.[19] It is composed of delegations from the National Societies, the ICRC and the International Federation with each having equal rights expressed by a single vote.[20] In general, it adopts its decisions, recommendations or declarations in the form of resolutions[21] and endeavors to adopt its resolutions by consensus.[22] The Council does not take final decisions on any matter which, on the basis of the Movement Statutes, "is within the sole competence of the International Conference" of the Red Cross and Red Crescent, nor "any decision contrary to the resolutions of [the Conference], or concerning any matter already settled by the Conference or reserved by it for the agenda of a forthcoming Conference".[23] In practice, the Council meets every two years.[24] Examples of more recent particularly important decisions of the Council of Delegates regulating the interrelationships between components of the Movement are Resolution 6 of the 1997 council containing the Agreement of the Organization of the International Activities of the Components of the International Red Cross and Red Crescent Movement (Seville Agreement),[25] Resolution 7 of the 2005 Council on Relations Between the Components of the Movement and Military Bodies,[26] Resolution 8 of the 2005 Council on Supplementary Measures to Enhance the Implementation of the Seville Agreement,[27] and Resolution 4 of the 2007 Council on Restoring Family Links.[28] Example of a recent particularly important decision of the Council of Delegates preparing decisions of the International Conference of the Red Cross and Red Crescent is Resolution 4 of the 30th International Conference 2007 on the Adoption of the Guidelines for the Domestic Facilitation and Regulation of International Disaster Relief and Initial Recovery Assistance.[29]

---

[17] International Conference (2006) Statutes of the International Red Cross and Red Crescent Movement and Rules of Procedure. https://standcom.ch/download/stat/Statutes-EN-A5.pdf. Accessed 1 August 2020.

[18] Rule 1 of the Rules of Procedure.

[19] Articles 12, 14 Movement Statutes.

[20] Article 13 Movement Statutes.

[21] Article 14 para 3 Movement Statutes.

[22] Article 15 para 5 Movement Statutes; Rules 27, 19 Rules of Procedure.

[23] Article 14 para 8 Movement Statutes.

[24] Details of its procedure are laid down in Article 15 Movement Statutes.

[25] IFRC 1997.

[26] ICRC 2005a.

[27] ICRC 2005b.

[28] IFRC 2007.The International Conference in 2007 explicitly "welcomed" the adoption of the RFL Strategy of the Movement and "call[ed] upon" State authorities "to continue their support for the activities (…) in the field of restoring family links, particularly by strengthening National Societies' capacities"; ICRC 2009a.

[29] IFRC 2007.

The International Conference of the Red Cross and Red Crescent brings together representatives of the States Parties to the Geneva Conventions of 1949 and the three components of the International Red Cross and Red Crescent Movement. The Conference is the supreme deliberative body for the Movement[30] and meets, as a rule, every four years.[31] It provides a non-political forum for dialogue on humanitarian issues, and representatives together examine and decide upon humanitarian matters of common interest "and any other related matter".[32] Delegations from the National Societies, the ICRC, the International Federation and the States Parties to the Geneva Conventions form the "members" of the International Conference.[33] Observers, usually governmental or non-governmental organizations and institutions, participate in the International Conference without voting rights.[34] Each delegation has equal rights expressed by a single vote.[35] Decisions, recommendations or declarations are adopted in the form of resolutions.[36] According to Article 11 para 7, the International Conference "shall endeavor to adopt its resolutions by consensus". Functions of the International Conference are to "contribute[s] to the unity of the Movement and to the achievement of its mission",[37] and to "contribute[s] to the respect for and development of international humanitarian law and other international conventions of particular interest of the Movement".[38] It does so "in full respect of the Fundamental Principles" of the International Red Cross and Red Crescent Movement.[39] All participants in the Conference, in particular members and observers, "shall respect the Fundamental Principles and all documents presented shall conform with these Principles".[40] Conference officers have the authority to ensure "that none of the speakers at any time engages in controversies of a political, racial, religious or ideological nature", and the same standard is to be applied to documents before authorizing their circulation.

In bringing together the States Parties to the Geneva Conventions of 1949 on a par with the three components of the Movement, the International Conference is a unique body in international relations and international law. Although the Movement and the International Conference do not constitute an International Organization, process and procedure of the Conference conform widely to those of a diplomatic conference, in particular in the framework of the Conference's Drafting Committee. The Conference represents the only specific and regular forum to discuss themes of a humanitarian nature and international humanitarian law issues. This characteristic is

---

[30] Article 8 Movement Statutes.

[31] Article 11 para 1 Movement Statutes.

[32] Article 8 Movement Statutes.

[33] Article 9 para 1 Movement Statutes.

[34] Article 11 para 5 Movement Statutes.

[35] Article 9 para 2 Movement Statutes.

[36] Article 9 para 2 Movement Statutes.

[37] Article 10 para 1 Movement Statutes.

[38] Article 10 para 2 Movement Statutes.

[39] Article 10 para 1 Movement Statutes.

[40] Article 11 para 4 Movement Statutes.

37 The International Red Cross and Red Crescent Movement

part of the ongoing debate on the potential for creating a new additional forum for a non-politicized, non-contextualized and non-selective effective debate on questions of international humanitarian law.[41]

States Parties to the Geneva Conventions of 1949 cooperate with the components of the Movement in accordance with these Conventions, the Movement Statutes and the resolutions of the International Conference.[42] Within the framework of the International Conference of the Red Cross and Red Crescent, they exercise their responsibilities under the Conventions and support the overall work of the Movement.[43] They promote the establishment of a National Red Cross/Red Crescent/Red Crystal Society on their territory and encourage its development[44] and "support, whenever possible, the work of the components of the Movement" which "in their turn and in accordance with their respective statutes, support as far as possible the humanitarian activities of the States".[45] Integral part of this relationship between States Parties to the Geneva Conventions and Movement components is the legal obligation of States Parties to "at all times respect the adherence by all components of the Movement to the Fundamental Principles".[46] This legal obligation of States Parties accords with the legal status of National Red Cross and Red Crescent Societies as "voluntary aid societ[ies], auxiliary to the public authorities in the humanitarian field" according to Article 4 para 3 Movement Statutes. The 2007 International Conference and its members have confirmed the details of such relations of auxiliarity and have characterized the relationship as a "balanced relationship with clear and reciprocal responsibilities, maintaining and enhancing a permanent dialogue at all levels within the agreed framework for humanitarian action".[47] Members of the Conference reaffirmed that it is "the primary responsibility of States and their respective public authorities to provide humanitarian assistance to vulnerable persons on their respective territories".[48] They recognized a "specific and distinctive partnership, entailing mutual responsibilities and benefits, and based on international and national laws"[49] between public authorities of the States Parties to the Geneva Conventions and National Societies. On that basis, public authorities and the National Society "agree on the areas

---

[41] International Conference (2015) Resolution 2. http://rcrcconference.org/wp-content/uploads/2015/04/32IC-AR-Compliance_EN.pdf. Accessed 1 August 2020.

[42] Article 2 para 1 Movement Statutes.

[43] Article 8 Movement Statutes.

[44] Article 2 para 2 Movement Statutes.

[45] Article 2 para 3 Movement Statutes.

[46] Article 2 para 4 Movement Statutes.

[47] International Conference (2007) Resolution 2, OP 2. https://www.icrc.org/en/doc/resources/documents/resolution/30-international-conference-resolution-2-2007.htm. Accessed 1 August 2020.

[48] International Conference (2007) Resolution 2, OP 1. https://www.icrc.org/en/doc/resources/documents/resolution/30-international-conference-resolution-2-2007.htm. Accessed 1 August 2020. Correlating, it is "the primary purpose of National Societies as auxiliaries to the public authorities in the humanitarian field (...) to supplement them in the fulfilment of this responsibility".

[49] International Conference (2007) Resolution 2, OP 3. https://www.icrc.org/en/doc/resources/documents/resolution/30-international-conference-resolution-2-2007.htm. Accessed 1 August 2020.

in which the National Society supplement or substitutes for public humanitarian services".[50]

The so called Standing Commission of the Red Cross and Red Crescent is the trustee of the International Conference of the Red Cross and Red Crescent.[51] As such, it makes arrangements in particular for the International Conference, e.g. in terms of place and date, programme and provisional agenda.[52] It is the one body, on a permanent basis for the Movement, where all components are represented and which meets regularly. Between Conferences, the Standing Commission settles potential differences of opinion regarding, e.g., the interpretation and application of the Movement Statutes or its Rules of Procedure.[53] The Commission generally provides strategic guidance in the interest of all components of the Movement, "promote[s] harmony in the work of the Movement and (...) coordination among its components", "encourage[s] and further[s] the implementation of resolutions of the International Conference", "examine[s], with these objects in view, matters which concern the Movement as a whole"[54] and takes "any measures which circumstances demand, provided always that the independence and initiative of each of the components of the Movement, as defined in the present Statutes, are strictly safeguarded".[55] The Standing Commission consists of nine members, five of whom are elected by the International Conference in a personal capacity, "taking into account personal qualities and the principle of fair geographical distribution".[56] Both the President of the ICRC and the President of the IFRC together with one additional representative each are members *ex officio* according to Article 17 para 1b and c.[57]

Name and emblems of the International Red Cross and Red Crescent Movement go back to the diplomatic conference of 1864 adopted a red cross on a white background,[58] the reverse colours of the Swiss flag, as the distinctive sign for the protection of volunteers taking care of casualties in times of war. A diplomatic conference of 1929 recognized the red cross and red crescent as emblems to be used for that purpose.[59] A diplomatic conference in 2005 adopted Additional Protocol III (AP III)

---

[50] International Conference (2007) Resolution 2, OP 3. https://www.icrc.org/en/doc/resources/doc uments/resolution/30-international-conference-resolution-2-2007.htm. Accessed 1 August 2020.

[51] Article 17 Movement Statutes.

[52] Article 18 para 1 Movement Statutes.

[53] Article 18 para 2 Movement Statutes.

[54] Article 18 para 3 Movement Statutes.

[55] Article 18 para 8 Movement Statutes.

[56] Article 10 para 4, 17 para 1 a Movement Statutes.

[57] For the present composition see Members of the Commission. https://standcom.ch/members-of-the-commission/. Accessed 1 August 2020.

[58] Haug 1986, p. 130.

[59] Bugnion 2007, p. 11. Also recognized was the emblem of the red lion and sun. '(...) By a note dated 4 September 1980, the Islamic Republic of Iran [the only State using this emblem] declared that it was waiving its right to use of the red lion and sun and would thenceforth use the red crescent as the distinctive sign of its armed forces medical services, while reserving the right to return to the red lion and sun should new emblems be recognized.'; Ibid. p. 16 f.

37 The International Red Cross and Red Crescent Movement

to the Geneva Conventions of 1949[60] and recognized a "red frame in the shape of a square on edge on a white ground"[61]—"red crystal"[62]—as a distinctive emblem with equal status.[63] According to Article 2 AP III, the red cross, red crescent, and red crystal are the distinctive devices of the medical service of the armed forces. A use by components of the Movement is enabled in Articles 3 and 4 AP III, and the International Conference of the Red Cross and Red Crescent proposed in June 2006 respective amendments to the Movement Statutes.[64] The Conference also decided that the name of the Movement and respective references were not to be modified from "Red Cross and Red Crescent".

All three emblems serve two purposes and may be used in two different ways: as a protective emblem as well as an indicative emblem. In armed conflicts, the protective emblem is the visible sign of the protection granted by the 1949 Geneva Conventions and their 1977 (2005) Additional Protocols to medical personnel, medical facilities, and medical means of transport of the armed forces, as well as on civilian medical units with the due authorization of competent governmental authorities. In such cases, the emblems should be as large as possible and should be displayed with no other information.[65] Outside armed conflict, medical services and religious personnel of the armed forces can use the protective emblem,[66] as well as National Society medical facilities and means of transport that are to function as such in the event of armed conflict, with the authorities' consent. Both within and outside the context of armed conflict, indicative devices show the link which a person or an object has to a component of the International Red Cross and Red Crescent Movement.[67] In such cases, the emblem should bear additional information, e.g. the name or the initials of a National Society. The indicative emblems generally are of relatively small dimensions and may not be placed on armlets or on the roofs of buildings,[68] in order to avoid any confusion with the emblems being used as protective devices.

For the purpose of enhancing a "collective brand" of the International Red Cross and Red Crescent Movement a specific Movement logo has been developed. This logo consists of the red cross and red crescent emblems side by side, together with the words "International" and "Movement" arranged in a circle and either in Arabic, Chinese, English, French, Russian or Spanish as the official languages of the International Conference of the Red Cross and Red Crescent. The logo is meant as

---

[60] Protocol Additional to the Geneva Conventions of 12 August 1949 and relating to the Adoption of an Additional Distinctive Emblem—AP III—(8 December 2005), 2404 UNTS 261.

[61] Article 2 para 2 AP III.

[62] International Conference (2006) Resolution 1, para 2. https://www.icrc.org/en/doc/resources/doc uments/resolution/29-international-conference-resolution-1-2006.htm. Accessed 1 August 2020.

[63] Article 2 para 1 Additional Protocol III.

[64] International Conference (2006) Resolution 1 para 2. https://www.icrc.org/en/doc/resources/doc uments/resolution/29-international-conference-resolution-1-2006.htm. Accessed 1 August 2020.

[65] Cauderay 1990.

[66] Articles 24, 44 GC I.

[67] Bouvier 1989.

[68] Article 19 of the Regulations, see ICRC 1991.

providing a visual identity for indicative use to enhance the positioning and visibility of the Movement as a relevant and essential humanitarian network present and active throughout the world, and to strengthen the ability of the Movement and its components to communicate, promote their work and maximize funds raised on a national and global level. For these purposes, the logo is used with regard to contexts which concern National Societies, the ICRC and the International Federation. The Movement logo aims to complement the Movement components' existing individual logos and is used exceptionally for representation, communication, global fundraising and promotional activities only to represent the Movement components collectively. Specific conditions and rules for such use have been determined by the Council of Delegates of the Movement in 2015,[69] including, e.g. a specific body for the determination whether the logo may be used in a specific context.

37.3 National Red Cross and Red Crescent Societies

At present[70] 192 existing[71] National Red Cross and Red Crescent Societies "form the basic units and constitute a vital force"[72] of the International Red Cross and Red Crescent Movement. National Societies support the public authorities in their humanitarian tasks, "according to the needs of the people of their respective countries".[73]

37.3.1 Recognition of National Societies

An entity becomes a National Red Cross or Red Crescent Society by recognition by both the home government of the country on whose territory the Society is expected to work according to Article 4 para 3 Movement Statutes and by the ICRC on the basis of Article 5 para 2b. Article 4 lists the following ten conditions for recognition of National Societies:[74]

The first condition requires that a National Society "be constituted on the territory of an independent State where the Geneva Convention for the Amelioration of the Condition of the Wounded and Sick in Armed Forces in the Field is in force".[75] It

---

[69] RCC 2015.

[70] As of August 2020.

[71] At present (August 2020) 192 National Societies are members of the International Federation of Red Cross and Red Crescent Societies.

[72] Article 3 para 1 Movement Statutes.

[73] Article 3 para 1 Movement Statutes.

[74] Article 4 Movement Statutes: "In order to be recognized in terms of Article 5, para 2b) as a National Society, the Society shall meet the following conditions: (…)".

[75] Article 4 para 1 Movement Statutes.

37 The International Red Cross and Red Crescent Movement

is thereby clarified that a National Red Cross or Red Crescent Society can only be established in an entity qualifying as a State, i.e. availing itself of full legal personality under international law. Cases where the fulfilment of this condition has been debated are, e.g. the institution of a National Society in Kosovo before the recognition of full international legal personality of Kosovo and the Palestinian Red Crescent Society.[76]

Article 4 para 2 postulates that the National Society to be recognized "be the only National Red Cross or Red Crescent Society of the said State and be directed by a central body which shall alone be competent to represent it in its dealings with other components of the Movement". In other words, there can only be one National Society in each State.[77] An organization like a 'Kurdish Red Crescent Society', for example, cannot be recognized in Germany since the German Red Cross has been recognized as the—only—German National (Red Cross) Society.[78] The German Red Cross has taken legal action in such cases.

The third requirement for the recognition of a National Society is to "be duly recognized by the legal government of its country on the basis of the Geneva Conventions and of the national legislation".[79] A National Society is thus to be recognized both by its Government and, on this basis, by the ICRC.[80] The National Society is to be recognized as a "voluntary aid society, auxiliary to the public authorities in the humanitarian field". The Movement Statutes clarify that National Societies "support the public authorities in their humanitarian tasks"[81] as well as "cooperate with the public authorities" in certain fields and "organize, in liaison with the public authorities" certain activities and services.[82]

The fourth condition for recognition provides that National Societies "have an autonomous status which allows [them] to operate in conformity with the Fundamental Principles of the Movement". The Fundamental Principles of the International Red Cross and Red Crescent Movement are: humanity, impartiality, neutrality, independence, voluntary service, unity, and universality. Together with a definition of

---

[76] The Palestinian Red Crescent Society (PRCS) was recognized in 2006. At the closing of the 29th International Conference on 22 June 2006 the ICRC announced the recognition. The subsequent General Assembly of the International Federation admitted the PRCS as a member of the International Federation of Red Cross and Red Crescent Societies; cf. International Conference of the Red Cross and Red Crescent Movement (2006) Resolution 1. https://www.icrc.org/en/doc/resour ces/documents/resolution/29-international-conference-resolution-1-2006.htm. Accessed 1 August 2020.

[77] The International Federation of Red Cross and Red Crescent Societies adopted a Guidance document for National Society Statutes and a model law on the recognition of a National Society in 1999/2000.

[78] Cf. Sect. 1 Act on the German Red Cross (2017):'The Deutsches Rotes Kreuz e.V. (German Red Cross, registered society) is the National Red Cross Society on the territory of the Federal Republic of Germany and Voluntary Aid Society, auxiliary to the German authorities in the humanitarian field.' https://www.drk.de/en/the-grc/mission/grc-act/. Accessed 1 August 2020.

[79] Article 4 para 3 Movement Statutes.

[80] Article 5 para 2 lit. b Movement Statutes.

[81] Article 3 para 1 Movement Statutes.

[82] Article 3 para 2 Movement Statutes.

their substance, these principles were proclaimed by the 20th International Conference of the Red Cross in 1965[83] and adopted in their present form by the 25th International Conference in 1986.[84] These International Conferences, i.e. the international community/States together with the components of the Movement, have not only determined the terms of these principles, but have also defined the content and substance of the seven principles.[85]

Article 4 para 5 stipulates that a National Society "use[s] a name and distinctive emblem in conformity with the Geneva Conventions and their Additional Protocols"—i.e. the red cross, the red crescent or the red crystal.[86]

Further recognition conditions stipulate that National Societies "be so organized as to be able to fulfil the tasks defined in its own statutes, including the preparation in peace time for its statutory tasks in case of armed conflict"[87,88] "extend [their] activities to the entire territory of the State"[89,90] "recruit [their] voluntary members and [their] staff without consideration of race, sex, class, religion or political opinions",[91] and "adhere to the present Statutes, share in the fellowship which unites the components of the Movement and cooperate with them".[92] This fellowship and cooperation form part of the statutory basis for international activities and operations of National Societies. Finally, Article 4 para 10 of the Statutes reiterates the requirement that National Societies are bound to "respect the Fundamental Principles of the Movement and be guided in its work by the principles of international humanitarian law" (see also the recognition requirements in Article 4 paras 3 and 4 above).

---

[83] International Conference (1965) Resolution 8.

[84] International Conference (1986) Resolution 31. https://www.icrc.org/en/doc/resources/documents/article/other/57jme2.htm. Accessed 1 August 2020.

[85] For a comprehensive analysis and evaluation of the Fundamental Principles cf. Pictet 1979, p. 93.

[86] See above, Sect. 37.2.

[87] Article 4 para 6 Movement Statutes.

[88] See also the Guidance for National Societies Statutes and Model Law on the Recognition of National Societies (2000). Unfortunately, these documents are not publicly available. Internally, they may be accessed under https://fednet.ifrc.org/en/resources/ns-development/national-society-development/legal-base-of-national-societies/national-society-statutes/guidance-document; https://fednet.ifrc.org/PageFiles/82735/model-law-on-ns-recognition-english%5b1%5d.pdf. Accessed 1 August 2020.

[89] Article 4 para 7 Movement Statutes.

[90] This requirement has been debated with regard to recognition of the Palestinian Red Crescent Society and the Cyprus Red Cross Society. On Northern Cyprus see for example Lanord 2000; see also ICRC 2012. Other debated situations have been, e.g. the Provisional Revolutionary Government of the Republic of South Sudan and Somaliland.

[91] Article 4 para 8 Movement Statutes.

[92] Article 4 para 9 Movement Statutes.

37 The International Red Cross and Red Crescent Movement

37.3.2 *Mandate, Role and Tasks*

The international community has assigned specific tasks, functions, and duties to be fulfilled by National Red Cross and Red Crescent Societies. The Geneva Conventions of 1949 and the Additional Protocols of 1977 assign, in particular,[93] the following tasks: rendering assistance to the regular medical service of the armed forces as defined in Article 26 GC I, including the utilization of hospital ships; providing for an official Information Bureau pursuant to Article 122 of the Second Geneva Convention of 1949 (GC II)[94] and Article 136 of the Fourth Geneva Convention of 1949 (GC IV);[95] conveying correspondence under the preconditions stipulated by Article 25, para 2 GC IV; and providing tracing services according to Article 26 GC IV as well as Article 33 para 3, 74 of the First Additional Protocol (AP I).[96] Further tasks stemming from international humanitarian law treaties are: to disseminate knowledge of international humanitarian law. This obligation is allocated to States Parties under Article 83 AP I and Article 3, para 2, subpara 3 Movement Statutes which mandates National Societies to disseminate and assist their Governments in disseminating international humanitarian law; to take initiatives in this respect; to disseminate the principles and ideals of the Movement and to assist those Governments which also disseminate these; and to cooperate with their Governments to ensure respect for international humanitarian law and to protect the distinctive emblems.

The Movement Statutes as negotiated, agreed, and adopted by the international community of States define the mandate of National Societies in more detail, both on the domestic as well as on the international level.[97] Beyond the assignment of tasks through the Geneva Conventions and their Additional Protocols, the Movement Statutes provide authorization for National Societies to become active in those areas and to proactively pursue activities in these fields. They do so within their respective framework of available resources as well as existing capabilities and capacities.

---

[93] Further tasks stem from explicit references in e.g. Articles 30, 63, 59, para 2 GC IV; Article 17 AP I; Article 25, para 2 GC IV; Article 81, para 2 AP I; Article 6, para 1 AP I, and implicit references in e.g. common Article 3 GC; Articles 10 GC I, II, III, 11 GC IV, Article 61, para 1 GC IV, as well as from international customary law.

[94] Convention (II) for the Amelioration of the Condition of Wounded, Sick and Shipwrecked Members of Armed Forces at Sea (12 August 1949), 75 UNTS 85.

[95] Convention (IV) Relative to the Protection of Civilian Persons in Time of War (12 August 1949), 75 UNTS 287.

[96] Protocol Additional to the Geneva Conventions of 12 August 1949, and Relating to the Protection of Victims of International Armed Conflicts—AP I—(8 June 1977), 1125 UNTS 3.

[97] Article 3 paras 2 and 3 Movement Statutes. Domestically, National Societies 'cooperate with the public authorities in the prevention of disease, the promotion of health and the mitigation of human suffering by their own programmes in such fields as education, health and social welfare, (. . .) and organize, in liaison with the public authorities, emergency relief operations and other services to assist the victims of armed conflicts as provided in the Geneva Conventions, and the victims of natural disaster and other emergencies'. Internationally, they 'give assistance for victims of armed conflicts, as provided in the Geneva Conventions, and for victims of natural disasters and other emergencies'.

The Statutes do not create international legal obligations in terms of National Societies being legally obliged to actually become active in all field of activities. Beyond international humanitarian law treaties and on the domestic level, States have the option of establishing mandatory tasks within the limits provided by international humanitarian law and the Statutes, in particular with regard to guaranteeing impartiality, neutrality, and independence of National Societies.[98] Within the assigned tasks which delineate the 'humanitarian field' National Societies have the right to initiate a dialogue with Governments on issues pertaining to this area.

37.3.3 Auxiliarity

In addition to the tasks National Societies have to fulfil, i.e. the content of their mandate, two requirements determine the manner in which they have to fulfil it. Like all components, they have to respect the Fundamental Principles of the International Red Cross and Red Crescent Movement. In contrast to the International Committee of the Red Cross and the International Federation of Red Cross and Red Crescent Societies, a National Society has to be constituted as a "voluntary aid societies, auxiliary to the public authorities in the humanitarian field".[99,100] This concept comprises to 'support the public authorities in their humanitarian tasks' and to 'cooperate with the public authorities' in certain fields, as well as to 'organize, in liaison with the public authorities' certain activities and services. States explicitly recognized and affirmed that 'the public authorities and the National Societies as auxiliaries enjoy a specific and distinctive partnership, entailing mutual responsibilities and benefits'. These are based on 'international and national laws, in which the national public authorities and the National Society agree on the areas in which the National Society supplements or substitutes for public humanitarian services'.[101] States and National Societies agreed that as an integral part of this specific and distinctive partnership 'the National Society must be able to deliver its humanitarian services at all times in conformity with the Fundamental Principles, in particular those of neutrality and independence'.[102] National Societies have a duty to consider seriously any request

---

[98] The German Red Cross Act, e.g., refers to 'tasks being allocated to [The German Red Cross] by federal or state law', in particular in the area of domestic disaster management on state (Länder) level; Section 2 para 3; see also Act Amending the Regulations on the German Red Cross 2008. https://www.drk.de/en/the-grc/mission/grc-act/. Accessed 1 August 2020.

[99] Article 4 para 3 Movement Statutes.

[100] Cf. voluntary service as principle 5 of the Fundamental Principles of the International Red Cross and Red Crescent Movement; Pictet 1979, pp. 49–50.

[101] International Conference (2007) Resolution 2, para 3. https://www.icrc.org/en/doc/resour ces/documents/resolution/30-international-conference-resolution-2-2007.htm. Accessed 1 August 2020.

[102] International Conference (2007) Resolution 2, para 3. https://www.icrc.org/en/doc/resour ces/documents/resolution/30-international-conference-resolution-2-2007.htm. Accessed 1 August 2020.

37 The International Red Cross and Red Crescent Movement

by their public authorities to carry out humanitarian activities within their mandate' while 'States must refrain from requesting National Societies to perform activities which are in conflict with the Fundamental Principles of the Movement Statutes or its mission.' 'National Societies have the duty to decline any such request' and public authorities need to 'respect such decisions by the National Societies.'[103] States and National Societies are committed to 'consolidate a balanced relationship with clear and reciprocal responsibilities, maintaining and enhancing a permanent dialogue at all levels within the agreed framework for humanitarian action'.[104]

National Red Cross and Red Crescent Societies thus are neither Non-Governmental Organizations (NGOs) nor part and parcel of civil society.[105] National Red Cross and Red Crescent Societies are, e.g. neither totally free with respect to the content of their statutes nor to the form of their organization and structure. Recognition by the Government of a National Society is an indispensable requirement, as is the fulfilment of the additional conditions for recognition.

37.4 The International Committee of the Red Cross—ICRC

The International Committee of the Red Cross (ICRC) is an impartial, neutral and independent organization whose exclusively humanitarian mission is to protect the lives and dignity of victims[106] of international and other armed conflicts or internal strife[107] and to provide them with assistance. The ICRC also endeavors to prevent suffering by promoting and strengthening international humanitarian law and universal humanitarian principles.[108]

37.4.1 Origin

It was on the initiative of the ICRC that States adopted the first Geneva Convention for the Amelioration of the Condition of the Wounded in Armies in the Field of 1864. The ICRC was founded in 1863 in Geneva, Switzerland, as the "Committee of Five" of the "Geneva Public Welfare Society" by a group of five Swiss citizens.[109] Among those five was the Geneva-based businessman Henry Dunant who in 1862 had published

---

[103] Ibid., para 4.

[104] Ibid., para 2.

[105] The term 'civil society' is not legally defined. Very often, a use of the term refers to nature and character of actors, i.e. their self-management and self-foundation. In contrast to such self-organization, recognition of National Societies by their respective Governments is required.

[106] ICRC undated.

[107] Article 5 para 2 lit. d Movement Statutes.

[108] ICRC undated.

[109] Louis Appia, Guillaume-Henri Dufour, Henry Dunant, Théodore Maunoir, Gustave Moynier.

a book called *A Memory of Solferino*[110] based on his personal experiences from the battle of Solferino between Austrian and Franco-Sardinian armed forces of 24 June 1859,[111] calling for improved care for wounded soldiers in wartime.[112] Along with his vision to establish national relief societies to support military medical services, Dunant and the other four Committee members initiated Government representatives to agree on the first Geneva Convention[113] in 1864. The "Committee of Five" in 1863 evolved into the "International Committee for Relief to the Wounded" which in 1876 became the "International Committee of the Red Cross"—ICRC.[114]

On 25 August 1863, the International Committee decided to convene an international conference in Geneva, under its own responsibility, to study ways of overcoming the inadequacy of army medical services at that time.[115] The conference was opened on 26 October 1863 with 36 participants, including 14 government delegates, six delegates of various organizations and seven private individuals. The 1863 conference took as a basis for discussion a draft convention prepared by the International Committee. A diplomatic conference adopted the first Geneva Convention in August 1864. This Convention in particular obliged armed forces to care for wounded soldiers[116] and introduced the sign of a red cross on a white background as the unified emblem for the protection of medical personnel and institutions.[117] By the end of 1864, the Convention was ratified by France, Switzerland, Belgium, the Netherlands, Italy, Spain, Sweden, Norway, Denmark and the Grand Duchy of Baden.[118] It constitutes the first multilateral international treaty of modern international humanitarian law.

37.4.2 Legal Basis and Mandate

The ICRC is an impartial, neutral and independent organisation with a humanitarian mission to protect the lives and dignity of victims of war and internal violence and to provide them with assistance. It directs and coordinates in situations of conflict the international relief activities conducted by the Movement. It takes action in response to emergencies and endeavours to prevent suffering by promoting and strengthening

---

[110] Haug 1986, p. 129. See also above under Sect. 37.1.

[111] For a more detailed description of the battle and its aftermath see, e.g., ICRC 2004.

[112] See above Sect. 37.1.

[113] Convention for the Amelioration of the Condition of the Wounded in Armies in the Field of 22 August 1864.

[114] See e.g. ICRC 2016. See also Schomann 2013, p. 53 ff.

[115] ICRC 2004.

[116] Article 6 Geneva Convention of 1864.

[117] Article 7 Geneva Convention of 1864.

[118] ICRC 2004.

37 The International Red Cross and Red Crescent Movement

international humanitarian law and universal humanitarian principles.[119] The main legal basis of actions of the ICRC today are the four Geneva Conventions of 1949, the Additional Protocols to the Geneva Conventions of 1977 and 2005, the Statutes of the International Red Cross and Red Crescent Movement and the Statutes of the International Committee of the Red Cross.

First and foremost, the ICRC is a private law association governed by Article 60 and following of the Swiss Civil Code[120] with its headquarters in Geneva, Switzerland.[121] It comprises 15–25 members, co-opted from among Swiss citizens.[122] Further characteristics and assets in relation to its legal personality[123] under the Swiss Civil Code including, in particular, its statutory bodies and relations within and outside the International Red Cross and Red Crescent Movement are regulated in the Statutes of the ICRC. According to Article 15 para 1 of the Statutes of the International Committee of the Red Cross [ICRC Statutes], major financial assets of the ICRC are contributions of governments and National Societies, funds from private sources and income from securities. Other main donors are the European Commission, federal, cantonal and municipal bodies, as well as international organizations, including UN agencies, the World Bank Group and non-governmental organizations.[124]

Article 1 of the ICRC Statutes determines the ICRC as "an independent humanitarian organization having a status of its own". In addition to its legal personality under domestic law, the International Committee of the Red Cross is an entity with partial/restricted/limited international legal personality.[125] Rights and obligations directly conferred by international law derive mainly from the Geneva Conventions and the Additional Protocols and are complemented, as the case may be,[126] by domestic law.

Of special importance is the right to visit prisoners of war on the basis of GC III and civilian internees under GC IV. In international armed conflicts, Article 126 GC III grants delegates of the International Committee of the Red Cross, appointed upon approval of the Detaining Power,[127] the "permission to go to all places where prisoners of war may be, particularly to places of internment, imprisonment and labour" and "access to all premises occupied by prisoners of war".[128] They shall also be "able to interview the prisoners, and in particular the prisoners' representatives, without witnesses, either personally or through an interpreter". ICRC delegates further have

---

[119] ICRC 2009b; Standing Commission of the Red Cross and Red Crescent. Components of the Movement. https://standcom.ch/components-of-the-movement/. Accessed 1 August 2020.

[120] Article 2 Statutes of the International Committee of the Red Cross [ICRC Statutes].

[121] Article 3 para 1 ICRC Statutes.

[122] Article 7 para 1 ICRC Statutes.

[123] Cf. Article 2 ICRC Statutes.

[124] ICRC 2019.

[125] Gasser 2016, para 43; Wilms 2010, para 5.

[126] See, e.g., Debuf 2016, pp. 319–321, 331 f.

[127] Article 126 para 4 GC III.

[128] Article 126 para 1 GC III.

"full liberty to select the places they wish to visit. The duration and frequency of these visits shall not be restricted" and "visits may not be prohibited except for reasons of imperative military necessity, and then only as an exceptional and temporary measure".[129] With a more general view, Article 9 GC III provides for the provisions of GC III not constituting an "obstacle to the humanitarian activities which the International Committee of the Red Cross (...)[130] may, subject to the consent of the Parties to the conflict concerned, undertake for the protection of prisoners of war and for their relief".

GC IV provides for a similar regime with regard to the visit of civilian detainees. Article 143 para 5 GC IV regulates that delegates of the ICRC, appointed upon approval of the Power governing the territories where delegates will carry out their activities, "have permission to go to all places where protected persons are",[131] that they "have access to all premises (...) and shall be able to interview (...) without witnesses",[132] that "such visits may not be prohibited except for reasons of military necessity, and then only as an exceptional and temporary measure" and that duration and frequency of visits shall not be restricted,[133] and that delegates "have full liberty to select the places they wish to visit".[134] For persons protected under GC IV, Article 76 para 6 establishes the "right to be visited by delegates (...) of the International Committee of the Red Cross, in accordance with the provisions of Article 143".

Article 81 para 1 AP I broadens the scope of this scheme of detention visits. First, it obliges Parties to the international armed conflict to "grant to the International Committee of the Red Cross", i.e. to the institution and not (only to individual delegates), "all facilities, within their power so as to enable it to carry out the humanitarian functions assigned to it by the [Geneva] Conventions and this Protocol in order to ensure protection and assistance to the victims of conflicts". Second, it introduces a right of initiative for the ICRC with regard to especially prisoners of war and protected civilians. It provides that the ICRC "may also carry out any other humanitarian activities in favour of these victims, subject to the consent of the Parties to the conflict concerned". Under international customary law,[135] "the ICRC must be granted regular access to all persons deprived of their liberty in order to verify the conditions of their detention and to restore contact between those persons and their families".[136]

For non-international armed conflicts, treaty law is restricted to the simple provision of common Article 3 para 2 GC that "an impartial humanitarian body, such as the International Committee of the Red Cross, may offer its services to the Parties to the conflict". International customary law is a little, though not substantially, broader

---

[129] Article 126 para 2 GC III; emphasis added.

[130] "Or any other impartial humanitarian organization".

[131] Article 143 para 1 GC III.

[132] Article 143 para 2 GC III.

[133] Article 143 para 3 GC III.

[134] Article 143 para 4 GC III.

[135] Henckaerts and Doswald-Beck 2009.

[136] Rule 124 A of the Customary International Humanitarian Law Study [CILS].

in that it provides that "the ICRC may offer its services to the parties to the conflict with a view to visiting all persons deprived of their liberty for reasons related to the conflict in order to verify the conditions of their detention and to restore contacts between those persons and their families".[137]

Outside treaties of international humanitarian law, the Statutes of the International Red Cross and Red Crescent Movement—which have been adopted not only by components of the Movement but also by the States Parties to the Geneva Conventions[138]—extend the rights bestowed on the ICRC by the international community. Article 5 para 3 establishes the right to "take any humanitarian initiative which comes within [the role of the ICRC] as a specifically neutral and independent institution and intermediary, and may consider any question requiring examination by such an institution". This so-called right of initiative extends in particular to all types of detainees being detained in relation to international or non-international armed conflict or internal strife.

37.4.3 Functions and Role

The Movement Statutes contain a list of roles which the States Parties to the Geneva Conventions and the other components of the Movement expect the ICRC to fulfill. The first role is "to maintain and disseminate the Fundamental Principles of the Movement" (Article 5 para 2 lit. a Movement Statutes). An additional role in the context the Fundamental Principles and international humanitarian law is specified in lit. c "to undertake the tasks incumbent upon it under the Geneva Conventions, to work for the faithful application of international humanitarian law applicable in armed conflicts and to take cognizance of any complaints based on alleged breaches of that law". Last but not least in this field, the ICRC has been assigned "to work for the understanding and dissemination of knowledge of international humanitarian law applicable in armed conflicts and to prepare any development thereof" (lit. g). It is not least on the basis of these functions that the ICRC's role has been described as "guardian" of international humanitarian law.[139] Since 2010 roughly, States have very much emphasized their responsibility to monitor and further develop international humanitarian law.

With a view to the ICRC's characteristic as a neutral intermediary, Article 5 para 2 lit. d Movement Statutes formulates the role "to endeavour at all times – as a neutral institution whose humanitarian work is carried out particularly in time of international and other armed conflicts or internal strife – to ensure the protection of and assistance

---

[137] Rule 124 B CILS.

[138] Cf. https://ihl-databases.icrc.org/applic/ihl/ihl.nsf/vwTreaties1949.xsp. Accessed 1 August 2020.

[139] Sandoz 1998. Sandoz identifies the following sub-functions: "monitoring", "catalyst", "promotion", "guardian angel", "direct action", and "watchdog". See more recently Lavoyer and Vité 2018, p. 549.

to military and civilian victims of such events and of their direct results". Article 10 para 3 GC I, II, III and Article 11 para 3 GC IV foresee that the ICRC may offer to assume "the humanitarian functions performed by Protecting Powers" under the Geneva Conventions. Additional Protocol I differs somewhat from the option of the ICRC acting as protecting power in that Article 5 para 4 stipulates the obligation of parties to the conflict to accept an offer of the ICRC to "act as a substitute" for protective powers. Article 5 para 3 AP I, however, indicates a connected, but distinctly different role of the ICRC as "impartial humanitarian organization" offering its good offices to the parties to the conflict. Today, the ICRC has shaped its characteristics as a neutral intermediary in contrast to a functioning as (substitute) protecting power. A protecting power is a state or organization which has been designated by a party to the conflict and accepted by the adverse party[140] and which is—or actually very often at least is being perceived as—representing only the interests of the conflict party having designated it. The ICRC therefore has focused on fulfilling the functions of, e.g., visiting protected persons, supervising relief missions and evacuations, receiving applications by protected persons, assisting in judicial proceedings against protected persons, transmitting information, documents and relief goods, and offering good offices as without being designated by only one party to the conflict. It has rather emphasized its role as neutral and impartial independent humanitarian actor whose action is accepted by all parties to the conflict.[141]

An additional operational role of the ICRC is the one "to ensure the operation of the Central Tracing Agency [CTA] as provided in the Geneva Conventions".[142] Although Article 123 GC III and Article 140 GC IV only mention the option to "propose to the Powers concerned the organization of such an Agency",[143] the Central Tracing Agency has been organized as an institution of and by the ICRC.[144] It fulfils the functions of both the Central Prisoners of War Information Agency[145] and the Central Information Agency.[146,147] Hence, the Central Tracing Agency collects and transmits information on protected persons, who are kept in custody for more than two weeks, who are subjected to assigned residence or who are interned, to their country of origin.[148] Thus, it acts as a neutral and impartial intermediary between Parties to the armed conflict.[149]

States Parties to the Geneva Conventions and the other components of the Movement further entrusted the ICRC with the role "to recognize any newly established or reconstituted National Society, which fulfils the conditions for recognition set

---

[140] Cf. Article 2 lit. c and d AP I.

[141] See also Sassòli et al. 2011.

[142] Article 2 lit. e AP I.

[143] Giladi and Ratner 2015, p. 532.

[144] Spieker 2015, p. 1113.

[145] Article 123 GC III.

[146] Article 140 GC IV.

[147] Spieker 2015, p. 1113.

[148] Ibid.

[149] Lavoyer and Vité 2018, p. 547; Spieker 2015, p. 1113.

37 The International Red Cross and Red Crescent Movement

out in Article 4 and to notify other National Societies of such recognition".[150] The most recent National Society having been recognized by the ICRC is the Marshall Islands Red Cross Society.[151] Concluding, Article 5 para 2 lit. h assigns the ICRC the role "to carry out mandates entrusted to it by the International Conference".[152] An example of an International Conference mandating a specific task of the ICRC is the Customary International Law Study[153] mandated by the 26th International Conference in 1995.[154]

37.4.4 Tasks and Operations

Already before the adoption of the first Geneva Convention in August 1864, the International Committee decided earlier in 1864 to send two delegates to the field in the German-Danish war after Austrian and Prussian armies had invaded Denmark on 1 February 1864. These two delegates' task was to care for the wounded and to study the possibilities of implementing the draft Convention. Deploying delegates on each side of the front line of the armed conflict, the International Committee for the first time took the role as a neutral intermediary between belligerents.[155] During the Franco-Prussian war 1870–71 the International Committee established the first Information Agency for families of wounded or captured soldiers. A series of conflicts, known as the Eastern crisis (1875–1878), took the delegates of the International Committee to the Balkans, followed by the Serbo-Bulgarian war (1885–1886) and the Balkan wars (1912–1913).[156] At the same time, the ICRC expanded its

---

[150] Article 5 para 2 lit. b Movement Statutes.

[151] Recognition of 20 December 2017.

[152] For the characteristics of the International Conference of the Red Cross and Red Crescent see in particular above Sect. 37.2.

[153] Henckaerts and Doswald-Beck 2009.

[154] Meeting of the Intergovernmental Group of Experts for the Protection of War Victims; Geneva, 23–27 January 1995; Recommendations, II. "The Experts recommend that the ICRC be invited to prepare, with the assistance of experts in international humanitarian law representing various geographical regions and different legal systems, and in consultation with experts from governments and international organisations, a report on customary rules of international humanitarian law applicable in international and non-international armed conflicts, and to circulate the report to States and competent international bodies."; ICRC 1996; International Conference (1995) Resolution 1. https://www.icrc.org/en/doc/resources/documents/resolution/26-international-conference-resolution-1-1995.htm. Accessed 1 August 2020; "International Humanitarian Law: From Law to Action – Report on the Follow-up to the International Conference for the Protection of War Victims", OP 4: "also endorses the Recommendations drawn up by the Intergovernmental Group of Experts, which aim at (…)". https://www.icrc.org/en/doc/resources/documents/report/57jmru.htm. Accessed 1 August 2020.

[155] ICRC 2010.

[156] ICRC 2004.

work in undertaking new activities such as visiting prisoners of war and transmitting lists of names of prisoners of war.[157]

Detention visits aim at three directions: first, they are undertaken with a view to preventing or putting an end to disappearances and summary executions, torture and ill-treatment; second, they restore contact between detainees and their families; and third, they search to improve conditions of detention when necessary and in accordance with the applicable law. In the area of detention visits, the ICRC visited 1,020,088 detainees in 2018 in 1352 places of detention. It conducted 3773 visits to detainees, and 31,531 detainees received individual visits and follow-up from the ICRC.[158] In its confidential approach to authorities, the ICRC visits places of detention and, if necessary, provides material or medical assistance. It does not take a position as to the reasons for arrest or capture of detainees and focuses on the factual and psychological conditions of detention only. Conditions for ICRC visits[159] are that the ICRC is granted to see all detainees falling with the mandate of the ICRC and to interview in private, i.e. without any witness. It must get access to all places where detainees are held and be able to repeat visits to detainees of the choice of the ICRC, as frequently as deemed necessary. During visits, the ICRC draws up lists of detainees with its mandate or receives such lists from the authorities to be verified or, as the case may be, completed by ICRC delegates.

On the basis of the ICRC's function "to endeavour at all times – as a neutral institution whose humanitarian work is carried out particularly in time of international and other armed conflicts or internal strife – to ensure the protection of and assistance to military and civilian victims of such events and of their direct results",[160] the ICRC's humanitarian action focuses on providing assistance and providing protection.[161] In order to cover contexts of activities which do not qualify as armed conflicts but have or may have humanitarian consequences, the ICRC has been using the term "other situations of violence" since 2009.[162] Both the term and ensuing consequences have been the object of debate within and outside the Movement.[163] Protection aims to ensure that authorities and other actors fulfil their obligations and uphold the rights of individuals, in order to preserve the lives, security, dignity, and physical and mental well-being of victims of armed conflict and "other situations of violence". It also tries to prevent or put an end to actual or probable violations of international humanitarian law or other bodies of law or fundamental rules protecting people in these situations. It focuses first on the causes or circumstances of violations, addressing those responsible and those who can influence them, and second on the consequences

---

[157] Ibid.

[158] ICRC 2019.

[159] ICRC 2015.

[160] Article 5 para 2 lit. d Movement Statutes.

[161] Cf. the mission statement, reiterated in ICRC 2018.

[162] ICRC 2009b, p. 3.

[163] For the ICRC's definition and its criteria to conduct a humanitarian operation in such circumstances, see ICRC 2014.

of violations.[164] The aim of ICRC assistance is to preserve life and/or restore the dignity of individuals or communities adversely affected by armed conflict or "other situations of violence". Assistance covers the unmet essential needs of individuals and/or communities as determined by the social and cultural environment. These needs vary, but responses mainly address issues relating to health, water, sanitation, shelter and economic security by providing goods and services, supporting existing facilities and services and encouraging the authorities and others to assume their responsibilities.[165]

Within its core mandate, the ICRC conducts and directs and otherwise, as appropriate and required by the exigencies of the situation, coordinates humanitarian action conducted by components of the International Red Cross and Red Crescent Movement. The division of work between the components[166] is implemented on the basis of the 1997 Seville Agreement,[167] the 2005 Supplementary Measures thereto[168] and the ongoing process on Strengthening Movement Coordination and Cooperation (SMCC).[169] In addition, the Movement Statutes include the function "to contribute, in anticipation of armed conflicts, to the training of medical personnel and the preparation of medical equipment, in cooperation with the National Societies, the military and civilian medical services and other competent authorities".[170]

37.5 The International Federation of Red Cross and Red Crescent Societies

Founded in 1919, the International Federation of Red Cross and Red Crescent Societies (IFRC) works on the basis of the Principles of the Red Cross and Red Crescent Movement to inspire, encourage, facilitate and promote at all times all forms of humanitarian activities carried out by its member National Societies, with a view to preventing and alleviating human suffering.[171] Its aim is to "thereby contributing to the maintenance and the promotion of peace in the world".[172] The International Federation is an "independent humanitarian organization which is not governmental, political, racial or sectarian in character"[173] and "acts under its own Constitution with all rights and obligations of a corporate body with a legal personality".[174]

---

[164] Ibid., p. 14.

[165] ICRC 2009b, p. 15.

[166] Cf. Article 5 para 4 Movement Statutes.

[167] IFRC 1997.

[168] ICRC 2005b.

[169] Compare the SMCC Progress Report; RCC 2017.

[170] Article 5 para 2 lit. f Movement Statutes.

[171] Article 6 para 3 Movement Statutes.

[172] Ibid.

[173] Article 6 para 2 Movement Statutes.

[174] Ibid., para 1.

The IFRC is the umbrella organisation of today[175] 192 National Red Cross and Red Crescent Societies. Its headquarters is also located in Geneva, Switzerland. The major functions of the International Federation are to "act as the permanent body of liaison, coordination and study between the National Societies and to give them any assistance they might request"; to "encourage and promote in every country the establishment and development of an independent and duly recognized National Society"; to "bring relief by all available means to all disaster victims"; to "assist the National Societies in their disaster relief preparedness, in the organization of their relief actions and in the relief operation themselves"; to "encourage and coordinate the participation of the National Societies in activities for safeguarding public health and the promotion of social welfare in cooperation with their appropriate national authorities", to "assist the International Committee in the promotion and development of international humanitarian law and collaborate with it in the dissemination of this law and of the Fundamental Principles of the Movement among the National Societies", and to "be the official representative of the member Societies in the international field, *inter alia* for dealing with decisions and recommendations adopted by its Assembly and to be the guardian of their integrity and the protector of their interests".[176] In other words, the International Federation's main functions focus, as appropriate, on the coordination of international actions and on the assistance to domestic activities of its members. Whereas the ICRC's mandate relates to situations of armed conflict, the mandate of the IFRC applies particularly to situations of natural and technological disasters, development cooperation and health emergencies.

It has been a continuous debate whether the International Federation's only or at least major focus should be the support and assistance to its Member Societies or whether it should be operative and conduct its own operations in emergency situations within its mandated areas. The 1997 Seville Agreement,[177] concluded between the Movement components, assumes the possibility of the International Federation being the lead agency in specific situations, including in particular natural or technological disasters and other emergency and disaster situations in peace time which require resources exceeding those of the operating National Society.[178] Although reconfirming and emphasising the role of National Societies on whose territory an

---

[175] For a list of IFRC members, compare https://www.ifrc.org/Docs/ExcelExport/NS_Directory. pdf. Accessed 1 August 2020.

[176] Article 6 para 4 lit. a, b, c, d, f, j and k Movement Statutes. Additional references are "to organize, coordinate and direct international relief actions in accordance with the Principles and Rules adopted by the International Conference" (lit. e)— i.e. the "Principles and Rules for Red Cross and Red Crescent Humanitarian Assistance" endorsed by the 32nd International Red Cross and Red Crescent Conference 2015, "to encourage and coordinate between National Societies the exchange of ideas for the education of children and young people in humanitarian ideals and for the development of friendly relations between young people of all countries" (lit. g), "to assist National Societies to recruit members from the population as a whole and inculcate the principles and ideals of the Movement" (lit. h), "to bring help to victims of armed conflicts in accordance with the agreements concluded with the International Committee" (lit. i), and "to carry out the mandates entrusted to it by the International Conference" (lit. l).

[177] IFRC 1997. See also above under Sect. 37.2.

[178] Article 5.3.2 Seville Agreement.

37 The International Red Cross and Red Crescent Movement

international Red Cross/Red Crescent Operation is being conducted, both the 2005 Supplementary Measures to the Seville Agreement[179] and the ongoing process on Strengthening Movement Coordination and Cooperation (SMCC)[180] confirm this option. However, in particular Member Societies with strong international cooperation portfolios closely monitor both effectiveness and efficiency of international operations coordinated by the International Federation of Red Cross and Red Crescent Societies.

37.6 Fundamental Principles of the International Red Cross and Red Crescent Movement

The Movement and all its components are legally bound to be guided by seven Fundamental Principles of the International Red Cross and Red Crescent Movement, i.e. humanity, impartiality, neutrality, independence, voluntary service, unity and universality.[181] All components—National Societies, the ICRC and the International Federation of Red Cross and Red Crescent Societies—are legally obliged to observe the fundamental principles when deciding on how to fulfil their respective mandate. For National Societies, observance of and adherence to the fundamental principles is also a condition for recognition (Article 4 para 10 Statutes of the Movement).[182] Proclaimed in Vienna in 1965 and adopted in their present form and integrated into the Statutes of the International Red Cross and Red Crescent Movement in 1986, the origins of the fundamental principles go back to Henry Dunant who elaborated on impartiality and voluntary service, but also on unity and universality in his book *A Memory of Solferino*.[183]

The Fundamental Principles are broader in scope than the so-called principles of humanitarian assistance or humanitarian principles. In the field of humanitarian action, a series of Non-Governmental or Governmental Organizations have voluntarily subscribed to the 'humanitarian principles', in particular within the framework

---

[179] Articles 1.4, 1.11, 1.15 Supplementary measures to enhance the implementation of the Seville Agreement; ICRC 2005b.

[180] Compare the SMCC Progress Report; RCC 2017.

[181] PP 2 Movement Statutes.

[182] For the interpretation of the fundamental principles and their relevance see, e.g., ICRC (2020), Connecting with the Past: The Fundamental Principles of the International Red Cross and Red Crescent Movement—A Critical Historical Perspective. https://www.icrc.org/en/publication/4258-connecting-past-fundamental-principles-international-red-cross-and-red-crescent. Accessed 10 August 2020; and Pictet (1979), The Fundamental Principles of the Red Cross—commentary. https://www.icrc.org/en/doc/resources/documents/misc/fundamental-principles-commentary-010179.htm. Accessed 10 August 2020.

[183] Haug 1986, p. 129. See also above Sects. 37.1 and 37.4.1.

804 H. Spieker

of the Code of Conduct for the International Red Cross and Red Crescent Movement and NGOs in Disaster Relief.[184] Donor institutions very often require humanitarian operations to be implemented on the basis of the 'humanitarian principles'.[185] Whereas "humanitarian principles' consist of 'humanity', 'impartiality', 'neutrality', and 'independence',[186] the Fundamental Principles of the International Red Cross and Red Crescent Movement additionally contain the principles 'voluntary service', 'unity', and 'universality'. Further, the Fundamental Principles are stricter in their applicability than the humanitarian principles in that they are legally binding on all activities and positions of all Movement components, without exception. National Societies' auxiliary status and role does not defer from their obligation to observe the Fundamental Principles. On the basis that public authorities and the National Society "agree on the areas in which the National Society supplement or substitutes for public humanitarian services", the National Society "must be able to deliver its humanitarian services at all times in conformity with the Fundamental Principles, in particular those of neutrality and independence, and with its other obligations under the Movement Statutes".[187]

The fundamental principles of the International Red Cross and Red Crescent Movement are also the basis for shaping and developing relations with Movement components and military bodies. Since the beginning of the 1990s, armed forces have become increasingly involved in multidisciplinary and multifaceted missions and operations abroad. They exercise military, law enforcement and civilian functions—including humanitarian tasks and functions—in various contexts and complex situations involving a multitude of actors, both national and international, governmental and nongovernmental, State and non-State, as well as components of the International Red Cross and Red Crescent Movement.

The presence of various actors with different mandates, objectives, and motivations and at the same time overlapping tasks and functions in the same environment automatically raises questions with regard to the relationship between these actors, as well as the potential for and limits to their cooperation and collaboration. Components of the International Red Cross and Red Crescent Movement act with, alongside or in parallel to military actors in different forms. Possibilities, limitations and extent of cooperation have been intensely debated within different circles over the last 25 years.[188] The debate has centred mainly on the issue of safeguarding the respective roles of actors. A primary concern has been to avoid a *'blurring of the lines* between

---

[184] IFRC/ICRC 1994.

[185] Cf. e.g. European Consensus on Humanitarian Aid, OJ C 25 (30.01.2008), pp. 1–12, para 10.

[186] Cf. IFRC/ICRC 1994.

[187] International Conference (2007) Resolution 2. https://www.icrc.org/en/doc/resources/docume nts/resolution/30-international-conference-resolution-2-2007.htm. Accessed 1 August 2020.

[188] See e.g. Steering Committee for Humanitarian Response (2010) SCHR Position Paper on Humanitarian Military Relations. https://reliefweb.int/sites/reliefweb.int/files/resources/C05620 DB85A3AD42C12576D200383803-SCHR_Jan2010.pdf. Accessed 1 August 2020.

37 The International Red Cross and Red Crescent Movement

the military, political and humanitarian functions of the international response to different crises'.[189]

When fulfilling their mandates, components of the Movement frequently interact with armed forces and military bodies. They do so in non-emergency peacetime, armed conflict, internal strife, and natural or other disasters, both in national and in international contexts. Major areas of contact and interplay include civil defence, disaster management, tracing, humanitarian assistance and protection, social welfare services, first-aid training, and dissemination. In order to facilitate interaction between components of the Movement and military bodies, components generally maintain a dialogue with them and at the same time ensure that they are clearly distinguishable from military and other governmental bodies. In order to streamline decisions taken by the Movement and to render such decisions more predictable and reliable to third parties and in particular military bodies, components of the Movement agreed on a guidance document in 2005, defining guiding principles for the implementation of such relationships.[190]

The guiding principles are legally binding on the components of the Movement which are required to base their decisions on interaction with military bodies on these principles with a view to safeguard components' independence, neutrality, and impartiality:

- While maintaining a dialogue with armed forces at all levels, the components of the Movement preserve their independence of decision-making and action, in order to ensure adequate access to all people in need of humanitarian assistance.[191]
- When establishing and maintaining relationships with military bodies, the components of the Movement ensure that such relationships seek to enhance effective assistance to and protection of the victims of armed conflict and vulnerable people.
- All components of the Movement ensure that their decisions are taken with due consideration for potential consequences for other components and the positioning of the whole Movement.
- All components of the Movement ensure that they act and are perceived as acting in accordance with the Fundamental Principles, in particular independence, neutrality, and impartiality.

---

[189] Oxfam International (2012) OI Policy Compendium Note on the Provision of Aid by Military Forces. https://oxfamilibrary.openrepository.com/bitstream/handle/10546/115031/hpn-provision-aid-military-forces-010412-en.pdf. Accessed 1 August 2020.

[190] ICRC 2005a.

[191] A different scenario is the constellation provided for in Article 26 Geneva Convention I: National Societies' personnel and materiel may be provided to and integrated in the medical services of the armed forces of a State Party to the Geneva Conventions. In consequence, a National Society's personnel is subject to military laws and regulations. But even in these situations a National Society "must respect the Fundamental Principles, including that of neutrality, and at all times maintain its autonomy and ensure that it is clearly distinguishable from military and other governmental bodies"; International Conference (2007) Resolution 2, OP 6. https://www.icrc.org/en/doc/resources/documents/resolution/30-international-conference-resolution-2-2007.htm. Accessed 1 August 2020.

806   H. Spieker

- Each component favours a clear distinction between the respective roles of military bodies and humanitarian actors, paying particular attention to perceptions locally and within the wider public.
- In their relations with military bodies, the components of the Movement ensure that their activities do not amount to a contribution to the military effort and are not perceived as such.
- The more military bodies are perceived as party to an armed conflict, the more the components of the Movement weigh the intensified need for interaction with those bodies against the consequences of such relations on their observance of the Fundamental Principles.
- The Movement's components always take care that their relationship with military bodies does not negatively affect the safety and security of beneficiaries and humanitarian personnel.

Decisions taken by components of the Movement on how to interact with military bodies and whether to engage in a specific relationship are taken on the basis of a case-by-case assessment and evaluation. Special emphasis merits the fact that an interaction not only complies with this guidance and, in particular, with the Fundamental Principles, but actually is perceived as such, in order to maintain access to the most vulnerable and to maintain the ability to fulfil the components' mandates. Experience shows that actors involved in a situation will most probably deny and/or impede humanitarian access and assistance in cases where they perceive a behaviour as taking place beyond a component's mandate, task or role and in particular as being partial and/or not neutral. The agreed guiding principles therefore generally presume that 'where there is a trend towards integrating humanitarian action into a wider political and military framework, components of the Movement promote and safeguard a clear distinction between their humanitarian work and the military/political actions of others'.[192]

37.7 Conclusion

The International Red Cross and Red Crescent Movement is the largest humanitarian network in the world and its central purpose of the Movement and its components is to help without discrimination those who suffer. Its mission is "to prevent and alleviate human suffering wherever it may be found, to protect life and health and ensure respect for the human being, in particular in times of armed conflict and other emergencies, to work for the prevention of disease and for the promotion of health and social welfare, to encourage voluntary service and a constant readiness to give help by the members of the Movement, and a universal sense of solidarity towards all those in need of its protection and assistance". Its supreme deliberative body, the International Conference of the Red Cross and Red Crescent, provides a

---

[192] ICRC 2005a.

non-political forum for dialogue on humanitarian issues, and it examines and decides upon humanitarian matters of common interest and any other related matter.[193] The Conference represents the only specific and regular forum to discuss themes of a humanitarian nature and international humanitarian law issues. This characteristic is part of the ongoing debate on the potential for creating a new additional forum for a non-politicized, non-contextualized and non-selective effective debate on questions of international humanitarian law.[194]

If the International Red Cross and Red Crescent Movement would not exist—would something be lacking? Would there be a lacuna in international relations in general and in international humanitarian law in particular? One might easily be inclined to answer these questions in the affirmative. However, given the reinforcement of considerations of domestic interests and national sovereignty in international relations it is a tough question whether the International Red Cross and Red Crescent Movement has anything to offer to the international community and whether what it has to offer actually meets the interests of the international community—at present and in the foreseeable future.

To date, the International Red Cross and Red Crescent Conference constitutes the only forum on a global and regular basis to discuss questions of international humanitarian law. At the same time it presents a global and regular forum for the discussion of humanitarian issues at large. For the time being, the creation of an additional forum does not seem feasible. In the framework of deliberations during the State process on Strengthening Respect for International Humanitarian Law 2011–2015, 2015–2019,[195] States discussed ways to enhance the implementation of IHL using, in particular, the potential of the International Conference. It seems that a considerable number and representation of States confirmed and emphasized the relevance, importance and potential of the International Conference. If the International Conference would not exist, the international community, States and components of the International Red Cross and Red Crescent Movement would be deprived of this unique opportunity to tackle legal and operational humanitarian needs pressing today's world. States and Movement components have the responsibility, the opportunity and the space to enrich debates and outcomes of the International Conference in the upcoming Conference in December 2019 and in following International Conferences.

The International Red Cross and Red Crescent Movement provides a reliable, feasible predictable and secure opportunity for both States and Movement components to achieve progress in international humanitarian law and humanitarian issues. Today's complexities do not allow for losing this unique asset and do not warrant sufficient potential for advancing and making progress. States and Movement components have a joint history and, in particular, joint experience in working together and making progress together. They also have sufficient joint success to reinforce joint

---

[193] See above Sect. 37.2.

[194] International Conference (2015) Resolution 2. http://rcrcconference.org/wp-content/uploads/2015/04/32IC-AR-Compliance_EN.pdf. Accessed 1 August 2020.

[195] Cf. Intergovernmental Process on Strengthening Respect for International Humanitarian Law (IHL) 2019.

efforts. And States have reiterated that they recognize and appreciate the results of this unique undertaking and that they desire to continue the joint effort. States and Movement components have the responsibility, the opportunity and the space to prove that they can achieve together what they would not be able to achieve alone.

References

Books, (Online) Articles and Chapters in Books

Bouvier A (1989) Special Aspects of the Use of the Red Cross or Red Crescent Emblem, IRRC 272:438–458

Bugnion F (2007) Red Cross, Red Crescent, Red Crystal. https://www.icrc.org/en/doc/assets/files/other/icrc_002_0778.pdf. Accessed 1 August 2020

Cauderay G C (1990) Visibility of the Distinctive Emblem on Medical Establishments, Units and Transports, IRRC 277:295–321

Debuf E (2016) Tools to Do the Job: The ICRC's Legal Status, Privileges and Immunities. IRRC doi:https://doi.org/10.1017/S181638311500051X

Directory Red Cross Red Crescent. https://www.ifrc.org/Docs/ExcelExport/NS_Directory.pdf. Accessed 1 August 2020

Dunant H (1862) A Memory of Solferino (reprint 1986). https://www.icrc.org/en/publication/0361-memory-solferino. Accessed 1 August 2020

Gasser H-P (2016) International Committee of the Red Cross (ICRC). In Max Planck Encyclopedia of Public International Law. https://opil.ouplaw.com/view/10.1093/law:epil/978019923 1690/law-9780199231690-e310. Accessed 1 August 2020

Geneva International Conference (1863) Resolutions of the Geneva International Conference, Geneva, 26–29 October 1863. https://ihl-databases.icrc.org/ihl/INTRO/115?OpenDocument. Accessed 1 August 2020

Giladi R, Ratner S (2015) The Role of the International Committee of the Red Cross. In: Clapham A et al (eds) The 1949 Geneva Conventions: A Commentary. Oxford University Press, Oxford, pp 524–547

Haug H (1986) Dunant's ideas-the test of time. In: Dunant H (ed) A Memory of Solferino. https://www.icrc.org/en/publication/0361-memory-solferino, pp 129–136. Accessed 1 August 2020

Henckaerts J-M, Doswald-Beck L (2009) Customary International Humanitarian Law. https://www.icrc.org/en/doc/assets/files/other/customary-international-humanitarian-law-i-icrc-eng.pdf. Accessed 1 August 2020

ICRC (Council of Delegates of the International Red Cross and Red Crescent Movement) (1991) Regulations adopted by the 20th Red Cross and Red Crescent International Conference (1965, revised by the Council of Delegates 1991) Regulations on the use of the Emblem of the Red Cross or the Red Crescent by the National Societies. https://www.icrc.org/en/doc/resources/doc uments/article/other/57jmbg.htm. Accessed 1 August 2020

ICRC (1996) Annex II: Meeting of the Intergovernmental Group of Experts for the Protection of War Victims, Geneva, 23–27 January 1995: Recommendations. https://www.icrc.org/en/doc/res ources/documents/article/other/57jmvt.htm. Accessed 1 August 2020

ICRC (2004) From the battle of Solferino to the eve of the First World War. https://www.icrc.org/en/doc/resources/documents/misc/57jnvp.htm. Accessed 1 August 2020

ICRC (Council of Delegates of the International Red Cross and Red Crescent Movement) (2005a) Resolution 7. https://www.icrc.org/eng/resources/documents/resolution/council-delega tes-resolution-7-2005.htm. Accessed 1 August 2020

37 The International Red Cross and Red Crescent Movement

ICRC (Council of Delegates of the International Red Cross and Red Crescent Movement) (2005b) Resolution 8. https://www.icrc.org/eng/resources/documents/resolution/council-delega tes-resolution-8-2005.htm. Accessed 1 August 2020

ICRC (2009a) Restoring Family Links. https://www.icrc.org/eng/assets/files/other/icrc_002_0967. pdf. Accessed 1 August 2020

ICRC (2009b) The ICRC: Its Mission and Work. https://www.icrc.org/en/doc/assets/files/other/ icrc_002_0963.pdf. Accessed 1 August 2020

ICRC (2010) Founding and early years of the ICRC (1863–1914). https://www.icrc.org/en/doc ument/founding-and-early-years-icrc-1863-1914. Accessed 1 August 2020

ICRC (2012) Interview with Philip Spoerri. Cyprus Red Cross Society: the Movement's 188th National Society. https://www.icrc.org/eng/resources/documents/interview/2012/cyprus-interv iew-2012-02-23.htm. Accessed on 1 August 2020

ICRC (2014) The International Committee of the Red Cross's (ICRC's) role in situations of violence below the threshold of armed conflict. IRRC doi:https://doi.org/10.1017/S1816383114000113

ICRC (2015) What we do for detainees. https://www.icrc.org/en/document/what-we-do-detainees. Accessed 1 August 2020

ICRC (2016) History of the ICRC. https://www.icrc.org/en/document/history-icrc. Accessed 1 August 2020

ICRC (2018) ICRC Strategy 2019–2022. https://www.icrc.org/en/publication/4354-icrc-strategy-2019-2022. Accessed 1 August 2020

ICRC (2019) Annual Report 2018. https://www.icrc.org/data/files/annual-report-2018/icrc-annual-report-2018.pdf. Accessed 1 August 2020

ICRC (undated) The ICRC's mandate and mission. https://www.icrc.org/en/mandate-and-mission. Accessed 1 August 2020

IFRC (Council of Delegates of the International Red Cross and Red Crescent Movement) (1997) Agreement on the Organization of the International Activities of the Components of the International Red Cross and Red Crescent Movement. https://www.ifrc.org/Global/Governance/Pol icies/Seville_Agreement.pdf. Accessed 1 August 2020

IFRC (Council of Delegates of the International Red Cross and Red Crescent Movement/International Conference of the Red Cross and Red Crescent) (2007) Resolutions. https://www.ifrc.org/Global/Governance/Meetings/International-Conference/2007/30IC-CoD-en.pdf. Accessed 1 August 2020

IFRC/ICRC (1994) The Code of Conduct for the International Red Cross and Red Crescent Movement and Non-Governmental Organisations (NGOs) in Disaster Relief. https://www.ifrc.org/Glo bal/Publications/disasters/code-of-conduct/code-english.pdf. Accessed 1 August 2020

Intergovernmental Process on Strengthening Respect for International Humanitarian Law (IHL) (2019) Factual Report on the Proceedings of the Intergovernmental Process on Strengthening Respect for IHL. https://www.eda.admin.ch/dam/eda/en/documents/aussenpolitik/voelkerrecht/ respect-ihl/6-Respect-IHL-Factual-Report_en.pdf. Accessed 1 August 2020

Lanord C (2000) The Legal Status of National Red Cross and Red Crescent Societies. IRRC 840:1053–1077

Lavoyer J-P, Vité S (2018) The International Committee of the Red Cross: Legal Status, Privileges, and Immunities. In: Fleck D (ed) The Handbook of the Law of Visiting Forces. Oxford University Press, Oxford, pp 545–557

Oxfam International (2012) OI Policy Compendium Note on the Provision of Aid by Military Forces. https://oxfamilibrary.openrepository.com/bitstream/handle/10546/115031/hpn-pro vision-aid-military-forces-010412-en.pdf. Accessed 10 August 2020

Pictet J (1979) The Fundamental Principles of the Red Cross. Henry Dunant Institute, Geneva

RCC (Council of Delegates of the International Red Cross and Red Crescent Movement) (2015) Resolution: International Red Cross and Red Crescent Movement Branding Initiative: Adoption of the International Red Cross and Red Crescent Movement Logo. http://rcrcconference.org/app// uploads/2015/03/CD15-AR-MBI-adoption-of-the-Mvt-logo_EN.pdf. Accessed 1 August 2020

RCC (Council of Delegates of the International Red Cross and Red Crescent Movement) (2017) Strengthening Movement Coordination and Cooperation (SMCC). Progress Report. http://rcr cconference.org/app//uploads/2017/08/CoD17_5-SMCC-Progress-Report-final-clean-with-ann exes-EN.pdf. Accessed 1 August 2020

Sandoz Y (1998) The International Committee of the Red Cross as guardian of international humanitarian law. https://www.icrc.org/en/doc/resources/documents/misc/about-the-icrc-311298.htm. Accessed 1 August 2020

Sassòli M, Bouvier AA, Quintin A (2011) How does law protect in war? https://casebook.icrc.org/law/implementation-mechanisms#iv_1. Accessed 1 August 2020

Schomann S (2013) Im Zeichen der Menschlichkeit. Geschichte und Gegenwart des Deutschen Roten Kreuzes. DVA, Munich

Spieker H (2015) Family Links and Transmission of Information. In: Clapham A et al (eds) The 1949 Geneva Conventions: A Commentary. Oxford University Press, Oxford, pp 1089–1121

Steering Committee for Humanitarian Response (2010) SCHR Position Paper on Humanitarian Military Relations. https://reliefweb.int/sites/reliefweb.int/files/resources/C05620DB85A3AD4 2C12576D200383803-SCHR_Jan2010.pdf. Accessed 1 August 2020

Wilms H-C (2010) International Red Cross and Red Crescent Movement. In: Max Planck Encyclopedia of Public International Law. https://opil.ouplaw.com/view/10.1093/law:epil/978019923 1690/law-9780199231690-e493?rskey=80kXbs&result=1&prd=OPIL. Accessed 1 August 2020

Other Documents

Act on the German Red Cross and other voluntary aid societies as defined in the Geneva Conventions (adopted 5 December 2008; amended 17 July 2017). https://www.drk.de/en/the-grc/mission/grc-act/. Accessed 1 August 2020

Convention for the Amelioration of the Condition of the Wounded in Armies in the Field of 22 August 1864

Convention (II) for the Amelioration of the Condition of Wounded, Sick and Shipwrecked Members of Armed Forces at Sea (12 August 1949), 75 UNTS 85

Convention (IV) Relative to the Protection of Civilian Persons in Time of War (12 August 1949), 75 UNTS 287

ICRC (2013) Statutes of the International Committee of the Red Cross. https://www.icrc.org/en/doc/resources/documents/misc/icrc-statutes 080503.htm. Accessed 1 August 2020

International Conference of the International Red Cross and Red Crescent Movement (1965) Resolution 8.

International Conference of the Red Cross and Red Crescent Movement (1986) Resolution 31. https://www.icrc.org/en/doc/resources/documents/article/other/57jme2.htm. Accessed 1 August 2020

International Conference of the Red Cross and Red Crescent Movement (1986, 1995, 2006) Statutes of the International Red Cross and Red Crescent Movement and Rules of Procedure. https://sta ndcom.ch/download/stat/Statutes-EN-A5.pdf. Accessed 1 August 2020

International Conference of the International Red Cross and Red Crescent (1995) Resolution 1. https://www.icrc.org/en/doc/resources/documents/resolution/26-international-conference-res olution-1-1995.htm. Accessed 1 August 2020

International Conference of the Red Cross and Red Crescent Movement (2006) Resolution 1. https://www.icrc.org/en/doc/resources/documents/resolution/29-international-conference-res olution-1-2006.htm. Accessed 1 August 2020

International Conference of the Red Cross and Red Crescent Movement (2007) Resolution 2. https://www.icrc.org/en/doc/resources/documents/resolution/30-international-conference-res olution-2-2007.htm. Accessed 1 August 2020

37 The International Red Cross and Red Crescent Movement

International Conference of the Red Cross and Red Crescent Movement (2015) Resolution 2. http://rcrcconference.org/wp-content/uploads/2015/04/32IC-AR-Compliance_EN.pdf. Accessed 1 August 2020

Joint Statement by the Council and the Representatives of the Governments of the Member States meeting within the Council, the European Parliament and the European Commission (2008) European Consensus on Humanitarian Aid, OJ C 25, 30 January 2008, pp 1–12

Protocol Additional to the Geneva Conventions of 12 August 1949, and Relating to the Protection of Victims of International Armed Conflicts—AP I—(8 June 1977), 1125 UNTS 3

Protocol Additional to the Geneva Conventions of 12 August 1949 and relating to the Adoption of an Additional Distinctive Emblem—AP III—(8 December 2005), 2404 UNTS 261

Standing Commission of the Red Cross and Red Crescent. Members of the Commission. https://standcom.ch/members-of-the-commission/. Accessed 1 August 2020

Standing Commission of the Red Cross and Red Crescent. Components of the Movement. https://standcom.ch/components-of-the-movement/. Accessed 1 August 2020

Heike Spieker is Doctor of Law and currently the Deputy Director of International Cooperation and National Emergency Services at the German Red Cross Headquarters. She is Adjunct Lecturer at University College Dublin, Ireland, and a Member of the Council of the International Institute of Humanitarian Law, San Remo, Italy, and served in various Official Delegations—German Government and German Red Cross—to international conferences and bodies.

Chapter 38
Human Rights NGOs and Humanitarian NGOs

Nataliia Hendel, Tymur Korotkyi and Roman Yedeliev

Contents

38.1 Introduction 814
38.2 The Legal Nature of NGOs 814
38.3 History of Human Rights and Humanitarian NGOs 816
38.4 Key Tasks of Human Rights and Humanitarian NGOs 820
38.5 Human Rights and Humanitarian NGOs and International Law Development 822
38.6 Human Rights and Humanitarian NGOs International Legal Obligations
Monitoring 827
38.7 Activities of NGOs in Humanitarian Assistance 828
38.8 Human Rights and Humanitarian NGOs and COVID-19 Pandemic 831
38.9 Conclusion 833
References 833

Abstract The chapter considers the influence of human rights NGOs on protecting human rights and the development of international human rights law. The chapter analyses the activities of Amnesty International and Human Rights Watch in prosecuting those responsible for war crimes, crimes against humanity and genocide. The activities of Médecins Sans Frontières, the World Medical Association, the International Council of Nurses, and the European Public Health Alliance in the provision of humanitarian aid, including healthcare, are explored. The chapter explores the activities of human rights NGOs and humanitarian NGOs aimed at ensuring peace and security through the rule of law, the implementation of the principle of humanity, the fight for justice and the provision of legal and humanitarian assistance in the most difficult situations.

N. Hendel (✉)
International Law and Comparative Law Department, International Humanitarian University, Odessa, Ukraine

T. Korotkyi
Department of International Law and Comparative Law, National Aviation University, Kyiv, Ukraine

R. Yedeliev
International Law Department, Taras Shevchenko National University of Kyiv, Kyiv, Ukraine
e-mail: yedeliev@knu.ua

© T.M.C. ASSER PRESS and the authors 2022
S. Sayapin et al. (eds.), *International Conflict and Security Law*,
https://doi.org/10.1007/978-94-6265-515-7_38

813

Keywords Amnesty International · Human Rights Watch · Médecins sans Frontières · World Medical Association · International Council of Nurses · European Public Health Alliance · Humanitarian aid · Human rights

38.1 Introduction

The chapter is devoted to the activities of human rights and humanitarian NGOs to ensure peace and security through the rule of law, the implementation of the principle of humanity, the fight for justice and the provision of legal and humanitarian assistance in the most difficult situations. The chapter describes the history of the creation and activities of Amnesty International, Human Rights Watch, Médecins Sans Frontières, the World Medical Association, the International Council of Nurses and the European Public Health Alliance. There is an overview of key tasks of NGOs in human rights protection and their activities in protection of human rights, using both the mechanisms of international governmental organisations such as the UN and the Council of Europe, and the mechanisms of the international justice system. The chapter also provides a legal assessment of NGOs' documents and their significance for the protection of human rights. Particular attention is paid to the monitoring activities of NGOs concerning the implementation of international human rights law, opportunities and procedures for such monitoring, and recommendations after the monitoring has taken place. The possibilities for states to consider the results of such monitoring, and its significance for the development of legal standards for the protection of human rights, are disclosed.

The authors also examine medical and humanitarian assistance by NGOs during conflicts and emergencies, in the reconstruction and development of national health systems, and in developing healthcare standards based on uniform ethical principles. Also, there is a role for NGOs to play in the recovery from the COVID-19 pandemic. In connection with the pandemic, human rights NGOs have stepped up their activities, as the pandemic not only exacerbated health problems but also increased the problem of human rights, including the prohibition of discrimination and torture, freedom of speech and others.

38.2 The Legal Nature of NGOs

International NGOs undoubtedly have a tremendous impact on international relations and international law. International NGOs work closely with international governmental organisations and international judicial bodies. Paradoxically, while states have increasingly incorporated NGOs into structures and procedures of global governance, it remains unclear what characterises NGOs and what status they officially have under international law. Although states welcome NGO contributions to international negotiation processes and have granted 'private associations' some recognition at the national level, they have not yet agreed on a standard for NGOs operating in the transnational sphere.[1]

Dr. Matthias Herdegen emphasizes that "[i]n practice, it is common to understand NGOs as international organizations that do not have an international legal agreement. These include private legal organizations with a sphere of activity extended beyond state borders and international membership".[2] Aslan Abashidze and Marianna Ilyashevich define "[a]n international non-governmental organization [as] an organization operating at the international level, independently of any government, created by individuals and/or legal entities of different states to achieve certain goals that are not related to the extraction of commercial profits."[3] Hilary Binder-Aviles defines non-governmental organizations as being independent from government and business.[4] Ali Mostashari indicates that NGOs only must be independent from government control, not seeking to challenge governments either as a political party or by a narrow focus on human rights, non-profit-making and non-criminal.[5] The constituent documents of the NGOs establish the structure, membership, functions, directions and principles of activity. International NGOs are effective because they base their activity on the principles of legitimacy, governance, transparency and accountability.[6] Ali Mostashari distinguishes two types of NGOs: operational and advocacy.[7]

After World War II, not only did the era of international governmental organisations begin, but international NGOs also became active actors in international relations and international law. International NGOs cooperate with the UN and UN specialised agencies. International NGOs have consultative status in cooperation with international governmental organisations. The legal basis for the UN's interaction with NGOs is Article 71 of the UN Charter, which determines, "The Economic and Social Council may make suitable arrangements for consultation with NGOs which are concerned with matters within its competence. Such arrangements may be made with international organizations and, where appropriate, with national organizations after consultation with the Member of the United Nations concerned". Article 11 of the UNESCO Constitution regulates cooperation with international NGOs. A similar provision is contained in Article 71 of the WHO Constitution and para 3 Article 12 of the ILO Constitution.

International NGOs are key contributors to the development and implementation of international human rights protection by informing people about specific facts of human rights violations. For example, the American Convention on Human Rights in Article 44 establishes that, "… any non-governmental entity legally recognised in one or more member states of the Organization, may lodge petitions with the

---

[1] Kerstin 2003, p. 23.

[2] Herdegen 2011, p. 122.

[3] Abashidze 2014, pp. 357–348.

[4] Binder-Aviles 2016, p. 3.

[5] Mostashari 2005, p. 2.

[6] Binder-Aviles 2016, p. 3–4; Stillman 2006, p. 9–10.

[7] Mostashari 2005, p. 3.

Commission containing denunciations or complaints of violation of this Convention by a State Party". The Convention for the Protection of Human Rights and Fundamental Freedoms in Article 34 stipulates that "[t]he Court may receive applications from ... non-governmental organisation ... claiming to be the victim of a violation by one of the High Contracting Parties of the rights in the Convention or the Protocols thereto. The High Contracting Parties undertake not to hinder in any way the effective exercise of this right". International NGOs influence the creation of international standards, including human rights and the humanitarian field. Although their recommendations are 'soft law', they serve as a good foundation for the development of 'hard law' documents by international government organizations.

38.3   History of Human Rights and Humanitarian NGOs

One event, one reflection, can create a whole movement and philosophy in the name of human rights. For example, British lawyer Peter Benenson was outraged by the arrest of two Portuguese students just because they raised a toast to freedom in 1961.[8] He wrote an article in the newspaper The Observer and launched a campaign that caused incredible resonance and became a call to unite in solidarity for justice and freedom. Indeed, one publication can change the course of history, including the history of international law. For example, the book by Henry Dunant, *A Memory of Solferino*, was the impetus for the creation of the International Committee of the Red Cross and the humanisation of the law of war. In 1961, nine states abolished executions because of Amnesty International campaigns against the death penalty. Amnesty International began its first campaign against torture in 1972 and after 12 years, the Convention against Torture was adopted in the United Nations. In 1977, Amnesty International was awarded the Nobel Peace Prize for its contribution to "securing the ground for freedom, for justice, and thereby also for peace in the world",[9] in recognition of the role and significance of Amnesty International's work in human rights, justice and peace. By 2014, 140 states had abolished the death penalty as a capital punishment. Since 1964, Amnesty International has held special consultative status at the UN.[10] Since 1993, Amnesty International has campaigned for the creation and activities of the International Criminal Court (ICC) to bring to justice those responsible for genocide, war crimes and crimes against humanity.[11] In 1962, Amnesty International sent a lawyer to oversee the trial of Nelson Mandela in South Africa. Nelson Mandela was the Amnesty International Ambassador of Conscience.[12] In 2007, Amnesty International's fight for free speech around the world moved to the internet. The Global Arms Trade Treaty entered into force on 24 December 2014,

---

[8] Amnesty 2021a.

[9] Amnesty 2021b.

[10] Amnesty 2021c.

[11] Amnesty 2021b.

[12] Ibid.

38 Human Rights NGOs and Humanitarian NGOs

after 20 years of the Amnesty International campaign, which aims to combat the flow of weapons that fuel conflicts and tensions around the world. Since its inception, Amnesty International's activities have expanded from abolishing the death penalty to protecting sexual and reproductive rights, from fighting discrimination to protecting the rights of refugees and migrants.[13] In addition to the areas of activity, the geography of Amnesty International's activities was also expanded. Regional offices operate in Africa, Asia-Pacific, Central and Eastern Europe, Latin America and the Middle East.[14] The new regional offices strengthen the work of companies that are already operating at the national level in over 70 states.[15] Currently, Amnesty International is a global movement of more than 10 million people.

Human Rights Watch was created in 1978[16] to monitor human rights violations in countries—especially behind the 'Iron Curtain'—that signed the 1975 Helsinki Final Act.[17] Human Rights Watch investigated mass killings, including genocide, government seizure of control over the media, and groundless arrests of activists and oppositionists. Human Rights Watch protects victims of war crimes, crimes against humanity, and genocide through the international justice system. The area of activity is the protection of the most vulnerable groups, for example, the protection of the rights of women, children, LGBT people, people with disabilities, refugees and labour migrants. Human Rights Watch is committed to combating discrimination, including discrimination against women, LGBT people and people with disabilities. Human Rights Watch advocates for freedom of speech, the fight against torture, the fight against terrorism, strengthening national health systems and realising the right to health. The primary method of Human Rights Watch's work is face-to-face interviews (documentation), and later, satellite images and other data and technologies were added to monitor human rights violations. Human Rights Watch is guided by a commitment to justice, human dignity, compassion and equality. Human Rights Watch actively cooperates with the UN system and the international justice system.

Médecins Sans Frontières (Doctors without Borders (MSF)) is a nongovernmental international humanitarian medical organisation providing medical help to people affected by armed conflicts and natural disasters, epidemics.[18] Founded in 1971 in Paris, MSF aimed to help victims of the armed conflict in Nigeria in 1967–1970. MSF is a non-profit, self-governing organisation of 23 associations based in Switzerland. In 1999, MSF was awarded the Nobel Peace Prize. MSF provides medical humanitarian aid to save lives and ease suffering in crisis situations in more than 70 states.[19]

The first MSF mission was carried out in Managua, the capital of Nicaragua, after the earthquake in 1972.[20] Since 1972, MSF has provided humanitarian and

---

[13] Amnesty 2021d.

[14] Amnesty 2021e.

[15] Ibid.

[16] The organization was originally called 'Helsinki Watch'.

[17] Human Rights Watch (HRW) 2021a.

[18] MSF 2021a.

[19] MSF 2021b.

[20] MSF 2021c.

medical help in situations of armed conflict and crisis. MSF organised a mission to help Honduras after Hurricane Fifi caused severe flooding and killed thousands in 1974. MSF created its first large-scale medical programme during the refugee crisis, providing medical help to Cambodians seeking asylum from the despotic rule of Pol Pot in 1975. From 1976 to 1984, MSF was present in Beirut and other cities in Lebanon, helping the wounded. In December 1992, the MSF published a report describing the ethnic cleansing policy of the Bosnian Serbs. MSF teams witnessed the massacre of patients and staff in Rwanda in 1994. In May 1994, the MSF asked the French government to help end the Rwandan massacre. MSF spoke to the UN Commission on Human Rights, hoping to provoke a reaction from member states to the situation in Rwanda on 24 May 1994. After the massacres of more than 800,000 Tutsis and Hutus, MSF accepted demands for international military intervention. The MSF team provided medical support in highly volatile conditions during the First Chechen war in 1994. Two years later, MSF called on the international community to force the Russian government to stop massive human rights abuses in Chechnya and systematic attacks on civilians. MSF provided healthcare to displaced persons in Kosovo and refugee camps in Albania, Macedonia and Montenegro, and civilians in Serbia in 1999. During the Second Chechen War, MSF called for access to Grozny and condemned the massive use of violence against civilians by Russian troops in 1999. MSF began antiretroviral therapy for people living with HIV in seven states in 2001, and started providing assistance to Afghan civilians in 2002. MSF launched the largest relief operation in its history just a day after the earthquake in Haiti on 12 January 2010. In the following October, after cholera hit Haiti, MSF mobilised hundreds of staff to help. Since 2012, MSF has been on a mission in Syria. On 22 March 2014, Guinea officially declared the largest Ebola outbreak in history. At the peak of the epidemic, MSF had about 4000 national staff and over 325 international staff. In May 2015, MSF and other non-governmental organisations began search and rescue operations for refugees and asylum seekers in the Central Mediterranean. In response to the Rohingya refugee crisis, MSF expanded its activities in the region to include water, sanitation and health services for refugees in 2017.[21]

During World War II, the British Medical Association House was a centre where doctors from allied states gathered to discuss the problems of medical practice and compare the conditions of medical care and medical education. In July 1945, an unofficial conference of doctors from several countries was held in London to discuss the creation of an international medical organization that would replace the 'Association Professionnelle Internationale des Médecins' (APIM), which was founded in 1926. The second conference, in which medical associations from 31 states participated, took place in London in September 1946.[22] At the 1946 conference, an organising committee was appointed that was entrusted with developing a constitution and a plan for the first general assembly. The conference decided that the name of the new organisation should be the World Medical Association and that it should have a

---

[21] MSF 2021d.
[22] WMA 2021a.

38 Human Rights NGOs and Humanitarian NGOs

broader scope and membership than the former APIM. The APIM delegates attending the conference decided to dissolve APIM, create WMA, and transfer WMA funds.

The second meeting of the organising committee took place in Paris in November 1946, during which progress was made in the constitution's drafting and the statutes.[23] The final draft of the constitution and statutes was approved at the third meeting of the organising committee, held in London in April 1947, and in September 1947, the first general assembly was planned to be held in Paris.[24] The fourth meeting of the organising committee was held in Paris on 16 September 1947, and the first session of the general assembly was convened on 17–18 September 1947. The constitution and the charter were adopted with minor amendments on 17 September 1947. The 27 represented national medical associations at the general assembly became Founding Associations. The first 10-member council was elected, and the World Medical Association began its work.

For economic reasons, in July 1964, the WMA was registered as a non-profit educational and scientific organisation under the laws of the State of New York, USA. In 1962, the annual meeting of delegates was changed to the World Medical Assembly' following the revision of the Constitution and Statutes at the 16th General Assembly.[25] The WMA headquarters from the moment of its foundation until 1974 were in New York (USA) and from 1975 to the present in Ferney-Voltaire (France).

The International Council of Nurses[26] is an association of national nursing organisations from 130 countries. The council was founded in 1899 and became the first professional international organisation in health. The purpose of the council was to promote the improvement of the quality of nursing care and the development of the scientific foundations of nursing. The Council reviewed the basic concepts used in nursing in 1973 and approved the Nursing Code. This is the most important ethical document that defines the norms and rules of the professional behaviour of nurses in relation to society and patients in their practice and intercollegiate relationships.

The Council of National Nursing Association Representatives (CNR) is the governing body of the ICN and develops organisational policy and direction, including membership, board election, charter amendments, and establishment of contributions.[27] The CNR meets every two years. The ICN's board of directors comprises 14 members, including a president and three vice presidents, who are elected by voting. All members should meet the ICN nurse definition and be in good standing with the ICN. The ICN board of directors sets and implements policies under CNR standards. The ICN's official language is English. Working languages are English, French and Spanish.[28]

The European Public Health Alliance (EPHA) represents more than 100 nongovernmental and other non-profit organisations working on public health issues

---

[23] Ibid.

[24] Ibid.

[25] Ibid.

[26] ICN 2021a.

[27] ICN 2021b.

[28] International Council of Nurses Constitution, Article 5.

in Europe.[29] The EPHA was founded and registered in Belgium in 1993 as an international non-profit association.[30] The EPHA is regulated by statutes and bylaws. The EPHA operates on a non-discriminatory basis.[31]

38.4 Key Tasks of Human Rights and Humanitarian NGOs

The goal of Amnesty International is to fight injustice, achieve peace, and protect human rights, including the abolition of the death penalty. The principles of the organisation's activities are independence, neutrality, non-discrimination and impartiality.

Amnesty International campaigns through petitions, letters and protests to protect human rights and promote justice. Lawyers without Borders Canada, the International Federation for Human Rights, the Malian Association for Human Rights and Amnesty International are implementing a project to strengthen the fight against impunity in Mali.[32] Amnesty International has advocated a full extension of the mandate of the UN Human Rights Commission in South Sudan at the 46th session of the UN Human Rights Council (22 February–23 March 2021).[33] Amnesty International is independent of the policies of states; therefore, it can require states to change their policies and practices in human rights. Human rights NGOs use the mechanisms of international governmental organisations to bring to justice states that violate international obligations in human rights.

The activities of Human Rights Watch are the study of the right to health and a healthy environment, the right to be free from discrimination and arbitrary detention, and the right to information, freedom of speech and expression, and freedom of assembly as essential tools for achieving health. Human Rights Watch works on communicable (infectious) diseases, environmental pollution and remediation, sexual and reproductive health issues, and noncommunicable diseases, including access to palliative care for the incurable.[34] A broad approach to the right to health allows for its effective implementation. Many factors are important for health, both in a healthy environment and in the fight against communicable (infectious) and noncommunicable diseases.

Human Rights Watch investigates human rights violations in connection with the economic activities of corporations, governments and international institutions, such as the World Bank. Human Rights Watch documents human rights violations

---

[29] EPHA 2021a.

[30] EPHA 2021b.

[31] EPHA 2021c.

[32] Amnesty 2021f.

[33] Amnesty 2021g.

[34] Human Rights Watch (HRW) 2013.

and the destruction of healthcare and education systems because of corruption in resource-rich states.[35]

Human Rights Watch considers international justice as an integral part of ensuring respect for human rights through the means of individual criminal responsibility for genocide, war crimes and crimes against humanity. Human Rights Watch cooperates with the International Criminal Court, international tribunals and national courts (including those in Guinea, Côte d'Ivoire, the Democratic Republic of Congo and Bosnia) to prosecute genocide, war crimes and crimes against humanity.[36] Human Rights Watch also supports the efforts of national courts to enforce national law against such individuals, regardless of where the crime was committed. Bringing perpetrators to justice for crimes under international law is a central element of post-conflict regulation and the restoration of peace.

Human Rights Watch's Refugee Rights Programme aims to protect the rights of refugees, asylum seekers and displaced persons. Human Rights Watch responds to both crisis and chronic situations by focusing on documenting government attempts to block access to asylum, deny asylum seekers the right to a fair hearing of their claims, and forcibly return people to places where their lives and freedom will be threatened.[37] Human Rights Watch conducts field research, interviewing refugees and displaced persons and documenting violations of their rights.

MSF was founded with the belief that all people should have access to health care regardless of gender, race, religion or political affiliation.[38] MSF is guided by medical ethics and the principles of impartiality, independence and neutrality in its activities.[39] MSF adheres to the principles of human rights law and international humanitarian law in its activities, which include: (1) the duty to respect the fundamental rights and freedoms of everyone, including the right to physical and mental integrity, and freedom of thought and movement, as set out in the 1949 Universal Declaration of Human Rights; (2) the right of victims to receive assistance, and the right of humanitarian organisations to provide assistance.[40] The following conditions must be ensured: free needs assessment, free access to victims, control over the distribution of humanitarian aid and respect for humanitarian immunity. Under the MSF Charter, members are committed to upholding their professional code of ethics and to maintaining complete independence from all political, economic or religious powers.[41]

The aim of the WMA is to ensure the guarantee of the independence of doctors and the high standards of their ethical work. Funding comes from the annual contributions of its members. Areas of activity are medical ethics, medical education, patient rights, human rights in health, patient safety, human research, caring for the sick

---

[35] Human Rights Watch (HRW) 2010.

[36] Human Rights Watch (HRW) 2011.

[37] Human Rights Watch (HRW) 2014a.

[38] MSF 2021e.

[39] MSF 2021f.

[40] MSF Médecins sans Frontières (MSF) 1995.

[41] MSF 2021g.

and wounded during armed conflict, public health policies and projects,[42] torture of prisoners, drug use and abuse, planning families, pollution[43] and transplant issues.[44] The General Assembly of the WMA adopted a strategic plan for the next five years, from 2020 to 2025, which identified priority areas: medical ethics, universal health insurance, human rights and health, and the potential of the organisation in Tbilisi in 2019.[45]

Under the Constitution of the International Council of Nursing 2019, the objectives of the organisation are: (1) influence on nursing, medical and social policy, professional and socio-economic standards around the world; (2) assisting National Nursing Associations (NNAs) to raise standards of nursing care and professional development; (3) promoting the development of strong national nursing associations; (4) represent nurses internationally.[46]

The EPHA's mission is to promote and protect interests related to the health of the population of Europe, and to strengthen cooperation between civil society and NGOs in EU countries, aimed at supporting effective public health policies. The EPHA performs the following functions: (1) oversees the policy development process of the EU institutions and ensures that information on health improvement and changes in public health policies is maximised to all stakeholders; (2) informs the public and non-governmental organisations about health policy changes and programme activities affecting the health of the European population, so that they can take part in the policy-making process and in the practical work of the respective programs; (3) supports cooperation and partnerships of non-governmental organisations and other non-profit organisations that are actively involved in public health issues at European, national and local levels; (4) informs about access to quality and affordable medicines.

38.5 Human Rights and Humanitarian NGOs and International Law Development

There is no reason why NGOs cannot draft and propose treaties. As A. Clark states, "NGOs press states to create binding norms for themselves. NGOs take advantage of the cognitive effects of norms when they highlight the difference between words and action. By invoking public opinion, they implicitly appeal to a wider audience. By offering information and expertise pertaining to departures from principle, NGOs highlight the contrast between ideals and practice. They also forge productive links

---

[42] Tobacco control, immunization.

[43] WMA 2021b.

[44] Kuroyanagi 2013, Historical Transition in Medical Ethics—Challenges of the World Medical Association, https://www.med.or.jp/english/journal/pdf/2013_04/220_226.pdf.

[45] WMA 2020.

[46] International Council of Nurses Constitution, Article 4.

38 Human Rights NGOs and Humanitarian NGOs

with sympathetic states that are committed to fostering new norms' emergence and enhancing the impact of existing norms."[47]

These functions of NGOs show that the concept of state-centred international relations is essential for understanding the establishment and maintenance of international norms. The importance of third parties does not lie in arguing that actual issues have passed or that the state can no longer be understood as a selfish actor. When normative issues are mainly represented by non-governmental organisations or other third-party actors through communication mechanisms, they change the environment in which the state must act. By advocating for ever-changing international human rights norms, NGOs help shape expectations for international behaviour and require countries to comply with international human rights norms.

Amnesty International provided a driving force behind the emergence of norms on torture. The Torture Convention has been described as "one of the most successful initiatives ever undertaken by an NGO" and is a landmark in the contemporary history of NGO law-making.[48]

NGOs' attention was focused on the need to develop an international regime of inspection of prisons and other centres of detention as a means of preventing torture. NGOs, including Amnesty International, the International Commission of Jurists and the Association for the Prevention of Torture, pushed for this goal despite the initial lack of any government support and they gradually built up a further coalition around the issue. Lobbying became a two-way process as NGOs lobbied governments to support the inspection regime and like-minded governments lobbied NGOs to back a compromise text.[49]

The Campaign for the Abolition of Torture was a new kind of endeavour for Amnesty International, and its success provided a blueprint for the emergence of norms in the United Nations.[50] Torture is a concealed practice and a severe accusation against the government that requires an absolute standard of information accuracy. The traditional technology of Amnesty International relies on speaking to the government on specific cases. Therefore, when investigating torture, it must be able to determine the possibility or threat of a particular torture case, for to propound poorly founded allegations in communications from its membership to government officials would impugn AI's credibility and endanger its ability to come to the aid of torture victims.[51]

Establishment of the Ottawa Convention Banning Landmines was regarded by many international law scholars, international activists, diplomats and international organization personnel as a defining, 'democratizing' change in the way international law is made. As Kenneth says, "By bringing international NGOs—what is often called 'international civil society'—into the diplomatic and international law-making process, many believe that the Ottawa Convention represented both a democratisation

---

[47] Clark 2001, p. 141.

[48] Korey 1998, p. 171.

[49] Boyle and Chinkin 2007, p. 103.

[50] Clark 2001, p. 68.

[51] Ibid.

of, and a new source of legitimacy for, international law, in part because it was presumably made 'from below'."[52]

Amnesty's collection and publication of the facts surrounding disappearances in Argentina helped lead to international recognition that a method to grapple with disappearances was needed at the UN.[53]

It cannot be claimed that NGOs legislated the Rome Statute, but NGO influence on the process and outcome was considerable. A. Clark finds three ways in which NGOs influenced the establishment of the International Criminal Court. First, many observers and commentators have concluded that without NGO participation, the ICC could not have come into existence. Second, some causes that NGOs especially promoted that had not been in the ILC draft statute were included in the text adopted in Rome, for example, an independent prosecutor with the power to initiate investigation subject to the permission of a pre-trial chamber. Third, special interest NGOs were instrumental in securing attention to their concerns. For example, the Rome Statute provides for jurisdiction over crimes against women (Articles 7(1)(g)(h), 8(b)(xxii), 8(e)(vi)); a 'fair representation' of women and men on the court (Article 36(8)(a)(iii)) and a definition of gender (Article 7(3)).[54]

NGOs made communicatively rational arguments in favour of a strong effective court that ultimately were persuasive for the negotiators of the statute and the state decision makers who chose to sign and ratify the Rome Statute. Their participation contributed to a statute that embodied a set of rules that were fair and potentially effective.[55] They presented their own arguments on the legal details of how to create a court and who to sue. The impact of NGO discourse on the ICC is profoundly significant because it shows that transnationally organised NGOs can play a role in determining what ends states pursue and, consequently, what outcomes are produced in the international system.[56]

Amnesty International educates people about their rights and ensures that states that practice torture are punished for it. Amnesty International is committed to the adoption and implementation of measures to protect people from torture and to bringing those responsible to justice, specifically: (1) independent checks of places of detention; (2) monitoring the interrogation; (3) prompt access to lawyers and courts; (4) visiting and communicating with family members; (5) thorough and effective investigation of allegations of torture. Amnesty International is campaigning for the adoption of international norms prohibiting the manufacture and sale of unscrupulous equipment and regulating the trade in goods that may be misused—that is, prohibiting the sale of 'instruments of torture'.[57]

---

[52] Anderson 2000, p. 91.

[53] Clark 2001, p. 99.

[54] Boyle and Chinkin 2007, p. 111.

[55] Struett 2008, p. 6.

[56] Ibid., p. 7.

[57] Amnesty 2021h.

38 Human Rights NGOs and Humanitarian NGOs

Amnesty International runs campaigns to protect the rights of refugees, asylum seekers and migrants.[58] Amnesty International is committed to ensuring that governments properly process asylum applications from asylum seekers. States shall comply with international standards for the rights of refugees, asylum seekers and migrants. Amnesty International is also joining with other organizations to ensure that migrants are protected from exploitation and abuse by their employers or traffickers.

Amnesty International campaigns on behalf of everyone's right to control their sexual and reproductive choices.[59] Reproductive rights are a component of the right to health. When realising reproductive human rights, both ethical principles, including bioethics and legal ones, must be considered.

MSF conducts educational activities and has produced The Practical Guide to Humanitarian Law, which was first published by Françoise Bouchet-Saulnier in 1998, and the last edition was reissued in 2013.[60] The Practical Guide presents the rules of humanitarian law applicable to the protection and assistance of victims of conflicts and crises. The Guide analyses how international humanitarian law has developed in the face of new challenges to international peace and human security associated with the war on terror, novel forms of armed conflict and humanitarian action, and the emergence of international criminal justice.

In the period after World War II and immediately after its founding, the WMA developed ethical principles for doctors around the world intended to contribute to raising the standards of professional behaviour and form professional consciousness, with elements of legal awareness and humanity. To achieve this goal, a research committee was formed to prepare the Charter of Medicine. The Research Committee developed a modernised formulation of the ancient Hippocratic Oath, which was reviewed and adopted by the General Assembly of the WMA in Geneva in 1948 and renamed the Geneva Declaration.[61] The Geneva Declaration was recommended for use by all medical schools and faculties of WMA members.

The report 'War Crimes and Medicine' was considered at the II General Assembly and prompted the Council to create another research committee to prepare an International Code of Medical Ethics. The draft was presented at the 1949 interannual session of the Council, which was supplemented by the text of the Geneva Declaration.[62] The revised draft was reviewed by the III General Assembly and the International Code of Medical Ethics was adopted with minor amendments.

From 1949 to 1952, the WMA received reports of medical ethics violations and crimes committed by doctors during World War II. Ethics, responsibility, and protection of patients' rights in connection with experiments on people was sharply raised. A separate problem during this period was the creation and activity of incompetent organisations to develop standards in medical ethics and medical law. These circumstances in 1952 prompted the creation of a permanent Committee on Medical

---

[58] Amnesty 2021i.

[59] Amnesty 2021j.

[60] The Practical Guide to Humanitarian Law, 2013.

[61] WMA 2021a.

[62] Ibid.

Ethics.[63] Through the development of unified medical ethics and the development of standards, professional consciousness was formed and complex regulatory legal acts in medicine and health care were developed in the states.

The WMA has developed a significant number of declarations and regulations, including the 1948 WMA Geneva Declaration; the 1964 WMA Declaration of Helsinki, Ethical Principles for Medical Research involving Human Subjects; the 1981 WMA Declaration on Principles of Health Care for Sports Medicine; and the 1987 WMA Declaration of Madrid on Professional Autonomy and Self-Regulation.

The Tokyo Declaration contains guidelines for doctors to prevent torture. The Taipei Declaration focuses on research on health databases and biobank. The WMA adopted a declaration on euthanasia and physician-assisted suicide, which reflects the organisation's stable and consistent position in its anti-euthanasia and physician-assisted suicide stance in terms of medical ethics in October 2019.[64] The declarations are advisory in nature, although they are the basis for regulating bioethics and international health law. With the adoption of domestic acts that implement declarations and international regional agreements, these standards become obligatory.

The normative activity of the WMA is also aimed at protecting the rights of the patient. In this area, the WMA develops guidelines, recommendations and methodological materials on medical ethics, paying special attention to medical ethics in scientific research, on the rights of patients, on the rights of doctors, on caring for the wounded and sick during armed conflicts, on the maintenance of prisoners, on the use of medicines, family planning, environmental pollution, public health and many other issues related to the principles and rules of organising medical activities. Recommendations are developed based on democratic principles for medical associations that represent developing countries.

The ICN collaborates with the specialised agencies of the United Nations system, especially the World Health Organization, the International Labour Organization and the World Bank, and several international nongovernmental organisations.

The ICN implements campaigns with partners, including International Nurses Day, Nursing Now, Fight the Fakes, Health Care in Danger, Safeguarding Health in Conflict Coalition, Deliver for Good, Childhood and Early Parenting Principles (CEPPs) Global Initiative, Global Coalition on Circulatory Health.[65] The ICN works to achieve the Sustainable Development Goals,[66] primarily Goal 3: good health and well-being.

The ICN has established a Nurse Practitioner/Advanced Practice Network (NP/APN Network) to facilitate communication on general professional issues. The network is an international resource for practicing nurses and aims to provide wide access to relevant and timely information on practice, education, research development, policy and regulatory developments in the health sector, providing a forum for

---

[63] Ibid.

[64] WMA 2019.

[65] ICN 2021c.

[66] ICN 2021d.

38 Human Rights NGOs and Humanitarian NGOs

the exchange of knowledge and experience, and access to international resources in the health sector.[67]

38.6 Human Rights and Humanitarian NGOs International Legal Obligations Monitoring

NGOs might be asked to provide advice on new national legal instruments, which is an opportunity to insert their own thinking on policy structures. Although NGOs are not traditionally the author of national constitutions and every nation's tradition will be different, the authors tend to lean on the side of recommending a written constitution and suggest that when NGOs are involved in any aspect of nation building, they take the opportunity to influence this process, even to the point of recommending language to government decision makers. There are plenty of examples like that of Syria, where written rights are ignored; still, a written document is a contract with the people that lays down basic rights and obligations.[68]

NGOs could not be directly involved in actual norm construction because of the difference in authority between NGOs and states at the international level. Technical expertise mattered most during the norm construction phase, when NGOs had to work with governments to achieve new formal norms. The contacts formed with elites during consensus-building activities also enhanced NGO ability to promote norm emergence. In the final phase, norm application, governments learned from the techniques developed by NGOs in their struggles to promote human rights.[69]

Amnesty International regularly monitors human rights violations through its field staff, who question the witnesses and victims of such cases. It cooperates with humanitarian missions and uses its facilities as a safe place for talks. Researchers also studied case issues based on official documents from the state and other organisations. The information obtained from both sources then served Amnesty International as a "springboard" for defending cases by lobbying influential actors. For South Sudan, these actors included the African Union and the United Nations. For this reason, Amnesty is in constant contact with them through oral and written statements, including cases of human rights violations and subsequent recommendations to improve the situation in the state. Amnesty International also uses the public to spread its influence. By sharing cases of victims of violence, it arouses emotions in people, which motivates them to get involved in defending these victims. They sign petitions, send letters and share cases on their social networks. In all these activities, Amnesty's ability to reach important national and international actors and use their influence for its goals can be observed.

---

[67] ICN 2021e.

[68] Roeder and Simard 2013, p. 164.

[69] Clark 2001, p. 69.

Amnesty International conducts research on human rights violations.[70] Amnesty International stated that the Russian Federation and China actively sought to undermine the international human rights system and the institutions empowered to protect it in the 2019 annual report.[71] Amnesty International uses research data for advocacy and promotion of human rights and justice to influence the government, companies and decision-makers.

Amnesty International has identified the following human rights trends in Eastern Europe and Central Asia: (1) the attitudes of women, anti-corruption and environmental activists have become more effective in collective action and protest; (2) there has been a regression of regional systems of human rights protection.[72]

Amnesty International has identified the following human rights violations in Eastern Europe and Central Asia: (1) declining living standards; (2) forced evictions; (3) rigging elections; (4) restriction of the right to freedom of assembly and association; (5) encroachments on freedom of speech; (6) restriction of travel abroad; (7) discrimination; (8) domestic and gender-based violence; (9) torture and other ill treatment; (10) restriction of freedom of movement.[73]

Human Rights Watch monitors how governments and intergovernmental organisations work to combat violent extremism to ensure that such struggles do not lead to infringement of the right to life, the right not to be tortured or ill-treated and the right to a fair trial.[74] Human Rights Watch also examines the use of prohibited means and methods of warfare by conflict participants in populated areas.[75] Human Rights Watch monitors compliance with IHL to protect civilians by parties to the conflict. The protection of war victims depends on the extent to which the parties to the conflict apply IHL. Human Rights Watch advocates for the need to stop the development of military robots in which the selection and defeat of the target is fully automated.

38.7 Activities of NGOs in Humanitarian Assistance

Amnesty International is campaigning to stop the unregulated flow of all weapons. Amnesty International takes the position that arms sales exacerbate conflicts. Arms trafficking undermine peace and security, and achieving peace is impossible in a

---

[70] Annual Report 2019: Eastern Europe and Central Asia 2020.

[71] Ibid.

[72] The resumption of the Russian delegation to the Parliamentary Assembly of the Council of Europe five years after its voting rights was suspended due to the illegal annexation of Crimea. See Annual Report 2019: Eastern Europe and Central Asia 2020.

[73] Annual Report 2019: Eastern Europe and Central Asia 2020.

[74] Human Rights Watch (HRW) 2021b.

[75] Human Rights Watch (HRW) 2021c.

38 Human Rights NGOs and Humanitarian NGOs

world where states are economically interested in the sale of arms. Amnesty International has stated that a number of states continue to supply arms to Saudi Arabian-led coalition forces largely fuelled the conflict in Yemen.[76] For example, Amnesty International and other human rights NGOs supported the Campaign against Arms Trafficking to prevent the UK government from supplying arms to Yemen. In June 2019, the UK Court of Appeals ruled that the UK government's decision to continue licensing the export of military equipment to Saudi Arabia was illegal.[77] Amnesty supported a joint appeal by the European Centre for Constitutional and Human Rights to the International Criminal Court to investigate the role of European arms companies in aiding and abetting alleged war crimes in Yemen.[78] Amnesty International successfully campaigned for an arms embargo in South Sudan, documenting violations of the arms embargo in Libya as well as civilian casualties from United States drone strikes in Somalia.[79]

Amnesty International supports the International Campaign to Abolish Nuclear Weapons to help states become parties to the 2017 Treaty on the Prohibition of Nuclear Weapons and to monitor its implementation. Nuclear weapons pose a global threat to the global security system.

Amnesty International documents violations of international humanitarian law during armed conflict. Amnesty International conducts campaigns against violations of international humanitarian law and international human rights law during armed conflict. For example, Amnesty International is demanding full humanitarian access to Tigray, where conflict continues between the Ethiopian federal government and the Tigray regional government ruling party, the Tigray People's Liberation Front.[80]

Amnesty International and its partners are launching the Campaign to Stop Killer Robots, calling for a new international treaty that guarantees meaningful human control over the use of force by robots and prohibits the development, production and use of fully autonomous weapons.[81] They demand that during an armed conflict, the rules of international humanitarian law, which limit the methods and means of warfare, should be respected.

Amnesty International participates in the prosecution of crimes against humanity, war crimes and genocide by: (1) campaigns for the creation and effective functioning of the ICC; (2) calling on states to exercise universal jurisdiction over crimes under international law; (3) a call for the creation of *ad hoc* international or mixed courts; (4) strengthening international, regional and national law to combat crime under international law.[82] Amnesty International's work in international justice is based on justice, truth, full reparation and guarantees of non-recurrence. Justice, truth,

---

[76] Amnesty 2021k.

[77] Ibid.

[78] Ibid.

[79] Ibid.

[80] Amnesty 2021l.

[81] Amnesty 2021k.

[82] Amnesty 2021m.

full reparation and guarantees of non-recurrence are the foundation in post-conflict settlement and peace restoration.

Amnesty International campaigns against "police brutality". Torture is absolutely prohibited under international law. For more than 50 years, Amnesty International has documented torture, exposed perpetrators and helped victims achieve justice.[83] In 2011, Amnesty International expressed concern about a lack of responsibility in France for the deaths of prisoners Ali Ziri, Mohammed Boukrourou, Lamine Dieng, Abou Bakari Tandia and Abdelhakim Ajimi, men from ethnic minorities.[84] Following the fight for justice in France, three of these cases were referred to the European Court of Human Rights, which found that the French police violated Ali Ziri's right to life and that their treatment of Mohammed Boukrourou amounted to inhuman and degrading treatment.[85]

Human Rights Watch documents violations based on sexual orientation and gender identity: torture, killings and executions, arrests under unfair laws, unequal attitude, censorship, medical violations, discrimination in health care, employment and housing, domestic violence, violations against children and refusal in the right to a family and recognition.[86] Human Rights Watch works to promote the dignity and gender equality of women and girls, protecting their rights and improving their lives.[87]

Human Rights Watch documents cases of torture or ill treatment around the world. Human Rights Watch is committed to encouraging states to take action to prevent torture and to hold those responsible for torture accountable. Human Rights Watch works to ensure that victims of torture receive reparations, including the right to fair and adequate compensation and full rehabilitation.[88]

Human Rights Watch investigates violations of human rights that arise when the state tries to restrain or redirect the flows of migrants, refugees and asylum seekers and detain them in special centres, camps that do not respect human rights.[89]

The Médecins Sans Frontières, the International Union against Tuberculosis and Lung Diseases, and the Union for International Cancer Control arc involved in direct activities related to the organisation of medical care and the fight against individual diseases.

In human rights, the WMA implements the following campaigns: the right to health—a comprehensive right for all; supporting doctors and patients at risk; doctors—key players in the fight against torture; a woman's right to the highest standard of health; and the right to health of LGBT people.[90] The WMA carries out information activities; for example, it holds the following companies: Global

---

[83] Amnesty 2021h.

[84] Amnesty 2021n.

[85] Ibid.

[86] Human Rights Watch (HRW) 2021d.

[87] Human Rights Watch (HRW) 2014b.

[88] Human Rights Watch (HRW) 2012.

[89] Human Rights Watch (HRW) 2014c.

[90] WMA 2021c.

38 Human Rights NGOs and Humanitarian NGOs

Communication Campaign on Influenza Immunisation, Consensus Framework for Ethical Collaboration, Protecting Healthcare Workers from Violence, and WMA African Medical Initiative.[91] The WMA collaborates with the WHO, the World Health Professions Alliance and other government and nongovernmental health organisations.

The ICN conducts its activities under the Universal Declaration of Human Rights, the International Covenants on Human Rights and the CESCR General Comment No. 14: The Right to the Highest Attainable Standard of Health (Article 12).[92] Nursing is inherent in respect for human rights, including the right to life and the right to choose, the right to dignity and the right to respectful treatment.[93] Nursing care is provided based on the principle of non-discrimination. The ICN is committed to the position that handles their actions and inaction in protecting human rights, while National Nursing Associations (NNAs) take part in the development of health and social protection policies and legislation related to patients' rights. Through professional medical activity, which is carried out with respect for and in the name of human rights, nurses contribute daily to the realisation of the right to health, the rights of patients, and the right to medical care.

The EPHA advocates for policies that address common risk factors for noncommunicable diseases and promote the transition to sustainable food systems with healthy food environments.[94] Noncommunicable diseases represent the major health threat of the 21st century and are responsible for the vast majority of premature death and illness.[95]

38.8 Human Rights and Humanitarian NGOs and COVID-19 Pandemic

Human Rights Watch examines the impact of the COVID-19 pandemic on the deterioration of human rights worldwide. According to Human Rights Watch research, several political parties and groups, including in the United States, Great Britain, Italy, Spain, Greece, France and Germany, have used the pandemic to promote all sorts of anti-immigrant, ultra-nationalist, anti-Semitic and xenophobic agendas and conspiracy theories.[96] Anti-immigrant, ultra-nationalist, anti-Semitic and xenophobic agendas and conspiracy theories lead to discrimination, infringement of human rights and are a threat to peace and security at the national, regional and

---

[91] WMA 2021d.

[92] ICN 2011.

[93] Ibid.

[94] EPHA 2021d.

[95] Noncommunicable diseases (NCDs) kill 41 million people each year, equivalent to 71% of all deaths globally. See WHO 2021.

[96] Human Rights Watch (HRW) 2020.

global levels. Discrimination and racism always lead to human tragedy. Discrimination and racism endanger the safety of the individual, the safety of the group, the safety and soundness of the state. Human Rights Watch calls on states to harmonize their anti-discrimination legislation with international standards, such as the practical guide *Developing National Action Plans to Combat Racial Discrimination*,[97] considering the realities and trends of the COVID-19 pandemic to exacerbate the human rights situation. According to Human Rights Watch, the situation with freedom of speech and peaceful assembly has also worsened in the world in connection with the COVID-19 pandemic.[98]

MSF teams are responding directly to the COVID-19 pandemic in more than 40 states. MSF's response to COVID-19 is focused on three key priorities: supporting national health systems by providing care to patients with COVID-19; protecting people who are vulnerable and at risk; maintaining essential health services.[99] For example, MSF is helping to combat the coronavirus pandemic in Malawi.[100]

A separate area of the EPHA's work is to improve the physical, mental, and social well-being of the Roma people, including access to medical care, health care systems and humanitarian assistance.[101] The coronavirus pandemic has exacerbated the plight of the Roma, and they are also not included in national COVID-19 vaccination plans. In the EU, only Slovakia has included the Roma in the national COVID-19 vaccination plan.[102]

The EPHA's EU International Trade Policy Campaign aims to protect and promote public health and ensure policy coherence between trade and public health.[103] With the coronavirus pandemic, trade and public health interdependence has only intensified. The coronavirus pandemic has also become a threat to the economic security of states.

The EPHA points out that COVID-19 is one of several common challenges facing Europe, for example: fighting the revival of infectious (communicable) diseases; direct and indirect health consequences of a climate emergency, such as alarming levels of air pollution; drug resistant infections; rising prices for medicines; an epidemic of noncommunicable diseases; and growing inequalities in health within states and across the EU.[104] Regarding COVID-19, EPHA states the need for a long-term EU strategy to combat infectious (communicable) diseases in Europe.[105] Indeed, the international community needs to develop a global strategy for dealing

---

[97] Ibid.

[98] In at least 83 states, governments have used the COVID-19 pandemic as a pretext to curtail freedom of speech and peaceful assembly. See Human Rights Watch (HRW) 2021e.

[99] MSF 2021h.

[100] MSF 2021i.

[101] EPHA 2018, 2017.

[102] EPHA 2021e.

[103] EPHA 2021f.

[104] EPHA 2020a.

[105] EPHA 2020b.

38 Human Rights NGOs and Humanitarian NGOs

with pandemics and epidemics within the WHO framework, and regional and national action plans based on it.

38.9 Conclusion

Human rights NGOs were created to fight for justice and respect for human rights. The principle of promoting and developing respect for human rights and fundamental freedoms is the foundation of the modern international legal order. However, international governmental organisations, whose competence includes issues of human rights protection, cannot always act promptly. The effectiveness and efficiency of the activities of international government organisations depends on the will and policy of the member states, as well as on their determination to fight for human rights. Human rights NGOs are independent of the state, they can oppose a state that violates human rights, and they can fight for justice even when the state is against it. Human rights NGOs fight for justice and defend human rights through universal mechanisms (the UN and its specialised agencies), regional (European Court of Human Rights, Inter-American Court of Human Rights and others) and national. Human rights NGOs help develop civil society in post-totalitarian and post-authoritarian states, where it is necessary to "vaccinate" the promotion and respect for human rights. Human rights NGOs operate where international government organisations cannot operate because of the bureaucratic mechanism and their legal nature. Human rights NGOs work to ensure personal safety through the rule of human rights.

Humanitarian NGOs operate in the most difficult situations, namely in times of armed conflict or emergencies. The credibility of humanitarian NGOs lies in their many years of activity and in the principles of their work. Humanitarian NGOs are the last hope for the survival of individuals who face armed conflict, epidemics and pandemics, natural disasters. Humanitarian NGOs are committed to human health and well-being. Humanitarian NGOs develop standards for medical and humanitarian action during emergencies that are put into practice. The activities of humanitarian NGOs are aimed at ensuring the biological safety of individuals.

References

Abashidze A (2014) Pravo mezhdunarodnykh organizatsiy [Law of international organizations]. Publishing house. Yurayt, Moscow

Amnesty (2020) Annual Report 2019: Eastern Europe and Central Asia, https://www.amnesty.org/en/latest/campaigns/2020/04/air2019-eeca/, accessed 16 February 2021

Amnesty (2021a) Where it all began, https://www.amnesty.org/en/who-we-are/, accessed 16 February 2021

Amnesty (2021b) Our story, https://www.amnesty.org/en/who-we-are/, accessed 16 February 2021

Amnesty (2021c) United Nations, https://www.amnesty.org/en/what-we-do/united-nations/, accessed 16 February 2021

Amnesty (2021d) Amnesty evolves, https://www.amnesty.org/en/who-we-are/, accessed 16 February 2021

Amnesty (2021e) Amnesty today, https://www.amnesty.org/en/who-we-are/, accessed 16 February 2021

Amnesty (2021f) Mali: New project makes the fight against impunity a priority, https://www.amn esty.org/en/latest/news/2021/02/mali-new-project-makes-the-fight-against-impunity-a-priority/, accessed 16 February 2021

Amnesty (2021g) South Sudan: Re: Extend the mandate of the UN Commission on human rights in South Sudan, https://www.amnesty.org/en/documents/afr65/3638/2021/en/, accessed 16 February 2021

Amnesty (2021h) Torture, https://www.amnesty.org/en/what-we-do/torture/, accessed 16 February 2021

Amnesty (2021i) Refugees, asylum-seekers and migrants, https://www.amnesty.org/en/what-we-do/refugees-asylum-seekers-and-migrants/, accessed 16 February 2021

Amnesty (2021j) Sexual and reproductive rights, https://www.amnesty.org/en/what-we-do/sexual-and-reproductive-rights/, accessed 16 February 2021

Amnesty (2021k) Arms control, https://www.amnesty.org/en/what-we-do/arms-control/, accessed 16 February 2021

Amnesty (2021l) Ethiopia: Government must honour promise of humanitarian access to Tigray, https://www.amnesty.org/en/latest/news/2021/02/ethiopia-government-must-honour-pro mise-of-humanitarian-access-to-tigray/, accessed 16 February 2021

Amnesty (2021m) International Justice, https://www.amnesty.org/en/what-we-do/international-jus tice/, accessed 16 February 2021

Amnesty (2021n) Police violence, https://www.amnesty.org/en/what-we-do/police-brutality/, accessed 16 February 2021

Anderson K (2000) The Ottawa Convention Banning Landmines, The Role of International Non-governmental Organizations and the Idea of International Civil Society. European Journal of International Law. 11. https://doi.org/10.1093/ejil/11.1.91

Binder-Aviles H (2016) The NGO Handbook. Bureau of International Information Programs. United States Department of State

Bouchet-Saulnier F (2013) The Practical Guide to Humanitarian Law, https://guide-humanitarian-law.org/content/index/, accessed 16 February 2021

Boyle A, Chinkin C (2007) The Making of International Law. Oxford University Press

Clark A (2001) Diplomacy of Conscience: Amnesty International and Changing Human Rights Norms. Princeton University Press, Princeton/Oxford

EPHA (2017) EPHA's Response to EU Evaluation of the National Roma Integra-tion Strategies, https://epha.org/ephas-response-to-eu-evaluation-of-the-national-roma-integr ation-stategies/, accessed 16 February 2021

EPHA (2018) Five key recommendations for better health, https://epha.org/post-2020-eu-framew ork-for-national-roma-integration-strategies/, accessed 16 February 2021

EPHA (2020a) COVID-19 reveals urgent need for a common European public health approach, https://epha.org/covid-19-reveals-urgent-need-for-a-common-european-public-health-app roach/, accessed 16 February 2021

EPHA (2020b) EPHA Statement on COVID-19, https://epha.org/epha-statement-on-covid19/, accessed 16 February 2021

EPHA (2021a) European Public Health Alliance (EPHA), http://www.epha.org/, accessed 16 February 2021

EPHA (2021b) Transparency Statement, https://epha.org/transparency-statement/, accessed 16 February 2021

EPHA (2021c) Health inequalities and Roma health, https://epha.org/health-inequalities-and-roma-health/, accessed 16 February 2021

EPHA (2021d) Food Systems & NCD Prevention, https://epha.org/food-drink-and-agriculture/, accessed 16 February 2021

38 Human Rights NGOs and Humanitarian NGOs

EPHA (2021e) Should governments consider Roma a priority in their COVID-19 vaccination roll-out plans? https://epha.org/should-governments-consider-roma-a-priority-in-their-covid-19-vaccination-roll-out-plans/, accessed 16 February 2021

EPHA (2021f) Trade for health, https://epha.org/trade-and-health/, accessed 16 February 2021

Herdegen M (2011) Mizhnarodne pravo [International law]. Publishing House "K. I. S. ", Kyiv

Human Rights Watch (HRW) (2010) Business, https://www.hrw.org/topic/business, accessed 16 February 2021

Human Rights Watch (HRW) (2011) International Justice https://www.hrw.org/topic/international-justice, accessed 16 February 2021

Human Rights Watch (HRW) (2012) Torture, https://www.hrw.org/topic/torture, accessed 16 February 2021

Human Rights Watch (HRW) (2013) Health, https://www.hrw.org/topic/health, accessed 16 February 2021

Human Rights Watch (HRW) (2014a) Refugee Rights, https://www.hrw.org/topic/refugee-rights, accessed 16 February 2021

Human Rights Watch (HRW) (2014b) Women's Rights, https://www.hrw.org/topic/womens-rights, accessed 16 February 2021

Human Rights Watch (HRW) (2014c) Migrants, https://www.hrw.org/topic/migrants, accessed 16 February 2021

Human Rights Watch (HRW) (2020) COVID-19 Fueling Anti-Asian Racism and Xenophobia Worldwide, https://www.hrw.org/news/2020/05/12/covid-19-fueling-anti-asian-racism-and-xenophobia-worldwide, accessed 16 February 2021

Human Rights Watch (HRW) (2021a) About us, https://www.hrw.org/about/about-us, accessed 16 February 2021

Human Rights Watch (HRW) (2021b) Terrorism/Counterterrorism, https://www.hrw.org/topic/terrorism-counterterrorism, accessed 16 February 2021

Human Rights Watch (HRW) (2021c) Arms, https://www.hrw.org/topic/arms, accessed 16 February 2021

Human Rights Watch (HRW) (2021d) LGBT Rights, https://www.hrw.org/ru/topic/prava-lgbt, accessed 16 February 2021

Human Rights Watch (HRW) (2021e) COVID-19 Triggers Wave of Free Speech Abuse, https://www.hrw.org/news/2021/02/11/covid-19-triggers-wave-free-speech-abuse, accessed 16 February 2021

ICN (2011) Nurses and human rights, https://www.icn.ch/sites/default/files/inline-files/E10_Nurses_Human_Rights%281%29.pdf, accessed 16 February 2021

ICN (2012) The ICN Code of ethics for nurses, https://www.icn.ch/sites/default/files/inline-files/2012_ICN_Codeofethicsfornurses_%20eng.pdf, accessed 16 February 2021

ICN (2019) International Council of Nurses Constitution, https://www.icn.ch/sites/default/files/inline-files/ICN%20Constitution%202019.pdf, accessed 16 February 2021

ICN (2021a) International Council of Nurses, http://www.icn.ch/, accessed 16 February 2021

ICN (2021b) Council of National Nursing Association Representatives (CNR), https://www.icn.ch/who-we-are/council-national-nursing-association-representatives-cnr, accessed 16 February 2021

ICN (2021c) Campaigns, https://www.icn.ch/what-we-do/campaigns, accessed 16 February 2021

ICN (2021d) Projects, https://www.icn.ch/what-we-do/projects, accessed 16 February 2021

ICN (2021e) ICN Nurse Practitioner/Advanced Practice Network (NP/APN Network), https://www.icn.ch/who-we-are/icn-nurse-practitioneradvanced-practice-network-npapn-network, accessed 16 February 2021

Korey W (1998) "To Light a Candle": Amnesty International and the "Prisoners of Conscience". In: Korey W (ed) NGOs and the Universal Declaration of Human Rights. "A Curious Grapevine". Palgrave Macmillan, New York. https://doi.org/10.1057/9780230108165_8.

Kuroyanagi T (2013) Historical Transition in Medical Ethics—Challenges of the World Medical Association, https://www.med.or.jp/english/journal/pdf/2013_04/220_226.pdf

Martens K (2003) Examining the (Non-)Status of NGOs in International Law. Indiana Journal of Global Legal Studies: Vol. 10: Issue 2, Article 1

Mostashari A (2005) An Introduction to Non-Governmental Organizations (NGO) Management. Iranian Studies Group at MIT

MSF Médecins sans Frontières (MSF) (1995) Who are the Médecins Sans Frontières, http://association.msf.org/sites/default/files/documents/Principles%20Chantilly%20EN.pdf, accessed 16 February 2021

MSF (2021a) Médecins sans Frontières http://www.msf.org/, accessed 16 February 2021

MSF (2021b) Where we work, https://www.msf.org/who-we-are, accessed 16 February 2021

MSF (2021c) MSF's first mission, https://www.msf.org/who-we-are, accessed 16 February 2021

MSF (2021d) Our history, https://www.msf.org/who-we-are, accessed 16 February 2021

MSF (2021e) Why we started, https://www.msf.org/who-we-are, accessed 16 February 2021

MSF (2021f) We are Médecins Sans Frontières, https://www.msf.org/who-we-are, accessed 16 February 2021

MSF (2021g) The MSF Charter, https://www.msf.org/who-we-are, accessed 16 February 2021

MSF (2021h) Coronavirus COVID-19 pandemic, https://www.msf.org/covid-19, accessed 16 February 2021

MSF (2021i) Malawi is overwhelmed by second wave of COVID-19, https://www.msf.org/malawi-overwhelmed-second-wave-coronavirus-covid-19, accessed 16 February 2021

Roeder LW, Simard A (2013) Diplomacy and Negotiation for Humanitarian NGOs. Humanitarian Solutions in the 21st Century. Springer, New York, NY

Stillman GB (2006) NGO Law and Governance. A Resource Book. Asian Development Bank Institute, Tokyo

Struett MJ (2008) The Politics of Constructing the International Criminal Court. Palgrave Macmillan, New York, https://doi.org/https://doi.org/10.1057/9780230612419.

WHO (2021) Noncommunicable diseases, https://www.who.int/news-room/fact-sheets/detail/noncommunicable-diseases, accessed 16 February 2021

WMA (2019) Position of the World Medical Association (WMA) on euthanasia and physician-assisted suicide, https://www.ieb-eib.org/en/newsletter/position-of-the-world-medical-association-wma-on-euthanasia-and-physician-assisted-suicide-chron-561.html, accessed 16 February 2021

WMA (2020) The World Medical Association Inc. Strategic Plan 2020–2025, https://www.wma.net/wp-content/uploads/2020/02/2020-2025-Strategic-plan-1.pdf, accessed 16 February 2021

WMA (2021a) Background and Preliminary Organisation, https://www.wma.net/who-we-are/history/, accessed 16 February 2021

WMA (2021b) WMA's mission, https://www.wma.net/who-we-are/about-us/, accessed 16 February 2021

WMA (2021c) Physicians as Human Rights Advocates, https://www.wma.net/what-we-do/human-rights/, accessed 16 February 2021

WMA (2021d) Outreach Activities to Implement WMA Policies, https://www.wma.net/what-we-do/campaigns/, accessed 16 February 2021

Nataliia Hendel holds a PhD in International Law, and is Professor of the International Law and Comparative Law Department at the International Humanitarian University, Ukraine.

Tymur Korotkyi holds a PhD in Law, and is Professor of the International Law and Comparative Law Department at the National Aviation University, Vice-President of the Ukrainian Association of International Law, Ukraine.

38 Human Rights NGOs and Humanitarian NGOs

Roman Yedeliev holds a PhD in International Law, and is Associate Professor of the International Law Department at the Taras Shevchenko National University of Kyiv, Ukraine.